The Psychology Almanac

The Psychology Almanac

Howard E. Wilkening

*California State University
at Los Angeles*

in collaboration with
Gregory Wilkening
and
Peter Wilkening

**BROOKS/COLE PUBLISHING COMPANY
MONTEREY, CALIFORNIA**
A Division of Wadsworth Publishing Company, Inc.

ISBN: 0-8185-0020-4
L.C. Catalog Card No.: 72-86775
Printed in the United States of America
3 4 5 6 7 8 9 10—77 76 75 74

Manuscript Editor: Jean Schuyler
Production Editor: Micky Lawler
Interior & Cover Design: Linda Marcetti
Illustrations: John Foster
Typesetting: Design Service, Fullerton, California
Printing & Binding: Malloy Lithographing, Inc., Ann Arbor, Michigan

Preface

This book is a dictionary of psychological and psychology-related terms. It also contains a number of other helpful features, such as a list of the ethical standards of psychologists, a description of professional journals, several sections on the language of psychology, an explanation of the symbols and notations used in statistics, and more than 70 pages of statistical tables.

The book is designed primarily for the psychology major, both undergraduate and graduate. It should also be popular with the beginning student in psychology who is taking the required introductory course either as a tolerant and reluctant participant or as a deeply involved and dedicated neophyte preliminary to majoring in psychology. Faculty members will also find it valuable for purposes of review and ready reference.

Most of the dictionary entries have a vein of history running through them, including brief etymologies, origins of the terms, and names of people closely associated with the terms or concepts. I have attempted to make the definitions as simple and operational as possible. In most instances I have avoided token definitions. Some definitions are rather elaborate, either because a shorter treatment would have been misleading or frustrating or because it would have been necessary to make several referrals to other sources.

In planning for the inclusion of material in this book, my associates and I adopted the following procedures:

An alphabetical card file was made for every item listed in the indexes of all books of a psychological nature located in college libraries and cooperative professors' offices for a period of over three years. The same procedure was followed in extracting entries from dictionaries in education, statistics, sociology, psychiatry, and psychology. However, no definitions were borrowed from any other dictionary, although in spot checks made after the definitions for this book were written there were some striking similarities between definitions, probably attesting to a hoped-for agreement in meaning among some terms at least. More than 800 books and approximately 500 periodicals were examined. The books referred to most frequently are listed in the References at the end of this handbook. More than 26,000 different entries were collected, and a record was kept of their frequency count up to 15 (a cut-off point arbitrarily arrived at mainly because of sheer ennui).

Although frequency count was at first given major consideration in reducing the unwieldy number of terms, it was not the only means of selection. For example, more than 50 entries mentioned fewer than three times in the compilation of entries from all source material have been retained because they were judged to have longevity or to have some usefulness, according to the opinions of various students and faculty members. In general, however, terms with a frequency count of less than three were automatically eliminated, as were terms with highly specialized or restrictive usages. This process brought the list down to a practicable 7500. Other strong persuasions (personal and editorial) helped stabilize the total number of entries at approximately 5000.

Naturally, a work like this would lack considerable authenticity if other professional persons with conceptual insights, extensive experience, and disciplined psychological knowledge had not contributed to its making. Foremost in line must stand Roger E. Kirk of Baylor University, who read not only every word of the statistical section but every digit as well, making many valuable suggestions, clarifications in expression, and corrections of errors. His gentle, objective criticism was most welcomed and deeply appreciated. Of course, any remaining errors must be attributed to my oversights or stubbornness. My deep gratitude is also expressed to the two people who helped initiate this project more than four years ago, Terry Hendrix, psychology editor of Brooks/Cole Publishing Company, and Edward L. Walker of the University of Michigan, consulting editor for Brooks/Cole, who also made numerous and detailed suggestions on organization and content. Special thanks are due as well to the youthful, spirited, but appropriately disciplined staff of Brooks/Cole, especially Micky Lawler and Bonnie Fitzwater.

Many professors played a significant role in the development of this book. Michael Gaston, Solomon Diamond, John Lamont, and Irwin Lublin from the psychology department at California State College at Los Angeles (now California State University at Los Angeles) were of considerable assistance in helping modify and clarify some of the entries. Charles L. Clark, professor of mathematics at California State University at Los Angeles, made several valuable suggestions on the accuracy of mathematical expressions. Norman Ahern, instructor of mathematics at West Los Angeles Community College, was very cooperative in continually checking details and mathematical concepts as well as in participating in writing some of the table descriptions. Sally Haralson of California State University at Long Beach raised some questions about point of view that helped clarify some entries.

Many graduate students, especially Alice Chang and Kathryn McCreary, helped in gathering material and presenting some of it from the student's viewpoint. Ray Weiss and John Zuehlke gave invaluable assistance in offering suggestions and criticisms on computer terminology. The Bobrick Corporation was of considerable assistance in providing me, from time to time, with the opportunity to use the facilities of their duplicating services. Nina Zuehlke, who not only typed the first draft but acted as critic and questioner of all details, deserves special mention. The dozen or more typists (especially Susan Knox, for her dedication and cooperation under most adverse circumstances) deserve praise. The constant assistance, direct and indirect, of Laura De Lacy can never be forgotten and is deeply appreciated.

I also offer many thanks to dozens of librarians at various libraries: the University of California at Los Angeles, particularly those at the Bio-Med Library and the Research Library; the University of Southern California; the University of California at Berkeley; the New York Public Library; the Los Angeles Public Library; the Smithsonian Institution at

Washington, D. C.; and especially to Miss A. Hawk, librarian at the John F. Kennedy Memorial Library at California State University at Los Angeles.

I am indebted to the Literary Executor of the late Sir Ronald A. Fisher, F.R.S., to Dr. Frank Yates, F.R.S., and to Oliver and Boyd, Edinburgh, for permission to reprint Tables 6a, 8, 10, 12, 15, 16, and 34 of this book from Tables III, IV, VI, VIII, XIII, XXIII, and XXXIII, respectively, of their book *Statistical Tables for Biological, Agricultural, and Medical Research* (6th edition, 1963). I am also indebted to Emeritus Professor Egon S. Pearson for his permission to reprint Tables 13a, 13b, 18, 19, 20, and 21 of this book from Tables 15, 18, 29, and 31 of *Biometrika Tables for Statisticians*, by E. S. Pearson and H. O. Hartley (Vol. 1, 3rd edition, 1966).

To all of these people, and to my special loved ones who not only put up with me but encouraged me to go on, I owe a real debt of gratitude. Thanks again, Barbara Ahern, Carol Vilas, Peter, Gregory, and Mary Louise for all your research, typing, clerical work, consulting assistance, and love.

Howard E. Wilkening

Acknowledgments

Table 1a: From *Statistical Inference* by Helen M. Walker and Joseph Lev. Copyright 1953 by Holt, Rinehart and Winston, Inc. Reprinted by permission of Holt, Rinehart and Winston, Inc.

Table 1b: From *Introduction to Statistical Analysis*, Third Edition, by Dixon & Massey. Copyright © 1969 by McGraw-Hill, Inc. Used by permission of McGraw-Hill Book Company.

Table 1d: Reproduced by permission of E. S. Pearson and *Biometrika*.

Table 2: From Richard P. Runyon and Audrey Haber, *Fundamentals of Behavioral Statistics*, 1967, Addison-Wesley, Reading, Mass.

Table 3: From *Fundamental Statistics in Psychology and Education*, 4th Edition, by J. P. Guilford. Copyright © 1965 by McGraw-Hill, Inc. Used by permission of McGraw-Hill Book Company.

Table 4: From The Psychological Corporation, Test Service Bulletin No. 48, 1955. Reprinted by permission.

Table 5: From *Statistical Analysis* by E. Vernon Lewis, Copyright © 1963 by Litton Educational Publishing, Inc.

Tables 6a, 8, 10, 12, 15, 16, and 34: Taken from Tables III, IV, VI, VIII, XIII, XXIII, and XXXIII of Fisher & Yates: *Statistical Tables for Biological, Agricultural, and Medical Research*, published by Oliver & Boyd, Edinburgh, and by permission of the authors and publishers.

Table 6b: From Sandler, *British Journal of Psychology*, 46, 225-226, 1955. Reprinted by permission of the British Psychological Society.

Table 7: From Kirk, Roger E., *Experimental Design: Procedures for the Behavioral Sciences*. Copyright 1968 by Wadsworth Publishing Co., Inc. Reprinted by permission of the publisher: Brooks/Cole Publishing Company, Monterey, California.

Table 9: From Newman, Edwin B., Computational Methods Useful in Analyzing Series of Binary Data, *Journal of Psychology*, 1951, 54, 252-262. Reprinted by permission.

Table 11: From Table XVII of W. V. Bingham, *Aptitudes and Aptitude Testing*. Copyright 1937 by Harper & Row Publishers, Inc., New York. Reprinted by permission.

Tables 13a, 13b, 18, 19, and 20: From E. S. Pearson and H. O. Hartley, *Biometrika Tables for Statisticians*, Vol. 1, 3rd edition, 1966. Reprinted by permission.

Table 14: From Davidoff, M. D., and H. W. Goheen, *Psychometrika*, 1953, 18, 115-121. Reprinted by permission. See also M. D. Davidoff, "Note," *Psychometrika*, 1954, 19, 163.

Table 17: From *Techniques of Statistical Analysis*, edited by C. Eisenhart, M. W. Hastay, and W. A. Wallis. Copyright © 1947 by McGraw-Hill, Inc. Used by permission of McGraw-Hill Book Company.

Table 21: From E. S. Pearson and H. O. Hartley, *Biometrika Tables for Statisticians*, Vol. 2, 1972. Reprinted by permission.

Table 22: From "Multiple comparisons among means," by Roger E. Kirk, *Journal of the American Statistical Association*, 1961, 56, 52-64. Reprinted by permission of the publisher.

Table 23: Abridged from D. B. Duncan, Multiple range and multiple *F* tests, *Biometrics*, 1955, 11, 1-42. Reprinted by permission of the author and the publisher.

Table 24: Reproduced from C. W. Dunnett, New tables for multiple comparisons with a control, *Biometrics*, 1964, 20, 482-491. Reprinted by permission of the author and the publisher.

Table 25a: Adapted from Miller, Leslie H., Tables of percentage points of Kolmogorov statistics, *Journal of the American Statistical Association*, 1956, 11-121. Reprinted by permission.

Table 25b: One-tailed test column is abridged from L. A. Goodman, "K-S test for psychological research," *Psychological Bulletin*, 1954. Copyright 1954 by the American Psychological Association and reproduced by permission. Two-tailed test column is derived from Massey, F. J., Jr., The distribution of the maximum deviation between two sample cumulative step functions, *Ann. Math. Statist.*, 1951, 22, 125-127. Reprinted with the permission of the Institute of Mathematical Statistics.

Table 25c: From Smirnov, N., "Table for estimating the goodness of fit in empirical distributions," *Ann. Math. Statist.*, 1948, 19, 279-281. Reprinted with the permission of the Institute of Mathematical Statistics.

Table 26: From Eisenhart, C., and Swed, F. S., "Tables for testing randomness of grouping in a sequence of alternatives," *Ann. Math. Statist.*, 1943, 14, 66-87. Reprinted with the permission of the Institute of Mathematical Statistics.

Table 28: From Wilcoxon, Katti, and Wilcox, "Critical values and probability levels for the Wilcoxon Rank Sum Test and the Wilcoxon Signed Rank Test." Copyright 1963 by American Cyanamid Co., New York. Reprinted by permission of Lederle Laboratories, a division of American Cyanamid Company.

Table 29: From Mann, H. B., and Whitney, D. R., "On a test of whether one of two random variables is stochastically larger than the other," *Ann. Math. Statist.*, 1947, 18, 50-60. Reprinted with the permission of the Institute of Mathematical Statistics.

Table 30: From Olds, E. G., "The 5 percent significance levels for sums of squares of rank differences and a correction," *Ann. Math. Statist.*, 1949, 20, 117-118. And from Olds, E. G., "Distribution of the sum of squares of rank differences for small numbers of individuals," *Ann. Math. Statist.*, 1938, 9, 133-148.

Table 31a: From Friedman, Milton, "A comparison of alternative tests of significance for the problem of *m* rankings," *Ann. Math. Statist.*, 1940, 11, 86-92.

Table 31b: Reproduced from *Rank Correlations Methods* (First edition, 1948; fourth edition, 1970) by M. G. Kendall, by permission of the publishers, Charles Griffin & Company Ltd., London.

Table 32: Adapted and abridged from W. J. Kruskal and W. A. Wallis, "Use of ranks in one-criterion variance analysis," *Journal of the American Statistical Association*, 1952, 47, 614-617. (The corrections made by the authors in Errata, *Journal of the American Statistical Association*, 48, 910, have been incorporated.) Reprinted by permission.

Table 33: From *CRC Standard Mathematical Tables*, 18th edition, 1970, S. M. Selby, Editor. The Chemical Rubber Co., Cleveland, Ohio.

Contents

Ethical Standards of Psychologists[1]

Principle 1: Responsibility. The psychologist[2] . . . places high value on objectivity and integrity, and maintains the highest standards in the services he offers.

Principle 2: Competence. All psychologists have responsibility of maintaining high standards of professional competence in the interest of the public and of the profession as a whole.

Principle 3: Moral and Legal Standards. The practicing psychologist shows sensible regard for the social codes and moral expectations of the community in which he works, recognizing that violations of such standards may personally damage his clients, students, or colleagues and impugn his own name and his profession's reputation.

Principle 4: Misrepresentation. The psychologist avoids misrepresentation of his own as well as his employer's professional qualifications, affiliations, and purposes.

[1] Modified and condensed from *Casebook on Ethical Standards of Psychologists*, 1967, pp. 64f. Copyright 1967 by the American Psychological Association, and reproduced by permission.

[2] A student of psychology who assumes the role of psychologist shall be considered a psychologist for the purpose of this code of ethics.

Principle 5: Public Statements. Modesty, scientific caution, and due regard for the limits of present knowledge characterize all statements of psychologists who supply any information to the public.

Principle 6: Confidentiality. Safeguarding information about an individual that has been obtained by the psychologist is a primary obligation of the psychologist.

Principle 7: Client Welfare. The psychologist respects the integrity and protects the welfare of all with whom he is working.

Principle 8: Client Relationship. The psychologist informs his prospective client of various aspects of the potential relationship that might affect the client's decision to enter the relationship.

Principle 9: Impersonal Services. Psychological services for the purpose of diagnosis, treatment, or personalized advice are provided only within a professional relationship, and not through public channels (radio, TV, magazines, etc.).

Principle 10: Announcement of Services. A psychologist adheres to professional standards in making known his availability for professional services.

Principle 11: Interprofessional Relations. A psychologist acts with integrity concerning colleagues in psychology and other professions.

Principle 12: Remuneration. Financial arrangements must meet professional standards that safeguard the best interests of client and profession.

Principle 13: Test Security. Psychological tests and other assessment devices are not described in popular publications so as not to invalidate the techniques. Access to such devices is limited to persons with professional interests who will safeguard their use.

Principle 14: Test Interpretation. Test scores, like test materials, are released only to persons qualified to interpret and use them properly.

Principle 15: Test Publication. Psychological tests are offered only to commercial publishers who present their tests professionally and distribute them only to qualified users.

Principle 16: Research Precautions. The psychologist assumes obligations for the welfare of his research subjects.

Principle 17: Publication Credit. Credit is assigned only to those who have contributed to a publication, in proportion to their contribution.

Principle 18: Responsibility Toward Organization. A psychologist respects the rights and reputation of his affiliated institute or organization.

Principle 19: Promotional Activities. The psychologist associated with the development or promotion of psychological materials for commercial sale is responsible for ensuring that such devices, books, or products are presented professionally and factually.

Description of Selected Journals in Psychology and Related Fields

Most journal information merely lists current editors, addresses, and other data that are soon outdated. In this section, journal contents are briefly described, enabling the interested reader to quickly determine if the journal might be of value as a medium of publication or might warrant further reading. Naturally, not all relevant journals for all readers can be described here, but the following selection represents a fair sampling of most of the journals in and related to psychology.

In general, the journals are alphabetized according to their subject matter as mentioned in the title (for instance, the *Journal of Abnormal Psychology* is found under *Abnormal Psychology, Journal of* rather than under *Journal of . . .*; *The British Journal of Educational Psychology* is described under *Educational Psychology, The British Journal of* rather than under *The British Journal of . . .*, etc.). Cross references to journals of a similar nature or to those fitting under a special category (such as journals published by the American Psychological Association, Japanese journals, British journals, etc.) are indicated with numbers in parentheses at the end of the journal description.

1. *Abnormal Psychology, Journal of* (APA journal). Devoted to basic research and theory in the broad field of abnormal behavior, its determinants and its correlates. Articles generally cover psychopathology, normal processes in abnormal individuals, atypical behavior of normal persons, experimental studies on animal or human subjects relating to atypical behavior, social or group effects on adjustment and pathological processes, etc., including case studies and other related material.

2. *Acta Paediatrica Scandinavica* (Published bimonthly in Sweden). Contains research articles on medicine, including clinical case reports, chromosomal studies, epidemiology, and treatment.

3. *Acta Paedopsychiatrica The International Journal of Child Psychiatry.* (Basel, Switzerland; text in English, French, German, and Spanish). Publishes articles and abstracts dealing with child psychiatry, having special reference to autism, dyslexia, diagnosis of mental deficiency, etiology, metabolic disorders, growth, etc.

4. *Acta Psychologica: European Journal of Psychology* (Netherlands: text in English, French or German). Articles of general nature covering research material, opinions, and reports of studies.

5. *Aging and Human Development* (An International Journal of Psychosocial Gerontology). Publishes research and clinical studies on the interaction of psychological and social factors with the biological processes of aging. (See 63.)

   American Psychological Association journals (See 1, 10, 35, 36, 37, 41, 45, 54, 115, 125, 140, 141, 146, 147, 156.)

6. *Analytic Psychology, Journal of* (London). Papers pertaining to subject matter on any phase of analytical psychology, especially those having direct bearing on its clinical application.

7. *Animal Behavior* (London, England: Association for the Study of Animal Behavior, U. K. and American Behavior Society). Original papers and critical reviews on all aspects of animal behavior and related subjects from contributors in many countries. Reports of researches, book reviews, and correspondence are included, as are reports of the Proceedings of the Association for the Study of Animal Behavior and the Section of Animal Behavior and Sociobiology (Ecological Society of America and American Society of Zoologists), of which it is the official journal.

8. *Anthropological Forum* (University of Western Australia). An international journal of social and cultural anthropology and comparative sociology.

9. *Applied Behavioral Science, Journal of* (National Training Laboratories Institute in conjunction with NEA). Articles concerned with action groups, problem solving, leadership training, communication with managerial groups, etc.

10. *Applied Psychology, Journal of* (APA journal). Articles on the application of psychology to business and industry, with special emphasis on original investigations that contribute new knowledge and understanding to any field of applied psychology, except clinical psychology.

11. *Art Therapy, American Journal of* Art in education, rehabilitation, and psychotherapy.

    Australian journals (See 8, 148, 153.)

12. *Behavioral Biology, Communications in* Research reports, review articles, theoretical statements, methods, and apparatus papers which represent original contributions to scientific literature, primarily physiological in nature. Provides rapid and efficient publication of articles by psychologists, physiologists, pharmacologists, biochemists, ethologists, and biologists concerned with biological bases of behavior.

13. *Behavioral Research, Multivariate* Substantive, methodological, and theoretical articles and brief reports on new findings, new equations, and new lines of behavioral research.

14. *Behavioral Science.* Articles on general theories of behavior based on empirical evidence. Interdisciplinary approach

stressed, with special emphasis placed on applied research in mental health and disease.

15. *Behavior Genetics.* (An International Journal Devoted to Research in the Inheritance of Behavior in Animals and Man). Studies the inheritance or evolution of behavioral characteristics in man and in infrahuman species through publication of relevant original material in such diverse fields as anthropology, animal behavior, demography, ecology, evolution, mental retardation, physiological psychology, psychiatric genetics, and twin research. (See 60.)

16. *Behavior Therapy.* An interdisciplinary journal. Publishes original research articles of experimental or clinical nature that contribute to behavior theory or behavior modification. Occasionally publishes critical evaluations of new books, films, and problems in the field and of theoretical, social, or ethical issues raised by the theory or practice of behavior therapy.

17. *Behavior Therapy and Experimental Psychology, Journal of* Publishes descriptions of new procedures, disquisitions on theory of behavior disorders in particular and behavior change in general, as well as accounts of experimental studies, both animal and human, relating to change in neurotic, psychotic, and psychopathic subjects.

18. *Behavior Today* (The Human Sciences Newsletter). A professional newsletter designed to present current information on the people, institutions, ideas, research, writing, jobs, grants, problems, politics, protest movements, splinter groups, social implications and radical criticism in the behavioral sciences.

19. *Biochemical Pharmacology* An international journal devoted to research into the development of biologically active substances and their mode of action at the biochemical and subcellular level.

20. *Biochemistry and Biophysics, Archives of* An international journal dedicated to the dissemination of fundamental knowledge in all areas of biochemistry and biophysics. In general, articles present new information of general interest to workers in these fields.

21. *Biological Psychology, The Journal of* (or The Worm Runner's Digest). A joint publication in one volume, consisting of a manual of psychological experiments on planarians, and including satirical and whimsical reports and cartoons.
Biophysics (See 20.)

22. *Biosocial Science, Journal of* Publishes original papers, reviews, lectures, proceedings and major book reviews. The scientific approach is interdisciplinary. Articles are concerned with social aspects of human biology, including reproduction and its control, gerontology, ecology, genetics, and applied psychology; with biological aspects of the social sciences, including sociology, social anthropology, education and criminology, and with biosocial aspects of demography.

23. *Brain* (A quarterly publication, New York) Research articles on medical aspects of the brain and nervous system.

24. *Brain: A Journal of Neurology* (London). Technical papers on scientific reports of research on the brain and the nervous system, including clinical neurology.
British journals (See 6, 7, 24, 30, 39, 44, 55, 68, 81, 85, 86, 100, 108, 130, 154, 177, 188, 192.)
Canadian journals (See 90, 127, 149, 155.)

25. *Child Development.* General articles dealing with child development, and with more specific studies on birth order, under-and-over achievers, creativity in children, etc.

26. *Child Development Research, Review of* Collates and interprets current research in child development and scientific knowledge about children obtained from reports and investigations from social workers, child psychologists, child psychiatrists, educators, etc.

27. *Child Psychiatry and Human Development* Serves the allied professional groups represented by the specialties of child psychiatry, pediatrics, psychology, social science, and human development in the task of defining the developing child and adolescent in health and in conflict. (See 3.)

28. *Child Psychiatry Journal, American Academy of* Original articles based on research and experiments dealing with treatment of psychiatric problems of children and adolescents, including such diverse topics as asthma therapy, stuttering, fixations, suicide, depressions, nostalgia, etc.

29. *Child Psychology and Psychiatry and Allied Disciplines, Journal of* Primarily concerned with child psychology and child psychiatry, including experimental and developmental studies. Also publishes relevant papers on animal behavior, anthropology, education, family studies, pediatrics, physiology and sociology.

30. *Child Psychotherapy, Journal of* (London). Exchanges ideas and methods of understanding personality of the child and processes at work in treatment relationships.

31. *Clinical Psychologist.* Manuscripts published on all phases of clinical psychology. Newsletter of Division 12, APA.

32. *Clinical Psychology, Journal of* Original papers concerning clinical problems, treatment, research and therapy; emphasis on psychological testing. Also deals with psychodiagnosis, psychopathology, clinical-practice problems, and includes editorial opinion. (See 177.)

33. *Cognitive Psychology.* Publishes original empirical, theoretical, and tutorial papers, methodological articles, and critical reviews dealing with memory, language processing, perception, problem solving, and thinking. Emphasis placed on the organization of human information processing.

34. *Communication Disorders, Journal of* (Amsterdam). Articles on problems related to anatomical, physiological, psychopathological, psychodynamic, diagnostic, and therapeutic aspects of communication disorders.

35. *Comparative and Physiological Psychology, Journal of* (APA journal). A continuation of The Journal of Animal Behavior, Psychology, and the Journal of Comparative Psychology. Begins with vol. 40, 1947. Publishes original research reports in the field of comparative and physiological psychology, including animal learning, conditioning, and sensory processes. Articles favored that report studies of substantial scope, usually involving series of related experiments.

36. *Consulting and Clinical Psychology, Journal of* (APA journal). Devoted to the area of clinical psychology, both child and adult. It covers a wide range of topics, including personality assessment and diagnosis, theories and techniques of behavior modification, community mental health concepts and techniques, etiology of behavior, structure and dynamics of personality, and clinical psychopathology. Publishes original research papers, major formulations of clinical theory or concepts, and significant applications of psychological principles to clinical practice.

37. *Counseling Psychology, Journal of* (APA journal). Theoretical and research articles on counseling and related activities carried on by counselors and personnel workers. Particular attention given to articles about diagnostic, remedial, therapeutic, and developmental aspects of counseling.

38. *Creative Behavior, Journal of* Information on current developments in creative behavior.

39. *Developmental Medicine and Child Neurology.* (Spastics International, London, England; also serves as the official journal of The American Academy for Cerebral Palsy). Publishes original articles, annotations, book reviews, and abstracts dealing with birth defects, palsy, seizures, phenylketonuria, autism, epilepsy, etc.

40. *Developmental Psychobiology.* Publishes papers dealing with physiological, behavioral, or genetic studies of the developing organism, including research reports, theoretical treatises, notes on apparatus of methodology, proceedings of symposia, and monograph supplements.

41. *Developmental Psychology.* (APA journal). Articles represent the broad range of growth and development and their major associated variables (sex, socioeconomic status, chronological age, etc.). Although adolescence and the aging population are emphasized, cross-species articles concerning developmental research with retardates are also included.

42. *Economics and Sociology, American Journal of* Published quarterly in the interest of constructive syntheses in the social sciences. Nature of articles: descriptive and research.

43. *Educational Measurement, Journal of* Publishes original measurement research and reports of applications of measurement in an educational context.

44. *Educational Psychology, British Journal of* (London). Publishes theses, abstracts, research notes, book reviews, and general articles on educational psychology.

45. *Educational Psychology, Journal of* (APA journal). Original investigations and theoretical papers dealing with problems of learning and teaching, and with the psychological development, relationships, and adjustment of the individual. Preference is given to studies of the more complex types of learning and behavior, especially in or relating to educational settings. Articles pertain to all levels of education and to all age groups.

46. *Educational Research, Journal of* Publishes research articles and critiques designed to advance the scientific study of education and to improve field practice. (See 190.)

47. *Experimental Education, Journal of* Specialized or technical education studies, treatises about the mathematics or methodology of behavior research, and monographs of major research interests.

48. *Endocrinology* (Published monthly for The Endocrine Society). Publishes original articles that contribute significantly to fundamental knowledge of the endocrines. Articles that deal primarily with human material are not necessarily rejected in this journal, but they do receive preferential consideration in the related journal *The Journal of Clinical Endocrinology and Metabolism.* (See 49.)

49. *Endocrinology and Metabolism, The Journal of Clinical* (Published monthly for The Endocrine Society). Research articles dealing primarily with the medical aspects of endocrinology and metabolism, including clinical observations, with emphasis on studies in man.

50. *Engineering Psychology, Journal of* A quarterly professional periodical containing articles that report the results of research in human processes in man-machine systems—information displays, speech communications, human motor activities, controls and related devices;

space and arrangement; atmospheric conditions; personnel and system integration—human factors in system development, simulation, etc. No theoretical articles, evaluative reviews, or reviews of research.

51. *Exceptional Children.* Deals with all areas of teaching and teaching with all children. Nature of articles: research and descriptive.

52. *Existential Psychology and Psychiatry, Review of* Articles that advance the understanding of human existence and that use the data of psychology and psychiatry to advance the science of man.

53. *Experimental Analysis of Behavior, Journal of the* Original publication of experiments relevant to the behavior of individual organisms.

54. *Experimental Psychology, Journal of* (APA journal). Original contributions of an experimental character, intended to contribute toward development of psychology as an experimental science. Studies of normal human subjects are favored over those of abnormal subjects.

55. *Experimental Psychology, Quarterly Journal of* (Cambridge, England). (Experimental Psychology Society). Devoted to general articles on experimental psychology (perception, laboratory studies, etc.). Includes book reviews, publications received, and author index.

French language journals (See 4, 70, 89, 90, 145, 155, 159, 180.)

56. *General Psychiatry, Archives of* (Published monthly by the American Medical Association). Articles cover a broad field of psychiatric information, including biological, psychological, sociological, medical, and mental health problems related to psychiatry.

57. *General Psychology, Journal of* Devoted to theoretical, experimental, historical, and physiological psychology with briefly reported replications, refinements, and comments.

58. *Genetic Psychology, Journal of* Publishes articles concerned with evolutionary processes, child behavior, comparative behavior, and ethology. Nature of articles: research.

59. *Genetic Psychology Monographs.* Devoted to developmental, comparative, and clinical psychology.

60. *Genetics, The American Journal of Human* (The American Society of Human Genetics). A record of research and reviews relating to heredity in man and to the applications of genetic principles in medicine, anthropology, psychology, and the social sciences. (See 15.)

61. *Geriatric Psychiatry, Journal of* Articles of psychiatric, psychological, and sociological issues dealing with the aging population.

62. *Geriatrics Society, Journal of The American* (Official monthly journal of The American Geriatric Society). Includes articles on various research aspects of developing problems in the elderly.

German language journals (See 4, 70, 107, 145, 180.)

63. *Gerontology, Journal of* (Quarterly journal of The Gerontological Society). Publishes original research in biological sciences, clinical medicine, psychological and social sciences, social research, planning, and practice. Preference is given manuscripts containing observational data. (See 5.)

64. *Group Psychotherapy.* Articles published on all methods of group psychotherapy and psychodrama.

65. *Group Psychotherapy, International Journal of* General articles on group therapy, plus book reviews. Also considers case histories and specific approaches to therapy.

66. *Health and Social Behavior, Journal of* (American Sociological Association, continuation of the *Journal of Health and Human Behavior* since 1967). Publishes papers that analyze those aspects of social life that bear on human health and welfare. Its central approach is sociological in nature, defining and analyzing problems of human welfare and the institutions and occupations devoted to diagnosing and managing them.

67. *Heredity, Journal of* (Published bimonthly by the American Genetic Association). Articles must be original in nature and slanted toward promoting a knowledge of the laws of heredity and their application to the improvement of plants, animals, and human welfare. (See 60.)

68. *History of Science, The British Journal for The* (Published by The British Society for the History of Science and is the official organ of the Society: Oxford, England). A journal designed to further the study of the history of science, often presenting new information about historical events and/or people. (See 77.)

69. *History of the Behavioral Sciences, Journal of* Articles on general theories of behavior and on empirical research specifically oriented to such theories. Interdisciplinary approach to problems of behavior is stressed with special emphasis placed on mental health and disease.

70. *Human Development: International Research Quarterly* (Formerly, *Vita Humana,* Basel, Switzerland, text in English, French, and German). An international research journal publishing material relating to mental and physical growth and general development from infancy to old age.

71. *Human Factors* (Human Factors Society). Original articles relating man to the machine, and environmental factors in all their ramifications, pure and applied. Evaluative reviews of pertinent literature, definitive articles on methodology and procedure, quantitative and qualitative approaches to theory, technical articles of original research, specific and unusual case histories and articles that stress utilization of information.

72. *Humanistic Psychology* Concerned with the publication of sophisticated experiential reports, theoretical papers, research studies, applications of humanistic psychology, and humanistic analyses of contemporary culture. Topics of special interest: authenticity, encounter, self-actualization, creativity, personal growth, search for meaning, love, identity, and commitment.

73. *Human Relations, Journal of* Interdisciplinary approach toward scientific research, psychosocial awareness, and practical programs.

Indian journals (See 157, 185.)

74. *Individual Psychology, Journal of* Adlerian emphasis on holistic, phenomenological, teleological, field-theoretical, and social approaches to psychology.

75. *Industrial Psychology, Journal of A* quarterly professional periodical containing articles reporting the results of research on personnel selection and placement, executive and supervisory development, employee training, human errors and accidents, worker morale and motivation, and psychological aspects of consumer behavior.

76. *Interpersonal Development* An international journal for humanistic approaches to group psychotherapy, sensitivity training, and organizational development.

77. *Isis* (Official journal of the History of Science Society of The Smithsonian Institution). An international review devoted to the history of science and its cultural influence. (See 68.)

Japanese journals (See 145, 160.)
Jewish journals (See 192.)

78. *Language and Language Behavior Abstracts* A multidisciplinary quarterly reference work providing access to the current world literature in language and language behavior.

79. *Learning and Motivation.* Original experimental theoretical papers addressed to the analysis of basic phenomena and mechanisms of learning and motivation. Studies involving infra-human subjects favored over those on human subjects.

80. *Learning Disabilities, Journal of* Multidisciplinary. International in scope. Includes articles concerned primarily with children's difficulties in learning school subjects, but also serves as a clinical exchange.

81. *Life Sciences* (Oxford, England). Provides an international medium for the rapid publication of preliminary communications in the Life Sciences. Its primary aim is to link research workers in many disciplines by presenting their findings to other workers in the same or related fields. Papers are published in two parts: 1. pharmacology and physiology; 2. biochemistry, general biology, and molecular biology.

82. *Marriage and the Family, Journal of* (formerly *Marriage and Family Living*). A medium for presentation of original theory, research interpretation, and critical discussion of materials related to marriage and the family.

83. *Mathematical Psychology, Journal of* Publishes papers describing original theoretical and empirical research in all areas of mathematical psychology.

84. *Mathematical Statistics, The Annals of* (The Official Journal of the Institute of Mathematical Statistics). The Institute encourages the development, dissemination, and application of mathematical statistics, the Annals being a major force in this purpose.

85. *Medical Genetics, Journal of* (Published quarterly by the British Medical Association). Articles are primarily research-oriented and concerned with the medical aspects of genetic problems.

86. *Medical Psychology, British Journal of* (The medical section of the *British Journal of Psychology*.) Original technical articles on schizophrenia, therapeutic techniques, hysteria, suicide, alcoholism, etc.

87. *Mental Deficiency, American Journal of* (Published bimonthly by the American Association on Mental Deficiency). An endeavor is made to select articles that will provide opportunities for presentation of new points of view concerning mental retardation.

88. *Mental Deficiency Research, Journal of* (Published quarterly by the National Society for Mentally Handicapped Children). Articles, primarily research in nature, are concerned with the education and psychological treatment of mentally deficient children.

89. *Mental Health Bulletin, World Federation for* (Switzerland, text in English and French). Articles about mental health collected from throughout the world, including original articles. Also publishes papers presented at its annual meeting.

90. *Mental Health, Canada's* (Published bimonthly in both English and French by the Department of National Health and Welfare, Ottawa). Directed to professionals and informed laymen to assist in the further development and improvement of Canadian mental health facilities and services. Descriptive articles dealing with clinical psychology, education, social work, vocational training and rehabilitation; also includes reviews, news items, general information, and statistics.

91. *Mental Health Journal, Community* Devoted to emergent approaches in mental health research, theory, and practice as they relate to the community, broadly defined. Mental health is seen as more or less congruent with the general concept of social well-being.

92. *Mental Hygiene* (National Association for Mental Health). An interdisciplinary journal concerned with all aspects of prevention and treatment of mental illness and promotion of mental hygiene.

93. *Mentally Retarded, Education and Training of the* (Published quarterly by the Division on Mental Retardation, The Council for Exceptional Children, NEA). As the official journal of the Division, it proposes to advance the education and welfare of the mentally retarded and to support research in the education of the mentally retarded.

94. *Mental Retardation* (American Association on Mental Deficiency). Various articles on mental retardation in general, child welfare programs for the mentally retarded, film reviews, rehabilitation programs, and material on the adult retarded. Also contains convention and seminar news, and other Association business.

95. *Mental Retardation Abstracts* (Published quarterly by the Superintendent of Documents, Washington, D. C.). Includes abstracts, annotated bibliographies, and reviews of the literature in the fields of medicine, clinical psychology, social work, education, language and speech, and includes information on vocational training and rehabilitation, institutional programs, and recreation.

96. *Motor Behavior, Journal of* Deals exclusively in motor behavior, and organized to provide understanding of human motor performance upon which solutions to problems in industry, psychology, and sport must ultimately depend.

97. *Music Therapy, Journal of* Quarterly publication. Original investigations and theoretical papers, descriptive or statistical, that will bring something new to music therapy.

98. *National Education Association Journal* Articles of a descriptive nature concerned with education and community programs; includes general information.

99. *Nervous System, Diseases of the* A practical journal on psychiatry and neurology. Includes experimental studies and discussions on biochemical, neurological, and psychiatric aspects of nervous system diseases.

100. *Neurochemistry, Journal of* (Oxford, England). Devoted to original findings in neurochemistry, favoring those with a direct bearing on the chemistry of the nervous system; also considers any paper containing new information of potential interest and value to neurochemists.

101. *Neurological Sciences, Journal of the* (Official Bulletin of the World Federation of Neurology).

102. *Neurology and Psychiatry, Digest of* Abstracts and reviews of selected literature in psychiatry, neurology, and their allied fields. (See 39.)

103. *Neurology, Archives of* (Published monthly by the American Medical Association). Includes articles on medical research and clinical observation of neurological phenomena.

104. *Neurology, The Journal of Comparative* Publishes original articles on the anatomy and physiology of the nervous system. Includes clinical neurology, neuropathology, psychiatry, and introspective psychology unless these bear on the anatomy and physiology of the nervous system.

105. *Neuropharmacology* An international journal with articles concerning studies of actions of drugs and biologically active substances on the central and peripheral nervous systems of animals and man.

106. *Neurophysiology, Journal of* (Published bimonthly by The American Physiological Society). Aims to provide a channel for publication of original contributions on the function of the nervous system, peripheral and central Papers on pure morphology or neuropathology are not acceptable. Psychological and zoological studies will be considered only if primarily experimental in character.

107. *Nordisk Psykologi* (psychological societies in Denmark, Finland, Norway, and Sweden; text in Danish, English, German, and Norwegian). Operates as a clearing house for publishing articles of Scandinavian countries, primarily in the areas of general, theoretical, and experimental psychology.

108. *Occupational Psychology* (London). General articles on occupational training, programmed instruction, and managerial studies.

109. *Occupational Therapy, American Journal of* Published bimonthly by the American Occupational Therapy Association. Articles are descriptive in nature covering such material as psychology, sociology, recreation, and institutional programs as relating to occupational therapy.

Oriental journals (See 139, 145, 160.)

110. *Orthopsychiatry, American Journal of* Dedicated to fostering the better understanding and effective treatment of human behavior disorders as well as improving community mental health. Articles are selected on basis of originality, adequacy of method, significance of findings, contribution to theory, and clarity and brevity of presentation. Includes special sections on opinions, theory and reviews, research articles, and clinical material.

111. *Parapsychology, International Journal of* (text in English; summaries in French, German, Italian, and Spanish). Publishes laboratory experiments concerned with extrasensory perception and psychokinesis, as well as so-called spontaneous phenomena (telepathy, clairvoyance, and precognition).

112. *Parapsychology, Journal of* A scientific quarterly dealing with extrasensory perception, the psychokinetic effect, and related topics. Also publishes reviews of literature relevant to parapsychology, criticisms of published works, proposals for research, theoretical and philosophical discussions, and new methods of mathematical analysis, as space allows.

113. *Pastoral Psychology.* Practical synthesis of concepts of counseling, dynamic psychiatry, and psychology with spiritual and religious values.

114. *Perception and Psychophysics.* Experimental investigations of sensory processes, perception, and psychophysics.

115. *Personality and Social Psychology, Journal of* (APA journal). Theoretical and research papers on personality dynamics, group processes, and the psychological aspects of structure.

116. *Personality, Journal of* Devoted to scientific investigations in the field of personality. Current stress is upon experimental studies of behavior dynamics and character structure, personality-related consistencies in cognitive processes, and the development of personality in its cultural context. Although scope of the journal is not fixed, most of its contributions are empirical in nature. (See 126.)

117. *Personality, Journal of Experimental Research in* Experimental studies in the field of personality and related fields basic to the understanding of personality.

118. *Personnel and Guidance Journal.* Articles dealing with current problems and trends in personnel and guidance work. Includes significant practical and critical attempts at synthesizing research and theory.

119. *Personnel Psychology.* Accepts manuscripts on research methods, research results, or the application of research results to the solution of personnel problems in business, industry, and government.

Pharmacology (See 19, 105.)

120. *Physiology, American Journal of* (Published monthly by the American Physiological Society). Articles deal with significant new research in some area of physiology. (See 35, 106, 123.)

121. *Physiology and Behavior.* An international journal. Original work which relates behavior and neurophysiology, reflects current trends and techniques in research.

122. *Physiology, Annual Review of* Abstracts of articles, primarily concerned with pain, vision, central nervous system studies, endocrine glands, cell membranes, and gross visceral physiological functioning.

123. *Physiology, Journal of Applied* (Published monthly by the American Physiological Society). (See 120.)

124. *Physiology, The Journal of General* (Official monthly organ of the Society of General Physiologists). Publishes technical articles on general physiology, but does not publish notes or brief communications.

125. *Professional Psychology* (APA journal). A publication responsive to concerns of students, educators, researchers, and practitioners whose work involves meeting human needs on an individual, group, or community basis. Devoted to the application of principles and skills in a wide variety of settings: clinics, hospitals, schools, industry, government, and independent practice.

126. *Projective Techniques and Personality Assessment, Journal of* (official organ of the Society for Projective Techniques and Personality Assessment, Inc.). Devoted to study and advancement of projective and other assessment techniques.

127. *Psychiatric Association Journal, Canadian.* Original articles of a technical nature on interviewing techniques and therapy, clinical notes, EKG studies, suicide problems, schizophrenia, and medication for psychiatric conditions.

128. *Psychiatry* (Journal for the Study of Interpersonal Processes). Articles provide a medium for communication between psychiatry, the social sciences, and all other branches of the study of man. Presents accounts of clinical and field observations, reports of original research, surveys, and critiques of scientific literature, as well as studies concerning methodology, epistemology, and philosophy.

129. *Psychiatry, American Journal of* (American Psychiatric Association). Publishes papers from the diverse reports, theoretical and applied, made at the annual meeting of the Association. Nature of articles: research and descriptive.

130. *Psychiatry, British Journal of* (official organ of the Royal Medico-Psychological Association; formerly *Journal of Mental Science*). Technical articles on clinical psychiatry, biochemical and metabolic disorders, organic psychoses, personality disorders, and some general topics on psychiatry; theoretical papers.

131. *Psychiatry Digest* (incorporating the *Journal of Clinical and Experimental Psychopathology*, and *Quarterly Review of Psychiatry and Neurology*, and *Psychiatry Abstracts*.) A monthly summary of the world's psychiatric literature for psychiatrists and other professionals in related fields.

132. *Psychical Research, The Journal of the American Society for* Publishes research and investigations of claims of telepathy, clairvoyance, precognition, retrocognition, veridical hallucinations, dowsing, and other forms of parapsychological, psychic, or paranormal phenomena.

133. *Psychics International.* An international quarterly of psychic and yogic research.

134. *Psychoanalysis, American Journal of* Dedicated to communicating modern concepts of psychoanalytic theory and practice and related investigations in allied fields. Addressed to everyone interested in the understanding and therapy of emotional problems.

135. *Psychoanalytic Association Journal, American* (Official organ of the American Psychoanalytic Association). Publishes papers from diverse reports of its members.

136. *Psychoanalytic Review.* An American journal of psychoanalytic psychology devoted to the understanding of behavior and culture. Articles are general in nature.

137. *Child, Psychoanalytic Study of the* Articles on mental retardation, memory, developmental processes, child psychoses, ego development, drug-taking adolescents, children's reactions to trauma, etc.

138. *Psychobiology, International Journal of* Original papers, critical reviews, and reports or proceedings of international conferences serve as a forum for the accelerated publication of multidisciplinary studies of the biophysical, biochemical, and neuro-endocrine mechanisms underlying the development of integrated adaptive reactions for psycho-environmental changes.

139. *Psychologia* An international journal of psychology in the Orient. As a channel of communication and feedback from the East to the West and as a forum for international discussion, *Psychologia* publishes symposia, general surveys, reviews, brief reports, notes and discussion, world news, as well as some representative original works in very broad fields of psychology.

140. *Psychological Abstracts.* (APA journal). Noncritical abstracts of the world's literature in psychology and related subjects. Published monthly with an Annual Cumulative Index. Approximately 20,000 abstracts published annually.

141. *Psychological Bulletin* (APA journal). Evaluative critical reviews and summaries of research literature, discussions of research methodology in psychology. Articles intend to bridge gap between the technical statistician and the typical research psychologist. Articles feature new and creative methodology.

142. *Psychological Issues.* Publishes diversified source materials that may contribute to a general psychoanalytic theory of behavior; controlled developmental studies, from clinical or experimental investigations, or from the genetic explorations of psychoanalytic therapy.

143. *Psychological Record.* A quarterly journal in theoretical and experimental psychology, with commentary on current developments in psychology and description of research planned or in progress. Papers favored that develop new approaches to the study of behavior, and which undertake critiques of existing approaches and methods.

144. *Psychological Reports.* Encourages scientific originality and creativity in the field of general psychology. It is primarily for the researcher who is first a psychologist, then a specialist. Carries experimental, theoretical, and speculative articles of scientific merit. Also publishes comments and special reviews, with a listing of new books and other material received.

145. *Psychological Research, Japanese* Original experimental articles (with text in English, French, and German) contributed by members of the Japanese Psychological Association, the only representative organization of Japanese psychologists in all fields.

146. *Psychological Review.* (APA journal). Original contributions of a theoretical nature.

147. *Psychologist, American* (APA journal). Includes official papers of the Association, archival documents, comments, notes and news, convention calendar, and timely articles of broad interest to psychologists.

148. *Psychologist, Australian* Devoted to the general activities of the Australian psychologist, including business reports, convention calendars, and topics of general concern to the profession.

149. *Psychologist, The Canadian* (Official papers and proceedings of the Canadian Psychological Association), with notes and comments on psychological affairs, evaluative reviews likely to be of general interest, and psychological theory of technical significance. Resembles *American Psychologist* in content.

150. *Psychologist, Counseling* (Division of Counseling Psychology of the APA). Quarterly journal of professional opinion dealing with contemporary issues in counseling; each issue being devoted to a major statement or problem (such as campus unrest), which is subjected to a critical analysis by prominent scholars or practitioners, with the lead writer then given a chance to respond.

151. *Psychology, American Journal of* Oriented toward and largely devoted to experimental psychology, but includes material in all fields of scientific psychology. Also contains book reviews, book listings, discussions, and notes on and descriptions of apparatus.

152. *Psychology, Annual Review of* Prepared by highly qualified specialists in each selected field for those engaged in teaching and research. Each review endeavors to offer a critical evaluation of current research on the subject covered.

153. *Psychology, Australian Journal of* (Published by Australian Psychological Society). Articles of general nature, concerning learning theory, sensory experiences, spatial discrimination, personality studies, etc. Also contains a review section.

154. *Psychology, The British Journal of* Contains diverse articles of general interest, ranging from such topics as serial learning and psychological effects of food to brain studies.

155. *Psychology, Canadian Journal of; Revue Canadienne de Psychologie* (published by the Canadian Psychological Association). Experimental and theoretical articles of general nature in all recognized fields of psychology. Also printed in French.

156. *Psychology, Contemporary* (APA journal). Critical reviews of books, films, and research material in the field of psychology.

157. *Psychology, Indian Journal of* (official organ of the Indian Psychological Association). Original articles either applied or experimental, dealing with motivation, neuropsychological factors, social psychology, and sensory investigations.

158. *Psychology in the Schools.* A journal devoted to research, opinion, and practice. Articles range in appeal from the theoretical and other problems of the school psychologist to those directed to others in the teaching profession.

159. *Psychology, International Journal of/ Journal International de Psychologie* (Paris). Devoted to cross-cultural, comparative, and cooperative research in general, genetic, and social psychology throughout the world. Interested in laboratory or field studies of comparative nature, surveys, and experimental replications. Its emphasis is on basic research and theory rather than technical or applied aspects, but its theoretical or methodological orientation is toward cross-cultural research. Also includes an international platform for psychologists, providing mutual exchange of news and opinions on psychology.

160. *Psychology, Japanese Journal of* (A journal of Japanese Psychological Association). A representative bimonthly journal of psychology in Japanese with English summaries.

161. *Psychology, Scandinavian Journal of* (Psychological Associations of Scandinavia; text in English). Original scientific contributions in all fields of psychology.

162. *Psychometrika* Devoted to the development of psychology as a quantitative rational science.

163. *Psychonomic Science.* Provides a medium for the publication of brief reports of research. Much of the work reported will subsequently appear as longer, more formal articles in archival journals. Contributions limited to approximately 1200 words or their equivalent in illustrative material. Subject matter includes significant, scientific contributions in any area of psychology, but the principal emphasis is on general experimental psychology.

164. *Psychophysiology* (formerly *Journal of Objective Research in the Physiology of Behavior*). Fosters original research relating to psychology and physiology.

165. *Psychosomatic Medicine* (Journal of the American Psychosomatic Society). A bimonthly publication with articles related to the psychological aspects of physical illnesses; covering the broad spectrum of medical practice and of interest to all physicians, psychiatrists, psychologists, and other professionals who wish to deal with their patients in a more psychologically sound manner.

166. *Psychosomatics* (Official publication of the Academy of Psychosomatic Medicine). An international journal exploring the role of psychiatry in the daily practice of comprehensive medicine.

Psychotherapy (See 11, 64, 65.)

167. *Psychotherapy, Journal of Contemporary* Brief, original papers in individual and group psychotherapy, psychiatry, psychoanalysis, casework, and allied mental health disciplines.

168. *Psychotherapy: Theory, Research and Practice* (The quarterly journal of the Psychotherapy Division of the American Psychological Association). Research articles, but also specializes in direct description of cases with emphasis on the therapist describing the problems and choices he was up against.

169. *Psychotherapy, American Journal of* (Official Organ of the Association for the Advancement of Psychotherapy). Contains articles dealing with various aspects of psychotherapy, including book reviews, abstracts of forthcoming articles as well as some on foreign publications.

170. *Reading Research Quarterly.* General articles dealing with testing and diagnosing reading abilities and problems (with emphasis on experimental testing and research programs).

171. *Rehabilitation, Journal of* (official publication of the National Rehabilitation Association). Concerned with problems of a medical and psychological nature,

speech therapy and social work, the blind, the deaf, and the crippled. Also outlines state and federal programs.

172. *Rehabilitation Literature* (Published monthly by the National Society for Crippled Children and Adults). Descriptive articles pertaining to rehabilitation problems, including vocational outlook and contributions from clinical psychology, medicine, and social work. It is intended for use by professional personnel and students in all disciplines concerned with the rehabilitation of the handicapped. As a reviewing and abstracting journal it identifies and describes current books, pamphlets, and periodicals pertaining to the care, welfare, education, and employment of handicapped children and adults.

Scandinavian journals (See 2, 107, 161.)

173. *Science.* (Published weekly by the American Association for the Advancement of Science). Brief articles on research reports covering entire field of science, plus letters to the editor and reviews.

174. *Scientific American.* A monthly publication that serves a dual purpose: (1) as a scientific journal for fellow scientists; and (2) as a magazine of science that fills the "gap between the specialized journal of the professional press and incidental coverage of science in the general press." Articles usually provide the background of a scientific investigation and explain how the scientists framed their theories, designed their experiments, applied their methods, and arrived at their conclusions.

175. *Scientist, American* (Published bimonthly by the Society of the Sigma Xi in the interest of scientific research). Articles are broad in scope including all the sciences.

176. *School Psychology, Journal of* Publishes articles on research, opinion, and practice in school psychology, with aim of fostering its continued development as a science and profession.

177. *Social and Clinical Psychology, British Journal of* Publishes articles dealing with group and social interaction, attitude studies, learning and motivation, as well as those in the clinical area of mental disorder, therapy, personality dimensions, and gerontological and delinquency research. Nature of articles: research and descriptive.

178. *Social Casework.* (Published by the Family Service Association of America). Descriptive articles on casework, social work and institutional and community programs.

179. *Social Issues, Journal of* Publishes articles in an attempt to bring theory and practice into focus on human problems of the group, the community, and the nation as well as the increasingly important ones that have no national boundaries. Each number is devoted to a single topic and has as its goal the communication of scientific findings and interpretations in a relatively non-technical manner but without the sacrifice of professional standards.

180. *Social Psychiatry* (Germany; text in English, French, and German). Provides medium for the prompt publication of scientific contributions concerned with the effects of social conditions upon behavior and the relationship between psychiatric disorder and the social environment.

181. *Social Psychology, Journal of* Devoted to studies of persons in group settings and of culture and personality, special attention to cross-cultural studies and to briefly reported replications and refinements.

182. *Social Psychology, Journal of Experimental* Scientific investigation of social interactions and related phenomena, reflecting current significant research in various areas of social psychology. Preference given to experimental studies and to theoretical analysis closely related to empirical data.

183. *Social Work* (Published quarterly by the Journal of the National Association of Social Workers). Descriptive articles on problems faced in social work and discussions on programs of an institutional and community nature.

184. *Social Work, Journal of Education for* (Council on Social Work Education). Concerned with education for the field of social welfare--trends, new developments, issues, problems--at the undergraduate, master's degree, and post-master's levels.

185. *Sociological Bulletin, Indian* An international quarterly of sociology and social science. Publishes results of various studies of current social problems, and original articles and research papers of reputable social scientists.

186. *Sociological Review, American* (official journal of the American Sociological Association). Articles of general sociological significance and those that pertain strictly to the Association and its members. Includes book reviews, opinions, etc.

187. *Sociologist, The American* (Publication of the American Sociological Association). Articles are general in nature, opinions primarily professional in attitude, dealing with ASA news, employment bulletin, calendar of annual meetings, etc.

188. *Sociology* (Journal of The British Sociological Association). Publishes papers which, reflecting the interest of the Association, range over a wide field, covering the sociology of economic development, education, the family, race relations, industry, leisure, rural and urban life, etc.

189. *Sociology, American Journal of* Articles are broad in scope, primarily research-oriented but also descriptive. Includes book reviews, commentaries, and editorial opinions. (*See* 42.)

190. *Sociology of Education* Provides a forum for studies of education by scholars in all the social sciences from all parts of the world. Dedicated to fostering this interdisciplinary approach in analyzing educational problems and institutions and in making constructive recommendations for improvement.

191. *Sociology, Rural* (Official journal of The Rural Sociological Society). Attempts to promote development of rural sociology through research as expressed in the journal.

192. *Sociology, The Jewish Journal of* (London). Published twice yearly on behalf of the World Jewish Congress. Articles, primarily descriptive in nature, must be original; also includes book reviews, a chronicle of Jewish events of a sociological nature, and biographical material on contributors.

193. *Sociometry.* Concerned with the entire range of interests and problems in social psychology. Central focus is upon the investigation of processes and products of social interaction and the subsequent development of significant empirical and theoretical generalizations.

194. *Soviet Psychology.* Selected articles from Soviet scholarly journals, translated in unabridged form into English and taken mainly from eight Soviet publications, but from others as well if the articles are considered to be of sufficient general interest.

195. *Soviet Psychology and Psychiatry.* A quarterly journal in translation which contains unabridged articles from all major Soviet journals in the fields of psychology and psychiatry which best reflect Soviet development in these areas, and which are of most interest to those professionals concerned with these fields.

196. *Special Education Review* Descriptive articles and reviews on special education in the United States.

197. *Speech and Hearing Disorders, Journal of* (Published quarterly by the American Speech and Hearing Association). Articles report educational and psychological research on hearing problems and language and speech.

198. *Speech and Hearing, The Journal of* Articles concerned with clinical research, case studies, remedial procedures, counseling and re-education methods, techniques of evaluation, and related matters in the field of speech pathology and audiology. Articles of opinion and "critical" and "tutorial" articles of a scholarly nature are also encouraged.

199. *Statistical Association, Journal of the American* (Official journal of the American Statistical Association). Articles apply statistical methods to practical problems, stressing the development of more useful methods and in publishing material that helps improve basic statistical data.

200. *Statistician, The American* (Published by the American Statistical Association). A journal devoted to the statistical profession. Includes articles of a technical and semi-technical nature, with personal news and notes, letters to the editor, and questions and answers concerned with a discussion of conceptual and measurement problems.

Therapy (See 16, 17, 97, 109.)

201. *Verbal Learning and Verbal Behavior, Journal of* Laboratory studies of human learning, psycholinguistics, and related disciplines. Main emphasis is on experiments and experimental studies.

Worm Runner's Digest (See 21.)

Foreign Alphabets

GERMAN Upper and Lower Case		GREEK Print and Script		RUSSIAN Upper and Lower Case	
А а	(a)	Α α Alpha	(a)	А а	(a)
Ӓ ä	(e)	Β β Beta	(b)	Б б	(b)
В b	(b)	Γ γ Gamma	(g)	В в	(v)
С с	(k, ts, s)	Δ δ Delta	(d)	Г г	(g)
Ch ch	(H, kh)	Ε ε Epsilon	(e)	Д д	(d)
D d	(d)	Z ζ Zeta	(z)	Е е	(ye)
E e	(e, a)	Η η Eta	(a)	Ж ж	(zh)
F f	(f)	Θ θ Theta	(th)	З з	(z)
G g	(g, kh)	Ι ι Iota	(e)	И и	(i, e)
H h	(h)	Κ κ Kappa	(k)	Й й	(e) 2
I i	(i, e)	Λ λ Lambda	(l)	К к	(k)
J j	(y)	Μ μ Mu	(m)	Л л	(l)
K k	(k)	Ν ν Nu	(n)	М м	(m)
L l	(l)	Ξ ξ Xi	(ks)	Н н	(n)
M m	(m)	Ο ο Omicron	(o)	О о	(o, o)
N n	(n)	Π π Pi	(p)	П п	(p)
O o	(ō, ö)	Ρ ρ Rho	(r)	Р р	(r)
Ö ö	(o)	Σ σ ς Sigma	(s) 1	С с	(s)
P p	(p)	Τ τ Tau	(t)	Т т	(t)
Qu(u) qu(u)	(kv)	Υ υ Upsilon	(u, oo)	У у	(oo)
R r	(r)	Φ φ Phi	(f)	Ф ф	(f)
S ſ s	(s, z) 1	Χ χ Chi	(H)	Х х	(kh)
Sch ſch	(sh)	Ψ ψ Psi	(ps)	Ц ц	(ts)
T t	(t)	Ω ω Omega	(o)	Ч ч	(ch)
U u	(oo)			Ш ш	(sh)
Ü ü	(u)			Щ щ	(shch)
V v	(f)			Ъ ъ	3
W w	(v)			Ы ы	(e)
X x	(ks)			Ь ь	4
Y y	(e, u)			Э э	(e)
Z z	(ts)			Ю ю	(u)
				Я я	(ya)

(Approximate sounds of the letters are shown in parentheses.)

[1] The final form is used only as the last letter of a word.

[2] Used only as the second vowel in a diphthong.

[3] Indicates nonpalatalization of a preceding consonant.

[4] Indicates palatalization of a preceding consonant.

The Language of Science

The language of psychology, like any other scientific language and indeed a vast portion of the English language in general, is primarily built from word elements (the root bases with prefixes and suffixes attached), originally Greek and Latin.

Column one of Table A contains a select list of these elements, sampled from the glossary of this book. Column two provides one or two literal meanings for the specific application to the key words given in the third column.

Refinements of inflection or word form in the original language are not explored. No distinction is made between Latin and Greek origins, nor are finer differences indicated between affixes and combining-forms. It seems unrealistic to labor over the mood of a Greek verb or the case of a Latin noun that enters into a modern compound. The intention of the list is to supply a practical ready-guide to a likely meaning of a word.

Knowledge of the meanings of word elements should help students recall the sense of a word temporarily forgotten or furnish a clue to the meaning of a word newly encountered. As practice, select some of the example words given in the third column of Table A and form your own literal meaning from the supplied word elements in the first column. Then compare with the more complete meanings given in the main body of the dictionary. There is no better reinforcement for learning word meanings and concepts, however, than to practice using them in context.

Prefixes as used in the **International System of Units (IS)** are included in the prefix table on p. 166.

Table A

Word Element*	Literal Meaning (Denotative)	Key Word to Check in Main Entry	Word Element*	Literal Meaning (Denotative)	Key Word to Check in Main Entry
a-	lacking; without	achromatism	-caud-	tail	cephalocaudal
ab-	away from	abnormal	ceph(alo)-	head	cephalocaudal
ac-	to; toward	acquisition	-cept-	received	perception
-aceous	in the nature of	camphoraceous	cerebr(o)-	brain	cerebrotonia
acet-	vinegar	acetylcholine	-chol-	bile	acetylcholine
acou(st)-	hearing	acoustic nerve	-chondr-	cartilage	hypochondria
acro-	height; extremity	acrophobia, acromegaly	chrom(o)-	color	chromosome
			chron(o)-	time	chronoscope
act(u)-	a doing	self-actualization	-cip(a)-	receive; take	anticipatory
ad-	toward, adjacent to	adrenal	-clis(is)	lean	anaclisis
-ad	pertaining to	monad	co-	together; equal	co-twin
aden(o)-	gland	adenohypophysis	cogn-	know	cognition
aesthes(io)-	See esthes-		collic-	hill	colliculus
af- (from ad-)	toward	afferent	con-	with	contiguity
ag- (from ad-)	toward	aggression	contra-	opposite	contraharmonic
-agog(ue)-	leading to	hypnagogic	corp-	body	corpus
agor(a)-	open place	agoraphobia	cort-	outer layer	cortex
-al	pertaining to	adrenal	counter-	opposite	counter-transference
alb-	white	albedo			
ald(o)-	aldehyde	aldosterone	-creas	flesh	pancreas
-alg(es)-	pain	algolagnia	-crin(e)	separate	endocrine
alien(at)-	foreign; strange	alienation	crypt(o)-	hidden	cryptomnesia
allo-	another	allokurtic	-cumul-	a heap	accumulator
amaur(o)-	dark	amaurotic	cycl-	circular	cycloscope
ambi-	both; around	ambivert	cyt(o)-	cell	cytoarchitectonics
ambly-	dim	amblyopia	de-	away from	decortication
ampli-	spacious; maximum	amplitude	dendr-	tree	dendrite
amygdal-	almond	amygdala	deuter(o)-	second	deuteranope
an-	without	anosmia	dextr(o)-	right	dextroamphetamine
an(a)-	up; upon	anabolism			
anankast-	fate	anankastic	di-	two	dichromatism
-ance	quality of	luminance	di(a)-	between	diencephalon
-and	one subjected to	analysand	dipl-	double	diplopia
andr(o)-	man; maleness	androgen	-dips-	thirst	adipsia
anomal(o)-	irregular	anomalous	dis-	opposite of; absence of	disinhibition
ante(ro)-	prior	anterograde	dolicho-	long	dolichocephalic
anthrop(o)-	man; human being	anthropomorphism	dom-	condition	dominant
anti-	against	antidromic	-drom(e)	a running	syndrome
apo-	away; offshoot	apoenzyme	-duc(t)-	leading	abducens
-apse	fasten	synapse	du(o)-	two	dualism
apti-	fitness	aptitude	dura	hard	dura mater
arachn-	spider; spider's web	arachnoid	dy-	two	dyad
arche-	primitive	archetype	dynam(o)-	power; energy	dynamics
arc(u)-	a bow	arcuate	dys-	bad; faulty	dyslalia
-ar(y)	situated at; related to	basilar; binary	eco-	home	ecological
asthen-	weak	asthenia	ecto-	outside	ectoderm
-ate	processing	caudate	-edo	quality of being	albedo
-ation	process	fixation	ef- (from ex-)	outside	efferent
audi(o)-	hearing	audiogenic	-ellum	diminutive	cerebellum
-aur-	ear	binaural	em-; en-	in	empathy; enzyme
aut(o)-	self; itself	autism, autochthonous	-(h)em-	blood	anoxemia
			-ence	process; quality of	transference
-bas-	step	astasia-abasia	encephal(o)-	brain	encephalé
bi(n)-	two; twice; double	bilateral, binary	end(o)-	within	endoderm
bi(o)-	life	biodynamic	-ent	one who	client
-bol-	throwing	metabolism	ep(i)-	upon	epilepsy
bou-	ox; cattle	boulimia	-er	one who; that which	transducer
-boul-	will	aboulia	erg(o)-	work	ergograph
brachy-	short	brachycephaly	-esis	process	amniocentesis
brady-	slow	bradycardia	esthes(io)-	feeling; sensitivity	esthesiometer
bu-	variant of bou-		eth-	custom; behavior	ethology
-card-	heart	bradycardia	eu-	good; well	euphoria
cat(a)-	down	catabolism	ex(o)-	external	exocrine
	lower	catelectrotonus	extra-	outside	extrapyramidal
cathex-	holding fast	cathexis	-fec(t)	make	affect

Table A (Continued)

Word Element*	Literal Meaning (Denotative)	Key Word to Check in Main Entry	Word Element*	Literal Meaning (Denotative)	Key Word to Check in Main Entry
-fer-	bear; carry	transference	lumin-	light	luminance
fili(a)-	son; relation	filial	lute-	yellowish	luteinizing
-fiss-	cleft	fissure	-lys(is)	dissolve; loosen	analysis
foll-	bellows	follicle	macr-	large	macrocephaly
-fract-	break	refractory	-mate-	act; move	automated
galact-	milk	galactosemia	mater	mother	dura mater
gam-	marriage	gamete	med-	middle; marrow	median, medulla
gangl-	knot	ganglion	-meg(al)-	large	acromegaly
-gen(e)	producing	androgen	mei(o)-	less	meiosis
gen(o)-	ancestry	genotype	melan-	black	melancholia
gloss(o)-	speech; language	glossolalia	menin-	membrane	meninges
-glyph	relief carving	anaglyph	-ment-	mind	amentia
gno(s)-	knowledge	agnosia	-ment	act, result	assessment
gonad-	testis, ovary	gonadotrophic	meso-	middle	mesoderm
gracil-	slender	gracile	met(a)-	change	metabolism
-gram-	record of	electroencephalogram	-metr(y)	measurement	psychometry
-graph	writing; writer	electroencephalograph	micr-	tiny	microcephaly
-greg-	flock; collection	aggregate	-mim(e)	imitator	psychotomimetic
-gress-	going; walking	aggression	-mne (m or s)-	memory	amnesia
gyr-	circular	gyrus	-mod-	measure, manner	bimodal
haben-	rein	habenula	mono-	one	monocular
hapt-	touch	haptometer	-morph	form; shape	ectomorph
heb(e)-	youth; puberty	hebephrenia	my(o)-	muscle	myogram
helic(o)-	a spiral	helicotrema	-nat(e)	born	neonate
hemi-	half	hemianopia	neo-	new	neologism
heter(o)-	other; different	heterozygote	neur(o)-	nerve	neurosecretion
hol-	complete; whole	holistic	-noi-	mind; thought	paranoia
hom(e)o-	resembling	homeostasis	-nom-	custom; law	autonomic
homo-	earth, soil; man	homunculus	-nom(i)-	name; term	binomial
homo-	identical, same	homozygous	ocul(o)-	eye	oculomotor
hydr(o)-	water	hydrocephaly	-oid	resembling	thyroid
hyper-	excessive	hyperalgesia	-ology	science of	psychology
hypn-	sleep	hypnosis	-om- (from [h]om-)	even; same	anomalous
hyp(o)-	under, below; deficient	hypothalamus; hypomania	-one	indicates ketone	aldosterone
hyster-	womb	hysteria	onto-	being; existing	ontogenesis
-ia	disorder, condition	hemianopia	-op(ia)	eye condition; vision	hemianopia
iatr(y)-	physician; healing	psychiatry	opistho-	behind	opisthotonus
-ic(al)-	pertaining to	prototaxic; psychological	-or	one who; that which	accumulator
-icle	little	utricle	-orex-	appetite	anorexia
-ic	relating to	psychogenic	orth(o)-	straight; correct	orthopsychiatry
-ics	study or practice	dynamics	-ory	having function of	anticipatory
-id	particle of; body structure	chromatid	-os(e)-	sugar; carbohydrate	galactosemia
ideo-	idea	ideokinetic	-osis	abnormal condition	psychosis
idio-	individual; personal	idiopathic	-osm-	sense of smell	anosmia
-ig(u)-	to drive	ambiguous	oss-	bone	ossicle
-il(e)	pertaining to	percentile	-otic	similar to; relating to	neurotic
im-; in-	in	imprinting; induction	ot(o)-	ear	otolith
-in(e)	extract (loose usage)	cortin	-ous	characterized by	anomalous
infra-	below	infrahuman	-ox(y)-	oxygen	anoxemia
insul(o)-	island	insulin	paleo-	ancient	paleocerebellum
inter-	between	interview	pan-	all	pancreas
intr(o)-	within	introjection	par(a)-	abnormal; beside	paranoia
-iod-	violet	iodopsin	-path(o)	suffering; disease	psychopath
-ion	act; process	regression	per(i)-	around	peripheral
-ism	doctrine; condition	animism; hypertelorism	-phag-	eat; hunger	aphagia
iso-	equal	isoscope	-phas-	speech	aphasia
-ist	one who practices	psychologist	phen-	appear	phenotype
-ite	segment; part of bodily process	dendrite	pher(o)- (cf. fer-)	carry	pheromone
-ity	condition	authenticity	-phob(o)-	fear	acrophobia
-jec(t)-	throw	projection	phon-	sound	phonometer
-jus(t)-	correct	adjusting	phot-	light	photopia
juxta-	near; beside	juxtallocortex	phren(o)-	mind	phrenology
kin(es)-	action; movement	kinesimeter	physi(o)-	growth; nature	physiological
kurt-	curved	kurtosis	pia	soft	pia mater
-lagn-	lust	algolagnia	pituit-	phlegm	pituitary
-lal-	speak	glossolalia	-plasm	formative material	endoplasm
-lat-	removing	ablation	platy-	broad; flat	platykurtosis
-later-	side	bilateral	pons	bridge	pons
-leps(y)	a seizure	catalepsy	potenti-	power	action potential
lept(o)-	peaked; thin	leptokurtosis; leptosome	-prax-	performance	apraxia
leuc(o)-	white	leucotomy	pre-	before	prefrontal
levo-, levu-	left	levorotatory	presby-	old person	presbyopia
-lex-	word; speech	alexia	prim-	first	primitivation
-lim-	hunger	boulimia	pro-	forward; in front of	projection
limin-	threshold	subliminal	proprio-	one's own	proprioceptor
-lith(o)	stone	otolith	prot-	first; primary	protanopia
lob(o)-	lobe	lobotomy	proxim-	nearest	proximal
-logy	study of	psychology	pseudo-	false	pseudoscope
			psych(o)-	mind; personality	psychergograph
			pykn-	thick	pyknic
			quadri-	four	quadrigeminal
			-quis(i)-	get; gain	acquisition
			re-	back; again	reaction

Table A (Continued)

Word Element*	Literal Meaning (Denotative)	Key Word to Check in Main Entry	Word Element*	Literal Meaning (Denotative)	Key Word to Check in Main Entry
-ren-	kidney	suprarenal	tel(e)-	far	telepathy
ret-	net; network	reticular	tele(o)-	end; purpose	teleology
retro-	backward; behind	retroactive	tetra-	four	tetrachoric
-rrhe(o)-	flowing	antirrheoscope	-therapy	treatment	psychotherapy
scala	scale; ladder	scala	therm(o)-	heat	thermesthesiometer
schiz(o)-	split	schizophrenia	-thyr-	shield	parathyroid
-sciss-	cut	abscissa	-tion	condition	reaction
-scop(e)	viewer	stroboscope	-tom(y)	cutting; surgery	lobotomy
scot(o)-	darkness	scotopic	-ton-	muscle tension	catatonia
sema-	sign	semantics	top-	region	topectomy
semi-	half	semicircular	toxic-	poison	aggregate
sial(o)-	saliva	sialometer			toxicity
-soci-	companion	association	trans-	across	transducer
-solut(e)	dissolved, loose	absolute	troph-	nourishment	trophotropic
som(at)-	body	somatotonia			function
-spect-	look; view	introspection	trop(o)-	turn; bend	tropostereoscope
-stas-	stable; fixed	homeostasis	-tude	quality of being	attitude
-ster-	site	allosteric	-ula	little	habenula
stere(o)-	three-dimensional	stereoscope	val-	worth; strength	valence
-sthen-	strength	psychasthenia	vect-	carry	vector
-stra(ct)-	draw	abstraction	veri-	truth	veridical
strepho-	twisted	strephosymbolia	-vers-	turn	introversion
sub-	less than; under	subvocal	vir-	man; adult male	eviration
super-	above; higher in quality, quantity, or degree	superego	viscer-	internal organs	viscerotonia
			vitr(o)	glass	in vitro
supra-	above; higher than	suprarenal	-y	condition; sickness	acromegaly
syn-	together	syndrome	-yl-	organic acid	acetylcholine
tach(isto)-	very rapid	tachistoscope	zyg(o)-	yoke; union	zygote
-tax-	arrangement	ataxia			

*Note: Certain liberties have been taken with the hyphenization of the word elements, some of them being made to relate to the position of the word element as found in the examples given in column three. Prefixes are hyphenated after the word elements, suffixes before: e.g., ad- is a prefix, but -ad is a suffix. Stems or stem-forms that have both prefixes and suffixes are hyphenated both before and after the word element.

Latin Words and Phrases Used in Psychology

The following list has been obtained from an examination of over 500 books, journals, and other publications of a psychological nature dating only from 1955.

Literal meanings or those not completely naturalized into English are italicized. Commonly used abbreviations precede their respective entries.

Latin phrases and abbreviations are most often found in footnotes and special citations. Although some Latin phrases are rapidly being replaced by English equivalents (such as *above* for *supra; in place cited* for *in loco citato*), they are described here because of their still frequent appearance.

Greek is not specially listed as most of these terms have become Latinized or absorbed into English. However, a number of Greek words (as well as French and German) are listed in the dictionary section of this book.

Table B
Latin Terms and Abbreviations

ab extra	*From without.* From the outside.
ab intra	*From within.*
ab ovo	*From the egg.* From the beginning; from inception.
ad hoc	*For this;* with respect to this. Referring to a special committee set up *for this* one purpose, or *with respect to this* (particular problem).
ad hominen	*To the man;* for personal reasons. An appeal based on a personal involvement or selling point.
ad litteram	*To the letter.* Exactly, literally.

c., ca.	*Circa, circiter; about.* Approximately, referring to dates that are uncertain (e.g.: Galen, A.D., *ca.* 130-*ca.* 200), but *ca.* dates are more exact than dates marked ?.
cet par.	*ceteris paribus; other things being equal.*
cf., cfr.	*Confer,* imper. of *conferre, to compare.* To compare or contrast with another term so as to weigh their parallel features. Contrast refers usually to a comparing of differences.
cit.	*Citatus;* cited.
corrigendum (pl. *corrigenda*)	A corrected error or one to be corrected. *Corrigenda* are usually inserted as an extra sheet or list in a book after its printing.
c.s.	*Cum suis: with collaborators.*
de facto	*In fact.* As it actually is, regardless of legal or moral considerations. Distinguished from *de jure.*
de gustibus (non est disputandum)	*There is no disputing one's tastes.*
de jure	*By law, by right.* In accordance with the law. Distinguished from *de facto.*
de novo	*Anew.* Once more, again, fresh. From the beginning.
e.g.	*Exempli gratia: for example.*
ejusd.	*Ejusdem: of the same author.*
entia non sunt multiplicanda praeter necessitatem	Concepts (descriptions) should not be multiplied unnecessarily. See **Occam's razor.**
e.p.	*Ex parte: from the side.*
ephialtes	*Nightmare.* See dictionary section.

et al.	*Et alibi: and elsewhere, Et alii: and others.*
et alibi	*And elsewhere.*
et alii	*And others.*
et seq.	*Et sequens: and the following.* See *ff.*
et seqq., et sqq.	*Et sequentes; et sequentia: and those that follow.*
et sic porro	*And so on.*
et ux	*Et uxor: and wife.*
exempli gratia;	*For example. By way of,* or for the sake of example.
ex mero motu	*Of one's own free will.*
ex parte	*From the side.* A one-sided statement; interested in one side only.
f. (pl. ff.)	*Folio: and the following page.*
f., fig., Fig.	*Figura; figure,* illustration. E.g.: t.4, f.3 = Plate 4, Figure 3.
fil.; F_1, F_2, etc.	*Filius: son:* filial generations (genetics).
ib., ibid.	*Ibidem, in the same place.* Usually abbreviated in a footnote to avoid duplication of source data (as author, title) in a reference immediately preceding.
ic.	*Icon:* illustration.
id.	*Idem: the same.*
idem quod	*The same as.*
id est	*That is; namely.*
i.e.	*Id est: that is;* namely.
index locorum (nominum, rerum)	*Index of places* (names, references).
ined.	*Ineditus: unpublished.*
in esse	*In existence.*
infra	*Below.*
in init, in initio	*In the beginning.*
in limine	*On the threshold;* at the limits.
in loc. cit.	*In loco citato: in the place cited.*
in loco parentis	*In place of a parent.*

Table B
Latin Terms and Abbreviations (Continued)

in re	*In reference to; in regard.*	*p.* (pl. *pp.*)	*Pagina;* page.	*s.l.*	*Sensu lato: in a broad sense; sine loco: no place.*
in situ	*In its original place.* See dictionary section.	*pari passu*	*At an equal pace;* with equal speed. *At an equal step;* at a like distance.	*s.n.*	*Sine numero: without a number,* unnumbered.
inter alia	*Among other things.*	*pars pro toto*	*A part for the whole.* See dictionary section.	*s. str.*	*Sensu stricto:* in a narrow sense.
inter vivos	*Among the living.*				
in toto	*In all;* completely.	*passim*	*Throughout.* In various parts, as of a book. Here and there. (Use sparingly.)	*sic*	*Thus, precisely as given.* Generally used within brackets to show that a quoted passage is verbatim, even including errors.
in utero, in ventre	*In the womb.*				
in vitro	*Inside glass; within glass.* Observable in a test tube.	*per se*	*By itself.* By, in, and of itself. Inherently.		
		post partum	*After birth,* a bringing forth.	*sine qua non*	*Without which, not.* An indispensable condition; absolutely necessary.
ipse dixit	*He himself said so.* An appeal to authority, since it is an assertion made but not proved.	*p.r.n.*	*Pro re nata:* as the thing is born. On prescriptions—as the occasion or need arises; said of therapy need.		
				sphalm	*Sphalmate: by mistake,* mistakenly.
ipsissima verba	*The identical words;* verbatim.	*proximo*	*In the next* (month). In or of the next month.	*ssp*	*Subspecies.*
ipso facto	*By the fact itself;* by the very nature of the case.	*p.m.*	*Plus minusve: more or less.*	*stet*	*Let it stand* (from *stare, to stand*). A printer's direction indicating that a word or other material previously marked out should be restored to its original condition and position.
i.q.	*Idem quod:* the same as.	*p. mag. p.*	*Pro magna parte:* for the great part.		
l.c., loc. cit.	*Loco citato:* at the place cited.	*p.p.*	*Pro parte:* partly, in part.		
mens sana in corpore sano	*A sound mind in a sound body.* A concept popularized by the Roman poet Juvenal (c. 60-140 A.D.) but held by many earlier philosophers.	*q.e.*	*Quod est:* which is.		
		Q.E.D.	*Quod erat demonstrandum;* that which is to be demonstrated or proven.	*stridor dentium*	See **bruxism** in dictionary section.
		qua	*As; in the character or quality of.*	*sui generis*	*Of his or her own kind.* Individual, unique.
modus operandi	*Mode of operation.* Method of doing things.	*quae vide*	*Which see.* Pl. of *quod vide.* A direction to look up the items referred to elsewhere in the work. See *q.v.*	*summum bonum*	The ultimate, ethical ideal or goal of human behavior.
modus vivendi	*Mode of living.* Temporary way of life while waiting for a permanent settlement.			*supra*	*Above.*
				t., tab	*Tabula:* plate.
MS, MSS.	*Manuscriptum, manuscripta: manuscript, nanuscripts.* No period after MS unless it refers to a specific manuscript.	*quid nunc*	*What now?* Often combined as one word in referring to a busybody or gossip.	*t. tom*	*Tomus:* volume.
				terminus ad quem	The end to which; aim; goal, such as Sherrington's use of it in referring to the final common path or terminal path—"the limb muscle is the *terminus ad quem* of nervous arcs.'
		quid pro quo	*Something for something.* Tit for tat; substitute.		
multum in parvo	*Much in small.* A condensation or digest.	*q.v.*	*Quod vide:* which see.		
		R, R	*Recipe; take.* Supposedly a distortion of Jupiter's sign, χ, which had been used to influence the gods to write prescriptions.		
N.B.	*Nota bene; note well.* Pay particular attention.			*U. i.*	*Ut infra: as below,* as cited below.
ne plus ultra	*No further.* The summit of achievement.			*undulatis reflexa*	Nervous action, as used by **Descartes.** *See* nerve.
nom.	*Nomen:* name.	*re*	*In the matter or case of.* As regards.	*U. s.*	*Ut supra: as above,* as cited above.
obiter dictum	*Said in passing.*	*s.a.*	*Sine anno: without date of publication.*	*V.*	*Vide.* See or consult.
o.d.	*Omni die:* every day.			*Vade mecum*	*Go with me.* A handy volume; an easy reference book.
op. cit.	*Opere citato,* or *opus citatum;* in the work cited.	*sc., scil.*	*Scilicet:* from *scire licit:* it is *permitted to know;* namely; to wit; that is to say.		
oxon.	*Oxoniensis; Oxonia:* of Oxford. Noted after degrees granted by Oxford University of England.			*Verisim.*	*Verisimiliter: probably*
		s.d.	*Sine die:* no date.	*V. g.*	*Verbi gratia: as for example.*
		sec.	*Secus, secundum:* following, according to; section.	*vide supra*	*See above.* See previous reference.
		sequitur	*It follows.*	*viz.*	*Videlicet:* namely.

Word Association List

In 1910, a list of 100 stimulus words was published, which since that time has become known as the **Kent-Rosanoff Word Association List.** This list was often used by psychiatrists and psychologists as a test for studying verbal behavior resulting from the responses made by patients or other subjects. As a means of obtaining valuable information about the personality, it seemed to be particularly promising, but other than providing some interesting exercises in experimental and clinical psychology, few studies of significance emerged over the years.

In 1964, Palermo and Jenkins published a study on word association norms from grade school through college, using the 100 words on the original Kent-Rosanoff list and adding 100 new stimulus words of their own. Their objectives were to "broaden the scope of the norms available at the college level . . . (to study the development and changes of language and associative habits), and to enable a clinical evaluation of the associative norms" over a wide age range, and to provide raw data for studying "recall, learning, perception, and generalization."

Since the Kent-Rosanoff list consists mainly of singular nouns and simple adjectives,

Palermo and Jenkins (to fulfill the need of greater flexibility and of broadening the noun base), in their additional "100 words, systematically sampled verbs, pronouns, adverbs, etc., which occur at relatively high frequency levels in the speech and writing of children and young adults." They placed emphasis and importance upon responding with: (*1*) only one word, (*2*) the first response that came to mind, (*3*) no concern about spelling, and (*4*) speed of responding.

Table C

Stimulus Words, with Parts of Speech *

1.	Table (noun)
2.	Dark (adjective)
3.	Music (noun)
4.	Sickness (noun)
5.	Man (noun)
6.	Deep (adjective)
7.	Soft (adjective)
8.	Eating (verb, participial form)
9.	Mountain (noun)
10.	House (noun)
11.	Black (adjective)
12.	Mutton (noun)
13.	Comfort (transitive verb)
14.	Hand (noun)
15.	Short (adjective)
16.	Fruit (noun)
17.	Butterfly (noun)
18.	Smooth (adjective)
19.	Command (transitive verb)
20.	Chair (noun)
21.	Sweet (adjective)
22.	Whistle (intransitive verb)
23.	Woman (noun)
24.	Cold (adjective)
25.	Slow (adjective)
26.	Wish (transitive verb)
27.	River (noun)
28.	White (noun)
29.	Beautiful (adjective)
30.	Window (noun)
31.	Rough (adjective)
32.	Citizen (noun)
33.	Foot (noun)

*From *Word Association Norms: Grade School Through College*, by David Palermo and James J. Jenkins. Copyright 1964 by the University of Minnesota Press and reprinted by permission.

34. Spider (noun)
35. Needle (noun)
36. Red (noun)
37. Sleep (intransitive verb)
38. Anger (noun)
39. Carpet (noun)
40. Girl (noun)
41. High (adjective)
42. Working (verb, participial form)
43. Sour (adjective)
44. Earth (noun)
45. Trouble (transitive verb)
46. Soldier (noun)
47. Cabbage (noun)
48. Hard (adjective)
49. Eagle (noun)
50. Stomach (noun)
51. Stem (noun)
52. Lamp (noun)
53. Dream (noun)
54. Yellow (noun)
55. Bread (noun)
56. Justice (noun)
57. Boy (noun)
58. Light (noun)
59. Health (noun)
60. Bible (noun)
61. Memory (noun)
62. Sheep (noun)
63. Bath (noun)
64. Cottage (noun)
65. Swift (adjective)
66. Blue (noun)
67. Hungry (adjective)
68. Priest (noun)
69. Ocean (noun)
70. Head (noun)
71. Stove (noun)
72. Long (adjective)
73. Religion (noun)
74. Whiskey (noun)
75. Child (noun)
76. Bitter (adjective)
77. Hammer (noun)
78. Thirsty (adjective)
79. City (noun)
80. Square (noun)
81. Butter (noun)
82. Doctor (noun)
83. Loud (adjective)
84. Thief (noun)
85. Lion (noun)
86. Joy (noun)
87. Bed (noun)
88. Heavy (adjective)
89. Tobacco (noun)
90. Baby (noun)
91. Moon (noun)
92. Scissors (noun)
93. Quiet (adjective)
94. Green (noun)
95. Salt (noun)
96. Street (noun)
97. King (noun)
98. Cheese (noun)
99. Blossom (noun)
100. Afraid (adjective)
101. Dogs (plural noun)
102. At (preposition)
103. Sell (transitive verb)
104. Always (adverb)
105. And (conjunction)
106. That (adjective)
107. Cry (intransitive verb)
108. Only (adjective)
109. Doors (plural noun)
110. Hotter (adverb)
111. On (preposition)
112. Is (intransitive verb)
113. Quickly (adverb)
114. A (adjective, indefinite article)
115. Carry (transitive verb)
116. However (adverb)
117. Very (adverb)
118. Appear (intransitive verb)
119. You (pronoun)
120. Salty (adjective)
121. Cars (plural noun)
122. Because (conjunction)
123. Oh (interjection)
124. Running (verb, participial form)
125. He (pronoun)
126. Find (transitive verb)
127. Of (preposition)
128. Then (adverb)
129. People (plural noun)
130. Although (conjunction)
131. What (pronoun)
132. Live (intransitive verb)
133. Broader (comparative adjective)
134. There (adverb)
135. Get (intransitive verb)
136. Why (adverb)
137. For (preposition)
138. Was (intransitive verb)
139. Or (conjunction)
140. Hardly (adverb)
141. Children (plural noun)
142. It (pronoun)
143. In (preposition)
144. Sit (intransitive verb)
145. Younger (comparative adjective)
146. With (preposition)
147. Take (transitive verb)
148. Easier (comparative adjective)
149. Go (intransitive verb)
150. How (adverb)
151. But (conjunction)
152. Lift (transitive verb)
153. They (pronoun)
154. Guns (plural noun)
155. Who (pronoun)
156. If (conjunction)
157. Come (intransitive verb)
158. Thinner (comparative adjective)
159. From (preposition)
160. Kittens (plural noun)
161. Me (pronoun)
162. Now (adverb)
163. See (transitive verb)
164. Faster (comparative adjective)
165. Playing (verb, participial form)
166. I (pronoun)
167. Farther (adjective)
168. Speak (intransitive verb)
169. Where (adverb)
170. As (adverb)
171. Shoes (plural noun)
172. To (preposition)
173. Am (intransitive verb)
174. Clearer (comparative adjective)
175. Ah (interjection)
176. Become (intransitive verb)
177. The (adjective, definite article)
178. By (preposition)
179. Stand (intransitive verb)
180. His (pronoun)
181. Make (transitive verb)
182. Closer (comparative adjective)
183. So (adverb)
184. Numbers (plural noun)
185. We (pronoun)
186. Over (preposition)
187. Slowly (adverb)
188. Jump (intransitive verb)
189. My (pronoun)
190. This (pronoun)
191. Tell (transitive verb)
192. An (adjective, indefinite article)
193. Buying (verb, participial form)
194. Here (adverb)
195. Fingers (plural noun)
196. Us (pronoun)
197. Therefore (adverb)
198. Have (transitive verb)
199. Quietly (adverb)
200. Him (pronoun)

Explanatory Notes on the Organization and Form of the Dictionary Entries

Main Entries

All dictionary entries have been entered in strict alphabetical order and as such also serve as an index. Entry words containing an Arabic numeral are alphabetized as if they were spelled out (1 as one, 5 as five, etc.). Main entries are usually in the noun or substantive form. In a term like coefficient of correlation the definition is given at the entry point rather than under a cross referral at correlation, coefficient of.

Boldfaced type within a definition indicates a main entry word that can be found in its proper alphabetical order in this book. The name of a person important in the development of a concept, an inventor of an instrument, etc., also appears in boldfaced type referring the reader to his brief biography in the regular alphabetical listing.

In general, terms are defined organizationally in the following manner:

a. *Etymology.* Scientific terms of Latin or Greek origin usually have a brief, literal translation immediately after the entry to reinforce the meaning of the more extensive psychological definition that follows. If applicable, the psychological definition may also include the cue words from the etymology. The English literal translation is followed in parentheses with its Latin or Greek origin.

b. *Body of the definition.* Sometimes, in those cases where such information has been available, the earliest definition historically of the word is listed first, otherwise a general description is given. In either case, the introductory definition is followed by the more specific and limited use of the term in psychological literature.

c. *Historical and biographical information*— including first usage of the term, person(s) responsible for term or concept, appropriate date(s), change in meaning—is usually placed in a separate paragraph at the end of an entry.

d. *References or citations.* There are two forms of references, both enclosed within parentheses. A parenthesis within the body of a definition refers only to the word, phrase, or quotation immediately preceding it. Parenthetical references at the end of an entry refer the reader to either (1) a more elaborate treatment of the subject or a major source of the information contained within the entry (in which case the reference is fully described) or, (2) a mention of only the author's last name and page number(s), the full reference being found in the reference list at the end of the book.

Abbreviations

Usually, except to prevent confusion, abbreviations appear in unspaced capital letters. They are listed alphabetically with reference made to the expanded term for definition. In those few instances where the abbreviation is more readily recognized than the full term (LSD rather than lysergic acid diethylamide, for example), the abbreviation is defined.

Variants

When there are two or more variants of a term, the one first mentioned is preferred. For example, the preparation of the anterior pituitary hormone is correctly spelled *corticotrophin*, but the misspelling of *corticotropin* seems to be even more frequently used. Here, however, although the purity of the hormone is not threatened, the purity of the literal meaning definitely is, and therefore the spelling of *corticotrophin* is preferred.

Combining Forms

Table A lists most of the Greek or Latin combining forms used in this book for etymological purposes, also giving an example word for reference.

Cross References

Cross references, indicated by boldfaced type, implicate words that may (1) occur within the definition; (2) follow the verb *see*, referring to another entry in this book that has some relation, direct or indirect, to the original entry; (3) follow *compare*, for a term that is similar or parallel in meaning; (4) follow *same as*, indicating that the word or term is identical in meaning to and therefore defined at the original entry; or (5) follow *contrast with*, signifying that careful distinctions are to be made between one entry and another of somewhat similar but crucially different meaning. In order to save space and reduce repetition, words or terms within the body of an entry are cross-referenced to the singular noun entry, regardless of whether they are in the possessive case, in the plural form, or in some other part of speech.

Acronyms and Portmanteau Words

Acronymic words, such as *WISC* (for *W*echsler *I*ntelligence *S*cale for *C*hildren), have the first letters of the critical words in italics to indicate the derivation of the acronym.

Portmanteau words, such as FORTRAN, have the segments of the words making up the new word italicized (*for*mula *trans*lator), indicating origin.

Foreign Word Entries

Entries specifically foreign in nature (other than Latin) are followed by a parenthesis indicating the language origin (e.g., *Fr., Ger.,* etc.) with a brief literal meaning preceding the more extended definition.

Eponymous Terms

Terms that have become identified with a person's name (such as Down's syndrome and Pearson's *r*) are first defined conceptually and then followed by brief, identifying information about the person.

Special Usage

Sometimes, a word has several interpretations in various disciplines as well as different meanings within psychology itself. In such cases, immediately following the main entry the specialized origin or use of such a term appears within parentheses; for example, a term limited to its psychoanalytic meaning is indicated as (Psychoanal.), and a term strictly defined in its existential sense is set off as (Exist.). Terms that have been derived from such specialized usage but that have become accepted and adopted as part of the general vocabulary are not so marked off.

Biographical Information

Biographical information is provided in several ways:

1. Eponymous terms, whether classical or contemporary (such as Skinner box, Down's syndrome, Occam's razor), have biographical information described at the end of the appropriate entry. Material elsewhere relating to the biographee is referred to the eponymic term instead of the man.

2. Contributors to the history of psychology who are not necessarily professional psychologists (Aristotle, Freud, Hobbes, etc.) are listed under their respective names with references to their special contributions that are described elsewhere in this book.

3. Contemporary psychologists (dating from about 1900) are identified briefly if their contributions to psychology are mentioned prominently in the psychological literature and if their names, concepts, or theories are referred to in this book.

Dictionary of Terms

A

a

AAAS **American Association for the Advancement of Science.**

AAAS **Socio-Psychological Prize** An annual prize of $1000 granted by the AAAS for a meritorious essay in sociopsychological inquiry. The prize was established in 1952 by the late Arthur F. Bentley and "is offered to encourage studies and analyses of social behavior based on explicitly stated assumptions or postulates which lead to experimentally verifiable conclusions or deductions" and which is intended to encourage "the development and applications of dependable methodology analogous to the methods that have proved so fruitful in the natural sciences." The contribution should "further the comprehension of the psychological-social-cultural behavior of human beings—the relationships of these hyphenated words being an essential part of the inquiry." Purely theoretical and empirical studies are not eligible. Further information may be obtained from AAAS Socio-Psychological Prize, 1515 Massachusetts Avenue, NW, Washington, D. C. 20005.

Prize Winners (Psychologists)

1956   Herbert G. Kelman (born 1927). Ph.D. Yale 1951. For his essay "Compliance, Identification, and Internationalization: A Theoretical and Experimental Approach to the Study of Social Influence."

1957   Irving A. Taylor (born 1925). Ph.D. NYU 1954. For his essay "Similarities in the Structure of Extreme Social Attitudes."

1959   Stanley Schachter (born 1922). Ph.D. Michigan 1950. For his essay "The Psychology of Affiliation."

1960   Robert Rosenthal (born 1933). Ph.D. UCLA 1956. For his essay "Three Experiments in Experimenter Bias," written in collaboration with Kermit Fode (born 1934), Ph.D. N. Dakota 1967.

1961   Morton Deutsch (born 1920). Ph.D. MIT 1948. For his essay "Experimental Studies of Interpersonal Bargaining," written in collaboration with Robert M. Krauss.

1963   William J. McGuire (born 1925). Ph.D. Yale 1954. For his essay "Immunization against Persuasion."

1964   Stanley Milgram (born 1933). Ph.D. Harvard 1960. For his essay "Some Conditions of Obedience and Disobedience to Authority."

1967   Irving Janis (born 1918). Ph.D. Columbia 1948. For his essay "Effects of Fear Arousal on Attitude Change: Recent Developments in Theory and Experimental Research."

1970   Elliot Aronson (born 1932). Ph.D. Stanford 1959. For his essay "Some Antecedents of Interpersonal Attraction."

abaissement (Fr., abasement, humiliation.) **Janet**'s term for the inability, because of physical or psychological exhaustion, to obey the **id**'s demands.

abasement Quality of (-ment) increasing (a-, French prefixes only) one's feeling of lowness (-base-). One of **Murray**'s psychogenic needs, driving a person to feel guilty, submissive, sorry for himself, inferior, and to be resigned to his fate (Murray, 1938, pp. 152-226).

ABBA order (ABBA sequence) An experimental method involving the comparison of only two values (A and B) of the **independent variable** that are compared with one another in the following balanced order ABBA. Basic is the assumption that a constant change (increase or decrease) in the successive positional order of the independent variable will influence the **dependent variable** so that order effects are neutralized.

For example, in an experiment to determine whether a sequence of seven telephone digits (839-1607) can be learned as readily as those preceded by letters (VE9-1607), the two values of the independent variable "telephone numbers" are A for the numbered sequence and B for the prefixed digits. Then, two similar lists of A values and two of comparable B values are constructed, with the subject being required to learn in order a number sequence A, a prefix sequence B, the other prefix sequence B, and the other number sequence A, thus ABBA, assuring that order effects will be neutralized over the two values of an independent variable (D'Amato, 1970, pp. 49-51).

abducens nerve Either one of the pair of **cranial nerve** VI, consisting of **motor** fibers that arise from the **pons** and lead (-duc-) to the rectus lateralis muscle which pulls the eye's pupil away from (ab-) the midline of the body.

Discovered in 1564 by **Eustachius**. Named abducent nerve (1713) by William Derham (1657-1735), English biologist and physicist.

ablation Act of (-ion) excising or removing (-lat-) an organ or part away from (ab-) the complete body; excision of part of the brain; removal of an animal's **sensory** receptors so as to observe his behavior. Suction is the preferential method today for ablation of any neural tissue that can be reached by a pipette (a glass or metal tube through which tissue is sucked by means of a vacuum pump).

abnormal psychology Referring to (-al) that area of **psychology** concerned with behavior that deviates away from (ab-) the norm (-norm-), such as studying the theoretical aspects of mental and **personality** disturbances (by diagnosis, definition, and prognosis), and serving as the framework for the practice of **clinical psychology**.

aboral Pertaining to (-al) that which is away from (ab-) or opposite to the mouth (-or-). *See* **anatomical directions.**

aboulia, abulia A chronic disorder (-ia) of having no (a-) will (-boul-); indecision, loss or lack of ability to concentrate or "will" to do something.

Term apparently coined in 1833 by English surgeon Robley Dunglison (1798-1869), who included the word in his *New Dictionary of Medical Science and Literature*. **Janet**, in his lectures, began (1903) using the term as a feeling of helplessness, associated with **psychasthenia**.

ABPP American Board of Professional Psychology.

abreaction An emotional reaction occurring in time and place away from (ab-) the original action or **stimulus**, produced by intensely reliving the initial situation in feeling, action, or imagination. The conscious recollection, release, or resolution of repressed emotional tensions (through verbalizing, acting out, etc.), aided by a **psychotherapist**, that enables the patient to become aware of the nature of the conflict that produced the **repression**.

The term was first used (1892) by **Freud** in a letter to his friend Wilhelm Fliess (1858-1928), the German physician (Josef Breuer and Sigmund Freud, Studies on Hysteria, *Basic Books*, 1957, p. 8n).

Abschlussexamen Final (Abschluss) examination. *See* **Vorexamen.**

abscissa That part of the infinitely long horizontal reference axis in a two-dimensional chart that is cut (-scissa) away (ab-) by a plotted point; by extension, the horizontal axis. *See* **polygon.**

When data are plotted on a two-dimensional graph, such **independent variables** as time and number of trials are scaled on the horizontal axis or abscissa; and such **dependent variables** as scores and numbers of responses are scaled on the vertical axis or ordinate; the measures written in the order (X, Y) that locate the point on these two scales are called the co-ordinates of a point.

Originally, the word, resembling its present meaning, was used by the Italian mathematician, Stephano degli Angeli, 1623-1697.

Absicht (Ger. purpose, intention.) A certain purposeful relationship between what **Narziss Ach** called **Bezugsvorstellung** (idea of objects) and **Zielvorstellung** (idea of goal or purpose).

absolute frequency distribution. *See* **frequency.**

absolute limen *See* **detection threshold.**

absolute luminosity The quality of being able to radiate or reflect light, expressed in absolute terms, such as **lumens** per watt.

absolute number *See* **real number.**

absolute refractory (period) phase The momentary interval, accompanying the passage of the **spike potential**, during which time a nerve fiber cannot transmit another impulse regardless of the strength of the stimulus.

absolute threshold *See* **detection threshold**, the more modern term.

absolute value The number of units that a point on a number scale deviates from the zero point, regardless of its direction. The value of a quantity disregarding its sign, as opposed to an algebraic value. The absolute value, for example, of a **real number**, a, written $|a|$, equals a if a is positive and $-a$ if a is negative. Whether a is -3 or 3, its absolute value is the magnitude 3. An *absolute value computer* processes all data in absolute values.

Concept devised and named (1881) by English mathematician, Arthur Cayley (1821-1895).

abstraction The process through which generalizations are formed from properties of things or conditions held in common. It results in loss of information whether a set of **data** is described or a distribution itself is grouped or simplified. Abstraction ability is often defective or missing in brain-injured people who have a difficulty seeing relations. In **statistics**, abstraction is the basic process for recording and communicating information. In **learning**, the generic aspect of abstraction emphasizes the common essentials of the material at the expense of the details.

Académie de Médecine A select French organization whose medical members can be elected to membership only after having achieved distinction.

Académie des Sciences The highest academic honor in France. An exceptionally select organization of scientists whose members can only be selected for membership after having achieved "immortality."

acceptance region A prescribed area in statistical decision-making into which a set of **outcomes** falls, indicating acceptance rather than rejection of the **null hypothesis.**

accessory nerve Cranial nerve XI, the spinal accessory nerve of **Willis**. Part of its **efferent** fibers originate in the **medulla**, while an additional **accessory** root originates in the **anterior** grey column of the cervical spinal cord. The nerve innervates muscles of the neck, shoulder, soft palate, and vocal organs. Some of its fibers join the **vagus nerve.**

Both **Vesalius** and **Eustachius** mentioned the nerve, but Willis named and better described it in 1664.

accessory structure Unique body, belonging to any of certain receptors, that assists or may take over a specific function of that receptor. Examples are the **Pacinian corpuscle** the pressure receptor of the skin and jelly-like **tectorial membrane** of the ear, both of which mediate, complement, and implement a particular stimulus. The Pacinian corpuscle itself has no intervening receptor cell; however, either the stimulus alone or the accessory structure can activate the receptor cells (such as the retinal **rods** and **cones** or the **cochlea**'s hair cells). Transduction for the Pacinian corpuscle is mechanical; that for the rods and cones is photochemical.

a

accidental sampling A **sampling** procedure whereby sampled individuals are selected from the **population** without attempting to make the sample either purposive or **random**. For example, if all pupils in a school constitute a population, an accidental sampling would be obtained if an investigator took the pupils found in the lunchroom at a chance moment during the meal period or a crowd of pupils in the northeast corner of the playground or the pupils sitting in the back row of the auditorium. Accidental samples of this sort are also called **chunk samples** and opportunistic samples.

accommodation Act or process (-tion) of being fitted (-commoda-) to (ac-) something. In physiology, an automatic adjustment of the curvature of the lens by the ciliary muscles so that light rays are focused on the **fovea** for continual sharp images. Such change compensates for the distance of the object from the observer, the lens becoming more convex for near objects and flattening out for far objects. As an aid in depth perception, accommodation is effective up to about 20 feet. It also refers to the adjustment of a nerve fiber to a constant **stimulus**, and to the changes in cells that permit them to live under altered conditions.

In 1637, **Descartes** explained accommodation as resulting from changes in the crystalline lens, comparing the eye to a **camera obscura**. In 1801, Thomas Young showed that changes in the curvature of the lens accounted for the eyes' accommodation factors.

According to **Piaget** (1950), accommodation as a process occurs when new environmental demands cause the child to alter his cognitive structures while attempting to cope with his experience. *See* (3) *under* **cognitive growth theories**.

accumulator (Comput.) A specialized register or part of the logical-arithmetic unit in the **processor** (the actual site of the computations performed by the computer) that serves as temporary storage; basic computer instructions relate to the accumulator. In general, often used for storage of intermediate operations (e.g., forming algebraic sums).

acetyl Acid (acet-) stuff or matter (-yl from "hule"); the hypothetical, univalent radical (CH_3CO) of acetic acid.

Term coined in 1839 by **Liebig**, but for a different radical.

acetylcholine (ACh) The **acetyl** derivative of **choline**. A chemical transmitter substance liberated at effector terminals of the **parasympathetic** and **sympathetic** divisions of the **autonomic nervous system**. Its liberation to skeletal muscles by somatic **motor** nerves at endplate terminals **(synaptic knobs)** enables transmission of nerve impulses to muscle fibers, and presumably from one **neuron** to another; also, along with **dopamine** and **serotonin**, acetylcholine plays a neurotransmitter role in the **limbic system**. Medicinally, ACh stops hemorrhaging and induces labor.

Acetylcholine was synthesized by **Baeyer** in 1867. In 1914, it was identified in certain extracts of ergot (ACh being its active principle) by the English physician, Arthur James Ewins (born 1882). **Loewi** and **Dale** shared the Nobel prize in 1936, primarily for showing the role of acetylcholine in the chemical transmission of the **nerve impulse**. *See* **acetylcholine esterase, cholinergic, cholinesterase, Vagusstoff, transmitter substance**.

acetylcholine esterase (AChE) A family of enzymes (-ase) that speeds destruction or inactivation of the ester of acetylcholine so that acetylcholine can be hydrolyzed to **choline** and acetic acid at the **synapse**, enabling the synaptic mechanisms to rest and be recycled again for future use. Acetylcholine esterase limits the duration of neuronal response to the chemical transmitter released at synapses (Thompson, 1967, pp. 12, 122-123).

Ach, Narziss (1871-1946) German experimental psychologist. Associated with **Würzburg School**. Characterized own work as "systematic experimental introspection." Scientifically studied elements and activities of consciousness. Used **determining tendency** to describe way his subjects seemed to acquire an unconscious set after receiving instructions. Concerning nonverbal and non-sensory thought processes, he used the term **Bewusstheiten** (awareness), to show that they were the conscious aspect of memory contents. In general, Ach believed that thought contains unconscious and unanalyzable components. *See* **Absicht, Brentano, Ehrenfels, Külpe**.

achievement motivation An inferred specialized characteristic of a human being that is learned early in life, causing him to strive for bigger and better accomplishments. Achievement is generally considered to be a significant social goal and, as such, an incentive that pressures people to strive for higher standards.

To measure achievement motivation, a group of Harvard psychologists carried on research using a modified **thematic apperception** technique. Subjects were asked to create stories about sets of pictures presented to them. From their creations a **need achievement score** was obtained, indicating a measure of the strength of their achievement motivation. Lack of high achievement motivation probably indicates the subject's low need for successful accomplishment as well as his high need either to avoid failure or to forget failure experiences (McClelland, et al, 1953).

achievement test A standardized examination (such as the American College Testing Program, ACTP, used for college admission purposes) that assesses the proficiency level already attained in specific performance (grades in school subjects, for example). The effects of past training (schooling) or experience may be inferred from the results.

Joseph Mayer Rice (1857-1934), American physician and practicing psychologist, coined "achievement test" in 1897.

Achillini, Alessandro (1463-1512) Italian anatomist who, in addition to other work, discovered (c. 1503) the **malleus, incus,** and **labyrinth**. *See* **olfactory nerve, trochlear nerve**.

achromatism (achromatopsia) Condition (-ism) of not (a-) being able to see color (-chromat-). Total color blindness; incapability of distinguishing between different hues of same brightness and saturation (such as red, green, blue, yellow). Only rod vision exists.

Terms first used in 1757 by English self-educated astronomer and optician, John Dollond (1706-1761), which he derived from "achromatics," a name previously coined in 1752 by British astronomer John Bevis (1693-1771).

acoumeter A hearing (acou-) meter. (Outmoded term for audiometer.) Acoumeter was coined (1878) by German physician, Arthur Hartmann (1849-1931).

acoustic nerve (acoustic-vestibular nerve, auditory nerve, stato-acoustic nerve) Relating to (-ic) the nerve of hearing (acoust-). Cranial nerve VIII, composed of two distinct divisions, carrying both vestibular (balancing) and cochlear (auditory) impulses. It is attached at the junction of the **pons** and the **medulla**. Specifically, the vestibular branch nerve fibers go from the semicircular canals to the vestibular ganglion in the internal auditory meatus while the cochlear branch carries fibers from the **organ of Corti** to their termination in the cochlear nuclei situated between the medulla and pons.

First noted by **Erasistratus**. **Marinus**, about 50 A.D., listed it as one of his seven cranial nerves. **Fallopius** described it briefly in 1561. In 1778, **Soemmering** identified and named it, adopting the term "acoustics" for this use, a term coined (1696) by the French physician Joseph Sauveur (1653-1716).

acquisition stage The process (-ion) of trying to (ac-) get (-quisit-) or acquire something. That stage of a learning experience in which an organism shows evidences of acquiring a new habit or mode of response. (E.g., the dog, in the acquisition stage of **classical conditioning**, shows such behavior when he salivates in response to a tone instead of to food.)

acromegaly A condition (-y) of bone enlargement (-mega-) of extremities (acro-), such as of the hands, feet, face, etc., after normal growth has stopped. Results from hypersecretion of the **somatotrophic** hormone by the pituitary's anterior lobe. Former wrestler Marcel Tillet (the "French Angel") and former boxer-wrestler Primo Carnera suffered from acromegaly.

In the Bible, II Samuel (XXI:20), an apparent case of acromegaly was described at a battle in Gath, "where was a man of great stature, that had on every hand six fingers, and on every foot six toes, four and twenty in number . . ." **Saucerotte** observed a case in 1772 and gave first medical description of the condition in 1801. In 1886, French physician, Pierre Marie (1853-1940), defined the condition in his "Essay on Acromegaly" as "characterized chiefly by hypertrophy of the feet, hands, and face, which I propose to call 'acromegaly,' that is to say, hypertrophy of the extremities."

acrophobia Fear (-phobia) of high (acro-) places. A morbid or pathological fear of high or elevated places, evidenced by the panic and vertigo some people experience while looking off roofs or cliffs, but not necessarily while peering out airplane windows.

Term coined (1842) by Andrea Verga (1811-1895) Italian neurologist.

ACTA Official acts or recorded proceedings of a scientific group or organization.

ACTH Adrenocorticotrophic hormone.

acting out *See* **ego**.

action potential (Action current, nerve impulse.) Localized sequence of voltage changes in the electrical potential (lasting between 0.5 and 5 msec.) existing between the inner and outer portions of an excitable nerve cell membrane or along a nerve fiber carrying an impulse. The action potential propagates itself wave-like from the point of original stimulation to the next point, repeating itself in fuse-like fashion, thus creating the passage of an impulse. Specifically, the membrane of a resting **neuron** (not conducting impulses) is polarized, the outer surface of the membrane being positive to the inner surface as a result of ionization. An **adequate stimulus** applied to a neuron greatly increases the membrane's permeability to positive sodium ions which then pour in at the point of stimulation causing a momentary local depolarization with the negative ions now flowing to the outside and the positive ones inside. At this point of interchange the resting potential (50 to 100 mV) proceeds through zero to about 30-50 mV in the opposite direction and then returns. *See* **potentials in the nervous system**.

The action potential was discovered and the term introduced in 1848 by German physiologist **DuBois-Reymond**. In 1875, **Caton** recorded action currents for the first time from an exposed animal's (rabbit's) brain. *See* **brain waves**.

action specific energy *See* **ethology**.

active therapy Ferenczi's directive form of therapy whereby the therapist actively encourages or discourages the patient to perform certain acts. **Ferenczi** believed in trying to create emotional tension in the patient because he considered it to be important for the patient to experience deep emotion during the therapeutic period.

Named and developed (1921) by **Sandor Ferenczi**.

activity cage A recorder-equipped enclosure designed for measuring gross movements of rats and other animals (sometimes including children) while engaged in laboratory experiments.

act psychology A system of psychology resulting from a revolt against **structuralism**. In contrast to **Wundt's** view that psychological processes themselves are the contents of consciousness or experience, act psychology emphasized "acts" or activities of consciousness stating that the act itself is mental or psychological and that the content is physical. For example, the hearing of a tone is a psychological act, or process; the tone that is heard is the content or end result of the act.

Although **Brentano** is recognized as the pioneer in **act psychology** with his *Psychologie vom empirischen Standpunkte* (1874), its origins lay in the concepts of **Leibniz, Kant,** and **Herbart. Mach, Ehrenfels, Külpe,** and Karl Bühler were leading followers of Brentano.

actualizing tendency *See* **self-actualization.**

acute hallucinatory mania *See* **Ganser syndrome.**

A/D (also **ADC**) Analog/digital computer. *See* **analog computer.**

AD Average deviation.

adaptation *See* **dark and light adaptation.**

adaptation level The reference point for judging a stimulus value (e.g., loudness, coldness), based on the neutralizing effect of past similar experiences or specialized learning. (Everything above is "too much, too heavy," while everything below this neutral value is "too little, too light," etc.) In **social psychology** the perceiver of a social event tends to adapt his level in terms of his own self-concept (usually considering himself as an objective, middle-of-the roader), although others may judge him to be a reactionary or radical.

The adaptation level concept was proposed by **Harry Helson,** who first expressed his views in the article "Adaptation-Level as a Basis for Quantitative Theory of Frames of Reference," *Psychological Review,* 1948, 55, 297-313, which he more fully explained in his book *Current Trends and Issues in Adaptation-Level Theory,* 1964.

adaptation syndrome *See* **general adaptation syndrome.**

adaptive reaction That generalized desensitizing reaction of an organism that serves to reduce harmful effects of environmental change (such as shivering in cold weather or perspiring in hot weather). Often follows the **orienting reflex,** and is opposed to it. Also refers to a sense organ's change of response as a result of prolonged or repeated responding.

Aubert introduced (1865) the term in referring to the adjustment of the eye to varying intensities of light.

adaptometer An instrument that measures (-meter) sensory adaptation (adapto-), such as in dark adaptation, whereby **limen** sensitivity to light is measured after varying intervals of darkness.

addictions Alcoholic addiction involves excessive intake and dependence on alcohol, leading to disruption of health and economic functioning and poor social adjustment. **Drug addiction** involves a reliance upon drugs associated with physical or psychological dependence.

Addison's disease An insidious and usually progressive disease of the **adrenal glands,** symptomatized by general weakness, skin pigmentation, dehydration, loss of weight, fatigability, **anorexia,** and gastrointestinal upsets.

In 1855, Thomas Addison (1793-1860), an English physician, wrote *On the Constitutional and Local Effects of Disease of the Suprarenal Capsules.* In 1856, French physician, Armand Trousseau, 1801-1867, suggested this disease be named after Addison.

additive color mixture The intermixture of colors by either mixing lights or rotating a **color wheel,** resulting in a new color perception created from lights of different wave lengths (colors) simultaneously exciting the retina. For example, when red and green lights are mixed, the eye sees "yellow"; when red, blue, and green are mixed in proper proportions a "white" is perceived. Contrasted with **subtractive color mixture,** characteristic of paint mixing.

address (comput.) A **number,** symbol, name or label that represents a location in memory storage designating where certain information may be found; the location of a station in a communication network. For example, let a, b, c, be addresses. The computer instruction, c=a+b, causes the contents of address *a* to be added to the contents of location *b* and the results placed in address location *c*. Note that the contents of the address are added, not the addresses themselves.

adenine One of the naturally occurring amino (-ine) purines extractable from a gland (aden-). One of the bases (as opposed to acids) in a DNA molecule that always pairs off with **thymine,** another base. In addition to DNA, it is also found in **RNA** molecules, **adenosine,** and other living tissues.

It was isolated from beef pancreas in 1885 by **Kossel.** *See* **chromosome, deoxyribonucleic acid, genetic code.**

adenohypophysis The anterior portion of the **hypophysis** (pituitary gland), derived embryologically from gland (adeno-) tissue, that secretes **somatotrophic, adrenocorticotrophic,** and **gonadotrophic** hormones.

adenosine A crystalline **nucleoside** and component of deoxyribonucleic acid, derived by partial hydrolysis of ribonucleic acid from yeast, yielding **adenine** (aden-) and **ribose** (-os+ine); found in various animal and vegetable tissues. In vertebrates, it acts as a vasodilator.

Adenosine was isolated from nucleic acids (primarily muscle tissue) by **Leven(e).**

adenosine diphosphate (ADP; also called adenosine diphosphoric acid). An intermediate product between **adenosine triphosphate** and **adenylic acid,** being an ester of adenosine and a phosphoric acid. It is formed from living cells, transferring energy during glycolysis (carbohydrate metabolism by enzymes, causing release of energy and production of such acids, as lactic).

adenosine phosphate (also called adenosine phosphoric acid and adenylic acid). Any of various esters (-ate) of adenosine and a phosphoric (phosp-) acid, including **adenosine triphosphate,** and especially **adenylic acid.**

adenosine triphosphatase An enzyme (-ase) that catalyzes the splitting of **adenosine triphosphate,** liberating inorganic phosphate and **adenosine diphosphate** in the process.

adenosine triphosphate (ATP; also called adenosine triphosphoric acid, and adenylpyrophosphate). An amorphous ester of **adenosine** and triphosphoric acid. ATP is a carrier of biological energy, expressed in the action of muscles and nerves that use ATP as a direct source of energy. It is produced in the **mitochondria** by the breakdown of glucose and other carbohydrates, forming **adenylic acid** and **adenosine diphosphate,** releasing phosphate and available energy for most biological processes.

In 1953, German-born American chemist, Fritz Lipmann (born 1899) received the Nobel prize, particularly for his discoveries concerning **adenosine triphosphate.**

adenylic acid Adenylic acid of forms "a" and "b" occur in nucleic acid hydrolysates. *See* **adenosine phosphate, adenosine triphosphate.**

adequate stimulus A stimulus that characteristically and typically stimulates an end organ especially adapted for such reception (light is an adequate stimulus for vision).

Sherrington introduced the concept and the term in 1906.

ADH Antidiuretic hormone. *See* **pressor substance.**

adiadochokinesis Loss of (a-) the power for rapid successive or alternating (-diadocho-) movement (kinesis), such as not being able to twist the forearm as rapidly from pronation to supination as before having a cerebellar disorder.

The term diadokokinesia was proposed (1892) by German neurologist, Ludwig Bruns (1858-1916) in reference to the ability of performing successive movements. Babinski (1902) added the prefix "a-" to this term so as to express a loss or change in this function, thus adiadochokinesis.

adipsia Disorder (-ia) of no (a-) thirst (-dips-). Absence of thirst, with special reference to experimental animals that consume no water; lack of a thirst drive, even when body water supply is low. Lesions in the lateral **hypothalamus** often produce adipsia in animals.

adjusting reinforcement schedule A complex **operant** reinforcement schedule in which each successive ratio's size is determined by some prior characteristic. *See* **complex reinforcement schedule, schedule of reinforcement.**

Adler, Alfred (1870-1937). Austrian psychiatrist (M.D., Vienna, 1895) and onetime colleague of Freud. Rejected Freud's extreme emphasis on sexuality, broke with him in 1911, and founded his own "school" of **individual psychology.** For him, an individual's **'life style'** is developed by the way he seeks solutions to problems of love, society, and occupation; man is a creative person; the struggle for power is pre-eminent in personality dynamics. He said (1922) that children should be prepared and educated for the *community* (Gemeinschaft) and that those with this *community spirit and feeling* (Gemeinschaftsgefühl) will be leaders of the future. After initially considering man as a lustful animal, Adler later recognized him as a socially responsible animal. He called experienced feelings of inferiority the inferiority complex and the struggle against these feelings **compensation;** to him, **aggression** was a overcompensation for felt inferiority, such inferiority being at the root of all personality difficulties. He left Vienna in 1936, during the Nazi regime, and lectured and practiced in the United States throughout the latter years of his life. (*The Individual Psychology of Alfred Adler* (Basic Books, 1956); also Bischof, 1964, pp. 231-261; Maddi, 1968, pp. 89-94; and Vinacke, 1968, p. 415).

ADP Adenosine diphosphate.

adrenal Pertaining to (-al) an organ above (ad-) the kidneys (ren-).

adrenal androgens Adrenal cortex hormones regulating development (-gen) of secondary sex characteristics, primarily of the male (andro-).

adrenal glands (suprarenal glands). Paired endocrine glands, one located over each kidney. The reddish central part (**medulla**) secretes **adrenalin** and **noradrenaline,** while the yellowish outer part (**cortex**) secretes cortical steroids (**cortin,** etc.). The principal function of the adrenal cortex is to maintain a general **homeostatic** balance. Also, by helping to regulate volume and composition of body fluids, it is essential in the organism's survival responses to stress conditions.

Eustachius first mentioned the gland in 1563, but not until 1855 did **Addison** adequately describe its function. Czechoslovakian physiologist, Arthur Biedl (1869-1933), reported in 1910 the need of the adrenal cortex for sustaining life. *See* **Addison's disease.**

adrenalin(e) (epinephrine, adrenine) A chemical compound (-in) or hormone secretion of the adrenal medulla that prepares the body for physical and emotional arousal by stimulating the liver to produce blood sugar, increasing the coagulation rate of the blood, increasing the rate and strength of the heart beat, controlling carbohydrate metabolism, etc. Adrenalin is the most potent of all **catecholamines.** Adrenalin is sometimes used as a collective term for all adrenal medulla extracts; also as a trade name. *See* **adrenal glands.**

a

In 1856, French physician, Edme Felix Vulpian (1826-1887), reported finding in the adrenal medulla a substance, demonstrated later to be adrenalin. The adrenal medulla's active principle was first isolated in 1901 by the Japanese-American chemist, Jokichi Takamine (1854-1922), who then named it adrenaline (still the most frequently used term). John J. Abel (1857-1938), American chemist and pharmacologist, gave it the official name (USP) of *epinephrine* in 1902. In 1904, Abel, Takamine, and Friedrich Stolz (1860-1936), crystallized and purified the substance.

adrenergic Referring to (-ic) the liberation of adrenaline (adren-) or an adrenaline-like substance that produces an effect or work (-erg-) somewhere else. For example, chemical transmitter substances released by **autonomic** axon terminals carry impulses across synapses and neuro-effector junctions. *Adrenergic fibers* (those axons that release norepinephrine and some adrenaline) are principally sympathetic postganglionic **axons** except for those few that go to sweat glands, skeletal muscles, blood vessels, etc., which are **cholinergic** (those that release **acetycholine**). An adrenaline-releasing nerve cell that stimulates other nerve cells is an *adrenergic cell. Adrenergic receptors* are classified as *alpha* (concerned with excitatory responses) and *beta* (for inhibitory responses).

The term "adrenergic" was coined by **Dale** in 1935. (Thompson and Schuster, 1968.)

adrenochrome An indole breakdown-product of adrenaline (adreno-) with a pinkish color (-chrome), known chemically for many years but never found **in vivo**. Reportedly, it produced hallucinations, among other effects, when given intravenously. *See* **adrenalin metabolite theory** under **biochemical theories of psychosis.**

adrenocorticotrophic hormone, ACTH (also called corticotrophin). Relating to (-ic) the hormone of the anterior **pituitary** gland that nourishes (-troph-) or stimulates the adrenal cortex (adrenocortico-) to release glucocorticoids. These corticoids, in turn, accelerate the hydrolysis of tissue proteins to **amino acids**, tending to increase blood glucose concentration. Under stressful situations, ACTH is released through the action of **neurosecretions** (released by hypothalamic cells) upon the anterior pituitary. Administration of ACTH has been reported to enhance fear reactions, but generally its effect upon human beings varies from little or no effect on some people to the full range from euphoria to depression on others.

The pure hormone was first isolated in 1943 by Choh Hao Li, a Chinese (Canton) American chemist (born 1913), and also by the American chemists H. M. Evans (*see* **chromosome**) and Miriam E. Simpson, anatomist and physician (born 1894). The Nobel prize in medicine was jointly awarded in 1950 to the following three scientists for work leading to the synthesis of ACTH and cortisone: Phillip S. Hench (1896-1965), an American research physician; E. C. Kendall (born 1886), American biochemist; and Tadeus Reichstein (born 1897, Poland), Swiss inorganic chemist who also synthesized ascorbic acid in 1933 and isolated **aldosterone** in 1953.

Adrian, Edgar Douglas (born England, 1889). Awarded Nobel prize (1932) in physiology (along with **Sherrington**) for his work on the physiology of the nervous system, including the **all-or-none law, alpha blocking response,** and function of the **neuron.**

aerial perspective One of the **monocular cues** used in determining relative clearness in depth and distance perception. Desaturation of colors makes distant scenes appear hazy, the apparent distance seeming greater.

aesthesiometer *See* **esthesiometer.**

affect Any prolonged feeling, emotion, mood, drive, or temperamental state generally not associated with thought processes, intellectual functioning, or with the physiological changes resulting from emotion. *Affect hunger* is a craving for affection and attention by children who have been deprived of love and close contact from parents (usually from the mother).

affective-arousal theory A motivational theory, developed by McClelland, that states that an individual tends to learn to seek anticipated pleasure and to avoid anticipated pain. (D. C. McClelland, *Personality*, 1951; **Paul Thomas Young**, "Affective Arousal: Some Implications," *American Psychologist*, 1967, **22**, 32-40).

David C. McClelland (born 1917), an American (New York) psychologist (Ph.D., Yale, 1941).

affective personality *See* **cyclothymic personality** under **personality disorders.**

affective psychoses (disorders) (major affective disorders). Characterized by either extreme **depression** or elation that dominates the patient's mental life, resulting in loss of contact with his environment. Onset of mood related directly to a precipitating life experience, thereby distinguishing it from **psychotic depressive reaction** and depressive **neurosis**. Includes **manic-depressive illness** and **involutional melancholia.**

afferent fiber A sensory nerve fiber that transmits or carries (-ferent) nerve impulses toward (af-) the central nervous system from the periphery or sense organs.

Afferent is translated from the German *aufleitend*, as coined by **Unzer** in 1771.

afterdischarge The phenomenon produced when a single stimulus causes a motoneuron to discharge for several seconds after cessation of stimulation.

afterimage (successive contrast). A sensory experience that persists or reappears after the external stimulus ceases. Visual afterimages occur when a person stares fixedly at an object in a strong light and then turns away with eyes closed; or, with color, when the eye is successively stimulated by different colors. Such afterimages may be opposite or complementary (*negative afterimage*), or similar (*positive afterimage*).

Aristotle described the phenomenon, but the term dates from approximately 1879, when it was translated into English from the German *Nachbild(er)*.

AGCT Army General Classification Test. *See* **group test.**

aggregate toxicity In animal drug-tolerance studies, the relative degree of toxicity tolerated by aggregated (grouped together) experimental animals. For example, the LD-50 (or *median lethal dose*) of **amphetamine** administered to animals in groups is lower (more toxic) when they are aggregated in one cage than in control animals housed individually. Room temperature, cage size, and fluid deprivation also influence aggregate toxicity.

aggression Act (-ion) of going (-agress-) toward (ag-); a series of hostile acts directed toward some thing or person (including one's self). Aggression may be overt or internalized, slow to progress or immediate. (It is considered a need by **Murray**.) In experimental conditions, an *operant aggression* usually indicates destruction of the source of irritation or punishment, while *respondent aggression* refers to generalized reaction against any convenient organism but not necessarily the culprit. (For example, nonaggressive caged rats that are electrically shocked will attack one another although the painful stimulus originates from the experimenter.) Respondent aggression does not reduce or eliminate the aversive stimulation as in operant aggression. Other forms of aggression involve receiving positive reinforcement by punishing others (**sadism**) or punishing oneself (**masochism**).

Aggression directed against the self is sometimes also called **autoplastic** (such as in conversion symptoms), while such behavior expressed toward the external situation is **alloplastic** behavior (as in delinquency).

aging disorder Brain cell and arterial damage resulting from deterioration associated with aging, such as from atherosclerosis but not necessarily arteriosclerosis. *See* **senile psychoses.**

agnosia A disorder (-ia) of not (a-) knowing (-gnos-) or not recognizing. A type of **aphasia** in which it is not possible to synthesize and interpret simple sensory impressions; the counterpart of **apraxia** in the motor sphere. Also, an inadequacy of perception, or inability to attach meaning to sensory stimuli, usually resulting from damage to visual association neurons—sometimes called "object blindness." Although the subject actually "sees," he cannot identify objects by visual cues alone. Or he may retain sensitivity to touch, but be unable to recognize by touch alone parts of the body or formerly familiar objects. *Visual agnosia* relates to disorders of perceiving objects, pictures, color, space, etc., and is further differentiated by form, distance, and direction. *Auditory agnosia* manifests itself by music deafness or psychic deafness for specific noises. (J. M. Nielsen, *Agnosia, Apraxia, Aphasia*, Hoeber, 1946.)

In 1864, Hughlings **Jackson** introduced the idea of imperception which Freud used (1891) in his prepsychoanalytic discussions about aphasia and agnosia. In 1900, H. J. Liepmann merely described motor aphasia, but in 1908 in his *Drei Aufsatze aus dem Apraxiegebret*, he specifically differentiated between apraxia and agnosia.

agoraphobia Morbid or neurotic fear (-phobia) of open areas (agora-). Apparently associated with the need for security and closeness of mother and home, as well as fears of molestation in open places or of being tempted to "run away from it all" with so much freedom.

In 1871, German neurologist Karl F. O. Westphal (1833-1890), clinically described the condition, coining the term in 1873.

agraphia A disorder (-ia) characterized by partial or no (a-) recall of writing (-graph) skills; a form of **aphasia**, usually caused by brain damage in the cortical area near the second frontal convolution, causing interference with memorized skill for written language.

First medical reference (1867) to the condition was made by German clinician, John Wilhelm Ogle (1822-1883) who coined the term in 1871. In 1884, French physician Jean Albert Pitres (1848-1928) gave first thorough description of the condition.

aha experience *See* **kairos.**

alanine [*al*(dehyde)] + *an*(for euphony) + *ine* Any of several isomers of a crystalline **amino acid** found naturally in proteins and also produced synthetically.

Discovered (1849) and named (1850) by **Strecker.**

albedo Quality of being (-edo) white (alb-); the whiteness of a surface. The percentage or fraction of incidental light or radiation reflected by a surface (as the moon, the ground, or snow). An albedo of 50 percent refers to a surface that reflects 50 percent of the light falling on it.

Coined (1760) by German mathematician and philosopher Johann H. Lambert (1728-1777) who said that albedo was the refractive quality of light that was diffusely reflected by a body.

Alcmaeon of Croton (fl. 6th century B.C.) Greek physician. Considered by some authorities to be founder of **empirical** psychology. Probably first to dissect animals and to have observed nerves. Apparently recognized brain as main organ for sensation and thought. Averred that man's power of understanding is what basically differentiates him from lower animals. *See* **optic nerve.**

alcoholic psychoses A psychotic condition resulting from poisoning with alcohol, including **delirium tremens, Korsakow's syndrome**. *See under* organic psychosis.

alcoholism A chronic compulsive disease characterized usually by excessive and continuous use of alcoholic drinks, often accompanied by mental, physical, and social malfunctioning resulting in evidences of sacrificing eating for drinking, with consequent malnutrition and possible cirrhosis of the liver, alcoholic psychosis, and eventual death; usually addictive. Some authors (such as Elvin M. Jellinek (1890-1963), American biometrician did in 1960), classify alcoholism as a disease and break it down into subtypes: *alpha type* (an apparently controlled form of drinking: psychologically determined reliance on alcohol for relief from psychic stress or physical discomfort), *beta type* (heavy social drinking but no psychological dependence evident), *gamma type* (psychological and physical dependence evident with withdrawal symptoms), *delta type* (psychological and physical dependence with incapability of abstaining from alcohol), and *epsilon type* (drinking bouts that last days or weeks spaced by periods of complete abstinence). For further information on alcoholism contact the following organizations: The National Council on Alcoholism, Inc., 2 East 103rd Street, New York, New York 10029; Rutgers Center of Alcohol Studies, Rutgers University, New Brunswick, New Jersey 08903; The Alcoholism and Drug Addiction Research Foundation, 24 Harbord Street, Toronto, Ontario, Canada.

alcohol paranoid state (alcoholic paranoia) A paranoid condition that develops generally in male chronic alcoholics; characterized by irritability, sullenness, and unusual fits of jealousy and delusions of infidelity by the spouse. Suggestive of homosexual patterns.

aldosterone A hormone produced by the cortex of the adrenal gland, chemically derived (-one) from sterols (-ster-) and aldehydes (ald-), and that helps regulate sodium and potassium metabolism. *Aldosteronism* is a condition of increased activity of aldosterone that causes excessive loss of potassium in the body, intermittent paralysis, hypertension, and edema.

Aldosterone was isolated in 1953 by Polish chemist Reichstein. *See* **adrenocorticotrophic hormone**.

alexia A cerebral disorder (-ia) of not (a-) being able to understand or read visual symbols as written words (-lex-); **word blindness** form of sensory **aphasia**. **Dyslexia** sometimes used as synonym. An idiopathic ("specific") dyslexia indicates an unknown cause.

Symptoms of condition often mentioned throughout history, but first adequately described in 1874 by **Wernicke** in his *Der Aphasische Symptomencomplex*, in which he classified alexia under aphasia. A more thorough treatment was given by the German physician, Ludwig Lichtheim (1845-1915), in an article, "On Aphasia," *Brain*, January, 1885.

ALGOL *Algorithmic Language*; sometimes *algebraic oriented language*. An international data processing language in which problem-solving formulas are treated for machine solution. ALGOL, similar to **FORTRAN** as an algebraic language, is the term primarily used in Europe.

algolagnia A sexual disorder (-ia) characterized by a lustful (-lagn-) desire to inflict pain (algo-) on others (**sadism**) or to enjoy receiving pain or punishment from others (**masochism**).

Albert Schrenck-Notzing (1862-1929), German psychiatrist, coined the term in 1897.

algorithm A well-defined systematic procedure for attacking all possibilities in mathematical and **computer** problems that guarantees the eventual solving of a problem within a finite number of steps (but may be prohibitively expensive both in expenditure of time and money). A simple algorithmic example is that of long division. *See* **model**.

Euclid's algorithmic method arrived at the highest common factor or greatest common divisor of two numbers. In algebra, the same process can be used for polynomials.

The term has nothing to do with "rhythm," but originates from "algorism"—system of Arabic numerals, or the **decimal number system** of counting—derived from the name of a Persian mathematician, Al-K(ho)warizm, native of K(h)warizm, fl. 925 A.D. (Contrast **heuristic** method.

alias In a fractionally replicated design, the term given to the two or more designations that are assigned to the same sum of squares, thus making one effect indistinguishable from another. Aliases are also known as generalized interactions in the **confounding** of block effects when **treatment combinations** requiring certain satisfactions are divided. (Kirk, 1968, pp. 385-387, 1962, pp. 426-433.)

alienation Condition (-ion) of being strange (alienat-); estranged: a feeling of having lost the awareness of self and the power to originate action. From sociologist Seeman's viewpoint, alienation is five-pronged: as *powerlessness*, it refers to the capitalist worker who is unable to engage in decision-making; as *meaninglessness*, to the person who is incapable of finding meaning in life; as *normlessness*, to the person who feels bereft of guidelines ("anomie"); as *isolationism*, to the one who so demeans his own society's values that he becomes estranged from that society; and finally, as *self-estrangement*, to the person whose attitude of "the world owes me a living" keeps him from participating in society. (Melvin Seeman, "On the Meaning of Alienation," *American Sociological Review*, 1959, 24, 783-791.) Melvin Seeman (born 1918), American sociologist (Ph.D., Ohio State 1947).

alienation, coefficient of *See* **coefficient of alienation.**

alienist One who (-ist) helps the mentally **alienated**, particularly a psychiatrist who specializes in testifying in court about psychiatric problems, serving as a general consultant or in defense of his own patients. Term is seldom used in the U.S. now, but it still has prominent usage in Great Britain.

Term is derived from "mental alienation," which was the term applied (1864) by French psychiatrist Jean Pierre Flaret (1794-1870) as a substitute for the opprobrious terms of "imbecility," "dementia," "furor," etc.; those physicians attending the mentally alienated became known as alienists during the nineteenth century.

alkaloid Similar to (-oid) alkali; an organic base related to nitrogen-ring compounds. Many alkaloids (e.g., **curare, nicotine, morphine,** etc.) are used in psychophysiological experimentation.

allele (short for allelomorph) Any of several forms of alternative **genes** identically located in homologous chromosomes that account for hereditary variation. From all the alleles in any one total group (population) a haploid organism has only one representative allele, and a diploid has two. *Identical alleles* may consist of either two dominant or two recessive genes. One of two or more contrasting genes containing both a dominant and a recessive gene is called an *unlike allele*. *See* **homozygote, heterozygote.**

allelomorph A gene of another (allelo-) shape (-morph) or form. *See* **allele.**

alley maze In psychological experimentation, an intricate network of pathways including various blind alleys leading to a goal. Animal learning can be measured by the time taken to overcome the obstacles (the series of pathways) before reaching the goal or reward (food).

allocortex (archipallium) The ontogenetically older (as opposed to the other [allo-], the newer and thinking aspect) area of the **cerebral cortex**; that cortical portion not laminated, comprising the **hippocampus**; primarily concerned with smell. *See* **archipallium, juxtallo cortex, limbic system;** Cf. **rhinencephalon, paleocortex.**

Term introduced by the **Vogt's** in 1903.

alloerotocism *See* **cathexis.**

allokurtic Pertaining to (-ic) another (allo-) curve (kurt-) or to the other array in a double entry table. *See* **kurtosis.**

alloplastic Pertaining to (-ic) behavior that is molded or directed (-plast-) toward others (allo-), or toward society or the environment. *See* **aggression.**

Ferenczi considered alloplastic adaptation to be that which man adapts to his needs, while autoplastic refers to the animal altering his own self to fit or adapt to his environment. In order to achieve an equilibrium between instinct and reality in the resolution of conflicts, it is necessary to change reality, or instincts, or neither, necessitating denying one or the other. (R. Waelder, The Structure of Paranoid Ideas: A Critical Survey of Various Theories. *International Journal of Psychoanalysis*, 1951, 32, 167.)

all-or-none law (all-or-nothing law). The principle that a stimulated single **neuron**, nerve fiber, or muscle fiber responds with all its intensity or not at all (being dependent upon the maximum **polarization** change permitted by its chemical reaction). There is no gradation of response; the intensity of the stimulus does not affect the magnitude of the response.

Concept was first demonstrated (1871) not in the nerve but in the heart muscle by American physiologist Henry P. Bowditch (1840-1911). In 1902, English physiologist F. Gotch (1835-1913) detected evidence of the all-or-nothing effect in nerve, but it was not proven until **Adrian** did so, publishing his work in the *Journal of Physiology*, London, 1913-14, 47: 460-474. However (since 1903), **Lucas** had performed many studies on the nerve impulse leading to Adrian's conclusive work, but his death precluded his sharing his findings. Lucas named the law in an article: "The All or None Contraction of the Amphibian Skeletal Muscle Fibre," *Journal of Physiology*, London, 1909, 38, 113-133.

allosteric enzyme Referring to (-ic) another (allo-) site (-ster-). A regulatory enzyme with two specific locations: one for the catalytic site (the enzyme's substrate) and the other for the effector site (which may either activate or inhibit an action).

The term allosteric was coined by M. Cohn, J. Monod, M. R. Pollock, S. Spiegelman, and R. Y. Stanier. *See* "Terminology of Enzyme Formation," *Nature*, 1953, 172, 1096.

Allport, Gordon Willard (1897-1968). American psychologist. Ph.D., Harvard 1922. Received **Gold Medal Award** 1963. Authority on personality theory, expressive movement, and the psychology of rumor and prejudice. Developed (with P. E. Vernon and G. Lindzey) the Allport-Vernon Study of Values, a scale based on **Spranger's** classification of value-types. Primarily concerned with developing a personality theory based on the normal person. In contrast to **Freud**, he objected to a concept of the unconscious, feeling that conscious factors are of more importance in determining behavior. He considered traits (as an initiator and determiner of behavior) to be functionally autonomous and not related to biological needs. He also felt (like **Jung**) that man's intentions rather than his past actions are of more importance in determining his present actions. *See* **proprium, trait, functional autonomy of motives, idiopathic.**

alpha (α) The first letter of the Greek alphabet, often used in the sciences to indicate the first of a series. In statistics, some uses of alpha are: (*1*) it designates the significance level (probability of rejecting a **null hypothesis** when it is true, a **type I error**, and is generally set equal to .05 or .01); and (2) it represents an absolute measure of **skewness** that cannot be used to compare the skewness of different distributions. Therefore, an adjustment must be made by dividing it by α^3, which is equal to the 3rd moment about the mean. The chance of making a type I error can be made as small as desired by changing the level of significance. If H_O is correct, alpha and the probability of a type I error are identical. Alpha is often called the *level of significance*. The value of alpha must be stated or specified before the study begins, the investigation always taking the risk of drawing a wrong conclusion.

alpha block conditioning *Conditioning* the alpha block response to a stimulus not ordinarily producing the *alpha blocking*, resulting in the **conditioned stimulus** itself producing the **alpha blocking response**.

alpha block response The process of responding to a desynchronization of the regular 8-13-per-second **alpha (wave) rhythm** by arousal, concentration, flashing lights, or other alerting stimuli.

This process was first studied and described by **Adrian** and co-workers. (E. D. Adrian, and B. H. C. Matthews, "The Interpretation of Potential Waves in the Cortex," *Journal of Physiology*, 1934, 81, 440-471.)

alpha error (type I error). That error resulting when the experimenter rejects the **null hypothesis** when it is true.

alpha fiber A main **motor** nerve fiber that supplies contractile muscle fibers.

alphameric (Comput.) A portmanteau word telescoping the two words *alpha*bet and nu*meric*. See **alphanumeric**.

alpha movement *See* **apparent movement**.

alphanumeric (Comput.) Refers to the combined use of letters (*alpha*bet) and numbers (*numeric*) in the same computer or machine operation. The term *alphameric* may be used as a shortened form of alphanumeric but it is more commonly used (especially in keypunching) to indicate the alphabetic section of data, not including numbers and special symbols (such as punctuation).

alpha receptors Adrenergic receptors most sensitive to **adrenalin**.

alpha (wave) rhythm The first (*alpha*) electrical impulse or wave of relatively low amplitude discovered in the brain, as observed on the **electroencephalogram**, (EEG). These waves have a frequency of about 8 to 13 per second and an amplitude between 5 and 15 microvolts at the scalp. Usually, the waves are apparent on the EEG during the waking state when the subject is mentally inactive, with the eyes closed, but disappear either when he falls asleep or when he becomes alert, uses his eyes functionally, or becomes mentally active in any way.

Discovered and named in 1929 by Hans **Berger**.

alpha risk (α) The risk of making a **type I error** (rejecting a true **null hypothesis**).

alpha tests of intelligence A set of verbal group tests devised 1917-18, by a number of American psychologists during World War I for screening Army recruits. The sub-tests consisted of arithmetical reasoning, directions, analogies and synonyms and antonyms, number series completion, practical judgment, disarranged sentences, and information. In the revised form, Alpha Examination Modified Form 9, eight tests yield subscores for numerical and verbal ability as well as a total score. Percentile norms are for grades 7-12 and some adult groups. See **beta tests**.

alternation response Tendency to not repeat the same response immediately, even if rewarded.

alternative hypothesis (H_1) The secondary hypothesis remaining operable after the **null hypothesis** has been rejected.

Alzheimer's disease A relatively rare organic disorder involving progressive cortical atrophy and occurring usually between the ages of 50 to 60. **Apraxic** and **aphasic** conditions may occur along with depression, deterioration of intellect, and loss of contact with reality. Prognosis is not good, with patient becoming a veritable "vegetable" within about ten years.

Named after the German neurologist, Alois Alzheimer (1864-1915), who first (1907) adequately described the disease. *See* **substantia nigra**.

amacrine cell Unipolar nerve cell that is without (a-) an axon or long (macr-) fiber (-ine). Such cells are found in the **olfactory bulb**, the cerebellar Purkinje cells, and the retinal cells that interconnect bipolar **neurons**.

amaurotic family idiocy Relating to (-ic) impaired or dim (amaurot-) vision or blindness associated with idiocy that tends to run in families.

Term now practically obsolete in favor of **Tay-Sachs disease**, one of the infantile forms of the condition known as **cerebral lipoidosis**. Cullen used the term "amaurosis" to mean a total loss of sight without visible injury to the eye.

The first case was apparently first reported by A. Stengel in 1826 in the Norwegian magazine, *Eyr*, in which he described four siblings with the condition. In 1903, **Batten** gave a more accurate description and in 1904 Mayou reported retinal changes, distinguishing his findings from those formerly described by listing a later onset of the disease, slower progress, and definite dementia. In 1905, Spielmeyer and H. Vogt confirmed earlier findings by Batten and Mayou by their pathological studies and clinical observations, which distinguished the condition from Tay-Sach's disease. In 1908, W. Stock, studying three of Spielmeyer's cases, made first thorough study of the retinal histopathology. In 1909 Jansky and in 1913 **Bielchowsky** described the late infantile variety of the disease (with the onset being at three to four years of age and lasting for about three or four years). See **Bielchowsky-Jansky disease**.

ambiguous figure A figure or visual **stimulus** that, primarily because of an unstable **figure-ground** relationship, may be perceived several ways. For example, in the accompanying drawing of a flight of stairs, a reversal **illusion** takes place despite efforts to keep the figure constant. Provided that the viewer fixates somewhere on the middle of the figure he sees the stairs alternatively, that is, at one time he perceives them as if looking from underneath and at other times from above. Blinking helps create the illusion.

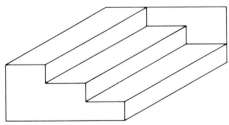

The Schröder staircase, pictured here, developed out of H. Schroder's study of visual relief (1858).

The term "ambiguous figure" was first used about 1912 by the Danish psychologist Edgar Rubin (1886-1961).

ambivalence Quality of (-ence) simultaneously having both (ambi-) negative and positive feelings or evidence of contradictory strength (-val-) toward a person, object, or idea, such as having love and hate or attraction and repulsion for the same person or object. For example, a child may have generalized feelings of love for his parents at the same time he has a specialized hatred for them for some act of commission or omission. *See* **approach-avoidance conflict**, **valence**.

In 1930, **Bleuler** used the term "ambivalence" to describe the presence of two strong opposing tendencies in psychotics.

ambivert A **personality** type that turns (-vert) or swings toward both (ambi-) the **introvert** and the **extrovert**, managing to attain a wholesome balance by avoiding the extremes.

amblyopia A disorder (-ia) involving dim (ambly-) sight (-op-); blurring of vision, accompanied often by **strabismus** and inability to focus. Commonly seen in alcoholics, drug users, those suffering from nicotinic poisoning (toxic amblyopia), dietary deficiencies, or from extreme eye-fatigue caused by overuse (as with students cramming for examinations).

Hippocrates described the term in referring to dimness of vision to which all elderly people are subject.

amentia Disorder (-ia) of being without (a-) a mind (-ment-); mental deficiency. Lack of development of intellectual capacity. Madness. To **Meynert** (1884) amentia was a psychosis with hallucinatory confusion, accompanied by functional loss due to cerebral exhaustion.

Term used by **Cullen** who classified it under a neurosis, defining it as imbecility of the intellect.

American Association for the Advancement of Science An organization founded in 1848 that developed out of the Association of American Geologists and Naturalists "to further the work of scientists, to facilitate cooperation among them, to improve the effectiveness of science in the promotion of human welfare, and to increase public understanding and appreciation of the importance and promise of the methods of science in human progress." *See* **AAAS Socio-Psychological Prize; Newcomb Cleveland Prize**.

American Association on Mental Deficiency (AAMD) An interdisciplinary association of physicians, psychiatrists, educators, social workers, psychologists and other professional people working in the field of mental retardation. The Association assists the **American Psychiatric Association** in setting standards for hospitals and schools for the mentally retarded.

American Board of Professional Psychology The organization, incorporated in 1947 as the American Board of Examiners in Professional Psychology (ABEPP), was established to set standards for the practice of psychology, corresponding to the various "Boards" of the American Medical Association. In 1969, the present name was adopted although its acronym ABPP is still pronounced "ABEPP." In its reorganization, the Board has become more flexible and realistic in its testing of candidates without relaxing its high standards.

Professional psychologists, aspiring to become diplomates of the ABPP in any of its various disciplines (industrial, counseling, clinical, and school psychology), must pass individualized examinations (covering knowledge, skills, attitudes, and values). Psychologists may apply for admission to candidacy at any time after experience requirement of five years is met. (Four years shall be postdoctoral). A diplomate has been judged to be a highly competent and well-trained professional psychologist in his chosen field of specialization, and may be relied upon as an ethical member of his community.

American Orthopsychiatric Association (AOA) An association of psychologists, psychiatrists, social workers, educators, sociologists, and other professional people working in a collaborative approach to the analysis, study, and treatment of people in psychological trouble.

It was founded in 1924 primarily to study juvenile delinquency. The organization is now the professional group for child guidance workers.

American Philosophical Society The first scientific society organized in the United States, founded in Philadelphia in 1743. Its transactions date from 1771.

American Psychiatric Association (APA) An association of psychiatrists dedicated to furthering the study of all phases of mental disorders. It helps regulate standards of practice and service in various psychiatric hospitals and clinics; and promotes education and research for greater understanding of mental illness.

It had its beginnings in 1844 when the thirteen hospital superintendents (the "Original 13")—called the Association of Medical Superintendents of American Institutions for the Insane—held their first meeting. For further information contact: *American Psychiatric Association,* 1700 18th Street, N.W., Washington, D. C. 20036.

American Psychoanalytic Association (APsaA) An association of analytically trained **psychiatrists** which sets and enforces standards for the training of **psychoanalysts**, as well as supervises the program and the individuals in training at its affiliated Institutes in various parts of the country.

The first association was founded as the New York Psychoanalytic Society in 1911 by Austrian-American psychoanalyst A. A. Brill (1874-1948), and the American Psychoanalytic Association was also founded in 1911 in New York. The first psychoanalytic institute in the United States was established in New York (1931). For further information, contact: *American Psychoanalytic Association,* One East 57th Street, New York, New York.

American Psychological Association (APA) On July 8, 1892, the APA was "founded" by G. Stanley Hall, the psychologist-President of Clark University, at an informal get-together. Of the twenty-six charter members in addition to Hall, some who later became famous in psychology and related disciplines were: James McKeen Cattell, James M. Baldwin; W. L. Bryan, John Dewey, and William James.

The APA was incorporated in 1925 "to advance psychology as a science, and as a means of promoting human welfare. It attempts to furnish these objectives by holding annual meetings, publishing psychological journals, and working toward improved standards for psychological training and service." From the article by Wayne Dennis and Edwin G. Boring, "The Founding of the APA," *The American Psychologist,* 1952, **8**, 95-97. For additional information, contact: *Board of Professional Affairs, American Psychological Association,* 1333 16th Street, N.W., Washington, D. C. 20036. *See* **awards of the American Psychological Association.**

American Psychological Foundation Established in 1953 to "receive gifts and bequests from psychologists wishing to make financial contributions toward the development of psychology as a science and as a contribution to human welfare."

A major use of Foundation funds has been in support of psychology in other countries (via journal subscriptions to foreign libraries or financial help for foreign psychologists to start research programs). The Foundation established two awards: a **Gold Medal Award,** given to senior North American psychologists "in recognition of distinguished and long-continued record of scientific and scholarly accomplishment, and a National Media Award for outstanding popular presentations of psychology in mass media."

American Sociological Association An association of sociologists, educators, social scientists, and other professional persons interested in the research, teaching, and applications of sociology.

It was founded in 1905 at Baltimore, Maryland, as the American Sociological Society to encourage "sociological research and discussion and the promotion of intercourse between persons engaged in the scientific study of society."

Ames' Distortion Room A specialized room designed in 1935 by the American educator and specialist in physiological optics, Adelbert Ames (1880-1955), for purposes of studying the retinal image distortions associated with **aniseikonia** and stereoscopic vision. *See* **distortion room.**

ametropia A disorder (-ia) of vision or sight (-op) caused by the eye not (a-) being able to measure (-metr-) correctly the refraction of light rays. **Hyperopia** is the most frequent form of ametropia, but other varieties are **myopia,** astigmatism, and **presbyopia.**

Donders made original studies on ametropia and hyperopia in 1860.

amine Any one of several organic compounds (-ine) derived from ammonia (am-), NH_3, by replacing one of its hydrogen atoms with a hydrocarbon radical (NH_2R) or other non-acidic organic radical.

Originally, in a letter dated September 2, 1832, to German chemist Frederick Wöhler (1800-1882) and Liebig, Berzelius referred to the NH_2 radical as "amid," but in 1848 the French chemist Charles Adolphe Wurtz (1817-1884) changed amid(e) to amine when he discovered the primary aliphatic amines.

amine pathways Specific neuroanatomical pathways in the brain as determined by precise histochemical localization of the **amines** that are sensitive to certain amines only and which allow for transmission of impulses along these paths. Modification of these pathways has been shown to be of some value in treating psychoses. A biochemical classification of brain pathways has resulted from the fluorescence studies mentioned under **biogenic amines.** The principal monoaminergic pathways thus far identified are outlined here:

A. *Dopaminergic pathways*
1. **Substantia nigra** to **caudate and putamen (corpus striatum)**
2. **Midbrain** to nucleus accumbens and tuberculum olfactorium
B. *Noradrenergic pathways*
1. **Reticular formation** to **neocortex**
2. Reticular formation to **hypothalamus** and limbic forebrain
C. *Serotonergic pathways*
1. **Raphe nuclei** to hypothalamus and limbic forebrain
2. Raphe nuclei to neocortex

See **adrenergic, cholinergic.** (From McGeer, Patrick L., The Chemistry of Mind, *American Scientist,* (March-April 1971, **59**, No. 2, pp. 221-229). Patrick McGeer (born 1927), Canadian physician and physiologist.

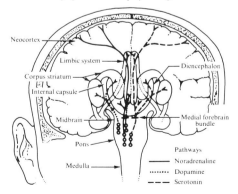

Approximate Locations of Amine Pathways in the Brain

amino acid An organic *acid* in which one or more *amino* groups (NH_2 or substitute) has replaced a portion of hydrogen in the formula, being thereby both basic and acidic. Most amino acids have the basic formula $RCH(NH_2)COOH$, and are considered to be the building blocks of proteins and necessary for metabolic and all related processes.

Various protein products (including **adenine, alanine, cystine, glycine, leucine, lysine, phenylalanine,** and **tyrosine** which are defined in this book) were categorized by Berzelius, naming them amino acids in 1848. Emil Fischer showed that amino acids are primary decomposition products of protein.

amnesia An organic or functional disorder (-ia) often caused by shock, cerebral trauma, or extreme repression, resulting in partial or complete memory (-mnes-) loss (a-) for events as well as for identity. *Anterograde amnesia* refers to the loss of memory for events going (-grade) forward (antero-) from or since the time of a precipitating event, not being able to recognize any person or event in the present time, any input being forgotten as soon as experienced; and *retrograde amnesia* referring to memory loss for events going (-grade) backward (retro-) or prior to the precipitating event.

Term used in ancient Greece for loss of memory, but apparently not used again in this sense until Broca referred to a condition of verbal amnesia in 1861, the same time he introduced the word "aphemia."

amniocentesis Surgical puncture (centesis) of the amnion; a surgical procedure in which a hollow needle is inserted into the amniotic sac surrounding the fetus and withdrawing a sample of amniotic fluid from the "bag of waters." Cells shed by the fetus and found in the fluid are cultured and tested to determine if any genetic disease is present. It is then a problem for the genetic counselor to advise the parents about the probabilities of genetic disease in the offspring.

By amniocentesis procedures, it is possible to determine the presence of approximately 40 serious genetic diseases, including **Down's syndrome** and **Tay-Sach's disease.** Once it is ascertained whether an unborn baby conceived by known carriers will become a postnatal victim of the disease, it is a matter of choice for parents and/or doctors to decide whether the fetus should live or be aborted. The decision, one way or the other, always brings with it a feeling of guilt. And subsequent problems, legal, moral, individual freedom, and financial, always ensue.

amobarbital A crystalline barbiturate used mainly as a sedative; also known as sodium amytal, Amytal Sodium and Amytal (tradenames).

Introduced as an anesthetic in 1931 by the American physician, Irvine H. Page (born 1901).

ampere (A) The SI unit of electric current equal to that constant electric current which, if maintained in two straight parallel conductors of infinite length, of negligible cross section, and placed 1 meter apart in vacuum, would produce between these conductors a force equal to 2×10^{-7} **newtons** per meter of length. *See* **International System of Units.**

Named after Andre M. Ampère (1775-1836), French physicist.

amphetamine An acronym constructed from α + *methyl* + *phenyl* + *ethyl* + *amine.* Commercial name for the sulphate is *Benzedrine,* while its more potent "dextro" form is called *Dexedrine;* another form is *Methedrine.* Its effect upon individuals is highly variable. Amphetamine is a **sympathomimetic** drug, similar in pharmacological effects to and related structurally to **epinephrin(e),** but acts as a greater stimulant to the cortex, keeping some persons "high" for hours. It arouses euphoric feelings, reducing depression, fatigue, and often weight because it is an appetite depressant. Large dosage can result in hallucinations and psychotic-like delusions, while prolonged use may produce depression and extreme fatigue. It is considered intoxicative rather than *addictive.* In addition to promoting **arousal,** it is also peripherally vaso-constrictive, often used to stop sniffling in colds. More recently it has been used medically as a drug to control **hyperkinesis** in children. Slang terms: bennies, dexies, speed, pep pills, copilots, wake-ups, lid-proppers.

a

First described by Russian-American physician George Piness (born 1891), H. Miller, and American chemist Gordon Alles (1901-1963) in, "Clinical Observations on Phenylaminoethanol Sulfate," *Journal of the American Medical Association*, 1930, *94*, 790-791. See **drugs.**

amplitude Quality (-tude) of being ample (ampli-). In general, starting from zero, amplitude refers to maximal displacement by a fluctuating quantity from any mean position to the midpoint of a wave. Amplitude is the height of maximum ordinate, or one-half the distance between highest and lowest points of any periodic (sine) curve. In *time-series analyses*, amplitude of a fluctuation refers to the value of the ordinate at its peak, or also to total differences between extremes in cyclic values. The amount of energy carried by a sound wave is proportional to the square of its amplitude, thus its loudness is a function of the amplitude.

ampulla A flask-like (ampulla) dilation of a canal (e.g., in the *semicircular canals* of the ear or the lactiferous ducts of the breast). Each of the three semicircular canals forms a curved arc lying in a plane approximately at right angles to the other two. The three canals open into the vestibule, which contains the **utricle** and the **saccule.** From the posterior wall of the utricle extend five semicircular ducts, each ending in an ampulla, which bears a small elevation or ridge called the **crista ampullaris.** Consisting of a group of hair cells (the sensory receptors) covered by a mass of gelatinous material (cupola), the crista is a receptor that signals head positions and sense of equilibrium.

About 1804, the Italian anatomist and surgeon Antonio Scarpa (1752-1832) referred to the ampulla as the dilated portions of the membranous semicircular canals.

amygdala (amygdaloid nucleus) An almond-shaped (amygdal-) nuclear structure of the forebrain; a portion of the **limbic system** buried in the base of the **temporal lobe.** It has two areas, the centromedial region, which receives direct input from the olfactory bulb and the basolateral region which receives input from the basal temporal cortex. It also has some direct connections with the **reticular formation.** Amygdaloid outputs go to, among others, the **hypothalamus,** the **caudate nucleus,** and limbic portions of the **cerebral cortex.** The amygdala functions in the arousal and control of emotional and motivational behavior through the limbic system, and it is also apparently a receptive center for such reinforcing stimuli as pain, food, etc. Destruction leads to elimination of rage reactions in animals which become abnormally tame.

Amytal Sodium (sodium amytal) Lilly tradename for **amobarbital.**

anabolism The process (-ism) of building (-bol-) up (ana-) or synthesizing relatively simple substances (e.g., **amino acids**) into complex organic compounds and living tissue (e.g., the healing process in a wound, protoplasm, etc.); constructive metabolism. Opposed to **catabolism.**

Term first used by **Galen** about 180 A.D.

anaclisis A leaning (-clisis) upon (ana-). (Psychoanal.) The tendency of an individual to lean or depend upon an earlier love object in making decisions, or the process one goes through in requiring physical and emotional support. For instance, a man may have an anaclitic dependence upon his mother, physically or psychologically. *Anaclitic depression* (extreme sadness and withdrawing), as used by René Spitz (born 1887), Austrian-American psychiatrist, is often noted in the infant who has been separated from the love or support of the mother for considerable periods of time. *Anaclitic identification* (crying and clinging to mother, doll, etc.) occurs when there is threatened loss or withdrawal of a love object.

anaglyph To carve (-glyph) up (ana-); a low relief carving. A *three-dimensional* depiction, obtained by looking through spectacles with lenses of corresponding colors to superimpose two pictures (usually one in red, the other in blue). Used to determine depth perception through retinal disparity.

First developed and named (1651) by d'Almeida (1619-1670), Portuguese physician, and further improved by French physicist Louis Ducos du Hauron (1837-1920).

anal character (anal personality, anal syndrome). See **character types.**

analeptic drug Referring to (-ic) a drug that takes (-lept-) up (ana-) or is restored. Any drug that has a stimulating effect upon the **central nervous system** (CNS), such as **amphetamine,** which has an **adrenergic** action. Analeptics have an antagonistic effect upon drugs that depress the CNS.

The term "analeptic" was introduced in 1671 as a medical term in referring to an aliment or restorative.

analog and digital data See **computer data.**

analog computer A **computer** dealing with *analog*ous data, such a control system using direct measurement of physical variables (e.g., voltage, position, distance) to represent corresponding numerical values. It translates physical attributes (temperature, pressure, etc.) into related mechanical or electrical values that are analogs for the phenomena under consideration.

Generally, an analog computer uses an analog for all variables and produces analogs as output, or processes continuous (graded) data as opposed to the **discrete** data processed by a **digital** computer. However, it is limited to the solution of problems that are easily represented by physical analogs; whereas the more versatile digital computer may be programmed to solve problems using mathematical methods. Thus, when a problem is easily simulated by some set of analog devices, the analog computer is used; when the problems require general solutions or the handling of large masses of data (test scores, results of polls, etc.), the digital computer is the method chosen. (Brown, 1967, pp. 482-485.)

analogy tests See **Miller Analogy Test.**

analysand The patient, client, or anyone (-and) who is analyzed (analys-).

analysis of covariance A statistical technique combining advantages of linear regression analysis with **analysis of variance** methods.

Analysis of covariance allows the **dependent variable** to be adjusted so that the effects of the uncontrolled error variance can be removed from the concomitant variable. Thus, it helps control **nuisance variables.** Analysis of covariance, however, requires not only the usual assumptions necessary for the analysis of variance approach but also demands progressively more involved assumptions concerning the **regression** effects. Additionally, it is more laborious to compute. (Winer, 1962, pp. 586-590, 600-603; Kirk, 1968, pp. 455-489.)

analysis of variance (anova) A statistical procedure that involves partitioning the total sum of squared deviations of scores into components, each part being associated with some experimental variable or with chance. In the simplest case, analysis of variance involves the ratio of two sources of variation: (1) the variation of scores around their **sample** means and (2) the variation of sample means around the **population** mean. This ratio, called an *F* ratio, is given by

$$F = \frac{MS \text{ among-groups}}{MS \text{ within-groups}}$$

If the preceding two variance estimates are really estimates of the same population variance, the *F* approaches 1.0. If the sample variance of means around the population mean is greater than the score variance around the sample means, the samples probably do not represent random samples from the same population. In this case the *F* ratio is greater than 1.0. In general, analysis of variance is used to test statistical hypotheses concerning two or more population means. (For other uses and definitions of analysis of variance see Guilford, 1965, pp. 268-302; Hays, 1963, pp. 368-378; Kirk, 1968, pp. 35-67, Snedecor and Cochran, 1967, pp. 258-379; and Walker and Lev, 1953, pp. 196-229.)

analyst One who (-yst) analyzes (anal-), or is skilled in analysis of any kind; a shortened form of **psychoanalyst.** In computer work, an analyst examines, evaluates, and defines problems, then develops **algorithms** and procedures for their solution.

analytic psychology Technically, **Jung's** conception of the personality structure, which he divided into consciousness and unconsciousness. The self (being both conscious and unconscious) acts as the integrator between them and includes the **ego** and persona (man's superficial nature) as well as his uninhibited natural self.

Jung viewed the unconscious as a many-layered accumulation of past experiences, consisting of the more recent state of man's personal life (including forgotten memories) and the more deeply hidden, ancestral experiences that mankind has constantly faced and responded to (such as fear of snakes). These experiences, continually repeated, become somewhat crystallized and form what Jung called **archetypes.** He considered religion to be man's major source in his search for fulfillment and the development of his spiritual self.

Generally, analytic psychology refers to any systematic approach to analyzing and hopefully solving psychological problems.

anamnesis The process (-sis) of writing a case history so as to be able to call up (ana-) a remembrance or restore memory (-mnes-). See **associative anamnesis.**

To Plato, in his *Dialogues*, anamnesis meant the process of recalling previous experienced ideas of the soul that existed in another life.

anankastic Relating to (-ic) or tied to fate (anankast-), or to the experience of feeling helpless about escaping from any reality, or to a feeling of inevitability about what is to happen with no way out. An *anankastic psychopath* exhibits complete hopelessness about himself and everything else. See **anankastic personality** under **personality disorders.**

anaphase A phase of **mitosis** in which the chromosome halves move upward (ana-) to the spindle-poles.

anatomical directions The *anatomical position* is a formalized, universally-used posture for presenting anatomical man in reference to the relative position of his appendages, thus, his body is erect with the arms hanging at the sides, palms facing forward in a ventral aspect, with the little fingers adjacent to the thighs. Sometimes called "erect man."

Areas of the body are central (or deep) in that they pertain to underlying structures, such as bones are central but their marrow is even more central; or areas are *superficial* (or **peripheral**) in that they refer to points on or near the body surface or its parts, such as skin is superficial. Peripheral is also distinguished from central in referring to being on the edge or external to another area. The point of attachment of an anatomical structure is its *proximal* end, the free end is *distal*.

In describing the following aspects, axes, and planes, some confusion in terminology arises because of the postural differences between man and quadrupeds. It is therefore important to know which animal is under discussion.

Aspects are named in reference to the direction from which a body is observed, such as:

caudal refers to the tail, but sometimes the term posterior and even **inferior** is used in reference to man's tail region, or *posterior* for reference to the tail in comparative anatomy.

cranial refers to *head*, but sometimes in man *inferior* is used while **anterior** is used in comparative studies.

dorsal (back), but for man **posterior** is often adopted. The back or bottom (when sitting) of the thigh corresponds to the dorsal aspect (or caudal in the quadruped).

dorsum refers to back of the palm.

lateral (side), usually refers to both sides (bilateral).

palmar or volar refers to palm surface of hand, wrist, and forearm.

plantar refers to sole of foot and corresponding aspect of lower leg.

radial (thumb aspects of the forearm).

rostral (pertaining to the nose in animals); in man, anterior.

ulnar (little finger aspects of forearm).

ventral (belly), but in man *anterior* is often used. The front or top (when sitting) of the thigh corresponds to the body's ventral aspect.

In referring to *anatomical positions*, it is sometimes convenient to refer to the adverbial form (-ad) ending rather than adjectival (-al). In general:

dextrad (toward the right).

distrad refers to a point farther away from the center of the body or midline than some other point· distally. The knee is distad to the hip.

mediad (in quadrupeds) refers to the surfaces on appendages that are nearest the midline of the body, i.e., they are mediad to their opposite (the lateral aspect).

proximad refers to a point nearer the center of the body or midline than some other point (the wrist is proximad to the fingers).

sinistrad (toward the left).

More specifically:

caudad (the coccyx is caudad to the atlas)

craniad (the shoulder is craniad to the knee)

dorsad (the vertebrae are dorsad to the sternum).

An axis is one of several imaginary lines assumed in describing the positions of planes passing through two aspects:

anterior-posterior (front to back), *dorsoventral* (back to belly), or *ventrodorsal* (belly to back); in quadrupeds from top to bottom or vice versa.

bilateral (of and relating to the right and left sides of a central organ or plane).

cephalocaudal, craniocaudal, or *vertical:* (from head to tail, head to toe, or up-down) in man.

contralateral (on the opposite side).

dextrosinistral, lateral: from right to left; extending from one side to the other.

ipsilateral (on the same side).

lateral (from side to side), *dextrosinistral.*

rostral-caudal (nose to tail).

vertical (from head to toe in erect man); see **cephalocaudal.**

Anatomical sectional planes are imaginary plane surfaces used to identify the position of a bodily organ and usually pass through four aspects of the body:

coronal: any plane in the human head lying at right angles to the vertical axis, passing through the dorsal, lateral (two), and ventral aspects. See **horizontal.**

frontal: any plane in bilaterally symmetrical animals that is perpendicular to the anterior-posterior axis, passing through the caudal, cranial, and two lateral aspects.

horizontal: a plane of the body that is parallel to the horizon, passing through the dorsal, two lateral, and ventral aspects. See **coronal.**

medial (mesial): the median vertical longitudinal plane that divides a bilaterally symmetrical animal into right and left halves, passing through the caudal, cranial, dorsal, and ventral aspects. Distinguished from **sagittal.**

sagittal: divides the body into any number of symmetrical right and left medial aspects, passing through the caudal, cranial, dorsal, and ventral aspects. Distinguished from **medial.**

transverse: a crosswise cut through the body passing through the dorsal, ventral, and lateral aspects and dividing the body into upper and lower parts.

AND connective *See* **Boolean algebra.**

AND-GATE A module (signal receiving and emitting device—the output being influenced by the input) that consists of one output lead (active only if all input leads are active simultaneously) and at least two input leads.

androgen A generic name for the sex hormones (e.g., **androsterone, testosterone**) produced (-gen) in the male (andro-). These hormones, secreted mainly by the testes (others by the *adrenal cortex*), influence sexual desire and stimulate development of secondary sexual characteristics.

Hippocrates used term "androgenia," referring to development of the male sex.

androsterone The male (andro-) sterol (-ster-) + -one, the suffix ending for a ketone. The hormonal secretion of the interstitial cells of the testes.

A relation between the testes and secondary sexual characteristics has long been assumed. The first article on gonadal transplantation showing its hormonal effect was published in 1849 by A. A. Berthold (1813-1861), German physiologist. In 1927, the testicular secretion from the interstitial cells was demonstrated to be a male sex hormone by three American scientists: (1) biochemist Fred Conrad Koch (1876-1948), (2) zoologist Carl Richard Moore (1892-1955), and biochemist Thomas F. Gallagher (born 1905). Koch named the testicular hormone "androsterone" in 1927. In 1931, androsterone was isolated in its crystalline form by the German biochemist, Adolf Butenandt (born 1903).

anechoic chamber Pertaining to (-ic) a chamber that is without (-an-) echoes (-echo-), such as an experimental room used for psychoacoustic research. Sound waves are absorbed within the chamber walls by fibrous structures that muffle echo and standing waves, with sound wave reflection being negligible.

anelectrotonus The lessened conductivity and tension (-tonus) of a nerve near an anode (an-) as an electrical (-electro-) current passes through it (with consequent increase in cell-membrane polarization). *See* **electrotonus.**

Term coined (1859) by Eduard F. Pflüger (1829-1910), German physiologist, who described it as meaning "a self-propagating condition carried from one ... (nerve section) to the next by a sequence of decreased excitability."

Angell, James Rowland (1869-1949) American psychologist. Student of **William James** and **Külpe.** At the University of Chicago from 1894 to 1920, later president of Yale University (1921-1937). Angell was a leading spokesman of the so-called Chicago school of **functionalism,** which he described as the "psychology of mental operations in contrast to the psychology of mental elements," as is found in **structuralism.** Furthermore, functionalism incorporated all body-mind relationships. Editor of the *Psychological Monographs,* 1912-1922. President of the APA, 1906. See **K. Bühler.**

Angst (G. anxiety-dread, anxiety-fright, a fear that erupts from the marrow of the bones, Angst deriving from an Old High German word (Engin) meaning "marrow"). **Freud, Goldstein,** and **Kierkegaard** have all used the term Angst, which often has been weakly translated into English as anxiety, losing some of its Teutonic emotional power in the process.

angular transformation Same as **arcsin transformation.**

anima, animus In Jungian personality theory, the repressed "other-sexed" aspects or soul (anima) of each sex: the **repressed** feminine nature of man is called his anima, and the repressed masculine side of woman, her animus.

animal care and use As approved June 26, 1968, by the Council of Representatives, American Psychological Association, the following principles amended apply: (1) All animals must be lawfully acquired, and their care and use in research shall be in compliance with Federal and local laws and regulations. (2) Care of all animals shall be in accordance with generally accepted laboratory practices, with appropriate considerations for bodily comfort, humane treatment, and sanitary environment. (3) Every effort must be made to avoid unnecessary discomfort to animals. Research procedures subjecting animals to discomfort shall be conducted only when such discomfort is required, and is justified by the objectives of the research. (4) Surgical procedures shall be done under appropriate anesthesia. Generally acceptable techniques to avoid infection and minimize pain must be followed throughout. The postoperative care of animals must minimize discomfort in accordance with generally accepted practices. (5) The disposal of animals must be done in a humane manner. (6) The use of animals by students shall be under the supervision of a qualified teacher or investigator and shall be in accordance with these Principles. (7) A qualified individual for each psychology department shall be designated as the responsible agent for implementing these Principles, and he shall see to it that a copy of these rules shall be posted in every room where animals are housed or where animal research is conducted.

Violations of these Principles shall be reported promptly to the designated individual. Repeated violations may be called to the attention of the *American Psychological Association.*

Copyright 1968 by the American Psychological Association, and reproduced by permission.

animal electricity Electricity generated by specially adapted organs of some fishes (the eel) and apparently used chiefly in attack or defense.

Stephen Hales (1677-1761) mentioned in 1732 that probably currents of an electrical nature were responsible for nerve transmission. A method for detecting animal electricity was not possible, however, until the galvanometer was invented by the Danish physicist Hans Christian Oersted (1777-1851) and by Johann Salomo Christoph Schweiger (1779-1857). Identified 1774 in the electric eel by John Walsh (1725-1795). Galvani had started his experiments on electricity by about 1780, which led to the development of electrophysiology and to the acceptance of "animal electricity as a biological phenomenon." Such studies slowed down for about 50 years, but when Italian physicist Leopoldo Nobili (1784-1835) developed the astatic galvanometer in 1825, studies again perked up, with Italian mathematician and physicist, Carlo Mateucci (1811-1868) leading the way. Soon du Bois-Reymond, Helmholtz, and other physiologists from Germany, England, and the United States stimulated research to its present stage of development with nerve transmission thought of as electro-chemical in nature. (Clarke and O'Malley, pp. 175-236, passim).

animal magnetism A dynamic spiritlike force reputedly possessed by some individuals who can utilize their power in a quasi-hypnotic manner so as to control and influence the thoughts and actions of others.

The idea was reportedly introduced (1666) by the Irish conjurer and healer **Valentine Greatrakes.** It was not heard of again until 1774 when Father Hehl, a Viennese Jesuit priest, reintroduced the practice, demonstrating it to his friend **Mesmer** who had written about astral magnetism in 1766. Mesmer broke from Hehl, practicing animal magnetism on a wide scale and writing about it in 1779. An American by the name of Jacob Perkins (1766-1849) invented a metallic

a

tractor for collecting, condensing, and applying animal magnetism, which had very successful sales for numbers of years. In an investigation by a commission of the French Academy of Sciences during 1837-38, animal magnetism was considered "disproved" and closed by a "dead letter" in 1840.

animism Soul (anim-) doctrine (-ism). A word used with related but not identical meanings in anthropology and philosophy, and often in the history of psychology.

Anthropology: Man's primitive inclination to ascribe living attributes to inanimate matter, having an existence similar to that found in an animate being; accordingly, a rock, river, etc., has irritability, malice, purpose, desire, etc. Nature-religions are characterized by animism and elements of animism remain even in more highly developed religions.

This type of animism is associated mainly with the name of Edward B. Tylor (1832-1917), British anthropologist, but it has its origins in the writings (1767) of Nicholas-Sylvestre Bergier (1718-1790), French antiquarian and theologian.

Philosophy: The doctrine that employs the immortal soul to explain the differences between a dead animal and a living one, the vital processes, etc.—a concept philosophers have resorted to from earliest time in answering such questions. Animism in this sense was first put in writing (1707) in *Theoria Medica Vera* by George Ernst Stahl (1660-1734), German physician.

In the psychological sense, the clinical psychologist encounters the two previous concepts of animism in his clients and observes many persons resorting to animism to explain the environment. Jean **Piaget** has called attention to animistic reasoning in children. Animistic explanations may appear in neurotic responses to problem situations. William **McDougall**, presenting his "interaction theory" of mind as a separate factor cooperating with the brain, employed the concept in his *Body and Mind: A History and Defense of Animism*, 1911.

aniseikonia A disorder (-ia) of binocular vision in which the images (-eikon-) are not (an-) equal (iso-). A visual anomaly in which the image projected on the retina of one eye is larger than the other, resulting in distorted depth perception (Woodworth and Schlosberg, 1965, pp. 487-488).

Anlage, (pl. **Anlagen**) (Ger., a beginning, arrangement.) A laying on, foundation. Biologically, an *Anlage* is the inherited organization (primordium) of an individual forming the basis for a later development; rudiment. **Jung** referred to the *Anlage* as the basic, usually unconscious element in each personality representing the opposite sex. Genetically, the *Anlage* (*Erbanlage* or hereditary factor) is the individual's basic self that predisposes the organism to develop certain traits or characteristics. *Anlage functions* are those early tendencies to act (span of apprehension, retention, etc.) that indicate the developing intelligence.

In 1892, Bernhard Sigismund Schultze (1827-1919), German obstetrician, referred to the points on the embryonic milkridge (precursor to milk glands) as *Anlagen*, which is the first recorded use of the term prior to Jung's use of it in psychology.

Anokhin, Peter Kuzmich (born 1898) Soviet physiologist and research physician. Did laboratory work with **Bekhterev** and **Pavlov**. Carried on many studies on cybernetics, conditioned reflexes, neurophysiology, and psychology. Developed a sensory-motor method of conditioned reflexes.

anomaloscope An optical instrument for viewing (-scope) **anomalous color vision**. The **Rayleigh equation** (which determines the proportions necessary for mixing red and green lights of constant intensity) is used to enable the observer to match a monochromatic yellow light. The proportions read off a scale indicate the degree of **deuteranopia** or **protanopia**. The anomaloscope demonstrates that yellow is not pure but always a balanced mixture of red and green.

anomalous color vision Color vision characterized by (-ous) an irregular (anomal-) responsiveness to certain colors; ability to discriminate vivid colors but not poorly saturated ones. Although people with this defect require three-colored lights for spectral vision, as is normal, they demand different proportions to see well. Specifically, the varied conditions are **protanopia, deuteranopia,** and **tritanopia**.

Lord Rayleigh (John William Strutt, 1842-1919, English physicist), discovered (1881) that those who confuse red with green require a greater intensity of either red or green to match yellow. Thus, the degree of color anomaly can be determined by the proportion of red and green light necessary for matching a monochromatic yellow.

anomie (anomy) Condition of (-ie or -y) being without (a-) a law (-nom-); lawlessness; normlessness. A condition of the individual or of society in general, characterized by weakening or disappearance of moral guidelines, resulting in a feeling of social isolation, anxiety, and disorientation in the individual, or in a chaotic society.

The term anomy first appeared (1591) in English meaning disregard of divine law. In 1755, it had the added meaning of lawlessness. *Anomie*, according to the French sociologist, Emile Durkheim (1858-1917), is a form of **alienation** in which "the social norms regulating individual conduct have broken down or are no longer effective as rules for behavior." He considered anomie to be a major cause of suicide, resulting when the person feels that his once secure society has disintegrated and become undependable. (Emile Durkheim, *The Division of Labor in Society*, 1933; Simon Markson [Ed.] *Automation, Alienation, and Anomie*, Harper and Row, 1970, pp. 377-442.)

anorexia A disorder (-ia) of partial or complete loss (an-) of appetite (-orex-) for food, generally psychogenic in nature, and most often found in children, young single women, and senile patients. *Anorexia nervosa*, of hysterical origin, is characterized by aversion to food with accompanying nutritive deficiencies and emaciation. Progression to chronic mental illness sometimes occurs, although the patient, despite weighing often less than ninety pounds and exhibiting a slow heart rate and fairly common vomiting, shows amazingly good nature and energy.

Galen referred to the term *c.* 190 A.D., as did Paul of Aegina *c.* 675 A.D. The word "anorexia" first appeared in English *c.* 1548, as *anorexie*. Anorexia nervosa was first described and named in 1873 by the English physician, William Gull (1816-1890).

anorthographia *See* **motor agraphia**.

anosmia Disorder (-ia) involving loss (an-) of the sense of smell (-osm-). Defective sensitivity to smell stimuli, which may be due to a lesion of the olfactory nerve, to an obstruction of the nasal area, or to a functional condition.

Galen was first to mention the condition. The term itself was originally recorded (1845) in Hooper's Medical Dictionary.

anosognosia Disorder (-ia) of not (a-) admitting one's knowledge (-gnos-) of his own obvious disease (-noso-), such as denying the existence of hemiplegia; refusal to acknowledge one's own sensory or motor defect(s), such extreme denial of illness being considered a distortion of body perception.

First described in 1914 by **Babinski** and so named by him in describing behavior of two patients suffering from left hemiplegia. (E. A. Weinstein and R. L. Kahn, *Denial of Illness*, 1955).

anoxemia Disorder (-ia) of being without (an-) sufficient oxygen (-ox-) in the blood (-em-); poor aeration of blood with accompanying symptoms of disturbance in mental functioning, or subsequent organic damage. Anoxemia, as a result of prolonged labor, may lead to brain damage in the new-born child.

anoxia Disorder (-ia) of being without (an-) sufficient oxygen (-ox-) in the body tissues to maintain homeostatic balance and normal **metabolism**. The neonate particularly needs oxygen to help brain cells develop. Anoxia results in severe mental and physical disturbances and if continued, death results.

ANS Autonomic nervous system.

Anschauung (Ger., intuition, in a broad sense). Immediate and direct effect of the impact of sensory experience upon the formation of perception or intuition.

Kant used the term (1781) in his "Critique," referring to the impact of space and time upon the intellect.

Antabuse (or **Disulfiram**) Tradename for tetraethylthiuram disulphide. A drug whose revulsive effect turns the chronic alcoholic against (ant-) the abuse of alcohol. If the patient takes alcohol within 24-72 hours after ingesting Antabuse, normal alcohol oxidation is interfered with, resulting in acetaldehyde poisoning with subsequent symptoms of headaches, flushed face, labored breathing, dizziness, chest pains, palpitation, apprehension, fear, nausea, and vomiting. Antabuse is not a cure but does make the patient more receptive and amenable to therapy.

Drug discovered (1946) by two Danish pharmacists (Jens Hald and Erik Jacobsen), and the term coined then by the drug firm of Medicinalco. The drug was first reported in an article, A Drug Sensitizing the Organism to Ethyl Alcohol, *Lancet*, 1948, **225**, 1001.

anterior Situated further (-ior) toward the front (anter-) of the head. Synonymous with ventral (in man) and cephalic (in lower animals). *See* **anatomical directions**.

anterior pituitary hormone One of several different hormones found to be active in the anterior pituitary lobe.

In 1930, Canadian biochemist and physician James B. Collip (1892-1965) reported that he had discovered an ovary-stimulating hormone in the placenta which he called the "anterior pituitary-like factor," and later **parathormone**.

anterior-posterior axis From the front (anterior), belly, or chest to its corresponding area in the back (posterior). *See* **anatomical directions**.

anterograde amnesia *See* **amnesia**.

anthropomorphism The doctrine (-ism) that God exists in the form (-morph-) of man (anthropo-). The ascription of human traits (especially mental) to God, deities, animals, or inanimate objects. The interpretation of the behavior of lower animals in terms of human feelings, motives, and behavior.

Term coined (1664) by Henry Moore (1614-1687), English writer and philosopher. Compare **animism**; *see* **theriomorphism**.

antianxiety drugs Term introduced about 1965-66 to describe drugs that have a quieting effect upon disturbed people.

anticipation learning method Testing rote learning by permitting the scoring of successes and failures throughout memorization, while providing a running record of the subject's progress. The method, presenting a list of items appearing consecutively in the aperture of a memory drum, is appropriate to either serial memorization or paired-associates learning, whereby the subject learns to anticipate a stimulus item or respond to it with the response item next to appear.

anticipatory response A response preceding or occurring before the expected one. A response made in anticipation of a stimulus or to an appropriate stimulus. For example, a subject instructed to press a key in response to a light may anticipate the signal and press the key prematurely, or press it in response to a sudden sound rather than a light. *See* **fractional anticipatory response**. (Sidney D. S. Spragg, "Anticipatory Responses in Serial Learning by Chimpanzees," *Comparative Psychology Monographs*, 1936, **13**, No. 2.)

antidepressant *Same as* **stimulant.**

antidromic activation of nerve impulses Referring to (-ic) the conduction of nerve impulses that run (-drom-) against (anti-) or are opposed to the normal manner of conduction. For example, using direct electrical stimulation of the **motor neuron's axon** to produce a so-called "backward" stimulation of the cell body. Opposed to **orthodromic activation.** (Thompson, 1967, p. 173.)

antilogarithm Opposed or against (anti-) the method used in finding **logarithms.** A natural number corresponding to a given logarithm. Antilogarithms are found by reversing the procedure used in finding logarithms. For example: given that 2 is the log of 100 (to the base 10), then the antilog of 2 is 100.

antisocial personality *See* **personality disorders.**

antisocial reactions (psychopathic personality) Disorders marked by lack of responsibility, poor judgment, absence of moral values, inability to learn from experience, or unwillingness to postpone gratifications.

Antrittsvorlesung The inaugural (Antritts) lecture (vorlesung) given, for example, by a German (medical) student on his procedural way through the **Habilitation** toward achieving the **venia legendi.** *See* **German higher education.**

anvil To hit or beat; the incus. One of three bones in the middle ear (the others are the **hammer** and the **stirrup**) that, as a system of levers, transmit and amplify vibrations from the eardrum to the fluid in the **inner ear.**

anxiety Distressed or painful (anxie-) condition (-ty). A complex, intense emotional pattern of behavior with apprehension or fear as its most prominent symptom. Chronic anxiety feelings are usually generated by dread of the past (reliving of a traumatic experience) or apprehension of the future (associated with fears of the unknown). Anxiety may be precipitated by diffuse factors within the psyche or in the environment, and may be identified with specific aspects of the organism, such as heart, lungs, and sex glands. *Psychoanalytically*, anxiety is the take-off point for the study of psychopathology (involving repression and neurotic formation). According to psychoanalysts and some learning theorists, the potential for anxiety lies within the nervous system. However, it can be learned from previously neutral cues. Anxiety also has drive-function in that it can motivate learning and performance. Sometimes, anxiety is differentiated from fear by being considered a reaction to subjective changes while fear relates to objective danger, their physiological effects being identical, however. To **Freud,** anxiety precedes **repression** and is an unpleasurable state accompanied by motor discharge along definite pathways. Freud considered anxiety as being of three types: objective (fear); neurotic (symbolically displaced); and social (interpersonal or cultural). *Free-floating anxiety* is not identifiable with any particular cause, usually occurring in periodic, acute attacks. Probably a reaction free of ego defenses. An anxiety reaction is a neurotic pattern marked by feelings of imminent, impending danger, uneasiness, obsessional behavior, extreme apprehension and dread; often associated with heart palpitations, cold sweats, tenseness, irritability, etc. Anxiety reaction may take the form of asthenic, hypochondriacal, or phobic reactions. *See* **asthenia, hypochondria, neurosis, phobia.**

AOA American Orthopsychiatric Association.

APA American Psychological Association; also American Psychiatric Association and American Philosophical Association. *See* **APsaA.**

APA Distinguished Scientific Contribution Award *See* **Distinguished Scientific Contribution Award.**

apartness (Exist.) The quality of experiencing the simultaneous feeling of being like yet different and apart from others; the vague feeling of belonging to some vast mass (the human race) without any close identification with or ties to any individual or group. Compare **alienation, anomie.**

aphagia A disorder (-ia) of having no (a-) desire to eat (-phag-); loss of appetite. Lack of a hunger drive, particularly in experimental animals. The condition is related not to drive level but to the palatability of the food. It is apparently due to lesions in the lateral area of the **hypothalamus,** such defect having an inhibitory effect upon the animal's appetite. Contrasted with **anorexia** and **hyperphagia.**

aphasia A disorder (-ia) of being without (a-) speech (-phas-). Inability to use or comprehend language, resulting from **functional disturbance** or presumed brain lesions. Aphasia is basically a disorder in ability to translate experiences into verbal symbols rather than actually involving organs of speech. Many clinicians eschew an etiologic classification, preferring a symptomatic one such as the following:

1. *Sensory*
   a. Auditory (word deafness): inability to understand meanings of the spoken word or language. Words are heard but not understood.
   b. Visual (**alexia** or word blindness): inability to perceive or comprehend written language.
2. *Motor* (inability to use spoken language; speech sounds have no meaningful combinations.)
   a. *Manual* (**agraphia**): inability to form written language.
   b. *Speech* (word muteness): inability to express language vocally.

Although it had been recognized in classical times, and Linnaeus (Carl von Linné) (1707-1778), Swedish naturalist and physician, had described a similar condition in 1745, Jean Baptist Bouillaud (1796-1881), French physician, was the first (1824) to adequately describe the condition.

In 1861, **Broca,** referring to it as "aphemie" or motor aphasia, pinpointed the third frontal convolution of the left cerebral hemisphere as the area involved in the disorder (**Broca's speech area**). In 1864, Armand Trousseau, upon learning that "aphemia" also meant "infamy" in Greek, substituted the name "aphasia" for the condition. In 1874, **Wernicke** divided aphasia into motor and sensory aphasia.

aphemia *See* **aphasia.**

apoenzyme The protein compound or *enzyme* that is different from (apo-) but combined with a **coenzyme** to form a complete enzyme.

a posteriori From (a) what comes later (posteriori). Reasoning backwards, from effect to cause. Proceeding from the particular to the general; inductive thinking. Conclusions, principles, or proportions based upon or having had experience or actual experimentation. Sometimes contrasted with **a priori.**

An example of an *a posteriori* statistical test is that of **Tukey's HSD test** used to examine experimental data for possible sources of treatment effects. (Kirk, 1968, pp. 88-90; Winer, 1962, p. 870.) *See* **multiple comparison test.**

apparent movement The **illusion** of movement produced by: (a) different but stationary views of an object presented in the proper order and (b) the presentation of visual stimuli at sufficient speed (as with a **stroboscope**) and at sufficient illumination.

In 1913, F. Kenkel, under **Koffka's** direction, developed the first three following categories of apparent movement, and in 1915, A. Korte added the fourth: (1) *alpha movement*: apparent change in the size of an object under successive presentation; (2) *beta movement*: apparent movement of an object from one position to another; (3) *gamma movement*: the apparent expansion and contraction of an object as illumination is increased or decreased; and (4) *delta movement*: a reversal of movement, seen under very limited conditions. *See* **phi phenomenon.**

apperception The process (-ion) of forming a new perception by consciously assimilating new sensations and meanings and adding them to (ap- from ad-) the already existing mental context.

The term was introduced by **Leibniz** in his *Principles of Nature and of Grace* (1714), who distinguished between perception (the inner self representing external factors) and apperception (the inner self being consciously aware of itself). To **Herbart,** too, any idea that reaches consciousness is apperceived, but for him the idea must also be absorbed into one's conscious nexus of previous ideas and experiences (the "apperceptive mass"). Herbart believed that unconscious ideas continually struggled to reach consciousness through apperceptive attention. **Wundt,** in his *Physiologisch Psychologie,* 1911, considered apperception to be an activity (act) in the focus of consciousness with cognitive and phenomenological aspects, actually setting up experiments to measure apperceptive phenomena.

applied psychology *See* **fields of psychology.**

approach-approach (positive-positive) conflict An anxiety-producing situation in which a person is motivated toward mutually incompatible but equally desirable goals. One solution is to make a choice. For example, a girl is invited to the same event on the same night by two equally attractive men, A and B. She chooses A for this occasion, but asks B for a "rain check" for another time, thus eliminating her conflict, at least temporarily, providing B gives her a rain check and that it doesn't "rain" again.

Concept and term developed by **Lewin** in 1933 and published in *A Dynamic Theory of Personality,* 1935.

approach-avoidance (positive-negative) conflict An anxiety-producing situation in which a person is simultaneously attracted and repelled by the same goal. For example, a man feels motivated to study for a doctor's degree, but because of the many sacrifices he must make, he is also repelled by the idea. One solution lies in weighing the ultimate and lasting values of each choice, then committing himself to his decision. *Compare* **approach-approach conflict;** *see* **ambivalence.**

Developed by **Lewin,** 1933.

apraxia A disorder (-ia) in which no (a-) action (-prax-) is taken. Inability to perform purposeful motor responses through loss of memory rather than because of a true paralysis; often caused by brain lesions. For example, a victim of apraxia unable to "remember" how to coordinate his own swimming movements may well remember intellectually the process of swimming. An apraxic no longer able to swim can teach others to do so.

Apraxic people exhibit motor handicaps in several ways: (1) difficulty or inability in constructing objects from a design (as required, for example, in the block design test of the **WISC** or **WAIS,** or in following directions of the **Bender-Gestalt Test**); (2) incapability of forming ideas so as to perform a given test; (3) incapability of carrying out complex forms of movement despite the ability to comprehend completely the directions.

In 1866, Hughlings **Jackson** made one of the first descriptions of apraxia, but German neurologist, Hugo Carl Liepmann (1863-1925) gave the first (1900) adequate description of the condition, indicating various forms of the disease. *See* **agnosia.**

a priori From (a) the first (priori). Reasoning forward, from cause to effect; *this* condition should produce *that* result. Innate, universal knowledge. Proceeding from a generalization to a particular instance. Conclusions deduced from previously known theories, assumed premises, or hypotheses. Reasoning based on "self-evident truths" that is logically prior to

a

experience or experiment; sometimes contrasted with **empirical** and **a posteriori**. *A priori* or planned hypotheses are those used in an experiment that is designed to test a specific set of hypotheses. *See* **multiple comparison test**.

aprosexia A disorder (-ia) in which attention (-prosex-) is lacking (a-). A perceptual deficit, an inability to form the whole from the sum of its parts, or incapability of maintaining one's attention.

APsaA American Psychoanalytic Association.

aptitude test Quality (-tude) of being fit (apti-). A written, oral, or performance test designed to measure a person's potential ability for performing well in some future selected skill or activity. Tests for musical aptitude, clerical aptitude, and mechanical aptitude are common. Aptitude tests measure aptitude indirectly by exploring correlated abilities that are assumed to indicate disposition toward some untried talent, profession, or job; usually used in education or personnel work. *See* **attitude**.

arachnoid layer (arachnoid membrane) Membrane resembling (-oid) a spider web (arachn-); the vascular middle layer of the **meninges**.

Hippocrates (c. 410 B.C.) used the term in referring to the scum on urine that appeared in the chamber pot each morning. Herophilus used it to describe the ventricles of the brain, since they resembled a spider's web to him. In 1650, it acquired its present meaning, but it was not until 1800 that French histologist, Marie Francois Xavier Bichat (1771-1802), in his *Treatise on the Membranes* described these membranes in rigorous detail.

Aranzi, Giulio Cesare (1530-1589) Italian physician. In 1587 he named and gave the first description of the **hippocampus**. He also named the aperture connecting the third and fourth ventricle the "aqueduct," later called the aqueduct of Sylvius.

ARAS Ascending reticular activating system.

arbitrary constant An assigned quantity that remains fixed for a particular statistical analysis.

arbitrary origin Any selected point from which all scale values are expressed as deviations; often the midpoint of a **class interval**.

archetype Primitive (arche-) mold or type. The original model, prototype. In **Jungian** psychology, a concept representing the most ancient and most universal thought-forms that transcend a man's experience. An archetype is evident in deep religious thought, in classical art, literature, mythology, and folklore. These expressions emerge from the depth of the psyche, being unconscious, inherited predispositions to specific reactions, usually creative in nature. The archetypes themselves are not inherited, but the capacity to create concepts is. An archetype is also a trace of the collective experience of the human race, which is continued on and expressed through the individual's unconscious. An archetypal experience occurs in the presence of great emotional or spiritual feelings, during psychotic episodes, and also in response to the stimulation of **psychotherapy**. Jung considered the Mother, the Great-God-Mother, as an archetypal concept: the giver of life, the mistress, the compassionate, the cruel one, etc.

Archetype was introduced (1605) into the English language as meaning prototype, which was similar to Plato's usage in referring to the idea or form that was in the divine soul before creation. Jung developed his concept in 1924. *See* **analytic psychology**.

archipallium The original or primitive (archi-) part of the pallium (the entire **cerebral cortex**), including the **hippocampus** and evolving earlier than the neocortex.

Meynert coined the term, describing it and neo-pallium in an article published 1867-68. The term is generally synonymous with the olfactory cortex, **Vogt's allocortex**, or **Koelliker's rhinencephalon**.

arcsin transformation (Also known as angular transformation and inverse sine transformation.) A nonlinear transformation that converts proportions or percentages into corresponding angle values in degrees of arc, varying from $0°$ to $90°$. These values are normally distributed in sampling, but not so for extreme proportions. Such a transformation tends to reduce heterogeneity of **variance**, but it does not remove irregularities in variance, as the n values differ.

Statistically, it is a procedure whereby one variate (say X) is transformed into another variate, X', whose distribution is more nearly normal. It is often best to transform proportions into angles by the following procedure:

$$X' = 2 \arcsin \sqrt{X},$$

where X is expressed as a proportion. See Table 7; also Walker and Lev, 1953, pp. 423-424; Kirk, 1968, pp. 63-67.

arcuate nucleus Having a nucleus shaped like (-ate) a bow (arcu-). That bowlike part of the ventrolateral nucleus of the **thalamus** where second order **neurons** excited by **sensory** nerves from the tongue and face terminate; a part of the nerve pathways serving taste and somesthetic sensations.

German anatomist Friedrich Arnold (1803-1890) first described the arcuate nuclei in 1838.

area sampling A relatively inexpensive form of **cluster sampling** used in making attitude and opinion surveys. The survey-respondents are selected randomly from clusters based on an arbitrary geographic area (city block or larger residential section, rural areas, etc.) in an attempt to obtain a cross-section of the total population. Used extensively by the U.S. Bureau of the Census. *See* **attitude scale**, **quota sampling**, **random sampling**, **representative sample**, and **sampling**.

areas of psychology *See* **fields of psychology**.

area under the normal curve In fitting a curve to a **histogram**, it may be assumed that the **normal curve** (despite its theoretical asymptoticity) has a finite area measurably the same as the area of the histogram to which it was fitted. The area under the entire curve is represented as 1.00, and any portion of it may be indicated in percentage terms. *See* **normal curve distribution**, Table 2.

Areteaus of Cappadocia (?81-138?), physician and anatomist of Asia Minor; in his textbook described frenzy, **epilepsy**, mental deterioration, **hysteria, mania,** and **melancholia,** among other mental terms. He believed that mania and melancholia were different symptoms of the same basic illness. Apparently never dissected a human being but did perform numerous dissections on animals. Differentiated between nervous diseases and mental disorders. Described aura and hallucinatory state preceding **epilepsy**. Apparently knew of **Galen's** decussation exposition, as he described the crossing over in the brain of nerves as "decussating each other in the form of the letter X." (Clarke and O'Malley, pp. 281-282).

Aristotle (384-322 B.C.) Greek philosopher. Student of **Plato** for about twenty years. An early empiricist, he taught that man's mind is a "**tabula rasa**" or blank tablet at birth, and that all knowledge comes from experience. He believed in Plato's idea that the intellect (nous) had a divine origin; considered the **brain** to be the interpreter of consciousness, but considered the heart to be the locale for thought and feelings of sensation; described the **meninges** as well as the five senses (touch, taste, smell, sight, and hearing). He believed that **epilepsy** was caused by brain disease. Aristotle wrote the first specifically psychological treatise, *De Anima*.

His extant books are essentially made up of the courses he gave in the Lyceum. They include Logic, Ethics, Politics, Rhetoric, Aesthetics, Metaphysics, Physics, Ontology, Cosmology, Biology, and Psychology. His

ideas on sensation, memory, and knowledge contributed to the **associationist** psychology of the seventeenth century. *See* **Bacon, Bain, humors, marasmus, nerves**.

arithmetic average (arithmetic mean) Often referred to as the mean, and unless otherwise specified the terms "mean" and "arithmetic mean" are synonymous. The mean is that point about which the sum of all deviations from the mean is zero, and is also the center of gravity of the distributions depicted on a histogram; it is the "least squares" solution for a central value (sum of squared deviations is at a minimum).

Two methods of calculating the arithmetic mean are:

1. In a listing of individual scores or values, the mean is the sum (Σ) of the scores (X) divided by the number (N) of cases:

$$\bar{X} = \frac{\Sigma X}{N} \quad \text{or} \quad M = \frac{\Sigma X}{N}$$

where: $\bar{X}$ (X bar) or M = mean, X = any score or measurement, N = number of cases, Σ = summation sign.

2. With the frequency distribution in class interval units, the value of X for any class interval is taken as the average of all the frequencies in that class interval and is conveniently set at the midpoint of each class interval, and multiplied by the frequency (f) in that class interval:

$$\bar{X} = \frac{\Sigma fX}{N} \quad \text{or} \quad M = \frac{\Sigma fX_c}{N}$$

where X_c = midpoint of a class interval and f = number of cases within the interval. The expression fX means the frequency times the X value for the interval. All such products must be found first, then summed.

Army alpha *See* **alpha tests of intelligence**.

Army General Classification Test *See* **group test**.

arousal A condition of excitability of the organism whose arousal level for emotion and motivation is dependent upon the behavioral efficiency of the organism. Arousal is controlled by the **RAS**. The level of arousal is on a continuum, lowest during sleep states and highest when the organism is alert and activated. The arousal concept helps integrate drive theory and other motivational concepts.

arousal system A diffuse network of nerve cells, extending from the **medulla oblongata** through the **thalamus**, involving organs controlled by both the **central nervous system** and the **autonomic nervous system**. The reticular core mediates cortical arousal. Since a well-functioning arousal system keeps the **cerebral cortex** at a highly alert level, it plays a large role in the intensity level of a drive or motivation. Naturally, during sleep a person's arousal level is low. *See* **reticular activating system**.

Arterenol Tradename for norepinephrine.

articuleme A basic structural unit (-eme) or motor schema of articulate speech sound. *See* **speech mechanisms of thinking**.

artificial intelligence *See* **intelligence**.

Arztliche Approbation A rank in Germany attained by the medical (arztlich) student after obtaining his M.D. degree and his medical license. *See* **German higher education**.

ascending reticular activating system (ARAS) The part of the **reticular activating system** that relays sensory impulses upward to the **cerebral cortex**. Midbrain transection results in somnolence, a condition related to the functions of the ARAS.

ascending tract *See* **nerve tract**.

ASCII *American Standard Code for Information Interchange*. A universal eight-bit code in digital systems that allows data to be transmitted from one manufacturer's equipment to another. The code can represent the decimal digits 0-9, the upper- and lower-case alphabet, and such special characters as *¢*, $, etc. Each group of eight bits is generally referred to as a **byte**. *See* **binary digit**.

Asclepiades of Bithynia (c. 124 B.C.) Father of psychiatry. Opposed **humoral doctrine** of diseases. Classified psychoses into febrile and non-febrile (from abuse of drugs, e.g., **opium**, mandragora) diseases. Differentiated between **delusions** and **hallucinations**. Also, first to divide diseases into acute and chronic conditions. *See* **insanity, methodists**.

asiles d'aliénés A French asylum for the alienated; a mental hospital, administered by the region *départements* (in Paris, the Département de la Seine). *See* **French higher education**.

aspects In anatomy, surfaces facing a particular direction and named with reference to the direction from which a body is viewed. *See* **anatomical directions**.

aspiration level The maximum goal, either general or specific, that a person strives to attain at any given time. For example, a student with a motivation for only average achievement may be satisfied with a "C" average, whereas another "C" average student, whose level of aspiration is to obtain an "A," may very well be miserable.

F. Hoppe developed the concept of aspiration level in the late 1920's while a student of Lewin's. In *Dynamic Theory of Personality*, 1935, **Lewin** abstracted Hoppe's article on success and failure (*Erfolg und Misserfolg*) which had been published originally in *Psychologische Forschung*, 1930, **14**, 1-62. Hoppe pointed out that success and failure determinants must include the subject's attitudes toward the value of a particular task as well as the task difficulty and eventual outcome. In other words, the subject's *level of aspiration* had to be considered in any such evaluation.

Asratyan, Ezras Asratovich (born 1903). Soviet physiologist, specializing in traumatic shock effects, reflex activity, and physiological studies on the central nervous system.

assassin *See* **hashish**.

assembler (assembly program, assembly routine) A **computer program** that translates, on a one-for-one basis, a programmer's symbolic **code** instructions (such as: "ADD," "SUBTRACT," "Left Shift Accumulator, Skip on Minus Accumulator") into the numerical codes that the particular computer can understand, producing as an **output** an identical number of instructions as there were in the **input** symbolic codes. An assembler also assigns memory locations.

assembly language A machine-oriented language for programming a particular assembly system. *See* **assembler, machine language**.

assessment A result of (-ment) sitting (assess-) in judgment or setting values upon. The use of any "procedure for making meaningful evaluations among human beings with respect to any characteristic or attribute."

According to American psychologist E. Lowell Kelly (born 1905), assessment first occurred as a psychological term "during World War II to describe the procedures used by a group of psychologists and psychiatrists to select individuals specifically qualified for demanding 'cloak and dagger' assignments essential to the worldwide wartime efforts of the Office of Strategic Services." It first appeared in psychological literature in the title of the book describing this unique program of personnel selection, *The Assessment of Men, OSS Staff*, 1942. (Kelly, 1967, p. 1.)

assimilation A term used in several ways in psychology: in *learning*, a process in which recall is aided by one's motivational and attitudinal characteristics; in **social perception**, a selective process in which the person tends to perceive a stimulus, through his own experience, as more conforming and similar (and thus assimilated) than it really is. For example, a literarily unsophisticated person assimilates into his perceptual pattern the certainty, based upon his limited previous experiences, that the English novelist George Eliot must be a man. To Piaget, assimilation pertains to the child's ability to relate his **cognitive** structure to the environment. *See* **contrast**.

assimilation effect A listener or reader distortion whereby the meaning of a message is absorbed as part of the receiver's preferred attitude; that is, he tends to perceive what he hears or reads (from a source whose beliefs are relatively like his own) as being closer to his own viewpoint than it actually is. A person opposed to the message tends to interpret it as even more distant than the actual discrepancy. Such refusal of assimilation is called the **contrast effect**, which also has other meanings.

Assistance Publique The public welfare and hospital administration run by the local authority (in Paris, for example, or one of the *départements* in the provinces).

Assistent The beginning rank for a German physician who aspires to a university appointment, usually begun by working in a university clinic or institute. He serves in this position doing scientific work and becomes, upon publication of original research, eligible for appointment by his professor to the rank of *Privatdozent*. *See* **German higher education**.

assistant des asiles d'aliénés A position in France equivalent to senior physician in most American state hospitals. *See* **French higher education**.

association Act of (-ation) joining (-soci-) to (as-) something. Formation of bonds between items of experience; a connection between a **stimulus** and a **response** or between two successive responses or ideas. *See* **Meynert**.

association areas of the brain Portions of the cerebral cortex (other than the **projection areas**) that do not directly control **sensory** or **motor** functions (such as hearing, vision, motor coordination) but presumably are involved in the more complex cortical functions of integrating the sensory and motor areas. *See* figure under **speech aphasia**.

Flechsig began studies in 1870 at Leipzig that resulted in his thorough description of the association areas in 1920. The term "association" was first used (1872) by **Meynert** in referring to the brain.

associationism Doctrine (-ism) of association. Used particularly in regard to **association** of ideas (1690). In *psychology*, the concept pertains to connecting one idea with another in learning, ideas being determined by one's experiences.

Associationism set the foundation for modern **learning theory** by reducing the complex functioning of the mind to a simple process of forming associative bonds between stimuli and responses. Contrast with **nativism**.

British associationism, stimulated by such thinkers as **Hobbes, Berkeley, Hartley, Hume, James Mill,** and **Bain,** held that all consciousness stems from simple elements derived from sense experience, a concept that helped lead to the development of **physiological psychology**.

Elements of *associationism* can be traced back to both **Aristotle** and **Plato**. In *Phaedo*, Plato discusses the ideas of contiguity and similarity, and in the *De Memoria et Reminiscentia*, Aristotle mentions three laws of association: similarity, difference, and contiguity (in both time and space). *See* **autochthonous laws of cognitive order**.

association neuron (internuncial neuron) A type of neuron in the **central nervous system** that completes the **reflex arc** by relaying impulses between **sensory** and **motor** neurons.

association psychology A **tabula rasa** approach to human behavior, in which behavior and mental activity are explained by the building up of associations between experiences and ideas. *See* **Aristotle, associationism**.

association value The value attached to the "meaningfulness" of **nonsense syllables**, measured by the percentage of subjects who respond with a meaningful association.

associative anamnesis (sector therapy) A therapeutic approach, developed by Viennese psychosomatist, Felix Deutsch (1884-1964), that concentrates on specific problems or conflicts which the client brings up in the interview (such as an emotionally laden word or strong term, e.g., "always hated her," or "could have killed him") and then probes into what these words "hated" and "killed" really mean, thus getting into the personal and family history (the anamnesis) of the client without making it obvious. (Deutsch, F., *Applied Psychoanalysis*).

assumed mean (same as guessed average or guessed mean) In computing the **arithmetic mean**, the assumed mean is an arbitrary origin guessed to be near the middle of a **frequency distribution**. Serves as an aid or short-cut in calculation.

astasia-abasia A functional disorder (-ia), hysterical in nature, in which the patient professes inability (a-) to stand (-stas-) or take a step (-bas-). Leg muscles, even after long periods of apparent disuse, show no atrophy and are also responsive to electrical stimulation, indicating that the muscles can be functionally useful. Some of these patients (schizophrenic and obsessive-compulsive types) contend that if they stand or walk something catastrophic will happen to a friend or loved one.

A-statistic *See* **Sandler's A-statistic**.

astereognosis A defect of **perception** (sometimes caused by brain damage) evidenced by the loss (a-) of ability to recognize (-gnosis) solid (-stereo-) objects through touch. *See* **agnosia**.

The condition was first described in 1888 by French physician, Paul Oscar Blocq (1860-1896).

asthenia Disorder (-ia) of having no (a-) physical or mental strength (-sthen-) to maintain a drive or interest in anything. The asthenic person feels chronically tired, lacks dedication and concentration, and suffers from mild physical symptoms in absence of known **organic** pathology. *Kretschmer's* asthenic body-type describes a frail, thin, long-limbed, flat-chested, short-trunked person who is also shy, sensitive, and withdrawn—symptoms that are often associated with dementia praecox (1888). Comparable to **Sheldon's** ectomorph type, but contrasted with Kretschmer's pyknic type.

John Brown (1735-1788), Scottish physician, apparently introduced (1780) the term "asthenic" in his *Elementa Medicinae* by referring to those with insufficient "excitability" in their personality as being subject to "asthenic maladies," such as lacking ambition and suffering from nervous exhaustion. **Heinroth** introduced the term asthenia in 1839, which **Beard** and **Janet** used as a model in coining respectively **neurasthenia** and **psychasthenia** in later years.

asthenic personality *See* **personality disorders**.

asthenopia A disorder (-ia) in which the eyes (-op-) become easily fatigued and function feebly or without (a-) strength (-sthen-), often resulting from psychic stress and symptomatized by back pains, neck tension, and headache.

Term and concept introduced (1830) by Scottish ophthalmologist, William Mackenzie (1791-1868).

astrocyte *See* **neuroglia**.

asymbolia A disorder (-ia) caused by brain lesions, in which there is a loss (a-) of ability to comprehend previously understood symbols.

First described (1870) by F. C. M. Finkelnburg.

asymmetrical confidence levels *See* **confidence level**.

asymmetrical contingency A form of dyadic interaction in which one person's planned responses in an interaction determine the unplanned reactions of the second person in the **dyad**.

a

asymmetry Not (a-) measured (-metry) together (-sym-). A lack of going together; a lack of expected conformance. *Algebraically*, if one variable *A* has more of the quality than *B*, then *B* cannot have more of the quality than *A*. If $A > B$, then $B < A$.

asymptote Not (a-) falling (-ptote-) together (sym-). A straight line that a theoretically unending curve approaches but never reaches, except at infinity. An asymptote to a curve is a straight line cutting the curve in two at an infinite distance from the origin. The *X* axis is the asymptote to the **normal probability** curve. An asymptote on a learning curve is the point of leveling off of performance during trial sequences; the level a variable tends to assume after a period of time (e.g., the final response strength after an extended period of acquisition; also called the limit of learning).

ataractic drugs (ataraxics) Relating to (-ic) drugs that cause no (a-) disturbed (-taract-) state; used of drugs that tranquilize in the treatment of anxiety, tension states, and other excitable mental illnesses.

Ataraxia (as freedom from disturbances of mind or passion) was a goal sought by Epicurus (342-270 B.C.), Greek philosopher, as well as by the Stoic philosophers. Recent usage, as applied to drugs that sedate or tranquilize, was introduced (1955) by the American psychiatrist, Howard D. Fabing (born 1907).

ataxia An impairment or disorder (-ia) characterized by a loss (a-) of steadiness or order (-tax-) associated with poor coordination of voluntary movements (involving striate muscles); usually indicative of pathology of the brain or spinal cord, as in **locomotor ataxia**.

Both **Hippocrates** and **Galen** used the term to describe any disordered condition. It entered English usage in 1615 to describe irregularities of function, such as persons with a strange gait. **Flourens** gave a classical description of cerebellar ataxia in 1824, and French physician Paul Bricquet (1796-1881) described ataxia analgica hysterica (anesthesia of skin and leg muscles), while French neurologist Pierre **Marie** (1853-1940), first described hereditary cerebellar ataxia in 1893.

ataxiagraph A device (-graph) for studying ataxia, such instrument measuring the degree and nature of muscle coordination.

ataxiometer A recording device for measuring (-meter) unsteadiness (ataxi-o-) and involuntary sway while the subject is attempting to maintain an erect posture.

athetosis Condition of (-osis) not (a-) being able to maintain a fixed posture (-thet-). A neurological disorder (due to brain damage), seen mostly in children, and characterized by involuntary, slow, spasmodic, vermicular movements of hands, feet, and digits. Often seen in **cerebral palsy** and in certain choreic conditions. *See* **Parkinson's disease**.

Silas Weir Mitchell coined the term **hemichorea** for this condition, referring to chorea-like movements on one-half (hemi-) the side of the body. American neurologist William A. Hammond (1828-1900) wrote an editorial on athetoses in the *Medical Times and Gazette*, 12-16-71, **2**, 747-48, in which he reported the condition and coined the term "athetosis," describing it as an "inability to retain the fingers and toes in any position in which they may be placed . . ."

athletic body type One of **Kretschmer's constitutional types**, having a well developed muscular and skeletal system. Limbs are strong, hands and feet large. Generally, this physique corresponds to the **mesomorphic** type of **Sheldon**.

atomism In philosophy, the view that reality consists of indivisible particles that may be either material (exceedingly minute and infinite in number) or spiritual. A stand by some psychologists (early behaviorists, and associationists, for example) emphasizing the productive and economic values of analytically reducing psychological phenomena to their basic components, disregarding the total or whole.

Atom coined by **Democritus** in meaning a thing so small it could not be cut.

ATP Adenosine triphosphate.

attenuation Process (-ion) of making thin (attenuat-). A statistical process of reducing or weakening a **statistic**. *See* **correction**.

attic children Children kept in isolation (in attics, cellars, etc.) with little or no chance to associate with others socially; minimal stimulation resulting from minimal human contact. Usually, such children have been rejected by adults and hidden from public contact because they are either illegitimate or mentally defective. (K. Davis, "Extreme Social Isolation of a Child," *American Journal of Sociology*, 1940, **45**, 554-565).

attitude Quality of (-tude) being fit (atti-, from apti-). A learned and relatively enduring **perception**, expressed or unexpressed, influencing a person to think or behave in a fairly predictable manner toward objects, persons, or situations. **Cognitive** (conceptual) and emotional (motivational) factors are involved when they direct behavior. Attitudes are derived from childhood internalizations of a vivid experience or from other meaningful and impressive values. In general, both attitudes and values are acquired from one's culture, but values are likely to be stabler and continuing. An *attitude system* contains a cluster of attitudes, all of which share and constantly overlap similar concepts, beliefs, motives, etc. The total collection or grouping of one's attitudes is labeled an *attitude constellation*. An *attitude cluster* consists of a set of readily distinguishable interrelated attitudes shared by a population.

Term entered English in 1668 to define the posture of a painted figure, replacing **aptitude** (coined in 1548) in that sense, and becoming general in usage about 1710. In 1862, Herbert Spencer (1820-1903), English philosopher, used the term in the sense of "attitude of mind."

attitude scale A means of making approximately quantitative measurement of subjective reactions, such a scale usually consisting of a set of items concentrating on one issue or a group of issues (social conformity, communism, birth control, etc.). Persons rate each item in terms of their own preferences. The techniques used for measurement are designed to achieve information primarily about two dimensions: direction (favorability-unfavorability) and intensity (strength of feeling).

The majority of attitude scales follow the construction methods of the American psychologists **Louis Thurstone** or **Rensis Likert**. However, there are many other ways used to measure attitudes (analysis of documentary material, personal interviews, projective tests, etc.). *Thurstone*'s method (in order to achieve equal intervals) utilized 20 or more statements which empirically were assigned scale values running from 0.0 for extremely unfavorable opinions, through 5.5 for neutral statements, to 11.0 for extremely favorable attitudes. *Likert*'s technique resembles simple questionnaires, but each statement is rated on a five-degree scale: "strongly agree," "agree," "undecided," "disagree," "strongly disagree." These ratings are weighted for favorable and unfavorable attitudes, with high scores indicating favorable attitudes. *See* **Guttman's Scalogram Analysis**.

attribute To (at-) bestow (tribute). A quality or characteristic of a person or thing being measured which may, by certain treatments, take on a quantitative score. It is also a dimension of sensory experience, such as **brightness** is an attribute of visual experience and **pitch** is an attribute of auditory experience.

Aubert, Hermann (1826-1892) German physiologist and inventor who developed a diaphragm for his studies on visual adaptation and reported on it in 1865, the same time he described the **Aubert illusion.** He also coined the term **adaptive reaction** in 1865.

Aubert diaphragm A device (sometimes provided with a scale for measuring passage of light) with two adjustable plates that can be moved over a square opening, thereby controlling the aperture size and thus the amount of light transmission.

Aubert illusion An optical illusion in which a vertical line seems to incline in a direction opposite from that in which the head inclines.

audiogenic seizure Seizure relating to (-ic) the kind produced (-gen) by sound (audio-). In laboratory experimentation (usually on rats), a seizure, epileptoid in nature, brought on by auditory stimulation, customarily by a very high pitched sound.

audiogram Chart or record (-gram) of a hearing (audio-) test, obtained on the **audiometer**. Audiograms indicate in **decibels** the sound-pressure level required to make tones of various pitches heard by the subject, or to show how **absolute thresholds** for pure tones vary with vibrational frequency (pitch).

audiogravic illusion Relating to (-ic) an illusion of sound (audio-) localization. An error in auditory localization resulting from a subject experimentally being deprived of visual cues so that he interprets sounds to be localized in the same manner as the illusion he has of his body being tilted relative to gravity (-grav-). *See* **audiogyral illusion**.

Experiment reported and term coined (1951) by American physician Ashton Graybiel (born 1902).

audiogyral illusion Relating to (-al) an illusion or error in sound (audio-) localization experienced by a blindfolded subject when he is rapidly rotated (-gyr-).

Experiment reported and term coined in 1949 by B. Clark and American physician Ashton Graybiel (born 1902).

audiometer (acoumeter, phonometer) An electronic device for producing varied tones used in measuring (-meter) the frequency limits of hearing (audio-), as well as for detecting hearing acuity anomalies. Sound frequencies can be varied in intensity from inaudibility up to a level capable of producing spasms resembling an **audiogenic seizure**.

The first audiometer (called acoumeter) was introduced in 1879 by Arthur Hartmann (1849-1931), German physician, although it was also reported on May 15, 1879, that a Professor Hughes of England described his similar instrument to the Royal Society. The modern audiometer is traceable to the work in 1922 of engineers at the Bell Laboratories, particularly acoustical engineer Harvey Fletcher (born in Utah, 1884). Obtained Ph.D. (physics), Chicago, 1911. Received **Presidential Certificate of Merit**, 1945, for his research on sound. Discovered critical bands of frequency in hearing mechanism.

audiometry Process of (-y) measuring (-metr-) hearing (audio-), such as determining the **absolute threshold** of the ear by testing for tone-hearing ability at various frequencies from 125 to 8,000 cycles per second. Pure tone threshold measurements can be made by air conduction or bone conduction hearing tests.

auditory agnosia *See* **agnosia**.

auditory aphasia *See* **aphasia**.

auditory area of the brain (auditory projection area) Cortical area (No. 41), in the wall of the **fissure of Sylvius** on each temporal lobe, where fibers of the auditory pathway end.

auditory localization The process (-ation) of localizing sound; ability of the ears to locate the source of sounds from any direction. Generally, two ears are required to efficiently determine the direction of sounds. Sound sources close to either side of the head are easier to locate than others, whereas sounds from above the head or from the front or rear are much more difficult to localize.

The first person to investigate the phenomenon of why separated receivers (ears) localized sound was the Italian physicist Giovanni Battista Venturi (1746-1822), who published his work in 1796. See **pseudophone**.

auditory nerve Same as **acoustic nerve**.

auditory ossicles See **ossicles**.

Aufgabe (pl. *Aufgaben*; Ger., purpose, conscious task, instruction) Relates to a person's readiness or attitude (originally set by specific directions or instructions) in preparing himself to solve a task or problem. The *Aufgabe* predisposes one toward an unconscious set (*Einstellung*). In computer terminology, *Aufgabe* means *output*. Compare **Bereitschaft**. (Also see Boring, 1957, pp. 404, 716.)

Augustine (St. Augustine: Aurelia Augustinus) (354-430 A.D.) Born near Carthage. Used and developed the process of **introspection** through self-analysis and autobiographic confession while reviewing (in *Confessions*, about 400 A.D.) what he considered his previous sinful life. Only by Divine Grace could man return to his original state of free will, able to choose between right and wrong. He expressed an early **faculty psychology** by his three divisions of the mind. Anticipated **Husserl's phenomenology**, psychoanalytic thought, and **existentialism** in his emphasis on self-awareness.

aura A sensation so wispy, so much like air (aura) that it often goes unnoticed by the inattentive. A premonitory perception (as of visceral disturbances, numbness, colored lights) experienced by the sufferer of **epilepsy**, **migraine** and other nervous disorders which presages the coming of an attack.

In his tract, "On the Sacred Disease," about 400 B.C., **Hippocrates** refers to the aura experienced by persons with epilepsy who then, before the attack, "flee from men either to their homes or to a deserted place and cover themselves up." They flee not because of a "fear of the divinity as many suppose," but because they have a "shame of the affection."

Ausfragemethode (Ger., interrogation, problem method.) **Buhler's** "Ausfragemethode" (1907), involved a free interchange of communication between experimenter and observer in an experiment in which the subject was presented with thought-provoking questions, detailing his thought-process as he progressed. Occasionally, the experimenter interjected questions to help clarify his method and the process.

Aussage test (Ger., testimony.) An appraisal, often in questionnaire form, of one's ability to make an accurate report of what has been seen or heard briefly, actually involving a study of retrospective distortion in reporting briefly-observed events (such as when a witness attempts to relate any event he has seen).

Developed by **Wilhelm Stern**.

ausserordentlicher Professor Outside (ausser) the ordinary or regular (ordentlicher) provisions usually given to the German professor.

ausserplanmassiger Outside (ausser) the plan of the German university system (massig); planmassiger—according to plan.

authenticity (Exist.) Relating to (-ity) the quality (-ity) of being able to accomplish (-hent-) oneself (aut-). The characteristic of being genuine, involving self-awareness and relationships to others. The authentic person is not only real, but accepts reality and the process of choice making. He is thoroughly prepared to take responsibility for his decisions, dropping all trickery and "phoniness" from his makeup.

authoritarianism The doctrine (-ism) advocated (-arian) by one who controls individual or group behavior by command or authority. Dictatorship. A perceptual way of viewing the world, characterized by the setting of specific directives for behavior, not permitting group decisions or individual initiative.

Adorno et al. (1950), in *The Authoritarian Personality*, describe the authoritarian personality as being extremely conventional, rigid, and resistant to change, with rigidity of thinking, dependence upon authority, strong ethnocentric feelings, and a general overcontrol of feeling and impulses.

autism A mental condition (-ism) of being morbidly preoccupied with one's self (aut-), evidencing no concern with or interest in life's realities, and tending to retreat into pathological phantasies or dwell in wishful thinking.

In the early infantile type of autism, the condition is characterized by withdrawal, language difficulties, inability to relate to others and general unavailability. In 1912, referring to schizophrenic symptoms, **Bleuler** said the most severe cases of **schizophrenia** "withdraw completely and live in a dream world. I call this symptom autism." In 1932, Bleuler gave the name "autistic" to the very illogical, personalized style of thinking involving phantasy and withdrawal from reality "since it was encountered first and in clearest form in the autism of schizophrenia." But because the term was misunderstood, "I (Bleuler) was constrained to rename it." He therefore coined the word "dereistic" (derived from "de-" meaning "away from" and "reor" indicating "reality"); therefore dereistic thinking "disregards reality." **Piaget**, 1932, said that autistic thought obeyed "a whole system of special laws (laws of symbolism and of immediate satisfaction . . . and is tied to imagery" as well as to "organic activity and organic movements." In 1933, E. Minkowski used the term *autisme pauvre* to describe behavior that is bereft of all meaning and without strivings; reality has become dry and boring, resulting in restlessness, a feeling of emptiness, and loss of contact with the environment.

autochthonous ideas Thoughts that apparently originate from some external source rather than from the individual himself, such as observed in the schizoid personality.

Term coined by **Bleuler**.

autochthonous laws of cognitive order Cognitive laws so indigenous that they possess the very qualities (-ous) of the earth (-chthon) itself (auto-). Those innate "laws" or behavior **drives** which an individual obeys without understanding the motivational precursors or reasons for his action. These autochthonous laws are considered basic to man's behavior and for all practical purposes exclude the role of the unconscious as a behavioral determinant. Some **Gestalt** laws considered autochthonous are: (1) *closure*, relating to those experiences that integrate and make meaningful other experiences (such as a cognitive insight in therapy); (2) *continuity*, pertaining to experiences that have carry-over value in either space and/or time; (3) *proximity*, in which experiential conditions are close to one another; and (4) *similarity*, in which experiences share common properties. (McDavid, 1967, p. 31.)

autoclitic responses Referring to (-ic) verbal responses that incline (-clit-) toward giving one's self (auto-) away: ("I *think* that," "I have no *doubts* about," etc.), which predict how strongly a person feels about his forthcoming statement. Autoclitic behavior refers to action(s) based upon or dependent upon verbal behavior. (B. F. Skinner, *Verbal Behavior*, 1957.)

autoeroticism See **cathexis**.

autokinetic illusion (also autokinetic effect, movement or phenomenon) The **illusion** of **apparent movement** originating from a small single point of emitted light observed in an otherwise dark room; the apparent erratic motion of an actually stationary pinpoint of light observed when there are no other reference points.

Astronomers, while staring at a single star at night, have reported this phenomenon for centuries, but Sherif (*Psychology of Social Norms*, 1936) was the first to investigate its properties in the laboratory. Without a **frame of reference**, subjects' estimates of the distance the light moved varied considerably. Furthermore, the observed autokinetic effect is influenced by *social pressure*, that is, the perceptions of a cultural group determine how the individual perceives.

Muzafer Sherif (born 1906, Turkey.) American social psychologist. Ph.D., Columbia, 1935. Received **Distinguished Scientific Contribution Award**, 1968; see Vinacke, p. 327.

automated training Self (auto-) motivated (-mated) or self operated type of training (such as flight trainers), which approximates the actual task to be performed with little but token participation (regulating controls, etc.) by an instructor.

automatic programming (Comput.) Any technique, using a **digital computer**, for transforming programming from a form that is humanly easy to produce into a form that is efficient for computer operation.

autonomic nervous system, ANS (involuntary nervous system) That nervous system which purportedly relates to (-ic) a self (auto-) operating law (-nom-), controlling automatic responses of the body (heart beat, respiration, etc.). Although the autonomic nervous system is often described as a **peripheral** system (being outside the brain and spinal cord), it is nevertheless controlled by the **brainstem** and the hypothalamus, functioning independently of conscious attention. Through **efferent** neurons it innervates and regulates internal organs controlled by muscles and glands, helping to maintain **homeostasis** and the vital functions of the body.

Anatomically, the ANS is divided into two main divisions: (1) the thoracico-lumbar (or thoracolumbar) division (more popularly **known as the sympathetic nervous system**), and (2) the craniosacral division (or the **parasympathetic nervous system**).

Functionally, *parasympathetic* action (**cholinergic** in nature) is concerned with such functions as constricting the lungs, slowing the heart, expelling feces, constriction of pupils, erecting the penis, etc., while *sympathetic* action (**adrenergic** or noradrenergic in nature) is depressive in slowing secretions, contracting blood vessels, decreasing the tone of smooth muscles, etc.

Eustachius knew of the ANS, actually making illustrations of it. **Remak**, however, was the first to demonstrate that certain nerve fibers were unmyelinated, thus introducing the modern concept of the ANS in 1838. In 1845, two brothers, E. F. and E. H. *Weber* (see **Weber's Law**), both physiologists, introduced inhibitory concept of nervous system. In 1886, Walter Holbrook Gaskell (1847-1914), English physiologist, said that this system was antagonistic in function, one being excitatory and the other inhibitory. In 1894, the English physiologist, John Newport Langley (1852-1925), under the impression that it functioned autonomously, changed the name of the involuntary nervous system to that of the autonomic nervous system, dividing it into sympathetic and parasympathetic divisions.

autoplastic behavior Relating to (-ic) behavior that is molded (-plast-) toward fitting oneself (auto-) to the environment. See **aggression**, **alloplastic**.

autoradiography A process (-y) of photographing radioactive material by itself (auto-). A radiographic technique in which tissue slices, obtained from an animal that has been fed or injected with radioactive atoms (such as carbon 14), are treated with a photographic emulsion so that, in time, it can be determined by examining the slowly developed film what neural tissue has taken up the tracer element (Milner, pp. 53-54).

a

autoscopy Watching (-scopy) the self (auto-) in action; self-seeing. A form of hallucination; the so-called phenomenon of the double in which a person sees a mirror image of himself, the confrontation being so real and vivid that the person is shocked by the experience. It has also been called the "astral body" of oneself, and has been described by such prominent writers as Daphne du Maurier, Goethe, Maupassant, and Dostoevsky. Some neurologists claim that such perceptions result from brain lesions or that they are sequelae of nervous system illnesses, such as epidemic encephalitis. (McCurdy, 1961, pp. 484-490.) Originally, the term referred to hallucinatory or illusory behavior in which the patient seemed to meet himself. In 1920, ego psychoanalyst Paul Schilder (1886-1940) broadened its meaning to include self-aspects, in which the "individual experience of his own body is redoubled and projected," the duplicate undergoing "transformation according to affective principles."

autosomal dominant gene Referring to (-al) a dominant gene associated with a non-sex-determining chromosome only—that is, one of a pair of alternative **alleles** present in the same cell that masks the effect of the other allele. *Compare with* **autosomal recessive gene**. *See* Pick's disease.

autosomal recessive gene Referring to (-al) a recessive gene associated with a non-sex-determining chromosome only—that is, one of a pair of alternative **alleles** present in the same cell whose effect is diluted (masked) by the other allele. *Compare with* **autosomal dominant gene**. *See* **microcephaly, phenylketonuria, trisome**.

autosomal trisomy of group G. *See* **trisome**.

autosome An ordinary **chromosome** that determines all body (-some) characteristics by itself (auto-), and has no influence upon sex determination.

autostasis A condition of light that appears stationary (-stasis) by itself (auto-) but actually is in motion. *See* **apparent motion, autokinetic illusion**.

average A not very precise term but usually referring to the **arithmetic mean**. A measure of **central tendency** or position in a **frequency distribution** around which other values are dispersed. *See* **median** and **mode**.

average deviation (AD) Mean deviation; mean variation. A measure of dispersion equal to the **mean** of the sum of absolute deviations from the mean. In a normal distribution the *AD* is related to the **standard deviation** by the *AD* = .7979σ.

In non-normal distributions (*U* and *J* types), the *AD* is sometimes used in place of the standard deviation. In general, the average deviation, when the mean is allowed to represent every score in the distribution, is given by the formula

$$AD = \frac{\Sigma |D|}{N}$$

where |*D*| is the absolute value of the deviation from the mean, or

$$AD = \frac{\Sigma |\lambda - \overline{X}|}{N}$$

where |*X* − *X̄*| means the absolute value of the difference between some score, *X*, and the mean, *X̄*.

average error, method of *See* **methods of psychology, psychophysical**.

averaging computer (computer of average transients; neurological signal processing device; signal averager. Sometimes called a boxcar correlator.) A memory device which accentuates, separates, and extracts repetitive events (such as low-level **evoked responses**) from a masking background of non-repetitive "noise," correlating and sampling incoming signals over a pre-determined time interval with memorized signals previously received over similar time intervals. In **EEG** activity

studies (as an example of a specialized use), the so-called computer of average transients (CAT) "sums in" code information (voltages) from the tape, averaging, plotting, and storing the voltage's average value in a special memory bin, allowing obtained values to be separately retrieved.

aversion therapy A therapy process (-sion) of avoidance or not (a-) turning (-ver-) toward; avoidance therapy. A therapeutic procedure such as behavior modification, based on **operant conditioning** principles, that pairs undesirable (negative) behavior with an aversive stimulus (e.g., shock), thereby conditioning the client to avoid such behavior. Also, a **classical conditioning** procedure of pairing an attractive stimulus (e.g., alcohol or cigarettes) with an already-learned distasteful stimulus (e.g., biting fingernails), resulting in the formerly attractive object also becoming unattractive.

aversive behavioral repertoire *See* **behavioral dysfunction classification**.

aversive center Nerve center in the brain especially reactive to or involved in noxious stimuli and experiences.

aversive conditioning Any conditioning in which some habit or activity (such as cigarette smoking or **enuresis**) is paired with some kind of punishment (such as shock) as an aid in learning to eliminate that habit.

aversive event An unpleasant and undesirable occasion that when reduced or terminated tends to increase occurrence of responses that preceded the termination. Aversive events elicit reflex **motor** responses, fear, and newly learned responses. *See* **escape learning**.

avoidance-avoidance (negative-negative) conflict A conflict situation in which both choices available are negative. The person tries to either escape from the problem or to alter the situations causing his conflict. For example, a student wants to avoid the draft but also wants to avoid a difficult required course necessary to qualify him to remain in school. The conflict can be reduced by passing the course, wangling a substitute course, or escaping the draft entirely (possibly by marrying a divorced woman with eight dependents). *See* **Lewin**.

avoidance learning A learning situation controlled by a warning signal or by the threat of punishment, wherein the necessary **operant** response must be made on schedule in order to avoid the aversive stimulus. The threat arouses anxiety; when the threat is avoided anxiety is reduced. For example, a rat is placed in a **Miller-Mowrer shuttlebox** equipped with a buzzer that can signal a coming electric shock on the grid floor. To avoid shock, the rat must learn to run to the opposite end of the box within a specified time interval (say, 5 seconds) after the buzzer sounds. Other studies show that when rats running a maze are shocked for wrong turns they tend to avoid the wrong turns thereafter. Thus, avoidance facilitates learning. (O. H. Mowrer. "A Stimulus-Response Analysis of Anxiety and its Role as a Reinforcing Agent," *Psychological Review*, 1939, **46**, 553-565).

awards and prizes of a psychological nature In addition to the various awards and prizes granted by the **American Psychological Association** or one of its divisions, or the **American Psychological Foundation**, there are several others given by organizations not specifically organized for professional psychologists. The **American Association for the Advancement of Science** is foremost in the granting of such awards, several psychologists being successful in winning the **Newcomb Cleveland Prize** and the **AAAS Socio-Psychological Prize**.

awards of the American Psychological Association The Association itself as well as many of its divisions has established awards for deserving persons. Two awards granted annually by the APA are: **Distinguished Scientific Contributions to Psychology**, and the **Richardson Creativity Award**. Additionally, the **American Psychological Foundation**

presents a **Gold Medal Award** as well as one for **Distinguished Contributions to Psychology in Education**. Various divisions of the APA provide the following special awards: **G. Stanley Hall Award in Developmental Psychology** (Division 7: Developmental Psychology); **Gordon Allport Award** (Division 8: Personality and Social Psychology); **Kurt Lewin Memorial Award** (Division 9: Psychological Study of Social Issues); **Distinguished Contribution to the Science of and Profession of Clinical Psychology** (Division 12: Clinical Psychology); **Cattell Fund Award** (Division 13: Consulting Psychology); **James McKeen Cattell Award** (Division 14: Industrial Psychology and Business Organization); **Edward Lee Thorndike Medal for Distinguished Psychological Contribution to Education** (Division 15: Educational Psychology); **Harold M. Hildreth Memorial Award** (Division 18: Psychologists in Public Service); a professional award for outstanding professional contributions in the field of rehabilitation (Division 22: Psychological Aspects of Disability); and an award granted to the member presenting the best paper on **psychopharmacology** at the annual APA meeting (Division 28: Psychopharmacology).

awards to psychologists *See* **National Medal of Science, awards and prizes of a psychological nature, awards of the American Psychological Association**.

axes and planes *See* **anatomical directions**.

axis In anatomy, an imaginary line around which the body can be rotated like a wheel on an axle (axis) and that passes through two aspects. Axes are named **craniocaudal** (cephalocaudal) or longitudinal, **dorsoventral** (anterior-posterior ventrodorsal), and **bilateral** (dextrosinistral). Axial refers to the axial skeleton (head and trunk) or the spinal axis. *See* **anatomical directions**.

axiology Study of (-logy) worth or values (axio-). A branch of philosophy that systematically studies values, primarily intrinsic values, but also deals with value-systems as proposed by man and those value concepts that are supposedly innate and basic (knowing the difference between right and wrong; that it is naturally wrong in our society to kill a human being for food but permissible to kill and eat a lower animal).

Although the concept of value is traceable to Plato's Idea of the Good, the term apparently was coined and first used in 1902 by the French philosopher Paul Lapie in his book *Logique de la Volunté*.

axis cylinder Same as **Remak's band**. *See* **axon**.

axon (axis cylinder) One of the fibrous processes of a **neuron**, usually longer (sometimes three feet or more in length) than the **dendrite**. It is attached to the slightly prominent area of the cell body called the *axon hillock*. An axon transmits nerve impulses away from the nerve cell to other neurons or to glands and muscles. Its connecting terminals are called end brushes. Axons are of uniform diameter, usually carrying side processes called collaterals, and are generally enclosed in one or more sheaths, a **myelin sheath**, a **neurilemma**, or both. In peripheral **ganglia**, axons form bundles called **nerves**. Bundles of axons within the central nervous system are called tracts or *fasciculi*.

Felix Fontana (1730-1805), Italian anatomist, referred to nerve fibers during 1780's as being transparent cylinders filled with a fluid. About fifty years later, **Purkinje** and Friedrich C. Rosenthal (1780-1829), German anatomist, named the long nerve fiber the axis cylinder, since being encased in its tubular sheath it resembled the axis of the neurone. In the early 1860's, Otto F. K. Deiters (1834-1863), German anatomist, demonstrated that individual nerve cells had one axon and several dendrites. In 1873, **Golgi** described the complete nerve cells for the first time. In 1884, the term "axis cylinder" was changed to axone to conform to the ending of neurone.

Babinski, Joseph F. (1857-1932) Polish-French neurologist who investigated various areas of the brain, particularly the **cerebellum**. In 1902, he thoroughly described and named the condition known as **adiadokokinesia**. In 1896, he reported noting in pyramidal tract diseases the reflex that now bears his name. The *Babinski reflex* is the automatic upward dorsiflexion or extension of the great toe and spreading or flexing of small toes upon lightly stroking the middle of the sole of the **neonate's** foot. It disappears later in infancy and for the rest of one's life except in cerebrospinal tract involvements and stupor; the reflex also serves to distinguish between organic and hysterical hemiplegia. In normal individuals, stroking of the sole of the foot causes the toes to curve downward.

Bachelor of (Medicine) Surgery In Britain, a degree from a university entitling the holder to be eligible to receive a license to practice medicine. This is a preliminary degree to that of obtaining the M.D. (requiring additional examination, passing of a thesis and member-ship requirements of one of the Royal Colleges of Physicians (honored by M.R.C.P.) and after at least five years elevation to Fellowship status (F.R.C.P.). Traditionally, all surgeons are called "Mr." instead of "Dr."

back solution One of two routines (back and front solutions) used as a time-saving compu-tational method for solving first-degree equa-tions (such as normal equations). *See* **Doolittle method**.

backward association An **association**, often found in paired-associate learning, whereby a secondary (or response) term evokes a preceding (or stimulus) term. If a person who has learned to follow the word *rat* with *pack* responds later to *pack* followed by *rat*, he is backward-associating.

backward conditioning In **classical condition-ing**, the process whereby the **conditioned stimulus** (CS) follows the presentation of the **unconditioned stimulus** (US).

Bacon, Francis (1561-1626) English philoso-pher. Introduced in his various books, particularly *Advancement of Learning* (1605) and *Novum Organum* (1620), concepts con-cerned with his new systematic analysis of knowledge based on the inductive method. Bacon was opposed to the deductive logic of **Aristotle** and the Scholastics; his method did not exclude **deduction** but rather deempha-sized it. He believed that truth could be best discovered by **empirical** observation, analyzing the observed data and deriving hypotheses from them. Finally, these hypotheses should be tested by further observation and experi-mentation.

Baeyer, Johann Adolph von (also Bayer), 1835-1917. German (Berlin) chemist. Synthe-sized **acetylcholine** in 1867 and **barbiturates** in 1883.

Baillarger, Jules G. (1806-1890) French physi-cian and psychiatrist. Studied **hallucinations** and **aphasia**, and made contributions to nomenclature of mental disorders. He was the first (1840) to definitely establish that the **cerebral cortex** has six layers. He was a strong supporter of Gall's **phrenology**. *See* **cortical layers, manic-depressive illness**.

Bain, Alexander (1818-1903) Scottish philoso-pher, physiological psychologist. Close friend of **J. S. Mill** and consequently influenced by his **associationism**, from which he later broke away, shifting toward a more scientific psychology. Bain's main writings, *The Senses and the Intellect* (1855) and *The Emotions and the Will* (1859) were on the senses. To Aristotle's five he added an "organic" sense or sense of movement (kinesthesis), which he held to be important psychologically, since movements are involved in associations. He was first in Great Britain and among the first

in psychology to study mental life in relation to physiology; among the first to appreciate the importance of the genetic and evolu-tionary approach (Boring, 1957, pp. 233-240, 245).

balance *See* **Mosso**.

balance theory In the perception of interper-sonal relations, a compensatory theory main-taining that a person with two conflicting attitudes (or unbalanced cognitive systems) strives to seek consistency and reduce tension by balancing positive and negative forces. In making such adjustment he may change one of the attitudes, redefine its meaning, or ignore the conflict (at least superficially). Balance exists when the net product of the competing forces is positive, or when the person tends to "feel" that his interpersonal relations are consistent or balanced. **(Fritz Heider**, *The Psychology of Interpersonal Relations*, 1958).

Baldwin, James Mark (1861-1934) American philosopher, theoretical and experimental psychologist. Ph.D. in philosophy, Princeton 1889. Emphasized evolutionary development, the study of individual differences, **reaction time**, and the functional approach to psy-chology (Boring, 1957, pp. 529-532; Vinacke, p. 28).

Bales, Robert Freed Born in Missouri, 1916. American sociologist, specializing in small-group processes and personality studies. Ph.D., Harvard, 1945. *See* **interaction process analy-sis, category-system method** (also *Psychology Today*, p. 668).

bang *See* **bhang**.

Bárány, Robert (1876-1936) Austrian otologist (M.D., Vienna, 1900), received the Nobel prize in 1914 for his work on the physiology of the vestibular apparatus. He also developed what has become known as the *Barany chair* which revolves as the subject is spun around. It was designed to determine effects of circular motion on the inner ear. Used in testing aircraft pilots, but especially during World War II by the OSS in studying adaptation of individual to various stresses.

barbital (barbitone) *See* **Veronal**.

barbiturate Salt or ester (-ate) derived from barbituric acid, used as a sedative and hypnotic. Barbiturates (such as phenobarbital, nembutal, seconal, amytal) act as a depressant on the **central nervous system** inducing relaxation. *Barbiturism* is an addictive con-dition that occurs when dosage is increased because of greater tolerance, symptomatized by slurring of the speech, confusion, **amnesia, ataxia**, drowsiness, weight loss, and appear-ance of intoxication. Addicts may commit crimes and yet have no memory of them. Sudden withdrawal often leads to epileptiform seizures in less than a week. *See* **drugs**.

First synthesized in 1883 by **Baeyer**. Origin of the term "barbituric" has been variously and curiously listed, one story being that it was synthesized on St. Barbara's day and Baeyer named it in her honor; another is that barbituric acid was named after Barbara, a Munich cafe waitress who gave valiantly and copiously of her urine (barbituric acid being a urea derivative) for the experiments. Slang terms: "barbs," "blue devils," "blue heavens," "candy," "peanuts," "yellow jackets."

Two German chemists, **Emil Fischer** and Josef von Mehring (1849-1908) introduced (1902) the first clinically useful barbiturate, which they named **Veronal**.

bar chart A graphic presentation of data in which a series of horizontal or vertical bars of equal width and of proportionate length represent magnitudes, quantities, or indi-viduals of the various classes.

Barker, Roger G. (Born 1903, Iowa). Ph.D. in psychology, Stanford, 1934. Child psycholo-gist during earlier years, observing children's behavior in natural settings. Later, made studies on structure of behavior, psychology of physical disability and **ecological psychol-ogy**. Received **DSC Award** in 1963. *See* **behavior setting**.

basal ganglia (Basal nuclei, a more appropriate term).

A group of deep grey nuclei surrounding the **thalamus** and located in the basal portion of each cerebral hemisphere. The subcortical nuclei comprising the **extrapyramidal system** are divided into diencephalic nuclei (consisting of the **corpus striatum** and various thalamic nuclei) and the mesencephalic nuclei (con-sisting of the **reticular formation**, the red **nucleus**, and **substantia nigra**). They derive from the original corpus striatum, consisting of two portions: dorsal (the **caudate nucleus**) and ventral (the **lentiform nucleus**) which is subdivided into the **putamen** and the **globus pallidus**. The caudate nucleus and the putamen are separated by the **internal capsule**. Lateral to the lentiform nucleus is the external capsule, a band of fibers that separates it from the claustrum (fence or barrier), a nearly vertical layer of grey matter between the **cortex** and the lentiform nucleus. Basal nuclei are apparently involved with controlling movements and maintaining posture. The **amygdala** is sometimes included with the basal nuclei, but it is classified in this book as part of the **limbic system**.

Known to and illustrated by the earliest anatomists. Fully described first by **Vieussens** (1685), although **Willis** (1664) had previously named the optic thalamus, the corpus striatum, and the lentiform bodies, all structures associated with the basal ganglia. The term was probably first used in 1879 by English physiologist, Sidney Ringer (1834-1910), who wrote that "Athetosis is due to atrophy and degeneration of the basal ganglia."

basal metabolic rate (BMR) The rate of oxygen intake and energy discharge of an organism under certain standardized conditions, includ-ing complete physical rest (not sleep), a fasting period, and an ambient temperature that does not require energy expenditure for physiological temperature regulation.

basal year (basal age) In an individual intelligence test, the base age at which a subject can pass all the tests within that age-level, especially in the **Stanford-Binet**, or any other test similarly based on age levels.

base A molecule (as ammonia) or ion that takes up a proton from an acid, according to the Danish chemist, Johannes Brønsted (1879-1941) who first (1923) espoused the idea of describing acids and bases in terms of proton membership.

base number The **radix** or fundamental number in any numerical scale. Ten is the base (radix) in the standard decimal system, 2 in the **binary system**, 8 in the octal notation system, etc.

basic anxiety The feelings of helplessness, loneliness, frustration, etc., found in children or traceable to early childhood, that result from the individual's confrontation with a continually threatening environment.

basilar membrane A delicate fibrous membrane or tissue sheath located within the coils at the base of the **cochlea** of the inner ear. The basilar membrane consists of approximately 24,000 tightly stretched, stiff fibers of increasing and varying width from one end of the cochlea to the other, and narrower at the cochlear base where sound enters. Resting on the basilar membrane is the **organ of Corti**, the hair cells of which, by movement of the basilar membrane, act as the **receptor** for hearing by transducing the mechanical energy of sound waves into the chemical (electrical) energy of the nervous impulse. *See* **place theories** under **hearing theories**.

basket nerve ending Specialized structure at roots of hairs on body, regarded as sense organ for pressure or touch.

Batten-Mayou disease A juvenile form of amaurotic family idiocy, reported in 1903 by Batten and 1904 by Mayou, and now grouped as one of the sub-diseases of **cerebral lipoidosis**.

b

Frederick Batten (1865-1918), English neurologist; Marmaduke Stephen Mayou (1876-1934), English physician.

battered child syndrome A pattern of behavior (lack of relatedness, feelings of rejection) associated with infants or young children who have been physically abused by parents or others in charge. Usually, the child is physically mistreated (sometimes suffering from permanent brain damage) because he is considered to be mentally retarded, unhealthy, or intractable (Katherine Bain, "The Physically Abused Child," *Pediatrics*, 1963, **31**, 895-897; David Bakan, *Slaughter of the Innocents*, 1971; J.M. Cameron, H. R. Johnson, and F. E. Camps, "The Battered Child Syndrome," *Medical Science Law*, 1966, **6**, 2-21).

Bayesian approach to statistics Complex procedures involved in practical studies about **probability** and decision-theory, primarily used in market research and analyses but now finding more frequent use in the social sciences. Bayes' approach to decision-making transforms **uncertainty** problems into risk problems. The decision-maker's judgments, based on his personal confidence in the truth of a specific proposition, are used to determine the likelihood of possible events and the expected payoff of a strategy employed in decision-making. Bayes' theorem is concerned with the calculation of certain conditional probabilities. It enables **a posteriori** probabilities to be expressed in terms of **a priori** probabilities, thus making it possible to revise probabilities in the light of new evidence. (Hays, 1963, pp. 113-116, 298; for marketing applications, see Green and Tull, pp. 465-494.)

Named after Bayes, an eighteenth century English clergyman.

Bayley Scales of Infant Development Mental and motor scales for the assessment of early mental and psychomotor development of infants up to 2-1/2 years of age. May be used as "extension-downwards" of the Binet test. In addition to the scales, forms are provided for a standardized interview with the mother concerning various mother-child relationships. It was standardized on a stratified sample of more than 1,200 children, and controlled for age, sex, color, urban-rural residence, and education of head of household. Norms are based on standard scores for each of fourteen age groups from 2 to 30 months.

Devised by Nancy Bayley, born 1899, American (Oregon) developmental psychologist. Ph.D., Iowa, 1926. Recipient of the **Distinguished Scientific Contribution Award**, 1966.

BCD system Binary coded decimal system.

Beard's disease *See* neurasthenia.

behavior The observable and recordable goal-directed responses of an organism or its parts. Behavior may be overt (speaking, muscle contraction, blinking, etc.) and/or covert (electronic evidences of thinking); it may be verbal (communicating intentionally by words) or nonverbal (communicating by gestures and bodily movements).

behavioral baseline The stabilized measurable behavior of any organism, subject to **operant conditioning** techniques under specified conditions, making it possible to compare this baseline with the reversible effect of an experimental manipulation.

behavioral deficit A deficit or seldom appearing pattern of responses (such as shallow or no reaction to kissing or other emotional stimuli, absence of skills, etc.), according to the social learning theory classification of behavioral disorders. *See* **behavioral dysfunctions classification.**

behavioral disorder Personality or mental disorder that is primarily outgoing or activist in nature, usually referring to children who have temper tantrums and rebel outwardly against parents and teachers. *See* **behavior modification.**

behavioral dysfunctions classification An attempt at developing a social learning classification of psychopathology (involving stimulus control over behavior) that relates to the interaction between stimulus events and their behavioral predispositions. It explains the course of deviant response patterns, sets up guides for therapeutic practices, and tries to avoid dependency upon disease entities.

The phrase *functional* mental disease is replaced by the term *behavioral dysfunctions* that includes: (1) **behavioral deficits** (evidenced by absence of verbal or physical skills as seen in the autistic child, the deaf child, in delayed speech, etc.); (2) *defective stimulus control of behavior* (involving failure to respond discriminatingly to different cues, as not distinguishing between the sound of a rattle from a snake or a toy, or between established laws and personal wishes, etc.); (3) *inappropriate stimulus control of behavior*, (in which a neutral stimulus, e.g., a plastic flower, acquires substitute value in being able to elicit a response, such as psychosomatic sneezing in response to the plastic flower); (4) *defective or inappropriate incentive systems*, evidenced by (a) breakdown of rewards previously serving as behavioral incentives, which is a defective incentive system (such as in schizophrenic withdrawal from society and reality); or (b) evolvement of reward value from events ordinarily not having reinforcement value, which is an inappropriate incentive system (such as in *transvestism* or *fetishism*); (5) *aversive behavioral repertoire*, in which the person persists in resorting to behavior that has aversive consequences to others (such as temper tantrums, aggressive business practices, attention-getting actions, etc.); and (6) *aversive self-reinforcing systems*, in which the person resorts to self-transmitted reinforcement or self-evaluation (through self-rewards), or instead to the setting of too high a personal standard that can only lead to self-depreciation (such as in persons having feelings of low personal worth, depressed persons, etc.) (Albert Bandura, A Social Learning Interpretation of Psychological Dysfunctions. In P. London and D. Rosenhan (Eds.), *Foundations of Abnormal Psychology*, 1968; Arthur and Carolyn Staats, *Complex Human Behavior*, 1963).

behavioral theory A viewpoint expressed by American learning theorist Spence, emphasizing immediate relations to the environment by using stimulus and response variables. (K. W. Spence, *Behavior Theory and Conditioning*, 1956).

behavior chain A sequence of movements (responses) linked together, each link playing a specific role in the totally integrated behavior toward achieving a goal. For example, the baseball batter takes a particular stance at the plate, bearing in mind the coach's signals, eyes the pitcher's movements hoping to observe a cue that will tell him whether a fast ball or a curve is coming, gets set for the coming ball, and then strikes at the pitch. All are complex movements, but are reduced to habit through feedback; through practice the behavior chain tends to become a single unified response. (Frank A. Logan, *Learning and Motivation*, 1970, pp. 30-31).

behavior disorders of childhood and adolescence Reactions related to various areas of behavior, such as: hyperkinesis, withdrawal, overanxiety, unsocialization (hostile disobedience, destructiveness, etc.), and group delinquency (stealing, skipping school, as a member of a gang, etc.).

behavior exchange theory An attempt at developing a unified approach to understanding human behavior by using accumulated experimental data and information gathered from observing interactions of people for its studies. Specifically, in a dyadic relationship, behavior exchange takes place when one person's intrinsic pleasures are affected by another's simultaneous extrinsic displeasures resulting from such pleasures. A husband may derive satisfaction from playing golf as well as being away from home responsibilities, while his wife is experiencing punishment by passively allowing him to do it. If the wife shows hostility, her husband's pleasure is reduced. Mutual interaction leads not only to behavior exchange but to behavioral change, which eventually may provide adjustments resulting in mutually satisfying payoffs. One of the aims of behavior exchange theory is to maximize one's personal satisfactions while minimizing dissatisfactions for others. (K. S. Gergen, *The Psychology of Behavior Exchange*, 1969).

behaviorism A methodological approach in psychology that insists upon the objective observation, description, and prediction of behavior of organisms, rather than upon the subjective study of states of consciousness. Behaviorism deals only with measurable and observable phenomena suitable for operational definition and public verification, stressing overt behavior and including even highly abstract speech but ignoring consciousness and ruling out introspection.

J. B. Watson first used the term in an article called "Psychology as the Behaviorist Views It." (*Psychological Review*, 1913, **20**, 158-177). The Russian physiologists Sechenov, Pavlov, and V. M. Bekhterev laid the foundation for Watson's behaviorism. Some behaviorist theories are identified with the following American psychologists: E. C. Tolman (purposive behaviorism); C. L. Hull (systematic behavior theory); B. F. Skinner (descriptive behaviorism); E. R. Guthrie (contiguity theory of learning). All are largely concerned with learning theory and animal experimentation.

behavior model A view of psychopathology in which symptoms are assumed to be treatable directly by suitably reinforced learning processes and changes of environment without seeking deep or hidden causes. *See* behavior modification.

behavior modification (behavior therapy) A systematic approach to applying conditioning procedures to modification of human behavior. Whereas the traditional psychoanalyst treats neurotic behavior by trying to unearth the deeper-lying causes, the behavior therapist attempts to remove the symptoms of anxiety responses, believing that such procedures do not result in symptom substitution or later recurrence of the same symptom, but rather that the removal of one symptom tends to have a wholesomely "contagious" effect upon other undesirable symptoms.

Behavior therapists assume that behavior disorders are learned maladjustments and can consequently be treated by: (1) classical- and operant-conditioning techniques, and (2) reciprocal inhibition (including systematic desensitization).

Systematic desensitization refers to behavioral responses (involving emotional reactions or feelings) conditioned by the classical method, involving: (1) training in relaxation of muscles, (2) development of anxiety hierarchies through client interviews to help determine anxiety-producing situations, and (3) muscle relaxation combined with imagining anxiety-arousing situations, proceeding from least to most disturbing so that the client may gradually become accustomed to the progressive simulated anxiety situations.

Behavior modification can be traced to the classical conditioning experiments of Pavlov and the work of Thorndike (law of effect) during the early years of this century. In the 1920's, Watson applied these earlier techniques to conditioning and counterconditioning experiments on phobic children. About 10 years later, O. H. Mowrer developed a classical conditioning method (bell and pad) for treatment of enuresis. During the 1950's, Joseph Wolpe, South African psychiatrist, used classical conditioning experiments in the development and extinction of phobic reactions in the cat. His systematic desensitization process utilized *reciprocal inhibition* by conditioning the more favorable responses of two mutually incompatible responses (such as relaxation vs. anxiety), resulting in the elimination of the undesirable one. From these successful animal experiments, Wolpe easily made the transition to working with human beings (Joseph Wolpe, *Psychotherapy by Reciprocal Inhibition*, 1958; also, *The Practice of Behavior Therapy*, 1969).

behavior sampling Technique for measuring personality traits in which the examiner observes the subject's behavior in a specified situation without the subject's knowledge.

behavior setting According to **Barker**, a behavior setting "has both structural and dynamic attributes." Structurally, this consists of: (1) *standing patterns of behavior* (such as motor units, reflexes, group activity), (2) *standing patterns of behavior-and-milieu* (in which manmade and natural environment "compose the milieu which operates independently of the standing pattern of behavior"), (3) the *milieu is circumjacent* (encompassing) to the behavior, (4) the *milieu is synomorphic* (similar in structure) to the behavior. Dynamically, the behavior-milieu parts are called synomorphs, which have a "specified degree of interdependence" (knowing, for example, the foolhardiness of scheduling a teenage dance on a Saturday night in an Indiana town where the high school basketball championship game is also scheduled).

Influenced considerably by Lewin's book *Principles of Topological Psychology* (1936), Barker concluded that every situation carries some culturally defined meaning of importance to the individual to which he reacts (Barker, 1968, pp. 18-20).

behavior theory *See* Hull's behavior system.
behavior therapy *See* behavior modification. (*See* journal 17 under journals.)

Békésy's traveling wave theory of hearing A "place" theory of pitch discrimination. Airborne sound waves, after setting off sequential vibrations from eardrum to **stapes**, are converted to pressure waves that "travel" along the **basilar membrane** toward the **helicotrema**, where the hair cells (as auditory receptors) are maximally stimulated, thus initiating the neural sequence for hearing.

Georg von Békésy, Hungarian-born (1899-1972), but later United States physicist. Received Ph.D. (chemistry), Budapest 1923. First reported his concepts on the wave theory in 1928, refining them in 1960. In 1955, he received the **Warren Medal** for his "program of research, imaginatively conceived and rigorously executed, that has made an outstanding contribution to the psychology of hearing." Received the Nobel prize in medicine and physiology (1961) for his study of the cochlear waves in the **basilar membrane** and for research on how the human ear hears. *See* **hearing theories**.

Bekhterev, Vladimir Mikhailovich (1857-1927) Russian neurologist and physiologist. Introduced the term **reflexology** in 1917 and the concept of the "defense reflex" or **instrumental conditioning**. Argued for an objective psychology, defended **behaviorism**, and took a stand against the use of mentalistic terminology. To him, all higher mental processes could be reduced to "symbolic responses based on conditioning." In his book **Objective Psychology**, translated in 1913, he introduced **Pavlov's** work to America. Watson valued Bekhterev's thinking because his *motor* conditioned response was free of **introspectionism**, and his psychoreflexology destroyed the pure psychology of consciousness. (Boring, 1957, pp. 637-638, 661).

bel A unit of measurement of sound threshold intensity when the base of the **logarithm** is 10. Bel is used only in measuring the relative intensity of power, relating to sound; 1 bel = 10 decibels.

After Alexander Graham Bell (1847-1922), Scottish born inventor of the telephone; naturalized American citizen, 1882.

Bell, Charles (1774-1842). Scottish neurologist, surgeon, and physiologist. In his *Anatomy of the Brain,* 1811, he published his belief that **sensory** nerves enter the dorsal side of the spinal cord, and **motor** nerves leave on the ventral side, (confirmed in 1822 by French physiologist **Magendie**). Bell described in 1830 a case of facial nerve paralysis (Bell's palsy). Made partial experimental clarification of the principles J. Müller later formulated as the doctrine of **specific nerve energies**, proving that each nerve has its own special sensory or motor function. *See* **brainstem, Bonnet.**

Bell-Magendie law The statement specifying that the ventral spinal nerve root is **motor** only, and that the dorsal spinal nerve root is **sensory** only.

bell-shaped curve A symmetrical unimodal curve belonging to a whole family of curves, following the general outline of a bell. *See* the **normal curve**, a more precise term.

Bender Visual-Motor Gestalt Test A widely used test of spatial relations, often of some value in helping diagnose brain damage and **schizophrenia**. Nine standardized cards of geometric design are shown in sequence, and discrepancies in copying them may be indicative of difficulties in concept formation and abstract thinking, according to Gestalt concepts of perception and organization. Designed by Lauretta Bender (born 1897), American child psychiatrist (M.D., Chicago 1923, Iowa 1926). *See* **apraxia.**

Bentham, Jeremy (1748-1832) English utilitarian philosopher. Considered pleasure and pain as ultimate motives of man. Happiness is the major motive, with pleasure being the essence of happiness. *See* **dynamics, hedonism, psychopathology.**

Benzedrine Tradename for **amphetamine.**

Bereitschaft (Ger., anticipatory mental set or attitude; readiness). Similar to **Einstellung** and mental set, except that there is more of an anticipatory readiness involved.

Berengario da Carpi, Giacomo (?1480-1550?) Italian anatomist and surgeon. In 1521, he became the first to raise doubts about the existence of the **rete mirabile** in man. Described in 1523 the **thymus, corpus striatum, pituitary gland** and walls of lateral **brain ventricles.** Noted olfactory and other **cranial nerves.** Also known as Berengarius and Jacob Berenger. *See* **malleus.**

Berger, Hans (1873-1944) German (Thuringia) **psychiatrist** and neurologist; often considered founder of psychophysiology. *See* **alpha rhythm, alpha blocking, beta waves, brain waves, electroencephalogram.**

Beritashvilli, Ivane Solomonovich (born 1884). Soviet physiologist. Member of the Academy of Sciences and winner of the Pavlov Prize. Performed many studies on the central nervous system, including specifically neural mechanisms.

Berkeley, George (1685-1753) Irish-born philosopher. Influenced by writings of Malebranche, Descartes, and Locke, although he opposed Locke by saying that nothing exists but mind. He gave a psychological interpretation of three-dimensional space perception (kinesthetic-visual sensations) in his "Essay Towards a New Theory of Vision," (1709). Believed that the appearance of constancy in perception is not in the object but an attribute given by the mind of the perceiver. *See* **Reid** (also Boring, 1957, pp. 179-186).

Berlin, Rudolf (1833-1897) German anatomist. In 1858, classified cells into a few common functional groups, thus inaugurating the development of **cytoarchitectonics.**

Bernard, Claude (1813-1878) French physiologist, M.D. 1843. Introduced term "internal secretion" resulting from his studies on glycogenic function of liver (1848). Demonstrated vasomotor functioning, and was the first to reason after his observations that the transmission across the neuromuscular junc-

tion was more likely pharmacological in nature than chemical. In his investigations with **curare** he showed that the paralysis in animals was caused by motor nerve rather than by sensory nerve involvement, as had been suspected.

Bernoulli Name of a Belgian-Swiss family of outstanding mathematicians and scientists, consisting of two brothers (both **Leibniz** pupils), Jacques or Jakob (1654-1705), and Jean or John (1667-1748); and Jean's two sons: Daniel (1700-1782) and Nicolaus (1695-1726). Various scientific eponymic terms honor the Bernoulli name, some of which are:

Bernoulli's theorem (Bernoulli's law) There is not one Bernoulli theorem, but two. One is a law of hydrodynamics developed by Daniel, while the **probability** principle was demonstrated and proved by Jacques. The probability law states that "If the probability of occurrence of the event X is $p(X)$, then if N trials are made independently and under exactly the same conditions, then the probability that the relative frequency of occurrence of X differs from $p(X)$ by any amount, however small, approaches zero as the number of trials grows indefinitely large." (Hays, p. 59.) As N becomes larger the value of the variance of the distribution of P must become smaller, other things remaining equal, which is basic to proving Bernoulli's theorem.

A *Bernoulli distribution* (after Jacques) consists of a plot of two events and their associated probabilities. A *Bernoulli trial* refers to a simple experiment (tossing of a coin) in which only one of two possible outcomes (heads or tails) can occur. *See* **binomial distribution, Euler diagrams, law of large numbers** (also Bell, 1937, pp. 131-138).

Berzelius, Jöns Jakob (1779-1848) Swedish physician and chemist. Introduced system of chemical symbols, leading to those in use today. Discovered several chemical elements. Named **amino acids** in 1848, organic and inorganic chemistry in 1807, and many other chemical terms (catalysis, **cystine**, isomer, etc.)

Besetzung (Ger., a taking possession of) *See* **cathexis.**

Bessel, Friedrich Wilhelm (1784-1846) Prussian astronomer and mathematician. Invented mathematical functions (Bessel functions), and introduced concept of the **personal equation** of observers.

best estimate *See* **sufficient estimate.**

best fit A fit of a straight line to a set of observations so that the sum of the squares of the deviations of the original observations from the line is at a minimum. The **least squares method** is such a fit.

bestiality *See* **zoophilia.**

beta (β) Second letter of the Greek alphabet, often used in the sciences to represent the second item of a series. In chemical notations, the second in a series of compounds. In statistics, the probability of accepting the null hypothesis when it is false.

beta coefficient (beta regression coefficient). A **regression coefficient** expressed in comparable units so that its effect on the **dependent variable** is indicated by its relative size.

beta (β) The error of the second kind or the so-called *type II error*, in which the null hypothesis is accepted when actually it is false or some alternative is true.

beta examination Revision of the earlier Army Beta Test provides a measure of mental ability without requiring the subject to read. Six subtests: mazes, digit-symbol substitution, pictorial absurdities, paper form board, picture completion, and perceptual speed. The restandardization permits securing of a Beta IQ that has statistical similarities to the Wechsler IQ. Norms provide intelligence quotients for ages 16-59. A French-Canadian edition is also available.

beta movement *See* **apparent movement.**

beta receptors Adrenergic receptors primarily concerned with inhibitory functions.

beta risk The probability of making a beta error, or failing to reject a false null

b

hypothesis. The beta risk increases as the **alpha risk** is decreased.

beta waves The second (Gr. beta) type of brain waves to be discovered, having a frequency of about 13-25 **Hertzes**, with relatively low voltage. Beta waves arise from the electrical energy or nerve impulses, and are readily observed on the **electroencephalograph**. They are characteristic of the awake, alert individual, but also occur during **paradoxical sleep**. In infants, they appear before **alpha waves**.

Hans **Berger** identified these waves in 1929 as having frequencies between 20 and 50 cycles per second.

between variance The **variance** between samples; also an estimate of the **population** variance based upon variances due to random effects and to the **independent variable**.

Bewusstheit (Ger., conscious attitude) Experiences that break all rules of conventional psychological analysis, obviously not sensory or perceptual in nature; conscious attitudes, awarenesses, or sets. Vague, imageless feelings, such as being uncertain, or at a loss for words. A special form of **Ach**'s *Bewusstheiten*.

Bezold-Brücke phenomenon A predictable condition involving the principle of color conversion that occurs when intensity of light (**luminance**) is sharply increased causing a hue-shift in red or green toward yellow or blue. Also, if the wave length is kept constant and illumination diminished the tendency of spectral hues to shift from yellow or blue toward red or green. Bezold noted (1873) and described the phenomenon in 1874 briefly, but Brücke (1878) made a more thorough study of it. (Purdy, *American Journal of Psychology*, 1937, 49, pp. 313-315).

Wilhelm von Bezold (also spelled Beshold, Bezhold, Bezhol) (1837-1907) German physician and meteorologist. In 1874, he wrote "*Die Farbenlehre im Hinblich auf Kunst und Kuntsgewerbe*," containing his observations on color conversion.

Wilhelm von Brücke (1819-1892), German physician and neurophysiologist, outstanding student of **Johannes Müller**.

Bezugsvorstellung (Ger., idea of objects) *See* **Absicht**.

bhang (Hind.) Larger leaves and tops of the **cannabis sativa** plants. The term as bang or bhang also means mainlining heroin by direct injection into a vein.

bias In general, a predisposition, conscious and/or unconscious, to lean toward one specific **attitude** or direction; giving undue weight to facts supporting one's personal opinion so as to bend the result to one's advantage.

In research, bias is any effect that systematically distorts the **outcome** of an experiment.

Avoiding bias is one of the first requirements of an adequate sampling study. A **statistic** may differ from its **parameter** because of sample-selection bias and random errors. Random errors decrease as the sample size increases, but this is not true for sample bias, which is equivalent to a constant error.

In electronics, bias refers to voltage or current applied to the input of a circuit in order to shift it into the desired range of operation.

biased estimators Sample statistics that are larger or smaller than their corresponding **population** parameters. An **estimator** is biased if its expected value does not equal the **parameter** it is intended to estimate.

Bielchowsky-Jansky disease One of the conditions classified as **cerebral lipoidosis, late infantile**. It occurs between 2-4 years of age, differing from **Tay-Sachs disease** by having retinal optic atrophy instead of the "cherry-red spot" on the **macula**, and is also found more commonly in non-Jewish families.

Named after the Czechoslovakian neuropsychiatrists Max Bielchowsky (1869-1940) and Jan Jansky (1873-1921).

bilateral transfer Pertaining to (-al) a transfer of an activity from one side of the body to the other, making it an activity of both (bi) sides (later-). The carryover to the unpracticed hand (or foot) of a skill achieved by trial or practice with the other. For example, in an incapacitated, ordinarily righthanded person, the ability to write can be transferred to the untrained left hand.

bimodal curve Referring to (-al) a curve with two (bi-) high values or modes (-mod-). A graphic representation of a bimodal **distribution** in which the cases cluster about two relative maxima.

bimodal distribution A frequency distribution having two (bi-) modes or peaks (-mod-), as in the figure following. Such distributions often result from continuing two heterogeneous sets of data.

binary Relating to (-ary) the integer two (bin-); composed of two elements or components. The **binary number system** uses 2 as its base. A *binary choice* is a choice between two alternatives.

binary arithmetic An arithmetical system developed (1703) by **Leibniz** using only 0 and 1. All numbers are represented in terms of powers of 2 (or with a number system to the base 2) as compared to the decimal system in which numbers are represented in terms of powers of 10 (base 10). *See* **binary number system**.

binary bit Any binary digit (0 or 1).

binary code A code in which each allowable position has one of two possible states. A common symbolism for binary states is 0 and 1. The **binary number system** is one of many binary codes.

binary coded decimal (BCD) system A coding system using four binary digits that allows for easy representation of a single decimal digit. Each contiguous set of four bits represents a numeric digit, a minimum of four bits being necessary to represent 10 decimal values (four-bit set having 2^4 or 16 combinations). *See* **binary number system**. One commonly used code is as follows:

Binary Digit	Decimal Equivalent
0000	0
0001	1
0010	2
0011	3
0100	4
0101	5
0110	6
0111	7
1000	8
1001	9

binary digit (binit; bit) A digit in the **binary number system** with one of two values, a zero (0) or one (1), as opposed to a digit in the familiar decimal notation which can have ten values: 0, 1, . . . 9. *See* **bit**.

binary notation The writing of numbers with a base of 2. The first dozen numbers, 0 to 11, are written: 0, 1, 10, 11, 100, 101, 110, 111, 1000, 1001, 1010, 1011. *See* **binary number system** and table under **binary coded decimal system**.

Bacon (1605), in his bilateral cryptographic system, anticipated the binary notation for numbers.

binary number system Pertaining to (-ary) the number system with the base (radix) of two (bi-) rather than ten as in the decimal system, the digits having absolute values of 0 or 1, the only two coefficients necessary to express any number. The binary system makes use of positional notation, each succeeding column to the left of the decimal point being reserved for the number of times the radix is taken to each succeeding power, beginning with 0 (thus, the first column is taken to 0 power, the second column to the 1st power, etc.). The decimal number 1764, as an example, designates a sum of 4 tens to the 0 power, 6 tens to the 1st, 7 tens to the 2nd, and 1 ten to the third. A *binary-to-decimal conversion device* is one that accepts binary-coded signals at its **input** and converts them into decimal-coded signals at its **output**.

Napier (1617) apparently provided the first use of the binary system for calculation purposes. *See* **logarithm**.

binaural Referring to (-al) the functioning, use, or simultaneous stimulation of two (bi-) ears (-aur-), such as with a binaural stethoscope.

Binet, Alfred (1857-1911) French psychologist. Wrote extensively on **hypnosis**, pathological phenomena, **intelligence**, **individual differences**, and mental fatigue. He made use of inkblots to study imaginative and perceptual processes twenty years before **Rorschach**. Binet considered intelligence to be not merely the sum of many different aspects of intelligent behavior but an interlocking process involving judgment, problem solving, and reasoning. When the Parisian school commission asked him to seek means of classifying school children (particularly feeble-minded ones), Binet put his ideas into practice.

In 1905, in collaboration with psychiatrist Theodore Simon (1873-1962), he published *Etude Experimentale de l'Intelligence*, the **Binet-Simon Test of Intelligence**. Binet obtained performance **norms** on his test for different age groups that became known as mental ages. Graded tests gave the **mental age** of a person in relation to growth and intellectual development, adult performance even being classified by mental age levels: 1-2 years, idiot; 3-7 years, imbecile; 8-12 years, moron; etc.

In 1910, American educator and psychologist, Henry H. Goddard (1866-1957), introduced the Binet-Simon type of test into the U.S. at the Training School for Feebleminded in Vineland, New Jersey, which he had founded in 1909. Later, **Terman** and associates of Stanford University revised the French edition for American usage, thus the **Stanford-Binet test**, first published in 1916 (revised in 1937 and 1960) resulted. *See* **fetishism, Gestalt, intelligence quotient** (also Boring, 1957, pp. 573-74, Vinacke, p. 648).

binit Contraction of *binary digit*. Binits have special application in decoding of linear systematic codes. For example, the binits x_1, $x_2 \ldots x_k$ of x (the code word) may be arbitrarily chosen, hence being called information **bits**. Upon selection of the information bits, so called parity-binits are specially determined.

binocular cues. *See* **distance cues**.

binocular disparity (retinal disparity) Relating to (-ar) the disparity or difference in vision that exists between the images projected onto the retinas of both (bin-) eyes (-ocul-), resulting when a person tries to fixate on a solid object. The disparate picture received from a near object by each eye, produced by the different angle of viewing (**parallax**).

Demonstration of binocular disparity was first made by Sir **Charles Wheatstone** in using a stereoscope. See his "Contribution to the Physiology of Vision, Part the First. On Some Remarkable and Hitherto Unobserved Phenomena of Binocular Vision." *Philosophical Transactions*, Royal Society of London, 1838.

binocular parallax *Same as* **binocular disparity**.

binomial An algebraic equation referring to (-al) two (bi-) terms (-nomi-) connected by plus or minus signs, thus $(a + b)$, $(x - 4y)$, and $(6x^3 - 3a^2 b)$ are examples of binomials; any sum or difference of two quantities.

binomial coefficient *See* Table 1c.

binomial curve The curve representing the plot of the successive terms of the expansion $(p + q)^n$ with $p + q = 1$, n having any positive integral value, where: p = probability of success of an event, q = probability of p's alternative or failure, and n = number of times an event can occur.

binomial distribution (Bernoulli distribution) A suitable model for events that can result in only two outcomes, e.g., "heads or tails," "true or false," etc. One of these two is called a "success" and its **probability** is symbolized by P. The other **outcome** is a "failure" or "nonsuccess" and is symbolized by $Q = 1 - P$. While using the same mathematical rule for determining probabilities, the particular probabilities worked out for a given problem depend on the **parameters** N and P.

Binomial distributions compose a family of theoretical distributions that associate a probability, $p(x)$, with each value of random variable X according to the rule

$$p(x) = \left(\frac{N}{x}\right) p^x q^{N-x}, \; 0 < X < N$$

with parameters of N (the number of independent trials) and p (the probability of observing exactly x successes in N independent trials). The binomial distribution is also interpreted as the sampling distribution of the proportions that might be observed in **random** samples drawn from a two-class **population**, giving the various values possibly occurring under H_O, (H_O here being the hypothesis that the population value is P). Therefore, when "scores" are in two classes, the binomial distribution may be used to test H_O. The test is of the **goodness-of-fit** type, helping to determine whether it is reasonable to believe that the proportions (or frequencies) observed in the sample could have been drawn from a population having a specified value P.

binomial expansion The expansion of a binomial to a given power, which can be used to determine the **probability** of obtaining a score as large as or larger than any given score. The expression $(a + b)^n$, for example, can be expanded by the following rule:

$$(a + b)^n = a^n + \frac{n!}{(n-1)!1!} a^{n-1}b$$
$$+ \frac{n!}{(n-2)!2!} a^{n-2}b^2 + \cdots$$
$$+ \frac{n!}{1!(n-1)!} ab^{n-1} + b^n.$$

For example, $(a + b)^3 = a^3 + 3a^2b + 3ab^2 + b^3$ according to this rule. The various probabilities in the binomial distribution are simply terms in such a binomial expansion. Thus, $a = p$, $b = q$, and $n = N$; therefore

$$(p + q)^N = p^N + (N) p^{N-1}q$$
$$+ \left(\frac{N(N-1)}{2}\right) p^{N-2}q^2 + \dots q^N.$$

Since $p + q$ must equal 1.00, then $(p + q)^N = 1.00$, and the sum of all the probabilities in a binomial distribution is 1.00.

Further information on the binomial is given in most algebra books as well as in the statistical books listed in the bibliography.

binomial probability (*See* Tables 1a, 1b.)

binomial test (*See* Tables 1a, 1b.)

binomial theorem A general formula, dealing with **probabilities**, for expanding the power of any binomial $(p + q)^n$ without performing the successive multiplications.

For positive integral powers the binomial theorem was known to Omar Khayyam (c. 1100). Isaac Newton (1642-1727), in 1664-1665, extended use of it to all values of n including fractional and negative values. The Norwegian mathematician Niels Henrik Abel (1802-1829), showed that the theorem holds for all values of n, including imaginary numbers. *See* **numbers.**

biochemical theories of psychosis Theories about **psychosis** that assume bizarre behavior to be caused by chemical factors, the basics of such an idea being traceable to the early humoral theories. Since the Second World War, advances in studies of **brain** metabolism led to many investigations on the biochemistry of psychoses. Two prominent but controversial theories of the many proposed are neuro-humoral in content: (*1*) *Serotonin theory.* An assumption that certain persons are predisposed toward and eventually develop **schizophrenia** because of abnormal brain metabolism of **serotonin.** Excessive serotonin may produce agitation and hallucinations resembling acute schizophrenia while a deficiency may result in catatonic-like depression. Since **LSD** ingestion results in psychotomimetic behavior and since serotonin resembles LSD in chemical structure, it is assumed that serotonin functions similarly to LSD. (*2*) *Adrenalin metabolites theory.* A working theory in which it is assumed that in schizophrenia an aberrant enzyme (probably **taraxein**) converts excess **adrenalin** (resulting from stress) into the chemical unstable metabolite which then is immediately converted to another metabolite, adrenolutin. In this theory, presence of both metabolites (considered as psychotomimetics) indicates the faulty hereditary factors predisposing to schizophrenia.

biodynamics Characteristic actions (-ics) of the powerful (-dynam-) forces of life (bio-); that aspect of physiology dealing with the active vital processes of a biological organism and its interrelationships with the environment.

bioenergetic analysis A therapeutic procedure that considers all emotional states as being reflected in the structuring and functioning of the body, these reflections (like an encoded language) being capable of analyses and interpretation by a skilled practitioner of bioenergetic analysis. Character traits and personality characteristics can be read by analyzing a person's posture, the way he walks, his handwriting, etc. It is felt that the physical posture, during rest and movement, is the most significant key in helping open the door of understanding about a person's inner problems. Therapeutically, the neurotic may be requested to express his repressed feelings by yelling, pounding a couch or stomping the floor, and by the assumption of various postures all leading toward relaxation and feeling of release.

Alexander Lowen, American psychiatrist, developed his program out of various practices and ideas, integrating them into a theory.

bio-feedback training A therapeutic approach (using a closed circuit electronic **feedback** system consisting of a **polygraph**, **oscilloscope**, and other recording devices) in which the subject is taught to control his physiological processes consciously by observing the output of his own brain waves and other autonomic functionings (heartbeat, pulse rate, etc.). For more striking results self-hypnosis is sometimes combined with bio-feedback, since **alpha** brain **waves** are faster and stronger in people subject to hypnosis. Adherents claim that the system has great promise for a new practical therapy and may even make *ESP* more available to broader scientific investigations. Since such autonomic controls are similarly found in Zen masters and yogi practitioners (achieving self-discipline, bodily control, and relaxation only after many years of practice), the relatively new and quickly learned bio-feedback approach is referred to as **electronic yoga.**

biogenic amines Those amines relating to (-ic) biological (bio-) effects which originate or derive (-gen-) from naturally occurring **amino acids**, such as those found in meat and other proteins or manufactured in the body. Biogenic amines (such as **acetylcholine, serotonin, dopamine, and norepinephrine**) probably serve as synaptic transmitter substances in the **brain.**

Spectrophotofluorometry in the mid 50's made precise chemical assays possible by showing that these amines are highly associated with appetite, mood fluctuations, sex demands, and primitive motor functions.

The Finnish investigators O. Eranko and L. Raisanen, writing in the *Journal of Histochemistry and Cytochemistry*, 1961, 9, 54, were first to show that fluorescence could be produced when **catecholamines** from the **adrenal glands** were reacted with formaldehyde. Later studies showed that the biogenic amines were localized in **axons** and nerve terminals.

biological drive A physiological pressure resulting from basic tissue **needs**, usually directing the organism toward certain types of behavior, such as the drive for sleep when exhausted or the drive to drink when dry.

biological transducing system A highly specialized and highly ordered biological system that converts energy or information from one form to another. For example, the **rods** and **cones** of the eye's retina convert light energy into nerve impulses; muscle fibers convert chemical energy into mechanical energy; the **mitochondria** in the **cytoplasm** of all cells help convert the chemical energy of food into a form directly usable by the other components of the cell.

biological world (Ger., *Umwelt*) The natural world around us; the intimate feeling of closeness to our environment. All organisms relate to the world about them. In addition to the world environment, the biological world of all animals includes biological **needs, drives,** and **instincts.**

bionics Portmanteau word for *bi*ology and elect*ronics.* Science of simulating the action in biological systems with electronic and mechanical devices. Often used to describe equipment made to **interface** with the biological system, such as prosthetic appliances (artificial limbs, etc.).

biosocial theory The viewpoint that interprets behavior as an integration of *biol*ogical (organismic) and *social* (environmental) forces.

biotransformation The transformation of a biologically active **drug** into a form that either is inactive or that produces different effects.

biotrope One whose mind is turned (-trope) toward biological (bio-) issues, or whose judgment and decision are based upon individual needs.

biserial coefficient of correlation (r_{bis}, or r_b). A statistical technique used when one of two traits is measured on a continuous scale and the other on a dichotomous scale.

bit (binary digit, binit) A portmanteau word combining the first and last letters of *binary digit*; an index of information transmission. One bit is the amount of information that reduces the number of alternatives in half; also, one of the characters of a language employing only two distinct characters. (In this connotation sometimes called "binit.") A bit can be equivalent to an *on* or an *off* condition, a *yes* or a *no* condition, or it can even be the absence or the presence of a hole in a piece of paper tape in coding information. Coded cards, punch tape, and magnetic tape depend upon binary digits (bits) information. A punched hole in a card is referred to as a "one," no punch as a "zero."

Bits are pure number units (single binary characters) that can be used as measurement units for psychological work in, say, choice-reaction time experiments that involve uncertainty ($\hat{H}$) or unpredictability of a distribution. Related to ($\hat{H}$) is a measure of uncertainty reduction ($\hat{T}$) that provides information as to how much a knowledge of one variable reduces the uncertainty ($\hat{H}$) of another **variable.** *Zone bits* are two bits combined to the four bits in a binary coded decimal system so that the group may represent alphabetic and special characters.

b

bivariate analysis Analysis of statistical data relating to (-ate) two (bi-) variables (-vari-), such as height and weight of individuals.

bivariate frequency distribution (scatter plot, contingency table) A joint distribution of two **random variables** showing the frequency of cases in each category of two scales. For example, in a height-weight bivariate scale, the distribution tells how many individuals fall into the mutual cell of a certain weight with a certain height. For qualitative categorical data, bivariate distributions are called **contingency tables**, for quantitative data, they are known as **scatter plots** or diagrams.

bivariate population A **population** of two variables, both normally distributed. In continuous bivariate populations, the bivariate scales have two coordinate axes, each pair of scores for one individual locating a point in the plane of those axes.

blackbody (complete radiator) An idealized perfect radiator (opaque to all wavelengths) that absorbs all the radiant energy to which it is exposed and whose surface would appear black if its temperature remained low enough so as not to be self-luminous. Since no material surface can absorb all the radiant energy incident upon it, blackbodies are construed only as approximations. A popularly conceived and almost perfect blackbody is that of a tiny opening in the wall of a rough, blackened enclosure or box, through which radiant energy may enter. Part of the radiant energy entering the opening is continuously absorbed and reflected by the inner walls until a uniform density of radiation exists. Blackbody radiation emitted from the hole (of the cavity) increases rapidly with increased temperature. If the temperature of the blackbody is that of melting platinum (*see* **candela**), a blackbody radiator of 1 cm^2 surface area has a light intensity of 60 candelas. Blackbody radiation is an electromagnetic field in a space that is surrounded on all sides by matter and in which there are no light sources. The spectrum of blackbody radiation is determined solely by the temperature of the surrounding material.

The determination of the candela, as the SI unit of luminous intensity, is arrived at by recourse to the use of a blackbody.

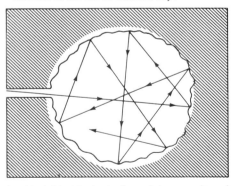

An ideal blackbody is formed by a cavity of rough internal surface with a very small opening.

blast olfactometer A device from which a blast of graded amounts of pressurized, odorous gas is released up the nostrils, designed for measuring (-meter) smell (olfacto-) thresholds.

Bleuler, Eugen (1858-1939) Swiss psychiatrist. By substituting his concepts and the term **schizophrenia** for **dementia praecox** in 1911 he led the way to a more dynamic consideration of the disease; he also imbued **psychiatry** with a more hopeful and constructive attitude toward psychotic patients. He coined the terms **autism, autistic thinking, autochthonous ideas** and schizoid personality, as well as introducing the term **ambivalence** (1911) to describe a variety of emotional pulls and pushes.

blind spot Exit point in the retina of the **optic nerve** where the absence of **rods** and **cones** makes the area insensitive to light; also that part of the visual field corresponding to this point where there is no vision because images are projected onto the optic disk.

Discovered and described in 1668 by French physicist Edme Mariotte (1620?-1684).

blocking The cutting off of a word or an association due to mental conflict. Involuntary inhibition (or repression) of recall, ideation, or communication. For example, one may forget or "block" on well known material during an examination when the test is threatening, or one may block on recalling a familiar person's name when he would rather not think of him.

block maze A maze in which all paths to the goal are equally correct and all of the same length. Error occurs only when the animal deviates from the direction of the goal or enters a blind alley. The block may have been used for testing cortical damage effects on spatial discrimination.

block sampling *See* **area sampling.**

blood-brain barrier(s) A physiological process that sets up a barrier preventing the passage of some diffused substances from blood plasma to the brain. The barrier's function seems to take place somewhere between blood plasma and nerve cells. It apparently serves to protect the brain from substances that would not ensure a stable neuronal environment. The barrier is extraordinarily discriminating with chemicals, passing freely such substances as anesthetics, water oxygen, carbon dioxide, and the precursor (5HTP) of **serotonin**, but locks out serotonin itself; it resists passage of sodium and potassium electrolytes for a time but finally lets them through.

Presence of the blood-brain barrier was first demonstrated (1885) in animals by **Paul Ehrlich**, who showed that all tissues except the brain and spinal cord are affected by vital staining. It was Edwin E. Goldmann (1863-1913), South African physician, however, who developed the concept (1913) of the blood brain barrier out of his brain researches. *See* **brain barrier systems.**

blood-cerebrospinal fluid barrier *See* **brain barrier systems.**

blood-sugar level A physiological measurement or standard of sugar content in the blood, below which **hypoglycemia** results and above which **hyperglycemia** develops. Sugar (glucose) in blood is a necessary characteristic of health and life. Each 100 centimeters of whole blood requires between 50 and 90 milligrams of glucose for a normal existence. Below this lower level (*hypoglycemia*), cells become deprived of the carbohydrates they need and suffer extinction. This is particularly true of nerve cells because they have no adequate means for storing carbohydrates. Extended hypoglycemia results in coma and death. *Hyperglycemia* (elevation of blood sugar above 90 milligrams), however, has no such disastrous effects, but can lead to diabetic conditions and other metabolic disorders. *See* **catechol amines.**

BMR Basal metabolic rate.

body build *See* **constitutional types, Kretschmer, Sheldon, somatotype.**

body image The mental image of our bodies that we live with, that we feel attitudinally, that we "see" internally and that helps dictate our **life style.** Anxiety, insecurity, and low self-esteem, for example, are associated with a poor body image. Our body image, however, also consists of a projected ideal body image and a fantasy-image (the Walter Mitty daydream image).

Paul Schilder (1886-1940), German **psychiatrist**, elaborated upon the body image concept by investing the **ego** with a structure, an irreducible entity that tended to remain constant.

body-sense area A projection area of the **cerebral cortex**, lying behind the fissure of Rolando, which helps determine the position of the body in space.

body-type theories Theories that attempt to relate the individual's body build to attributes of his **personality.** *See* **constitutional types, Kretschmer, Sheldon, somatotype theory**; also Bischof, 1964, pp. 93-123).

Bonferroni t test *Same as* **Dunn multiple comparison test.**

Bonnet, Charles (1720-1793) Swiss naturalist and philosopher. Anticipated **act psychology** and the discovery of **specific nerve energies** by stating that each quality of **sensation** depended upon a special area of the **brain** that had been stimulated. Considered memory to be a function of activities in nerve fibers.

Boolean algebra (Set algebra) A branch of **symbolic logic** that deals with the truth of logical propositions; the algebra of proportions, only two possibilities being allowed: on or off, true or false, yes or no, etc. All propositions expressing relationships among binary variables can be obtained with one or more of only three "operators" or connectives: AND (expressing conjunction), OR (expressing disjunction), and NOT (expressing negation). Other connectives (such as "either ... or," "neither ... nor," "if," "whether," etc.) can be reduced to these three (AND, OR, NOT) or constructed from a combination of the three. These operators are used analogously to mathematical signs.

The usual laws of algebra hold for set algebra, but supplementary postulates are added, such as: *commutative laws* ($A \cup B = B \cup A$; $A \cap B = B \cap A$); *associative laws* [$(A \cup B) \cup C = A \cup (B \cup C)$]; [$(A \cap B) \cap C = A \cap (B \cap C)$]; *distributive laws* $A \cup (B \cap C) = (A \cup B) \cap (A \cup C)$; $A \cap (B \cup C) = (A \cap B) \cup (A \cap C)$, and several other even more specialized laws.

Such a mathematical technique makes it possible to combine, manipulate and reduce the number of propositions to a more workable few.

Mathematical logic was first outlined by **Leibniz** about 1700 and later systematized (1847) by English mathematician and logician Augustus de Morgan (1806-1871) and by George Boole (1815-1864), English mathematician, who in 1848 developed symbolic logic in his work *An Investigation of the Laws of Thought.* Boole also discovered "invariants," a necessary "ingredient" for relativity theory. (Bell, 1937, pp. 433-447.)

borborygmus Rumbling sound in the bowels. Gas in the stomach; a rumbling or gurgling in the intestines, sometimes initiated by an emotional upset. *See* **emotion.**

botryology The intuitive or statistical study (-ology) of separating interconnected objects (such as body typing of individuals, speech sounds, words) into groups or clusters (botry-), such as in constructing a psychiatric nomenclature, developing a thesaurus or dictionary. (I. J. Good, "How Much Science Can You Have at Your Fingertips?" *IBM Journal of Research and Development*, 1958, *2*, 282).

boulimia A disorder (-ia) of having an appetite (-lim-) like an ox (bou-). Abnormal increase in hunger; ravenous hunger satisfied only temporarily by huge portions of food. Observable in hebephrenic conditions, and also in certain brain disorders. Psychoanalytically, a symbolic indication of a hunger for love, stability, and support; associated with an infantile **oral character** trait. *Opposed to* anorexia, *compare* **hyperphagia.**

Term found in **Aristotle's** writings.

Bourneville's disease *See* **tuberous sclerosis.**

bouton terminaux (Fr. terminal buttons, end bulbs, end feet, synaptic bulbs). Club-shaped swellings of **axon** endings at the **synapse** whose function is to send nerve impulses across the synapse to other **neurons.** In the central nervous system (CNS) neurons, the boutons are assumed to hold fluid-filled sacs containing a chemical substance that transmits a signal from one cell to the next, facilitating or inhibiting the function of each cell. Actually, the concept of chemical transmission in the CNS is inferred from the findings on peripheral structures rather than coming from discoveries about the CNS itself.

The German physiologist Hans Held (1866-1942) was the first (1897) to demonstrate that there were swellings at the end of axons. English neurologist Thomas R. Elliott (1877-1961) in his preliminary article, "On the Action of Adrenalin," *Journal of Physiology*, 1904, **31**, XX-XXI, was the first to suggest (for the autonomic nervous system) that a chemical agent probably was released at the nerve endings, accounting for the transmission of excitatory or inhibitory stimuli.

boxcar correlator *See* **averaging computer.**

brachycephaly A condition (-aly) of shortness (brachy-) of the head (-ceph-). *See* **cephalic index.**

Braconnot, M. Henri (1781-1855) French chemist, specializing in studies on cellulose, sugars, and amino acids. In 1820, he isolated and named both **glycine** and **leucine.**

brain The brain, weighing approximately three pounds [77% water, 23% solids (lipids about 10%, and proteins 8% etc.)] is that part of the **central nervous system** enclosed within the cranium, consisting mainly of the **cerebrum, cerebellum,** and **brainstem.**

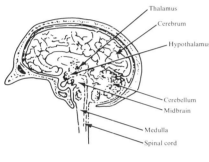

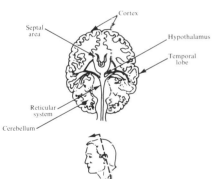

Major parts of the brain and their location within the shell. From Psychology: A Scientific Study of Man, 3rd Ed., by Sanford and Wrightsman. Copyright 1970 by Wadsworth Publishing Company, Inc. Reprinted by permission of the publisher, Brooks/Cole Publishing Company, Monterey, California.

The major parts of the brain are derived from the three divisions of the embryological neural tube and are as follows:

1. **Prosencephalon** (forebrain) is divided into two parts:
    A. **Telencephalon** (the end-brain) consists of:
    Cerebral hemispheres (cerebrum)
    Basal ganglia
    Corpus striatum
    Caudate nucleus
    Lentiform nucleus
    Putamen
    Globus pallidus
    Amygdala
    Claustrum
    Cerebral cortex
    Corpus callosum
    Lateral ventricles
    Rostral portion of third ventricle
    Limbic system (involving circuits concerned with olfaction, memory, emotional control, homeostatic regulation of behavior, and regulation of factors concerned with sequential movement)
    Olfactory bulb and tract
    Hippocampal formation
    B. **Diencephalon** (the between-brain) located between telencephalon and mesencephalon:
    Thalamus
    Lateral geniculate body
    Medial geniculate body
    Hypothalamus (primary control center for autonomic functions)
    Mammillary bodies (influence sleep)
    Pituitary body and infundibulum
    Optic tract and retina
    Third ventricle
2. **Mesencephalon** (midbrain) connects forebrain and hindbrain by a stalk or bridge
    Tectum (sensory in nature)
    Superior colliculi (one pair)—primitive visual center
    Inferior colliculi (one pair)—primitive hearing center
    The two pairs of colliculi (4 in all) are also known as the **corpora quadrigemina.**
    Floor of the midbrain, acting as passageway for ascending sensory tracts and descending motor tracts
3. **Rhombencephalon** (hindbrain)
    Metencephalon
    Pons
    Cerebellum
    Fourth ventricle
    Myelencephalon
    Medulla

Terms boldfaced above are described more fully at respective entries in this almanac. Because of much overlapping between various systems, the above classification is somewhat arbitrary and not always consistent. For example, sometimes the amygdala is included under basal ganglia (as here) but other times it is grouped in the limbic system.

The first reference to a word expressing the meaning of "brain" is found in the **Edwin Smith Surgical Papyrus,** a manuscript dating from 3500 B.C. It also mentioned the brain coverings (**meninges**) and fluid beneath them (**cerebrospinal fluid**).

In 1522 **Galen** discarded **Hippocrates'** idea that the brain is a gland, describing it as resembling bone marrow and continuous with spinal cord, with the frontal lobes being the seat of the soul (pneuma) and source of animal spirits.

For information pertaining to the brain and the nervous system, contact the following: UCLA Brain Information Service, School of Medicine and Biomedical Library, Los Angeles, California 90024; American Academy of Neurology, 7100 France Avenue, South, Minneapolis, Minnesota 55435; and the New York Association for Brain Injured Children, 305 Broadway, New York, N.Y. 10007 for information relating to perceptually handicapped.

brain action currents *See* **action potential.**

brain barrier systems Physiological processes that, because of differences in ionic composition and permeability rates between one brain fluid and another, prevent or delay the exchange of fluids, solutes, or ions throughout the brain. The **blood-brain barrier,** for instance, prevents or delays the direct transfer of many substances and ions from blood plasma to brain tissue because brain blood capillaries appear to be less permeable to solutes and ions than other capillaries. The *blood-cerebrospinal fluid barrier* acts to separate cerebrospinal fluid from the blood plasma because of the differences in ionic composition. Yet, despite similar ionic composition, the *cerebrospinal fluid-brain barrier* delays only slightly the interchange between cerebrospinal fluid and brain extracellular fluid, apparently with the ependyma (epithelial cell layer), covering the walls of the brain, acting as the barrier.

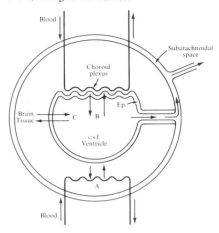

From "The Chemistry of Mind," by Patrick L. McGeer, *American Scientist*, **59**, 1971. Reprinted by permission.

brain localization *See* **localization of brain function.**

brain mapping A method of laying out the brain's anatomy according to specific functions, assumed or known. *See* **homunculus, Brodmann.**

Probably the first example of cranial-cerebral topography was drawn in 1316 in the anatomical manual by the Italian physician Mundinus [Mondino de Luzzi], (1275-1326).

brainstem The stalk-like portion of the **brain** below the level of the **telencephalon,** comprising the **rhombencephalon** or hindbrain (**medulla, pons, cerebellum,** and part of the

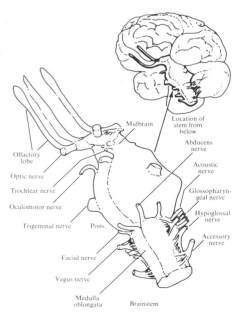

From The Human Brain, by Isaac Asimov. Copyright 1967 by Houghton Mifflin Company. Reprinted by permission.

b

fourth ventricle), the **mesencephalon** (the midbrain floor and the dorsal portion of the **tectum** containing the **corpora quadrigemina** or four **colliculi**), and the **brainstem reticular formation** (located largely within the hindbrain but whose projections extend into the midbrain and the **hypothalamus** of the **diencephalon**. In general, the brainstem contains the cranial nerves (except **olfactory** and **optic**) and all nerve fiber systems interrelating the higher brain structures in the diencephalon with the spinal cord. The brainstem passes through the foramen magnum at the base of the skull and enters the neural canal where it merges with the spinal cord.

Gross studies of the brainstem were first reported by **Sir Charles Bell**, but microscopic studies not until late 19th century.

brainstem reticular formation (BSRF) *See* **brainstem**.

brainstorming A technique for stimulating creativity in group or individual problem solving, sometimes using a "green light" stage in which solutions are suggested without criticism or comment, and a "red light" stage in which they are evaluated and criticized.

brain ventricles Four hollows or little (-icles) belly-like (ventr-) chambers in the brain. Ventricles are derived from the embryonic medullary canal. They are numbered from those lying forward of the brain to the one at the base. Thus, the *fourth ventricle* is the lowermost and is located where the central canal of the spinal cord merges with the **brain**. The *third ventricle* is relatively long and thin and connects through a narrow aperture with the fourth ventricle below it as well as with the two foremost ventricles that lie within the cerebrum, one on either side of the midline (thus being named the *lateral ventricles*). The lateral ventricles are by far the largest of the ventricles. The ventricles and the central canal of the spinal cord are filled with **cerebrospinal fluid**, which originates from the intricate network of blood vessels called choroid plexuses.

From *The Human Brain*, by Isaac Asimov. Copyright 1967 by Houghton Mifflin Company. Reprinted by permission.

Erasistratus mentioned the ventricles as early as the 3rd century B.C. as did **Herophilus**. **Galen** gave the name of ventricles to the cavities, saying that they were fashioned from the choroid plexus or the **rete mirabile** and that they served as a reservoir for animal spirits. **Mondino** supported the idea in 1316 that the ventricles were the center of mental functions, but **Vesalius** disagreed and both he

and **Aranzi** contributed more realistic descriptions of them. Da Vinci made a wax cast of the ventricles in 1504, indicating the general interest in the subject.

brainwashing An intensive and coercive form of persuasion or propaganda carried out on individuals who lack strong leadership qualities, resulting in almost complete control of the influenced person. Often, the American prisoner of war in Korea was so brainwashed that he was ignored and isolated by his buddies. Sometimes this social deprivation resulted in severe depression and death. [I. E. Farber, Harry F. Harlow, and Louis Jolyon West, "Brainwashing, Conditioning, and DDD: (Debility, Dependency, and Dread)."] *Sociometry*, 1957, **20**, 271-283. For further information, contact *Group for Advancement of Psychiatry*, Public Affairs, 104 East 25th Street, New York, N.Y. 10010 for publications.

The word was derived by an American journalist from the Chinese term for "thought reform."

brain waves Spontaneous generation of small amounts of electricity in the **brain**, mainly in the **cerebral cortex**. Brain waves are measured by the **electroencephalograph**, and can be recorded from the depths of the brain by using implanted electrodes.

As early as 1875, English physiologist R. Caton (*see* **cathode**) had observed fluctuations of electrical **action potentials** in the brain while using galvanometric electrodes attached to the exposed cortex. V. J. Danilewski, a Russian physiologist, observed the same phenomenon in 1891. However, these researchers and several others following them were unable to record the oscillating brain potentials until, with newer refinements in instrumentation, **Berger** did so in 1929, using electrodes placed on the scalp.

Brentano, Franz (1838-1917) German philosopher. He and his followers comprised the **Würzburg School**. In 1874, Brentano published *Psychology from an Empirical Standpoint*, emphasizing that all psychological activity consists of functions or acts and that the content of experience is physical. Psychology, he said, need not study the color "red," for example, but should investigate the process of "experiencing red." He thus pioneered the development of **act psychology**, opposing **Wundt**'s emphasis on "content." **Freud, Angell, James**, and Woodworth took sides with him against **Wundt** and **Titchener**. (Boring, 1957, pp. 356-358).

Breuer, Josef (1842-1925) Viennese neurologist and physiologist. Instrumental in helping **Freud** establish concepts of the **id, ego, superego, catharsis**, and the unconscious. Breuer also discovered (1874) the function of the **semicircular canals**.

Briggsian logarithms *See* **logarithm**.

brightness Psychological attribute of lightsource **color** perceptions, whereby "light" stimuli may be ordered on a scale from dim to bright, or from black through gray to white, measurable in **lambert** or millilambert units. This subjective visual sensation is determined by the **amplitude** (intensity) of light waves, greater amplitude causing brighter (lighter) color.

brightness constancy The tendency to perceive familiar visual objects as always having the same consistent brightness regardless of the amount of light and shadow they actually reflect under differing conditions of illumination. For instance, snow in dim illumination at night is perceived to be as white as it was during daytime brightness. Although the retinal image here corresponds to the **stimulus**, a perceptual correction is made to compensate for the apparent disparity so that the object can be seen in its familiar light, thus helping make the perceived world relatively stable and constant. *See* **perceptual constancy**.

bril A subjective unit of light on the scale of brightness, contrasting with millilamberts, the physical units.

American psychologist Randall M. Hanes (born 1920) in his article (A Scale of Subjective Brightness. *Journal of Experimental Psychology*, 1949, **39**, pp. 438-452) adapted the word from "brill," previously used by Wright. William D. Wright (born 1906), an English optics specialist, in his book *Researches on Normal and Defective Color Vision*, 1946, had used his word to define "an arbitrary subjective brightness function to correspond to the way in which the difference limen for brightness varies with intensity" (Hanes, p. 451). Hanes felt that the different spelling was warranted in order to clarify the meanings.

British associationism A philosophical movement or doctrine (thriving from about 1650 to 1850) that emphasized the importance of the senses and experience in learning, while also explaining the process of how ideas combine to influence and form other ideas. Its tenets led into the development of associationist psychology. The leaders in the movement were **Hobbes, Hartley, Locke, James Mill** and son **John Stuart Mill**.

British higher education University studies usually are organized in three steps. The first level lasts for three or four years (five or six for medicine), culminating in a Bachelor of Arts or Bachelor of Science degree. A bachelor's degree with honors usually signifies a higher level of degree, indicating that the student intends to teach or carry on research. The next stage takes approximately two years or less, the successful student being awarded the Master's degree (M.A. or M.Sc.), provided he also passes additional work and submits a thesis. The final stage results in the granting of a Doctor's degree, usually given after additional studies and publication of original research.

Broca's speech area A convolution of the left cerebral hemisphere situated above the **fissure of Sylvius**, in front of the **optic tract** and behind the *gyrus rectus*. Its function is to control **motor** speech. *See* **aphasia, cerebral cortex**; figure under **speech aphasia**.

Named after Pierre Paul Broca (1824-1880), French surgeon who discovered the articulate speech area in 1861. However, about 1850, French neurologist, Jean Baptist Bouillard (1797-1881), in his studies on inflammation of the brain, had indicated that the temporal lobe contained the speech area.

Brodmann, Korbinian (1868-1918) German physician. Studied medicine in Münich, Würzburg, Berlin, and Freiburg, receiving his medical license in 1895 and his M.D. 1898, at Leipzig. In 1908, Brodmann published a cortical map describing the 52 occipital and pre-occipital areas of the **cerebral cortex**, grouping them into eleven major areas, which became known as *Brodmann's area*(s). His numbering of each of the six cortical layers based on the thickness of cellular structure was adopted from a diagram first presented (1878) by English pathologist William Bevan-Lewis (1847-1929), whose concepts (Brodmann's) were also adopted by his mentor **Oskar Vogt**. He also believed that evolutionary progress was associated with increasing differentiation. Brodmann's system of brain architectonics was published posthumously in 1925.

Brown, Thomas (1778-1820). Scottish metaphysician. Although his psychology has often been called **associationism** he preferred the term "suggestion." He believed that the mind functions unitarily rather than in separate units. To him, one idea suggested another rather than one idea sequentially following another, as might be assumed with associationism. *See* **kinesthesis**.

Bruner, Jerome S. Born, New York, 1915. American psychologist (cognitive processes, opinion and attitude research, perception and learning, social psychology). Received **Gold Medal Award**, 1962. APA President 1965. (J. S. Bruner, "The Course of Cognitive Growth," *American Psychologist*, 1964, **19**). *See* **symbolic mode; (1)** under **cognitive growth theories**.

bruxism (stridor dentium) The act (-ism) of compulsively gnashing the teeth (brux-) during sleep, but also at other times when under either physical or emotional stress. More severe and prolonged cases are evident in psychotic conditions.

Bryan, William L. (1860-1955) American (Indiana) psychologist (physiological, learning; classical telegraph studies). Ph.D., Clark, 1892. APA President 1903. *See* **plateau, American Psychological Association.**

Buber, Martin (1878-1965) Born, Vienna. Philosopher, theologian. Ph.D., Vienna 1904. Professor of social philosophy at Hebrew University, Jerusalem, and at several universities in the United States. *See* **I-Thou relationship.**

bufotenin(e) Derived from poisonous secretions of tendon-like (-ten-) skin glands of toads (bufo-). A crystalline toxic alkaloid from indole. Resembles **serotonin** structurally and has biological action like **epinephrine**. Raises blood pressure, and induces hallucinations; a **psychotomimetic.**

Bühler, Karl Ludwig (1879-1963) German-born American clinical psychologist. In investigating thought processes, he used Woodworth's technique of recording the steps involved in reaching answers to thought-provoking questions.

Bühler considered "thought elements" to be the content of the thinking process, an idea somewhat similar to **Angell's. Titchener** in 1909 criticized the Würzburg School for its "conscious attitudes" and Bühler, in particular, for his "thought elements." To Titchener, imageless thought did not exist. Bühler's work, along with **Brentano's,** did much to break the authority of **Wundt** and Titchener. *See* **act psychology, Ausfragemethode.**

bulimia Variant of **boulimia.**

byte Usually shorter than a **word** and operated upon as a unit in a digital system; a group or series of ordered **binary digits** that may represent a character (see **ASCII**); also refers to the space on the tape (in punched-tape programming) normally filled with one **character.** The byte in some computers refers to eight information **bits** but may consist of any number (for example, a 4 bit byte is a digit; a 6 bit byte is known as a character)—bit bytes, for example, are somewhat less common.

C

C. A. Chronological age

Cabanis, Pierre Jean George (1757-1808) French physician and philosopher. After studying the bodies of the guillotined during the French Revolution, he concluded that the **brain** is the organ of consciousness; also, that body movements after execution were pain-free reflex actions on the lowest level. Considered the body and soul as two "aspects of one faculty," but just perceived differently. Added the principle of developmental levels to the mechanism of **Condillac.** In *Traite due Physique et du Moral de l'Homme* 1802, he approached psychology from a physiological standpoint, becoming a pioneer in the development of physiological psychology. *See* **fields of psychology; Hartley.**

CAI Computer assisted instruction.

camera acustica A device or chamber (camera) for hearing (acustica) purposes, consisting of a water-filled box with various physical counterparts of the ear, designed to reproduce the vibrations of the cochlear partition.

Julius Richard Ewald (1855-1921), German physiologist, developed this box in line with cameras of the day.

camera obscura A darkened box-like enclosure having an aperture and lens through which light enters to form an image on the opposite surface, used for drawing exact pictures or taking photographs.

Invented in 1588 by Giovanni Battista della Porta (1536-1617), of Naples. *See* **accommodation.**

camphoraceous Of the nature of (aceous) camphor. One of seven primary qualities of the **stereochemical smell theory.**

campimeter An instrument for measuring (meter-) or mapping out the visual field (campi-) and determining peripheral visual perception of **color** and/or form.

camptocormia A hysterogenic static disorder (-ia) or deformity in which there is constant forward bending or flexion (campto-) of the trunk (-corm-). Such a posture seems to be associated with some deep psychoneurotic conditions, as well as with some forms of **catatonia.**

In 1915, this condition was first well described and named by French neurologist, Achille Alexander Souques (1860-1944), although English surgeon Sir Benjamin Brodie (1783-1862) had mentioned the condition in 1837.

canalization A concept by **Janet** describing the progressive narrowing of drives that structures perceptions by bringing them into its schema, including the assimilation processes of conceptual organization and commonality of schema. Related to **Freud's cathexis** and **Piaget's** sensory motor scheme of intelligence.

canal sickness A form of motion sickness created experimentally in a specially contrived **slow rotation room,** which appears "normal" to the subjects who may continuously live in the room for weeks in a homelike atmosphere. Room rotation provides a gravity-supplementing force, centrifugal in nature. Head turning or tilting movements not in line with the room's rotational axis disturb the fluid in **semicircular canals,** causing the so-called canal sickness. (Weintraub and Walker, pp. 71-73.)

candela The **SI** unit of luminous intensity, an arbitrary source of light consisting of a glowing **blackbody** cavity at the temperature of freezing platinum. Technically, a candela represents the luminous intensity of 1/600,000 of a square meter of a radiating cavity (a blackbody), subjected to the temperature of solidifying platinum (2042 K). A one-candela light source emits one lumen per steradian, the lumen being the SI unit of light flux. A source with an intensity of one candela in all directions (a highly idealized state) would radiate a light flux of 4π lumens. A lighted 100-watt bulb emits about 1700 lumens. *See* **luminous flux, International System of Units.**

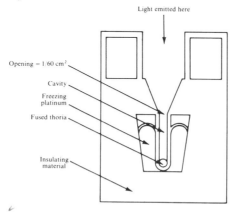

Light emitted here

Opening = 1/60 cm²

Cavity

Freezing platinum

Fused thoria

Insulating material

A schematic diagram of the international standard light source: candela. The diagram depicts a cylindrical tube of thorium oxide, surrounded by pure platinum at its freezing point and with powdered thorium oxide in the bottom. The tube is open only at the top, where a tiny hole, 1/60 cm² in area, permits radiant energy to enter.

cannabis (L. hemp. Synonyms: *cannabis indica, guaza, ganjah,* **hashish,** Indian hemp, **marijuana;** Ger., *Hanf;* Fr., *chanvre*). A tall, roughish, annual herb that thrives in any kind of soil, including desert land. It is known botanically as *cannabis sativa,* which is grown in temperate countries for its fibers (hemp) and for its fruit (hemp seed). Its dried leaves and young twigs constitute the drug "bhang," while its resin is marketed in India as "churrus" or "chares." The dried flowering tops constitute "guaza" or "ganjah," in which the tops are kneaded into rounded resinous masses. American cannabis is less resinous than the Indian variety (*cannabis indica*).

Cannabis contains up to 20 percent of a brown, amorphous resin called cannabin (cannibone) that itself contains a toxic, reddish oily substance called cannabinol, as well as **choline,** calcium carbonate, and other substances. The drug deteriorates gradually.

Linnaeus (Carl von Linné) (1707-1778), Swedish botanist named the drug *cannabis sativa* in 1745.

Cannon-Bard theory of emotion A neurophysiological theory holding that environmental stimuli set off patterns of activity in the lower brain centers of the **hypothalamus** and **thalamus;** these patterns are then relayed simultaneously to the **autonomic nervous system,** where they trigger the bodily changes of emotion, and to the **cerebral cortex,** where they result in the feelings of emotion. *Contrasted with* the **James-Lange theory.**

Walter Bradford Cannon (1871-1945), performed extensive researches on physiological factors in emotion. In *The Wisdom of the Body* (1932), he applied the term **homeostasis** to the complex interaction of autonomic, chemical, and endocrine functions that maintain optimal conditions of the internal environment and protect the organism from danger. He modified the James-Lange theory by relating emotions to the **hypothalamus** rather than to the periphery. Cannon's dispute with James' point of view is merely academic, for James was talking about feeling and Cannon about behavior. Cannon's stand, however, played a significant role in psychology's shift of emphasis from feelings to behavior. He demonstrated vital importance of the **adrenal glands** in emotion, and generally influenced psychologists to study the physiological basis of behavior. (Vinacke, p. 55.)

Philip Bard (born 1898) American physiologist, developed Cannon's theory, demonstrating that full rage could not be elicited in cats if the hypothalamus was removed. Hypothalamic cats (those with all neural tissue above the hypothalamus removed but with the hypothalamus intact) showed rage, such as spitting, biting, clawing, hair erection, etc., which Bard called "sham" rage, not because it was false but apparently because he felt that a true rage could be shown only with higher centers able to function. Bard concluded from his studies that the hypothalamus was necessary for emotional expression, thus complementing Cannon's theory.

cannulation The process (-ion) of acting upon (-at-) or inserting a small (-ula-) cane (cann-), or tube (cannula), into body cavities or glands (e.g., salivary) for purposes of drainage; also for channeling the fluid into other areas or containers for examination and chemical analysis. Generally used in animal experimentation.

cardinal number in a set *See* **set.**

Cartesian coordinate system Relating to (-an) the coordinate system of Renatus Cartesius, Latinized form of **René Descartes,** that fixes any point in a plane by stating its distance from each of the two intersecting lines called the coordinate axes. If axes intersect at right angles the coordinates are rectangular; if not, they are oblique. Descartes also developed the grid system for constructing graphs and charts (utilizing similar concepts in geometry and algebra). He used algebraical and numerical quantities in a geometrical coordinate system, often called a rectangular system.

c

C

case-history method The procedure of interviewing a client or patient for purposes of gathering information about his childhood, his family, and various social, educational, and vocational situations. *See* **methods of psychology: clinical.**

catabolism The process (-ism) of breaking (-bol-) down (cata-) food components or living tissues into their elements as part of the life process. Destructive metabolism. Physiological waste products are some results of catabolism. *See* **anabolism.**

catalepsy A seizing (-lepsy) down (cata-); a sudden seizure. A mental condition in which the person assumes a trancelike state, characterized by prolonged maintenance of waxlike muscular rigidities (**cerea flexibilitas**). Associated with **hysteria** and the catatonic type of **schizophrenia.**

Hippocrates used the term for a sudden attack of illness, hysterical or otherwise.

catalytic site Referring to (-ic) a site involved in catalysis, or to the change in a reaction facilitated by a chemical substance that itself does not change chemically by the end of the reaction. *See* **allosteric enzyme.**

catatonia Disorder (-ia) of having low (cata-) muscle tone (-ton-). A schizophrenic reaction alternating between motor inhibition and excitement or between emotional stupor and excitement. *See* **catatonic type** under **schizophrenia.**

Karl Kahlbaum (1828-1899), German **psychiatrist** introduced the term and the modern clinical picture of catatonia in 1874.

cat-cry syndrome (*cri du chat*) A high-pitched cry, weak but prolonged, of a child suffering from a special and severe form of **mental retardation.** Upon being disturbed, the child mews like a suffering cat. Other characteristics of the syndrome are slanting eyes and marked **hypertelorism** accompanied by pronounced reduction in the size of the brain (microcephaly). It is associated with a chromosomal anomaly in which there is a deletion of the short arms of the fifth chromosome (Jèrome Lejeune, et al: *Trois cas de deletion partielle du bras court d'un chromosome 5.* C. R. *Académie de Science.* Paris, 1963, 257, 3098).

catecholamines Those amines akin to extracts from a Malaysian tree (Catechu) with an alcohol (-ol) base. A collective name for the closely related **hormones** released by the adrenal medulla, two in number: **epinephrin(e)** and **norepinephrine** (or respectively, adrenalin and noradrenalin). Both hormones raise blood pressure—epinephrine by increasing heart output, norepinephrine by general vasoconstriction. The catechol amines also release glycogen from the liver, raising blood-sugar levels.

category-system method A method proposed by **Bales** describing group interaction in which an observer classifies group actions into sets of mutually exclusive categories. *See* **interaction process analysis.**

catelectrotonus Electrical (-electro-) change in a nerve's sensitivity, resulting in lower (-cat-) tonus. Reduction in cell membrane's polarization without impulse excitation; nerve depolarization with increased irritability near the cathode area.

catharsis (purification, purgation). Relief of emotional tension by re-establishing the association between the present emotion and the past causal event. A talking-out process (ventilation) in **psychotherapy** in which previously unpleasant memories lose their intensity because they are brought to consciousness, the therapist explaining the significance of the present insights in terms of past causal factors.

Aristotle used the term in his "Poetics" to describe the purpose of dramatic tragedy.

Freud credited **Breuer** (1895) with discovering the value of catharsis or talking-out under hypnosis in the treatment of **hysteria.** According to English psychoanalyst Ernest Jones, Freud's biographer, Breuer named his technique "catharsis," although he received the idea from his patient Anna O.

cathexis (Gr., holding; act of occupying). A charge or investment of energy in an object, idea, or person having special significance or feeling tone. The concentration of psychic energy on a particular idea, memory, or action.

Freud had first used the term in 1893 but it was not published until Freud's and **Breuer's** *Studies on Hysteria* (1895), in which cathexis was defined as "a rendering of the German *'Besetzung'* to express physical energy, akin to an electric charge, being attached to a mental process." Freud originally conceived of *Besetzung* as of purely physiological origin, but it has come to mean the charge of one's psychic energy on to some particular person, thing, idea, or experience. *Object cathexis*: when the **libido** is directed outwardly or toward others (alloeroticism); *subject or ego cathexis*: when the libido is directed inwardly or toward oneself (autoeroticism).

cathode [Way (-hode) down (cat-) east. From early belief that electric current passes from east to west.] The negatively charged electrode or the one at which electrons enter an electrical device. A *cathode-ray oscillograph* is an electrical recording device that translates an electrical wave into a visual pattern capable of being photographed for detailed analysis. It is used for recording sound waves of frequencies involving thousands of cycles per second, for observing bursts of impulses in nerve fibers (of more than 500 frequencies per second), etc.

Richard Caton (1842-1926) English physiologist demonstrated direct recordings from animal brains. *See* **action potential, brain waves.**

Cattell, James McKeen (1860-1944). American (Pennsylvania) psychologist. Ph.D., Leipzig 1886. Interests and research: various studies on reaction time, perception, individual differences, mental testing (coined term "mental test"), and psychophysics in general. APA President 1895. *See the* **James McKeen Cattell Award.** (Bischoff, pp. 532-535, 548-549; Vinacke, p. 693).

Cattell, Raymond B. Born England, 1905. Originally had majored in chemistry and physics at Kings College, but switched to psychology (Ph.D. and D.Sc., London, 1929). To U. S. in 1937. Diverse research interests—general, social, experimental, statistical, personality and mental testing. *See* **ipsative unit, normative unit, synergy, syntality, t-technique.**

Cattell Fund Award of Division 13, Consulting Psychology, is "given for the most fruitful completed research concerned with problems of special interest to the division." First prize is a certificate and $500; second prize $300. *See* **awards of the American Psychological Association.**

caudal Pertaining to (-al) or located in the tail or rear (caud-) of an animal. *See* **anatomical directions.**

caudate nucleus Characterized by (-ate) having the nucleus toward the end or tail (caud-). One of the three (along with the **lentiform nucleus** and the **amygdaloid body**) main **basal ganglia** lying deep inside the **cerebrum.** It is an area of grey matter in the **corpus striatum,** composed mainly of cell bodies and **dendrites,** that suppresses movements and excitatory processes in the **cerebral cortex.** Recent research implicates the caudate nucleus in memory storage.

Avicenna (Ibn Sina) (980-1037), Persian physician, translator of **Galen,** used Arabic equivalent of "tailed nucleus" from which Italian surgeon and anatomist M. V. G. Malacarne (1744-1816) derived the term caudate nucleus.

causation and correlation A positive **correlation** between two sets of **data** does not, of itself, indicate a causal relationship. A causal relationship may be involved in negative and positive correlations, but this cannot be determined merely from the presence of a relationship between the **independent variable** and the **dependent variable.** *See* **Hume.**

C. C. Coefficient of contingency.

CD$_{50}$ Median curative dose (that which abolishes symptoms in 50% of test cases).

CE Constant error.

ceiling age In **intelligence tests** of the **Binet** type (in which test items are arranged by age-levels), the age-level at which the testee fails all the test items. That is his ceiling—that level for which he receives no credit.

cell body The main portion of the **neuron** including nucleus and cytoplasm but excluding collateral branches such as the **axon** and **dendrites.** *See* **synaptic cleft, synaptic knob.**

cell theory *See* **Purkinje.**

Celsius scale *See* **centigrade.**

Celsus, Aurelius Cornelius (?25 B.C.-50 A.D.). Latin medical writer. *See* **insanity, lemniscus.**

centile score The point on a measurement scale below which and above which a certain percentage of the cases in a distribution fall. For example, the **median** is the fiftieth centile or percentile, as 50% of the cases are above and 50% are below the median. *Centile* is the same as **percentile.**

central effector neuron *See* **neuron.**

central fissure (central sulcus, fissure of Rolando). *See* **cerebral cortex** figure; **fissure.**

central limit theorem Regardless of the shape of the **population** distribution, if relatively large (more than 30) randomly selected samples of n independent observations are drawn from a population with mean μ and variance σ^2, the sampling distribution of the means approaches a normal distribution with mean μ and variance σ^2/n, provided the sample size continually increases. And because the shape of the **population** distribution may be normal or non-normal, this theorem enables the experimenter to apply the **normal probability** distribution in testing hypotheses about any form of population distribution. *See* **inferential statistics.**

The concept was first developed by the French mathematician Rene La Place (1749-1827) but it was further developed and proved by I. Liapounoff (1857-1918), Russian mathematician who coined the phrase in 1901.

central lobe (insula of Reil). A **lobe** of the **cerebral hemisphere** that lies deeply within the **fissure of Sylvius** and is not visible on the cortical surface.

central nervous system The **brain** and **spinal cord** exclusive of **efferent** and **afferent** nerves and distinguished from the **autonomic nervous system.**

central processing unit (CPU), main frame (Comput.) That part of a computer containing the circuits (arithmetic unit, control unit, and main memory or storage unit) controlling the interpretation and execution of instructions.

central sulcus (central fissure, fissure of Rolando). *See* **cerebral cortex** figure; **fissure.**

central tendency (central value, measures of location) Statistically, the tendency of numerical **data,** especially in **normal distributions,** to fall about a central datum; a middle value between extremes of a set of measures. The **arithmetic mean** (average), the **median** (middle) and the **mode** (most numerous) are measures of central tendency, but even when using the same scores these measures may not give identical values, except in a perfectly symmetrical frequency curve.

central theory (centralist position) The concept that thinking processes occur centrally (in the brain and nervous system), being relatively independent of input from the environment. Muscular movements, as such, are only accompaniments of the central process. **Cognitive** theories of learning are centralist in their emphasis upon learning and organizational processes as occurring primarily within the individual.

The centralist theory of emotion considers the brain and neural processes to be central to the emotional experience. The concept was espoused first by Cannon in 1927 and later by Bard in 1934 (**Cannon-Bard theory**). Klüver and Bucy (1937), by showing that monkeys became placid and unemotional upon removal of the temporal lobes, also demonstrated centralist function. Papez, in 1937 was centralist in proposing specific circuits in the **limbic system** as having the major role in emotion. MacLean (**Papez-MacLean theory**) in 1960 stated that the limbic system possibly serves as a "visceral brain" where experiences are recorded and expressed as "feeling" or "organ language." **Pribram** (1967) showed that brain lesions, other than in the limbic system, also affect emotion, leading him to propose a computer programming type of operation concerned with organizing and processing data; with sensory input interrupting plans, the interruption being the emotion.

centrifugal Relating to (-al) anything that recedes or flees (fug-) from the center (centri-). *Opposite to* **afferent, centripetal.**

Centrifugal impulses are those feedback impulses that pass from the **cerebral cortex** down to the relay stations of the sensory pathways and in some cases out to the sense organs; serve to filter out certain messages, probably playing a role in selective attention.

Centrifugal pathways are those feedback pathways that help filter out and select certain messages for acceptance or rejection, the filtering process being mediated by efferent fibers arising in higher order sensory levels and often terminating in the peripheral sense organs. *See* **gating.**

centripetal impulse Impulse seeking (-petal) the center. A system of impulses that course from the sense organs toward the brain centers.

centromere A central (centro-) part (-mere). *See* **chromosome.**

centrosome A minute protoplasmic body (-some) in the cytoplasmic center (centro-) of a cell that plays an important part in **mitosis.** Belgian embryologist Pierre Edouard van Beneden (1809-1894), reported the first (1876) observation of the structure in an ovum. **Walther Flemming**, later in the same year identified the body in other cells. In 1888, it was named centrosome by German zoologist Theodore Boveri (1862-1915).

cephalic Pertaining to (-ic), situated or directed toward the head (cephal-) or head-end of an animal. *Contrasted with* **caudal.**

cephalic index A ratio indicating the relation between the maximum breadth of the head and its length (measured in centimeters), obtained by multiplying the breadth of the skull by 100 and dividing by the length. There are three well-known terms for various head shapes: *brachycephalic*—broad or *short* (brachy-), with an index of 81.0 and over; *dolichocephalic*—*long* (dolicho-), with an index up to 75.9; *mesocephalic* (or mesaticephalic)—*medium* (meso-) with an index between 76.0 and 80.9.

Anders Adolf Retzius (1796-1860), Swedish anatomist coined the terms in 1838. This anthropometric scale is virtually outmoded, except in some European countries and South America.

cephalocaudal axis Pertaining to (-al) or passing from head (cephalo-) to tail (-caud-); in man called vertical axis. Opposed to the proximo-distal axis. *See* **anatomical directions.**

cephalocaudal sequence Relating to (-al) a sequence of maturational development of bodily control progressing from the head (cephalo-) to the tail (-caud-). The development of walking in the human, for example, is in cephalocaudal sequence: starting at one month the baby lifts its head, then its chest, then sits alone, then stands—first with help and then alone, etc. *See* **mass action.**

First described by Coghill in his studies on amblystoma, a salamander tadpole.

cerea flexibilitas Waxy (cerea) flexibility, the pliable, malleable condition of the extremities as seen in **catalepsy.** The patient, resembling a wax museum figure, maintains fixed,

and often bizarre positions (self-imposed or fashioned by others) for seemingly interminable periods of time. *See* **catatonic type** under **schizophrenia.**

cerebellum The little (-ellum) brain (cereb-). The **hindbrain** portion of the human **brain** above the **medulla oblongata** connecting with the spinal cord and the cerebral hemispheres. It coordinates "postural" voluntary movements initiated in the motor areas of the cortex.

Apparently **Aristotle** was the first to mention the cerebellum and to also differentiate it from the **cerebrum. Erasistratus** not only differentiated between them but also named them. **Galen** was the first to describe the cerebellum, considering it to be the source of motor nerves. The term "cerebellum" entered the English language in 1565. Although other physicians and philosophers mentioned the organ, it was not until 1664 that **Willis** drew attention to it prominently by saying that it was the seat of involuntary movements. Twenty years later **Vieussens** was the first to mention a "rhomboid body" (the dentate nucleus). Almost a hundred years later (1776) **Malacarne** wrote the first book solely on the cerebellum. During 1807-1809 **Reil** made a thorough study of the brain possible by soaking the brain in alcohol to harden it. **Flourens** updated (1823) the cerebellum's role in coordination, but it took **Rolando** to definitively indicate its **motor** nature. Both **Ramon y Cajal** and **Golgi** demonstrated that the cerebellum was relatively simple structurally in comparison to the cerebrum, some of their conclusions helping support Luciani's earlier ideas about the unitary nature of cerebellar function. **Magendie** conceived the idea (1824) that the cerebellum may be the equilibrium center and experiments (1914) by **Magnus** led to further studies to help confirm this concept. In 1895, German physician Max S. Löwenthal (1867-1960) and **Horsley**, English neurophysiologist, found the cerebellar cortex to be responsive to electrical stimuli. Studies by **Berger** (1929) and **Adrian** (1934) helped pioneer the field of brain **electrophysiology.** In 1944, the findings on the reticular system by American anatomist Howard W. Magoun (b. 1907) and his colleagues inaugurated literally hundreds of studies in this field. Thus far, studies do not seem to indicate that the cerebellum functions in a localized manner similar to the cerebrum. (Clarke and O'Malley, pp. 628-707 *passim*).

cerebral cortex Relating to (-al) the outer area or bark (cortex) of the brain (cereb-); also neopallium. The largest portion of the **forebrain** consisting of a mass of gray matter (mostly neuron **dendrites** and cell bodies) arranged in folds covering the cerebral hemispheres and functioning mainly in coordinating higher mental activity.

A highly schematic lateral view of the brain dominated by the cerebral cortex. The lobes of the cerebral cortex—temporal, frontal, parietal, and occipital—are shown; the central sulcus and the lateral fissure are prominent landmarks of the lateral cerebral cortex.

In 1586, Piccolomini (*see* **cerebrum**) distinguished between the **cerebral cortex** and the underlying white matter, but not until 1861 did **Broca** discover some indications of brain localization in the cerebral cortex (Broca's speech area). **Fritsch** and **Hitzig** also observed certain specific areas of localization within the pre-central cortex in 1870. **Ferrier** published *The Functions of the Brain* in 1876, in which he made a topographic numbered map of the brain, indicating specific localization of the cortical areas. A chart of the sensory and motor areas of the cortex was also made in 1876 by **Flechsig.**

cerebral dominance *See* **motor dominance.**

cerebral dysrhythmia *See* **epilepsy.**

cerebral hemisphere Either of the twin lateral brain masses of higher mammals that originates from the forebrain and overlies most lower brain areas as two symmetrical protruding pouches. Both hemispheres together form the largest part of the human brain, having a cortex and medulla of white matter (interlaced nerve tracts).

cerebral lipoidosis (amaurotic family idiocy) A condition (-osis) caused by a single recessive autosomal gene, in which a fat- (lip-) like (-oid) substance accumulates in the cerebral cells. There are two major forms of the disease:

1. Infantile
   a. **Tay-Sach's disease**
   b. **Bielchowsky-Jansky disease**
2. Juvenile
   a. **Batten-Mayou disease**
   b. **Spielmeyer-Vogt disease**

cerebral localization *See* **localization of brain function.**

cerebral palsy A muscle disturbance caused by brain damage and originating from various causes during fetal development or at the time of birth. For detailed information contact the *United Cerebral Palsy Association, Inc.,* 66 East 34th Street, New York, N. Y. 10016.

cerebral peduncle *See* **mesencephalon.**

cerebral vesicle *See* **diencephalon, rhombencephalon.**

cerebrospinal fluid (CSF, c.s.f.) A clear watery liquid surrounding the brain and spinal cord and filling the four **brain ventricles.** The fluid is formed by a secretory process on the ventricular walls (epithelial cells) of the choroid plexus, flows through openings in the fourth ventricle to circulate over the brain and the spinal cord in the subarachnoid space, finally entering the blood system.

The fluid was noted by ancients. **Galen** thought of it as a humoral excrement and **Soemmering** as the seat of the soul. It was mentioned in the **Edwin Smith Surgical Papyrus.**

Italian physician Nicolo Massa (1485-1569), first clearly described it in 1536. About 1674, an experimental physiologist Richard Lower (1631-1691), investigated the circulation of the CSF. In 1721, Italian physician Antonio Pacchioni (1665-1726), considered it to be secreted by the arachnoid granulations. It was frequently described and observed but only in the **brain ventricle**, that is, until **Cotugno** discovered (1764) it in both the ventricles and subarachnoid space. Cotugno concluded that the spinal fluid was continuous with ventricular and cerebral fluids.

Magendie coined the term in 1827, saying, "I have named ... my fluid ... céphalespinal," also giving full credit to Cotugno for his findings in 1764. Walter Edward Dandy (1886-1946), American physician was able to produce experimental **hydrocephalus** in animals to demonstrate that the CSF was probably produced by the choroid plexuses. *See* **brain ventricles.** (Clarke and O'Malley, pp. 721-22).

cerebrospinal fluid-brain barrier *See* **brain-barrier systems.**

cerebrotonia A condition (-ia) of the brain (cerebro-) having tone (-ton-). One of the human temperament components, according to **W. H.** **Sheldon**, whose characteristics are evident in the shy, aloof, thoughtful, re-strained, and hypersensitive person. For example, the cerebrotonic temperament is ascribed to the stereotype of the research scientist in his lonely laboratory. Associated with the **ectomorph** physique. *See* **constitutional types, somatotonia, viscerotonia.**

cerebrum The brain; that part usually considered to be the upper and anterior portion of the brain, consisting of the two hemispheres and the fibers of the **corpus callosum** connecting them. Each hemisphere is divided into five **lobes**: frontal, **central**, occipital, parietal, and temporal. Convolutions of the cerebrum are technically called gyri (**gyrus**), and **fissures** are known as **sulci** (sulcus), although sometimes the word "fissure" is restricted to meaning "deeper crevices."
Erasistratus described the cerebrum as consisting of the two **cerebral hemispheres**, and **Galen** did the same. Cerebrum first appeared in English in 1615, 50 years after **cerebellum**. The distinction between the grey and white matter of the cerebrum ("I call the cerebrum that whole ashen-colored body and the 'medulla' is the whole of the white.") was first clearly made (1586) by Archangelo Piccolomini (1526-1586), Italian anatomist and physician.

certificat preparatoire aux études médicales A certificate from a French medical school indicating that the medical student has passed his first year's training (corresponding to the propédeutique of the science faculties) and is eligible to pursue medical studies for the next five years (with an additional six months hospital training), hopefully resulting in the granting of the doctor of medicine degree.

cerveau isolé Fr., isolated or detached (*isolé*) brain (*cerveau*). In animal experimentation, the procedure of transecting the **brainstem** at the level of the **superior colliculus** of the **mesencephalon**. The preparation of the *cerveau isolé* was made to study sleep characteristics, and particularly EEG sleep. In the transection all afferent **cranial nerve** inputs to the brain, except olfactory and visual, are cut off with a subsequent interruption of all brain motor outputs except some eye movement control. Symptoms resembling normal sleep occur.
First described by the Belgian F. Bremer in 1935. Later experiments by W. H. Magoun (*see* **cerebellum**) and his associates at the UCLA Brain Institute pointed to the **reticular formation** as probably being more involved in *cerveau isolé* effects than the classical sensory pathways (F. Bremer, "*Cerveau Isolé et Physiologie du Sommeil,*" Comp. Rend. Soc., Biol., 1935, pp. 118, 1235-1241; Thompson, 1967, pp. 429-434).

Cf Cumulative frequency.

CFF Critical flicker frequency.

cgs Centimeter=gram=second system, in which these units represent, respectively, the units of length, mass, and time.

chad Code to *H*andle *A*ngular *D*ata. The small pieces of paper or disks resulting from punching out holes in paper tapes or cards. *Chadless* refers to the punching of tape in which chad does not occur.

chain schedule (chaining) In a **schedule of reinforcement** the learning of a sequence of **responses** in a fixed order so that one event serves to elicit the next event, and so on. For example, the first response is reinforced on a set schedule by producing a second **stimulus**, and the next response is rewarded by a third stimulus, etc., eventually leading to unconditional **reinforcement** (or the final primary reinforcement).

character A term that has gone through a series of meanings: first, it was an engraving tool (*A*); then added to the tool were the marks (numbers, letters, etc.) made by the tool (*A+B*); then it became the total characteristics and traits (*C*) distinctive of the person who used the tool to make the characters (*A+B+C*);

then taxonomy was used to classify the "hereditary" traits possessed in common (*D*) by individuals who no longer used a tool (*B+C+D*) but did use the modifications (*E*) acquired in the course of ontogeny (*B+C+D+E*). *Psychoanalytically*, character is practically synonymous with **personality** when it refers to the individual's total habit patterns.
In *electronic data processing*, one of a set of marks or events that may be combined to give information. A character includes all marks, such as a grouping of holes in a paper tape. The characters normally used in a numerical control system include the grouping of holes that spell out decimal digits from 0 to 9, the letters of the alphabet, or some binary-coded symbol (parenthesis, comma, period, asterisk, etc.). Normally, a character occupies one **byte** on a tape.

character disorder (personality disorder) A disorganized conduct reaction that forms a lifelong pattern of socially deviant behavior (alcoholism, drug addiction, stealing, embezzling, sexual excesses, general psychopathic reaction, etc.). People with character disorders are not considered neurotic or psychotic but do show a conscious amoral attitude with an apparently deep involvement and aggressive behavior against society or the symbols of society and the "establishment." They show little ability to profit by experience or to stand stress. They also lack moral standards, show little or no evidence of experiencing deep emotion, and tend toward habitual behavior without conscious feeling of anxiety.

characteristic *See* **logarithm.**

character types Adult patterns of behavior, according to **Freud**, formed during infancy and early childhood in progressive stages of psychosexual development: *oral, anal, phallic,* and *genital.* Unresolved conflicts resulting from poor adjustment to psychosexual crises lingered on as fixations, symbolized in adult life as character types:
The *oral character*: extremely dependent on others; loves food and love; mouth important for drinking smoking, kissing, and oral movements; insatiable need for reassurance; gifts disproportionately important as token of affection, overcompensates for dependency role by becoming active, demanding, authoritarian, and masculine. Traits probably develop during the oral stage (before age of 2) when there is often overemphasis on food intake and talking.
The *anal character*: overly frugal, obstinate, perfectionistic, punctual, neat, and planconscious. May vary from hoarding to wasteful extravagance. Such traits supposedly originate during the anal stage (from about 2 to 4 years of age) because of conflicts over elimination and retention of feces.
The *phallic character*: may evidence castration anxiety and is penis-oriented. Appears self-assured, reckless, courageous, and adventurous. Phallic men are vain, exhibitionistic, sensitive, and overly proud; tend to be hostile and contemptuous toward women; they are Don Juan seducers, and incapable of deep love. The phallic female lords it over men and becomes quite masculine, trying to resolve her penis envy. In the child, the phallic stage (from about third to fifth year) is marked by genital exploration and manipulation, with libidinal attachment for opposite-sex parent.
The *genital character*: the supposed culmination of successful progression through all the psychosexual crises, resulting in a mature human being.

Charcot, Jean-Martin (1825-1893) French neurologist. Especially studied **hysteria**, which he treated by hypnosis. Both **Freud** and **Janet** studied with him at the Salpetriere, a mental hospital in Paris. His presentation of the symptoms of hypnosis in physiological terms led to some acceptance of it as a "respectable" method of treatment. Described characteristics of **tabes dorsalis.** Freud credited Charcot

with having considerable influence in laying the groundwork of early psychoanalytic concepts. *See* **Bekhterev.**

chef de clinique Similar to an assistant professorship in an American university hospital, with duration of service unlimited. Includes status of university rank plus municipal hospital recognition. Also, provides an opportunity for following an academic career at the university. Competitive examinations and successful completion of a **thèse d'agrègation** lead to the next university rank—*professeur agrégé* (associate professor).

chef de laboratoire à la faculté In French education, equivalent to rank of assistant professor, with responsibilities beyond the rank of **préparateur.**

chef des travaux à la faculté In French education, equivalent to rank of assistant professor, with responsibilities beyond the rank of **préparateur.**

Cheiron The name of a scholarly historical society (*The International Society of the History of the Behavioral and Social Sciences*) whose name was borrowed from Greek mythology. Cheiron, son of the Titan Cronus, was a wise and beneficent centaur, and an outstanding teacher, some of whose pupils were Jason, Asclepius, Hercules, and Achilles. Upon being mortally wounded when struck with a poisoned arrow by Hercules, he bequeathed his immortality to Prometheus, who had been suffering in Hades. After death Cheiron became the constellation Sagittarius, and was later reborn at the charter meeting of the society hosted by the University of Akron, May 8-10, 1970.

chemical methods of brain study Methods of studying brain function that use three general types of preparation: (1) the *in vivo* method, analyzing chemical processes in the alive, functioning, intact brain (2) the *in vitro* method, maintaining portions (slices) of brain tissue in nutrient solutions (3) the processed tissue method, in which neural tissue is ground up for chemical analysis.

chemical senses Smell, common chemical sensitivity, and taste, as chemical senses, require a dilute solution of chemical molecular substances (acids, alkalies, and salts) in order to function effectively, interactive effects from each sense often producing one perceptual experience. Smell receptors (unique neurons) and taste receptors (consisting of epithelial cells) are highly specialized, while the common chemical receptor is a relatively free nerve ending (Morgan, pp. 109-128).

chemical transmitter substance See **bouton, transmitter substance.**

chiasma *See* **optic chiasma.**

childhood schizophrenia A psychotic condition of childhood (generally ranging from 6 months of age to adolescence but more often occurring after 5 years of age), characterized by passivity, disorientation, confusion, and incapability of establishing interest in people or objects. Children with **schizophrenia** may stare blankly at objects or people for hours, and demonstrate bizarre motor behavior (such as continually turning around in circles). They tend to have low frustration tolerance and disorganized thought processes. Possible causes: undetermined organic involvement, overprotective parents.
When childhood schizophrenics become adults, they cannot solve their own problems and are constantly in need of assistance. From an hereditary point of view, in those cases where one member of a twin pair is diagnosed as having preadolescent schizophrenia the chances are much greater for the other to be so diagnosed than in fraternal twins. *See* **infantile autism.**
Earliest recognition of childhood schizophrenia is traceable to the observations of Benjamin Rush (1745-1813), American physician. He wrote the first American textbook on psychiatry in 1812, describing his observations on childhood insanity.

C

chimerism A condition (-ism) of being like a goat (chimer-); a monster. A chromosomal anomaly, similar to **mosaicism**, except that the two different cell populations arise from two different **zygotes**. The organism is composed of two genetically distinct tissues (such as partly male, partly female); it may also be an artificial organism having tissues consisting of several distinctly different other tissues.

chi square (χ^2) A useful **statistic** for **data** in frequency form enabling the making of statistical inferences about categorical data (or data that can be reduced to this level), some of which are mentioned here: The distribution of χ^2 depends upon only one **parameter**, the **degrees of freedom**. In the use of χ^2 each observation or frequency must be independent of all other observations. Dependence upon observations leads to an inflated N, which can cause rejection of the **null hypothesis** when it is in fact true.

The *chi-square statistic*, like the F, is used to test hypotheses about **variance** as well as about **central tendency**. Although chi-square has been used as a **parametric test** it now serves more often as a **nonparametric** test. There are many formulas and uses for chi-square.

As a *parametric test*, chi-square is defined as

$$\chi^2 = \frac{(n-1)\hat{\sigma}_l^2}{\sigma_O^2}$$

where σ_O^2 = variance value under the null hypothesis. The above formula may be one- or two-tailed.

As a *non-parametric test*, chi-square has several applications, two of which are:
(1) For testing **goodness of fit** (or one-variable chi-square tests), it is used to determine whether an observed frequency distribution departs significantly from a theoretical one. The data should be at least on a **nominal scale** and require fairly large samples (in which 80% of the cells in a **contingency table** have an expected frequency of >5). This severe restriction of minimum expected frequency may be overcome, in some instances, by use of the **binomial probability distribution** or the Kolmogorov statistic (if data are **ordinal** and continuously distributed, but not if data are grouped or there are too many tie scores). For goodness of fit, χ^2 is calculated as follows:

$$\chi^2 = \sum_{j=1}^{k} \frac{(O_j - E_j)^2}{E_j}$$

where

O_j = observed frequency for the *j*th cell
E_j = expected frequency for the *j*th cell
k = number of cells
$\sum_{j=1}^{k}$ directs summation of this ratio over all *k* categories.

(2) As a *test of independence*, chi-square is a valuable non-parametric procedure for determining whether paired measures that are at least nominally ordered are related. Data are organized into a contingency table to determine the **significance** of the relationship between row and column variables, i.e., whether they are independent of each other. The calculation of χ^2 for a contingency table is similar to that for goodness of fit. The difference between each observed (O) and expected (E) value is squared, then divided by the expected (E) value and finally summed over all cells, as

$$\chi^2 = \sum \frac{(O-E)^2}{E}$$

This formula may be expressed, for computational purposes, as

$$\chi^2 = \sum \frac{O^2}{E} - N$$

It is customary to refer to the symbol χ^2 for the quantity calculated from the observed data as well as to denote the test of significance, whereas the term "chi-square" refers to the theoretical chi-square distribution.

See the chi-square table (that is, Table 8), which gives the sampling distribution of chi-square as well as the probability of obtaining various values of chi-square.

Friedrich R. Helmert (1843-1917), German astronomer and mathematician devised the chi-square distribution in 1875-76, and **Karl Pearson** used it first in 1900 as a means of testing hypotheses.

Because of the many uses of chi-square and the complexities that sometime occur, it is desirable to refer to various texts for more complete information. (See, for instance, Ferguson, pp. 192-213; Kirk, pp. 35-9; Hays, pp. 336-348, 352-355; Runyon and Haber, pp. 204-211; and Siegel, pp. 104-111, 175-9.)

chlordiazepoxide hydrochloride A compound (-ide) consisting of a *diazo* group (the bivalent group combined with a hydrocarbon group and another atom or group) and an *epoxy* group (an oxygen atom bound to two other carbon atoms to form a ring) and related to *chlorine* (chlor-), such as **Librium**, a therapeutic agent for the relief of anxiety and tension. Side effects are rare, but withdrawal symptoms, similar to those observed with meprobamate or barbiturates, have been produced after lengthy usage (300-600 mg. daily for more than five months).

chlorpromazine CPZ (tradename: Thorazine) A crystalline salt derived from **phenothiazine** and administered as the hydrochloride to control agitation, tension, confusion, and related symptoms observed in neuroses, schizophrenias, manic-depressive states (manic phase only), severe personality disorders, and senile psychoses. Its effects, without loss of consciousness, create a somnolent disinterest about problems that usually created fear or terror.

CPZ was synthesized and named in 1950 by French chemist Paul Charpentier, who was assisted in his research by French pharmacologist Simone Courvoisier.

choline A crystalline base (-ine) and vitamin B constituent found in most animal tissues and originally in the bile (chol-).

Strecker, about 1854, demonstrated that lecithin contained the as yet unnamed choline as well as a fatty acid and other chemicals. In 1861, he discovered this substance in bile, naming it choline in 1869. In 1914, **Dale** showed that "certain esters of choline are **muscarinic** in nature and inhibit cardiac rate." In 1926, **Loewi** presented evidence of cholinesterase in the nervous system.

cholinergic Relating to (-ic) being worked up or activated (-erg-) by **acetylcholine**, or simulating the physiological action of acetylcholine on the **central nervous system**. *Cholinergic fibers* are those axons whose terminals release acetylcholine as a transmitter substance at their synapse with other nerve cells.

cholinesterase An enzyme (-ase) that accelerates the synthesis of choline (cholin-) esters, as well as assisting **acetylcholine** in its role of transmitting nervous impulses.

chorea Sporadic dance-like (chor-) movements. Any of several diseases of the nervous system, symptomatized by involuntary, jerky movements, mainly of the arms, legs, and face.

Chorea Sancti Viti was the term applied to the hysteroid dancing mania in Europe during 15th and 16th centuries, pilgrimages being made to the shrine of St. Vitus to cure it. Thomas Sydenham (1624-1689), English

physician, gave the name "chorea" in 1686 to the nervous disease because the twitching suggested a wild or grotesque dance, this more moderate form of chorea being called *Sydenham's chorea*. Although Charles Oscar Waters (1816-1892), first described the condition, it was not until 1842 that American physiologist, Robley Dunglison (1798-1869), gave first recorded description of chronic hereditary chorea. This was later more fully described by American physician George Huntington (1851-1916), the condition becoming known as *Huntington's chorea*, characterized by twitchings of the head and extremities, progressive dementia, paranoid reactions, irascibility, destructiveness, memory and judgment impairment, irregularity of movement, and speech disturbances, followed by severe intellectual deterioration.

choreiform movement *See* **Parkinson's disease.**

choroid plexus A vascular fringe in each of the four **brain ventricles** consisting of tufts of blood capillaries covered by a layer of epithelial cells, the cells acting as a barrier between the blood and CSF (the Na+ concentration of the CSF being considerably higher and its K+ concentration considerably lower than the blood plasma concentration for these ions). *See* **Herophilus.**

chromatic Referring to (-ic) color (chromat-), or to variations in visual experiences when some **color** is present. *Chromatic adaptation* is the process by which the visual mechanism achieves equilibrium under the influence of a stimulus of non-daylight chromaticity. Complete chromatic adaptation is the apparent absence of hue in monochromatic light. Also refers to a retinal phenomenon that occurs when one fixates on a particular hue, causing the hue to appear progressively less saturated until it seems to be grey or greyish. *Chromatic color* refers to all colors (not black, grey, or white) perceived to have a *hue*, such as red, yellow, blue, etc.

chromaticity diagram A three-dimensional geometrical model that combines the various facts about color mixture so that the viewer can grasp the principles of "mixing" more readily. The specific proportions of the three primaries in a mixture are determined for matching the **hue** and **saturation** of any color stimulus. (R. C. Teevan and R. C. Birney (eds.), *Color Vision*, 1961). *See* **Maxwell triangle.**

chromaticness Pertaining to (-ic) that quality (-ness) of a color (chromat-) perception that is determined by combining its hue and saturation; psychological correlate of chromaticity.

Term coined in 1943 as "chromie" by French physicist Henri Pieron: became chromaticness upon translation.

chromatid Particle or structure (-id) of chromosomes. Newly formed chromosome; a particular strand of a **chromosome**.

chromatin Readily stainable (chromat-), granular protoplasmic material (-in) in cell nuclei. *See* **Flemming.**

chromatolysis Loosening or dissolution (-lysis) of the chromatin, so that it no longer stains with usual dyes; the breaking up of the Nissl granules (mainly RNA nucleoproteins) in the nerve cell body that occurs when a nerve axon fiber has been cut. Chromatolysis involves a gradual change in appearance of the nerve cell body, leading to proximal (or retrograde) degeneration.

Georges Marinesco (1864-1938), Rumanian neurologist, coined term chromatolysis in 1909.

chromosomal map A diagram or photograph showing the number and arrangement of **chromosomes** for a given individual.

First such map was drawn up on the fruit fly by American geneticist T. H. Morgan (1866-1945).

chromosome Color (chromo-) body (-some). One of the microscopically minute, stubby-looking, rod-, j-, or v-shaped bodies in the cell capable of being stained for viewing under a

C

microscope. Between successive cell divisions they appear as deeply stained granules (chromatin granules). Chromosomes contain the genes which are the hereditary determiners for each individual.

Chemically, chromosomes consist of two materials: a giant helical-shaped molecule called **deoxyribonucleic acid** (DNA) and proteins. DNA (within the nucleus of the chromosome) is a "master blueprint of life" inherited from one's parents that carries the instructions of numerous proteins needed by the cell to function, and which emerge out of the nucleus into the cytoplasm.

In the human being, half (23) of an individual's chromosomes come from the father, half (23) from the mother, totaling 46 in the fertilized egg cell. This arrangement is repeated by **mitosis** in every cell of the body that grows from this cell. DNA duplication occurs during the interphase of mitosis, in which each coiled DNA molecule uncoils and separates where the base pairs were joined. Each half DNA molecule duplicates itself to form a whole new DNA molecule, with each original chromosome becoming two (called **chromatids**). The juncture of the chromatids is called the **centromere**.

During the next stage of **mitosis (anaphase)**, one set of chromatids moves to the opposite cell poles where the chromatids now become known as chromosomes. Then, one set of chromosomes each enters the two new cells when the parent cell divides, thus assuring a complete set of genes identical to those in the parent cell.

Friedrich Arnold (1803-1890), German anatomist and histologist, first clearly reported presence of chromosomes in 1879. In 1888, **Waldeyer** coined the term "chromosom." In 1902, Clarence E. McClung, American zoologist discovered X and Y chromosomes (so-called sex chromosomes). Herbert McLean Evans (b. 1882) an American (California) physician charted 48 chromosomes in man (1918).

New techniques developed in 1952 by geneticist Tao Chinh Hsu (born 1917, China) allowing simpler identification of individual chromosomes enabled Finnish geneticist J. H. Tijo and Swedish geneticist J. A. Levan (born 1905) to determine in somatic tissue (of aborted embryos) that there were only 46 chromosomes, as they reported in "The Chromosome Number of Man," *Hereditas*, 1956, **42**, 1-6. A few months later geneticists C. E. Ford and J. L. Hamerton found the chromosome number in sex cells to be also 46.

In 1959, the study of chromosomal aberrations was sparked by the discovery of trisomy 21 in mongolism by the French geneticists J. J. Louis Marie Lejeune (born 1926), Raymond Turpin (born 1895) and co-workers. Also in 1959, Turpin and his group reported the first example of translocation in man. Soon afterward the XXY sex-determining mechanism in **Klinefelter's syndrome** was reported by English biologist Patricia Ann Jacobs (born 1934) and her colleague J. A. Strong. Other chromosomal aberrations have been reported consistently since then (X haploidy in the Turner syndrome, the XXX syndrome, etc.).

chronaxie Time (chron-) value (-axie). A numerical index expressing the excitability of tissue, especially of nerve fibers. It is determined by ascertaining the shortest duration of an electrical current (of double the threshold voltage) required to produce an excitation or muscular contraction.

In 1850, **Helmholtz** first estimated the speed of the nervous impulse, but not until 1903 was it systematically studied by Louis Lapicque (1866-1952), French physiologist. He measured the peripheral neural reaction time, or the duration of time a current twice as strong as the galvanic threshold takes to excite the test tissue. In 1909, he called "this duration the chronaxie," in his book *Definition Experimentele de l'Excitabilité.*

chronograph A recording instrument (-graph) (with revolving drum and stylus) for measuring precise time (chrono-) intervals.

chronological age In psychological testing, the actual living time of the person in years and months. For example, the notation 5-3 means 5 years and 3 months old.

chronoscope A viewing instrument (-scope) (fitted with a precise chronometer) for measuring and recording small intervals of time (chrono-). *See* **Hipp chronoscope.**

Wheatstone presumably invented the first chronoscope in 1840.

Ch'uan *See* **T'ai Chi Ch'uan.**

C.I.E. (CIE) **Commission Internationale de L'Eclairage.**

cinematograph A recording instrument (-graph) that projects still pictures in series at regulated times, making possible analysis and evaluation of photographed movement (cinemato-).

cingulate gyrus A circle (gyrus) having (-ate) a girdle (cingul-) of transverse bands. The cortex of the cingulate gyrus is a part of the **cerebral cortex** included in the **limbic system**, the cingulate gyrus lying in the longitudinal fissure above the **corpus callosum**. Stimulation of this area elicits reactions of fear and rage in experimental animals. Removal of the cingulate gyrus with all the **neocortex** results in increased ferocious behavior, but removal of cingulate gyrus alone shows no marked change in emotional behavior, indicating that the inhibitory action of the cingulate gyrus does not function when the rest of cortex is intact.

The cingulate gyrus was named and described by Karl Friedrich Burdach (1776-1847), German anatomist and physiologist.

circadian rhythm Pertaining to (-an) a rhythm that lasts for about (circa-) a day (-di-), emphasizing daily as opposed to other periodic rhythms, e.g., yearly. Internally regulated natural cycles (bodily rhythms in temperature or ability to tolerate drugs, alcohol, food, etc., at one time but not at another) that influence an organism's behavior. For example, **chlorpromazine** and similar drugs are affected by internal temperature of an organism, low temperatures tending to induce depression and high ones hyperexcitability and greater toxicity. Amphetamine toxicity can vary considerably throughout the day. In rats, far more histamine is excreted and greater quantities of water are needed at night than in the daytime. Aschoff believes that all physiological functions can be described by circadian rhythms (J. Aschoff, "Circadian Rhythms in Man," *Science*, **48**, 1965, 1427-1432).

Term proposed (1959) by Austro-American chronobiologist and physician Franz Halberg (born 1919, Roumania) in his article "Physiologic 24-Hour Periodicity: General and Procedural Considerations with Reference to the Adrenal Cycle," *Zeitschrift für Vitamin, Hormon und Fermentforschung*, 10:225-296, 1959.

circular insanity (manic depressive-insanity) Swings in mood from euphoria to depression and back again.

Condition first described in 1853-54 by J.P. Falret.

cis (on this side) In *genetics*, two or more genes on the same **chromosome** of a homologous pair. In *chemistry*, a form of isomerism with attachment of similar groups on the same side of two carbon atoms. Term was introduced into chemical usage by **Baeyer** in 1892. The term entered psychiatry in the form of *cisvestitism* (as a contrasting term to transvestitism) meaning the condition of dressing "on this side of" one's sex but inappropriately so (such as a grandmother dressing in the style of her children or a girl like her grandmother, etc.).

clairvoyance (Fr., to see clearly). The action (-ance) or power of a person (the clairvoyant) to be able to see (-voy-) clearly (clair-) those things others are not able to perceive, such as

discerning objects concealed from sight, relating distant happenings, etc.

Term coined by the French mystic Marquis Puysegur in the 18th century, who became a disciple and later rival of **Mesmer.**

classes There are two special types of classes: the universal class, 1, containing all things, and the null class, 0, which contains no members.

class frequency Number of cases or observations in a **class interval.**

classical conditioning (or Pavlovian conditioning) Conditioned response involving pairing of stimuli in close time-proximity, as produced in experiments conforming to the classical experiments of **Pavlov**. The type of learning involved in making a **response** to a new (or neutral) **conditioned stimulus** (CS) that previously was elicited only by the original or natural **unconditioned stimulus** (US). The response to the unconditioned stimulus is duly elicited by a conditioned stimulus, thus becoming a conditioned response (CR). For example, a subject is subjected to a shock and buzzer simultaneously. The shock causes the subject to jump (unconditioned response). After pairing the stimuli a number of times (reinforcement), the buzzer (conditioned stimulus) is sounded alone: the subject jumps (conditioned response) at the buzzer sound without the shock (I. P. Pavlov, *Conditioned Reflexes*, 1927).

classification of mental disorders The amended outline of the following diagnostic nomenclature is based upon the *Diagnostic and Statistical Manual of Mental Disorders*, Second Edition (DSM-II), 1968, of the American Psychiatric Association.

Mental Disorders

   I. **Mental retardation**
  II. Psychoses associated with organic brain syndromes (**organic psychoses**)
 III. Psychoses attributable to conditions other than determinable organic causes (**functional psychoses**)
    A. **Schizophrenia**
    B. **Affective psychoses**
    C. **Paranoid states**
    D. **Reactive type of psychoses**
 IV. **Neuroses**
  V. Personality disorders and other nonpsychotic conditions
    A. **Personality disorders**
    B. **Sexual deviations**
 VI. **Psychophysiologic disorders**
VII. Special symptoms not elsewhere classified (tics, enuresis, encopresis, disturbances of sleep, learning, speech, etc.)
VIII. **Transient situational disturbances** (including adjustment reactions of infancy, childhood, adolescence, adult life, and late life.)
 IX. **Behavior disorders of childhood and adolescence**
  X. General maladjustment problems (not necessarily psychiatric) which include maladjustments in marriage, social maladjustments, occupational maladjustments, and dyssocial behavior.

The first classification of mental illness was devised in 1583 by the Swiss physician Felix Plater (1536-1614), who considered illness to originate with the devil.

class interval (step interval, class size). An arbitrary **range** of values into which **frequency distribution** scores are grouped. Class intervals are usually selected so that between 10 and 20 of them will cover the total range of observations. For example, if the smallest observation in a set is 3 and the largest 56, a class interval of 5 may be selected with the data arranged into 12 intervals extending from 0-4, 5-9, 10-14, etc., on up through 55-59.

class limits The upper and lower limits of a **class interval.**

claustrophobia Morbid fear (-phobia) of an enclosed (claustro-) place, or of being suffocated in confined places (rooms, closets, etc.). Psychoanalytically, it is considered a physiological manifestation of unexpressed aggression or sexual excitement. *See* **phobia**.
Term introduced (1879) by Andrea Verga (1811-1895) Italian neuropsychiatrist.

claustrum *See* **basal ganglia**.

Cleveland award *See* **Newcomb Cleveland Prize**.

client-centered therapy (nondirective counseling; nondirective therapy). A type of psychotherapy in which the central role is played by the client rather than the counselor or therapist. The counselor's role is a permissive one, radiating acceptance and reflecting verbally the feelings implicit in the client's expressions. He does not question the client about doubtful statements, nor does he pass judgment or give interpretations or advice. It is considered a testable theory of psychotherapy using empirical research.
This nondirective therapeutic process, according to **Rogers**, follows five steps: (1) the individual, recognizing his need, seeks the therapist's help; (2) the therapist encourages the client to express his hostility and other feelings freely with the client being permitted to choose his own topic for discussion; (3) with release of pent-up feelings the client develops different perceptions, attains insight, and gains a truer perspective of himself and his problems; (4) following insight comes decision-making and plans for new courses of action, with subsequent self-assurance and definite growth toward positive goals; (5) finally, the client, more secure and independent, becomes aware of the reduced need for help and moves toward termination of the therapy.
It is an application of Rogers' view that: (1) every individual has a natural tendency toward growth, health, and adjustment; (2) emotional blocks against integration of the personality need to be removed; (3) the present rather than the past is to be stressed; (4) the counseling process itself is a growth process; and (5) the counselor's function is neither to interpret nor to direct but instead, by reflecting the client's feelings, should serve as a catalyst in the resolution of conflicts. *See* **counseling**; (also Bischof, pp. 423-449; Maddi, pp. 66-80; Vinacke, p. 278).

climate counseling A counseling approach in industry whereby both the individual and the organizational climate (consisting of those qualities unique to the organization that are fairly predictable and constant, and that influence people in an organization) are taken into consideration for matching men and jobs (Rensis Likert, *The Human Organization: Its Management and Its Value*, 1967).

clinical interview *See* **methods of psychology: clinical**.

clinical method Referring to (-al) the method used at the bedside (clinic-). By extension, the method of gathering data from actual cases, patients, or clients by means of **interview**, case history, autobiography, testing, and/or observation. Distinguished from experimental method. *See* **methods of psychology**.

clinical psychologist A **psychologist**, using the clinical method, who works with an individual in helping him to adjust more adequately to his environment. Through psychological tests, **counseling**, and reports of behavior he reaches a working diagnosis from which he plans and works out a treatment program. In psychiatric hospitals, child-guidance clinics, etc., he serves as a member of a team including **psychiatrists** and psychiatric social workers. The clinical psychologist, however, never treats psychological problems with medical involvement unless under the supervision of a psychiatrist or physician. A marriage counselor, a school psychologist, or anyone doing professional work of a psychological nature in courts, civil

service agencies, and charitable organizations, is sometimes loosely called a clinical psychologist.
Strictly, however, a professional clinical psychologist must have a Ph.D. degree in clinical psychology from an accredited university, and also must have at least one year's internship training in a recognized clinical facility. The Ed.D. (Doctor of Education) degree, with a major in clinical psychology, is acceptable in lieu of the Ph.D. The **American Board of Professional Psychology** awards its diploma to clinical psychologists who pass their specially tailored written examination and oral interview, and who otherwise meet their standards of skill, experience, and ethical practice.
Although modern-day clinical psychology received its impetus as a result of rewarding work done by clinicians during World War II, it is generally accepted that in 1896, Lightner Witmer (1867-1956), American experimental psychologist, started the first clinical laboratory in the United States at the University of Pennsylvania. Witmer had worked for years with **G. S. Hall** in the study of developmental problems before becoming interested in setting up a study-laboratory for handicapped and retarded children.

Clinical Psychology Award of Division 12, Clinical Psychology, presented to one of its members for **Distinguished Contribution to the Science and Profession of Clinical Psychology**. *See* **awards of the APA**.

clock (Comput.) Any internal timing device that keeps all functions within the **computer** operating in proper sequence. The "real time" clock found in some computers allows the program to record (in memory) the actual time of occurrence of some event.

clone (graft, twig, or slip) The sum of individual organisms descended by asexual reproduction from a single sexually produced individual (such as with aphids that reproduce parthenogenetically, with hydras by budding, or with plants by budding or by cutting). Experiments on cloning have been successfully conducted on frogs and attempts are being made on mammals. Once cloning is possible on the human being there exists the possibility that cells will be taken from an adult who possesses desirable genetic traits and such cells reproduced in great numbers of people, the cells eventually developing into a complete human being with the same genetic endowment of the donor.

clonus Rapid, alternating violent motions (clonus) in which spasmodic muscular contractions (limb-jerking) and relaxation serially follow one another, generally occurring after the tonic phase in **grand mal epilepsy**.

closure Translated from *Zusammenfassung*, literally *summation* or *cohesion*. A **Gestalt** principle of perceptual organization. Percepts, memories, actions, etc., attain stability by the subjective closing of gaps or the subjective completion of incomplete forms. For example, closure takes place when separate arcs in a circular pattern are seen as a broken circle. Closure also applies to the experience of tension-relief when a problem is solved or a task completed—the satisfying feeling of completion that allows the person to dismiss the problem and attend to something else.
Coined by **Koffka** as meaning "good form."

cluster analysis An analysis of trait intercorrelations, based on clustering those traits (or items) showing similar patterns of inter-item **correlation**. The method is more superficial than **factor analysis**, for which it sometimes substitutes.

cluster sampling A procedure for restricted random sampling that involves dividing the population into clusters and then taking a **random sample** from each cluster or from different clusters. If all pupils of a school constitute the population, clusters might be obtained by putting every pupil's name on a card, shuffling the cards, and piling them in groups of equal numbers, each pile being a

cluster. Clusters need not be equal; thus, it differs from a stratum in that its essential quality is its concern with a homogeneous group of individuals. Generally, a cluster sampling is considered an integral part of area sampling. *See* **stratified sampling, sampling**.

CM Contraharmonic mean.

CNS Central nervous system.

coactive group task Performance by a group in which individuals do not interact but work singly or in parallel fashion, the group performance being measured by a summation of each individual effort. For example, in a coal-shoveling operation, if one man can shovel so much coal in an 8-hour day, then it is expected that 8 men can do 8 times as much, or the same amount in one hour. Such tasks seldom take individual differences into consideration.

COBOL COmmon Business Oriented Language. A **computer** language designed for commercial or business data processing uses.

cocaine A bitter crystalline alkaloid (-ine) derived from coca bean, whose leaves were long chewed by natives of Chile and Peru to relieve fatigue and hunger. It is a cortical stimulant. When taken as a stimulant and drug-kick it makes the user euphoric and hyperactive, with sleeplessness and sexual excitement emphasized. Prolonged and excessive dosage results in early symptoms of headache, dizziness, restlessness, hallucinations, and depressive feelings, followed by feelings of peace and contentment. Although labeled as an addictive drug by the World Health Organization, it is technically not so. Withdrawal symptoms of the *coquero* (an addict, from the Spanish of South America where cocainism was common), if any, are not severe, although there have been some reports in which the symptoms were similar to the effects of chronic **alcoholism** or even **heroine** or **morphine** discontinuance. Slang: snow, speed balls, star dust, coke, gold dust, flake. *See* **drugs**.
Cocaine was first isolated by Gadeke in 1855, but Albert Niemann in 1859 first described it after isolating it from Peruvian coca leaves (from the Aymara Indians who called it "khoka" meaning "the plant"), naming it cocaine in 1860. Cocaine had been prescribed to relieve fatigue by physicians as early as 1870. By 1878, coca leaves were publicly chewed in London, New York, and other large cities for purposes of stimulating the brain and body to greater accomplishments. Introduced as an anesthetic by Russian physician Vasili K. Anrep (1852-1927) during 1879-1884, and Freud published a paper on his research with cocaine in 1884. First used as a local anesthetic in 1884 by Austro-American ophthalmologist Karl Köller (1857-1944), who used it to deaden the eye for an operation.

cochlea The primary receptor organ of hearing shaped like a spiral shell (cochlea). The base of the cochlea has a broad end, and its coiled structure, in about two and three-quarter turns, becomes smaller and narrower as it winds toward its apex. The cavity of the bony cochlea is divided into three fluid-filled triangular-shaped tubes or canals: the **scala media** (cochlear duct), the **scala tympani** (tympanic canal), and the **scala vestibuli** (vestibular canal). Reissner's membrane, which is the roof of the scala media, separates the scala media and the scala vestibuli while the floor of the cochlear duct separates the scala media from the scala tympani. However, the scala tympani and the scala vestibuli are linked together by a small hole called the **helicotrema**.
Békésy has shown that acoustic stimulation generates pressure changes in the **cochlea** that, transformed into traveling waves, propagate themselves at about 0.9 mile per second along the **basilar membrane**, proceeding from the less resilient basal portion to the more flexible **helicotrema**, where, since frequence of traveling waves is dependent on flexibility, maximal bulge and hence maximal stimulus to the hair cells (hearing receptors) are induced.

C

Empedocles of Agrigentum first described the resemblance of this spiral shaped organ of the inner ear to a snail shell. **Eustachius** correctly described and illustrated it in 1552. Named cochlea by **Fallopius** in 1561. Entered English in 1688 as meaning the "spiral cavity of the internal ear."

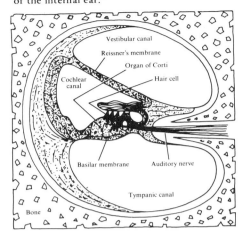

From *Psychology: A Scientific Study of Man*, by Sanford and Wrightsman. Copyright 1970 by Wadsworth Publishing Company, Inc. Reprinted by permission of the publisher, Brooks/Cole Publishing Company, Monterey, California.

Cochran's C Test A nonparametric statistical test for detecting heterogeneity among k population variances. The test statistic C is given by:

$$C = \frac{\hat{\sigma}_j^2 \text{ largest}}{\sum_{j=1}^{k} \hat{\sigma}_j^2}$$

where

$\hat{\sigma}_j^2$ largest = largest of k treatment variances,

$\sum_{j=1}^{k} \sigma_j^2$ = the sum of all the variances,

k = number of variances, and

j = variable subscript that ranges over the $1, \ldots, k$ treatment levels.

The **degrees of freedom** are equal to k and $n - 1$, n being the number of observations within each treatment level. If the treatment level N's differ only slightly, the largest N can be used to determine the degrees of freedom for this test. This tends to reject the hypothesis of homogeneity more frequently than it should be rejected. (See Table 17.) The C test, unlike the F_{max} statistic, uses all of the k population variance estimates and is the preferred test unless the N's are radically different. (See Table 17.)

cocktail *See* **lytic cocktail, Synanon.**

co-counseling (peer counseling) A form of counseling using peer partners to counsel each other in discharging emotionally upsetting feelings (shame, frustrations, etc.), thereby hopefully enabling each to gain greater clarity and insight into his overall functioning. Methods used are noninterpretive.

coded-decimal code A decimal number system in which each decimal digit is expressed by a code consisting of a system of characters representing information.

codeine A white, bitter, crystalline alkaloid or compound (-ine) obtained from the poppy head ([kode] or code-); a derivative of **opium** used as an analgesic, sedative, or hypnotic; also a cough inhibitor.

coding scores Scores that are a linear transformation of the original scale of measurement. One coding method assigns 0 to the **arbitrary origin**, which is either the midpoint of the lowest **class interval** or the class interval nearest the middle of the distribution. Intervals above the arbitrary origin are coded 1, 2, 3, ... and those below $-1, -2, -3, \ldots$ Coding reduces the size of numbers and hence the amount of computational labor.

coefficient A "dimensionless" description of a set of data. Also, any constant factor such as 5 in the term $5y$. *See* **coefficient of correlation.**

coefficient of alienation A measure of the lack of linear association between <u>two variables</u>, X and Y, given by $R = \sqrt{1 - r^2}$ where r represents the **Pearson product-moment correlation** coefficient. The term under the radical indicates the portion of the Y variance that is not associated with the variance in X.

Attributed to Truman L. Kelley (1884-1961), American psychologist and statistician. Ph.D. Columbia, 1914.

coefficient of concordance Same as **Kendall's coefficient of concordance.**

coefficient of contingency (mean square contingency) A measure of the degree of association between two **variables** (usually qualitative in nature), often used to measure the correlation for a general **contingency** table. If X^2 has been found to be significant, so is C. Its formula is $C = \sqrt{2/N + X^2}$.

First developed and used by **Karl Pearson** in 1887.

coefficient of correlation (r) An index of the tendency of two **variables** to vary concomitantly. The coefficient can assume values from +1.00 (perfect positive correspondence between the two variables) through 0.00 (no correspondence) to −1.00 (perfect negative correspondence), which indicates an inverse relationship between the variables. *See* **Pearson product-moment correlation** (also Hays, 1963, p. 496; Hays, 1967, p. 99).

The coefficient of correlation was so named (from Galton's function) by Francis Ysidro Edgeworth (1845-1926), British economist and statistician.

coefficient of curvilinear correlation (E) An index of the degree of **correlation** between **variables** when the distribution is curvilinear. It is often used when two variables stem from **interval** or **ratio scales**. When the **curvilinear correlation** is for a sample, the correlation ratio, η is used. *See* **eta coefficient.** (Senders, pp. 229-242).

coefficient of determination (r^2) The square of the **coefficient of correlation** (r), which indicates the proportion of the total **variance** explained by the relation of x and y, or the relative value of the correlation coefficient. The r^2 gives information about the relative validity of the obtained prediction. In formula form: $r^2 =$ Explained variance/Total variance.

The r^2 is always positive since it is the ratio of two sums of squares. It indicates the strength of linear relationship in a given set of **data**.

coefficient of intraclass correlation (ρI) A statistic that estimates strength of relationship (linear and non-linear) between X and Y when the **independent variable** is qualitative. Intraclass correlation is useful for studying grouped observations from different investigators. With the observations combined into one total sample, ρI is then used as a means of measuring the extent of the bias existing between subsamples, or classes of the same sample (Hays, 1963, p. 513; Kirk, pp. 126, 199).

coefficient of mean square contingency Same as **coefficient of contingency.**

coefficient of multiple correlation (multiple correlation coefficiency) $R_{0.1,2,3,\ldots n}$ A pure number lying between limits of 0.00 and +1.00, indicating strength and direction of the relationship between the **criterion** and **dependent variable** and the best combination of many other **independent variables**, the independent ones being so weighted as to make the **coefficient of correlation** a maximum. It also tells how much weight should be given to each of the many variables from which the criterion is being predicted.

coefficient of non determination (k^2) The proportion of the **variance** in the **dependent variable** not accounted for by **independent variable**(s); the complement of the **coefficient of determination.** Represents the square of the **coefficient of alienation.** It is the ratio of the unexplained variance to the total variance. Interpretation is similar to r^2, the coefficient of determination, except for k^2 showing lack of association.

coefficient of partial correlation A correlational measure of the degree of association between two **variables** with the effects of one or more other variables partialled out or held constant statistically.

coefficient of rank correlation *Same as* **Spearman rank difference method.**

coefficient of reliability A method of determining **reliability** by dividing **data** (questions from a test, e.g.) into two equal parts and then applying the **coefficient of correlation** to the scores obtained from two applications of the same measuring instrument. The reliability of a test may be increased by using the Spearman-Brown formula: $r_n = n r_{11}/[1 + (n - 1) \ r_{11}]$ where $r_n =$ the increased reliability coefficient resulting from increasing the length of the test n times or repeating it n times, and $r_{11} =$ coefficient of reliability for the original test.

coefficient of variation (V) The ratio of the **standard deviation** to the mean. It relates the standard deviation to the absolute size of the objects being measured. Unlike the S.D., it permits comparisons between different scales or units because it expresses the S.D. as a percentage of the mean. As V decreases, its distribution becomes more concentrated. Since it is a pure number, V can be compared to any other V. Its formula is:

$$V = 100 \frac{s}{\overline{X}}$$

where $s =$ the sample standard deviation, $\overline{X} =$ the mean.

coenzyme An enzyme working together (co-). The smaller of the two (the other being the **apoenzyme**) usually distinct nonprotein parts that make up an enzyme system. The coenzyme, of low molecular weight, activates the apoenzyme by combining with it and endowing it with catalytic qualities.

COEPS Cortically originating extrapyramidal system.

Coghill, George Ellett (1872-1941) American (Illinois) anatomist whose experiments with the larval amblystoma (species of salamander) reinforced **Gestalt** theory. In studying **motor** behavior and neural growth he discovered that total or mass movements appear first, and that specialized movements (including reflexes) develop with maturation of the nervous system. Coghill called his process **individuation.** *See* **cephalocaudal sequence.**

cognition Process or act (-tion) of knowing (-gni-), perceiving, or of gathering knowledge together (co-). The faculty of apprehending, knowing, thinking, and of information-processing. Cognition covers the various intellectual aspects of knowledge, such as reasoning, remembering, attitudes, motives, values, etc.

James Ward (1843-1925), English philosopher-psychologist, introduced the term in 1886, relating closely to its present-day meanings.

cognitive balance An aspect of Heider's social theory of **interpersonal perception.**

cognitive change therapies Therapeutic approaches to people's problems that deemphasize unconscious processes in the attempt to make changes, directly or indirectly, in a person's **cognitive system** (thoughts, values, concepts, beliefs, and assumptions). **Adler's individual psychology** apparently has supplied the fuel for such therapies, since his psychology explained many of man's neurotic difficulties as being due to his mistaken ideas, assumptions, and false logic. **Reality therapy** and **rational-emotive therapy** are two of the more prominent approaches along these lines.

cognitive consonance (cognitive consistency) A characteristic of a **cognitive system** referring to internal consistency or harmony among the various cognitions in that system. When congruence exists among the total cognitions, the cognition is considered high in consonance; when contradictory or incongruent elements exist, the consonance is low. *See* **balance theory, cognitive dissonance theory.**

cognitive development theory *See* **Piaget.**

cognitive dissonance theory A motivational theory (based on **Lewin's aspiration level** experiments) proposed by **Festinger** in 1957. It states that two or more concurrent, mutually dissonant ideas, attitudes, or facts of knowledge (cognitions in general) will "drive" people to resolve these contradictions because they cannot tolerate the state of tension that exists. The drive is toward consistency and away from dissonance, such drive occurring because of an actual cognitive attitudinal change. In actuality, people tend to reject or deny information that may be in conflict with their prior beliefs. Festinger lists some sources of dissonance as: new information, logical inconsistency, uncontrollable circumstances, cultural mores, and events inconsistent with past experiences. Such dissonances may be reduced by changing behavior, attitudes, conditions of the environment, etc. *See* **insufficient deterrance hypothesis** (also Leon Festinger, *A Theory of Cognitive Dissonance*, 1957).

cognitive growth theories Three basic theories are described here: (*1*) Bruner's *instrumental conceptualism.* A theoretical assessment of **cognitive** processes in which the child passes through three stages for representing information: (a) the *enactive stage* or *mode* in which the child thinks in terms of the usability of things; (b) the **iconic mode** in which his visual-spatial imagery becomes predominant, and finally (c) the stage when the child learns to symbolize things, at about the age of 2, and begins to use and understand grammatical concepts. In instrumental conceptualism, man grows by the process of internalizing his ways of acting, creating images, and symbolizing those things that are in his **phenomenal field.** Self-discovery enables him to develop his intellectual capacities. **Actualization** results as a function of the uses to which he puts himself, thus becoming fully functioning. Development of cognitive powers depends upon the supply of the cultural stock, the nature of the individual's life, and the extent of his desire for a meaningful open life experience. (Jerome S. Bruner, et al., *Studies of Cognitive Growth*, 1966). (*2*) Guilford's *structure-of-intellect theory.* Intelligence is basically problem-solving and made up of a number of factors, possibly 120, that can be classified under *five major operations* including **cognition**, memory, convergent thinking or utilizing logical procedures, divergent thinking involving creative endeavors, and evaluative decision-making; *six products* consisting of single experiences, relational effects between units and classes, a composite of experiences, changes in experiences, implications, and systems; and *four contents* including figural, symbolic, semantic, and behavioral aspects of one's exposure to experiences. Man can achieve the ultimate in intellectual performance by proceeding toward maximizing himself and achieving personal adequacy (J. P. Guilford, *The Nature of Human Intelligence*, 1967). (*3*) **Piaget's** *cognitive development theory.* Piaget utilizes concepts of biology,

psychology, and logic for studying the origin of **intelligence** in children. His theories are perceptual and experiential-phenomenological in nature. Piaget's basic premise is to learn how the child adjusts himself to his real world. To understand the child one must enter his world and live as he does. To Piaget, intelligence derives from and thrives on action, which is the catalyst that makes the intellectual potential a reality. Intellectualization never occurs in isolation, but only in reference to a total system's organizational scheme. *Two processes* are necessary for development of intelligence: (a) **assimilation** (incorporation of a new **experience** into old structure; (b) **accommodation** (adjustment of structure itself to new experience). In preparing for adult thinking the child goes through *four stages*: (a) sensori-motor stage from birth to 2 years; (b) operational stage (2-6 years)—someone causes things to happen (a fire occurs because the fire engine brings it); the child's logic is irreversible; (c) the period of carrying out concrete operations (7-11 years)—the child becomes capable of performing reversible logical processes; (d) **formal operations** behavior (12-15 years) as opposed to concrete—the child is capable of understanding and making hypothetical constructs. (Jean Piaget, *The Language and Thought of the Child*, 1959).

cognitive learning theories Theories that consider learning as a process of making new discriminations or reorganizing old material into new patterns. Instead of learning responses (as conditioning theorists imply), the person responds to **cognitive structures** (knowledge, ideas, etc.). Furthermore, cognitive or **sign learning** theorists emphasize the knowledge of location, as in the case of a rat constructing a **cognitive map** of his **maze** so that he can make faster trips to the goal. Such cognitive mapping involves changing perceptions and reorganizing knowledge. There also must be understanding, cognitive-feedback trial, acceptance, and rejection, goal-setting, and divergent thinking (leading to creative adjustments).

Cognitive theories are concerned primarily with how the individual organizes his subjective experiences, and how he gains information about the world for an understanding of it. An experience can be fully appreciated only in terms of its meaning to the individual, of how he perceives experiences. **Bruner**, for example, believes that the perceptual process is selectively organized into specific categories, enabling the individual to be less surprised by new experiences, particularly by those that are relatively congruent with past experiences. (J. S. Bruner and C. C. Goodman, "Value and Need as Organizing Factors in Perception," *Journal of Abnormal and Social Psychology*, 1947, *42*, 33-44).

cognitive map A term applied by **Tolman** (1932) to a "mental" outline developed by the individual to assist him in any goal-seeking behavior, thereby relieving him of making so many trial and error motions. It usually involves storage of information for use in making decisions about various responses under different situations. *See* **cognitive learning theories.**

cognitive structure The pattern of paths, sequences, and signs resulting from experience and learning, e.g., the learned paths an individual uses in finding his way about the house in the dark. In general, cognitive structures are the patterns followed when performing complicated activities with very reduced cues. The term is used primarily in **Gestalt psychology.** *See* **cognitive learning theories.**

cognitive system The formation of separate **cognitions** into a meaningful and functioning complex. Such generalizing must derive from experience (whereby only a person who knows the game can generalize that cactus,

raspberry, and rhubarb belong as much to baseball as they do to the vegetable kingdom) as well as from stimulus determinants involving similarity and proximity (such as grouping Chinese and Japanese together as Oriental).

cognitive theory of developmental behavior *See* (3) under **cognitive growth theories.**

cohesiveness *See* **group cohesiveness.**

collator (Comput.) A device for merging different pieces of information or two or more sets of items into one ordered set or sequence. One such device collates **Hollerith** or IBM cards into a sequence.

collective unconscious According to Jung, "the all-controlling deposit of ancestral experience from untold millions of years, the echo of prehistoric world events to which each century adds an infinitesimally small amount of variation and differentiation" (*Contributions to Analytical Psychology*, 1928). But the unconscious psyche, this collective experience of the human race "is not only immensely old, it is also able to grow increasingly into an equally remote future." (*The Integration of the Personality*, 1939).

Collège de France A research and teaching institute only, not a college for students.

colliculus (pl. colliculi) Little (-ulus) hill (collic-) or prominence. The four (two pairs) sensory centers of the **corpora quadrigemina** that form pea-shaped enlargements on the **tectum of the midbrain**, near the **pineal gland.** The two *superior colliculi* represent primitive visual centers serving as relay centers for visual reflexes involving skeletal muscle, while the two *inferior colliculi* are concerned with the auditory reflex centers.

color Any visible characteristics, other than spatial and temporal inconsistencies, of reflecting light waves of a particular length. Refers also to variation in **hue** (the wavelength), **saturation** (the degree of pure color), and to **brightness** (the lightness or darkness of a color). All colors of the **visible spectrum** are produced when a prism is used to separate white light into its components extending from about 380 **nanometers** (for violet light) to 780 nanometers (for red light).

color blindness (Daltonism) Visual defect in which the person is unable to distinguish between **hues** that appear different to people with normal color vision. The severity may vary from **achromatism** to **dichromatism** (inability to distinguish between some hues). Other color defects are **deuteranopia, protanopia,** and the rare **tritanopia** (the blueblind). *See* **sex-linked characteristic.**

Color defects had been noted as early as 1684, but it was not until 1794 that color-blind John Dalton (1766-1844), English chemist and physicist, first described color blindness scientifically (published in Manchester in 1798). Later, **Helmholtz,** Goethe, and **Thomas Young** carried on similar discussions.

Alarik Frithiof **Holmgren** (1831-1897), Swedish physiologist, in 1878 introduced colored wools for testing color blindness. **Ishihara** developed his test for color blindness, using color plates. Many other color charts have been introduced in recent years.

color circle Chromatic colors (**hues**) and their corresponding wavelengths arranged around a disk in their natural spectral order, with the addition of nonspectral reds and purples; hues opposite one another are complementary in **additive mixture.** When rapidly rotated, the disk will give a grey or colorless field. The color diagram, expressing the same idea, takes various and usually more complicated forms, one of them having the wavelengths arranged in a parabola with the hues represented as a straight line connecting the wavelengths that produce them.

C

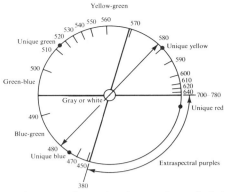

Points opposite each other on the unshaded sectors represent complementary hues in the **visible spectrum.** Those on the lightly shaded sector have no complementary wavelengths in the visible spectrum.

color constancy See **perceptual constancy.**

color diagram See **color circle.**

color formula A scheme of predicting how the seven primary qualities of vision mix to form secondary qualities: C = (R or G) + (B or Y) + (Wh or Bl) + Gr.

colorimeter A device for measuring (-meter) color, used to determine, specify, and match colors, especially of liquids, so that an unknown color may be compared to a standard color mixture; a device in which lights of a predetermined wavelength and intensity may be blended through a series of lenses and prisms.

colorimetry The measurement (-metry) of color specifications for the purpose of providing standard color information and eliminating as many subjective experiences as possible.

color mixture laws Rules that have been found to apply in the mixing of colors, the mixing of wavelengths requiring a different set of rules than for those in mixing paints. There are three principal *psychological laws of color mixture* (not pigment mixture): (1) For every color or hue there is a **complementary color,** or **hue.** If complementary hues are mixed by rotating a disk marked with proper color proportions, the two hues will cancel each other out and give a neutral grey. (2) The mixture of any two uncomplementary colors will produce an intermediate hue, which varies with the relative amounts of the two colors and whose **saturation** varies according to its nearness to grey. Mixture involves a loss of saturation. The elements of these first two laws were laid down in 1704 by Isaac Newton (1642-1727), English natural philosopher and mathematician. (3) If both of two color mixtures arouse a certain visual response, a mixture of them will also arouse the same visual response.

In general, laws of psychological color mixture show that all variations in hue are matched by mixing red, green, and blue, yellow apparently not being a primary visual quality, but a function of red and green. If yellow and blue, for example, are spun on a **color circle,** the human eye perceives it as a whitish grey. If blue and yellow paints are mixed, however, the eye perceives green. This is so because paint-mixing involves both subtraction (absorption) and addition (reflection), each paint absorbing its part of the spectrum, the reflected remaining wavelength producing color perception.

Blue absorbs red, orange, and yellow but reflects yellow, green, and blue, while yellow tends to absorb violet and blue wavelengths but reflects mostly yellow and green wavelengths, and since vision is partially a function of reflectance, the color green becomes apparent because most of the wavelengths refelcted from mixing blue and yellow are green. See **color vision theories.**

color-mixture triangle See **chromaticity diagram.**

color pyramid (color solid, color spindle) A solid figure, shaped either as a double pyramid with a trapezoidal base or as a double cone, representing the visual sensations in all degrees of **hue, saturation,** and **brightness.** The double cone (actually an extension of the color diagram with brightness added as a dimension) classifies colors three-dimensionally: with points along the vertical axis representing degrees of brightness, points along any radius (from the center to the periphery) representing degrees of saturation, and points around the circumference representing the different hues. See **color circle.**

In 1810, P. O. Runge, an artist, made the first color pyramid that accounted for the position of the four principal colors. Modern double pyramid was introduced (1902) by **Ebbinghaus.**

color subtraction The mixture of pigments that are illuminated by a white light; the pigments absorb certain colors and reflect others to the observer.

color triangle See **Maxwell triangle.**

color vision theories Several theories of color vision which follow (arranged alphabetically) have been developed but no one satisfactorily explains all phenomena. (See **Munsell color system**). However, there are strong indications that two major types of opposite-sign summators operate in color vision—the red vs. green and the blue vs. the yellow.

Dominator-modulator theory. **(Granit theory).** A visual theory based on the assumption that a separate dominating retinal ganglion cell exists for the **brightness** aspect of vision with chromatic distinctions introduced by receptors modulating the dominant response. Ganglion cells that respond over the whole **visible spectrum** of wavelengths "produce" a dominator curve ("dominators"), while cells responsive to a narrower band of wavelengths produce modulator curves ("modulators").

The theory was first expressed about 1923 as a so-called "stage theory" by E. Q. Adams, but the term dominator-modulator was not applied to it until **Ragnar Granit** (in his work on cats) did so in his article ("A Physiological Theory of Colour Perception," *Nature*, 1943, **151,** 11-14). Also see his *Sensory Mechanisms of the Retina,* 1947. Granit has continued to carry on much research in this area as have many others, particularly C. R. Michael (1966), who showed that some optic nerve fibers are fired by green or yellow light and inhibited by blue light, while other fibers responded in reverse fashion.

Duplicity (duplex) theory. In 1866, Max Schultze (1825-1874), German anatomist, laid the groundwork for this theory by concluding that the **cones** are the mediators of color. In 1894, Johann von **Kries** (1853-1928), German physiologist, formulated what is now known as the *duplicity theory,* emphasizing the importance of the **rods** as primitive brightness receptors. Unlike cones, which operate in daylight vision, stimulation of rods by appropriate light stimulus gives no perception of color. However, under the influence of **rhodopsin,** they function with great sensitivity low illumination. Thus color vision is duplex in that the cones mediate color and daylight vision, the rods achromatic and twilight vision; that is, rods are sensitive primarily to intensity of light waves and cones to differences in wavelength.

Hecht's theory. Selig Hecht (1892-1947), American physiologist, developed a theory of retinal excitation that is consistent with recent knowledge of neural action. It uses the principle that light as a stimulus decomposes retinal photosensitive substances, and that recomposition takes place after the **stimulus** ceases. Aided by catalytic action, the originally decomposed products excite the neural impulse.

Hering theory. In 1874, Ewald **Hering** (1834-1918), German physiologist, suggested that the retina contained three visual substances, each being capable of constructive and destructive processes, which he called "assimilation" and "dissimilation." He proposed black-white, blue-yellow, and green-red substances with pure colors being dependent upon the six processes: three assimilations, three dissimilations. All other colors are mixed colors. The Hering theory explains **color blindness, negative afterimages,** and retinal color-zones, but not the appearance of neutral grey or the fusion of red and green into yellow. See **opponent-process theory.**

Ladd-Franklin theory. In 1892, Christine **Ladd-Franklin** (1847-1930), American psychologist and logician, combined the concept of an evolutionary difference between **rods** and **cones** (rods had been considered more primitive, according to Max Schultze, 1866) with that of **Donders,** involving the decomposition of a retinal color molecule whose product stimulates the nerve fibers selectively. Red, green, and blue are the basic colors. The advantages and disadvantages are similar to those of the Hering theory (C. Ladd-Franklin, *Colour and Colour Theories,* 1929).

Opponent-process theory. A theory that assumed, in its original form (Hering), that there are three different sets of **cones** with color-vision processes opposed to one another. More recently (Hurvich and Hurvich) it has been postulated that there are four (two pairs) spectrally sensitive retinal units, each pair opposing the other (yellow vs. blue receptor, red vs. green, black vs. white, white vs. black) in its effect upon **neurons** or possibly bipolar cells. There is apparently a direct inhibitory interaction between the pairs of color-sensitive members. And since the pairs oppose one another only one pair-member can be effective at a time. Apparently, the so-called opponent-process takes place not in the cones but further toward the brain in the **lateral geniculate body.** (L. M. Hurvich and Dorothea Jameson, "An Opponent-Process Theory of Color Vision." *Psychological Review,* 1957, 64, pp. 384-404). In 1971, both L. M. and D. Hurvich received the **Warren Medal** for "studies that have given quantitative substance to the Hering model of opponent processes in the visual system."

Young-Helmholtz theory. In 1802, Thomas Young (1773-1829), English physician, in "On the Theory of Light and Colours" explained color sensation in relation to the presence in the retina of structures sensitive to red, green, and violet (utilizing Newton's principles of color mixture). In 1852, **Helmholtz** rediscovered the theory. It received more recognition because it fitted **Johannes Müller's** concept of nerve specificity and was correspondingly understandable. The Young-Helmholtz theory sets up three different photoreceptor processes, each one specifically sensitive to red, green, or blue (violet). Appropriate mixing of these three gives the entire spectrum but does not explain yellow.

Recent research suggests that color vision is based on a combination of variations in the physical relationships of cone cells to bipolar cells, and not on three cone photopigments. E. H. Land, inventor of the Polaroid Land camera, discovered in 1959 that varied colors could be produced by mixing only two lengths—black and white covered by colored filters, with the sensitive transparencies being further exposed and overlapped with other colors (E. H. Land, "Color Vision and the Natural Image," *Proceedings of the National Academy of Sciences,* 1959, 45, 115-129, 636-644; J. J. Sheppard, Jr., "A Critical Review of the Experimental Foundation of Human Color Perception" [Santa Monica, California: *The Rand Corporation*]).

color wheel A device that blends color segments into a uniform mixture of the component colors by rotating interlaced colordisks rapidly. A schematic cross-section of the color solid, showing relationships between **hues**. See **color pyramid**.

combination A term used in mathematics and **probability** theory referring to the number of ways that *r* things could be chosen from among *N* things, irrespective of order. Or, what are the number of combinations possible from *n* objects taken *r* at a time? The general equation for determining such probabilities is:

$$C(n,r) = \frac{n!}{r!\,(n-r)!}$$

The following symbols are also used to represent various combinations:

$C\binom{n}{r}$ = the number of combinations of *n* things taken *r* at a time

$C\binom{N}{r}$ = the number of combinations of *N* things taken *r* at a time

Commission Internationale De L'Eclairage (The International Commission of Illumination). A group of scientists stationed in France dedicated to standardizing degrees of illumination. The Commission derived a curve as a standard (based on a combination of the concepts involved in the **Young-Helmholtz, opponent-process theories** and scientists' measurements in various parts of the world), to which all attempts of assessing quantity of illumination must be compared. See **color vision theories**.

commissure(s) Act of (-ure) sending (-miss-) together (com-); connecting. Long, connective nerve fibers passing between the two hemispheres of the **brain**, or crossing from one side of the spinal cord to the other.

common chemical sense Sensitivity to pain of the mucous membranes (e.g., of the eyes, nose, and mouth) when stimulated by various chemical substances in solution.

communication net The involved pattern of information-exchanging channels among group members, commonly used to study effect of internal communication on group behavior (H. J. Leavitt, "Some Effects of Certain Communication Patterns on Group Performance." *Journal of Abnormal Social Psychology*, 1951, 46, 38-50).

comparative judgment law See **scaling technique**.

comparison level (CL) The self-imposed level or standard a person uses in comparing any **outcome**, such standard being dependent upon past personal or closely observed experiences. Outcomes that fall below the comparison level are dissatisfying, while those above give satisfaction. Dissatisfying outcomes, however, do not necessarily produce hostile or escapist behavior in the person.
A term coined by John W. Thibaut (born 1917), Ph.D., MIT, 1949, and Harold H. Kelly (born 1921), Ph.D., MIT, 1948, American social psychologists. See **comparison level for alternatives**.

comparison level for alternatives (CL alt) The particular standard of judgment that a person postulates in comparing his present negative situation with the one he would expect to achieve if he changed. For example, a person may choose to remain in a present dissatisfying situation (such as an unhappy marriage) if the compared alternatives (being alone, preparing his own meals, and keeping house, etc.) seem to be less attractive (Gergen, p. 32).

compensation A **defense mechanism** designed to overcome feelings of inferiority by making a special effort to eliminate a real or imagined physical deficiency or personality defect, so that the person may achieve social rewards or some form of self-satisfaction. Many successful athletes have compensated for a previously handicapping ailment (such as polio) and proved to all that "it can be done."

compiler A program that translates statements written in a high level source language (such as FORTRAN) into the numeric object code to be entered into the **computer**.

complement The quantity or number needed to complete something else, usually in the mathematical sense. The portion of a **set** that, when included with the remainder of the set, makes the combination equal to the set. In binary arithmetic, 1001 and 0110 are complemented because their combination (sum) fills the set 1111 (1001). In **Boolean algebra**, for example, the complement of set *A* (denoted variously as $\bar{A}$, $\sim A$, A', $-A$, $\acute{A}$ etc.) is the set of all elements in the universe (U) that are not members of set *A*. When the set *A* and its complement $\bar{A}$ are united, they comprise the whole universal set (*U*), since only two values are allowed. In **computer** terminology a complement refers to either of two numbers derived by rule from a given number expressed to the base *N*. In arithmetic, the complement of a number *n* is another number *m* such that their sum *n* + *m* is some specially defined number *k*. Two types of arithmetical complement are in common use: (1) the radix complement where *k* = radix (the 10's complement in decimal arithmetic, the 2's complement in the **binary** system); and (2) the radix minus-one complement where *k* = radix −1 (the 9's complement in decimal, the 1's complement in binary).

complementary classes In **symbolic logic** and **Boolean algebra**, two groups that have no members in common but divide the universe between them (*A* and −*A*, *X* and −*X*), since each needs the other to complement the **universe**.

complementary colors Pairs of colors (**hues**) that lie exactly opposite each other on the color circle, which if properly mixed together will result in the sensation of an achromatic grey or white. For example, red and blue-green, yellow and bluish green, primary yellow and primary blue. If opposite hues do not produce grey, then they will produce the hue (in desaturated form) of the dominant member of the pair. See **color mixture, primary colors**.

completely connected network See **group network**.

complex number Any number of the form (*a* + *bi*), where *a* and *b* are **real numbers** and *i* = $\sqrt{-1}$.

complex reinforcement schedule A schedule of **reinforcement** in which ratio and interval contingencies either (1) remain constant regardless of the subject's behavior (e.g., a conjunctive schedule) or (2) vary as a function of the organism's previous behavior (e.g., an **adjusting schedule**).

compound action potential A recording of several **action potentials** (usually spikes) in the nerve fibers obtained by placing one electrode on a nerve and another electrode (the ground) somewhere else on the body and recording the results of the nerve's excitation. See **evoked potentials**.

compound reinforcement schedule A schedule of **reinforcement** in which several simple schedules are programmed sequentially or concurrently (e.g., chained, tandem, multiple, mixed schedules).

compulsion Act (-sion) of driving (-pul-) together (com-); an irresistible inner force compelling the performance of an act (such as over-concern with order, regularity, etc.) even against the "will" of the individual. The act (for example, in counting the lines on the sidewalk, or repeatedly washing the hands) has no rational purpose other than to reduce the rising tension. According to **Freud**, compulsion neuroses result from prohibitions or atonements and are consequently negative, or they are substitute gratifications, often symbolic. See **obsession**.

computer One who or that which (-er) reckons (comput-). In modern times, an intricate electronic calculating machine designed to solve complex mathematical problems rapidly. Usually consists of **input** and **output** devices, as well as storage, arithmetic, and logical units coordinated by a control unit.
The abacus was the earliest form of computer (Chinese in the sixth century B.C. and Mediterranean cultures in 450 B.C.). In 1614 John Napier (1550-1617), Scottish mathematician, developed a logarithmic system, and in 1617 he invented mechanical computing devices. In 1850 an American inventor, D. D. Parmalee patented a set of keys, pushing down a marked key with the finger that turned the wheels of a calculator to the correct number, thus making it possible for the invention of the adding machine, cash registers, and other key-machines. The American William S. Burroughs (1857-1898), invented the first successful adding machine in 1885. Then, Herman **Hollerith** of the United States Census Bureau developed the punched card system for recording and analyzing data for use in the 1890 decennial census (modified from the French punched cards for weaving purposes used in 1728), and now the basis of the on-off language of present-day electronic computers, which are programmed on the **binary** system of counting.

computer-assisted-instruction (CAI) Instruction or teaching of a course through progressive units electronically manipulated. CAI can include audio as well as video presentation. Generally, each learner has his own cubicle and console. He responds to each question presented, and the questions are repeated, with added hints of the correct response, until a correct answer is given. Then the machine goes on to the next unit.

computer data The basic information that is used to feed information to computers or control systems. Many signals can be used in either the analog or digital sense.
The information content of an analog signal, such as the running graphic trace of an oscillogram, is conveyed by the value or magnitude of some continuous characteristic of the signal—such as the **amplitude**, phase, or frequency of a voltage, or the pressure of a fluid. To extract the information, it is necessary to compare the value of the signal's magnitude to a standard.
The information content of a digital signal is concerned with discrete states of the signal—such as relays which are open or closed, or have a hole or no hole in certain positions on the IBM card. The signal is made meaningful by assigning numerical or other values to the various possible combinations of the signal's units.

computer language A language used in and for computers. Early devices used numbers almost exclusively so that the machine could process all the **data** in numerical form. From this type of "language" the trend has shifted to high-level languages, the first being **FORTRAN** (FORmula TRANslator), which was developed to translate formulas into machine-readable form. FORTRAN led to COBOL (COmmon Business-Oriented Language), developed primarily for business applications. Both these computer languages continued to develop and improve, but a multipurpose problem-oriented language was obviously needed. Thus evolved PL/1, which can be used by commercial and scientific programmers.

computer of average transients (CAT) See **averaging computer**.

computer operation (computer organization) The total process involved in the operation of a computer, covering five basic functions: (1) *inputting data* through a device, such as a punch card or paper tape reader, teletype, etc.; (2) *processing of the data* by the **central processing unit**; (3) *outputting of data* through output devices, such as card punch, paper tape punch, page printer, etc.; (4) *memory*, **such as** disks, drums, magnetic tape,

C

etc., allowing for storage of the program the computer is to follow, for the data it is operating on, and for other information useful in computation, such as sine and cosine tables and subroutines; and (5) *control functions* or that part of the computer that directs and coordinates all the operations listed above.

computer program A precisely stated plan or routine specifying a sequence of instructions for the **computer** to follow, indicating how to use given **data** and how to function in a certain order so as to provide an answer to some problems. The writing of a computer program may be enhanced by drawing a **flow chart**, which delineates in logical order the sequence of operations a computer is to take, graphically outlining the flow of information through a particular system (such as in an **information-processing** system used in **psychology**).

In a psychological application, a computer has been programmed to handle the role of the therapist in a clinical first interview with a patient. In order for the computer to respond to the patient's written comments, it was necessary for the therapist to anticipate the possible situation and to program the computer with certain key words, such as "love," "hate," "mother," etc. (K. M. Colby and H. Enea, "Heuristic Methods for Computer Understanding of Natural Language in the Context-Restricted On-Line Dialogue," *Mathematical Biosciences*, 1967, **1**, 1-25).

Comte, (Isadore) Auguste (1798-1857) French social reformer and philosopher; opposed to **introspectionism**. Founder of positivism, a philosophy denying transcendent metaphysics and emphasizing the positive and the scientific while denouncing the negative and unprovable. As American psychologist Gardner Murphy (1895-1971) said, "if he had offered a program of research, he might fairly be called the first behaviorist." He coined the term "sociology" in his work, *Cours de Philosophie Positiv*, 1830-1842.

conation The process (-ation) of striving or attempting (con-), including desire and volition, and with or without a conscious goal. *See* **redintegration**.

concept formation A cognitive process in which perceptual experiences are classified, sorted, and given more elaborate and symbolic meanings.

concordance In twin studies, concordance refers to the sharing of a common illness (usually of mental illness) so that genetic influence can be posited. The *concordance ratio* is the percentage of relatives (including siblings) of a subject who show the same trait as the person being studied. For statistical meaning, see Table 31a; **Kendall's coefficient of concordance.**

concours A unique characteristic of a French medical school in which the future progress of the students is coursed or planned after he passes a competitive examination in prerequisite courses, making him eligible after his first year for an appointment as **externe des hôpitaux.**

concrete operations of Piaget The fourth stage (7-11 years of age) of the mental development of the child, in which the child gathers many concrete concepts previously unable to grasp (such as idea of conservation of material—one shape of clay twisted into another has neither gained nor lost material). He can also appreciate points of view different from his own. *See* **cognitive growth theories**.

concurrent validity Validity determined by the internal consistency of different parts of a test battery, all scores obtained at the same testing; or the validity measured by the **correlation** of a test with another one of known validity.

Condillac, Etienne Bonnot de (1715-1780) French philosopher. Exponent of **empiricism**, mechanism, and developer of sensationalism. Started where **Locke** left off on sensation as the source of ideas. His writings upheld the view that ideas and all conscious experience are derived from passive sensations. He retained **Descartes'** dichotomy of body and soul, however. Condillac used the analytic method of imagining a statue endowed with only one sense, smell, and then gradually building up the mind by adding the other senses. Thus he avoided mysticism, the problem of the soul, and the necessity for laws of **association**. *See* **Hartley**.

conditional response *See* **conditioned reflex**.

conditioned avoidance response (CAR) Any learned **response** performed to avoid punishment, pain, or an otherwise stressful situation.

conditioned discrimination The combining of acquisition and **extinction** procedures for training an organism to respond to a **conditioned stimulus** and not to a generalized one. Performed by pairing the conditioned and unconditioned stimuli and presenting the generalized stimulus alone.

conditioned inhibition Process by which the organism becomes conditioned *not* to respond, one example being when a **conditioned stimulus** (CS) and a neutral stimulus are presented together and not followed by an **unconditioned stimulus** (US). The neutral stimulus becomes the suppressor. This is not the same as simple extinction because the CS alone still elicits the CR. *See* **reactive inhibition**.

conditioned operant Behavior (response) learned through **operant conditioning**; a type of behavior with which the organism "operates" in its environment to obtain a desired result.

conditioned reflex *See* **conditioned response**.

conditioned reinforcement *See* **secondary reinforcement**.

conditioned response (CR) A newly learned **response** (such as salivation) to a stimulus not originally capable of arousing the response; or, that response made to a neutral **conditioned stimulus** (CS) after the CS has been repeatedly paired with an **unconditioned stimulus** (US), and which through repeated association becomes adequate thereafter to evoke the same response.

For example, a child, after some unpleasant exposure to a doctor's needle, may develop crying or withdrawing as a CR to the presence of the doctor or the needle only, without being pricked. *See* **classical conditioning**.

Johann August Unger (1727-1799), German neurophysiologist, described many of the conditioned reflexes of Pavlov without fully understanding them. Concept developed by Pavlov in his 1928 Lectures on Conditioned Reflexes. Pavlov used the term "ooslovny" ("conditional") in Russian but which became "conditioned" in English usage (1927). Pavlov also first used the phrase "conditional response."

E. R. Guthrie and S. Smith introduced the term "conditioned response" in 1921, to describe all learning by association, which they claimed Pavlov's "conditioned reflex" did not do.

conditioned stimulus (CS) In classical conditioning, a previously neutral stimulus (such as a sound) that, through pairing in close temporal proximity with (usually but not necessarily) an unconditioned "natural" stimulus (such as food), acquires the ability to elicit a CR or reflex behavior (such as salivation). *See* **Pavlov**.

conditioning The process of acquiring new stimulus-response relationships under either of the two systematic learning techniques: (1) in **classical conditioning** (Pavlovian), a stimulus that originally elicits a certain response is paired with a stimulus that originally did not elicit that response so that the new **conditioned stimulus** (CS) comes to produce the **conditioned response** (CR); (2) in **instrumental conditioning**, reward is contingent upon the occurrence of some response so that the subject learns to produce reinforcement by his own act.

conditioning, Type R R refers to a **response** being correlated to the controlling stimulus and not to a **stimulus** as in Type S.

conditioning, Type S S refers to a stimulus being correlated to the controlling stimulus and not to a response as in Type R.

conditioning apparatus A laboratory device (usually for administering a mild electronic shock) used in simple Pavlovian psychological experiments whereby an auditory (e.g., a buzzer) or visual stimulus and a mild "shock" are administered simultaneously to produce a **conditioned response.**

conduct disorder Behavior (such as **alcoholism**, drug addiction, and sociopathic behavior) that is characterized by violation of society's standards of conduct.

cone A retinal cone-shaped photo-receptor (with a higher **detection threshold** than the **rod**), that responds in daylight vision. Cones are densely packed in the **fovea** and absent in the retinal periphery. They mediate color vision. On the average it is estimated that there are about six and a half million cones in the human eye.

The retinas of some species—dogs, for example—have no cones, only rods, such animals being presumed to see no colors but only shades of gray. *See* **duplicity theory** under **color-vision theories**.

In one study (MacNichol), three kinds of light-sensitive cone pigments were differentiated by using a **microspectrophotometer**. One type of cone substance has an absorption peak at 447 nanometers (a violet-blue on the color circle, with blue being perceived by the retina when stimulated at wavelengths of 477 nanometers), another at a peak approximating 540 nanometers (perceived as green), and a third cone at 577 nanometers (perceived as yellow) but also extending into and being sensitive to the longer "red" wavelengths (E. F. MacNichol, Jr., "Three Pigment Color Vision," *Scientific American*, 1964, **211**, 48-56).

Conférence Générale des Poids et Mesures (General Conference on Weights and Measures) An international regulating body responsible for maintaining standards of measurements. At the Eleventh General Conference in 1960, the metric system of units (based on the **ampere, candela, kelvin, kilogram, meter,** and **second**) was approved as the eventual universal currency of science, industry, teaching, and technical practice, and given the name **Les Système International d'Unités (International System of Units)**, establishing the abbreviation "IS" as the standard for all languages. At the Twelfth Conference in 1964, among other actions, the liter was redefined to be a special name for the cubic centimeter. At the Thirteenth Conference in 1967, the ephemeris definition of the **second** was abrogated and replaced by the atomic definition, while **candela** was redefined and the **kelvin** redesignated.

confidence belts *See* Table 1d and Table 1e.

confidence (level) interval A range of values, considering all possible samples, within which a statistical **parameter** may be expected, or where there is a probability of locating the true **population** value.

confidence limits The upper and lower boundaries of the **confidence level**. *See* **Neyman** under **likelihood ratio test**, Table 13a (p. 187), and Table 13b (p. 188).

configuration Act (-tion) of forming (-figura-) together (con-). A *Gestalt* term emphasizing organization of experience, indicating that a part of any perception influences every other part, and that the whole pattern or configuration is more than the sum of its parts. For example, a group of dots in a circular pattern is seen as a circle rather than as a group of dots.

Titchener suggested the term "configuration (ism)" as an equivalent for the German word *Gestalt*. The word was originally introduced into English in 1559.

conflict A condition of an organism that is simultaneously attracted to and repulsed by a person, thing, or some **cognitive** experience.

To **Jung**, conflict was not only the basic motivator of life, but it was only through conflict that mental progress was possible. **Horney** felt that in order to resolve conflicts, a neurotic may react by being helpless, or all powerful, or by removing himself, both physically and mentally, from the conflicting situation. To Gardner Murphy (1895-1971), American psychologist, the opportunity of choice means conflict, and from conflict comes a learning experience. Psychological conflict is the only true conflict, whereas physiological conflict has to resolve itself or perish. **Lewin** conceived of conflict in three ways: **approach-approach** types; **avoidance-avoidance**; and **approach-avoidance**. Many other **psychologists** and **psychiatrists** have somewhat similar ideas about the role of conflicts in personality development.

In consideration of a conflict model, the assumption is that man is continuously and ineluctably caught between opposing forces. In this sense, conflict is both psychosocial, with one force coming from within the individual and the other from society in general, and intrapsychic, with both opposing forces originating within the individual (Maddi, pp. 17-64).

conformity A social phenomenon in which behavior tends to follow a uniform pattern, conventionally expected in a particular society; an expected standard of conduct. This is *congruence conformity*. Another form is *movement conformity*, in which experimental subjects prefer a socially prescribed standard in preference to their own preferred one.

confounding (Stat.) A procedure whereby **treatments** are assigned to subjects so that certain effects cannot be distinguished from other effects. Confounding reduces number of treatment combinations that must be assigned to blocks of subjects.

congruence The quality of melding together; understanding or a coming together in mutual respect and feeling. **Carl Rogers** believes that the therapist (in the client-therapist relationship) should show congruence by allowing his feelings to be available to the client, and to be able to live these feelings, "be them and able to communicate them if appropriate." *See* **client-centered therapy, free.**

congruence conformity *See* **conformity.**

congruity model A behavioristic schema for placing any object (persons, publications, etc.) on a generalized **attitude scale** ranging from −3 to +3, and rating them accordingly. It has general application for problems of cognitive interaction and attitude change. *See* **model.** (American psychologists, Charles Osgood [born 1916] and Percy Tannenbaum [born 1927], "The Principles of Congruity in the Prediction of Attitude Changes," *Psychological Review*, 1955, 62, 42-55).

congruity theory A behavioristic theory related to **Heider's balance theory** but permitting better prediction of direction and degree of attitude change. The more extreme an **attitude** the less likely it will change when related to an attitude of opposite **valence.** For example, people who had a very high personal regard for President Kennedy and only a moderately favorable feeling toward Cuba's struggles, were more likely to accept Kennedy's decision about Cuba rather than lower their regard for him. *See* **congruity model.**

conjunction The AND function in **Boolean algebra.**

conjunctive reinforcing schedule *See* **complex reinforcement schedule.**

connectedness The relationship stated as: if A is different from B, then A has either more or less of the quality than B. If $A \neq B$, then either $A > B$ or $A < B$.

connection Pavlovian term for a **conditioned reflex.**

connectionism Thorndike's theory that all psychological functions are the result of the mediation of stimulus-response (S–R) bonds, learned and unlearned; that learning takes place when such connections are reinforced. All behavior is a function of S–R combinations, with **intelligence** considered as a function of number and availability of connections. *Compare* **associationism.**

consistency principle in attitude change For three systematic uses of this principle, see **balance theory, congruity theory,** and **dissonance theory.**

constancy, object *See* **object constancy.**

constancy, perceptual *See* **perceptual constancy.**

constant (Stat.) In a **regression** equation, if with subscripts, the first subscript is the predicted **variable**, the second the observed one, then a_{xy}. Also, any property that is the same for all groups under consideration is a constant.

constant error In **psychophysics**, the tendency of a judgment to persist or be constant on observations where physical equality does not exist, such as in judging the magnitude of **illusions.**

constant-stimulus method (constant stimuli) A method whereby a series of stimuli is presented repeatedly to an observer, whose task is to determine a difference, if it exists, between that **stimulus** and some standard. *See* **methods of psychology: psychophysical.**

constitutional psychopathic inferiority Old term for **conduct disorders.**

constitutional types (typology) theories Theories that human beings are classifiable into homogeneous, small groups with specific characteristics (body build, temperament) held in common, and from such grouping certain predictions can be made. **Hippocrates**, about 400 B.C., was supposedly the first to classify people according to types (although many historians claim that it was **Galen**, living 500 years later, who actually devised the first such scheme. Nevertheless, the Galen-Hippocratic typology listed four kinds of humors (body fluids) with parallel temperaments:

Humor	Temperament
Blood	Sanguine (optimistic)
Phlegm	Phlegmatic (listless)
Yellow bile	Choleric (irritable)
Black bile	Melancholic (maudlin)

About 1400 years passed before **Kretschmer** presented his four types of body build in 1929: (1) *pyknic*—short and squat in general, barrel-chested; mental illness tends toward manic-depressive psychoses; (2) *athletic*—well developed and proportioned, muscular; tends toward schizophrenia and epilepsy; (3) *leptosome*—tall and slender, narrow chest, long bones; tends toward schizophrenia; (4) *dysplastic*—disproportionate mixtures of other three types.

In 1940, **Sheldon** offered his theory holding that a person's body build is correlated with specific temperaments. In 1942, he listed dimensions of body build with corresponding temperaments:

Physique	Temperament
Endomorphy—large viscera, soft and round, flabby	*Viscerotonia*—sociable, love of eating and good times; relaxed in behavior
Mesomorphy—muscular, strong	*Somatotonia*—energetic, adventurous, courageous; assertive in nature
Ectomorphy—long, fragile, large brain and nervous system	*Cerebrotonia*—restrained, nervous, introvertive

Sheldon uses a numerical system to show the relationships between his body-temperament types, ranging from the extremes of 1 to a maximum of 7. In theory this would lead to 343 different somatotypes, but actually less than 100 have been identified. As an example of the three-digit numbering system, a rating of 7-1-1 would depict a person very high in endo/viscerotonia and very low in both meso/somatotonia and ecto/cerebrotonia. See figure.

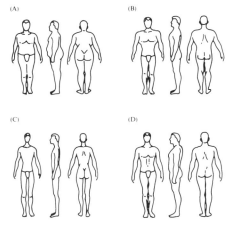

Characteristic body types. (A) is the endomorph, (B) the mesomorph, (C) the ectomorph, and (D) is the combination. Donald L. Lewis, Scientific Principles of Psychology, © 1963. Reprinted by permission of Prentice-Hall, Inc., Englewood Cliffs, New Jersey.

construct A concept, defined and inferred from observable events, used to summarize or to account for relationships between a stimulus situation and a special response or two or more experimental variables. The concept of habit, for example, is a theoretical construct. Experimental facts, without the conceptual glue of a construct, can remain only as isolated and relatively meaningless facts. Constructs enable the investigator to articulate what he is attempting to describe, and make possible a certain degree of prediction. A poorly made construct, however, not only may cause confusion but can stop creative thinking. A famous construct in physics, tongue-in-cheek in origin, is that of the "quark," which is posited as being any one of three types of elementary particles that form the basis of all matter. It was named by physicist W. Gell-Mann (born 1929) after the elusive quark in *Finnegan's Wake* by James Joyce.

constructive apraxia *See* **apraxia.**

construct validity The degree to which the defined construct (temperament, intelligence, etc.) actually meets the criteria established by judges, experience, experimental conditions, or other relevant information. Such validity is determined by complex inferential and hypothetical procedures (L. J. Cronbach and P. E. Meehl, "Construct Validity in Psychological Tests," *Psychological Bulletin*, 1955, 52, 281-302).

content validity *See* **validity.**

context In **perception**, context refers to the background or **frame of reference** against which a perception is judged.

contiguity theory Condition (-ity) of keeping in touch (-tigu-) with (con-). A principle of **learning theory** that states that if two or more events occur together in time and space, the later presentation of one will reinstate the other. In this context, learning takes place by a contiguous relationship between sensory and motor events in the learning situation (as the sight of lightning gives rise to an expectation of thunder) rather than by reinforcement. Contiguity is the central principle of **Guthrie's** theory of learning. *See* **Mill, John S.**

contingency The dependency of one event upon another. The **coefficient of contingency**, being roughly comparable to a **coefficient of correlation**, expresses the strength of associa-

C

tion between phenomena that have not been numerically measured but simply classified as belonging or not belonging in certain qualitative categories. A *contingency table* is a multidimensional tabular presentation of frequencies by categories. The simplest, four-cell contingency table (called a fourfold table) results when observations are classified into just two categories of each of two dimensions. For example, each person may be classified as male or female, employed or unemployed. The *contingency test of association* is a variant of the chi-square (X^2) test. It may be used to test the **null hypothesis** of independence or the hypothesis of zero correlation. In **operant conditioning**, contingency refers to the conditions under which responses are followed by reinforcing or punishing stimuli or by the elimination of either of them, while in respondent conditioning, contingency refers to the conditions operating while conditioned and unconditioned stimuli are paired. *See* **elicited behavior.**

continuity law *See* **autochthonous laws.**

continuous reinforcement (Crf: regular reinforcement) Reinforcement of every response.

continuous variable A **variable** whose **range** is an interval or a set of intervals on the real axis. Measurements of heights, weights, etc., are examples of continuous random variables. *See* **discrete data (variable).**

continuum An uninterrupted flow of basic elements so that no dividing line may be made, such as the continuum of space, or the normal-abnormal continuum.

A concept developed mainly by James Ward (1843-1925), British psychologist, in opposition to the atomistic views of **Condillac** and of the associationists.

contourogram A compressed graphic record of signals (e.g., those produced by an EEG or EKG) used to show cycle-by-cycle variations.

contractility of cells The ability of the cytoplasm to shrink or to draw into a more compact form, one of three general properties of cytoplasm (the other two being secretion and metabolism). Resulting from chemical reaction, contractility involves molecular change causing cell and membrane alteration in shape. It makes possible the movement of cells and eventually the movement of the total organism.

contrast An enhancement of a perceived difference between two stimuli when closely presented together, or when stimulus differences among parts are noticeably large. Small differences create an opposite phenomenon called *assimilation.*

In color vision, the simultaneous or successive influence of one color upon another. *Successive contrast* (or temporal induction), for example, occurs by staring at a bright red light and then looking at a white wall: the afterimage of the light appears green. *Simultaneous contrast* (spatial induction) occurs by looking at a grey square on a black background, which looks brighter than a grey square on a white background.

Contrast effect, in taste perception, occurs when relatively sour things taste even more sour when sweet items have been tasted first—a reason why dry, tart wines are never sampled after sweet, dessert wines. *See* **assimilation effect.**

control functions *See* **computer operation.**

control group For experimentation purposes, a group subjected to essentially the same conditions as the **experimental group** (the **independent variable**) except for the change in the variable under study (the **dependent variable**). Also, the control group may be the body of subjects from whom the independent variable is withheld in an experiment. For example, in an experiment to study the effects of **Benzedrine** on learning, the experimental group would be administered the drug, one control group might be given nothing, and another control group might be given **placebos**, being told they were Benzedrine.

The results from the experimental group could then be checked against the control groups of no-drug and imagined-drug. *See* **proactive inhibition.**

convergence, visual *See* **visual convergence.**

conversion (hysteria) reaction A neurotic reaction in which the organic (somatic) symptoms are "converted" into paralysis of the limbs, insensitive areas of the body (anesthesias), uncontrolled emotional outbursts, or related bodily symptoms—all without apparent organic basis. Such conditions supposedly stem from **repressions.** *See* **hysterical neurosis** under **neurosis.**

converted scores Scores that are changed from one form to another, such as converting **IQ** scores into **percentiles**, or numeric test scores into letter grades.

convolution (gyrus) A sinuous fold or ridge of the brain surface, covering both the **cerebrum** and **cerebellum.** The cerebral convolutions are separated by furrows, the deeper ones called fissures and the shallower ones sulci.

Convolutions were first mentioned by Praxagoras of Cos (fl. 300 B.C.). **Erasistratus** referred to the cerebral convolutions as analogous in appearance to the spiral form of the small intestine, also indicating an association between the greater complexity of the convolutions of man and his intellect.

convulsive (disorders) reactions Brain damage associated with epileptic seizures.

convulsive seizure *See* **epilepsy.**

coordinates The values, X (the **abscissa**) and Y (the **ordinate**), of a point. The positions of points on planes usually refer to the **Cartesian coordinate system** in which the three basic planes are designated x, y, and z.

coping behavior Behavior that tends to be positive rather than escapist or defensive in action (-ing), dealing with threatening situations involved in fighting or meeting (cop-) problems.

Introduced (1956) by Lois Murphy, an American psychologist, in her book *Personality in Young Children*, in referring to the schizophrenic child and his poor ability to cope with life's situations.

coprolalia A disorder (-ia) in which "filthy" words relating to excrement or dung (copro-) are obsessively spoken (-lal-). *See* **Gilles de la Tourette.**

coronal plane Pertaining to (-al) the upper portion or crown (coron-), such as the top of the head; any plane in the human head lying at right angles to the **cephalocaudal** (vertical) **axis** or lying in the direction of the coronal suture; relating to the frontal plane that passes through the vertical axis of the body. *See* **anatomical directions.**

corpora quadrigemina Four (quadri-) twin (gemina) bodies (corpora): one pair being the **inferior colliculi**, and the other the **superior colliculi.** *See* **mesencephalon.**

Galen originally described these bodies about 170 A.D.

corpus callosum Hard (callosum) body (corpus). A large nerve tract (or band of white matter) connecting the right and left **cerebral hemispheres** and enabling the two hemispheres to share functions, which are, however, not entirely clear: apparently it is involved during the first learning experience in the transfer of **memory traces** from the hemisphere receiving the **input** to the other. *See* **raphé.**

In 1543, the complete term first appeared in print in *De Humani Corporis Fabrica* by **Vesalius**, but **Galen** had called this nerve tract "callosus" about 170 A.D.

corpus luteum Yellow (luteum) body. A mass of yellowish tissue formed in the ovary. After the Graafian follicle has ruptured and ovulation has taken place, the follicle, under the influence of the **luteinizing hormone** (LH) starts anew becoming the corpus luteum. The corpus luteum secretes **estrogen** and develops a new hormone **progesterone**, which prepares the uterine lining for implantation of a fertilized egg (Morgan, p. 402).

First mentioned by **Fallopius** in 1561, and later investigated by Marcello Malpighi (1628-1694), Italian anatomist.

corpus striatum (pl. corpora striata) Either of two striated (striata) masses or bodies (corpora) of white nervous tissue passing to and from the **cortex** (which envelopes it) and situated in front of the **thalamus** in each half of the **brain.** It is one of the main subcortical nuclei comprising the **basal ganglia** portion of the **extrapyramidal system.** Some confusion exists about terminology, since the **caudate nucleus**, the **lentiform nucleus** (consisting of the **pallidum** and **putamen**), and the **internal capsule** are technically known as the corpus striatum, but the caudate nucleus and putamen together are sometimes called the striatum or striata.

Called "striated" because of passage of whitish-grey fibers through it. Noted as early as 1524 by Jacob Berenger (Berengarius) (1480-1550), Italian anatomist and physician, who said that the corpus housed the soul. **Willis** in 1664, as reported by **Vieussens**, was first to use the terms "corpus striatum" and "lentiform bodies" for the basal ganglia, although Willis, in his own writings, seemed to use "corpora striata" familiarly, as if the term were in common usage at the time.

correction A term affixed to a **statistic** indicating an adjustment that must be made to account for exaggerations or underestimates caused by, say, the small number of cases, age factors, unreliability of measures, etc. *Correction for attenuation* is a statistical procedure for correcting the **product-moment correlation coefficient** for the unreliability of the measures used. It furnishes an estimate of the expected correlation if the measures were perfectly reliable, and is given by

$$r_c = \frac{r_{xy}}{\sqrt{r_{xx}r_{yy}}}$$

where

r_c = the correlation between X and Y corrected for attenuation

r_{xx}, r_{yy} = the reliability coefficient of test X and criterion Y, respectively

r_{xy} = the computed validity coefficient

correlation Relation or degree of correspondence (or of covariance) between two or more **variables**, or between two sets of paired measurements. A correlation is positive or negative according to whether one variable changes in the same way as the other or in an opposite way. Correlation is evidence of relationship but does not necessarily indicate a cause-and-effect relation.

The term correlation was introduced into mathematics in 1708. Auguste Bravais (1811-1863), French mathematician, worked out the theorems of correlation in 1846; Galton used "co-relation" concepts from 1877 to 1886 and particularly in 1885 in his **regression** studies; **Karl Pearson** developed mathematical concepts of correlation in 1896. *See* **coefficient of correlation, causation and correlation.**

correlation, multiple *See* **coefficient of multiple correlation.**

correlation, partial *See* **coefficient of partial correlation.**

correlation coefficient *See* **Pearson product-moment correlation;** Table 10.

correlation ratio *See* **coefficient of curvilinear correlation.**

correlation table A work sheet, with rows representing a Y **variable** and the columns representing an X variable, generally designed to simplify computations for the **Pearson product-moment correlation.**

correlator (Comput.) A device for determining the coincidence or noncoincidence of two signals and then signalizing the results of the comparison.

cortex The outer layer or "bark" of an organ; for example, the cortex of the **adrenal glands**, cerebellum or cerebrum.

Although several extracts had been obtained from the adrenal cortex it was not until 1927 that American physiologist F. A. Hartman and co-workers were successful in extracting the substance now known as **cortin**.

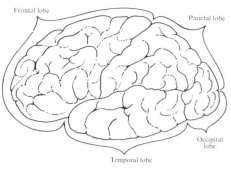

The cerebral cortex. From Psychology: A Scientific Study of Man, *by Sanford and Wrightsman. Copyright 1970 by Wadsworth Publishing Company, Inc. Reprinted by permission of the publisher, Brooks/Cole Publishing Company, Monterey, California.*

cortical activation Referring to (-al) activation of the cerebral cortex (cortic-). A shift in the electrical activity of the **cerebral cortex** from the 30-60/sec. **alpha rhythm** to 1 to 3 per second rhythms. Such changes may arise because of environmental stimulation or the injection of **epinephrine** into the **reticular activating system**.

cortical area *See* **Brodmann, cerebral cortex**.

cortical centers Referring to (-al) neural centers of the **cerebral cortex**.

Cortical motor centers were described in 1877 1878, and 1883 by French neurologists Charcot and Jean Albert Pitres (1848-1928). The cortical visual center was discovered and reported in 1888 by Swedish pathologist, Salomon Eberhard Henschen (1847-1930). The sensory cortex subdivisions (on the rhesus monkey) were first described in 1924 by Dutch physiologist, Johannes G. Dusser de Barne (1885-1940).

cortical layers Referring to (-al) neural layers of the **cerebral cortex**.

An indication of the irregularity of the cortex was first described (1776) as a *lineola albidior* (white line) in the **occipital** area by Italian anatomist, Francisco Gennari (1752-1797), then by **Vicq d'Azyr** in 1781 and by **Soemmering** in 1784 who also referred to Gennari's observation. First detailed (before microscopy took hold) descriptions of the cortical layers were made in 1840 by **Baillarger**.

cortical localization *See* **localization of brain function**.

cortically originating extrapyramidal system (COEPS) Neurons of **extrapyramidal system**, originating in the **cerebral cortex**, which descend the **brainstem** and spinal cord to motor neurons.

cortical neuron *See* **neuron**.

corticoid Similar to or acting like (-oid) an extract from the adrenal cortex (cortic-), the term deriving from telescoping of adreno-*cortical* ster*oid*. Any of the various steroids, some being hormones (as **corticone**) that govern the sodium and potassium balance of the body.

corticone A **hormone** that promotes the storage of glycogen in the liver and helps control blood glucose level.

Isolated in 1936 by American chemist, Harold Lawrence Mason, with E. C. **Kendall**, and the English psychologist and physician, Charles S. Myers (1873-1946). Cortin had been isolated by the same men with assistance from B. F. McKenzie and American physician, G. A. Koelscke (born 1908).

corticosterone (changed to corticone in 1939).

corticotrophin A molecular fragment of **adreno-corticotrophic hormone** that has essentially the same *corticoid* (cortico-) stimulating or *nourishing* (-troph-) effect and value of natural ACTH.

cortin A general term for the hormonal secretions of the adrenal cortex. The individual secretions, known as cortical steroids, regulate salt, water, and carbohydrate metabolism, and thus provide proper **homeostasis** for withstanding periods of **stress**. In general, cortin has a regulatory effect upon both nerve and muscle tissues and also upon sex function. *See* **adrenal glands**.

Corti organ *See* **organ(s) of Corti**.

Cotugno, Domenico Cotunnius (1736-1822). Italian physician and anatomist. In 1761, he not only named the **helicotrema** but also described the labyrinthine system and its fluids. In 1764, he discovered and described the **cerebrospinal fluid**, mentioning that the spinal and ventricular fluids were continuous. This observation was ignored until **Magendie** (1827) mentioned Cotugno's finding.

co-twin control A method using complexities of one twin to clarify the complexities of the other twin under highly controlled situations, i.e., differential training in a specific function is confined to one of a pair of **identical twins** whose overall behavior is similar before training. A comparison between twins at the end of the training period can show what effect imposed training has had upon modifying the natural behavior of the experimental twin. This method is also used to compare the individual with himself as he would have been if not trained.

coulomb (C) The **IS** unit of quantity of electricity equal to the charge transported in 1 second across a conductor in which there is a constant current of 1 **ampere**. *See* **International System of Units**.

Named after Charles Augustin de Coulomb (1736-1806), French physicist and inventor.

counseling An interactional process, usually between two persons (*see* **group therapy**), in which the client or patient seeks out the professional counselor for assistance in helping him change his behavior so that a satisfactory resolution of his needs may be made. The process involves, implicitly or explicitly, the expression of goals of the relationship, the methods to be followed, and the setting of criteria for evaluation of the interaction. Technically, the term covers a relationship that is more involved than the interview but not as deep as therapy (which implies probing into the individual's unconscious). An **interview** may be conducted by a relatively untrained person, but a *counselor* (school, industrial, guidance, vocational, marriage counselor) is generally expected to have at least a master's degree and preferably an Ed.D. or Ph.D. Counseling may be directive or nondirective, each of these techniques being one phase of a continuum. Most ethical counselors in private practice have found it to be advantageous to have a member of the medical profession available for consultation on their cases. *See* **client-centered counseling**.

counterconditioning Strengthening responses that are incompatible with undesirable responses.

A term introduced by **Guthrie**.

countertransference (psychoanal.) A psychotherapeutic relationship in which the therapist becomes emotionally involved with his patient, bringing to the therapy session some of his own childhood conflicts, **defense mechanisms** and unconscious or repressed desires. (For example, while a female patient is evidencing a transference toward the therapist, flattering and teasing him, he may respond in kind toward her.)

Term first used by **Freud** in 1910.

covariance An expected value of the product of the deviations of two random variables from their respective means.

covert movement *See* **implicit movement**.

CPU Central processing unit.
CPZ Chlorpromazine.
CR Conditioned response.

cranial nerve One of the twelve specialized nerves that enters or leaves the **brain**, mediating a variety of **sensory** and **motor** functions. In numerical order (based on **Willis'** and **Soemmering's** classification using skull openings as criteria) they are: I **olfactory**, II **optic**, III **oculomotor**, IV **trochlear**, V **trigeminal**, VI **abducens**, VII **facial**, VIII **acoustic-vestibular**, IX **glossopharyngeal**, X **vagus**, XI **spinal accessory**, and XII **hypoglossal**. *See* **mnemonic system**. Organized on the basis of **sensory** and/or **motor** functions they are:
Sensory
I olfactory (smell); *II* optic (vision); and *VIII* acoustic-vestibular (hearing and balance).
Motor
III oculomotor (eye movement, regulation of size of pupil, accommodation, coordination of eye and head position); *IV* trochlear (eye movement, proprioceptive awareness); *VI* abducens (abduction of eye, proprioception); *XI* spinal accessory (neck, head, and shoulder movements; peristalsis; vocalizing); and *XII* hypoglossal (tongue muscles).
Sensory-Motor Action
V trigeminal (sensory:face and tongue sensitivity; motor:chewing movements); *VII* facial (sensory:taste; motor: facial movements); *IX* glossopharyngeal (sensory: taste, tongue and pharynx sensitivity; motor:swallowing movements, salivary secretion, assists reflex control of blood pressure and respiration); and *X* vagus (sensory and motor combined functions with autonomic impulses to and from heart which it slows, but increases peristalsis and contracts voice muscles).

All cranial nerves from *VI* to *XII* originate or terminate in the **medulla**, including the sensory part of *V*, while *III*, *IV*, and motor part of *V* end in the **midbrain**, with *II* in the **thalamus**, and *I* in the ventral part of **cerebral hemisphere**.

Galen listed seven pairs of cranial nerves, while **Willis** listed nine (olfactory, optic, oculomotor, trochlear, trigeminal, abducens, facial and auditory (7th), and combining the glossopharyngeal, vagus, and spinal accessory into the 8th, with hypoglossal as 9th. **Soemmering** named the facial and auditory nerves, splitting into the 7th and 8th, and separated Willis' 8th into the glossophryngeal (9th), the vagus (10th), the spinal accessory (11th), and listing the hypoglossal as 12th. (Soemmering, *The Brain and the Origin of the Cranial Nerves*, 1778).

craniology The study of (-ology) a skull (crani-) and its characteristics. *See* **phrenology**.

craniosacral division *See* **autonomic nervous system**.

creativity The dynamic process of pursuing, discovering, and achieving new perceptions and solutions of problems. **Moreno** classified creativity into: (1) chance acts (those that come about by accident or luck and are seldom duplicable); (2) spontaneous creativity (resulting from a creative attitude with a specific purpose in mind); (3) conservable creativity (not designed for an immediate purpose, such as in painting, writing, etc.). **Maslow** considered creativity (to be able to apply new approaches to old things) one of the absolute essentials for a self-actualized person.

Measured intelligence correlates only about .40 with creativity, but the more intelligent person will produce the more complex and more lasting work. The creative child tends to be more active and less controllable, more of a problem to adults. Creative people generally are freer and less rigidly controlled, less subject to making black and white decisions or to being held down, less likely to be on time for appointments, but more likely to have a sense of humor. (D. W. MacKinnon, "The Nature and Nurture of Creative Talent," *American Psychologist*, 1962, **17**, 484-495).

C

creativity awards See **Richardson Creativity Award**.

cretinism The condition (-ism) of being an idiot or dunce (French-Swiss, *crétin*), usually caused by chronic and extreme **hypothyroidism**. Cretinism is often divided into two categories: *endemic*—common in certain regions where dietary supply of iodine is low (the thyroid may be nonfunctioning or atrophied); *sporadic*—occurs universally, due to defect of the **thyroid gland** (either prenatal atrophy or poor embryological development). Symptoms in both conditions, however, are identical, and can be recognized when the infant is about 3 months of age. The child is dwarfed, with large head, short extremities, thick lips and tongue, puffy face, apathetic expression, and pale yellow complexion. Normal mental and physical development is possible if thyroid therapy is started within the first year but preferably before 6 months.

Ancient Christian refugees who settled in remote areas of the Pyrenees developed hypothyroidism because of lack of iodine in the water. Their goitrous condition, with open mouths and slow thinking, caused the natives to contemptuously label these foreigners "Chrétien," which became "cretin" over the years. In 1603, **Paracelsus** was first to describe endemic goiter and to relate cretin-children with goitrous parents. Wolfgang Hoefer (1603-1661), German physician, was first (1657) to describe the condition using the term cretin.

In 1883, Felix Semon (1849-1921), indicated relationship of loss of thyroid function to cretinism.

crista ampullaris A jug-shaped (ampulla) enlargement at the end of each semicircular canal in the **labyrinth** of the ear containing a crest or ridge (crista) consisting of hair cells embedded in a gelatinous bud-shaped mass.

criterion A standard selected as the goal to be achieved in a task. A set of scores or some other measure of performance against which the success of a productive test is verified or compared. For example, a supervisor's rating of a worker's performance on the job is a criterion for judging the **validity** of an **aptitude test**.

critical flicker frequency (CFF) Critical fusion frequency. The minimum frequency of intermittent light flashes necessary to eliminate flicker and to create **fusion** or the sensation of continuous light without flicker.

CFF requires the intermittent stimulation of the eye by use of either rotating black and white disks or an **episcotister**. A light is seen as flickering at low rates of flicker and gradually loses its flicker (by fusing) as the flicker rate is increased, resulting in a perception of steady light.

The CFF is a function of many different characteristics (e.g., size of pupil, body temperature, age, use of drugs, **hyperventilation, IQ**) of the perceiving organism. It is an index of the eye's ability to discriminate between various visual sensations.

critical ratio (C.R.) The ratio of any normally distributed variate to its estimated **standard error**. The t-ratio is used with small samples.

In statistical notation, $D/\sigma d$ is a ratio whose numerator is the difference between an obtained **statistic** and the **parameter** expected under the **null hypothesis**; the denominator is the standard error of the statistic under the null hypothesis. $D/\sigma d$ is used in determining the significance of the difference between various statistics, such ratio being evaluated by comparison with the critical value in the **normal distribution**. The critical ratio provides information concerning the degree of confidence one can have (say at the 1 percent or 5 percent level) about an observed difference not being due to chance. See **critical region**.

The term was introduced by McGaughy, who originally applied it to a particular value of *t*.

critical region The area (region) of a sampling distribution into which a **statistic** or set of **outcomes** of a statistical test must fall in order for the **null hypothesis** to be rejected. A *critical value* is one that relates to a given significance level obtained from its sampling distribution. See **one-tailed test, tails of a distribution, two-tailed test**.

critical value See **critical region**.

cross-cultural research (or method) The systematic analysis, description, and comparison of human societies in an attempt to identify significant principles that may account for their similarities and differences. Specifically, each "culture" is given a score on different selected dimensions and its patterns are then compared with others. Social psychologists often use this approach in making comparative studies among various societies, including their individual members, but there are many experimental pitfalls in the technique (McDavid and Harari, pp. 40-41; 409-410).

cross education The positive **transfer** of a skill acquired by one part of the body to another part (usually from practiced to the unpracticed hand).

crossover The twisting of a pair of **chromosomes**. As a result the final cell division producing reproductive cells may contain **genes** from both chromosomes of a pair.

cross products, sum of Use of the **summation** sign, such as in Σxy, to indicate that the products x and y are to be summed.

cross-sectional (analysis) method A research approach to the relationship between variables, such as age and intelligence, in two or more groups simultaneously available; or a systematic investigation of samples of behavior at different ages, and comparing one sample with another. Contrasts with the **longitudinal studies** method, in which relationship is studied in the same group (same individuals) over different time periods.

Cross-section study of intelligence test scores as a function of age and education shows rapid growth of intelligence at first and then slow decline to about the twenties, continuing on a downward trend until death.

cryptomnesia A disorder (-ia) in which the memory (-mnes-) appears to be hidden or concealed (crypto-), habitual experiences being reacted to as if they were new.

CS Conditioned stimulus.

Cullen, William (1710-1790), British physician (M.D. Glasgow 1740). In his book *Synopsis Edinburgh Methodicae*, 1769, he introduced into English the word **paranoia** which the German physician R. A. Vogel had been using. Cullen also introduced the term "dementia," which he described as representing disproportionate emotions resulting from imagination or false recollections. He coined the term **neuroses** as one of the subheads in his classification of diseases, considering mental diseases as being primarily **endogenous** in nature.

cultural lag The delay between changes in custom and the carrying on of a cultured act, or the preservation of cultural elements after environmental changes have outmoded the custom (such as not eating meat on Friday, not eating pork, etc.). The term represents the idea that man has developed his intellect at the expense of developing the emotions.

First developed in 1922 by American sociologist William Ogburn (1886-1959) in his book *Social Change*; concept further refined by Franz Alexander (1891-1964), German-American psychoanalyst.

culture-free (culture-fair) intelligence test Any test that strives for measurement of pure innate **intelligence**, independent of experience; that tries to assure all test items "equally difficult for all races, social classes, religions, nationalities, etc." so that specialized education (North vs. South, rural vs. urban, black vs. white) does not prejudice the results. Such tests "avoid language often using spatial

analogies or other such material relatively new to testees. Even these tests present problems concerning specialized training necessary for certain space percepts, etc."

J. E. Milholland, "Review of Culture Fair Intelligence Tests." In O. K. Buros (Ed.) *The Sixth Mental Measurements Yearbook*. (1959-1965), pp. 719-721. In his 1959 Yearbook, Buros claimed that there were no such tests as "culture-free," only that some did not systematically favor members of one culture over another. In that sense, they were "culture fair."

culture shock The shock effect experienced by an unprepared, unsuspecting traveler who is suddenly dumped (by a jet plane, for example) into a strange culture and is almost immediately exposed to cultural and psychological cues that are entirely opposed to or at least culturally different from his own. These strange, incomprehensible, and meaningless foreign cues result in communication chaos, misinterpretations of reality, and an inability to cope with the present culture efficiently. For example, on a minor scale, culture shock is felt by the traveler who has to adjust to the intricacies of foreign money exchange, the foreign language itself, and the strange customs in eating, dress, and transportation. If he is to become more deeply immersed in the foreign culture the shock deepens with time until he becomes acclimated to the new culture.

cumulative curve A graphical representation of a learning experience (recorded while the behavior is in progress) that shows the number of responses made plotted against time.

cumulative distribution A **distribution** obtained by cumulating the frequencies of a **distribution** in one direction. A cumulation upwards from the lowest to highest value gives the total number of observations lying below the upper limits of each **class interval**. A downward cumulation is the converse of this. The **graph** of a cumulative frequency distribution is an **ogive**.

cumulative record An **operant** behavior graphic record (similar to a kymographic recording) of all the instrumental responses emitted during the conditioning session. The slope of the cumulative response curve is proportional to the rate of responding.

cuneate nucleus Wedge-shaped (cuneate) nucleus. See **gracile nucleus**.

curare (Spanish term for "urary" meaning "arrow poison" in Tupi (Amazon) Indian language). Any one of several drugs with paralyzing actions on the heart and neuromuscular skeletal junction. It inhibits preganglionic sympathetic fibers without affecting striated muscle or blocking neuromuscular transmission completely. The poison had been used by South American Indians, who tipped their arrows with it, to kill or paralyze animals or enemies.

It also has been used in measured doses to prevent surgical shock and to lower incidence of dislocations and fractures from **electroconvulsive shock therapy** by reducing intensity of convulsions. Its effects (paralysis of differing degrees) on **conditioning** have also been studied.

Sir Walter Raleigh (1552-1618), brought curare to Europe from Guiana in 1595, reporting on it in his *Discovery of Guiana* (1596). Curare was first described in writing (1777) in *History of America* by William Robertson (1721-1793), a Scottish historian.

Claude Bernard was the first (in 1850 and 1857) to show that curare blocked the nerve stimulation of muscle rather than paralyzing the muscle itself. Clinical use dates from R. West, Curare in Man, *Procedures of the Royal Society of Medicine*, 1932, **25**, 1107-1116, who used it for patients with tetanus and spastic disorders. In 1946, American researcher Richard C. Gill brought in authentic samples of curare for study. "Curare: Misconceptions Regarding the Discovery and Development of the Present Form of the Drug." *Anesthesiology*, 1946, 7, 14-23.

curve, exponential *See* **exponential curve.**

curve, logarithmic *See* **logarithmic curve.**

curve, normal *See* **normal curve.**

curves of returns (decreasing, equal, and increasing) Those curves or graphic representations of learning situations in which: (*1*) the greatest improvement in performance occurs during the early trials with a consequent trailing off (*decreasing returns*); (*2*) early trials yield the same amount of improvement as later trials (*equal returns*); (*3*) improvement is greater in later trials than in early trials (*increasing returns*).

curvilinear correlation *See* **coefficient of curvilinear correlation.**

curvilinear regression The fitting of a **regression** line to a nonlinear relationship.

cut-off point (score) A certain point, score, or composite score that has been agreed upon, subjectively or objectively, systematized or arbitrarily, as the decisive mark by which persons either fail or succeed in any given contest.

cybernetics Study or practice (-ics) of behavior (mechanical or animal) that is controlled by a governor or steersman (cybernet-); science of communication, especially between man and machine or machine to machine.

A field of study involving an analysis and investigation of complex electronic calculating and computing machines in comparison with the human brain and nervous system, so as hopefully to better explain human brain functioning. Also, a study of **information-processing** and control systems in higher animals so as to design better mechanical control systems. *See* **feedback, input.**

Norbert Wiener (1894-1964), American mathematician, who was professor at M.I.T. for years, developed the concept, naming it cybernetics which he described as "the entire field of control and communication theory, whether in machine or the animal." The term previously had been used in 1834 by French scientist, physicist Andre Ampère (1775-1836), in reference to a specialized example. See Wiener's book *Cybernetics: Or Control and Communication in the Animal and the Machine*, 1948.

cyborg The cybernetic (cyb-) organization (-org) or fusion of man and machine; machines embodying biological components and men incorporating sensors and mechanical organs as part of their symbiotic selves.

cycloscope Cyclic (cyclo-) wave viewer (-scope) for studying intracerebral wave patterns. Originally, an astronomical instrument, but adapted for **electroencephalographic** and psychophysiological use.

cyclothymia A cyclic (cyclo-) personality (-thym-) disorder (-ia). *See* **Kahlbaum manic-depressive psychosis.**

cyclothymic personality (affective personality) *See* **personality disorders.**

cystine A colorless crystalline compound (-ine) or **amino acid** found in most proteins but originally discovered in a bladder (cyst-) stone.

English physiologist and physician, William Hyde Wollaston (1766-1828), first isolated (1810) this substance from a bladder stone. Wollaston called it cystic acid but **Berzelius** later renamed it cystine.

cytoarchitectonics The systematic study (-ics) of the architecture (-architecton-) of cells (cyto-), enabling the further study of cellular form and function through mapping of cerebral surfaces.

The beginnings (1903) of cytoarchitectonics may be found in the investigations of, for example, **Meynert, Brodmann,** and the **Vogts.**

cytoplasm The formative material (-plasm) of cells (cyto-). *See* **ectoplasm, endoplasm.**

cytosine One of the four (the others being **adenine, thymine,** and **guanine**) pyrimidine bases occurring in **nucleic acids** that play a vital part in the formulation of the **genetic code.** In the DNA molecule, the four bases form complementary pairs across each strand of the double helix, with cytosine joined to guanine and adenine to thymine. *See* **chromosome, deoxyribonucleic acid.**

D

D In calculus, derivative. A critical value in the **Kolmogorov-Smirnov test** for two large samples. See Table 25c.

D/A (also DAC) Digital/analog converter.

Dale, Sir Henry Hallett (1875-1968) English physician and physiologist. In 1929, he and his colleagues isolated **acetylcholine.** Dale proposed (1935) the terms **adrenergic** and **cholinergic** as applying to classes of nerves (now, also referring to types of effector cells and responses as well as to autonomic drugs). In 1936, he received the Nobel prize in physiology and medicine. *See* **Loewi.**

Daltonism *See* **color blindness.**

dancing mania (*Danse de St. Guy*, St. Vitus' dance, epidemic chorea) *See* **chorea.**

dark and light adaptation A photochemical process in the **rod** cells of the retina, involving progressive adjustment of the building up and breaking down of **rhodopsin.** During the first 30 minutes exposure to darkness, as the photosensitive substance is being reconstituted, the eyes become slowly but increasingly more sensitive to light (for example, when adapting to dim light in a theater). Upon leaving a dark theater and being exposed to bright sunshine, the eyes become less sensitive to light; the photosensitive material is being broken down.

Darwin, Charles (1809-1892) English naturalist. His theory of evolution greatly influenced the development of psychology because its implied continuity between man and animals stimulated the study of animal behavior. His ideas on **instincts** and **emotions,** somewhat similar to **Gall's,** also contributed to psychological thinking. *See* **Baldwin, Hull, Ladd-Franklin.**

Dasein (Exist.) A compound word consisting of the German *Sein* (to be) plus *Da* (here and now); "being here," with a sensation of **existence** and a complete awareness of being here and now, which implies a knowledge of existence. Actually, man's phenomenological experience of being aware (his "beingness") is the **essence** of his existence.

Dasein analysis (The "being here" analysis of existential analysis.) A technique of **psychotherapy** (often called insight therapy) that has borrowed its framework from compatible elements in **psychoanalysis, phenomenology,** and philosophical **existentialism** while adding new insights and an open attitude toward the therapeutic relationship. It involves an encounter between two equal people (therapist and patient), the resulting interaction hopefully resulting in each person experiencing life itself and not just life in the protective environment of an office.

data Any information (measurements, observations, or estimates) that can be collected, stored for review, analyzed, evaluated, and interpreted. Data may be a series of numbers, group qualitative information subjected to some form of arithmetical or statistical treatment, or any facts or information taken in, operated on or put out by a machine for handling information.

Data are classifiable into two categories: *quantitative data*: events with certain well defined, limited values expressed numerically for any set of values (even qualitative data, such as maleness, femaleness) when assigned a numerical equivalent in data-processing; *qualitative data*: all data not expressed as

quantities; those qualities or characteristics determining distinctions, for example, between males and females or between animals and plants.

data handling system (sometimes data reduction system). A coordinated method for automatic sorting, decoding, or storing of information. *See* **computer operation.**

Daytop Village *See* **Synanon.**

debug (Comput.) To isolate and remove malfunctions or mistakes from a control system or data input program.

decerebration *See* **decortication conditioning.**

decibel One-tenth (deci-) of a **bel.** The unit used for measuring, on a logarithmic scale, relative intensities (as of a sound wave or electricity), signifying a change of 26 per cent (a **just noticeable difference**). For example, if the lesser stimulus has an absolute intensity value of 1.00, then to be perceived as louder the stimulus must be increased by 26 percent—to an absolute intensity value of 1.26. The next detectable increase is 26 percent of 1.26, increasing the absolute intensity to approximately 1.59. Ten such increases (ten decibels) comprise one bel. In considering the ratio of two intensities, the number of decibels is given by 10 times the **logarithm** to the base 10 of the ratio of the stronger to the weaker intensity. Hence, 10 decibels above a reference level of 1 unit is 10 units; 20 decibels above the reference level is 100 units; 30 above is 1000, etc. *See* **intensity.**

Some recognizable sounds and their decibel measurements are indicated in the following table:

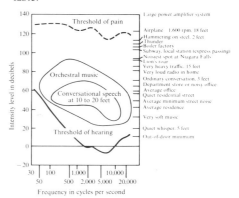

Approximate Intensity Levels of Common Sounds Represented in Decibels. (Decibels (dB) with respect to 10^{-16} Watt/centimeter². This reference is for acoustic measurements in air only.) Donald J. Lewis, Scientific Principles of Psychology, © 1963. Reprinted by permission of Prentice-Hall, Inc., Englewood Cliffs, New Jersey.

decimal number system (Arabic system) A **number system** with real numbers in terms of place values for multiples of ten including digits 0 through 9. Decimals or decimal fractions always have a denominator of ten or a power of ten, such as 10, 100, 1000. Fractions become decimal fractions by dividing the numerator by the denominator: 1/2 = .50; 1/4 = .25; etc.

decision-rules One of the predetermined rules (derived from decision theory in mathematics) for making a decision in the face of uncertainty. Criteria for choosing decision-rules are: (1) the extent to which expected loss is minimized, (2) the extent to which subjective loss is minimized. *See* **Bayesian approach to statistics;** also Hays, 1963, pp. 247-266.

decoding (Comput.) Translation, without significant loss of information, from a coded form to an analog or other easily recognized form. *See* **computer data.**

d

decortication conditioning The process (-ation) of taking away (de-) or removing the cortex (-cortic-). **Conditioning** that takes place in a *decorticated animal* (one whose entire **cerebral cortex** has been destroyed or removed).

In 1869, decerebration experiments were carried out by German physiologist, Friedrich Leopold Goltz (1834-1904), who showed that decerebrate frogs could perform motor acts. **Flourens, Rolando** and others had performed similar experiments earlier, but no one approached Goltz' thorough and graphic description. In 1911, the Russian physiologist G. P. Zelinii, **Pavlov**'s colleague, failed in attempts to condition totally decorticated dogs, leading to the belief that conditioning was purely a function of the cerebral cortex. In 1930, however, Zelinii and associates succeeded in their experiments on differential conditioning on decorticated dogs. Later studies have shown that classical and avoidance conditioning, plus differential conditioned responses, can be initiated in such animals.

decreasing returns *See* **curves of returns.**

decussation The act (-ation) of crossing (decuss-) over in the form of an X, a term used often in anatomy and neurology in referring to nerve fibers, for example, crossing over to the opposite side of the body.

About 132 A.D., *Aretaeus* in referring to paralysis occurring on the side opposite to the lesion, described the motor pathway in the form of the letter X. Cassuis Andreas (1640-1673), German physician and chemist, is credited with first observing (about 1670) that the cerebrospinal path crosses. Antonio Maria Valsalva (1666-1723) showed (1704) that in apoplectic hemiplegia the lesion occurs on the opposite side of the brain. In 1710, **Pourfoir du Petit** observed decussation in the pyramidal tracts, as did Italian anatomist, Giovanni Santorini (1681-1737), but it was not until 1721 that French anatomist Joseph G. Duverney (1648-1730) clearly showed the decussation of the cerebrospinal path. Italian anatomist Giovanni Battista Morgagni (1682-1771) presented evidence (1761) that in apoplexy the lesion is on the side opposite to the paralysis, substantiating theories of Pourfoir du Petit and others back to Aretaeus. Morgagni credited Valsalva, however, with the first demonstration.

dedifferentiation *See* **differentiation.**

deduction Act or process (-tion) of leading (-duc-) down (de-) or away; tracing the derivation of; deducing. In logic, the process of reasoning in which a conclusion is based on the premises only so that the conclusion cannot be false if the premises are true. *Compare* **induction.**

defective incentive system *See* **behavioral dysfunctions classification.**

defective stimulus control of behavior *See* **behavioral dysfunctions classification.**

defectology The study (-ology) of defects. A broad term in Russian psychology referring to any behavioral or physiological defect (such as **mental retardation**). Defectology emphasizes the comparative psychophysiological approach and the importance of studying behavioral defects in relation to the person's accomplishments within his milieu, and always with the hope of adapting maximally (Cole and Maltzman, p. 302).

defense mechanism Any of several unconscious **ego** devices or reactions to frustration and conflict (**rationalization, compensation,** etc.) that the individual uses to protect or enhance his self-concept and image. It is generally self-deceptive in nature and anxiety-and-tension-reducing in purpose.

defense reflex *See* **Bekhterev.**

degree of freedom (df or DF) The number of available independent observations upon which a **parameter**'s estimate is based; the number of free (unrestricted, independent observations unhampered in the sense of random sampling) variables entering into a statistic minus the number of independent restrictions estimated in computing the variation.

The degrees of freedom associated with a given sample or the variability in a set of scores is the number of scores (N) minus the number of restrictions placed upon the variables.

In a sum of three scores (51, for instance), if the mean of the set is known, only two of the three numbers are free to vary independently and to take any value (17 and 14, for example). The third value is now automatically known as 20 since the sum is equal to its given value. The degrees of freedom are then equal to two, the N of 3 minus the one restriction.

For small samples, df is a correction term used with the number of estimates when the **S.D.** of the **population** is not known but must be estimated from a sample. In estimating S.D., regardless of sample size, one degree of freedom is lost in estimating the value of the mean, so for computing the variance the df is $n - 1$.

In evaluating a t statistic, the number of degrees of freedom equals the number of pairs of observations minus 1.

dehumanization (Exist.) The process of mechanizing man, of giving him a number instead of a name, of reducing his choices, of making him conform because it is logical and can be proved to be good for him. Dehumanization reduces the intimacy of making personal errors and subjects man to predictable, mechanical outcomes, eventually depriving him of human contact and involvement.

deindividuation In social psychology, the process whereby inhibitions are weakened as a person loses his identity, resultant behavior being impulsive, aggressive, or regressive. For example, an army recruit aided by the anonymity of his uniform may perform unpredictable and antisocial behavior while away from his hometown; members of a cult may engage in bizzare and violent behavior, since being dressed alike they feel unidentifiable and thus free of guilt.

(Term introduced in this sense by L. Festinger, A. Pepitone, and T. M. Newcomb, "Some Consequences of Deindividuation in a Group," *Journal of Abnormal and Social Psychology,* 1952, **58**: 203-210).

Deiters, Otto F. K. (1834-1863) German (born) physician who was a pioneer in the microscopic study of nerve tissue (published posthumously 1865). Showed (1865) that the **nerve fiber** and **cell body** are in contact.

déjà entendu (Fr. already heard). **Illusion** of having heard something before.

déjà vecu (Fr. already lived). An impression (though not as strong as the déjà vu experience) that the "now" experience has been lived through before. *See* **epilepsy.**

déjà vu (Fr. already seen, unoriginal). A time and space **illusion** of falsely perceiving a new scene or experience as a familiar one. Sometimes, the illusion occurs in normal people under stress, but it frequently occurs in schizophrenics who tend to look upon everyone and everything as familiar. Psychoanalytically, déjà vu is an unconscious defense-response to an **id** wish that has been provoked by a real situation. *Compare* **paramnesia, pseudomnesia.** *See* **epilepsy.**

de Lange syndrome A clinical entity (possibly of autosomal recessive origin) in which there is usually severe retardation of mental and physical development and associated with synophrys (confluent eyebrows), long eyelashes, low-set ears, small extremities, hirsutism, and webbing of second and third toes.

Named after the Dutch pediatrician Cornelia de Lange (1871-1950), the first to report on such a condition.

delayed conditioning A variation in **classical conditioning** in which the **unconditioned stimulus** (UCS) is delayed for a period of time (generally five seconds or longer) during which the **conditioned stimulus** (CS) is continually present.

delayed-reaction method (delayed-response problem) A type of experiment (designed to test an animal's capacity for symbolic representation) in which, after a planned and timed waiting period, a subject must respond to a **stimulus** after its removal. (E.g., the dilemma faced by an animal in having to choose between two identical closed containers in one of which he had previously seen a reward placed.)

delirium tremens A variety of acute **brain** syndromes characterized by delirium, coarse tremors, and frightening visual **hallucinations.** Unless otherwise qualified it is considered to be due to or associated with **alcoholism.** If symptoms are due to a nutritional deficiency rather than to alcohol poisoning, it is classified under **psychosis associated with metabolic or nutritional disorder.** *See* **Korsakow's syndrome.**

In 1813, English physician, Thomas Sutton (1767-1835), described the condition and named it; more fully described in 1831 by American physician, John Ware (1795-1864).

delta (Δ) mean-square successive difference method A technique that indicates the presence but not necessarily the degree of relationship between successive observations in the same series of **data.** It can detect both linear and nonlinear serial **correlation.**

delta movement *See* **apparent movement.**

delta waves High voltage (about 150 μV at skull surface) slow (low) frequency (1-3 **Hertzes**) EEG waves, characteristic of stage 4 (deep sleep) but also evident in stage 3 (low arousal). *See* **paradoxical sleep, sleep stages.**

delusion A persistent and often consistent false mental concept not amenable to logic or persuasion. Delusions are usually associated with **schizophrenia,** the most common ones being *delusions of grandeur* (in which the person has exaggerated ideas about his importance in history or about his wealth) and *delusions of persecution* (in which the person feels others are plotting against him or are planning on hurting or killing him). *See* **dementia praecox.**

dementia praecox A mental disorder (-ia) of early or precocious (praecox) madness (dement-), characterized primarily by withdrawal from reality with associated **delusions** of grandeur and persecution.

In his book *De Anima Brutorum* (1672), **Thomas Willis** coined the term in describing a mental condition. And Viennese psychiatrist, Benoit Augustin Morel (1809-1873), used the term démence précoce in his "Traité 'des Digenerescences Physiques, Intellectuelles, et Morales,'" 1860. Because of his observation that this condition seemed to worsen in late adolescence, **Kraepelin** used the term in 1896. In 1930 **Bleuler,** suggested that the term dementia praecox be replaced by **schizophrenia.** *See* **Cullen.**

Demerol Tradename for **meperidine.**

Democritus of Abdera (c. 450-380 B.C.) A Greek philosopher and naturalist. Believed that the brain was the center for thinking. Considered matter to be composed of atoms, the smallest indivisible parts of matter. *See* **determinism, monism.**

dendrite The receiving end of a **neuron,** usually a branched tree-like (dendr-) process (-ite), thick and short. It transmits impulses to the **cell body** from an external **stimulus, receptor,** or by a neural impulse from a presynaptic **axon.** *Dendritic potential* refers to the electrical charge constituting the constant state of excitation of the dendrite.

Named (1889) by Swiss neurologist, histologist, Wilhelm His (1831-1904).

denial of reality *See* **ego.**

density functions (probability density function, sometimes called frequency functions) A statistical or mathematical derivative in which the **frequency** of a **random** variable, as a function of X, represents the proportion of the total frequency or unity.

Denver system *See* **Down's disease.**

deoxyribonucleic acid (DNA) A ribonucleic acid that has less (de-) oxygen (-oxy-) than another. A complex acid compound in the nucleus of each of man's trillions of microscopically tiny cells. DNA's material is inherited half from the father's sperm and half from the mother's egg, which provides the cell with instructions on not only how many **amino acids** (over twenty thus far found in nature) are needed to construct a specific protein but which variety of amino acid should follow which in the protein.

Each DNA compound consists of genes with alternating sugar and phosphate groups. Each sugar group (deoxyribose) has a nitrogen-containing material (base) attached to it. Which base (**adenine, thymine, cytosine,** or **guanine**) follows which in a DNA-gene sets the position of the amino acids. Three bases in a DNA-gene determine the selection of one other amino acid in a protein to become the fourth member of their team. Four bases arranged in groups of three at a time ($4 \times 4 \times 4$) will give 64 possible base triplets, and in each of the 64 are the protein-producing instructions—the entire **genetic code.**

In 1953, Drs. James D. Watson, American geneticist, and Francis H. C. Crick and Maurice H. F. Wilkins, British geneticists, discovered the basic structure of the DNA molecule, for which they received the Nobel prize in medicine in 1962. For their work on DNA, Drs. H. Gobind Khorana of the University of Wisconsin, Marshall W. Nirenberg of the National Institute of Health, and Robert W. Holley of Cornell University and Salk Institute shared the 1968 Nobel prize in physiology and medicine.

dependent variable The observed and expected behavioral change (response of subjects, etc.) that is dependent upon changes resulting from manipulation of the **independent variable**(s). In behavioral studies, the dependent variable is almost always related to rate of response or the amount of response during a certain time period. For example, the dependent variable can be the amount of learning one achieves during various measured degrees of time spent under muscular tension, the independent variable. *See* **graph.**

depersonalization A defense reaction that not only masks anxiety but serves to insulate the person from bothersome people. Allied to the protective device of "playing dead." To **Freud,** it had its origins in early infantile traumata. The depersonalization neurosis involves a sense of detachment of the self from the body; a bodiless feeling. *See* **neurosis, psychasthenia.**

depolarization Process or act (-ation) of negating (de-). Neutralization of opposite charges, such as when stimulation causes the membrane of a nerve cell to become semipermeable, allowing positive **ions** to pass through and thereby neutralize negative ions.

depressant An agent (-ant) that depresses the **central nervous system,** causing reduction in **anxiety,** insomnia, and psychological stress. Depressants produce sedation in low doses; sleep in larger doses. Depressants (such as **Librium, Doriden,** and **Amytal**) are often used both pre-operatively and post-operatively to relieve apprehension and to relax the muscles. The barbituric depressants (Amytal, **Luminal, Nembutal,** and **Seconal**) may become habit-forming, and also require increased dosage for continued satisfaction. Withdrawal convulsions tend to be more fatal than those from **heroin** withdrawal. Symptoms from abuse are variable: some users may become sleepy, act like happy drunks, or become belligerent.

However, there may also be **ataxia,** memory loss, slurring of speech, delirium, respiratory depression, lowered body temperature, and coma. Excessive dosage may cause death, especially when taken with other **sedatives** (alcohol, **barbiturates,** etc.). *See* table of drugs, under **drugs,** for names of some of the more popularly used depressants.

depressive neurosis *See* **neurosis.**

depth interview (qualitative interview) A technique that developed from depth-psychology (or the **unconscious**), referring particularly to the **id** and **superego** in **psychoanalysis** and to the **collective unconscious of Jung.** In therapeutic relationships, such an interview is concerned with probing into the unconscious motivations of the patient. In its general sense, it has become a much used practice in **motivational research** as an unstructured, informal interview aimed at exploring the basic **needs,** desires, feelings, and **emotions** of a consumer toward products and services.

depth perception apparatus A device used to determine the subject's spatial relationships or **perception** of objects in terms of distance and angle away from the observer. *See* **Howard-Dohlman apparatus.**

depth psychology *See* **depth interview.**

dereistic thinking Relating to (-istic) a type of thinking, usually schizophrenic in nature, that is away from (de-) or ignores reality (-re-) and logical organization. Unrealistic thinking (including fantasy), thinking unchecked by reality-testing. *See* **autism.**

dermo-optical perception (DOP) Eyeless vision; skin vision. A supposed ability to "see" with one's fingers, toes, skin, etc. (Martin Gardner, "Dermo-Optical Perception: A Peek Down the Nose," *Science,* Feb. 1965, 654-657).

Descartes, René (1596-1650) French philosopher, mechanistic physiologist, mathematician and scientist. Attempted to make metaphysics a logical certainty by applying mathematical principles to its use. By his rigorous thinking he initiated the scientific tone of modern philosophy. His *De Homine* (1662) is considered the first European physiology text and was probably written even 25 years earlier. His **dualism** separated the mind from the body (which he considered to function like a machine). The **pineal body** held the rational soul, the soul interacting with the body (interactionism). His explanations followed the prevailing **iatrophysical** influences of using physical and mechanical laws to explain natural phenomena.

He developed what has become known as the **Cartesian coordinate system.** He was a pioneer (1649) in developing work on **reflex** action, saying that a "reflexion" of animal spirits were sent back to the **brain** through the nerves when a person sighted an approaching object. *See* **accommodation, ego, Hobbes;** (also Boring, 1953, pp. 160-165; Bell, 1952, pp. 35-55).

descending nerve tract *See* **nerve tract.**

descending reticular activating system (DRAS) That part of the **reticular activating system** (RAS) that relays impulses downward to the spinal cord, serving to increase muscle tone which in turn mobilizes the **brain** for arousal. *See* **brainstem, reticular formation.**

descriptive statistics A method of describing, summarizing, or condensing **data.** Examples of descriptive statistics are measures of **central tendency (mean, median,** and **mode)** and measures of **variability (range** and **standard deviation).**

desensitization Process (-tion) of desensitizing. A therapeutic process by which traumatic experiences are reduced in intensity through repeated exposures to them in reality or in fantasy. For example, in **psychotherapy,** retelling certain painful associations until they are no longer painful (1904). An aspect of **behavior therapy** (J. Wolpe, 1958) whereby the therapist appraises **anxieties** and fears, and

then systematically desensitizes (by **reciprocal inhibition**) the patient to his problems by applying **conditioning** concepts. *See* **behavior modification.**

desynchronization The process or act (-ation) of removing (de-) or changing certain simultaneous (-syn-) time (-chron-) factors, such as the shift from high-voltage slow activity to low-voltage fast activity seen on the **EEG** which accompanies the transition from sleep to wakefulness.

desynchronized sleep (DS) *See* **sleep stages.**

detection threshold The more modern term for absolute threshold; also known as differential or difference-limen, difference threshold, **just noticeable difference.** The point, value, or measurement of the intensity at which a stimulus becomes strong or effective enough to produce a response (in practice, the minimal amount of stimulation needed to make a receptor respond 50 percent of the time); the lowest intensity or minimal value of a physical stimulus that can be reliably detected under optimal conditions of experimentation. It also refers to the degree to which a stimulus must be varied (increased or decreased) in order to be discriminated from another **stimulus.** Experimentally, it has been determined under special conditions that the sense **modalities** have the following approximate detection threshold values: *hearing* (ability to hear the tick of a watch under quiet conditions at 20 feet); *smell* (ability to detect the odor of a drop of perfume diffused into the entire volume of a three-room apartment); *taste* (ability to detect a teaspoon of sugar stirred into 2 gallons of water); *touch* (ability to feel a bee wing falling on one's cheek from a distance of one centimeter); and *vision* (ability to see a candle flame from 30 miles on a dark clear night). (Morgan and King, p. 609).

determining tendency (set) A concept developed by **Ach** in which an act serves as a reinforcing agent in determining a person's association, if that person is given instructions or directions to select one of several choices. For example, if given a series of numbers (say 4, 5, 6, and 9) without any instruction a person may multiply or add the numbers; but if a direction is given to select the odd numbers, one's determining tendency is to eliminate the even numbers and concentrate on or associate with the odd numbers. Ach thought of determining tendency as originating in the task (*Aufgabe*) assigned to the person. Basically, a determining tendency, although a specific form of **Einstellung,** is a more persistent and lasting characteristic, tending toward solidifying personality patterns.

determinism A cosmological doctrine (-ism) of complete (de-) limits (-termini-), stating that all natural occurrences are determined by prior events or occur according to universal, natural laws. In an applied sense, with a complete knowledge of conditions given, it is possible to predict precisely how a person will—must—act. Also, a philosophical and psychological theory that the specific sequences of phenomena are the determining causes for later change in one's life or in the behavior of a group. Early determinism was opposed to free will.

Psychological determinism (empirical determinism) stresses the importance of biologically determined forces that dictate the direction of one's subjective life (ideas, fantasies, and so on). There is no action without a preceding cause.

Aristotle opposed *ethical determinism* (espoused by **Socrates** who believed that man automatically seeks out the good if he knows what is good), in saying that man's emotions were often in conflict with his reason. The fatalistic Stoics followed more closely the original determinism of the **atomism** of **Democritus** (who allowed only for mechanical causation) by believing that the world was controlled by a world intelligence and that one might as well submit willingly to the laws

d

of the universe; man behaved according to the dictates of a higher power.

Moral determinism developed from man's interest in the goodness of God (according to **Spinoza** and **Leibniz** the world was basically good because God made it so).

Physical determinism developed out of the progress of the physical sciences, emphasizing that all physical facts are absolutely dependent upon and conditioned by their causes. **Hobbes'** materialism emphasized that an act of will was all that was necessary for a resultant action. Sir **William Hamilton** called Hobbes' philosophy (so as to distinguish it from fatalism) determinism, and from this emerged psychological determinism that became the guiding force in **psychoanalysis** and all **dynamic psychology** (that is, that the will was not free but was caused by psychical or physical factors).

detour problem (*Umweg* problem) One of the "natural" problem-situations used by **Köhler** who placed an animal on one side of a short fence and food on the other side, the problem being for the animal to solve how to reach the goal (food). Chimps and dogs solved the problem readily but chickens could not reason that they could reach the food by running to the end of the fence and around to the goal, plunging into the fence repeatedly. Detour behavior is, therefore, that behavior (at first often random and indirect) eventually leading toward a goal after direct access has been blocked.

deuteranomaly An irregular (anomal-) condition (-y) involving the second (deuter-) primary color: green, a trichromatism in which there is a red-green **hue** weakness.

Term first used in the visual nomenclature of Polack.

deuteranope One who (-e-[r]) is not (an-) able to see (-op) the second (deuter-) primary color: green; a form of **dichromatism**. A deuteranope has no difficulty in making brightness discriminations, but lacks ability to distinguish red and green hues, confusing them with bluish and yellowish greys. Possibly due to insensitivity toward blue-green light.

developmental psychology A specialized area of **psychology** concerned with the psycho-biological life-span development of an organism, the evolution of mankind, and his place in nature.

developmental schedules A series of perceptual-motor growth progressions in the child, primarily dating from birth. A sampling of such a schedule follows:

Behavior	*Age in Months*
Lies on stomach, lifts head	1/2
Grasps ring	3/4
Sits with support	3-1/2
Turns from back to side	5
Sits alone	6
Walks alone	13, etc.

Numbers of researchers have produced developmental schedules, some of the better known being by **Arnold Gesell, Nancy Bayley**, and M. M. Shirley. Such schedules are of some value in comparing the individual child's progress with established norms, but they can often be alarming to those parents who fail to realize the considerable differences between normal individuals. *See* **motor development**; also Arnold Gessell and Frances L. Ilg, *Child Development: The Infant and Child in the Culture of Today*, 1949.

deviation The difference between an item of **data** and some measure of the series of data, usually in respect to the **arithmetic mean**; the interval between a point in a distribution (such as the arithmetic mean) and some other point, such as a particular score. The term d, or x', or y' represents the deviation of a score (in terms of **step intervals**, or d' for the midpoint of a class) from an **arbitrary origin**. The **variable** expressed as deviation from the $A.M. = x$ or y.

Dewey, John (1859-1952) American (Vermont) pragmatic philosopher, psychologist, and educator. Ph.D. (philosophy), Johns Hopkins 1884. Stimulated by **James'** *Principles of Psychology* toward **functional psychology**. In earlier years he was influenced by German philosopher **Hegel**. Dewey's article "The Reflex Arc Concept in Psychology," in 1896, departed sharply from the elementarism of contemporary psychology and became the definite starting point of functional psychology. He believed in purposive total coordination in behavior, pointing toward a dynamic approach, and emphasized learning through experimentation and practice. Dewey was essentially a humanist and philosopher of social change (Boring, 1952, pp. 552-554).

Dexedrine The Smith, Kline and French tradename for **dextroamphetamine sulphate**. Slang: dexies, copilots. *See* **amphetamine**.

dextral Pertaining to (-al) the right (dext-) side of the body; contrasted with **sinistral**. *See* **anatomical directions**.

dextr(o)- Located on the right (dextr-) side; toward the right. With chemical compounds dextro (dextrorotatory) refers to the property of certain solutions that twists the plane of polarized light toward the right.

dextroamphetamine sulphate (Dexedrine tradename) The isomer of **amphetamine** that rotates chemically toward the **right** (dextro-). A stimulant of the **CNS**, causing hyperexcitability; also serves as an antidepressant.

dextrosinistral axis (same as lateral axis) Pertaining to (-al) a line which extends from the right (dextro-) to the left (-sinistr-) side of the body. *See* **anatomical directions**.

d.f., D.F. (df, DF) *See* **degree of freedom**.

diagnostic test A test designed to discover, describe, and predict emotional or behavioral problems, based upon an **empirical** correspondence between the test items and the behavior (such as skills, etc.) that the test is to predict. A diagnostic test is often classified under **achievement tests**.

dialectical materialism The philosophy of Karl Marx and Friedrich Engels, holding that the ultimate reality is material and that the objective reality of matter is foremost in time and logic over that of mind. There is always a constant struggle of opposites, only temporary peace can exist. All sciences, including psychology, have had to function under this philosophy in Socialist countries. Dialectic generally refers to the critical examination of principles so as to ascertain their meaning and implications; the art of reasoning and argumentation.

Dialectic, according to **Aristotle**, began with Zeno of Elea (c. 490-430 B.C.) who argued against the atomistic idea that motion was able to explain all phenomena. **Socrates** used dialectics in his Platonic dialogs (dispensing with hypothesis and thus getting, for him, at true knowledge). **Kant** considered dialectic as dealing critically with phenomena in space and time, while **Hegel** described it as being the prime aspect of speculative thought. Marx and Engels developed dialectical materialism to refer to matter (including space and time) that is prior to and therefore more important than mind, and to their dialectics that referred to the universality of change, thereby denying most of metaphysical and mechanistic theories. Everything must be examined in terms of their histories and changes that are going on, thus rejecting *a priori* thinking and theory without practice and practice without theory. In general, social institutions must be reconstructed so that a classless society can assure "productive employment" and security for all.

diazepam derivatives *See* **drug interactions**.

dibit Any pair (di-) of **bit** or binary signals (00, 01, 10, etc.), understood to be part of a more complex signal. Derived by analogy from digraph (any pair of written characters extracted from a sequence of characters).

dichromatism Two (di-) color (-chromat-) condition (-ism). The most common variety of partial **color blindness** in which color perception is limited to two **hues**, there being an inability to distinguish between either red and green or blue and yellow. All hues may be matched by a mixture of two hues, with so-called dichromats seeing all hues as shades of but two hues.

There are three groups of dichromats: **protanopes, deuteranopes**, and **tritanopes**.

diencephalon The between (di-) brain (-encephalon) or cerebral vesicle, located between the **cerebral hemispheres** and the **mesencephalon** A subdivision of the **prosencephalon** that includes the **thalamus** and the **hypothalamus** with various substructures—the pineal **gland**, the **pituitary gland**, and the **optic chiasma**—serving different functions. *See* **ergotropic activity, epithalamus**.

diestrus *See* **estrus**.

difference between means The application of **inferential statistics** to differences between means of **samples** representing two **populations**. It is used for making comparisons of two or more samples so as to ascertain the likelihood of the samples being drawn from the same population. In making an inference from an obtained sample difference, the best estimate an experimenter can make is that the true difference between population means are as different as the sample means. Large sample distributions of differences between sample means can be determined by the **standard error of estimate**.

The application of the t distribution to small sample differences, involving a difference between means, requires making two assumptions: (1) the populations must have a normal distribution, and (2) the population variances are homogeneous.

difference limen *See* **detection threshold, limen**.

difference threshold *See* **detection threshold**.

differential diagnosis Determining and considering all possible **dynamic** factors in evaluating a person so that he might be compared to and differentiated from some standard or reference.

differential high rate conditioning (drh) *See* **rate conditioning**.

differential low rate conditioning (drl) *See* **rate conditioning**.

differential reinforcement Reinforcing one stimulus while extinguishing another stimulus or at least not reinforcing it. Such reinforcement depends upon the presence of (1) a unique characteristic of a stimulus that enables the organism to discriminate and respond more rapidly (the **operant** discrimination process), (2) a unique property of a **response** that causes a change in the relative frequency of responses that have the special property (the differentiation process), and (3) a given rate of responding. *See* **discrimination learning, rate conditioning, reinforcement**.

differentiation The developmental modification of the body which progresses from making random, generalized, gross movements to those less diffuse, more specific, and more purposeful. Also, a social process in which a culture becomes more complex, more specific, and more specialized in its functions (such as the development of various religious sects and political subgroups from larger, more generalized groups). In **Lewin's** social psychology, differentiation refers to the "depth and richness of experience," meaning the application of intelligence to one's learning experiences, which invariably leads to better personality development. *De-differentiation* takes place when the disparate parts return to a condition of balance and homogeneity. *See* **differential reinforcement**. (Kurt Lewin, *A Dynamic Theory of Personality*, 1935).

diffuse thalamic projection system (DTPS) A thalamic extension of the **reticular formation** that "projects" to the **cortex**, and is active in **arousal** functions.

d

digital computer A computer that performs mathematical and logical operations with information in digital form, such as with discrete numbers (5, 27, −3, etc.) as contrasted with the **analog computer** that operates by generating a continuous non-numerical analog of the problem being computed.

digital input data Information supplied to a machine-control in the form of digits, quantized pulses, or some other coding elements. These **data** can take on only discrete values.

digitizer (quantizer) A device that converts an analog input of a physical **variable** into discrete output signals (such as having a number expressed in digits).

digraph A written (-graph) pair (di-) of characters. *See* **dibit.**

Dilantin A synthetic drug (sodium diphenyl-hydantoin) isolated from **phenobarbital** that has been found useful in conjunction with other drugs (such as phenobarbital) as a corrective for **epilepsy**, particularly **grand mal** seizures.

It was discovered (1936) by two American neurologists, Tracy J. Putnam (born 1894) and Hiram H. Merritt (born 1902).

diode A device for sending electrical current flow into two (di-) paths (-ode), one path facilitating the current to flow through it in one direction while inhibiting its flow in the other direction. In **computers,** diodes are usually made of germanium or silicon crystal.

diplacusis Double (dipla-) hearing (-cu-) action (-sis). A phenomenon in which apparent pitch is perceived differently in each ear when exactly the same frequency (tone) is presented simultaneously to both ears.

diplegia Disorder (-ia) of paralysis (-pleg-) on both (di-) sides of the body, such as both legs.

Diplom The German student's official degree and title given in conjunction with licensing (to practice psychology, for example). *See* **German higher education.**

diplopia A double (dipl-) vision (-op-) disorder (-ia) or derangement of the visual axes causing the image of objects to fall upon noncorresponding portions of each retina, resulting in one object being seen as two. It may be caused by hereditary paralysis of eye muscles, or by accident, disease, or poison.

direct-access data Information stored in a direct-access device (see **input-output devices**) that can be found directly and read into the **computer** without sequential searching. Preceding data need not be read in sequence.

direct cortical response A response activated by direct electrical stimulation of cortical nerve tissue.

directive counseling A therapeutic approach in which the counselor or therapist plays a dominant role, supplying direct answers to problems and assuming most of the responsibility for the progress of therapy. *See* **counseling.**

directrex *See* **parabola.**

discrete data (variable) Separate, distinct, discontinuous material (such as individual people, tools, and horses) that assumes only a finite set of values which can be divided into equal parts without fractions. A *discrete variable* is one of two kinds of variables (the other being a **continuous variable**).

discriminant function A multivariate technique for evaluating degree of similarity of different populations. It is useful for purposes of classification and diagnosis. *See* **multivariate analysis.**

discrimination learning Learning evidenced by the ability to make perceptual distinctions and to choose between two or more stimuli or between stimulus and no stimulus, such choice being dependent upon previous **differential reinforcement.**

discriminatory (or discriminative) stimulus A stimulus that calls for an **operant** response, e.g., the ringing of the bell that conditions a person to answer the telephone.

diseases of adaptation *See* **general adaptation syndrome.**

disinhibition Process (-tion) of opposing (dis-) inhibition. Inhibition (external) of an inhibition (internal); the temporary restorative effect (or reappearance) of an extinguished response occurring when a new stimulus accompanies the **conditioned stimulus** (CS). For example, one may learn to extinguish the fear of darkness, but a strong emotional reaction or shock may temporarily disinhibit the organism so that it will show the same response (fear of darkness) that was thought to have been forgotten, indicating that a habit is never really forgotten.

In Pavlovian theory, disinhibition involves augmentation of a partially suppressed **conditioned response** (CR) or the return of a CR that has been extinguished. **Pavlov** considered experimental **extinction** to be an inhibition of the response, with the extraneous stimulus operating as an inhibition of the inhibition.

Disinhibition also refers to the condition in which the Pavlovian dog responds indiscriminately to any stimulus, all conditioned inhibitions having been lost. There is often, during the experimental **extinction** process, a temporary reappearance of an inhibited conditioned response resulting from an extraneous stimulus. *See* **displacement.**

Herbart used the concept of disinhibition in 1823 and the Scottish physician Sir Thomas Brunton (1844-1916), recognized (1814) disinhibition as the basis of many "released" responses (I. P. Pavlov, *Experimental Psychology and Other Essays*, 1957).

disjunction The act of (-ion) disjoining or separating (disjunct-). In genetics, the normal separation of both chromosomes during the reduction division in meiosis. In **Boolean** algebra, the logical operation requiring the presence of one or more **variables** so as to show their relationship (the OR function).

disparity Same as **binocular disparity.**

dispersion measure Information about the spread or **variability** of observations throughout the **distribution**. Scores that cluster closely around a measure of **central tendency**, for example, represent a low degree of dispersion; widely scattered scores indicate a high degree of dispersion. Measures of dispersion most widely used are **range** and the **standard deviation.** Same as **variability.**

displacement Act (-ment) of placing or taking (-place-) out (dis-). The process of associating with an inappropriate object the feelings proper to another object. Discharging usually hostile feelings onto less threatening objects than those originally involved. The Freudian term for a thwarted or repressed impulse that receives temporary satisfaction through an alternative outlet. Hence, a **defense mechanism** involving transfer of an emotional attitude, feeling, or symbol from one attachment to a psychologically more available and specific substitute. For example, an executive who holds unexpressed anger toward his wife may displace his hostility onto his subordinates in the office.

In some **learning theories,** displacement is related to **disinhibition.** Punishment not only develops a tendency for the individual not to respond to the original **stimulus** but also leads him to generalize his **responses** and, more likely, respond to (or displace his actions to) a different stimulus. Thus, a child punished at home not only tends to stop performing his unwanted behavior but also becomes predisposed to generalize and displace his bad behavior with good behavior in places other than home.

display Any device that converts (transduces) **data** not readily assimilated by the human being into a format that a person can easily and rapidly understand. Displays may be *pictorial* (a map or chart), *symbolic* (dials, lights, etc.), *audio* (buzzers, bells, etc.), or *tactile* (vibrators, "tinglers," etc.). Displays often combine a variety of these forms to prevent *sensory overloading* (or reliance upon one sense).

dissimilation *See* **color vision theories:** *Hering theory.*

dissociation A splitting up or severing of ideas or desires from their appropriate emotion (such as compartmentalizing ideas from feelings and emotions to achieve objective decision-making).

Concept of dissociation was developed (1906) by American psychiatrist Morton Prince (1854-1929), who described dissociation in terms of multiple personalities.

dissociative reactions A neurosis involving disturbances of consciousness and memory (such as **amnesia, fugue** states, somnambulism, and multiple personality). Conflicts are sometimes temporarily avoided by the person becoming amnesic and escaping from familiar scenes. *See* **hysterical neurosis** under **neurosis.**

distal Referring to (-al) something distant (dist-), or away from the center, such as an anatomical region or area. A distal **stimulus,** for example, is outside the body, an environmental event; the fingers are distal to the elbow. A *distal response* refers to the organism itself changing the environmental situation. *See* **anatomical directions.**

distance cues In *vision,* distance cues consist of both the **monocular cues** (such as superposition of objects, perspective, light and shadow, and relative movement) by which the distance of objects is perceived, and the **binocular cues** used in stereoscopic vision; in *audition*, the corresponding cues (such as intensity and time differences of sound reaching the two ears) governing perception of distance and direction.

Distinguished Contributions to Education in Psychology Awards In 1970, the American Psychological Foundation gave its first awards for distinguished contributions in education in psychology. The award recognizes individuals who have made "unusual contributions to instruction in psychology either through their own teaching or through other instructional functions, such as the development of new courses or execution of creative work in evaluation of research in the teaching of psychology." The first (1970) recipients of this award were the American psychologists: Fred S. Keller (born 1899), Ph.D., Harvard U., 1931, and Freda G. Rebelsky (born 1931), Ph.D., Harvard U.-Radcliffe College, 1961. The awards were granted in 1971 to American psychologists Theophile S. Krawiec (born 1913), Ph.D., N.Y.U., 1945, and Jack Michael (born 1926), Ph.D., U.C.L.A., 1955. *See* **American Psychologist,** January issues for 1971 and 1972.

Distinguished Contribution to the Science and Profession of Clinical Psychology Award, consisting of a scroll and $100 awarded annually to one of the members of the Division of Clinical Psychology (12). *See* **awards of the APA.**

Distinguished Scientific Contribution Award of APA. At the **APA** meeting in San Francisco, 1955, it was decided to "establish a continuing program to honor those of its members whose scientific contributions are regarded as outstanding." Each year, starting in 1956, three psychologists have been selected to receive a Distinguished Scientific Contribution Award. The award consists of a scroll inscribed with a citation describing the contribution for which the $1,000 award is made, and an invitation to deliver a lecture on APA Day the following year.

The recipients of the Award and year granted are listed here with parenthetical reference made to the issue of the *American Psychologist* that includes brief biographical sketches of these psychologists.

1956 (Mar., 1957)
Wolfgang Köhler
Carl R. Rogers
Kenneth W. Spence

1957 (Apr., 1958)
Carl I. Hovland
Curt P. Richter
Edward C. Tolman

1958 (Dec., 1958)
Frank A. Beach
Paul E. Meehl
B. F. Skinner

1959 (Dec., 1959)
Leon Festinger
Donald B. Lindsley
Neal E. Miller

1960 (Dec., 1960)
Harry F. Harlow
Charles E. Osgood
S. Smith Stevens

1961 (Dec., 1961)
James J. Gibson
Donald O. Hebb
Henry A. Murray

1962 (Dec., 1962)
Jerome S. Bruner
William K. Estes
Harry Helson

1963 (Dec., 1963)
Roger G. Barker
George A. Miller
Carl Pfaffmann

1964 (Dec., 1964)
Gordon W. Allport
Wendell R. Garner
J. P. Guilford

1965 (Dec., 1965)
Floyd H. Allport
Fritz Heider
Paul Thomas Young

1966 (Dec., 1966)
Nancy Bayley
Clarence H. Graham
Richard L. Solomon

1967 (Dec., 1967)
Solomon E. Asch
Ernest R. Hilgard
James Olds

1968 (Dec., 1968)
James E. Birren
Eleanor J. Gibson
Muzafer Sherif

1969 (Jan., 1970)
Jean Piaget
Stanley Schachter
Herbert Alexander Simon

1970 (Jan., 1971)
Donald T. Campbell
David Krech
R. Duncan Luce

1971 (Jan., 1972)
Roger William Brown
Harold H. Kelley
Roger Wolcott Sperry

distortion room A life-sized model of a bare room so constructed that an observer, peering into a peephole with one eye, sees size distortions of figures; for example, two men known to be six feet tall appear disproportionate in size when viewed standing in the room, one seeming unusually larger than the other. The three dimensional **illusion** is caused by means of misleading monocular depth cues and the absence of binocular and other depth cues (objects in room); the room and windows are assumed to be rectangular in shape, windows appear to be equally distant, and the slanted floor seems level. The retinal images created by the distortions give the illusion that instead of a person's head actually appearing closer it is perceived as larger. *See* **Honi phenomenon, Ames' distortion room.**

distributed practice A type of practice in learning in which the subject has relatively frequent rest periods so that the practice is spread out. Distinguished from **massed practice,** which goes on for longer periods, uninterrupted. Both methods have been the subject of innumerable studies. Distributed practice is often more effective, especially in learning motor skills.

distribution Any set of **data** that is presented according to its magnitude in a systematic or tabular summary form, as in a **frequency distribution.**

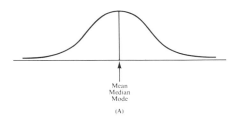

Mean
Median
Mode

(A)

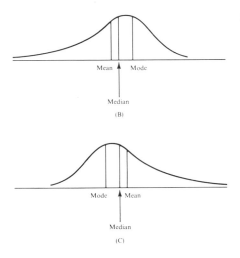

Mean | Mode

Median

(B)

Mode | Mean

Median

(C)

Three distributions: (A) normal, (B) negatively skewed, and (C) positively skewed.

distribution curve The graphic representation of a **frequency distribution.** Although the original **data** were continuous the curve is discontinuous since it consists of a series of connected straight lines rather than a smooth curving line.

distribution-free test A statistical test that makes no assumptions regarding the form of the underlying distribution. *Same as* nonparametric statistics.

distribution frequency *See* **frequency distribution.**

divisions of psychology *See* listing of divisions in current APA directory, **awards of the APA** for divisional recognition of its members.

dizygotic twins Referring to (-ic) twins who develop from two (di-) **zygotes.** Fraternal twins, developing from two separate but simultaneously fertilized eggs. *Compare* **identical twins.**

DL Difference limen.

DNA Deoxyribonucleic acid.

doctorat de specialité The third cycle doctorate conferred on a French student upon satisfactorily serving two years in school after obtaining his license and having submitted an acceptable thesis.

doctor d' état The state doctorate in the arts and sciences, obtainable in French universities after a minimum of five years research following granting of the *license* and defense of an original dissertation. The degree provides access to university teaching and research.

dolichocephalic Relating to (-ic) a long (dolicho-) head (-cephal-). *See* **cephalic index.**

Dolophine Lilly tradename for **methadone.**

dominant gene A **gene,** such as the one for brown eyes, that always appears as a **phenotype** and prevails over a recessive gene, such as the one for blue eyes.

dominant wavelength Wavelength of the spectral band that when mixed with some aribtrary choice of achromatic **color** produces a match for the chromatic color, or yields a hue compatible with any given hue.

dominator-modulator theory *See* **color vision theories.**

Donders, Franciscus Cornelius (1818-1889) Dutch ophthalmologist and physiologist. Known to psychologists for his work in the 1860's on reaction time. He measured not only "simple" reaction time, or direct response to a stimulus, but also the reaction times involved in choice and discrimination. Anticipated (1881) **Ladd-Franklin's** basic assumption that color vision is caused by decomposition of a color molecule. *See* **ametropia, color-vision theories, hypermetropia.**

Doolittle method A rapid and systematic tabular arrangement for solving the unknowns in a first-degree equation (normal). The Doolittle method (with operations similar to conventional methods of algebraic substitution) proceeds in cyclic fashion with the so-called *forward solution* successively eliminating one unknown after another until a value is found for one of the unknowns. The *back solution* takes the value of those unknowns already found and substitutes them in equations to obtain values of the remaining unknowns.

This method was first published (1878) by M. H. Doolittle, geometer of the U. S. Coast and Geodetic Survey. A modification of a similar system earlier used by **Gauss,** it is simpler and more practical, particularly when three or more equations are to be solved simultaneously. It is especially useful in multiple correlational studies and in curve fitting. **Fisher's** modification is an often used variation of this technique. (*See* P. S. Dwyer, "Recent Developments in Correlation Technique," *Journal of the American Statistical Association,* No. 218, 1942, **37,** 441-460, for advantages and disadvantages of the many techniques).

dopa (acronym for *d*ihydroxyphenylalanine). A catechol biogenic amine precursor for **dopamine** and **noradrenalin** that can cross the **blood-brain barrier,** whereas dopamine cannot. It is released at certain sites in the **central nervous system** as an intermediate product in the oxidation of **tyrosine.** Dopa apparently plays a critical role in **Parkinson's disease,** since it is absent or decreased in the **basal ganglia** in such cases. It is also a direct precursor of the natural **adrenergic** transmitter **levarterenol.** There are also some astounding reports of its aphrodisiacal effects.

dopamine The product of the decarboxylation (removal of CO_2) of **dopa,** an intermediate product in synthesis of **norepinephrine,** dopamine itself being formed from **tyrosine.**

Dopamine has been used successfully for increasing cardiac output and in treating **Parkinson's disease** and depression. There are some questions about its use, however, since with **L-dopa,** long-range toxicity may sometimes result, and there are reports of mental depression with increased tendency toward suicide.

dopaminergic pathways *See* **amine pathways.**

Doppler effect (or principle) The apparent change (increase or decrease) of frequency of sound or light waves, varying with the relative velocity of the source as it approaches or recedes from the observer. If the source and the observer are approaching one another, the wave frequencies are increased rapidly so that there is noticed for light waves a change in hue, for sound waves a change in pitch.

After Christian Doppler (1803-1853), Austrian mathematician and physicist.

Doriden The Ciba tradename for **glutethimide.** Slang: dori.

dorsal Pertaining to (-al) the back (dors-) of an animal; in man, the middle of the back, below the neck. Opposed to **ventral.** *See* **anatomical directions.**

dorsal column system An older term for the **lemniscal system.**

dorsomedial nucleus Relating to (-al) the nucleus located toward the back (dorso-) and in the median (-medi-) plane. An important association nucleus of the **thalamus** that projects to the frontal **cortex** and not to any specific **sensory** region. It is associated with **anxiety** and fear, and when the area is stimulated the animal drops into a fear-crouching response.

dorsoventral Pertaining to (-al) a straight line from the back (dorso-) to the belly (-ventr-) in man; sagittal direction or anterior-posterior axis. *See* **anatomical directions.**

double alternation method (D.A. test) A type of animal experiment (considered as a test of symbolic **intelligence**) in which the sub...

required to make a sequence of turns, such as right, right, left, left, right, right, left, left, etc. Credit is not given for solving the problem if the subject responds only to the cue from the last turn. *See* **delayed-reaction method.**

double aspect theory A doctrine (espoused by **Spinoza** in his posthumous *Ethica*, 1677) that describes the material (body) and the mental (mind) as contrasting aspects of one universal, ultimate "substance." Body and mind are double aspects of God. According to Klein (p. 233) the double aspect theory and **psychophysical parallelism** should not be confused. Double aspect implies a "fundamental identity between neural events and conscious events while psychophysical parallelism assumes nothing about a causal relationship between conscious events and concomitant brain events—neither affirming nor denying identity of mind and body."

double bind hypothesis A situational "trap" in which an individual ("the victim") finds himself "damned if he does and damned if he doesn't"; receiving equal disapproval for doing something or not doing it. Panic, rage, conflict, and sometimes schizoid behavior (particularly in **schizophrenogenic** children) may result from the double bind situation caused by inconsistent and contradictory remarks made by one person to another; usually the conflict arises from the incongruities that exist between verbal and nonverbal communication. For example, one may well understand the resulting conflict in a husband when he hears his wife say, "You know, darling, I love you very much" as she turns her head away as he tries to kiss her.

The term and concept was advanced by Gregory Bateson, Don Jackson, Jay Haley, and J. Weakland, Toward a Theory of Schizophrenia. *Behavioral Science*, 1956, 1:251-264.

double blind An experimental design, often used in drug research, in which neither the administrator of the drug nor the patient(s) knows which subjects are in the treatment (the **experimental group**) and which in the nontreatment condition (the **control group**) until the experiment has been completed.

double helix The formal arrangements of **DNA** chemical components. *See* **cytosine.**

double punch (Comput.) The punching of more than one numeric punch in any one column of a Hollerith card. *See* **Hollerith code.**

double subscripts More than one subscript (a figure, letter, or other symbol written underneath and to the right of a value to indicate its attachment or relation to some other value). Double or multiple subscripts classify an observation on two variables simultaneously. For example, the symbol $X_{1\,2}$ is read as "X one-two" or "X sub-one-two."

Down's disease or syndrome (mongolism) A child's disorder characterized by flattened skull and slanted eyes (which led to the name of mongolism or mongolian idiocy), plus rubbery limbs and small genitals. Frequently, such children are the last born in large families (six or more children). They are generally institutionalized but are amenable to training and are agreeable and cooperative.

Down's disease is a congenital genetic defect whose cause is not thoroughly understood, but the evidence does seem quite conclusive that an extra chromosome (a so-called **trisome**) produces a "mongoloid" child. This trisome has been labeled number 21 (according to the Denver System of classifying hormones), and is supposedly caused by a genetic process, called **nondisjunction** (when chromosome 21 fails to divide properly), resulting in 47 chromosomes in the **diploid** process (having twice the number of chromosomes present in typical gametes) rather than the normal 46 (23 from each parent). In addition to nondisjunction there is another type of chromosomal abnormality known as **translocation,** in which the right number (46) of chromosomes is present but the genetic

material of one of them is broken off and translocated elsewhere, causing excess genes and again resulting in Down's syndrome.

After John Haydon Langdon Down (1828-1896), English physician.

Dozent University teacher or lecturer. One of the steps in the German scholar's education coming after the **Wissenschaftlicher Assistent** and provided his **Habilitationsschrift** has been accepted. When the *Dozent* receives his "**Ruf**" or call from another university he becomes a recognized professor. *See* **German higher education.**

DRAS *See* **descending reticular activating system.**

dread (Exist.) Terror or apprehensive feeling about facing the future. To dread something encompasses feelings of uselessness, estrangement, blame, powerlessness, and general frustration.

According to **Heidegger,** "dread differs absolutely from fear." Fear is usually specific in nature, whereas dread is concerned with something vague. "The indefiniteness of what we dread is not just lack of definition; it represents the essential impossibility of defining the 'what.' Dread reveals Nothing."

dream analysis (Psychoanal.) The interpretation of dreams as a means of gaining access to the unconscious, usually utilizing **free association** by the patient. *See* **psychoanalysis, Traumdeutung.**

dream content (Psychoanal.) The makeup of a dream, comprising the **manifest content** (recalled images and events of a dream) and the latent content (the symbolic or indirectly expressed meaning of a dream, emerging from repressed wishes).

Dr. habil. The second doctorate (level) degree in Germany, equivalent to the French **doctor d'état** and the Russian federal doctorate. *See* **German higher education.**

DRH schedule Differential reinforcement of high rates. *See* **rate conditioning.**

drinkometer A laboratory device that provides a signal for recording or measuring (-meter) an animal's physical contact with various aspects of the experimental environment (such as his rate of ingestion of food, the occurrence of licking the fluid in a liquid dispenser, etc.).

drive The motive power behind behavior; an **arousal** state of the organism. Drives may be *acquired* or *learned* (fear, approval, aggression, etc.) depending upon individual experiences, or they may be *innate* or *unlearned* (sexual drives, thirst, hunger, etc.) that impel the organism to make responses to satisfy or relieve these physiological deprivations. Anxiety-arousing stimuli (fear, aggression, approval, etc.) also augment drive in addition to tissue needs. A *primary drive* (e.g., pain) is one in which the organism is aroused to action without any special training or experience. A *secondary drive* (fear, avoidance), arises from the arousal of the organism to action because of prior association with some **aversive** situation. Generally, drives are only a part of the total motivational system of man (or an organism). *See* **motive.**

drive-reduction theory A behavioristic concept evolving out of food-deprivation studies and indicating that behavior exists because its very action leads to a satisfying reduction of some drive condition, whose reduction makes possible learning and/or performance. Drive reduction considers the basic source of an organism's energy to be an undifferentiated drive (similar to **libido**), which is eventually directed by tissue needs toward a goal. Generally, learned drives depend upon responses that create strong stimuli. A so-called primary drive must precede a secondary drive before such response can be acquired.

The theory of drive-reduction is one of the keynotes of **Hull's** concept of **reinforcement** in learning. Although "Skinnerians" accept the goal-directedness of behavior they consider its consistent direction to be merely an

assumed rewarding condition. *See* C. L. Hull, *Principles of Behavior: An Introduction to Behavior Theory*, 1943.

DRL schedule Differential reinforcement of low rates. *See* **rate conditioning.**

Dr. phil., *doctor philosophiae* (Ph.D.)

Dr. rer. nat., *doctor rerum naturalium* (Dr. Sc. or Sc. D.) *See* **German higher education.**

drug addiction, drug dependence, and drug habituation *Drug addiction*, according to a committee of the World Health Organization is a ". . . state of periodic or chronic intoxication, detrimental to the individual and to society, produced by the repeated consumption of a drug (natural or synthetic)." Other characteristics of drug addiction are a driving compulsion to obtain the drug at any cost, an increasing usage and dosage of the drug, and a psychological and/or physical dependence upon the effects of the drug.

Drug dependence is often used medically to refer to psychiatric patients addicted to or dependent on drugs other than alcohol, tobacco, ordinary caffeine-containing beverages or medically indicated drugs. Diagnosis requires evidence of habitual use or craving need for the drug in question (opiates, **barbiturates, hallucinogens,** etc.). Withdrawal symptoms are always present when opium derivatives are withdrawn but they may be and usually are absent upon **marijuana** or **cocaine** withdrawal.

Drug habituation is distinguished from drug addiction in that habituation is habit-forming but non-addictive (such as the habitual use of caffeine in coffee, tea, and Coca Cola and that of nicotine in cigarettes). One habituated to a drug has a desire (but no compulsion) to continue taking the drug for its obvious effects. There is little or no tendency to increase the dosage, nor is there any physical dependence upon the drug's effects. Detrimental effects, if any, are on the individual only.

For further information concerning drug use and abuse, contact one or all of the following agencies:

American Pharmaceutical Association, 2215 Constitution Avenue, N. W., Washington, D. C. 20037; *American Social Health Association, Inc.*, 1740 Broadway, New York, N. Y. 10019; *Bureau of Medicine, Food & Drug Administration*, Washington, D. C. 20204; and *Pharmaceutical Manufacturers' Association*, Public Information Office, 1155 15th Street N. W., Washington, D. C. 20005.

drug interactions Many people unknowingly or unthinkingly take two or more drugs, each alone safely having its intended effect, but in combination producing unwanted results and perhaps death. The following table gives a brief listing of the effects produced by combining some of the more common drugs.

1. Effect of each drug is increased by the following combinations:
    a. Tranquilizers and diazepam derivatives (Librium, Valium, Serax, etc.)
    b. Meprobamates (Miltown, etc.) and alcohol
    c. Tricyclic antidepressants (Tofranil, etc.) combined with phenothiazine tranquilizers (Compazine, Thorazine, etc.), or with **barbiturates,** or with MAO (**monoamine oxidase**) inhibitors (Marplan, Nardel, Parnate, Eutonyl, etc.), or with diazepam derivatives.
2. Sedation increased by combining phenothiazine derivatives with alcohol or with **Demerol** or with barbiturates.
3. Antidepressant action increased by combining phenothiazine derivatives and MAO-inhibiting antidepressants.
4. Effect of barbiturates, **amphetamines,** diazepam tranquilizers are increased when combined with MAO-inhibitors.

5. Alcohol not only depresses the central nervous system but also has the additional effects mentioned when combined with the following drugs:
   a. Antidepressants (increases alcoholic effect)
   b. Tranquilizers (affects coordination perceptibly)
   c. Sedatives and hypnotics (causes over-sedation)
   d. Antihistamines (causes sleepiness and dazed condition)
   e. MAO inhibitors (causes confusion, sleepiness)

drugs For definitions and general conditions occurring with use of **stimulants, depressants, hallucinogens,** and **narcotics,** see the respective terms in the dictionary section of this handbook. The following drugs are listed according to popular or tradename.

Stimulants	*Hallucinogens*
1. **Benzedrine**	1. **Hashish**
2. **Dexedrine**	2. **Lysergic acid**
3. **Methedrine**	**diethylamide**
4. **Cocaine**	3. **Marijuana**
5. **LSD**	4. **Mescaline**
See **hallucinogens.**	5. **Peyote**
	6. **Psilocybin**
Depressants	
1. **Amytal**	*Narcotics*
2. **Luminal**	1. **Pantopon**
3. **Nembutal**	2. **Morphine**
4. **Seconal**	3. **Heroin**
5. **Librium**	4. **Laudanum**
6. **Doriden**	5. **Codeine**
7. **Miltown**	6. **Paregoric**
8. **Equanil**	7. **Percodan**
	8. **Demerol**
	9. **Dolophine**

DSC Award *See* **Distinguished Scientific Contribution Award** of APA.

DTPS Diffuse thalamic projection system.

dualism The theory or doctrine (-ism) that divides a given realm of phenomena into two (dual-) mutually irreducible elements, as in (1) the viewpoint in philosophy, psychology, medicine, that mind and body are two separate entities, but are able to interact upon one another (the term psychosomatic retains the dualistic approach), and (2) the belief that events in the world consist of two radically opposed and absolute elements (e.g., good and evil). The dividing of reality into mind (spirit) and matter is called *metaphysical* or *ontological dualism* while *epistemological dualism* refers to a distinction between the real object (the experiencing of a sensation) and the image (the idea of the object).

Dualism is traceable to pre-Aristotelian times such as the dualistic religion of the Persians (during the middle of the second millennium) who worshipped Ormuzd, the god of goodness and light who created the world, and also to ancient Chinese philosophy and religion in which two principles ruled the world: the **Yin** (being negative, dark and feminine) and the **Yang** (positive, bright and masculine). However, **Aristotle** integrated some of the concepts of religious and philosophical dualism along with that approaching a "scientific" dualism by declaring that the soul is free. Aristotle could not dispose of **Plato's** concept of being and nonbeing, of form and matter, thus following in his footsteps, as did **Descartes** who believed in the dualistic free soul and a completely determined human body. **Kant** reemphasized Descartes' view in founding German idealism (his noumenal vs. the phenomenal). In the 17th century advances toward science, philosophy was dualistic in emphasizing on one hand the deductive-mathematical approach (as espoused by Descartes, **Hobbes,** and **Spinoza**) and the inductive-empirical method (followed by **Locke** and **Francis Bacon**). **Leibniz** and his **psychophysical parallelism** (of the actual and possible worlds) was another form of dualism. *See* **double aspect theory.**

Dualism has been consistently associated with religion, the term first appearing in English (1700) in that context in a religious history book by Thomas Hyde, and later used in the same sense (good vs. evil) by Leibniz in *Théodicée* (1710). In its psychophysical sense, however, **Christian Wolff** was responsible for such an emphasis. Contrasted with **monism.**

Du Bois-Reymond, Emil (1818-1896) A German-born physician (M.D. Berlin) born of Swiss-French extraction. He devoted his life to the field of electro-physiology (which he created), probably being the main influence in making the break from the ancient concepts of nerve function. Coined term **electrotonus** in 1843. *See* **action potential.**

duct gland (exocrine gland) A gland that secretes its product through ducts onto the surface of the body (tear gland) or into the body cavities (salivary gland) but not directly into the bloodstream.

ductless gland (endocrine gland) A gland (**thyroid, pituitary, adrenals,** etc.) concerned with energy **metabolism** that secretes its chemical substances directly into the blood, lymph, or other body fluids.

Duncan new multiple range test A multilple comparison test for carrying out all pairwise comparisons among **means.** *See* Table 23 for additional information.

David Beattie Duncan. Australian born (1916), naturalized American 1948. Ph.D., mathematical statistics, Iowa State College 1947. Major research in biostatistics, and development of linear theory and methods, time series analyses, and multiple comparisons.

Dunlap chronoscope (Johns Hopkins chronoscope) A time measuring instrument using a clockwork system to stop when each time interval has been measured.

Named after Knight Dunlap (1875-1949), American (California) psychologist, while he was professor at Johns Hopkins (1906-1936). Received Ph.D., Harvard, 1903. Studied primarily psychophysics, psychobiology, visual perception, and learning (specifically on the making and unmaking of habits). APA President 1922. *See* **negative practice.**

Dunn multiple comparison test Also called Bonferroni *t* test. A versatile test for performing *a priori* comparisons among **means.** The test is based on **Student's** *t* distribution. It splits up the level of significance (α) among a set of planned comparisons. Its assumptions are identical to those for a *t* statistic. (*See* Table 22.)

Olive Jean Dunn. (Born Canada 1915) Ph.D., mathematics, U.C.L.A. Major field of interests: confidence interval estimation, statistics.

Dunnett's multiple comparison test A test designed for making comparisons among *k*–1 treatment level means and a control **mean.** Also called Dunnett's *t* statistic. For *k*=2, the sampling distribution of Dunnett's and Student's test statistics are identical. For *k*>2 the critical values for Dunnett's test are larger than those for the *t* test. (*See* Table 24.)

Charles William Dunnett. (Born Canada 1921). D.Sc., Aberdeen 1960; Columbia (mathematics). Major fields of interest: biometrics, statistics applied to biological and physical sciences, statistical methodology.

duplicity (duplex) theory *See* **color vision theories.**

dura mater Hard (dura) mother (mater). A tough, fibrous membrane forming the outer covering (**meninges**) of the brain and spinal cord.

"Mother" was often used by the Arabs in naming vital or intimate parts of the body. Since the Arabs apparently had exposed the meninges earlier than the Greeks, they had names for two of the layers (the arachnoid membrane was not recognized at the time): the "thick mother" and the "thin mother," since they believed that the meninges were the origin or "mother" of all membranes. The

anatomy text of the 10th century by Hali (Haly ben) Abbas (936-994) had described and referred to the meninges as "mother." When translated into Latin in 1127 A.D. by Stephen of Antioch, a twelfth-century monk, the thick harder membrane became "dura mater" and the soft, thinner one, "pia mater."

dwarfism *See* **pituitary gland.**

dyad Pertaining to (-ad) two (di- or dy-) individuals in a sociopsychological relationship, who may be engaged in a **sensitivity** experience or confrontation. Pairs (dyads) may work together on a special project (sexual or otherwise), designed, by exposure or disclosure, to reveal dynamics of a person-to-person relationship. A *dyadic unit* describes the interaction of two or more persons (such as parent-child, husband-wife). A *dyadic approach* indicates mutual give and take interchange of two persons over a given period of time.

dynamic psychology Psychology that emphasizes **drives** and **motives** as determinants of behavior. It is concerned primarily with change and causal factors related to change.

The term "dynamic" had been used by **Dewey** (1884), **James** (1908), and **Woodworth** (1918) in various ways, all of them, however, pertaining to motivation in some form or other. **Freud's** concepts are often considered to be the epitome of dynamic psychology. *See* **dynamics.**

dynamics (psychodynamics) Force or energy in motion; the science of forces acting in any field. The term dynamics is used in various sciences, but is most frequently applied in *physics* (where, as a branch of mechanics, it relates to the motion and equilibrium of systems as effected by external forces) and in the *social sciences* (particularly in psychology and sociology where it often refers to a theory, such as Freud's, that is a reaction against one that has apparently outlived its usefulness, such as **structuralism**). Basically, dynamics pertains to considering and including all possible factors (unconscious as well as others) before reaching a conclusion.

A term sometimes used synonymously with *dynamism,* which more strictly relates to a process of achieving interaction with another personality, so as to produce certain behavioral consequences. A dynamism may be thought of as a discrete overt measurable unit of behavior (grimaces, posture, laughing patterns, etc.) or as a covert activity (thinking, reasoning, etc.). Dynamisms are relatively enduring behavioral patterns, manifested by one person's attitudes, habits, or feelings in relation to another. A dynamism is modified and enhanced by experience and as such is a social-psychological interaction.

The concept of dynamics is traceable to Heraclitus (c. 540-475 B.C.) and his principle of universal flux (relating to motion, dynamic energy, and forces operating everywhere). In his *Chrestomathia,* English philosopher Jeremy **Bentham** (1748-1832), introduced (1817) the phrase *psychological dynamics* into psychological literature, by which he meant application of the method of observation and induction in analysis of behavior. *Dynamic psychology* developed from this point of view.

dysfunction Abnormal, defective, or impaired (dys-) functioning of any organ.

dyskinesia A disorder (-ia) manifested by impaired (dys-) motion (-kines-), usually in reference to bodily movement associated with **cerebral palsy.** Such diverse motor activities as tremors and rigidity, plus rapid, jerky, random, involuntary (choreic), and wormlike but slow movements (athetotic) are characteristic of dyskinesia. *See* **athetosis, chorea.**

Term apparently first used (1872) in the article "On Chorea," written by American neurologist, George Huntington (1862-1927).

dyslalia A disorder (-ia) manifested by difficult (dys-) speech (-lal-). Any one of the disorders in speech articulation not due to **central nervous system** involvement.

d

dyslexia A disorder (-ia) in which a person evidences extreme difficulty (dys-) in being able to read words (-lex-) or sentences; persistent inability to spell or read with comprehension more than a few lines at a time regardless of intellectual level. Other symptoms may also be evident: word reversals, poor phrasing or rhythm in reading, mispronunciations, and malapropisms. *See* **word blindness.**

dysphasia A disorder (-ia) manifested by defective (dys-) language (-phas-) ability, including difficulties in expression (speaking or writing) and in receiving information (reading or understanding the spoken word). *See* **aphasia.**

dysphoria A disorder (-ia) in which a person bears or carries (-phor-) abnormal (dys-) feelings, such as those associated with being uncomfortable, gloomy, anxious, or depressed. (Opposed to **euphoria**).

dysplastic type of body build Relating to (-ic) an impaired (dys-) form or shape (-plast-). One of **Kretschmer's** body types, representing incompatible mixtures of his other three types: **pyknic**, short, stocky, and barrel-chested; **athletic**, well developed and proportioned; and **leptosome**, tall and slender with long, skinny extremities.

dyssocial reactions Disorders characterized by strong loyalties to subgroup values that conflict with the larger societal values, such as observed in gang loyalties and in hippie revolts against the "establishment."

E

E Experimenter; environment.

e The base of the natural system of logarithms; the limit of $(1 + 1/n)^n$, as n increases without limit. Its numerical value is approximately 2.71828 . . .

ear The organ of hearing. *Anatomically*, the human ear has three major parts: (1) the *external ear* consisting of the pinna and the auditory canal; (2) the *middle ear*, separated from the external by the eardrum, which consists primarily of the **tympanic membrane** and an air-filled chamber lined with a mucous membrane that contains the **ossicles** (**stapes, malleus,** and **incus**); and (3) the *inner ear*, consisting of a bony **labyrinth** (composed of **semicircular canals**, a **vestibule**, and the **cochlea**) that embraces a membranous labyrinth. *Functionally*, the auditory canal conducts air pressure changes to the eardrum which is set into vibrations, the vibrations then transmitted to and amplified by the ossicles which, in turn, push on the **oval window** and are transformed into waves of pressure in the fluid-filled cochlea. By distorting the **organ of Corti** on the **basilar membrane**, the cochlear fluid waves stimulate the membrane's hair cells, and after traveling through the cochlea, the pressure is relieved by bulging of the **round window.**

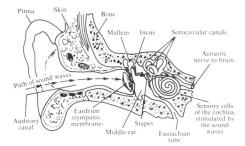

Schematic Diagram of the Ear. From Psychology: A Scientific Study of Man, by Sanford and Wrightsman. Copyright 1970 by Wadsworth Publishing Company, Inc. Reprinted by permission of the publisher, Brooks/Cole Publishing Company, Monterey, California.

Ebbinghaus, Herman (1850-1909) German philosopher, psychologist, and researcher in **psychophysics**. Developed **nonsense syllables** for use in studies of learning and memory so as to reduce the influence of past associations. Proved that "higher" mental processes could be brought under experimental control. In 1885 he published *Memory: A Contribution to Experimental Psychology*. In 1897 he devised the completion test in carrying out fatigue studies. Also pioneered in measurement of **intelligence**; and in studies on forgetting. The *Ebbinghaus curve of forgetting*, for example, indicates that forgetting takes place rapidly in the first few hours after learning and proceeds gradually after that. (Boring, 1952, pp. 386-391: **American Psychologist**, March 1968, 149-157).

Eccles, Sir John Neurophysiologist. He shared the Nobel prize in 1963 for contributions demonstrating the chemical basis for **synaptic transmission**. (*See* Eccles' article on "The Synapse," *Scientific American* (January) 1965, **112**, 56).

Eccles-Jordan circuit *See* **flip-flop.**

echolalia A disorder (-ia) in which a person echoes the speech (-lal-) sounds of another, often meaningless; involuntary and unaware repetition of another's speech, often repeating only the last word or two of a sentence. Frequently found in autistic children who parrot whatever they hear; also observed in catatonics. Echolalia also refers to one of the three types of **Piaget's egocentric speech** in which there is "repetition of words and syllables for the pleasure of talking, with no thought of talking to anyone, nor even at times of saying words that will make sense." (Jean Piaget, *The Language and Thoughts of the Child*, 1926). *See* **autism, catatonic type**, *under* **schizophrenia.**

Echolalia, along with other conditions (such as **coprolalia**) was first recorded in 1884 by French neurologist, **Georges Gilles de la Tourette** (1857-1904).

echolocation The ability of some animals (such as bats and porpoises) to emit sounds and use the reflected echoes as distance cues for locating prey or determining their own location. Bats, in particular, emit a series of brief pulses of high frequency sound enabling them, by the returning echoes, to identify direction, distance, speed, and even partial size and shape of various stimuli. The so-called "facial vision" of the blind is an example of echolocation. (*American Scientist*, 197, 59, No. 2, 198-209).

Echo phenomena was so-named in 1851 and an article on the subject was published in England (1853) by German physiologist, Moritz Heinrich Romberg (1795-1873).

echopraxia Automatic echoing or repeating (echo-) the actions (-praxia) of others; a compulsion to imitate movements or postures of others, most often seen in **catatonics.**

ecological psychology Referring to (-ical) the area of psychology concerned with the study of (-log-) its relationships to the environment (eco-). Ecological psychology embraces the **molar** behavior of man in relation to all possible factors that might affect him. **Barker** considers the basic problem of ecological psychology to be the manner in which psychology copes "with nonpsychological inputs." The ecological environment is the natural, objective real-life setting within which each living organism behaves.

Whereas a person's life space determines his momentary behavior, the ecological environment provides the situational context necessary for him to behave meaningfully as a total human being. According to Barker and his **behavior setting theory**, "the environment is a set of homeostatically governed eco-behavioral entities consisting of nonhuman components, human components, and control circuits that modify the components in predictable ways to maintain the environmental entities in their characteristic states." (Barker, 1968, p. 186).

Lewin as early as 1936 suggested that the "real" environmental situation and the individual's experience of his own environment might be studied under what he called "psychological ecology." But he made no further reference to this relationship in his **field theory.** *See* **environmental psychology.**

ecology Study of (-ology) all interrelated factors pertaining to the environment or habitat (ec-). Originally only of biological significance the concept has become of increasing psychologic import in the study of animal psychology and ethology. *See* **ecological psychology.**

Ernst Heinrich Haeckel (1834-1919), German biologist, coined (1868) the German equivalent of the term in his work, *Natürliche Schopfungsgeschlicte.*

ectoderm External (ecto-) skin (-derm) or layer of the three primitive germ layers of the developing **zygote**, from which the **central nervous system** as well as the skin, hair, external sense organs (eye, ear, etc.) and other structures develop. *See* **ectomorph.**

Karl Ernst von Baer (1792-1876), Esthonian zoologist, advanced the germ layer theory during the years 1828-1834. However, **Remak** reduced Baer's four germ layers to three and in his *Neurologische Erläuterungen*, 1844, he named them ectoderm, **endoderm**, and **mesoderm**. *See* **Remak's band.**

ectomorph Shape (morph-) derived from the outer (ecto-) embryonic layer or **ectoderm**. According to **Sheldon's** system of **constitutional types**, a body build characterized by long fragile bones and highly developed nervous system, associated with **cerebrotonia**, or extrasensitive and introspective personality characteristics. *See* **somatotype theory.**

ectoplasm Formative material (-plasm) located toward the outer (ecto-) portion of the cell. *See* **endoplasm.**

Ed.D. Doctor of education degree. *See* **clinical psychologist, educational psychologist.**

ED$_{50}$ Median effective dose.

educable-mentally-retarded child (EMR) A **mentally retarded** child (classified by certain school systems as those with an IQ roughly between 50 and 75) who is able to be educated in the three R's up to about the fourth grade level, occasionally to the sixth grade. When adult he is likely to be socially adequate and capable of most semiskilled work. Roughly comparable to the formerly popular term of **moron.** *See* **mentally subnormal.**

educational psychologist A professional person, usually with an **Ed.D.**, whose interest lies in the research and application of psychological principles to the education of children and adults in schools. Often a specialist in test construction, he is most of the time engaged in teaching in universities and colleges. (Cf. **school psychologist.**)

Edward Lee Thorndike Medal for Distinguished Psychological Contribution to Education Awarded by Division 15, Educational Psychology, for "outstanding contribution to the body of psychological knowledge relevant to education in the form of research or theory with achieved or potential impact on the conduct and study of education." The award is a bas-relief of **Thorndike** on a plaque and a monetary award "sufficient to cover the expenses involved in bringing the recipient and spouse to the Awards Ceremonies at the regular APA convention." *See* **awards of the APA.**

Edwin Smith Surgical Papyrus A papyrus containing records and clinical cases of medical illnesses that was probably written in the 17th century B.C., but whose contents relate to the age of the Pyramids (c. 3000-2500 B.C.). *See* **brain, cerebrospinal fluid.**

EEG Electroencephalogram, electroencephalograph.

e

effect In **analysis of variance**, an indicator of a difference between population means. *See* **treatment.**

effect, law of *See* **law of effect.**

effector Any agent (-or) that produces a result or effect. Term applied by **C. S. Sherrington** to nerve endings that stimulate organs, glands, or muscles; a responding organ. *See* **receptor.**

effector site *See* **allosteric enzyme.**

efferent nerve fibers Nerve fibers that conduct (-ferent) impulses outward (ef-) from the **central nervous system** to peripheral muscles and other **effector** mechanisms. In perception, efferent signals (efference) are those cues issued from the **brain** to the motor system, there being an efferent readiness to issue such signals. *Opposite of* **afferent.**

ego (L. *ego* = I) Concept of self (psychoanal.). The controlling and integrating core of the **personality** in actual contact with the external, real world, serving to mediate between the primitive, instinctual **id** needs, reality, and the civilized, moralistic, **super-ego.** Also, the largely conscious, logical, executive aspect of the personality, organized, derived from, and separated out of the id, corresponding most nearly to the perceived self. The part of the psyche forced upon the id because of reality demands (**Freud**). Neopsychoanalysts lean toward the concept that the id and ego are gradually formed together. *See* **Heinroth; identification.**

In attempting to protect itself, the ego, according to psychoanalysts, sets up various **defense mechanisms,** such as *acting out* (reduction of anxiety by expression); **compensation;** *denial of reality* (protection from unpleasant reality by escaping or denying pains of reality); **displacement;** fantasy; **identification; intellectualization; introjection; projection; rationalization; reaction formation; regression; repression; sublimation;** and *undoing* (atoning for immoral acts or thoughts).

Introduced into philosophy by **Descartes** in referring to the whole man, body and mind. Freud introduced his concept of the ego into psychological terminology in his book *The Ego and the Id* (1923), viewing the ego as an "internal regulatory mechanism to maintain a stable, constant condition." **Schizophrenia** was first expressed as a disorder of the ego by psychoanalyst Paul Federn (1872-1950), who also developed the phrase "ego boundary" in 1952 to refer to the ego structure that is maintained when the ego remains interested in some object and which loses its form when the ego withdraws its emotional investment.

ego boundary *See* **ego.**

egocentric speech In **Piaget's** terminology, the child's difficulty or inability to understand the adult's viewpoint primarily because of lack of self awareness rather than because of environmental influences. Consequently, when his speech (using special referents and associations that have meaning only to him) is misinterpreted or uncomprehended by the adult, he is shocked and surprised at his own failure to communicate and the adult's incapability of seeing things in the only way possible (the childs' limited way). To Piaget, infantile egocentrism does not imply selfishness or self-consciousness but is strongly tinged with anthropomorphic thinking (**animism**). *See* **echolalia.**

ego ideal (Psychoanal.) The human being's conception of what he wants to be. Usually a standard of perfection (a value system) formed in childhood through identification with love-objects, or the picture of himself according to his parents' expectations. It is the positive, nonpunitive aspect of the **super-ego.**

ego involvement (Psychoanal.) Commitment to and absorption in a task so that success in it becomes vital to self-esteem, and failure leads to chagrin, disappointment, and loss of **ego strength;** placing oneself completely in a situation without regard to personal damage, physical or psychological.

ego psychology Psychological theories of the **personality** that emphasize the independent functions of the **ego** as against the earlier depth psychology of **psychoanalysis.** Ego psychology is primarily concerned with reality testing (through various forms of existential confrontation), **defense mechanisms, transference** processes, and the eventual attainment of the **ego-ideal.**

Pioneering in this field, during the 1940's and 1950's, three psychoanalysts, Austro-American Heinz Hartmann (born 1894), Ernst Kris, and Polish-American Rudolph Loewenstein (born 1898), developed the foundation-stone for ego-psychology by many of their "ego" papers in psychoanalytic literature. Erik Erikson (born 1902), another early (1950) ego-psychologist, considered ego-identity "as a polarity of what one feels one is and of what others take one to be." In the 1960's, ego-psychology became so personal and individualistic that it was virtually impossible to set up general principles about the field.

ego strength An attitudinal **variable** that determines a person's response in problem situations; high ego strength connotes realistic, efficient, and well-controlled coping with life's realities.

ego structure The composition of the **ego,** resulting from the interaction between **needs** and environment. Typical defensive reactions and other aspects of the self are considered as the integrating core of the **personality.** According to **psychoanalysis,** the ego structure undergoes gradual evolution from its **id** beginnings to its more mature facing of reality as one grows older.

Ehrenfels, Baron Christian von (1859-1932) Austrian philosopher. Student of **Brentano.** Anticipated **Gestalt** psychology by publishing a paper in 1890 on "Gestaltqualität" which was a reaction against the elementarism of **Wundt.** Gestaltqualität held that each person adds a unique "quality" to his own **sensory** entities, resulting in what is known as **perception.** *See* **Ach, Kulpe.**

Ehrlich, Paul (1854-1915) German bacteriologist and physician (M.D., Leipzig 1878). Contributed to the development of the **neuron** theory by discovering (1885) and later (1886) describing his *intra vitam* technique of staining nerve tissue with methylene blue, that is, in being able to distinguish the tissue in its natural condition because the acidic dye stained all organs except those of the nervous system. Also recognized as the founder of chemotherapy.

eidetic imagery Referring to (-etic) that kind of mental imagery that, upon recall, is as intensely physical and vivid as a statue (eid-), retaining its clearness for long periods of time. Such imagery is usually visual, but acoustic, tactual, olfactory, gustatory, and proprioceptive images of the same nature have been reported. An *eidetiker* is one who has such powers of imagery. Eidetic imagery is more frequently reported by children under the age of 6.

The German philosopher-psychologist Erick Rudolf Jaensch (1883-1940), performed pioneer studies in this area, describing the phenomenon as early as 1907. He developed an eidetic typology, reporting his results in *Eidetic Imagery and Typological Methods of Investigation,* 1930. (See **Kluver, Stilenheit**).

Eigenwelt (Exist.) One's "own world." A German concept that presupposes self-awareness and self-relatedness, bringing all things in one's environment up close for examination, appreciation, and reappraisal, so as to see the real world more nearly in its true perspective.

eikonometer *See* **space eikonometer.**

Eindringlichkeit (Ger., forcefulness, insistence) A specific characteristic or quality of a perceived sensory dimension (such as color, brightness, or size) that is, by its insistence, forced into one's attention.

The German-trained Swedish psychologist David Katz (1884-1953) used the term in 1911 to describe the awareness an observer has about the brightness and stimulus intensity of a color. The observer particularly notices this lack of insistence after being trained to observe colors subjectively as the painter does instead of seeing the colors naturally and objectively as he had seen them before. After the shift in attitude from seeing object colors to that of seeing the stimulus colors of a painter, a white object looks faded or whitish in dim light. (Woodworth and Schlosberg, 1965, p. 446; David Katz, *The World of Colour,* 1935).

In 1913, Max Meyer used *Eindringlichkeit* to describe the intense nature of the stimulation that held one's attention. Ebbinghaus had previously called this characteristic *Aufdringlichkeit.*

Einfuhling *See* **empathy.**

Einstellung (Ger., mind set, mental set). A momentary mind-set or **attitude** in which a person persists with an obviously inappropriate (even to him) method when a more efficient one is available; behaving in a set way to expected relationships and experiences.

Wertheimer (1923) said that *Einstellung* was both subjective (in which the observer sets his mind for certain expectancies and ignores similarity and proximity) and objective (in which the observer retains his previous judgments or perseverates in his previous perception). *See* **Bereitschaft.**

EKG Electrocardiogram. **Electrocardiograph.**

élan vital Vital spurt (élan), impetus, or spark. Creative or life force. **Bergson** believed that the source of evolution in the biological sense was represented by the élan vital, an original life force that is carried "mystically" from one generation to the next, enabling the universe to move forward without a fixed beginning or end, the future being determined by decision-making in the present.

Jung identified **libido** with élan vital, but Freud had implied the same thing earlier with the use of "libidinal charge" according to Jones (1953-57).

Elavil One of the trade names for **imipramine hydrochloride.**

Electra complex According to **Freud,** the **libidinal** attachment or suppressed sexual love that a daughter develops for her father (as the boy does for his mother in the **Oedipal complex**); usually accompanied by a concomitant hostility toward her mother. The Electra complex supposedly occurs during the latter portion of the **phallic stage.**

Classical mythology, from which Freud borrowed his term, relates that Electra deeply loved her father, Agamemnon, a Greek hero. Upon the killing of Agamemnon by his wife Clytemnestra and her lover, Electra and her brother Orestes avenged their father's murder by slaying Clytemnestra. Plagued by the crime of matricide, Orestes became raving mad while Electra grew into a despondent and moody woman for the rest of her life, finding no marriage mate fit to compare with her ideal and beloved hero-father.

electro(a)esthesiometer An electronic (electro-) instrument for measuring (-meter), one's sensitivity (-[a]esthesio-) to determining spatial thresholds.

electrocardiogram, electrocardiograph (EKG, from *Elektrokardiogram,* original spelling.) The tracing or graphic record (-gram) of the heart's **action potential** as shown by the electrocardiograph, which is an electronic (electro-) apparatus that records (-graph) changes in the electrical **potential** of the heartbeat, enabling interpretations to be made of irregularities in heart (-cardio-) action.

William Einthoven (1860-1927), Dutch physician (M.D., Utrecht 1885) invented the string **galvanometer** in 1902, making it possible to record cardiac heart currents (1903), producing what Einthoven called "telegrams from the heart." such "telegrams" named "electrokardiograms" by him in 1904. The electrocardiograph was developed later in the same year. Einthoven received the Nobel prize in 1924.

electroconvulsive shock therapy (EST) Electrotherapy. A medical form of shock treatment for mental illness (mainly for depressive states), in which high-voltage current is passed briefly through the brain producing instant but temporary unconsciousness and epileptiform convulsions. Its use has been considerably curtailed and modified in recent years. Used in psychological laboratories for learning and memory experiments, indicating that shock tends to impair recent memory in rats.

As early as 47 A.D., Roman physician Scribonius Largus used an electric eel for nonconvulsive electrotherapy on his emperor for relief of his headaches.

Probably the first use of EST for mental illness (psychogenic blindness) was that by French physician Jean Baptiste LeRoy (1720-1800), in 1755. Faradic current for diagnosis and treatment was introduced in 1855 by French neurologist, Guillaume B. A. Duchenne (1806-1875), leading to his being considered the founder of electrotherapy. Hungarian neurologist Karoly Schaffer (1864-1939), and Dutch physician Anton de Haen (1704-1776), helped pioneer electrotherapy.

In 1938 it was reported by Italian neuropsychiatrist Ugo Cerletti and his collaborator neuropsychiatrist Lucio Bini (1908-1964), Italian psychiatrist, that they had successfully used electric convulsive therapy on a schizophrenic patient.

electrocorticogram (ECoG) An electronic (electro-) tracing (-gram) of the summed signals of the brain's activity, obtained from electrodes placed directly on the cortex (-cortico-) rather than on the scalp, as is usually done with the **electroencephalograph.**

electroencephalogram (EEG) The graphic chart or record (-gram) of the electrical (electro-) currents developed in the cortex by brain (encephalo-) activity. These minute electrical changes are amplified about a million times and recorded on tape.

In 1929, **Berger** gave the name "electroencephalogram" to the recordings obtained from the **electroencephalograph.** *See* **alpha waves, beta waves, brain waves, cathode.**

electroencephalograph (EEG) Apparatus consisting of a cathode-ray oscillograph that records (-graph) electrical (electro-) activity in the brain (-encephalo-) by means of electrodes placed on the scalp or sometimes the **brain** itself. The actual record or chart obtained from the EEG is called the **electroencephalogram.** Psychologists in psychophysiological laboratories use the EEG primarily for brain studies on lower animals, such as **central nervous system** disorders and learning problems. *See* **cathode.**

electromagnetic spectrum *See* **visible spectrum.**

electronic yoga *See* **bio-feedback training.**

electrophysiology A branch of physiology devoted to the investigation of electric phenomena within the living body (nerve and muscle tissue), particularly the role of electricity in nerve transmission and conduction. *See* **animal electricity, nerve impulse.**

electroretinogram (ERG) A graphic record (-gram) of retinal (retino-) electrical (electro-) activity consisting of a series of waves resulting from light illuminating the eye; often used in diagnosing retinal disorders.

electro-shock treatment *See* **electroconvulsive shock therapy.**

electro-stimulator An instrument for producing electrical shocks when administered under controlled duration, intensity, or frequency Usually applied in nonconvulsive doses for sensory stimulation.

electrotonus The altered tone (-tonus) or change in polarization of a cell membrane or nerve resulting from being constantly stimulated by an electrical (electro-) current.

In 1843, **du Bois-Reymond** described and named this condition that occurs when a galvanic current is applied to a portion of the length of a nerve or muscle.

elicited behavior Behavior that is lured or brought (-licit-) out (e-). In respondent conditioning, the application of an **unconditioned stimulus (US)** to a habituated response that can be reliably counted upon to respond to that specific **stimulus** as the experimenter wills.

emergency reaction The physiological correlate of intense emotional excitement interpreted (by **Cannon** and others) as an adaptive preparation of the organism to meet emergencies; the **alarm reaction** state of the **general adaptation syndrome.**

emitted behavior Behavior that is sent (-mit-) out (e-) or discharged by the organism in **operant conditioning.** The organism itself dictates when an experimental trial begins and ends, the conditioning being subject-controlled.

Emmert's law A finding in perceptual studies on **size constancy,** indicating that the perceived size of a projected **afterimage** on the retina varies in direct proportion to its apparent distance from the observer. In other words, an inverse relation exists between size and distance; the afterimage projected on a wall five times as distant as the original stimulus appears five times as large (due to constancy-scaling), despite the retinal image remaining the same.

Emil Emmert (1844-1913), German physiologist, formulated this geometric law of after-images in 1881.

emotion Quality (-tion) of moving (-mo) out (e-). A stirred up condition or complex response of the organism producing internal (diarrhea, **borborygmus,** tachycardia, etc.) or external (such as swearing, striking out randomly) disruption, abortive actions (e.g., panic reactions, **stuttering**), or generally atypical and inappropriate behavior. Emotional experiences are patterns of diverse and complex feelings, their variations often referred to as having **hedonic tone** (the degree of fluctuation between pleasantness and unpleasantness).

Emotions are sometimes classified as: (1) *primary* (joy, fear, anger, grief); (2) *sensory stimulative* (pain, disgust, horror, delight); (3) *provoked by self-appraisal* (shame, pride, guilt); (4) *generated by interrelationships* (love, hate, pity); (5) *appreciative* (humor, beauty, wonder); and (6) *moods* (sadness, anxiety, elation).

In trying to explain these interactions and reactions, psychologists and physiologists have developed certain **emotion** theories over the years, which tend to be variations of one or all of the **James-Lange theory,** the **Cannon-Bard theory,** the **Papez-MacLean theory,** the **Lindsley activation theory,** or the **Pribram** memory-based theory. *See* **central theory, peripheral theory.**

empathic understanding *See* **free.**

empathy Feeling (-pathy) into (em-); fellow feeling. Translated from the German *Einfuhlung* (1912). Taking into oneself the feelings, sensations, or attitudes of another person or object; the capacity for experiencing vicariously the feelings, thoughts, or posture of another. For example, a father at a track meet watching the high jump may, in empathy, lift his own foot as his son attempts to clear the bar. However, if his son breaks his arm and the father's eyes fill with tears, that's sympathy and not empathy.

In another aspect of empathy Theodor Lipps (1851-1941), German philosopher, in his *Psychologische Untersuchungen*, (Vol. I, 1907) claimed that empathy was stimulated even by the esthetics of architecture and simple lines; that a vertical line (because of the person's feeling that it is struggling to stand up) is interpreted as being longer than an equally long horizontal line. *See* **mimpathy.**

Empedocles (c. 495-435 B.C.) Greek philosopher and statesman. Proposed four irreducible substances (air, water, fire, and earth) to complement the four basic elements (cold, moisture, heat, and dryness). For him, there were also four humors of the body: blood (from the heart); phlegm (from the **brain**); yellow bile (from the liver); and black bile (from the spleen). The humors had to remain in proper balance or else disease would result. Proper drugs could restore balance only if they complemented the four basic elements. *See* **Galen, Hippocrates, cochlea.**

empirical Referring to (-al) experience (empiric-), or to knowledge obtained from experience, evidence, or direct observation. Based on experiments, surveys, and facts. Referring to **induction** as opposed to argument, opinion, and **deduction.** *See* **empiricism, intelligence tests, Herbart.**

The term "empirical psychology" was introduced and defined by **Christian Wolff,** who considered empirical and rational psychology to be equivalent.

empirical determinism *See* **determinism.**

empirical (true) validity *See* **validity.**

empiricism The philosophical doctrine (-ism) or approach to knowledge holding that all information is derived from sensory perceptions and experience (empiric-), and that all *a priori* knowledge or innate ideas should be rejected; epistemologically, the only valid source of knowledge is experience. Especially associated with the British philosophers: **Locke** holding that there is nothing innate about ideas, which can only come from experience; **Berkeley** affirming mind as the immediate reality; **Hume** saying that the mind is capable of knowing only its own processes, ideas being reducible to sensations only; **Hobbes** applying deductive logic to new facts, saying that all events are caused only by motion; **Reid,** in opposing Berkeley and Hume, was nevertheless an empiricist in emphasizing the obvious and readily experienced consciousness of man. **Condillac** and **Bonnet,** influenced by Locke and **Malebranche,** developed empiricism in France. **Hartley, Helmholtz,** and **Wundt** set the stage for the heavily oriented empiric-sensationistic psychology of the 19th century.

More recently, in perception theory, empiricism refers to perceptual organization as being learned from experience, and that the study of natural and not experimental behavior is the productive area for the advancement of psychology. *See* **syndrome.**

Originally, *Empirics* were medical followers of **Erasistratus** who believed that clinical practice (experience) was all important, but the **Methodists** (who practiced medicine by reason and theory rather than observation of the patient's condition) considered the Empirics to be trial and error doctors and charlatans, Empirics and charlatans becoming synonymous. *Empiricism* was introduced into English in 1657 as meaning "quackery or ignorant practice." *See* **Aristotle.**

EMR Educable-mentally-retarded.

enacted role *See* **role.**

enactive mode *See* 1. under **cognitive growth theories.**

encephalé isolé (Fr., isolated brain.) An experimental procedure of isolating the **brain** by severing the **brainstem** at the juncture of the spinal cord and the brain. Sensory input from the face and head remains intact, but sensory input from the body is eliminated. *See* **cerveau isolé.**

In 1935, Belgian research physician, Frederic Bremer (born 1892), was the first to describe the preparations known as encephalé isolé and the cerveau isolé. (Thompson, pp. 429, 430-431, 437-441.)

encephalon That which is in (en-) the head (-cephalon) or the **brain;** the whole brain.

encoding (enciphering) (Comput.) Translation, without significant loss of information, to a coded form from an analog or other easily recognized form.

encopresis Process (-esis) of defecating (-copr-) involuntarily in (-en) the clothing; bowel incontinence. A technical term for soiling. Encopresis in children may be due to (1) **feeble-mindedness**, (2) poor toilet training, (3) **neurosis**, or (4) poor sphincter musculature and control. Encopresis rarely occurs during sleep (Kessler, 1966, pp. 123-125). **Behavior therapy** treatment by Neale, rather than using a negative approach, places the child on a toidy or toilet seat four times a day, reinforcing him with praise and rewards (e.g., candy). No punishment for soiling. (Neale, D. H., Behavior Therapy and Encopresis in Children, *Behavior Research and Therapy*, 1963, I, 139-149).

encounter group *See* **intensive group experience.**

end brain *See* **telencephalon.**

end brush (end plate) The mass of branching terminal fibers of the **axon**, or the region of a neural cell that joins and stimulates other neuronal **dendrites**; also, the area where excitation is transferred from nerve to muscle cells.

endocrine gland A ductless gland of internal (endo-) secretion (-crine), whose substance is absorbed by capillaries in the gland and passed directly into the bloodstream or tissue fluid, thereby influencing the nervous system, other glands and organs, and eventually the total behavior of the organism. For hormones, function, and dysfunctions of individual glands see specific entries.

endoderm Inner (endo-) skin (-derm). The internal layer of the developing **zygote** from which the respiratory tract (except nose), digestive tract, bladder, and other visceral organs develop. *See* **ectoderm, endomorph.**

endogenous factor Any substance, object, or determiner originating from within or caused by heredity. *See* **Cullen, Kraepelin.**

endolymph The inner (endo-) lymph fluid of the **semicircular canals** (membranous labyrinth) of the **inner ear.** *See* **ampulla, ear.**

endomorph A type of body shaped (-morph-) by the endoderm (endo-). A body build or shape, which **W. H. Sheldon** believed to derive from the **endoderm**, thus denoting the fatty, visceral type and correlating highly (.79 in Sheldon's study) with **viscerotonia**, a temperament characterized by relaxed posture, love of physical comfort, etc.

endoplasm The inner (endo-) fluid part or formative material (-plasm) of the cytoplasm located near the cell center; distinguished from **ectoplasm**, which is located near the peripheral portion of the cell.

endoradiosonde A sounding line (Fr., *sonde*) or miniature radio transmitter capsule implanted or ingested into (endo-) an organism for studying its internal reactions. In physiological psychology, this biotelemetric device is important for obtaining information about the internal behavior of animals.

Named by R. Stuart Mackay. See his book, *Biomedical Telemetry: Sensing and Transmitting Biological Information from Animals to Man* (Wiley, 1968).

enelicomorphism (adultomorphism) A practice or belief (-ism) in attributing the structure (-morph-) of the mental processes of adults (enelico-) to small children; interpreting children's behavior in terms of adult behavior, such as believing that an infant's frown means he is angry, or that he is thinking hard when he stares off blankly into space.

energizer (antidepressant) A **drug** (such as pep pills, **iproniazid** and **imipramine**) that makes the individual more responsive, sleepless, and alert. When used to excess and without controls an energizer may necessitate taking depressant drugs to counterbalance its effect, thus producing an unwanted cyclic action going from alertness to somnolence and depression and back again; as used in chemotherapy, energizers are aids in reducing depression and creating alertness so as to make the patient more amenable to **psychotherapy.**

engram Written (-gram) in (en-). A permanent **memory trace** or impression supposedly formed in living protoplasm or neural tissue by any **stimulus** that, when regularly repeated, forms a habit.

The term, after being threatened with extinction as a result of its flamboyant use in dianetics (a quack therapeutic technique propagandized by a science-fiction writer in the late forties and 1950's), is now being used in the phrase *engram-code*, as applied to **long-term memory**'s stability and durability. As encoded representations, engrams "have a static or spatial organization that makes them independent of the dynamic factors and able to survive periods like those of deep anesthesia, **electroconvulsive shock**, and cerebral **anoxia**, in which all dynamic organization fades out or is violently disrupted. The memory traces may be dormant . . . for years before the particular experience involved is recalled into activity" (Quarton, et al. pp. 714-723).

Defined by Richard Semon (1921) in *The Mneme* as the "change left behind in the irritable substance of the brain after excitation has died down." According to J. M. Nielsen, an American neurologist who has used the term frequently in his various books, an engram is "a previously existing set of cells, axons, and dendrites trained by practice to form a 'beaten pathway' over which impulses travel with greater ease than over untrained pathways; sometimes called a neurogram." (*A Textbook of Clinical Neurology*, 1951, 3rd edition, p. 242). *See* **mneme.** (David Wechsler, "Engrams, Memory Storage and Mnemonic Coding," *American Psychologist*, 1963, **18**, 149-157).

enuresis Involuntary process (-esis) of urinating (-ur-) while asleep in (en-) the bed; bedwetting by a child of about 3 years of age or over. It may be **functional** (e.g., caused by poor toilet training, emotional instability, poor adjustability), or **organic** and due to disease (cystitis, urethritis, various systemic diseases, **mental deficiency, epilepsy**, etc.). **Behavior therapists** claim unusual success in treating enuresis. Meinhard von Pfaundler, German physician (1872-1939), devised an electrical appliance (prior to 1910) for warning parents that sleeping children had wet diapers, incidentally finding that children seemed to anticipate the signal and often stopped wetting the bed.

In 1938, the **Mowrers** reported on the first use of learning techniques in treating nocturnal enuresis (with bladder tension as the **conditioned stimulus**). They used an electrical wire mesh apparatus for the child to sleep on, and when he urinated, the moisture completed an electric current setting off a slight shock (O. H. and W. Mowrer, "Enuresis: A Method for Its Study and Treatment," *American Journal of Orthopsychiatry*, 1938, **7**, 436-459).

In 1963, Lovibond reported that a twin signal technique (in which an apparatus was designed to make a loud noise, startling and awakening the child) caused a reflexive tightening of the sphincter muscle. After sufficient pairings, contraction aborted urination, followed by the child awakening and going to the bathroom.

environmental psychology The study of behavior in relationship to its environmental influences (considering constraints on ranges of behavior as well as freedom to operate), involving such specifics as climate extremes, crowding, etc. and their effect on setting patterns of behavior (e.g., the behavioral pattern of a taxi driver in Tokyo, Mexico City, or New York). Environmental psychology also studies why persons move toward or away from some aspect of a geographical or environmental location (the **approach-avoidance** conflict of persons who try to decide about living in the sun-smog environment of Los Angeles). Considered synonymous with

ecological psychology. (Joachim F. Wohlwill, "The Emerging Discipline of Environmental Psychology," *American Psychologist*, 1970, **25**, 303-311).

enzymes Leavening (-zyme) in (en-). A chemical protein substance (catalyst) found in the body in many forms; originally called a ferment, whence the nomenclature referring to leavening or yeast. Digestive enzymes are necessary for **metabolism.** An enzyme cycle in nerve fibers (the breakdown and buildup of **acetylcholine**) is thought to furnish the biochemical energy for the electrical potential of the **nerve impulse.**

In 1876, Wilhelm Kühne (1837-1900), German physiologist, coined term "enzyme" to replace "ferment" so as to avoid confusion.

ependyma *See* **neuroglia.**

ephedrine The plant of the genus *Ephedra*, meaning the buttocks, where one sits (hedr-) upon (ep-); the horsetail plant as described by Pliny. The alkaloid (-ine) was obtained originally from the leaves of this plant.

Isolated in 1885 by Yamanashi. In 1924 it was introduced therapeutically, and in 1928 it was produced by Ko Kuei Chen (born 1898, Shanghai, China), American physician (M.D., Johns Hopkins 1927). Used beneficially at first for myasthenia, but replaced by prostigmine. Now used for asthma, nasal congestion, and relief of hay fever. *See* **amphetamine, drugs.**

ephialtes Nightmare. *Ephialtes vigilantum* pertains to upsetting dreams or "nightmares" during the day; a daymare, such as those suffered by Ephialtes, son of Poseidon, who is doomed forever to suffer such agony in Hades.

epicritic sensation (epicritic sensibility) Relating to (-ic) a sensation felt about (epi-) something; the ability to accurately determine (-crit-) or discriminate between the degrees of light touch and to sense its specific localization. It is often determined by light application of hairs or fine hair brushes; epicritic relates to sensory nerve fibers in the skin only.

Epicritic, along with **protopathic**, was coined by **Henry Head** and described in the article "A Human Experiment in Nerve Division," *Brain*, 1908, **31**, 323-340, written by Head and W. H. R. Rivers (1864-1922), British experimental psychologist. *See* **somatic sensory system.**

epilepsy Seizure (-lepsy) upon (-epi-). A condition characterized by periodic loss of consciousness with convulsions; in fact, a variety of seizures that may differ greatly in severity. Epilepsy may be caused at birth by brain damage, or later by brain injury or disease. Seizures may be minimized by soothing drugs (such as **Dilantin**) and special diets. The terms *convulsive seizure* or *cerebral dysrhythmia* are often used in place of epilepsy. Typical **electroencephalogram** patterns appear in many persons prone to epilepsy, and an electroencephalogram taken during an attack will usually show extremely marked disturbance of cortical electrical activity.

Two types of epilepsy are usually differentiated: (1) **grand mal seizures.** A major form of epilepsy often preceded by an **aura** but may also occur without warning. It is characterized by extensive, severe convulsions and prolonged loss of consciousness that may pass into normal sleep. A post-convulsive period may last for days accompanied by mood changes, clouding of consciousness, fear, anxiety, and distorted perceptions, including **déjà vu** and **déjà vecu** phenomena. The condition may occur at any age and is often associated with organic brain damage. Grand mal attacks can be controlled in more than 50% of the cases by **Dilantin** and other drugs (e.g., **phenobarbital**); (2) **petit mal seizures.** A relatively minor form of epilepsy, usually beginning between four to eight years of age. No aura is associated with the condition, although there may be signs of a coming attack by loss of muscle tone (such as noticed in stumbling). The child may suddenly become immobile, stare off into space, and then lapse briefly into unconsciousness. There is usually no post-convulsive period as found in grand mal. Approximately two out of three petit mal cases develop into grand mal if the condition persists beyond the age of 20. Petit mal may be due to birth injury, encephalitic viral conditions, middle-ear and brain infections, etc.

Petit mal and psychomotor seizures often respond well to Phenurone, Primodone, and Tridione (which unfortunately may sometimes cause other types of seizures.)

Epilepsy (as a seizure) is an old term, having been used by **Hippocrates** in his book, *Sacred Disease* (c. 400 B.C.), to describe a single attack; also being the first to describe childrens' epilepsy. The term came into English in 1578 as "epilepsie." (For further information, contact the *National Epilepsy League, Inc.,* 203 N. Wabash Ave., Chicago, Ill. 60601, and *Epilepsy Foundation of America*, 1419 H Street N.W., Washington, D. C. 20005).

epileptoid personality disorder *See* **explosive personality** under **personality disorders.**

epiloia A disorder (-ia) in which epileptic (-epilo-) convulsions may be the first indication of the disease, the seizures occurring usually before the end of the second year of life. Lesions are of unknown origin.

Named by American physician Sherlock. *See* **tuberous sclerosis.**

epinephrin(e) The basic compound (-ine) derived from the **adrenal glands** situated upon (epi-) the kidneys (-nephr-). The noncommercial, technically proper name for a synthetic preparation chemically identical with the active principle of the adrenal **medulla**; also prepared from adrenal extracts. Used chiefly as a heart stimulant and vasoconstrictor for surface blood vessels.

In 1901, the chemical formula was devised by Thomas Bell Aldrich (1861-1938), American chemist, after Takamine had isolated it in crystal form. *See* **adrenalin** for more details.

epiphenomenalism A doctrine (-ism) relating to (-al) phenomena that depends upon (epi-) other phenomena: mind-body relation, with the mind regarded as a by-product of the **brain** processes but which cannot, in turn, influence or interact with the brain; also, consciousness considered as an epiphenomenon of physiological processes without having any influence upon them. *Opposed to* **interactionism.** *See* **Descartes.**

Hobbes (1658) considered consciousness, in his form of epiphenomenalism, to result from nervous impulses. Shadworth Hodgson (1852-1913), English writer and philosopher, and English scientist Thomas H. Huxley (1825-1895), advanced epiphenomenalism in articles and lectures.

episcotister That which (-er) resembles (-ist) darkness (-scot-) over (epi-) a specified area. A rapidly rotating disk with adjustable open and closed or opaque and transparent sectors for reducing the brightness (brilliance) of light in a known ratio. Used often in **flicker** studies.

epistemological dualism *See* **dualism.**

epistemological loneliness Relating to (-ical) the study (-olog-) of knowledge or understanding (epistem-) about loneliness. (Exist.) A loneliness that has arisen because of man's feeling of futility of trying to discover both the meaning of life and the extent of his knowledge about his universe. This feeling of isolation and **alienation** is the ultimate consequence of subject Man being separated repeatedly from object World, and man's feeling of despair and frustration. *Epistemology*, basically, is the study of man's way of acquiring knowledge about his world and the validity of such.

epithalamus Near or about (epi-) the **thalamus.** The most dorsal section of the **diencephalon**, containing the **pineal gland** and the **habenula.**

EPS Experimental Publication System.

EPSP *Excitatory postsynaptic potential.*

equal returns *See* **curves of returns.**

Equanil (The Wyeth tradename for **meprobamate**).

equation Process of (-tion) equating or equalizing. An algebraic statement of equality between two expressions, consisting of two sides or members separated by an equal sign (=). A simple rule exists for performing equation operations: whatever is done to one side of the equation (addition, subtraction, or other use of a number or other symbol) must be done to the other side (Edwards, 1961, p. 28, and 1967, p. 393 f., gives ten examples of this rule).

equipotentiality The quality (-ity) of having equal (equi-) potential, or power. A principle, based on studies of cortical-damage-influence on behavior, indicating that within large areas of the **brain** one region can effectively substitute for another; also, that all parts of the **cerebrum** are equally important in respect to their specific functions.

The term "equipotential" dates from 1678. It was used frequently during the 1880's in electricity and physics. **K. Lashley** first made reference to "equipotentiality" as it related to brain function in his book *Brain Mechanisms and Intelligence*, 1929.

ER Educable-retarded.

Erasistratus (c. 310-250 B.C.) Greek physician. Many of the ideas of Erasistratus and **Herophilus** overlapped (such as they both believed that the soul resided in the brain) but it was understandable since both men studied together at the Alexandrian school of medicine. Erasistratus made many anatomical studies, mainly of the nerves, being the first to distinguish between **sensory** and **motor** nerves. He also concluded that the degree of man's **intelligence** was related to the number of cerebral convolutions. *See* **cerebrum, cerebellum, auditory nerve, meninges, empiricism.**

Erbanlage *See* **Anlage.**

ERG *Electroretinogram.*

ergograph A recording apparatus (-graph) for measuring work (ergo-) capacity of muscle by exercising to exhaustion one muscle or restricted muscle group (as a finger or a hand), and measuring the declining rate of responses as an indicator of muscle fatigue. *See* **Mosso**; *compare* **dynamometer.**

ergonomics The application of scientific laws (-nomics) to human factors in work (erg-), machine design, and operation. A term used in Great Britain and Western Europe that is roughly comparable in meaning to **human engineering**; an ergonomist being a human factor specialist.

ergotropic activity Relating to (-ic) an activity system that centers or turns (-trop) around work (ergo-), preparing the body for interaction with the environment. The type of activity associated with the posterior **hypothalamus** that, upon stimulation, activates the **sympathetic nervous system**, raises the heart rate and blood pressure, and produces results similar to those resulting from heavy work. **Dopa** has produced **EEG** activity and a syndrome similar to that found in ergotropic activity.

Ergotropic and **trophotropic** were coined by German neurologist, Walter Rudolph Hess, and used by him in 1948 in a German article and later (1957) in his book: *The Functional Organization of the Diencephalon*. Hess received the Nobel prize in physiology and medicine in 1949.

error In inferential **statistics**, a product of chance, with variability among observations resulting from innumerable uncontrolled influences upon experimental results.

error, type I (error of first kind) *See* **type I error.**

error, type II (error of second kind) *See* **type II error.**

error of anticipation In psychophysical measurements, the tendency to anticipate a **stimulus** and respond too soon.

error of habituation (Psychophysics) The error resulting from habit, or from resistance to changing a **response.**

error of judgment The error any person makes in attempting to rate performance or pass judgment on other people's traits or characteristics. Error in judging tends to be "averaged out" toward greater **reliability** and **validity** as more judges are used. For instance, in a study of judging, personality traits, the averages of the judges' ratings were consistently shown to be more valid and reliable. (Kelly, 1967, p. 62).

error of measurement (Error of observation) The amount by which a measurement deviates from the true value due to uncontrolled or poorly controlled experimental conditions. In general, measurement error approximates a **normal distribution.**

error rate The expected number of errors per experiment, the rate usually being defined in terms of the probability of its being falsely declared significant.

In hypothesis testing an experimenter may make a **type I error** (in which the **null hypothesis** H_O is falsely rejected), a **type II error** (or failing to reject the null hypothesis when in fact it is false), a correct decision, or he may delay decision-making altogether. Prior to his experiment the researcher must choose a test statistic that will give him the protection he desires in terms of the error rate selected and the probabilities of committing either of the two types of errors (Kirk, 1968, pp. 82-86).

error variance Any nonsystematic variation in response that occurs in an experimental situation despite the use of appropriate controls.

escape learning (escape conditioning) A form of negative **reinforcement** in which an acquired **response** removes an individual from the painful stimulus (such as a rat frantically hopping off a charged grid), but the removal from punishment does not alter the situation if it occurs again. Escape learning becomes **avoidance learning** if **conditioning** to a cue has taken place so that in anticipation of punishment the animal avoids the punishing stimulus, thus having no need to escape. An escape response is one that terminates an aversive event. (G. H. Bower, "Partial and Correlated Reward in Escape Learning," *Journal of Experimental Psychology*, 1960, 59, 126-130).

ESP *Extrasensory perception.*

essence (Exist.) The necessary basic quality or nature of anything that distinguishes it from something else, including all dimensions and characteristics that give it substance; contrasted with nonessential qualities or accidents and regarded separately from its **existence.** An abstract idea, concept, or knowledge of a desk for instance, demonstrates its essence in the mind; the desk one is writing on is material evidence of its existence. "Everything that exists," said **Plato**, "is the reflection of an essence." And Jean Paul Sartre (born 1905), French philosophic existentialist and writer, claims that "Essence is not the object, it is the sense of the object." **Martin Heidegger**, German phenomenologist, with his philosophy of let things be, has the final word when he asks: "Isn't the question of essence the most unessential and arbitrary one that can be raised?"

EST *Electroshock therapy.*

Estes, William K. Born 1919, Minnesota. Ph.D., Minnesota 1943. Received the **Distinguished Scientific Contribution Award** 1962. In 1963, he was awarded the **Warren Medal** for his "development of a mathematical theory of learning which he has painstakingly tested and which has proved to be a powerful tool for analyzing the role of stimulation in both

e

human and animal learning." *See* **stochastic learning theory**; also William K. Estes, "All or None Processes in Retention and Learning." *American Psychologist*, 1964, **1**, 16-25 .

esthesiometer A calibrated device (-meter) with hairs of varying diameters, used to measure sensitivity (esthesio-) or thresholds of touch in cutaneous experiments.

The original esthesiometer was invented and named by **E. H. Weber** in 1834.

estimation The prediction of a **population parameter** (specifying margin of error) from knowledge about a **sample**.

estimator That which estimates from a **sample** (such as a sample mean) what the **population parameter** (the population mean) should be. The numerical value obtained is the estimate. An estimator is either biased or unbiased. A good estimator of a population parameter should be consistent, unbiased, sufficient, and efficient.

Estradiol A crystalline chemical compound containing two hydroxyl groups (-diol) found in estrogens (estra-). Estradiol is one of the two (the other being **estrone**) most active of the estrogens produced by follicular fluid of the ovaries and also possibly by the placenta. Used to treat **melancholia** in menopausal conditions and other human female disorders.

estrogen Producing (-gen) estrus or heat (estro-) in animals. Estrogen is the uterus-growth hormone produced by the ovaries. It is known chemically as 17-beta-estradiol, and belongs to the class of chemical substances called **steroids** (as do cortisone, **progesterone**, **testosterone**, etc.) The hormone **estrone** is one of the estrogens.

Upon leaving the ovaries, estrogen causes the uterus to grow by a rather complex procedure. Reaching the uterus (via the blood stream) it enters into each of the uterine cells, travels through the cytoplasm, penetrates the nucleus and attaches itself to **chromosomes** and nucleoli, which in turn produce increased amounts of **RNA** (particularly the r-RNA by the nucleolus). This allows more **r-RNA** in combination to get out of the nucleus into the cytoplasm to produce more **ribosomes** and consequently more protein. The additional protein and r-RNA make an increase in cell size and number with a subsequent increase in the size of the uterus.

Name coined in 1926 by English biologist, Alan Sterling Parkes (born 1900), Ph.D., Manchester 1923 and physician Charles William Bellerby (born 1902), who also introduced term "estrin" for estrogenic hormones.

estrone A female hormone (-one) that stimulates physiological changes characteristic of estrus (estr-) and induces growth of the female sex organs. *See* **estradiol**.

In 1927, two gynecologists, German-born Israeli Bernhard Zondek (born 1891) and German-born Solomon (Selmar) Ascheim (born 1878), discovered that female mice were aroused to sexual heat by the injection of extracts from pregnant women's urine, leading to the isolation in 1929 of pure samples of the hormone by German chemist Adolf Butenandt (born 1903) and American biochemist Edward Doisy (born 1893) which they named estrone. Doisy received the Nobel Prize in 1943. Butenandt received the Nobel Prize in 1949.

estrus (L. *gadfly*, symbolic of frenzy or intense desire; heat). A specific period of time in the sexual cycle of all mammalian females (except for the higher primates), during which they permit copulation. Estrus may be *shortlasting* (10 to 20 hours and recurring every four to five days throughout the year, such as is found in hamsters, mice, rats, etc.), or *long-lasting* (about a week, as in dogs, repeated semi-annually; and in foxes, annually). Estrus may be considered one of four phases of the estrous cycle: (1) *proestrus* (prior to estrus), during which time numerous graafian follicles develop within the ovary in response to **FSH** and **LH**, preparing for the implantation of a

fertilized egg; (2) *estrus*, in which the follicles are maximally developed and the time when ovulation usually occurs; (3) *metestrus* occurs in the absence of fertilization and when the organs begin to adjust themselves to the beginning of a new cycle; and (4) *diestrus* refers to the short intervals of quiescence separating the estrous cycles of polyestrous animals.

eta coefficient (Stat.) Correlation ratio. A measure of association between two continuous variables where the **regression** is curvilinear. Curvilinear correlation assumes that the relation between the two variables can best be described by the equation of a curve rather than the equation of a straight line. It is essentially a negative type of coefficient, being neither an equation for line of best fit nor one that gives any picture of its shape. Eta determines the average variance within each column (row) in a scatter diagram. It is computable for either grouped or ungrouped data. *See* **coefficient of curvilinear correlation** (also Guilford, pp. 310-317).

ethereal Relating to (-al) ether or the air. In the **stereochemical smell theory**, one of the seven primary smell qualities.

ethical determinism *See* **determinism**.

ethogram A written record (-gram) of animal behavior (etho-). A completely documented report on all behavior of a species throughout its life cycle; a procedure recommended by ethologists before any analytical and interpretive studies are made on any specific qualities of behavior. *See* **ethology**.

ethology Study of (-logy) behavior or character (etho-) in animals (of a given species) in their natural environment. Generally conducted by zoologists (specializing in behavioral studies and hence called ethologists), studies are primarily directed toward instinctive behavior, and through them the concept of **instinct** has been revived in psychology. European ethologists consider instinctive behavior to relate to behavioral or physiological patterns that are primarily innate or maturational in nature, and **species-specific**. Most research has been conducted on insects, birds, and fishes rather than mammals, although Pronko reports some recent studies on the gorilla. (*See* **ethogram**, also N. H. Pronko, 1969; R. F. Ewer, "Ethological Concepts," *Science*, **126**, 1957, 599-603; and many articles and books by K. Z. Lorenz and particularly N. Tinbergen's *The Study of Instinct*, 1951).

The term "ethologie" was used in France as early as 1762 in reference to studies of animal activity. In 1842, **J. S. Mill** used the term ethology in his *System of Logic, Ratiocinative and Inductive*, referring to what he called a "science of character" in which behavior should be studied in relation to its environment, the idea eventually developing into social psychology and present-day ethology. Mill, in referring to character, was using the Ionic form of Greek for ethos, which meant character, behavior, or moral disposition resulting from habitual use. In Homerian Greek, ethos developed into what has come to be associated with the term ethical—relating to acceptable behavior or moral action.

Euler diagram A diagram of concentric circles or some variation of them designed to show relationship between **sets** and subsets. A set within a larger set is represented as a circle within a larger circle. Independent sets are shown by separate circles.

Named (about 1774) after Swiss mathematician Leonhard Euler (1707-1783) who popularized the diagrams by writing about them in *Letters to a German Princess* (1772). Student of **Jean Bernoulli**. Euler diagrams set the stage for Venn diagrams (John Venn (1834-1923), English logician) with each circle representing one set. Two or more may overlap, the overlapped areas indicating subsets that may contain elements common to both or all of the individual sets. Venn diagrams represent infinite sets.

There are many variations of the Euler and Venn diagrams used in psychology. One of the more intricate ones appears below; taken from an article by Paul J. Woods, "Psychological Organizations: Their Nature and Membership Patterns," *American Psychologist*, 1964, **19**, 663-669. Copyright 1964 by the American Psychological Association, and reproduced by permission.

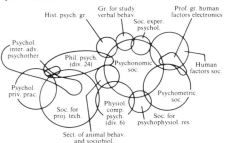

Approximation of the relative sizes and major overlaps of psychological organizations in the spring of 1962.

euphoria A condition (-ia) in which one seems to bear (-phor-) up well (eu-), to have a sense of well being—often false or put-on or resulting from the effects of a drug. It is frequently associated with elated states or episodes of mania.

Hippocrates used the term for those who were able to bear themselves well and also in the sense of being productive or fertile.

Eustachius, Bartolommeo Eustacheo (1524-1574) Italian anatomist and illustrator. In 1564, he reported his description of the **abducens** and **optic nerves**, as well as the **adrenal glands**. *See* **cochlea, ear.**

event A fundamental concept in probability theory. Every possible **outcome** of an experiment is called an elementary or simple event, elements that are completely abstract. Compound events are constructed from simple events, the outcome of the elements of the experiment (Hays, 1963, pp. 9, 48-63).

eviration The process (-ation) of depriving (e-) the male (vir-) of his manhood or virility; castration; emasculation. Also, the assumption by the male of the feminine role in sexual relations (in position, submission, or passivity, or in all).

evoked potential A potential experimentally produced in the brain by various stimuli (a sound click, a light, etc.). An electrical discharge that occurs in the nervous system other than at its original stimulation site, such discharge being recordable by an **averaging computer**, which can average many independent **EEG** records. The recording of evoked potentials is used in the study of mapping of sensory pathways. On the EEG, the evoked potential is observed first by a positive curve deflection followed by a negative deflection and other less pronounced waves. Most studies of attention in human beings indicate that evoked potentials are larger while paying attention.

evoked response (ER) A predictable response in the nervous system of constant pattern brought forth usually by some **sensory stimulus**. In more subtle electrophysiological experiments in which the response is not overt (such as in nonexpressed emotional responses), an evoked response can be determined on the EEG by noting the characteristic wave-form produced or by detecting minor changes in visual and/or aural **displays**.

examens d'état (final examinations) French. The period of examination during which time (and after five years at the **Faculté de Médicine** plus the required 2 years of clinical experience), a sifting of the students is carried on (regardless of whether they have been **externes** or **internes**). If successful, they are permitted to present a doctoral thesis before a commission of professors appointed by the Dean. After successful defense of the thesis and after its publication a diploma of the Doctor of the University of Paris (or some other recognized French university) is granted. *See* **French higher education.**

excitatory postsynaptic potential (EPSP) Relating to (-al) the power (-potenti-) of certain forms of signals (**inputs**) to cause a depolarizing potential to augment the excitatory level and thus increase the likelihood of firing a nerve impulse. Synapses can be either excitatory or inhibitory.

In the **synaptic transmission** of a neural impulse, it is assumed that there is a proclivity toward change (being actually different from the nerve impulse itself) in the next neuron's membrane. The **all-or-none law** does not operate here, but when the ionic exchange is sufficiently strong to pass the threshold it activates an impulse in the second **neuron** which then carries on to its **effector.** The potential change (or partial depolarization of cell bodies and dendrites) responds to release of a so-called excitatory **transmitter substance** by **synaptic knobs.**

Each neuron is a cell specialized to: receive stimuli or inputs, respond with certain outputs (such as any **motor response**), conduct impulses, and make "functional contacts with other neurons or with receptors or effectors." Each cell membrane changes its resistance or "conductance to one or more species of ions . . . resulting in a **gating** of current that can represent a large power amplification. Of several types of active potential involved in cell membrane change, the **exogenic** type (responses to environmental stimuli or from other neurons) is the one concerned with excitatory postsynaptic potential (EPSP) and **inhibitory post-synaptic potential (IPSP).**" (Quarton, et al , pp. 348 f., and 408 f.)

Both the excitatory postsynaptic potential and the inhibitory postsynaptic potential were so-named by J. S. Coombs, J. C. Eccles, and P. Fatt in their article: Excitatory Synaptic Action in Motoneurons, *Journal of Physiology*, 1955, 130, 374-395.

executive program (Comput.) A permanently stored program that provides a master control over all the system's functions.

exercise, law of *See* **law of exercise.**

exhaustion *See* **general adaptation syndrome;** also **Hans Selye.**

existence The quality of being; the awareness of knowing that life is an ongoing process. Kierkegaard, a Danish pioneer in existential thinking, said that ". . . existence is precisely the opposite of finality . . . Existence separates and holds the various moments of reality discretely apart."

Martin Heidegger, German philosopher (influenced by Nietzsche), gave an existential twist to **Husserl's phenomenology.** Heidegger believed that reality derived its meaning strictly from self and that the only being that exists is Man. "God is, but He does not exist . . . To be a self is admittedly one feature of the nature of that being which exists; but existence does not consist in being a self, nor can it be defined in such terms." Sartre said that "Every existing thing is born without reason, prolongs itself out of weakness, and dies by chance." See **dread.**

existential anxiety A feeling of restlessness and dissatisfaction stemming apparently from one's inability to find **closure** and satisfaction in his way of life.

existentialism Relating to (-al) a doctrine (-ism) about the existence (existenti-) of man. A philosophical attitude expressing the idea that man, far from being a machine, has the freedom to make choices and must not only take the responsibility for his own existence but also for achieving some degree of **self-actualization.** Man must create values for himself through action.

There is no essential human nature common to all men, each individual finding it necessary to create his own essence by his choice of interests, actions, and **life style. Existence** therefore precedes **essence,** since essence is not completed until life ceases. The existential nature of **Titchener's** concept of the task of psychology (that it was limited to observation and description of contents of experience) led to the term of *existential psychology.* (Rollo May, et al., eds., *Existence: A New Dimension in Psychiatry and Psychology* (Basic Books, 1958); and Hazel E. Barnes, *Humanistic Existentialism*, University of Nebraska Press, 1965.)

existential therapy A form of therapy or attitudinal stance of a therapist that deals with the "here and now" of the total situation rather than with the client's past as emphasized in the Freudian approach. Resolving present conflicts prepares one for **self-actualization** in the future. Ludwig Binswanger (1852-1929), a Swiss existential psychoanalyst deeply influenced by **Husserl** and **Freud,** considered the patient's whole mode of consciousness, his existential presence, as most important in treating him. *See* **existence, existentialism, logotherapy.**

exocrine gland A gland that secretes (-crine) outwardly (ex-). A gland whose fluids are secreted through a duct leading to the outside, as in the case of the salivary glands, sweat glands, etc. *Opposite of* **endocrine gland.**

exogenic (exogenous) Related to (-ic) those factors produced (-genous) or generated (-gen-) externally (exo-), such as those caused by external events or the environment. Distinguished from **endogenous.** *See* **excitatory postsynaptic potential, Kraepelin.**

expected value (Stat.) The mean value of a **random** variable over an indefinite number of samplings. The expected value $E(X)$ of a discrete random variable X is given by $E(X) = \Sigma Xp(X) = $ mean of X, the sum being taken over any value of X. In all **probability** distributions, the computation of a **mean** is based on probabilities from a table (the value of the **population** proportion), this mean being called the expected value of p, or $E(p)$.

The concept of an expected value originated in games of chance where it referred to expected long-term **outcomes** (winnings or losings) over repeated play (Walker-Lev. 1953, p. 27; Hays, 1964, p. 167; Kirk, 1968, pp. 509-512, 554).

experiment A situation in which an observer tries to control various factors (variables) while manipulating other **variables** so that he can objectively study relationships between them. The factor introduced into the experiment is called the **independent** (experimental) **variable,** while the one observed is the **dependent variable.**

experimental control The type of control necessary in experiments, whereby all **variables** (other than the **independent variable**) that might affect the results are held constant. *See* **proactive inhibition.**

experimental design The plan of an experiment arranged to produce the most advantageous analysis of the results. It is a guideline for experimental action covering the selection of the **independent variable,** selection of the experimental units, randomization procedures, and analysis of data (Edwards, 1967, p. 9; Hays, 1964, p. 457; Winer, 1962, Chapters 3, 5; Kirk, 1968, pp. 1, 12, 20-22).

experimental error Any error that occurs in **parameter** estimation resulting from sampling variations. Determination of such errors is based on the estimated differences that would occur if repeated **samples** were taken from the same **population. Reliability** measurements help give an indication of the extent of experiment error.

experimental extinction Disappearance of the **conditioned response** in **conditioning** experiments when, after the conditioned response has been established, presentation of the

conditioned stimulus is continued without reward (the **unconditioned stimulus**). For example, if an animal has been conditioned to respond (salivate) to a bell (the conditioned stimulus) in lieu of food (the unconditioned stimulus), it will in time cease to respond if the food is withheld entirely. The conditioning has been experimentally extinguished. *See* **extinction.**

experimental group The unit of subjects in an experiment subjected to the experimental conditions, for which the **independent** (experimental) **variable** is manipulated by the experimenter.

experimental method *See* **methods of psychology: experimental.**

experimental neurosis Experimentally induced **neurosis** or emotionally disturbed behavior of laboratory animals when they are subjected to conditions beyond their capacities to make discriminations or adjustments.

The term was introduced by **I. P. Pavlov** in 1927 while training dogs to salivate by feeding them as they viewed a luminous circle projected on a screen and not feeding them as an ellipse was shown. A dog learned to discriminate between the circle and the ellipse, but when the ellipse was made to approach a perfect circle the dog's powers of discrimination broke down and it became frantic. Pavlov said that the experimental conditions had produced neurosis by bringing the dog to the limit of its ability to discriminate between stimuli.

Since Pavlov's early work (*Conditioned Reflexes*, 1927), many psychologists have reproduced similar results on sheep, rats, cats, etc.

Experimental Psychologists, Society of *See* **Society of Experimental Psychologists.**

experimental psychology A specialized area of psychology concerned with the investigation and study of psychological phenomena, using controlled, scientific methodology to help arrive at logical, well-documented conclusions that are replicable.

Albrecht von Haller (1708-1777), Swiss philosopher and physician, is sometimes considered to be the first "experimental" psychologist because of some of his studies on tissue irritability and sensibility (concerning tissues supplied with nerves). *See* **Wundt.**

Experimental Publication System (EPS) An experimental program, instituted by the **American Psychological Association,** designed to explore the advantages and disadvantages of an early publication system; a phase of the **National Information System for Psychology.**

experimenter bias The tendency for an experimenter to allow his own prejudices (in ideas, feelings, or slant as to how he would like the experiment to turn out) to interfere with his objectivity in collecting and interpreting **data,** as well as in the procedures used in the experiment.

explosive personality (epileptoid personality disorder) *See* **personality disorder.**

exponent An index or indicator of the power to which a quantity is raised. The number or symbol in the superscript position, at the right and above a base number (a) indicating the power to which a is raised. For example, a^3 indicates that a is to be cubed or raised to the third power; $(ab)^2 = a^2 b^2$; $4^3 = 4 \cdot 4 \cdot 4 = 64$.

exponential curve A graph of an exponential function in which an **independent variable** appears in one of the **exponents.**

external capsule *See* **basal ganglia.**

external memory A storage medium outside the **computer system,** such as a punched card, a magnetic tape, or some form dictated by the computer.

externe des hôpitaux A part-time, non-resident hospital position in France.

externeship The beginning of the formal medical training of the student at the hospital services—quite distinct from the formal medical education at the Faculté de Médicine. The externeship (length of time served dependent

e

upon individual medical student, although it generally lasts about two years) is prerequisite to the student's eligibility for competitive examination for an appointment as *interne* at one of the municipal hospitals (*interne des hôpitaux*). *See* **French higher education.**

exteroceptor A sense organ or (re)ceptor (such as skin pressure receptors, **rods** and **cones,** taste buds) stimulated by physical changes or events outside (extero-) the organism.

This term, along with **interoceptor** and **pro-prioceptor,** was introduced by **Sherrington** in *The Integrative Action of the Nervous System,* 1906.

f

extinction (ext.) Act (-ion) of making extinct. In **operant conditioning** the elimination of a **conditioned response** learned under conditions of reinforcement when the reinforcing stimulus is discontinued; also, the tendency to stop a learned response no longer reinforced. Resistance to extinction varies under different **schedules of reinforcement,** partial reinforcement or intermittent reward seeming to promote the strongest resistance. Extinction also refers to the strength of a response that immediately follows elimination of the reinforcement.

Operant extinction refers to either *operation* (in which a reinforcer previously dependent upon an operant is withheld) or *process* (making less likely the rate of occurrence of a previously reinforced operant). *Respondent extinction* also refers to *operation* (with the **conditioned stimulus** occurring without the **unconditioned stimulus**) and to *process* (with a reduction in any dimension of the response elicited by the conditioned stimulus).

In therapeutic situations, extinction of **anxiety** has played a major role in **behavior therapy** as well as in Estes' applications of extinction principles in the study of punishment. *See* **experimental extinction;** (also, W. K. Estes, "An Experimental Study of Punishment," *Psychological Monographs,* No. **263** [1944] **57,** 37-38; and J. Wolpe, *Psychotherapy by Reciprocal Inhibition,* 1958).

extirpation experiments Experiments involving the act (-tion) of rooting (-tirp-) out (ex-). Surgical removal, destruction, or amputation of part of the brain for experimental purposes in order to determine brain function. *See* **ablation, localization of brain function.**

extrapyramidal system All the cortical descending neural pathways that are outside (extra-) the **pyramidal system** (which consists of cortical motor neurons destined for the **brainstem** and spinal cord). The relatively short extrapyramidal neurons, as they descend through the brainstem, connect with subcortical nuclei and motoneurons, involving the **basal ganglia** (including the **corpus striatum** and the **brainstem reticular formation** in their reversible projections). It is theorized that the extrapyramidal system promotes and maintains movement and posture.

Because of overlapping areas and functions the extrapyramidal system definition is only a token one. It may be best to consider for a definition only **basal ganglia** considered as part of the extrapyramidal system (excluding the **amygdala,** the **thalamus** and other parts associated with the **rhinencephalon**).

Samuel Alexander Kinnier Wilson (1878-1937), English neurologist, coined the term *extrapyramidal system* in 1924.

extrasensory perception (ESP) The process of becoming aware of or otherwise responding to an external object, event, or situation that is unavailable to ordinary sensory processes. *Psychokinesis* (telekinesis) involves exerting an influence upon an outside physical object, event, or situation without the direct use of the muscles or any other physical device. Three subheads of ESP are distinguishable: *Telepathy* is the ESP of another person's thoughts or purely subjective state. *Clairvoyance* is the ESP of a physical object, event,

or situation that is known to any person at the time. *Precognition* is the ESP of a future event that is beyond the reach of logical inference and that is not in any way later influenced or produced to make the target fit the prediction (J. Gaither Pratt, *Parapsychology: An Insider's View of ESP* [Dutton, 1966], pp. 33-34).

extrinsic cortex Pribram's term (1958) for cortical areas that receive stimuli directly from the environment. A substitute term for sensory area. *Compare with* **intrinsic cortex.** (Milner, p. 112).

F

F (For any F statistic, see respective alphabetical listing); frequency in a **population.**

f Frequency in a **sample** (or event class).

face validity The degree to which a test appears to measure the situation or phenomenon being tested, such observation assumed to be valid simply by definition or acceptance of what a measuring instrument is called. It is the assumed **validity** of a test because it resembles the **criterion** measure. Face validity is not an adequate index of "true" (or empirical) validity.

facial nerve Cranial nerve VII of vertebrates, functioning mainly as a motor nerve in mammals. It innervates muscles of the face, salivary glands, and the taste buds on the frontal two-thirds of the tongue.

Galen listed seven pairs of cranial nerves, the fifth pair combining the facial and auditory. **Willis** listed nine pairs, dividing his seventh into facial and auditory. **Soemmering** separated the facial and auditory as seventh and eighth in 1778, actually naming the seventh as facial. In 1822-23, the first adequate description of the nerve's function was given by the English physician, Herbert Mayo (1796-1852), in which he described the **motor** function of the nerve (as well as the sensory function of the fifth—the **trigeminal**).

facial vision *See* **echolocation.**

factor An **independent variable** that is investigated in an experiment; a quantity that will divide into another quantity exactly without remainder; one of two or more quantities that, when multiplied together, produce a given quantity; any **trait** or **variable** that accounts for **correlations** among variables.

factor analysis One of several mathematical-statistical procedures involving a large number of sets of intercorrelations or matrices of numbers. Factor analysis starts with locating a model that must agree with the **data** and when it does, estimating its **parameters.** It is aimed at discovering, isolating, and analyzing the minimal number of common factors (determiners) that can account for the observed **correlation** (community) among a set of variables (items on a test, etc.). Factor analysis shows in summary form the relative importance of each factor sorted out of a more complex **population,** the factors being preferably fewer in number than the original variables.

In using factor analysis for experiments there are definite *advantages,* such as enabling efficient use and evaluation of all subjects and resources as well as of experimental and interaction effects. *Disadvantages* are in the prohibitive number of subjects required if many treatments are demanded; the large number of experiments required; and the complex interpretations needed when interactions evolve.

Factor analysis is an outgrowth of **Spearman's** research on **g** and his **tetrad difference method** as elaborated by **Thurstone** in his search for **primary mental abilities.**

factorial A symbol (!) denoting the product of consecutive integers beginning with one and continuing to the given number. Thus, 4! =

$1 \cdot 2 \cdot 3 \cdot 4 = 24$ is called factorial 4 or 4 factorial. Factorials are often used in problems involving permutations, combinations, and **probability** theory.

factorial design (More correctly factorial type experiments). An experimental plan used to study simultaneously the effect of several **independent variables** (including all combinations of levels of the variables) upon a **dependent variable.**

factorial validity *See* **validity.**

Faculté de Médécine An academic institution run by the central government in France.

faculty (facultas=facility) In American and English colleges and universities, the teaching personnel. In European academic institutions, faculty signifies a division or department of the university (such as *Faculté de Médécine* means School of Medicine of a French university).

faculty psychology A pre-experimental psychology that viewed the mind as possessing a number of separate powers or faculties, including intellect, feeling, attention, memory, will, etc., which produce and are responsible for the various mental activities. Faculty psychology had its origins with **Saint Augustine,** who posited three faculties of the mind: reason, memory, and will. *See* **Aristotle, Descartes, Hamilton.**

FAE Figural aftereffects.

FAGR Fractional anticipatory goal response.

Fakultät In Germany, full status of a faculty member, including tenure rights; faculty in a university. *See* **German higher education.**

fall chronometer In reaction-time experiments, an instrument used to measure (-meter) time (chrono-) intervals, consisting of a weight that either makes or breaks contact with an electrical recording device when it falls or is allowed to drop.

Fallopius, Gabriele Fallopio (1523-1563). Italian anatomist, studied under **Vesalius.** Introduced terms **cochlea** and **labyrinth** to anatomy in 1561. His thorough description of the uterine tubes in 1561 in his only book, *Observationes Anatomicae,* led subsequent authorities to refer to the human oviducts as Fallopian tubes. *See* **corpus luteum, malleus, trigeminal nerve.**

false negative numbers (or cases) The proportion of individuals falling below a critical score in a certain group (e.g., on an **aptitude test** or on college entrance examination), which arbitrarily eliminates them from passing or entering school. The false negatives are the ones who would have been successful if the cut-off point or **criterion** had not been used to exclude them.

false positive numbers (or cases) Cases that are passed or admitted into a program by passing the **criteria,** but then fail the program.

family therapy (family-centered therapy) A method of **group** psycho**therapy** in which as many members of a patient's family as considered desirable or practicable are brought together to discuss, clarify, and resolve their problems as a unit with a marriage counselor, social worker, clinical psychologist, or **psychiatrist** or with two of them acting as the catalyst in the same room at the same time.

American psychiatrist John Bell was one of the first so-called "family therapists," followed in 1934 by American psychiatrists Clarence Oberndorf (1882-1954) and Nathan Ackerman (born 1908, Russia).

FAP Fixed action pattern.

farad (F) The SI unit of capacitance, equal to the capacitance of a capacitor (condenser) between the plates of which there occurs a potential difference of 1 volt when it is charged by a quantity of electricity equal to 1 coulomb. *See* **International System of Units.** Named after Faraday.

Faraday, Michael (1791-1867) English physicist and chemist. In 1833, he, among his other contributions to electricity, introduced various electrical terms often used in experimental psychology and psychophysiology: **anion, anode, ion, cathode, cation, electrode.**

f

farsightedness Deficient visual acuity in which distant objects seem to be seen more clearly than near ones. There are two types of farsightedness: (1) **hyperopia** and (2) **presbyopia**.

fasciculus (fascicle) A small (-culus) bundle (fasci-), as of nerve fibers.

F distribution The sampling distribution expected from a large number of *F* ratios, its form depending upon the number of **degrees of freedom** of the two **variance** estimates. The *F* ratio is technically an *F* test **statistic** whose sampling distribution is the *F* distribution, which actually is a function of the sizes of two samples. For every *F* ratio there are degrees of freedom associated with the numerator as well as with the denominator. *F* curves tend toward symmetry as the values of *df* become larger. The *F* distribution is used to test hypotheses of the form

$$H_0 : \mu_1 = \mu_2 = \cdots = \mu_k$$

(which involves analysis of variance),

$$H_0 : \sigma_1^2 - \sigma_2^2 = 0$$

(which doesn't involve analysis of variance). One formula for computing *F* is as follows:

$$F = \frac{est\ \sigma_1^2}{est\ \sigma_2^2} = \frac{s_1^2}{s_2^2}$$

where s_1^2 is the larger variance.

The *F* distribution was so named in 1934 by G. W. Snedecor in tribute to **R. A. Fisher**, who developed the distribution in 1924 (Hays, 1964, 348-355; Kirk, 1968, 39-41. *See* Table 20.

Fechner, Gustav Theodor (1801-1887) German physicist and philosopher. He published *Elements of Psychophysics*, 1860 (in two parts), expressing relationship between psychology and physics, thereby formulating the **Weber-Fechner law**. He attempted to express a relation between mind and body, claiming that they were not separate entities but actually one (often called the identity hypothesis or panpsychism).

In reformulating Weber's law, Fechner indicated that, within limits, the sensory intensity increases arithmetically as stimulus intensity increases geometrically, or that the magnitude of a sensation is roughly proportional to the **logarithm** of stimulus intensity.

$$S = k\ log\ \mathbf{R}$$

where *S* = magnitude of a sensation, measured in number of **jnd**'s above threshold, **R** = magnitude of stimulus intensity, measured in terms of **detection threshold**, and *k* = some arbitrary constant. Boring indicates several restrictions in the use of $S = k\ log\ \mathbf{R}$ (p. 289).

Fechner also defined the **constant-stimulus method**, the **average error method**, and the **method of limits**, all used in psychophysics.

See **Herbart**, **methods of psychology** (also Hays, 1963, p. 27; Boring, pp. 275-283).

feeblemindedness An obsolete term for **mental retardation**, considered as a lack of mental capacity or as a defect in the **brain cells**. In the *social sense*, a feebleminded person is one who is unable to care for himself, requiring constant supervision and control. In the *psychological sense*, the feebleminded person customarily falls below 70 in **intelligence quotient**, with a mental age not progressing beyond that of the average child of 11. *Idiot* is the extreme on the scale of feeblemindedness (IQ 0-25); *imbecile* next (IQ 26-50); and *moron* nearest normal (IQ 51-70). These labels and intelligence quotients are merely historical carry-overs of an outmoded means of classification, and should not be used in a diagnostic sense.

feedback Knowledge of results. The returning to a control center (servomechanism or nervous system) of the error-correcting informa-tion about events maintained under its control. In psychology, the sensory return of information from the periphery used for controlling movement and analogous processes; in learning, knowledge fed back to the learner on how well he is progressing. A *feedback system* is self-regulating (e.g., kinesthetic sensitivity, thermostatic control of room temperature) in that it uses its information from one event to control related subsequent events. *See* **biofeedback training**.

feeding center An area in the lateral hypothalamic region that is involved in food and water intake, particularly in the process of starting to eat. Lesions in this hypothalamic area produce **adipsia** and **aphagia**. *See* **glucostatic theory**, **lipostatic hypothesis**, **thermostatic theory**, and **ventromedial nucleus**.

Fellowship of the Royal Society (F.R.S.) The most coveted scientific honor by an English scientist, attained only by election.

femto (Danish.) One-quadrillionth.

fenestra Window (fenestra), referring particularly to the **round window** (*fenestra rotunda*) or to the **oval window** (*fenestra ovalis*). *Fenestra cochlea* is a term sometimes used for fenestra rotunda.

In 1645, Italian anatomist, Cecilio Folli (1615-1660), described these ear structures.

feral child Relating to (-al) a wild (fer-) child, or to human offspring reportedly raised by animals. Such reports have not been well authenticated. Behavior is similar to any child who has been found to be suffering the effects of severe isolation from human contact (R. M. Zingg, "Feral Man and Extreme Cases of Isolation," *American Journal of Psychology*, 1940, 53, 487-515; K. Davis, "Final Note on a Case of Extreme Isolation," *American Journal of Sociology*, 1947, 53, 432-437; Bruno Bettelheim, "Feral Children and Autistic Children," *American Journal of Sociology*, 1959, 63, 455-467).

Ferenczi, Sandor (1873-1933) Hungarian pioneer psychoanalyst and friend of **Freud**. Developed **active therapy** and coined terms **alloplastic** and **autoplastic adaptation**. *See* **introjection**, **relaxation therapy**.

Ferrier, David (1843-1928) British neurologist (born in Scotland). M.D., Edinburgh 1868. Used the faradic current to repeat and confirm experiments of **Fritsch** and **Hitzig** (who had used the galvanic current) on cortical localization. Ferrier mapped the **cerebral cortex** of the monkey, showing that the excitable areas were limited to various **gyri** in the cerebral cortex, and indicating the regions of the **motor cortex**.

Festinger, Leon (born New York, 1919). Ph.D. (psychology), Iowa 1942. Theorist and experimenter in social psychology, especially in studies on prejudice, communication of humor, and the development of a theory on **cognitive dissonance**. Received **DSC Award** 1959.

fetishism Practice or belief (-ism) in a fetish ("magic," from Portuguese). A perverse attachment or fixation on what is ordinarily a nonsexual object (pair of sox, finger ring, etc.) but may also be an appendage or part of the human body itself (such as the hair, the feet, etc.). Often, erotic feelings to the point of orgasm are achieved by the fetishist. In anthropology, fetishism involves the veneration of inanimate objects that are believed to have magical powers.

The term was introduced into psychology by **Binet** in reference to those who derived sexual gratification directly or indirectly from the collection and possession of various items.

fetus (A bringing forth, offspring). Any vertebrate but especially the unborn human organism in the womb from about the eighth week after conception until birth.

FI Fixed interval schedule.

field, phenomenal or phenomenological *See* **phenomenal field**.

fields of psychology There are two major areas or fields of psychology: (1) *theoretical* (including experimental, abnormal, social, comparative, statistical, physiological); and (2) *applied* (vocational and industrial, including personnel, educational, criminal, correctional, and legal; and clinical, including testing, counseling, and therapy of the child, adolescent, and adult).

Testing and social psychology are both theoretical and applied. The distinctions between theoretical and applied psychology are merely traditional, for scientific psychology could not be conscientiously applied without adequate theoretical backgrounds.

field theory A social-psychological theory associated with personality and social psychology. It was developed by **Kurt Lewin** who was concerned with the subject's present psychological states (immediate perceptions) as they affect his responses. "Every psychological event" he said "depends upon the state of the person and at the same time on the environment, although their relative importance is different in different cases." *See* **monad**, **topological psychology**; also K. W. Lewin, *Principles of Topological Psychology*, 1936, p. 12.

fifth cranial nerve Trigeminal nerve. *See* **cranial nerves**.

figural aftereffect (FAE) Distortion or illusion (usually a change in apparent shape or location of a visual figure) produced as a result of fixation on a previous **illusion** or pattern. Figural aftereffects may be classified as: *rotational aftereffect*, in which illusions of movement are created after actual rotation has stopped, and **kinesthetic aftereffect**, involving a muscle-sense awareness of changes in one's experiences of width (Weintraub and Walker, 1968, Chapter 6).

figure-ground effect The tendency of one part of a perceptual configuration (or an event) to stand out distinctly against its background.

This concept was expressed in 1915 by the phenomenologically-oriented Danish psychologist Edgar Ruben, who had begun his research in 1912. Goldstein used the term *figure* in 1934 as an essential character of all physiological processes. Ruben was the first to differentiate between figure and ground by using figures in black and white (see figure in **figure-ground relationship**) and classifying their phenomenal differences.

figure-ground relationship The Gestalt concept that visual perception is divided into two parts, figure and ground. The figure or object attended to is seen "in focus" and as a whole, while the rest of the visual field, less clearly seen, is the ground or background. By a shift in attention or perception different objects in the field may become figure and the former figure may become part of the ground. For example, the ambiguous figure pictured may be seen either as black faces on a white background or as a white vase on a black background. *See* **illusion**, **figure-ground effect**.

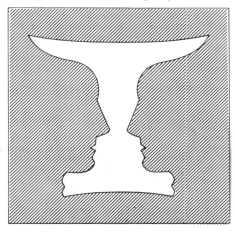

f

file (Comput.) An organized set of collected **data**, items, or records (all having something in common), generally stored on a peripheral device (such as a magnetic tape) and treated as a unit.

filial regression Relating to (-al) the **regression** involving a son or daughter (fili-). A principle developed by Galton (1869) stating that offspring tend, as a whole, to approach the average of their parents' general group; also that offspring of gifted parents tend to regress to the average. For example, the offspring of two very intelligent (or very tall) parents will tend toward the parents' **mean** in **intelligence** (or in height).

final common path The "funnel" or pathway, particularly in the function of the spinal cord, through which many different nerve impulses meet and which is in direct control of musculature.

Sherrington introduced the phrase in 1904, saying that "The terminal path may, to distinguish it from internuncial common paths, be called the final common path, with the motor nerve to a muscle being a collection of such paths." (Sherrington, p. 116).

finger maze A maze, often used to test blindfolded human subjects, in which the path to the goal is traced by hand.

first moment The first moment about a **mean** is zero. See **moments**.

first order neuron A myelinated preganglionic neuron whose cell body lies in the **central nervous system**. Their **axons** (preganglionic fibers) pass through cranial or spinal nerves to **ganglia**, where they terminate.

first signal (system) stimulus Any or all stimuli that are basically non-verbal in nature. Even though a word is verbal in context it "initially emerges as a first signal system stimulus" (Cole and Maltzman, p. 178). Pavlov attributed "our perceptions and concepts" to the first signal system, transmitting not only "sensory material to the second signal system" but "also performs initial, elementary forms of analysis and synthesis characteristic of clear thinking." (Cole and Maltzman, p. 533). See **second signal system**.

Fischer, Emil (1852-1929) German chemist. Investigated **purines**, synthesized dextrose and levulose. Isolated many new compounds including **Veronal** (1902) and **barbiturates**. Nobel prize in 1902.

Fisher, Sir Ronald Aylmer (1890-1962) English statistician; innovator of many unique approaches in statistical theory. The use of *F* in statistics usually refers to a specialized **statistic** developed by Fisher, who first applied his statistics in agricultural research and later in genetic studies. The following three statistical procedures are named after Fisher.

Fisher's distribution See **F distribution**.

Fisher's exact test A test used with a two-by-two **contingency table** to compute the exact **probability** of a "sample's showing as much or more evidence for association than that obtained, given only the operation of chance." (Hays, 1964, p. 599).

Fisher's r to Z transformation. A statistical technique involving a nonlinear transformation of *r*, used for handling sampling errors for high values of *r*. Used to test hypotheses about ρ_{XY} and to establish confidence intervals for ρ_{XY}. The function relating *r* to *Z* is given by

$$Z = \frac{1}{2} \log_e \left(\frac{1 + r_{XY}}{1 - r_{XY}} \right)$$

(Hays, p. 530; see Table 12.)

fissure A cleft, crack, or groove in any organ, especially one of the deep folds on the surface of the **cerebral cortex**; also called a *sulcus*. Two principal fissures are: (1) the **fissure of Sylvius** (or lateral fissure); named after the Prussian anatomist, Franciscus Sylvius, pseudonym of Franz de la Boes (1614-1672), who published (1641) a description of the lateral fissure, which separated the anterior

lobe of the **cerebrum** from the middle lobe. The largest of the cerebral fissures, it begins about halfway between the front and center side of the cerebrum, angling back and upward, terminating toward the back and side of the cerebrum. See **Broca's speech area, central lobe, frontal lobes**. (2) Fissure of Rolando (or central fissure); named after Luigi Rolando (1773-1831), Italian anatomist, who described this sulcus as lying between the parietal and frontal lobes. It runs laterally across the top of the **cerebrum**, then proceeds downward and slightly forward toward the ears. It is apparently concerned with body awareness. The area of this fissure, however, was first described in 1781 by **Vicq d'Azyr**. However, another French anatomist, **Francois Leuret**, not knowing of Vicq d'Azyr's earlier work, named (1839) this fissure after Rolando.

fistula A small (-ula) tube or pipe (fist-). Usually, an abnormal hollow passage from an abcess or cavity to the exterior; in physiology and psychology, a surgical canal not permitted to heal, such as the fistula created in the cheeks of **Pavlov**'s dogs for purposes of collecting and measuring salivary flow under varying conditions.

fit, goodness of See **goodness of fit**.

five HTP (5HTP) Technically known as 5-hydroxytryptophan, the chemical precursor to 5-hydroxytryptamine or **serotonin**. It is possible for 5HTP to cross the **blood-brain barrier** freely (which serotonin cannot do) and be converted to serotonin in the brain tissue. (Thompson, pp. 116-125).

fixation Process or act (-tion) of fixating. In *psychoanalytic theory*, the arresting of emotional development at an early psychosexual stage, making possible the gratification of needs through behavior that is appropriate to a developmental stage ordinarily previously outgrown. For example, a mature man may, in periods of stress, suck his thumb. In 1915, Freud said "A particularly close attachment of the instinct to its object is distinguished by the term fixation; this frequently occurs in very early stages of the instinct's development and so puts an end to its mobility, through the vigorous resistance it sets up against detachment" (Instincts and Their Vicissitudes, in *Collected Papers*, Hogarth, 4, pp. 65-66).

In *learning theory*, fixation may refer simply to a well-conditioned response (Mowrer 1940), but it also connotes the persistence of a response in conflict situations, the endurance of an unchanging habit developed by repeated partial reinforcement, frustration, or continual punishment, and the unwillingness to relinquish old habits for new, more reinforcing experiences (O. H. Mowrer, "An Experimental Analogue of 'Regression' with Incidental Observations on 'Reaction-Formation,'" *Journal of Abnormal Social Psychology*, 35 (1940), 56-87; I. E. Farber, "Response Fixation Under Anxiety and Non-anxiety Conditions," *Journal of Experimental Psychology*, 38 (1948), 111-131).

Fixation also refers to eye-convergence (with eyes fastened to a specific point in space), in which an object's image is projected onto the **fovea**.

fixed action pattern (FAP) A basic behavior pattern that is presumed to be encoded in the genes, its programmed sequential order being controlled by a neurological center. The FAP is neither a reflex, an instinct in the ordinary sense, nor a learned act. Its uniqueness is further emphasized in that it follows stereotyped behavior invariably and predictably, it is independent of learning and from external control, and it is spontaneous in action. Examples of FAP behavior are: the egg-retrieving behavior of the grey-lag goose, the human neonate's side-to-side movement of its head, the zigzag sex dance of the stickleback, etc. (H. Moltz "The Fixed Action Pattern: Empirical Properties and Theoretical Implications," in J. Wortis [Ed.], *Recent Advances in*

Biological Psychiatry Vol. 4, 1962; H. Moltz, "Contemporary Instinct Theory and the Fixed Action Pattern," *Psychological Review*, 1965, 72, 22-47).

fixed effects model An experimental design model that assumes that all treatment levels about which inferences are to be drawn, including those in replication experiments, are necessarily included in the experiment.

fixed interval schedule (FI) An operant **conditioning** technique (involving a simple intermittent **schedule of reinforcement**) requiring the passage of a constant predetermined fixed-time interval (e.g., 2, 5, 10 minutes), measured from the preceding reinforced response before reinforcing the new response. A given interval schedule is indicated by adding the number of minutes to the letters FI, thus FI2 is a reinforcement schedule with the first response occurring 2 minutes after the previous reinforcement has been reinforced.

fixed ratio schedule (FR) An operant conditioning technique (involving a simple intermittent **schedule of reinforcement**) in which a response is reinforced only after a predetermined fixed number of correct responses have been counted since the preceding reinforcement, the ratio referring to responses/reinforcement. A fixed ratio schedule is given by adding to the letters FR a number designating the ratio, thus FR50 is a reinforcement schedule in which the 50th response after the preceding reinforcement is reinforced.

fixed-role therapy A specialized type of therapy in which the patient and therapist(s) jointly construct and write out a fixed-role sketch for the patient, who practices the new role continuously (both in and out of the office), after the therapist has demonstrated the new forms of behavior he wants him to play. Roles vary from time to time, enabling the neurotic patient to "test out" his limits in new experiences. The aim of fixed-role therapy is to help the patient change his undesirable personal constructs.

Fixed-role therapy is an outgrowth of **Kelly**'s personality theory asserting that people tend to behave in the manner in which they construe, interpret, and anticipate coming events (George A. Kelly, *The Psychology of Personal Constructs*, 1955).

flaccid See **muscle tone**.

Flechsig, Paul Emil (1847-1929) German physician (M.D. Leipzig 1865) and **psychiatrist**. His myelogenetic studies (based on myelinization of neural fibers maturing at different times in different cerebral pathways) led to many discoveries in the brain and spinal cord (such as being able to trace the pyramidal tract to the cortex, and in being able to make various discriminations between cortical areas). See **association areas of the brain**.

Flemming, Walther German anatomist (1843-1905), the first to describe the **centrosome**. Named **chromatin** and **mitosis**.

flexibilitas cerea Same as **cerea flexibilitas**.

flicker A wavering, unsteady light. Rapidly recurring changes in visual or auditory perception resulting from an intermittent flashing on and off of a light stimulus. See **critical flicker frequency, episcotister**.

flicker fusion See **fusion**.

flip-flop (bistable multivibrator or Eccles-Jordan circuit). A monostable or bistable electronic circuit and trigger that maintains one of two stable states enabling the storage of one bit of information; the context, however, should clarify which alternative has been selected.

floral Relating to (-al) flowers (flor-). A flowery smell, one of the seven primary qualities of the **stereochemical smell theory**.

Flourens, Pierre (1794-1867) French physician and neurophysiologist who carried out many investigations on the **central nervous system**. He is thought of as the pioneer in developing the holistic theory of brain function, but he handicapped the development of cortical localization by vigorously opposing Gall's teachings on this matter. He taught that the **cerebral hemispheres** were the center of **intelligence** and sensation and the **cerebellum** of **motor** function. *See* **ataxia.**

flowchart A chart that graphically depicts the sequence of operations, events, or flow of data in logical order from the beginning to the end of a procedure. Flowchart symbols (squares, triangles, etc.) must be labeled to indicate their meanings. Flowcharts are useful for laying out the sequence of operations in a **computer program** and for planning psychological experiments, particularly in the area of social psychology, such as in **information processing.**

Fmax statistic A test for detecting heterogeneity among k **population variances.** The test statistic F_{max} is given by:

$$F_{max} = \frac{\text{largest of } k \text{ variances}}{\text{smallest of } k \text{ variances}} = \frac{\sigma_j^2 \text{ largest}}{\sigma_j^2 \text{ smallest}}$$

where k = the number of variances, n = the number of observations within each treatment level, and σ_j^2 = unbiased estimate of population, variance for the jth population, and with degrees of freedom = to k and $n-1$.

If treatment level n's differ only slightly, the largest n can be used to determine the degrees of freedom, this procedure leading to a positive bias in the test. *See* Table 19.

Test designed by Herman O. Hartley (born Berlin 1912). Received Ph.D. (mathematics), Berlin 1934 and Ph.D. (statistics), Cambridge 1940. Became British citizen and later migrated to the United States, where he became a professor of statistics at Iowa State and Texas A and M.

focal motor seizure Convulsive movement that occurs only in the part of the body controlled by a damaged part of the **brain.**

focus *See* **parabola.**

folie Madness. A special class (the eighth) of nervous disorders as classified (1750) by French physician, Francois Boissier de Sauvages (1706-1767). From this term various others developed, such as:

Folie à deux. Madness (*folie*), or delusional ideas supposedly transmitted to and shared by two (*deux*) and sometimes more intimately associated persons (spouses, friends, etc., but not blood-relations). The condition is primarily paranoidal, seeming to propagate itself more favorably in a religious medium and with very suggestible persons, often taking the form of suicide pacts and criminal acts performed together.

The condition was described and named in 1867 by two French psychiatrists, Jean Pierre Falret (1794-1870), a pupil of the French psychiatrist Jean Esquirol (1772-1840), and Ernest Charles Lasègue (1816-1883).

Folie de doute. Madness (*folie*) of (*de*) doubt (*doute*). Pathological indecision involving generally simple choices.

follicle Any small (-cle) sac-like (folli-) gland producing a secretion or excretion.

Term introduced by Linnaeus (*see* **aphasia**).

follicle stimulating hormone (FSH) One of the three **gonadotrophic hormones** composed of protein-carbohydrate molecules and produced by the **adenohypophysis** or anterior pituitary gland that stimulates appropriate follicles to produce sperm cells and ova. The other two are a **luteinizing hormone** transmitted to the gonads and a **lactogenic hormone, prolactin,** that goes to the gonads and mammary glands.

foot-candle power The **illuminance** produced by one standard candle on a surface every point of which is one foot away from the source. *See* **intensity.**

foot-lambert A unit of measurable brightness. One foot-candle has a **luminance** of one foot-lambert from any angle of observation, provided that the surface is perfectly diffusing and reflecting. *See* **lambert.**

force *See* **newton.**

forced-choice method A method in which the rater or testee is forced to choose from various fixed alternatives of seemingly equal attractiveness. It is designed to reduce faking on **personality** inventories and similar rating devices.

forebrain *Same as* **prosencephalon.**

Forel, August-Henri (1848-1931) Swiss physician, neuroanatomist, and psychiatrist. Studied with **Meynert** and **Gudden.** He used Gudden's technique of **retrograde degeneration** to conclude that nerve fibers originate from cells and that fibers, therefore, will degenerate upon cell damage.

formal operations of Piaget The fifth stage of Piaget's mental development in which adult thought and abstractive ability take place. *See* **cognitive growth theories.**

formant Relating to (-ant) the concentrated formation (form-) of energy in a relatively narrow frequency band as differentiated by a **sound spectrograph,** and characteristic of a specific musical instrument (representing its timbre) or a speaker's voice.

formboard A board with depressed spaces into which various appropriately sized and shaped blocks are to be fitted. Used for testing speed and accuracy of manual dexterity.

FORTRAN (Comput.) A portmanteau word for FORmula TRANslator. An artificial programming language of the algebraic procedure-oriented type. It translates, through a compiler, standard algebraic and arithmetic equations into **machine language** for the purpose of solving scientific problems.

forward solution *See* **Doolittle method.**

fourfold coefficient (fourfold point coefficient, phi coefficient) A measure of **correlation** for two dichotomized **variables,** computed for a 2×2 (fourfold) **contingency table.** The sample value of phi is given by

$$\phi = \frac{(bc - ad)}{\sqrt{(a + c)(b + d)(a + b)(c + d)}}$$

where r = the fourfold point coefficient or phi coefficient, bc = the product of the entries in cells b and c, and ad = the product of entries in cells a and d.

The terms in the denominator are the marginal sums of the 2×2 table. (Edwards, pp. 185-188; Walker-Lev, p. 272; Hays, 1963, pp. 604-606).

Fourier series An expansion for a periodic function. In psychophysiological experiments, amplitude linearity, adequate bandwidth, and phase linearity are necessary for faithful reproduction of a physiological event. The bandwidth and phase linearity can be determined only if a relationship between sine waves and waves of nonsinusoidal form can be established. The Fourier series, according to Brown (p. 434), shows that "any periodic wave can be dissected into the sum of a series of sine and cosine waves which, when added in the correct proportions, will reproduce the original event."

In psychophysics, the Fourier series is applied mathematically to any complex tone with a fundamental frequency n, which can be analyzed into certain sine waves (where the overtone frequencies are always a simple multiple, $2n$, $3n$, etc., of the frequency of the lowest tone or fundamental).

Named after Jean Baptiste Joseph Fourier (1768-1830), French mathematician and physicist, who used the series as a base for his mathematical theory of heat. *See* **harmonic analysis.**

fourth ventricle *See* **brain ventricles.**

fovea centralis A centrally (centralis) located, slight pit or indentation (fovea) in the **macula lutea** of the retina containing long, densely packed cones but no rods; the point at which fixated images fall, with daytime vision being most acute for clarity, detail, and color. The fovea is so small (0.25 mm in diameter) that

eye motion is necessary for focusing clearly on two points as close together as the dots in a colon (:). For proper vision it is necessary for the eye muscles to rotate the eyeball until the object's image falls directly on the fovea.

FR Fixed ratio schedule.

fractional anticipatory goal response; fractional antedating goal response (FAGR) In **Hull's systematic behavior theory,** an inferred mechanism that integrates the various alternatives into a **habit-family** as the organism pursues different routes on its way to a common goal. Apparently the FAGR is always present as each alternative choice is made (C. L. Hull, "Mind, Mechanism, and Adaptive Behavior," *Psychological Review,* 1937, 44, pp. 1-32).

fractional replication designs An experimental design that includes only a fraction of all **treatment combinations** in the factorial **set,** such as using only 1/2, 1/3, or 1/4 of the total number of treatment combinations available. Such a procedure reduces cost and labor for the experimenter and makes possible many other replicative studies that would ordinarily be discouraged by the vast amount of work required. *See* **alias.**

The theory of fractional replication was developed by D. J. Finney and extended by O. Kempthorne (Winer, 1962, pp. 447-455; Kirk, 1968, pp. 385-421).

frame of reference A much (ab)used term in the social sciences, referring to the standard(s) that one uses in arriving at conclusions or making perceptual judgments.

For instance, Sherif found (1936) that subjects' estimates of the distance a light supposedly moved varied considerably because, as Sherif put it, they had no "frame of reference." But the introduction of judgments from an instructor led them to accept the frame of reference of the instructor and their judgments were influenced considerably (Muzafer Sherif, *The Psychology of Social Norms,* 1936).

Franz, Shephard Ivory (1874-1933) American (New Jersey) physiological and experimental psychologist. Ph.D., Columbia 1899. His investigations in 1902 of animal behavior during extirpation experiments were pioneering work in this field, which **Lashley** later refined, emphasizing quantitative aspects. Best known for his work on **localization of brain function.**

fraternal twins (dizygotic twins) Twins, unlike **identical twins,** that have developed from separate simultaneously fertilized eggs. They are no more alike genetically than ordinary siblings and can be of the same or different sexes.

F.R.C.P. Fellow of Royal College of Physicians. *See* **Bachelor of Medicine.**

free Not subject to an arbitrary external power, compulsion or determination but still not exempt from all restraints. To be free can also mean to have the independence and lack of fear to impose restraints and discipline upon oneself. *Free will* is the doctrine that man's will to choose is independent of all prior conditions and any causal principle that binds the rest of the universe.

In **Rogers'** psychotherapeutic concepts there are at least three qualities involved in the process of not only learning to be free but in promoting personal change and a feeling of freedom in a relationship. These qualities are: (1) *congruence* in which the therapist is genuine and "unphony," being completely aware of these feelings; (2) *unconditional positive regard,* in which there is an "outgoing positive feeling without reservations, and without evaluations"; and (3) *empathic understanding,* in which the therapist can internally sense or feel what the client is experiencing and communicate to the client this understanding, verbally or nonverbally (Rogers and Stevens, *Person to Person,* pp. 53-55).

f

free association A **psychoanalytic** technique, originated by **Freud** in 1895, designed to encourage the patient to respond freely and immediately to any association he makes (relevant or irrelevant); used to unearth and study **repressions**, thus leading to therapeutic insights and future beneficial action. In later adaptations in **psychology** it is used in testing behavior by asking a subject without directive instructions to respond to a stimulus (word, person, phrase, or picture) with the first idea that comes to mind. *See* **mondo, word association.**

freedom The state or quality of exercising one's own choices or decisions without external or internal constraint. The use of such freedom implies the practice of wholesome responsibility and constructive action. But the French philosopher Sartre says the "Respect for another's freedom is an empty phrase ... There is no given freedom. One must win an inner victory over his passions, his race, his class, and his nation, and must conquer other men along with himself. But what counts ... is the particular form of the obstacle to surmount, of the resistance to overcome. That is what gives form to freedom in each circumstance." *See* **existence.**

To **Carl Rogers,** freedom "is the quality of courage which enables a person to step into the uncertainty of the unknown as he, himself, chooses. It is the burden of being responsible for the self one chooses to be. It is the recognition by the person that he is an emerging process, not a static end product." (Rogers and Stevens, *Person to Person*, p. 52).

free-floating anger Chronic reaction pattern in which hostility becomes so generalized that even neutral situations are met with anger.

free-floating anxiety Chronic reaction pattern of fear or foreboding in which **anxiety** becomes generalized and the patient feels a sense of impending doom for no specific reason; may become fixed on specific objects in the form of **phobias.**

free nerve endings Nonmyelinated **sensory** fibers (in skin, mucous and serous membranes, blood vessels, etc.) that do not appear to be structurally differentiated (unassociated with any special **receptor** structures). They divide repeatedly, their fine branches being distributed among the epithelial cells. These endings serve as pain and probably pressure and temperature receptors.

free operant An **operant** by which an organism re-emits a **response** immediately following **reinforcement**, to be reinforced again. (Opposed to **maze,** runway, or other spatially restricted situations where behavior and reinforcement are independent of each other.) Free operant action is random, purposeless action, such as the movements of an infant in his crib.

French higher education Details as presented here are primarily associated with the traditional approach. Present day education in France may be radically different (especially since the draft reform program of 1966-67), but these changes are of little importance for reference in this book, since educational material discussed here usually relates to years prior to 1965.

As in many European programs, scientific studies proceed through three cycles. The first cycle (**propédeutique**) of one year's duration, leads to the second cycle lasting for two or three years and the granting of the first university degree (the **licence**). The third cycle entails advanced studies in a given specialty and an introduction to research, culminating in a **lycée agrégation** examination, marking the end of introductory research. A student is then eligible to take the special examination for teaching in a **lycée.**

In medicine, studies begin also with a one-year course similar to the **propédeutique**, which prepares for the **certificat preparatoire aux études médicales.** After obtaining this certificate, the student studies medicine for five years and also spends at least six months interning in a hospital, then becoming eligible for a doctor of medicine degree. Clinical training usually begins in the first year of medicine. At the end of his first year the student is eligible for a competitive examination in anatomy, medicine, and surgery, a **concours** for an appointment as **externe des hôpitaux.** Unsuccessful students on this examination nevertheless are required to complete their clinical training before graduation. The externeship begins the student's formal medical training, which is distinct from his class work at the **Faculté de Médecine.** After satisfactory clinical training and schooling the student is eligible for the highly competitive examination for internship appointment at one of the municipal hospitals (**interne des hôpitaux**). An *interne* does not have his medical degree yet, however. All aspiring medical students (even those never having been *externes* or *internes*), after completing their clinical experience and five years at the *Faculté de Médecine*, are eligible to take the final examinations (**examens d'état**). Success here means that the student may then present a doctoral thesis before a commission, which, if successfully defended, results in a Doctor's diploma being granted.

An *interne*, aspiring to the academic life, may become eligible to become **chef de clinique** (similar to assistant professor in an American university. Upon successfully passing a competitive examination and presenting an acceptable thesis (**these d'agrégation**), the **chef de clinique** may become a **professeur agrégé** (associate professor). The rank of full professor is extraordinarily difficult to achieve.

In the non-clinical areas of teaching (anatomy, physiology, etc.), a medical instructor in a school of medicine is called a **préparateur**, an assistant professor—either a **chef des travaus à la faculté** or **chef de laboratoire à la faculté.**

The clinical physician reaches his highest clinical appointment when he is made a **médecin** (or *chirurgien*) **des hôpitaux**, but it carries no university status. A distinguished physician may be elected to the **Académie de Médecine**, and an exceptional one to the **Académie des Sciences**—the highest academic honor in France.

Psychiatrists in France proceed through similar appointments or elective posts. See **interne des asiles d'aliénés, assistant des asiles d'aliénés, médecin des asiles.** (*Founders of Neurology*, pp. ix-xii; *Education and Development in Western Europe*, pp. 160-62).

frequency The number of times a specified event occurs; statistically, the number of measures that fall at a given point in a **distribution** or in a given **set** or category.

In areas of audition and vision frequency refers to the number of cycles per unit of time that can be counted in a periodic vibration, although light is generally represented by its **wavelength** (distance between two repetitive events rather than its frequency). However, in electromagnetic radiation, the rate of vibration is often referred to as frequency. For example, under ordinary conditions, the highest frequency to which the eye responds is that corresponding to $380\,\mu$ (about 790×10^{12} cycles per second); the lowest frequency to $780\,\mu$ (or about 385×10^{12} cycles per second). *See* **micron (μ).**

frequency curve *Same as* **frequency polygon.**

frequency distribution (frequency table) A tabulation of a set of measurements or scores arranged in **class intervals** in order of magnitude from the lowest to the highest. Also, a compilation of the absolute or relative happenings of all possible values of the **variable** under consideration. If frequencies are in absolute terms, it is an *absolute frequency distribution*; if in percentage terms, it is a *relative frequency distribution*.

frequency functions *See* **density functions.**

frequency polygon (frequency curve) A graphic representation of a **frequency distribution** in which the frequency (represented by the vertical axis) for each class or score is plotted at the midpoints of the intervals on the horizontal axis with successive points connected by straight lines.

frequency theory *See* **hearing theories.**

Freud, Sigmund (1856-1939) Viennese physician and neurologist. Student of **Charcot, E. W. von Brücke,** and **Meynert.** Founder of the psychoanalytic movement, which includes a **personality** theory, explanations of normal as well as abnormal behavior, and a method of **psychotherapy.** For Freud, all behavior is dependent upon past experience which although relegated to the unconscious still affects present behavior and feelings. Every person's life history is in stages of **psychosexual development** corresponding to erogenous zones on which attention is currently focused. His basic concepts deal with **infantile sexuality, conflict, repression,** and manifestations of unconscious activity, revealed through dreams and **free association.** *See* **Adler, Breuer** (also Boring, pp. 702-712; Maddi, pp. 19-38, 229-243).

Friedman test for J matched groups A test similar to the **Wilcoxon signed ranks test** serving as an alternative to the matched groups **analysis of variance**; it is appropriate when each of r sets of matched individuals contain j individuals assigned at **random** to experimental **treatments** or when each of r individuals is observed under each of j treatments in random order.

Milton Friedman, Polish-born (1911) American mathematician. Ph.D. (mathematics), 1952 Chicago.

Fritsch, Gustav (1838-1927) German naturalist, physician, histologist, whose research with **Eduard Hitzig** instigated experimental neurophysiology. *See* **localization of brain function.**

Fröhlich's syndrome (adiposogenitalism) Rare condition marked by obesity and hypogenitalism, resulting from a hypothalamic-pituitary disorder interfering with brain centers that regulate food intake and disturb gonadotrophic function of the **pituitary.** Also associated with **mental retardation.**

Fromm, Erich (born 1900, Germany). Ph.D., Heidelberg, 1922; studied at Psychoanalytic Institute (Berlin). A neo-Freudian who stresses the importance of social factors on emotional development. *See* **love** (also Bischof 651-660; Maddi, 292-301).

frontal lobes Pertaining to (-al) the forehead (front-). The area of the **cerebral hemispheres** lying in front of the **central lobe** and the **fissure** of Sylvius.

Considered by **Galen** to be the seat of the soul (pneuma).

frontal lobotomy *See* **lobotomy.**

frontal plane Pertaining to (-al) the front or forehead; any plane in bilaterally symmetrical animals that is perpendicular to the **dorsoventral** axis, passing through the **caudal, cranial,** and two **lateral** aspects.

FSH Follicle stimulating hormone.

F statistic (F ratio) A test **statistic** in **analysis of variance** that is equal to the ratio of two **variance** estimates where the larger variance is the numerator of the ratio. It provides a test of the H_0 that all treatment **population** means are equal. It is distributed as the **sampling distribution** of F, such distribution sometimes being called the **F distribution** or the variance-ratio distribution. It assumes that the two variances are based on independent samples drawn at random from a normal population (McNemar, 1962, pp. 246-250; Kirk, 1968, pp. 39-41, 59).

fugue Type of **dissociative-reaction** in which the person takes actual flight (fugue) from his threatening or undesirable life situation and establishes a different mode of life, which may last for many years. He has extensive **amnesia** for his past but otherwise appears normal, retaining his memory for skills and habits. Sometimes, fugue states occur after episodes of erotic escapades and also apparently have been set off by acts of rage or blind panic.

function (f or F) In the algebraic sense, two sets of elements (**variables**) with an element of the first **set** x being so related to an element of the second set y that for each element x there corresponds one and only one element y. *Function of* means that the value that depends on and varies with that of another quantity or quantities. For example: $f(a)$ = function of a; or $b = f(a,c) = b$ is a function of the two variables a and c. Other symbols (Greek alphabet letters, such as T, γ), may be used to indicate functions.

functional Relating to disorders of a psychological nonorganic basis.

functional autonomy of motives A theory of **R. Woodworth** and **G. W. Allport**, holding that an activity that originally was a means to an end (such as earning money to live) frequently acquires an independent function (a self-sustaining motive), becoming an end in itself (such as collecting and valuing money for its own sake). In human learning theory, functional autonomy refers to the indefinite longevity of **instrumental behavior** after the initiating reinforcer is withdrawn.

functional fixedness; functional fixity A fixed point of view, as being unable to see a new use for a familiar tool. In problem-solving studies, a "set" induced by the method in which certain stimuli are introduced, making it difficult or impossible for the subject to see different or unique solutions for the stimulus objects.

functional psychology (functionalism) A movement in psychology whose adherents are primarily interested in finding the answers to the "how" and "why" of psychological phenomena. Originating about 1896, it was sparked by **James Rowland Angell** and **John Dewey** of the University of Chicago, after **William James** and others had gathered the fuel. Functionalism was a revolt against the **structuralism** of **Titchener** and **Wundt**, studying mental processes as activities leading to practical results. It utilized common sense as part of its field. It was concerned with the active, adaptive, and functional processes of mental life (conscious experience), not solely the conscious "structures," such as thoughts, feelings, and sensations. Functionalism, therefore, led naturally into applied psychology, primarily **educational psychology** (testing, grading, etc.).

The term presents confusion, however, when considered internationally. The schools called "structural" in Europe correspond to those called "functional" in the United States. In Germany, for instance, "functional psychology" and "act psychology" are practically synonymous, with "mental acts" producing "content." German structural psychologists have attacked the very concepts that United States "structural psychologists" have defended. *See* **Buhler, fields of psychology.**

functional psychosis A psychotic disorder of **psychogenic** origin (believed to be a learned response to psychological stress) without clearly defined or obvious organic involvement. **Manic-depressive illness, schizophrenia,** and **paranoia** are generally considered functional psychoses, but numerous investigators feel otherwise. *See* **biochemical theories of psychosis.**

funneling A neural process by which auditory sensations are sharpened, primarily by **inhibition** of excited fibers. Peripheral fibers intensify the sensation without altering the frequency (being that of the tone conducted by the central fibers).

Fürsorge (Ger., care for). Concern for someone's welfare. *Fürsorge* is often used interchangeably with *Sorge* (care). **Heidegger** considered *Sorge* the most important structure of human consciousness and the basis of all "being." Medart Boss, Swiss psychiatrist and a

convert from Freudian and Jungian analysis to Heideggerian **existentialism**, believed *Sorge* to be an all-inclusive vector of care (love and hate, hope and despair, etc).

fusion A process (-ion) of melting together (fus-); a blending. A visual phenomenon of a continuous sensation that gradually appears when a series of discrete, successive stimuli is presented at a constantly increasing frequency. For example, the visual fusion of colors seen on a **color wheel** whose rotation speed is gradually increased so that **flicker** (except for brightness differences) disappears when the critical speed is attained. Fusion frequency is the frequency, in cycles per second, at which all flicker disappears. Once the critical speed is reached for fusion frequency, no increase in frequency produces any improvement in the quality of fusion. *See* **summation.**

future shock Psychological shock of facing the reality of the future now, with feelings of confusion, alienation, and disorientation. The panic that hits a person when he becomes suddenly aware of the "racing rate of change that makes reality seem sometimes to be like a kaleidoscope run wild . . . compelling the individual to act out new roles . . ." The rapid changes occurring in one's own society or from a new culture being superimposed over an old one, produce a vague realization that future time has arrived prematurely before one's own personal lagging system is ready for it. With future time compressed into one's present time, mass **neurosis,** irrational behavior, **free-floating anxiety,** and violence result. It is a form of **culture shock** occurring within one's own culture that is leaving him behind and unidentifiable, with frightening feelings of hopelessness about ever seeing the "good old days" again, of having lost a dear friend, of being unable to return to the familiarity and safety of his lost culture. (From *Future Shock,* by Alvin Toffler, 1970. A Bantam Book, published by arrangement with Random House, Inc.)

G

G, g General factor; **geometric mean**; also difference in rank on one test versus rank on another test.

GA Guessed average.

GABA Gamma *amino butyric acid.*

galactosemia Disorder (-ia) of milk (galact) sugar (-ose-) in the blood (-em-). Galactose (a monosaccharide sugar but less soluble and less sweet than glucose) accumulates in the blood of infants because of the absence or inactivity of a transfer(ase) enzyme (galactokinase) that normally converts a galactose phosphate into a glucose phosphate. Like **phenylketonuria,** galactosemia is a recessively inherited defect (or **inborn error** of **metabolism**) marked by an abnormal accumulation of galactose metabolites in body cells (resulting in tissue damage).

Most infants with galactosemia fail to survive. Those who do, run through a series of ailments such as jaundice, edema, tendency to infection, vomiting, poor appetite, and eventually cataracts with accompanying physical and mental retardation.

Transferase deficiency can be detected at birth by a specialized procedure (enzyme fluorescence spot test) on umbilical cord specimens. Lack of milk and all foods containing galactose and lactose for the first three years of life will prevent the symptoms mentioned above. Even if the symptoms have already appeared, elimination of all milk and milk products will bring about noticeable improvement in the child.

In 1908, Austrian physician A. von Reuss first recognized the condition as a defect in metabolism of galactose. In 1935, Harold L.

Mason and C. Donnell Turner decided that the primary defect was failure of the liver to convert galactose to **glycogen.**

Galen of Pergamum (ca. 130-200 A.D.) Roman physician of Greek origin who classified the medical and physiological knowledge of his day, relying upon animal dissection for observations and conclusions. Influenced considerably by **Hippocratic** medicine and **Aristotle's** biology, although he strongly opposed Aristotle's idea that the heart was the center of intelligence and sensation. Reformulated theory of temperaments (doctrine of four humors), applying ideas to psychopathology. He established that arteries carry blood instead of air; distinguished **motor** and **sensory** nerves as had **Herophilus** before him; traced and classified **7 cranial nerves.** He wrote extensively on the **brain ventricles,** saying that they served as the reservoir for animal spirits. Until the Renaissance his teachings, much of which were dogma without evidence, were considered unimpeachable authority.

He espoused many sophisticated ideas about the nervous system (such as nerves relaying impulses from brain and spinal cord), some of which probably found their way to J. **Müller's** and **Bell's** concepts about **specific nerve energies.** Differentiated the **dura mater** and **pia mater.** Named the **corpus callosum,** the four ventricles, **corpora quadrigemina, pineal** and **pituitary** glands. *See* **ganglion, glossopharyngeal, Empedocles, Hippocrates, humoral doctrine of diseases,** and **hypophysis.**

Gall, Franz Joseph (1758-1828) German physician and founder of **phrenology.** Studied brains and skulls of men and animals in an attempt to find a relation between "mental faculties" and cranial conformation. Despite the exaggerated claims of phrenology, Gall's scientific standing as an anatomist stimulated others to investigation, leading to genuine advances in the anatomy and physiology of the brain.

Galton, Sir Francis (1822-1911) In his studies of heredity, particularly concerning characteristics of family stature, Galton observed the phenomenon of **regression:** children of tall parents were likely to be taller than average, but they were less likely to be as much above average as their parents. As Galton said, following a similar line of thinking in his studies on intelligence and talent: If the law of regression "discourages the extravagant hopes of a gifted parent that his children will inherit all of his powers, it no less discountenances extravagant fears that they will inherit all his weakness and disease," Boring, 482-488).

Galton called this phenomenon "regression towards mediocrity," introduced the term "regression line," and later referred to the mutual relationship between two variables as "co-relation." Additionally, he performed original experiments in mental imagery, in **reaction time** in producing associations, and "mental" testing, as well as inaugurating the family history and biographical method in his studies. He initiated the eugenics (his term) movement, and developed the (1) *Galton bar,* an instrument for measuring thresholds (limens) for visual linear distances by having the subject try to match a standard line to a movable line; used in **psychophysics** for determining average error or **just noticeable difference;** and the (2) *Galton whistle,* a cylindrical whistle with a variable high pitch used to determine the upper limit of hearing; because of inaccuracies, it is now used experimentally for only the simplest demonstrations in tonal hearing, but its high tones still have value for calling dogs. *See* **coefficient of correlation.**

Galvani, Luigi A. (1737-1798) An Italian philosopher and physician. Started experiments on electricity (with animals) about 1779-80, demonstrating that animal tissues possess electricity but material not published until 1791. The galvanic skin response was named after him. *See* **psychogalvanic reflex.**

g

galvanic skin response (GSR, gsr) *See* **Galvani; psychogalvanic reflex.**

galvanometer An instrument for measuring (-meter) galvanic current, or for determining a current's presence (direction) by observing movements of a magnetic needle in a magnetic field. *See* **psychogalvanic reflex, psycho-galvanometer.**

Invented (and first named multiplier) by J. Christoph Schweiger (1779-1859), which was improved upon in 1825 by the Italian physicist, Leopoldo Nobili (1784-1835), who introduced the astatic galvanometer.

game *See* **Synanon.**

gamete (Gr.: Wife; husband; marriage) A mature reproductive or germ cell whose nucleus (sometimes the cytoplasm) fuses with that of another gamete (constituting fertilization), the resulting **zygote** becoming a new individual. Gametes are **haploid**, and are usually differentiated into male (sperm) and female (ovum) gametes.

Term introduced by Gregor Johann Mendel (1822-1884), Austrian monk and botanist who set up a mathematical law of inheritance (based on his observations on plants and peas).

game theory A branch of mathematics applied to any kind of competitive situation (social behavior, business management, etc.), in which from several available strategies one is chosen that will lead to a maximum gain or at least a minimal loss. In most such games, each player's strategy is made without knowing his opponent's choice. The foremost objective in game theory is to determine what choice of strategies will be most profitable for each player (arrived at by listing the "moves" available to each player with corresponding payoff amounts). One of the popular games is called a "2-X-2 zero-sum two person game," in which two players oppose each other with each player having the choice of two possible strategies (2-X-2) and accepting that whatever is won by one is lost by the other (zero-sum). There is no so-called "housecut" and no accumulation of capital. There are variations in which a player chooses a strategy that would, in one game, minimize his maximum losses (**minimax strategies**) and, in another game, maximize the minimum amount he can win (**maximin strategies**). (For elementary presentation of game theory, see John E. Freund and Frank J. Williams, *Elementary Business Statistics: The Modern Approach*, 1964, pp. 162-175; Ernest R. Hilgard and Gordon H. Bower, *Theories of Learning*, 1966, pp. 399-408).

Hungarian mathematician, John von Neumann (1903-1957), first wrote on game theory as a new branch of mathematics in 1928. The idea had only limited appeal but then gained favor when with German born (1902) American (1944) Oskar Morganstern, von Neumann subjected man's problem-solving techniques to the rigors of mathematics, jointly publishing the book *The Theory of Games and Economic Behavior* in 1944. *See* **model.**

gamma Third letter of the Greek alphabet, used sometimes to indicate the third function, operator, or item in a series (after alpha and beta).

gamma amino butyric acid (GABA) An inhibitory chemical transmitter that increases dendritic polarization. Thompson, however, states that "direct evidence at present indicates that it is not a specific inhibitory transmitter substance in the mammalian nervous system" (Leukel, p. 65, and Thompson, p. 125).

gamma efferent fiber Motor nerve fiber connecting with the muscle spindle and affecting the receptor's sensitivity so as to "provide a feedback loop regulating the input of kinesthetic information" (Morgan, p. 274; Leukel, p. 163).

gamma movement *See* **apparent movement.**

gamma phenomenon The **apparent movement** of a light perceived as drawing closer when the light brightens or as moving away when it dims.

ganglion (pl. ganglia) Tumor or knob of nerve cells associated with nerve fiber bundles. A collection of nerve cells (or bodies) and synapses, constituting a form of nerve center lying outside the **central nervous system**, as in the sympathetic ganglia; also, the cluster of grey matter within the **brain** and spinal cord. Ganglion cells (in the third layer of the retina) receive stimuli from the bipolar neurons, their axons making up the **optic nerve.**

Hippocrates used the term to describe a tumor under the skin, while **Galen** limited its meaning to a nerve swelling. In its neurological sense (as a collection of nerve cell bodies) it was not described as such until French anatomist Raymond Vieussens (1641-1716), did so in his work, *Neurologia Universalis*, 1685.

Ganser syndrome (acute hallucinatory mania; prison syndrome; syndrome of approximate answers) A pattern of hysteroid behavior in which the person simulates confusion, disorientation, lack of insight or may appear to be suffering from more seriously involved mental illness when faced, for example, with a lie or if involved in a traffic violation. He characteristically gives seemingly senseless answers to questions (such as repeatedly saying that 5 and 5 are 11 even though he is corrected and intelligent enough and schooled enough to know otherwise) and may also show incongruous, absurd behavior (such as crying at a joke or laughing at sad news). Other symptoms may be loss of personal identity, **fugue** states, conversion, **anxiety**, and **depression**. Most authorities agree that the patient plays a **role**, that he is "putting on an act." The condition is apparently sparked by having to face some reality situation, resulting in the behavior that is either unconsciously motivated or designed purposely to avoid embarrassing questions. It has been particularly noticeable among prisoners, soldiers, or those who get into continually difficult situations.

Originally described in 1898 by a German prison psychiatrist, Sigbert Ganser (1853-1931).

Ganzfeld (Ger., whole field) Upon continual visual bombardment (such as being exposed to ongoing psychedelic lighting effects or to the sensation of seeing countless snowflakes in a blizzard) the perception of color soon fades into a completely uniform, homogeneous, colorless, gray blur, without background, without figure (such as in snow blindness or "white out" of the Arctic. (W. Cohen, "Color Perception in the Chromatic Ganzfeld," *American Journal of Psychology*, 1958, 71, 390-394).

gargoylism *See* **Hurler's disease.**

G.A.S. General adaptation syndrome.

gate (Comput.) A device, circuit, or module of switches and relays providing one **output** signal dependent upon one or more (past or present) **input** channel states; controls flow of a signal through a system. Logically, there are only two kinds of gate, the AND and the OR, which, however, can be assembled with inverters and other gates to produce other gating functions. An AND gate (gate, AND) with two or more input wires and one output wire, permits signals from an output wire only if there is an input pulse on all input wires. An OR gate (gate, OR) permits an output signal or pulse to occur as long as any input signal is present on any input line. A NOR gate is an OR gate with an inverted output (or with an inverter attached to its output), which generates an output when no input is energized.

gating Process performed by the **centrifugal** nerve fibers of inhibiting certain stimuli so that others may pass, one at a time, through

the "gate of admission," making specific or greater attention possible. As applied in electronics, *see* **gate.**

Gauss, Karl Friedrich (1777-1855) German astronomer and mathematician who discovered many mathematical theorems and concepts. In 1809, he published *Theoria Motus Corporum Coelestrum* in which he expressed principles dealing with **normal distributions** and normal curve of errors (which were called Gaussian distributions and curves for almost 150 years, and still are in some texts). He also devised solutions for **binomial** equations. In *electricity*, a Gauss is the unit of measurement of magnetic induction, equal to one line of magnetic force per square centimeter (Bell, pp. 218-269).

Geheimrat Ger., privy (*geheim*) councillor (*Rat*). An honorary title conferred by the German government on a senior professor.

Gemeinschaftsgefühl (Ger., feeling [*Gefühl*] of good fellowship [*Gemeinschaft*]; a community spirit). The process of trying to achieve a oneness, a feeling of belonging, of being close to the breast and the mother's warm, protective embrace. Supposedly, mankind continually strives to return to this primal *Gemeinschaftsgefühl*. This primal drive may be related to Janov's primal screaming. *See* **primal therapy.**

Contrary to Nietzche's "will to power," **Adler** developed and emphasized importance of *Gemeinschaftsgefühl*, saying that only through good will could man achieve his full potential.

In 1887, a German social philosopher and sociologist, Friedrich Tönnies (1855-1936) differentiated between *Gemeinschaft* and *Gesellschaft* (association) in his book, *Gemeinschaft and Gesellschaft* (translated by C. P. Loomis under the title *Fundamental Concepts of Sociology*, 1940). *Gesellschaft* refers to idiosyncratic relationships, utilitarian in nature (such as in a pact or a contract) whereas in a *Gemeinschaft* relationship a sharing of advantages and disadvantages (as between parent and child) is implied. Tönnies believed that as man moves toward mechanization the more community structure disintegrates.

gene Born; to become. The essential unit of hereditary transmission, arranged linearly in the **chromosomes** and capable of reproduction and mutation. *See* **alleles, mitosis, deoxyribonucleic acid, ribonucleic acid, genetic code.**

The term gene was coined in 1898 by the Danish botanist Wilhelm Ludwig Johannsen (1857-1927), who concurrently also coined genotype and phenotype (phänotype). American geneticist, Thomas Hunt Morgan (1866-1945), was the first (1909) to use *gene* in describing the unique parts of chromosomes.

gene linkage A tendency for all the genes (DNA molecules) in the same **chromosome** to be inherited together, except for crossing-over (involving exchange of homologous segments of **chromatids**).

general adaptation syndrome (G.A.S.) A group of reactive patterns that react to stress. A controversial theory, but according to **Selye**, a three-stage complex physiological response to severe physical or psychological stress. The *first stage* (**alarm reaction**) consists of typical emotional bodily changes; the *second stage* is resistance to stress, in which the organism attempts to adapt itself by physiological changes, but organic pathological damage occurs (ulcers, etc.). The recurrence or persistence of stress brings the **syndrome** to the *third stage*, exhaustion. *See* **adrenocorticotrophic hormone.**

General Conference on Weights and Measures *See* **Conférence Générale des Poids et Mesures.**

general factor (G, g) An assumption that a general factor g determines one's ability to adapt to new situations.

Spearman, who advanced the idea in 1904, considered *g* a mathematical quantity that explained the correlations existing between diverse aspects of cognitive performance. In the hypothesis, it underlies all other factors that make up intelligence, especially in intelligence tests, as distinct from special abilities unique to each test. Since Spearman's time, however, *g* has come to mean more than a mathematical construct; according to **Wechsler**, general intelligence involves much more than a *g* factor or just the capacity to do intellectual work. **Thurstone** used the term as a general ability to which each of the primary factors correlates. *See* **two-factor theory.**

general intelligence A postulated basic intellectual factor or trait which some factor analysts believe operates in all situations demanding **intelligence**, accounting for positive relationships existing between many different kinds of tests of abilities and achievements.

generalization In **concept formation**, problem-solving, and **transfer of training**, the ability of the learner to derive principles from a class of objects, events, or problems. In therapy, the ability of a client to transfer his learning experiences from the "protective" environment of the therapy situation to the general world of reality outside the therapy room. *See* **generalization of response, generalization of stimulus.**

generalization of response The act of responding to a new **stimulus** in similar fashion to the familiar one, if that one is blocked. A principle of **conditioning** stating that once a conditioned response has been established, similar stimuli may evoke the same response; the more similar the stimuli, the greater the generalization of response. *See* **transfer.**

generalization of stimulus In learning, elicitation of responses by stimuli (or general classes of stimuli) similar to the specific stimulus. It is common in early stages of learning, dropping out as discrimination improves.

general paralysis A condition characterized by physical signs and symptoms of syphilis of the **central nervous system**; may simulate other **psychoses** and brain syndromes. *See* (3) *under* **organic psychosis, paresis.**

general psychotherapy An eclectic **psychotherapeutic** approach using a variety of techniques (e.g., reassurance, **relaxation therapy**, and **play therapy**).

general-to-specific-sequence Maturational development of responses from undifferentiated general movements to specific and detailed movements. *See* **individuation.**

generative theory of language acquisition A linguistic proposal claiming that children gain language comprehension by intuitively generating meaning out of experience with proper word sequences, while the brain assimilates and organizes the material like a computer (by information-gathering and interpreting, for example). Continuous environmental feedback (such as learning grammar rules in school) is considered not essential.

Theory proposed by Russian-American linguist Noam (Avram) Chomsky (born 1928). *See* **transformational grammar, stratificational grammar.** The term "generative," as used by Chomsky and other grammarians and psycholinguists, derives from its use by E. Post (1944), a mathematician (*Bulletin of the American Mathematical Society*, 1944, **50,** 284).

genetic code The specific and predictable rules by which **deoxyribonucleic acid** (DNA) or **ribonucleic acid** genetic information is translated into **amino acids**. Specifically, the information stored in the DNA molecules as a linear sequence of the bases (**adenine, cytosine, guanine,** and **thymine**) is translated into a complementary base sequence of uracil, guanine, cytosine and adenine within the **messenger RNA** (mRNA) molecules. The genetic message is encoded in the DNA molecules in the cell nucleus. The DNA molecule acts as a template for the production of mRNA molecules, which carry the messages as marked to protein factories in the cell cytoplasm, activating production of a specific kind of protein.

genetic counseling Counseling of persons with a poor genetic history who plan to marry, or of those who are married and are thinking of having children. For example, **phenyl-ketonuria** (PKU) is a relatively rare **inborn error** disorder (occurring about once in 12,000 cases), and until recently such afflicted individuals did not reproduce. But now that PKU can be effectively treated by dietary control, persons with PKU can grow to adulthood with little or no signs of **mental retardation**, and thus become more eligible for marriage. If these people were to marry unrelated individuals **homozygous** (genes of the same allele) for the normal **allele** (each different form of a **gene**), all the offspring would be carriers of the defect. There are, of course, many other combinations possible, but the need for counseling such prospective parents is evident.

The risk of having defective children in consanguineous marriages is, of course, much greater; in first cousin matings, the chances of producing a PKU child are about five times greater than for unrelated persons.

As genetic knowledge increases, a greater need for genetic counseling is expected.

The word genetics was introduced in 1905 by English biologist William Bateson (1861-1926).

genital stage In classical **psychoanalysis**, the final stage of **psychosexual development** consisting of a mature pattern of traits, marked by realism in coping with problems (sexual and otherwise) and directed toward constructive goals, including a mature heterosexual love relationship.

The original concept of the genital period was presented by **Freud** in 1905 as the *third stage* in libidinal development (from 3 to 5 years) but he altered it in 1933 to be the fourth and final stage of libidinal development, representing the unification and maturation of all erotic functions.

genotype The genetic (geno-) characteristics or mold (-type) directly inherited by an individual or group that is transmitted to descendents despite acquired characteristics. A genotype, not necessarily observable, is the sum of inheritable underlying genetic information (a set of **alleles** or potential present in the cells) as contrasted with the characteristics manifested by the organism (**phenotype**). Organisms may have the same genotype but different phenotypes (due to environmentally produced variations) or the same phenotypes with different genotypes.

The term was coined by Danish botanist, Ludwig Johannsen. *See* **gene.**

Lewin used the term to include all the factors causing a phenomenon, saying that the ultimate aim of "all sciences is to find the 'genotypes' of the observed 'phenotypes.' " Some phenotypes of the thinking process (such as attention, inductive and deductive reasoning, creative thinking, and humor) have barely been investigated.

geometric mean The geometric average of all the observations. Algebraically, it is the *N*th root of the product of the *N* observations or values of a **variable.** It is very useful for averaging ratios, and is more appropriate than the **arithmetic mean** as a measure of **central tendency** when a **distribution** is log-normal. In psychophysics, the geometric mean is preferred for averaging in some scaling procedures, such as when the subject's variability tends to be proportional to the size of the judged sensations.

geriatrics Study or practice (-ics) of medical (-iatr-) care of the aged (ger-).

A London physician, John Smith (1630-1679), wrote a book on *Distress of Mind in Old Age*, 1666. In 1724, John Floyer (1649-1734), English physician, wrote *Medicina Gerocomica*, the first book on the aging man's health. The German physician, Carl F. Canstatt (1807-1850), wrote in 1839 on general geriatric problems.

(For information, contact: *National Council on the Aging, Inc.*, 315 Park Avenue S., New York, N. Y. 10010; *Administration on Aging,* U. S. Department of Health, Education and Welfare, Washington, D. C. 20201; and *American Geriatrics Society, Inc.*, 10 Columbus Circle, New York, N Y. 10019).

Gerlach, Joseph von (1820-1896) German physician. He described a nerve net theory that **Golgi** opposed. *See* **sensorium commune.**

German higher education Although many of the titles and degrees have changed during the 1960's, the following information is included because reference to university degrees in this book relate to information of an historical nature.

In medicine, upon obtaining his M.D. and medical license (being granted **Ärztliche Approbation**), a physician interested in a university appointment serves first as an **Assistent,** then, after serving for several years and writing original research publications, his professor may then sponsor him as **Privatdozent.** As *Privatdozent* he is eligible for permission to lecture in his chosen field (**venia legendi**), but first he must proceed through the rituals of **Habilitationsschrift, Habilitation,** and the **Antrittsvorlesung.** The *Privatdozent* upon recommendation by the faculty, is further given the title of professor, sometimes with and sometimes without a salary. A successful professor was often rewarded by the government with the honorary title of **Geheimrat** (privy councillor), or a higher title of **Wirklicher Geheimer Rat** (actual privy councillor) which may also carry the title of *Exzellenz* (your excellency).

All German universities are State institutions, and there has been no distinction between undergraduate and graduate levels. In psychology, for instance, the student's first major examination is called the **Vor-diplom,** while the **Diplom** is his official degree and title. Six years after acceptance of his doctoral dissertation, the German *Assistent* submits another thesis, the *Habilitationsschrift.* Acceptance of this thesis enables the **Wissenschaftlicher Assistent** to become a *Dozent,* which also entitles him to change his title from *Dr. phil.* or *Dr. rer. nat.* to **Dr. habil.** (a second doctorate). The *Dozent,* however, does not obtain tenure status (**Fakultät**) until he receives an appointment from another university (his **Ruf**), one in which he makes his first breakaway from his sponsoring professor (*Founders of Neurology*, pp. ix to xvi; *Education and Development in Western Europe,* pp. 157-163); Frank Wesley and Gerald M. Murch, Psychological Studies and Careers in the United States and Germany, *American Psychologist.*

germ cell A specialized reproductive cell (sperm and ovum), which as a mature **gamete** unites with a reproductive cell of the opposite sex to produce a new organism. Germ cells contain half the number of **chromosomes** of somatic cells, so that, upon egg and sperm fusion, a single cell results with the total number of general body cells restored in the organism (46 in the human being).

germinal period In human beings, the first two weeks of prenatal development, during which time the **zygote** develops by division into a hollow sphere of cells.

gerontology Study of (-ology) the general problems of old age (geront-). (For information, contact *Gerontological Society, Inc.*, 660 S. Euclid Avenue, St. Louis, Missouri 63110).

Gesell Developmental Schedules A clinical method for the study of sensori-motor growth of the preschool child. Qualitative measurements in the form of normative tables of

g

motor development, adaptive behavior, language development, and personal-social behavior are provided.

Named after Arnold Gesell (1880-1961), American physician and child psychologist.

Gesellschaft See **Gemeinschaftsgefühl.**

Gestalt (Ger., configuration, total structure, good form, or shape.) An object of **perception** (such as squareness, roundness) that cannot be expressed in terms of its parts since it is simultaneously the object itself and the form qualities of that object; an integrated organized, articulate "whole" or unit in experience or behavior that cannot be achieved by the mere addition of individual elements because each element depends on its relation to the whole. See **Binet.**

Term adopted in 1910 by **Wertheimer** for application to his concepts.

Gestalt psychology A group of related psychological ideas, developed about 1910-1912 by the German psychologists **Wertheimer, Köhler,** and **Koffka,** emphasizing **holistic** concepts, or the unity of an individual or group rather than analysis of the parts or elements. Especially concerned with **perception,** stressing the importance of "**set**" and meaning. In Gestalt psychology, the decisive factor in learning and problem-solving is insight rather than trial and error. See **Coghill.**

According to Köhler, Gestalt psychology depends upon the trace theory which is a dynamic description of hypothesized electrochemical potentials.

Gestaltqualität (Ger., Gestalt quality.) The attribute of mind-content recognizable as having a special characteristic or manner by which its elements are combined. Gestaltqualität held that the experiencing person always adds an extra "quality" to sensory entities resulting in **perception.** See **Ach, Külpe, act psychology.**

Gestalt therapy A therapeutic procedure that uses **Gestalt** concepts in perceiving human life processes and man's attempts to adjust to problems. Techniques may alter from session to session as long as the basic philosophy of being concerned with the awareness of the immediate moment is adhered to. Communications must involve direct confrontation between sender and receiver. No anonymous "it" or "they" or third person language is permitted, and distinctions between "talking to" and "talking at" must be understood and controlled by the therapist. Emphasis is on the "here and now." The client is led to see himself as a doer rather than one to whom things always seem to happen. Psychoanalytic approaches are rarely employed. Always, the patient must be made aware of the what and how of behavior rather than the why. Gestalt therapy openly admits the use of game playing as part of its "existential continuum."

Although there are many Gestalt therapists, the one best known for his contributions to the approach is the psychiatrist-psychologist Frederick R. (Fritz) Perls (1893-1970).

GG Goal gradient.

giantism (gigantism) A growth disorder of the anterior lobe of the pituitary resulting from overfunctioning of the eosinophilic cells of the **pituitary gland,** probably caused by a pituitary tumor. Characterized by overgrowth of the long bones before the epiphyses close. Arm span is usually greater than one's total height. See **acromegaly.**

Gilles de la Tourette, Georges (1857-1904) French neurologist. The Gilles de la Tourette syndrome, described by him in 1884, is a pattern of behavior involving motor action (as in tics) and verbal behavior (as in stuttering, and **echolalia** which he named), with overreaction to sudden stimuli (startle response) followed by a grunt leading to an obscenity (which he called **coprolalia**). He also published a treatise on **hypnotism** in 1887 and one on **hysteria** (1891-5).

glia cells Neuroglia cells proper.

glioma Tumor (-oma) of glia (gli-) cells. See **neuroglia.**

gliosis A glue-like (gli-) condition (-osis). An overgrowth or tumor of the **neuroglia** (glia cells).

global intelligence See **Binet test.**

globus pallidus (pale mass) The pallidum. One of the two parts (the other being the larger **putamen**) of the **lentiform nucleus,** being paler and situated more medially than other parts of the nucleus. The *pallidum* "feeds into the subthalamic and other **brainstem** nuclei in which there are apparently innate connections capable of producing basic **motor** patterns . . . as well as strong connections" with thalamic nuclei that project to the premotor and motor cortex. (Milner, p. 88). See **basal ganglia.**

Vesalius clearly showed it (along with the putamen) as being a division of the lentiform nucleus.

Named (c. 1825) by German anatomist and physiologist, K. F. Burdach (1776-1847).

glossolalia Disorder (-ia) of having the tongue (glosso-) get in the way of speech (-lal-). Gibberish. Word salad; unintelligible neologisms, generally uttered during sessions of religious fervor.

glossopharyngeal nerve Relating to (-al) the nerve supplying the tongue (glosso-) and pharynx. **Cranial nerve** IX of vertebrates. In mammals, concerned mainly with **sensory** and **motor** actions of the swallowing reflex, the taste buds at back of tongue, and tongue movements.

Included in the 6th pair of cranial nerves (with vagus X and spinal accessory XI) by **Galen.** In 1561, **Fallopius** described the nerve as separate and not paired. **Soemmering** (1778) separated it from the **vagus** (which Willis had grouped it with), listing it as the 9th cranial. German anatomist Carl D. Andersch (1732-1777) described it independently in 1774.

glucagon Hormone secreted by the alpha cells of the islets of Langerhans that activates (-agon) the muscles and liver to release stored blood sugar (gluc-) into the blood supply. By increasing blood sugar (glucose) its action is opposed to **insulin,** thereby operating with insulin to provide a balanced blood-sugar level. When blood sugar falls, glucagon secretion increases while insulin decreases.

glucostatic theory A theory relating to (-ic) the stabilizing of blood sugar (gluco-) through control processes in a hypothalamic regulatory mechanism (-stat). A **centralist position,** maintaining that the **homeostatic** balance in the brain, arteries, and veins primarily provides the signals to the **hypothalamus** for the starting and ending of feedings; animals eat (feel hungry) because of a low rate of glucose utilization and stop eating because of a high rate. (*Compare* **thermostatic theory, lipostatic hypothesis**).

(J. Mayer, Regulation of Energy Intake and the Body Weight. The Glucostatic Theory and the Lipostatic Hypothesis. *Annals of the New York Academy of Science,* 1955, 63.)

glutamic acid Relating to (-ic) the crystalline amino (-am-) acid of the gluey or glutinous (glut-) material of wheat and other grains. Glutamic acid maintains **brain** oxygen intake, and with aspartic acid accounts for most of the **amino acid** metabolism in the body. Also plays a major role in developing free amino acid composition of brain tissue. See **synaptic transmission.**

Glutamic acid has been used experimentally on animals and human beings to elevate sensory awareness and intellectual responsiveness. Although IQ's reportedly have been sometimes strikingly raised by its administration, the effects have not been lasting.

glutethimide (Tradename: Doriden) A white crystalline water-insoluble powder used as a hypnotic, sedative, and depressant; an *organic compound from ammonia* a(mide), derived from sulphur (-the[o]) and a nitrogenous gluey (glute-) substance.

Obtained (1872) by German chemist K. H. L. Ritthausen.

glycine A sweet (glyc-) chemical compound (-ine) or crystalline acid obtained from proteins. See **synaptic transmission.**

Braconnot at first named it *sucre de gélatine,* but **Berzelius** renamed it glycine.

glycogen Sugar (glyco-) producer (-gen). Animal starch. An insoluble starchlike substance (the main polysaccharide stored in animal cells) transformed from blood glucose for storage in the liver and muscles, the liver being by far the major resource for sugar need.

Claude Bernard demonstrated the glycogenic (and carbohydrate storage) function of the liver, naming this form of carbohydrate "glycogen" in 1848.

gnostic cells Relating to (-ic) those cells that are concerned with knowledge (gnost-) or concepts; single **neurons** in the cerebral **cortex** functioning from time of birth, that are assumed to be coded to respond to certain categories of stimuli or to specific forms (such as the hand, angles, etc.) or to the more generalized concepts (such as number concept).

The term "gnostic cells" was originated by the Polish neurophysiologist Jerzy Konorski (born 1903) and published in his book, *Integrative Activity of the Brain: An Interdisciplinary Approach,* 1967. A group of Dutch neurologists (Brouwer and Kappers, for example) have referred to certain sensations as gnostic, indicating deep and epicritic sensations as opposed to protopathic sensations.

gnothi seauton (Gr., know thyself). A maxim on the walls of Apollo's temple at Delphi, attributed to various Greek philosophers, mainly **Socrates,** but it is more appropriately attributed to **Thales.**

goal gradient (gradient of reinforcement) In **conditioning** experiments, there are two primary time gradients to consider: (1) those based on time-elapse between the **conditioned stimulus** (found mainly in **classical conditioning**), and (2) those based on time-elapse between the response to be strengthened and the reinforcement (found principally in **instrumental conditioning**). Also, the tendency for response-strength to change progressively as the organism approaches the goal (Hilgard and Bower, 1966, pp. 166-168; C. L. Hull, "The Goal Gradient Hypothesis and Maze Learning," *Psychological Review,* 1932, 39, 25-43).

Goclenius Latin name of Rudolph Goeckel (1547-1628). German philosopher and logician. In 1590, his *Psychologia Hoc Est de Hominis Perfectione* ("Psychology, or On the Improvement of Man") was the first time the word "psychology" appeared in a manuscript.

Goeckel, Rudolph See **Goclenius.**

Gold Medal Award An award granted as part of the **American Psychological Foundation's** program to develop **psychology** as a science. In 1955 the Gold Medal Award was established to be "given to an American psychologist with a distinguishing and protracted history of scientific and scholarly accomplishments." The Award is limited to North American psychologists, 65 years of age or older. **Robert Woodworth** received the first award. Parentheses below refer to the issues of the *American Psychologist* in which biographical information about recipients is given.

1956 Robert S. Woodworth (November, 1956)
1957*
1958 Edwin R. Guthrie (December, 1958)
1959 Edwin G. Boring (December, 1959)
1960 John Dashiell (December, 1960)
1962 Walter Miles (December, 1962)
1963 Gordon W. Allport (December, 1963)
1965 Heinrich Kluver (December, 1965)
1966 Karl M. Dallenbach (December, 1966)
1967*

*Missing years indicate that no award was granted. In 1957 and 1967, however, the awards would have been granted respectively to Lewis M. Terman and Wolfgang Kohler if they had lived.

1968 Floyd H. Allport (December, 1968)
1969 Henry A. Murray (January, 1970)
1970 Sidney L. Pressey (January, 1971)
1971 Burrhus F. Skinner (January, 1972)

Goldstein, Kurt (1878-1965) German neuro-psychiatrist, immigrated to the United States in 1933. His theory of **personality** is organismic and **holistic** in nature, with an overlay of **Gestalt** influences; claimed that the only motive in life is to actualize oneself. Also made numerous studies on **aphasia**, language problems, and development of tests on abstract impairment behavior. *See* **self-actualization** (Bischof, pp. 630-635).

Golgi, Camillo (1844-1926) Italian histologist and physician (M.D., Padua, 1865). As a result of his silver staining method (1873) the tracing of nerve fibers became possible, making structures visible that had never before been seen or imagined. He presented the theory of the **nerve net** (as opposed to the dendritic plexus theory of **Gerlach**) in which the net consisted of **axons** of two types of cells: *type I* having a long axon, and *type II*, with a short axon. He also concluded that nerve cells could not act in isolation and that specific cerebral localization was not possible. When he received the Nobel prize in 1906 (along with **Ramon y Cajal**) he still said he could not abandon his ideas about the unitary action of the nervous system (despite Cajal's overwhelming evidence to the contrary). In 1883 he published *Sulla fina Anatomia de la Sistema Nervosa*, summarizing much of his work. Many present-day terms reflect his influence: *Golgi apparatus*--a network of threadlike substances in a nerve cell, first mentioned by Golgi in 1896; *Golgi cells* (astrocytes)--two types of neurons (described in 1880 and 1885 respectively): *Golgi type I neuron*, multipolar in nature, carrying a long axon that emerges from gray matter and conducts impulses from one **CNS** area to another, and *Golgi type II neuron*, also multipolar, but with a short, branching axon that excites nearby neurons; found in but do not emerge from cortical gray matter.

gonadotrophic hormone (GTH), Gonadotrophin. Relating to (-ic) a **hormone** that stimulates or nourishes (-troph-) the gonads. Any of the various hormones (**follicle-stimulating, luteinizing**) of the anterior pituitary gland (**adenohypophysis**) that activate the gonads to produce their own hormones and reproductive cells as well as regulate the female menstrual cycle. *See* **neurosecretion**.

goniometer An instrument for measuring (-meter) angles (gonio-); in psychology, a device used to measure the range of motion in a joint or the tendency of the body to sway.

goodness of fit A type of statistical test based on a single sample **distribution**. A **chi-square** test of **goodness of fit** that may be carried out for any specified hypothetical population distribution, "provided that the **population** distribution is discrete, or is thought of as grouped into some relatively small set of **class intervals**." *See* Table 8 (also Hays, pp. 579-588).

Gordon Allport Award ($500) is granted annually by the Personality and Social Psychology Division (8) for the best manuscript printed during the preceding year in the Journal of Personality and Social Psychology. *See* **Awards of the American Psychological Association**.

gracile nucleus A slender (gracile) nucleus along the dorsal aspect of the **medulla** which, with the **cuneate nucleus**, contains synapses between first- and second-order neurons. Cell bodies of second-order neurons from the cuneate and gracile nuclei send axons up to the **thalamus**, whereas long fibers (kinesthetic) of the dorsal columns terminate in these nuclei, giving origin to a part of the **medial lemniscus**, a somatic pathway to the thalamus. Both gracile and cuneate nuclei are involved in relaying **proprioceptive** impulses destined for the thalamus.

gradient of avoidance The changing strength of the tendency to avoid an unpleasant (negative) incentive or goal, dependent upon distance from the goal, among other factors.

gradient of generalization The greater a test stimulus is different from the original one the less the tendency is to make a newly learned **response**; often plotted as a curve.

gradient of reinforcement Same as **goal gradient**.

gradient of texture A surface perceived visually as having a noticeably grainy substantial texture (hard, soft, smooth, rough, etc.) tends to become finer in appearance as the surface recedes from the viewer, producing a gradient of texture that is important in judgments of slant and distance. (*Compare* **distance cues**.)

Graeco-Latin square design An experimental design that takes its name from the arrangement of two superimposed Latin squares, one square containing small Greek letters (α, β, etc.) and the other Latin letters, patterned so that the same Latin letter is never paired more than once with the same Greek letter. Two superimposed squares that fulfill the above conditions are called orthogonal Latin squares. A **Graeco-Latin analysis of variance** design permits the isolation of three nuisance variables. A hyper-Graeco-Latin square consists of three superimposed orthogonal squares.

$A\alpha$	$B\beta$	$C\gamma$
$C\beta$	$A\gamma$	$B\alpha$
$B\gamma$	$C\alpha$	$A\beta$

grand mal seizures *See* **epilepsy**.

Granit theory Named after the Finnish-Swedish physiologist (born 1900) who shared the 1967 Nobel prize (with two others) for his work on vision. He discovered inhibitors in the retina and color specific modulators and dominators in the **optic nerve**. *See* **dominator-modulator theory** under **color vision theories**.

graph A means of illustrating the relationship between two or more **variables**. Generally, the **independent variable** is plotted on the x-axis with values increasing left to right, and the **dependent variable** on the y-axis with values increasing as they go up the scale.

grapheme A basic structural unit (-eme) of written (graph-) speech; a minimal unit of a writing system representing all characteristics of written symbols used to denote a single **phoneme**. *See* **speech mechanisms of thinking**.

graphic rating scale One of several kinds of measurement used when one person rates another. The rater records his judgment by placing a mark at some scaled point along a printed line, generally ranging from a low degree of the trait at one end to a high at the other end with intermediate points in between.

Gratiolet, Louis Pierre (1815-1865) French physician (M.D., Paris 1845). Studied the cerebral convolutions, comparing the appearance of **gyri** in increasing complexity from the lower order of primates to the chimpanzee and man. He delimited each cerebral lobe and named them in terms of the overlying bone: the **central lobe**, the **frontal**, the **parietal**, the temperosphenoidal, and the **occipital** lobe.

Greatrakes (Gratrux, Gratrix, Greatarick, Greatrake), Valentine (1629-1683), an Irishman who, after serving in Cromwell's army, returned home saying that he was blessed with the "king's touch,"--a touch of his divinely inspired hands would cure anyone of his ailments. He supposedly cured thousands with his "blessed" hands. He first wrote (1666) of his "blessing" and success in a letter to British physicist and chemist Robert Boyle (1627-1691); also published a report in Dublin, 1668. *See* **animal magnetism**.

Grieg's disease *See* **hypertelorism**.

Griesinger, Wilhelm (1817-1868), German psychiatrist. Fought for a "physiological medicine." His concept of mind was an adaptation of **Herbart's** psychology (that the mind was composed of mental images--**Vorstellungen**--in a condition of dynamic equilibrium). Furthermore, the mind was essentially unconscious. **Ego** development resulted from the progressive combination and amassing of mental images which helped maintain the mind's dynamic equilibrium in health. He wanted psychological and neuropathological research to complement one another.

GRIT strategy (GRIT = Graduated Reciprocation in International Tension-reduction.) A suggestion by **Osgood** indicating that international conflicts, which create tension and mutual distrust, can be reduced by announcing and carrying out small conciliatory acts on a unilateral basis, which may be considered as "playing from strength" since such acts are voluntary and are the gesture only of a prestigious and powerful nation (C. E. Osgood, *An Alternative to War or Surrender*, 1962).

group abilities or group factors Terms used interchangeably with **primary mental abilities**.

group cohesiveness An index of the overall solidarity, unity, or attractiveness of a group to its members. A multidimensional composite characteristic of a group's structure symbolizing all the field forces acting together to hold each member within the group.

Individual motivations are highly important for a sense of group cohesiveness. **Lewin** considered group cohesiveness and group locomotion (or movement toward a desired goal) to be important factors for understanding group dynamics.

In industry, group cohesiveness does not necessarily guarantee more production, since such solidarity can also be present in slowdowns or where union workers resist management standards (D. R. Cartwright and A. Zander (Eds.), *Group Dynamics: Research and Theory*, 1968, 2nd ed. [Harper and Row], p. 74).

group distribution The **distribution** grouped as a result of numerical values, within a certain range, to form a single **class interval**.

grouping A scheme or method of compressing **distributions** (especially those with wide ranges) by clustering several measurement units into intervals.

group networks In social psychology, a specialized organizational system devised for use with groups involved in problem solving. In one group of five members, called a *wheel network*, four of the subjects must communicate and interrelate only with and through an assigned hub-man but not with each other. The arrangement is designed to centralize information and to delegate responsibility through this hub-man of the network. A *completely connected network* permits and encourages free communication with all group members, allowing them to decide on their own organizational and communication processing procedures. (A. M. Cohen and J. R. Foerst, Jr., "Organizational Behaviors and Adaptations to Organizational Change of Sensitizer and Repressor Problem-Solving Groups." *Journal of Personality and Social Psychology*, 1968, 8, 209-216).

group scores Separate values in a **distribution** grouped into a number of equal intervals, classes, or steps along a scale to form a **frequency distribution**.

group test Paper-and-pencil test of **intelligence, personality, aptitude**, etc., designed to be administered simultaneously to a group. Examples are the AGCT--Army General Classification Test (a screening intelligence test used by the U. S. military services during World War II)--and most college entrance examinations.

g

group therapy A psychotherapeutic technique whereby members of a group of patients (generally fewer than ten) discuss their problems freely with each other; the therapist may play a relatively inactive role, guiding and directing the group tactfully into interpersonal relationship. Group therapy provides reality testing, enabling the individual in the group to recognize that his problems are not unique and that he does not have to become dependent upon the therapist, as so often happens in individual therapy. Group therapy with children is closely allied to **play therapy**.

Although group therapy was first used by Pratt in 1903 in his work with tuberculosis patients, and group activities for physically ill persons for instructional purposes had been organized in 1906, and forms of group counseling had been in use since the early 1900's, it was not until 1931 that **J. L. Moreno** labeled group treatment methods as "group psychotherapy." *See* **psychodrama, psychotherapy, role playing** (also Joseph I. Meirs, "Origins and Development of Group Psychotherapy" in J. L. Moreno, *Group Psychotherapy: A Symposium* Beacon House, 1945).

G.S.R. Galvanic skin response.

G. Stanley Hall Award in Developmental Psychology (Division 7) is awarded annually at the Division's business meeting to those judged as contributing significantly to the field. The award is a medal, selection being made by the Executive Committee of the Division. *See* **awards of the APA, Hall, G.S.**

guanine A colorless, crystalline chemical base or substance (-ine) found in guano and in liver, muscle, and pancreas of animals; a decomposition product of yeast nucleic acid. *See* **deoxyribonucleic acid, nucleotide.**

Discovered (1844) in guano by **Unzer**.

Gudden, Bernhard Aloys von (1824-1886), German psychiatrist and neuroanatomist (M.D., Halle 1848). He developed a new technique to study the brain (starting in 1849 and publishing in 1870), especially the optic and olfactory pathways. By removing a sense organ (such as the eye) of newborn animals he was able to "produce secondary atrophy of nerve centers and their connections" and thus was able to trace the nerve fiber **fasciculi** by their degenerated **axons**. He also demonstrated (Gudden's law) that "lesions of the cerebral cortex do not cause atrophy of peripheral nerves" (Clarke and O'Malley, p. 606).

guessed average (guessed mean) An arbitrary starting point for using the short method in calculating the **arithmetic mean** for grouped **data.**

Guilford, Joy Paul (Born, Nebraska 1897). Ph.D., Cornell 1927. Conducted **factor analysis** investigations of **personality**. Development of psychometric methods and personality and temperament scales. APA President, 1950. Received DSC Award 1964. *See* **cognitive growth theories** (also Maddi, pp. 366-374).

Guilford-Zimmerman Temperament Survey A single inventory of ten major personality traits identified through **factor analysis** by **Guilford** and associates.

The 300 items are expressed as affirmative statements, 30 for each of the following ten traits: G (general activity); R (restraint); A (ascendance); S (sociability); E (emotional stability); O (objectivity); F (friendliness); T (thoughtfulness); P (personal relations); and M (masculinity). Each one of the ten categories has its opposite pole as well (for example, a high score on E indicates relative emotional stability whereas a low score points to emotional instability). *See* **psychograph.**

guilt (Exist.) The feeling resulting from a willful or intentional commission or omission of some act, knowing it to be a crime or violation of law or established code (religious, for example). In acts of omission, guilt feelings may result from not having prevented something harmful from happening or not

h

doing what may be expected of the person. Man is faced with hope and the process of trying to fulfill his hopes and dreams. When he is challenged to try to realize his potentialities, or fails to fulfill his ambitions, he becomes absorbed with guilt and self-recrimination. James Bugental, California existentialist-psychologist, says that guilt need be neither crippling nor depressing, since it is a part of the dignity of being a man. According to **G. A. Kelly**, guilt involves the person's awareness about having strayed from playing the role he is expected to play with other persons. Thus, guilt is not a reaction to having done wrong nor is it a result of the Freudian **superego** punishing the person for committing an evil deed.

gulp (Comput.) Several **bytes** or parts of words.

gustation Act or process (-tion) of tasting (gusta-). Sense of taste, involving all combinations of sweet, sour, salt, and bitter, with receptors in the mucous membrane of the tongue and soft palate.

Guthrie, Edwin Ray (1886-1959) American psychologist. Known for his **contiguity theory** of learning, which holds that learning takes place, not by **reinforcement**, but by an association or contiguity between **sensory** and **motor** events in the learning situation. He introduced the term "**conditioned response**" in 1921.

Guttman's Scalogram Analysis A unidimensional **attitude scale** for measuring favorability or unfavorability of attitudes constructed according to Guttman's method. The emphasis is upon "internal consistency as evidence that the different items do represent different quantitative positions on the same basic dimensions." It makes attitude measurement amenable to **ordinal** scale interpretations and sets up fairly consistent sets of items. Intended as a "pure scale, so that a subject with a specified attitude who answers a certain question favorably will be favorable to all questions less **extreme** and unfavorable to all questions more extreme." (Hays, 1964, pp. 70, 71, 75; also L. Guttman, "The Third Component of Scalable Attitudes," *International Journal of Opinion and Attitude Research*, 1950, 4, 285-287).

Louis Guttman (born, New York 1916). Ph.D., sociology, 1942 Minnesota. Major research interests: public opinion, psychometrics, research methodology, structure of attitudes and intellect.

Gymnasium In Germany, a secondary school of the highest grade that stressed the classics, mathematics, history, and language in preparing the student for the university.

gyrus A circle. In the **cerebral cortex**, a convoluted ridge on the surface between two sulci or fissures.

Term entered medical terminology about 16th century, although German anatomist and physiologist, K. F. Burdach (1776-1847), is credited with having introduced the term in 1820. Many of the gyri were named by German anatomist Alexander Ecker (1816-1887)--Ecker's gyrus cuneatus, gyrus fornicatus, gyrus medius, gyrus inferious--and by English naturalist Thomas Henry Huxley (1825-1895)--gyrus angularis, gyrus dentatus, and gyrus frontalis, among others.

H

habenula Little (-ula) strap (haben-) or bridle reins. Refers particularly to the so-called habenular trigone and nucleus of the **pineal body** and the thalamic wall.

Since the anthropomorphic-minded early anatomists believed the **pineal gland** to carry the soul, it was easy for them to picture the gland as the driver who used his "reins" (habenula) to control the brain and behavior. *See* **epithalamus.**

Habilitation The inauguration of a scholar into his academic career. The process (involving a second thesis) by which a candidate advances in German institutions of higher education. For example, a medical student proceeds, after obtaining his medical experience (M.D. and license), to his **venia legendi**, which required, as a prerequisite, the **Habilitationsschrift** and a lecture and questioning period before the faculty. Upon passing this hurdle he was eligible to give the **Antrittsvorlesung** (a lecture before students, public, and faculty members), and after this the *venia legendi* was granted. The *Habilitation* provides access to university teaching and research. The *habilitationsschrift* refers to the scholar's inaugural (habilitation) dissertation (schrift). *Habilitieren* indicates that the scholar qualifies to start his academic career as a lecturer.

Habilitationsschrift An extended dissertation submitted by the German assistant to his professor approximately six years after acceptance of his doctoral dissertation. If accepted, the **Wissenschaftlicher Assistent** becomes a *Dozent*, entitling him to change his *Dr. phil.* (Ph.D.) or his **Dr. rer. nat.** to **Dr. habil.**

habit disorders Characterized by repeated, maladaptive spasms or actions (such as tics, habitual acts, and habits which interfere with biological functioning).

habit-family hierarchy A principle in C. L. Hull's behavior system. In a learning situation, an organism forms a habit family by learning routes to a goal. With **reinforcement**, some routes come to be preferred over others, and a hierarchy varying in degrees of strength thus develops in the habit-family as a result of the organism's tendency to eliminate unnecessary movements and eventually adopt the shortest and easiest path to the goal. *See* **fractional anticipatory goal response.**

habituation The tendency of a response's effect to be reduced temporarily because of repeated elicitation, often used in learning experiments as a precursor to **classical conditioning**. The **stimulus** of a bell or a buzzer may stimulate and excite an animal or human at first, but repeated, seemingly senseless repetition creates disinterest or an habituation to the stimulus.

habitus Appearance, character, condition. The overall body build (**somatotype**) and general constitution considered as a predisposition toward a certain disease, habit, or mental condition; a mental faculty.

Hackordnung *See* **pecking order.**

hair esthesiometer A measuring device (-meter) for determining degree of sensitivity (esthesio-) to lightly applied pressure necessary to bend a hair encased in a frame with a chemical balance. *Compare* **haptometer.**

Hall, Granville Stanley (1844-1924) American (Massachusetts) psychologist and educator. Harvard Ph.D., 1898, after studying at the Union Theological Seminary. Student of **James** and **Wundt**. In 1882, founded the first American formal psychological laboratory at Johns Hopkins. In 1887, founded the American Journal of Psychology, the first psychological journal in the United States. Organized the **American Psychological Association**, becoming its first president in 1892. Instrumental in initiating the child-study movement in the United States. As first president of Clark University (1889-1920), he brought **psychoanalysis** to American attention when he invited **Freud** and **Jung** to Clark in 1909 for a series of lectures. In his later years he became interested in the psychology of religion. *See* **experimental psychology** (also Boring, pp. 518-521, 845; Vinacke, p. 366).

Hall, Marshall (1790-1857) English experimental neurologist and physiologist. In 1826, he described the concept of the **reflex arc** and introduced the noun "reflex" in a rough approximation to its present meaning, although **Whytt** had used it previously in a different context. In 1832 and 1833, he briefly reported on reflex action but did not firmly establish the concept until 1850.

Hall Award *See* **G. Stanley Hall Award** in Developmental Psychology.

hallucination Wandering in the mind (hallucinatio). A perception of any of the senses (touch, hearing, smell, etc.) for which there is no appropriate external **stimulus**. For example, a person in a paranoid state may hear the voice of God giving him advice, or may feel a sympathetic pat on the back from Moses. *See* **paranoia**.

Word entered into English about 1650.

hallucinogen (psychotogenic; psychotomimetic drugs) An agent or substance that generates (-gen) dreams (hallucino-) or induces hallucinations (e.g., **psilocybin**, **marijuana**, **mescaline**, **LSD**). Hallucinogens magnify the emotions, such as fear developing into panic. Feelings of confusion, disorganization, and lack of reality are common. Visual and auditory hallucinations, altered perceptions, impaired judgment, anxiety, and paranoid feelings occur frequently. The use of hallucinogens leads to a strong psychological dependence. Most of these drugs have little medical use, except for some experimentation. *See* table of drugs, under **drugs**, for names of some of the more popularly used hallucinogens. *See* **drug addiction**.

Term coined by **Osmond** in 1954, referring to drugs with mescaline-like effects.

halo effect The influence that a general impression makes upon judgment of a specific quality. In trait ratings, the halo effect results in spuriously high intercorrelations. The effect is evident in a tendency to assign high or low ratings in most or all other traits because of one's general reputation, or to rate him on specific traits because of his general impression, or even to rate him generally because of the relative strength of one trait or characteristic. For example, a teacher may believe a child to be brighter than **intelligence tests** show because he has a pleasing personality, or because he can readily identify musical compositions; or less so because he articulates poorly, or isn't dressed neatly.

hamartia (Gr., an error). A defect of character; the making of a tragic error in judgment.

Hamilton, Sir William (1778-1856) Scottish philosopher. Much influenced by German philosophy while studying in Germany in 1817 and 1820. Accepted **Kantian** faculty psychology, holding unity of mind as most important. Contributed theories on the association of ideas, of unconscious mental modification of perceptions, and the inverse relation of **perception** and sensation. Developed and named the process of **redintegration** in 1836. *See* **law of parsimony**.

hammer *See* **malleus**.

haploid cell A cell resembling (-oid) the basic single (hapl-) condition in **chromosomes**, or half the **diploid** number; a single set of unpaired chromosomes in each nucleus. *See* **gamete**.

haptometer A device for measuring (-meter) sensitivity to pressure or touch (hapto-) employing a system of counterbalanced weights and levers that vary the pressure applied to the skin. *Compare* **hair esthesiometer**.

hardware The mechanical, magnetic, electrical, and electronic components that when assembled constitute a system, such as a **computer**. The functions of hardware and software often overlap. In psychology, **phi phenomena** apparatus, **Skinner box**, etc., are also considered hardware. (*Contrasted with* **software**).

Harlow, Harry F. Born Iowa, 1905. American comparative psychologist. Ph.D. Stanford, 1930. He has carried out many studies on learning, love, exploration and manipulative motives, and analysis of stimulus relationships. Received the **Warren Medal** in 1956 for his ". . . brilliantly conceived experiments on the behavior of monkeys, including studies of motivation, learning, and problem solving." Recipient of the **Distinguished Scientific Contribution Award** in 1950. APA President 1958. Awarded the **National Medal of Science**

by President Johnson in 1967 (Vinacke, p. 435). *See* **brainwashing, mother surrogate**.

harmonic analysis The process of finding and expressing functions in a series of sines and cosines. The terms $c_1 \sin (x + \alpha_1)$ and $c_2 \sin (2x + \alpha_2)$ are the first (fundamental) and second harmonics of the basic radial frequency X. It is the mathematical treatment of Fourier's theorem. *See* **Fourier series, set**.

harmonics Components of complex tones that are multiples or partials of the fundamental frequency. Each partial has its own pitch, which is known as a harmonic or overtone. The harmonics heard with the fundamental tone give a distinct timbre to the sound of a musical instrument.

Harold M. Hildreth Memorial Award of Division 18 (Psychologists in Public Service) awarded annually to psychologists who have made outstanding contributions to public service. *See* **awards of the APA**.

H. M. Hildreth (1906-1969). Received Ph.D., Syracuse 1935. Clinical psychologist. Served as consultant to the Community Service Bureau, NIMH, for a number of years after 1956.

Hartley, David (1705-1757) English physician, philosopher, and psychologist. Formulated the doctrine of **associationism** by integrating the associationist concepts of **Locke, Berkeley, Hobbes, Hume**, and others in his book *Observations on Man, His Frame, His Duty, and His Expectations* (1749). He admittedly gained many of his ideas from the *Dissertation Concerning the Fundamental Principle of Virtue or Morality*, written by John Gay (1669-1745), an English clergyman and scholar. Hartley applied his medical knowledge to a physiological explanation of some of Gay's ideas, thus acting as a fillip to physiological psychology. He helped popularize **Leibniz**'s idea that the body and the mind are parallel but definitely distinct (**psychophysical parallelism**). Applied Newton's concept of "vibratory action" to nerve action, instead of the contemporary idea of "animal spirits" running through tubelike nerves. He held that vibrations for ideas are miniatures of the vibrations for sensations and that they run parallel; are similar but do not interact. He considered mental activity a result of the association of simple sensations, somewhat similar to the concepts of **Condillac**. *See* **Bentham** (also Boring, pp. 193-95).

Hartley oscillator A bio-telemetric technique in which an encapsulated, ingestible tiny transmitter is swallowed for purposes of determining pressure changes within the viscera.

Ralph Vinton Lyon Hartley, American physicist (born 1888, Nevada), BA (Rhodes Scholar) Oxford 1912, Bsc 1913. Made many studies on the oscillator circuit, binaural sound localization, and information theory.

Hartley statistical test *See* F_{max} **statistic**.

hashish The concentration of THC (tetrahydrocannabinol which is the intoxicant of **marijuana**). A narcotic drug derived from the dark-brown resin that is collected from the tops of potent **Cannabis** sativa (or indica) hemp plants. Hashish is estimated to be at least five times stronger than marijuana. Most of the hashish is processed in the Near East and is smuggled into the United States. An indication of the effects of hashish can be gleaned from the origin of "assassin" and the relationship of use of such drugs to the idolatrous and "follow-the-leader" mania of the followers of Charles Manson in their ruthless assassination of people in the Los Angeles Tate-La Bianca murders in 1969. Slang: hash, sandstone, gum.

A Moslem sect (gathered together by Hassan-Ben-Sabah about 1090 A.D.) in a mountain stronghold in Persia during their religious ceremonies took hashish that gave them the illusion of the paradise they would go to after death. They obeyed any command of their leader, called the Old Man of the Mountains, to receive this key to the heavens.

His commands sometimes ordered them to kill enemy rulers and hostile Moslem government officials, giving rise to the word "assassin" from "hashishin" (a user of hashish).

Head, Henry (1861-1940) English neurologist. *See* **epicritic sensation, protopathic sensation**.

hearing theories Although the **receptors** for hearing are believed to be hair-cells of the **organ of Corti** in the **cochlea**, the exact mechanism for discrimination of the frequency, intensity, and complexity of sound waves is less clearly understood. Several theories of hearing (E. G. Boring mentions 21) have been advanced to explain auditory phenomena, but no single one is completely satisfactory. The theories fall into two major types: place theories and frequency theories, with the volley theory a refinement of frequency theories:

1. *Place theories* always involve the principle of specificity and make the nerve fiber the determiner of quality. Every tone has a specific place within the cochlea that is sensitive and responsive to that particular tone only. In this theory, the **basilar membrane** plays an important role in that the different transverse fibers, acting like piano strings, vary in mechanical properties, giving progressive tuning from high to low. The basilar membrane at any given place supposedly excites the proper nerve fibers, resulting in the hearing of a given pitch. Place theories are classified as resonance and wave theories:

a. In the *resonance theories*, the basilar membrane and affiliated structures are regarded as a series of resonators. A tone sets up vibrations, which stimulate corresponding hair-cells, thus generating impulses in auditory nerve fibers.

b. According to the *wave theories*, sound waves of a given pitch stimulate a particular area (involving frequency-scale placement along the membrane), which determine perception of pitch. *See* **Békésy's traveling wave theory of hearing**.

2. *Frequency theories* hold that the frequency of the **stimulus** is transmitted as a rate of impulse in the **auditory nerve**, with the ear serving as a relay center for the stimulus. Much evidence supports the frequency theories (except that the frequency of neural impulse in single fibers cannot exceed 1000 cycles per second). Frequency theories are sometimes referred to as telephone theories, since the nerve itself, like a telephone line, carries frequency messages to the brain.

The *volley theory* was developed mainly to remedy the inadequacies in frequency theories, such as the nerve fibers being unable to vibrate as frequently as the fastest sound waves travel. It attempted to account for the difficulty at frequencies exceeding 1000 cycles per second by assuming that the fibers of the auditory nerve work in squads, different squads firing their volleys alternately at each condensation of the external stimulus, so as to carry the total surge of the impulse. Thus pitch above 1000 c.p.s. is perceived as the total frequency of volleys rather than as the frequency of impulses transmitted along any single nerve fiber.

The volley theory was first presented in 1930 by two American experimental psychologists, specializing in hearing and learning studies: Charles William Bray (born 1904), Ph.D., 1928 Princeton, and Ernest Glen Wever (born 1902), Ph.D., 1926, Harvard. In 1936, both Wever and Bray received the **Warren Medal** for "their studies of auditory nerve responses in reptiles and insects, following their similar work on mammals, the whole research constituting an outstanding contribution to the study of auditory function."

hebephilia Pathological disorder (-ia) of loving (-phil-) a youth (hebe-) or comparatively young person: sexual activity carried out by an adult on an adolescent, such as described in Nabokov's novel *Lolita*. Such adults are usually aggressive, impulsive, and schizoid.

h

hebephrenia A subclass of **schizophrenia** characteristic of youth (hebe-) and marked by giggling, **hallucinations**, and emotional deterioration.

Hypothalamic lesions were discovered in the postmortem brains of hebephrenics. There are indications that the diencephalic area is a center for such psychotic conditions as hebephrenia and **manic-depressive psychoses**. C. Vogt, and O. Vogt, 1948 *Uber anatomische Substrate-Bemerkungen zum pathol-anatomische Befunden bei Schizophrenen,"* *Arztliche Forschung*, 1948, **2**, 101 ff.

Etienne Gorget (1795-1828) a French clinician, described (1827) what later became known as hebephrenia. Ewald Hecker (1843-1900) a German psychiatrist and student of **Kahlbaum** described the condition more thoroughly in 1863, but did not publish his material until 1871, at which time he also coined the term. Kahlbaum improved on the description.

hebephrenic schizophrenia *See* **schizophrenia.**

Hecht's theory *See* **color vision theories.**

hedonic theory Relating to (-ic) pleasure (hedon-). An attempt to explain behavior simply by the pleasantness or unpleasantness of its consequences.

hedonic tone The simple pleasantness-unpleasantness dimension (quality) accompanying certain sensory experiences.

hedonism Pleasure (hedon-) doctrine (-ism). The view that a person seeks or should seek the most satisfying things in life. It considered pleasure as the highest good, and as a concept can be traced back to the Greek philosophers Aristippus (435-356 B.C.) and Epicurus (341-210 B.C.). Hedonism varies in meaning from the simple pleasure-pain principle to that of utilitarianism--the greatest good to the greatest number.

For **Bergson** and his *élan vital* concept, one should actively search out pleasure, whereas for de la Mettrie, one should be impulsive and risk-taking, eliminating reflections. **La Mettrie's** hedonism held that pleasure is the end of life and all motivation is selfish.

Jeremy Bentham (1748-1832) represented the utilitarian hedonistic approach applying it to the community--each individual must accept the common goals, else conflict results, bringing more pain than pleasure; hence pleasure instead of pain is associated with those actions that lead to the common goal--altruism.

Herbert Spencer (1820-1903) related hedonism to the evolutionary stage where sensations are more important than ideas. Freud looked to the hedonism of the past and Thorndike's experiments with the puzzle boxes pointed to the law of effect. For psychological hedonism, *see* **law of effect.**

Heidegger, Martin (1889-1919) German existential philosopher. *See* **dread, essence, existence, Fursorge.**

Heider, Fritz (Born 1896, Austria). Received Ph.D., University of Graz 1920. Developed **balance theory** in social psychology; made many studies on **interpersonal perception**; also studied psychology of the deaf. Received DSC Award 1965. (Vinacke, p. 308).

Heinroth, J. C. H. Christian (1773-1843) German psychiatrist. Coined the term **asthenia** in 1830. He also divided psychological processes into: (1) the lowest level of instinctual forces (now, the **id**) striving for pleasure; (2) the **ego** (ich) guided by the intellect; and (3) the conscience (or *Gewissen*). He believed that mental illness had a moral basis.

helicotrema A spiral or coiled (helico-) hole or opening (-trema), connecting the **scala tympani** and **scala vestibuli** at the apex of the **cochlea.**

First described in 1761 by **Cotugno** but not named until 1834 by French anatomist Gilbert Breschet (1784-1845).

helix A spiral or spiral in form. *See* **cytosine.**

Helmholtz, Hermann Ludwig von (1821-1894), German anatomist, physician, physiologist, and physicist. Studied with **Johannes Muller.** He published, during the years of 1856-1866, his *Handbook of Physiological Optics* and, in 1863, *Sensations of Tone* (*Tonempfindungen*), dealing with acoustics. His *Optics* contained the extension of **Thomas Young's** theory, now known as the Young-Helmholtz theory of perceptual color vision (retinal cones are responsive to red, green, and blue colors). He made many other physiological studies related to **psychology**: determination of the speed of nerve impulses (1850); investigation of the mechanisms of vision; investigation of mechanisms of hearing, development of the resonance theory, etc. He also invented the **ophthalmoscope**. *See* **opponent process theory** under **color vision theories, hearing theories, reaction time** (also Boring, p. 298-301).

Helson, Henry (Harry) Born 1898, Massachusetts. Received Ph.D., Harvard 1924. Studies on perception and sensory phenomena. Received **Warren Medal** 1959 for "his development of the concept of **adaptation-level** and his demonstration of its power to encompass many empirical findings, to reconcile conflicting results, and to point to new investigations." Recipient of the **Distinguished Scientific Contribution Award** 1962.

hemeralopia Disorder (-ia) of obscure (-al-) day-(hemer-) vision (-op-). Day blindness; difficulty in seeing except in dim light or darkness, resulting from lack of retinal **cones.**

hemianopia (hemianopsia) A disorder (-ia) in which there is blindness or no (-an-) vision (-op[s]) in one-half (hemi-) of the visual field in one or both eyes.

hemiballismus Jumping about (-ballismus) on one side or half (hemi-) of the body. An involuntary flailing of the arms and legs, probably caused by lesions of the **extrapyramidal tract** on the opposite side of the body from the site of the lesion.

hemicrania A disorder (-ia) on half (hemi-) of the side of the cranium (-cran-); *See* **migraine.**

henry (H) The SI unit of inductance, equal to the inductance of a closed circuit in which an electromotive force of 1 **volt** is produced by a current in the circuit which varies uniformly at a rate of 1 **ampere** per second. *See* **International System of Units.**

Named after the American physicist Joseph Henry (1797-1878).

Heraclitus *See* **dynamics.**

Herbart, Johann Friedrich (1776-1841) German philosopher, psychologist, and educator. Influenced by **Leibniz**, Johann Pestalozzi (1746-1827), the Swiss educational reformer, and John Fichte (1762-1814), German philosopher. Called the father of scientific pedagogy. Decried the relevance of physiology and the experimental method in **psychology.** For Herbart, psychology should be defined in three ways: *empirical*, based upon experience and observation; *metaphysical*, as opposed to the methods of natural science; *mathematical*, in that measurement of experience is possible, as in determining a limen.

His concept of **apperception** was that ideas rise to consciousness and are then assimilated into what he called the "apperceiving mass," or totality of conscious ideas. His concepts were transitional between the speculative psychology of philosophers and the experimentalism of **Fechner** and **Wundt**, having a direct influence on the latter two. *See* **act psychology** (also Boring, pp. 250-261).

Hering, Ewald (1834-1918), German physiologist and psychologist. Proposed a theory of color vision that called for substances in the retina which react to colors. Hering was a forerunner of the Gestaltists in his insistence on the phenomenological viewpoint. Contrary to **Helmholtz**, Hering believed that space perception is an innate ability, as did **Kant.** *See* **color-vision theories, mneme, phenomenology** (also Boring, pp. 352-354).

heroin(e) and morphine The principal derivatives of **opium**; addictive drugs. Heroin is the German tradename for diacetylmorphine: a synthetic derivative of **morphine.** Heroin is more potent than morphine, but in the United States it is still only 4-5 percent pure. Its manufacture and importation are prohibited by law in the United States and most Western countries. Immediate effects upon introduction into the body (by eating, smoking, or injection by hypodermic needle) are: sexual drive decreased, pain relief, **euphoria** with attendant feelings of relaxation, contentment, reverie or daydreaming, shrinkage distortion in time and distance, drowsiness but clear mind. Continual usage of over about 30 days results in **drug addiction.** Heroin is the addict's main choice and is most dangerous in the form of capsules (caps) or packages (decks). If the addict does not take heroin or morphine within about 6-12 hours he begins to suffer withdrawal symptoms (severity depending upon frequency, duration of drugs used, personality characteristics, etc.), becoming quite severe within 48 hours. Some symptoms are: **anorexia**, violent sneezing, and sweating, followed by craving for drug with feelings of restlessness, irritability, impending doom, delirium, hallucinations, with manic activity possibly resulting, gradually getting worse and developing into sweating, flushing, chills, abdominal cramps, diarrhea, vomiting, severe tremors, etc. May lose an average of 10 pounds a day because of dehydration resulting from sweating, diarrhea, and refusal to take water. Withdrawal symptoms reach a peak in about 3-4 days, then begin decreasing by the 5th day, and phase out by the 8th day. As soon as heroin or morphine is taken, symptoms subside usually within a half hour.

Addict shows physical, moral, and mental deterioration, resulting in social ostracization, lying, conniving and resorting to crime to obtain his drugs. Heroin, morphine, and opium are considered addictive because users develop a tolerance for them requiring increased dosage, and because the addict is compelled to take the drug to escape the agony of withdrawal symptoms. Slang: *H, deck, horse, junk, skag, smack, cap* for a capsule. A *speedball* is a mixture of heroin and **cocaine** injected by an addict.

The term heroin(e) was introduced in 1898 by the German chemist Hermann Dreser.

Herophilus (c. 335-280 B.C.) A Greek physician of Alexandria (founded by Alexander the Great in 332 B.C. who had brought **Aristotle** there to help establish the medical school) where it was possible to actually dissect the human body. In his medical studies he was primarily interested in investigating the **brain**, which he felt to be the main organ of the nervous system and the seat of **intelligence.** He believed that the soul was located in the **brain ventricles** and that animal spirits emanated from the **cerebrum.** He coined and described the **rete mirabile** and the **choroid plexus**, among several other anatomical structures (prostate, duodenum, etc.). He also differentiated between the **sensory** and **motor** nerves. *See* **Erasistratus, arachnoid layer.**

hertz (Hz) A frequency unit equal to one cycle per second; the frequency of wave vibrations that determines pitch, the more hertzes the higher the pitch. Human hearing ranges from about 20 Hz to a high of 20,000 Hz.

After Heinrich R. Hertz (1857-1894), German physicist.

heteronymous reflex arc Characterizing (-ous) a reflex arc that affects a differently (heter-) named (-onym-) muscle. A reflex resulting from a **sensory** impulse that originates in one muscle but causes another one, similar in function (synergistic), to contract instead.

Heteronymous excitation refers to the excitation of motor neurons from muscles not controlled by those motor neurons (Thompson, 1967, p. 378). *Contrast with* **homonymous reflex arc.**

heterophoria A tendency (-phoria) for the lines of vision to deviate from one to the other (hetero-). *See* **strabismus.**

heterozygote A contrasting or different (hetero-) **zygote.** An organism possessing two of a pair of unlike **alleles** for a particular **trait,** making it possible to transmit either of the two genes to offspring. Also, a hybrid, not breeding true to type as a result of having one or more recessive characteristics.

heuristic method A nonrigorous method (usually trial and error) related to (-ic) discovering (heurist-) the answer to problems by which approximations to the correct answers are obtained (using shortcuts, rules of thumb, analogies, etc.) without exploring more scientific possibilities. Often used to conduct empirical research, but without much hope of obtaining proof. Heuristic thinking leaves problems for others to prove or for someone else to discover for himself. Computing machines can be programmed to use such methods. (*Contrasted with* **algorithm.**)

hexadecimal system *See* **number systems.**

hierarchy of needs *See* **needs.**

higher-order conditioning A classical conditioning procedure in which a previously established **conditioned stimulus** (CS) functions as an **unconditioned stimulus** (UCS), thereby establishing a new second-order **conditioned response.** Also, **conditioning** in which a CS precedes a stimulus that elicits a response because of prior conditioning. Higher-order conditioning demonstrates how a neutral stimulus can become a secondary reinforcing agent, or how the UCS acquires its reinforcing strength through having been previously a CS.

higher-order reinforcement Reinforcement provided by value-rewarding stimuli through association with secondary reinforcing stimuli or with a reinforcement even further removed from the primary reinforcement.

Hildreth award *See* **Harold M. Hildreth Memorial Award.**

hindbrain The posterior one of the three primary divisions of the developing **brain** in the embryo. Same as **rhombencephalon.**

HIOMT *Hydroxy Indole-O-Methyl Transferase.* An enzyme necessary for stimulating the **pineal gland** in producing the hormone melatonin (Leukel, pp. 47-48).

Hipp chronoscope (Wheatstone-Hipp chronoscope) An electrically operated clock used to measure small fractions in time (in 1/1000 of a second), formerly used in **reaction-time** experiments.

After Sir **Charles Wheatstone** who developed a chronoscope in 1840, which was improved in 1842 by Mathias Hipp (1800-1867), an English watchmaker and mechanic.

hippocampus A ridge or convolution along each lateral ventricle of the brain that, to its discoverer, resembled a small sea (-campus) horse (hippo-); in **Vogt's** terminology, most of the **allocortex,** the subcortical curved ridge of grey matter covering the floor, ruglike, of the descending horn of each lateral **brain ventricle,** which literally and phylogenetically is "buried" in the **cerebral hemispheres.** An area considered crucial for recalling recent events.

Aranzi, in 1587, named and gave the first account of the hippocampus as a whitish substance that "has an uneven, bent form which resembles the appearance of a hippocampus, that is, a sea horse . . ." First (1786) accurately described by **Vic d'Azyr** in his atlas (Clarke and O'Malley, pp. 718-720).

Hippocrates (c. 460-377 B.C.) Greek physician. Denounced the demonic explanation for physical and mental illnesses, claiming they were due to natural causes; believed that **epilepsy** was caused by **brain** disease. Emphasized the importance for physicians to closely observe the patient for symptoms rather than depending upon hearsay. Considered brain as

interpreter of consciousness, and (following **Alcmaeon**) as the central organ of reason. Hippocratic physicians recommended sexual intercourse as cure for hysteria (hyster-uterus) or "wandering uterus." The Hippocratic (or medical) oath, still in use, probably represents his ideals, but cannot necessarily be attributed to him.

Also attributed to Hippocrates, but more rightly probably belonging to **Galen,** is the revision of **Empedocles'** theory that the human body is composed of four humors. The predominant influence of any one humor was held to be responsible for a characteristic **temperament:** excess of yellow bile, choleric; excess of black bile, melancholic; excess of phlegm, phlegmatic; and excess of blood, sanguine. Medical treatment was aimed at restoring proper balance among them. Such classification served for more than two thousand years as a means of typing men according to their temperament. *See* **catalepsy, constitutional types, euphoria, ganglion, hormone, humoral doctrine of diseases, meninges, opisthotonus, tabes dorsalis.**

His, Wilhelm (1831-1904) Swiss neurologist, student of **Remak.** His observations about **axons** helped lay the groundwork for the embryological aspects of the **neuron doctrine.** He also coined the terms **dendrite,** neuropil, neuroblast among others.

histamine The tissue (hist-) amine. Technically known as β-iminoazolylethylamine, histamine is formed *in vivo* from histidine, an **amino acid,** but is also found in brain tissue. When pain receptors are stimulated, histamine is released, some theorists claiming it to be the **adequate stimulus** for pain.

Histamine was isolated in 1907 by two German chemists, Adolf Windaus (1876-1959) and Karl Vogt (born 1880). Antihistamine was discovered in 1937 by the Hungarian-American Georges Ungar (born 1906).

histogram Loom (histo-) picture (-gram). A graphic presentation of a **frequency distribution** in which the classes of **data** are represented by a series of rectangles or vertical bars. The number of cases falling within each class interval corresponds to the height and the size of the **class interval** to the width of the rectangle. *See* **area, sample,** and figure in Table 1b.

histrionic personality disorder *See* **hysterical personality** under **personality disorders.**

Hitzig, Eduard (1838-1907) German neuropsychiatrist (M.D., Berlin 1862). With **Fritsch,** he was responsible for demonstrating experimentally Jackson's surmise that the **cerebral cortex** induced motor activity. In 1870, they showed that electrical stimulation on one side of the **brain** caused the opposite side to twitch (indicating that there were specific **sensory** and **motor** areas in the brain, thereby establishing electrical excitability of the brain). Their research instigated experimental neurophysiology. *See* **localization of brain function, Jacksonian epilepsy.**

H₀ Symbol for **null hypothesis.**

Hobbes, Thomas (1588-1679) English political philosopher. In *Leviathan,* published in 1651, he claimed that man is naturally self-seeking and hostile. In order to protect himself, however, he makes a *social contract* (the basis of group life) in order to respect the rights of others. To him, man's behavior is dictated by the self-preservation instinct and a hedonistic need. Although Hobbes' interests in **psychology** were secondary to his interests in political philosophy, he helped initiate English **empiricism;** espoused **epiphenomenalism.** Realistic and cynical, he drew his materialistic conclusions from **Bacon** to whom he had been an assistant. Hobbes was an empiricist, referring the content of the mind to sense-experience rather than to innate ideas like his contemporary **Descartes.** His mechanistic approach offended churchmen in France, causing him to return to England.

Influenced by Galileo, he became a strict sensationist (believing that all ideas consist of sensory experiences). He anticipated some aspects of **associationism,** saying that **similarity** and contiguity are basic principles for associating ideas.

hodology The study of (-ology) the pathways (hod-) of behavior. **Lewin** applied the term to his construct of circles, elliptical shapes, vectors, etc., to indicate paths of energy. It is more a tri-dimensional than a two-dimensional concept, since it also uses depth to help explain the paths of various forces acting either toward or away from an object.

Hofrat Ger., court or privy (Hof) councillor (Rat) An honorary title conferred by the Austrian government (in old days) on a professor after having served successfully for a number of years.

holistic theories Pertaining to (-istic) **cognitive learning theories,** emphasizing the importance of the wholeness (hol-) of the individual and the unity and organization of behavior in shaping the parts of the whole. Those with a holistic orientation believe that all properties of a living organism must be described in terms of its totality and not in isolated parts. *See* **Flourens, Goldstein.**

The concept of holism was expressed by **G. W. F. Hegel,** who said that phenomena could only be understood by studying the whole.

Hollerith code A code developed by Herman Hollerith in 1889 that combines "zone" punches (top three positions) with digit punches (1 through 9) on a punch card to allow coding of letters, numbers, and special symbols (**alphanumeric**). In recent years, "Hollerith code" has been applied to diverse **computer** and communication codes.

Holmgren wools Differently colored skeins of wool that are used to match against three standard skeins (in helping determine **color-blindness**).

After Alarik Frithiof Holmgren (1831-1897), Swedish physiologist, who introduced his test in 1874.

holography The process (-y) of obtaining a full-color, three-dimensional photographic whole (holo-) image. It is taken without a lens, preserving the original **parallax** as well as the original depth. The object photographed can be seen from all angles, giving the viewer the impression of looking into a window. The film itself is called a *hologram,* and is usually made by photographically recording wave-fronts of laser light reflected from a real object. Every part (broken pieces, snipped parts, etc.) of the hologram retains complete information about the original, total scene. Ordinarily, most holograms must be viewed with a laser (limiting its usefulness somewhat), but special processes make some holograms viewable under an ordinary incandescent bulb. Holography is expected to revolutionize the storage of research data, since, for example, the bulk of the Bible can be reduced to a one-inch square hologram. Holography has been used in medicine to photograph a tumor extradimensionally as an aid in determining possible malignancy. It also has possible use as a memory core in computers, and for adding perspective to television and to movies.

Lashley's model of learning (wave interference pattern, 1951), and other psychological models are being re-examined in terms of holography.

The term "holograph" was adopted from its legal use by British physicist Dennis Gabor (born 1900 in Hungary) who conceived of the idea in 1947, but was unable to develop it at the time because there was no coherent light (intense direct light needed for illumination of the interference patterns produced by intersecting light waves). Gabor received the Nobel prize in physics in 1971.

homeostasis Standing or staying (-stasis) the same (homeo-). The tendency of an organism to maintain a condition of physiological

h

h

dynamic equilibrium, according to **W. B. Cannon** who first used this term (1929). Also, the organism's "steady states" of blood-sugar level, blood acidity, and balance of physiological and chemical needs and drives. Man's restoration of his own psychological and physiological equilibrium by manipulating his environment, as when he uses artificial means to maintain temperature, weight, or body chemistry; also the maintenance of the proper balance between psychological and biological functioning. *See* **adrenocorticotrophic hormone, Cannon-Bard theory.**

homeostat A mechanism that controls (-stat); a specific portion or mechanism of the brain (**hypothalamus**) that is sensitive to and regulates the homeostatic (homeo-) balancing of internal bodily systems.

hominology The study of (-ology) Hominidae (homin-), the family of mammals (order of primates) to which man and his ancestors belong; the non-disciplinary, non-specialized approach to the study of the whole man, including ontogeny and phylogeny. Hominology emphasizes "mankind emerging" and is concerned with abstractions (ethics, values, morality), human universals but not differences, and self-understanding through studying mankind as a whole. It offers "models and perspectives" for the person to discover his own answers to the meaningful problems he must face. Hominology has goals that transcend **self-actualization** (Theodore C. Kahn, Hominology Instead of Humanistic Psychology, *American Psychologist*, Vol. 26, **12**, 1971, p. 1162; T. C. Kahn, *An Introduction to Hominology: The Study of the Whole Man.* Springfield, Illinois: Charles C. Thomas, 1970).

homogenetic cortex *See* **isocortex.**

homogeneous test *See* **performance test.**

homoiotherm An animal (mammal, bird) capable of maintaining its body temperature or heat (-therm) at a relatively similar or constant (homoio-) degree (Milner, p. 301 f.).

homolateral Referring to (-al) that which is on the same (homo-) side (later-), such as a lobe is homolateral if it is in the same cerebral hemisphere with another lobe or area.

homonymous reflex arc A reflex arc that affects a muscle characterized by (-ous) the identical (hom-) name (-onym-); a reflex initiating in and contracting the same muscle. *Homonymous excitation* refers to stimulation of motor neurons that originates from a muscle controlled by the same motor neurons. *Contrast with* **heteronymous reflex arc.**

homoscedasticity A quality (-ity) relating to (-ic-) the same (homo-) amount of scatter (-scedast-), or equal **variance.** In a **bivariate distribution** one of the **variables** is homoscedastic if, for given values of the second variable, the variance of the first variable is the same. In a product-moment scatter diagram, homoscedasticity is apparent if an assumption is made that array dispersions are all equal.

homosexual panic Overwhelming anxiety evident in persons whose latent homosexual tendencies, formerly repressed, threaten to emerge into consciousness as a result of being exposed to dormitory, camp, or military situations that demand physical proximity (such as sleeping in one room, showering together) to members of the same sex. The threatened person may attempt to escape his anxiety by running away, hallucinating, or trying to commit suicide.

homozygote Identical (homo-) zygote or cell formed by two **gametes.** An organism possessing similar **alleles** concerning a given character or trait. *Homozygous* refers to identical alleles as being in the two corresponding **loci** (place occupied by a gene or allele) of a pair of **chromosomes;** possessing genes for one member of at least one pair of alleles. *Homozygous recessive* is a condition in which the corresponding loci of a pair of chromosomes have identical recessive genes.

homunculus Little (-unculus) man (hom-). A chart (figure) constructed from mapping out various portions of the **brain** (somatic sensory and motor areas) showing that brain space utilization is directly proportional to the precision and skill of movements (in the motor areas) rather than upon relative size and gross activity of a particular body part (Morgan, pp. 285-286; Thompson, pp. 314-316).

From pre-Christian times up to about the eighth century A.D., some alchemists attempted to transmute various chemicals in their alembics into a miniature man (homunculus). In 1937, Canadian neurosurgeon Wilder Penfield (born 1891) applied this term to a schematic representation of what roughly appeared to be "little men" in his brain mapping.

H₁ Alternate hypothesis. *See* **null hypothesis.**

Honi phenomenon Failure to experience the distortion of apparent size when one views a familiar face in the so-called **distortion room.** Instead, the room itself appears distorted while the familiar, more valued, face tends to remain stable.

As Wittreich reports: "In 1949 a woman observed the faces of her husband and another man through the rear windows of the smaller room. The face of the other man was described as distorted in the usual manner, but no size changes whatsoever were reported for the husband; his face was described as being perfectly normal no matter which window it appeared in. Similar results were obtained in the large room. Again the other man was described in the usual manner: he appeared to grow or shrink and looked large or small, depending upon the corner in which he was observed. But again no such size changes were reported for the husband. No matter which corner he stood in, he was reported as looking perfectly normal—his usual size. This unusual observation was named the 'Honi phenomenon' following the family nickname for the woman who first experienced and reported it") W. J. Wittreich, "The Honi Phenomenon: A Case of Selective Personal Distortion," *Journal of Abnormal and Social Psychology*, 1952, **47**, 705-712).

honorary physician In Great Britain, the highest status of a physician at one of the leading hospitals where he is in charge of internal medicine. The physician proceeds from assistant physician to physician-to-outpatients and finally to full visiting physician, all appointments being honorary. Higher honors are conferred by the government, such as various orders of knighthood (such as Sir William Gowers, 1897, and Sir David Ferrier, 1902). The Order of Merit, established 1902, is granted for outstanding achievement (such as that given to **Adrian, Penfield,** and **Sherrington**). Beyond this is that of Barony (such as Lord Adrian).

hook order A hierarchy of social dominance in which any one member within a herd of cattle may hook one of lower status with its horns, without fear of retaliation, and may, by the same pattern, submit to hooking without retaliation from one of higher rank. *See* **pecking order.**

Hoppe-Seyler, Felix (1825-1895) German physiological chemist. First to discover lecithin in its pure state; contributed much to the fields of **metabolism** and blood chemistry. *See* **Sechenov.**

hormism A doctrine (-ism) of goals or purpose (horm-). *See* **McDougall.**

hormone Urge on; arouse. Complex chemical substance secreted directly into the bloodstream or lymph by the endocrine glands, which promotes or controls many kinds of bodily activities and behavior.

Hippocrates used the term in the arousal sense, apparently also regarding phlegm and other bodily excretions and secretions as hormones. In 1902, two English physiologists, W. M. Bayliss (1860-1924) and E. H. Starling (1866-1927), announced that a chemical messenger or "hormone" had been discovered. As a result of his work on secretin in 1903, Starling suggested in 1906 that the meaning of the term hormone be restricted to secretions.

Horney, Karen (1885-1952) Born in Germany of Dutch and Norwegian parents. A **psychoanalyst** who emphasized social rather than biological factors in mental illness. *See* **conflict** (also Vinacke, p. 230).

horopter That which (-er) looks (-opt-) at a boundary (hor-). The visual field area where all points in space, because they fall on corresponding positions on the two retinas, are seen singly and in focus by the two eyes.

Horsley, Sir Victor A. Hadden (1857-1916) English physician. In 1897, he presented a paper with Max Sally Löwenthal (1867-1960) German-born English physician that indicated the likelihood of the **cerebellum** having some form of localization of function. In 1905, in conjunction with R. H. Clarke (1845-1909), he developed what has come to be known as the Horsley-Clark instrument, a stereotaxic device in which an electrode can be maneuvered to any desired depth or horizontal plane, used in controlled stimulation and destruction of brain tissue. It has been modified many times since.

Howard Crosby Warren Medal *See* **Warren Medal.**

Howard-Dohlman apparatus A depth perception apparatus consisting of a box with an opening in which two upright metallic rods are to be lined up by the subject.

HSD test *See* **Tukey's honestly significant difference test.**

hubris (Gr., Hybris: insolence; pride) A form of **hamartia** in which overweening pride or smugness causes one impulsively to "sin" or ignore better judgment (such as that provided by a divine warning in ancient times).

hue A psychological dimension of color vision associated with variations in wavelength of the light stimulus, represented perceptually by differences in color (red, yellow, blue, etc.). The scientific term for color. *See* **achromatic color, deuteranomaly.**

Hull's behavior system A logically rigorous scientific system set forth in a series of postulates from which conclusions and hypotheses may be drawn. As expressed in his book, *Principles of Behavior*, 1943, Hull based his theory on evolution, emphasizing the emergence of behavior as having survival value for the organism and for the species. It stresses the role of **reinforcement** in learning, and considers "habit strength" as well as tendencies not to respond. *See* **reactive inhibition, intervening variable, behaviorism, monad, habit-family hierarchy.**

Clark Leonard Hull (1884-1952), American (New York) psychologist. Ph.D., Wisconsin 1918. Specialized in learning theory but also carried on research in aptitudes, testing, and hypnosis. In 1945, he received the **Warren Medal** for "his careful development of a synthetic theory of behavior." APA President 1936 (Vinacke, p. 547).

human engineering (engineering psychology, human factors research) A branch of applied psychology (participated in jointly by engineers and psychologists) concerned with increasing the efficient operation of man-machine systems by designing safe and comfortable machines and equipment to fit the size, strength, and capabilities of the operator or worker. *See* **fields of psychology.**

humanistic psychology (Exist.) A form of **psychology** that seeks the elevation of human interests, values, and dignity above what the humanists call the two dominating forces in psychology (behaviorism and psychoanalysis). Humanistic psychology, the new "third force," strives to integrate related disciplines (psychology, **sociology, psychiatry,** and education) for the betterment and understanding of people. *See* **existentialism, hominology.**

human relations training Programs designed to train personnel to deal effectively with interpersonal relations through various forms of interaction, such as sensitivity training programs and communication and interaction groups. *See* **intensive-group experience.**

Hume, David (1711-1776), Scottish philosopher and historian. Known for his skepticism, he restricted human knowledge to experience and impressions of experience. He denied the possibility of any ultimate verification of knowledge. Everything, to him, must have a cause and similar causes must produce similar effects. He was careful to point out that because two events were correlated it did not necessarily mean that cause and effect were operating.

He published *A Treatise of Human Nature* in 1739, which contains many of his psychological thoughts, some of them stemming directly from **Berkeley** (for example, cognition derives from sensation and reflection). He was even critical of his own skepticism. His questioning attitude stimulated both **James Mill** and **Bain** to do likewise later, a stance that helped establish guiding principles of modern psychology. *See* **Bentham, causation and correlation, Mach, Reid** (also Boring, pp. 186-193).

humoral doctrine of diseases A belief of the ancient anatomists that various organs secreted liquids, or humors—the liver producing blood, the lungs phlegm, the brain mucus, the gall bladder yellow bile or choler, and the spleen black bile or melancholia. The proportion of the four humors determined a person's complexion or temperament (temperamentum: mixing the humors). When properly balanced, the state of health was good; if improperly mixed, a distemper resulted.

Apparently, the origins of the theory stem from **Empedocles,** but **Hippocrates, Aristotle,** and **Galen** all undoubtedly participated in modifying the concept. When **Virchow** concluded that each cell comes from another cell, utilizing the cell theory of German botanist Matthias Schleiden (1804-1881) and German physiologist Theodor Schwann (1810-1882) the humoral doctrine of the ancients lost favor.

Hurler's disease (gargoylism) A medical condition (**lipochondrodystrophy**) including dwarfism, large head, short extremities, kyphosis of spine, congenital eye defects (cataracts), and **mental retardation.** (Enid F. Gilbert and Grace H. Guin, "Gargoylism: A Review Including Two Occurrences in the American Negro," AMA *Journal of the Disturbed Child,* 1958, **95,** 69-80).

After Gertrud Hurler, Austrian pediatrician, who first (1920) described the condition.

Husserl, Edmund (1859-1938) German phenomenologist, who originated the philosophy of **phenomenology,** a form of realism concerned with the analysis of immediate data.

In his *Logische Untersuchungen* (1900-01), he defined phenomenology in a manner similar to **Hamilton,** that is, as an analytic description of subjective experiences. Thus, to him, phenomenology was the basic theme of **psychology.** *See* **existence.**

hybrid computer A combination of the best characteristics of the analog and digital **computers.**

hydrocephaly (hydrocephalus) A relatively rare condition (-y) in which drainage of spinal fluid (hydro-) is blocked and accumulates in the ventricles of the brain (-cephal-), causing brain atrophy, abnormally enlarged skull, and consequent **mental retardation.** With early diagnosis and treatment, the condition can usually be arrested with a minimum of brain damage.

The condition was first described by Latin encyclopedist Aulus Cornelius **Celsus** about 23 A.D. Also described in 1808 by Scottish physician John Cheyne (1777-1836), who wrote the first work on hydrocephaly.

hyoscine Derived from *Hyoscyamus,* a poisonous Eurasian herb of the nightshade family. A **psychotomimetic** drug (form of scopolamine) with anticholinergic actions, depressing the **central nervous system** causing feelings of fatigue and sleep. Also has been used as a withdrawal treatment in drug addiction and alcoholism.

hyperalgesia Disorder (-ia) of excessive (hyper-) or increased sensitivity to pain (-alges-).

hyperesthesia A hysterical disorder (-ia) in which a person reports excessive (hyper-) sensitivity (-esthes-) to touch or to any sense perception; may be caused by some undetermined neural defect.

Term coined in 1849.

hyperglycemia A disorder (-ia) of abnormally high (hyper-) blood (-em) sugar (-glyc-), often caused (among other factors) by secretion of **adrenalin.**

hyper-Graeco-Latin square *See* **Graeco-Latin square design, Latin square design.**

hyperkinesis (hyperkinesia) A behavioral disorder (-is or -ia) of increased (hyper-) movement (-kines-), observed more frequently in boys than in girls, characterized by restlessness, talkativeness, inattention, and tendency to disrupt discipline in the home or classroom. Individual behavior is unpredictable since the child may be manic one day and very conforming and cooperative the next. The condition probably results from damage or disease to the **basal ganglia** (the **caudate nuclei** and **putamen** in particular).

Researchers estimate that up to 15 percent of all elementary school children suffer from this "learning malady." Some neurologists hypothesize that hyperkinetic children have a faulty **reticular activating system,** which ordinarily controls **motor** behavior. Since about 1965 some of these children have been treated by drug therapy hopefully to improve classroom deportment and increase learning ability. Usually, the drug of choice is **amphetamine,** which, as a stimulant would seem to exacerbate the child's hyperactivity. It does for a time, but, because amphetamine stimulates the reticular system, the resulting effect is to increase the control mechanisms of the system, which then brake the child's activity. Such drug treatment seems to work on some children but not on others. *See* **circadian rhythm.**

hypermetropia, hyperopia A disorder (-ia) of the eyes (-op-) enabling them to see at excessive (hyper-) distances. The most frequent error of refraction in which the image is focused behind the retina either because the eyeball axis is too short or the eye's refractive power is too weak. *See* **farsightedness.**

The disorder was first described during 1858-60 by **Donders,** and more specifically defined by him in 1864. The term hypermetropia was introduced in 1884. *See* **Maurolyco.**

hyperphagia A disorder (-ia) of constant and excessive (hyper-) appetite (-phag-), seemingly without satiation regardless of amount of food intake. *Hypothalamic hyperphagia* is a syndrome of overeating and extreme obesity, produced by lesions of or damage to the ventromedial portion of the **hypothalamus** (which apparently normally functions as an inhibitory mechanism in eating). There are no observable metabolic disturbances. Experimentally, bilateral electrolytic lesions can produce the same condition. Some experimenters have found that hyperphagic rats are influenced in their overeating only by the availability and palatableness of food and not because of hunger drive. Other researchers claim that ordinarily truly hyperphagic animals eat ravenously and unselectively. *See* **boulimia, satiety center** (also P. Teitlebaum, "Sensory Control of Hypothalamic Hyperphagia," *Journal of Comparative and Physiological Psychology,* 1955, **48,** 156-163; and

"Random and Food-Directed Activity in Hyperphagic and Normal Rats," *Journal of Comparative and Physiological Psychology,* 1957, **50,** 486-490).

hyperplasia Disorder (-ia) of excessive (hyper-) change (-plas-). Increase or growth in the size of an organ or tissue because of an abnormal increase in the number of cells. (*Compare* **hypertrophy.**)

hypersynchrony Condition (-y) of excessive (hyper-) discharge happening at the same (-syn-) time (-chron-). Mass synchronous discharge of electrical energy as pictured on the **electroencephalogram.**

hypertelorism (Greig's disease) A condition (-ism) of excessive (hyper-) separation (-or-izo) or distance (-tel-) between two paired organs, such as in *ocular hypertelorism,* where there is an abnormally large distance between the eyes, somewhat resembling "mongolism." The condition is often associated with severe **mental retardation.** *See* **cat-cry syndrome.**

First described and named in 1924 by Scottish scientist and physician, David Middleton Greig (1864-1936).

hypertrophy A condition (-y) of excessive (hyper-) increase in the size of an organ or part because of growth (-troph-) in the size of its individual cells. (*Compare* **hyperplasia.**)

hyperthyroidism Condition (-ism) of excessive (hyper-) thyroid secretion. *See* **thyroid gland.**

hyperventilation Excessive (hyper-) ventilation or airing of the lungs; episodic rapid and abnormally prolonged and deep breathing, indicated by fast, shallow panting with mouth wide open, leading to unusual loss of carbon dioxide from the blood, supplanted by hyperoxygenation. Hyperventilation, other than upon a physician's request, is associated with attacks of anger, anxiety, panic, or hysterical episodes, with concurrent excessive activity of the **sympathetic nervous system.** Other symptoms are tingling of extremities and buzzing in head, with occasional fainting.

hypnagogic Pertaining to (-ic) the state leading (-agog-) into or out of sleep (hypn-), with drowsiness and attendant **illusions** and **hallucinations,** such as might occur under **hypnosis.**

hypnosis A condition (-osis) of sleep (hypn-). An artificially induced dreamlike and trancelike condition in which the subject is made susceptible to suggestions from the hypnotist. Such suggestions may be carried out immediately or posthypnotically.

James Braid (1795-1860), British surgeon and writer, changed the name of mesmerism to neurohypnotism (1842) and then to hypnotism after his scientific investigation showed that mesmeric effects were not magnetic in nature.

For further information on hypnosis, contact: *American Society of Clinical Hypnosis,* 800 Washington Ave., S. E., Minneapolis, Minn. 55414; *Society for Clinical and Experimental Hypnosis,* 353 West 57th Street, New York, N. Y. 10019.

hypochondria (hypochondriasis) Under (hypo-) the cartilage or rib case (-chondr-). A neurotic reaction characterized by excessive concern about one's health in the absence of related organic pathology. An escape mechanism in which the individual has excessive and abnormal anxiety about minor aches and pains. *See* **Minnesota Multiphasic Personality Inventory.**

The name refers to the chest region formerly supposed to have been the seat of melancholy (1563). Hypochondria was first described in 1711 by English satirist and physician Bernard de Mandeville (1670-1733), referring to disorders of the spleen as hypochondria.

hypoglossal nerve Referring to (-al) the nerve located under (hypo-) the tongue (-gloss-). Cranial nerve XII, functioning in movements of the tongue.

hypoglycemia Disorder (-ia) of abnormally low (hypo-) blood (-em) sugar (-glyc-) content, in which the symptoms may resemble anxiety

h

states (sweating, flushing or pallor, trembling, increase in blood pressure, apprehensiveness, emotional instability, negativism, and disorientation). Caused by overdose of insulin or from organic or functional causes (**anorexia nervosa**, extreme muscular exertion, etc.). Sometimes, hypoglycemia leads to epileptoid convulsions and mental defect in the infant.

hypomania Less (hypo-) than madness (-mania). Mild manic symptoms, sometimes described as including a mild degree of insanity, characterized primarily by an excessive amount of often impracticable ideas and great plans for doing things but with little or no accomplishment. According to the **Minnesota Multiphasic Personality Inventory**, the hypomanic personality tends to be charming, aggressive, expansive, confident, and hypersensitive, in addition to having the previously listed characteristics.

Henry Johnson (?1805-1877) English physician, proposed in his book (*On the Arrangement and Nomenclature of Mental Disorders*, 1843, pp. 18-19) "to discard the term Monomania (coined by **Esquirol**) and substitute for it that of Hypomania, as signifying a slighter form or lower grade of Mania," considering both daemonomania and melancholia as forms of hypomania.

hypophysis cerebri Under (hypo-) growth (-physis) of the brain (cerebri); the **pituitary gland**, which hangs from the base of the brain. *See* **adenohypophysis** and **neurohypophysis**.

The term "hypophysis" was known from **Galen's** time as anything beneath something else. In 1913, the American anatomist Burt Green Wilder (1841-1925) first used the phrase hypophysis cerebri in referring to the pituitary body.

hypothalamus Part of the **diencephalon**. A group of nerve centers (gray matter) under (hypo-) the thalamus and connected to the **pituitary gland**, which integrates autonomic function into patterns of activity that adjust the internal environment of the body. It has been established experimentally that the hypothalamus contains nuclei controlling sleep, hunger, body temperature, sexual activity, respiration, heartbeat, and glandular function. Generally, it involves motivational and emotional behavioral components. *See* **hyperphagia, prosencephalon**.

In 1888, English physician Byron Bramwell (1847-1931), first described the functions of the hypothalamus, and the effect of tumors on them, as well as coining the word. In 1909, the first experimental work on the hypothalamus was reported by two Austrian physiologists, Johann Paul Karplus (1866-1936) and Alois Kreidl (1864-1928).

hypothesis An idea placed or set down (-thesis) under (hypo-) another as a temporary support. A tentative theory or supposition provisionally adopted to account for certain facts and to guide in the investigation of others. *See* **hypothesis testing**.

hypothesis testing A procedure for choosing, on the basis of sample **data** and a set of **decision rules**, between two mutually exclusive and exhaustive statistical **hypotheses**. Kirk (1968, pp. 25-27) outlines the conventions involved in hypothesis testing, these being listed in a slightly modified form: Step 1: State a **null hypothesis** H_0, and an alternate one, H_1; Step 2: Decide on an appropriate **sample** statistic and a test statistic; Step 3: Decide on a **level of significance** (alpha) and a sample size N. Alpha, N, and the sampling distribution of the test statistic under the null hypothesis determine the region for rejecting H_0; Step 4: Obtain the sample statistic and compute the test statistic.

hypothetical construct *See* **construct**.

hypothyroidism A condition (-ism) of under (hypo-) secretion of the **thyroid gland**. *See* **myxedema**.

hysteria Disorder (-ia) associated with the womb (hyster-). The exhibition of symptoms (conversion-type) in the absence of any related organic pathology. For example,

hysteria is associated with neurotic conditions characterized by vague pains, paralysis, seizures, etc., and by dissociation and emotional instability, such as uncontrolled laughing or crying.

Hysteria was named by early physicians (reportedly coined about 400 B.C. by **Hippocrates**) on the mistaken assumption that it was an abnormal condition caused by the womb's malfunction and consequently found only in women. *See* **Charcot**.

In 1671, **Willis** described hysteria in the more modern sense, and about 1750, English neurologist Robert Whytt (1714-1766) divided the neuroses into three categories (hysteria, hypochondriasis, and nervous exhaustion).

hysterical neurosis *See* **neurosis**.

hysterical personality (histrionic personality disorder) *See* **personality disorders**.

Hz hertz.

I

iatrochemical school of thought In the 17th century, one of the two major materialistic beliefs about neural physiology, which treated physiological phenomena as resulting from chemical changes. *Compare with* **iatrophysical**.

Swiss physician Philippus Paracelsus (1493?-1541) for example, was an iatrochemist in that he introduced new medicines into practice, such as **opium**, mercury, and arsenic.

iatrogenic addiction Drug addiction initiated (-gen-) by use of narcotics under treatment of a physician (iatro-) for an unrelated condition.

iatrophysical Resulting from physical laws, or applying the laws of the physical sciences to functioning of animal and human nerves. **Descartes** was a so called iatrophysicist in viewing the physical world as mechanistic and separated from the mind, as well as interpreting emotion as basically physiological in nature. *Compare* **iatrochemical**.

iconic mode (ikonic memory) Relating to (-ic) a very short-term imagelike (icon) memory or visual-spatial imagery that, according to **J. S. Bruner** (*Studies in Cognitive Growth*, 1966), is characteristic of his second stage of the child's linguistic development. The child is perceptually capable (through imagery or iconic representation) of recognizing and reproducing objects but cannot apply language abstractions to create new forms. Related to **Piaget's** stage of formal operations. *See* (1) under **cognitive growth theories**.

iconic sign A representation relating to (-ic) its image (icon-). An indicator that is similar to what it denotes (such as a good likeness of a photograph to the person).

Term introduced (1946) by American philosopher and linguist Charles Morris.

ICSH *I*nterstitial *c*ell *s*timulating *h*ormone. *See* **gonadotrophic hormone**.

ictus A stroke or blow, as in sunstroke or an epileptic seizure.

id The singular neuter pronoun in Latin. In the evolutionary theory of German biologist August Weissman (1834-1914) a unit of germ plasm (1893). In Freudian theory (1923-24), the process within the human psyche that is governed by the pleasure principle. It is the least accessible and the most primitive aspect of the mind, purely hedonistic (blindly seeking gratification of its impulses and primitive needs) and is without conflict. As the reservoir of the **libido**, of instinctive drives, the id knows no logic and has no sense of morality, values, or time. To **Freud**, the infant personality is all id and the **ego** and **superego** are built out of it.

Freud, in 1923, said he borrowed the term "id" from George Groddeck, whose "id" was identical to the creative life force or the

unconscious of Karl Gustav Carus (1789-1869), indicating that from the id (Das Es—Groddeck's id) all bodily processes derive.

identical components (or elements) theory Thorndike's transfer of training theory specifying that new tasks are easier to learn when they consist of some of the same elements found in tasks already learned.

identical twins (duplicate or monozygotic twins) Two siblings who have developed from one fertilized ovum. They are always of the same sex, same blood type, etc., and because of their identical heredity they are valuable subjects for scientific research.

identification Act of (-tion) making (-fic-) the same (identi-). The normal childhood process of becoming emotionally attached to significant adults by imitating them and acquiring appropriate social roles. Psychoanalytically, the resolution of the child's **Oedipus complex** by absorbing his parent's role into his own.

A defense mechanism by which a person puts himself in the same role with some other usually successful or illustrious person or group, thereby enhancing his self esteem and reducing his own anxieties and conflicts. An unconscious striving to make one's own **ego** and behavior the same as that of the model. *See* **introjection**.

identity (Exist.) The condition of being one's unique self with the concomitant feeling of recognizing this self. A person with identity feels in close juncture with everything of the moment; he has roots; he "belongs" without being a joiner; he feels that he supplies some meaning to life; he is able to relate to others with a suitable degree of assertiveness; and he is capable of intimacy of closeness.

identity formation The process of achieving a consistent, well-integrated, and mature personality as an outgrowth of earlier positive **identification** and other influences.

identity hypothesis *See* **Fechner**.

ideokinetic *See* **apraxia**.

idiocy, mongolian *See* **Down's syndrome**.

idioglossia A disorder (-ia) characterized by inventing or using a unique or peculiar (idio-) tongue (-gloss-); own-tongued. Same as **idiolalia**.

idiographic approach Relating to (-ic) an approach that studies a unique or individual (idio-) record (graph-) of someone. A psychological viewpoint in which the unique individual is the only proper and final unit of analysis. The clinical psychologist, psychiatrist, social worker and others using a case-study method employ the idiographic approach.

In 1921, German philosopher Wilhelm Windelband (*see* **nomothetic**) coined the terms idiographic and nomothetic in his book, *An Introduction to Philosophy*. He proposed that idiographic be used to gain an appreciation of the single event as not being an example of a scientific or natural law. *Idiographic psychology*, for example, is the art of understanding people in their uniqueness.

Initially (1937), Allport considered this method the most productive and reasonable one to use for developing true concepts and laws about behavior. In 1962, however, he selected the term **morphogenic** to replace idiographic, since it did not have the stigma of being so extreme and restrictive in its focus on uniqueness (G. W. Allport, *Personality: A Psychological Interpretation*, 1937, pp. 3-23; G. W. Allport, "The General and the Unique in Psychological Science," *Journal of Personality*, 1962, 30, 405-422).

idiolalia A disorder (-ia) characterized by a unique, peculiar, or private (idio-) form of unintelligible chatter or speech (-lal-), invented and/or used by children in close contact, such as twins.

idiopathic Relating to (-ic) a diseased (-path-) condition unique (idio-) to an individual. A condition arising spontaneously or from unknown causes, such as in *idiopathic epilepsy*, which cannot be attributed to any known organic cause.

idiosyncrasy credit Condition (-y) of building up credit when one's distinct (idio-) behavior is blended (-cras-) together (syn-). A term proposed by Hollander in an attempt to explain that a leader's behavior frequently shows deviance from group norms, while in general, status depends on conformity to norms. For services rendered by a leader to his group he accumulates certain "units" of idiosyncrasy credit. The more conforming and competent he appears to his group the greater the amount of credit he builds up and consequently the greater amount of freedom and nonconformity he is permitted by that group. If he varies too greatly from the group's expectancies and accepted norms, however, he loses idiosyncrasy credit and consequently some of his leadership control. His role ceases when his credit reaches zero (E. P. Hollander, "Conformity, Status and Idiosyncrasy Credit," *Psychological Review*, 1958, 65, 117-127).

idiot An outmoded term. *See* **mental retardation.**

Originally, in Greek society, an ordinary civilian as contrasted with a soldier was an *idiotes* (from *idios*, meaning personal and private). Historically, the term became progressively a layman (versus a professional); a commonplace fellow; an uneducated illiterate person; a mentally defective illiterate person; and (according to older classifications in psychological testing), a person with an intelligence quotient of less than 25, the lowest grade of mentally retarded (unable to guard against common dangers or learn connected speech), now often classified as severely retarded (IQ 20-35) and profoundly retarded (IQ below 20). Less than 100,000 are so classified in the United States. They have a high susceptibility to disease, and are able to relate to others only at a most superficial level. Most have to be institutionalized, requiring lifelong custodial care and supervision. The term idiot is frowned upon by most professional people.

idiot savant (skilled or wise idiot) A mentally subnormal person (in general knowledge and adaptation to life) who has unusual ability in one or more specialized activities, usually of the rote-memory type (in recalling musical compositions or performing arithmetic calculations), but who may lack social awareness and ability to think abstractly. May be considered **autistic** by some clinicians (M. Scheerer, E. Rothman and K. Goldstein, "A Case of Idiot Savant: An Experimental Study of Personality Organization," *Psychological Monographs*, No. 4, 1945, 58, 63).

illuminance (formerly, illumination) The **intensity** of light energy falling upon a surface; its most common unit is the **foot-candle.**

illuminant color Color perceived as belonging to a self-luminous object, a glowing color (not reflected).

illusion A mocking (illusio). A false perception; misinterpretation of sensory **data**; a subjective perversion of actual sense data. For example, in the **Müller-Lyer illusion**, line A appears to be shorter than line B. Measurement, however, proves that their lengths are identical.

The **Necker** (illusion) **cube** was derived in 1832 by L. A. Necker, a Swiss naturalist who observed "that a transparent rhomboid spontaneously reverses in depth." The first (1860) special distortion figure published was that by German astronomer Johann Zollner (1834-1882), which gave the impression that straight equidistant diagonal lines were converging upon one another or were not equally distant. Johann Poggendorff (1796-1877) later in the same year published his illusion in which "the two segments of the diagonal line seem to be offset." In 1889, Müller-Lyer published his double-headed arrow illusion in 15 variations.

The Hering illusion was published in 1861 by **Ewald Hering**, in which two exactly parallel

lines cross lines radiating outward from a central spot, creating the illusion that the parallel lines bulge in the middle.

(For further history of illusions, paradoxical pictures, distortion figures, impossible figures, and a theory of illusions see Richard L. Gregory, "Visual Illusions" in *Contemporary Psychology, Readings from Scientific American*, San Francisco; W. H. Freemand and Company, 1971, pp. 167-177).

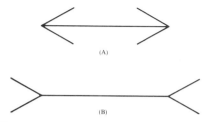

illusory motion The perception of motion in an unchanging **stimulus**, such as in the **autokinetic illusion.** (*Compare* **apparent movement**).

imageless thought A controversial theory that considered thought to occur on an unconscious level, and to be an abstract, imageless activity, completely lacking in sensory content and not available for **introspection**. *See* **Bewusstseinslage** (conscious attitude) as an imageless aspect of mind, vague and intangible, but a conscious element that is neither image nor sensation.

In 1894, Külpe went to Würzburg where he developed the basis of imageless thought from 1901-1909. He, as well as **Woodworth** in America, held that imageless thought is the process by which problems are solved. They were opposed to the idea of an imaginal process that could be observed step by step, as was held by the introspectionists. Opponents of imageless thought contended that even though some memory images were too weak to be identified they could readily be made meaningful when taken together.

imaginary chromaticity Relating to (-ic) the quality or degree (-ity) of color (chromat-) unproducible by the spectrum; chromaticities corresponding to some one visual process in the absence of activity of other processes are usually imaginary.

imaginary number *See* **complex number, real number.**

imago Image or **archetype** from man's **collective unconscious**, such as God, Devil, heroes, villains, et cetera. Used primarily in **Jungian** psychology. An imago usually carries with it strong emotional connotations.

imbecile Weak (imbecillus) of mind; weak-minded. Former term for persons with an IQ of 25 to 49, who are generally unable to earn a living but able to protect themselves against common dangers and exist under supervision. They do not develop mentally beyond the level achieved by a normal 6 to 8 year-old child. *See* **mental retardation.**

imipramine hydrochloride (Marketed under name of Elavil and Tofranil).

A psychic energizer, used in treatment of depression, feelings of incapacity, unworthiness, guilt, and inferiority, suicidal thoughts, and **hypochondria**. It is not, however, a stimulant nor **amphetamine** nor does it function as a MAO inhibitor. Has been useful in making patients more amenable to psychotherapy or shock treatment. High dosage may produce epileptiform seizures. The drug is anticholinergic in action. Speeds up heart rate, blood pressure, and respiration. Side effects: increased agitation and anxiety.

The antidepressant quality was discovered by the Swiss psychiatrist Roland Kühn (born 1912), much of his research being stimulated by the success of **chlorpromazine.**

implicit movement (covert movement) A muscular contraction (e.g., that which occurs in the speech organs during thought) so faint that it can be detected only by sensitive recording and measuring instruments.

impossible figure A contrived two-dimensional picture or figure, designed to confuse one's perception by presenting clearly incompatible distance information to the eye, creating the **illusion** of seeing a third dimension.

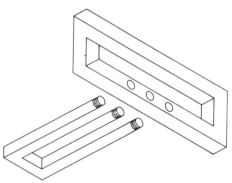

imprinting A specific strong attachment to an object, person, or member of its own species by a particular species (such as chicks, ducklings, birds), during a critical limited period of time soon after birth and then is highly resistant to **extinction**. Such response is relatively unmodifiable thereafter. Lorenz (1935) named this tendency to follow at a critical period in life "imprinting." *See* **ethology.**

In Sir Thomas More's *Utopia*, written in 1515, the phenomenon of imprinting was reported: "The farm workers . . . breed an enormous number of chickens by a marvelous method. Men, not hens, hatch the eggs, by keeping them in a warm place at an even temperature. The chicks, as soon as they come out of the shell, recognize and follow men instead of their mothers." (According to Margaret Altmann in *American Psychologist*, page 684, Vol. 19, 8, 1964, referring to page 29 of T. More, In H. V. S. Ogden (Ed.) *Utopia*. Book 2. New York: Appleton-Century Croft, 1949).

Imprinting observations were noted by D. A. Spalding in 1873 ("Instinct, With Original Observations on Young Animals." Reprinted in *British Journal of Animal Behavior*, 1954, 2, 2-11 from *Macmillan's Magazine*, 1873, 27, 282-293).

inadequate personality *See* **personality disorders.**

inappropriate incentive system *See* **behavioral dysfunctions classification.**

inappropriate stimulus control of behavior *See* **behavioral dysfunctions classification.**

inborn error Variation from the normal number of genetic errors likely to occur in any organism from the time of conception to actual birth.

The term "inborn errors of metabolism" was originated in 1908 by English geneticist Sir Archibal Garrod (1857-1936), and published in 1923 in his book, *Inborn Errors of Metabolism.*

incompatible response method Habit-breaking technique in which a new, more desirable **response**, but incompatible with the previous one, is substituted for an undesirable one; a response incapable of being elicited simultaneously with another response.

increasing returns *See* **curves of returns.**

incremental learning Learning that occurs in a series of steps; the amount of learning increasing irregularly because the pace depends upon the subject's ability to cope with each phase of the assignment.

incus Anvil. The middle one of a chain of three pairs of hinged ear bones called the auditory **ossicles**: **malleus**, incus, **stapes**—six in all, located in the tiny epithelial-lined tympanic cavity, hollowed out of the temporal bone. The incus conducts sound vibrations from the malleus to the stapes. *See* **Achellini**.

Term coined by **Vesalius**, 1543.

independent variable An experimental condition or variable directly controlled or manipulated by the experimenter so that its effects on the **dependent variable** can be measured or determined. The choices made by the experimenter and the kinds of conditions he imposes upon the experiment constitute various levels of the independent variable. Stimulus, organismic, and response variables are three classes of independent variables, responses to which are the dependent variables under investigation. *See* **graph**.

individual differences *See* **J. McK. Cattell**, **personal equation**.

individual psychology Adler's approach to **psychology** emphasizing that what motivates man is his striving for power and need to be superior. Contrary to his earlier view (that man is an aggressive, lustful animal) he felt that man is a socially responsible animal and that he was born with social awareness. Adler, himself, named his psychology "individual." (Heinz and Rowena Ansbacher, *The Individual Psychology of Alfred Adler*, 1956).

individual test Any test (verbal or performance) that can be administered (by tester) to only one subject (testee) at a time. Individual tests may sample **intelligence, aptitude, personality**, etc. Examples: **Stanford-Binet** and **Wechsler tests of intelligence; Rorschach** for exploring the personality.

individuation Becoming (-ation) not (in-) divisible (-dividu-). Differentiation or emergence of specific and undividable activities out of general mass activity. For example, the process of a baby learning to reach with his hand instead of wriggling all over when he wants to touch something. To **Jung**, individuation involved the complete development of all parts of man, conscious or unconscious, psychic or organic, and was thus the true goal in life. *See* **Coghill**.

induction (generalization) Act of (-tion) leading (-duc-) into (in-), or introducing. A type of reasoning that leads from the observation of events into some general rule or class. A scientific method (or experimental procedure) dependent upon the accumulation of specific evidence or **data**, observing regularities and differences, and from them making inductions about principles involved. The method of induction is the basis of **inferential statistics**. *See* **empirical**; *compare* **deduction, inference**.

industrial psychology The application of psychological principles and skills to problems in industry, including the specialties of personnel evaluation and testing, **human engineering**, job analyses and placement, etc.

inequalities The relation between two quantities, usually expressed by a sign of inequality, indicating that the quantities are not equal, or that one quantity is more than or less than some other quantity or characteristic. For example, $5 < 9$ indicates that 5 is less than 9; $9 > 5$ shows that 9 is greater or more than 5; and $a \neq b$ indicates that whatever the quantity a symbolizes it does not equal that of b. The symbols used for inequality indicate only position and do not tell "how much" or to what degree there is a difference. The three signs of inequality are: $\neq$ does not equal or is not equal to; $<$ is less than; and $>$ is more than or greater than. Used to state the levels of significance in **hypothesis testing**. *See* **null hypothesis**.

infantile autism A disorder that may occur before six months of age, characterized by apathy and preoccupation with objects and apparent rejection or ignoring of people. *See* **childhood schizophrenia, autism**.

inference The process of reaching conclusions or generalizations by **deduction** or **induction** from sampling evidence rather than from direct observation of all of the **data**.

inferential statistics A **probability** technique that enables an experimenter to arrive at general conclusions from sample evidence and to calculate the risks of drawing erroneous conclusions. The computation of averages, percentages, etc. (so-called **descriptive statistics**) is preliminary to the computation of inferential statistics about **population** parameters. Inferential statistics utilizes two important theorems for its operation: the **central limit theorem** and the law of large numbers.

inferior Lower or inferior part of the human body; away from the head (e.g., the foot is part of the inferior extremity). *See* **anatomical directions**.

inferior colliculi *See* **corpora quadrigemina**.

inferiority complex According to **Adler**, strong, repressed feelings of inadequacy and insecurity that color a person's entire behavioral and adjustive efforts, leading to neurotic behavior and to **compensation**. Such "feelings of inferiority" (the preferred term) may accompany defeat, organ inferiority, or low social status. *See* **individual psychology**.

Adler introduced the concept of inferiority in 1910 referring to the child's feeling of inferiority to adults and attempts to correct or balance his feelings by resorting to temper tantrums, crying, and other physical expressions.

information Information in a **computer** may take one of three forms: (1) **data**—the actual numbers to be entered into the computer through the **input device**, operated upon, and outputted through the output device; (2) format—information that tells the computer in what form to expect the incoming data and specifying the form of the **output** data; and (3) control or program—the information telling the computer how to process the input data

information processing A complex process in which **cognitive** events are considered as **input** and behavioral responses as **output**. This model is especially associated with **computer** simulation and theorizing about verbal learning although it also appears in approaches to **perception** and **intelligence**, or in the flow of information in the nervous system itself. Information processing has been arbitrarily divided into five stages: (*1*) sensory transduction, involving the transformation of sensory data into usable physiological energy for transference to the brain where (*2*) conscious attention is paid to incoming stimuli and decisions made as to whether (*3*) short-term memory or (*4*) long-term memory should be called upon. Stage (*5*) concludes the process in which retrieval involves the selection of only one correct item from perhaps billions of others stored (*Psychology Today, An Introduction*, CRM, 1970, 342-343).

Garner makes a special plea that factors other than just processing be considered in the study of information processing. He believes that the stimulus itself and the nature of the input have been practically ignored in such studies. He calls for a greater maturity on the part of experimentalists in asking "where and under what circumstances does the organism process information in a particular way?" *See* **flow-chart, short-term memory** (also W. R. Garner, "The Stimulus in Information Processing," *American Psychologist*, 1970, **25**, 350-358).

information theory The study of communication systems, their transmission, and the principles that make for understanding, control, and predictability in communication; a measurement framework specifying the amount of information contained in an event relative to the proportion of **uncertainty** reduced; a mathematical description of the units of information contained in a particular message form, and the relations between such symbols and other events in information transmission. In its elementary form, information theory is concerned only with the

relationships between communication signs (Morse code signals, noise level, etc.) and not with their meanings. *See* **Bayesian approach to statistics**.

infrahuman Below (infra-) the human being on the evolutionary scale.

in-group Any group to which a person belongs or feels he belongs and with which he identifies himself. A group whose members feel loyalty to each other and tend to view outsiders (out-group) with disinterest, suspicion, or hostility.

inhibition Act of (-ition) holding (-hib-) in (in-). Blocking of one process by another. An increase in a **neuron**'s resting **potential** above its usual one. Also, a response reduction caused by an incompatible response being activated. In learning, an assumed process believed to occur during **extinction**. A tendency to suppress impulses or desires, or prevent certain modes of expression that would expose the individual to social or self-censure. For example, very young children behave spontaneously, but as they mature, social, cultural, and parental pressures cause them to become inhibited, or to develop inhibitions. In brain damage, the inhibitory function may be impaired and the child may not be able to control his impulses. To **Freud**, inhibition is the expression of a functional limitation of the **ego**. *See* **inhibitory postsynaptic potential, disinhibition** (also Butter, 1967, p. 23; Thompson, 1967, pp. 180-183).

The process of inhibition (in discussing relaxation of antagonistic muscles) was first referred to by **Galen** in "The Movement of Muscles," and a similar point was made by **Descartes** in 1649. The first description of nervous inhibition of a specific organ (the heart) by stimulating a peripheral nerve (the **vagus**) was made by A. W. Volkmann in 1838, later demonstrated experimentally in 1845-46 by E. and **E. H. Weber**. In 1863, **I. M. Sechenov** was first to observe inhibition in the central nervous system (spinal reflex inhibition in a frog). In 1886-87, **Gaskell** explained that vagal inhibition, as had been reported by Volkmann, was due to the heart muscle being hyperpolarized. He also showed (in 1886 and 1916) that the **autonomic nervous system**, in controlling involuntary muscular activity and glandular secretion, functioned in both an excitatory and inhibitory manner.

inhibitory postsynaptic potential (IPSP) Eccles' (1958) term for the brief hyperpolarization of the neuron's postsynaptic membrane, with resulting heightened threshold for the depolarization that initiates **neuron** excitatory response. This hyperpolarization follows release in the **synapse** of an inhibitory **transmitter substance**. Excitatory transmitter substances tend to produce depolarization of the postsynaptic membrane or **excitatory postsynaptic potential** (EPSP). Although each neuron discharges only one kind of transmitter substance, neurons of different types may have presynaptic membranes forming synapses with a third neuron in close proximity, hence tending to have IPSP and EPSP counterbalance one another.

inkblot test *See* **Rorschach**.

innate releasing mechanism (IRM) A concept developed by **Tinbergen** relating to the existence of a coordinating unit in the nervous system. The IRM is the "special neurosensory mechanism that releases the reaction to certain cues or **sign** stimuli and is responsible for its selective susceptibility to special combinations of sign stimuli." **Lorenz** and others believe that human beings have a definite IRM to snakes and possibly to mice, indicating that the sign stimuli here may be the appearance of leglessness (Nikolaas Tinbergen, *The Study of Instinct* [Oxford University Press, 1951] p. 41).

inner ear (or labyrinth) The portion of the ear inward from the **oval window**, comprising two major parts: (a) a bony labyrinth (consisting of the vestibule, cochlea, and semicircular canals) that encases (2) a membranous labyrinth (containing the **saccule** and **utricle** inside the vestibule, the cochlear duct inside the **cochlea**, and the membranous semicircular canals).

inoculation theory The process of (-tion) providing (-at-) a bud or eye (-ocul-) for insertion into (in-) a stem or trunk; engrafting. In medical terminology, inoculation is the injection of a disease virus into the body so as to cause a mild form of the disease and thereby build up resistance to a stronger attack. The inoculation theory of McGuire is analogous to medical inoculation in that he believes **attitudes** can be made resistant to change by desensitizing the person (against an eventual or expected major attack upon his beliefs) with the inoculation of unconvincing, weaker arguments so that adequate defenses and arguments can be gradually built up (William J. McGuire, "Persistence of the Resistance to Persuasion Induced by Various Types of Prior Belief Defenses," *Journal of Abnormal and Social Psychology*, 1962, 64, 241-248).

William James McGuire. Born, New York 1925. Ph.D., Yale 1954. Major research interests: personality and social psychology, communication, selective perception studies.

input In **cybernetics** and **computer language**, the **stimulus** that initiates activity of a machine or living organism; the **data** to be processed; process of transferring data from external to internal storage.

input device A means (magnetic tape, punched cards, typewriter keyboards, etc.) of transferring **data** and program information into a **computer** or other such device. *See* **computer operation**.

input-output device An instrument that introduces **information** into laboratory computers (usually magnetic tapes and keypunched cards) and obtains information from them by printers, typewriters, or oscilloscopes. Two such instruments are: (1) *direct access devices* (such as magnetic disks, magnetic drums, data cells) and (2) *sequential devices* (such as card readers, magnetic tape units, paper tape units), which require rewinding or restarting once the device passes the **data** they are seeking.

INRC (*Identity, Negation, Reciprocal* and *Correlative* transformations) In **Piaget's** conceptual description of the intellectual stage of development for bright adolescents, the four transformations in the symbolic logic system that form the basis of a structural group permitting the operation of highest intellectual thought. (Barbel Inhelder and J. Piaget, *The Growth of Logical Thinking from Childhood to Adolescence*, 1958).

insanity A medico-legal concept applied to any grave mental condition rendering the individual incapable of intent and thus not legally responsible for his actions. Not properly a synonym for **psychosis**. **Psychiatrists** and **psychologists** frown upon the term because of its dichotomous nature (sane-insane); but psychiatrists have been, in a sense, forced (because of their medical training and acceptance by the legal profession) to testify about an individual's "sanity."

Insanity was first described by primitive Greeks who believed that the chthonian gods (those deities reigning under the earth or in the underworld) were responsible for the affliction. **Hippocrates** described 3 types of mental conditions (feverish delirium, nonfeverish delirium, and **melancholia**) sometimes classified as **paranoia**. **Asclepiades** distinguished between **hallucination** and **illusion**, and between acute and chronic diseases.

The term insanity (as "insania") was first used (about 35 A.D.) by **Celsus**, who wrote on nervous diseases, insanity, and epilepsy.

insight Sudden awareness or intellectual penetration. In *problem solving*, perception of relationships and the relatively sudden and permanent solution to a problem or puzzle, the parts of which have been previously seemingly unrelated. In *psychotherapy*, insights are illuminations or the bringing to awareness of hitherto unsuspected motives, desires, and feelings: the inner views of processes in the **personality**, which can enable a patient to view his problems in a new light. *See* **kairos, Köhler**.

insight therapy *See* **Dasein analysis**.

insistence An attribute of color perception associated with **luminance**, that has to do with impressiveness; sometimes considered to be synonymous with **brightness**. *See* **Eindringlichkeit**.

in situ A manner of lying, the local position, the site; situated in its natural or original position. In medicine and physiology, an undisturbed object in position, referring to various anatomical structures.

instinct Pricked (-stinct) in. An inherited, unlearned, coordinated, complex, species-specific response pattern or chain of behavior elicited largely by physiological stimuli: for example, nest-building in birds. The role of instincts or unlearned behavior patterns in human beings has been hotly debated. **Freud** considered instinct to be an irreducible component of man's personality. Psychoanalytic theory today uses the concept of instinctual drives. The template idea, that is, a passive translation from genetic encoding, is apparently implicit in most instinct theories. (*See* the selection on instinct from Vernon L. Kellogg's *Mind and Heredity* condensed in Pronko, pp. 107-110; Solomon Diamond, "Gestation of the Instinct Concept," *Journal of the History of the Behavioral Sciences*, Vol. VII, 4, 323-336; also Bischof, 1964, pp. 47-49, on Freud's concept of instinct).

instrumental activity In motivation, an activity that precedes and makes possible consummatory activity, not only persisting but even increasing in intensity (such as the persistence a lone person might demonstrate in searching for water during the summertime in the desert).

instrumental behavior Behavior that is a means for accomplishing a purpose or satisfying a need, such as changing the environment, whereby the change reinforces the individual by reward or by providing escape routes from unwanted stimulation.

instrumental conceptualism *See* (1) under **cognitive growth theories**.

instrumental (or operant) conditioning Conditioning in which a learned response is instrumental in receiving a reward, resulting from performing a reinforced response in preference to many other responses not so reinforced. *See* **instrumental learning, behavior therapy, Bekhterev, instrumental behavior, operant conditioning**.

instrumental learning An outcome of **instrumental conditioning** methods; a type of learning by trial and error in which the subject learns a response which is instrumental in achieving an end, accomplishing a purpose, or receiving **reinforcement** (such as learning to acquire food or avoiding pain). In instrumental learning, the response is **operant**, that is, the **stimulus** is not specific and the **response** may simply be emitted. The reinforcement cannot be called the stimulus, since it follows the instrumental response. *See* **law of effect**.

instrumental response A **response** supported by environmental reinforcement contingencies, for example, rewards or avoidance of pain.

insufficient deterrence hypothesis The severity of a minimally sufficient deterrent is inversely related to the degree of internalization of the prohibition. That is, the milder the threatened punishment, assuming the individual refrains from the forbidden behavior, the more likely that the prohibitions will be internalized.

Derived from **Festinger's** theory of **cognitive dissonance**.

insula (island) of Reil A group of convolutions located at the base of the **lateral fissure**. *Same as* **central lobe**.

Named after Johann Reil (1759-1813), German physician.

insulin One of two sugar-regulating hormones (the other, **glucagon** from the alpha cells). Insulin is produced in the **pancreas** by the beta cells of the islets of Langerhans, which inhibit blood glucose release by the liver and muscles and increase the activity of the enzyme glucokinase (necessary for glucose catabolism). Commercially, insulin is prepared from pig or ox pancreas and is used in control of diabetes mellitus by lowering sugar content of blood and urine and by having other metabolic effects not well known as yet.

Insulin(e) was first suggested as a name in 1909 by a British physician Albert Sharpey-Schäfer (1850-1935) when he surmised that the islets of Langerhans were producing the anti-diabetes hormone, but the name was not in print until 1916. It was not isolated until 1921 by the Canadians Sir Frederick Banting (1891-1941) and C. H. Best (born 1899) at Toronto, Canada. First synthesized in 1964. The islets of Langerhans are named after Paul Langerhans (1847-1888), German physician and anatomist, who in 1869 described the small cluster of cells scattered like tiny islands throughout the pancreas.

insulin shock A syndrome (anxiety, sweating, tremor, vertigo, **diplopia**, and hunger, followed by emotional upset, delirium, convulsions, and collapse into a coma) occurring when an oversupply of insulin causes a sharp reduction in the amount of blood sugar that excites the **central nervous system**. May result in death due to extreme reduction in brain activity.

insulin shock therapy An almost obsolete type of therapy developing from the observation that psychotic patients who were also diabetic seemed to become more psychologically normal if they survived an unintentional insulin shock resulting from diabetic treatment. After the shock, schizophrenic patients have sometimes become more realistic and amenable to psychotherapy.

Manfred Sakel (1900-1957), Viennese physician, initiated treatment 1929-1933.

integrity therapy O. H. **Mowrer's** form of psychotherapy using the concept of neurosis as a form of moral failure, advocating that the client or parishioner should commit himself to take responsibility for his actions and for living up to his moral code (or values). A therapeutic procedure accepted widely by **pastoral counselors**.

intellectualization A defensive, verbalizing reaction in which the person attempts to ward off or drive (explain) away his anxieties by intellectually analyzing his troublesome and painful situations; by coldly naming and defining; by resorting to **rationalization**; by theorizing and talking unemotionally about his problems rather than dealing with them directly on a feeling level; or by dismissing them objectively as intellectual exercises. A reduction of an emotional charge from painful events by constructing logic-tight arguments. Obsessive-compulsive persons may exaggerate their intellectualizations by being so concerned with details that they bury their problems in trivia. *See* **ego**.

intelligence An abstract **construct** or conceptualization of many different abilities and ways of thinking and believing. Also considered as a relative ability to succeed in activities that are characterized by difficulty, complexity, abstractness, need for planning, problem-solving, arriving at concepts, maintaining a directed effort, emergence of original thought, self-criticism, by being able to adapt appropriately to environmental demands, etc. This wide range of correlated abilities is usually measured by intelligence tests such as the **Binet** and the various **Wechsler** tests. Intelligence, operationally, according to Wechsler, "is the aggregate capacity of the individual to act purposefully, to think rationally, and to deal effectively with his environment." **Piaget** is not concerned with the content of intelligence nor its performance but looks upon it as an adaptive process, as a complex act of inference, constantly changing throughout life (qualitatively and quantitatively), and proceeding through four periods of development: (1) *sensorimotor intelligence* (without representational thought); (2) *operational stage*; (3) *functioning of concrete operations* (development of child's language and representational thinking); and (4) *formal operations* (development of abstract and logical systems). Described here are but a few brief concepts about intelligence, no one of which is completely satisfying to other practitioners and theoreticians. *See* (3) *under* **cognitive growth theories**.

Any type of intellectual functioning, modeled after higher animal or human intelligence (such as solving problems by a digital computer) is sometimes called *artificial intelligence*. The TOTE is a cybernetic type of artificial intelligence.

intelligence quotient (IQ) An expression of relative ability in general intelligence. On a **Binet**-type standardized test of intelligence, it is the ratio between a person's mental age (MA) and chronological age (CA) multiplied by 100. The computing equation is: IQ = $100 \times MA/CA$. Thus, a child of mental age 10 and chronological age 8 has an IQ of 125; that is, $100 \times 10/8$ (MA/CS) = 125. IQs centering about 100 (from 84 to 116 on the Terman scale) are considered average or normal, whereas IQs below 70 are inferior and those above 130 are very superior. For subjects older than 15, the revised formula is: IQ = $MA/15 \times 100$.

Wechsler's classification of intelligence does not use the mental age, but determines how much an individual's test score deviates from the average of the total population. The IQ provides a measure for comparing the intelligence or mental function of persons who differ widely in chronological or mental age, as parent and child.

The following table is based on Cronbach's table (p. 174 of the 1960 edition) and on other sources:

IQ	Competence represented (and some famous men with estimated equivalent IQs)
190-200	(Galton, J. S. Mill)
180-189	(Goethe, Leibniz, Macaulay, Pascal)
170-179	(Voltaire)
160-169	(J. Q. Adams, A. Pope)
150-159	(Tennyson, Bryant, Wordsworth, Mozart, Longfellow, V. Hugo)
140-149	(Jefferson, Emerson, Franklin, Galileo, Milton, La Place, Carlyle, Kepler)
130-139	(Darwin, Kant, Napoleon, Newton, Spinoza)
130	Mean of persons receiving Ph.D.
125	(Washington, Lincoln, Linnaeus)
120	Mean of college graduates (Haydn, John Adams).
115	Mean of freshmen in typical 4-year college; mean of children from white-collar and skilled-labor homes (Goldsmith, Swedenborg).
110	Mean of high school graduates; has 50-50 chance of graduating from college (U. S. Grant).
105	About 50-50 chance of passing in academic high school curriculum (Michael Faraday).
100	Average for total population.
90	Mean of children from low-income city homes or rural homes. Adult can perform jobs requiring some judgment (operate sewing machine, assemble parts).
75	About 50-50 chance of reaching high school. Adult can keep small store, perform in orchestra.
60	Adult can repair furniture, harvest vegetables, assist electrician.
50	Adult can do simple carpentry, domestic work.
40	Adult can mow lawns, do simple laundry.

In 1912, the German psychologist L. Wilhelm Stern (1871-1938) in his book, *The Psychological Methods of Testing Intelligence*, introduced the concept of the intelligence ratio, which later became the "intelligence quotient" that Terman adopted. *See also* **Aussage test, intelligence tests**.

intelligence tests A standardized means of measuring some or all of the abilities (memory, reasoning, recall, symbolic thinking, visual-motor performance, etc.) that make up the capacity called **intelligence**. They may be **group tests**, or **individual tests**, and may call for verbal or performance responses, or both. Intelligence tests consist of a graded series of tasks that attempt to evaluate the person's ability to use his acquired knowledge or to demonstrate his flexibility in adjusting to new problems. Subject's responses are scored and compared with those established by **empirical** methods as normal for persons of his age, sex, social status, economic status, or other characteristics. The most commonly used individual intelligence tests are the **Stanford-Binet Intelligence Scale** and the **Wechsler tests** (Cronbach, 1970, pp. 197-308).

intensity The measured degree or amount of some quality, condition, or force. A unit of light intensity (measured by its energy level) is the **foot-candle**; a unit of sound intensity (measured by its pressure) is the **decibel**. Intensity is also one of the dimensions of sensory experience, representing the magnitudes of a physical stimulus acting upon a sense organ.

intensive group experience A general term for various group practices in which the individuals are exposed to and taught to be aware of the group interactions, especially their own roles in them, for purposes of self-evaluation, analysis, interpretation, and ultimate self-fulfillment and understanding. Specific practices have their own names: **T group, sensitivity training**, and encounter group.

An outgrowth of **Kurt Lewin**'s ideas that led to the development of the T group training programs (T for "training") for the National Training Laboratories at Bethel, Maine, in 1947. Although at first the approach was oriented toward developing human relations skills and understandings for people in industry, it has become very popular with the general population.

interactionism *See* **Descartes**.

interaction process analysis (IPA) Bales' procedure for coding, recording, and analyzing of social interaction processes in a discussion group. An observer records interactions (verbal and nonverbal) of people in a group, placing each comment into the appropriately classified content category, of which there are twelve. "These data are then analyzed, hopefully to reveal the group role structure and various interaction trends" (Jones and Gerard, pp. 657-663); first described by R. F. Bales, in *Interaction Process Analyses: A Method for the Study of Small Groups*, 1950.

interaction profile A chart portraying the relative incidence of acts in the twelve categories of the Bales' system of **interaction process analysis**.

interactive explanation Explanation of behavior dealing with the **arousal** and control of immediate behavior according to stimuli that are currently responded to, motives that are active, and possibilities of open response; every effect has a cause, in interactive, and is related.

interactive theory *See* **animism**.

intercalated neuron *See* **interneuron**.

interest inventory (test) A psychological scaling technique (for example, **Kuder Preference Record, Strong Vocational Interest Blank**) designed to measure preferences (likes or dislikes) for various kinds of activities (art, music, literature, science, hobbies, goals, etc.), the results of which can be interpreted as patterns that characterize certain occupational fields (Anastasi, 1968, pp. 466-479; Cronbach, 1970, pp. 455-488).

interface In a *physico-chemical system*, the shared boundary between two phases. In a **computer** system, the common boundary between different data-processing systems or between the parts of a single system; also refers to an input/output connection, or by extension to specific changes demanded (code, format, speed, etc.). The total set of equipment used for establishing communication between a man and a machine is a *man-machine interface*. A *standard interface* is one in which differently designed systems can be readily interconnected.

interference theory of forgetting In human learning, a theory indicating that forgetting occurs either because of interference from earlier learned materials (proactive interference) or from later learned materials (**retroactive inhibition**).

The basic idea of the theory was first expressed in 1932 by the American psychologist J. A. McGeoch (born 1897), and was later refined by various psychologists, including Benton J. Underwood (born 1915) in 1957 and also Underwood with Leo Postman (born 1918) in 1960. These later experimenters have introduced new experimental techniques and developed the theory to consider the factor of unlearning as well as the proactive effects of forgetting.

interferometer *See* **meter**.

interitem consistency A statistical method for determining **reliability** or consistency among (inter-) all items when using a single administration of one form of a test, which is "based on the consistency of subjects' responses to all items in the test." (Anastasi, p. 84).

interitem interval Time between presentation of successive items in a learning situation.

intermittent reinforcement (noncontinuous reinforcement, partial reinforcement) Irregularly occurring rewards occurring after an activity. An intermittent reinforcement schedule with reinforcements programmed by a timing device is known as an **interval reinforcement schedule**.

internal capsule A large irregular mass of white matter (consisting of a group of **sensory** and **motor** projection tracts) that lies within the **cerebrum** separating the **thalamus** on one side from the caudate and lentiform nuclei on the other. *See* **basal ganglia**.

Recognized and described by **Vesalius** in 1543. **Willis** observed that capsular lesions produce hemiplegia.

internal environment The bodily state of an organism, including all conditions and factors that affect it from within, such as amounts of oxygen in the blood, **pH** and **blood-sugar level** water content of cells, temperature, and endocrine secretions.

The term was introduced by Claude Bernard (1813-1878), French physician and physiologist in referring to the fluid environment of the cells (interstitial fluid and blood) in contrast to the external environment.

International System of Units (*Système International d'Unités*).

The International System of Units emerged from the creation of the **meter** and the **kilogram**, units adopted by the National Assembly of France in 1795. Eventually, these and other recognized units became known as the metric system. On July 28, 1866, the United States Congress legalized the use of the metric system in the United States. Since April 5, 1893 all legal units of measure in the

United States have been metric units or their exact numerical multiples. On May 20, 1875, the United States (with sixteen other nations) signed the Treaty of the Meter providing for: (1) an International Bureau of Weights and Measures to be established on neutral ground at Sèvres, France; (2) an International Committee on Weights and Measures; and (3) a General Conference on Weights and Measures, all dedicated to devising, refining, and maintaining precise, internationally uniform standards of measure. The voting members of these organizations are professional metrologists, generally representing national bureaus of standards from member countries.

By agreement, the International System of Units is referred to worldwide as *SI* (from *Système International d'Unités*). SI represents an extension and refinement of the traditional metric system. Multiples of units are normally restricted to steps of a thousand and fractions to steps of a thousandth, and are indicated by prefixes. Larger and smaller units relate to the standard units in powers of 10. The **kilometer** therefore, is 1000 m., and the millimeter is 0.0001 m. (*American Scientist*, 1968, 56, **22**, pp. 159-164; *American Psychologist*, 1971, 26, **12**, p. 1099). The basic SI units follow:

Name of unit and symbol	Physical quantity
ampere (A)	electric current
candela (cd)	luminous intensity
degree kelvin (**K**)	thermodynamic temperature
*kilogram (kg)	mass
meter (m)	length
**second (s)	time

*Until such time as a new name may be adopted for the kilogram as the basic unit of mass, the gram will often be used, both as an elementary unit (to avoid the absurdity of mkg) and in association with numerical prefixes, e.g., μg.
**Common units of time (second, hour, year) are to be used as heretofore.

Much of the material referred to above and included in the definitions of units used in the **SI** system has been adopted from the following sources: The International System of Units. Physical Constants. Conversion Factors. Revised, 1969. NASA, Washington, D.C.: National Bureau of Standards Special Publication 304 (for sale by the Superintendent of Documents, U.S. Government Printing Office, Washington, D.C. 20402—price 50 cents. This is a pictorial chart useful for classroom demonstrations); NBS Handbook 102, ASTM Metric Practice Guide, 40 cents; NBS Misc. Pub. 247, Weights and Measures Standards of the United States, A Brief History, 35 cents; and NBS Misc. Pub. 286, Units of Weight and Measure, Definitions and Tables of Equivalents, $1.50.

interne des asiles d'aliénés de la Seine A psychiatric training appointment at the **asiles d'aliénés**. *See* **French higher education**.

interne des hôpitaux A medical position in France (lasting from one to four years) equivalent to that of a full-time resident house officer in American hospitals. Not yet qualified to have M.D., a physician in name only. A qualified interne (with his doctorate) has the opportunity to advance to **chef de clinique** of the hospital service of a faculty professor in charge of the service, and is privileged to see private patients outside the university. An interne's duties also include supervision of the facilities, and the teaching of internes, externes and medical students. *See* **externeship, French higher education**.

interneuron (internuncial or intercalated neuron) A nerve cell, lying entirely within the **central nervous system**, with many short **dendrites** and a short **axon** that conduct impulses from one **neuron** to another.

internuncial neuron *Same as* **interneuron**.

interoceptive conditioning Classical conditioning of the body's internal organs, such as the kidneys.

interoceptor Taker (-ceptor) within (intero-). C. S. Sherrington's term (1905) for **receptors** sensitive to conditions within the body, especially in the alimentary canal, the viscera, and the smooth musculature of the body. (*See* **exteroceptor**).

interpersonal perception An involved process of perceiving, evaluating, and interacting directly with one another in terms of the situation-background. **Perceptual constancy**, imbeddedness, **closure**, and causality all play a prominent part in such interrelationships.

interpersonal theory H. S. Sullivan's concept of interpersonal relationship, involving interaction of the growing **personality** with the culture. An individual differs from time to time, both to himself and to others as he interacts with other people and situations. A person alters a joke, as well as himself, when he relates it to his father, to his mother, to a priest or rabbi, to a college roommate, or to a girl friend. Human behavior, according to Sullivan, seeks two basic goals: physical satisfactions and security. The child's self-concept emerges from his perception and appraisal of the world and significant others in his life.

interpersonal therapy A psychotherapeutic approach (using communications as a major focus) and Sullivan's **interpersonal theory** that stresses interpersonal interactions in conjunction with the environmental impact.

interphase *See* **mitosis**.

interphase analyzer A means of analyzing and scoring **EEG**'s and correlating results in relation to the various phases of **brain** activity.

interpolation The process of (-ation) polishing (-pol-) up so as to find the correct number between (inter-) two widely spread given numbers. For example, in finding the 5 percent significance level of κ^2 for 48 degrees of freedom, it is necessary to turn to Table 8, and locate there the probability (*P*) value of 0.050. There are no values given for 48 d.f., but there are values at 40 (55.76) and at 50 (67.50). By inspection alone it can be figured that the difference between 67.50 and 55.76 is 11.74, and, since this difference value occupies 10 degrees of freedom, each degree of freedom is then valued at 1.17. Since 48 d.f. is 2 d.f. less than 50, it follows that their total value is approximately 2.34. And 2.34 from 67.50 gives 65.16, which should be the approximate P value of the 0.050 level for 48 degrees of freedom.

To calculate the same values:

$$(48\text{-}40)/(50\text{-}40) = \frac{8}{10} = 0.8.$$

The required value of κ^2 is:

$$55.76 + 0.8\,(67.50 - 55.76) = 55.76 + 0.8$$
$$(11.74)$$
$$= 55.76 + 9.392$$
$$= 65.152$$

approximately the same as that obtained by inspection (65.16).

interposition A **monocular** stimulus **cue** for visual depth perception occurring when a near object (or contour) partially obscures a more distinct object (or contour) in the same line of vision by positioning itself between the distant object and the viewer's eyes.

interpretive therapy A form of **psychotherapy** (effective with verbal children and adults) in which the therapist encourages the subject to resolve his conflicts by verbalizing his problems and attempting to understand their symbolic meanings.

interquartile range (Q) The range in scale units between (inter-) the quartiles (first and third), $Q = Q_3\text{-}Q_1$. Also, the range from the end of the first to the beginning of the third quartile, indicating that chances are equal for a score to fall within its limits or outside those limits. *See* **semi-interquartile range**.

interstitial cell stimulating hormone (ICSH) *Same as* **luteinizing hormone**.

interval *See* **class interval, frequency distribution**.

interval reinforcement schedule A schedule of **reinforcement** in which **reinforcement** is administered on a subject's first response following a predetermined fixed time interval; reinforcement schedules programmed by a clock. Even though it is *time* that determines the appearance of the reward, reinforcement must be made contingent upon a response. Examples are **fixed interval** and **variable interval** schedules (E. L. Walker, 1967, p. 100).

interval scale A scaling technique in which equal differences between measurements stand for equal differences in the amount of the attribute being measured. The numbers in an interval scale have an arbitrary zero rather than an absolute zero.

interval timer A device that automatically provides an audible or visible signal at the end of the period for which it is set, making it especially convenient for timing **group tests**, or any tests that have time limits. Such timers may be either electronic or of the spring-wound mechanism type.

intervening variable An inferred variable or process (-ing) that comes (-ven-) between (inter-) the experimenter's **independent variable** (experimental condition) and the **dependent variable** (behavior, or change in behavior).

If the subject demonstrates that he has mastered a new task as shown by performance, learning is presumed to have taken place; this learning is an *intervening variable*. Critical articles over the past two decades have debated the point as to whether an intervening variable is a hypothetical **construct** or an as yet undiscovered inherent physiological process that influences behavior in an experiment.

The process (intervening variable) that happens between **stimulus** and **response** (thus supposedly accounting for different responses to the same stimulus) may be a function of **personality** traits, the internal environment, attitudes, "mind-sets" of individuals, etc. In laboratory jargon, the term intervening variable is usually restricted to logical constructs that are relatively constant and measurable.

Hull's intervening variables are symbolic constructs hypothesized to bear functional relationships to both antecedent conditions (conditions affecting strength of variables) and consequent actions. However, research has shown that another intervening variable, incentive motivation (K), was introduced into Hullian theory as a determinant of action. Thus, two energizing sources, drive and incentive, act to effect action.

Tolman (1930) built his theoretical framework on six intervening variables—demand, appetite, hypothesis, differentiation, motor skill, and bias. Demand is defined in terms of a deprivation schedule of the organism; appetite, in terms of appropriateness of the goal object; and hypothesis, in terms of the effect of the nature and number of trials in the organism's past history. The three basic antecedents—deprivation, type of goal object, and previous learning—are concomitant in both Hull's and Tolman's theories.

interview The procedure in which one person (the respondent) asks questions of or gives answers to another (the interviewer). The interview is generally simple, straight-forward, and non-probing into personal problems, as when a person applies for a job. Market-research organizations have introduced the so-called "depth" of therapy (with the emphasis on "why" and not "how much") into their interviewing techniques so as to probe into respondents' qualitative reasons for buying articles or listening to programs, etc.

In personnel and industrial relations work, there are several types of interview, such as:

employment, disciplinary (usually of a corrective nature conducted by the supervisor with an employee), grievance, progress, and termination interviews.

In the initial interview with a patient, a **psychiatrist** may utilize the following approaches: (1) the **anamnestic**; (2) the **client-centered**; (3) the modified diagnostic interview concerned primarily with a systematic inquiry; and (4) the interaction interview, concerned with the nature of the complaint, the motivations for therapy, capacities of the patient to respond, and the external conditions affecting treatment.

intragroup process A behavioral characteristic (such as responses to decision-making) among (intra-) or between persons in social groups. The dynamic behavior that takes place as a result of interactions within a social group.

intravert, introvert Turned (-vert) inward (intra-, intro). A person whose mind, attention, emotions, etc., have strong reference to himself. One of the two personality types (extrovert being the other) into which **Jung** (1916) classified individuals, claiming that the intravert directs his **libido** inward because of his feelings of inferiority and "will to power," an idea reminiscent of **Adler's** beliefs. The intravert tends to withdraw into himself (especially in times of stress), to avoid other people, and to be interested primarily in his own inner world of experience. He leans toward self-sufficiency while the extrovert tends to need people around him.

intra vitam Referring to that which is performed upon or during (intra) life (vitam) or where one is alive, in particular reference to *intra vitam* staining (such as **Ehrlich's** methylene blue technique) in which living cells can be stained without killing them, enabling them to be studied while fully functioning.

intrinsic cortex Cortical areas that receive signals from nonsensory thalamic nuclei.

Term proposed in 1958 by **Pribram** as preferential to association areas, on the assumption that they have integrative functions in mediating complex activities without necessarily involving learned associative links. *Contrast with* **extrinsic cortex**.

intrinsic force Influence on behavior originating in the biological system (such as organic disturbance, homeostatic imbalance, etc.), as opposed to environmental or extrinsic forces.

intrinsic motivation A drive that is organically or inherently initiated, as distinct from action that is motivated by promise of reward or threat of punishment (for example, writing poems or stories, or creating paintings for the sheer joy of creating, without the thought of financial return); self-reinforcing motivation (or responses).

introjection Act of (-ion) throwing (-ject-) within (intro-). A process in the unconscious by which a person makes an **identification** with other persons or institutions by incorporating their attributes within himself. Integration of external values into one's ego as a protection against external threats. Also, the adoption of symbolic meaning attached to various religious practices (such as dietary observances) into one's everyday behavioral modes in attempts to achieve spiritual union. In psychoanalytic theory, a child develops social values, including a conscience or **superego**, by introjecting parental standards for behavior. *Opposed to* **projection**.

Psychoanalytic concept put forth by Ferenczi in 1903, using the term "introjected" which he later changed to the noun form.

Berkeley, Descartes, and **Locke** used the term to describe their epistemological theory that the external world (including other results) is known only by projecting our inner ideas and symbols onto something else, an idea similar to projection of today. German philosopher Richard Avenarius (1843-1896) objected to this concept in 1888, substituting the idea that introjection related to pure experience that was essential in integrating knowing man and known object.

introspection Act of (-ion) looking (-spect-) inward (intro-). Examination or observation of one's own thoughts. The study of one's own experience by analyzing it into its component parts, such as sensations, images, feelings.

Introspection has been practiced since very early times; **Saint Augustine** (354-430) reports on it in his *Confessions*, about 400 A.D. **Hobbes, Locke, Berkeley,** and **Hume** also discuss it.

introspectionism Doctrine (-ism) of introspection. An early psychological approach to mental life, considering it to be the basic method for investigation in psychology. Behaviorism considered introspection nonscientific, claiming that it should be excluded from scientific study. *See* **Bekhterev**.

Modern introspectionism was founded by **Wundt**.

introversion-extroversion Process (-ion) of turning (-vers-) either inward (intro-) or outward (extro-). A **Jungian** concept that the human **personality** moves or is directed in bipolar fashion, either extrovertively (toward others or outward and involved in action) or introvertively (away from the outside world, centering on subjective experiences). *See* intravert, extrovert, (also C. G. Jung, **Psychological Types**, 1933).

intrusion error An inappropriately substituted response in serial learning that was either not in the original learning list or that was in the original list but placed wrong (for example, responding with the fifth item instead of the sixth).

inverter A logic device, digital in nature, that provides at its **output** the complement of the logic introduced at its **input**.

investigatory reflex Pavlov's term (1927) for the highly adaptive tendency in mammals to orient the appropriate sense organs to the slightest change in surroundings.

in vitro In (in) glass (vitro). Outside the living body. *See* **chemical methods of brain study**.

in vivo In that which is alive (vivo). *See* **chemical methods of brain study**.

involuntary nervous system (INS) *See* **autonomic nervous system**.

The involuntary nervous system was so named by the Italian born English physiologist, Walter H. Gaskell (1847-1914).

involutional melancholia (involutional psychotic reaction) Referring to (-al) the melancholic process (-tion-) of turning (-volut-) inward (in-). A psychotic reaction similar to but differentiated from the depressed reaction of the **manic-depressive** by there being no previous history of such episodes. It is characterized by abnormal anxiety, guilt feelings, agitation, **delusion**, and severe insomnia and **depression**. Involutional melancholia may occur in some women during menopause, when marked changes in endocrine functioning are taking place, without previous history of psychosis.

Described and termed so by **Kraepelin** as a separate form of **melancholia**.

I/O input/output *See* **input, output, input/output device**.

iodopsin A photosensitive violet-(iod-) colored neutral chemical pigment (-in) in the eye (-ops-), located specifically in the **cones** of the retina of mammals. Iodopsin breaks down upon exposure to light into **retinene** and **photopsin**, a protein. It is important in adjustments to daylight vision. Chemically, reactions are similar to **rhodopsin**.

ion Move; to go. A charged particle. An ion is negative (*cation*) if the electrons are in excess; it is positive (*anion*) if the electrons are deficient. Term coined by **Faraday**.

The phenomenon of interchange between the potassium and sodium ions in the transmission of a nerve impulse was first demonstrated by the English physiologist Ernest Overton (1865-1933).

ipsative unit Relating to (-ative) itself (ips-). The amount of variation in which raw scores are expressed as **standard scores** to reflect fluctuations (mood, anxiety, etc.) within the person himself rather than represent a **population** of persons (as in normative scores, such as percentiles). R. Cattell's **P-technique** is ipsative in that it is concerned with the factoring of the unique structure of the single person. In the ipsative method, a person is compared against his former record of idiosyncrasies to help determine growth or **regression** from time to time. However, self-comparisons may lead to comparisons of built-in mediocrity or below-normal behavior.

The ipsative unit and the P-technique were developed concurrently by R. B. Cattell.

ipsilateral (ipselateral) Referring to (-al) the same side (-later-) of the body, such as the knee jerk is an ipsilateral reflex, since the impulses that mediate it go and come from the same side of the body. *Contrast with* **contralateral**.

IPSP Inhibitory postsynaptic potential.

IQ Intelligence quotient.

iris Colored portion of the eye consisting of circular and radial smooth muscle fibers resembling a doughnut-shaped structure (the hole being the pupil). The iris, attached to the ciliary body, adjusts in size (by contracting and expanding) so as to regulate the amount of light entering the eye (the pupil becoming smaller in bright light and larger in dim light).

IRM Innate releasing mechanism.

irradiation Process of (-ion) radiating (-radiat-) or spreading from within (ir-); mass action; the sluggish,irregular, widespread movement characteristic of the fetus; a process whereby, as more sensory fibers are activated by a stronger stimulus, more **motoneurons** are stimulated and a larger part of the body reacts.

A term originally postulated by **Pavlov** to account for **stimulus generalization**, or spread of excitation from the **conditioned stimulus** (CS) located in the **brain** to others associated with it, helping form the CS.

irrational number *See* **real number**.

irreal A term used by **Kurt Lewin** to describe an unrealistic aspect of a person's psychological environment (life space). Irreal behavior obtains gratifications considered unrealistic by the society of which the individual is a member. For example, daydreaming, fantasying, fabricating.

Ishihara color test A test for the detection of **color blindness** (hue sensitivity). Assorted geometric numerals (perceived as an **array** of colored dots) are mixed into a background of different hues and saturations on color plates which can be detected by those not color-blind. *See* **pseudo-isochromatic plates**.

After Shinobu Ishihara (1879-1967), Japanese ophthalmologist. The test was a modification of Stilling's Color Table (Jacob Stilling (1842-1915), German ophthalmologist) and of Reuss's Color Tables or charts.

islets of Langerhans *See* **insulin**.

isocortex (homogenetic cortex) The portion of the **cerebral cortex** consisting of new cortical formations that pass through a developmental six horizontal-layered stage of nerve tissue (each layer having certain predominant cells), which develop between 6-8 months of fetal life. *See* **Vogts, allocortex**.

isolation Defense **mechanism** in which life experiences are compartmentalized. *See* **alienation**.

isolation effect *See* **von Restorff effect**.

isometric myograph *See* **myograph**.

isomorphism In body-image **Gestalt** studies, a belief or hypothesis (-ism) that the form (-morph-) of a figure drawing is a projection approximately like or equal (iso-) to that of the person's actual body.

isoscope A viewing apparatus (-scope) for judging equal or parallel (iso-) lines, in which two vertical wires are placed in front of one eye and a single vertical wire in front of the other. The single wire, seen binocularly with the other two, can be adjusted so that it appears parallel to the others.

isotonic myograph See **myograph.**

IS Unit See **International System of Units.**

item analysis Any one of various methods used to select items for tests or **personality** inventories, as well as for quizzes and examinations in classroom use. Items can be analyzed qualitatively (considering content validity) and quantitatively (statistical measurement of item difficulty and item validity) (Anastasi, pp. 158-184).

I-Thou-relationship (Exist.) A term that has been borrowed from the book **I and Thou,** 1958, by Jewish theologian Martin Buber (1878-1965), who espoused the idea that man must not only have complete faith and confidence in himself (the "I"), but must also fully accept and understand others ("Thou") for what they are—unique beings. The I-Thou relationship is much talked about and often practiced (to varying degrees) in the therapeutic setting. It involves a disclosure, an openness on the part of those in any dyadic relationship. You can "know" someone only if he permits you to learn of his "secrets"; only if he wants you to. Any misunderstanding between two people (I and Thou), any difficulty in communication, arises because of lack of adequate relationship between the two. One person of the pair can never solely be at fault.

J

Jacksonian (seizure) epilepsy Spasms or convulsions (without loss of awareness) confined at first to a relatively small group of muscles, but which may progress to larger areas of the body.

After English physician John Hughlings Jackson (1834-1911).

jamais vu (Fr., never seen). An error of recognition or a feeling that what should be a familiar situation, object, or person is strange, unknown, and has never been seen before.

James-Lange theory of emotion A combined physiological theory independently put forth by the psychologists **James** (1884) and **Lange** (1885), holding that stimuli in the environment precede or set off physiological changes (visceral and motor responses) in the individual, that the changes in turn stimulate **sensory** nerves inside the body, producing messages, the awareness of which leads to the subjective recognizable experience perceived as **emotion.** The sensory source for emotions, (as James puts it in *Psychology*, 1890), makes us "feel sorry because we cry, angry because we strike, afraid because we tremble, and not that we cry, strike, or tremble because we are sorry, angry, or fearful..." Lange's theory stressed that being aware of vasomotor changes is the emotion itself.

Who was first, James or Lange? Neither one, said **Titchener** and others, for the germ of the so-called James-Lange theory could be traced to French philosopher-psychologists **La Mettrie** and **Malebranch.**

James, William (1842-1910) American (New York) psychologist, physiologist, and philosopher. M.D., Harvard 1869. APA President twice, in 1894 and 1904. He called **psychology** a "nasty little science" and returned to his beloved philosophy in 1890. He considered **introspection** (but not Wundt's and Titchener's laboratory introspection) to be the basic method in psychology. Yet he was a pioneer in general and experimental psychology (had an informal "demonstration" laboratory at Harvard in 1875). In philosophy, a pragmatist. In personal relations a true individualist. Considered consciousness as only one type of relationship within experience itself and not separate from experience.

James McKeen Cattell Award of Division 14 (Industrial and Organizational Psychology) is granted to the psychologist presenting the best research design (not a completed project) "in which basic scientific methods are applied to problems concerning human behavior in organizations." The award is symbolized by an appropriate certificate, and $500.00 for the winner, with those getting honorable mention receiving $100.00 each. Studies should involve a *bona fide* **organization** (or suitable laboratory model), directed toward facilitating interaction between scientific knowledge and practice in some substantial segment of industrial and organizational psychology. The design should be feasible, preferably involving studies of a longitudinal nature. Although completed projects cannot be considered, the Division feels that the "major reward to the recipients is the support of Division 14... in obtaining the necessary funding and cooperation for the completion of the projects." *See* **awards of the APA.**

Cattell Award Winners

1964 Ernest J. McCormick (born 1911). Ph.D., Purdue 1948.

1965 (Two awards) Marvin Dunnette (Born 1926). Ph.D., Minnesota 1954; Milton Hakel (born 1941). Ph.D., Minnesota 1966. Also Robert M. Guion (born 1924). Ph.D., Purdue 1952.

1966 Claude J. Bartlett (born 1931). Ph.D., Ohio State 1958 and Benjamin Schneider (born 1938). Ph.D., Maryland 1967. Honorable mention: Dallis K. Perry (born 1929). Ph.D., Minnesota 1953.

1967 George Graine (born 1934). M.A. Alfred, 1956. Honorable mention: John P. Campbell (born 1937). Ph.D., Minnesota 1964.

1968 Anthony J. Reilly Ph.D. Honorable mention: C. Jack Bartlett and George Graine.

1969 Lyman W. Porter (born 1930). Ph.D., Yale 1956, and Frank J. Smith (born 1937). Ph.D., IIT 1960.

1970 Victor Vroom (born 1932). Ph.D., Michigan 1958, and Phillip Yetton. Honorable mention: Daniel Tear (born 1926) Ph.D., Penn. St., 1955.

1971 Lyle Schoenfeldt (born 1939). Ph.D., Purdue 1966.

Janet, Pierre (1859-1947) French neurologist and psychologist. Student of Charcot. Studied **hysteria, dissociation,** and psychopathology generally. He described hysteria as a splitting of the personality. Janet started a movement to bring academic and clinical psychology closer together. First (1903) to describe and name **psychasthenia** (Janet's disease) in *Les Obsessions et la Psychasthenie* (Boring, pp. 699-700, 730-731).

Jaspers, Karl (Born 1883). German existential philosopher. Emphasized the importance of the individual. Purely personal and subjective in approach. *See* **love, subject-object dichotomy.**

JND, jnd Just noticeable difference.

Johns Hopkins chronoscope See **Dunlap chronoscope.**

Jones, Ernest (1879-1958), born Wales; M.D., 1904 University of London, D.P.H. 1905 Cambridge. Psychoanalyst; professor of psychiatry. Freud's major biographer. *See* **élan vital, rationalization.**

joule (J) An SI unit of work or energy, equal to the work done by the force of 1 **newton** when its point of application is displaced 1 **meter** in the direction of the force. *See* **International System of Units.** Named after the English physicist, James P. Joule (1818-1889).

J-shaped curve A strongly skewed curve in the shape of a J or reversed J, with many cases falling at the **mode,** others occurring clustered on one side and close to the mode. **Frequency distribution** of scores (based on institutional behavior that is greatly influenced toward conformity by social pressure) tend toward a J-type of curve or its reversal. For example,

one study of drivers, where traffic was regulated by highway stop signs, showed almost 85 percent compliance in stopping, a small amount of semi-compliance (rabbit-hop-stopping), and a minute amount of violation. Plotted on a graph, this distribution approximates a J shape.

judgment sampling See **purposive sampling.**

jumping apparatus See **Lashley jumping stand.**

Jung, Carl Gustav (1875-1961) Swiss psychiatrist. While **Bleuler's** assistant he first learned of **Freud's** methods and later (1911) both he and Freud organized the first psychoanalytic society with Jung as first president. After breaking with Freud in 1913, he founded **analytic(al) psychology.** Jung's system is considered verbally complex and mystical. He modified the psychological **determinism** of Freud into a generalized racial unconscious; originated the terms **intravert** and **extrovert** to describe the types into which he divides mankind; developed **word association** tests; considered the **libido** as basic nonsexual energy similar to the **élan vital** of **Bergson.** Jung's unconscious consists of, (1) the personal, or repressed events of one's own life and (2) the archeracial or collective. *See* **conflict** (also Bischof, pp. 178-223; Vinacke, p. 215).

just noticeable difference (JND, jnd) A quantitative method of determining the smallest perceptible difference between stimuli. The jnd or difference limen is the change (increase or decrease) in intensity, location, quality, etc., of a stimulus that is just sufficient for differentiation from another stimulus. *Same as* **detection threshold.**

The jnd concept was derived from an empirical observation by E. H. Weber after he had made an assumption that to judge a stimulus as being jnd from the standard depended "directly on the intensity of the standard." Became known as **Weber's law.** *See* **Fechner.**

juxtallocortex Near (juxt-) the allocortex. A transitional zone of the **archipallium** or "old cortex" (developmentally and in the adult brain), that includes the **cingulate gyrus** and lies between the allo- and isocortex (4 or 5 cell layers) along the entire length of their interface. (I. N. Filimonoff, "A Rational Subdivision of the Cerebral Cortex." *Archives of Neurology and Psychiatry*, 1947, **58**, 296).

In 1954, Pribram and Kruger used the term to refer to certain portions of the **limbic system.** *See* **intrinsic cortex.**

K

KAE Kinesthetic aftereffect.

Kahlbaum, Karl Ludwig (1828-1899) German psychiatrist. Introduced the term **cyclothymia** (alternating moods) in 1861, and described **hebephrenia** in 1863 and **catatonia** in 1874.

kairos (Gr., fitness, opportunity, time) The moment when a person gains insight into the meaning of an important event, past or future. It is never an intellectual act alone; the grasping of the new meaning always implies some personal decision, some shift in **Gestalt,** some new orientation toward the world and future. For most people it is the moment of most heightened awareness; referred to in psychological literature as the "aha" experience. *See* **insight.**

On the philosophical level, German-American theologian Paul Tillich (1886-1965) describes **kairos** as the moment when "eternity touches time;" as "time fulfilled."

Kant, Immanuel (1724-1804) German philosopher and metaphysician. Developed a critical philosophy (stimulated by **Hume**) that sought to elucidate the laws and limitations of human knowledge. Kant merged the two diverse streams of thought of **Bacon** and **Descartes.**

k

He believed that all knowledge begins with experience but does not necessarily come from experience. *See* **act psychology, Hamilton**, **noumenon**(also Boring, pp. 246-250).

karyotype In the design or model (type) of a kernel or nucleus (karyo-). The total chromosomal constitution of the cell nucleus, being characteristic of an individual, species, or genus.

K-complex *See* **sleep stages.**

K_D critical values *See* Table 25a.

Keeler polygraph *See* **lie detector.**

After Leonarde Keeler (1903-1949), American criminologist, lawyer, and inventor, who originally utilized a combination of various instruments for testing physiological changes occurring in guilt-ridden persons.

Kelley, Truman Lee (1884-1961). Originally majored in mathematics then turned to **psychology**, receiving his Ph.D., Columbia 1914. Experimental and statistical methods, **factor analyses**, and influential in introducing statistics into psychology and in developing measurement of interests and aptitudes test construction (psychometrics). *See* **coefficient of alienation.**

Kelly, George Alexander (1905-1966) Ph.D., psychology, State University of Iowa 1931. Clinical psychologist and theoretician; **personality** theory and **psychotherapy**. *See* **guilt**; **fixed role therapy** (also Maddi, pp. 111-126, 362-364).

kelvin (K) The SI unit of thermodynamic temperature. Its zero point is at absolute zero with a fixed point at the triple point of water defined as 273.16 kelvins. The triple point is defined as 0.01°C on the Celsius scale and approximately 32.02°F on the Fahrenheit scale. When the triple point cell (an evacuated glass cylinder filled with pure water) is cooled until a mantle of ice forms around the re-entrant well, the temperature at the interface of solid, liquid, and vapor is 0.01°C. *See* **International System of Units.**

Named after Lord Kelvin, William Thompson (1824-1907), English physicist and mathematician.

Kendall, Maurice George Born 1907. Sc.D., Cambridge 1943. Has written many papers and books (including a dictionary on statistics) primarily on rank correlation methods, **multivariate analysis** and geometrical probability. Professor of Statistics, London University, 1949-1961. Developed, among other tests, both the *coefficient of concordance* and *rank correlation coefficient (tau)*.

Kendall's coefficient of concordance A measure of the degree of agreement among rankings by judges of events or conditions. The value of the coefficient ranges from 0 (indicating complete randomness in allocation of rankings) to 1 (signifying complete agreement among judges). It cannot be negative. The statistic, symbolized by W, is given by

$$W = \frac{12\Sigma D^2}{m^2(N)(N^2-1)}$$

(Hays, pp. 656-658; Downie and Heath, p. 210; Kirk, pp. 498-500; and Table 31A).

Kendall's rank-correlation coefficient (tau) A measure of rank correlation that applies to the same type of **data** as the **Spearman rank-difference method (rho)**. Both *tau* and *rho* have equal power since they will reject a false **null hypothesis** at the same **level of significance**. Tau can be adjusted to measure partial correlation. Tau is based on the number of inversions (interchanges of rank) required to make one ranking agree with another.

The formula for *tau* uses the statistic S, which symbolizes the disarray in a set of ranks. The obtained value of S divided by its maximum possible value gives

$$\tau = \frac{S}{\frac{1}{2}N(N-1)}$$

where N = the number of individuals ranked

on both X and Y. (*See* Table 31b; also Hays, 1964, p. 647f).

keypunch A mechanical device that records information by punching holes in a deck of cards. The position of the hole(s) in each column specifies an alphabetic, numeric, or special character.

Kierkegaard, Søren (1813-1855) Danish religious existentialist. Placed emphasis on the unique value of the individual, teaching that only **existence** itself has reality and that existence precedes essence.

kilogram (kg) The SI unit of mass, equal to 1000 (kilo-) grams, and equivalent to 2.2046 pounds avoirdupois. It is standardized on an established cylinder of platinum-iridium alloy preserved in a vault at Sèvres, France by the International Bureau of Weights and Measures. *See* **International System of Units.**

kinephantoscope A viewing instrument (-scope) used to make motion (kine-) visible (-phanto-). A projector used in presenting shadows or silhouettes so as to study optical **illusions** or directions of movement.

kinesimeter A device for measuring (-meter) the threshold for sensation of movement (kinesi-).

kinesis Process (-sis) of moving (kine-) from place to place, such activity being elicited by the avoidance of an undesirable environment (as in the case of a spider avoiding light) or the approach toward a desirable environment (as in the case of the wood louse seeking out moist areas in order to survive). Kinesis tends to be random behavior, but it can be indirectly orienting—as indicated by the examples of animal behavior above. *Compare* **taxis.**

kinesthesis (kinesthesia, kinesthetic sense) Sensitivity to or feeling of (-esthesis) movement (kin-). The muscle sense. Sensations within the muscles, joints, and tendons that provide **perception** of bodily movement, position or weight. For example, the feeling of bending the arm or moving the fingers, perceived independently of the sense of touch.

Shortly before his death, the Scottish philosopher **Thomas Brown** advanced the idea of an inner muscular sense, but it was not until 1826 when **Charles Bell** wrote about the existence of an independent muscle sense which was thereafter known as the sixth sense. H. C. Bastian (1832-1915) the British neurologist, introduced the term kinesthesis in 1880 and in 1906 **Sherrington** proposed **proprioception** as a more inclusive word.

kinesthetic aftereffect (KAE) An **illusion**, involving the muscle sense, whereby apparent weight or width, for example, is influenced by shifting from an accustomed weight or width to a heavier or wider one in order to create the experience of comparative lightness or narrowness in the previous object (such as the batter who swings an overweighted bat on his way to the plate so that his own bat will seem lighter). *See* **figural aftereffect.**

kinesthetic receptor Sense organ located in the tendons, muscles, and most importantly, in the joints. *See* **proprioceptor.**

Klinefelter's disease (Klinefelter's syndrome) **Mental retardation** associated with a genetic anomaly in the number of sex chromosomes (47 instead of 46), with the usual two female (XX) chromosomes but only one male (Y) sex chromosome, resulting in a sterile male (eunuchoid), with atrophic testes.

After American physician Harry F. Klinefelter, Jr., born in 1912, who first described the condition.

Klüver, Heinrich Born 1897, Germany. Received Ph.D., Stanford 1924. **Gold Medal Award** 1965. Influenced by **Wilhelm Stern** and **Max Wertheimer**. Studied eidetic imagery (1926), effects of mescal, and psychophysiology of the **temporal lobe**. He collaborated with the American neurosurgeon Paul C. Bucy (born 1904) in brain research, results from one of their studies becoming known as the **Kluver-Bucy syndrome**: a pattern of symptoms

("psychic blindness" or visual **agnosia**, **boulimia**, perverted and excessive sexual behavior, mouthing, visual distractibility) occurring in rhesus monkeys after having had a bilateral temporal **lobectomy** (Heinrich Kluver and Paul C. Bucy, "An Analysis of Certain Effects of Bilateral Temporal Lobectomy in the Rhesus Monkey with Special Reference to Psychic Blindness." *Journal of Psychology*, 1938, **5**, 33-54).

koan A public (ko-) plan (-an) or procedure in Zen Buddhism whereby a Zen master forces a student or monk to meditate over nonsensical questions so that greater reliance is placed upon intuition and less dependence upon reason is emphasized. The stress of meditation often leads to greater insights.

Koenig (König) cylinders A group of short, solid metal cylinders suspended by threads, the cylinders emitting high frequency tones when struck by a rod. Used for testing upper auditory limits for pitch.

Karl Rudolph Koenig (1832-1901), German-born French physicist and acoustical authority.

Koffka, Kurt (1886-1941) German-born American psychologist. With **Köhler** and **Wertheimer**, developed **Gestalt psychology**. His paper in the *Psychological Bulletin* (1922) "Perception: An Introduction to Gestalt-theories" introduced Gestalt concepts to the United States, which helped make it possible for him to obtain a professorship at Smith College in 1928. He held **insight** to be an important factor in learning and criticized **Thorndike's trial and error** theory as mechanistic.

Köhler, Wolfgang (1887-1967) An Esthonian-born American psychologist. Ph.D., Berlin 1909. Made many studies on tonal acoustics and **Gestalt** principles. Demonstrated that chimpanzees solved problems by **insight** and not just by **trial** and error. In 1947, he received the **Warren Medal** for "his studies on figural after-effects and an approach to a more general theory of perceptual responses." Received the **Distinguished Scientific Contribution Award** 1956. APA President 1959. In 1967 he was selected to receive the **Gold Medal Award** but he died before he could accept it since the award is not granted posthumously. (Boring, pp. 595-7, 616-17; Vinacke, p. 498).

koinonia (Gr., association, communion) Spiritual relationship and sharing in a common commitment, formerly in a religious sense but now also used in an existential commitment.

Kollectivgegenstand (Ger., collective-object [*Gegenstand*]). **Fechner's** "finite collective," that later became known as *Kollectivmasslehre* (theory of finite population) which was closely related to the frequency theory of **probability**.

Kölliker (Koelliker), Rudolf Albert von (1817-1905) Born Zürich, Switzerland. Histologist and biologist. Ph.D., 1842 (Zürich) and M.D., 1843 (Heidelberg). Published first book ever written on comparative anatomy. Anticipated, before adequate staining methods could demonstrate it conclusively, that spinal nerves led to the **brain**, leading to the concept of the **neuron doctrine** (1853) later expressed (1889-90) by **Ramon y Cajal** and **Waldeyer**, 1891. Proved (1845) continuity of the nerve cell and its fiber but failed to give recognition to **Remak's** prior research. Helped reinforce cell theory of animal life.

Kolmogorov-Smirnov Tests Two related nonparametric tests that are sensitive to differences between two cumulative distributions. Three different tables have been constructed for their use. (See Tables 25a, 25b, 25c).

1. The K-S one-sample test is a test for **goodness of fit**. It is concerned with the degree of agreement between the distribution of a set of sample values (observed scores) and some specified theoretical **distribution**. Under H_O that the sample has been drawn from the

specified theoretical distribution, it is expected that the difference between the distribution and the H_O will be small and within the limits of the random errors. The largest value of the deviations is symbolized by D, the maximum deviation. If the observed D exceeds the tabled value for the desired **significance** level and sample size, the **null hypothesis** is rejected. The procedure involves comparing the empirical cumulative distribution function of the sample with the known and specified cumulative distribution function.

If the **data** are continuously distributed, the K-S test is superior to the **chi-square** goodness of fit test, since the K-S test has more rigorous assumptions. For the K-S test, there is no provision for estimating **parameters** from sample data and the **hypothesis** must completely state the hypothesized distribution.

2. The K-S two-sample test is an extension of the K-S one sample goodness of fit test, and is concerned with the degree of agreement between two observed cumulative distributions. This test requires **ordinal scale** measurement, continuously distributed **data**, and two independent random samples of equal size. The largest of the differences in the cumulative frequencies is designated as K_D. Table 25b provides values of N from 3 to 40, where N equals the size of each sample. Table 25c is used for large samples, that is, when both n_1 and n_2 are larger than 40. In the latter case, it is not necessary that n_1 equals n_2.

Andrey Nikolaevich Kolmogorov. Born 1903. Graduate, University of Moscow 1925. Russian mathematician: specialist in theory of real variable functions.

Nikolay Vasilevich Smirnov (Smirnoff). Born 1900. Graduate, University of Moscow 1926. Russian mathematician: specialist in probability theory and mathematical statistics.

Kopfermann cubes A series of line drawings that can be perceived tridimensionally (in which each pattern appears to be a cube from a different viewing angle) as well as bidimensionally. (Woodworth and Schlosberg, 1965, pp. 410-411).

Devised by Hans Kopfermann (born 1895), German physicist and experimental psychologist, and reported by him in 1930.

Korsakow's syndrome A pattern of symptoms exhibited most often by chronic alcoholics, especially after **delirium tremens.** It is characterized by loss of memory for recent events, auditory hallucinations, extensive peripheral nerve irritation (polyneuritis), disorientation, and unsystematic confabulation. However, the symptoms may also occur in non-alcoholics suffering from vitamin B deficiency, metallic poisoning, or various infections. *See* (2) *under* **organic psychosis.**

Sergei S. Korsakow (Korsakov, Korsakoff) (1854-1900), Russian neuropsychiatrist, who described the condition only as it affected alcoholics.

Kossel, Albrecht (1953-1927) Swiss chemist. Received the Nobel prize in physiology and medicine in 1910. Discovered nucleic acids and their breakdown products (**purine and pyrimidine**); isolated **guanine** and **adenine** and with Stendal discovered **thymine**, 1900.

Kraepelin, Emil (1856-1926) German psychiatrist. Student of **Wundt.** Pioneer in experimental **psychiatry.** Devised a classification and diagnostic system for mental disease in 1896, coining the terms **dementia praecox** and **manic-depressive** psychoses for his two main types. Held the manic-depressive type to be "exogenous" in origin and likely to recover, and the dementia praecox type "endogenous" and likely to deteriorate. Performed many experiments on effect of drugs and fatigue. *See* **paranoia.**

Krasnogorskii, Nikolai Ivanovich (born 1882). Soviet pediatrician and physiologist. Studied under **Pavlov.** Research primarily in pathophysiology of intellective functions of children.

Krause's end bulb (K's corpuscle, K's ending) One of the special structures of the skin (mainly in the lips, the skin of the nipples, the genitals, and conjunctiva of the eyes). Serves as special receptor for cold stimuli.

Named after Wilhelm Krause (1833-1910), German anatomist, who was first (1860) to describe these corpuscles.

Kretschmer, Ernst (1888-1964) German psychiatrist, developed body-type classification as reported in *Körperbau and Charakter*, 1921 (translated in 1925 as *Physique and Character*). He classified people into four general body types: (1) *asthenic* or *leptosomatic*—tall and thin, lean appendages, with long, narrow chest, and inclined toward being introverted, maladjusted, **autistic** with tendency toward **schizophrenia** if **psychosis** develops; (2) *pyknic*—short and plump, fat-faced, chesty, with inclination toward being outgoing and temperamentally well-adjusted but may alternate between exhilaration and depression, with predisposition toward **manic-depressive psychosis;** (3) *athletic*—muscular, well-developed chest with tapered trunk, no dominant predisposition toward psychosis; and (4) *dysplastic*—a variable type, differing markedly from other body types. *See* **constitutional types.**

Kries, Johann von (1853-1964) A German physiologist who had specialized in studies on vision, making many contributions in this area: in 1882, determining the **detection thresholds** for **hue**; in 1894, indicating the role of retinal **rods** to twilight vision and of **cones** to daylight vision (as reported in his duplicity theory of color vision); and also coining various terms such as **protanope, protanopia, deuteranope,** and **deuteranopia.** *See* **duplicity theory** under **color vision theories.**

Kruskal-Wallis ranks test A one-way **analysis of variance** by ranks test for determining if k independent samples are from the same or different populations. The test assumes that the **variable** under study is at least **ordinal** in nature and continuously distributed. If the **null hypothesis** is true (that is, if the k independent samples have been drawn from a common population) then H, as in the formula below, is distributed as a **chi-square** statistic with df = $k-1$, provided that the number of samples (k) are not too small (>5). The null hypothesis is rejected for large values of H. H is given by:

$$H = \frac{12}{N(N+1)} \sum_{j=1}^{k} \left(\frac{R_j^2}{n_j}\right) - 3(N+1)$$

where k = number of independent samples, n_j = number of cases in jth sample, $N = \Sigma n_j$, the number of cases in all samples combined, R_j = sum of ranks in jth sample (column), and $\sum_{j=1}^{k}$ directs the summing over of the k samples (columns O).

In cases where the $n_j > 5$, the chi-square values in Table 8 may then be used. However, for k = 3 and the $n_j < 5$, the chi-square approximation is not sufficient, and exact probabilities are obtained from Table 32 (Siegel, pp. 184-193; Ferguson, pp. 362-363; Downie and Heath, pp. 246-247).

Kruskal, William Henry. Born 1919, New York. Ph.D. mathematical statistics, Columbia, 1955.

Wallis, Wilson Allen. Born 1912. American statistician, economist. Professor at Yale, Stanford, and Chicago. Major studies in time series analyses, test of randomness and general statistical techniques.

Kuder Preference Record-Vocational A self-scoring, forced choice, self-report **interest inventory** used in vocational **counseling;** the test provides a profile by which appraisals can be made of the relative strength of ten areas (such as scientific, musical, clerical, and artistic).

George Frederic Kuder. Born 1903, Michigan. Ph.D. (psychology) Ohio State 1937. Fields: psychological measurement, vocational and aptitude testing.

Külpe, Oswald (1862-1915) German philosopher and psychologist. His psychology was dualistic in nature. In 1893 he wrote the first psychology text completely devoted to the experimental approach. At first, under **Wundt** and **J. Müller,** he was an experimentalist on "content" and esthetics. Later, chosen as head of the experimental laboratory at **Würzburg,** he became influenced by **K. Bühler** in integrating thoughts of **Brentano, Husserl, Ehrenfels,** and others into a system. Külpe's efforts were directed mainly against Wundt's **structuralism,** resulting in many studies on thought processes, notably those by **Ach** and Bühler. Similar studies were being carried on independently by **Binet** in France and **Woodworth** in the United States. *See* **act psychology, Angell,** (also Boring, pp. 397-399, 401-402).

Kupalov, Petr Stepanorich (born 1888). Russian physiologist and physician. A student of **Pavlov** and founder of a school of physiology emphasizing Pavlov's teachings. Specialized in studies on the physiology of higher nervous activity and in experimental animal neuroses.

Kurt Lewin Memorial Award is given annually by the Society for the Psychological Study of Social Issues (Division 9) for "outstanding contributions to the development and integration of psychological research and social action." *See* **awards of the American Psychological Association.**

kurtosis Condition (-osis) of being convex or peaked (kurt-); the height of a distribution relative to the size of the **standard deviation.**

A *mesokurtic* (medium) curve is normal; a *platykurtic* (flat) curve has an abnormally flat peak; and a *leptokurtic* (tall and thin) one has an abnormally high peak.

The kurtosis of a normal distribution is 3. Anything lower than this indicates a platykurtic curve; anything higher is representative of a leptokurtic curve. One measure of kurtosis:

$$\alpha_4 = \frac{\text{fourth moment of the sample about the mean}}{\sigma^4}$$

The more of a peak in a distribution the greater is α_4, or the kurtosis. *See* **allokurtic.**

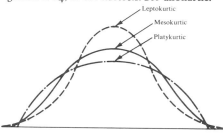

Three degrees of kurtosis.

kymograph Wave (kymo-) record (-graph). An electrically controlled recording instrument essentially consisting of a sensitized paper-covered rotating drum on which a tracing point (stylus) or pen draws a record, indicating changes in intensity or frequency of response. Thus it furnishes a direct record of changes over time, as of blood pressure, skin temperature, respiratory movement, heart action, or other observed **variable.**

Said to be invented in 1847 by German physiologist Karl F. W. Ludwig (1816-1895). Actually it was a modification of French physiologist Jean Marie Poiseville's (1799-1869) hemodynamometer (for determining blood pressure) invented in 1828, to which Ludwig added a revolving cylinder and a float on which a stylus "wrote" on a recording cylinder.

L

L Limen; as L- the levorotatory form of a chemical compound denoting a substance that rotates the plane of polarized light to the left (levo-), such as **L-dopa**.

l- Rotatory form of a chemical compound.

la belle indifférence **Janet's** phrase for a patient's complete and inappropriate indifference to his disability, regardless of seriousness of the condition. This symptom helps distinguish the hysteric from the **hypochondriac**, the hysteric showing unusual optimism about his condition, feeling confident that he can be cured medically.

labyrinth Double ax or maze. The bony structure containing the **inner ear**, consisting of the **cochlea, semicircular canals,** and the vestibular sacs. The *labyrinthine sense* (or **vestibular sense** since its organs are located in the vestibular area of the inner ear) is sensitive to pressure changes and is related to body balance and position or direction of movement. In learning studies, the labyrinth refers to a structure devised to test a subject's skill in working his way from the maze entrance through a series of intricate passageways to a specified goal. *See* **Cotugno.**

The ear labyrinth was discovered in 445 B.C. by **Empedocles** of Agrigentum, and mentioned by **Galen** and **Vesalius.** It was first adequately described in 1503 by **Achellini,** and named by **Fallopius** in 1550.

Lacroix, Sylvestre-Francois (1765-1843) French mathematician who investigated theory of functions of a real variable, and introduced various terms into mathematics, such as Napierian **logarithms,** differential coefficient, and **variable.**

lactogenic hormone Relating to (-ic) the hormone of the anterior pituitary gland that stimulates ovarian progesterone and the production (-gen-) of milk (lacto-); also helps in the maturation process of the **corpus luteum.** *See* **follicle stimulating hormone, neurosecretion.**

Ladd-Franklin, Christine (1847-1930) American psychologist and logician. Student of **G. Müller** and **Helmholtz.** Developed a theory of color vision (1892) that reconciled the **Hering** and **Helmholtz** theories and which is consistent with the evolutionary development of the neural mechanisms of vision. *See* **color vision theories, Donders.**

lag The continuance of physiological activity in a **receptor** or in the **brain** itself after cessation of the **stimulus:** for example, an **afterimage.** The delay in the beginning of physiological activity after the application of the stimulus. The period of time elapsing between the change of stimulus and the change of response. *See* **cultural lag, reaction time.**

lambert The cgs unit of **luminance** equal to the **brightness** of a perfectly diffusing surface that reflects one **lumen** per square centimeter.

After Johann Heinrich Lambert (1728-1777), German physicist, mathematician, and astronomer. Discovered method of measuring intensity and absorption of light.

La Mettrie, Julien Offray de (1709-1751) French physiologist and philosopher. He theorized that thought as well as the soul is the result of mechanical action of the **brain** and nervous system. He offered objective and physiological explanations of behavior, explaining man and the universe on a purely mechanistic basis and denying the reality of the mind. Some of his ideas purportedly led to the formulation of the **James-Lange theory of emotion.** *See* **hedonism.**

Land camera *See* **Young-Helmholtz theory** under **color vision theories.**

Landolt ring One of a series of c-shaped rings used for the study of visual acuity or discrimination. The ring can be rotated into various positions to see whether the subject can locate the gap.

After Hans Landolt (1831-1910), Swiss chemist.

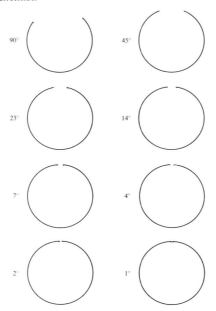

From *Psychology: A Scientific Study of Man,* by Sanford and Wrightsman. Copyright 1970 by Wadsworth Publishing Company, Inc. Reprinted by permission of the publisher, Brooks/Cole Publishing Company, Monterey, California.

Lange, Carl Georg (1834-1900) Danish physician and physiologist. In 1885, Lange published his *Om Sindsbevaegelser* in Denmark, which considered **emotion** to be a result rather than the cause of specific body reactions, an idea strikingly similar to James'. *See* **James-Lange theory.**

Langfeldt, Gabriel A Norwegian physician and psychologist, born 1895. Developed concepts of the **schizophreniform state** (1937) and **process schizophrenia.**

large numbers law *See* **law of large numbers.**

Lashley, Karl Spencer (1890-1958) American (West Virginia) comparative psychologist. Received Ph.D. (genetics) Johns Hopkins 1914, but turned to **psychology,** 1915, as a result of studying with **Watson** and **Adolph Meyer.** Watson influenced him in an early stand for **behaviorism,** but Lashley changed (1947) from this view as a result of his own experiments. Instrumental (after visiting Russia) in pointing out the value of **Pavlov's** experiments. Noted for his work on brain localization, genetics, and instincts. Trained rats with varying amounts of surgical brain damage to learn **mazes** and discovered that, although all the rats learned the maze, errors increased as brain damage increased. From these results Lashley formulated his law of **mass action:** the more brain tissue available the more rapid and accurate the learning. Also demonstrated his principle of **equipotentiality:** one part of the cortex is equally potential (in rate) to another in its capacity to learn a skill.

In 1937, he received the **Warren Medal** for "his distinguished work on the physiological basis of learning and on the neural mechanisms involved in vision." *See* **Franz.**

To develop his research on two-choice learning situations he invented what has become known as the *Lashley jumping stand,* a device for testing discrimination in rats and other small animals. The animal is placed on the stool (S), required to jump at either L or R. If the experimenter wants L, for example, to be the correct stimulus, L flips back, allowing the animal access to P where he can eat. If L is wrong, it remains immobile and the animal falls to the net (N). In recent modifications, if the rat chooses the wrong **stimulus** he is spared falling to the net by being able to jump to a ledge under L and R.

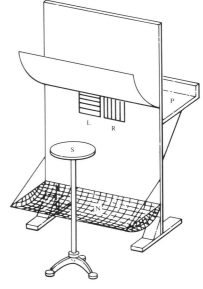

Donald J. Lewis, *Scientific Principles of Psychology,* © 1963. Reprinted by permission of Prentice-Hall, Inc., Englewood Cliffs, New Jersey.

latency period The quality or state (-cy) of being hidden (laten-) for a period of time. A time of dormancy in **personality** development. In Freudian theory, the period of middle childhood (from about 4 to 12 years) following the suppression of the **Oedipus** conflict when sex interests are relatively dormant, sublimated, or subordinated. Also, the time elapsing between **stimulus** presentation and the start of a **response,** as seen in a muscle twitch or **reflex.**

latent content of dreams *See* **dream content, manifest content of dreams.**

latent learning Unexpressed or hidden (laten-) learning. Learning, not coincidently apparent but assumed to have taken place in the absence of **reinforcement,** that becomes evident only when reinforcement is introduced (in the form of special incentives or increased motivation).

In 1930 E. C. Tolman gave an example of latent learning from one of his experiments: "Rats in unrewarded tours of the maze were picking up 'sign-Gestalt-expectations' which were utilized when food was placed in the goal-box." *See* **sign learning.**

lateral Pertaining to (-al) the side (later-), or away from the midline of the body. The lateral axis lies away from the medial plane of the body, and is identical to the dextrosinistral axis.

latent type of schizophrenia. *See* **schizophrenia.**

lateral fissure (fissure of Sylvius) *See* **fissure.**

lateral geniculate (nucleus) body (LGN) One of two small terminal swellings of the **optic tracts** in the **thalamus** that receives nerve fibers of the optic nerves passing from the retinal cells through the **optic chiasma,** fibers from the right half of each retina entering one tract and those from the left halves entering the other. The LGN is organized topographically, that is, for each point on the retina there is a corresponding point in the LGN and another in the striate cortex. The anatomy of the LGN has been primarily determined by the **retrograde degeneration technique**. *See* **occipital lobe**. (Morgan, pp. 156-157).

lateral lemniscus *See* **lemniscus**.

lateral ventricles *See* **brain ventricles**.

Latin square design An experimental design in which each **treatment** (indicated by a letter) appears only once in each row and once in each column. For example:

ADCB   ABCD
BADC   CADB
CBAD or DCBA
DCBA   BDAC

Latin squares permit an experimenter to isolate variation due to two **nuisance variables** in evaluating treatment effects. A Latin square design is simple to use for **data** analysis but inappropriate when there are interactions among **variables**. If interaction effects are assumed to be negligible, a Latin square design may be used to reduce the number of observations ordinarily required in a complete **factorial design**. A hyper-Graeco-Latin square (three or more orthogonal squares combined) may be obtained from complete sets of orthogonal squares. *See* **Graeco-Latin square design**, Table 15 for orthogonal Latin squares (also Kirk, pp. 16-17, 151-169).

laudanum (from *labdanum,* a rock rose) Any of various **opium** preparations; a tincture of opium.

Paracelsus (1493?-1541), Swiss physician, used the word as a name for a remedy based on opium. It was introduced in more modern times (about 1672) by Thomas Sydenham. *See* **chorea**.

law of comparative judgment *See* **Thurstone scales, scaling technique**.

law of disuse *See* **law of exercise**.

law of effect Thorndike's main learning law: success is self-rewarding and tends to repeat itself while unsuccessful events tend to be eliminated. Basic to the law is the satisfaction one has in a learning experience. Those responses tend to be learned that are associated with pleasure; the end results of an activity determine its learnability. All trial and error learning seems to follow this law. In modified forms, it is virtually synonymous with **operant conditioning**, since it now means that responses followed by reinforcers or rewards (good results) are more likely to occur again. Sometimes called the *law of psychological* **hedonism** or the *law of selection* (E. L. Thorndike, "The Law of Effect." *American Journal of Psychology*, 1927, *27*, 212-222).

law of exercise Thorndike's laws of use and disuse combined into one: "When a modifiable connection is made between a situation and a response, that connection's strength is, other things being equal, increased" (the *law of use*) and, when such a connection is not made during a certain time period, that "connection's strength is decreased" (*law of disuse*). Thorndike considered this law, as well as his others, to be a corollary of the **law of effect**.

law of large numbers The larger the **sample** size, drawn from any-shaped **population**, the more likely it is that the sample mean will approach the population mean, the **variance** of the sample means $\sigma_{\bar{X}}^2 = \alpha^2/N$, and a standard error $\sigma_{\bar{X}}$ of $\alpha/\sqrt{N}$. *See* **inferential statistics**.

Jacques Bernoulli expressed this law in his book, *Ars Conjectandi* (1713), after "meditating on the idea for more than twenty years."

law of least effort *See* **law of parsimony**.

law of parsimony In considering scientific formulations and constructs, the simplest approach is the best, all other things being equal. The law represents a generalization of numerous statements dealing with economy of action or thought, such as expressed in **Occam's razor**, **Morgan's canon** or *law of least effort* (in which an organism will expend only a minimal amount of effort in exploratory behavior in order to survive).

Term first used by Sir **William Hamilton**, probably in 1853, renaming Occam's razor.

law of proximity The process by which viewed objects tend to fuse or form a new group through closer spatial relationship.

law of psychological hedonism *See* **hedonism, law of effect**.

law of readiness "When any conduction unit is in readiness to conduct, for it to do so is satisfying," and when it is not ready it is annoying. *See* **Thorndike**.

law of use *See* **law of exercise**.

laws of learning *See* **Thorndike, learning theory**.

LD₅₀ (LD-50) Median lethal dose.

L-dopa The levorotatory (L- or l-) form of **dopa**.

learning disorders Learning problems associated with scholastic or communication skills (e.g., **stuttering, aphasia**, delayed speech, poor articulation, **dyslexia**, and other disorders of reading and arithmetic).

For information on learning disorders, contact the *National Easter Seal Society for Crippled Children and Adults*, 2023 W. Ogden Avenue, Chicago, Illinois 60612.

learning set Faster learning of new material by organisms that have been previously exposed to similar material.

learning theory Any theory advanced to explain the process of learning or the acquisition and extinction of knowledge, skills, and habits.

Theories about the learning process were pioneered by **Ebbinghaus, W. L. Bryan**, and N. Harter (see **plateau**), **Thorndike**, others. Stimulus-response (S-R) theories, based on ideas of Thorndike and Pavlov, consider learning as a result of changes in association between S. and R. Cognitive theories derived from **Gestalt psychology** (such as Lewin's **field theory** and Tolman's **purposive behaviorism**) conceive of learning as a change in **perception**. Learning theories have taken little or no account of activities or changes in the **central nervous system, B. F. Skinner** claiming that any consideration of the central nervous system is unnecessary; that research should consist of varying the experimental conditions and of observing the resultant behavior. Of the leading theorists, only E. C. Tolman introduced **intervening variables**, presumably occurring in the central nervous system and contributing to learning, such as "expectancy."

Major learning theorists are: Thorndike—connectionism or bond psychology; Skinner—descriptive behaviorism, emphasizing reinforcements that strengthen responses; Hull—systematic behavior theory (drive reduction); Tolman—**sign-Gestalt** motivational theory, sign learnings; **Guthrie—contiguity theory** or contiguous conditioning (emphasizing stimuli that evoke responses); and **Lewin**—field theory, or topological and vector psychology. There are also many other modifications of Gestalt and field concepts in learning theory. *See* **stochastic learning theory**.

least squares method A technique for obtaining the regression coefficients (unknown parameters of *a* and *b* in fitting a regression equation) such that the sum of the squares of the deviations from the regression line is less than from any other straight line.

The least squares method was developed and refined by Müller in 1904 and by F. M. Urban in 1909, 1912 from one (the constant method) of the three fundamental methods of measurement established by **Fechner**: (1) j.n.d.; (2) method of constant stimuli or constant method; and (3) average error. *See* **Müller-Urban method**; also Senders, pp. 136, 283; Walker-Lev, p. 325; Hays, 1963, p. 496; Kirk, pp. 204-208; and Lewis, p. 301.

Legion of Merit An award, created by President Roosevelt and passed into law on November 5, 1942, granting recognition to those of any nationality who have made outstanding contributions to their occupational field.

This decoration is similar to and is based upon the Badge for Military Merit, established by George Washington in 1782, but differs from it in that it may be granted to civilians. Most recipients, however, have been associated with the military effort.

J. P. Guilford received the Legion of Merit in 1946, for developing psychological tests used in the selection of Air Force personnel during World War II.

Leibniz, Gottfried Wilhelm (1646-1716) German philosopher and mathematician. His philosophy differed from that of **Descartes** and **Spinoza** in claiming that substance cannot have any extension but can have thought. "There is nothing in intellect," he said, "which was not first in sense, except intellect itself." In his *Monadologie* (1714), he conceived of a dominant "monad," the soul, with many lower monads in attendance. Superior to them all rules the supreme monad, God, who permits free will. His doctrine of *petites perceptions* is virtually one of the unconscious. In his *Nouveaux Essais,* published posthumously in 1765, he said that the body and mind are completely separate but that they function harmoniously like, for example, two separate orchestras playing the same piece. They might serve parallel functions but they are nevertheless distinct, requiring unique concepts and terms to describe each one. *See* **psychophysical parallelism** (also Boring, pp. 165-8; Bell, pp. 117-130).

lemniscal neurons *See* **neuron**.

lemniscal system Relating to (-al) the system with a ribbon-like (lemnisc-) band of nerve fibers. One of the two pathways (the spinothalamic system being the other) in the spinal cord and **brainstem** that carries cutaneous sensations to the **cerebral cortex**. The lemniscal system is apparently concerned with touch and kinesthetic sensations. (Butter, pp. 79-85; Thompson, pp. 233, 235).

The lemniscal system derives its name from the midbrain pathway of the medial **lemniscus**.

Apparently, Celsus first used the word lemniscus, but in the sense of bandage. **Reil** was first to outline the structure of **lentiform nuclei** and the lemniscal system.

lemniscus Ribbon. A band of nerve fibers of the **second order neurons** in the sensory path ending in the **thalamus**. The *lateral lemniscus* is the auditory pathway that ascends the **brainstem medial geniculate body** (on the surface of the thalamus) from cochlear nuclei, while the *medial lemniscus* (a flat band of sensory fibers) transmits proprioceptive impulses from the **medulla** through the **pons** and **midbrain** to the thalamus.

leniency error Tendency by judges to rate most subjects at the top (most favorable rating) of a scale. **Forced-choice** scales help minimize such distortions.

lentiform (lenticular) nucleus A nucleus shaped (form) like a lens; the ventral portion of the **corpus striatum** divided into the **putamen** and **globus pallidus**. *See* **caudate nucleus, basal ganglia**.

leptokurtosis Condition (-osis) of a thin (lepto-) peaked (-kurt-) curve, which occurs when samples of **data** produce relative degrees of peakedness in a frequency polygon. *See* **kurtosis**.

leptosomatic, leptosome. *See* **Kretschmer, constitutional types**.

lesbianism (Sapphism) Female homosexuality; a term derived from Lesbos, Greek island in the Aegean Sea, which was the home of Sappho (fl. about 600 B.C.), Greek lyric poet and her cult of female lovers. She was more likely bisexual, since she supposedly leaped to her death from the high Leucadian rock because of unrequited love for Phaon, a Mytilene (male) boatman.

Le Système International d'Unités *See* **International System of Units**.

leucine A white (leuc-) crystalline **amino acid** (-ine) obtained from proteins and by synthesis; essential in the nutrition of man and lower animals in its L-form (levorotatory).

Noted (1818) in rotting cheese by French chemist Joseph Louis Proust (1754-1826). Identified and named by **Braconnot** in 1820 because of the whiteness of its crystals.

leucotomy See **lobotomy**.

Leuret, Francois (1797-1851) French anatomist and psychiatrist. In addition to contributions on psychotherapy, he proposed that the "variations in convolutional patterns from species to species could be used as a criterion of differentiation." Named the **fissure** of Rolando in 1839 (Clarke and O'Malley, p. 399).

Levarterenol, l-arterenol, l-norepinephrine, l-noradrenalin The levorotatory form of Arterenol (a tradename) or **norepinephrine** that occurs as a hormone with epinephrine. It differs from epinephrine by absence of methyl substitution in the amino group. Possesses excitatory action of **epinephrine** (tending to increase blood pressure) but is limited in inhibitory effects. It also serves as an **adrenergic** mediator in maintenance of internal economy of body, useful in shock.

level of aspiration See **aspiration level**.

level of confidence See **confidence level**.

level of significance (α) The likelihood of rejecting the **null hypothesis** when it is true. See **significance**.

Leven(e), Phoebus (Fishel) 1869-1940. Russian-American physiologist. See **adenosine, nucleus, purine**.

levorotatory Characterized by (-ory) rotating (-rotat-) the plane of polarized light counter-clockwise or toward the left (levo-).

Lewin, Kurt (1890-1947) Born in Prussia, but became naturalized American. Received Ph.D. (psychology) University of Berlin 1914. From his background in **Gestalt psychology**, he advanced his **field theory** which considered a person to be continually interacting within a field of psychological forces. He developed **topological psychology**, and introduced many ideas and terms into psychology, such as **ecological psychology, intensive group experience, psychological field, irreal**, and made other contributions to learning theory.

To Lewin, all behavior is motivated toward goals within defined regions of **life space**. He believed that a genetic approach to behavior, as in **psychoanalysis**, is unnecessary and that a full understanding of a person's life space (including all the **valences**, goals, and barriers) would provide all the description and explanation necessary to understand his behavior. (Boring, pp. 723-8; 733-4; Bischof, pp. 575-585; and Vinacke; p. 173).

Lewin Memorial Award See **Kurt Lewin Memorial Award**.

LGN Lateral geniculate nucleus.

LH luteinizing hormone.

libido Lust, passion, sexual hunger, life energy, or the energy of the sexual instinct. More broadly conceived, libido is psychic energy irrespective of the object upon which it acts. In **Freudian** theory, it is the dynamic manifestation of sexuality, as well as the unifying and constructive element of the organism leading to the preservation of the species; the energy provided by the generalized sexual instinct or affiliative needs.

Term first used by **Freud** in 1895, but not until 1905 did he adequately define what he meant by it.

library routine Pre-written "off the shelf" program sections (including mathematical and statistical information) to be spliced into any program designed for solving computational problems.

Librium The Roche tradename for **chlordiazepoxide hydrochloride**.

licence In French **higher education**, the first university degree granted after satisfactory completion of the first cycle (**propédeutique**) and preliminary to the **lycée** examinations.

Liebig, Justas von (1803-1873) German chemist. Discovered, among other chemicals, chloroform, aldehyde, and acetyl acid. In 1846, isolated a substance from cheese that he named **tyrosine**.

lie detector (Keeler polygraph) A device used to register physiological changes in blood pressure, pulse beat, respiratory rate, and increased perspiration occurring under emotional arousal or tension, often believed to be associated with lying under questioning.

Liepmann, Hugo Carl (1863-1925) German neurologist. See **agnosia, apraxia**.

life space In **Lewin's field theory**, the totality of the individual existing in his perceived environment (both psychological and physical) at any given time. See **irreal**.

life style (style of life) A compensatory, dynamic, goal-oriented way of behaving that characterizes a person's consistent and expected mode of response under differing circumstances. For example, a person's life style might dictate that after committing an impulsive act—insulting someone, proposing marriage, buying a car—he talk his way out of his difficulty, while another might say that fate made him act that way. Under different and threatening situations, similar behaviors may be repeated and expected as dictated by one's style of life, which consists of all aspects of living, oriented toward achieving one's goal of life. **Adler** believed that one's life style becomes set in about the fifth year.

The term "style of life" had been first used in 1915 by German sociologist Max Weber (1864-1920) in discussing the way of life practiced by people living in subcultures. Adler first used the phrase in his lectures in 1926 and in his book *The Science of Living*, 1929. The phrase lost favor for a number of years but regained popularity during the 1960's as part of the existential terminology.

likelihood ratio test A general approach for locating a good test statistic for purposes of testing any of a broad class of hypotheses. A form of hypothesis testing initiated by **R. A. Fisher** but developed by Neyman and E. S. Pearson during the late 1920's and early 1930's. (Hays, 1964, p. 287).

Jerzy Neyman. Rumanian-born (1894) American statistician. Ph.D., Warsaw 1923. Spent much of American academic life at University of California (Berkeley), since 1938. Devised and named **confidence limits**. Egon Sharpe Pearson. Born 1895, England. D.Sc., Trinity College, Cambridge. Biometrician and mathematical statistician.

Likert Summated Scale An ordinal measurement device for discriminating between different attitudes being measured. The subject indicates his feeling on a 5-point scale from "strongly approve" to strongly disapprove" for every item under consideration. The items finally selected are those that have discriminated best between high and low scores. See **attitude scale; ordinal scale; scaling technique**.

Rensis Likert born 1903. An American (Wyoming) social scientist and statistician. Received Ph.D., Columbia 1932. A professor of both psychology and sociology at Michigan for a number of years, specializing in attitude and motivation measurement, leadership, management, and public opinion studies.

limbic system Relating to (-al) parts of the brain considered as a borderline (limb-) nervous system interconnecting phylogenetically newer (cortical) and older (subcortical) pathways around the **corpus callosum**; a system including an older region of the **cerebral cortex** (the **cingulate gyrus**) and portions of the **reticular formation**, the hypothalamus, hippocampus, the amygdala, the **septum**, olfactory projection areas and other structures important for emotion and motivation. It is apparently also concerned with sequential behavior wherein one activity depends upon another. Disorders of the limbic

system lead to assaultive behavior (e.g., by stimulating the amygdala, some patients have become uncontrollable). The limbic system is a major feature of the **Papez-MacLean theory of emotion**. Evolutionarily, the limbic system arises from olfactory structures, and was formerly known as the **rhinencephalon**. See **central theory**. (P. D. MacLean, "The Limbic System with Respect to Self-preservation and the Preservation of the Species," *Journal of Nervous and Mental Diseases*, 1958, **127**, 1-11).

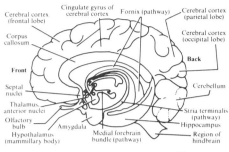

A schematic drawing of the limbic system with its structures indicated by darker shadowing (with the exception of the cerebellum).

limbkinetic Referring to (-ic) motions (-kinet-) of limbs. See **apraxia**.

limen (Ger., *Schwelle*, threshold.) The point at which a certain effect takes place, usually referring to the threshold level below which nothing happens and above which the effect occurs (as in the **all or none law** in which a sufficiently strong stimulus will produce a response in the nerve fiber but a stimulus not strong enough to reach the **limen** or trigger point produces no reaction). *Absolute limen* (see **detection threshold**) is the detection criterion above which a stimulus becomes effective or below which it is ineffective; the running energy required to cause a response. For example, the wavelengths of infrared light are too long and those of ultraviolet light too short to be perceived by human vision; they are beyond the absolute limens. *Difference limen* is the smallest difference that can be perceived between a pair of stimuli (such as recognizing two sounds as different tones) under experimental conditions.

limits A psychophysical method for determining **just noticeable differences** and other constants. Subjects are presented varying degrees of stimuli (values) and are asked to compare these with standard stimuli or to report absence or presence of same; also used to obtain **audiograms**. See **methods of psychology: clinical**.

limits, central theorem of See **central limits theorem**.

limits, class See **class limits**.

limits, confidence See **confidence limits**.

limulus A small (-ulus) crab that progresses in a sidelong (lim-) manner; a horseshoe or king crab frequently used for research in psychology, particularly in vision (brightness discrimination) experiments (Morgan, pp. 198-200).

Lindsley, Donald Benjamin Born Ohio, 1907. Received Ph.D. in psychology, Iowa 1932. Major researches in physiological psychology, primarily electroencephalographic applications to physiological phenomena. In 1951, as a result of his earlier work on the **reticular formation**, he showed the importance of the reticular activating system in emotion, linking emotion to a general **arousal** process, which has become known as the *Lindsley activation theory*. A member of the **National Academy of Sciences** and a recipient of the **Presidential Certificate of Merit**. Received **DSC Award**, 1959. See **beta waves**.

linear equation A mathematical statement of equality between known and unknown quantities which when represented as a **graph** is one of the first degree, a straight line. For example, $y = ax + b$.

linear function A mathematical function of the first degree ($y = ax + b$) whose mean rate of increase is constant, and which can be combined only by addition and subtraction.

linear perspective A **monocular cue** to visual depth perception or distance, produced, for example, when two lines perpendicular to the observer and equally spaced apart are perceived as converging to a point on the horizon as their distance from the observer increases.

linear programming model See **model.**

lipidhistiocytosis (Niemann-Pick disease) Condition (-osis) of fatty (lipid-) tissue (histio-) or "foam" cells (cyt-) in the spleen, lymph, or marrow, the enlargement of the liver and spleen distinguishing the condition from **Tay-Sach's disease.**

lipochondrodystrophy A condition (-y) of poor (dys-) growth (-troph-) resulting from fat (lipo-) metabolism disturbances in the granules (-chondro-) of the Golgi body (lipochondrion). *Same as* **Hurler's disease.**

lipostatic hypothesis A proposition relating to (-ic) the control of long term feeding patterns through processes in a hypothalamic regulatory mechanism (-stat), involving the circulation of blood metabolites concerned with the storage of fat (lipo-) in the system. *See* **thermostatic theory, glucostatic theory.**

lithium carbonate A pharmaceutical rediscovery used to treat **manic-depressive illness,** apparently restoring normal behavior in many extreme cases, particularly in acute mania. The level at which it produces toxic results, however, is dangerously close to its level of efficiency.

Apparently had been used as treatment for mania by Soranus, Greek physician of early second century A.D., who had his patients take mineral baths containing lithium salts.

lobe Lump or pod (lobos). A curved or rounded division of an organ, separated from each other by a **fissure**, such as the five **lobes** of the **cerebral cortex**: frontal, parietal, central, temporal, and occipital.

lobectomy Excision (-ectomy) of the lobe of an organ (such as the **brain** or gland).

lobotomy The cutting (-tomy) of nerve-fiber tracts connecting the **thalamus** and the **frontal lobes.** Moniz reasoned that separation of the brain's emotional center (the thalamus) from the thinking area (prefrontal lobes) would result in reducing the patient's anguish and suicidal and homicidal tendencies. Patients did become calm after the operation but they were seldom more than "vegetables," and consequently the technique lost favor.

Prefrontal lobotomy separates the prefrontal areas from the thalamus. *Prefrontal topectomy* involves the cutting out (-ec-) of small places (top-) or pieces from the prefrontal cortex of the **cerebrum.** *Thalectomy* requires using an electric needle on the **thalamus** and searing out part of it. *Leucotomy,* which necessitates cutting the white (leuco-) nerve fibers, is another term for prefrontal lobotomy and is the one more frequently used in Great Britain.

Egas Moniz (1874-1955), professor of neurology at the University of Lisbon, performed the first frontal lobotomy on a psychiatric patient in 1935. Prior to this, however, lobotomies had been performed on monkeys by researchers Fulton and Jacobson at Yale University, who found that the postoperative monkeys were more tractable and less subject to frustration. Moniz said in 1954 that in his first publication on the subject (1936) his "decision to perform the surgical operation which I named the 'prefrontal leukotomy' did not come (from) some sudden burst of inspiration." Rather, it was due to the considerable influence of "the doctrines of **Ramon y Cajal**" (Sahakian, p. 372).

localization of brain function The assignment of specific **motor** and/or **sensory** functions to certain areas of the brain. Such localization has been made possible by observing the results of brain injuries in human beings and of surgery in animals, especially in brain studies performed by **Fritsch, Franz, Lashley, Penfield,** and **Olds.** Functions of many areas have been identified, although not for such complex activities as memory.

Probably from the time of the first recorded mention of the area later to become known as the **brain** (dating from about 1550 B.C. according to the **Edwin Smith Surgical Papyrus**), man has been interested in assigning specific functions to certain brain areas. At first, it must have seemed natural to locate the seat of the soul in the brain, which Pythagoras did (530 B.C.). **Plato,** like Pythagoras, stated that reasoning was located in the brain, with the senses originating in the heart and vegetative functions stemming from the abdomen. The Hippocratic writers (400 B.C.) thought of the brain as the site for all mental phenomena. **Herophilus** favored the ventricles as the site. **Aretaeus,** probably the first to become more specific, reported that spasms on one side of the body were caused by lesions on the opposite side of the brain. Apparently, the concept of the **sensus communis** sprung from the brain of Poseidonius (fl. 370 A.D.) surgeon of Byzantium, claiming that mental functions had specific brain locations, placing the seat of imagination in the frontal region, understanding in the middle, and memory in the rear. Nemesius of Emesa (fl. 390 A.D.), elaborating upon the idea, located the *sensus communis* along with imagination in the lateral ventricles.

Interest in brain localization was scattered throughout the following centuries (even the drawings of Albertus Magnus [1193-1280] show crude attempts at indicating cerebral localization), but mainly the cerebral hemispheres were considered, even during the 17th and 18th centuries, to have little use other than being the focus and locus of the **sensorium commune.** Vesalius, by positing the pineal gland as the seat of the soul, not only opposed the ventricular concept but also Plato's three seats of the soul. **Descartes** preferred to think of only a single soul, his ideas diverting attention from the cortex as a possibility. Actual experimentation of localization sites probably began about 1670 with **Willis** and 1673 with G. J. Du Verney (1648-1730), who excised the human brain for study. Willis' observations led him to conclude that the motor processes of circulation, digestion, and respiration were centered in the **cerebellum,** and that the **cerebral hemispheres** contained three centers: the **corpus striatum** as the seat of the *sensus communis*; the **corpus callosum** (which then included all parts of the white matter as well as the present anatomy of the structure) as the seat of imagination; and the cortex as the site of memory.

In 1784, **Prochaska** said that the *sensorium commune* was comprised of the **medulla oblongata,** spinal cord, and nerves, and that the rest of the brain functioned as the faculty of the intellect with many functional units, thereby helping lead to the **phrenology** of Gall and **Spurzheim.** Gall's ideas (although based on erroneous observations), by delineating areas of language and speech, led to the modern concept of cortical localization. In 1812, French physiologist Julien C. Legallois (1770-1814) claimed that the medulla oblongata was the center of respiration. Pierre Flourens (1794-1867), most influential in causing phrenology to be ridiculed, pinpointed the cerebral hemisphere as the seat of intelligence and sensation; the cerebellum of motor function; and the medulla oblongata of vital functions. His ideas (1822-23) anticipated the holistic theory of brain function. In 1825, Jean Baptiste Bouillaud (1796-1881) linked phrenology and cortical

localization by observing that loss of speech was associated with the anterior lobes of the brain. Ernst Auburtin (1825-?1893) held that speech function was centered in the anterior lobes (as had his father-in-law Bouillaud) and that the brain should be studied for its local functions rather than *in toto*, thereby helping crystallize the concept of cerebral localization, an idea often attributed mainly to **Broca. Fritsch** and **Hitzig** (1870) demonstrated that electrical stimulation of the cortex induced motor response, thereby opposing Flourens. **Ferrier** confirmed Hitzig's findings in 1873, defining a motor area of the cerebral cortex. Bartolomeo Panizzi (1785-1867), Italian anatomist, was first to demonstrate (1855) with animals that the **occipital lobe** was necessary for vision, and German physiologist Hermann Munk (1839-1912) not only confirmed Panizzi's findings but also located auditory functions in the **temporal lobes.** Other experimenters soon crystallized ideas about localization; namely Salomen Eberhard Henschen (1847-1930) a Swede; the Polish physician Mechyslav Minkowski (born 1884); Flechsig with his myelogenic technique; Brodmann and his brain mapping; Lashley and his integrative action of the cerebral cortex; and many others. (Clarke and O'Malley, pp. 297-299; 391-394; 463; 484-488; passim).

loci See **homozygote.**

Locke, John (1632-1704) English philosopher and founder of British empiricism, and of the empirical approach to psychology. Spurned Aristotelianism in favor of **Descartes'** and **Bacon's** inductive methods of experimental science. His ideas (in the social and practical sense) were similar to those of Spinoza, Bacon, and **Hobbes.** Locke and Hobbes approached an objective viewpoint (claiming that association of ideas came through reflection), which helped lead to **Pavlov's** conditioned responses. Locke was primarily interested in the validity of knowledge, holding that knowledge is derived solely from experience (the senses); that ideas, which may be simple or complex, are the elements of the mind. For him, objects had both *primary* qualities (those perceived by the senses, like shape or solidity), and *secondary* qualities (derived from the primary ones, like color and taste). Locke, advancing Hobbes' ideational concepts, believed (like Aristotle) that the mind at birth is a *tabula rasa* or blank tablet on which experiences are recorded. The period of the Enlightenment is usually dated from Locke's *Essay Concerning Human Understanding* (1690) and ending with Kant's *Critique of Pure Reason* (1781). See **Berkeley, Malebranche** (also Boring, pp. 169-76, 178).

locomotor ataxia A disorder (-ia) of unsteadiness (atax-) upon attempting locomotion. See **ataxia.**

Jean Cruveilhier (1791-1874), French physician, described the condition first in 1830 and gave the name to it shortly after. **Remak** renamed it **tabes dorsalis** in 1836.

Loeb, Jacques (1859-1924) German-born American physiologist. Advanced a theory of **tropism** to explain animal behavior. His "associative memory" which "tied an old response to a new stimulus," was one of the forerunners of **Pavlov's** conditioning. He felt that physico-chemical methods were adequate for study of both physiology and behavior. *See* **Locke.**

Loewi, Otto (1873-1961) German pharmacologist and physician (Dr. med., Strasbourg 1896). Shared with **Dale** the 1936 Nobel prize for physiology and medicine. Discovered **acetylcholine.** See **Vagusstoff.**

logarithm The exponent to which a fixed number (the base) is to be raised to produce a given number. The logarithm of a number usually contains an integer and a decimal. For example, $\log_{10} 200 = 2.3010$. The integral part (2) is called the *characteristic*, and the decimal tail (.3010) is the *mantissa*.

In the *Briggsian system* of common logarithms the base is *10*. An example: log *a* = log$_{10}$*a*, which is the common logarithm of *a*, or log *a* to the base 10. To convert common logarithms to natural, multiply the common by 2.3025850930.

After Henry Briggs (1556-1631), English mathematician who proposed common logarithms in his book *Arithmetica Logarithmica*, 1624.

In the *Napierian system,* the base is 2.718818, symbolized by *e*. Any positive number except 1 can be used as a base. Example: 4^3 = 64, 4 is the logarithm of 64 to the base 3, meaning that 4 must be raised to the third power to produce 64, or $1_n a = \log_e a$, which is the natural log of a^n to the base *e* (equaling 2.718818). To convert natural to common logarithms, multiply the natural by 0.4342944819. *See* **computer, Lacroix.**

After John Napier (1550-1617), Scottish mathematician, who proposed his system of logarithms in 1614.

logarithmic curve A curve similar to the exponential curve except that the **dependent variable** appears as the **exponent.**

logotherapy A form of **existential therapy** emphasizing man's search for meaning (logo-).

Developed by a Viennese psychoanalyst, Victor Frankl, born 1905, after his experiences as a World War II prisoner in a concentration camp in Germany. Preparing to die, he was faced with trying to discover the "why" of life. After the war he integrated his thoughts with those of his patients who also were searching for a meaning of life (Victor E. Frankl, *The Doctor and the Soul, An Introduction to Logotherapy*, 1955).

longitudinal fissure The groove that divides the right and left **cerebral hemispheres.**

longitudinal studies Studies concerned with the changes occurring in individuals over extended periods of time, or in which samples of a **population** are selected and then studied intensively as age and experience increase.

In his **personality** theory, **Murray** applies the longitudinal principle by considering the ideal case study to be an exhaustive investigation of all the person's experiences from birth to the present.

long-term memory (LTM) A theory that conceives of a storage mechanism in the brain, which permanently preserves or records certain types of frequently required information useful for self-preservation. Memory that tends to persist for a relatively long period of time or for life. It is probably resistant to spontaneous decay and to interfering associations, probably because it is associated with permanent changes in the brain (primarily) and the rest of the nervous system. *See* **information processing, short-term memory.**

loop (reverberatory circuit) A closed path or circuit over which a signal can circulate, as in a **feedback** control system, which provides a flow of information back to a source, thereby allowing a comparison with an input command signal. Loop also refers to a series of instructions that predictably repeat a set of computations, modifying some variable each time.

Lorenz, Konrad Zacharias Born 1903, Austria. Received his medical degree (Vienna 1928) but turned to **ethology** as a profession soon afterward. He considers animals' behavior to be a product of adaptive evolution.

Lotze, Rudolph Hermann (1817-1881) German philosopher, physician, and artist. Helped establish physiological psychology. Although his psychology was physiological and mechanistic, his philosophy, in respect to the essence of reality, was metaphysical. Lotze's theory of space perception, antedating functionalism, considered that perception of distance and movement were made possible by "local signs" or learned cues used unconsciously. He was also a pioneer in studying the subconscious. *See* **Dewey** (also Boring, pp. 261-5).

loudness *See* **sound.**

love (Exist.) The profound and reciprocal feeling of affection and attachment toward another human being, which is so individual that it defies generalization. It is known only to the person who experiences it and demands complete commitment to that other person and vice versa. Love cannot exist when subjected to analysis and definition; it is either then destroyed or never comes into being. Any reference to such feelings for lower animals should be preceded by a qualifying term, such as dog-love, cat-love, etc.

Søren Kierkegaard, Danish theologian, said that "Love is not like art, jealous of itself, and therefore poured out on only a few. Everyone who wishes to love, to him it is given."

And **Karl Jaspers** said: "He does not love at all who loves mankind only; he does who loves one specific person."

Friedrich Nietzsche, German philosopher, and Kierkegaard both affirmed the necessity for one to be sufficient within himself in order to love another person.

To **Erich Fromm**, love needs four interdependent basic elements: care, responsibility, respect, and knowledge. He believes in five types of love: brotherly love; motherly love; erotic love; self-love, which is necessary if one expects to love others; and the greatest love of all, the love of God. Love is an art and must be practiced and worked at seriously, if one hopes for success in love.

There is homosexual love, puppy love, romantic love, fictional love (in which the reader falls in love with the heroes and heroines), and then there is the cloth surrogate love of **Harry Harlow**'s monkeys. In 1958, Harlow, one of the few researchers ever to conduct experiments on love, introduced a cloth surrogate and its wire surrogate sibling in attempting to discover the nature of love. He found that body contact was of utmost importance (even though the cloth mother was inanimate) in providing the infant monkey with emotional security.

In 1970, Harlow simplified his aims so that the only role for the surrogate mother was to provide "early social support and security to infants." His observations pointed to the infant, not the mother, as "the primary attachment object even where the mother locomotes."

Harlow's previous experimental mothers have been "of the cloth"—terry mostly—so he has not had much of a chance to experiment with a "red hot mama." By 1970, however, he was getting closer—at least, as he reported, he had a "swinging" mama. (Harry F. Harlow, "The Nature of Love," *American Psychologist*, 1958, 13, 673-685, and "Nature of Love—Simplified," *American Psychologist*, 1970, 25, 161-168).

LSD-25 Dextro-lysergic acid diethylamide. A psychotomimetic drug or **hallucinogen**, about 400 times more potent than **mescaline**. A dose of 100 micrograms lasting for 10 hours, causes hyperexcitability and rambling speech. Some "trips" last as long as 48 hours. Existing psychotic conditions may be intensified by the drug and depressed people may be brought to suicide. It may also result in mania and aggressive psychopathic behavior. Because of its unpredictable nature the U.S. Food and Drug Administration has severely limited manufacture and use of LSD, even for medical research, and classified it as a narcotic. Those caught using it are subject to legal penalties similar to those dealt to users of **opium** derivatives. Slang parlance: acid, the chief, big D, hawk, sugar, mind-benders, and trips. *See* **drugs.**

LSD was discovered in 1943 by Albert Hoffman (born 1906), a Swiss chemist; the discovery was not published until 1947. Introduced into America in 1950 by German-American psychiatrist Max Rinkel (born 1894). Up to about 1950, LSD had been used only therapeutically in treating disturbed and/or schizophrenic persons. Then, apparently as a result of Aldous Huxley's vivid descriptions of his hallucinatory experiences (described in *Doors of Perception*, 1954), while experimenting with a related drug mescaline, plus the lectures and articles by two psychology professors at Harvard— Timothy Leary and Richard Alpert—the college and high school student craze for LSD from about 1955 through the 1960's took hold, and so-called "wild trips" began.

LTM-STM theories (long-term memory-short-term memory theories)

lumen (lm) The SI unit of *luminous flux* (the rate of transmission of luminous energy), equal to the luminous flux emitted in a unit solid angle of 1 steradian by a uniform point source with an intensity of 1 **candela**. *See* **International System of Units.**

Term coined in 1891 by André Eugene Blondel (1863-1938), French engineer and physicist, specializing in studies on electricity, and founder of oscillographic techniques.

Luminal (Winthrop tradename for **phenobarbital**). Slang: barbie doll.

luminance A physical measure expressing the quality (-ance) of brightness (lumin-) on a surface that is radiating or reflecting light. Luminance is described in **candelas** per square meter, 1 cd/m^2 giving about the same light as a standard candle. Luminance is also expressed as foot **lambert**, which is 3.426cd/m^2.

luminosity The condition (-ity) of being luminous or bright. The perceived brightness of any visual stimulus. In psychophysics, the ratio of light to heat in radiant energy (or luminous efficiency).

luminous flux The flow (flux) of bright (luminous) light. That part of the *radiant flux* (the electromagnetic radiation streaming out from a source), visible to the unaided eye, as viewed from directly overhead. The luminous flux of the standard light source, under such conditions, is one **lumen** per *steradian* (the solid angle subtended by 1 m^2 of the surface of a sphere of 1 meter in radius). The *luminous intensity* of the standard source of light, therefore, is one **candela**. The lumen is the unit of light flux. A lux is equal to one lumen per square meter. *See* **International System of Units.**

luminous intensity *See* **candela.**

Luria (Luriya), Aleksandr Romanovich (born 1902) A leading Russian psychologist and physician. Graduated University of Kazan 1921, and First Moscow Medical School (M.D. 1936) and Dr. of Science (psychology). Head of neuropsychology at University of Moscow. His point of view about psychology is broad. He emphasizes that, despite his physiologically oriented research and his psychoanalytic readings, he nevertheless remains "withal a psychologist." Nor does he claim to be a behaviorist in his approach to various problems.

Least of all is he interested in deducing "the laws of higher activity from simple neurodynamical processes." He does not believe that complex problems of human behavior "can be solved by the laws of the dynamics of tendency nor by the analysis of the **conditional reflex** connections playing a role in the nervous system; the solution of this problem will be attained only by a careful description of the specific systems of behavior produced in the process of the social historical development. . . ." *See* **tremorgraph.** (A. R. Luria, *The Nature of Human Conflicts*, New York: Washington Square Press, 1967, from The Liveright edition, 1932).

luteinizing hormone (LH) Also called interstitial cell stimulating hormone (ICSH). A hormone, deriving from the anterior pituitary gland, that stimulates production of sex hormones, particularly the estrogens from the **corpus luteum** of the ovaries and androgens from the interstitial cells of the testes. LH also instigates the release of the ovum from the mature ovarian follicle, causing the follicle to change into the corpus luteum. *See* **follicle stimulating hormone.**

lux A unit of illumination or light (lux) that is equal to one **lumen** per square meter.

LVFW *Low Voltage Fast Wave. See* **sleep stages.**

lycée The third cycle program of studies in French universities, coming after the **licence** and consisting of certificates of advanced studies (first year after the *licence*) and the **doctorat de specialité** (third cycle doctorate granted two years after the *licence* and presentation of a satisfactory thesis); a French college (*lycée*) that grants bachelors' degrees. *See* **French higher education.**

lycée agrégation An examination held at the end of the *lycée* period, marking the end of introductory research. *See* **French higher education.**

lysergic acid *See* **LSD-25.**

lysine A crystalline amino-acid (-ine) obtained by hydrolysis (lys-) from many proteins (as from blood) and by synthesis; essential in nutrition of man and the lower animals.

Described (1889) by Swiss chemist Edmund Drechsel (1843-1897).

lytic Relating to (-ic) the loosening of (lyt-) or the remission of fever, particularly by an autonomolytic drug or antonomic inhibiting agent. A *lytic cocktail* is a mixture of two or more active synergic drugs in reduced amounts that complement and potentiate each other's effects upon target organs and reduce their total toxicity, such as is given to counteract the negative effects of **methadone.** *See* Synanon.

Coined (1950-51) by French surgeon Henri Laborit (born 1914) and French anesthesiologist Pierre Huguenard (born 1921). American physicians Vincent P. Dole and Marie Nyswander were the originators of the lytic cocktail, as reported by them in 1965. (Dole, V. P. and M. Nyswander: A medical treatment for diacetylmorphine (heroin) addiction. A clinical trial with methadone hydrochloride. *JAMA*, 193 (No. 8), 80-84, 1965.)

M

M micron; mean.
M.A. mental age.

Mach, Ernst (1838-1916) Austrian physicist and philosopher. His philosophy generally followed that of Comte's early positivism, but he also tended to agree with **Hume** in believing that correlation is only concomitance. Mach reduced all the **data** of physics and psychology, including space and time, to the immediate data of their observation or sensation, thus pointing to present-day logical positivism. He advanced the idea that the scientist must use the simplest means available in arriving at his results and should exclude all metaphysical thinking on any data not perceived by the senses. Any *a priori* assumptions should be rejected. His work directly influenced **Kulpe** and **Titchener** and **K. Pearson** indirectly (Boring, p. 393). Mach developed many instruments, the two following having been used in psychological research.

Mach bands (Mach rings). A visual phenomenon of contours (resulting from retinal inhibition) in which an observer perceives a narrow bright band on the lighter side of the boundary between two areas of markedly different light intensities, and a narrow darker band on the other side. (F. Ratliff, *Mach Bands: Quantitative Studies on Neural Networks in the Retina*, 1965).

Mach rotation frame. A large rectangular frame that is pivoted at the top and bottom on a vertical axis, with the subject's chair mounted at one end in a smaller frame, and in which the chair may be tilted. Devised by Mach in 1875, for the perceptual study of bodily movement.

machine language A lower level programming language in which the programmer must consider the actual machine structure of the **computer** used. In contrast, the higher level language, such as **FORTRAN** or **COBOL** is essentially independent of the machine. An **assembly language** is dependent upon the machine and therefore it is a machine language. Machine language is also interpreted as the set of symbols, characters, signs and the rules for combining them, which conveys instructions or information to be processed.

macrocephaly (megalencephaly) The condition (-y) of having an exceptionally large (macr-) head (-cephal-) and **brain** in both size and weight due partially to proliferation of **glia.** Severe **mental retardation,** convulsions, headaches and impaired vision are common.

macula A little (-ula) spot or stain (mac-), referring to various anatomical sensory structures, particularly of the ears and eyes. The *maculae acusticae* (consisting of the macula sacculi and the macula utriculi) are small areas of sensory hair cells, **otoliths,** and gelatinous material inside the inner ear sacs; associated with perception of equilibrium. The *macula lutea* (yellow spot), is the small central retinal area, containing mainly retinal **rods** where maximum visual acuity occurs.

In 1668, French scientist Edme Mariotte (1620-1684), was first to describe macula lutea but it was later better described and named in 1791 by German anatomist Soemmering, and recorded between 1795-98.

Maddox rod test A transparent cylindrical glass rod, or one of a parallel series of such rods mounted on a disk, used for diagnosing eye muscular imbalance or latent **strabismus.**

Ernest Edmund Maddox (1860-1933). Scottish ophthalmologist. Performed research on relation between eye accommodation and convergence, developing the Maddox rod test as well as inventing various other devices for eye operations.

Magendie, François (1783-1855) French physiologist. Pioneer in French experimental physiology; demonstrated spinal nerves' functions. Introduced **morphine** into medical practice. Showed first (1824) specific but crude evidence of the role of the **cerebellum** in equilibration. His pioneer work on the **cerebrospinal fluid** (a term he introduced) in 1825 has been the spark for all future research in this area. He credited **Cotugno** with making prior discoveries about the fluid. *See* **acromegaly, Bell, James-Lange theory of emotion.**

magnetic flux *See* **weber.**

magnetic tape (Comput.) A magnetic metal or plastic coated strip that can store information.

Magnus, Rudolf (1873-1927) German physician and physiologist. Experimented on equilibration reflexes and the effect of drugs on the nervous system.

maieutic Relating to (-ic) being a midwife (maieut-) or nursing one along, as practiced by **Socrates** in his dialectical method of helping a student clarify his ideas.

maintenance synergy *See* **synergy.**

major affective disorders *See* **affective psychoses.**

Malacarne, Michele V. G. (1744-1816) Italian comparative anatomist and surgeon. Made contributions to knowledge of **cretinism,** and published (1776) the first book devoted completely to the **cerebellum.** Introduced term pyramid as applied to the area of the **brain.**

Malebranche, Nicolas de (1638-1715) French metaphysician, follower of **Descartes.** He said that the mind cannot have knowledge of anything external to itself except through its relation to God. Even more than Descartes, Malebranche stressed the duality of mind and body, to the extent that any interaction was completely impossible. His thorough understanding of Descartes' mechanistic "reflex response" and belief in the physiological basis of emotion may be considered as antedating the **James-Lange theory of emotion.** *See* Locke, Berkeley.

malleus (or hammer) The first of three hinged ear bones that together transmit vibrations from the eardrum to the **oval window** of the cochlea. The "handle" of the malleus attaches to the inner surface of the **tympanic membrane,** and the "head" attaches to the **incus,** which, in turn, attaches to the **stapes.**

Fallopius credits Berengarius (Jacopo Berenger) (1480-1550), Italian physician as first to describe this bone, although it is usually attributed to Alessandro Achellini (1463-1512), Italian anatomist who, in his book, *Corporis Humane Anatomia* (1503 and later in 1516), noted and described the incus, malleus, and **labyrinth.** It was not until 1543, however, that **Vesalius** named the malleus as well as the incus.

Malpighi, Marcello (1628-1694) Italian physician, anatomist and microscopist. Made many explorations of tissue with the microscope and was first to publish a microscopic study of the **cerebral cortex.** He discovered the capillaries in 1661. *See* **corpus luteum.**

mammillary body Old name for **olfactory** bulb.

manic-depressive illness (manic-depressive psychosis) A psychotic complex of mental illnesses characterized by severe mood changes varying from frenzy (mania) to deep depression, with a tendency to remission and recurrence. There are three major subtypes: the *manic episode* (with flight of ideas, irritability, nervous chatter, elation, and increased motor activity); the *depressed episode* (with a marked depressed mood accompanied by mental and **motor** retardation with occasional stupor); and the *circular episode* (in which an attack of both a depressed and a manic episode occur). Considered by many authorities to be **functional** in origin. The classic alternating form of this psychosis is rarely seen: when such diagnosis is made it is often given as *manic-depressive reaction, manic type* (where excited behavior predominates), or *depressive type* (where depression and self-accusation predominate). Sometimes called **cyclothymia** and **circular insanity.** *See* **affective reaction, lithium carbonate.**

There are indications that **Aretaeus** first described the condition, and that his ideas were incorporated into a description of the illness (1747) by French psychiatrist, André Piquer (1711-1772). Independently, two French psychiatrists, Jean P. Falret (1794-1870) in 1851 (*la folie circulaire*) and **Jules Baillarger** in 1854 described the condition in modern concepts. The term was coined as manic-depressive insanity in 1898 by **Kraepelin.**

manifest content of dreams In **Freudian** theory, the remembered superficial or verbalized content of a dream, (such as the characters and their actions), as distinguished from the inferred, emotionally painful **latent content.** *See* **dream content.**

manipulandum That which is manipulated. A response-detecting mechanism in **operant conditioning** experiments that the subject must manipulate to obtain reinforcement. In social psychology, the stimulus condition systematically controlled and varied by the experimenter.

man-machine interface *See* **interface.**

Mann-Whitney test for two independent variables A test that uses the actual ranks of the various observations directly as a device for testing **hypotheses** about the identity of two **population** distributions. Used as an alternative to the *t* test for equality of means. Any probability statements refer directly to all possible randomizations of the same sample of *N* subjects among the various treatments. The test assumes that the underlying **criterion** variable is continuously distributed.

Henry Berthold Mann. Born 1905, Austria; naturalized American (1938) mathematician.

m

Ph.D., Vienna 1935. Specialized in number theory, group theory, and mathematical statistics.

Hasler Whitney. Born 1907; American mathematician, Ph.D., Yale 1928. Research and publication on basic mathematical theory and statistics.

manoptoscope A truncated cardboard cone adjusted by hand (man-) to view (-scope) and measure eye (-opto-) dominance.

mantissa (*See* **logarithm**.)

manual aphasia Disorder (-ia) of not (a-) being able to form words (-phas-) with the hands (manual). Difficulty in writing language. *See* **agraphia**.

MAO Monoamine oxidase.

mapping of brain *See* **cerebral cortex, homunculus, topographic mapping**.

marasmus Wasting away, withering. Progressive emaciation, usually in the infant, resulting from faulty nutrition or metabolic disorders. In psychology, the term refers to psychological deprivation characterized by negativism, apathy, refusal to suck, depression, **autism, anorexia**, constipation, decrease in reflex responses and muscle tonus, and regressive tendencies. Attributed to emotionally disturbed or unresponsive mothers who do not give their children sufficient tactual, kinesthetic, or auditory stimulation.

Word used by both **Aristotle** and **Galen**, and came into English usage during the 17th century.

marathon group therapy An extension of **group therapy** into a longer period of time (sometimes around-the-clock without sleeping until exhaustion sets in, but usually for 24 hours or over a weekend with short periods of sleep), and always with the same members of the group. The leader is usually a neutral behind-the-scenes "director"; sometimes, however, he takes a very active part in the involvement.

Marbe's law In word association tests, the speed of an association is related to or is a function of the frequency of occurrence.

Karl Marbe (1869-1951), German philosopher and psychologist.

Marie's disease *See* **acromegaly**.

marijuana (Mexican-Spanish mariguana or maraguango—any intoxicating substance. Translated often as Mary Jane or Mary John and thought of as an aphrodisiac.) A plant that grows wild in many parts of Mexico and throughout the southwestern part of the United States, as well as in the Eastern countries (where it is called **hashish**, ganga, or manzoul). The flowering resinous tops of the female plant contain the highest concentration of THC (tetrahydrocannabinol), which is believed to be the active ingredient in marijuana; the leaves have a smaller amount, while the stalks and seeds have little or none. The tops of the potent **canabis sativa** plant are collected for making hashish, as it is known in America.

Psychological effects of marijuana are variable. They may include visual, auditory, and temporal distortions. **Illusions** are often reported, but **hallucinations** and **delusions** are rare. Unfounded suspicion is not unusual, which may be accompanied by anxiety reactions and irritability. Generally, the feeling is one of passive euphoria or "high," with the tendency to withdraw after a while and become reflective and contemplative. Uncontrollable laughter or crying may occur in users inclined toward hysterical reactions.

Marijuana is not considered addicting (no physical craving), but it is habituating in that chronic users become dependent upon it for its psychological effects. There are no withdrawal symptoms. Most marijuana smokers do not progress to stronger substances, but there exists the danger of "graduating" to **heroin**. Slang terms: Acapulco-gold, M.J., pot. As a cigarette it is known as a "reefer" or "joint"; unrolled it is "grass." A butt is called roach, grass, tea, boo, weed, hemp, muggles, mary jane. Compare **bhang, hashish, cannabis**. *See* **drug addiction**.

mark sensing A method for detecting specially placed marks on a **computer** card, the marks being automatically translated into punched holes.

marriage and family relations For information relating to marriage problems and for reference to ethical counselors, contact the following: *Mental Research Institute*, 55 Middlefield Road, Palo Alto, California 94301; *American Association of Marriage Counselors, Inc.*, 3603 Lemman Avenue, Room 104, Dallas, Texas 75219.

Marsalid Tradename for a **psychic energizer**.

masking Tending to conceal or diminish the influence of something. In *psychophysics*, masking occurs when a higher intensity tone makes a lower tone inaudible, or one strong odor dominates another. In monaural listening experiments, with talking and wide-band noise occurring simultaneously, the masking effect makes the hearing of ordinary speech sounds extremely difficult. The masking effect tends to disappear, however, when the same noise is presented binaurally. Masking or concealing of figures is also a common phenomenon in human perception of form (usually achieved by removing portions of contour in a particular figure). In **computer** work, masking takes place when a group of characters is extracted from a computer **word**.

Maslow, Abraham H. (1908-1970) American (New York) psychologist. Ph.D., Wisconsin 1934. Theorist on mental health, mainly of the normal **personality**. Developed theories of motivation. *See* **self-actualization; needs, hierarchy of; Goldstein** (also Bischof, pp. 638-51; Maddi, pp. 80-88, Vinacke, p. 248; *Abraham H. Maslow, A Memorial Volume*, Brooks/Cole, 1972).

masochism Masoch condition (-ism). The perversion that the Austrian novelist Leopold von Sacher-Masoch (1836-1895) experienced, and also described in some of his novels. Sexual (erotic) gratification from suffering pain or in being beaten, whipped, or tortured by a loved one; a tendency to enjoy being a martyr.

Richard von Krafft-Ebing created the term in 1893, which soon replaced the word **algolagnia** for such gratification.

mass A property of matter in the body under consideration. The U.S. standard of mass is a standard **kilogram**, which is a platinum-iridium cylinder approximating 39 mm. in both height and diameter. The pound mass equals 0.45359237 kilograms.

mass action Movement of the organism as a whole. G. E. **Coghill** held that behavior of an organism begins as **individuation**, dependent on mass action of the nervous system rather than on individual parts, and that specific reflexes develop from diffuse responses (a theory developed from his work with salamanders). K. S. **Lashley** concluded (from maze-learning in rats with varying amounts of cortical **ablation**) that learning takes place not through specific cortical connections but by functioning of the **cortex** as a whole; that mass action in the cortex is indicated because learning seems affected (in rats) not by what cortical tissue is removed, but by how much is left. *See* **cephalocaudal sequence**.

The term was first used by Coghill in 1929, and the concept was emphasized by Lashley in the same year.

massed practice Learning **motor** skills or memorizing verbal material by repeated, uninterrupted practice over a relatively long period. Many experimenters have studied the value of this method as opposed to **distributed practice**. For most tasks, massed practice does not seem to be as effective as distributed, except possibly for learning mathematics.

MAT Miller Analogies Test.

Matched Pairs Signed Rank Test (*See* Table 27.)

matching An experimental method of control by which subjects under differing conditions are rendered similar on some **variable** other than the **independent variable**.

Mateson multistimulus olfactometer An odorant-mixing **olfactometer** designed to yield "information about and control of temperature, pressure, and humidity of the odorivector (odorant vapor)," to handle any odorant, and to perform liminal and supraliminal "work with pure chemicals and odorant mixtures" (Brown, p. 201-202; J. F. Mateson, "Olfactometry: Its Techniques and Apparatus," *Journal of the Air Pollution Control Association*, 1955, 5, 167-170).

After J. F. Mateson, American physiologist.

matrix (Comput. and math.) A rectangular array of numbers, such as

$$\begin{pmatrix} 1 & 2 & 3 \\ 4 & 5 & 6 \end{pmatrix}, \begin{pmatrix} 1 \\ 0 \\ 1 \end{pmatrix}, \text{ and } \begin{pmatrix} 8 & -8 \\ 0 & 2 \end{pmatrix},$$

which are subject to mathematical operations (addition, subtraction, etc.) and matrix algebraic laws; also, any statistical or mathematical table; a grid chart. In **computer** terminology, an array or logic network of circuit elements (**diodes**, relays, etc.) which serve a specific function (such as converting from one system to another).

Matteucci, Carlo (1811-1868) Italian physicist and electrophysiologist. In 1838 and 1843 he tetanized muscle by establishing difference of potential existing between a nerve and its damaged muscle. Made many studies on **animal electricity** with electric fishes.

maturation Act of (-tion) ripening (matura-). A genetically determined process that controls growth and development of the individual within the physiological limits of the species or organism. Anatomical, physiological, and neurological development of the organism, independent of changes that occur because of special experiences and training. For example, maturation in the nervous system and muscles enables an infant to sit up; he is not taught to sit. *See* **Coghill**.

Maurolyco (Maurolycus), Francesco (1494-1575) Italian geometer and physician, the first (1560) to describe the condition of **hypermetropia** and **myopia**.

maximin principle In **game theory**, a **saddle-point** in which a competitor achieves the *max*imum of the *min*imum rewards.

Maxwell triangle (chromaticity diagram; color triangle) A triangular diagram (for testing the chromatic aspects of **perception** as related to daylight adaptation) in which the apexes of the triangle represent the **primary colors**. Also, the base of the **color pyramid**, showing certain color relationships.

After James Clerk Maxwell (1831-1879), Scottish physicist.

maze A problem-solving device commonly used in the study of animal (rat) learning, in which the subject must select a correct path among numerous blind alleys in order to move from the start to the final goal. Its difficulty can be varied by increasing the alleys or changing the overall pattern of the maze. *See* **Porteus maze test**.

In 1901, Willard S. Small (1870-1943) published the second part of his doctoral dissertation that he had begun in 1898 at Clark University, revealing for the first time the use of a maze for animal intelligence studies. Small's small maze was inspired by the original maze at Hampton Court in England. (Willard S. Small. "An Experimental Study of the Mental Processes of the Rat," *American Journal of Psychology*, 1899, 11, 133-165; 1901, 12, 206-239).

McClelland, David Clarence Born 1917, New York. Ph.D. (psychology), Yale 1941. Studies in **motivation, personality**, and the achieving society. *See* **affective-arousal theory, need for achievement** (also Maddi, pp. 127-133, 304-316, 417-434).

McClung's hormone *See* **sex chromosome.**

McDougall, William (1871-1938) English psychologist. At first, physiological and experimental in interest, later a social psychologist. Called his purposive approach to mental life "hormism" (from Gr. *borme*, a goal). Held that individual and group behavior is determined by instinctual drives and that there are two overall impulses: (1) the self-regarding, and (2) the self-denying. Definitely opposed to **mechanism** and **behaviorism** (*see* Boring, pp. 465-67, 496-7; Vinacke, p. 288).

MD Mental deficiency; manic-depressive.

M.D., m.d Mean deviation; (capitals only) mean deviation in class intervals.

Md, Mdn Median; C_{50}.

mean A measure of **central tendency**, the most common one being the **arithmetic mean.** The words "average" or "mean" when used without specification usually refer to the arithmetic mean. *See* **median, mode, geometric mean.**

mean deviation Same as **average deviation.**

meaninglessness *See* **alienation.**

mean square The sum of the squares of the differences between the observations and the **arithmetic mean** divided by N (the number of observations). The root mean square is the square root of the **variance.**

measurement A refined form of classification in which **numbers** are assigned to certain traits, characteristics, or events according to certain rules. The most familiar scales of measurement are: **nominal, ordinal, interval,** and **ratio.**

In marketing research, measurements are pieces of information used for determining the value in comparison to the cost of obtaining information. Another approach to measurement is through *semiotics* (or the theory of signs), which embraces three fields of investigation: (l) *syntactics*, relationship among signs; (2) *semantics*, relationship between signs and objects; and (3) *pragmatics* relationship between signs and the users of signs (Green and Tull, 1966, pp. 184-190).

measurement synergy *See* **synergy.**

measure of central tendency *See* **central tendency.**

measure of dispersion (measure of variation) Any **descriptive statistic** that represents the scattering of a set of values in a **frequency distribution.** Examples are **range, variance,** and **standard deviation.**

measure of response A quantitative index of response strength, such as **amplitude, latency, probability,** and rate of response.

measure of variation Same as **measure of dispersion.**

mechanical aptitude test A specialized **performance test** in which the successful completion of certain skills by the testee is presumably predictive of comprehension and manipulation of mechanical devices on an actual job situation.

mechanical comprehension test A paper and pencil test consisting of diagrams, pictures, or other schemata setting up theoretical problems, which are given to a subject who must use his previous knowledge, training, or experience in solving the problems presented. It is concerned not with performance itself but with comprehension of the principles involved and the procedures used in solving problems.

The Bennett mechanical comprehension test (MCT) is one of the most widely used tests of mechanical comprehension. It is designed to measure one's practical **perception** and comprehension of the relationships between physical forces and mechanical factors.

mechanism In psychology or psychoanalysis, usually a mental mechanism (**rationalization, projection, identification,** etc.), which **Freud** constructed for his mental mechanistic theories. A mental mechanism supposedly determines behavior and operates unconsciously while the individual "defends" his self-respect and pride as he meets temporarily insurmountable obstacles.

Mecholyl Tradename for **methacholine.**

meconium *See* **mekonion.**

med. median.

médecin des asiles In France, a position equivalent to psychiatrist-in-chief at most American hospitals or to the **médecin des hôpitaux,** who may also serve as a professor at the **Faculté de Médecine.** *See* **French higher education.**

médecin (chirurgien) des hôpitaux The highest rank obtainable by a French physician requiring an appointment by the Assistance Publique, through a **concours** as well as passing a written and oral examination in clinical and academic areas, only after having achieved a high degree of personal and academic distinction. In actuality, he is a physician in chief of a service in a municipal hospital, having no rank in a university (such as professor) although he may have attained higher world recognition. For example, **Babinski** was *chef de clinique* of **Charcot** at the Salpetriere but never achieved rank of **professeur agrégé** or *medecin des hopitaux.* *See* **French higher education.**

medial geniculate body Slight enlargement (a nucleus) on the lateral surface of the **thalamus,** functioning as the final relay station through which inner ear impulses are relayed to the auditory cortex and other auditory centers, such as the **lateral lemniscus.** *See* **lateral geniculate body.**

medial lemniscus *See* **lemniscus.**

medial (or mesial) plane Pertaining to (-al) the midline (medi- or mesi-) of the body. In bilaterally symmetrical animals that plane located at right angles to the **dextrosinistral axis,** dividing the body into right and left halves. Distinguished from the **sagittal plane,** and opposed to **lateral.**

median That which is in the middle (from medianus). A measure of **central tendency** that locates the middle value in a series or in a **frequency distribution;** the point on a scale that divides the series, arranged in order of magnitude, into two equal parts coinciding with the 50th percentile (2nd quartile).

median effective dose (ED-50) The dose dividing the **population** into two equal groups. A dose may be a certain measurable amount of electricity, medicine, or a drug; for example, one at which 50 percent of the subjects fail to avoid a painful electric shock.

median lethal dose (LD-50) The dose at which 50 percent of the subjects die following drug administration.

mediate To be (-ate) in the middle (medi-). To serve as an intermediary, or to be between two events, ideas, or **data.** For example, two auditory nerves mediate to the auditory brain centers the sound waves received by the inner ear receptors.

mediated generalization Deriving a conclusion about two stimuli by the use of language, although their physical similarities are not apparent. For example, making a generalization that a tree and a fly are alike because they are both alive.

medulla Any soft marrow-like (medulla) substance, especially in the center of a part. Chronologically, it has meant substance of the brain (1651), its hindmost part (1676), a nerve's medullary sheath (1839) and in 1878 it was defined as the inner portion of an organ (as in the medulla of the spinal cord, or of the **adrenal gland,** or of the kidney), as differentiated from the **cortex.** It has been used synonymously with bone marrow, the spinal cord, and the **medulla oblongata.**

medulla oblongata The oblong or bulbous end of the spinal cord that protrudes into the **brain,** about an inch long, cylindrical or coneshaped. It is sometimes called the vital center of the brain, for it contains the autonomic centers concerned with heartbeat, respiration, blood pressure, and circulation. It also contains the nuclei of many of the **cranial nerves.**

In **Willis'** time (1664), the area referred to all "the deep white matter, the ventricles, the basal ganglia and thalami of the cerebral hemispheres, and the three parts of the brainstem" (Clarke and O'Malley, p. 582). In some classifications, considered as synonymous with **brainstem,** while in others it is a part of the brainstem.

Term introduced in 1740 by the German anatomist and surgeon Lorenz Heister (1683-1758).

medullary sheath *See* **myelin sheath.**

megabit One million **bits.**

megalencephaly *See* **macrocephaly.**

megalomania A type of **delusion** or mania in which the individual believes himself to be great (megalo-); the insanity of self-exaltation. The delusions of grandeur or omnipotence seen in manic and paranoid reactions, such as believing oneself to be God.

meiosis Condition (-osis) of lessening or reducing (mei-); the process in cell (nuclear) division whereby the chromosomal number is reduced to half the original number before the cell divides in two. Meiosis starts with two successive divisions of the diploid cell which differs from mitosis in that the chromosomes are duplicated only once (since the daughter cells are **haploid**).

Hippocrates described the reduction of fever as meiosis; then it became an "abatement of symptoms," finally assuming its present meaning as a result of the German biologist August Weismann's (1834-1914) work on genetics and evolution.

Meissner's corpuscles (tactile corpuscles) Small elliptical bodies found in the connective tissue papillae of the hairless portions of the skin. They contain encapsulated, specialized nerve endings believed to be receptors for pressure or touch.

After George Meissner (1829-1905), German physiologist.

mekonion (Gr., little poppy). Meconium. First fecal excrement of a new-born child. *See* **opium.**

mel Substitution of M (1000) for the b in bel. A mel is a subjective unit of pitch, perceived as being equal to 1/1000 of a tonal pitch having a standard tone of 1000 cycles per second.

melancholia (From Hippocratic Greek medicine), a disorder (-ia) of black (melan-) bile (-chol-) or biliousness, resulting in a deep **depression.** A mental condition marked by apathy, indifference, and depression, regarded chiefly as one of the phases of **manic-depressive psychosis.**

Galen's usage approximated its present meaning.

Melanchthon (Philipp Melanchthon Schwarzert) German scholar and religious reformer. *See* **psychology.**

melanin Any of various dark brown or black (melan-) pigments (-in), especially referring to those obtained through enzymatic action of **tyrosine** or **dopa,** and that may be found in hair or skin.

The term was first applied (1843) to the dark fluid in the ink bag of cephalopods by the Italian naturalist Giuseppe Vizio (1790-1851).

melatonin A chemical substance (-in) producing a black (mela-) or serious tone (-ton-) or tension. A **pineal gland** hormone inhibiting output of gonadal sex hormones, such a black and saddened condition probably being the inspiration for its coinage. *See* **HIOMT.**

memory Musing, brooding, or remembering. Memory applies to the process of remembering as well as to the contents or material remembered and held in storage for recall. In **computer** work, interchangeable with storage; a device or any assemblage of devices designed for **input** of information (usually binary-coded), its storage, and subsequent extraction. Holding information in **machine language** in electrical or magnetic form. *See* **computer operation.**

m

In Greek mythology, the mother of the Muses was Mnemosyne, the goddess of memory.

memory drum A rotating cylinder used in rote-learning experiments to present uniformly one set of verbal materials (such as **nonsense syllables**) at a time. The items to be memorized are exposed for a predetermined time on the revolving drum as successive items pass by a window or slot on a screen. Each syllable is usually announced before it appears.

Devised in 1894 by **G. E. Müller** (1850-1934), and Friedrich Schumann (1863-1940), German psychologists, and apparently first used by **Ebbinghaus** in the same year.

memory span The greatest amount of material (usually six to eight digits or letters when presented orally) that can be repeated accurately after a single presentation.

memory systems See **long-term memory, short-term memory.**

memory trace A hypothetical construct of that which is remembered, or that which a learning experience indelibilizes in the nervous system. Gestaltists say that the trace is subject to constant change and reorganization. See **engram, mneme, short-term memory.**

Mendel, Gregor See **gamete.**

meninges (plural of **meninx**) Membrane. The three distinct layers of tissues (the **dura mater, arachnoid membrane,** and **pia mater**) that envelop the **brain** and the spinal cord.

Hippocrates used the word for the membranes covering the brain, and **Erasistratus** used it to describe the membranes covering both the brain and spinal cord.

mental age (MA) The age appropriate to an individual on the basis of scores achieved or passed on a Binet type of **intelligence test** and determined by the degree of difficulty of the test items passed. It is one's intellectual accomplishment compared to a group's standard of performance of the same chronological age, with scores converted to a scale unit. Originally proposed by **Binet.** For example, a child who scores at the age norm of 10 on the **Stanford-Binet Test,** has a mental age of 10, regardless of his chronological age. Because of the developmental curve's characteristics, special corrections must be made to the mental age after the chronological age of 15.

mental deficiency See **mental retardation.**

mental disorders, classification of See **classification of mental disorders.**

mental hygiene The science concerned with the maintenance of mental health and the prevention of neuroses, psychoses, and mental illness in general. For specific information concerning mental health, contact any of the following groups: *American Mental Health Foundation,* 2 East 86th Street, New York, N.Y. 10028; *Mental Health Materials Center, Inc.,* 104 East 25th Street, New York, N.Y. 10010; *National Association for Mental Health, Inc.,* 10 Columbus Circle, New York, N.Y. 10019; *National Clearinghouse for Mental Health Information,* 5454 Wisconsin Avenue, Chevy Chase, Md. 20203; *National Institute of Mental Health,* Bethesda, Md. 20014; and *Neurotics Anonymous International Liaison, Inc.,* 1341 G Street N.W., Washington, D.C. 20005.

mentally subnormal Descriptive of a person whose intelligence is below that usually considered necessary for ordinary schooling, but with some chance for improvement indicated. Those with varying degrees of workable intelligence are classified as: the *educable* (with an IQ of about 50-70); and the *trainable* (at least 6 years of age with IQ's ranging from about 30-55). Generally, those with an IQ below about 30 are deemed not trainable and may have to be institutionalized. However, any such classification routinely causes reaction from academicians, teachers,

and parents. Despite much opposition to classifications, they still linger on if only to provide convenient coat hangers for budgetary cloaks.

mental retardation (mental deficiency) Mental retardation, as defined by the *American Association on Mental Deficiency* in 1960, is "sub-average general intellectual functioning which originated during the developmental period and is associated with impairment in adaptive behavior" (pertaining to maturation, learning, and social adjustment). The *American Psychiatric Association* has adopted the content of this definition in its 1968 revision of psychiatric terms, and has also developed a classification, presented here in a somewhat modified form:

Borderline	(IQ 68-83, can live independently and make living on minor skill jobs)
Mild	(IQ 52-67, fair degree of independent living, with some supervision and guidance)
Moderate	(IQ 36-51, semi-independent, self-care and partial financial support)
Severe	(IQ 20-35, capable of some self-help with complete supervision)
Profound	(IQ below 20, requires custodial care)
Unspecified	(Clearly subnormal but difficult to diagnose)

Where possible the above classifications should be qualified if the condition is associated with or has resulted from any of the following:

a. Cerebral damage caused by intracranial infections, serums, drugs, or toxic agents (such as from congenital syphilis or rubella, toxemia of pregnancy, lead, arsenic)

b. Trauma (pre- and postnatal injury, strokes, radiation, birth asphyxia, etc.)

c. Disorders of metabolism, growth or nutrition (**cretinism, Tay-Sach's disease, phenylketonuria, galactosemia**, etc.)

d. Gross brain disease (**epiloia,** neoplasms, etc.)

e. Conditions of unknown prenatal influence (**hydrocephalus, hypertelorism, macrocephaly,** etc.)

f. Chromosomal abnormality (trisomy 21, **Down's disease,** etc.) See **trisome.**

g. Prematurity (birth weight of less than 5.5 pounds and/or gestational age of less than 38 weeks, not classifiable otherwise)

h. A major psychiatric disorder

i. Psycho-social deprivation (no organic disease but with a hisotry of mental retardation in at least one parent and one or more siblings or evidence of early deprivation of normal environmental stimulation)

j. Intoxication (**alcoholism,** lead poisoning)

For further information, contact the *American Association on Mental Deficiency,* 5201 Connecticut Ave., N.W., Washington, D.C. 20015, and National Association for Retarded Children, 386 Park Avenue South, New York, N.Y. See **cat cry syndrome.**

As of January 17, 1970, the **American Psychological Association** adopted as a position statement their article "Psychology and Mental Retardation" (published on pp. 267-268 in the *American Psychologist,* March, 1970), which although not specifically defining mental retardation refers to the condition as "primarily a psycho-social and psychoeducational problem—a deficit in adaptation to the demands and expectations of society evidenced by the individual's relative difficulty in learning, problem solving, adapting to new situations, and abstract thinking."

This article represents an all-out move on the part of the APA "for a concentrated psychological approach to the problem of retardation." It suggests that at least one contribution psychologists might make in this

field would be to work "toward classifying those of below average capacity in ways differing from the traditionally stigmatizing influence of the label 'deficient,' 'defective,' or 'retardate." It has been demonstrated frequently that with the appropriate application of psychological principles of learning and rehabilitation, a significant percentage of those now called 'retarded' can become active, productive members of society, not considered a special 'out' group."

mental set Readiness of the individual to organize his **perceptions** and **cognitions** in a set manner, such inclinations being transient or persistent, which reflect the emotions, physiological conditions, and experiences of the individual.

meperidine (*methyl* pi*peridine*) A narcotic compound used in its hydrochloride form as an analgesic, sedative, and anti-spasmodic.

meprobamate Contrived from *me*thyl + *pro*pyl + dicar*bamate* (**Miltown,** Wallace tradename; Equanil, Wyeth tradename). A tranquilizer or depressant that acts on the **central nervous system,** used to relieve anxiety and tension; also for medical treatment of skeletal muscle spasm. See **drugs.**

The drug was synthesized in 1954 by American chemist Dr. Frank M. Berger of Wallace Laboratories, Milltown, New Jersey and introduced by Berger as Miltown.

Merkwelt (Ger., perception-world.) The way the world is seen, not necessarily the way it is. See *Eigenwelt, Mitwelt,* and *Umwelt.*

mesaticephalic See **cephalic index.**

mescaline (peyote) An alkaloid (-ine), structurally resembling the **catecholamines,** found in peyote (mescal), obtained from Mexcalli, native Mexican intoxicating drink distilled from *Lophophora williamsii,* the North American small, spineless dumpling cactus. Used medically as a **stimulant** and antispasmodic. An oral dose of 5 mgm per kilogram weight of the average person causes anxiety, tremors, vivid hallucinations (psychedelic lighting effects, constantly shifting animals and people, and distorted perceptions of space and color), and other varying symptoms. Usually, the person retains awareness and reportedly gains insight during the "trip" of about 12 hours. Its effects are similar to minute doses of LSD. Experimentally, mescaline has been used to investigate **schizophrenia** (particularly cataleptic conditions) and other hallucinatory experiences, and in inducing regressive behavior (read *Doors of Perception* 1954, by Aldous Huxley [1894-1963] for vivid description of its effects). Slang: cactus, buttons.

For celebrations, or just for the effects of hallucinations and ecstasy, indians of Mexico have eaten peyote "mescal buttons" (from the cactus, anhalonium) and drunk agave or maguey cactus stew for many centuries. The active principle was isolated in 1894 by A. Heffter, and was studied in 1895 for its hallucinogenic states for first time by American chemists D. W. Prentiss and F. P. Morgan. Its structure was determined and synthesized in 1919 by German-American organic chemist E. Späth (1860-1924?).

mesencephalon Mid (mes-) brain (-encephalon). One of the three embryological divisions of the **brain** lying below the inferior surface of the **cerebrum** and above the **pons,** and lying midway between and connecting the **prosencephalon** (forebrain) and **rhombencephalon** (hindbrain). It consists mainly of white matter (primarily myelinated axons). The ventral portion consists of the cerebral peduncles (tracts constituting the main connection between forebrain and hindbrain) while the dorsal part is formed of the **corpora quadrigemina** concerned with visual and auditory reflex centers. Cerebellar and cortical frontal lobe fibers end in the **red nucleus,** and the **rubrospinal tract.** Two main areas of the mesencephalon are the **tectum** or "roof" and a lower portion, the **tegmentum.**

m

The functions of the midbrain relate to sensations and postural changes (via the projection tracts) and to pupillary reflexes and eye movements (mediated by the **oculomotor** and **trochlear** cranial nerves). It is an important relay station and center for vision and hearing as well as for much of the **reticular formation.**

The word mesencephalon was suggested in 1807 by French physician Francois Chaussier (1746-1828) but it was not published until 1846.

mesial *See* **medial (or mesial) plane.**

mesmerism Originally a doctrine (created by Friedrich Anton Mesmer (1734-1815), Austrian-Swiss physician) that attempted to reconcile the old ideas of astrology with the then new discoveries in electricity and magnetism. Mesmer borrowed the term **animal magnetism** (first proposed in 1666 by **Valentine Greatrakes**) to describe his method of utilizing diffused fluids from the heavenly bodies, which supposedly acted upon one's nervous system. At first, he used metal plates and bath salts in conjunction with stroking the patients with magnets in order to achieve his striking effects. Later, however, he added hypnotism as an extra fillip. His successful use of hypnosis in reducing neurotic symptoms came to be called "mesmerism." But when his séances in Paris were investigated by a commission of physicians and scientists, he was denounced as a charlatan, and the use of hypnosis remained under a cloud for years because of its association with Mesmer.

Mesmer's memoirs on *Animal Magnetism* were published in 1779.

mesocephalic *See* **cephalic index.**

mesoderm The middle (meso-) skin (-derm) or layer (developing between the **ectoderm** and **endoderm**) of the growing **zygote**, which gives rise to the bone marrow, blood vessels, muscles, skeleton, generative glands, and kidneys. *See* **mesomorph.**

mesokurtosis The type of **kurtosis** in which the curve is considered normal or medium (meso-) without too much or too little peakedness (kurtosis).

mesomorph Shape (-morph) derived from the middle (meso-) embryonic layer or **mesoderm.** The **body type** (physique) characterized by prominent musculature and heavy bones. According to **Sheldon,** the mesomorph is highly correlated with **somatotonia** (or a temperament that is outgoing, aggressive, and relatively insensitive to people's feelings). *See* **somatotype theory.**

messenger-RNA (mRNA) The **ribonucleic acid** molecule (genetic code) that travels from the nuclear **deoxyribonucleic acid** molecules to the cell cytoplasmic **ribosomes,** where its pattern is formed for **transfer RNA.** In protein production, the mRNA activates the manufacture of specific kinds of proteins. Apparently, each **amino acid** sequence is specified by a different **gene,** this encoded information being directly transcribed into a messenger RNA according to base-pairing rules (**guanine** with **cytosine, adenine** with **thymine** of DNA or uracil of RNA, etc.).

metabolic or nutritional dysfunction disorders Brain damage resulting from vitamin or endocrine deficiency or malfunction.

metabolism Process (-ism) of change (metabol-). The sum of the positive and negative chemical and physicochemical activities in an organism, including the complex process of food utilization and all the energy changes implicit in **anabolism** (building up) and **catabolism** (tearing down). Metabolic disorders are apparently at the root of **cretinism** and **phenylketonuria.**

Earliest studies on metabolism were made by Italian physician, Sanctorio Sanctorius (1561-1636), who is credited with founding physiology of metabolism in 1615. Term coined in 1878.

metamerism Condition (-ism) of having parts (-mer-) come with or together (meta-). In color psychology, the property exhibited by a *metameric pair* (two stimuli having the same color but different spectral composition); a greater difference in spectral composition between the two colors indicates a higher degree of metamerism. Metamerism also has special meanings in biology and chemistry.

metamphetamine hydrochloride (Tradename: **Methedrine**) A sympathomimetic cerebral **stimulant** and appetite retardant. Decreases sense of fatigue. At first, produces manic-like state of **euphoria** in which the person may not sleep for days, but then irritability, depression, and exhaustion follow. Sleep helps, but hospital care is needed when **hallucinations** and schizoid behavior develop. Prolonged overdose is the only known method of stimulating schizophrenia through a drug-induced state. Slang: crystals, speed, greenies. *See* **drugs.**

metaphase The phase or stage of **mitosis** in which the chromosomes split, preceding the **anaphase** and coming after (meta-) the **prophase.**

metaphysics Subject matter that comes after (meta-) physics (referring to ontology and cosmology, since these subjects followed physics in **Aristotle's** list of books), therefore concerned with the study of being (ontology) and the nature of the universe (cosmology). *See* **redintegration.**

metapsychology Psychology that speculates on the associations between (meta-) mental and physical processes or on the role of the mind in the universe; that which goes to the core of a problem or to the basis of man and his universe. That which is beyond consciousness or psychology, such as in Freud's use of the word in writing to his friend Wilhelm Fliess: "I am going to ask you seriously whether I should use the term metapsychology for my psychology which leads me beyond consciousness," and also in his first use of the term on Feb. 13, 1896, in a letter to Fliess in which he said "I am continually occupied with psychology—it is really metapsychology." (*The Origins of Psychoanalysis: Letters to Wilhelm Fliess,* by Sigmund Freud, New York, N.Y., *Basic Books, Inc.,* pp. 157, 246).

metencephalon (hindbrain) The after (met-) brain (-encephalon). The anterior portion of the **rhombencephalon** from which rise the isthmus, **pons,** and **cerebellum.** Distinguished from **myelencephalon,** which is the posterior portion of the rhombenecephalon.

In 1871, Thomas Henry Huxley (1825-1895), English naturalist and surgeon, descriptively divided the rhombencephalon into metencephalon and myelencephalon.

meter (m) The fundamental **SI** unit of length, equal to a length $1,650,763.73$ times the wavelength, in vacuum, of the orange-red radiation emitted by the pure krypton isotope of mass 86 (atom), when excited in an electric discharge. Measurement of the meter is made by an *interferometer,* a sensitive instrument for measuring length by means of light waves. The meter is equivalent to 39.37 U.S. inches. The square meter (m^2) is the SI unit of area; the cubic meter (m^3) is the SI unit of volume. *See* **International System of Units.**

metestrus *See* **estrus.**

methacholine (Tradename: Mecholyl) A **parasympathomimetic** drug administered in its crystalline form as acetyl-β-methyl-choline or **acetylcholine.** Upon injection there is a drop in systolic blood pressure occurring probably only in those in an emotional state.

A favorable sign for prognosis in **schizophrenia** is for chills to develop after methacholine injection, as well as anxiety produced only by Mecholyl with small or decreased blood pressure. Increased blood pressure is an unfavorable prognostic sign.

Methacholine chloride was introduced in 1932 by American chemist Randolph Thomas Major, born 1901.

methadone Meth(yl) a(mino) d(iphenyl) (heptan)one. An analgesic drug synthesized in Germany and brought to United States after World War II. Pharmacological properties are qualitatively similar to those of **morphine,** but it blocks action of heroin, morphine, or other opiate drugs. The abstinence syndrome following methadone withdrawal is similar but less severe than in morphine withdrawal. It may have dangerous after-effects when administered to those addicted to **barbiturates.** It is of value in the therapy of morphine withdrawal, usually given in the form of a "cocktail."

The cocktail consists of methadone dissolved in a glass of orange juice given once a day. Usually, counseling is given along with the cocktail. Use of methadone is designed to substitute a lesser evil, methadone, for the greater one, heroin and morphine. However, methadone is no "cure," actually being as necessary to take for the addict as insulin is for the diabetic.

Discovered by American researchers Marie Nyswander and Vincent Dole (born 1913) of Rockefeller Institute.

Methedrine (The Burroughs Wellcome tradename for **metamphetamine hydrochloride**) Slang: crystals, speed. A "meth monster" demonstrates bizarre and uncontrollable behavior resulting from Methedrine abuse.

methodists A philosophical group organized about 50 B.C. by Themison (123-43 B.C.), a physician and former student of **Asclepiades;** opposed to **humoral doctrine of diseases** and Empirics. To these physician-philosophers, disease resulted from relaxation, constriction of the pores, or both. Treatment involved application of relaxing agents or constricting ones, depending upon need. *See* **empiricism.**

method of approximation An operant conditioning approach in which desired performance is encouraged by reinforcing those responses approximating the correct performance, in other words, reinforcing a good try. *See* **shaping of behavior.**

method of limits A method of **just noticeable differences** (or threshold measurement) in which an attempt is made to determine how small a difference (in a **stimulus,** for example) can be discriminated by a subject. A series of stimuli may be presented on a magnitude scale until the instructed observer's response changes.

methods of psychology In the various fields of psychology, many methods are used for establishing facts but the distinctions between them are primarily in purpose rather than approach. Psychological methods may overlap the categories listed here or in others not mentioned.

1. *Clinical.* Any technique, within ethical limits, which a professional psychologist uses to gain a better understanding of human behavior may be considered within the scope of clinical methods, such as: (*a*) *autobiographical method;* (*b*) *case-history method;* (*c*) the *clinical interview* (including **depth interviews, counseling,** and **psychotherapy**); (*d*) the *interview* (job interview, personal survey interview, etc.); (*e*) the *testing method;* and (*f*) one that might be included under all categories, the *existential confrontation,* which is more an attitude than a method.

2. *Experimental.* A method that reflects the scientific attitude. The scientist, in setting up an experiment, tries to maintain the following: experimental and control groups, repeatability of the experiment, limitation of the variables that may affect results, and an understanding of the limitations imposed upon the experiment and the experimenter. Some specific aids to the experimental procedure are listed under the following psychophysical methods.

m

3. *Psychophysical.* (*a*) *Adjustment* or *average error*: The average difference obtained between separate judgments by an observer who is required to adjust a variable stimulus until it appears to be equal to a standard or constant stimulus. (*b*) *Paired comparisons* (developed by **G. T. Fechner**): The subject judges which of each pair of presented stimuli is greater in some respect than the other pair. Used for rank order, equal intervals, etc. Another form of this method is constant stimuli, in which comparison stimuli are paired at random with a standard. The subject indicates whether differences exist from the standard. It is the method used to establish limens. (*c*) *Limits* (minimal change): As the experimenter varies the stimuli upward, downward, etc., the subject indicates relationship to a **criterion**. Used for determining thresholds and equality. (*d*) *Order of merit*: Subject places a presented group of stimuli into subjective rank order. Used to determine rank order in perceptions. (*e*) *Quantal*: Stated increments are added successively to a standard at various intervals. Subject indicates presence or absence of the increments. Used for difference limens. (*f*) *Rating scale*: Subject is "forced" to give each of a series of stimuli an absolute rating in terms of some quality. Used in determining rank order, in rating stimuli, etc.

Metrazol (Knoll tradename for pentylene-tetrazol; known in Europe as cardiazol). A synthetic compound that stimulates the cardiovascular and **central nervous systems**. When given in high dosage to animals it causes restlessness, excitement, increased **motor** activity, and **clonic** convulsions. A relatively non-toxic drug that has been used in the treatment of **schizophrenia, manic-depressive illness**, and other mental diseases, but because of the violent convulsions caused, it has been largely replaced by better controlled **electro-convulsive shock therapy**.

The Metrazol convulsive shock therapy was inaugurated by Lazlo Joseph Meduna (1896-1964), a Hungarian psychiatrist. His treatment was based on a report by two Czech physicians, Nyirö and Jablonzky, who found that "in cases of epilepsy combined with schizophrenia, the epileptic convulsions ceased or became rare." Meduna considered this to be evidence "of a biologic antagonism between the schizophrenic and the epileptic process" (Sahakian, p. 367).

Meynert, Theodore (1833-1892) German psychiatrist. A pioneer in the field of **cytoarchitectonics**. He also classified mental diseases and made the first detailed description of the **cerebral cortex**. In 1867-68, he divided the brain into the **neopallium** and the **archipallium** (both of which he named) and he also introduced (1872) the words "association" and "projection" in their modern neurological connotation.

miazine See **pyrimidine**.

microcephaly (microcephalia) Relating to (-y) a disorder (-ia) of an abnormally small (micro-) head (-cephal-) in which the cranium and **brain** fail to develop; associated with **mental retardation**. True microcephaly is probably caused by heredity (transmitted as a single autosomal recessive).

First described in 1473 by German pediatrician Bartholomaeus Metlinger (1422-1492), in a book on pediatrics.

microglia Small (micro-) glial (neuroglial) cells of the **central nervous system**

Discovered and named in 1921 by the Spanish neurologist Pio del Rio Hortega (1882-1945).

micron (M, mu) Something small (micron); the millionth part of a meter.

microsecond (Nsec.) One millionth of a second (10-6).

microspectrophotometer A spectrophotometer enabling the study of light transmitted by small (micro-) specimens (as in obtaining spectral-absorption of light through a single human retinal **cone** and computer-analyzing the energy transmitted).

midbrain See **mesencephalon**.

middle ear The tympanic cavity, fashioned out of the temporal bone, opening into the eustachian tube. It contains the three auditory ossicles (**malleus, incus, stapes**) that amplify and aid transmission of sound waves. The middle ear connects the tympanic membrane (eardrum) of the outer ear to the **oval window** of the **inner ear**.

Miescher, Johann Friedrich (1844-1895) Swiss biochemist. First (1869) to locate **deoxyribonucleic acid** in the cell nucleus. Discovered nuclein (1868) and named it (1869). Founder of cellular chemistry.

migraine A severe, paroxysmal headache usually occurring and recurring on one-half ([he] *mi*) of the head ([g] replacing c in *craine* or cranium); hemicrania. The "splitting" headaches are often accompanied by nausea and vomiting, followed by deep sleep. Causes are attributed to allergy, endocrine disturbances, cerebral edema, etc., any one of which may be the causative factor(s) in a person's attack, but definite causes have not been clinically affirmed.

Often found in women with a strong perfectionistic trend who fear being second best: may also have a demanding conscience. Emotional tension usually precipitates the conditions, often resulting from a showdown related to finances, social position, or some interpersonal conflict.

Descriptions of migraine were known at time of ancient Mesopotamia (c. 330 B.C.). Greek physician Soranus of Ephesus (fl. 2nd century) described the condition, as did **Aretaeus of Cappadocia** (Persia). **Galen's** term for it (*hemikranion*) was translated into hemicrania (1597), then becoming hemigranea, migranea, and migraine (French). In 1777, this "sick headache" was first adequately described by English physician John Fothergill (1712-1780).

milieu (Fr., environment) According to **Barker**, an "intricate complex of times, places, and things." See **behavior setting**.

milieu therepy An approach to the treatment of mental disorder whereby the home or the institution as a whole is made a therapeutic community, with every person (janitor, doctor, nurse, spouse, etc.) being made aware of the sensitive role he must play in the therapeutic process.

At a psychiatric hospital (Belmont, England), a *therapeutic community* was established and made famous by psychiatrist Maxwell Jones. Group meetings were held with as many as 100 patients and 25 staff present simultaneously, all attempting to work together in solving mutual problems (Bruno Bettelheim, "Closed Institutions for Children," *Bulletin of the Menninger Clinic*, 1948, **12**, 135-142; Bruno Bettelheim and Emmy Silvester, "Milieu Therapy," *The Psychoanalytic Review*, 1949, **36**, 54-68; M. Jones, The Concept of a Therapeutic Community, *American Journal of Psychiatry*, 1956, **112**, 647-650).

Mill, James (1773-1836) English historian, economist, and utilitarian philosopher. Father of **John Stuart Mill**. For James Mill, mental activity consisted of sensations and ideas; all consciousness, including volition and emotion, he explained by association of ideas. See **associationism, Brown** (also Boring, pp. 219-26).

Mill, John Stuart (1806-1873) English philosopher and economist. Son of **James Mill**. Sympathetic to the views of **Comte**. Developed laws governing the association of ideas, including **contiguity**, similarity, frequency, and intensity. He gave name of "mental chemistry" to the interaction of ideas making

up conscious states. Many of his psychological ideas were introduced into **Bain's** textbook, and these in turn were quoted by **James** in his *Principles of Psychology*, 1890 (Boring, pp. 227-33).

Miller, Neal Elgar Born, Wisconsin 1909. American psychologist. Ph.D., Yale 1935. Major fields of study: basic principles of learning, **motivation, personality** theory, conflict studies, clinical psychology, psychological mechanisms. In 1954, he received the **Warren Medal** for "his distinguished contributions to the scientific investigation of the relationships between learning and emotional behavior, leading to an increased understanding of the development and fixation of emotional attitudes." Recipient of the AAAS **Newcomb Cleveland Prize** in 1956 for "illuminating behavioral analysis of effects of direct electrical stimulation of the brain." Awarded **National Medal of Science** by President Johnson 1964. Recipient of **Distinguished Scientific Contribution Award**, 1959. Member **National Academy of Sciences**. President APA, 1960 (Vinacke, p. 237).

Miller analogies test A fairly widely used test for screening graduate students. Consists of 100 increasingly difficult verbal analogy items.

Devised by Wolford Stanton Miller, born, Indiana 1883. Ph.D., psychology, Indiana 1917. Specialized in mental tests for evaluating graduate students.

Miller-Mowrer shuttlebox In **avoidance learning**, a box with a grid floor through which electric shocks can be administered to the subject, usually a rat. The subject must learn to avoid the aversive stimulus on schedule, such as running to the opposite end of the box (where there is no shock) within, say, 5 seconds after the warning buzzer is sounded. See **Neal Elgar Miller, Orval H. Mowrer**.

millilambert One-thousandth (milli-) of a **lambert**. The most commonly used unit of **luminance**.

millimicron (mμ) Unit of length equal to one-thousandth (milli-) of a micron, or one-millionth of a millimeter, or one-billionth of a meter, or 10 angstroms; unit of length most frequently used with electromagnetic radiations to specify wavelength of visible radiant energy, extending from approximately 400 to 800 millimicrons. See **nano**.

milliphot One-thousandth (milli-) of a phot, or the unit of illuminance equal to one-thousandth of a **lumen** per square centimeter, or one-thousandth of a centimeter-candle.

millisecond (m sec.) One-thousandth of a second (10^{-3}).

Miltown Registered tradename for **meprobamate**. Name evolves from the town of Milltown, adjacent to the Wallace laboratories in New Jersey, where the drug was developed.

mimpathy (Ger., *Nachfühlen*: after (*nach*) feeling (*Fühlen*); after-experiencing. The type of sensation necessary for the novelist, the actor, or the historian in order to recreate the feeling-tone of the original incident (whether an historical event or a personal experience). It differs from **empathy** by being a re-creative act after the fact while empathy is a "feeling-in" with another person or an event at the time of its occurrence or the telling of an event. Neither empathy nor mimpathy implies any feeling of sympathy (involving sorrow, regret, or other strong emotional feelings of attachment).

minimax principle Minimizing risk; maximizing gain. A strategy in which the minimum number of procedures finds the maximum value of a function of one or more variables. In decision-making and **game theory**, a decision rule whereby an experimenter minimizes his maximum-expected loss over all possible true situations. *Minimax solution*: in a two-person **zero-sum game**, the best solution either player can achieve under the worst conditions created by the other.

Minnesota Multiphasic Personality Inventory (MMPI) An untimed psychodiagnostic test designed to detect abnormal patterns of behavior in older adolescents and adults.

Statements, printed on 3 x 5 cards, are limited to matters of "common knowledge." The items have been constructed entirely from clinical interviews. Subjects decide whether to answer "yes" or "no" (also "?" in individual form) to nearly 600 questions, and then place the card in the appropriate box provided.

Scores are assigned to a series of ten diagnostic categories, including: (l) **hypochondriasis** (Hs)—exaggerated anxiety about one's health, and pessimistic interpretations and exaggerations of minor symptoms; (2) **depression** (D)—feelings of pessimism, worthlessness, hopelessness; (3) **hysteria** (Hy)—various ailments, such as headaches and paralyses, without a physical basis; (4) psychopathic deviation (Pd)—antisocial and amoral conduct; (5) masculinity-feminity (Mf)—measure of masculine and feminine interests, especially a measure of feminine values and emotional expression in men; (6) **paranoia** (Pa)—extreme suspiciousness of other people's motives, frequently resulting in elaborate beliefs that certain people are plotting against one; (7) **psychasthenia** (Pt)—irrational thoughts that recur and/or strong compulsions to repeat seemingly meaningless acts; (8) **schizophrenia** (Sc)—withdrawal into a private world of one's own, often accompanied by **hallucinations** and bizarre behavior; (9) **hypomania** (Ma)—mild elation and excitement without any clear reason; and (10) social introversion (Si)—avoidance of other people and removal of oneself from social contacts.

Four other scores are obtained: the *Question* score, the *Lie* score, the *Validity* score, and the *K* score (a suppressor variable refining the discrimination of five of the clinical variables).

The patterns are based on psychiatric categories (depression, schizophrenia, etc.), with interpretation dependent upon interrelationships between categories and degree of variation from "normality." The major items covered by the inventory are, in frequency order: social attitudes; masculinity-feminity; political attitudes—toward law and order; morale; depressive characteristics; and delusions, hallucinations, etc. Although the inventory has been widely used, there are differences of opinion about its **validity**.

minty One of the seven primary qualities of the **stereochemical smell theory**.

mirror drawing (mirror tracing design) A skill test or experiment that requires the subject to trace a drawing (star or other figure) on a shielded board while viewing only the reflection of it and his drawing hand in a mirror. Often used to test eye-hand coordination, and the ability to reverse **responses** to visual cues (or to learn new sensorimotor coordination).

mirror writing A visual **motor** disturbance wherein a person writes script from right to left, which must be viewed in a mirror to be read normally. Such words as *retrography* and *palingraphia*, invented to lend supposed scientific dignity to the phenomenon, have not found favor.

mitochondrion A minute, folded, granular (-chondrion) thread-like (mito-) self-perpetuating **organelle** found in the cytoplasm of cells of animal and plant organisms. It functions in cellular metabolism, secretion, and respiration, creating biological energy (through reactions of oxidative phosphorylation) to help run the body. Its variable size and shape is bounded by a two-layered membrane. Mitochondria contain genetic material within a specific **deoxyribonucleic acid**, its inheritable makeup being independent of its nuclear system.

The mitochondrion has been studied for approximately a century, its similarity in form to bacteria being well recognized even before the invention of the electron microscope.

Functionally, its role as a "powerhouse" has been known since the late 1940's. *See* **biological transducing system, motor end plate.**

It was first observed by German histologist Richard Altmann (1852-1900) sometime between 1870-1880, and was further investigated (1902) by the German physician Carl Benda (1857-1933), who then coined the term in 1897. In 1914, the American histologist Margaret R. Lewis, with Warren Harmer Lewis, gave detailed description of mitochondria.

mitosis (nuclear division) Condition (-osis) of being like a thread (mit-). The process of cell division in which a cell doubles its number of **chromosomes** and then splits so that the newly formed cells contain the same number of chromosomes as the original one. The mitotic process occurs in five phases: *prophase* (in which DNA molecules coil up, causing chromosomes to shorten and thicken); *metaphase* (chromosomes line up along spindle fibers ready to split); *anaphase* (the **chromatids** of each chromosome separate from each other and form new chromosomes, twice as many as before mitosis began); *telophase* (new chromosomes start elongating and division of cytoplasm takes place); and *interphase* (the period between the telophase of one cell division and the prophase of the next).

In 1880, the term was introduced by German anatomist **Walther Flemming**, to describe changes in cell division. About 1884, German histologist, Eduard Adolf Strasburger (1844-1912), named and divided mitosis into 3 stages: prophase, metaphase, and anaphase.

Mitwelt (Ger., with-world). Being with the world; involved in the relationship of human beings in the world at large, with group meaning being influenced by one's own relationship with each and every one in the group. *See Eigenwelt, Merkwelt, Umwelt.*

mixed model An **experimental design** model in which the mixed **treatments** consist of some **fixed effects** and some **random effects**. *Mixed designs* are frequently used in psychological research; for example, in comparing group performance for a number of trials or a certain period of time and for comparison of test results between different groups.

mixed-motive game In decision-making or **game theory**, a game in which a competitor must choose between increasing his own immediate gain or increasing the overall gain of both players. His mixed motives relate to a decision as to whether he should be a competitor or a partner. In mixed strategy the competitor decides, in a pre-game plan, to choose a different course of action for each play.

mixed schedule (MIX) A combination of two or more simple **schedules of reinforcement**, programmed so that no cues are given as to which schedule is in effect at any given time but usually alternating at random.

MMPI Minnesota Multiphasic Personality Inventory.

mneme The basic principle indicating the capability of all living cells to remember; also the basic memory in the individual or race. A mnemic hypothesis, as proposed by Semon and **Ewald Hering**, stated that stimuli leave specific traces (**engrams**) on the protoplasm of the nerve cell and will produce a habit when regularly repeated.

Term introduced by Richard Semon (1859-1908), German naturalist.

mnemonic (device) system A memory aid, employing coding and decoding materials (a set of memorized symbols or an easy to remember sentence) used as a base for new stimuli and more effective memorization. For example, as a cue for remembering the cranial nerves in proper order: olfactory, optic, oculomotor, trochlear, trigeminal, abducens, facial, acoustic, glossopharyngeal, vagus, spinal accessory, and hypoglossal, try to recall the first letter of each nerve by resorting to the mnemonic device: On old Olympus' towering tops, a Finn and German viewed some hops. It is certainly easier to recall the more "meaningful" Olympian reference than each of the dissociated nerves in order. Loci experiments have demonstrated that the **experimental group** has recalled 2-7 times as much as the **control group**.

Cicero (106-43 B.C.) claimed in his handbook for orators, *De Oratore*, that the mnemonic "method of loci" originated with Simonides of Ceos (Greek poet of late sixth and early fifth centuries, B.C.). It seems that Simonides, while at a festive occasion, stepped outside for a few moments, and during his absence the roof caved in, mangling those inside beyond recognition. Simonides easily recognized the bodies by the places (loci) they were in, since he had total recall of the locations of all his friends before the disaster occurred.

Mo Mode.

modality Quality of (-ity) of being modal; manner (moda-) of perceiving. Any one of the principal senses (vision, audition, etc.). A group of **sensory** qualities with sometimes vague similarities or resemblances but generally classifiable under one of the main senses, as visual modalities, tactile modalities, etc.

The word was introduced into English in 1545, and had special meanings in logic (1628) and as used by **Kant** (1628). Helmholtz in 1878, used the word to define "a class of sensations connected by qualitative continua."

mode Generally, manner of appearance. *Musically*, the appearance of notes and intervals in a scale. *Statistically*, one of the three principal measures of **central tendency**. It is the most frequent value in a **frequency distribution**, or the **class interval** into which the greatest number of cases falls. If two separate values have the same maximum frequency, then the distribution is called **bimodal**.

mode of appearance The characteristic way in which a **sensory** phenomenon (such as visual sensation, including glow, bulk, volume, surface) is presented.

model A logical, mathematical, or mechanical miniature system that parallels some larger or more complex system. Models are used in simulation studies for predicting and comparing one system with another (such as comparing an electronic brain with the brain itself).

Psychology has borrowed the "model" concept in helping define, delimit, and express various problems in a more convenient and structured manner. Operations for an abstract model (e.g., an **attitude** change) are programmed as if for a computer. When certain information **bits** are relayed into the human psychological "machine," for example, only certain specific and predictable attitude changes can result. Some classes of models are: the *algoristic*, or descriptive, or deterministic type (involving certainty in outcome); *stochastic* or *probabilistic* (involving uncertainty in outcome); *predictive* or relative (for purposes of evaluating potential results); *normative* models or *gaming* models (for decision-making and development of strategies in which tentative guidelines can be devised and studied, such as in executive games with management and labor unions with various matrices describing the game and subsequent payoff); *linear programming* models (often used in operations research procedures for determining ratios and relative efficiency of one solution over another); congruity **models**, etc. *Stimulus-sampling* is a special example of use of the stochastic model, using a combination of set theory and probability theory. (E. L. Walker, 1968, pp. 124-134).

module A small (-ule) model (mod-). *See* **gate, AND-gate.**

Mo_E Empirical mode.

m

MOL Machine-Oriented Language.

molar Referring to (-ar) mass (mol-). In general, relating to something meaningful, connected, of the whole, or purposeful; often applied to situations, behaviors, objects of inquiry or research, etc.

Usually opposed to **molecular**. *Molar behavior* describes the larger units of behavior, such as **ego** functions, or the more abstract concepts such as the psychological over physiological analysis, etc. According to E. C. Tolman (1932), molar behavior is organized into meaningful sequences or patterns, described in terms of the ends it serves instead of detailed movement—for example, goal-seeking behavior.

molecular Referring to (-ar) a small (-cul-) mass (mol-). Limited, of a part, unconnected, special, and thus opposed to **molar**. An interest in only individual responses or certain special structural aspects of behavior, rather than goals, might be called a molecular approach. In physics and chemistry, refers to the molecule.

molecular model of memory A theory postulating that a **sensory** stimulus triggers an electrical impulse code to produce in turn a chemical agent, a specific **mRNA**, and then a protein, allowing for permanent memory recall through self-regeneration.

moment The descriptive constant of a **frequency distribution** that measures its average value, relative scatter of the observations, its symmetry, etc. It is the expectation (E) of different powers of the random variable, say X, and may be computed about any **arbitrary origin**. Actually, moments are a family of **descriptive statistics** and are closely related to the **mean** and the **standard deviation**. The first four moments about the **arithmetic mean** are:

$$m_1 = \frac{\Sigma(X - \overline{X})}{N} = \frac{\Sigma x}{N} = 0$$

$$m_2 = \frac{\Sigma(X - \overline{X})^2}{N} = \frac{\Sigma x^2}{N} = s^2$$

$$m_3 = \frac{\Sigma(X - \overline{X})^3}{N} = \frac{\Sigma x^3}{N}$$

$$m_4 = \frac{\Sigma(X - \overline{X})^4}{N} = \frac{\Sigma x^4}{N}$$

where $\overline{X}$ denotes the mean.

And the nth moment about the mean would be

$$m_n = \frac{\Sigma(X - \overline{X})^n}{N} = \frac{\Sigma x^n}{N}$$

A measure of **skewness** may be obtained from the second and third moments:

$$g_1 = \frac{m_3}{m_2\sqrt{m_2}}$$

A measure of **kurtosis** may be obtained from the second and fourth moments:

$$g_2 = \frac{m_4}{m_2^{\,2}} - 3$$

(Downie and Heath, p. 61; Ferguson, pp. 75-76).

monad A unit (-ad) of one (mon-). A term in philosophy and early physics and chemistry indicating specific, irreducible entities, each one serving a particular purpose.

For Giordano Bruno (1548-1600), Italian philosopher, a monad was a metaphysical entity. For **Leibniz**, the universe (reality) consists of a hierarchy of monads, or units of force ruled by the supreme monad (God), being an indestructible soul and power-source from whom all matter is derived. Monads, to Leibniz, lacked extension, shape, divisibility, and penetrability.

The term was introduced (1733) by Christian von Wolff (1679-1754).

Contemporary concepts, such as **Hull's** behavior sequence and **Lewin's field theory**, are in essence monadic units that conceive of the individual as so important that he can dictate general laws by his own behavior.

Monadic approach refers to the reaction of the individual organism to a single **stimulus** provided by the experimenter. *See* **act psychology, computer, psychophysical parallelism** (also R. R. Sears, "A Theoretical Framework for Personality and Social Behavior," *American Psychologist*, 1951, 6, 476-484).

mondo A procedure in Zen Buddhism in which a Zen master forces his students or monks to answer rapidly any question put to them. Spontaneity of response is emphasized, the aim being to lead the learner beyond the limits of ordinary conceptual thinking, which is usually logical and organized. *See* **free association, word association.**

mongolism A form of **mental retardation** genetic and congenital in nature. **Down's disease** is the preferred term. For further information check with: Inquiries Branch, Health Services and Mental Health Administration, Public Health Service, U.S. Department of Health, Education, and Welfare, Washington, D.C. 20420; Information Office, NINDB, National Institute of Health, Bethesda, Maryland 20014.

monism The **metaphysical** position that there is only one single principle or substance, which may be manifested as idealism, materialism, or neutralism (as in the neutral monism of **Spinoza**).

Berkeley held (1710) that nothing exists but mind (subjective idealistic monism), contrary to the materialistic monism of **Democritus** (only matter exists). *Contrasted with* **pluralism, dualism**.

Moniz, Egas (Antonio Caetano de Abren Freire) (1874-1955) Portuguese physician. Received Nobel prize in 1949. *See* **lobotomy.**

monoamine oxidase (MAO) An enzyme that attacks **biogenic amines**, particularly depleting **serotonin**; blockage of MAO by inhibitors potentiates the effects of the amines, resulting in mood enhancement. An antidepressant or psychic energizer. *See* **drug interactions.**

monocular cue A cue pertaining to (-ar) the use of one (mon-) eye (-ocul-). Any cue (e.g., aerial and **linear perspective, interposition,** relative size, light and shadow, movement) that enables a person with only one eye to perceive depth or distance. *See* **distance cues.**

Monod, Jacques Lucien Born Paris, France, 1910. Doctorate in Natural Science, Paris 1941. Nobel prize 1965. *See* **allosteric enzyme.**

monomania A mental disorder or mania of being obsessed with a single idea. *See* **hypomania.**

Monomania was coined by French psychiatrist Jean Esquirol (1772-1840) in 1823.

monosynaptic arc An arc involving a single (mono-) neural synapse. A simple two-neuron arc (or reflex pathway) usually consisting of one **sensory** neuron, one **motor** neuron, and a **synapse** between them, with no **interneurons** involved. It is likely, however, that more than one of each kind of neuron always functions in these arcs.

monosynaptic transmission Synaptic transmission in which nerve activity is relayed only once (mono-) from presynaptic to postsynaptic **neurons**. *Monosynaptic pathways* are found in sympathetic **ganglia** and in the stretch mechanisms of the spinal cord.

monozygotic Referring to (-ic) or developed from one (mono-) **zygote**; said of identical twins. Monozygotic twins are sometimes referred to as monozygotes.

Monte Carlo method A statistical procedure in which problems are solved by applying mathematical operations to random numbers; an empirical approach to studying the laws of chance under actual probability conditions,

such as at the gambling casinos at Monte Carlo, Reno, Las Vegas, etc. **Karl Pearson** himself used the facilities at Monte Carlo casinos to test out some of his statistical generalizations.

moral determinism *See* **determinism.**

Moreno, Jacob L. Rumanian-born (1892) American **psychiatrist** and group psychotherapist. M.D., Vienna 1917. Originated **psychodrama** form of **psychotherapy**. Moreno states that psychodrama is not based on **Aristotle's** concept of **catharsis** which dealt only with the depressive effect of tragedy on the actors playing such roles. He considers psychodrama to be a method of relating one person to others, making him an attracting or repelling force in a group.

Morgan's Canon A statement based on **Occam's razor** and **Leibniz'** concept of the "identity of indiscernibles," expressed in 1894 by C. Lloyd Morgan (1852-1936), English zoologist and comparative psychologist. Morgan's Canon, which combated anthropomorphic thinking about animal behavior, stated: "In no case is an interpretation to be interpreted in terms of higher psychological processes, if it can be fairly interpreted in terms of processes which stand lower in the scale of psychological evolution and development." Morgan strongly influenced **behaviorism**. *See* **law of parsimony** (also C. L. Morgan, *An Introduction to Comparative Psychology*, Walter Scott 1906, p. 59).

moron (*Moros* - stupid) The category of **feeblemindedness** now called mildly retarded. *See* **mental retardation.**

H. H. Goddard (*see* **Binet**) introduced the term "moron" in 1913, to mean a person of arrested intellectual development.

morpheme The smallest grammatical or linguistic unit (-eme) occurring either (1) in a free form (morph-), such as roughly in root words or nouns or (2) in a restricted form, such as in suffixes and prefixes; a combination of two or more phonemes. Often it is not possible to attach meaning to a morpheme.

The term was created by Beaudovin de Courtenay.

morphine A bitter crystalline, narcotic, habit-forming drug that is a 10-1 reduction of crude **opium**. *See* **heroin**. Slang: M, monkey, miss emma.

Extracted from opium in 1805 and isolated in 1806 by German pharmacologist Friedrich Wilhelm Adam Serturner (1784-1841) who named it after Morpheus, Roman God of sleep.

morphogenic method A method relating to (-ic) the normal development (-gen-) of man's form (morph-), particularly concerning the formation of his **personality**. *See* **idiographic, phenotype.**

morphology A study of (-ology) form or shape (morph-) in the biological and medical sense, particularly the overt physical structure of any part and the various factors that influence that form; the comparative structure and form of an individual; judging personality from physical appearance.

The term was invented by Johann Wolfgang von Goethe (1749-1832), German poet, in his *Zür Naturwissenschaft überhaupt, besonders zür Morphologie*, in 1830, but was not used in the zoological sense until about 1860.

mosaicism A rare condition (-ism) of **inborn error** in the division of an early embryonic cell, resulting in **nondisjunction** of chromosome #21, and producing eventually a daughter cell with 47 chromosomes. Afflicted persons sometimes are typically mongoloid with severe **mental retardation**, but others may appear normal. The condition is apparently related to maternal age, the risk being about fifty-five times as great for a mother 45 to 49 years of age to produce such a child than for one half her age.

Mosso, Angelo (1846-1910) Italian physiologist, especially known for his work on fatigue and blood circulation, showing in 1890 that toxic products in the blood cause fatigue resulting from muscular contraction. He invented a sphygomomanometer, ergograph, and balance, all at one time known by his name. The *Mosso balance*—a recording apparatus consisting of a variably inclined board upon which the subject lies while his different positions are noted and measurements made of the changes in his body's blood supply. The *Mosso ergograph*—an instrument for recording changes in the relative strength and movement of arm muscles resulting from repeatedly lifting a weight.

mother surrogate A substitute for a mother. More specifically, an object such as a wire or cloth model, devised and used by **Harlow** in his experiments on affectional responses in the infant monkey. *See* **love**.

motion parallax (movement parallax) Apparent (par-) change (-allax) in motion. A cue to depth of distance **perception**. It involves change in an object's apparent direction of movement in the visual field, resulting from a shift in the observer's position or as the point of view is shifted laterally. As the head moves, near objects appear to move across the field of vision faster than more distant objects.

motion perception Any perception in which visual factors (e.g., motion parallax and eye movements) produce or create motion that is apparent rather than actual, such as **apparent movement**, induced motion, and **autokinetic motion**.

motivation Act or process (-tion) of being moved (motiv-). That which provides an incentive for behavior; the operation of **drives**, inherent or acquired. Presumably all behavior is motivated, whether by **physiological needs**, such as hunger, by *psychological cultural needs*, such as the need for status in the community, or by **instinct**, with respect to goals (McDavid and Harari, pp. 42-75; Bischof, pp. 145-156, 456-463).

motivational conflict A conflict that arises in the individual because of inability to decide between two mutually attractive rival objects. *See* **approach approach conflict**.

motivational disposition The persistent and potential tendency of a diffused **motive** to become specific and aroused.

motivational research (MR) A market research program utilizing modified **projective techniques**. It has been carried out since World War II usually by or for advertising agencies, making studies on consumer motivation, selection of brand names, **attitudes** and opinions, etc. Its purpose is to unearth hidden or unexpressed motives as to why people buy or do not buy certain products. Generally, depth interview methods are used. **Word association** and sentence completion types of tests are also sometimes used.

motivational sequence A series of events (behavioral in nature) beginning with an observable **arousal** of a **motive**, and proceeding through goal-directed behavior to the goal itself. More specifically, there are four steps to this sequence: (*1*) the *antecedent condition*, either a need or a stimulus; (*2*) the *motive* or *drive*, as an energizer of behavior; (*3*) *instrumental behavior*, or the process involved leading to reduction of the drive; and (*4*) *drive-reduction* itself, achieved by reaching one's goal. The motivational sequence tends to be repeated upon a similar stimulus or need, and is thus cyclical in nature. (Richard C. Teevan and Barry D. Smith, *Motivation*, McGraw-Hill, 1967, pp. 1-18).

motive An inferred process (desire, need, drive, emotion) within a person that consciously or unconsciously propels him toward a specific value-oriented goal. A motive may be derived from a biological drive or established by learning, but it is not to be construed as synonymous with "cause."

Many attempts have been made to classify motives. One of the more elaborate ones is that of Murray (1938) but it fails to consider women's motives except by implication, since the study was limited to extensive tests and interviews only on young men. However, many of the motives he had described have achieved a prominent place in psychological terminology, such as **abasement**, **achievement**, **affiliation**, **aggression**, **deference**, **dominance**, **exhibition**, **play**, and **rejection**. There is much overlapping and confusion between the various terms (desire, want, need, drive, motive) that are used to try to describe the emotive dimensions of man.

motoneuron (Same as **motor** or **efferent** neuron). A **neuron** that transmits **nerve impulses** away from the **brain** or spinal cord.

motor Pertaining to (-or) movement (mot-) or to a structure or function concerned with muscle activity, or with the **response** of an organism to a **stimulus**. For example, motor (efferent) nerves are those that carry impulses away from the **central nervous system** to muscles and glands. *See* **Bell**.

motor agraphia (anorthographia) Disorder (-ia) of not (a-) being able to write (-graph-) because of **motor** incoordination.

motor aphasia Disorder (-ia) of having a complete or partial loss (a-) of ability for converting ideas into words (-phas-) because of **motor** handicap (probably due to left prefrontal **lobe** lesion(s) in the **brain**).

motor cortex The primary motor area of the **cerebral cortex** is the ascending precentral (pre-Rolandic) **gyrus**, the most posterior gyrus of the frontal lobe, which governs movement of the distal joints. The gyrus immediately anterior to it also contains motor neurons, which assist in activating muscle groups simultaneously. Motor centers control voluntary movements of skeletal muscles on opposite sides of the body. Direct stimulation of specific portions of the motor area can produce isolated body movements. Many **pyramidal** and **extrapyramidal** neurons originate here.

motor development Although motor development in babies is orderly, some infants reach each stage ahead of others while others are delayed in their development. The following figure presents various stages of motor development as determined in a study of 25 children.

Shirley, M. M., *The First Two Years: A Study of Twenty-five*. Vol II Intellectual Development. University of Minnesota Press, Minneapolis. © 1933 University of Minnesota.

In later studies the child shows ability at 18 months (to creep downstairs backward and to have good grasp); at 24 months (to walk stairs with one foot forward only and be able to run jerkily); at 30 months (to jump with both feet and stand on one foot for at least a second); and at 36 months (to walk stairs with alternating feet and tiptoe 3 yards).

motor dominance (cerebral dominance) The controlling influence of one **cerebral hemisphere** over another, shown in **motor** activity (preferential handedness in writing, throwing a ball, etc.).

motor end plate *See* **myoneural junction**.

motor incapacitation Ataxoid incoordination of striate muscular activity, referring usually to gross behavioral and **motor** changes. *See* **ataxia**.

motor (or skill) learning Acquisition of skills through coordinated sequence of movements involving primarily muscular action, as in learning to write, type, or swim.

motor neuron (motoneuron) An **efferent** neuron conducting neural impulses away from the **central nervous system** toward effectors (muscle and glands).

motor pathways One of the relatively complex neural pathways to skeletal muscles, classified as to their fibril location in the **medulla** and as to their influence on the lower **motoneurons** (as facilitatory and inhibitory tracts). Two major principles dictate the function of these pathways: convergence and the **final common path**.

motor primacy theory The concept that neuromuscular mechanisms for movement mature before the **sensory** mechanisms, and that their degree of maturation dictates their capability of responding to stimulation.

motor set The readiness of a subject to react in a predictable and specific manner upon presentation of an anticipated **stimulus**.

motor theory of thinking The process of thinking examined as a succession of implicit stimulus-response relations, that is, muscular **activity** occurs simultaneously with the thinking process. An opposing argument stresses that motor action is not essential for all thinking, since paralyzed people are not handicapped in thinking.

motor tract (pyramidal tract) Any **motor** **pathway** from the **brain** to the spinal cord.

motor unit A unified relation between a somatic motor neuron and the muscle cells in which its **axon** terminates. However, motor units may have one motor neuron and one muscle cell, or one motor neuron and hundreds of muscle cells (the fewer the number of muscle cells innervated the more precise are the muscle actions).

movement parallax *See* **motion parallax**.

movement perception *See* **motion perception**.

Mowrer, Orval Hobart Born, Missouri 1907. American psychologist. Ph.D., Johns Hopkins 1932. A learning theorist, and researcher in social and clinical psychology, and **personality**. President of APA 1953. *See* **behavior modification**, **integrity therapy**, neurotic paradox, **enuresis**, Miller-Mowrer shuttlebox (also Bischof, pp. 620-625; Vinacke, p. 552).

MP midpoint.

M.R.C.P. Member of the Royal Colleges of Physicians.

mRNA messenger RNA.

MS mean square, in the **analysis of variance**.

mu (μ) *See* **Greek alphabet**.

Müller, George Elias (1850-1934) German philosopher and psychophysicist. One of his studies in psychophysics (lifting weights) led to the development of **motor set** or immediate muscular reaction without intellectualization. He also helped develop the **memory drum**. According to Boring, Müller was second only to **Wundt** in the development of **experimental psychology**, and second only to **Fechner** as a psychophysicist. *See* **Ach**, **Müller-Schumann law**, **Müller-Urban method** (also Boring, pp. 371-9).

m

Müller, Johannes Peter (1801-1858) German physiologist and comparative anatomist. In his *Handbuch der Physiologie des Menschen*, 1838, he elaborated laws on the doctrine of **specific nerve energies**, proving Bell's contention that each nerve has its own specific sensory or motor function. From work on the problem of how nerve fibers code sensory experiences, he concluded that it was not how but which receptor or nerve was stimulated: ice that stimulates hot receptors feels hot. *See* **Bell** under **Bell-Magendie law.**

Müller-Lyer illusion A geometrical optical **illusion** of length or distance in which two equal lines are shown. However, at the ends one has arrowheads while the other has inverted arrows.

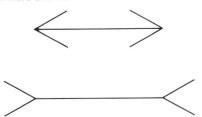

The perceptual distortion produced, in which the lines appear unequal (the enclosed line looks shorter while the one with inverted arrowheads looks longer), results in a **constant error** of estimating the length of the lines. The illusory effect diminishes with practice.

After Franz C. Müller-Lyer (1857-1916), German sociologist and philosopher, who described the illusion in 1896.

Müller-Schumann law Two items that have become associated through learning are difficult to dissociate and re-associate either item with another item.

After **G. E. Müller**, and Friedrich Schumann (1863-1940), German psychologist specializing in memory and visual space-perception.

Müller-Urban method A psychophysical procedure using the **constant stimulus method** to treat **data**. It purportedly accounts for sampling errors that may affect exact positions of data in a plotting diagram. *See* **least squares method.**

After **G. E. Müller** and F. M. Urban, German psychologists.

multimodal distribution A **distribution curve** containing several modes or humps, indicative of several classes or **class intervals** with high scores or great frequencies of observations.

multiple comparison test A test used for making comparisons among **means**. Usually, a distinction is made between **a priori** comparison, those made prior to an inspection of the **data**, and **a posteriori** comparison, those made after and possibly resulting from data inspection. A distinction is also made between **orthogonal comparisons**, which are independent of each other, and nonorthogonal ones. A simple *t* test or *F* test may be used for making certain orthogonal *a priori* comparisons, but these tests have limited value, since most comparisons of interest are not orthogonal. Various tests are available for making *a posteriori* comparisons, for example, the **Tukey** (defined only at its entry; Kirk, 1968, pp. 88-90), the **Duncan** (Table 23 and Kirk, 1968, pp. 93-94), the **Dunn test** (Table 22 and Kirk, 1968, pp. 94-95), and the **Dunnett comparison test** (Table 24 and Kirk, 1968, pp. 94-95).

multiple range test *See* Table 23.

multiple reinforcement schedule A compound learning schedule useful for analyzing behaviorally active drugs. It involves programming of a sequential arrangement of two or more simple schedules, alternating, usually at random, each being accompanied by a distinctive discriminative **stimulus** as long as the schedule remains in operation (Thompson and Schuster, pp. 153-157).

multiple personality A **dissociative reaction** to stress characterized by the person exhibiting two distinctly different aspects of himself, each aspect representative of and so considered by the observing public as a different personality. (The Dr. Jekyll-Mr. Hyde syn[1] drome, or the five distinct personalities as reported by Morton Prince about his patient Beauchamp.)

multiple response learning The process of acquiring response-sequences in learning to master a task (such as a specific skill).

multiple T maze A device for testing learning in laboratory animals. Usually consists of a series of interchangeable units, with junctions as well as one-way doors to prevent retracing in case of error. The pathways contain a number of blind alleys, which the animal learns to bypass as the shortest path to the reward. *See* **T maze.**

multiplex Many (multi-) networks (-plex); a multiplex system, relating to the transmission of multiple messages simultaneously over one circuit (e.g., telegraphy) or one channel (e.g., radio or television). Also, the process of transferring **data** from many low-transfer rate storage units to one high transfer rate device.

multipolar neuron A **neuron** with two or more dendrites and an **axon** arising from the **cell body**.

multivariate analysis The statistical analysis of **data** consisting of n-triples (pairs, triples, etc.) of observations, that is, the simultaneous analysis of data for two or more **dependent variables.** A *multivariate distribution* consists of data in which more than two measurements are taken for each individual.

Multivariate sampling-distribution theory had its origin in an article published in 1928 by U. Wishart. *See* **discriminant function.**

Munsell, Albert H. (1858-1918) American painter. Developed a color system in which color changes are based on their appearance. All **hues** appear equally spaced around a circle similar to a **color wheel.** The value of his lightness scale is compared to an axle through the wheel, while the saturation (which he labeled "chroma") compares to spokes radiating out from the axle to the rim. Reflected colors are determined by comparison with samples (varying independently in hue, saturation, and **brightness**). *See* **color-vision theories: Hecht's theory.**

Munsell book notation Munsell hue, value, and chroma of a color estimated by interpolation of and extrapolation from the color scales of the *Munsell Book of Color. See Webster's Third New International Dictionary, Unabridged*, 1965, pp. 447-449, including plates.

Munsell chroma Expression of the degree of departure of an object color from the nearest grey color on arbitrary scales defined in terms of its Y value (luminous reflectance, or luminous transmittance) and its chromaticity coordinates.

Munsell color system *See* Munsell, Albert H.

Munsell hue Correlate of **hue** on arbitrary scales defined in terms of Y value (luminous reflectance, or luminous transmittance) and chromaticity coordinates.

Munsell renotation Munsell **hue**, value, and chroma of an object color obtained by reference to the definition of the "ideal" Munsell system.

Munsell value Expression of the luminous reflectance, or transmittance, of an object on an arbitrary scale giving approximately uniform perceptual steps under usual conditions of observation; correlate of lightness.

Munsterberg, Hugo (1863-1916) German-born American psychologist. Received Ph.D. Leipzig 1885, and M.D., Heidelberg 1887. Often called "father of applied psychology." Stressed importance of values and social applications of psychology. APA President 1898. *See* **applied psychology** under **fields of psychology.**

Murphy, Gardner (1895-1971), American psychologist. Ph.D., Columbia 1923. Fields of interest: social, history, and parapsychology. *See* **Comte, conflict, need, neuron doctrine.**

Murray, Henry A. Born, New York 1893. Received M.D., Columbia 1919, and Ph.D. in biochemistry, 1927 from Cambridge, England. Influenced in 1920's by **Jung's** writings, he spent time with him in Zürich, resulting in changing his interests from medicine to **psychology** and **psychoanalysis.** Developed a motivational **personality** theory in which a person's **needs** may be positive or negative, **psychogenic** or **viscerogenic.** Received **Legion of Merit** (for assessment procedures and research for OSS during World War II) and also the **DSC Award** 1961. (Bischof, pp. 140-174; Maddi, pp. 38-44; Vinacke, p. 449).

muscarin(e) An alkaloid isolated from *amanita muscaria*, the brilliant red and white-dotted poisonous fly agaric (mushroom). It has been used extensively as a drug to activate the **parasympathetic nervous system** in animals and, as a **cholinergic** receptor, to demonstrate its action on smooth muscles and glands. Apparently it has no effect on autonomic ganglion cells. However, when ingested it produces marked salivation and sweating, abdominal spasms, blurred vision, and bradycardia. *See* **nicotinic receptor.**

In 1869, German physical-chemist Hermann Franz Moritz Kopp (1817-1892), and German pharmacologist Oswald Schmiedeberg (1838-1921), isolated a poison from the fungus "agaricus muscarius" (fly-like appearance = musca), which they named muscarine.

muscle spindle A **proprioceptive** sensory end organ located in striated muscle fibers richly supplied by **afferent** nerve endings, enclosed by a capsule of connective tissue. Such spindles are necessary for postural and stretch reflexes.

Term introduced in 1863 by German physiologist Wilhelm (Willy) Kühne (1837-1900).

muscle tone (tonus) A healthy condition of continual slight contraction or tension in a muscle that keeps it ready to respond instantaneously. Good tone is essential for maintaining posture. Muscles below normal in tone are called *flaccid*, those with exaggerated tone *spastic.*

music therapy The application of music for therapeutic means, with patients playing instruments and/or listening to music so as to gain emotional release and aid in self-development, ego building, and group participation.

For information concerning music therapy, contact: *National Association for Music Therapy*, P.O. Box 610, Lawrence, Kansas 66044.

musky One of the seven primary qualities of the **stereochemical smell theory.**

mutual contingency interaction A mutually dyadic interaction in which each person contributes to and responds to the other's actions and reactions.

myelencephalon (medulla) The brain (-encephalon) marrow (myel-). The posterior portion of the **rhombencephalon**, which connects the spinal cord to the **brain.** Believed to control breathing, blood pressure, and heartbeat.

myelin sheath (medullary sheath) Myelin: marrow. A white fatlike sheath covering white nerve fibers. Its formation (called myelination), some of which takes place after birth, supposedly is the result of secretion by the **glial** cells and the **neurilemma.** Myelinated or medullated nerve fibers are numerous in the white matter of the **brain** and spinal cord.

Rudolf Virchow (1821-1902), German anatomist, gave the name "myelin" to a fatty substance obtainable from various animal tissues.

myelinogenetic studies *See* Flechsig.

m

mylar tape A plastic tape made of polyvinyl chloride (PVC) or polyethylene terephthalate, characterized by flexibility, resistance to stretching and tearing, and immunity to humidity variations.

myofibril Muscle (myo-) fibril. The threadlike bundle within the muscle cell that is the contractile structure of the cell.

myogram A graphic record (-gram) of the velocity and intensity of muscular (myo-) contractions.

myograph A photographic or other type of graphic device (using levers and a **kymograph,** for example) for recording muscle (myo-) contraction and push or pull type forces. Myographs are either *isotonic* (which measure contractions against a relatively minor external resistance) or *isometric* (which measure contractions against a strong resistance).

myoneural junction (motor end plate, neuromyal junction) Relating to a (-al) neuromuscular or muscle- (myo-) nerve (-neur-) junction. The area of contact between the ending of each **motor** nerve cell (or nerve fiber) and each striate muscle cell (or muscle fiber) where muscle fiber sarcoplasm bulges forth as a small mound. The muscle cells supply the receptive material and the nerve cells add a transmission material, both of which are mediated by a material neither nerve nor muscle at the junction. There are numerous **mitochondria** and many sensory nerve endings in the skeletal muscles. *See* **curare.**

myopia Closed (my-) eye disorder (-opia). A symptom of straining to see objects in the distance. A disorder in which the light rays entering the eye are focused too near the lens (that is, in front of the retina) as a result of the lens being too thick or the eyeball too long from the front to the back. Nearsightedness, shortsightedness. *See* **hypermetropia, presbyopia.**

myxedema A condition of swelling (-edema) and excess phlegm or mucus (myx-). **Hypothyroidism** of adolescents (juvenile myxedema) and adults, marked by a dry, waxlike edema of the skin, loss of hair, labored speech, slowing of pulse rate, low basal metabolic rate, apathy, dulling of mental activity, and typically the abundant showing of nasal mucus or phlegm.

The condition was first described in 1873 by English physician Sir William Withey Gull (1816-1890), and it was named in 1878 by London surgeon William Miller Ord (1834-1902). **Horsley** in 1884 demonstrated that myxedema, as well as **cretinism,** resulted from thyroid deficiency. *See* **anorexia nervosa** (also W. M. Ord, "On Myxedema," *Medical Chirurigical Transactions,* 1878, 61, 57-78).

N

N number.

n number of instances in a subclass.

nAch need for achievement.

Nachfuhlen (Ger., after feeling), translated as **mimpathy**; mimicking feeling after it has happened.

nalline (Tradename: Nalorphine). A crystalline powder used for nullifying respiratory depression and other effects due to narcotic addiction, and for the diagnosis of addiction as well as checking to see if a "former" addict has resorted to **heroin** again (which would be symptomatized by pupillary changes). Nalline resembles **morphine** in its effects by producing analgesia, depression of spinal reflex activity, and lowering of body temperature. As used for the diagnosis of addiction to morphine or **methadone,** for example, nalline is administered subcutaneously, which is then followed by typical withdrawal symptoms: profuse perspiration, nausea, gastrointestinal disturbances, pupil dilation, excessively deep and rapid respiration, and horripilation. Nalline effects (pupil contraction, eyelid ptosis, slurred speech, and slow breathing) indicate that the patient is not an opiate addict; he is given methadone if other symptoms of withdrawal are present. Large doses of morphine are incapable of nullifying the effects of even small doses of nalline, indicating that nalline has chemical superiority over morphine in competing for the receptor sites involved.

Nalorphine Tradename for **nalline.**

NAND gate *See* **gate.**

nano A rapidly becoming standard prefix replacing millimicron for all physical measures, designating one-billionth (10^{-9}). *See* **nanometer,** table of prefixes, p. 166.

nanometer The billionth (nano) part of a meter.

Napierian system of logarithms *See* **computer, Lacroix, logarithm.**

narcissism Condition (-ism) like that of Narcissus. Self-love and preoccupation with oneself and one's own concerns. In psychoanalytic theory, narcissism is regarded as a normal early or infantile stage of **psychosexual development.** In such narcissism the **libido** is directed upon the person's own body, and may invest the **ego** as an object. Normally, this early stage terminates with the development of interest and love for others; when found in older persons, the condition is not normal.

In Greek myth, Narcissus was a handsome youth who fell in love with his own reflection in a pool but pined away and died of this unattainable self-love, turning into a flower which bears his name. The term was adopted by **Ferenczi** in 1921 to denote morbid self-admiration, although it had been used (1898) by the Russian-German psychiatrist Paul Näcke (1851-1924?) for the form of autoerotism that was generally exciting through imagery rather than by masturbation.

narcoanalysis (narcosynthesis, narcosis therapy) Therapeutic analysis while asleep (narco-), involving probing and exploring of usually unconscious mental processes. Sleep-producing drugs (primarily **thiopental sodium**) are used with control so that a "twilight-sleep" condition is maintained. The therapist encourages the patient (who is generally quite amenable to suggestion while under the drug) to discuss emotionally painful experiences that he either has been only faintly aware of or has repressed. Narcosis therapy is used principally to quiet agitated patients and to make them and other uncooperative ones more amenable to psychotherapy. Patients may sleep as long as 15-20 hours per day under the drug, but continuance is dependent upon the psychiatrist's evaluation of the success of the treatment and the health of the patient.

narcolepsy A transient condition (-y) of sleep (narco-) seizure (-leps-), often considered hysterical in nature, marked sometimes by uncontrollable and recurrent tendency to fall asleep for minutes or hours at a time; in emotional upsets, may be accompanied by sudden loss of muscle tone in extremities or trunk. Narcoleptoic behavior usually has been looked upon as an escape (defense) reaction from emotional problems, but there have been indications that some chemical imbalance may be partially responsible.

First described in 1862 by Casse and named in 1880 by French psychiatrist Jean Baptiste Edouard Gélineau (1859-1893), who gave the first clear description of this condition

narcotic Relating to (-ic) numbness (narcot-). A drug (such as **opium, morphine** and its derivatives: **heroin** codeine, **laudanum, Demerol,** etc.) that acts as a depressant, dulling the **CNS** and producing a decrease in pain, fear, sex drive, and hunger. Narcotics are used medically to relieve pain and produce profound sleep, but when used without medical control it often results in stupor, convulsions, and coma. Withdrawal symptoms are painful, often psychologically terrifying and fear-inducing. Toxicity is shown by coma, pinpoint pupils, and depressed respiration. *See* **drugs.**

National Academy of Sciences (NAS) Incorporated by act of Congress and approved by President Lincoln March 3, 1863, stipulating that the "Academy shall, whenever called upon by any department of the Government, investigate, examine, experiment, and report upon any subject of science."

In December 1964, the National Academy of Engineering was established under the charter of the National Academy of Sciences as a parallel organization of distinguished engineers. It shares with the NAS responsibilities for advising the federal government.

Membership in the NAS requires election by the Academy on nomination of the section of the Council of the NAS; limited to acceptance of 45 new members annually.

Address of the National Academy of Sciences, the National Academy of Engineering, and the National Research Council: 2101 Constitution Avenue, N.W., Washington, D.C. 20418.

National Association for Mental Health A national organization consisting of voluntary citizens dedicated to promoting a program of action for mental health and against mental illness. It was organized in September 1950 by a merger of three groups: the National Committee for Mental Hygiene (founded by Clifford Beers, 1909), the National Mental Health Foundation and the Psychiatric Foundation.

National Association for Retarded Children (NARC) A parents' association, established in 1950, dedicated to improving the public relations and the general welfare of mentally retarded children. The NARC was primarily responsible for substituting the term "mental retardation" for "mental deficiency." Members of the organization felt that mental deficiency held too much of a stigma because it connoted hopelessness.

National Association of Social Workers The official organization of social workers, established in 1955. Its membership consists of all professional social workers (medical social workers, psychiatric social workers, case workers, etc.), dedicated to improving the standards and public recognition of the field of social work as well as working cooperatively with other related professional organizations.

National Education Association Organized in Philadelphia as the National Teachers' Association on August 26, 1857 "to elevate the character and advance the interest of the profession of teaching and to promote the cause of popular education in the United States." The name was changed to NEA at a convention in Cleveland May 15, 1870.

National Information System for Psychology (NISP) A program, inaugurated by the American Psychological Association and with authority and sponsorship from the National Science Foundation, to spend about $2.4 million over a 25-month period to "plan and develop improvements and innovations in communications." This plan is a direct outgrowth of the concern the APA has had about information exchange in psychology since 1960. A related program is the **Experimental Publication System.** (*American Psychologist,* 1970, nos. 4 and 5; 1971, no. 4, pp. 325-362).

National Institute of Mental Health (NIMH) A Federal agency responsible for conducting a comprehensive and integrated attack on mental illness by providing grants to states for consultation, supporting research, and training of mental health workers (psychiatrists, psychologists, psychiatric social workers, psychiatric nurses). It emerged from the Mental Hygiene Division of the Public Health Service (established 1930), eventually leading to the passage of the National Mental Health Act 1946 and the development of the NIMH.

n

n

National Medal of Science Award An award established in 1959 to be granted by the President of the United States to persons "deserving of special recognition by reason of their outstanding contribution to knowledge in the physical, biological, mathematical, or engineering sciences." It is the Federal Government's highest award for distinguished achievement in these fields. *See* **N. E. Miller.**

National Rehabilitation Association (NRA) An organization of educators, counselors, and therapists, physicians, social workers, and psychologists concerned with rehabilitation of the physically and mentally handicapped. The association periodically makes recommendations for improved rehabilitation programs.

National Research Council An organization, established September 20, 1916 to promote wartime research, and perpetuated by order of President Wilson May 11, 1918 to stimulate all kinds of scientific research and programs and to expedite scientific information.

National Science Foundation An independent agency of the United States Government, established by the NSF Act of 1950 to strengthen basic research and education in the United States. The Foundation consists of a National Science Board of 24 members and a Director, each appointed by the President with advice and consent of Senate. Some activities are: (1) award of grants and contracts to universities and other nonprofitable institutions for basic research; (2) support of national centers for research; (3) granting of graduate fellowships; and (4) granting of funds for improving the teaching of science. Contact National Science Foundation. 1800 G. Street N.W., Washington, D.C.

nativism The doctrine (-ism) that emphasizes the inborn (nativ-) or innate characteristics (such as certain aspects of knowledge), rather than those acquired or learned; the point of view that elevates heredity over experience, particularly in regard to fundamental perceptual relations, which are inborn and not dependent upon prior experience or learned.

The concept of innate ideas as expressed by **Descartes** led to nativistic theories, such as the epistemological one put forth by **Helmholtz** (inherent in the definition above), who was the first to use the term in this special sense (1887).

naturalistic observation Scientific and objective observation of events as they occur in nature without experimental control or manipulation of behavior or the situation. For example, studying animals in their natural habitat or observing natural behavior of human beings without their knowledge.

natural logarithm Same as Napierian **logarithms**. Logarithms to base *e*.

Necker's cube(s) A line drawing of a transparent cube or **ambiguous figure** that, when viewed, alternates in depth, creating the illusion of reversible perspective. When the circle is fixated upon, it may appear to be sometimes in the front of the cube, sometimes at the back.

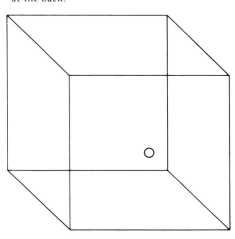

Louis A. Necker (1786-1841), Swiss naturalist, first observed this phenomenon in 1832, and described the phenomenon in a letter to the Scottish physicist Sir David Brewster (1781-1868).

need A feeling of unfulfillment or deprivation in the biological system (produced by either physical or environmental imbalances) evidenced by a drive to satisfy the need or complete such lack (one's tissue need for moisture may be satisfied by drinking water, which also reduces the drive or desire for something to drink). Loosely, any specific **motive**. *See* **motive, drive.**

In **H. A. Murray's** system, need represents an individual's motivational trait (such as any psychological or physiological motive). He defined need in 1938 as "a construct which stands for a force in the **brain** region which organizes action so as to transform in a certain direction an existing unsatisfying situation." His original (1938) list of needs included, among others, **abasement, achievement**, affiliation, rejection, **aggression**, autonomy, and sex. (Bischof, pp. 140-141, 146-152, 640-642).

Kurt Lewin defined need as "any desire for object possession or any desire to achieve a goal."

Gardner Murphy lists four inborn organic needs: *visceral* (food, air, etc.); *activity* (exploration and manipulation); *sensory* (openness to and awareness of sensory stimuli); and *preservation* (avoidance of pain and death).

need achievement score A measure of the strength of the individual's motivation to achieve. *See* **need for achievement.**

need for achievement (achievement motive; nAch) **McClelland** operationally defined achievement motive as a need that leads the organism to seek high standards of performance, or to compete with a standard of excellence. (David C. McClelland, born 1917, an American psychologist. Ph.D., Yale 1941).

McClelland's technique (using a modified **thematic apperception** approach) for measuring nAch combines objective scoring with the subject's revelations while writing an imaginary story about each of several (usually four) ambiguous pictures. His story must be framed within the context of four basic questions asked of him (dealing with the persons in the pictures, the circumstances surrounding the present situation, the psychological climate of the participants, and a prediction as to the future). The scoring is based on an 11-point scale. Results from use of this approach are inconclusive. (D. C. McClelland, J. W. Atkinson, R. A. Clark, and E. L. Lowell, *The Achievement Motive*, 1953).

needs, hierarchy of Preferential order (hierarchy) in satisfying needs. According to **A. H. Maslow**, needs arrange themsleves in a rank or hierarchy of prepotency, and "the appearance of one need usually rests on the prior satisfaction of another more prepotent need." He lists five needs: (1) *physiological*: for food, water, oxygen, constant temperature; (2) *safety*: for avoidance of pain, threats, and danger; (3) *love*: to belong, to be wanted, to be loved by friends, relatives, and family; (4) *esteem*: for self-respect, strength, achievement, adequacy, prestige attention, and appreciation; and (5) *self-actualization*: one must do what he can do.

neencephalon Phylogenetically, the newest (ne-) part of the brain (-encephalon); the **cerebral cortex**. *Compare* **paleencephalon.**

negative afterimage The visual sensation (usually less bright and in complementary hue) that appears in rhythmic fashion after the initial stimulation has ceased, such as seeing the negative (blackish or grayish) aftersensation when a stared-at bright light has been turned off, or of seeing red after stimulation with a blue-green color.

negative conditioned stimulus In **classical conditioning**, a stimulus that is presented repeatedly without reinforcement following, tending to inhibit conditioned responses.

negative-negative conflict *See* **avoidance-avoidance conflict.**

negative-practice The treatment of undesirable behavior (errors) by having the client voluntarily repeat undesirable responses until they are weakened or eliminated by satiation. The object is to bring the undesired behavior to the attention of consciousness. For example, purposely typing a word wrong (as hte for the) when one has previously been making that mistake.

Knight Dunlap, American psychologist, developed concept in 1928. *See* **Dunlap chronoscope.**

negative reinforcement A response closely followed in time by the reduction or termination of an aversive condition (ceasing to shock a rat, for example), resulting in a tendency for an organism to seek more of that response in the future, such increase being proportional to the degree of reduction. Termination, or even reduction, of an unpleasant experience is itself reinforcing and makes behavior experienced prior to unpleasant **stimulus** more likely. Negative reinforcement usually results in the **organism's** responding reluctantly, grudgingly, or with hostility. A society is usually built upon negative reinforcement (punishment, legal fines, and threats) in order to achieve a desired effect.

Nembutal (Abbott tradename for **pentobarbital sodium**) Slang: yellow jacket.

neocerebellum The phylogenetically newest or youngest (neo-) part of the **cerebellum** (containing most of the cerebellar hemispheres) acting with the **cerebral cortex** in integrating limb movements.

neocortex The new (neo-) cortex. The phylogenetically youngest part of the **cerebral cortex**, comprising six layers.

neo-Freudian theories Theoretical modifications of **Freud's** original theory developed by some of his disciples (**Fromm, Horney, Sullivan**, etc.), which include greater emphasis upon cultural influences as against instinctual tendencies (**libido**, for example). Such theories also attempt to reconcile the existential present with the typically Freudian unconscious processes and childhood **psychosexuality** and experience.

neologism The habit or practice (-ism) of using new (neo-) words (-log-), especially words coined by the user, or of using existing words in new senses invented by the user. Systematic and frequent neologism is often a symptom of **schizophrenia**.

neopallium The phylogenetically new (neo-) part of the **cerebral cortex** (-pallium), comprising the nonolfactory area of the **cortex**.

The neopallium was named by **Meynert** in an article published in 1867-68, at which time he also named the **archipallium**. The neopallium has also been known as the nonolfactory cortex or the **pallium** (as named by **Koelliker**), and is now more familiarly known as the **isocortex** (named by the **Vogts**).

nerve A cord-like band of nervous tissue composed of bundles of nerve fibers enclosed in a connective tissue sheath that conducts nervous impulses to or away from various organs.

The Greek word for nerve is **neuron**, which meant not only nerve but tendon, vein, and ligament as well. **Alcmaeon, Aristotle**, and **Galen** had taught that a nerve was a tube that transmitted nervous fluid from the sense organs to the **sensorium commune. Herophilus** and other physicians of the Alexandrian school differentiated tendons from nerves as well as making a distinction between sensory and motor nerves. **Descartes** called nervous action *undulatio reflexa*, with its center in the pineal gland, which he considered to be the seat of the soul.

nerve cell *Same as* **neuron.**

nerve fiber A polarized cable-like structure such as the **axon** or **dendrite** that may be bare (as in the grey matter) or covered with both a **myelin sheath** and **neurilemma** (as in the **peripheral nervous system**) with a myelin sheath only (as in the **central nervous system**) or with a neurilemma only (as in the sympathetic system). The nerve fiber "transmits potential changes resulting from the movements of sodium and potassium across its boundary membrane. The ions move along electrochemical gradients..." providing "the electric currents that determine the farther spread of the impulse," resulting in a self-regenerative depolarization process. Synaptic transmission can be either a chemical or an electrical phenomenon and synapses have been identified that transmit electrically, chemically, or in both ways. (Clarke and O'Malley, 1968, pp. 29, 258-59, 576).

The nerve fiber was first identified in 1781 by **Fontana**. Prior to this time, the word fiber had been used to describe a bundle of axons.

nerve impulse (or current) The self-propagated change that occurs, for example, in the protoplasm of a stimulated nerve fiber after its stimulation, accompanied by a wave of alteration of electrical potential enabling conduction to take place by the release of stored potential energy, thereby converting it into the kinetic energy of the moving impulse. Nerve cell communication embraces two processes: (1) conduction of a message along and within continuous portions of the cell itself and (2) transmission across a gap from one cell to another.

Conduction involves the passage of a self-propagated wave of membrane collapse and restoration (being the conducted nerve, muscle, or gland cell impulse). *Transmission* revolves around the diffusion of the cell chemical secretions across intercellular gaps. Conduction in the cell takes place because of the unequal distribution of ions (with potassium concentration being about 27 times higher on the inside of the cell than outside while sodium is about 10 times higher outside than inside) such differences occurring because of the selectivity of the permeable membranes, resulting in **polarization.** The voltage reading of the difference between potential recordings on the inside and outside of the cell membrane is called the **resting potential.** The modified **potential** is the source of the impulse that enters into the point of dropped potential at the site of stimulation, eventually causing **depolarization,** with the diffusion of ions across the cell membrane carrying the current into the cell, such action stimulating the surrounding membrane, which is then depolarized, drawing current from other regions adjacent to the new stimulus sites, *ad infinitum,* the original sites recovering in the process.

Transmission of an impulse across an intercellular gap (such as interneuronal, synaptic, etc.) comprises both excitatory (depolarizing) factors—such as **acetylcholine,** and inhibitory (hyperpolarizing) chemicals—such as **noradrenalin, adrenalin, serotonin,** and histamine. An excitatory impulse is transmitted across the gap by the intervention of a chemical diffusion process, while the inhibitory **biogenic amines** combine specific receptors to initiate further action.

nerve net theory *See* **Golgi.**

nerve spike The unit of neural activity represented by a "transient change in voltage of about 60 mv. and lasting for about 0.4-2 sec." The amplitude of the spike potential is constant for any given nerve. (Deutsch and Deutsch, pp. 446-47).

nerve tract A bundle of **axons** within the **central nervous system.** A tract's name indicates its origin, the direction in which the impulses travel, and its destination. For example, the corticospinal tract originates in the cortical area and descends to the grey matter of the spinal cord. *Ascending tracts* contain afferent fibers that carry impulses toward the brain and *descending tracts* contain efferent fibers that carry impulses from the brain to the spinal cord.

neurasthenia (Beard's disease, nerve weakness) Disorder (-ia) marked by no (-a-) strength (-sthen-) of the nerves (neur-). Functional nervous weakness; nervous debility. Neurotic reaction characterized by chronic mental and physical fatigue, headaches, photophobia, backaches, dizzy spells, listlessness, and sometimes by the presence of **phobias** and **hypochondriasis.** *See* **asthenia reaction.**

Described in 1860 as *nervosisme* by Paris physician Jean Antoine E. Bouchut (1818-1891). In 1869, New York physician George Miller Beard (1839-1883) grouped the symptoms of nervous exhaustion into an entity, and named the condition in a journal article "Neurasthenia, a Nervous Exhaustion."

neurilemma (sheath of Schwann) Nerve (neuri-) covering or sheath (-lemma); a continuous sheath surrounding the segmented **myelin sheath** that plays a vital role in peripheral nerve regeneration. *See* **neuron.**

The neurilemma was discovered in 1811 by German histologist G. G. T. Keuffel. **Reil** first used the term in 1825 in referring to a different nerve covering, but it was not used in its approximate present sense until 1838. In 1839 Schwann defined and described the structure more accurately.

neurofibrils *See* **neuron.**

neurofibromatosis (neurofibroblastomatosis, Recklinghausen's disease) A condition (-osis) transmitted by a dominant autosomal gene, characterized by cutaneous pigmentation and fibrous tumors (-fibromas) primarily around nerve (neuro-) sheaths with intellectual capacity varying from normal to severely retarded.

neuroglia Nerve (neuro-) glue (-glia). Non-neural supporting cells of the vertebrate **central nervous system** consisting mainly of long fibrous processes, derived from embryonic neural tissue, lying between the neurons. Recent speculation suggests that the neuroglia plays a role in neuron metabolism and in the storage of memory functions. They are active in degenerative and regenerative processes after injury, as well as in the formation of brain tumors (**gliomas**), which result in paralyses of the 5th, 6th, 8th, and 10th **cranial nerves** and in inability to gaze laterally.

The term neuroglia causes some confusion because in a general sense it applies to cells comprising the interstitial tissue of the nervous system but it also refers to specific cells. Generally, neuroglia cells include *ependyma* (membranous cells that line brain ventricles and the spinal cord's central canal), *neuroglia* proper (often called *glia cells* to differentiate them from the generic neuroglia), *satellite cells* (those that encase cell bodies of sensory neurons in peripheral ganglia), and neurilemma.

There are three types of *glia cells* (neuroglia proper): (*1*) *astrocytes*—star-shaped cells with numerous processes; (*2*) *migroglia*—tiny cells whose main function seems to be concerned with destroying foreign material in nerve tissue; (*3*) *oligodendroglia*—cells that support neurons and connect them to blood vessels within nerve tissue. Glia cells make up about half the brain mass (there being about 100 billion glia cells to approximately 10 billion cerebral nerve cells).

In addition to supporting nerve cells and serving a defense or protective function, neuroglia apparently are also involved in forming the **myelin sheath** of brain and spinal cord neurons.

German pathologist **Virchow** observed this supporting tissue of the CNS in 1846, naming it in 1854 and calling tumors of these cells "gliomas" in 1869. The astrocytes were described and reported posthumously (1865) by German anatomist Otto F. K. Deiters (1834-1863), and described more clearly by Ramon y Cajal in 1881.

neurogram Nerve (neuro-) record or writing (-gram); the anatomic basis of memory, according to J. M. Nielsen, the American neurologist. *See* **engram.**

neurohypophysis Posterior portion of the pituitary gland (hypophysis) carrying nerve (neuro-) cells from the **hypothalamus.** Secretes **oxytocin, vasopressin,** and antidiuretic hormone.

neuroleptic drug Referring to (-ic) a drug (e.g., **chlorpromazine**) that results in a slight seizure (lept-), temporary change, or reduction of nervous (neuro-) tension.

Term proposed in 1955 by French psychiatrist Jean De Lay (born 1907) as a borrowed suffixal reference to **Janet's** term of psychelepsy (reduced psychological tension).

neurological signal processing device *See* **averaging computer.**

neurologist One who (-ist) practices **neurology;** a medical specialist skilled in the knowledge, diagnosis, and treatment of diseases, abnormalities, and injuries of the **brain** and nervous system.

neurology The scientific study (-logy) of the nervous (neuro-) system, including its anatomy, physiology, and neuropathology.

The term was coined by **Willis** and reported in his *Cerebri Anatome,* 1664, which was translated in 1681 from the Latin by Samuel Pordage and referred to as "doctrine of the nerves."

neuromyal Referring to (-al) nerve (neuro-) muscle (-my-) functions. *See* **myoneural.**

neuron (nerve cell: Gr., equivalent of Latin — nerve derived from Sanskrit *snavara*—string, cord—or tendon, the original meaning of nerve) The neuron is the basic structural and functional unit of the nervous system, consisting of a cell body (soma) containing protoplasm, a nucleus and one or more fibers attached to the cell body. There are several structural characteristics of a neuron: **dendrites; axon; myelin sheath; neurilemma; neurofibrils** (fiberlike threads) found in dendrites, cell bodies, and axons which form an interlacing network in neuron cytoplasm; and intracellular Nissl bodies (consisting of flat membranous reticular sacs and **ribonucleic acid** granules), which specialize in protein synthesis as well as serving other functions in the neuron. A neuron also has other less unique structures, such as a cell membrane, vesicles, **mitochondria,** and Golgi membranes.

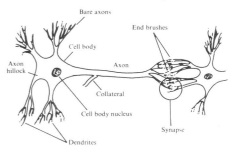

A simplified diagram of a single neuron. An impulse is normally received by the dendrites, passes along the axon, and produces action at the end brushes which potentially stimulate firing of other neurons.

Neurons may be classified structurally as: (*1*) *multipolar* (with only one axon but several dendrites); (*2*) *bipolar* (with only two fibers, one axon and one dendrite; and (*3*) *unipolar* (with only one process or fiber extending from the cell body).

Another method of classification indicates the estimated number of **inputs** (variety of sources for receiving stimuli from dendritic branching) they receive. For example, **central nervous system** (CNS) neurons (with cortical neurons at the top) have greater magnitude of inputs than peripheral ones. CNS neurons are

n

organized as: *cortical neurons* (in the **cerebrum, cerebellum,** and **optic lobes**); *interneurons* (of secondary sensory cells and the short axon types); and *central effector neurons* (motoneurons, autonomic neurons, and hypophyseal neurons). *Peripheral neurons* are divided into: *sensory neurons*—bipolar type (auditory, olfactory, and cutaneous); *motor neurons* (invertebrate and autonomic ganglia). *Functionally,* neurons may be classified as: (*1*) sensory (afferent), (*2*) motoneurons (efferent), and (*3*) interneurons (internuncial or intercalated). The specific function of a neuron is to conduct impulses, providing the means for communication and integration.

Neurons have various qualifying terms to help locate or describe them, such as *lemniscal neurons,* which precisely code touch sensations and kinesthetic experiences, and *postganglionic neurons,* located in *ganglia* outside the CNS, which innervate effector organs (Butter, p. 14).

neuron doctrine (or neuron theory) A proposal made by **Waldeyer** in 1891 that the nervous system consisted of numerous nerve cells or structural units called **neurons,** with nervous energy being relayed by contact only from one to the other. Previously, the idea had prevailed that the nervous system consisted of a continuous tubelike network, similar to the vascular system, through which electricity or some fluid could flow.

American psychologist Gardner Murphy (born 1895) considered the neuron theory "one of the most important neurological contributions for the history of psychology. . .as it gave both the theory of learning. . .and association a much more definite and usable form." Boring claimed that the neuron theory with its "association and synapses" led to Ebbinghaus' experiments on memory. *See* **chromosome, Ehrlich, Ramon y Cajal, Sherrington.**

In 1891, German anatomist **Waldeyer-Hartz** gave the name of neuron to the nerve cell and its process. In 1899 the Russian neurologist and histologist Alexander S. Dogiel (1852-1922), classified neurons into "spinal, sympathetic," etc. In 1887, Wilhelm His, père (1831-1904), Swiss anatomist, showed that nerve fibers originated from a single nerve cell, which was also the functional and nutritive center of the fibers, thereby proving the independence of the neuron and its process. Later in the same year, August H. Forel (1848-1931), Swiss psychiatrist, by using **Gudden's retrograde degeneration technique,** demonstrated that no nerve network existed, contrary to **Golgi's** belief. He also showed that neurons and their fibers degenerated as a unit, complementing his findings that they grew as a unit. (Clarke and O'Malley, p. 100).

neurosecretion A chemical transmitter substance released from neuronal mechanisms, such as from axons in certain parts of the **hypothalamus,** into the blood supply (the hypophyseal or pituitary portal system). The neurosecretions travel from the hypothalamus to the *anterior lobe* of the *pituitary gland* where they stimulate its cells to secrete various hormones (for one, the **corticotrophin**-releasing factor, which stimulates the release of *ACTH* into the blood); other neurosecretions probably also control secretions of **gonadotrophins, thyrotrophins** and **lactogenic** hormones of the pituitary gland's anterior lobe.

neuroses and neurotic patterns A functional personality disorder without evidence of organic involvement or gross personality disorganization, and not requiring hospitalization. Its major characteristic is anxiety which may be overtly expressed (such as in nervous mannerisms, fears, obsessive-compulsive behavior) or it may be controlled unconsciously or automatically and expressed as conversion **hysterias,** displacement, etc.

Neurotic symptoms, contrasted with those of **psychoses,** are not manifest in gross distortions or misinterpretations of external reality. Neurotics are aware that there is a disturbance in their mental functioning. Some of the major subheads of neuroses with their symptoms are: (*a*) **anxiety** (anxious overconcern extending to panic and often with somatic symptoms); (*b*) **hysteria** including the conversion type (**paresthesia,** anesthesia, **ataxia, dyskinesia,** etc.) and dissociative type (**fugue, amnesia,** multiple personality, somnambulism); (*c*) **phobia** (intense fear, apprehension, palpitation, nausea, tremor, and panic); (*d*) *obsessive—compulsive type* (persistent unstoppable intrusion of unwanted thoughts, urges, or actions); (*e*) *depressive type* (resulting from internal conflict or loss of love object or possession); (*f*) *neurasthenia* (chronic weakness, fatigability, exhaustion); (*g*) *depersonalization* (estrangement from self, body, or environment); and (*h*) *hypochondria* (preoccupation with body and fear of presumed diseases).

In 1769, the Scottish physician William Cullen (1710-1790) was the first to use the word neurosis in describing the condition as a functional disorder, possibly of organic origin. In 1796, **Reil** described more thoroughly the neurotic personality, referring to cases of depersonalization and double personality as examples.

neurotic paradox Neurotic behavior that is apparently unreinforcing and punishing (such as the alcoholic who seeks out more drinking episodes despite disgrace, vomiting, and hangovers). **Mowrer** states that the neurotic paradox refers to behavior that is simultaneously self-perpetuating and self-defeating. Lundin believes that the "neurotic is reinforced because his symptoms allow him to escape or avoid an aversive stimulus. By the elimination of these aversive stimuli and the reduction of anxiety that they generate. . . the reinforcing effects are far more powerful than the punishing consequences of his acts" (Lundin, 1969, pp. 365-366).

neurovesicle A microscopic sac (vesicle) in an **axon** terminal that contains neuro-transmitter substances.

Newcomb Cleveland Prize Granted by the American Association for the Advancement of Science since 1923, when the award was established by Newcomb Cleveland (1867-1951), of New York. It is given for a noteworthy paper representing an outstanding contribution to science.

The first psychologist to receive the Cleveland Prize was Norman R. F. Maier (born 1900), Ph.D., Michigan 1928, for his article "Experimentally Produced Neurotic Behavior in the Rat," 1938. In 1956, Neal E. Miller shared the prize with **James Olds.** Although technically not a psychologist, **Jerzy Neyman** (who has made contributions to psychological and statistical theory) won the prize (along with Elizabeth L. Scott) for the article "On Certain Stochastic Models of Population Dynamical Phenomena."

newton (N) The SI standard unit of force which gives to a mass of 1 **kilogram** an acceleration of 1 **meter** per second. *See* **International System of Units.**

Named after the English mathematician and philosopher, Isaac Newton (1642-1727).

Newton, Isaac *See* **color mixture, Hartley** (also Bell, pp. 90-116).

Neyman-Pearson likelihood ratio test *See* **likelihood ratio test.**

nichtbeamteter Not (*nicht*) on the official (*beamteter*) staff; not officially credited. Refers to appointments to a lectureship post in a German university.

nicotine Chemical substance (-ine) named after Nicot. A poisonous volatile alkaloid that acts with the rapidity of cyanide and is considered one of the most toxic of all drugs. The nicotine content of one cigar, if injected into the bloodstream, approximates two lethal doses for man.

After Jean Nicot (1530-1600), French diplomat and scholar who introduced use of tobacco from Portugal into France in 1560. Nicotine was first isolated from leaves of tobacco in 1828 and named after Nicot.

nicotinic acid (Niacin, tradename) An acid derived from the oxidation of nicotine but which has none of its pharmacological properties. In a therapeutic dose it produces vasodilation in man, causing him to flush, which may be accompanied by itching and burning. It is a member of the vitamin B complex and found in blood, liver, yeast, and bran. Functioning in the body as nicotinamide, it does not have the vascular action of the acid, and is therefore the preferred preparation for treating dietary conditions, such as **pellagra.**

Casimir Funk, a Polish biochemist, born in 1884, identified (1913) nicotinic acid in England before migrating to Cornell University, New York, for a year's research. The complexities of vitamin B were not known at that time, and thus it took about a dozen years, from 1913-1925, for Joseph Goldberger (1874-1929), Austrian-born American physician, to discover the nature of pellagra and its remedy (nicotinic acid).

nicotinic receptor One of two types of **receptors** for **acetylcholine** injections, so named because when antagonized by **curare** it produces conditions similar to those following nicotine injection in experimental animals—sympathetic ganglionic and skeletal muscle stimulation.

In neurohumoral transmission experiments, it is assumed that the **brain** is the basic site of action of most behaviorally active drugs, although such drugs exert both peripheral and central effects. In experiments in 1914 using acetylcholine injections, **H. H. Dale** found that "two types of receptors for acetylcholine are found in different effectors and that one type is antagonized by atropine" (producing effects similar to **muscarine** and hence called muscarinic receptor) while the other is antagonized by curare (producing effects similar to those after nicotine injection and thus called nicotinic receptor) (Thompson and Schuster, p. 32f.).

Niemann-Pick disease A disorder of lipoid **metabolism.** Onset usually in infancy with weight loss, dehydration, and progressive paralysis, and marked by fatty deposits in spleen. *See* **lipid histiocytosis.**

German physicians Albert Niemann (1880-1921) and Ludwig Pick (1868-1935) first described the condition.

night terror *See* **pavor nocturnus.**

NIMH National Institute of Mental Health.

Nissl bodies After Franz Nissl (1860-1919), German neurologist. *See* **neuron.**

noise (Comput.) An unwanted, meaningless, stray signal in a control system, similar to radio static. When excessive, it can interfere with normal operation or cause a malfunction.

nomenclature of mental disorders *See* **classification of mental disorders.**

nominal aphasia *See* **speech aphasia.**

nominal scale A **scaling technique** (on the nominal, ordinal, interval, ratio scale system) that consists of assigning different numerals to represent categories. Nominal scale measurements distinguish between two or more mutually exclusive categories, but the numerals cannot be mathematically manipulated.

nomograph (nomogram) Written (-graph) law or system (nomo-). A scaled graph (chart) representing values of related variables (organized) along parallel straight lines; use of a straight-edge enables reading off of a **dependent variable** when the value of two or more **independent variables** is known.

nomothetic approach Relating to (-ic) the search, discovery, and establishment (-thet-) of general laws (nomo-) to explain behavior. An approach to **personality** study emphasizing measurement or statistics to describe general principles about individual differences. Used by educators in studying, for example, large groups of "underachievers," by sociologists in their statistical emphasis upon studying people, and by psychologists (such as McClelland with his need for achievement) in developing concepts designed to predict the average score. *Opposed to* **idiographic approach.**

Although "nomothetic" as *nomethete* was used as early as 1586 and in the legislative sense in 1619, it was not until 1921 (*An Introduction to Philosophy*) that Wilhelm Windelband (1848-1915), a German philosopher, introduced the word in reference to the sciences—a *nomothetic science,* (for example, physics, chemistry, astronomy) seeking general laws to explain individual events while *nomothetic psychology* also sought generalizations about human nature or mental life. In 1937 Allport introduced it into psychological usage (G. W. Allport. *Personality: A Psychological Interpretation*, Holt, 1937, p. 4).

nomothetic description The means (formal or informal norms) by which an individual is characterized as being different from others.

non-directive counseling, therapy, or technique *See* **client-centered counseling.**

nondisjunction The non-separation (disjunct-) of two homologous chromosomes of a pair during the reduction division, with one daughter cell holding both chromosomes and the other neither. Normally, following the metaphase period, the two chromosomes do separate.

Nondisjunction accounts for most chromosomal aberrations in which extra chromosomes are present in the body cells. So-called mongolism is a manifestation of a trisomy of autosomal chromosome #21, which usually develops from a normal sperm combining with an egg heavily endowed with chromosome #21. Nondisjunction during the first division (**meiosis**) of sperm production results in two kinds of sperm cells, those with both X and Y chromosomes and those with no sex chromosomes at all. An XXY male (**Klinefelter's syndrome**) develops from the fertilization of a normal ovum by an XY sperm. *See* **Down's disease.**

nonparametric statistics (distribution-free tests, order statistics) Statistical techniques for testing **hypotheses** that make no explicit assertions about a **parameter.** Examples are the **runs test, sign test,** and Spearman rank difference method. These tests make fewer assumptions about the population than **parametric** tests and can be used when the latter tests' assumptions are not fulfilled. See any of the tables numbered from 25a to 32 inclusive for descriptions.

nonreversal shift In discrimination studies, an experimental technique requiring the subject to shift his response to a previously irrelevant one, such as after being rewarded for choosing a specific color he is then not reinforced unless he ignores color and selects a ball or a cube. *See* **reversal shift.**

nonsense syllables Relatively meaningless syllables composed of two consonants and a vowel (for example, zal, dal). They are devised to avoid any resemblance to real words so that previous associations will not interfere in learning "new" material. Used as items in verbal learning experiments.

First used by **Ebbinghaus** in studies of retention, with himself as subject, demonstrating that "higher" mental processes could be brought under experimental control.

nonzero-sum game A game with no "winner-take-all" conclusion, but rather a give and take situation in which various response combinations lead to a result other than zero, the strategy depending upon each player evaluating another's behavioral patterns under the stress of the game and making his moves on the basis of how his opponent (or even colleague) might behave. The **mixed-motive game** is a type of nonzero-sum game. Such a game is considered a "model" for studying social relationships involving competition and cooperation (Jones and Gerard, p. 561 f.).

nor- In chemical nomenclature, a compound derived from a parent compound in the normal form: as a prefix for norepinephrin and noradrenalin it represents an acronymic formation for the German, *Nitrogen ohne Radikal.*

noradrenalin(e) *See* **norepinephrin.**

noradrenergic pathways *See* **amine pathways.**

NOR circuit (Comput.) A circuit that will not produce an output signal when any of its input signals is present. Inverse of AND circuit. *See* **Boolean algebra.**

norepinephrin(e) (also noradrenalin, arterenol). A crystalline compound occurring as a hormone with **epinephrin** mediating transmission of sympathetic nerve impulses to effector organs. It is highly concentrated in the hypothalamus. As a hormone, norepinephrine is secreted by adrenergic nerve endings of the adrenal **medulla**, participates with epinephrin in emotional responses of fear and anger, and helps to constrict superficial blood vessels; also serves as a transmitter substance at postganglionic endings of the **sympathetic nervous system** *See* **nor-.**

NOR gate *See* **gate.**

norm The rule (norm) or standard of reference existing within a group to which individual performance can be compared. For example, the norms of social behavior accepted in one culture may differ sharply from what is acceptable in another.

normal curve (normal probability curve) A bell-shaped curve that is the **graph** of a unimodal perfectly symmetrical distribution of data whose **mean, median,** and **mode** are identical. Its function rule is:

The normal curve is a mathematical entity and is represented by the following formula:

$$Y = \frac{N}{\sigma \sqrt{2\pi}} e^{-(X-\mu)^2 / 2\sigma^2}$$

where

Y = height of curve for particular values of X

π = a constant = 3.1416

e = base of Napierian logarithms = 2.7183

N = number of measures, indicating that the total area under the curve is N

μ and σ = mean and standard deviation of the distribution, respectively

(Downie and Heath, p. 69).

The normal curve most nearly describes many physical and psychological variables outlined in a distribution. It represents a constellation of possible curves rather than one curve, for there can be enormous variation in "height" and "breadth." The bell shape of the curve does not necessarily make the distribution normal.

In a practical application, an intelligence test given to a very large unselected group of school children with the resulting IQ's arranged in a distribution, the mean, median, and modal IQ's would be expected to approximate 100. About 68 percent of them would fall within one **standard deviation** (S.D.) above and below the mean, about 95 percent within two S.D.'s above and below, and over 99 percent within three S.D.'s above and below. Thus, the great majority of scores would cluster about the middle values and a smaller percentage would be very high or very low, corresponding to the shape of the normal curve.

Although many **frequency distributions** are normally distributed, the statistical importance of this distribution stems from the sampling distribution of most statistics (mean, standard error, etc.) being normally distributed. *See* Tables 2, 3, and 4.

The normal curve equation was developed in 1733 by Abraham De Moivre (1667-1754) in his book *The Doctrine of Chances*, which dealt with probability theory. *See* **area under the normal curve, Karl Pearson.**

normal distribution *See* **normal curve.**

normative approach A specific, clearly defined evaluative standard as contrasted to a cognitive judgment in measuring individual differences or psychological maturity. The **Gesell Developmental Schedule** pertaining to the maturing child is one of the better-known examples of a normative approach. *See* **model.**

normative model *See* **model.**

normative unit According to **R. Cattell**, the amount one individual varies from another. *See* **ipsative unit.**

normlessness *See* **alienation.**

norms *See* **Binet.**

nosebrain *See* **rhinencephalon.**

NOT connective *See* **Boolean algebra.**

noumenon (plural **noumena**) That which is apprehended or conceived. **Kant's** term (1798) for denoting the "thing in itself," an object of purely intellectual intuition that is really unknowable. Opposed to phenomenon, which is something that is seen or perceived.

nous (Gr., mind, intellect.) *See* **Aristotle.**

NREM-sleep Non-Rapid Eye Movement sleep. The period of sleep in which rapid *eye* movements (REMs) are not apparent, immediately following wakefulness and preceding the deep sleep of REM.

nuclear vs. peripheral forms of schizophrenia *Nuclear schizophrenia* (primarily the simple and hebephrenic types) is a gradually developing but ever-increasing-in-severity form of probably biologically determined **schizophrenia** without apparent precipitating cause. Social inadequacy is its predominant symptom. It has an early and insidious onset of symptoms, with a poor prepsychotic personality and poor prognosis. **Process schizophrenia** is sometimes considered a nuclear form of schizophrenia.

In the *peripheral form* (catatonic and paranoid types) of schizophrenia, symptoms develop later with a more acute onset and from a better prepsychotic personality. There is usually a favorable response to treatment with better prognosis.

In an article "Mental Illness in Primitive Societies," *Psychiatry*, 1954, **17**, 377-389, P. K. Benedict and I. Jacks differentiate between nuclear and peripheral indicating that the nuclear type is more evident in primitive societies. Distinction between so-called true schizophrenia and schizophrenoform schizophrenia can be traced back to 1849. (*See* G. E. Vaillant, "An Historical View of the Remitting Schizophrenia". *Journal of Nervous and Mental Disease*, 1964, **138**, 48-56).

nucleic acid *See* **ribonucleic acid, nucleotide, deoxyribonucleic acid, nucleus.**

nuclein *See* **nucleus.**

nucleoside A phosphate-free crystalline compound (-ide), such as **adenosine**, formed from the partial hydrolysis of any **purine** or **pyrimidine** combined with a pentose sugar (-ose-; such as ribose or deoxyribose). Nucleosides appear in the nucleus (nucle-) of cells in all living tissue. The phosphorylated derivative of a nucleoside is a **nucleotide** (such as nucleic acids, which are poly-nucleotides).

nucleotide A chemical compound (-ide) or molecular complex of three units, consisting of a phosphate group (derivations of phosphoric acid), a pentose sugar (-ot-, a variant of -ose-; such as **ribose** or **deoxyribose**), and a nitrogen base (e.g., **adenine** or **thymine**). The nitrogen base in a ribose nucleotide usually is either **uracil** or **cytosine** or **adenine** or **guanine**; a deoxyribose nucleotide typically contains either **thymine** or cytosine or adenine or guanine. Uracil occurs only in ribose series;

n

thymine only in deoxyribose series; adenine, guanine, and cytosine in both series. Nucleotides appear as **adenosine triphosphate** in the *nucleus* (nucle-) of cells in all living tissue. As building blocks or larger molecules, nucleotides serve as energy carriers, as coenzymes (most of these being chemical derivatives of nucleotides) or as a genetic system in itself. As energy carriers, nucleotides are able to link up serially with one or two additional phosphate groups (e.g., if to adenosine monophosphate (AMP) one more phosphate is added, then **adenosine diphosphate** (ADP) is formed; if a third phosphate is added to ADP, then **adenosine triphosphate** (ATP) is formed). Nucleic acids are polynucleotides (extended chains of up to thousands of joined nucleotide units), and of two types: (1) a chain consisting of ribose nucleotides (ribotides) or **nucleic acid** and (2) a chain of deoxyribose nucleotides (deoxyribotides) or **deoxyribonucleic acid.**

Albrecht Kossel (1852-1927), Swiss chemist, discovered nucleic acids. Isolated adenine and guanine, and (with Stendal) thymine, 1900. Recipient, Nobel prize (medicine and physiology) 1910.

nucleus A kernel or cluster (nucleus); a spherical body located in the center of a cell, separated from the cytoplasm by a double-layered porous membrane. Within the nucleus are located **chromosomes** and one or more dense bodies called nucleoli. A nucleus is also a group of neuron cell bodies (grey matter) in the **brain** or cord, composed mainly of neuronal cell bodies and **dendrites.** The cell nucleus consists largely of a phosphorus containing substance (nuclein—later renamed nucleic acid). *See* **ganglion.**

Reference to the term nucleus first appeared in English in 1704, but it was not mentioned until 1823 as a dense spot in cell protoplasm. The term nucleolus was coined in 1836 by German physician Gabriel G. Valentin (1810-1883), who also discovered and described this spot within the nucleus. Nuclein was so named in 1869 by the Swiss biochemist **Friedrich Miescher** and the name changed to nucleic acid in 1871 by **Hoppe-Seyler** who isolated nucleic acid from yeast cells, which were later, after studies by **Levene,** found to contain ribose—thus by name **ribonucleic acid** (RNA), and thymus nucleic acid (Miescher's nuclein) lacking one oxygen atom became known as **deoxyribonucleic acid** (DNA).

nuisance variable Any variable that is an undesired factor of possible variation in an experiment. It may affect the **dependent variable** and the total experiment unless it is controlled. Some nuisance variables in an experiment may be an undetected disease (for example, a heart or kidney condition), temperature variations in different rooms, or cages used for research, etc. *See* **analysis of variance.**

null hypothesis (H$_0$) A statistical statement of one or more **parameters** subjected to statistical testing indicating that **variables** under study are independent. Also, a statistical hypothesis stating that the difference between experimental **treatments** occurs by chance and does not reflect a true difference between the corresponding parameters. If the null hypothesis is rejected (based upon statistical evidence), it is assumed that the difference is not due to chance. In forming hypotheses it is assumed that it is known what to expect if they are true and to hypothesize the exact opposite of what needs to be proved. The assumption is that there is no difference between the regular and the predicted value. By rejecting equality it is stated that there is a difference. The hypothesis is never proved or established but may be possibly disproved. Guidelines in testing hypotheses: (1) formulate a null hypothesis so that the probability of a **type I error** can be calculated and also an alternative hypothesis so that rejection of the null hypothesis is equivalent

to acceptance of the alternative hypothesis; (2) specify the probability of committing a type I error at the 0.05 or 0.01 level; (3) set up statistical criteria for testing the null hypothesis; and (4) indicate whether the alternative to rejecting the null hypothesis is to accept it or reserve judgment. (Lewis, 1960, p. 134; Runyon, 1968, p. 136; Guilford, 1965, pp. 205-207).

		The Decision	
		Accept H$_0$ as True	Reject H$_0$ as False
The Fact	H$_0$ is True	Decision Correct	Decision Incorrect Type I Error, Alpha Risk
	H$_0$ is False	Decision Incorrect Type II Error Beta Risk	Decision Correct

Possible Results of Testing a Hypothesis, H$_0$

number A concept of quantity or of combined units. A number utilizes digits such as 1, 2, 10, or 1000, which are called simple natural numbers. Numerals are symbols or groups of symbols that represent categories. For any number there is an infinite amount of numeral expressions. For example, the number three can be numeralized as: 3, three, III, 9/3, 27/9, etc.

All Numbers

Pure Real Numbers	Pure Imaginary Numbers	Complex Numbers
$\frac{a}{3}$	$\frac{bi}{3}$	$a + bi$ (where a & b are not 0)
2.71828	$-2/3\sqrt{-1}$	$3 + 3\sqrt{-1}$
$-2/3$	$3^7\sqrt{-1}$	$\frac{-27}{5} - \sqrt{-1}$
$27\sqrt{5}$	$\sqrt{-1}$	$-3 + 7\sqrt{-5}$
3^7	i	$8\sqrt{9} + 3i\sqrt{5}$
π	$\frac{a}{i}$	

Note: As used above, a and b are real numbers and i equals $\sqrt{-1}$.

Our customary method of writing numbers is of Hindu origin. It combines the positional principle, and the method of ciphers, arithmetically the most advanced of all number systems. The old Babylonians, whose number base was 60, anticipated the Hindus in the positional principle but they had no ciphers. They used the iterative principle in writing digits. The same principle, but without the positional idea, was used by the Romans and Egyptians.

number system A means of using various numbers and combinations of numbers to arrive at a desired result. The decimal system (base 10) is one of these systems, each position in a number being assigned a value ten times the value of the position on its right. The **binary number system** (base 2), however, is more convenient for use with **computers,** since the information handled is in binary form—on or off, present or absent, etc.—which needs only two different symbols, 0 and 1. Another important number system for modern computers is the hexadecimal system (base 16), which uses the first ten symbols (0-9) of the decimal system plus letters of the

alphabet to extend the notation to the required sixteen characters (A for 10, B for 11, etc.). By using the hexadecimal system only two digits are required to write the equivalent of eight binary digits.

number system bases In **computer** or data processing several different bases have been used:

Name	Base
binary	2
biquinary	2 and 5
octal	8
decimal	10
sexidecimal or hexadecimal	16

number 21 *See* **Down's disease.**

nystagmus (Gr., to nod in sleep.) A rapid, rhythmic, vertical or horizontal oscillation of the eyeballs caused by spasms.

o

O (pl. Os) observer(s).

object constancy An unconscious assumption or tendency to perceive objects as relatively unchanged in color, size, or shape despite varying conditions of illumination, distance, and viewing position. In **Gestalt** theory, one of the organizing processes of **perception,** which insures meaningfulness to the data.

objective data Data not influenced by the bias or interpretation of the observer. For example, in learning experiments, such quantitative data as number of responses, time of trial, etc., are objective.

objective psychology A behavioristic viewpoint that accepts in psychological research any behavior that is publicly observable or capable of replication. Subjectivity and subjective judgments are rejected.

In 1907, **Bekhterev** used the term to explain his conditioning approach in his book *Objective Psychology,* his objective methods being used after 1915 by **Watson** when he became acquainted with Russian conditioning experiments.

objective test A test (personality inventory, paper-and-pencil, etc.) administered so as to be relatively free of examiner bias. It can be scored simply and systematically by equally trained personnel so that the results are universally the same (that is, a person could take a given test anywhere and theoretically achieve the same results no matter which examiner marked the test).

object language (Comput.) The actual numerical code used by and specific to each type of **computer;** the machine language that the computer obeys directly. A program written in a higher level language such as FORTRAN or ALGOL may be compiled by the computer and translated into the object language. If this object level program is in the form of a punch card deck it may be used to directly control the computer without the necessity of any further computer translation (compilation).

In psychology, an object language consists of stimuli and responses fitted to the organism rather than the experimenter.

object size The actual size of an object determined by physical and objective means. An observer tends to perceive the distant object as its object size, although the sense impression received is smaller.

obsession Besieged (obsess-) state (-ion). A persistent idea usually strongly tinged with emotion that resists attempts to dismiss from the mind; a recurring, irresistible impulse to perform an act. Obsession differs from a **compulsion** usually by the degree of overt action involved. For example, continual handwashing or constant fingering of an object is considered a compulsion, while inescapable preoccupation with morbid thoughts or counting people in a crowd is labeled an obsession.

obsessive-compulsive (neurosis) reaction An anxiety-laden, defensive behavioral pattern in which the person is plagued by **obsessions** (recurring, unwanted, intrusive thoughts, often senseless and disturbing), **compulsions** (irresistible urges to repeat ritualistic acts such as continually washing one's hands), or a combination of both. From a psychoanalytic point of view, such conditions arise from repressive and rigid toilet training during childhood. *See* **anankastic personality** under **personality disorders; obsessive-compulsive neuroses** under **neuroses.**

Occam's razor Concepts, principles, or factors should not be multiplied unnecessarily, a statement translated from *entia non sunt multiplicanda praeter necessitatem*, and attributed to William of Occam (1280?-1349?), an English political theorist and philosopher. Also, assumptions made about anything must be reduced or cut to a minimum, as if by a razor; thus, Occam's razor, supposedly expressed by him because of his resentment of the medieval scientists' tendency to explain simple things *ad infinitum*. Many others had voiced the same dissatisfaction but not in such timeless Latin. *See* **law of parsimony.**

occipital lobe Pertaining to (-al) the lobe in the back (oc-) of the head (-cipit-). One of the five sensory lobes of each hemisphere of the **brain,** where fibers from the **lateral geniculate bodies** terminate. Projection and association areas for vision are located here. It is marked off by the parieto-occipital fissure. (*Contrasted with* frontal). *See* **anatomical directions.**

Ockham's razor *Same as* Occam's razor.

octal number system A number system with base or **radix** of 8. Possible digits run from 0-7. Three **bits** make one octal digit.

oculogravic illusion Relating to (-ic) an **illusion** involving sight (oculo-) and gravity (-grav-) as reference points, such as when a subject, while sitting in a slowly rotating experimental room, finds that his judgment of the horizontal is perpendicular not to the force of gravity "but to the vector sum of gravity plus the centrifugal force." First evidence of this illusion resulted from research on visual perception in the **slow rotation room** of the U. S. Naval School of Aviation Medicine in Pensacola, Florida. (Weintraub and Walker, 1967, pp. 71-73).

oculogyral illusion Relating to (-al) an **illusion** involving the circular (-gyr-) motion of the eyeballs (oculo-). A **slow rotation room** illusion occurring while the rotation speed is increasing, whereby a stationary illuminated object otherwise in complete darkness appears to move inward toward the center of rotation, while in deceleration it appears to move outward (Weintraub and Walker, p. 73).

oculomotor cranial nerve The cranial nerve connected with eye (oculo-) motion (-motor). **Cranial nerve III,** whose fibers originate in the oculomotor nucleus in the ventral part of the **mesencephalon** and **extend** to various eye muscles (except superior oblique and lateral rectus). Autonomic fibers of the oculomotor nerve terminate in the ciliary **ganglia,** which eventually supply the intrinsic eye muscles (ciliary and iris). Also contains sensory fibers from proprioceptors in the eye muscles.

odorivector One of the vectors or qualities of odor (odori-); the odorant vapor. *See* **Mateson multistimulus olfactometer.**

Oedipus (conflict) complex A repressed emotional conflict named for the Greek mythic character Oedipus (meaning "swollen feet," since as a forsaken babe he had been found with his feet bound and swollen). In **psychoanalysis,** the usually unconscious repressed desire of the young son to possess and love the mother, accompanied with jealousy and hostility toward the father. These infantile feelings, if not resolved, lead to

neurotic conflicts about relations with other people. The concept has been extended to include an erotic attachment by the young child of either sex to the parent of the opposite sex, with **ambivalent** feelings of hostility and love directed toward the parent of the same sex.

Oedipus, not knowing his real parents, was told by a seer that he was fated to kill his father and marry his own mother. After fulfilling the prophesy and discovering the truth, he blinded himself, and his wife-mother Jocasta killed herself. The Oedipus legend, according to **Freud,** had its sources in dream material of immemorial antiquity. Freud himself, derived this complex after his experiences in analyzing his own dreams, putting his material into *Three Essays on the Theory of Sexuality* (1905). *See* **Electra complex.**

off-line processing (Comput.) **Data** processing not done in conjunction with the main program but usually by auxiliary computer equipment. An example is card to magnetic tape conversion.

ogive Shape of tub or trough. The **graph** of a cumulative **distribution,** which may be loosely described as S-shaped.

ohm (O) The **SI** unit of electrical resistance, equal to the electrical resistance between two points of a conductor in which one **volt** of potential difference produces a current of one **ampere.** *See* **International System of Units.**

Named after George S. Ohm (1787-1854), German physicist.

Olds, James (Born, Illinois 1922) Ph.D., social psychology, Harvard 1952. A pioneer in **brain** recording and brain manipulation in freely behaving animals. Received **Newcomb Cleveland Prize** in 1956. Received the **Warren Medal** in 1962 for "his development and effective exploitation of intracranial electrical stimulation as a fruitful method in the analysis of positive reinforcement." Recipient of **DSC Award** in 1967. *See* **reward center, septal area, Miller, N. E.**

olfaction Act of (-tion) smelling (olfac-); the sense of smell. *See* **stereochemical smell theory.**

olfactometer An instrument for measuring (-meter) the sense of smell (olfacto-) or smell sensitivity thresholds. *See* **Mateson multistimulus olfactometer.**

olfactory brain Relating to (-ory) the part of the brain that makes (-fact-) the sense of smell (ol-) possible. *See* **rhinencephalon.**

olfactory bulb A bulbous anterior portion of the **olfactory tract** that is really an extension of the **brain.** It is characterized by reticular fibers (glomeruli) leading into the brain, and also by a reverberatory circuit system, allowing for secondary impulses to continue fuselike after the initial **stimulus** has ceased. *See* **amacrine cell.**

olfactory cortex *Same as* archipallium.

olfactory epithelium A stratified yellowish membrane, approximately 500 square millimeters in size and having no blood vessels, that overlies the nasal connective tissue in the naso-pharyngeal area containing the smell receptors. The epithelium is constantly moistened by a mucous fluid, which apparently plays a role in gas-solubility for the purpose of exciting olfactory receptors.

olfactory nerve Cranial nerve I (for smell). One of a pair of **sensory** nerves consisting of **axons** whose cell bodies and **dendrites** lie high up in the nasal mucosa. These axons form about 20 small fibers, which pierce each cribriform plate and end in the **olfactory bulb,** where they synapse with other olfactory neurons whose axons comprise the **olfactory tract.** The nerve conducts smell stimuli from the olfactory organ to the brain.

Italian anatomist Achillini (1463-1512) is believed to be the first to recognize these nerves and to understand their function. In 1786, Scottish-English surgeon John Hunter (1728-1793) described them even more thoroughly.

olfactory neuron *See* olfactory sense organ.

olfactory prism A six-cornered diagram (representative of the six presumed olfactory qualities: burned, putrid, spicy, fragrant, resinous, ethereal) designed as a means of mixing these basic qualities. However, mixing odors has not proven to be satisfactory, nor do the descriptive terms meet agreement by various "experts." *See* **stereochemical smell theory.**

olfactory rods *Same as* **olfactory sense organ.**

olfactory sense organ A receptor for the fibers of the **olfactory nerve** lying almost hidden in the mucosa of the roof of the nasal cavity. *Olfactory neurons* consist of long hair cells that serve as receptors for smell, and, although extremely sensitive (stimulated by the slightest odor), they are also easily fatigued (a strong odor soon becomes unnoticeable).

olfactory tract A narrow, whitish band (bundles of fibers) extending from the olfactory bulb to a **sulcus** on the under surface of the **frontal lobes** of the **brain.**

oligodendroglia Small (oligo-) tree-like (-dendro-) glia cells. *See* **neuroglia.**

oligophrenia Disorder (-ia) of a small (oligo-) mind (phren-) or of little intellect. Term used primarily in Great Britain and Russia for the condition of neurologically damaged persons suffering from **mental retardation.** *See* **phenylpyruvic oligophrenia.**

Named by Fölling in 1934. *See* **phenylketonuria.**

one sample test *See* Tables 25a, 26.

one-tailed test A test of a statistical **hypothesis** in which the **critical region** (region of rejection) lies in either extreme (upper or lower tail) of the **sampling distribution.**

one-to-one correspondence *See* set.

on-line processing (Comput.) **Data** processing for a program done under absolute and direct control of a single operational unit.

on-off language *See* computer.

ontogenesis or ontogeny Origin (-genesis) of the being (onto-) or individual. The history of the development of the fertilized ovum through fetal life or of the individual organism, as distinguished from **phylogenesis** or evolution of the species.

ontological dualism *See* dualism.

ontology (Exist.) The study (-logy) of being (onto-), or the nature of being or existence. Ontology sometimes has been considered synonymous with **metaphysics,** but it is more appropriately a phase of metaphysics and was used by **Aristotle** to mean the science of the essence of things, the First Philosophy.

Introduced into philosophy by **Christian Wolff,** German mathematician and philosopher.

open shop (Comput.) A computer facility open to any qualified company employee so that he can **input** his own programs or use equipment.

operand(um) That which (-andum) is operated (oper-) upon. The quantity or symbol upon which a mathematical operation is performed; in **operant-conditioning** experiments, the environmental segment upon which an organism produces an effect (to secure reinforcement). For example, response keys and bars that animals press are operanda.

Coined by **Skinner** as substitute for the anthropomorphic term "manipulandum."

operand (Comput.) That which (-and) is operated (oper-) upon, usually identified by an **address** part of an instruction.

operant Work (oper-)-ing (-ant) or that which works. In **Skinner's** system of behavior, a term used to describe behavior in instrumental learning where an effective (operant) response develops through voluntary activity of the subject, as when a rat acquires a bar-pressing response in a **Skinner Box** and is rewarded by a food pellet. Thus the operant response first occurs as a random act and thereafter becomes related to a discriminated **stimulus**—a response "emitted" by the subject, not "elicited" by a specific, known external stimulus. It may produce reward or punishment, its rate of

O

occurrence depending upon the **schedule of reinforcement.** Operant behavior usually results in environmental change, such change reinforcing the operant behavior and making it likely to happen again.

According to Skinner, who invented the phrase and introduced it in 1937, operant distinguishes between reflexes and responses, emphasizing the "fact that the behavior operates upon the environment to generate consequences." (B. F. Skinner, Science and Human Behavior, [*Macmillan*, 1953]: "Two Types of Conditioned Reflex: A Reply to Konorski and Miller. *Journal of General Psychology*, 16, 272-279).

operant aggression See **aggression.**

operant avoidance (operant escape) The avoidance or escape from unpleasant circumstances by using behavior previously learned while exposed to **operant conditioning.**

operant behavior Any behavior that operates on or has an effect on the environment.

operant conditioning (instrumental conditioning) Systematic conditioning or strengthening of emitted behavior so that a desired response is selectively reinforced (strengthened by presentation of a reward following the response), thereby increasing the likelihood of the recurrence of the response.

operant extinction See **extinction.**

operant learning Learning that takes place as a result of presentation of a reward following the response to be strengthened.

operant level The observed rate or frequency of emitting an operant response (e.g., lever pressing) prior to **conditioning** or any reinforced training. Also, a **schedule of reinforcement** in which, prior to conditioning, each response is unreinforced.

operant response See **operant.**

operationism A system or doctrine (-ism) of developing definitions from the way things work (operation). A term first used (1927) by Percy Williams Bridgman (1882-1961), Harvard physicist, in *The Logic of Modern Physics.* He said that scientific concepts obtain their meaning from the methods used to arrive at them, and that objective standards lead to **validity.** For example, in an experiment on the effects of hunger on learning in rats, hunger, which is a subjective or private experience, cannot be measured, but hours of food deprivation can; the hunger is inferred. Learning itself must be inferred from number of responses, errors, etc. This method aims at objective description of events that other workers can verify and/or reproduce. Since operational definitions refer to concepts derived from the methods used, the definer must include specific descriptions, experimental operations and observable events, delimitations of procedures, and material used as well as find a high index of **reliability** for the definition.

ophthalmic nerve A division of the **trigeminal nerve,** described and named in 1664 by **Thomas Willis.**

ophthalmometer An instrument for determining the presence and amount of astigmatism in the eye (ophthalmo-) by measuring (-meter) the curvature of the corneal surface along different meridians.

ophthalmoscope A viewing instrument (-scope) with a built-in adjustable concave mirror with a hole in its center for reflecting a light beam directly into the interior of the eye (ophthalmo-) thus making visible a clear image of the *fundus* (part of the eye opposite the pupil).

opisthotonos Tetanic spasm or increased tone (-tonos) of the muscles of the back (opisthot-), resulting in retraction of the head and lower limbs. An extreme form of the condition results in the back being so arched that only the head and feet rest on the bed. Associated with **hysteria** but sometimes with other causes not easily identifiable.

The term was apparently first used by **Hippocrates** to describe limbs that were drawn back and stiffened. The French anatomist and surgeon Alexis Littre (1658-1728) revived the term about 1700. Examples of the condition are seen in the frescoes of Andrea del Sarto (*Annunziata,* Florence) and in Raphael's *Transfiguration* (Vatican).

opium A drug derived from the dried, coagulated milk of the unripe opium poppy pod. Opium is usually smoked and gives off pungent odor. True **hallucinations** apparently do not occur. No evidence of mental deterioration. Withdrawal agonizing: cold sweat, cramps, insomnia, uncontrollable yawning, retching, diarrhea, panic, suicidal attempts. Has been used throughout history as a pain-killer and treatment for severe diarrhea. *See* **heroin(e) and morphine, paregoric.**

Referred to in the 3rd century B.C. in the writings of the Greek naturalist and philosopher, Theophrastus (c. 372-c. 287 B.C.) who called opium *mekonion* (now *meconium*). In 1803, German pharmacist Friedrich Sertürner (1784-1841) isolated and described **morphine.**

opponent-process theory of color vision See **color-vision theories.**

optical scanner (Comput.) An on-line **input** device to a **digital computer** system that effectively "reads" various symbols such as handwriting on prepared forms, and converts the characters into **machine language.**

optic chiasma The crossover (chiasma) junction where the **optic nerves,** coming from each retina, unite at the base of the **brain,** with some of the fibers from each nerve crossing over to the opposite side and continuing in the **optic tract** of that side.

First described by the Roman physician, Rufus of Ephesus, fl. 100 A.D.

optic nerve Either of the two **cranial nerves II.** The nerves are composed of **axons** from the innermost layer (**ganglion** cells) of retinal neurons, and lead through the optic foramina to the cranial cavity, where they unite to form the **optic chiasma.** Beyond the chiasma the optic nerve is known as the **optic tract.** Each optic nerve has fibers only from the retina of the same side, and carries impulses from the **rods** and **cones** to the **thalamus.**

Discovered by **Alcmaeon** (fl. 6th century B.C.), Greek physician and Pythagorean philosopher.

optic tract A bundle of nerve fibers leading from the **optic chiasma** to termination in the **lateral geniculate** body in the **thalamus,** where a new relay of fibers then take off to the visual area of the **occipital lobe** cortex. Other tract fibers terminate in the **superior colliculi** of the **mesencephalon** synapsing with motor fibers on their way to the external eye muscles.

OR *See* **Boolean algebra, disjunction.**

oral character See **character types.**

ordentlicher öffentlicher Professor (or Ordinarius) The highest academic appointment, indicating that the holder is in charge of an established chair with additional duties of holding the directorship of a clinic or institute. The faculty originates the appointment which is usually approved by the government. *See* **German higher education.**

Order of Merit See **honorary physician.**

order of merit See **methods of psychology; psychophysical.**

ordinal scale A **scaling technique** relating to (-al) a system in which objects or persons are arranged or ranked in order (ordin-) on the basis of some attribute (like grades in school, or performance on a test).

ordinate Ordered or arranged (ordin-). The distance from a two-dimensional plotted point in a **graph** to the origin, measured on the scale of the Y, or vertical, axis. The vertical reference axis. *See* **abscissa, polygon.**

organelle Little (-elles) organ or body. A specialized structure (such as **mitochondrion,** the cell nucleus, the nucleolus, and the cell membrane) that serves specific functions (such as cell metabolism, cell respiration, cell reproduction, and synthesis of new chemicals).

organic (disorders) psychosis Pertaining to (-ic) a **psychosis** caused by a disorder of the organs or parts of the body. Mental disorder involving or based on structural changes in cells with impairment of **brain** tissue function, particularly of the **cerebral cortex.** An organic psychosis may be classified in the following manner:

1. *senile* (e.g., self-centeredness, childish emotionality) and **pre-senile dementia** (cortical brain diseases such as **Pick's** and **Alzheimer's** diseases)

2. *alcoholic psychoses* (caused by alcoholic poisoning) (a) **delirium tremens** (tremors, visual hallucinations, delirium); (b) **Korsakow's psychosis** (long-standing condition, with memory impairment, disorientation and confabulation); (c) alcohol paranoid state (alcoholic paranoia) such as having excessive jealousy and delusions of infidelity by spouse

3. *psychosis associated with intracranial infection* such as (a) **general paralysis** (may simulate other psychoses but is due to syphilis of the CNS)

4. *psychosis associated with other cerebral condition(s)* (a) cerebral arteriosclerosis (chronic; similar to pre-and senile dementia); (b) brain trauma (develops immediately after severe head injury, brain surgery); (c) epilepsy of idiopathic type

5. psychoses with other physical conditions (a) endocrine disorder (mainly from complication of diabetes); (b) metabolic or nutritional disorder (from **pellagra,** avitaminosis, etc.); (c) drug or poison intoxication; and (d) childbirth, etc.

organismic psychology The biological and embryological emphasis placed upon **Gestalt psychology** by such men as **Kurt Goldstein** (1918), J. R. Kantor (1924), and R. H. Wheeler (1929). By extension, it has come to mean **holistic** and antimentalistic (opposed to conscious phenomena). (J. R. Kantor, *Principles of Psychology,* 1924-25; Kurt Goldstein, *The Organism: A Holistic Approach to Biology Derived from Pathological Data in Man,* 1938; R. H. Wheeler, *The Science of Psychology,* 1929).

Gustav Fechner introduced the term "organismic" into psychology in 1873.

OR connective See **Boolean algebra.**

organ(s) of Corti Complicated cell structures within the **cochlea** in the inner ear, situated near the inner edge of the **basilar membrane.** They contain rows of fine hair cells in two groups, which are presumed to be the receptors for hearing centers in the brain. The hair cells (one group of internal hair cells in a single row and another group of external hair cells in rows of three or four) are stimulated by the fluidic motion in the cochlear canals, transducing mechanical energy into **nerve impulses.** See **acoustic, frequency theory** under **hearing theories.**

In 1851, Italian anatomist Alfonso Corti first described this organ of hearing, which later was named after him.

organ specificity The belief that the patient suffering from **psychosomatic disorders** unconsciously selects a particular organ or part of the body (such as stomach for ulcers, skin for hives) to be the physical manifestation of his stress or tension, which he has not been able to discharge otherwise.

OR gate See **gate.**

orienting reflex (orienting response) A set or series of nonspecific, original, innate physiological responses (attaining body balance and position, **galvanic skin response,** pupil dilation, sniffing by a dog, etc.) to external changes in stimulation. Of primary biological importance in enabling the organism to adapt to novel environmental changes through use of its past experience, orienting reactions prepare the organism for prospective action by receiving and processing information. Sometimes, the term **orienting reaction** is used to describe the behavioral fight or flight in an organism following the orienting reflex, involving heightened alertness and behavioral orientation to the total environment.

According to **Pribram**, this reflex is accompanied by behavioral arrest of movement except for head, eye, and perhaps body orientation toward the stimulating event (such as the posture of a baseball batter setting himself for the coming pitch).

For the infant, orienting reflexes convey his first response to unfamiliar and unexpected stimuli (e.g., postural adjustments necessary for being held upright; lips pursed for sucking). Later, between 2 and 5 weeks, they occur in response to sound and visual stimuli. The orienting reflex also plays an important part in **Piaget's cognitive development theory.**

Pavlov suggested the idea of an orienting reflex. More recent studies (by E. N. Sokolov, a leading Russian neurophysiologist) relate it to the neural basis of memory. Investigations in this field have become an important phase of Russian psychophysiological experimentation, even connecting the orienting reflex with perceptual illusions and "probabilistic prognosis" in **schizophrenia** (as being studied by Russian psychiatrist, I. M. Feigenberg). *See* **investigatory response**; (also J. Robinson and W. H. Gantt, "The Orienting Reflex [Questioning Reaction]: Cardiac, Respiratory, Salivary, Motor Components," *Bulletin of Johns Hopkins Hospital*, 1947, 80, pp. 231-253.

origin *See* **polygon.**

orthogonal coefficient *See* Table 16.

orthogonal comparison Relating to (-al) two mutually independent comparisons in which the products of their corresponding **coefficients** result in zero, since their intersections meet at straight (ortho-) angles (-gon-). *See* Table 16.

orthogonal Latin square *See* **Graeco-Latin square design**; also Table 15.

orthogonal polynomial Relating to (-al) an algebraic expression that has many (poly-) terms (-nom-) whose axes are at right (ortho-) angles (-gon-) with one another. An orthogonal polynomial is of particular use in the analysis of data for trend, in that orthogonal sets of **coefficients** (in which the sum of products is zero) are independent of each other, or uncorrelated. *See* Table 16.

orthopsychiatry Psychiatry for corrective (ortho-) purposes. A field of study associated with the growth of the American Orthopsychiatric Association, organized in 1924, incorporating the services (in a true Freudian sense) of social workers, anthropologists, psychologists, educators, probation officers, psychiatrists, nurses, as well as laymen, in an effort to unite the services of all professions engaged in the study of human behavioral problems. After first being concerned primarily with delinquency, orthopsychiatry branched out to investigate and treat all forms of maladaptive behavior.

oscillometer An instrument for measuring (-meter) oscillation, or change in arterial pulsation, primarily of the extremities.

oscilloscope A viewing instrument (-scope) for the temporary display of oscillation of an electrical quantity on the fluorescent screen of a cathode-ray tube.

Osgood, Charles Egerton Born, Massachusetts 1916. Ph.D., Yale 1945. Researcher in higher mental processes, psycholinguistics, and learning theory. Received **DSC Award** in 1960. President APA 1963. *See* **semantic differential, scaling technique.**

ossicle Little (-icles) bone (oss-). One of a chain of small bones (**malleus, incus,** and **stapes**) called auditory ossicles, located in the **middle ear** (tympanic cavity), which is a tiny epithelial-lined cavity hollowed out of the temporal bone. The ossicles amplify and transmit auditory vibrations from the eardrum (**tympanic membrane**) to the **oval window** into which the stapes fits.

Ossicles supposedly were first noticed by Empedocles of Agrigentum (490-430 B.C.).

otolith Ear (oto-) stone (-liths). A small particle of calcium carbonate embedded in the gelatinous membrane (also containing sensitive hair cells) of the macula, which is located within the **utricle** and **saccule.** When the head position changes the otoliths pull on the hair cells, stimulating adjacent receptors of the vestibular nerve to inform the brain about head position, changes in the pull of gravity, or changes in acceleration.

Otoliths were described and named by French anatomist Gilbert Breschet (*see* **helicotrema**).

outcome The end result of an experiment. In **game theory**, outcome determines a particular set of payments, one set being paid to each competitor. In experimental psychology, the **dependent variable** in an experiment indicating the degree of response (change of attitude, how much has been learned, etc.) basic to experimental prediction. Outcomes of an experiment (often denoted by the variable X) are also called elementary or simple **events.**

output Something produced; energy put out by a machine or system for storage or conversion purposes; in **cybernetics**, the **response** of a mechanism or organism; **data** that have been processed.

oval window (fenestra ovalis) A membrane-covered opening to the fluid-filled **inner ear**, separating the **middle** and inner ears, through which sound waves are transmitted from the middle ear bones to the **cochlea.** The oval window (attached to the **stapes**) is located at the base of the **scala vestibuli** (one of the three canals of the cochlea). Vibrations received from the auditory **ossicles** exert pressure on the oval window, causing the fluid to set up ripples with a subsequent bulging inside the cochlea. Once the energy is transmitted to the **scala tympani** canal, it becomes rapidly extinguished.

First adequately described by **Fallopius** in 1561.

ovarian hormone *See* **estrogen.**

overcompensation A sometimes unconscious exaggeration of a socially desirable trait in order to cover up real or imagined deficiencies. An exaggerated attempt to overcome threatened inferiority or threatened loss of self-respect (**Alfred Adler, 1917**). Overcompensation may be *positive* (wherein a person who "will never walk again" trains himself to become the world's greatest mile runner) or *negative* (wherein a person may overreact to criticism by trying to be so good as to avoid censure, thus destroying his human touch).

overlearning In memory experiments, learning a skill by practicing beyond or over the point necessary for immediate recall or immediate use. (**Ebbinghaus, 1885**).

overloading The act or process (-ing) of subjecting someone or an organism to excessive stress, as by forcing the organism to process an unusual amount of information.

overpunching (Comput.) The process of punching more than one character in a single column of an IBM card in order to form a special character. Same as **zone punch.**

overtone In a complex tone, one of the upper partials (along with the fundamental) that comprise a musical tone. *See* **Fourier series.**

oximeter A filter photometer attached to the ear and used to monitor or measure (-meter) changes continuously in arterial oxygen (oxi-) saturation without extracting blood. Two types are: *reflectance oximeter* in which the photodetectors are located on either side of the light source (usually the forehead); and *photoelectric oximeter,* which indicate changes in the blood's volume in the optical path (Brown, pp. 87, 391).

oxytocin Chemical substance (-in) that results in the quickening (oxy-) of childbirth (-toc-); quickbirth. One of the two (the other, **vasopressin**) hormones of the posterior pituitary gland (**neurohypophysis**) primarily responsible for stimulating smooth muscle and the alveoli of the breast to send milk into the ducts.

Term introduced in 1953 by American biochemist Vincent du Vigneaud (born 1901), who isolated bottle oxytocin and vasopressin in 1953. He received the Nobel prize in 1955.

P

P probability.

pacer stimulus A stimulus that becomes the ideal. In the theory of choice proposed in 1960 by American psychologists W. N. Dember (born 1928) and R. W. Earl (born 1920), perception is considered to be affected by stimuli and behavior is determined by perception. Each person automatically, in his choices, sets up an ideal or preferred level of complexity. Theoretically, he will never select any stimulus that is less complex than his ideal; however, he will choose one slightly more complex, and if given a free choice, he will select stimuli more continually complex.

Pacinian corpuscle An end organ in the skin, first described about 1740 by German anatomist Abraham Vater (1648-1751), and later (1840) more thoroughly by Italian anatomist Filippo Pacini (1812-1883)—the Vater-Pacini corpuscles. In 1844, the term Pacinian corpuscle was introduced by German anatomist, Friedrich G. J. Henle (1809-1885) and Swiss histologist **Kölliker.** *See* **accessory structure.**

paired associate learning A rote method used in verbal learning and retention studies whereby a subject must learn **stimulus-response** paired items, and later, upon request, reproduce the second item upon presentation of the first remembered item.

paired comparisons L. L. Thurstone's method (1927) that scales psychological judgments in terms of psychological distance. Mathematical assumptions are made from comparisons obtained from subjects who must, of two stimuli, choose one over the other—as the more preferred one, the more intense one, etc. *See* **methods of psychology: psychophysical** (also Hays, 1963, p. 30f).

paleencephalon The old (pale-) brain (-encephalon); the more evolutionarily ancient part of the **brain** in animals, including the **cerebellum** and other areas not related to the **cerebrum.** *Contrast with* **neencephalon.**

paleocerebellum From an evolutionary standpoint, the older more ancient (paleo-) part of the cerebellum (consisting of both the anterior and posterior lobes) which regulates postural tone.

In 1885, the distinction between paleo- and neocerebellum (as well as the paleo- and neocerebrum) was first made by German neurologist Ludwig Edinger (1855-1918).

paleocortex The evolutionarily ancient (paleo-) cortex, primitive in structure, with approximately four layers, and located mainly on the brain's ventral surface. The paleocortex is associated with the **hypothalamus** and the **limbic system,** playing a role in emotion and in the thirst reaction; sometimes called the olfactory cortex and **archipallium.**

palingraphia A disorder (-ia) of writing (-graph-) backward (palin-). *See* **mirror writing.**

pallidum Same as **globus pallidus.**

pancreas All (pan-) flesh (-creas). Endocrine gland lying along the lower wall of the stomach, near the duodenum. Contains **alpha** and **beta cells,** which release **glucagon** and **insulin,** controlling blood-sugar quantities.

p

Described by **Herophilus** about 300 B.C.; its function in digestion was described by **Claude Bernard**, 1849-56.

panpsychism The doctrine (-ism) that all (pan-) objects in the universe have an unconscious psyche (-psych-) or functioning mind. *See* **Fechner**.

Pantopon (Roche tradename for hydrochloride of opium alkaloids). A preparation consisting of alkaloids of opium in a highly purified form. It acts essentially the same as **morphine** and has the same addictive effects.

Papez-MacLean theory of emotion In 1937, Papez introduced the **limbic system** as the major site of emotional experience, but also accepting the **hypothalamus** as a center for bodily expression of emotion. MacLean in 1949, revised some of the details of the Papez theory, still clinging to the importance of the limbic system but suggesting the **amygdala** and the **hippocampus** as the mediating organs in emotional experience. *See* **central theory**. (J. W. Papez, "A Proposed Mechanism of Emotion," *Archives of Neurological Psychiatry*, 1937, **38**, 725-743; P. D. MacLean, "Psychosomatic Disease and the 'Visceral Brain.'" *Psychosomatic Medicine*, 1949, **11**, 338-353).

James Wenscelas Papez. Born, Minnesota 1883. M.D. 1911, Minnesota. Comparative neurologist specializing in cerebral mechanisms and thalamic evolution.

Paul Donald MacLean. Born, Phelps, New York 1913. Yale M.D. (*cum laude*) 1940. Neurophysiology and internal medicine.

parabola To throw (-bola) beside (para-), referring to the axis being placed parallel to the side of the cone. A type of curve whose general equation is: $y = ax^2 + bx + c$.

Although it has other meanings, the term usually refers to the locus of a point that moves, so that its distance from a fixed point (the focus) is equal to its perpendicular distance from a fixed straight line (the directrex). The standard form of the equation when the vertex of the parabola lies on the origin and the focus is on the positive x axis is $y^2 = 2px$, where $p/2$ is the distance between the fixed line of the focus.

Paracelsus (1493-1541) German-Swiss alchemist, philosopher, and physician. *See* **cretinism**.

parachromatism Condition (-ism) of seeing colors (-chromat-) with a distorted (para-) perception; type of **color blindness**.

paradigm A scientific model that can be shown (-digm) side by side (para-), designed to stimulate research questions, develop a methodology for gaining and classifying **data**, and secure standards necessary for evaluating evidence accumulated. Various paradigms exist in **psychology**, such as **behaviorism**, **psychoanalysis**, and **topological psychology**. In experimental social psychology, the S-O-R paradigm is a prominent approach to social problems. It entails the manipulation of social stimuli (S) so that they have some effect upon the organism (O), making it possible for relevant responses (R) to be observed (Jones and Gerard, pp. 46-58).

paradoxical Relating to (-ical) perverted or contrary (para-) thinking (-dox-).

paradoxical cold A sensation of cold aroused by a hot stimulus, instigated when such object (with temperature above 110°F.) stimulates any cold-sensitive skin receptor.

paradoxical sleep (PS) A stage of sleep characterized *physiologically* by cortical **beta** (awake cortical rhythm), **rapid eye movements**, and lack of muscle tone, *behaviorally* by difficulty in awakening, and frequent dreaming. Occurs about 1½ to 2 hours after sleep sets in, and alternates with slow wave (**delta** and **theta**) sleep. *See* **sleep stages**.

So-named because a paradox existed in which experimental cats produced a waking EEG while they were asleep. Many mammals and some birds have also demonstrated such a paradox.

Term introduced by the French research physician Michel Jouvet in an article "The States of Sleep," as published in the *Scientific American* (February 1967, pp. 62-72).

paradoxical warmth A feeling of warmth experienced even though a **stimulus** cooler than the body temperature (98.6°F.) is applied to the receptor cells for warm or hot sensations.

parageusia Disorder (-ia) of distorted (para-) taste (-geus-); taste hallucination.

parallax Distorted (para-) change (-allax). Any apparent displacement (or distortion) of an object due to the observer's position.

parallax shift *Same as* **binocular disparity**.

parallelism *See* **psychophysical parallelism**.

paralogical thinking A type of thinking characterized by (-al) a logic that is illogical or unreasonable (para-); involuntary false reasoning; in **schizophrenia**, a type of thinking that manifests logical fallacies, tending to identify objects on the basis of identical predicates so that two objects with a common property between them is perceived as the same, such as a schizophrenic person being told by his girl friend that she is pregnant, and since they have not had intercourse, he reasons that her conception was immaculate, therefore she is the Virgin Mary, and he necessarily God. (Ephraim Rosen. Ian Gregory, Abnormal Psychology, 1965, Philadelphia: *W. B. Saunders Company*, p. 306.

paralysis agitans *Same as* **Parkinson's disease**.

parameter An accessory (para-) or variable of some measurement (-meter) or equation; a **variable** given a constant value for a specific purpose. It is usually a fixed value but may be altered in special instances. In mathematics, usually some quantitative element of a curve or a system of curves; a characteristic of a **set** of scores that is dependent upon every element within that set, as distinguished from a **statistic** that is dependent upon a **sampling** of the elements. The term entered psychology and statistics when applied to the **normal curve** and to learning curves. Parameters are usually designated by Greek letters (such as μ for population mean and σ for the standard deviation).

Although a parameter is considered a constant, it is not a universal constant (such as pi), but is, as has been facetiously stated, a constant that varies: varies according to any given situation or change in experimental conditions. A parameter is also considered to be the true value of a statistic computed from all observations in a **population**.

parametric statistics Statistical techniques (based on the normality assumption) that are used to test **hypotheses** concerning **population** parameters or to establish confidence limits for **parameters**. They require a number of restrictive assumptions about the population(s) under investigation. *Compare* **nonparametric statistics**.

paramnesia Disorder (-ia) of distorted or perverted (para-) memory (mnes-); recalling events that never happened. *See* *déjà vu*.

paranoia An extremely rare disorder (-ia) characteristic of a deranged (para-) mind (-no[us]), with systematized, persecutory and/or grandiose **delusions** and **hallucinations** usually with absence of other emotional or intellective malfunctioning.

In *paranoid schizophrenia*, the delusions are not so classically systematized, but personality deterioration is more evident, with gross disturbances of the emotions and adaptive and intellective functioning. So-called *paranoid states* are characterized by hallucinations but with less systematized and less complex delusions than in paranoia, and without bizarre dissociation and deterioration of paranoid type of **schizophrenia**. *Paranoid disorders* (including paranoia and paranoid states) involve thought disturbances of a persecutory form but without gross personality disturbance.

In **Hippocrates'** time (ca. 400 B.C.) paranoia meant craziness, folly, general mental disorder. In 1764, R. A. Vogel (1730-1792) reintroduced the word to deal with disorders of thinking; in 1879, German neuropsychiatrist Richard von Krafft-Ebing (1840-1902) first applied the term to all forms of systematized delusional insanity, and in 1883, **Kraepelin** used it as a special form of insanity. Between 1887-1890, Russian psychiatrist Sergei Sergeivich (1853-1900), established basis of modern concept of paranoia. *See* **Cullen**.

paranoid personality *See* **personality disorders**.

paranoid states *See* **paranoia**.

paranoid type of schizophrenia *See* **schizophrenia**.

paraphemia Disorder (-ia) of distorted (para-) wording (phem-). An aphasic condition in which wrong words are used.

paraphilia A pathological disorder (-ia) of abnormal (para-) sexual desire; perversion; sexual deviation.

paraphrenia Disorder (-ia) of a distorted (para-) mind (-phren-).

The term was first used by French psychiatrist Joseph Guislain (1797-1860) as a synonym for folly, and reintroduced by Kraepelin in 1912 who applied it to paranoid disorders that are neither true paranoia nor paranoid schizophrenia. **Freud** used it to describe schizophrenia. Sometimes used synonymously for **schizophrenia**.

parapsychology (psionics) An area of psychology that conducts experiments beyond (para-) the ordinary concern of academic psychology. *See* **extrasensory perception**.

In 1893, the French mystic Boirac introduced the word.

parasympathetic division A phrase introduced in 1905 by English physiologist John Newport Langley (1852-1925) to represent the craniosacral portion of the **autonomic nervous system**. *See* **sympathetic division**.

parasympathomimetic drug Relating to (-ic) a drug that simulates (-mimet-) the action of the **parasympathetic nervous system**; an inhibitor, or having constrictive effects, such as **methacholine**.

parataxic thinking Related to (-ic) thinking that is beside (para-) the orderly (tax-) way of thinking, or beside the point. In **H. S. Sullivan's** theory of three hierarchical forms of thinking (the **prototaxic**, parataxic, and **syntaxic**) parataxic refers to a false belief that one of two associated events must be causative, or that correlation means causation, as is evident in children who believe that because firemen are associated with fires they must bring the fires. *See* **ego formation**.

parathormone A hormone secreted by the **parathyroid glands**. Isolated (1925) by Canadian biochemist, James B. Collip (1892-1965).

parathyroid glands One of four (sometimes more) pea-sized endocrine glands, two on each side (para-) of and embedded in the **thyroid glands**. Removal results in cramps, convulsions, tetany and death, since the parathyroids secrete a hormone necessary for regulating calcium metabolism as well as phosphate metabolism.

Described and named in 1880 by the Swedish anatomist Ivar Victor Sandström (1852-1889), the gland being functionally demonstrated to be independent of the thyroid in 1897 by the French physician, Gustav Moussu (1864-1919). The influence of the gland on the regulation of calcium concentration in mammalian blood was first recognized in 1909 by American pathologist William G. MacCollum (1874-1944) and American pharmacologist Carl Voegtlin (1879-1951).

paregoric Relating to (-ic) soothing speech held beside (par-) the marketplace (a[e]gor-), resulting from taking an anodyne such as paregoric, a tincture of **opium** that relieves pain; also helpful in checking children's diarrhea.

p

parergasic Referring to (-ic) psychotic disorders that are unusual or distorted (par-), characterized by incongruous, bizarre, and idiosyncratic behavior.

paresis Paralysis. A syphilitic brain involvement marked by degeneration of cerebral tissue resulting in mental and physical deterioration; an inflammation of usually the entire **cerebral cortex** causing atrophy of tissue in varying degrees. Onset usually insidious with headaches and memory changes, distractibility, and easy fatigability.

Called **general paralysis** of the insane and initially described in 1798 by J. Haslem, a London pharmacist.

paresthesia A disorder (-ia) of perverted (par-) feelings (-esthes-). Pathological skin sensations, such as of ants crawling on the skin or tingling, burning sensations; may be caused by certain drugs.

parietal See **anatomical directions.**

parietal lobe Referring to (-al) the wall-like (pariet-) division of the **cerebral cortex** lying between the **frontal** and **occipital** lobes and above the **temporal**, containing projection areas for the somesthetic sense and association areas for somesthetic, visual, and speech areas. Primarily association cortex. Plays a role in bodily sensations and movement.

Parkinson's disease A nerve condition, characterized by an expressionless face and **athetoid** (slow twisting motions of limbs) and *choreiform* movements (quick, jerky motions).

Many drugs have been used to treat the condition, most of them unsuccessfully. **L-dopa**, when first tried in 1961 with small doses, had little success, but larger doses were given in 1967 with such success that it has become the agent of choice in treating the disease.

In 1893, Rumanian neurologist Georges Marinesco (1864-1938) and French physician Paul Blocq (1860-1896) reported a lesion in the **substantia nigra** in persons having Parkinson's disease, leading French neurologist Eduard Brissaud (1852-1909) to develop the nigral origin of Parkinson's disease as reported in his textbook in 1899. In 1921 several experimenters, led by French neurologist Charles Foix (1882-1927), located the site of such lesions to be in the substantia nigra and **basal ganglia.**

Further information on the disease may be obtained at: *Parkinson's Disease Research and Information Center,* 640 West 168th Street, New York, N.Y. 10032; and *American Parkinson Disease Association,* 147 East 50th Street, New York, N.Y. 10022.

parorexia Disorder (-ia) of perverted (par-) appetite (-orex-) or desire for unusual food, such as the craving of some pregnant women for unusual dishes. *Compare* **pica.**

parosmia Disorder (-ia) of a perverted (par-) sense of smell (-osm-), sometimes seen in children or psychotics who perceive odors differently from others.

parsimony, law of See **law of parsimony.**

pars pro toto (Part of the whole). In psychology and psychiatry the part of a person (eyes, nose, voice, wearing apparel) that is substituted for the whole being, as in **fetishism.** First used in this sense by **Freud.**

partial correlation. See **coefficient of partial correlation.**

partial reinforcement An experimental condition in which subjects receive **reinforcement** not after every **response** but for only a portion of its occurrences (at various time intervals or after a certain number of responses). It is the type of reinforcement most often found in nature. Different schedules of partial reinforcement may lead to different response rates; for example, rats on a fixed time schedule may make few responses, while those reinforced after a certain number of responses may respond often and rapidly (D. J. Lewis, "Partial Reinforcement: A Selective Review of the Literature Since 1950," *Psychological Bulletin,* 1960, 57, 1-28).

Pascal's triangle A triangle of numbers based on the **binomial** coefficient. Its name derives from Blaise Pascal (1623-1662), French geometer and scientist, who did not invent the triangle but popularized it with ingenious and extensive uses in **probability** theory. *See* Table 1c (also Bell, pp. 73-89).

passive-aggressive personality *See* **personality disorders.**

pastoral counseling Relating to (-al) counseling by a pastor. A psychological approach to the presentation of spiritual values in a therapeutic relationship; religious counseling by a priest, rabbi, or clergyman. *See* **integrity therapy.**

Paul of Aegina (625-690) Alexandrian Greek physician and medical compiler from the island of Aegina. First to use the term hemiplegia. *See* **enuresis, stenopeic.**

Pavlov, Ivan Petrovich (1849-1936) Russian physiologist. Graduate of Medico-Chirurgical Academy, 1879.

After studying salivation in dogs for several years, he developed the concept and the term "conditional (conditioned) reflex." His dogs had developed an anticipatory response to the meat they expected and salivated before chewing. Any stimulus (footsteps, bells sounding, sight of food) acted as a conditioning stimulus, supplanting the need for supplying the original stimulus (food). Pavlov won the Nobel prize in 1904 for his contributions to medicine and physiology.

Although Pavlov received most of the credit for his reflex studies, there were others who set the stage for his work. **Sechenov** was one, as was another Russian physiologist, **V. M. Bekhterev** who, at first, worked under the banner of **objective psychology** but later shifted to reflexology and published *General Principles of Reflexology* (1932 English translation). His so-called "associated reflexes" were apparently similar to Pavlov's conditional reflexes. *See* **Locke, Loeb, classical conditioning, behaviorism, experimental neurosis, decortication conditioning, reinforcement** (also Boring, pp. 636-637; Vinacke, p. 517).

pavor nocturnus Night (*nocturnus*) terror (*pavor*). An extreme form of nightmare, most likely to occur between the ages of 3 and 12, in which the child suffers from panic reactions and has great difficulty in reorienting himself to reality. Usually, after a later sleep, he remembers nothing about his terrifying experience (Kessler, 1966, pp. 233-235).

payoff matrix The pattern of limitations (including rewards and/or punishments) explained to players in a game as a phase of the rules. The payoff is dependent upon the choice made between alternatives. *See* **game theory.**

peak experience An expression used by **Maslow** to describe the absolute feeling of happiness and fulfillment in having achieved the ultimate in experiencing one's "being"; of having been intimately acquainted with experience of wholeness, aliveness, beauty, truth, uniqueness, self-sufficiency, goal-attainment, or self-actualization (A. H. Maslow, "Cognition of Being in the Peak Experiences," *Journal of Genetic Psychology,* 1959, 94, 43-66).

Pearson, Egon Sharpe Born 1895, England. D.Sc. Trinity College, Cambridge 1926. Biometrician and mathematical statistician. Professor Emeritus, University College, London. Author of many books and papers on theory and application of statistics. For many years editor of *Biometrika. See* **likelihood ratio test.**

Pearson, Karl (1857-1936) English scientist and statistician. Developed statistical methods for studying biological distributions (from his studies on evolution and heredity). Worked with and was a disciple of **Galton.** Used for the first time the statistical terms of **normal curve,** and **standard deviation.** Developed the mathematical basis of **correlation** (Pearson **r**).

Pearson product-moment correlation (Pearson **r**) A method for computing the **coefficient of correlation** utilizing the products of the deviations of the **data** from their **means,** simply expressing the relation between two **variables.** It is designed for use only with **interval-** or ratio-**scaling techniques,** and reflects only linear relationship between two variables. The Pearson **r** represents the extent to which the same subjects are in the same relative position on two variables.

Correlation coefficient formula (Ungrouped data)

$$r = \frac{\Sigma xy}{\sqrt{\Sigma x^2 \, \Sigma y^2}}$$

where x and y are deviations from the means of X and Y, respectively.

For use with a calculating machine

$$r_{xy} = \frac{N\Sigma XY - (\Sigma X)(\Sigma Y)}{\sqrt{[N\Sigma X^2 - (\Sigma X)^2][N\Sigma Y^2 - (\Sigma Y)^2]}}$$

where X and Y are original scores in variables X and Y.

Product-moment formulas are so called because the value of r is a function of the **moment** or potency of these products. It involves computations between actual scores rather than between ranks on two measures.

As American psychologists M. D. Nefzger (born 1926) and James Drasgow (born 1924) point out, there is no necessity "to assume that each of the correlated variables, when treated as separate **frequency distributions,** is normal in form... for proper application of the Pearson technique." The assumption about normality was erroneously made by Karl Pearson himself in 1896, because he used a "bias-oriented example" to illustrate his point. **Fisher's** classic text perpetuated this error through eleven editions up to 1950, when British statistician George Udny Yule (1871-1951) objected to "Pearson's choice of a poor example and his failure to generalize beyond the restrictive limits of normal data." But Yule's criticism met deaf ears, thus accounting for much of the confusion in textbooks about the Pearson **r** (M. D. Nefzger and James Drasgow, "The Needless Assumption of Normality in Pearson's r," *The American Psychologist,* 1957, 12, 623-625).

pecking order (translation of Ger., *Hackordnung*) A hierarchical social system originally noticed in behavior of poultry: birds on a lower scale permit those on a higher scale to peck at them without retaliation, but these birds can likewise expect to peck at those below them without fear of counterattack. Pecking orders usually exist for each sex, and males usually dominate the females. In human social organizations (women's clubs, faculty groups) pecking orders also exist. (Also called prostasia; *compare* **hook order.**)

Term first used (1935) by Norwegian sociologist, psychologist, and educator Thorleif Schjelderup-Ebbe (born 1894), who was also the first to systematically describe such behavior.

pedomorphism Attributing childish limitations to the human adult; describing adult behavior in relation to child behavior. *Contrast with* **enelicomorphism.**

pedophilia A disorder (-ia) characterized by making love (phil-) to children (pedo-) or young adolescents, the pedophiliac being potent only with generally helpless children whose genitals he manipulates or may make partial and sometimes complete penetration. Usually, attack is forceful or done with threats.

pellagra A chronic condition or seizure (-agra) associated with vitamin B deficiencies and marked by skin (pell-) lesions, gastrointestinal disturbances, apprehension, fear, anxiety, insomnia, fatigue, and easy distractibility.

p

Greater severity evidenced by delirium, confusion, hallucinations, and disorientation. *See* **nicotinic acid.**

In 1771, Italian physician Francesco Frapolli (1711-1773), was first to describe the condition in Italy and derived the term from pellarella, a word used as early as 1590 to describe rough skin conditions.

pentobarbital (Tradename: Nembutal) A **barbiturate** (-barbital-) used mainly in its sodium or calcium salt as a hypnotic and as a sedative. Slang: nimbies, pink ladies, yellow jackets.

Pentothal Sodium Abbott tradename for sodium thiopental, a **barbiturate** used chiefly as a surgical anesthetic, usually administered intravenously.

Introduced in 1935 by American physician John Silas Lundy (born 1894).

pentylenetetrazol A white, crystalline powder, used as a respiratory and circulatory stimulant in treatment of, for example, barbiturate poisoning; also for inducing convulsions in certain psychoses.

perceived role *See* **role.**

percentage point A level of significance (α) expressed as a percentage.

percentile (centile) Pertaining to (-ile) percent or hundred (-cent-). A division of a group into 100 equal parts, the individuals having been arranged in order of magnitude. The group may be rats or students, and the magnitude may deal with **reaction times** or with examination grades. A percentile is one of these 100 equal parts.

A percentile is analogous to a **median** and a **quartile** (the 50th percentile is the median, while the first quartile and third quartile are identical with the 25th percentile and the 75th percentile, respectively). Subscripts, if any, indicate which percentile is meant. For example, P_{70} is that value in the **distribution** below which 70 percent of the values lies and above which 30 percent lie. *See* Table 2.

percentile rank The rank of an individual (or class of individuals) with reference to a **percentile** division of the group, indicating the percentage of scores in the entire **distribution** that lie below that rank. For example, an individual in the 90th percentile ranks higher than one in the 1st to 89th percentiles but lower than one in the 91st to 100th percentiles.

percentile score A converted score representing an individual's place on a percentile scale and relating to its group in a point on the scale. Percentile scores enable comparisons of results from different raw units.

perception Act of (-tion) perceiving (percep-). Awareness of having the senses stimulated by external objects, qualities, or relations. Immediate experiences, as opposed to memory; ability to select, organize, and interpret various sensory experiences into recognizable patterns. The interpretation placed upon a **stimulus** or experience, determined by general organization principles. A persistent condition of perceptual readiness for any kind of desired or expected goal is called a *perceptual set*. Perception, as defined by **Bruner**, a **cognitive** theorist, is "the construction of a set of organized categories in terms of which stimulus inputs (new experiences) may be sorted, given identity, and given more elaborated connotative meaning" (J. S. Bruner, "On Perceptual Readiness," *Psychological Review*, 1957, 64, 123-152).

perceptual constancy A person's tendency to perceive experience as expected; as being relatively stable under diverse conditions of stimulation, such as environmental variability. The tendency of perceptual responses to be relatively independent of environmental alterations, so that one perceives objects as constant (same size, shape, color, etc.) even though they stimulate sense receptors differently. Perception constancy does not operate if a **reduction screen** (which eliminates context cues) is used to view an object.

Because of color constancy, for example, hues tend to be correctly perceived in spite of changes in illumination; because of **size constancy**, background or foreground objects tend to be perceived in terms of their objective sizes. One tends to correct for illumination differences (**brightness constancy**), for angle of view (**shape constancy**), or for distance (**size constancy**). Perceptual constancy, in social psychology, has been studied in relation to expectancy of outcome. *See* **object constancy.**

First described by **Helmholtz** in 1867.

perceptual defense A perceptually selective process whereby a person defensively blocks or distorts (hesitates, misidentifies, adds material that isn't there, or acts ignorant of) perceptions that are threatening or disagreeable to him.

perceptual norm In social psychology, the socially approved and usually well-established, well-defined, traditional way of perceiving the environment, norms which members of the community are expected to observe.

perceptual set *See* **perception.**

perceptual vigilance The heightened sensitivity to need-related cues.

Percodan (Endo tradename for an opiate analgesic. It is less habit-forming than **morphine** but more so than codeine.

performance test A nonverbal **intelligence test** requiring the subject to manipulate materials or use muscular responses, such as completing pictures, assembling objects, placing blocks in a certain pattern, etc. The performances required on the paper-cutting subtest of the **Stanford-Binet test** and the "blocks" subtest used by **Wechsler** are examples of testing performance rather than verbality (vocabulary knowledge, word fluency). Such tests can employ either language or nonlanguage cues, using pictures or even pantomime for direction.

A test in which performance on any single item is predictive of the performance on any other item is said to be homogeneous.

perikaryon Situated around (peri-) a nucleus or nut (-karyon). The cytoplasmic cell body of a **neuron.**

perimeter Measuring (-meter) around (peri-). An instrument consisting of an adjustable sweeping arm with a fixation point for the eye and variable locations for the visual stimuli. It is used for optometric, clinical, and laboratory experimentation in mapping areas of the retina sensitive to differently colored lights. Auditory space perception is studied similarly.

peripheralist position (or peripheralist psychology) A point of view (such as the **James-Lange theory**) holding that many aspects of behavior (such as learning, thirst, thinking, need for eating) take place by action in the outer boundaries of the body (in **motor** activities, for example) and are not functions of the **central nervous system.** Thirst, accordingly, results from decreased salivary flow; hunger comes from an empty stomach and satiety from a full stomach; and the process of thinking amounts to small movements of the vocal apparatus. In learning, stimulus-response theories are called peripheralist in that they emphasize stimulation and reinforcement from the periphery or the environment. The peripheralist position applied to the emotions assigns the major role to the **autonomic nervous system.** However, it is claimed that visceral changes are not responsive enough to set off emotional feelings. Furthermore, animals experimentally deprived of sensory impulses still behave "emotionally."

Some theorists (**Watson** and **Skinner** among them) have presented the idea that thinking is also peripheral in that it is done with muscles, the central nervous system being important only in the formation of learned connections. Some evidence to support this idea comes from research that showed electrical potentials being recorded from the tongue when the subject was thinking. Furthermore, experiments on deaf-mutes who had learned a sign language showed that the subjects had electrical activity in their fingers but not tongues, while another experiment with deaf children who were taught to speak and also use a sign language showed electrical potentials in both tongue and hands. The extreme peripheralist stand is that thinking actually is small muscle movement while the moderate view assumes that muscle movement accompanies thinking. (Harlow, McGaugh, Thompson, pp. 383-84).

Peripherality, in a communication net, denotes the place occupied by a person in reference to other people (e.g., one with a high degree of peripherality is relatively farther away from others). *Contrast with* **central theory.**

peripheral nervous system Relating to (-al) the part of the nervous system that includes all the nerves and nerve **ganglia** lying outside the **brain** and spinal cord. Divisions include the **somatic nervous system** and the **autonomic nervous system.**

peripheral schizophrenia *See* **nuclear vs. peripheral schizophrenia.**

permutation The process (-ion) of thoroughly changing (permutat-), exchanging, or arranging some or all of a group of elements; the number of ways that objects may be arranged in order. There are only two ways of arranging AB, but there are six ways of ordering ABC: ABC, ACB, BAC, BCA, CAB, CBA. The number of permutations of n things taken r at a time is given by the formula:

$$P(n,r) = \frac{n!}{(n-r)!}$$

where
  P = number of possible permutations,
  n = number of arrangeable things,
  r = number of things in each group,
  $n!$ = (n factorial) = the product of all positive integers from 1 to the number denoted by n.
  Example: $5! = 1 \times 2 \times 3 \times 4 \times 5 = 120$
(Hays, 1964, p. 134; Lewis, p. 88).

perseveration The tendency to persist in repeating an activity (thoughts, words, or movements) after a stimulus has ceased. Inappropriate repetition of an act without any apparent associative stimulus. Perseveration tends to be common among mentally retarded and brain-injured persons, and those having difficulty in perceiving relationships. People with **schizophrenia** and **compulsion** and **anxiety** neuroses may perseverate on **motor** activities. *See* **sterotypy.**

persona *See* **analytic psychology, personality.**

personal equation The tendency to personal bias resulting in discrepancies between chronological measurements of different scientific observers (and between a person's own periodic observations) due to individual differences. The term proposed by Bessel for the personal adjustment needed to make one person's observation equal to the same datum reported by another person. Loosely, individual differences, especially in reaction time, for which such allowance must be made.

Friedrich Bessel (1784-1846), German astronomer, became interested in why Nevil Maskelyne (1732-1811) astronomer-royal at Greenwich, England dismissed his assistant, Kinnebrook in 1796. Maskelyne had accused Kinnebrook of making too many constant errors in comparing his observation of stellar transits with his own. Bessel made a study of observation times among many competent astronomers, discovering that individual variations occurred not only between all of them but also within their own observations periodically. By indicating the errors due to the personal equation, Bessel played a major role in helping psychology point out the importance of individual differences and

p

variability in **reaction time**. The personal equation is a recognized source of bias in all scientific measurements.

personality Etymologically, a mask (*persona:* through a mouthpiece) or facade that a person uses to camouflage his true self, as a male might use a female mask to enact the role of a woman, or even exchange masks during a play to denote different characters, such as the devil, or a god. The concept of role-playing may well have developed from this early use of the term.

Currently, personality is the distinctively different characteristic or sum total of a person, including his behavior, character traits (honesty, loyalty, etc.), physical appearance, and individual and social modes of adjustment.

As a cultural stereotype, personality refers to a behavioral pattern by which the person is known and from which mosaic certain predictions can be made about his future behavior. See **individual tests, personality inventory.**

personality disorders and other non-psychotic mental disorders Lifelong patterns of maladaptive behavior qualitatively different from **neuroses** or **psychoses**, such as those personality types called paranoid personality, cyclothymic, schizoid, explosive, hysterical, asthenic, antisocial, and obsessive-compulsive personality. Other recognizable types are the passive-aggressive personality (pouting, intentional inefficiency, or stubbornness) and inadequate personality (inept, poor judgment, generally ineffectual in meeting life's demands).

personality inventory (personality test) A standardized scale that assesses various aspects of the personality by having the testee respond to a listing of characteristics or situations. There are no right and wrong answers. It is mainly a self-appraisal inventory about certain traits and their application to the testee. See **projective techniques, Rorschach test, MMPI.**

personality structure The inferred unifying pattern in which personality characteristics are developed, organized, and integrated by the person but observed by others. If his so-called structure could really be known then a person's idiosyncrasies, contradictory traits and behaviors would become meaningful in terms of his total behavior.

personality syndrome The tendency of a person to behave in certain prescribed ways. Despite his idiosyncratic behavior or partial behavior, his personality becomes identified by the predominance of his behavior, such as the **authoritarian personality,** compulsive personality, impulsive personality.

petit mal seizures Epileptoid convulsions with minor and brief rhythmical movements. See **epilepsy.**

peyote (from the Nahuatl Indian-Mexican word *peyotl* meaning cactus). A cactus, *Lophophora williamsii,* containing the drug **mescaline** that has a narcotic and hallucinatory effect; also refers to the dried cactus buttons containing mescaline.

Pflüger, Eduard Friedrich (1829-1910) German physiologist, known for his work on metabolic processes, the nervous system, and especially for electrical stimulation of motor nerves (also coining in 1859 the terms **anelectrotonus** and **catelectrotonus,** following the model set by **Du Bois-Reymond** in coining **electrotonus** in 1849).

PGR *Psychogalvanic reflex.*

pH The degree of acidity or alkalinity of any solution measured by the amount of hydrogen ion present, its index being pH, which is equal to the logarithm of 1/(molar concentration of H+). The pH scale, ranging from 0 to 14, measures *acidity* (pH of 0 to 6.9, examples: gastric juice, pH of 2.0; wine, pH of 6.0) and *alkalinity* (pH of 7.1 to 14 – blood having a pH of 7.5, for example). A neutral solution (H_2O) has a pH of 7.0.

In 1909, Danish chemist Søren Peter Lauritz Sørensen (1868-1939), introduced the symbol pH for hydrogen ion concentration, and it was put into formula form by K. H. Hasselbalch in 1910 for pH of the blood.

phakoscope (phaco-) A viewing device (-scope) that uses reflected images from the surface of the lens (phako-) of the eye for observation of size changes during the accommodation process of the lens.

In 1851 **Helmholtz** invented an early form of this dark chamber for observing accommodation changes in crystalline lens.

phallic character Relating to (-ic) the phallus or penis, and by extension to the clitoris. See **character types.**

phenakistoscope A viewing device (-scope) causing (-isto-) a deceptive (phenak-) image; eye-deceiver. See **stroboscope.**

The first effort (1830) to show motion pictorially was with the phenakistoscope, invented by the Belgian physicist Joseph Antoine Plateau (1801-1883).

phenobarbital (Tradename: Luminal; phenobarbitone: British) A white, shiny (pheno-) crystalline barbituric (-barbit-) compound (-al), used usually in its sodium form as a hypnotic and sedative, and as an antispasmodic in **epilepsy.**

phenomenal field The perceptual appearance (phenomenon) in the **Gestalt** sense; the field (environment) perceived by the person, which guides behavior within the limits imposed by the physical world. In **Roger's** self-concept theory, the total realm of experience. See **field theory.**

phenomenal self In social psychology, the awareness each person has concerning his own **cognitions** (beliefs, values, attitudes, etc.), the relationships between them, and their possible effect upon his behavior.

phenomenal viewpoint An approach related to **field theory,** but emphasizing the existential here and now. In developmental studies, it is concerned with a descriptive recording of each stage of development, in and by itself. See **normative approach.**

phenomenology Study of (-ology) that which is seen (phenomen-), perceived, or appears to consciousness, as distinct from "being." Emphasis is placed upon the phenomena of direct sensory experience without analysis into discrete units.

Term used in philosophy since 1764 at which time philosopher J. H. Lambert (1728-1777) used the word in reference to observations or appearances basic to all empirical knowledge. **Kant** also used it in a similar sense.

According to **Husserl,** who applied the term ("phänomenologie") in 1920 to psychology, phenomenology is a form of realism that avoids the problem of mind and matter by relegating them to outside the "pure phenomena of experience." It attempts to deal only with consciousness, and to separate immediate data from all previous concepts before organizing them. See **Heidegger.**

phenotype The type that shows (pheno-); the actual physical impression a person makes, regardless of genetic origin. The physical, observable, or detectable characteristics of an individual; in genetics, the specific characteristics exhibited by an organism (such as eye color, hair color, etc.) as distinguished from the genotypical factors. **Sheldon** developed his **somatotype** as the integrating concept for both morphogenotype (man's organic past) and phenotype (man's observable presence). See **morphogenic method, recessive gene.**

phenylalanine (phenylamino propionic acid) A naturally occurring, water-soluble, crystalline **amino acid** necessary for man's nutrition. Phenylalanine is the starting compound in the synthesis of the hormones **adrenalin** and **thyroxine,** and is converted normally by a liver enzyme to the amino acid **tyrosine.** In **phenylketonuria,** the liver enzyme, phenylalanine hydroxylase, is either missing or inactive as a result of an **inborn error** of **metabolism,** thus creating a morbid accumulation of

phenylalanine in the blood and the **cerebro-spinal fluid,** which can eventually create **mental retardation.** See **alanine.**

Phenylalanine was discovered in plants during the years 1879-1881 by Ernst A. Schulze and J. Barbieri, but information was not published until 1882. It was synthesized by German chemist Friedrich Erlenmeyer (1864-1921) and published by him in 1893.

phenylketonuria (PKU) Disorder (-ia) of being unable to oxidize **phenylpyruvic acid,** a ketone (keton-) acid found in urine (-ur-). Phenyl is a derivative from benzene, while ketonuria is a condition of marked increase of ketone bodies in the blood, which are products of fatty-acid catabolism in blood and urine and found in diabetes mellitus as well as in phenylketonuria.

PKU is a genetically recessive, inherited, biochemical defect in which the defective recessive **allele** fails to produce an enzyme necessary for transforming phenylalanine into tyrosine, causing accumulation of **phenylalanine** in the body, which fortunately can be readily detected in the newborn's urine through chromatographic studies. The acid gives a telltale olive-green color in presence of $FeCl_3$. If undetected, phenylalanine is transformed into other chemical products, which adversely affect **central nervous system** development and result in **mental retardation** unless phenylalanine is greatly reduced in the diet of the affected child.

The condition is found in either sex and is transmitted by an **autosomal recessive gene** from **heterozygous** parents (carriers) with one defective gene, the patient being a **homozygote** with a pair of defective genes.

PKU children who are not started on a special diet in infancy are typically hyperactive, erratic, immature, irritable, and easily distractible. Those who develop mental retardation not only are verbally inadequate, but have poor **motor** coordination and suffer from visual-perceptual difficulties. Mental retardation usually appears in the latter half of the first year if the baby is not treated. Most diagnosed PKU children have IQ's below 50.

Phenylketonuria is relatively rare, occurring about once in every 12,000 births, primarily because such defective persons ordinarily do not reproduce (usually being institutional cases). But since about 10 out of every thousand people are carriers of the defective allele (with no mutations being heterozygous until one carrier mates with another), there exists the risk of one defective child being born out of every four in such a mating, the same risk remaining for each successive pregnancy. Thus the need for direction by a **genetic counselor,** particularly for closely related spouses (the chances being one in sixteen, for example, that two first cousins could carry the defective allele).

Phenylketonuria was first described in 1934 by Asbjorn Fölling, Norwegian chemist. The *Superintendent of Documents, Government Printing Office,* Washington, D.C. 20402, publishes several booklets on the subject.

phenylpyruvic acid A crystalline ketone acid (pyruvic acid) combination with the univalent radical C_6H_5 (phenyl-). Found in the urine of those who have had some metabolic malfunctioning of **phenylalanine,** an indicated condition in **phenylpyruvic oligophrenia** (or **phenylketonuria**).

phenylpyruvic oligophrenia Little (oligo-) mind (phren-) disorder (-ia-); same as **phenylketonuria.** The word **oligophrenia** was previously used alone to describe the mental condition before it was found to be caused by poor oxidation of **phenylalanine.** Term now seldom used.

pheromone A chemical substance bearing (phero-) hormones (-mone) that, when released by some animals, signals the animal's presence to a receptive individual of the same or closely related species. Pheromones serve as sexual attractants, may mark off territory as

p

already claimed, or may alert other animals of a predator's presence. An animal may respond to a pheromone through the sense of taste (by licking residue of a pheromone left by another animal) and/or by smell (olfactory receptors), often over great distances.

German biochemist Peter Karlson (born 1918) and Swiss zoologist Martin Lüscher (born 1917) suggested in 1959 that the term "pheromone" replace that of "ectohormone" as used by the German physiologist Albrecht Bethe (born 1872), since ectohormone was too broad, including insect repellents, phago-stimulants, scents of flowers, etc. (Peter Karlson and Martin Lüscher, "Pheromones; a New Term for a Class of Biologically Active Substances." Nature, 1959, Vol. 183, No. 4653, p. 55).

phi A Greek letter (ϕ) often used to indicate a function in mathematics.

phi coefficient A term sometimes used for the **Pearson product-moment correlation** computed for a pair of dichotomous **variables**.

phi phenomenon A term introduced by **Wertheimer** in 1912 and used by **Gestalt** psychologists as a construct for **apparent movement**. It refers to the simple **stroboscopic illusion** of motion of a rapid succession of images and lights that are actually stationary, or of one light appearing to "jump" between two locations when actually two lights are alternately flashed.

In his famous paper on the phi phenomenon, published in the *Zeitschrift für Psychologie*, Wertheimer indicated that perceived, apparent, or phenomenological movement under optimal conditions may be difficult if not impossible to distinguish from an actual physical movement. Therefore, he interpreted all perceived movements as phi phenomena, a special neutral name indicating the uniqueness of the phenomenon and avoiding the traditional limitations imposed by the concept of sensation. This concept was the framework of experimental **phenomenology**, the backbone of Gestalt psychology.

phobia Fear. An intense, neurotic, irrational fear of some object or situation often of morbid or pathological nature—for example, *fear* of *high* places (acrophobia); of *open* places (agoraphobia); of being shut in (claustrophobia). Phobias are thought to be acquired by simple **classical conditioning**, supposedly symptomatic of a basic anxiety. Childhood phobias are chiefly about dogs, other animals, school, and vehicles of transportation. *See* **phobic neurosis** under **neurosis** (also S. Rachman and C. G. Costello. "The Aetiology and Treatment of Children's Phobias: A Review," *American Journal of Psychiatry*, 1961, **118**, 97-106).

phonelescope (phoneidoscope) A viewing device (-scope), essentially like a telephone ([t]-ele-) receiver with a mirror, that reflects a light beam onto a photosensitive film for purposes of photographing, observing, measuring, and analyzing sound (-phon-) waves converted into visible phenomena.

phoneme A fundamental (-eme) structural unit of sound (phon-), audible speech, or group of speech sounds combined into syllables and words, each language having a limited number and each phoneme having relevance only for that language. English has 45 phonemes. (For example, phonemes p and b help distinguish the meanings between pull and bull). *See* **morpheme, speech mechanisms of thinking**.

phonometer (acoumeter) An instrument for measuring (-meter) one's auditory acuity for sound (phono-) intensity or its frequency vibration. (The phonometer and acoumeter have been generally superseded by more modern **audiometers**, vacuum tubes, and oscillators).

phonoscope Any instrument that makes sound (phono-) waves visible, specifically referring to a viewing device (-scope) for observing properties of sounding bodies.

phosphene To show (-phene) light (phos-). A sensation of light resulting from pressure placed on the eyeball when the lids are closed; also, the light streak surrounding the visual field as the eye adjusts in the dark.

phot A light (phot-) unit, the **cgs** unit of illumination equal to about 929 footcandles (10,000 **luxes**). *See* **lumen, milliphot**.

photochronograph A recording instrument (-graph) for determining sequential phases of movement by photographing (photo-) minute intervals of time (-chrono-) from a series of pictures of a moving object.

photoelectric oximeter *See* **oximeter**.

photokymograph A recording instrument (-graph) for photographing (photo-) waves (-kymo-) of movement, such as the rapid movement of the eyes while reading.

photometer A light (photo-) meter. An optical arrangement for measuring light intensity, luminous flux, illumination, or brightness by adjusting two unequal lights (in candlepower units) until they appear equal, and equating them with known brightness. If two sources of light have different colors, however, it is necessary to illuminate a screen first by one source and then by the other, making it possible to locate a frequency of alternation so that the color difference disappears. The observer can thereby adjust the source distance until each source produces equal illuminance. Such an arrangement is called a flicker photometer, used in flicker studies. *See* **wedge photometer**.

photopia Disorder (-ia) of light (phot-) vision (-op-). Daylight and color vision, or vision as it occurs under sufficient illumination to permit the discrimination of color. *See* **cones**.

Term coined in 1915 by British physician Sir John Herbert Parsons (1868-1957).

photopsin *See* **iodopsin**.

phrenology Mind (phren-) study (-ology). An idea developed in 1808 by **F. J. Gall**, a German physician, on the assumption that development of a trait is dependent upon the hereditary development of the appropriate brain area. To him, the mind consisted of a group of special faculties with each one located in a particular area of the **brain**. The degree of development of each separate faculty could be judged by the "bumps" or topography on the skull. His idea was exploited by the Austrian physician Johann Spurzheim (1776-1832), who, in 1815, gave the name phrenology to the concept (previously called craniology by Gall), and whose selling campaign of "bump psychology" led to its denunciation. Despite the exaggerated claims for his phrenology, Gall's scientific reputation as an anatomist stimulated others to investigation, leading to genuine advances in brain anatomy and physiology. *See* **localization of function**.

phrenotropic drug Relating to (-ic) a drug that alters, changes, or turns (trop-) the mind (phren-); a neurosedative drug that has a tranquilizing effect (such as **reserpine** and **meprobamate**).

physical determinism *See* **determinism**.

physiological drive *Same as* **physiological need**.

physiological limit The limit relating to (-ical) the study of (-log-) nature (physio-); the limit imposed on performance (learning, activity) by the characteristics of the current functioning of the organism.

physiological need Need arising from the physiological functioning of the organism (tissues, cells, organs, etc.); opposed to acquired or social need. Hunger is a physiological need; appetite is acquired. *See* **needs**.

physiological psychologist *See* **psychologist**.

physiological psychology The branch of **psychology** concerned with the physiological aspects of sensory-motor activity. the **brain**, and the nervous system. Also necessarily included are such correlative studies as neurology, endocrinology, anatomy, biology, and histology. *See* **Cabanis, Hartley, fields of psychology**.

Named by **Wundt**.

physiological zero or psychological zero The range of temperature (between about 85-90 degrees F.) of a **stimulus** (gaseous, liquid, or solid) that the skin does not feel as being either warm or cold, its sensation being a variable function of both body and environmental temperature.

Piaget, Jean Born 1896. Swiss developmental psychologist, originally a zoologist. Ph.D. in biology, Neuchâtel 1918. He has sought to discover an "embryology of intelligence." Worked at the University of Geneva with the famous Swiss anatomist and educator, Edouard Claparede (1873-1940). In 1940, succeeded him as director of the psychological laboratory there. Has conducted extensive experimental and observational studies on children, attempting to elucidate the emergence of intelligence, of symbolic behavior, and the development of logic. Piaget's **theory of cognitive development** lists several stages: (*a*) *sensorimotor* (birth to 2 years); (*b*) *preconceptual thought* (2-4 years); (*c*) *intuitive thought* (4-7 years); (*d*) *concrete operation* (7-11 years); and (*e*) *formal operation* (11-15 years). First European to be awarded the **DSC Award** by the APA (1969). *See* **accommodation, assimilation, cognitive growth theories, egocentric speech, INRC, intelligence, concrete operation** (also *American Psychologist*, 1970, **25**, No. 1, pp. 65-79; Vinacke, p. 381).

pia mater Tender (pia) mother (mater). The fragile, vascular innermost covering (**meninges**) of the **brain** and spinal cord. *See* **dura mater** for history of the term; **pineal gland**.

pica (From Latin meaning magpie, the bird famous for indiscriminate collection of food and other items). In children, a purposeful habit of ingesting usually inedible substances (plaster, ashes, wood, etc.). Pica is found more frequently in the lower economic groups, with poor nutrition being evident in some cases. However, other concomitant conditions are behavior disorders, family disorganization, and disciplinary problems (M. Gutelius, et al. "Nutritional Studies of Children with Pica," *Pediatrics*, 1962, **29**, 1012-1023).

Pick's disease Rare form of **presenile psychosis** in which focal progressive atrophy occurs in frontal and temporal areas of the **cerebral cortex**. It is caused by a single **autosomal** dominant **gene** with the particular gene often manifested by specifiable **phenotypic** behavior. Language facility and intellectual functions are impaired.

First described by Czechoslovakian physician Arnold Pick (1851-1924).

piezometer An instrument for measuring (-meter) pressure (piezo-) of liquids or gases. Piezo-electric crystals have been used as a more controlled device than the **sphygmomanometer** for measuring blood pressure in experimental animals and human subjects. The piezometer was invented in 1836 by Hans C. Ørsted (1777-1851), a Danish physicist. His researches initiated the study of electromagnetism.

pineal gland (pineal body) Relating to (-al) the nature of (-e[us]) a pinecone (pin-). A small pinecone-shaped body arising from the posterior **third ventricle** and enclosed by the **pia mater**. Originally believed to be the seat of the soul and a vestige of a third eye, it is now known to secrete **melatonin** (which inhibits sex hormones) and is thought to transform cyclic nervous energy from light into hormonal messages. *See* **Descartes, epithalamus, HIOMT**.

pipette *See* **ablation**.

pitch A psychological attribute of musical sounds, or highness or lowness of a tone, determined by the frequency of the vibrations that produce it. Some persons have the sense of absolute pitch, the ability to recognize the pitch of a tone without reference to other tones. *See* **sound**.

Pitocin *See* **pressor substance**.

Pitressin *See* **pressor substance**.

pituitary gland Hypophysis cerebri. (The name pituitary, dating from 1615, was applied to this gland under the misapprehension that it secreted phlegm or mucus [Gr., *pituita*]).

An endocrine gland situated at the base of the **brain**, near the **hypothalamus**, sometimes called the master or governor gland. Its two small oval lobes secrete vitally important hormones that regulate other glands, body weight, growth, skin color, and many other bodily functions. Among these, the smaller posterior lobe secretes a hormone (pituitrin) that raises blood pressure and hastens childbirth; the larger, anterior lobe secretes a hormone that influences growth. *See* **adaptation syndrome, oxytocin.**

Dysfunctions of the pituitary gland are **acromegaly,** dwarfism (from hormonal deficiency in early life preventing normal growth but body is correctly proportioned and general intelligence and emotional reactions are apparently not affected), and **giantism.**

Hippocrates felt that the brain was a gland that was cooled off by secreting phlegm, mucus, or pituita, which was formed during the process of change from vital to animal spirits and discharged into the pharynx and nose.

placebo (L., I shall please.) Originally a mild or inert, medicineless preparation administered to please or satisfy a person who needs to believe he is receiving treatment—substituted for medication either because the person had no need of a drug or because a proper drug was not available. A physiologically inert preparation administered to a control group in place of a drug being tested (for example, saline solution instead of vaccine), to help determine effects of suggestion.

In 1787, it was considered a "commonplace method of medicine," according to Quincy's Lexicon; in 1811, in *Hooper's Medical Dictionary*, it was described as "any medicine adapted more to please than to benefit the patient."

place hypothesis *See* **basilar membrane, hearing theories.**

place volley theory *See* **volley theory of hearing.**

Planaria Any of the genus *Planaria* (lying on one plane), a type of free-living, two-eyed flatworm having a nerve-net nervous system enabling them to regenerate missing parts. They are the highest level of animal that can regenerate as much as six or seven parts within a few weeks. Used frequently in studies on the role of **deoxyribonucleic acid and ribonucleic acid** in conditioning experiments (J. L. McConnell, A. L. Jacobson, and D. P. Kimble, "The Effects of Regeneration upon Retention of a Conditioned Response in the Planarian," *Journal of Comparative and Physiological Psychology*, 1959 52(1), 1-5).

plateau Flat place. A level portion or flattening out of a learning curve. A temporary stage in the learning process in which no apparent progress or learning takes place despite continued practice (commonly seen in learning motor skills).

William Lowe Bryan and N. Harter applied the term in 1897-1899 to learning, indicating that a plateau did not necessarily occur in learning telegraphy, however.

Plato (427-374 B.C.) Original name, Aristocles. Called Plato because of his "broad shoulders." Greek philosopher. Pupil of **Socrates,** teacher of **Aristotle.** Influenced greatly by the oriental (mystical) thinking of Greek philosopher Pythagoras (c.582-c.507 B.C.) who had spent years in the Orient. Believed the **brain** to be the site of the mind. His ideas, as expressed in the *Dialogues*, antedated many of the theories pertaining to sensation, memory, and association. Plato's psychology is speculative. He localized the three aspects of the soul (reason, feeling, and appetite) to be in the cerebralspinal marrow, with reason being closest to God—in the head. The soul itself was separate from the body.

platykurtosis A broad, flattened (platy-) peak (-kurt-) condition (-osis). Tendency for the distribution of cases to produce a relatively flattened distribution. *See* **kurtosis.**

play therapy A **psychotherapeutic** technique with and for children in which the therapist attempts (with games, toys, and game-stimulating tests) to set up and encourage the child to express himself verbally and nonverbally. Some therapists use it for symbolic interpretations of unconscious conflicts (Melanie Klein and her followers); others, simply as an indicator of the child's feeling (Allen); while Axline looks upon it as a procedure for nondirective therapy; and Anna Freud, differing from Klein by not being as classically psychoanalytic, allows for developing a good child-therapist relationship so that the child really desires therapy. (Frederick H. Allen, *Psychotherapy with Children, 1942;* Virginia M. Axline, *Play Therapy,* 1947; Melanie Klein, "The Psychoanalytic Play Technique," *American Journal of Orthopsychiatry*, 1955, **25**, 223-238; Kessler, 1966, pp. 376-377).

pleasure center *Same as* **reward center.**

plethysmograph A device (-graph) for measuring increases (plethysmo-) or volumetric changes in blood supply of various parts (organs) of the body.

P/L₁ Programming Language (Comput.) A higher level programming language combining some of the better features of FORTRAN and ALGOL. It is useful because of its flexibility and applications for information-retrieval and related control and command uses.

pluralism The doctrine (-ism) of establishing reality as being composed of many distinct, independent, and ultimate entities. Pluralistic systems may be material (as espoused by the atomists), spiritual (**Leibniz**) or neutral (**Herbart**). *Contrasted with* **monism.**

plurel (irregular form of plural) In social sciences, a generic term for any unsystematized collection of people grouped together for convenience in describing their specialized attributes. Such plurels may be: (*1*) classes (representing all registered Democrats or Republicans, or all members of the Catholic Church); (*2*) aggregates (representing a physical gathering of people in one place, such as a Holy Roller gathering or a Peace March on Washington).

pneumograph (pneumatograph) An instrument (-graph) filled with air (pneumo-). A flexible air-filled tube placed around the chest and connected to a **tambour,** which activates a stylus on a **kymograph** during the respiratory processes of expiration and inspiration, measuring subtle volume changes and overall respiratory movements.

pneumotachograph An instrument (-graph) consisting of a face mask, wire screen, and a differential pressure **transducer** that records speed or rate (-tacho-) of instantaneous air (pneumo-) flow during breathing (Brown, p. 89).

Poggendorff illusion *See* **illusion.**

poikilotherm An organism whose body heat (-therm) or temperature varies (poikilo-) with the environmental temperature; cold-blooded animals (snakes, paramecia) as opposed to **homoiotherms** (Milner, p. 301). Actually, poikilotherm is a misnomer, since, in a hot environment, cold-blooded animals have been found to have a high internal temperature.

point estimation Any estimation value of a **parameter** obtained by assigning to it a unique value, such as giving the **population** mean the same value as the obtained **sample** mean. Its merits are determined by evaluating the resulting point estimate's qualities, such as consistency, relative frequency, minimum variance and relative unbiased nature.

Poisson distribution An extremely skewed distribution associated with the number of times a very rare event occurs; a probability distribution that can be used when p is either very small or very large and N is large. In such instances, the agreement between the calculated values of the Poisson distribution and the **binomial distribution** will be fairly close. Actually, the Poisson distribution is a limiting form of the binomial distribution, but is much simpler to arrive at and actually improves as $P > .50$ and as N increases. It is best for $\mu = nP$ not to exceed 5.

Tests of significance for **means** of such distributions are made by substituting the **variable** (number of occurrences) by its square root. The table of chi-squares (Table 8), with various values of P, can be used to find the mean of a Poisson series of which the first $\frac{1}{2}n$ terms represent a portion of the whole, since the mean of the complete Poisson series $= \frac{1}{2}$ chi-square, its sum is unity, and its partial sum's number of terms $= \frac{1}{2}n$. The **variance** is always equal to the **mean.** The Poisson distribution treats statistically many items that occur randomly and independently over a definite period of time. *See* Table 5.

Named after Simeon D. Poisson (1781-1840), French mathematician and statistician.

polarization In neuro- and psychophysiology the semipermeable condition of membranes covering nerve fiber cells in the inactive state, the membrane having positively charged ions on the outside and negatively charged ones inside. The **nerve impulse** is activated when an **adequate stimulus** causes not only a change in permeability, but also a change in the membrane's electrical **potential** resulting in an interchange of ions leading to neutralization and a consequent loss of polarization. *See* **depolarization, potential.**

The theory of dynamic polarization was formulated by **Ramon y Cajal** in 1892 upon noting functions of **axons** and **dendrites** in relation to nerve impulses.

polarized membrane Usually, the membrane of a nerve fiber in which an electrical **potential** is created (with an excess of positive ions outside and an excess of negative ions inside the membrane).

polarized synaptic transmission The conductance of **nerve impulses** across synapses in one direction only (from **axon** to **dendrite** or to **neuron**).

polygon A geometrical figure having many (poly-) angles (-gon) and many sides. A frequency polygon is similar in construction to a **histogram** except that a point of several such points is located on the **graph** corresponding to the midpoint of the interval (on the horizontal axis) and the frequency (on the vertical axis). The horizontal axis is the X axis and is called the **abscissa.** It intersects the Y axis at right angles at a point called the origin (O). The vertical axis is labeled the Y axis and its values are called *ordinate values.*

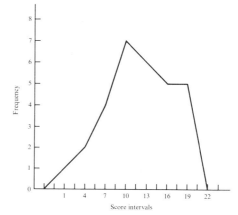

polygraph An instrument with a stylus that records (-graph) simultaneously many (poly-) mechanical or electrical impulses received from different physiological processes (respiration rate, heartbeat, muscular response, blood pressure, skin moisture, etc.) controlled by the

p

autonomic nervous system. A "lie detector" is a kind of polygraph.

In 1892, Scottish-English cardiologist James Mackenzie (1853-1925) produced the forerunner of the modern polygraph, and in 1902 improved it so as to record simultaneous readings of blood pressure, pulse beat, etc. *See* **Keeler polygraph.**

polyvinyl chloride *See* **mylar tape.**

pons Bridge. Any bridgelike anatomical formation. The pons Varolii is a broad transverse band of white fibers that connects the **cerebrum, cerebellum,** and **medulla oblongata** and contains the nuclei of several **cranial nerves.**

Named in 1693 after the Italian anatomist Contanzio **Varolio** (1543-1576). *See* **metencephalon.**

population Any group of individuals (persons, other organisms, objects, items of data) making up the total of all possible cases from which **samples** may be taken for measurement. The term *universe* is often used in the same sense. A given set of statistics (or observations) whose **data** have been obtained from each and every member of a particular group under study.

Porteus mazes A non-language test of mental ability used with the verbally handicapped, in anthropological studies, and in research on the effects of drugs and psychosurgery.

Prior to its first publicly described results at a meeting in 1914 in Australia (British Association for Advancement of Science) much work had been done on it with deaf and defectives. The tests published in 1915 and 1916 were first applied to delinquents and some normals.

Stanley David Porteus (born 1883). An Australian educator and psychologist.

Poseidonius (c. 135-50 B.C.) Greek Stoic philosopher.

positive aftersensation (Now often used interchangeably with positive afterimage although earlier there were differences). The sensation of the original **hue** that persists after stimulation ceases (or if the **afterimage** seems brighter than the background).

positive reinforcer An individual or object (such as food in **classical conditioning**) that upon presentation serves to reinforce or strengthen a stimulus-response association.

positive transfer The transfer of learned material from one experience to another. Common elements present in two or more situations promote generalization of response and facilitate more efficient learning in the second situation as a result of the prior learning. For example, a person who has learned to operate one brand of adding machine learns more readily how to operate another brand.

positivism A belief or doctrine (-ism) of being positive. It holds that the highest form of knowledge is the description of pure sensory phenomena, subjected, if possible, to the rigors of mathematical formulas. As indicated by **Comte** (1822), positivism was one of the stages (along with the theological and metaphysical) in his development of an evolutionary "law of three stages." He considered positivism to represent the full maturity of the mind, since it thought only in terms of phenomena, once it renounced speculative philosophy and became concerned only with the positive results of science.

posterior Behind or to the rear (post-); in lower animals the tail area or **caudal** region. *See* **anatomical directions.**

postganglionic neuron *See* **neuron, second order neuron.**

posthypnotic suggestion *See* **suggestion.**

post-partum reaction Emotional upset or reaction that occurs after (post-) birth (partum), sometimes bordering on psychotic behavior.

postsynaptic signal *See* **synapse.**

potential (E or V) A quantity expressed either as the **potential difference** between any point in an electrical field about a charged object and some reference point, or the energy per unit charge necessary for bringing a charged object to that point from where no potential field exists. Potentials are usually measured in volts (or subdivision thereof) with the polarity indicated (+ or -) and the reference specifically stated. **Neurons** develop electrical potentials, which when recorded are considered as evidence of bioelectric activity.

potential difference In psychophysiology, a relative difference between the electrical charges on the outer and inner surfaces of the neuronal membrane. Potential difference is measured in volts by a voltmeter, a millivoltmeter, a microvoltmeter. An electrostatic field enables charged objects to attract or repel each other without actually touching. Potential energy is converted into kinetic energy any time a charged object moves against either the force of attraction or repulsion. This change of energy causes those points (involved in the shifting of a charge between any two points in an electrostatic field) to be at different electrical potentials. Areas with relative electron excess (negative potential) tend to lose, by attraction of unlike charges, this excess to areas of relative electron deficiency (positive potential).

potentials in the nervous system An electrochemical potential occurs when, for example, nerve cell membranes become polarized (one side of the membrane having more positive ions than negative and vice versa). A **resting potential** exists when no **nerve impulse** is being carried, the outside of the neuron carrying a positive charge in relation to its inside. This condition presumably exists because in the resting state the semi-permeable membrane resists the passage of sodium ions, causing an excess of these positive ions to remain on the outside, thus polarizing the membrane. Experimental application of a weak chemical or electrical **stimulus** to a **neuron** changes the resting **potential** to an **action potential,** but it first passes through an intermediate change called an *excitatory potential* (in which there is a decrease recorded in the cell membrane's potential difference). The action potential occurs when a critical level of depolarization takes place (evidenced by a rapid voltage change on the voltmeter, indicating a reversal from the resting potential condition, that is, the membrane's interior becomes positively charged now because of the increased permeability of the membrane to potassium which has become relatively concentrated inside). Once the nerve impulse has passed a particular site along a nerve fiber, the original polarization and permeability are restored.

Neurons also exhibit *graded potentials,* which can be of any size and are considered to be responsible for evoking action potentials in normal cell functioning. Three kinds of graded potentials are: (*1*) *receptor,* proportional in size to their stimuli, each succeeding stimulus being cumulative; (*2*) *postsynaptic (PSP),* requiring a specific chemical stimulus for activation. These potentials may be excitatory (EPSP) or **inhibitory postsynaptic potentials** (IPSP); and (*3*) *subthreshold,* that may occur from an electrical stimulus, and which is proportional to the intensity of the stimulus but which can never develop into the all-or-none action potential. *See* **compound action potential, evoked potential, excitatory postsynaptic potential.**

potentiometer An electronic device for measuring (-meter) potential (potentio-) difference (EMF) by comparison with a known voltage. It has three terminals and a control. When two of the terminals are at fixed but different potentials, the control automatically sets the value of the third terminal potential at intermediate points between the other two.

Pourfour du Petit, François (1664-1741) French physician. Studied the **sympathetic nervous system,** described decussation in the **pyramidal system,** and contributed to the knowledge of spinal cord anatomy.

power function In psychophysics, a concept stating that relationships between physical stimuli and subjective experiences (tactile, auditory, and visual stimuli) show a mathematical relationship between **stimulus** and **response,** having the general form $\psi = k\phi^n$ where

ψ = psychological response of the subject
ϕ = actual stimulus intensity
k = numerical constant
n = exponent that depends upon type of stimulus used.

Apparently, the receptors are the loci for the transformation from the physical-stimulus scale to the subjective-experience scale. Experiences are not real, then, but only a power function, a mathematical relationship of those experiences. *See* Table 21.

powerlessness *See* **alienation.**

power of a test The **probability** of rejecting the **null hypothesis** when the alternative **hypothesis** is true. Once any true alternative hypothesis is designated, then β (the probability of making a **type II error**) can be determined, and power is equal to $1-\beta$.

power test A test of intelligence or aptitudes that contains items progressively increasing in difficulty so that the level achieved, rather than the speed of completion, is the performance **criterion.** For example, the **Miller Analogies Test** starts with simple comparisons and increases in power almost beyond solution. *Contrasted with* **speed test.**

Praegnanz (*Prägnanz:* Ger., precision; terseness; simplicity). A law in **Gestalt psychology** relating to perceptual organization that tends toward achieving equilibrium and balance in the simplest manner possible. For example, a symbol has *Praegnanz* when its meaningfulness is comprehended as a part of the total fabric; it is never an isolated concept. *See* **law of parsimony.**

pragmatics The study or practice (-ics) of being useful or practical (-pragmat-). *See* **measurement.**

pragmatism A movement or doctrine (-ism) that emphasizes the importance of the practical (pragmat-) as opposed to absolutism, particularly absolute idealism. It has been mainly associated with the philosophies of **John Dewey, William James,** and English philosopher Ferdinand C. S. Schiller (1864-1937). Its importance derives from its analyses and evaluation of the practical meanings of concepts; that truth is measured by the practical results of one's belief. Dewey's pragmatism considers thought, for example, to serve as an instrument of adaptation and as a guide to action.

precognition Prior (pre-) cognition. Foreknowledge of coming events. In **extrasensory perception** terminology, a type of **clairvoyance** that relates to a future existence or to an experience not yet available. *See* **psi phenomena.**

preconscious (psychoanal.) The feeling of "meness," the "tie that binds the memory-image to our me, by which we hold on to it and by virtue of which we can summon it from the depths of the subconscious" (Edouard Claparède, 1873-1940, Swiss psychologist). French **psychology** and **psychiatry** used the term subconscious for both the preconscious and unconscious.

Freud's term (1896) to indicate the third layer of his schematic system of the psychical mechanism, defining it not only as **Breuer** had done in 1895 as being whatever is "capable of becoming conscious" but adding ". . . easily and under conditions which frequently arise." However, preconscious processes vary considerably in their ease of emerging into consciousness, which then may be expressed through different degrees of emotional experiences. (Sigmund Freud, The Origins of Psychoanalysis, Letters to Wilhelm Fliess, New York: *Basic Books, Inc.*, p. 174; David Rapaport, Organization and Pathology of Thought. New York: *Columbia University Press*, p. 476-77).

predicted role *See* role.

prefrontal lobotomy *See* lobotomy. Type of psychosurgery involving severing of the nerve fibers connecting the **hypothalamus** with the prefrontal **lobes** of the brain, hopefully performed to reduce **psychotic** reactions by minimizing the effect of **cognitive** experiences (worry, guilt, thinking) upon the emotions. Generally, a last-resort technique.

preganglionic neuron *See* **first order neuron**.

pregenital stages A **psychoanalytic** concept embracing the three early stages of **psychosexual development**: (1) *oral* (gratification centered around mouth or eating activities); (2) *anal* (gratification centered around excretory functions); (3) *phallic* (gratification derived from genital-region stimulation). *See* **character types**.

Premack principle Of two behaviors with differing likelihood of occurring, the behavior more likely to occur may be used to reinforce the less likely behavior if it is made contingent upon it. In a laboratory setting in which a rat often voluntarily performed on a running wheel but ignored pressing a lever without food reinforcement, the wheel was braked, making its operation dependent upon pressing the lever. Once the rat learned the importance of lever pressing as a prerequisite for his wheel running, lever pressing increased much as if the rat were being reinforced with food. Thus, the high probability behavior (operating the running wheel) reinforced the low probability behavior (lever pressing) because it was made a reinforcing event. The Premack principle has been used successfully in helping eliminate bad habits (David Premack, "Reinforcement Theory," in *Nebraska Symposium on Motivation*, Marshall Jones, Ed., 1965).

David Premack (1925-1964), Ph.D. (psychology), Minnesota 1955. Research and interests in behavior theory and comparative verbal behavior.

préparateur In France, an academic position equivalent to instructor in the non-clinical fields of histology, anatomy, and physiology. Filled by appointment only.

presbycusis (presbyacusia) Old-age (presby-) type of hearing (-cusis). In older people, the gradually increasing loss for hearing high frequencies. At about the age of 70 a person may not be able to hear sounds above 4000 cps, whereas the average range of hearing is from 15 (the lowest frequency that sounds like a tone) to 15,000 cps.

presbyophrenia A disorder (-ia) of the mind (-phren-) occurring in the elderly (presbyo-) person, characterized by loss of memory, disorientation, and confabulation. Also called *Wernicke's syndrome*.

presbyopia Old (presby-) person's eye disorder (-opia). *See* **farsightedness**.

prescribed role *See* role.

presenile dementia Cortical brain disease in which the clinical picture resembles senile dementia, although the condition appears at a younger age. **Alzheimer's** and **Pick's** diseases are the two best known forms.

press According to **Murray**, some external quality that assists or handicaps a person in his attempts to satisfy his needs. *See* **motivation**.

pressor substance That which (-or) presses or constricts. A substance that causes an increase in blood pressure by constricting blood vessels leading from the arteries, such as *pituitrin* (an extract of the posterior pituitary gland) which has been synthesized into **vasopressin** and **oxytocin**.

In 1894, Sharpey-Schafer and his English physiologist associate George Oliver (1841-1915) reported the first pressor substance (later named epinephrine) to be in the adrenal medulla. In 1928, an extract from the posterior lobe of the pituitary gland was separated into two pressor factors, namely Pitressin (contracting blood vessels) and Pitocin (later named **oxytocin**) which stimulated uterine contractions.

presynaptic signal *See* synapse.

Pribram, Karl Henry Born 1919, Austria. Stanford neurologist and psychophysiologist. *See* **emotion, central theory, intrinsic cortex, allocortex, juxtallocortex**.

primal therapy A therapeutic approach in which the neurotic patient is required to regress to or relive his early childhood (primal) experiences so that he may gain emotional release and subsequent maturity.

The therapeutic procedure was popularized in 1969 when Beatle John Lennon and Yoko Ono undertook such treatment and subsequently referred to some aspects of primal therapy in their album John Lennon/Plastic Ono Band.

Artur Janov (born 1924), an American psychologist (Ph.D., Claremont, 1960), originated the term and the procedures during the late 1960's.

primary amentia Mental retardation caused by hereditary factors. *See* **amentia**.

primary color perceptions *See* **primary colors**.

primary colors A traditional term for the hue-triad—red, green, and blue (called additive primaries). They are considered fundamental because all or most other **hues** can be matched by pigment mixtures of these three. Although pure hues exist in an almost infinitesimally differing series ranging from red to violet, each being a specific frequency or wavelength of light energy, it is thought that the color receptors in the eye perceive all but a few of these hues as mixtures of a set of primary hues.

Primary color perceptions (psychological primary colors) are usually black, white, blue, yellow, green, and red. They are used as references for analysis of all other color perceptions, and considered primary because the observer tends to perceive them as "pure" rather than mixtures of other colors, although white and black (being "shades" and not "colors") are often excluded from primary color considerations. *See* **color-vision theories, color mixture**.

primary drive A physiologically consistent condition of the organism that has risen from a need produced by physiological imbalance. Drives are arousers both of general behavior and of specific actions to reduce specific drives. In **Hull's** theory, drive-reduction through need-reduction is an essential "need" for learning.

primary emotion An emotion (anger, fear, grief, or joy) judged to be primitive in its action, "pure" (undiluted by other feelings), spontaneous, genuine, and often involved with goal-seeking behavior and consequent explosion of tension.

primary mental abilities (PMA) tests A series of test batteries, for various age groups, constructed by the **Thurstones** (L. L. and T. G.) on a **factor analysis** basis. The tests consist of nine inferred, basic, measurable, intellectual abilities believed to underlie general intelligence-test performance: spatial, perceptual speed, number, verbal relations, word forms, memory, **induction**, **deduction**, and reasoning. Later, they became known as the SRA (Science Research Associates, the publisher) PMA tests. The test format is designed for simple administration and scoring (L. L. Thurstone, "Primary Mental Abilities," *Psychometric Monographs*, No. 1, 1938).

primary reinforcement In classical conditioning, the presentation (pairing) of the **unconditioned stimulus** (reward) immediately following the **conditioned stimulus**; in **instrumental conditioning**, the presentation of a reward immediately following the instrumental response. The reinforcing stimuli usually satisfy **physiological needs** (hunger, thirst, etc.) or reduce a homeostatic drive, without need of prior training. *Contrasted with* **secondary reinforcement**.

prime(s) Single ('), double ("), triple (''') primes are used to distinguish between different values of the same variable: e.g., a', a'', a''', etc., or to show the derivatives of a function: e.g., $f'(a)$; $f''(a)$, etc.

primitivation Process of reverting to a primitive (primitiva-) state (-tion) or to an earlier evolutionary type of behavior. *See* **regression**.

primus inter pares (Chief among equals). "As a method of treatment," **Freud** said about **psychoanalysis**, "it is one among many, though, to be sure, *primus inter pares*."

Prince, Morton (1854-1924) American psychiatrist and neurologist. *See* **hysteria, multiple personality**.

Prisoner's Dilemma Game (PDG) An experimental game involving a cooperative versus competitive relationship between two interacting persons, with a "payoff" matrix indicating the payoff for each choice made. In essence, the game requires a competitor, playing the role of a prisoner, to decide whether to confess to a "crime" without knowing whether his colleague in crime has already confessed. It is possible for one competitor to gain the most by not confessing if his partner has not confessed. On the whole, however, confession is the better strategy and returns the most rewards.

Privatdozent University lecturer in Germany. An appointive rank obtained by a medical or professional student after having served as Arzliche Approbation. After serving successfully as *Privatdozent*, he may, upon recommendation of the faculty, receive the title of a professor.

privileged communication Information judged to be so personal, confidential, and discriminatory that it is exempt from disclosure in court by those (lawyer, pastor, physician, and spouse) deemed legally privileged to not do so, providing the client claims such privilege.

Psychologists have attempted to gain equal privilege in this regard, primarily since the end of World War II when clinical psychology greatly increased in popularity. Thus far, they have had only limited success.

The concept of confidential or privileged communication is difficult to interpret and presents various problems even in the psychiatrist-patient relationship as indicated in a California court litigation case in 1969. The psychiatrist was held in contempt of court and sentenced to jail because he refused to testify even at pretrial hearings. The State Supreme Court's decision was summarized in this manner: "...No Constitutional right enables the **psychotherapist** to assert an absolute privilege concerning all psychotherapeutic communications. We do not believe the patient-psychotherapist privilege should be frozen into the rigidity of absolutism. So extreme a conclusion neither harmonizes with the expressed legislative intent nor finds a clear source in constitutional law. Such an application would lock the patient into a vise which would prevent him from waiving the privilege without the psychotherapist's consent. The question of whether such a ruling would have the medical merit claimed by petitioner... must be addressed to the Legislature; we can find no basis for such a ruling in legal precedent or principle."

p.r.n. On prescriptions, *pro re nata* = as the thing is born, or as the occasion or need arises, said of therapy need.

proactive inhibition (PI) Forward (pro-) acting (-active) inhibition. An example of negative transfer in which a recently acquired learning activity is inhibited by a previously learned activity. Proactive inhibition is tested experimentally as follows: an **experimental group**

p

learns task 1, then learns task 2, and is then tested on task 2. A **control group** learns only task 2, and is then tested on task 2. If the performance of the experimental group falls significantly below that of the control group, it may be inferred that proactive inhibition from learning task 1 interfered with the learning of task 2. In other words, prior learning presumably interferes with learning and recall of new material. *See* **reactive inhibition, retroactive inhibition.**

probability The quantitative measurement of expectation that any specified event (of a known and limited assortment of events) will occur by chance. Its extremes are impossibility and certainty, expressed as zero and one; intermediate degrees of probability are fractions. The computation of probability takes into account: p, the number of chances that a specified event will occur; q, the number of chances that some other event(s) will occur. The probability, P, that the event will occur is given by $p/(p + q)$. By this formula, the probability P that one specified face of a thrown die will fall uppermost is $P = 1/(1 + 5) = 1/6 = 0.166$. For computing probability in more complex situations recourse to other methods, chiefly statistical, is made. *See* **alpha, area sample, Bayesian approach to statistics, beta, confidence level, correlation, null hypothesis, regression, significance.**

The rudiments of probability theory were first expressed (1550) by the Italian physician and mathematician Jeromy or Jerome Cardanos (1501-1576). About 1636, French mathematician Pierre de Fermat (1601-1665) founded the calculus of probabilities. Pierre Simon de Laplace (1749-1827), French astronomer and mathematician, in his book *The Analytic Theory of Probability*, 1812, expounded the modern theory of probability, although **Pascal** had proposed the concept in 1654. (Bell, pp. 172-182).

probit transformation A transformation derived from a **probability** unit. A normal equivalent deviate increased by five for purposes, usually, of facilitating calculation by making all values positive (Fisher and Yates, 1963, pp. 10-14).

problem box In animal psychological experiments, a compartment of varying complexity and intricacy fastened with a system of bars and latches. Each time the animal opens a door (either by **trial and error** or as a result of learning the correct responses) he is rewarded or reinforced. *See* **Thorndike's laws of learning.**

problem-oriented language (Comput.) Any higher level source language that is designed and oriented toward facilitating the programming of certain classes of problems. Examples of these languages are: FORTRAN for scientific applications, and COBOL for business applications.

procedure oriented language A programming language designed for the convenient expression of procedures used in the solution of a wide class of problems.

processed tissue method *See* **chemical methods.**

processor (Comput.) The portion of a computer that operates upon the **input** data to produce the desired **output.** A term also used in the terminology of **hardware** (a data processor) and **software** (a computer program with its functions designed for a specific programming language, e.g., COBOL processor, FORTRAN processor). *See* **accumulator, computer operation.**

process schizophrenia A gradually developing, ever increasing in severity, insidious form of probably biologically determined **schizophrenia** without apparent precipitating cause and with poor prognosis. The diagnosis of schizophrenia is firm and unquestioned.

Process schizophrenia is one phase of a two-dimensional classification (the other being **reactive schizophrenia**), based not on apparent symptoms but on the patient's history of adjustability or lack of it (W. C. Herron, "The Process-Reactive Classification of Schizophrenia," *Psychological Bulletin*, No. 59, 1962, 329-342).

Gabriel Langfeldt, Norwegian psychologist and prominent spokesman for this type of classification, believes that the process involves: (1) adverse heredity, (2) ectomorphic (hypersensitive) constitution, (3) a schizoid temperament, (4) absence of psychogenic factors, and (5) massive **dereism**, depersonalization and inexplicable **delusions** leading to inevitable deterioration about 90% of the time. *See* **schizophrenogenic.**

Prochaska, (Jiri) George (1749-1820) A Moravian physician and anatomist. He used the term "**sensorium commune**" in 1784 for the basic "mechanism of the reflex. . . not related to the soul" (Clarke and O'Malley, p. 345-46).

prodrome A symptom that runs (-drome-) before (pro-) or precedes the disease (such as an aura is a prodrome of epilepsy).

product-moment correlation *See* **Pearson product-moment correlation.**

proestrus A preliminary (pro-) or preparatory period of **estrus.**

professeur agrégé (Fr., associate professor.)

Professor A rank in Germany which was perpetual, the holder only being relieved of his official duties at time of "retirement" but still retaining his full university salary as well as being able to receive pay from his lecture fees and private practice.

profile *See* **psychograph.**

progesterone A sterone that originates in the ovary's **corpus luteum** and precedes (pro-) pregnancy, acting as a precursor to other hormones. It inhibits production of the **follicle-stimulating hormone** by the **adenohypophysis**, but also prepares the female for pregnancy.

Discovered in 1929 by American physician Willard Myron Allen (born 1904) and American anatomist George Washington Corner (born 1889).

program (Comput.) A set of instructions that defines the desired sequence of events and operations required to perform the desired computation. In reinforcement studies, the interrelating factors in a set of reinforcing conditions (schedules, stimuli, etc.).

program library A collection of available **computer programs** and routines.

programmed instruction A **program** based on **instrumental conditioning** (usually in textbook form, but a computer can also be programmed for teaching), whereby material to be learned is presented in sequential order or "frames" with the student or subject not proceeding to the next frame until he checks his answer with that given in the instructional material, positive reinforcement resulting with a correct response. Programmed learning is sometimes used as a synonym for programmed instruction, but it more strictly refers to the process of learning by programmed instruction or teaching. The process not only involves the student in the learning process but also gives him immediate feedback of results.

projection Act (-ion) of throwing (-ject-) forward (pro-). A verbal **defense mechanism** (**Freud**, 1894) through which an individual represses or protects himself from awareness of his own undesirable characteristics by attributing them to others, or by accusing others of having the trait instead. A process by which anxiety-provoking elements in the personality are externalized and eliminated by unrealistically attributing them to others or to the environment. Deceptive behavior, in which the person deceptively accuses others of taking things he has stolen or lost, is a form of projection. *See* **projective technique.**

projection area A surface area of the **cerebral cortex** that connects with **peripheral** areas by means of projection fibers. Projection areas produce electrical **potentials** upon stimulation of sense organs, or produce somatic responses upon electrical stimulation. *See* **Meynert.**

projective technique (projective test) An indirect, standardized method for obtaining a diagnosis of personality organization by interpreting the subject's responses to relatively unstructured and ambiguous stimuli. The responses (fantasies, associations, etc.) are considered as **projections**, or the throwing forth in disguised fashion of unconscious attitudes, needs, or fears that ordinarily would not be expressed in direct, conscious, controlled language.

One of the best known projective tests is the **Rorschach Inkblot Test.** The subject is asked general questions about the inkblots, such as, "What do you see?" Scoring of projective tests follows a systematic procedure described in a manual. Interpretation of the response-patterns may be "read" fairly well by a number of different psychologists who have seen only the **protocol** (blind interpretation). However, the **validity** of these very costly assessments of human personality is much suspect. In projective tests, scoring technique is vastly more important than in other kinds of tests. Because only ten stimulus cards are used (and despite claims of Rorschach experts that these cards uniquely sample the total personality), it is extremely difficult to compare subject-to-subject behavior because of lack of structure.

Although inkblot interpretations of the personality were used as early as 1895, the first tests to use the psychoanalytic concept of projection were in England by R. B. Cattell in his *A Guide to Mental Testing*, 1936, by **H. A. Murray** in his "Techniques for a Systematic Investigation of Phantasy." *Journal of Psychology*, 1937, **3**, 115-143; and by R. R. Sears "Experimental Studies of Projection: Part I, Attribution of Traits." *Journal of Social Psychology*, 1936, **7**, 389-398.

The term projective testing was first named (1937), defined, and given a rationale by American psychologist Lawrence K. Frank (1890-1969), and published in "Projective Methods for the Study of Personality." *Journal of Psychology*, 1939, **8**, 389-413.

prolactin (lactogenic hormone, luteotropin) A pituitary hormone that is a precursor (pro-) to the development of maternal milk (-lactin).

propedeutique The first cycle (of three successive ones) in French higher education, lasting about a year and consisting of a generalized exposure to scientific understanding and accumulation of knowledge. It is roughly comparable to the general education program in colleges and universities of the United States (except that a demanding comprehensive examination must be passed before proceeding to the next cycle), usually lasting for about two or three years and leading to the first university degree, the **licence.**

Propf schizophrenia (Ger., grafted [*Propf*] upon) Schizophrenia that occurs in association with congenitally mentally retarded children, symptomatized by anxiety, irritability, excitement, or stupor. At times, the patient is mute and seems oblivious to his surroundings, with no signs of affect. Suddenly, he may change in behavior, becoming repetitive and hyperkinetic. Often associated with whatever structural damage has produced the mental deficiency but also related to the severe emotional deprivation such children have experienced.

Kraepelin used the term "*Propfhebephrenie*" in 1919 to describe those adolescent patients who developed **dementia praecox** after having already been diagnosed as mentally deficient (S. L. Garfield, "Abnormal Behavior and Mental Deficiency," in *Handbook of Mental Deficiency*, N. R. Ellis, Ed. [McGraw-Hill, 1963], pp. 574-601).

prophase An early or before (pro-) phase. *See* **mitosis.**

proprioceptor Receiver (-ceptor) of one's own (proprio-) sense of location. An internal **receptor** located in vestibular sense organs, muscles, tendons, and joints, and sensitive to body position and movements or to stimuli originating within the body. *See* **exteroceptor, interceptor, Sherrington.**

proprium (Property; attribute); selfhood. The process of **individuation** in personality development. According to **G. W. Allport** (*Becoming: Basic Consideration for a Psychology of Personality*, 1955), the core tendency of man is not **self-actualization** in itself but an individual's unique way of discovering his own personality. The proprium refers to those collective aspects of personality which "seem singularly one's own."

prosencephalon The most anterior or fore (pro-s-) part of the three primary embryological divisions of the vertebrate brain (encephalon), or the part of the adult brain derived from this tissue, including the **telencephalon** and **diencephalon**; the forebrain. It is concerned with functions of thought, perception, speech, and learning.

Francois Chaussier (*see* **raphé nuclei**) was the first to use this term for the forebrain or anterior brain vesicle of the embryo.

prosopagnosia A disorder (-ia) manifested by not (a-) being able to recognize or know (-gnos-) the face (prosop-) of intimate friends, even after having been recently in touch with them; visual **agnosia**. An extreme form of the condition may occur in which the person is incapable of recognizing his own face in the mirror or on a snapshot. The defect probably stems from an infant's inability to organize his visual perceptions (in particular, difficulty in forming a face **Gestalt**); may also result from genetic defects or from lesions or damage to the left parieto-occipital lobe.

prostasia State of standing (-stasia) first (pro-) in line. Social dominance. *See* **pecking order.**

protanomaly An anomaly about perceiving the first (proto-) or red end of the spectrum; a **trichromatism** in which large amounts of red are needed to match the spectrum; also, a red-green **hue** weakness.

protanope (protonope) A person suffering from **protanopia**; one who cannot (-an) recognize or see (-ope) red, the first (pro-) of the primary colors. *See* **deuteranope, dichromatism, Purkinje.**

protanopia Disorder (-ia) of not (-an-) being able to see (-op-) red, the first (prot-) of the primary colors. Red-green hue blindness. Partial color blindness is marked by faulty brightness discrimination and a relative insensitivity to the red end of the spectrum; a type of **dichromatism.**

protocol First (proto-) leaf or page glued (-col) to a papyrus. The original non-interpretive recorded clinical observations, notes of an experiment, direct quotations of an interview, or notes and verbatim responses to questions on a psychological test. *See* **projective technique.**

protopathic sensation Relating to (-ic) basic or first (proto-) pain or suffering (-path-). Responsive only to the basic or gross sensations, such as pain, heat, and cold. *See* **somatic sensory system, epicritic sensation.**

Named by **Head** in 1911.

protoplasm First (proto-) formative material. *See* **Purkinje.**

prototaxic experience Referring to (-ic) a response (-tax-), either negative or positive, that occurs in the first (proto-) year of life, in which the infant characteristically seems unaware of time, space, or self. According to **Sullivan**, such responses are on the lowest level of the child's hierarchical system of thinking in relating to other human beings. *See* **ego formation, parataxic thinking, syntaxic thinking** (also H. S. Sullivan, *The Interpersonal Theory of Psychiatry*, 1953).

proximal Pertaining to (-al) the nearest or proximate (proxim-) anatomical region; situated toward the point of origin. *See* **anatomical directions.**

proximal-distal sequence In physical development, the progressive tendency for organs and functions close to (proximal) an organism's center to develop sooner than those more peripheral or distant (distal).

A *proximal stimulus* affects a receptor directly, initiating sensation, while a *distal* one is of the environment. A *proximal response* requires muscular involvement, while a *distal response* necessitates that the organism alter the environment. *See* **anatomical directions, cephalocaudal sequence.**

proximity law *See* **autochthonous laws of cognitive order.**

Psa psychoanalysis.

pseudocyesis False (pseudo-) pregnancy (-cyesis), as sometimes reported by patients with a **conversion reaction.**

pseudofeeblemindedness Mental retardation as determined by poor performance on **intelligence tests** or school tests despite indications of normal intellectual achievement otherwise; believed to be due to emotional blockage rather than actual lack of capacity or brain cells.

pseudo-isochromatic plate Referring to (-ic) a color (chromat-) plate that deceptively (pseudo) appears to have equal (iso-) color intensity. One of a set of colored plates or pictures (with colored dots in the shape of numbers), such as the **Ishihara color test**, that appears to those with certain types of **color blindness** to have no number at all or to seem of a different number. Other tests, such as the Dvorine, use a combination of numbers and designs. Color-normal individuals "see through" the designs or numbers to the actual numbers presented.

pseudomnesia A disorder (-ia) of false (pseudo-) memory (-mnes-). *See* **paramnesia.**

pseudophone False or illusory (pseudo-) sounds (-phone). A device used in producing **illusions** of auditory localization where the auditory field is reversed—sounds normally reaching the right ear stimulate the left and vice versa.

Originally invented by British physicist, Silvanus P. Thompson (1851-1916) in 1899. A later modification was used by **P. T. Young** in his pseudophone studies.

pseudo random numbers (Comput.) A set of numbers created by a number generator operating on a "kernel" of numbers. While not a **random** selection, the set does possess the properties of such a selection.

pseudoscope An optical instrument (-scope), using prisms, that produces false (pseudo-) results (making a solid object appear hollow) by reversing normal optical relationships (up for down, right for left, etc.); useful for studying convergence and disparity in depth perception. The reversed depths are possible only when the depth is fairly ambiguous. The effects produced are opposite to those of the **stereoscope.**

The pseudoscope was invented by **Wheatstone** in 1852.

P-silocybin (Psilocybin) Bare, smooth (Psilo-) head (cyb- + in = a chemical suffix for neutral compounds). A crystalline alkaloid solid obtained from the Mexican mushroom *Psilocybe mexicana*; an **hallucinogen**. Usually self-administered, it produces nausea and vomiting for 6 to 8 hours, followed later by wild, frightening, psychedelic, hallucinogenic experiences, sometimes leading to suicide. Slang: silo, the barn.

Isolated in 1958 by A. Hofmann (see **LSD**). In 1960 he identified the psychoactive principle of *ololiuqui*, a Mexican morning glory (*Rivea corymbosa*), obtaining ergot alkaloids (such as d-lysergic acid amide).

psionics The body of knowledge (-ics) about psi (-on-as euphony). *Same as* **parapsychology.** *See* **psi phenomena.**

psi phenomena A non-theoretical approach to all parapsychological functions of the mind, consisting of **clairvoyance** (ability to discern objects hidden or at great distance), **extrasensory perception, precognition** (foreseeing the future), **psychokinesis** (ability to produce motion in another being or objects without direct contact), **telepathy** (direct mental relationship between two or more human beings), and **telekinesis** (ability to manipulate objects without directly touching them).

PSR Psychogalvanic skin reflex. *See* **psychogalvanic reflex.**

psychasthenia Disorder (-ia) of no (-a-) strength (-sthen-) of the mind (psych-); mind weakness (-asthenia). A type of **neurosis** marked by morbid fear and anxiety, **obsessive-compulsive reaction, fixed ideas**, feelings of inadequacy, irrationally expressed thoughts, unreality, and **depersonalization.**

Janet was the first (1903) to describe and name psychasthenia, in *Les Obsessions et la Psychasthenie*, referring to it as a "lack of psychic cohesiveness" which leads to "hysterical and dissociative phenomena."

psychedelic drug Relating to (-ic) a mind- (psyche-) manifesting (-del-) drug; **psychotomimetic**. Any of the consciousness-expanding drugs, like **LSD**, and **mescaline**, that produce such related but temporary symptoms of **schizophrenia** as visual **hallucinations**, detachment from one's own body, apparent sense of great insights and awareness of basic truths.

The term "psychedelic," upon a suggestion from Aldous Huxley, was introduced in 1957 by Humphrey Osmond (born 1917, England). He received a diploma in psychological medicine in England 1949, and a certificate in psychiatry (1952) from the Royal College of Physicians and Surgeons, Canada. (H. Osmond, "A Review of the Clinical Effects of Psychotomimetic Agents," *Annals of the New York Academy of Science*, 1957, 66, 418-434).

psychelepsy *See* **neuroleptic drug.**

psychergograph A recorder-equipped apparatus (-graph) that triggers successive stimuli when a correct response is given, used in fatigue discrimination studies and for determining psychological (psych-) work (-ergo-) output.

psychiatric diagnoses of mental disorders *See* **classification of mental disorders.**

psychiatry Medical care (-iatr-) of the mind (psych-). The branch of medicine dealing with the study, diagnosis, and treatment of mental disorders and personal adjustment. The practice of psychiatry is carried on by a psychiatrist, an M.D. specializing in psychiatry, with an internship in a psychiatric facility and a residency in psychiatry.

The word "psychiaterie" was used in 1808 by **Reil** and spelled "psychiatrie" by **Heinroth** in 1818. In 1845, the German physician Ernst von Feuchtersleben (1806-1848) used the term "psychiatrics" for the subject matter, later (1846) changing it to psychiatry. In 1847, he also introduced its adjective form—psychiatric.

psychic determinism *See* **Freud.**

psychic energizer *See* **monoamine oxidase.**

psychoanalysis Mind (psycho-) analysis. A dynamic system of **psychology** (basically nonexperimental except by some of the **neo-Freudians**). Its primary principle is psychic determinism. *See* **primus inter pares.**

Freud states in his *Autobiography* that he published his first tenets of psychoanalysis in an obituary for **Charcot** in 1883, but actually attributed the founding of psychoanalysis to Breuer. Freud used the term for the first time in 1896, centering on the explanation and relief of mental and emotional maladjustments. The exploration of unconscious mechanisms was aided by Freud's use of **free association** (1895), **transference**, and **dream analysis** (*Traumdeutung*, 1900).

psychoanalyst One who (-yst) analyzes the mind (psycho-) by practicing classical **psychoanalysis** or some modification of it, including the use of **free association, dream analysis**, and reliving of childhood conflicts and attachments. In the United States, a psychoanalyst must first attain the status of a **psychiatrist.**

p

During or shortly after his medical residency he must study at a psychoanalytic institute located in any one of several major cities, and be analyzed by a training psychoanalyst while receiving didactic analysis. His early cases in his practice are monitored and discussed, often in relationship to his own analysis and how his own problems might enter into his patients' problems. *Lay analysts* are usually professional people without medical training (educators, psychologists, etc.) who have been analyzed and specially trained by didactic psychoanalysts. Freud recommended wide use of lay analysts but such practice has been frowned upon by the AMA in the United States. There are some practicing in major cities, however. In loose usage, a psychoanalyst is anyone who practices some form of **psychotherapy.**

psychobiology The study (-logy) interrelating mental (psych-) functions with other life (bio-) processes and activities.

Friedrich Eduard Beneke (1798-1854), German philosopher-psychologist, and Friedrich Groos (1768-1852), German philosopher-psychiatrist, pioneered in development of the psychobiological approach. The use of the term in 1886 by Hippolyte-Marie Bernheim, (1840-1919) French psychiatrist, put emphasis on the mental processes. The *Objective Psychobiology* (1915) of Adolph Meyer (1866-1950) describes his form of therapy that stresses the patient's relation to his environment, using **distributive analysis** to study all factors (psychic, social, and biological) connected with his development. Insisting on the importance of synthesis in addition to the analysis, Meyer placed his therapy in opposition to **psychoanalysis. Harry Stack Sullivan,** however, developed his psychobiology along psychoanalytic lines.

psychodrama A group psychotherapeutic technique in which the patient acts out or dramatizes various roles and situations from real life in an attempt to gain insight and achieve **catharsis** See **group therapy, psychotherapy, role.**

In 1909, **Moreno** had Viennese schoolchildren act out prepared scripts based on their behavioral problems, but he soon learned that they preferred to be spontaneous in reacting to one another. He applied a similar technique to adults for both diagnostic and therapeutic purposes, using the name *sociodrama* (1922) when used to clarify social issues and psychodrama when applied to the individual.

psychodynamics Dynamics (various interacting forces or motivational sequences) in which past events influence the present and future behavior of the psychological (psycho-) self, or **personality.** See **dynamics.**

psychogalvanic reflex (PGR) Relating to (-ic) involuntary, physiological changes in the body resulting from reactions to emotional stress and measureable by the **psychogalvanometer.** Such changes are related to sweating, the skin, for example, being a better electrical conductor when wet. Thus, when a person is active or under stress the skin sweats, producing a change in electrical potential. The psychogalvanometer measures the lowered resistance to the passage of an electric current between points on the skin surface. The PGR is often used as an indicator of emotional arousal (such as in lie detection or experimental studies) and also as an aid in measuring responses to **sympathetic nervous system** activity. (Also known as galvanic skin response, psychogalvanic skin reflex, (Tcharnoff phenomenon).

First described in 1879 by Auguste Vigouroux (1841-1902), French neurologist, and more accurately described in 1890 by Ivan R. Tcharnoff (1848-1909), Russian physiologist. The term was first used in 1909 by Otto Veraguth, German neurologist.

psychogalvanometer A device used for measuring (-meter) the change in skin conductivity produced when a person sweats under emotional stress. The momentary decrease in the apparent electrical skin resistance is measured by a low amperage current when sweat glands (influenced by action of the **autonomic nervous system**) respond to stimuli. See **psychogalvanic reflex.**

psychogenic Related to (-ic) or caused by a stimulus (idea, fear, guilt) that originates (-gen-) in the mind (psycho-) rather than in the body; caused by emotional and psychological factors as distinguished from organic. See **Murray.**

psychograph (profile, test profile, trait profile) A means of picturing a person's relative standing on different tests, the scores being expressed in comparable units and with reference to a common norm. Also, a chart of relevant test scores (in comparable units, such as **standard scores**) from subtests (such as in the **Guilford-Zimmerman Temperament Scale**) or from various tests given to the same individual. The chart (scaled in centiles, etc.) has parallel rows, with scores connected by lines to form a profile of high and low scores.

psychokinesis An ability to move (-kinesis) physical objects by the mind (psycho-). *Same as* telekinesis. See **extrasensory perception, psi phenomena.**

psycholinguistics The study (-ics) of language (linguist-) or language behavior in relation to human psychological (psycho-) characteristics. Also, the coding and encoding processes involved in the speaker's and hearer's transformation of signals according to the culturally accepted code. See **transformational grammar, stratificational grammar.**

psychological awards and prizes See **awards and prizes of a psychological nature.**

psychological field The dynamic and amorphous field of psychological experience, including the individual and the mutual interaction he has with his environment. **Koffka** considered the psychological field to consist of the perceiving subject in terms of the perceived environment, and that both acted as a field of forces generated toward achieving an ideal balance. Koffka worked his concepts into **Gestalt** laws, especially **Praegnanz.** To **Lewin,** psychological field meant the Gestalt involved with psychological events that are coexisting and interdependent, all of which determine behavior. Interactions between one's personality and environment resulted in what **Lewin** called **life space.**

psychological hedonism See **law of effect.**

psychological laboratory The world's first formal psychological laboratory is generally accepted to have been established at the University of Leipzig in 1879. However, Robert Watson states that formal university recognition for an experimental course of a laboratory appropriation "did not come. . . until the winter of 1883. . . In this connection, 1879 is notable only for appearance of the first student to do publishable psychological research with Wundt." He claims that 1875 is more authentic, since in that year both James (with a small laboratory) and Wundt (with a special room for his own experimental work) established so-called laboratories. (R. I. Watson, *The Great Psychologists,* from Aristotle to Freud. J. B. Lippincott Company, 1963; R. S. Harper, "The First Psychological Laboratory" *Isis,* 1950, **41,** 158-161).

psychological primary colors See **primary colors.**

psychological zero point Point at which neither warmth-sensitive spots nor cold-sensitive spots are stimulated (or neither warmth nor cold is experienced by the subject); point of indifference; usually occurs at about 90°F., but can vary according to the organism's adaptive temperature.

psychologist One who (-ist) studies, teaches, or practices **psychology.** A psychologist's interest may be in any of the fields of psychology.

Most applied psychologists combine university teaching with part-time practice or full-time practice with part-time teaching at a college or university. In loose usage, many persons whose occupation is primarily in being of service to people are called psychologists, regardless of training or experience. Technically, however, a professional psychologist is research-oriented and must have a doctor of philosophy (Ph.D.) or doctor of education (Ed.D) degree with a major in psychology from an accredited college or university.

Many applied professional psychologists (sparked by clinicians and students interested in "human" psychology who had become disenchanted with so-called "rat psychology" and what some consider an inordinate and useless amount of time spent on foreign languages, research, and statistics) were instrumental in developing Doctor of Psychology or related degrees or even special "schools of psychology" to take care of those opposed to traditional graduate school degrees.

A *clinical psychologist* must have a doctorate as well as an internship in some recognized clinical facility in the area of "deviant behaviors." He performs research, diagnostic, and therapeutic work including mental and personality testing with patients in hospitals, clinics, or private practice. An *industrial psychologist* (specializing in industrial, personnel, engineering psychology, etc.) also must have a doctorate, generally working in industry or government or as a consultant in combination with teaching in a college or university. *Social psychologists* hold a Ph.D., primarily doing research and teaching in universities but may also work in social and governmental agencies. *Child psychologists* have a doctorate, usually conducting research, therapy, and testing on and with children at university clinics as well as serving as consultants at child guidance clinics. A "*statistical psychologist*" has a Ph.D., with heavy background in mathematics, theory of test construction, and applied statistics. He also carries out research and acts as consultant on experimental design and test construction. *Experimental* and *physiological psychologists* are heavily oriented toward research, conducting research and teaching functions at universities and frequently in governmental agencies and aircraft companies (aerospace activities).

Answers to specific questions concerning psychology may be obtained by enclosing a stamped, self-addressed return envelope in your request to the *American Psychological Association,* 1200 17th Street, Washington, D.C. 20036.

psychologistics The study (-ics) of the functions of a psychologist; also relates to the logistics employed by psychologists in carrying out their varied responsibilities.

As coined by American psychologist, Philip M. Carman (born 1925), Ph.D., Wash. 1955, it refers particularly to the "series of structured group programs" designed ". . .to assist disabled institutionalized veterans to develop more effective psychological strategies to deal with their medical, psychological, and social deficits—an all-inclusive term for what and how psychologists do things."

psychology Study or science (-logy) of the soul or the mind (psych-). The science that studies and measures the behavior and experience of living organisms, especially of human beings.

Philipp Melanchthon (1497-1560), German scholar and religious reformer, in his book, *Commentarius de Anima,* 1540, was the first to publish the term "psychologia" but in reference to the soul. The concept of "psychology" in relationship to man rather than his soul apparently was first used in 1590 when **Goclenius** wrote his *Psychologia—Hoc*

Est de Hominis Perfectione (Psychology, or On the Improvement of Man). (Francois H. La Pointe, "Origin and Evolution of the Term Psychology." *American Psychologist*, 1970, 25, 7, 640-645).

psychology divisions or organizations The APA directory lists the APA affiliated divisions for the current year. Some organizations not associated with the APA have been described by Paul J. Woods in "Psychological Organizations: Their Nature and Membership Patterns," *American Psychologist*, 1964, **19**, 663-669. Organizations and groups referred to even tangentially in this book are nevertheless briefly described under the appropriate alphabetical entry. *See* **Euler diagram** for an example of the number of psychological organizations that overlap one another.

psychometry (psychometrics) Process (-y) of measuring (-metr-) psychological (psycho-) factors. A branch of **psychology** devoted to measuring psychological **variables** within the field of testing. For test construction, considerable knowledge of logic and statistics is needed. However, in the lower levels of psychometry, such as in the administration and scoring of tests, relatively little knowledge of statistics is required.

The term was coined by **Christian Wolff** in 1736 in his attempt to give psychology meaning as a structural science of measurement. The term has also been used (1870) to describe the ability of some so-called sensitives to provide detailed information about an absent person while holding a personal object of that person.

psychomotor Pertaining to (-or) mind (psycho-) combined with movement (-mot-); motor activity induced by psychic action. A term applied to the combination of muscular activity and the psychological (cerebral or other neural) process that gives rise to it or controls it.

In *psychomotor seizure* (related to **epilepsy**), the person carries on repetitive behavior (such as running aimlessly or continually smacking the lips) without apparent logical reasons. **Amnesia** for such activity usually follows.

psychoneurotic (neurotic) disorder A **neurosis**, characterized by a general awareness of condition and a fair adjustment to life, but tending to over rely on defenses. Includes **phobias, obsessive-compulsive neurosis**, conversion reaction, and **hypochondriasis**. *See* **psychiatric nomenclature**.

The term psychoneurosis was first suggested in 1904 by the French psychiatrist Paul C. Dubois (1848-1918) in reference to psychogenic mental conditions.

psychonomics The study or practice (-ics) of the laws (-nom-) of the mind (psycho-). Relationship of the individual with its environment; the branch of **sociology** dealing with psychological factors and laws involved in social organization and development. In **psychology**, the disciplined application of rigorous scientific laws to the study of psychology, particularly experimental.

Psychonomic Society, The An organization whose object is "to promote the communication of scientific research in psychology and related sciences." It was organized on December 31, 1959, at the annual meeting of the AAAS. Members must hold the Ph.D. degree or equivalent and should have published significant research beyond the doctoral dissertation.

psychopath, psychopathic deviate Diseased (-path) mind (psych-). A person with a personality disorder, characterized by amoral, antisocial behavior with little tendency to learn by experience. *See* **Minnesota Multiphasic Personality Inventory**. (H. Cleckley, *The Mask of Sanity*, 1941).

psychopathology The science or study of (-o-logy) diseases (-path-) of the mind (psycho-).

The term psychopathology was coined (1817) by **Bentham** as "psychological pathology" but it was first used (1847) in its modern

sense by the German psychiatrist Feuchtersleben (1806-1848). *See* **psychiatry**.

psychopharmacology The science (-logy) that investigates the behavioral or psychological (psycho-) effects of alcohol, narcotics, tranquilizers, and the various hallucinogenic drugs (-pharmaco-). A relatively new field of study incorporating the disciplines of pharmacology and psychology in the study of behavior.

Term coined in 1920 by American chemist, D. I. Macht, after he had previously coined "psychopharmacological" in 1918 in reference to other drugs (e.g., aspirin) possibly having such effects. In 1935, psychiatrist N. W. Thorner first used the term in psychiatry, referring to effects of **sodium amytal**.

Psychopharmacology Award The Division of Psychopharmacology (28) sponsors this award, which consists of $300 granted to the one presenting the best paper at the annual APA meeting and $100 each awarded for the two next best papers.

psychophysical method An experimental procedure for treating **data** by which (1) **detection thresholds** are determined and (2) psychological scales are developed (measuring how changes in intensity or quality of a stimulus affect sensation). *See* **psychophysical** under **methods of psychology; psychophysics**.

psychophysical parallelism A dualistic concept about the body-mind connections indicating that physical and psychic (soul) or mental activities may parallel each other but do not necessarily interact or have causative effects upon each other.

Leibniz and **Descartes** were dualists in this sense, but Leibniz differed in rejecting interaction completely. In *A New System of Nature* (1695), he stated that the body follows its own mechanical laws and that mental activity (the soul) separately operates in its own fashion, neither entity acting upon the other. *See* **double-aspect theory**.

psychophysics The study (-ics) of psychology (psycho-) with the relation between a physical (-physics) stimulus and its perception by the subject. Although initiated by a physiologist (Weber) in his just noticeable difference observations, psychophysics has been absorbed into psychology, indirectly leading to the first **psychological laboratory** in 1879 and subsequently to experimental psychology. *See* **psychophysical method**.

Fechner considered psychophysics as the science of body-mind relationships. Today, however, it is primarily an experimental field of investigation specifying relations between stimulus-dimension and response variations of the subject. Its special methods are used in studying controlled sensory processes. *See* **psychophysical** under **methods of psychology**.

Historically, psychophysics translates physical characteristics of stimuli into corresponding psychological characteristics (**intelligence, attitude**, etc.).

Founded by German physicist **Gustav T. Fechner** in 1860.

psychophysiologic (psychosomatic) disorders Physical or structural changes in the body, presumably **psychogenic** in nature, that involve a single organ system usually under **autonomic nervous system** innervation, symptomatized by backache, tension headache, sighing, bronchial asthma, paroxysmal tachycardia, **migraine**, peptic ulcer, heartburn, constipation, impotence, menstrual disorders, etc.

psychosexual development Pertaining to (-al) the psychic or emotional (psycho-) aspects of sexuality. In **Freudian** theory, the progression of the child's **libido** through so-called **pregenital stages**: *oral, anal,* then *genital. See* **character types**.

psychosis Morbid condition (-osis) of the mind (psych-). Any kind of mental derangement. A severe mental disorder that interferes with the person's ability to function normally or to adjust to the ordinary demands of life,

symptomatized by autistic thinking, personality disorganization, loss of contact with or difficulty in recognizing reality (i.e., disorientation in time, space, and relationships), profound mood alterations, severe deficits in language, memory, and **perception**, and frequent **delusions** and/or **hallucinations**; for example, **schizophrenia**. A psychosis may be functional or organic.

Psychotic disorders are characterized by deep sensory and thought dysfunctions, lack of insight, and loss of contact with reality. (Includes **infantile autism, childhood schizophrenia, anaclitic depressions**, and **manic-depressive psychosis**).

psychosomatic (disorder) illness Pertaining to (-ic) mind (psycho-) body (-somat-) illness, in which the physiological condition (as in asthma, colitis, dermatitis) may be the consequence of emotional disturbance or personality disorder; that is, may be **psychogenic**, or precipitated by emotional arousal. The preferred term is now **psychophysiologic disorders**.

Heinroth first used the term in 1828. The word came into popular usage during the 1920's and 1930's due particularly to the many writings on the subject by American psychosomatic physician Helen Flanders Dunbar (1902-1959). It was given medical recognition as a distinct condition when the *American Journal of Psychosomatic Medicine* was founded in 1939.

psychotherapy Treatment (-therapy) of the mind (psycho-), specifically of an emotional disorder, psychosomatic illness, or other maladjustment by psychiatric or psychological means, involving personal consultation and interaction. Techniques include: **play therapy, client-centered therapy, psychoanalysis, psychodrama**, group therapy, **narcoanalysis, hypnosis**, and others. A practitioner of psychotherapy is usually expected to have high professional training (usually an M.D. or Ph.D.). A person may engage in counseling with less training.

psychotic depressive reaction (reactive depressive psychosis) A depressive mood traceable to some disturbing experience, and characterized by the person ordinarily having no history of repeated **depressions** or cyclothymic mood swings. Differentiation between this condition and depressive **neurosis** depends upon whether the reaction impairs reality testing or functional adequacy enough to be considered a **psychosis**.

psychotogen A drug that produces (-gen) psychosis (psychoto-). *Same as* **psychotomimetic drug**.

psychotomimetic drug A drug that mimics (-mimetic-) the effect of psychosis (psychoto-) by producing **delusions, hallucinations**, and generally bizarre sensations, all for relatively brief periods of time (hours or days) but generally not for a continuing state.

Term coined in 1955 by J. Gerard, but since such drugs do not always or really mimic psychoses, the term is losing favor.

psychotropic drug A drug tending to turn (-tropic) the mind (psycho-), such as a tranquilizer and psychotogen.

P-technique An experimental and statistical means of "measuring a set of variables on one person and repeating those measures on a sufficient number of occasions to provide a correlatable series; a correlation of occasions with behavior of a given kind." *See* **ipsative unit**. (R. B. Cattell, *Factor Analysis*, New York: Harper and Bros., 1952, pp. 102-3).

Developed in 1946 by **R. B. Cattell**.

punched card (Comput.) A **data** processing card of constant size and shape, suitable for punching, and capable of being handled mechanically. The punched holes are usually sensed electrically by wire brushes or by a photoelectric light beam process.

punched tape (Comput.) Paper or Mylar plastic tape punched in a pattern of holes so as to convey information.

p

pungent Acrid, irritating. One of the seven primary qualities of smell in the **stereochemical smell theory**.

pupillary reflex Relating to (-ary) the pupil reflex. Contraction of the pupil induced by light entering the eye, by change in the intensity of light, or by accommodation for distance.

The reflex was first described by **R. Whytt** in 1751.

pupillometer A device for measuring (-meter) the diameter of the pupil, the dilations and contractions being possible indicators of psychological change in the subject.

pupilloscope An optical instrument (-scope). A color vision efficiency testing device for measuring pupil size when the wavelength of light is varied.

pure strategy In **game theory**, a set of directions to be followed according to a pregame plan, in which one of the competitors makes a decision to play the game in the same way each time, for example, playing for the "least loss" on each play.

purine A pure crystalline compound (-ine); a double ring nitrogen base that includes two variants (**adenine** and **guanine**) and is also a component of **nucleotides** and **nucleic acids**.

Albrecht **Kossel** named both purine (a double ring formation of adenine and guanine) and **pyrimidine** (a single ring formation of **cytosine** and **thymine**) after he had isolated a series of nitrogen-containing compounds from nucleic acid. He received the Nobel prize in 1910. In 1911, **Leven(e)** extended Kossel's studies by showing that nucleic acids contained five-carbon sugar molecules and additionally had two varieties of nucleic acid: *yeast nucleic acid* containing ribose and *thymus nucleic acid* having one oxygen atom missing (deoxyribose), the two varieties of nucleic acid being named respectively **ribosenucleic acid** (RNA) and **deoxyribonucleic acid** (DNA). By 1934, Levene had shown that nucleic acids contained a purine or a pyrimidine, and either the ribose or deoxyribose sugar, as well as a phosphate group, which he named a nucleotide.

Purkinje shift (or effect) A shift in the perception of relative brightness of color upon reduced illumination, the retina adapting to twilight and night (rod) vision from daylight (cone) vision. At twilight, hues at the violet to short wave end of the spectrum (blues, greens) appear relatively brighter while those at the red or long wave end (reds, yellows) seem darker. During dark adaptation the eye loses sensitivity first to red, then to yellow, blue, and green.

Named for Jan Purkyně (Johannes Evangelista Purkinje) (1787-1869), Czech physiologist, noted for studies in ophthalmology and embryology. Proposed the word "protoplasm" (1839) for formative material of animal embryos, and also discovered **neurons** in the **cortex** of the **cerebellum**. *See* **axon**.

q

puromycin A compound (-in-) or **drug** derived from the pure (puro-) extract of actinomycete and that has the effect of inhibiting protein synthesis. Puromycin injected into the **brain** (for example, in the **hippocampus**) creates an impermanent **amnesia** for well-established habits, caused by indirectly reducing cholinesterase activity (preventing accumulation of **acetylcholine**).

purposive behaviorism *See* **Tolman's purposive behaviorism**.

r

purposive sampling A **sampling** procedure in which the investigator seeks to obtain representativeness in the **sample** by selecting the individuals according to his purpose or judgment rather than by **random** methods. It is sometimes called judgment sampling. If all pupils in a school constitute the population, an investigator will obtain a purposive sample by choosing the individuals who are, in his judgment, typical with respect to the purpose of the investigation. Or, he might formulate a description of the kind of person he deems

representative, then obtain a specified number of individuals who conform to the description; for example, ten pupils whose ages approximate the **median** for the **population**. Probability theory can be applied to random samples, but not to the analysis of purposive samples.

pursuit rotor (pursuit meter) A clock-and-motor-equipped device that challenges the subject to maintain the point of a hinged, hand-operated stylus in time-recorded contact with a spot target near the outer rim of a revolving turntable.

putamen (A cutting or paring; a nut shell.) The lateral part of the **lentiform nucleus** so-named because of its resemblance to the bark of a tree or the shell of a nut. *See* **globus pallidus, basal ganglia**.

Term introduced (1819-1826) by Burdach (*see* **cingulate gyrus**).

putrid (rotten) One of the seven primary qualities of smell in the **stereochemical smell theory**.

pyknic type Type relating to (-ic) being bulky (pykn-) or fatty. One of **Kretschmer's body types** (short, rounded, soft physique) with an inclination toward mood variations, but generally jovial, active, and outgoing: in mental illness, this type of person tends toward **manic-depressive** behavior. Comparable to **endomorphic**; *contrasted with* **asthenic**. *See* **dysplastic type of body build**.

pyramidal system Relating to (-al) the symmetrical wedge-shaped nerve pathway on the ventral surface of the medulla whose tracts descend on each side in the cortical white matter that helps make up part of the internal capsule. In the upper part of the brainstem most of the fibers decussate to form bundles of fibers called the lateral pyramids, from which the pyramidal system takes its name. The pyramidal system consists of four columns of motor fibers that run longitudinally in pairs (without synapses) from the medullary (or bulbar) pyramids down to the motor nuclei of the brainstem and to the spinal cord. The system is concerned with skilled and complex movements (primarily of the hands and mouth) as well as with such grosser body movements as those governed by the trunk muscles (Morgan, pp. 282-283; Butter, pp. 113-114).

The term pyramidal tract was first used in 1877 by the German neurologist **Flechsig**.

pyrimidine (miazine) An inorganic (pyr-) heterocyclic ring compound (-ine) derived from the ammonia group (-imid-), serving as an important constituent of various biochemical substances (such as thiamine). It is the parent substance of the **barbiturates** as well as being a component of **nucleotides** and **nucleic acids**, and includes three variants: **thymine, cytosine,** and **uracil**. *See* **purine**.

Q

Q Quartile; semi-interquartile range.

Q-sort A checklist **rating scale** in which the rater sorts out described general traits or characteristics printed on a stack of cards. *See* **forced-choice method, Q technique**.

Q-technique An ambiguous term, sometimes referring to **Q-sort** or transpose **factor analysis**, or both, but in general relating to factoring correlations between persons instead of between tests. William Stephenson (1953) originally called it "inverse factor analysis" because it was an "inversion of all previous work." Stephenson's objective was to compare individuals, considering "person-correlation" (*q*) statistically independent of "test-correlation" (*r*).

It was devised to aid in making comparative judgments regarding an individual's change in self-concept, particularly during psychotherapy. From this developed the Q-sort as a research tool. The subject sorts into piles a large number (usually five or seven in each category) of printed self-referrent statements, such as "I am generally moody"; "I am often critical of others"; etc. The piles range from "very characteristic" through "neutral" to "not characteristic." After finishing this so-called self-sort, the subject may then re-sort the statements, this time sorting them as the kind of person he would ideally like to be. There are many variations of the technique.

quadrigeminal bodies Relating to (-al) four (quadri-) twin (gemin-) bodies. *See* **corpora quadrigemina**.

quale The quality (*quale*) of a thing within itself; a particular quality that has no meaning or any external reference (such as the specific but nevertheless vague quality of heredity or of the vague form of spatiality). Quale emphasizes heredity or the soma as the determining factor in perception, attitudes, and behavior in general.

In perception, quale is the irreducible element of all spatial experiences, as ascribed by the **nativists** (Hering, Müller, Stumpf, and the **Gestalt** psychologists) to sensations.

qualitative variable Statistically, a **variable** not measurable by hard, fast rules of a number system. The **chi-square statistic** and its related C^2, indicating a strength of relationship or index of association, can be used to advantage with qualitative variables.

quantal Referring to (-al) an amount (quan-) of **data** in drug sensitivity experiments in which only two categories occur (all or none, dead or alive, etc.). Its use is log normally distributed. The *quantal dose-effect* is the degree to which an organism responds to an administered drug, that is, the relationship of the drug dosage to the individual's responsiveness. *See* **methods of psychology: psychophysical**.

quantitative variable A **variable** that relates (-ative) to a specific quantity. Statistically, a variable that can be subjected to mathematical treatment, such as using an index or **coefficient** to represent its numerical equivalent.

quantizer A feedback device that (-er) acts (iz) to convert a certain quantity (quant-) to a series of digital output signals. *See* **digitizer**.

quartile Pertaining to (-ile) a fourth (quart-) or quarter. One of the dividing points on a scale that separates a **distribution** into four equal parts. In this sense, analogous to a **median** and a **percentile**: the first quartile is the 25th percentile, the second quartile is the median (50th percentile), and the third quartile and the 75th percentile are identical. *See* **interquartile range**.

questionnaire A printed form consisting of a number of questions related to a specific subject (attitude, personality, opinions) that are to be answered by one or more persons. A well-constructed questionnaire usually bases its written items on questions tested-out beforehand, either by receiving suggestions from a personal interview or by refining the questions after feedback from extensive and repeated written questioning.

quota control In attitude and opinion polling, the control set up by a survey organization that directs the interviewer to select respondents, as under **quota sampling**. *See* **area sample**.

quota sampling A technique used in mass surveys (e.g., public opinion polling) to obtain a cross section of a **population**. It requires interviewers to choose respondents, within a certain quota, who have specified characteristics (in respect to age, education, income, etc.).

R

R Response.

r A symbol for the **Pearson product-moment correlation**.

radian The unit of measure of a plane **angle** with its vertex at the center of a circle and subtended by an arc equal in length to the radius (from which its name derives).

radiant flux *See* **luminous flux.**

radical Referring to (-al) the root (radi[x]). The root of a quantity or quantities, denoted by an expression written under the *radical sign*, $\sqrt{}$, such as $\sqrt{5}$, 5 being the radical, meaning the square root of 5.

radix (Root) The total number of characters or symbols for use in a digital position of a **number system.** Also, a quantity whose successive integral powers are the implicit multipliers of the sequence of digits that represent a number. For example, if the radix is five, then 143.2 means 1 times 5 to the second power, plus 4 times 5 to the first power, plus 3 times 5 to the zero power, plus 2 times 5 to the minus one power. The radix in the **binary system** is 2, since there are only two symbols (0, 1), while the **radix** in the decimal system is 10, since only 10 symbols (0 - 9) are used.

RAE Rotational After Effect.

Ramon y Cajal, Santiago (1852-1934) Spanish histologist and neurologist (M.D., Zaragoza 1873). Known especially for his work on isolating the **neuron**, and for discovering, in 1889, certain neuronal laws known today as the synapse theory (or **neuron theory**). Carried out researches on morphology and function of the nerve cell and of the **neuroglia.** He was the first to directly show that neurons are contiguous to but not continuous with each other (1888), confirming the work of **His** and **Forel** on nerve cell individuality and undermining the nerve net theory of **Golgi.** Ramon y Cajal's principal publication was *Histologie du Système Nerveuse de l'Homme et des Vertébrés*, Paris, 1909-1911. In 1906, he and Golgi shared the Nobel prize in medicine. *See* **Waldeyer.**

random An **event** that occurs by chance, that is, by the natural course of events, or by manmade design such as in the use of a random numbers table.

random effects model A model for an **experimental design** that assumes the experimental **variables** to be random; that is, that levels were selected from some larger population of **treatment levels** with the assurance that all units of the **population** have an equal chance of being chosen. (Subjects for most psychological studies are chosen randomly from a population.)

randomization Any method of assigning subjects to **experimental groups** using a **random sampling** approach so that subjective or unnoticed systematic selective factors do not enter into and influence the objectivity of an experiment.

random numbers table *See* Table 34.

random sample A sample obtained by chance methods so that each member (person or object) of the sampled population has the same **probability** of being selected. *Contrasted with* **biased sample.**

random sampling Any procedure for drawing samples so that each individual in the population has an equal chance of being selected for the **sample**, the selection of each individual being independent of any other member's selection. Such samples can be analyzed by probability theory techniques; hence they are also called probability samples. *See* **area sampling, cluster sampling, systematic sampling,** and **stratified sampling.** (*Purposive sampling* and *accidental sampling* are distinguished from random sampling.)

range A measure of **variability** indicating the difference between the highest score and the lowest score. For example, if on an examination the highest score is 95 and the lowest 53, the range is 42.

rank The ordinal position of an individual in a group whose members have been arranged in order of magnitude with respect to a certain **variable.** Individuals who are tied in rank are given the **mean** of their rank. For example, assume that the first five students (A through E) on an exam receive the following grades:

Student	Grade	Rank
A	95	1
B	92	2
C	85	3.5
D	85	3.5
E	84	5

There is no question about ranks 1, 2, and 5. Since students C and D are tied in grades they must also be tied in rank and since the difference between rank 2 and rank 5 is 3, it is averaged (1.5) and added to the last unchallenged rank (2) to give both C and D the tied rank of 3.5. *See* **percentile rank.**

rank correlation coefficient *See* **Spearman rank difference method,** Table 30, Table 31b.

rank difference method *See* **Spearman.**

Rankine (degree Rankine) An absolute scale of temperature in which the degree intervals are equal to those of Fahrenheit scales, $x°$ Rankine equalling $(x-459.7)°$ Fahrenheit.

Named after the Scottish engineer and physicist, William J. Macquorn Rankine (1820-1872).

Rank order correlation coefficient *Same as* **Spearman rank difference method.**

ranks test *See* Table 31b.

raphé nuclei A vertical group of cells (nuclei) that forms a seam or ridge (raphé) along the midline of the entire **brainstem**; apparently involved in regulating sleeping and waking. Cell bodies of the **serotonin** neurons in the **brain** are located in the raphé nuclei.

About 1807, French physician Francois Chaussier (1746-1828), first described the median raphé of the corpus callosum, as he found it in experiments on the cat. *See* **trigeminal nerve, prosencephalon.**

rapid eye movements (REMs) Eye movements associated with dreaming during the first deep stage of sleep, as determined by **electroencephalographic (EEG)** investigations. There is almost complete atonicity of muscles, except that eyes dart back and forth, and extremities may twitch. The EEG shows rapid, fast activity as if in a waking or alert state. This phase (sometimes referred to as the second stage of sleep) closely follows non-REM (NREM) sleep, during which there are no observable rapid eye movements. Customarily, there are considered to be three successive physiological states occurring each day: wakefulness, NREM sleep, and REM sleep.

In 1953, American physiologist Eugene Aserinsky (born 1921) and N. Kleitman (born 1895), Russian-American physiologist, started the considerable research on rapid eye movement by reporting their observations in the article "Regularly Occurring Periods of Eye Mobility and Concomitant Phenomena, During Sleep," *Science*, 1953, *118*, 272-274.

rapport The relationship that exists between any two or more people, particularly in reference to the mutual feeling between therapist and client, a good rapport facilitating the relationship and resulting in a more wholesome, revealing, and trusting milieu.

Mesmer borrowed the term from the French in reference to establishing a good relationship between two persons through the magic of human touch.

rate conditioning A type of **conditioning** dependent upon the setting of certain rate schedules that are variations of **ratio reinforcement schedules.** Reinforcement occurs when a **response** is obtained that is either higher or lower than a previously established rate.

In conditioning of the *differential high-rate* (drh) type, reinforcement occurs when a specific number of responses is made within a specified time interval after the last reinforcement. The number of responses and the time interval are specifically set so that the schedule differentially reinforces high rates of responding. For example, in a non-experimental situation, the relatively greater amount of work scheduled and expected of foreign language students over other students gradually forces them to approach their maximum performance ability.

In *differential low-rate* (drl) conditioning, reinforcement begins as soon as the first response occurs after a minimal interval. Premature responding restarts the interval. These contingencies differentially reinforce low rates of responding. In such cases, reinforcement is dependent upon spacing responses farther apart than usual. For example, bosses who space out their encouragement of employees over extended periods of time are unknowingly carrying out this schedule, generally resulting in poor morale (Lundin, 1969, pp. 99-100).

rating scale A scale for expressing judgments of raters or judges, generally from 1 to 5 or 1 to 7 with 3 or 4 the mid-rating or **average.** Also, a numerically scaled device on which a rater rates himself or others on special qualities, traits, or specified dimensions of behavior (group or individual). On *relative rating scales*, subjects are ranked in order from favorable to unfavorable; on *absolute rating scales*, they are judged on a scale with absolute values or scores (usually from 0).

Rating scales attempt to objectively and reliably describe many aspects of a person or a condition (from overt behavior to attitudes and opinions). **Factor analysis** is often used to help isolate, out of a vast number of **variables**, those that might particularly apply to the study in question. *See* **scaling technique.**

rational emotive therapy (RT) A type of **cognitive change therapy,** primarily therapist-oriented and didactically directed, in which the therapist attempts to educate and rationally manipulate the client out of his illogical ways of thinking about his problems. Each neurotic, according to this doctrine, continually reinforces himself falsely with internal dialog, saying, for example, "I masturbated several times today" (which may be accepted as a statement of fact), but then the neurotic feeds himself with something like "and because of that I am no good. I am immoral. I'll never be any good, I am bad, bad, I will go crazy," which is illogical and full of self-defeating verbalizations.

This approach emerged from the work of Albert Ellis (born 1913), American psychologist, whose first work on the subject was "Rational Psychotherapy and Individual Psychology," *Journal of Individual Psychology*, 1957, *13*, 38-44, followed by "Rational Psychotherapy," *Journal of General Psychology*, 1958, *59*, 35-49.

Ellis contends that those who oppose his approach as being too authoritarian and controlling do not consider that all therapies are actually this way since therapists themselves, by their very position, reputation, and training, are controlling and authoritative—at least to their clientele.

rationalization The act of (-tion) superficially making rational, reasonable, or intelligible. As a **defense mechanism,** the attempt to make justifiable and plausible excuses to oneself and others for socially unacceptable impulsive behavior or expressed attitude, the motivation being to maintain self-esteem and avoid anxiety and feelings of guilt and shame. As an example, the student who says that he failed the test because the teacher was unfair, or that the book was poorly written, the questions ambiguous, etc.

Rationalization is often used to camouflage real motives, the person being unaware or only dimly aware of the process he is using to justify his behavior.

The term was introduced into psychological literature in 1908 by **Ernest Jones.**

r

Rationalize, in **SI** terminology, means to round completely a converted value to a popular standard figure compatible with noncritical mating components, interchangeable parts, or other nominal sizes in a series.

rational number *See* **real number.**

ratio reinforcement schedule In learning experiments, a **reinforcement** procedure wherein the **response** is reinforced only after the subject has made a predetermined number of responses. *See* **schedules of reinforcement.**

ratio scale A **scaling technique** (height, weight, mensuration) that permits value-ratios to be directly interpretable as ratios of amounts of the property being measured. Of the four categorical scales (**nominal, ordinal, interval,** and **ratio**), the ratio is the most sophisticated and advanced since it measures arbitrarily the variation in a **variable** with equal units and also functions from an absolute zero.

rauwolfia A tropical tree or shrub of the genus *Rauwolfia*; an extract from the roots of *Rauwolfia serpentina* of India, containing alkaloids such as **reserpine.** Rauwolfia compounds apparently have their greatest effect upon the **hypothalamus** and the **autonomic nervous system.** It has been used mainly to reduce high blood pressure and as a sedative.

Since antiquity the plant has been prescribed for insanity (its name in one of the Indian dialects being *pagla-ka-dawa*, meaning insanity cure) and as an aid for epilepsy, headaches, dysentery, and insomnia, to name a few. In 1582, a German physician-botanist Leonhard Rauwolf (1541-1597), published an account of his travels in India during 1573-75, mentioning the values of the plant but his report was ignored. In 1703, Plumier a French botanist, described and named the plant *Rauwolfia serpentina*. In 1931, Indian researchers isolated five alkaloids from the root, leading to many other studies in Switzerland (1947), England and America. Reserpine was identified in 1952 in Switzerland. The first American physician to investigate the properties of the plant was Robert W. Wilkins of Boston in 1953.

raw score The actual and original numerical value of a score achieved on a test or examination. *Opposed to* **standard score** or **z-score.**

Rayleigh equation *See* **anomalous color vision; anomaloscope.**

reaction formation Excessive **conditioning** in **aversive** behavior, resulting from a previously positively reinforced response to an aversive stimulus. A two-step **defense mechanism** by which a person first represses or denies unacceptable traits or anxiety-producing motives, and then strongly manifests an opposite trait or conscious behavior and attitudes. For example, the mother who has guilt feelings about her unwanted child may become overindulgent to prove to herself, the child, and others that she loves him. Also, in calling for censorship of literature or movies, persons may be fighting against the publishing or showing of material that strongly arouses them.

According to **Freud** (1905) reaction formation is a lower form of **sublimation** that "begins early in the latency period of infancy, and may continue throughout life. . ." (A. A. Brill, *The Basic Writings of Sigmund Freud.* New York: The Modern Library, p. 625).

reaction time Interval between the application of a **stimulus** and the **response.** *See* **personal equation.**

Extensively studied by **Helmholtz** (1850), **Donders** (1868) on reaction time in mental processes, **Wundt** (1874), and **Titchener** and **Baldwin** (1890's).

reaction time apparatus A chronoscope-equipped apparatus for testing elapsed time between the **stimulus** application and the organism's immediate reaction to it. Often used with a reaction (tapping) key or with just two switches, one controlled by the experimenter and one by the subject.

reactive depressive psychosis (psychotic depressive reaction) A **psychosis** in which the **depression** apparently has been precipitated by an unhappy life experience.

reactive inhibition The reaction to effort; the aftereffect of a response to pain, fatigue, or shock. **C. L. Hull** (1943) used the term for the subject's progressive tendency not to respond (negative drive) at the same time he is making effortful responses. Such a habit dissipates with sufficient rest, Hull calling this phenomenon **conditioned inhibition** or learned tendency not to respond. He implied that reactive inhibition accumulates in the **effector** system. The generally higher efficiency of **distributed practice** over **massed practice** tends to verify the occurrence of some such process.

reactive schizophrenia An acute "attack" of **schizophrenia** (in reaction to a traumatic event) occurring late in life, with all the classifiable symptoms, but which may disappear as quickly as it occurs. Prognosis is good. *Compare* **process schizophrenia.**

readiness, law of *See* **law of readiness.**

reality principle As expressed by **Freud,** a recognition by the child, occurring sometime during the anal phase, "of the limitations on the pleasure principle due to punishment for inappropriate behavior by others with greater controls and power than he has." *See* **character types.**

reality therapy A "value" therapy, based on the assumption that every person learns his sense of morals and values early in life, thereby setting the model for his later behaviors, but often the neurotic finds it difficult to live with these early-set values. In reality therapy the therapist assists the client in clearly stating his values, acknowledging them for what they are, and setting up guidelines so that he can live responsibly and productively according to his own values. The therapy reportedly works well with adolescents and delinquents. Sometimes, reality therapy and rational-emotive therapy are called **cognitive change therapies** (William Glasser, *Reality Therapy,* 1965).

real limits The points on a scale that are located a half unit on either side of a given point and represent the actual interval on the scale to which the number refers. For example, a number, say 5, refers to the interval from 4.5 to 5.5.

real number A number represented by a point on a line, as in the **set** of all *rational numbers* (0, 1, 2, 3, -1/4. . .), all *irrational numbers* ($\sqrt{-5}$, π), *relative numbers* (those with a sign), and *absolute numbers* (those without their sign), but not *imaginary numbers* (those expressible as the square root of a negative number: $\sqrt{-1}$, $\sqrt{-15}$).

real time Basically, the actual time elapsed during which a physical process occurs; also, that time during which the computer system must perform tasks immediately, such as scanning of communication lines and communication time spent with the **central processor.** Also, the timing of signals from a rigid system (mechanical or regulated by man) and of return signals required by it. A **computer,** in a "real time" application, inputs, computes, and outputs data concurrently with the process it is monitoring or controlling, immediately accepting and processing incoming data. It will interrupt its operation to receive or simultaneously accept new data.

real time processing A **program** that processes **data** as it is generated, using **real time** as a **variable** and perhaps affecting the variable being controlled or monitored. Examples: a computer-controlled chemical reaction; a computer playing chess with a human being. *See* **clock.**

recall method A means of measuring retentive memory by requiring the subject to reproduce what he had learned. The recall score, percentagewise, is obtained by dividing the number of items previously learned into the number of items reproduced. *See* **remembering.**

receptor That which (-or) receives (recept-). The peripheral ending of a **sensory** neuron that receives stimuli. A single receptor is fired only by a specific **stimulus,** such as sound waves, light waves, or muscular tension. Specialized receptors are **exteroceptor, interoceptor, proprioceptor.** *See* **effector, senses.**

recessive gene A subordinate **gene** (such as for blue eyes) that tends (-ive) to recede (recess-) and that can be expressed only when paired with another recessive gene. When the gene for blue eyes is paired with one for brown eyes (a dominant gene), the **phenotype** is that of the brown eyes, blue eyes being masked.

reciprocal The number resulting when 1 is divided by a given number; or the number that, when multiplied by a given number, has 1 as a product. The reciprocal of 5 is 1/5. If 1 is divided by any number *n*, this fraction or its quotient is the reciprocal of *n*. Thus, 1/4 or .25 is the reciprocal of 4. The reciprocal of a fraction is the fraction inverted: the reciprocal of 3/4 is 4/3; of 7/8 is 8/7.

reciprocal inhibition *See* **behavior modification.**

reciprocal innervation Mutually opposing interaction of the **sympathetic** and **parasympathetic nervous systems.** As the sympathetic accelerates action, the parasympathetic decelerates it.

Sherrington was the first (1898) to study and name the phenomenon.

Recklinghausen's disease *See* **neurofibromatosis.** Named after Friedrich Daniel v. Recklinghausen (1833-1910) German pathologist.

recognition *See* **remembering.**

red-green color blindness A variety of **dichromatism,** the commonest form of color blindness.

redintegration Act or process (-tion) of making whole (-integra-) again (re[d]-); restoration, renewal. A process of cue-reduction, where only a portion of a previous stimulus becomes necessary to reestablish the previous response. The tendency for each impression to bring back into consciousness the total situation of which it had been a part.

Sir **William Hamilton** developed and named the process of redintegration in 1836, although the concept received little recognition until his book *Metaphysics* was published posthumously in 1858. To him, redintegration meant thoughts that suggested other thoughts, all of which had previously been parts of the same total act of **cognition.** He considered metaphysics as philosophical psychology (concerned with the mind, its laws and the results to be inferred from phenomena). He classified phenomena into **cognitions,** feelings, and **conation.** *See* **Bell, determinism.**

red nucleus A mass of greyish tissue located in the midbrain **reticular formation.** In the fresh brain it has a reddish hue. It is involved in exciting **interneurons** of reflex pathways. It serves as an important relay station for **afferent** and **efferent** impulses to and from the **cerebellum,** the **pons,** and the **medulla;** also contains cells of origin of efferent fibers in the **rubrospinal tract.** *See* **mesencephalon.**

In 1909, it was first described by the Russian neurologist Constantin von Monakow (1853-1930).

reduction screen A screen with a small aperture, permitting the viewing of a limited surface area only, the limited view lessening the effects of brightness and other constancies. In its simplest form, a piece of paper with a hole punched in it, allowing any object to be observed without its influencing background, so that the object can be seen more nearly like it should be, that is, coal looks blacker in a dark room than in sunlight and a shirt is darker in the evening than during the day.

The screen was invented by the German-Swedish phenomenological psychologist David Katz (1884-1953), who made many contributions to animal, child, and **Gestalt** psychology as well as to the development of **color** psychology.

reflectance oximeter *See* **oximeter.**

reflex Reflected. Involuntary automatic action of a muscle or gland, controlled by subcortical nerve centers, and originating in the excitation of a sensory nerve, the stimulus being transmitted to a nerve center and then reflected along efferent nerves to the proper organ, as in the knee-jerk reflex. An immediate and unlearned response to a specific stimulus elicited by an external stimulus, like the startle pattern in infants.

French physician Jean Francois Fernel (1506-1588) sparked the thinking about reflex action in 1571 by saying that not all motor activity (e.g., respiration) is voluntary. **Descartes** also mentioned reflex ideas. During the latter part of the 18th century and early years of the 19th century, the **sensorium commune** was considered the core mechanism of the reflex.

Reflex activity studies of the spinal cord were begun by **Bell** and **Magendie**, but later clarified by English physiologist and surgeon, Herbert M. Mayo (1796-1852). In 1833, English physiologist **Marshall Hall** introduced the concept and the noun "reflex" in the modern sense referring to the act of involuntarily pulling away from a hot flame. However, both **Robert Whytt** and the German physiologist **Unzer** had used the term previously, Unzer in referring to motor performance. In 1850, Hall first used the terms **reflex arc** and reflex action.

reflex arc The simplest nervous system pathway along which the **nerve impulse** travels from the **sensory neuron** (initial sensation) through a connecting neuron to a **motor** neuron (final response).

reflex theory of thinking See **speech mechanisms of thinking**.

reflexology The study of (-ology) reflexes.

Mentioned first by **Bekhterev** about 1927 when he referred to "collective reflexology" in his conditioning experiments on social group interaction.

refractory period Unresponsive (refractory) period. The short time interval immediately following the stimulation and firing of a nerve fiber during which, in the *absolute refractory period*, no stimulus, no matter how intense, will fire an impulse; as the sensitivity of the fiber begins to recover, it enters the *relative refractory period*, during which only a stimulus more intense than normal will fire it.

region In **psychology**, an area or section out of or part of **life space**. Statistically, there are several meanings, two of which are:

(1) *Region of (retention) acceptance.* The **set** of **outcomes** of a statistical test that lead to nonrejection, or retention of the **null hypothesis**. A sample whose representative statistic falls within this interval is considered to belong to the same **population** as any other **sample** whose statistic falls within the same interval, the difference between the sample and population values being attributed to chance sampling. In the first figure, the rejection region is relatively small, having been set by the researcher at the 1 percent level of significance so as to assure that there will not be more than one chance out of 100 of being wrong; that is, the null hypothesis can be rejected at the 1 percent level of significance. If the null hypothesis is $H_0: = \mu = 100$, then it can be said the H_0 can be rejected at 1 percent level; or, there is one chance out of 100 that the population mean, μ, does not equal 100.

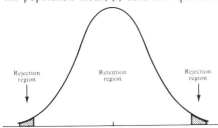

(2) *Region of rejection.* The area outside the retention region. The sample statistics lying within the rejection region are considered to be significantly different from their own population. This region is a range of values for a test statistic allowing for rejection of the H_0 being tested. In the second figure, if the null hypothesis is rejected, the risk is greater than in the example under the region of retention (only 1 percent) but still the risk here is only about 5 percent of being wrong; that is, there are only 5 chances out of 100 that the population mean, μ, does not equal 100.

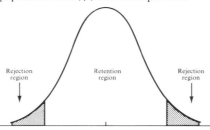

regression Process (-ion) of stepping (-gress-) back (re-) to a previous condition or place; reversion. In statistics, regression means reverting or going back toward the **mean**, referring to the **coefficient** of correlation as indicating that prediction is always in the direction of the mean. The term arises from **Galton's** studies of heredity, in which he found that stature tended to run in families. Although offspring of tall parents were likely to be taller than average, they were not likely to be as much above average as their parents. In other words, the children tended to regress. Thus, the coefficient measuring the relation of stature between parents and children (which was developed by **Karl Pearson** at Galton's urging) became a measure of "regression to mediocrity." It is still symbolized by *r* but is called the **Pearson product moment correlation**.

In **Freudian** theory, regression is a **defense mechanism** so often found in dreams. A person reverts to less mature, less realistic modes of response in attempting to escape from responsibility, stress, and anxiety, and to allow for self-indulgence. For example, an older child may regress to baby talk and bed-wetting under the stress of the birth of a new sibling. Such regression may result from influences of one's own earlier behavior or it may resemble **primitivation**, i.e., reverting to evolutionarily earlier behavior not necessarily like one's own.

Albertus Magnus first indicated the process of regression by saying that the imagination creates the dream out of tangible objects it has retained, the "converse of that operating in the waking state." Freud said "If we call the direction which the psychic process follows from the unconscious into the waking state progressive, we may then speak of the dream as having a regressive character... This regression is therefore assuredly one of the most important psychological peculiarities of the dream-process..." (A. A. Brill, *The Basic Writing of Sigmund Freud*, p. 492).

regression equation A formula for determining the most probable score on one **variable** (Y) from the known value of another variable (X).

Rehabilitation Award of Division 22, (Psychological Aspects of Disability), granted occasionally to those who have made outstanding professional contributions in the field of rehabilitation.

Reid, Thomas (1710-1796) Scottish philosopher. In *Essays on the Intellectual Powers of Man* (1785), he described his form of empirical psychology. In an earlier work, *An Inquiry into the Human Mind on the Principles of Common Sense* (1763), he opposed the influence of **Berkeley** and **Hume**, stating that mankind's common sense (as consciousness) was basic, thus, becoming the founder of the so-called Common Sense

school. He believed that **perception** is unconsciously performed.

reification The making (-ification) of a thing (re[s]); turning an abstraction into something concrete (for example, reifying culture into traditions, or making attitudes measurable). Using theoretical concepts, devised as hypotheses, to explain behavior as if they were entities, or reifying them, as in the case of "the unconscious."

reinforcement Process (-ment) or event that strengthens (-inforc-) or follows the response, increasing the likelihood that the response will occur again (re-). In **classical conditioning**, reinforcement is identical to the **unconditioned stimulus** (US), and means pairing of the US and the **conditioned stimulus**; for instance, buzzer and shock (I. P. Pavlov, 1902). In **instrumental conditioning**, once the operant response has appeared (meaning that the subject has made the appropriate response), reinforcement may be operationally defined as anything that serves to maintain the occurrence of the response: food, water, the avoidance of punishment, or an environmental change dependent upon the occurrence of an operant.

Adjectival or qualifying types of reinforcement should be looked up under their respective terms (negative, positive, partial, etc.).

reinforcement schedules See **schedule of reinforcement**.

reinforcement therapy Therapeutic techniques (**operant conditioning** using positive reinforcement) applied to initiating, maintaining, or modifying behavior. See **behavior modification** (also Lundin, 1969, pp. 417-422).

relationship therapy A therapeutic outgrowth from the **psychoanalytic**, non-medical approach of Otto Rank (1884-1939), maintaining that the values of therapy stem from the therapist's intelligent and constructive use of the patient's reaction to the therapeutic environment. The approach involves analysis, interpretation, and subsequent use of the **dynamics** of the therapist-patient relationship. It has been emphasized in child-therapy work primarily by American social worker Taft and psychiatrist Frederick Allen.

The phrase was originated by American psychiatrist John Levy in an article: "Relationship Therapy," *American Journal of Orthopsychiatry*, 1938, **8**, 64-69 (see also Jessie Taft, *The Dynamics of Therapy in a Controlled Relationship*, 1933, F. H. Allen, *Psychotherapy with Children*, 1942).

relative movement A monocular **cue** to distance. See **motion parallax**.

relative refractory (period) phase The period after the transmission of a **nerve impulse**, during which a very strong **stimulus** is needed to produce a **response** in the nerve fiber. See **refractory period**.

relaxation therapy A therapeutic method in which the patient is encouraged to become relaxed so that he can express himself freely through a form of **catharsis**. Opposed to **active therapy**.

Introduced in 1929 by **Ferenczi**.

relearning See **remembering**.

releaser A physiological, chemical, or sensory **stimulus** that is specific for the **arousal** of so-called instinctive patterns of behavior. For example, color changes in certain birds call forth or "release" courting behavior.

reliability The dependability or self-consistency of a test or method of measurement; the consistency of individual scores on the repetition of the same test or its equivalent. One common measure of reliability is the degree of **correlation** between test and retest scores on the same group of subjects (**stability coefficient**). Another is correlating the scores on two comparable halves of a test (**split-half technique**), or by correlating scores on alternate forms of the test.

reliability coefficient See **coefficient of reliability**.

r

Remak's band (axis cylinder) The core of the axon (axis cylinder) as identified and described in 1838 by the Polish-German physiologist and neurologist Robert Remak (1815-1865). His name for the axis cylinder was "the primitive band" (Remak's band). *See* **tabes dorsalis, ectoderm, endoderm, mesoderm.**

remembering A process of utilizing material that has been learned previously. Remembering usually involves three other but related processes: *recall*, or ability to reproduce, with a minimum of cues, previously learned material (such as recalling a poem learned in childhood); *recognition*, or ability to recognize and reproduce something instantaneously, such as recognizing a correct answer in a multiple choice test; and *relearning* or *savings method*, which involves learning again something previously learned and comparing how much time or how many trials have been saved by relearning, the difference between the learnings indicating the savings made, expressed on a percentage basis by:

$$\frac{\text{Original trials - Relearning trials}}{\text{Original trials}} \times 100$$

REM sleep Rapid eye movement sleep.

replication Process or act (-ion) of replying (replicat-) to a challenge, or of repeating an experiment under the same conditions (including time, place, and instrumentation) as a previous one; also, the collection of at least two observations under identical conditions

report program generator (RPG) A symbolic language designed to simplify the programmer's problem in writing programs that produce reports, adapted particularly for handling a large volume of preprinted forms. RPG eliminates the task of developing processing steps.

representative sample A sample of a population that accurately represents, on the basis of statistical sampling techniques, the significant characteristics of the larger group. *See* **area sample.**

repression Process or act (-ion) of being pressed (-press-) back (re-). Unconscious forgetting in Freudian theory (1900); the ego **defense mechanism** by which wishes, thoughts, or memories (which might provoke guilt feelings and conflicts with social values and taboos) are made inaccessible to consciousness except in disguised form, such as in a disease. Thus, salacious desires and intolerable memories are banished or temporarily forgotten (repressed) into the unconscious (the **id**), where, however, they still exert their influence and may result in **neurosis.**

In behavior modification, similar repressive behaviors are noted in that punished behaviors, as long as conditioned punishment is in operation, are not really forgotten, since when the punishment ceases the original response returns. In essence, behavior theory minimizes forgotten or extinguished responses, considering them to be interfered with primarily by alternate avoidance behaviors.

The term *Verdrängung* (as repression in mental illness) was used in 1846 by Wilhelm Griesinger (1817-1868), German psychiatrist and neurologist, a term borrowed from **Herbart.** In 1910, Freud said, "I called this hypothetical process 'repression' (*Verdrägung*), and considered that it was proved by the undesirable existence of resistance." (Freud, Sigmund, "The origin and development of psychoanalysis," *American Journal of Psychology*, 1910, **21**, 181-218).

reserpine A pure crystalline alkaloid, derived from **rauwolfia**, that lowers blood pressure by working on the **hypothalamus** and causes an increase in appetite by depleting **dopamine** and **serotonin** in the **corpus striatum.** Its Parkinson-like **extrapyramidal** effects with high doses was not recognized at first, but it was demonstrably noted when used with other antipsychotic agents, such as **phenothiazines.**

American cardiologist R. W. Wilkins (born 1906) introduced (1952) crude Rauwolfia into Western medicine, as a heart drug and for hypertension. Swiss chemists of Ciba isolated reserpine in 1952, and presented it under the tradename of Serpasil.

resistance (psychoanal.) The tendency of a patient to become increasingly uncooperative with his therapist during therapy sessions, of displacing responsibility, of confabulating, and of maintaining aloofness and alienation. An opposition to becoming involved. As **Freud** (1936) said, "The whole of psychoanalytic theory is in fact built up on the perception of the resistance exerted by the patient when we try to make him conscious of his unconscious."

resonance theory *See* **hearing theories.**

respondent aggression *See* **aggression.**

respondent behavior In B. F. Skinner's system of behavior, behavioral responses "elicited" by specific stimuli, such as a person's ducking to avoid a blow. Opposed to **operant** behavior, in which the response is "emitted" by the subject in the absence of a specific stimulus (B. F. Skinner, *The Behavior of Organisms; An Experimental Analysis*, Appleton-Century, 1938).

respondent conditioning *See* **elicited behavior.**

response Any kind of behavior, psychological event, or reaction produced by a **stimulus.** A response is determined directly by its physiological activity (movement, glandular secretion) or indirectly by its effect (e.g., tears after an insult), or even not overtly at all (images or fantasies which are reportable only by the experiencing person himself). In the pharmacological sense, a measurable change in the organism resulting from receiving a drug. For qualifying types of responses (e.g., **instrumental response**), see respective term.

response generalization *See* **generalization.**

response operating characteristic (ROC) In **psychophysics**, a characteristic often noticed in the tendency of a judge to be either very cautious or very careless.

resting potential The normal value of the **potential** difference across a cell wall (about 50 to 100 mV), the extracellular fluid being positive.

retarded children classification The terms idiot, imbecile, and moron formerly used for such classification in the United States have now been virtually abandoned. Often used in their places are: *educable* (mentally handicapped), *trainable* (mentally deficient), and *custodial* (of such low intelligence as to require constant care). *See* **classification of mental diseases, mental retardation.**

rete mirabile Wonderful (mirabile) network (rete). An assumed and presumed reticular network in the brain of man.

Herophilus applied "rete" to the vascular network of blood vessels around the pituitary gland and internal carotid artery (his **maximum miraculum**) which he and his followers observed in ungulates and falsely reasoned to be also in man. He considered nervous energy to originate in the "rete" where vital spirits were transformed into animal spirits, and stored in the ventricles. Both **Berengarius** (1523) and **Vesalius** (1543) contended that the rete mirabile could not be found in man. (Clarke and O'Malley, pp. 764, 767, passim).

retest reliability *See* **stability.**

reticular activating system (RAS) A diffusely organized network of neural nuclei lying largely within the brainstem, but extending into the **mesencephalon** and the **hypothalamus.** In general, it is situated outside the well-defined nerve pathways. It plays a significant role in arousal and alerting functions of the brain. Apparently, the posterior hypothalamic area and the brainstem portions of the **RAS** are involved in forming the so-called waking center of the brain.

Impulses continually lead into this reticular formation from various tracts (including auditory and visual) and leave for the cortex via long and multisynaptic routes (the **ARAS**), probably involving a relay system to the **thalamus** and **hypothalamus.**

Relative arousal or activation of the cortex and maintenance of consciousness are dependent upon impulses from the reticular activating system. Blocked conduction results in unconsciousness (for example, anesthetics inhibit such conduction). **Amphetamine** and **adrenalin**, on the other hand, stimulate the activating system, producing wakefulness. It is believed that the RAS contains noradrenalin neurons that play a role in consciousness. *See* **hyperkinesis.**

Nuclear complexes of reticular formation were described by **Bekhterev** in 1894. *See* **sensorium commune.**

In 1949, the Italian physiologist Guiseppe Moruzzi (born 1910) and the American neurophysiologist Horace W. Magoun (born 1907) discovered that the reticular formation acted like a sentinel in arousing the cortex to action. They named the system the reticular activating system. (G. Moruzzi and H. W. Magoun, "Brain Stem Reticular Formation and Activation of the EEG," *Electroencephalography and Clinical Neurophysiology*, November, 1949, Vol. 1, No. 4, 455-473; H. W. Magoun, *The Waking Brain*, 1963).

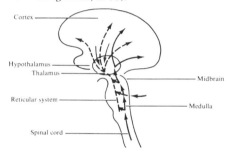

A schematic diagram of the reticular activating system. The system comprises an indirect sensory pathway to several areas of the cortex; it receives branches from the direct sensory pathway. Pathways also lead back from the cortex to the reticular system, thus forming a loop. From Introduction to Psychology, *4th Edition, by Morgan & King. Copyright 1971 by McGraw-Hill, Inc. Used with permission of McGraw-Hill Book Company.*

reticular formation Same as reticular activating system.

reticular hypothesis of Golgi Opposed to neuron doctrine. *See* **Golgi, Ramon y Cajal.**

reticular theory of Herophilus *See* **rete mirabile.**

retinal disparity Same as binocular disparity.

retinene A light yellow crystalline carbon compound (-ene) of the retina (retin-), produced by the photochemical reaction in the **rods** of the eye. When **rhodopsin** is shocked by light, it breaks down into retinene and **opsin.** Subsequently retinene may either join with opsin to reform rhodopsin or be converted to vitamin A (Morgan, p. 137).

retrieval *See* **information processing.**

retroactive inhibition (RI) Backward-acting (retroactive) inhibition. Negative transfer or interference with retention of previous learning by material learned more recently, especially when the content is similar. *See* **proactive inhibition, reactive inhibition.**

retrograde amnesia *See* **amnesia.**

retrograde degeneration technique An anatomical mapping of the infrahuman **cortex** made possible by the finding that some **neurons** degenerate if their **axon** terminals are separated from their **efferent** neurons by lesions or disease. Experimentally, it is possible to map out the areas that receive projections from the **thalamus** (for example, the occipital visual area receives projections from the **lateral geniculate nucleus**) and from many other areas that receive sensory projections. *See* **Brodmann's area.**

retrography The act or process (-y) of writing (-graph-) backward (retro-). *See* **mirror writing.**

retrolental fibroplasia (RLF; Terry's syndrome) A disorder (-ia) in which newly forming (-plas-) fibrous (fibro-) retinal tissues behind (retro-) the eye's lens (-lent-) are destroyed in prematurely born babies given an excessive and continual amount of pure oxygen to combat anoxia. Symptoms: head-banging and rocking, autistic language difficulties, blindness, and sometimes **mental retardation.**

In 1942, American ophthalmologist Theodor Lasater Terry (1899-1946) was first to describe the condition.

reversal shift (reversal learning) In discrimination studies, a technique in which the experimenter (after the subject learns to discriminate between pairs of stimuli; for example, white instead of black) changes previous experimental demands and forces the subject to learn (by rewards) that he must select an opposite or different quality of the same dimension (black instead of white). If the dimension (color) is shifted to another dimension (size or weight), the technique is then called a **nonreversal shift.**

reversibility (reversible figure) Ability to reverse itself. A perceptual quality (form of optical illusion) whereby the same figure may be seen as two separate and incompatible objects or perspectives. *See* **figure-ground relationship.**

reward center (pleasure center) A brain area where stimulation (electrical, chemical, etc.) arouses pleasurable sensations in man. According to **Olds**, reinforcers such as food, sex, water are learned for what they represent because they tend to excite sensory pathways that reward (reinforce) themselves by intracranial self-stimulation; that is, the animal will often prefer to be electrically self-stimulated at the so-called "reward center" than eat, drink, or be merry. (Olds, J., and M. Olds. Drives, Rewards and the Brain. In F. Barron, et al., *New Directions in Psychology*, Vol. II. New York: Holt, Rinehart and Winston, 1965).

rhinencephalon Nose (rhin-) brain (-encephalon). Area in the **brainstem** that contains both olfactory and emotional centers, and according to **Pribram**, includes the **allocortex** and **juxtallocortex.** Oldest area of the cerebral hemispheres. *See* **archipallium.**

Named by Geoffroy St. Hilaire (1772-1844), French naturalist and adopted by Rudolf von Kölliker (1817-1905), Swiss anatomist, who divided the cerebral cortex into rhinencephalon and **pallium.** Replaced by **limbic system.**

rho (ρ) The symbol for the **Spearman rank-difference method.** *See* **rank,** Table 30.

rhodopsin Purplish or red (rhod-) eye (-ops-) chemical (-in); visual purple. Reddish photochemical visual pigment, found in the **rods** of the retina, which is bleached by light to visual orange, to yellow, and then to white. Restored by darkness. Rhodopsin is necessary in twilight or night vision. *See* **dark or light adaptation, adaptation, duplicity, retinene.**

George Wald (born 1906), Harvard biologist, in 1938 began work on chemistry of vision in dim light, showing that light causes visual purple (rhodopsin) to separate into opsin and retinene (retinene always combining with opsin to form rhodopsin in the dark).

rhombencephalon The lozenge-shaped (rhomb-) brain (-encephalon). The posterior section of the three primitive cerebral vesicles (being respectively the **prosencephalon,** the **mesencephalon,** and the rhombencephalon).

ribonucleic acid (RNA) Nucleic acid that yields the sugar ribose (ribo-). Complex molecules that control cellular function, play a role in

memory, and carry genetic information. *See* **ribosomal RNA, messenger RNA, transfer RNA, deoxyribonucleic acid** (also Thompson, pp. 114-126; Butter, pp. 174-179).

ribose (From faulty transposition of letters in arabinose: solid principle of gum arabic.) A crystalline sugar found in many combinations.

ribosomal RNA (template RNA); The ribonucleic acid in a cell that is a normal structural unit of the **ribosomes.** It may be stored temporarily in the nucleoli of a cell nucleus, the nucleoli themselves possibly being involved in the assembling of ribosomes.

ribosome Ribose (ribo-) body (-some). An **organelle** in the cell cytoplasm that synthesizes proteins, assembles enzymes, and determines metabolic cell reactions. It is the smallest organized structure in the cell, so small as to even possibly appear on the surface of **mitochondria.**

Richardson Creativity Award The Council of the **American Psychological Association** delegated to the Committee on Distinguished Scientific Awards responsibility for selecting winners of the Richardson Creativity Award, established in 1965 by the Richardson Foundation. The Foundation was incorporated in 1935 to promote "the general welfare and improve the living conditions of the American people." Financial support is granted primarily for programs of citizenship education, creativity research, and historic restoration.

The award is to be granted for "the most outstanding contribution during the preceding year or recent years toward improving creative and innovative talents or developing or utilizing such talents." The recipient receives a citation and a check for $5,000. For biographical and other additional information refer to the appropriate volume of the *American Psychologist* indicated within parentheses after each recipient below:

List of Recipients

1967 Donald W. MacKinnon (December, 1967, pp. 1142-43)

1968 Anne Roe (December, 1968, pp. 870-1)

1969 Frank Barron (January, 1970, pp. 94-95)

1970 Calvin W. Taylor (January, 1971, pp. 96-99)

right tail of a distribution *See* **tails of a distribution.**

RNA Ribonucleic acid. *See* **deoxyribonucleic acid.**

ROC Response Operating Characteristic.

rod A low-threshold, achromatic, rod-shaped receptor (containing **rhodopsin**) for twilight or night vision. Located mostly in the retinal periphery, rods are responsive to **color** in intensity of light waves. Stimulation of rods results in experience of brightness but not **hue.** *See* **achromatism, duplicity theory** under **color-vision theories.**

In 1674, Dutch naturalist Anton van Leeuwenhoek (1632-1723), described the retinal rods that he saw through his microscope. Irish ophthalmologist Arthur Jacob (1790-1874) described the layer of the rods and **cones** in 1847.

Rogerian counseling or therapy *Same as* **client-centered therapy.**

Rogers, Carl Ransom Born Illinois, 1902, Ph.D. psychology, Columbia 1931. Received **DSC Award** 1956; President of APA 1947. Specialties: clinical psychology and the application of scientific principles to therapy. *See* **client-centered therapy, self-actualization.**

Rolando, fissure of *See* **fissure.**

role The identifying quality or characteristic of a person functioning in a specific setting with specific duties and responsibilities (the role of a professor, or a mother). Any person, however, may play different roles; that is, roles and personalities are mutually determinative, interlocking, and overlapping. As sets of norms or units of a social system, roles

prescribe behavior (expected patterns of actions, dress, etc.) and an established culture expects and sometimes demands them from members of its society. (A policeman is presumed to dress and play the role of a law-enforcing agent and not of a hippie.)

In **sensitivity training** groups, individual therapy, **psychodrama** and the like, participants may be expected to engage in role-playing, a method that simulates real-life situations by placing the person in another role and requesting him to act out how he would behave if he were confronted with the same or similar situation. Its purpose is to facilitate understanding of the problems involved.

Since the concept of role in social psychology is variable, it demands many interpretations, which may be grouped in four ways: (1) *enacted role*—actual overt behavior of a person in a specific position within a social group; (2) *perceived role*—selective perception of an individual's role within a group; (3) *prescribed role*—what a group expects of its members in conforming to its norms; and (4) *predicted role*—pattern of behavior an individual is expected to carry out as he has in the past (McDavid and Harari, 1968, pp. 267-278).

Romberg sign A diagnostic cue in which a person tends to sway sidewise with eyes closed and feet held together, indicative of **tabes dorsalis.**

Named after Moritz Romberg (1795-1873), German neurologist, who also wrote the first systematic book on neurology *Lehrbuch der Nervenkrankheiten* (1840-46).

root mean square *See* **mean square.**

root mean square deviation *Same as* **standard deviation.**

Rorschach Inkblot Test A psychodiagnostic, unstructured **projective test** introduced in 1921 by Rorschach, consisting of a series of simulated inkblots, some black, some colored. Originally it was only an **individual test,** but now it can also be group-administered, by using either cards or 2" × 2" Kodaslides for scoring on a multiple choice blank. By reporting what he perceives in these blots, the subject reveals significant patterns of his **personality,** since his perceptions are accepted largely as projections of his own fantasies. There are no right or wrong answers but the psychologist interprets the responses on the basis of other "normal" or popular responses. *See* **Binet.**

Hermann Rorschach (1884-1922) Swiss psychiatrist.

rostral Pertaining to (-al) an organ or part suggestive of a bird's beak (rostr-). A medial view, as when the **brain** has been cut in half along the longitudinal fissure, presenting the medial surface as if it were posted flat on the blackboard. *See* **anatomical directions.**

rotational aftereffect (RAE) *See* **figural aftereffect.**

round window (fenestra rotunda, fenestra cochlea). A round opening between the middle ear and the **cochlea,** covered by a thin membrane, which bulges in and out, permitting cochlear fluid to respond as wave motion.

Royal Colleges of Physicians Professional corporations entirely separate from any university affiliation. Its licentiates, however, are entitled to practice medicine. A physician can become a Member of the Royal Colleges of Physicians (M.R.C.P.) only after having passed a membership examination. After having served at least five years as a member, the physician is qualified to be elected to Fellowship of a Royal College of Physicians (F.R.C.P.). Primarily a British institution.

RPG Report Program Generator.

rRNA Ribosomal RNA, or template RNA.

rubrospinal tract Crossed nerve fibers that pass from the red (rubro-) nucleus to the spinal cord, relaying impulses from the corpora striata and cerebellum to the cord's motor neurons. It is not well developed in man.

r

Ruf Call (*Ruf*) or summons from another university. *See* **German higher education.**

run A single, continuous performance of a **computer** routine.

runs test A **nonparametric** test of the **null hypothesis** that two groups are **random samples** of the same **population**. The test is based on the sequence in which the scores originally were obtained. There are two runs-test statistical techniques: the one-sample runs test and the two-sample runs test.

In the *one-sample runs test* a run is defined as a succession of identical symbols preceded and/or followed by a different grouping of symbols. For example, MMMWWWBBBBBBMMGGGGGGW, where M = men, W = women, B = boys, G = girls, there are six runs in all. Since the total number of runs in a sample indicates the random pattern, it seems likely that the preceding distribution is random.

In the *two-sample runs test* (or **Wald-Wolfowitz test**) a run is defined as any sequence of scores from the same group. The **null hypothesis** states that two independent **samples** have been drawn from the same **population**, while the alternative hypothesis states that the two groups differ in some way. The null hypothesis is rejected if there are too few runs. (*See* Table 26.)

Rutherford theory *See* **hearing theories.**

S

S

S (plural, Ss) Subject, **stimulus.**

S.A. Social age. *See* **Vineland Social Maturity Scale.**

saccades (Fr., flicks of a sail). A series of very rapid involuntary flicks of the eyes, such as is observable in adjusting a contact lens. Saccadic movements are experimentally observed in the study of eye movements involving fixation on a specific point. Despite concerted efforts to fixate, there are slow shifts away from the point, this tendency to unfixate being compensated by saccades.

saddle points in **game theory,** the equilibrium points in which one competitor has reached the minimum of the maximum losses (**minimax**) and the other competitor has reached the maximum of the minimum rewards (**maximin**). In a **zero-sum** matrix, a saddle point is the entry that represents simultaneously the lowest value in a row and the biggest value in a column. Games without saddle points require more complicated strategy to arrive at a solution.

sadism Sexual gratification or excitation associated with the use of violence in inflicting pain, or in watching such activity.

Richard von Krafft-Ebing (1840-1902), German neurologist, adapted the term in 1888 from the name of Marquis Donatien de Sade (1740-1814), a French soldier and author of two novels judged obscene at the time. Krafft-Ebing defined sadism as "sexual emotion associated with the wish to inflict pain and use violence." De Sade himself is supposed to have derived great pleasure out of inflicting pain on others.

sagittal plane Pertaining to (-al) a lengthwise plane that runs like an arrow (sagitt-) through the **caudal, cranial, dorsal,** and **ventral** aspects, dividing the body or any part of it into right and left sides. Any plane parallel to the **medial,** lying either to the right or left of the center, in slices as it were. Sagittal sectioning in midline divides the body into symmetrical right and left medial aspects.

sample A subset of observations from a **population.** A sample is usually intended to be representative of the total population and is obtained for the purpose of ascertaining information about the population. For the kinds of samples and the methods of choosing individuals in samples, *see* **random, purposive, quota, stratified sampling; representative sample.**

sample bias A bias that occurs in sample **data** and is generally not detected until the sample has been collected. Such prejudices may occur because the sample is not representative or because the questions asked are poorly framed.

sample space The **set** of all sample points possible in a sampling experiment; the space, made up of all possible samples, that shows all the possible outcomes of variable X.

sampling The process (-ing) of obtaining a **sample.** The sampling method determines the type of sample and the degree to which it is representative of the **population** from which it is drawn. *See* **random sampling, purposive sampling, quota sampling, representative sampling, stratified sampling.**

sampling distribution A theoretical **probability distribution** that describes the functional relation between possible values of a statistic based on N cases drawn at random and the probability associated with each value over all possible samples of size N.

sampling error *See* **sample bias.**

Sandler's A-statistic A **parametric statistic** for testing the **null hypothesis** concerning two **population** means. It is mathematically equivalent to **Student's t-ratio** for correlated **data** and therefore has the same interpretation and probability values as Student's t. (*See* Table 6b.)

The A-statistic is given by:

$$A = \frac{\Sigma D^2}{(\Sigma D)^2}$$

where

ΣD^2 = the sum of the squares of the differences

$(\Sigma D)^2$ = the square of the sum of the differences

satiety center *Same as* **ventromedial nucleus.**

saturation *See* **Munsell.**

Saucerotte, Nicholas (1741-1814) French physician and neurologist. Observed (1801) **opisthotonos, hyperesthesia,** and **nystagmus** resulting from cerebellar lesions. In 1772, described giantism in **acromegaly.** In 1778, reported in an essay that injury on one side of the brain caused paralysis on opposite side. *See* **decussation.**

savings method *See* **remembering.**

scala media A structure located between the **scala vestibuli** and **scala tympani** of the bony cavity of the **cochlea**; the membranous middle (media) ear canal resembling a spiral staircase (scala).

scala tympani Scala of the **tympanum,** the lymph-filled spiral chamber of the **cochlea.** *See* **scala media, scala vestibuli.**

Antonio Maria Valsalva (1666-1723), Italian anatomist, introduced the terms scala tympani and scala vestibuli.

scala vestibuli Scala of the **vestibule,** the lymph-filled spiral canal of the **cochlea,** receiving vibrations from the **stapes.** *See* **scala media, scala tympani.**

scaling technique A method used in the social sciences for measuring and classifying **data.** The most frequently described general scales are: (*1*) *nominal* (in which numbers are used as labeling devices for identification—telephone numbers, social security numbers); (*2*) *ordinal* (ranking scales, or those that deal with ordering items, with statistical description limited primarily to summary statistics—**median, centiles**); (*3*) *interval* (with an arbitrary zero point, such as Fahrenheit and Centigrade scales); and (*4*) *ratio* (permitting all forms of arithmetic operation, with unique zero point on scales to measure loudness, length, or weight: 12 inches, for example, being in the ratio of 12:1, or twelve times as long as one inch).

Other scaling techniques are: *Thurstone's law of comparative judgment,* in which interval scales are derived from comparative judgments

(for example, A is better or happier or more religious than B); **Guttman's Scalogram Analysis** an illustration of the response approach, which attempts to predict responses from a person's rank order on a series of items; Osgood's **semantic differential,** which digs into the intensity and content of respondent's **attitudes** on various subjects; *Thurstone's differential scale,* which uses equal-appearing intervals to develop interval-scaled data; *Likert* summated rating scale, which assumes only ordinal properties in judging "favorable" or "unfavorable" feelings toward certain items; and the **Q-sort technique,** which compares individuals rather than deriving scales. (Green and Tull, pp. 185-213).

scalogram analysis *See* **Guttman's Scalogram Analysis, scaling technique.**

scapegoatism The process (-ism) of making a scapegoat (escape-goat); displacing **aggression** onto some person or thing, oftentimes irrationally or prejudicially, and many times for the purpose of fixing blame when no guilty party is readily available or if the cause of the frustration is too powerful to attack. Minority groups have often been made the object of scapegoating (such as Hitler accusing the Jews of creating Germany's problems).

Under Mosaic law (Lev. 16), part of the ancient ritual among the Hebrews for the Day of Atonement was for the high priest to bring two goats to the altar of the tabernacle. Lots were cast to see which goat would be unfortunately allowed to escape (the scape-goat)—unfortunate because forevermore it was doomed to carry the burden of all the people's sins as decreed by the high priest. (A. J. Yates, *Frustration and Conflict,* Methuen, 1962).

scatter The **dispersion** of **data** about its **mean.** Scatter is measured by the **range, variance, standard deviation,** etc.

scatter diagram (scattergram) The graphic representation of **scatter** in a **distribution**; used for depicting the relation between two sets of **data** and in computing a **correlation coefficient.** The diagram shows the scatter or dispersal of the separate points in relation to each other.

Introduced by **Wechsler** in 1941.

schedule of reinforcement A planned arrangement of reinforcements and responses in **instrumental conditioning** (the schedule being 100 percent when every **operant** response is reinforced) that sets up a time schedule for reinforcing desired responses. Basically, the various schedules may be reduced to two dimensions: (*1*) when the interval between successive reinforcements is set (such as **fixed ratio** and **variable ratio**); (*2*) when the interval between successive reinforcements is either regular (**fixed interval**) or irregular (**variable interval**), and is determined by the elapsed time.

In 1933 Skinner reported experiments in which reinforcements were intermittent and in 1938 showed that they may be scheduled in many ways, clearly showing (in only two types of schedules) that subtle similar differences in scheduling might generate dramatic differences in behavior. (The Abolition of a Discrimination. *Procedures of the National Academy of Sciences,* 1933 **8,** 114-129; *The Behavior of Organisms.* New York: Appleton-Century-Crofts, 1938; C. S. Ferster and B. F. Skinner, *Schedules of Reinforcement.* New York: Appleton-Century-Crofts, 1957, pp. 282-283).

schemata According to **Piaget,** schemata represent the "organizing frameworks of thinking, planning, and problem solving which are successively changed during the course of cognitive development."

schizoid personality A personality that resembles (-oid) the behavior of one with schizophrenia (schiz-). A character disorder distinguished by withdrawal, diminution of affect, protracted **introspection,** and sometimes a breaking away from reality, but without any evident intellectual or emotional deterioration. *See* **personality disorders.**

schizokinesis A splitting off or fragmentation (schizo-) of two or more acts or movements (-kinesis) that previously had been a complete **conditioned response**, each of the prior acts, however, having had a different result.

schizophrenia(s) A **functional** psychotic disorder (-ia) or group of disorders (the schizophrenias) in which a person suffers from a so-called split (schizo-) **personality** or mind (-phren-), characterized by disturbance of: (*1*) thinking (evidenced by alternations in concept formation, sometimes leading to **delusions**, **hallucinations**, and misinterpretations of reality); (*2*) behavior (with **regressive**, bizarre, and withdrawing tendencies); and (*3*) mood (shown by **ambivalence**, loss of feelings of empathy, and inappropriate emotional responses).

Generally, however, schizophrenia is considered to be primarily a thought disorder and should be distinguished from the **affective psychoses** (predominantly mood disorders of either **depression** or elation) and the *paranoid states* (in which disturbances of thought, mood, and behavior stem from delusion). There are several recognized subtypes of schizophrenia:

1. simple type—with gradual removal from outside contacts and interests, mental deterioration, inadequate adjustment to life's realities, apathy, and general impoverishment of interpersonal relations. Little or no tendency to progress to more involved and more dramatic types of schizophrenia, such as hebephrenic, catatonic, and paranoid types

2. hebephrenic type—with silly and regressive behavior, unpredictable giggling, exhibitionism; thinking and affective responses are shallow, disorganized, and inappropriate, with frequent **hypochondriacal** complaints. Any delusions and **hallucinations** tend to be temporary

3. catatonic type—with motor activity or lack of it being most prominent. Sometimes the condition is subdivided into:

   a. excited type—with patient exhibiting unusually excessive motor activity, general excitement, and impulsive, belligerent behavior

   b. withdrawn type—in which the patient is stuporous, mute, negative, inhibited, and may become immobilized—retaining self-imposed, bizarre, fixed postures (**catalepsy**) or those in which he is placed by someone else (**waxy flexibility**). Patient may also be **echolalic** and insensitive to pain, the more seriously involved cases deteriorating into a vegetative condition

4. paranoid type—hallucinations and delusions of grandeur and persecution are paramount; also, extremes of hostility, aggressivity, and religiosity are sometimes present. Differentiated from the severe condition of **paranoia**

5. childhood type—generally appearing before puberty, the patient being withdrawn, atypical, and **autistic**, with many evidences of immature and inadequate behavior.

Other types of schizophrenia, less well-defined and sometimes overlapping with other conditions are the *latent type* (in which there has been no history of a psychotic break although the patient shows schizophrenic symptoms); the *residual type* (in which some evidences of schizophrenic symptoms remain but the person is no longer classifiable as psychotic); and the *acute schizophrenic episode* (in which the acuteness is emphasized, distinguishable from simple schizophrenia, but there are also symptoms of confusion, fear, excitement, or **depression** and other schizoid tendencies).

Many dissatisfactions exist with a classification such as the foregoing (modified from the Diagnostic and Statistical Manual of Mental Disorders, prepared and published by the American Psychiatric Association in 1969),

resulting in the development of some other less-categorical, less medically-oriented types of groupings. One of these approaches is a two-dimensional classification (itself seriously criticized), labeled as *process-schizophrenia* and *reactive-schizophrenia* (the concept being inherent in Bleuler's works of 1911, 1930, and 1936).

In **reactive schizophrenia**, there is generally a good, early psychological history at home, school, and with peers. Parents are understanding and accepting. Youth shows normal heterosexual behavior, a good outlook on life, is extroverive, and has good socially acceptable behavior in general. But then during adolescence or early adulthood there is a sudden onset of the psychosis with much verbal but no physical **aggression** and hostility. The patient responds well to psychiatric treatment, necessitating only a short stay in the hospital. He recovers well and tends not to be plagued by the symptoms again. The condition is presumably caused by difficulties in responding to environmental stresses. Onset is acute; prognosis is favorable to good.

In **process schizophrenia**, the condition begins gradually and insidiously in socially inadequate persons, there being definite evidences of early psychological trauma, with school difficulties, **introvertive** behavior, lack of heterosexual interests, and physical **aggression** being prominent. Generally, the father rejected the child but the mother may have been rejecting or overprotective. The patient responds poorly to psychiatric therapy and consequently has a long stay in the hospital. As an adult, the patient's **paranoia** becomes full-blown and tends to have a biological basis (which may be neural, chemical, endocrine, enzymatic, or toxic in origin), and is considered by some investigators to be the "true" form of schizophrenia. (R. Kantor, J. Wallner, and C. Winder, Process and Reactive Schizophrenia. *Journal of Consulting Psychology*, 1953, **17**, 157).

Causative factors involved in schizophrenia have been attributed to: (*1*) *genetics* (see **concordance ratio**); (*2*) *biochemical substances* (see **biochemical theories of psychosis**); or to (*3*) *psychological stress* (see **double bind**).

Treatment of schizophrenia has been varied over the years, shock, of one kind or another being used from the earliest times. Since it had been discovered by accident that some mentally ill persons no longer acted peculiarly after being drowned and revived, some early Greek doctors apparently purposely drowned some people suffering from madness but sometimes they could be revived and other times not. Convulsions were induced by inserting camphor roots or bark into the blood circulation. In more modern times, insulin shock was used first by Austro-American psychiatrist Manfred Sakel (born 1900) in the years 1927, and 1929-1933, and by others. In 1934, Hungarian psychiatrist Lazlo de Meduna (born 1896) introduced the use of pentylenetetrazol (tradenames: Metrazol, Cardiazol). **Electroshock therapy** was first used by the Italian psychiatrists Ugo Cerletti and Lucio Bini, although there are reports that some English psychiatrist experimented with the early **Wheatstone** bridge in this regard. *See* **electroconvulsive shock, nuclear vs. peripheral schizophrenia, lobotomy.**

Bleuler introduced "schizophrenia" in 1911 as a more inclusive term than **dementia praecox** so as to make it a distinct diagnostic entity, limiting it primarily to adolescent disorders.

For additional information about schizophrenia, contact *The American Schizophrenia Foundation*, 305 S. State Street, Ann Arbor, Michigan 48108.

schizophrenic reactions A group of psychotic reactions in which the person's sense of reality is distorted or lost; associated with **autism**, **ambivalence**, and **dissociations**.

schizophreniform psychosis Having or taking the form of **schizophrenia** but not strictly classifiable as schizophrenia. Regardless of constitutional factors there is always environmental stress seen as precipitating cause (infections, intoxication, etc.). Symptoms: illusions, heightened perception, **hallucinations**, **delusions**, and multiple ideas of reference.

(G. Langfeldt, a leading Danish psychiatrist, has written extensively on schizophrenia, favoring the **reactive-process** viewpoint, and also refers to schizophreniform states. See his publications: The Prognosis on Schizophrenia and the Factors Influencing the Course of the Disease. *Acta Psychiatrica Scandinavia*, Supplement 13, 1937, 1-228; *The Schizophreniform States*, Copenhagen: E. Munksgaard, 1939; and The Diagnosis of Schizophrenia, *American Journal of Psychiatry*, 1951, **108**, 123.

schizophrenogenic parents Relating to (-ic) parents who produce (-gen-) or cause **schizophrenia** in their child(ren). In studying family interaction as a determiner of schizophrenia, many studies have been carried out on parents of schizophrenics. However, most studies lack adequate controls. Results are conflicting concerning the roles of parents in causing schizophrenia. However, the so-called *schizophrenogenic mother* is supposedly at the origin of the child's later psychotic break. Such mothers, according to the Danish psychiatrist Yrjö Alanen, leaned toward psychosomatic complaints, and were anxiety-ridden, depressed, insecure, aloof and cold, and tended toward **dereistic thinking**. These mothers tended to act possessively toward their sons and were hostile and ambivalent toward their daughters. Mothers were aggressive, overprotective, and rigid with their children rather than showing a warm and flexible mixture of affection, and fair, just discipline (Alanen, Yrjö O., *The Mothers of Schizophrenic Patients*. Munksgaard, 1958).

Studies on fathers picture them as being generally weak in their masculine role, in conflict with their wives, inconsistent and hostile with the children, a "nothing" in the home, tending to remain aloof and isolated from the family, but dominated by the wife (T. Lidz, Alice R. Cornelison, Dorothy Terry, and S. Fleck, The Intrafamilial Environment of the Schizophrenic Patient, I. The Father. *Psychiatry*, 1957, **20**, 329-342).

schizotaxia A peculiar genetic arrangement or order (-taxia) believed to be a necessary precursor for schizophrenia (schizo-) (P. E. Meehl, Schizotaxia, Schizotypy, Schizophrenia, *American Psychologist*, 1962, **17**, pp. 827-838).

scholastic aptitude tests A group of tests usually validated against measures of academic achievement. They are frequently used as a preliminary screening device in the testing of people for counseling, personnel selection, and other classification purposes. After a general classification has been determined, further and more specific **aptitudes** may be explored, such as engineering, medical, and law aptitudes.

These specialized tests do not tend to be any better predictors of professional success than previous academic record, interview ratings, or letters of recommendation, but they do serve to give convenient scores and comparative ratings.

Schwann sheath *See* **myelin sheath.**

Schwarzert (Melanchthon, Grecized surname), **Philipp.** *See* **psychology.**

scientific method A systematic method of investigation consisting generally of formulating a **hypothesis** (a trial idea) testing it by experiment or by gathering and classifying **data**, and revising, rejecting, or extending the hypothesis in light of the experimental findings. Then comes the basic method of science: generalization or induction, the process of drawing inferences about a whole

S

class from a sample observation. After induction comes logic in the form of deduction, more particularly symbolic-deductive logic. A researcher should have a clear understanding of the nature of objective observation, be able to predict or control certain events and deal reasonably with cause and effect, learn how to analyze the problem and practice simplification (*see* **law of parsimony**), and synthesize his material from relatively simple parts.

scopophilia (scoptophilia) Pathological disorder (-ia) of loving (-phil-) to view (scopo-) sexually stimulating scenes, or in a lesser sense, of viewing the nude body. **Freud** called it a paired instinct, being to exhibitionism what sadism is to masochism. (S. Freud, *Collected Papers*, Vol. 3. Translated by A. Strachey and J. Leonard and Virginia Woolf, London: Hogarth Press, 1925).

score Any numerical representation of the behavior of an individual or experimental unit. *See* **raw score, deviation, standard score, z-score, transformed score, rank.**

scotoma Darkness or dimness (scotoma) of vision. A partially or totally blind area in the visual field, that may be temporary or permanent and which may be caused by any of various conditions (overuse of tobacco or alcohol, destruction of part of visual sensory cortex, certain diseases, and overexposure to strong light). *See* **scotometer.**

scotometer A measuring (-meter) instrument for locating and mapping scotomata (the blind or partially blind areas of the retina). *See* **scotoma.**

scotopic vision Vision relating to (-ic) the eye (-op-) adapting to darkness (scot-) or to relatively low intensity illumination, mediated by the rods of the retina; twilight or **rod** vision. Scotopia is a term sometimes used for twilight or rod vision. *See* **achromatic.**

S.D. Standard deviation.

SE Standard error.

Sechenov, Ivan M. (1829-1905) Russian physiologist and physician (M.D., Moscow 1856). In his book *Reflexes of the Brain*, 1863, he showed that psychical activity had a physiological basis. Stated that reflexes are either innate or learned and that learning is associated in nature while thinking is an inhibited reflex (in that the **cerebral cortex** actually inhibits reflex action). He expanded the idea of Thomas Laycock (1812-1876), Scottish physiologist, which considered the nervous system as the center of reflex action, and subjected it to experimental proof. **Pavlov** called him the "father of Russian physiology." He indicated (1863) that higher brain functions were primarily reflex in nature, and showed for "the first time...reversible, central neural inhibition." Pavlov developed his "conditional" reflexes from Sechenov's proof that the functioning of the entire nervous system (cerebral or spinal) sprung from reflex responses. His work helped pave the way for **behaviorism.** Studied under or was associated with **Claude Bernard, du Bois-Reymond, Hoppe-Seyler, Johannes Müller,** and **Helmholtz** (Boring, pp. 635-636, 660-661).

secobarbital sodium (Tradename: Seconal) A white odorless bitter powder used medically as a sedative and hypnotic. *See* **drugs.**

Seconal (The Lilly tradename for secobarbital sodium). Slang: redbirds. *See* **drugs.**

second(s) The sixtieth part of a minute of time. At a meeting of the General Conference on Weights and Measures in 1967 the ephemeris definition of second was replaced by the atomic definition, which specified the second as the duration of 9,192,631,770 periods of the radiation corresponding to the transition between the two hyperfine levels of the ground state of the cesium-133 atom. *See* **International System of Units.**

secondary amentia Mental retardation due to environmental or external factors.

secondary drive A **motive** acquired through learning.

secondary reinforcement Reinforcement provided by an initially nonreinforcing **stimulus** that has been formerly paired with a rewarding event over many trials. Although not directly satisfying a biological need, it does acquire reward value, itself functioning as a reinforcer (such as when chimpanzees were trained first to perform a task with fruit as a reward, then to accept poker chips that they could exchange for fruit later). Secondary reinforcement may possibly be a stronger learning factor than is commonly realized. Analogous to higher-order conditioning in **classical conditioning** (W. N. Schoenfeld, J. J. Antonitis, P. J. Bersh, "A Preliminary Study of the Training Conditions Necessary for Secondary Reinforcement," *Journal of Experimental Psychology*, 1950, **40**, 40-45).

second order neuron An unmyelinated post-ganglionic neuron whose cell body lies in the ganglia outside the central nervous system. Their axons (postganglionic fibers) terminate in the heart, smooth muscles, or glandular tissue.

second signal system The signal system pertaining to man's speech, or to symbolic or linguistic stimuli. In modern Russian psychological studies of conditioning is a vital, important concept. Originally (1934), **Pavlov** said that "...speech constitutes a second signalling system of reality which is peculiarly ours..." In a posthumous publication (1949) he said that speech was the "signal of signals. It is the abstraction of reality which allows us to generalize ... the basis of our extra specifically human higher reason" (p. 68).

Normally, the second signal system protectively assumes the activity of the first signal system. The second signal system, being more mobile, "can exert a regulatory action on the first signal system" (Cole and Maltzman, p. 184). Speech serves as the basis for the second signal system, which represents the "new principle of nervous activity" and serves as the "higher regulator of behavior" (p. 144). For Pavlov, the second signal system "refers simultaneously to speech and thinking" (p. 593). *See* **speech mechanisms of thinking.**

sector therapy *See* **associative anamnesis.**

Sequin, Edouard Constant (1812-1880) French-American physician. Pioneer in devising methods for teaching and testing the mentally retarded.

self The summation of all living forces and interactions (positive or negative) acting upon a person. Loosely, the **ego** or the I of experience. Often used synonymously with the **personality** when viewed by others. Historically, the self has had **metaphysical** meanings (as the most valuable identity in the universe) and during the 1960's it has taken on many of its earlier subjective meanings. The development of the self proceeds slowly but gathers momentum and unification with age and experience. The self has many dimensions, some of which are: perception of one's specific skills and position in life; the transitory perception of self and one's values; the social being; and the self-fulfilling conception of the ideal self. Structurally, to **Jung**, the self is located "midway between the conscious and the unconscious," which seems to be about as good a place as any for giving equilibrium and stability to the personality.

self-actualization A process in **personality** theory concerned with the constant striving of man to make his true potential actual and to become a more complete person. Actualization is an important concept in the theories of **Maslow, Goldstein** (who originated the concept), and **Rogers** (Maddi, 1968, pp. 77-80).

The term self-actualization was constructed by **Jung** (1924), meaning the development of full individuality with all parts functioning harmoniously.

self-concept (self-perception) An attitudinal and conceptual self-image based on the person's **perception** and awareness of himself, especially his feelings of self-worth, values, and aspirations. Tests administered before and after therapy show that some people tend to have a more realistic and worthy self-concept after psychotherapy than before. Positive self-concept involves an awareness of one's functioning identity, with a satisfying feeling that he "belongs" and "knows what it's all about." He has self-esteem. *See* **phenomenal field.**

self-estrangement *See* **alienation.**

self-exciting circuit A fuselike circuit of **interneurons** that occurs when a neuron-discharged **nerve impulse** is transmitted from the main **axon** to a collateral then to a second **neuron** and back again to the original cell, exciting it a second time. This process may happen repeatedly without the instigation of a new external **stimulus.**

self-fulfilling prophecy The principle that the likelihood of achieving a certain goal or of behaving in a certain way is increased if the participating person believes or expects that event or behavior to occur. Related to **perceptual constancy** in that people tend to "see" experiences in the manner they expect to perceive them. It is often seen in paranoid people such as in a man predicting that his girlfriend will reject his marriage proposal, antagonizes her so that she must refuse him, then says "I knew it all the time," thus setting up a pattern of this or similar behavior for future girls.

Selye, Hans Austrian-born (1907) physician and research physiologist. In 1945, became director of the Institute of Experimental Medicine and Surgery, Université de Montreal. *See* **general adaptation syndrome, adrenocorticotrophic hormone.**

semantic aphasia *See* **aphasia, speech aphasia.**

semantic differential **Osgood's** term (1957) for his controlled association method for measuring *connotative meaning* (symbolic, emotional, and perceptive elaboration of a word) as opposed to *denotative meaning* (a specific and restricted reference to objects in the real world). Used for assessing interactions between people and situations and **attitude** measurement. This technique involves the use of **rating scales** (consisting of bipolar adjectives, like good-bad, cruel-kind) and **factor analysis** to measure connotative meanings.

semantic generalization Generalization between an object (such as a bell) and a word or phrase (such as "clang" or "ting-a-ling") that symbolizes the object. For example, generalizing based on a **conditioned response** to a bell sound, such response also being elicited by the word "bell," or from the word to the object, or between words themselves (homonyms, synonyms, and antonyms). Younger children tend to generalize more often between antonyms while adults do so more frequently between synonyms.

semantics Field of study (-ics) concerned with the meaning of signs (semant-). The study of the relation of symbols to objects and of the meaning and significance of words in human behavior. As a branch of general linguistics, semantics investigates meaning in language.

This term, introduced in 1900 as a translation of M. Bréal's "la semantique," replaced the earlier word "semasiology," introduced in 1877, meaning an overall historical view of word meanings.

General semantics was popularized by the Polish mathematician Alfred Korzybski (1879-1950) in his book *Science and Sanity* (1933), referring originally to the science of meaning through a non-Aristotelian approach, emphasizing the human tendency to substitute words for the person or thing itself. *See* **measurement.**

semasiology *See* **semantics.**

semicircular canals Any of three small, liquid-filled, semicircular structures in the bony **labyrinth of the inner ear**, situated in three planes roughly at right angles to one another (whose **receptors** distinguish between left-right, up-down, and forward-backward).

semi-interquartile range A measure of variation Q, that is equal to one-half of the distance between the 25th and 75th percentiles (the middle 50 percent of the cases). It is given by $Q = (Q_3 - Q_1)/2$.

The interval $Q_3 Q_1$ (or the interquartile range) contains the middle 50 percent of the measurements. It is used when the scores are evenly distributed on both sides of the **median**.

semiology Study of (-ology) signs (sem-).

semiotics Any study, practice, or system (-ics) of signs (semio-), including natural languages (such as Indian language). See **measurement**.

sensationism (sensationalism) The doctrine (-ism) that all knowledge is ultimately derived from the senses, or from the actual experiencing of life; there are no innate ideas. **Hobbes** is recognized as the founder of modern sensationism (*De Corpore*, 1655). Others who expressed similar ideas were **Berkeley, Condillac, Locke, Hume,** and **La Mettrie**.

sense modality The modal quality (-ity), attribute, or characteristic of one of the senses. The different modes or ways of perceiving the environment as determined by receptor specialization, each type of receptor responding only to specific stimuli. See **modality**.

sense modality	physical stimulus	receptor	cortical projection area	dimensions of the psychological experience
vision	Electro-magnetic waves	Rods and cones in the retina of the eyes	Occipital lobe	Hue Brightness Saturation
hearing (audition)	Compression and expansion in a medium such as air	Hair cells in the cochlea of the inner ear	Temporal lobe	Pitch Loudness Timbre
smell (olfaction)	Molecules in the air	Hair cells in the olfactory epithelium in the nose	None. The olfactory nerve terminates in lower centers	? (No simple dimensions)
taste (gustation)	Molecules in solution	Hair cells in the tastebuds on the tongue	Parietal lobe	Sweet Salty Sour Bitter
pressure	Mechanical deformation of the skin	Nerve endings in the skin	Parietal lobe	Extent Duration Intensity
temperature	Temperature changes from "physiological zero"	Nerve endings in the skin	Parietal lobe	Cold to warm to hot
pain	Intense stimuli; tissue injury	Nerve endings in the skin	Parietal lobe	Sharp Dull Throbbing
kinesthesia	Stretching of muscles and joints	Nerve endings in muscles and tendons	Parietal lobe	Position Load
equilibrium	Body movement and acceleration	Hair cell in the semicircular canals and vestibular sacs of the inner ear	?	Movement in three planes; body position

McKeachie-Doyle, *Psychology, Second Edition*, 1970, Addison-Wesley, Reading, Mass. Reprinted by permission.

senses Organs that respond to stimuli. The senses, with their adequate stimuli, are:
Vision—light waves 400-760 millimicrons in length. See **visible spectrum**.

Chemical senses, including: *smell*—gases, or particles of air; *taste*—chemicals in solution, and in some instances, electrical current.

Cutaneous senses, including: *touch*—objects that press, touch, wrinkle, pull the skin or mucous membrane, or touch a hair; *warmth*—heat radiations above 30° Centigrade; *cold*—heat radiation below 30° Centigrade; *pain*—objects that cut, prick, burn, or tear the tissues, or extremes of temperature that cause pain.

Common chemical senses—not yet identifiable but sensitive to acids, alkalies, and salts.

Hearing—for normal ear, sound vibrations that vary in pitch from a low of about 15 to approximately 20,000 vibrations per second.

Deep senses, including: *kinesthetic*—muscle sense—muscle contractions or movements of body parts that result in pulls on muscles, tendons, or joint surfaces; *vestibular*—(labyrinthine sense)—movements of the head; *organic*—hunger, thirst, and sex.

sensitivity In **computer** language, the degree of the response in any control unit (e.g., radio) that mediates change in the incoming signal, or the ability of such device to react to such signals, expressed as the minimum **input** signal necessary to produce a specified **output** signal with a given noise level; also, the ratio of the response to the magnitude of the input.

sensitivity training A widely used awareness-awakening training group method, often practiced in industry. It is primarily oriented toward an open confrontation with others, facing the existential reality of the "here and now" world and **self**. See **intensive-group experience**, (also *Psychology Today*, 1970, pp. 539-555).

sensor Detector or pickup. A **transducer** designed to respond to a physical stimulus (for example, temperature, flow, pressure) and transmit impulses for interpretation or for operating a control.

sensorimotor Feeling (sensori-) and moving (-motor). Relating to neural activity where both sensory and motor functions are involved. In **Piaget's** series of intellectual development, *sensorimotor intelligence* is the earliest stage.

sensorium commune (rendezvous of sensation). An Aristotelian phrase adopted and re-introduced (1780-1784) by **Prochaska**, to indicate a central area of the central nervous system where the "sensory and motor nerves run together. . ." and ". . .the impressions of the sensory nerves are reflected to the motor nerves. . ." **Gerlach** in 1871 developed the reticular concept maintaining that gray matter of the brain was composed of a reticulum (**rete mirabile**) of **dendrites**, considering the sensorium commune to consist of this network. Gerlach's ideas gained credence until **Waller** (1883) and **Forel** (1887) helped establish the concept of nerve cell individuality, with Waldeyer clinching the argument in 1891 by synthesizing much of the available (particularly **Ramon y Cajal's**) information which led to the **neuron theory**. (Clarke and O'Malley, p. 333, 346).

Aristotle used the term for the heart as being the center of sensations, as did **Vives**.

sensory Pertaining to (-ory) the senses or feelings (-sens-); the **receptors** and the **afferent** nerve mechanisms. Also, referring to direct experience perceived by the senses. See **Bell** under **Bell-Magendie**.

sensory adaptation The process by which **receptors** tend to become relatively insensitive when called upon to respond to the same kind of **stimulus** for a continued period of time, or to become more sensitive after the absence of stimulation. Temporal interaction in which immediate prior stimulation of a receptor modifies effectiveness of later stimuli (S. Hecht, "The Influence of Light Adaptation on Subsequent Dark Adaptation of the Eye," *Journal of General Physiology*, 1937, 20, 831-852).

sensory aphasia See **alexia, aphasia**.

sensory cortex See **cortex**.

sensory deprivation The process or act (-ion) of depriving (deprivat-) an organism of reinforcement values from ordinary **sensory** stimuli (visual, taste, hearing, etc.). People who live in restricted environments (such as attic children) tend to behave abnormally; those who are deprived of verbal contacts tend to talk to themselves. Monotonous tasks, working in windowless rooms, and facing brick walls have deleterious effects upon workers, contributing to frequent excuses to go to restrooms and poor morale. Some children in foundling homes suffer from relative sensory deprivation (P. Solomon, (Ed.) *Sensory Deprivation* [Harvard, 1961]).

sensory gating A neural process in which one **stimulus** is selectively chosen over another, such as when a stronger **input** blocks out a weaker input from another sensory channel. For example, concentrating on one object in preference to another, or when an athlete, during the heat of the game, is not aware that he has suffered an injury until the game ceases.

sensory input All neural **inputs** are "filtered" through a series of nuclei before reaching the **cortex**, thereby assuring that stimuli are selectively chosen before being transmitted to the **cortex**. *Acoustic impulses* travel to the spinal **ganglion**, the **cochlear** nuclei in the **brainstem**, the **superior olive**, the **inferior colliculi** in the **mesencephalon** and then to the gyrus of Herschl in the cortex. *Optic impulses* proceed to the cortical striate area after having passed through, among others, ganglion cells in the retina and the thalamic **lateral geniculate body**. *Pain and temperature impulses* are transmitted, in order, to the spinal ganglia, the posterior horn in the cord, and the **thalamus**. Some of these impulses branch off and certain aspects of touch (deep sensibility, for example) travel circuitous courses. *Smell* goes to the glomeruli of the **olfactory bulb**, contacting the mitral cells in relay fashion which then carry the impulses to the prepyriform area of the **brain** and then to the neocortex. *Taste* impulses enter the **ganglia** of the VIIth, IXth, and Xth nerves near the brainstem, then go to the nucleus and the thalamus.

sensory neuron See **neuron**.

sensory overloading See **display**.

sensory transduction See **information processing**.

sentence completion test A verbal **projective technique** in which only the opening words are provided (such as "I love. . ."; "My religion. . ."; etc.), the subject being required to complete the sentence.

septal area (septum of the brain) A wall-like (septum) region in the **limbic system**, located between the **amygdala** and **hypothalamus** with many interconnecting fibers. The septal area and the amygdala apparently have opposing effects upon each other since septal operations on animals produced aggressive and vicious behavior while an amygdaloid operation on these same animals caused them to become cooperative and passive. Electrical stimulation of the septum seems to produce a pleasurable emotion, as **Olds** (1956) has shown that rats will press a bar apparently just for the satisfaction of being electrically shocked in the septum again. See **reward center**.

sequential development See **general-to-specific sequence, individuation**.

serendipity The quality or faculty (-ity) of having the sagacity and good fortune of the three princes of Serendip; the discovery of a scientific or medical truth through the combined qualities of sagacious endeavor and fortuitious circumstance.

English novelist and essayist Horace (Horatio) Walpole (1717-1797) derived the name in 1754 from the Persian tale *The Three Princes of Serendip*, by Christoforo Armeno, published in 1557 in Venice under the title (translated) of *Peregrination of the Three Sons of the King of Serendip*. Serendip was the ancient name of Ceylon. On January 28, 1754, Walpole wrote to the English man of letters Sir Horace Mann (1706-1786), saying, among other things, that he had invented the word to signify the faculty of making happy discoveries by accident, such as the princes did in "always making discoveries, by accidents and sagacity, of things which they were not in quest of: for instance, one of them discovered that a mule blind of the right eye had travelled the same road lately, because the grass was

S

eaten only on the left side, where it was worse than on the right—now do you understand *serendipity?"*

The American physiologist Walter B. Cannon reportedly was the first to apply the word to scientific findings, mentioning several examples of serendipity in his autobiography, *The Way of an Investigator.* Ruch (pp. 48-50) indicates, as an example of serendipity close to psychology, Pavlov's "accidental discovery of 'psychic secretions' which led to the formulation of the basic principles of conditioning." (*See Serendipity and the Three Princes. From the Peregrinaggio of 1557.* Edited by Theodore G. Remer, Oklahoma Press, 1965).

serial learning list (serial memorization list) A verbal learning task in which a list of items (digits, syllables, or words) is presented in the same order on every trial and must be sequentially learned by rote so that each item is a cue to the one following (Hermann Ebbinghaus, *Über das Gedächtniss* [1885]; translated by H. Roger and C. E. Bussenius, 1913).

serial response In habitual behavior, a chain of responses that may become highly integrated (for example, learning the individual acts of operating a complicated machine and subsequently achieving smooth total operation).

serotonergic pathways *See* **amine pathways.**

serotonin A hormone-like, chemical compound (-in) found throughout the **central nervous system** and the blood serum (sero-), its vasoconstrictor action having a tonic (-ton-) effect, reducing hemorrhaging and blood pressure. It is formed in animal tissues from **tryptophane** (an amino acid essential in animal nutrition).

It is chemically related to adrenalin. Manufactured in the gastrointestinal mucosa, it passes into the circulating blood in the blood platelets. It is also found in many areas of the **central nervous system,** mainly in the **hypothalamus,** and is probably manufactured in the **raphé nuclei** and distributed throughout the brain by these cell axons. It acts as a powerful tranquilizer when injected directly.

Its amino acid precursor is 5-hydroxytryptophan (which has been found useful in treating hypotonia of **Down's disease**). Serotonin was discovered in the blood in 1948 and in the hypothalamic region by Twarog and Page in 1950. Resembling serotonin, and having a similar effect upon the central nervous system is **bufotenin,** a toad venom. **LSD** is a serotonin antagonist.

Serpasil *See* **reserpine.**

servomechanism (servo system) A system using little power to control much power in a prescribed pursuit of a goal. Any usually closed-loop, error-sensing, feedback-control complex or power device for producing machine motion. It may range from the well known room thermostat to a complicated electronic controlling device actuated and controlled by some low-energy feedback signal.

set(s) Fixed habit. An aggregate, herd, flock, or class. Set is used in different ways in psychology and the mathematical sciences, although meanings overlap in some applications.

In *psychology,* set refers to the readiness of an organism to respond in a fixed or determined manner. A subject may be prepared to get "set" to respond to a synonym, homonym, or antonym in word-association experiments. There are motor sets, mental sets, and perceptual sets. *See* **Einstellung.**

In statistics, a group or series of objects or ideas. For example, a set of sample points = (ABC).

In mathematical usage, sets may be finite (such as the set of all people in the room) or infinite (such as the set of all real numbers).

In set terminology, the word "equal" is restricted to mean "the same set as." Set A = set B, for example, means that there are two

different names for the same set. Set A contains the same elements as Set B. A *one-to-one correspondence between two sets* indicates that there exists an exact matching between the elements of one set and those of another set. The *cardinal number of a set* refers to the number of elements in its set. *Universal set* (U) is the set that contains all possible elements under consideration.

Set theory was developed by George Cantor (1845-1918), Russian-born, German mathematician, during the years 1874-1895, which gave an entirely new and revolutionary analysis of the role of infinity in mathematics.

seventh cranial nerve *Same as* **facial nerve.**

Motor function of this nerve was described (1822-23) by English physiologist Herbert M. Mayo (1796-1852), who also described the sensory function of the fifth.

sex chromosomes *See* **X-chromosome, Y-chromosome.**

sex-linked characteristic An hereditary factor (carried in the XY and XX chromosomes) controlled by a **gene** that determines an individual's sex. Hemophilia is a sex linked characteristic, as is red-green **color blindness.**

sexual deviation Sexual practice in which needs are gratified by acts ordinarily considered socially and legally taboo by a particular ruling society. Many but certainly not all groups or societies consider the following to be sexual deviations: homosexuality, **pedophilia, zoophilia,** fetishism, necrophilia, **sadism, masochism, transvestism,** exhibitionism, voyeurism, nymphomania, and satyriasis.

For information on sex and sex education, contact the following organizations: *American Social Health Association, Inc.,* 1740 Broadway, New York, N.Y. 10019; *Institute for Sex Research,* Indiana University, Bloomington, Indiana 47405; and *Sex Information and Education Council of the U.S.,* 1885 Broadway, New York, N.Y. 10023.

sham rage The rage responses that decorticated animals show when touched or stimulated. The rage appears to be unreal, generalized, and targetless. There is no apparent carryover of the "emotion," since as soon as the stimulus ceases the animal immediately returns to its former facies. *See* **Bard, decortication conditioning.**

shape constancy The tendency to perceive the shape of an object correctly or as being constant, regardless of the viewing angle. Shape constancy depends upon the relation of the shape of the retinal image to the apparent plane of the object. *See* **perceptual constancy.**

shaping of behavior (method of approximation, successive approximation) An animal-training method in **operant conditioning.** Complicated tasks are shaped out or differentiated by selectively rewarding responses that are successively more similar to the kind of behavior desired. Tolerably understandable mistakes barely approximating the final desired behavior are nevertheless **reinforced** as long as the person seems to be moving toward his goal, all other responses being extinguished. Shaping of skills by reinforcement or reward is also done, such as in shaping a child to learn not to be **enuretic,** or by showing social approval of a child's smile if smiling is desired.

shaping therapy A form of behavior therapy that uses shaping techniques to develop more acceptable forms of behavior in the patient.

Sheldon, William Herbert American psychologist and physician, born 1899. Ph.D. 1925 and M.D. 1933, both from Chicago. His research has attempted to type people (**somatotype**) by relating physique and temperament. Controversy has surrounded his findings and conclusions ever since he published his work. Diamond (1957) stated that Child's study (1950) constituted "an overwhelming confirmation of the general validity of Sheldon's theories." Hood's (1963) study of 10,000 male freshmen found practically no significance in relationship between body type and

temperament (Hood, A. B., "A Study of the Relationship between Physique and Personality Variables Measured by the MMPI." *Journal of Personality,* 1963, **31,** 97-107).

Sherif, Muzafer Born 1906, Turkey. Received Ph.D., psychology, Columbia 1935. A social psychologist specializing in social factors in **cognitive processes; attitudes.** Received DSC Award 1968. *See* **autokinetic, frame of reference.**

Sherrington, Sir Charles Scott (1857-1952) English physician and physiologist especially known for his work with the **reflex** and on the nervous system. Introduced the terms **proprioceptor, interoceptor, exteroceptor** in 1906. First to adequately study the **synapse** and introduce the term. He also was first to describe and name the **final common path.** Winner in 1932, with Adrian, of the Nobel prize in medicine for discoveries on the function of the **neuron.** *See* **Ramon y Cajal.**

shock therapy Any therapeutic technique (as insulin and electric shock) that induces a convulsive seizure in the patient. Primarily used for depressed patients who may experience temporary periods of lucidity, making them more amenable to **final** verbal therapeutic communications.

short-term memory (STM) A phase of memory that exists for a relatively short period of time (seconds or minutes), probably being stored by a so-called **memory trace,** the trace disappearing quickly (or decaying) if the information is not **reinforced** sufficiently. The set of memory traces stored in STM is called the rehearsal buffer. To delay decay, information must be rehearsed. If rehearsed enough, STM information may be recoded and transferred to the storage mechanism that holds **long-term memory.** *See* **information processing.**

SI *Système International d'Unités. See* **International System of Units**

sialometer A saliva (sialo-) meter. Originally, a rather simple apparatus for collecting and measuring salivary flow for experimental analyses and studies. Oscillographs, teflon tubing, and electronic recording devices have largely superseded the less sophisticated equipment.

Sidman avoidance technique The type of avoidance behavior conditioned to occur without a warning signal or cue. Sidman conditioned rats to press a lever as the avoidance response (being shocked unless they pressed the lever) with a following assured time period free from shock each time the lever was pressed. Thus, the animal could avoid being shocked indefinitely if he learned to press the bar before his time was up (Lundin, pp. 238-242; M. Sidman, "Avoidance Conditioning with Brief Shock and No Exteroceptive Warning Signal," *Science,* 1953, **118,** 157-158). Murray Sidman (born 1923). American psychologist. Ph.D. (psychology), Columbia 1952.

signal averager *See* **averaging computer.**

sign Gestalt *See* **Tolman.**

significance Statistically, the **reliability** of a finding or the dependability one can place on an obtained **statistic** as an indicator of reality. In determining the significance of a sample as to its representativeness of a total population, the **null hypothesis** provides the simplest criterion available. Significance always refers to **probability,** or how much an obtained value can be explained as a chance occurrence. Anything of statistical significance has a very low probability of having occurred by chance. *See* **significance testing.** (Walker-Lev, p. 46, and Edwards, pp. 257-270).

significance level *See* **level of significance.**

significance testing (hypothesis testing) A means of evaluating statements made about the **population,** particularly in terms of either retaining (nonrejecting) or rejecting the **null hypothesis** (H_0). Good hypotheses, if true,

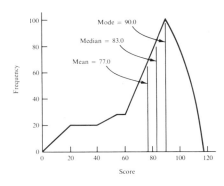

Mean, median, and mode in skewed distributions. In skewed distributions, the mean, the median, and the mode do not coincide.

make obtained **data** likely of occurrence and agree with the available evidence, indicating that the null hypothesis should be upheld or maintained.

If a **sample** is obtained that has a small probability of agreement with the null hypothesis, then the H_O is rejected and the sample result is said to be significant. If the probability indicates a relatively large chance of getting a sample value in disagreement with the null hypothesis, the hypothesis is not rejected, the result thus being significant.

sign learning An organism's learned expectation that one stimulus (the sign) will be succeeded by another (sign-significate) as long as a familiar behavioral pattern is followed. In this sense it does not form habits, which would only be learning a series of movements.

Concept presented by E. C. Tolman (1932).

sign stimulus According to **ethologists**, a specific **stimulus** in the environment that apparently signals an involved behavioral sequence.

sign test A procedure for testing the **hypothesis** that the parameter p in the formula $P(r) = [n!/r!(n-r)!]\ p^r(1-p)^{n-r}$ has the specified value p_O under the **null hypothesis**. The sign test is relatively easy to apply and understand.

The binomial $(p + q)^N$ with $p = 0.50$ is used to test whether there are more plus or more minus signs than reasonable on a chance basis. N is the number of pairs remaining after all pairs showing zero differences, i.e., tied scores, have been dropped from the calculation. Measurements must be at least **ordinal**, and the underlying variable is assumed to be continuously distributed. See Table 27.

The sign test is so-named because it uses plus and minus signs as data.

similarity See **autochthonous laws of cognitive order.**

simple event See **elementary event.**

simple type of schizophrenia See **schizophrenia.**

simultaneous contrast See **contrast.**

single blind (procedure) technique An experimental method in which only the experimenter knows what type of medication (or active drug or a **placebo**) is being given to the subject.

sinistrad Toward (-ad) the left (sinistr-); sometimes used to refer to the direction in which **mirror writing** proceeds. See **anatomical directions.**

sinistral Pertaining to (-al) the left (sinistr-) side of the body, contrasted with **dextral.** See anatomical directions.

SI units and symbols The SI system consists of six base units (**meter, kilogram, second, ampere, kelvin,** and **candela**), two supplementary units (**radian, steradian**), a series of derived units (meter per second squared, radian per second squared, **volt, ohm,** etc.) consistent with the base and supplementary units, and a series of approved prefixes for the formation of multiples and submultiples of the various units. See **International System of Units.**

size constancy A perceptual phenomenon in which familiar objects appear to remain the same size regardless of their true distance from the viewer; a compensatory perceptual adjustment by the viewer to relate other-sized objects to his accustomed one. See **object constancy.**

skewed distribution An asymmetrical (skew-) **distribution** in which the scores cluster around either end of the distribution. See **skewness.**

skewness The asymmetrical (skew-) quality or condition (-ness) of a **distribution.** Skewness is toward the longer tail. In a positively skewed distribution the scores cluster around the lower portion of the distribution; in a negatively skewed distribution, they cluster around the upper portion. See **moment.**

skin color Having the color of skin, whether black, brown, yellow, or white. Skin color is a function of "skin-color" genes, which are multiple in nature, each gene being able to assert itself in the production of pigment. A dark-skin gene is dominant over a light-skin gene, but two dark-skin genes will produce an even darker color. For example, a full black skin color is possible only from two pairs of different black genes, but one black gene coupled with a white gene will produce the mulatto shade. Other gradations in color depend upon the various linkage possibilities between black and white. A truly black-skinned child can result only if both parents carry black skin-color genes, and a truly white child could never develop from parents who were both genetically black.

Skinner, Burrhus Frederick Born Pennsylvania, 1904. Received Ph.D., psychology, Harvard 1931. Calls his experimental approach "descriptive behaviorism." He has argued that the present state of psychological knowledge does not warrant the formulation of **learning theories**; that present psychologists should mainly accumulate empirical data. His **operant** behavior approach has been used in pure science and industry. He has also studied verbal psychotic behavior. He believes that man has had too much individual freedom and needs controls to lead him on to more desirable and constructive behavior. In 1938, he reported his invention of the **Skinner box**, an operant conditioning laboratory enclosure designed so that caged experimental animals (rats, pigeons, etc.) must press a lever (or key, or button, or push a panel), in order to gain reward or avoid punishment. Member of the **National Academy of Sciences.** Awarded the **Warren Medal** in 1942 for "his experimental analysis of laws operating in one type of conditioning, furnishing a basis for a positivistic description of operant behavior," and the **Distinguished Scientific Contribution Award** in 1958 (Vinacke, p. 518).

sleep stages Particular phases of sleep as determined by **electroencephalographic** studies. Accordingly, the sleep process has been categorized into several stages: *stage 1*, characterized by disappearance of the **alpha rhythm** and replacement by **theta waves**, immediately follows quiescent wakefulness (stage 1 descending) or precedes awakening (stage 1 ascending); and *stage 2*, the "light sleep" as reported by subjects, and characterized on the EEG by appearance of the *K complex* (slow frequency, high amplitude waves) and *sleep spindles* (bundles of high frequency EEG waves). *Stages 3 and 4* are usually combined because of the minor differences between them but both show **delta waves** (in stage 3 occurring less than 50 percent of the time while in stage 4 they occur more than 50 percent of the time). The stages reverse themselves after 3 and 4, first to stage 2 and then stage 1, completing a sleep cycle from stage 1 (descending) through stage 4 and reversing to stage 1 (ascending).

Sleep periods have been given various names. Probably the most common name applied to the dreaming stage of sleep is that of rapid eye movement (REM) sleep. Other names are low voltage, fast wave (LVFW) sleep, **paradoxical sleep**, desynchronized sleep (DS), and low muscle tone (LMT) sleep. (Milner, p. 271).

For further information, write *Association for the Psychophysiological Study of Sleep*, Box 3415, University Station, Laramie, Wyoming 82070.

slow rotation room A completely enclosed circular experimental room, 15 feet in diameter, that rotates its vertical centerline. It was built to assess rotation effects upon the human being. In addition to gravity, "the rotation of the room provides. . . a force in a direction outward from the center of rotation and perpendicular to the force of gravity. . . Visually, the environment is at rest; vestibularly, the environment is not at rest." Most of the comforts of home are provided. Subjects can live in the room for several weeks at a time, but head turning or tilting causes a form of motion sickness called **canal sickness**. (Weintraub and Walker, *Perception*, pp. 71-73).

small sample theory A theory based on small **sample** investigations demanding that strict attention be paid to the sample size, the number of **degrees of freedom** to be used, and the nature of the unbiased estimates of the **population** parameters. See large sample theory, **sample theory**, and **t distribution** (also McNemar, 1962, pp. 98-108).

smell See **stereochemical smell theory.**

Smith papyrus See **Edwin Smith Surgical Papyrus.**

Snellen Test Chart A quick test for central visual acuity with rows of block letters in graduated sizes to be read at a standard distance.

After Herman Snellen (1834-1908), Dutch ophthalmologist, who devised such a chart about 1860 and reported on it in 1862.

social determinism The doctrine (-ism) of social laws determining and transcending individual consideration, including one's behavior.

social development. See **Vineland Social Maturity Scale.**

social dominance See **hook order, pecking order.**

social facilitation studies Investigations concerned with the influence of the group upon individual motivational behavior, such as: (1) *audience effects*—spectators tend to facilitate well-learned performances (such as the positive stimulation an audience provides a lecturer or musician when presenting well-rehearsed material), but tend to handicap performers in presenting unfamiliar material; (2) *coaction effects*—group participation facilitates mastery of well-learned material but impairs learning of new material, indicating that it is better for a study group to review "old" material and more efficacious for one person to study "new" material alone.

social introversion See **Minnesota Multiphasic Personality Inventory.**

social maladjustment A disorder associated with problems related to marriage, occupation, adjusting to a new culture (**culture shock**) or to the conflicts arising from divided cultural loyalties (such as rejection of family traditions by a second generation youth while making adjustments to his own new culture), or in dyssocial behavior (including gambling, prostitution and dope peddling).

social maturity scale See **Vineland Social Maturity Scale.**

social psychiatry A theoretical and practical approach to **psychiatry** in which social and cultural effects upon mental illness are emphasized, coordinating its efforts with the related disciplines of sociology, anthropology, education and often psychology.

S

social psychology The study of man's behavioral components (such as **personality**, **attitude**, and **motivation**), in relation to the social milieu and the effects of society upon the individual. Closely related to sociology, but psychologically oriented in concepts and terminology.

The publication in 1908 of **William McDougall**'s book *Introduction to Social Psychology* is generally conceded to mark at least the printed origins of the field.

social statistics (demography) The application of statistics to the study of social **data**, relating primarily to the development of the physical and intellectual qualities of man.

Founded in 1836 by Lambert A. Jacques Quetelet (1796-1874), Belgian statistician and astronomer.

social stimulus value The unique quality of a person in a social interacting situation that generates positive or negative social responsiveness in others; for example, a smiling baby attracts social contact whereas a grouchy baby repels it.

Society of Experimental Psychologists An organization of like-minded experimental psychologists, founded by **Titchener** in 1904 and formally organized in 1929 to "advance psychology by arranging informal conferences on experimental methodology." Through the granting of its Warren Medal "outstanding work in experimental psychology in the U.S. and Canada is recognized." *See* **Euler diagrams** for indication of the relative size of the society and how it overlaps with other psychological organizations.

sociogram A social map or diagrammatic research tool, using the **sociometric** method of indicating interactions (for example, interpersonal preferences and dislikes, choice and rejection patterns), among group members. One of the ways of revealing group structure, such as in clique formation and group cohesiveness. Patterns formed depend upon personal feelings, social standards, etc.

Developed by **J. L. Moreno** in 1934.

sociology The systematic study of (-ology) social (soci-) forces, institutions, relationships, and group processes. Sociology is primarily a theoretical science but also includes such practical branches as social welfare and social work.

Auguste Comte (1798-1857), French philosopher, introduced the term in his work *Cours de Philosophie Positiv*, 1830-1842, translated into English 1853.

sociometry Process of measuring (-metry) or describing the structure of a group (socio-), an outgrowth of Moreno's work in **psychodrama** and related practices. A procedure of social mapping in which functional relationship (through a so-called nominating technique) is shown among the group members, each member confidentially expressing his preference for other group members (to play, to live with, to work with, etc.). Results of the sociometric method (indicating attraction or repulsion bonds between people) are graphically shown in a sociogram.

Term coined by **Moreno** (1934).

sociopathic disorder Relating to (-ic) a social (socio-) illness (-path-) or disorder; lack of social responsibility occasioned by inability or unwillingness to conform to prevailing social norms. *See* **character disorder**.

sociotrope One whose mind is turned (-trope) toward social issues, or who allows social factors to influence his judgment and decisions. According to Boring, a sociotrope has a "fixation on human nature and citizenship," while a **biotrope** has a "fixation on research." (Boring, Edwin G., "Biotropes, Sociotropes, and Teaching," *American Psychologist*, 1966, No. 1, **21**, 80-83.)

Socrates (469-399 B.C.) Greek philosopher. Developed the technique of **maieutics** (drawing forth) in his discussions with students, which became known as the Socratic method.

Direct and indirect questioning (with Socrates seldom offering any answers) ferreted out objective differences between assumptions and principles. *See* **gnothi seauton**.

sodium amytal *Same as* **amobarbital sodium**.

sodium pentothal The sodium salt of thiopental, used often in psychiatric and psychological research to induce and control hypnotic trances.

Soemmering, Samuel Thomas von (1755-1830) Prussian anatomist, artist. Described and named **cranial nerves** in his work: *The Brain and the Origin of the Cranial Nerves*, 1778. *See* **acoustic nerve**, **glossopharyngeal nerve**, **macula lutea**, **substantia nigra**.

software Programming aids (symbolic assembly systems, library and utility program routines, compilers, etc.) developed for the most efficient use of a computer. Often refers to those programs that compile and provide diagnostic information on failures. *Contrasted with* **hardware**.

soma The body (soma) frame without viscera; the body except for the germ cells; the body as distinguished from the mind. A **dualistic** formulation, assuming that *psyche* (mind) and *soma* (body) are separate entities. *See* **psychosomatic illness**.

somatic nervous system The division of the **peripheral nervous system** that includes the 12 **cranial nerves** and the 31 **spinal nerves**. Through this system, **afferent** impulses are sent to the brain and **efferent** impulses are carried to the striped or voluntary muscles, which control the skeletal muscles.

somatic sensory system The areas of the **cerebral cortex** (primarily in back of the **fissure** of Rolando) concerned with **kinesthesis** and the cutaneous senses. *Anatomically*, skin **receptors** may be divided into two categories: **epicritic** (specific pressure, position, and touch sensations) and **protopathic** (relatively generalized pain, touch and temperature sensations). Pressure receptors are the **Pacinian corpuscles**, so specific that they are insensitive to thermal stimuli (Thompson, p. 323).

somatopsychological factors Factors of the body and physique (including physiological functioning) that affect the psychological (emotional) behavior of the person; the influence of body shape and body health upon individual behavior and **attitudes**. The term is often used to describe both behavior and conditions related to physically handicapped people.

somatotonia Condition or degree (-ia) of tone or tonus (-ton-) in the human body. **Sheldon's** term for a dimension of **temperament** (showing energy, risk-taking, muscularity, assertiveness, love of adventure) highly correlated with the **mesomorph** body build. Somatotonics, when mentally ill, are inclined toward **manic-depressive reactions**. *See* **constitutional types**.

somatotrophin (somatotrophic hormone). One of the six hormones of the **adenohypophysis** (anterior pituitary gland), concerned with controlling and promoting general body (somato-) growth (-troph) somewhat under control of blood sugar. Sometimes erroneously spelled "somatotropin"–(-trop-) = turn, not growth.

somatotype theory (somatotyping) Body (somato-) type theory. *See* **constitutional types**.

somesthesis Body (som-) feeling or sensitivity (esthesis), including **kinesthetic** and cutaneous sensations of cold, warmth, pressure, and especially deep pain. The somesthetic-sensory cortical area (lying directly behind the **central fissure** on the **brain** surface) is the termination center for somesthetic sense organs.

sonometer (audiometer) A sound (sono-) meter. A device used to measure auditory acuity by detecting deviations from one's normal hearing. A modification of the ancient monochord.

sophrosyne The quality (-syne) of having a sound (so-) mind (-phro-). State of being prudent, logical, reasonable, self-controlling. *Contrasted with* **hubris**.

SOR Stimulus-Organism-Response. *See* **paradigm**, **stimulus-response theory**.

Sörge (Ger., worry, care) **Heidegger's** term for care: "If man doesn't or can't care he is not man, he is animal." Sörge, for Heidegger, is the basis of all Being. Man overcomes everything because of his capacity for Sörge. *See* **Fürsörge**.

Sosein (Ger., content) of a psychosis. The term was applied to psychosis in 1954 by German psychiatrist Kurt Schneider (1890-1961).

sound The sensation produced in the organs of hearing, which depend upon various qualities, namely: **pitch**, relating to frequency of sound waves; *loudness*, referring to their amplitude; and **timbre**, pertaining to the quality or complexity of sound waves. *See* **hearing**.

sound spectrograph Graphically (-graph) a sound spectrum (spectro-), in which changes in the intensity-frequency pattern of sounds as a function of time are indicated. An electronic device that analyzes complex sounds into their component parts. Sometimes called "visible speech," since the spectrograph is used primarily in visual display of speech.

source language The language initially coded or written into a **computer program** by a programmer. For example, a FORTRAN statement (source) will be compiled into a set of numeric statements or object codes for entry and execution in the **digital computer** system.

sour-grapes reaction A form of **rationalization** in which a person asserts that he didn't want it anyway when he fails to achieve a goal. So called from Aesop's fable of the fox who could not reach some grapes on a vine, and therefore rationalized that they were sour and not worth striving for.

Soviet higher education University studies usually last four years (since 1964) and consist of cycles somewhat similar to the French system. However, the first cycle emphasizes the acquisition of general scientific knowledge in a selected area and the second cycle is devoted to specialization in that area. The first four years of successful study is rewarded by a qualification diploma. Students are then encouraged to pursue their studies further by obtaining a thesis fellowship (postgraduate course or *aspirantura*) enabling them to study an additional three years leading to the candidate degree (*Kandidat Nauk*), requiring the passing of special examinations and presenting a satisfactory thesis.

Passing the candidate degree makes the student eligible for original scientific research which may culminate (after about four more years) in the granting of a doctorate, leading to university appointments in teaching and research. (*Education and Development in Western Europe*, pp. 156-57).

space-eikonometer An instrument for measuring (-meter) space or depth cues of images (eikono-) or figures. Used for studying stereoscopic vision and **aniseikonia** (K. N. Ogle, "Theory of the Space-Eikonometer," *Journal of the Optical Society of America*, 1946, 36, 20-32).

space perception Vision in depth. In binocular vision, it is obtained from the stereoscopic effect of **binocular disparity**, relative size, lineal and aerial perspective, and relative motion. Ability to visualize the relations of objects in space (a **primary mental ability**) is called *spatial intelligence*.

spastic *See* **muscle tone**.

spatial induction *See* **contrast**.

spatial intelligence *See* **space perception**.

Spearman, Charles Edward (1863-1945) English psychologist-statistician. Applied statistical methods to individual differences in attempt to quantify the nature of **intelligence**. *See* **general factor**, **two-factor theory**.

Spearman has had several statistical procedures named after him, such as:

Spearman-Brown prophecy formula. A statistical technique for adjusting the **coefficient of reliability** (obtained by correlating scores on two-halves of a test) so that an estimate may be made of the **reliability** of the whole test. The prophecy formula predicts what the reliability would be if each half of the test (odd-and even-numbered items) were twice as long. The formula is

$$r_{tt} = \frac{2r_{oe}}{1+r_{oe}} \text{ or } r_{tt} = \frac{2r_{\frac{1}{2}\frac{1}{2}}}{1+r_{\frac{1}{2}\frac{1}{2}}}$$

where

r_{tt} = reliability of original test

$\left.\begin{array}{l} r_{oe} \\ \text{or} \\ r_{\frac{1}{2}\frac{1}{2}} \end{array}\right\}$ reliability coefficient obtained by correlating scores on odd (*o*) items with scores on even (*e*) items; or correlating scores on ½ of the test with scores obtained on the other ½.

This coefficient is referred to as the Spearman-Brown formula because articles by them appeared in the same issue of the same journal (William Brown, "Some Experimental Results in the Correlation of Mental Abilities," *British Journal of Psychology*, 1910, 3, 296-322 and Charles Spearman, "Correlation Calculated from Faulty Data," *British Journal of Psychology*, 1910, 3, 271-295). *See* **coefficient of reliability**; also Walker and Lev, 1953, p. 314.

Spearman rank difference method (rank-order correlation coefficient, rho). A **non-parametric** statistical method using differences in rank-order to determine relationship between two **variables**. Individuals who are tied with respect to the ranking variable are given the same rank, which is the **mean** of their ranks. When the ranks of the same individuals are established with respect to another variable (for example, age or quantity of practice), the **correlation** of the two ranks can be computed from ranked data, a comparison of ranked data, or two sets of ordered scores. Then Spearman's formula is applied, whose coefficient is given by rho (ρ)

$$\rho = 1 - \frac{6\Sigma D^2}{N(N^2 - 1)}$$

where

ρ = measure of correlation
D = difference between the two ranks for each individual on two sets of data
N = number of individuals

Like the coefficient of correlation, this coefficient ranges from 1.00 (perfect correlation), through 0.00 (both ranks independent of each other), to -1.00 (perfect negative correlation). *See* Table 30.

Spearman's *rho* is used primarily for studies involving small *N*, about 15 to 20 cases. *See* **percentile rank**, Table 30 (also Hays, 1963, p. 641).

Spearman also devised a "footrule" formula for a rough rank correlation:

$$R = 1 - \frac{6\Sigma G}{N^2 - 1}$$

where

G = positive differences in rank.

species specific behavior Behavior unique to one species of animal only.

specific energy of nerves *See* **specific nerve energies.**

specific energy of the senses A phrase considered by many neurophysiologists to be preferable to **specific energy of nerves**.

A. J. McKeag apparently first expressed such an idea in 1902 in his book *The Sensation of Pain and the Theory of Specific Sense Energies*. W. Riese and G. E. Arrington also stressed the point in 1963 ("The History of Johannes Müller's Doctrine of the Specific Energies of the Senses: Original and Later Versions," *Bulletin of the History of Medicine*, 37, 179-183) See Clarke and O'Malley, p. 204.

specificity A term applied by **Pavlov** (1890) to distinctions between stimuli. A classic specificity viewpoint (**Johannes Müller**, 1838) is the doctrine of **specific nerve energies**, indicating that the kind of **receptor** stimulated determines the nature of the sensation perceived; thus the skin has specific and separate receptors for heat, cold, pressure, and pain. Another specificity viewpoint is the Young-Helmholtz theory. *See* **color-vision theories.**

specific nerve energies (specific energy of nerves) The doctrine stating that sensation depends upon which nerve is stimulated rather than upon how the nerve is stimulated. Visual sensations occur not only from stimulation of light but also from electric shock or eye-ball pressure.

Johannes Müller (1801-1858). German physiologist, published his now famous theory in *Zür vergleichenden Physiologie des Gesichtssinnes*, 1826, which he later expanded upon in his *Handbuch der Physiologie des Menschen*, (1833-1840). *See* **specificity**, **Bell** under **Bell-Magendie law, Bonnet.**

spectrocolorimeter A device or meter for numerically measuring colors in the spectrum (spectro-) by a matching process, the results being analyzed for various purposes. Used in learning, attention, and **perception** studies.

A. W. Volkmann (1801-1877), German physiologist, first used the word in 1850.

spectrogram A spectral (spectro-) record (-gram); such as a photograph, map, or chart. *See* **sound spectrograph.**

spectrometer An instrument that measures (-meter) the index of refraction by wavelengths or spectral colors, analyzing white light into its component wavelengths.

spectrophotometer A device for measuring (-meter) and comparing light (-photo-) emissions from various parts of spectra.

spectroscope Spectrum (spectro-) viewer (-scope). An instrument for visually examining optical spectra and making them visible.

speech aphasia (word muteness) Inability to express language orally. **Head** listed four types of speech aphasia: (*1*) *verbal*, difficulty in forming words; (*2*) *syntactical*, in which certain parts of speech (usually articles and prepositions) are slurred or dropped out; (*3*) *nominal*, inability to name names; (*4*) *semantic*, difficulty in forming sequential language.

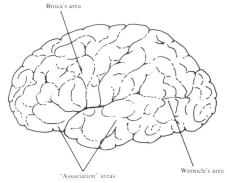

Broca's area

"Association" areas

Wernicke's area

From *Psychology: A Scientific Study of Man*, *3rd Edition*, by Sanford and Wrightsman. Copyright 1970 by Wadsworth Publishing Company, Inc. Reprinted by permission of the publisher, Brooks/Cole Publishing Company, Monterey, California.

speech mechanisms of thinking (reflex theory of thinking) A concept holding that the speech mechanisms involved in thinking are a central **brain** process. It reflects the "highest integration of all the stimuli impinging on the cortex by means of second-signal (speech) associations." Speech-motor stimuli "acquire their abstraction and generalization qualities only from their mutual associations in the brain." The interconnected "system of motor, auditory, and visual components of speech corresponds to the linguistic and psychophysiological concept of the **phoneme**, **grapheme**, and **articuleme** representing all of the elements of verbal and written speech as well as the means for all verbal-logical operations." (Cole and Maltzman, p. 533).

The reflex theory of thinking stems from the ideas of **Sechenov** and **Pavlov** and is opposed to the motor theory of thinking (the **peripheralist position**).

Spence, Kenneth (1907-1967) American psychologist. Ph.D., Yale 1933. Interests include formulation and testing of theories of discrimination learning, classical and instrumental learning, role of motivation in learning, neobehavioristic theory of learning. His so-called *Spence learning theory* is a modification of Hull's **stimulus-response theory** of learning, indicating that incentives as well as drives influence behavior. Received **Warren Medal** 1953 for "his persistent and rigorous theoretical and experimental work on fundamental problems of learning," and the **Distinguished Scientific Contribution** Award 1956. *See* **learning theory** (also Vinacke, p. 550).

sphygmograph An instrument that, when applied over an artery, produces a record (-graph) of the rate and force of the pulse (sphygmo-).

Introduced in 1850 by the German physiologist Karl Vierordt (1818-1884).

sphygmomanometer An instrument consisting of an inflatable rubber cuff connected to a pressure gauge and applied by hand (-mano-) over an artery. It measures (-meter-) the pulse (sphygmo-) or arterial blood pressure.

First practical one invented by the Italian physician Scipione Riva-Rocci (1863-1943).

Spielmeyer-Vogt disease A condition that occurs usually between the ages of five to ten, involving frequent motor or epileptic seizures, blindness, impairment of balance and coordination, and mental deterioration. Death usually follows within ten years of recognition of disease. A juvenile form of **cerebral lipoidosis**.

spike An analog signal shaped like a spike, with voltage plotted against time.

spike potential An extremely rapid change of **potential** or polarization reversal (going first in one direction, then in the other), returning to its resting position after carrying the **nerve impulse** down the **axon** of the nerve cell (Morgan, pp. 63-65).

spinal accessory nerve Cranial nerve XI, involved in neck movements.

spinal animal Any experimental animal whose spinal cord has been severed, enabling studies to be made on separate aspects of the nervous system, such as **reflexes**.

spinal conditioning Conditioning in animals where no nerve centers higher than those of the spinal cord are involved, achieved by cutting the nerve fibers immediately below the brain. Attempts at **classical conditioning** have been made on rats and dogs operated upon in this way, with conflicting and inconclusive results.

spinal nerves The 31 pairs of nerves connecting at intervals in the spinal cord. Classified by pairs according to the part of the cord from which they arise: 8 cervical, 12 thoracic, 5 lumbar, 5 sacral, and 1 coccygeal. *See* **Bell**, **sensory.**

English physician **Thomas Willis** made the first adequate description of the spinal nerves in 1671; published posthumously in 1684.

spinal shock *See* **Marshall Hall.**

Spinoza, Baruch (1632-1677) Dutch monist philosopher of Portuguese parentage. Rejected **Descartes' dualism**, claiming that God or Nature is substance which, in space is matter

S

and as thought it is mind. Reason sets man apart from other animals, with emotion, as a disturbing influence in life, needing to be controlled by reason.

split-brain animal An animal whose brain has been operatively split in two (such as **sagittal** sectioning of the **corpus callosum** and other **forebrain** commissures) for purposes of studying, in effect, two related but separate brains.

split-half technique A statistical method for determining the consistency or **reliability** of a test by correlating scores from comparable halves.

spontaneous recovery Reappearance of a **response** after a time lapse, following extinction of the **conditioned response** without any additional conditioning.

Spranger, Eduard (1882-1963) German philosopher-psychologist. Favored descriptive over explanatory psychology. Developed ideal types of mankind (theoretical, religious, political, esthetic, etc.) representing ultimate categories of value. To him, these types of personality are merely theoretical guides to understanding people. He defiantly called his psychology the "psychology from the standpoint of the cultural sciences" in opposing those who thought only the physical sciences could rightly be called "science." *See* **study of values.**

S.Q. Social quotient. *See* **Vineland Social Maturity Scale.**

squint glasses Eyeglasses composed of prismatic lenses, used for the study of **color vision.** *See* **stenopeic spectacles.**

SR, S-R Stimulus-response.

SR compatibility The psychological closeness of **stimulus** and **response.**

S-shaped curve A curve, graphically presented, showing the entire learning process: a period of *increasing returns* from practice during early trials, a period during which the rate of improvement remains *constant*, and finally, a period of *decreasing* improvement. *See* **rates of return.**

stabilimeter A meter for determining stability. An apparatus that records the actions of an animal or child. A stabilimeter crib contains an instrument for measuring bodily sway in a person who attempts to hold himself steady.

stability coefficient (retest reliability) An estimate of **reliability** determined by administering the same test to the same group of subjects on two different occasions and noting the consistency between the **sets** of scores. Stability is the correlation (r_{tt}) between the two resulting sets of test scores.

stammering (stuttering) A spasmodic speech condition marked by involuntary stops and blockings of utterances, involving a repetition of the initial syllable of a word or phrase (usually beginning with b, d, p, s, and t), and also including body mannerisms and facial grimaces. The condition usually becomes exaggerated when the person faces those with whom he feels inferior or embarrassed, but it reduces in intensity when with those younger or in inferior positions. Stammering is apparently as dependent upon speech perception as it is upon speech production.

Possible causes: heredity predisposition, brain damage, psychological trauma. There seems to be little or no relationship, however, to handedness or to changing from left handed to right handed.

Various methods have been applied in treating the condition. **Dunlap** tried (1932) a negative practice technique that had some success. **Shaping** has also been utilized, using the speech patterns (hesitancies, a-a-a-a, etc.) as **operants** that can be shaped, for example, by a controlled electric shock, shocking the person each time he stammered. Cherry and Sayers (1956), claiming that stammering is a perceptual disturbance rather than motor, trained the stammerer to mimic exactly what he hears but in slower tempo, thereby diverting his attention from his own speech.

Fluent speech then becomes a habit. (C. Cherry and B. Sayers. Experiments Upon the Total Inhibition of Stammering by External Control and Some Clinical Results. *Journal of Psychosomatic Research,* 1956, T, 233-246).

Psychoanalytically, stammering is due to libidinal fixation and emotional arrest at the oral stage. Psychologically, it is due to bad habits and emotional conflicts, such as an approach-avoidance one in which the stutterer has learned to fear and avoid speaking but because of its social necessity he feels compelled to talk but blocks; also stammering is reinforced by fear reduction once the stuttered word has been uttered, thus creating a vicious cycle with (*a*) fear leading to blocking, (*b*) stuttering reducing the fear, and (*c*) the accompanying feeling of relief being reinforced and sought for again.

standard deviation (root mean square deviation) A measure of the **variability** or scatter of statistical **data** around the **mean** of a **frequency distribution.** It is the square root of the mean of the squared deviations of the scores about the **sample** mean. In a **normal distribution,** 68.27 percent of the scores will fall within the limits of one standard deviation (S.D.) above and below the mean; 95 percent within 1.96 S.D.'s either side of the mean; and 99 percent within 2.58 S.D.'s of the mean. These points of reference are frequently used in tests of **significance.** In any distribution, the size of the S.D. is a function of the scatter of data; the greater the scatter, the larger the S.D. Its symbol is the lower-case Greek letter σ (sigma) and is given by

$$\sigma = \sqrt{\Sigma x^2 / N}$$

where *x* is the difference between a datum and the mean of the distribution.

standard error (S.E.) or standard error of the mean. The **standard deviation** of the **sampling distribution** of a **statistic.** Interpreted like other standard deviations, but measures the sampling errors that affect a statistic.

standard error of estimate The **standard error** of the differences between the predicted value and true value of a measure; the square root of the residual **variance.**

standard interface *See* **interface.**

standardization The process of transforming a **set** of scores into **standard scores;** the establishment of norms of achievement (standards) on tests by compiling reliable and **valid** results from sufficiently large and representative groups. For example, the principal normative sample in the 1955 standardization of the **Wechsler Adult Intelligence Scale** consisted of 1700 persons with an equal number of men and women distributed over seven age levels between 16 and 64 years, with an additional 475 male-female subjects aged 60-75 and over. *See* **Stanford-Binet test** (also Wechsler, 1958, pp. 86-92).

standardization group A **sample** of subjects that serves as a reference group against which the performance of other subjects is compared.

standardized interview A structured **interview** in which specific questions are asked in a standard order of all interviewees. Often, written directions are provided the interviewer on how to cope with the contingencies that might arise during such an interview.

standardized test A test whose items have been rigorously selected, and tested out; it is accompanied by directions for its administration, scoring, and interpretation.

standard (standardized) score A score converted from each value in any **distribution** that expresses the deviation from the **mean** in standard deviation units. *See* **z-score.**

standing patterns of behavior *See* **behavior setting.**

Stanford-Binet Test The modification of the original Binet-Simon test of intelligence. The Stanford-Binet test was first standardized (on approximately 1000 children and 400 adults)

for the American population by Terman of Stanford University in 1916. It was revised in 1937, consisting of two equivalent forms (L and M), and including 3184 subjects in the sample. The third revision (1960) condensed the two forms into one again, incorporating the best items of forms L and M. It is primarily an **individual test** of verbal intelligence, although in later revisions more attention has been paid to performance factors. *See* **Binet.**

stanine score A portmanteau word (*standard nine*) used to identify the compiled score obtained on the standard nine tests (running from 1 to 9) given by the Air Force during the Second World War. It is a type of standard score (with a **mean** of 5 and **standard deviation** of 2).

stapes Stirrup. Tiny stirrup-shaped **ossicle** of the **middle ear**, consisting of a hinged chain of bones that transmit vibrations from the **incus** to the oval window of the **cochlea.**

In 1546, Italian physician and anatomist Giovanni Filippo Ingrassia (1510-1580) discovered the stapes and made the first accurate description of it in 1557.

startle (pattern) response An extremely rapid and complex pattern of involuntary **motor** reactions to a sudden **stimulus,** such as a person's response (thrusting the head and neck forward, shutting the eyes, and widening the mouth) upon hearing the unexpected firing of a gun or other loud noise. It is not identical to a fear reaction; a person is startled, not scared, by a loud or unexpected sound.

statistic Any item, number, or measure representative of a certain property of **data.** A statistic is a quantity calculated from a sample only and is designated, for example, by English letters X for the **sample** mean and S for the **standard deviation** of a sample.

statistical control An experimental arrangement whereby **variables** may be controlled mathematically rather than experimentally.

statistical decision theory The branch of mathematics dealing with **uncertainty,** in which the decision-making process is studied and certain **decision-rules** are established.

statistical hypothesis A direct statement made only about one or more **population** parameters and never about a **sample. Null** and **alternative hypotheses** are two kinds of statistical hypotheses in that each is stated generally but can be deductively transformed into a statistical hypothesis.

statistical inference The process of drawing conclusions about **population** parameters from **sample data.**

statistical model A specific mathematical statement that can be used as a guideline for determining **outcomes** of experiments, particularly being concerned with sampling distributions of **random variables.**

statistical significance The degree to which an experimental **outcome** (result) contradicts the **null hypothesis.**

statistics A branch of mathematics; a tool used to evaluate experimental situations that involve an element of **uncertainty.** *See* **parametric statistics, nonparametric statistics, statistic, uncertainty.**

stenopeic spectacles or visors Spectacles with a narrow (steno-) opening (-peic) or slit, used to protect the eyes against snow-blindness.

Originally recommended by **Paul of Aegina.** It was first used in 1575 by French surgeon Ambroise Paré (1510-1590). **Donders** introduced a more perfected one in 1854.

steradian *See* **luminous flux.**

stereochemical smell theory A chemical smell theory based upon the spatial (stereo-) arrangement of atoms in molecules. A theory of olfaction listing seven primary odor qualities for man, each odor supposedly being associated with a typical change or shape of odorous molecules. The odors and their shapes are: (*1*) *camphoraceous* (spherical-shaped), whose odor is most typically stimulated by mothballs and camphor; (*2*) *ethereal* (small, flat, thin), whose common stimulus is dry-cleaning fluid; (*3*) *floral* (key-shaped), whose stimulus is roses; (*4*) *musky* (disk-shaped), stimulated by angelica root oil; (*5*) *minty* (wedge-shaped), with peppermint candy a typical stimulus; (*6*) *pungent* (shape undetermined), but stimulated by vinegar; (*7*) *putrid* (shape undetermined), with smell of rotten egg as stimulus.

The idea of odorous substances being molecular in nature was predicted by Amoore, himself, in 1952, although the resulting definitive research by him and his colleagues did not appear until 1964. (J. D. Amoore, J. W. Johnston, and M. Rubin, "The Stereochemical Theory of Olfaction," *Scientific American*, 1964, **210**, 42-49).

stereogram Three-dimensional (stereo-) picture (-gram). A flat photographic or drawn picture so arranged (by superimposing two stereoscopic images) that, when viewed binocularly through a *stereoscope*, gives the tridimensional effect of a solid object in relief.

stereopsis Three-dimensional (stereo-) vision (-opsis). *Same as* stereoscopic vision or **stereoscopic depth perception.**

stereoscope Three-dimensional (stereo-) viewer (-scope). A binocular device used for investigating depth perception. Prisms or mirrors are contrived, with the primary lenses separated by "a distance greater than the separation of the normal eyes," so as to increase the tridimensional effect of **stereograms**, which, when presented one to each eye, fuse into a single picture of depth and solidity. More modern, but basically similar, devices are the *stereoscopic camera* and *stereoscopic viewer* (Walker, 1967, pp. 29-32).

The first stereoscope was constructed, exhibited, and named by **Charles Wheatstone** in 1838.

stereoscopic depth perception (stereopsis) A phenomenon resulting from the two-dimensional projections of a three-dimensional object on the left and right retinas because of the difference in their horizontal positions. Stereopsis is the most powerful single depth cue.

stereotaxic (stereotactic) instrument Relating to (-ic) a framelike instrument that holds an experimental animal's head in a steady position, making it possible to arrange (tax-) the skull tridimensionally (stereo-); that is, along the **anterior-posterior,** **lateral,** and **vertical** axes.

stereotype A solid (stereo-) type, characteristic of the group. A biased generalization (social perception) of grouping a person in an established category that usually connotes an exaggerated or poor value of the group as a whole; for example, Scots are stingy; Irish are drunkards; rich people are ruthless and grasping. Stereotypic impressions are difficult to alter and are seldom accurate pictures of the person so classified.

Originally, stereotype referred to the solid metal duplicate of a relief printing surface for making a matrix. It was in use in 1711 but it was not named until 1798 by a Parisian printer, Henri Didot (1765-1852).

stereotypy Persistent repetition of senseless acts or words; a symptom in some schizophrenic reactions. Stereotyped behavior may also appear in experimental animals as a result of brain surgery, or in those animals suffering from **experimental neurosis.**

Stern, Wilhelm (Louis William, or sometimes, Ludwig W.) (1871-1938) German experimental psychologist noted for emphasis on individual differences. Studied with **Ebbinghaus.** Founder of differential psychology. In *The Psychological Methods of Testing Intelligence*, 1912, he introduced the concept and the term "mental quotient," which Terman and his associates renamed "intelligence quotient" in 1916. Stern also devised a measure of imagery called the **Aussage test.** Became an applied psychologist, working especially on testimony. Visiting professor at Duke University, 1934-1938.

steroid Like (-oid) a sterol (-ster-). A complex chemical substance, essential for human bodily maintenance, similar in structure to the sterols and including the sterols, certain hormones, and other specialized chemical substances. Steroids may be involved in the development of some mental illnesses. A *sterol* (such as cortisol, a stronger variant of cortisone, **corticone,** and **aldosterone**) is an alcohol, derived from plant and animal sources, with physical properties similar to the fats. *See* **androsterone.**

The term was first proposed in 1930.

Stevens, Stanley Smith Born Utah, 1906. Ph.D., Harvard 1933. Psychophysicist in areas of hearing and acoustics and theory of scaling. Exponent of **operationism.** Collaborated with **Sheldon** on physique and personality study. Member **National Academy of Sciences.** Awarded the **Warren Medal** in 1943 for "his analysis of psychological pitch which has revealed both its quantal structure and its functional relation to stimulus frequency." Received the Presidential Certificate of Merit in 1948 and the **Distinguished Scientific Contribution Award** in 1960.

STH *S*omato*t*rophic *h*ormone.

Stilenheit (Ger., unity of style) A term used by Jaensch to indicate that personalities exhibit a certain style of behavior, evidencing a Nordic-superiority form of **typology.** His S-type for example, was characterized by eccentricity, effeminacy, and indecisiveness, found prominently, he said, in such anti-types as Jews, Orientals, and Communists. On the other hand, his I or J type, was decisive, masculine, dependable, tough, and most likely Nordic and Jaensch. *See* **authoritarian personality.**

E. B. Jaensch, a German psychologist and Nazi, published *Der Gegentypus*, which contained the elements of his anti-type propaganda. Jaensch had also done work on **eidetic imagery.**

stimulant (antidepressant) An agent that produces a temporary increase in the functional activity of the **central nervous system**; a **sympathomimetic** cerebral (CNS) stimulant. In varying degrees, stimulants elevate mood, increase alertness, and reduce fatigue. Continued usage or overdosage produces insomnia, nausea, confusion, irritability, delirium, and unpredictable behavior (but often aggression). Psychological dependence is quick to develop. Slang terms: uppers, pep pills. (See **drugs** for names of some of the more popularly used stimulants.)

stimulus Goad. The cause of a **response.** Energy, or change in energy in the environment that is perceived through any **receptor,** internal or external, and which produces a response. Anything to which the organism responds, which may be as specific as the prick of a needle or as general as a seascape.

stimulus generalization The tendency of an organism to make a learned response to or be evoked by stimuli generally similar to the original **conditioned stimulus,** but only after a response has been made contingent upon a stimulus through conditioning. *See* **generalization** (also D. I. Mostofsky, Ed., *Stimulus Generalization* [Stanford, 1965]).

stimulus-response theory (S-R) The analysis of behavior in terms of a **sensory input** to the brain that elicits a **response.** Various **learning** theories (contiguity, for example) are based on this simple principle of association. However, although the S-R theory explains many of the problems of learning, its failure to explain numerous others (such as unrewarded responses) accounts for the insertion of the O (for organism) in the S-R paradigm—thus S-O-R.

Thorndike (1898) is credited with introducing the S-R paradigm (in "Animal Intelligence: An Experimental Study of the Associative Processes in Animals," *Psychological Review Monograph Supplements*, **2**, 1-109). However, the idea had been expressed

in various ways by many earlier philosopher-psychologists. **Pavlov's** studies helped reinforce the concept.

stimulus sampling theory *See* **stochastic learning theory.**

stirrup *See* **stapes.**

stochastic learning (model) theory A probabilistic model that uses chance and random considerations in attempting to predict behavioral irregularities and individual differences. The *stimulus sampling theory* of Estes, as one form of stochastic learning theory, utilizes a combination of mathematical probability and **set** theories. It is too intricate to describe here (See E. L. Walker, 1968, for further explanation and examples, and W. K. Estes in S. Koch, Ed., Vol. II., 1959).

strabismus Squint. A weakness of the eye muscles resulting in inability to focus both eyes on the same object, commonly recognized as cross-eye (in which lines of vision converge) and wall-eye (in which they diverge). *See* **Maddox rod test.**

A striking pictorial example of strabismus is evident in Raphael's portrait of Tommaso Inghirami, exhibited in the Pitti Palace, Florence, Italy. The word was first used in English in 1684.

strategy In **game theory,** a set of directions (pure or mixed) selected for a special course of action.

stratification A method of dividing a **population** into distinctive subpopulations (strata) according to such established **criteria** as educational level, sex, and race, with a selection made from each stratum. Usually, it is done in preparation for collecting a **sample** to insure that subpopulations are represented. This process is called *stratified random sampling*. *See* **cluster sampling.**

stratificational grammar A linguistic, theoretical model designed to explain the processes of acquisition and comprehension of a language, including a conceptual framework explaining the storage of information in cortical neurons and the subsequent outputting of such information to other receptors (including man and other animals) for communication purposes. The structure of language is conceived of as a network and comprising many layers (strata), the language processes involving the passage of impulses. Ramifications of the theory have led into perceptual, motor, and emotional correlates of **cognition.** The hypothesis hopefully bridges the gap between the linguists' knowledge about language and the neurophysiologists' and psychologists' understanding of the brain.

The concept, developed by the American linguist, Sydney Lamb, conceives of language as a mental communication system (not an accumulation of words and not including speech and writing which are merely manifestations of the language system.) To Lamb, "Language is a finite system of the brain that can be used for encoding (speaking or writing) and decoding (understanding) any of a number of texts in that language." Stratification grammar is limited to a consideration of units no larger than a sentence. (Sydney Lamb, *Outline of Stratificational Grammar*).

stratified sampling *See* **stratification.**

Strecker, Adolph (1822-1871) German chemist. About 1854 he showed that lecithin contained choline. He also discovered **alanine** in 1850.

strephosymbolia A disorder (-ia) of twisted (strepho-) symbols (-symbol-), or reversal of phrases, words, or symbols, especially in reading (mirror reversals), attributed to mixed cerebral dominance.

S. Orton, an American physician, introduced the term, describing it in "Specific Reading Disability: Strephosymbolia," *Journal of the American Medical Association*, 1928, **90**, 1095-1099.

stress A **stimulus** (intrinsic or extrinsic) that threatens damage to the organism, causing internal bodily reactions. Stress, in all, consists of the stressful situation, the resulting

S

physiological changes, and subsequent stressful behavior. *See* **general adaptation syndrome.**
Stress concept introduced by **Selye** in 1936.

stress interview A personal **interview** designed to test a person's ability to withstand emotional and intellectual stress, particularly by putting the subject on the defensive in answering embarrassing questions about himself and his attitudes.

stressor That which (-or) produces biological stress. Any such factor (extrinsic or intrinsic), according to **Selye.**

stroboscope Whirling (strobo-) instrument for viewing (-scope). Originally (1832), a toy that produced the **illusion** of motion by running a series of pictures in rapid succession through slits in a whirling disk or cylinder. Hence, any device used to provide intermittent views at short equal intervals. Additionally, a stroboscope can produce the illusion that a cyclically moving object is stationary or is moving in a direction contrary to its real motion. In psychology, stroboscopes are used to study **apparent movement.**
In 1832, a German ophthalmologist S. Stumpfer (1790-1857) modified the **phenakistoscope**, naming it "stroboscope," but it was still a toy.

Strong Vocational Interest Blank (SVIB) An inventory of interests and preferences intended as an aid in predicting chances of success and satisfaction in a variety of occupations. The occupational scales are based on the responses of men and women actually working in the various occupations. It was first published in 1927.
The 1966 revision of the SVIB for Men includes new and updated items, and several new occupational scales. The 1969 revision of the SVIB for Women similarly includes updated items and provides for 58 occupational scales. Range: Mature high school students, college students, and adults.
After Edward K. Strong (1884-1963), American psychologist. Received Ph.D., Stanford. Specialized in studies of vocational interests.

structuralism (structural psychology) Historically, a so-called school of **psychology** emphasizing **introspection** or the analysis of contents of consciousness (**Wundt**) and the structure of consciousness (**Titchener**). Titchener, founder of structuralism, considered sensations, images, and feelings the basic elements for mental states. However, the parts or elements were abstractions produced by analysis, answering the "what" of psychology. To Titchener, these elements were not "prior," and mind could not be explained as the sum of its parts. In general, the structuralists' emphasis was on sensation and **perception.**

structure of intellect theory *See* (2) under **cognitive growth theories.**

structuring Making, directing, or forcing something intangible or diffuse into something more rigid, definite, or structural. For example, in structuring an interview, the interviewer may so word questions (the "loaded" question) that it is possible to give only one answer. An **intelligence test** is considered structured, but a **projective test** is relatively unstructured.

studentized range statistic A **statistic** whose sampling distribution, based on the studentized range, depends upon the range of values and the **degrees of freedom** associated with the estimate of experimental error. *See* Table 18, **Student's** *t.*

Student's *t* A family of test statistics that are given by the ratio of a normally distributed deviation score to an independent estimate of experimental error. *T*-distributions compose an important family of symmetrical distributions which vary slightly from normal distributions, and are used as the basis for performing exact tests of **significance** when working with small samples.

The *t* was developed in 1908 by William Sealy Gosset (1876-1937), a British statistician who published under the name "Student."

Study of Values (Allport-Vernon-Lindzey) A scale for use with college students or adults who have college or equivalent education. It aims to measure six basic interests or **motives** in **personality**, the classification being based directly on ideal types as represented in **Spranger's** *Types of Men*. The *theoretical* man's primary interest is the discovery of truth; the *economic* man's interest centers about usefulness; the *aesthetic* man "sees his highest value in form and harmony;" the *social* man loves people; the *political* man seeks power; and the *religious* man "searches for mystical unity." (E. Spranger, Types of Men. Translated from 5th German edition of *Lebensformen* by Paul J. S. Pigors [Halle: Max Niemeyer Verlag; American Agent, Stechert-Hafner, Inc., 31 East Tenth Street, New York 10003]; G. W. Allport, P. E. Vernon and G. Lindzey, *A Study of Values*, 3rd edition [Boston: Houghton Mifflin, 1960]).

stuttering Same as stammering, both terms now commonly used for the same speech difficulty.

style of life *See* life style.

stylus maze A maze in which the path is a slot to be followed by the subject, using a pencil-like instrument (stylus).

subception (subliminal perception). The act or process (-ion) of responding to or perceiving (-cept-) an environmental cue that is below (sub-) the threshold for conscious detection.
In 1951, American psychologists Richard S. Lazarus (born 1922) and Robert A. McCleary (born 1923) introduced the term as a subliminal perceptive process.

subconscious Under (sub-) aware (-conscious). Partly or imperfectly conscious. A group of mental processes below the threshold of objective consciousness and beyond one's awareness; activities that are outside the field of **introspection** at the moment. Unconscious is the term more generally used.
The word was introduced into English in 1632, and **Lotze** used the term freely, beginning about 1852, in his discussions about unconscious and subconscious minds.

subitizing The process (-ing) of treating (-iz-) an instrument so that things can be seen quickly or suddenly (subit-); the quick perception of small numbers exposed briefly by a **tachistoscopic** technique (E. L. Kaufman, M. W. Lord, T. W. Reese, and J. Volkmann, "The Discrimination of Visual Numbers," *American Journal of Psychology*, 1949, 62, 498-525).
Term introduced in 1949. *See* Kaufman, et al, above.

subject-object dichotomy (Exist.) The split of the total Being into two parts; the cutting (-tomy) of man's Being into two (dicho-), the *subject* (man or person) and *object* (thing or environment). Existentially, man can never be separated from the object that he observes; the subject and object must be unified. Sören Kierkegaard, the Danish philosopher, stated that **existentialism** is the "endeavor to understand man by cutting below the cleavage between subject and object which has bedeviled Western thought and science since shortly after the Renaissance." The only solution then is to eliminate the dichotomy and consider the subject (man) and the object (that which man observes) as a relationship.
Karl Jaspers states: "Subject and object belong to each other; the one cannot exist without the other."

subject-oriented counseling An approach to counseling in which the counselor allows and stimulates the client to move toward self-understanding without direct intervention from the counselor. One of the major aims of such counseling is to assist the client in clarifying his self-concept through insight, self-understanding, and self-evaluation with subsequent self-reorganization. *See* **client-centered counseling.**

sublimation Act of (-ation) making sublime. According to **Freudian** theory (1900), an unconscious **ego** process by which **libido** is desexualized and channeled into other activities (partly responsible for a career choice as in the fields of art, medicine, or politics). A **psychoanalytic defense mechanism** that diverts unacceptable impulses or motives into higher (more sublime), more socially acceptable forms (1916), as when a person with hostile urges rechannels his aggressions into writing stories about criminals or other violence. An indirect substitute expression of a strong, unsatisfiable need.

subliminal perception *Same as* subception.

subliminal processes Relating to (-al) those processes occurring below (sub-) the perceptual threshold (-limin-), or one that is too weak to be identified clearly.

subliminal stimulus Pertaining to (-al) a stimulus of lower (sub-) intensity than required by the established threshold (-limin-), or to a stimulus so faint or brief that an observer is not aware of it. Energy or change in energy insufficient to fire a nerve impulse in a **receptor.**

subroutine (Comput.) A related set of logic and/or program central operations with definable limits. A separate block or section of a program usually written in machine code to direct the **computer** to perform a specific task or operation.

substantia nigra Black substance (Soemmering's ganglion). Markedly pigmented nerve cells in the gray matter of the **corpus striatum.** Polymerization of **dopa** or **dopamine** causes accumulation of this melanin-like substance. In cases of **Parkinsonism**, lack of dopamine in the corpus striatum and pale substantia nigra are possible indications that these nerve cells have been unable to metabolize catechol amines.
In 1798, **Soemmering** described and gave specific location of the substantia nigra. Jules Bernard Luys (1828-1897), French neurologist, whose studies on the nervous system in 1865 sparked further studies on thalamic function, postulated the idea that the substantia nigra was involved in body movement. Marinesco and Blocq, in 1893, by their discovery of a lesion in the substantia nigra of a Parkinsonism patient, set the foundation for Brissaud's theory (1895-1899) of nigral origin of this condition and for **Alzheimer's** conclusive description of the disease's pathology.

subvocal speech Below (sub-) voiced (-voc-) speech. Slight movements of the tongue and larynx that do not produce sound. Said by J. B. Watson (1913) to be the vehicle of thought.

successive approximation *See* **shaping of behavior.**

successive contrast *See* **contrast.**

sufficient estimator (best estimator) A **statistic** whose data are so complete (concerning a parameter) that it cannot be improved upon; for example, the sample mean is a best estimator of the population when its distribution is normal.

suggestion A socialization process, by which one person influences another. Communication that is accepted uncritically. Sometimes used in psychotherapy; largely used in advertising, propaganda and **hypnosis.** A suggestion that is made during hypnosis so as to be effective upon awakening is called a *posthypnotic suggestion.*

sulcus Furrow. A **fissure** or surface fold in the cerebral **cortex** separating adjacent **convolutions.**

Sullivan, Harry Stack (1892-1949) American psychiatrist. M.D., Chicago College of Medicine and Surgery 1917. Originally Freudian-oriented, but he developed an offshoot called the **interpersonal theory** of psychiatry, emphasizing the impact of society and culture upon the formation of man's personality and the interrelationships between personalities (Maddi, pp. 44-54; Bischof, pp. 267-307).

summated rating scale A method, devised by **Rensis Likert**, of constructing attitude scales. Subjects are asked to indicate on a five-step scale their degrees of agreement-disagreement on a number of items. *See* **Likert Summated Scale; rating scale.**

summation The process of adding together or combining. The Greek capital letter Σ (sigma) is used to denote the operation of summation. The **variable** being summed is placed after the summation sign Σ. The range of summation is indicated by adding a subscript to the variable, placing the number of the first variable to be summed under the summation sign and the last number to be summed over it. For example,

$$\sum_{i=1}^{7} Xi$$

means that the variable X is summed from its first value to its seventh value, inclusive (Walker and Lev, 1953, chapter 16).

In concept formation, summation is the use of an inductive approach in concept attainment. In physiology, it refers to the fusion phenomenon whereby two or more impulses, arriving within a short interval, will succeed in bridging a synapse to produce a reflex response when one impulse will not. Pharmacologically, the combined effects ot two or more drugs when they are equal to the sum of their individual effects. *See* **drug interactions, temporal summation.**

superego Above (super-) the ego or self. Analogous to conscience. In **Freud's** tripartite personality system (**id, ego,** and **superego**), the superego is that part of the ego emerging when the **Oedipus complex** is resolved, resulting in self-criticism and moral control (1923). However, other psychoanalysts claim that the emergence of the superego predates the Oedipal stage. Also, the dimension of **personality** that develops by internalizing parental authority and remains largely unconscious. It helps perpetuate moral and ethical standards by monitoring the ego, and in neurotic persons it may be very uncompromising and punishing. It is in constant conflict with the id, imposing restrictions upon its instinctual demands. (S. Freud, *The Ego and the Id*, 1923, Hogarth, 1957).

superior Upper or superior part of the human body; toward the head end of the body in man (e.g., the elbow is part of the superior extremity).

superior colliculus Prominence or little (-ulus) hill (collic-) toward the head end or anterior (superior) portion; any of the four prominences constituting the **corpora quadrigemina;** the **superior colliculus** is either of the two anterior prominences, which are concerned with primitive visual functions. *See* **optic tract.**

superior olive A small olive-shaped gray nucleus enclosing a white central core, and consisting of cells in the auditory pathways. Incoming auditory nerve fibers, after synapsing in the cochlear nuclei, are relayed directly or indirectly (through the superior olive) to form the lateral lemniscus, inhibitory neuronal interaction resulting in stimulation of both ears. *See* **lemniscus.**

suprarenal glands Glands above (supra-) the kidneys (ren-). *See* **adrenal glands.**

SVIB Strong Vocational Interest Blank.

Sydenham's chorea *See* **chorea.**

Sylvius, fissure of *See* **fissure.**

symbol Throw (-bol) together (sym-); token, sign. Something that stands for or represents another thing; a written or printed mark, letter or number, standing for an object; in **psychology**, an object, expression, or action that often is substituted for the thing itself. Words are symbols, standing for objects as well as ideas; gestures may also be symbols, as in waving goodbye. Especially in **psychoanalysis**, the concept of symbolism applies when an otherwise neutral person or object comes to have stimulus value or is the focus of repressed emotional reactions. Thus, a person may fear and hate his authoritarian employer who has become a symbol of a feared and hated father.

symbolic display *See* **display.**

symbolic logic (mathematical logic) The discipline of applying symbols to formal logic, thereby establishing an artificial language or symbolic calculus so precise as to avoid the ambiguities and logical inadequacies of ordinary languages.

symbolic mode A stage of development in **Bruner's cognitive** and linguistic system in which the child is able to combine and formulate words or concepts spontaneously by "sensing" their meanings through usage, although he has been previously unaware of them. Approximately at the end of the average child's second year, this striking change takes place in his sophisticated use of grammar and sentence structure.

symmetrical distribution A frequency distribution in which the cases fall equally in the **class intervals** on either side of the middle; hence, the **mean, median,** and **mode** have the same value. *Contrast with* **skewed distribution.**

sympathetic (thoracolumbar) division The division of the **autonomic nervous system** in which the first order **neurons** lie in the gray matter of the spinal cord in the thoracic and lumbar regions, their axons passing through the anterior roots and white rami of thoracic and lumbar spinal nerves to vertebral **ganglia**, where they **synapse** with second-order neurons. It acts in reciprocal coordination with the **parasympathetic** division, that is, nerve impulses carried by the fibers of one division are antagonistic to those of the other. For example, the heart beat is slowed down by the action of the parasympathetic whereas it is speeded up by the functioning of the sympathetic. Although, in general, the visceral effector organs are innervated by efferent fibers from both divisions, a few organs (sweat glands, erector muscles of hair follicles, and digestive tract blood vessels) receive fibers only from the sympathetic division. Sympathetic activity, usually in preparation to meet crises, sends blood to the brain, widens the pupils, speeds the heart beat, stimulates adrenal action so that blood-sugar level and tissue metabolism are increased.

In 1905, English physiologist John Newport Langley (1852-1925) introduced this term for the thoracolumbar portion of the autonomic nervous system.

sympathomimetic drug Relating to (-ic) a drug (such as **metamphetamine**) that simulates or mimics (-mimet-) in its action the effects of the sympathetic nervous system.

Synanon A group of anonymous people working together (syn-). A narcotic treatment center, originating (1958) in Santa Monica, California, based on a strong patriarchal system in which the father figure "dominates" his "family" of drug addicts with justice and a firm, loving concern for each one. Ex-addicts serve as therapists for addicts in trying to help them abstain from drug usage. Group therapy here, as well as at Daytop Village—a similarly designed organization—is referred to as "game." *See* **intensive group experience** (also D. Casriel, *So Fair a House: The Story of Synanon* [Prentice-Hall, 1963]).

synapse Binding (-apse) together (syn-). The functional area of contact between one neuron and another. nerve impulses passing in one direction through the dendrites of a neuron to its cell body and out through its axon to make connections with dendrites or cell bodies of other neuron(s). Synapses are characterized by a state of polarization, resistance to the passage of an impulse, and susceptibility to fatigue.

There is no cellular continuity at the synapse. Impulses can travel in only one direction. Synapses are denoted anatomically to be either *central* (brain and spinal cord) or *peripheral* (autonomic and sensory ganglia, for example). Physiologically, most synapses and all neuromuscular junctions are excitatory in action and transmit chemically (by **acetylcholine**, for example) in only one direction, while a few transmit electrically, usually in both directions.

Presynaptic signals are those that approach a synapse whereas *postsynaptic* refers to those signals leaving a synapse.

The term was introduced in 1897 by Sherrington and his English collaborator physiologist Michael Foster (1836-1907) upon the suggestion of Verral, a Greek scholar. In 1906, Sherrington described the synapse as the physiological (functional) relation or "electrical field" permitting the nerve impulse to pass from the axon of one cell to the dendrite of another.

synaptic cleft The space (approximately a millionth of an inch) between the **synaptic knob** and the **dendrite** and **cell body.**

synaptic knob (also end feet or end button) Rounded eminence, at the end of each branch of a neuronal end brush, that contacts either a **dendrite** or a **cell body** of another **neuron**, the contact point constituting a **synapse.** Each synaptic knob encloses numerous **mitochondria** and neurovesicles, closely packed together.

synaptic transmission The phenomenon by which a **nerve impulse** passes across the **synapse.** Up to about 1950, the means of transmission appeared to be primarily electrical in nature. The prevailing point of view now favors the chemical theory. This assumes that when the axon **spike potential** reaches presynaptic terminals (or the axon's **synaptic knobs**), some chemical transmitter substance (possibly **acetylcholine** and/or **norepinephrine**) is released into the **synaptic cleft**, making it possible for the **action potential** to regenerate itself as it comes in contact with the membrane of the postsynaptic neuron. Here the chemical transmitter substance serves as a threshold stimulus, lowering that neuron's membrane potential and thereby triggering impulse conduction by the postsynaptic neuron.

The three best known transmitter substances are **acetylcholine, epinephrine,** and **norepinephrine**, but others well identified are **gamma amino-butyric acid** (GABA), **glutamic acid,** and glycine. *See* **nerve fiber.**

Sir John Eccles, Australian contemporary neurophysiologist born in 1903, shared the Nobel Prize in 1963 for his contribution demonstrating the chemical basis for synaptic transmission (John Eccles "The Synapse," *Scientific American*, January, 1965, 112).

synaptosome (Nerve ending) Synapse (synapto-) body (-some); **axon** terminal knob (about 3 microns in diameter) filled with densely packed spherical vesicles (about 5 angstroms in diameter) purportedly carrying the neurotransmitter substance.

syndrome Running (-drome) together (syn-). The combination of several symptoms in a disease or other reaction. Traits organized into clusters; pattern of characteristics defining a personality disorder or mental disease. *See* **general adaptation syndrome.**

An ancient term, probably originating with the Empiric School of physicians (about 1st century, B.C.). It entered English in 1541 through the translation of **Galen** by the English printer and translator, Robert Copland (fl. 1508-1547).

synergy Working (-ergy) together (syn-). In social psychology, the collective energy available for use by the group as an organized system. Energy expended in group performance is divided into *maintenance synergy*, energy used to maintain the group's functioning and to keep individuals in the group, and

S

task synergy, energy expended to achieve group goals. (R. B. Cattell, "New Concepts for Measuring Leadership in Terms of Group Syntality," *Human Relations*, 1951, 4, 161-184).

synesthesia Feeling (-esthesia) with (syn-). A **sensory** phenomenon of secondary **perception** accompanying an actual perception, or the experience of perceiving the stimulation of one sensory organ modality in place of another (for example, colored hearing, in which a tone arouses an image of a color).

Condition first described by **Sir Francis Galton**, 1869, and term first used by **Fechner** in 1876.

synidetics The study (-etics) of conscious experience (synid-) relating to "awareness of events that are simultaneously (in the ongoing present) observable within the organism and the environment," its purpose being to "determine the physiological and psychological factors that affect and are affected by awareness."

The term was suggested by American psychologist Frank B. Jones.

synomorph Patterned or shaped (-morph) alike (syno-); independent. *See* **behavior setting.**

synophrys The growing together (syn-) of the eyebrows (-ophrys); confluent eyebrows. *See* **de Lange syndrome.**

syntactical aphasia *See* **speech aphasia.**

syntactics *See* **measurement.**

syntality The capacity (-tality) to function together (syn-). **R. B. Cattell** describes syntality as "the relevant characteristics of an entire group which leads to consistent behavior by that group, thereby leading to possible prediction of group performance." *See* **synergy** for reference.

syntaxic thinking Relating to (-ic) arranging (tax-) or putting things together (syn-), especially in the highest form of thinking as conceived by **H. S. Sullivan.** It refers to the use of publicly accepted and verifiable symbols, which makes it possible for man to carry on interpersonal relationships and communications. *See* **prototaxic experience, parataxic thinking.**

systematic behavior theory *See* **Hull's behavior system.**

systematic desensitization Gradual and planned exposure of an experimental subject or a client to previously tension-producing and feared situations while he is relaxed. *See* **behavior modification.**

systematic experimental introspection *See* **Ach, Titchener.**

Systéme International d' Unités The standard international system of measurement units, being an extension and refinement of the metric system. *See* **International System of Units.**

T

tab A nonprinting, spacing action on typewriters and tape-preparation devices, used to express a code necessary to the **tab sequential format.**

tab character *See* **tab sequential format.**

tabes dorsalis Locomotor ataxia. A wasting (tabes) disease originating in the dorsal region of the spinal column, involving destruction of the nerve pathways for **kinethesis**, serious impairment of control of muscular movements, and disorders of sensation, nutrition, and vision. Caused by syphilitic infection of the spinal cord (posterior columns) and sensory nerve trunks. *See* **Charcot.**

Hippocrates had used term *tekedon* (from *tekein*) for a general decline or wasting away, but the disease itself was first described in 1749 by Johann Gottfried Brendel. **Robert Remak,** German neurologist, changed name of locomotor ataxia to tabes dorsalis in 1836 because he thought it more appropriate to describe the wasting away

of the spinal cord's dorsal column. In 1858 and 1859, the most thorough description of tabes dorsalis up to that time was recorded by French neurologist Guillaume Benjamin Armand Duchenne de Boulogne (1806-1875). In 1876, Jean Alfred Fournier (1832-1914), French syphilologist reported that syphilis was the cause of tabes dorsalis.

tab sequential format (Comput.) The means for identifying a word by the number of **tab** characters in the block preceding the word. The first character in each word is a *tab character*. Words must be presented in a specific order but all characters in a word except the tab character may be omitted when the command represented by that word is not desired.

tabula rasa An erased (rasa) tablet. Clear or clean slate. **Locke's** image of the mind at birth, a blank tablet on which anything can be indelibilized (written) by learning and experience. *See* **Aristotle, association psychology.**

tachistoscope Rapid (tachisto-) viewing instrument (-scope). An electronic or manually operated apparatus that projects brief (usually 0.1 to 0.01 second) single-glance visual stimuli of images, objects, letters, or words. The exposure, controlled by the experimenter, is regulated by a time shutter, a falling screen, or some device to interrupt the viewing for a specified time. Used in learning, attention, and perception studies.

German physiologist A. W. Volkmann (1801-1877) used the word for the first time in 1850.

T'ai Chi Ch'uan A form of Ch'uan (indicative of one's power to control thoughts and actions) in which specific mind-exercises are used to implement and complement the body's activities.

T'ai Chi represents the continual interaction of two dynamic forces—the Yin (passive, female, and quietude) and the Yang (active and male). T'ai Chi begot Yin and Yang and everything else in the cosmos. Ch'uan symbolizes the integration of the mind and body—a sound mind in a sound body. A healthy mind, as the directive force, helps create a healthy body which recycles itself. *See* **dualism.**

tails of a distribution The upper and lower extremes of a sampling distribution that together or separately constitute the **region of rejection.** *One-tailed tests*, which are more powerful than two-tailed (both ends) tests, are used when the **alternative hypothesis** is directional, that is, when it states that a **population** mean is greater than or equal to, or that it is less than or equal to, another population **mean.** A *two-tailed test* is used when the alternative hypothesis states that two population means are equal.

In a two-tailed test the left tail indicates minus values; the right tail is positive or plus.

Rejection of a **null hypothesis** in either the one-tailed or two-tailed test must be described in terms of either the 1 or 5 percent level.

Two-tailed tests at .05 level (2.5% + 2.5%)

Left tail — 2.5%   Right tail — 2.5%

-1.96 $+1.96$

$H_0: m_1 = m_2$

One-tailed test at .05 level (directional)

5%

$H_1: m_1 \geq m_2$

talent *See* **ability.**

tambo(u)r A drumlike (tambour) recording device, consisting of a vessel or chamber closed at one end by a stretched elasticized membrane. Variations in pressure or other changes are transmitted by the diaphragm to a marking lever resting upon it.

tandem schedule (Tand) A single **reinforcement,** in a reinforcement schedule, that is programmed by two or more successive schedules.

tape feed (Comput.) A mechanism that feeds tape to be read or used by the machine.

taraxein A non-base compound (-ein) presumably a protein extract distilled from the blood serum of schizophrenic persons that when introduced into normal persons reportedly makes some so disturbed and confused (tarax-) that their extreme behavior (depersonalization, thought fragmentation, **autism,** apprehension, fear, and reduced attention span) approximates transitory schizophrenic reactions; supposedly acts upon a specific enzyme.

Term coined in the article by R. G. Heath, S. Martens, B. E. Leach, M. Cohen, and C. Angel, "Effect on Behavior in Humans with the Administration of Taraxein," *American Journal of Psychiatry*, 1957, 114, 14-24.

task synergy *See* **synergy.**

T(ar)chanoff phenomenon *Same as* **psychogalvanic reflex.**

TAT Thematic Apperception Test.

tau *See* **Kendall's rank correlation coefficient.**

tau effect Phenomenon by which timing of stimulation of sensory organs (skin surfaces, eyes, or ears) influences **perception** of the actual space involved. For instance, if the time between the first and second **stimulus** is shorter than that between the second and third, the first two stimuli are perceived as being closer together spatially. Such phenomena exist even when subject knows that stimuli are equally distant.

taxis Arrangement, order. Reflex movement in relatively simple organisms that respond positively or negatively to a **stimulus.** A taxis is set in motion for a specific action and ceases when its function is fulfilled, in that sense being more efficient than kinetic ones. A taxis is evident in the egg-retrieving behavior of the greylag goose. In trying to return an errant egg to its nest, the goose resorts to two movements: one that rolls the egg and the other that keeps the egg on course by a side-to-side tapping. The tapping movement is a taxis and ceases when the egg stops rolling. *See* **tropism.**

Tay-Sachs disease (amaurotic family idiocy) A rare genetic (single recessive anomaly) mental impairment in the infant, sometimes characteristic of destitute families in which several children of the same family may be afflicted. There is degeneration of cerebral neurons resulting in blindness (occurring after the characteristic "cherry-red spot" appears in the **macular** area of the retina), paralysis, deafness, and wasting away, with death commonly occurring before age of 4.

In such conditions, the human system has failed to produce an enzyme necessary for lipid **metabolism,** resulting in excess fats accumulating in brain cells and retarding normal development. The missing enzyme is HEX-A, one of two enzymes (the other, HEX-B) of hexosaminidase, which prevents metabolism of fats in brain cells. The HEX-A discovery makes possible identification of both carriers and victims of Tay-Sach's disease.

The reference to "family" in the syndrome is traceable back 500 years to the finding that such a condition seemed to run in the Ashkenazic Jewish families of Lithuania and Poland, and that this tendency occurred because the Jews were a close-knit, inbred group. Even today, in the United States, Tay-Sach's disease occurs once in every 5000

Jewish births, but only once in every 400,000 non-Jewish. If both parents carry a Tay-Sach's gene, a 1 in 4 risk exists for the children to have the disease.

Named after Warren Tay, English physician who first described the condition in 1881 (referring mainly to the eye defects), and Bernard Sachs, New York neurologist who, in 1887, extended Tay's description to include brain changes.

Tcharnoff phenomenon See **psychogalvanic reflex**.

t-distributions An important family of symmetrical distributions, which vary slightly from the normal distributions and are used as the basis for exact tests of **significance** when working with small samples. See **Student's t**.

tectorial membrane Of the nature of (-al) a covering (tectori-), a gelatinous adherent membrane in which hair cell endings of the **organ of Corti** in the cochlear duct of the **inner ear** are imbedded, by which sound is directly perceived.

tectum of the midbrain The dorsal stratified portion of the **mesencephalon** located at the *roof* (tectum) of the **brainstem** and traversed by a longitudinal and a transverse groove, which splits into two superior and two inferior colliculi, the four collectively known as the **corpora quadrigemina**.

tegmentum of the midbrain The dorsal portion of each of the cerebral peduncles, consisting of white matter (longitudinal and transverse fibers) and grey matter (nuclei and fiber tracts). The **red nucleus** is one of the nuclei in the grey matter, as are the motor nuclei of the **oculomotor** and **trochlear cranial nerves**.

telekinesis Motion (-kinesis) produced from afar (tele-). See **extrasensory perception, psi phenomenon**.

telencephalon The end (tel-) brain (-encephalon). The anterior subdivision of the **prosencephalon** comprising mainly the **cerebral hemispheres**, the two **olfactory** bulbs and tracts, and the **corpus callosum**. The medial portion of the cerebral hemispheres whose many structures are interconnected by fiber systems are collectively called the **limbic system**. (Butter, pp. 34-37, Morgan pp. 42-53).

teleology Study (-ology) of ends (tele-). The doctrine that nature shows knowledge of the end; purposefulness. A belief that everything has a definite purpose; also that adaptation and evolutionary processes are determined by their results (that birds, for instance, developed wings so they could fly). **Adler** used the term in reference to a final goal of mankind, the "ultimate, future life" for which present acts are the preparation.

telepathy Conveying feeling (-pathy) from afar or at a distance (tele-). See **extrasensory perception, psi phenomenon**.

telephone theory of hearing A frequency theory of hearing indicating that the perception of pitch depends upon the **basilar membrane** (acting like a telephone transmitter) to relay impulses of various frequencies to the **brain**. Such a theory cannot account for frequencies greater than 1000 cycles per second. See **Rutherford** under **hearing theories**.

telestereoscope (teleostereoscope) A binocular stereoscope for viewing distant (tele-) objects, useful for studying convergence and disparity in depth perception. It has a series of mirrors so placed that distant objects or pictures appear to be closer to the viewer than they actually are (as a result of exaggerated relief), thereby effectively increasing the viewing distance of the eyes. See **binocular disparity**. Described by **Helmholtz** in 1857.

teletactor That which (-or) teaches speech from afar (tele-) by touch (-tact-). An instrument used to convey and teach speech sounds to the deaf by transmitting amplified sound waves to the skin.

telophase The end or final (telo-) phase of **mitosis**, in which new nuclei are formed.

temperament A term surviving from the abandoned **humoral doctrine**, referring to the condition (-ment) resulting from the mixing (tempera-) of the humors to establish the individual's characteristic mode of behavior. The natural disposition, physical constitution, or habit of mind. A person's general, apparently innate, characteristic way of responding, or of experiencing mood changes. Temperament is frequently studied in connection with body build and temperament surveys and analyses. See **somatotype theory**.

temperature See **Kelvin**.

template RNA Same as **ribosomal RNA**.

temporal Pertaining to (-al) the temples (tempor-) or sides of forehead. See **anatomical directions**.

temporal induction See **contrast**.

temporal lobe The lobe of the **brain** beneath the temples (tempora). A sensory area located at the sides of the **cerebral cortex** below the **fissure of Sylvius** (lateral fissure) and in front of the **occipital lobe**. The lobe contains auditory projection areas and centers for speech perception and related functions.

temporal maze Any maze whose solution is dependent upon or related to (-al) a time (tempor-) factor; a maze requiring the subject to pass repeatedly through the same passages in order to learn a temporal sequence; a learning pattern in which different responses must be made successively to the same cues.

temporal summation The cumulative effect of repeated subthreshold stimuli reaching a neuron in a relatively short period of time (temporal). Successive stimulation may elicit a response by summation when single or widely spaced weak stimuli are incapable of doing so.

Terman, Lewis Madison (1877-1956) American (Indiana) psychologist. Ph.D., Clark 1905. Research interests: studies of individual differences, gifted children, and factors responsible for successful marriages. Adopted and adapted the Binet-Simon test for use in United States (the **Stanford-Binet** tests). In 1957 he was voted to receive the APF **Gold Medal Award**, although it is not conferred posthumously (Vinacke, p. 651).

Terry's syndrome See **retrolental fibroplasia**.

test battery The administering of several **individual tests** to one person for purposes of appraising individual differences for therapeutic purposes or of obtaining a conclusive psychological **profile** of a person for school or vocational guidance. For example, the **Rorschach**, the Strong Interest Inventory, the MMPI, and the WAIS may be given to one person, or other tests may be grouped for different purposes. Some tests (**Wechsler** tests) have built-in subtests, all of which may reveal a composite score or a total profile for helping determine a person's weaknesses or strengths.

testing method See **methods of psychology: clinical**.

testosterone A testicular (testo-) sterone or steroid hormone of the **adrenal cortex**, important in determining male physiology. See **androsterone**.

In 1934-35, testosterone was isolated by Dutch chemist Ernst Laquer (1880-1947). Later in 1935, it was first synthesized by German biochemist Adolf Friedrich Johann Butenandt (born 1903).

test profile Same as **psychograph**.

test-retest reliability See **reliability**.

tests and inventories Relatively few tests (individual or group) and personality inventories or interest surveys are mentioned in this glossary, since their number is vast and any adequate description of them would have to be extensive. See texts by both Anastasi and Cronbach, listed in the references section, for fairly complete treatments of scales and tests.

test statistic A **statistic** designed to provide a test of a statistical **hypothesis**. Test statistics (such as z- and t-ratios, with known sampling distributions) are not used for estimating

population parameters. However, as a probability statement they enable an experimenter to decide whether or not to reject a **null hypothesis**.

tetrachoric correlation A means of association that is appropriate when both the dichotomized variables in a fourfold table are actually continuous and normally distributed. The tetrachoric r provides an estimate of the **parameter** ρ and its interpretation is identical to that of Pearson's r. See **fourfold coefficient** (also Table 14; also the article by Karl Pearson, "On the Correlation of Characters not Quantitatively Measureable," *Philosophical Transactions*, Series A, 1901, 195, 1-47).

tetrad difference method A difference method for determining whether the correlations among four (tetra-) tests in a numerical group (-ad) can be accounted for by a single factor. Introduced into psychology by **Spearman**. See **factor analysis**.

tetrahydrocannabinol See **marijuana**.

T group See **training group**.

thalamus Inner chamber (thalamus) in the **brain**. A walnut-sized, ovoid structure at the base of the **cerebrum** (almost in the center of the brain) containing the endings of all sensory nerves (except those of olfaction), where synapses are made with other nerve fibers to carry the **sensory** impulses to cerebral centers; a relay center between spinal cord, **brainstem**, and **cerebral cortex**. The thalamus is responsible for pain sensations and some other less pronounced, more diffuse feelings. It also figures in theories of emotion, as in the **Cannon-Bard theory**.

Thalamus was called "glutae" (buttocks) by **Galen**, and **Berengarius** still referred to the thalami as buttocks (c. 1525), describing them as walls of the lateral ventricles. See **brain ventricles**.

thalectomy Cutting (-tomy) out (-ec−) of the thalamus (thal-). See **lobotomy**.

THC See **marijuana**.

Thematic Apperception Test (TAT) A semiprojective test developed by **Murray** in 1943, consisting of a set of 31 somewhat ambiguous black and white picture cards providing two series of ten each for boys, girls, men, and women, to which the subject responds by creating a story. The story themes are considered as expressions of deeply hidden **personality** needs and reveal to the trained interpreter some of the dominant drives, emotions and personality conflicts on a somewhat more conscious level than that evoked by the **Rorschach**. Scoring is complicated. See **projective technique**.

therapeutic community A social group whose members reside in a specific locale (such as a hospital) where the prevailing attitude is one of considering the total milieu in and about the hospital as a therapeutic unit, including not only the patient's direct treatment by a therapist but all other possibly related factors, both of space and time.

In 1946, T. F. Maine of Birmingham, England organized a mental hospital that he called "therapeutic community." The idea became world renowned through Maxwell Jones of the Dingleton Hospital, Melrose, Scotland through his writings. See **milieu therapy**.

theriomorphism (zoomorphism) A primitive belief (-ism) attributing alleged mental processes or characteristics of a lower animal or wild beast (therio-) to a human being; having the form (morph-) of beasts; the ascription of animal characteristics to man. Contrast with **anthropomorphism** which describes all behavior in terms of animal behavior.

thermesthesiometer A meter sensitive (-esthesio-) to heat (therm-) variation. A temperature-controlling instrument that can be regulated to provide continuous warm or cold stimuli (such as in tactile or skin experiments).

thermistor That which (-or) is sensitive to heat (thermist-). A **transducer** that translates temperature into an electrical resistance in a

t

predictable manner. Semiconductor material is often used for thermistors because its high temperature coefficient causes a large (and hence easily measured) resistance change with small changes in temperature.

thermostatic theory A proposal relating to (-ic) the stabilizing (-stat-) of heat (thermo-); a **contralist position**, in which the **brain** is considered to monitor the homeostatic balancing of the body with particular regard to body heat—an animal eats to keep warm and stops eating when too hot. *Compare* **glucostatic theory**. (J. R. Brobeck, "Food Intake as a Mechanism of Temperature Regulation." *Yale Journal of Biological Medicine*, 1947-48, 20, 545-552).

thèse d'agrégation Fellowship thesis, a necessary and all-inclusive dissertation indicative of the assistant professor's progress at a French university. If satisfactory, and after having passed his qualifying examinations he is eligible for promotion to **professeur agrégé** (associate professor). *See* **French higher education.**

theta effect Illusion of movement.

theta (rhythm) wave An electroencephalographic rhythm with a frequency of about 4-7 hertzes with greater voltage than the **alpha rhythm**. *See* **paradoxical sleep.**

thiopental A barbituric compound containing sulphur (thio-), an aldehyde (-al) and a pentyl (-pent-) group (C_5H_{11}), used mainly as an anesthetic.

third moment *See* **moments.**

third ventricle *See* **brain ventricles.**

thoracicolumbar, thoracolumbar *See* **sympathetic nervous system.**

Thorndike, Edward Lee (1874-1959). American psychologist and educator. Ph.D. Columbia 1898. His thesis, "Animal Intelligence: An Experimental Study of the Associative Processes in Animals," 1898, initiated the laboratory approach into animal psychology. Pioneered in the use of **problem boxes, mazes,** and other laboratory equipment to study learning in chicks, cats, and dogs, including the famous puzzle-boxes for cats. APA president 1912 (Boring, pp. 561-564, 580; Vinacke, p. 516).

Thorndike's laws of learning Learning laws, namely: the **law of exercise,** the **law of effect,** and the **law of readiness,** developed by **Thorndike** (1913).

threshold (limen) The point at which a **stimulus** becomes perceptible or at which it disappears; the minimal degree of change in stimulation to which a sensory **receptor** will respond. Usually stated as a **detection threshold.** In hearing, threshold relates to the "loudness level" at which a person can hear 50 percent of the sounds he is exposed to experimentally.

Thurstone, Louis Leon (1887-1955) American (Illinois) psychologist. Received Ph.D., Chicago 1917. Authority on mental measurements, **attitude scales,** and statistics. Played important role in the development of **factor analysis** as used in psychology. Introduced multiple factor analysis in 1931 (*American Psychologist*, November, 1968, pp. 786-802; Vinacke, p. 67).

Thurstone scales **Thurstone** did considerable research on mental measurements and attitude scaling. One of his techniques, called *law of comparative judgment*, provides a means of judging quantitative and qualitative attributes.

His differential scale assumes the use of the method of equal-appearing intervals. Thurstone conceived of the opinions to be judged as being on a continuum from a very favorable to a very unfavorable rating, which forms a rough scale in itself. He also used subjective judgments (as judged by typical people) to help define subjective statements, attitudes, or opinions. *See* **scaling technique.** (L. L. Thurstone, *The Measurement of Values* [University of Chicago Press, 1959]).

thymine A white crystalline basic chemical substance (-ine) derived from thymus (thym-) **deoxyribonucleic acid.** *See* **genetic code.**

Discovery of thymine reported in 1900 by **Kossel** and colleagues.

thymus A wart (thymos); warty growth, a glandular body. An **endocrine gland** in the lower part of the neck, most active in early life, that normally atrophies by the onset of puberty. Supposedly inhibits premature sexual maturation and plays a part in building up immunity to disease.

The term is derived from thyme, which was considered in early Greece as a sacrificial offering. Galen used the word signifying a warty growth resembling a bunch of thyme.

In 1522, **Berengaro da Carpi** was first to describe the thymus gland accurately. German physician Johann Kopp was first (1808) to discover an enlarged thymus and first (1830) to describe thymus death, but it was named status lymphaticus and clinically described by English clinician Richard Bright (1789-1858), and more fully in 1889 by Viennese physician Arnold Paltauf (1860-1893).

thyroid gland The shield- (thyr-) like (-oid), two-lobed **endocrine gland** located in the neck, essential to **metabolism,** involved in regulation of tissue growth, heart action, carbohydrate utilization, and protein synthesis. It is stimulated by the **thyrotrophic hormone,** which regulates its activity. The thyroid gland produces two hormones, the principal one being **thyroxin(e),** which governs the body's metabolic rate. If thyroxin(e) is overproduced, **homeostasis** is maintained by a decrease in production of the pituitary's thyrotrophic hormone. Congenital lack of thyroid function (**hypothyroidism**) causes **cretinism**; hypothyroidism in later life leads to a similar condition called **myxedema.**

The gland was first accurately described by **Vesalius,** and given its name in 1646 by the English physician Thomas Wharton (1614-1673). In 1896, the German chemist Eugen Baumann (1846-1896) discovered iodine in the gland.

thyrotrophic hormone (TTH) Relating to (-ic) the hormone of the **adenohypophysis** that nourishes (-trophi-) and stimulates the **thyroid gland** to secrete **thyroxin**; thyroid nourishing hormone. *See* **neurosecretion.**

thyroxin(e) A compound (-ine) or hormone of the **thyroid gland.**

Thyroxine, an iodine-containing amino acid resembling a hormone, was isolated from the thyroid gland and named thyroxine in 1915 by **E. C. Kendall,** American physiologist. In 1926, its molecular structure was described by English biochemist Charles Robert Harington (born 1897).

timbre Sounding, as by a drum (Fr., timbre). The unique tone qualities (psychological attributes) by which different instruments or voices vary when sounding the same note (or fundamental tone). They are caused by sound wave complexities involving the number, mixture, and strength of overtones or partials (and other impurities) that respond with the fundamental tone. Timbre is also considered a psychological dimension of hearing. *See* **sound.**

timers *See* **interval timers.**

Tinbergen, Niko(lass) Born Holland, 1907. Trained as zoologist (D.Phil., Leiden, 1932) and **ethologist.** Specialized in studies on instinct and social behavior of animals. His early work led to demonstration of the value of sign stimuli and to the motivation-specific gating of sensory input. *See* **innate releasing mechanism, sign stimulus, releaser mechanism.**

Titchener, Edward Bradford (1867-1927) English-born psychologist. Student of **Wundt.** Greatly influenced by **Mach.** Titchener and his students at Cornell (where he taught for 35 years) were the only ones in the United States to carry on Wundt's type of experimentation (dealing largely with the introspective analysis of feeling states, attention, and the careful measurement of **reaction time**). For him, the subject matter of psychology was consciousness (feeling, images, and sensations), the generalized normal human state that seems to be available to **introspection**. Titchener's methods were merely the extension of the scientific method into this new field, which became known as Titchenerian psychology, sometimes voiced sarcastically. He introduced the terms functional, in 1898, and structural in 1908, as they have been used in American psychology. *See* **functional psychology** (Boring, pp. 410-417, 435).

T-maze A system of alleys in an experimental box designed like the figure T. The animal (usually the white rat) is put into the start-box, the door is opened and clocks started to measure the running time of the rat from one place to another. Upon reaching a goal-box the rat is put in the start-box to begin another trial. Records are kept of its trials, errors, and successes (number of correct turns).

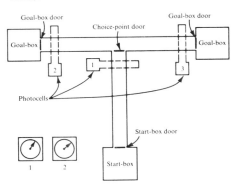

Donald J. Lewis, *Scientific Principles of Psychology*. © 1963. Reprinted by permission of Prentice-Hall, Inc., Englewood Cliffs, New Jersey.

Tofranil (Geigy tradename for **imipramine hydrochloride**).

Tolman's purposive behaviorism A behavioristic **Gestalt** approach oriented toward the study of purpose in all behavior. Tolman's purposivism eschewed **introspection** and all subjective data, placing them outside the realm of science since such phenomena could not be judged objectively. He stressed a **molar** approach to behavior, that is, purposive behavior must be seen as a whole and not as separate (**molecular**) responses. Only overt behavior is important, which must be objectively observed and operationally defined. Between stimulus and response he hypothesized **intervening variables** (such as cognition and demand), not necessarily physiological but probably necessary to produce goal-directed behavior. *See* **behaviorism, cognitive map, latent learning** (also E. C. Tolman, 1932, Schultz, 1969, pp. 219-223).

Edward Chace Tolman (1886-1959) American psychologist. Ph.D., Harvard 1915. APA President 1937. Received the **DSC Award** 1957.

Tonempfindungen (Ger., tone; tonal sensation.) *See* **Helmholtz.**

tonus Tone. A tense, muscular, spasmodic contraction of the body or limbs (usually referring to the tonic phase symptoms in **epilepsy**), lasting usually less than a minute, during which time pupils dilate, eyes become bloodshot and unresponsive to light, and the face suddenly blanches then turns dark blue. Tonus also refers to the steady activity of neural tissue and normal protoplasm.

topectomy Surgical excision (-ectomy) of a certain local area (top-). *See* **lobotomy.**

topographic mapping of brain *See* **cerebral cortex, Brodmann's area.**

topological psychology Relating to (-al) the psychology that uses **topology** to study behavior. An approach to the study of motives and behavior proposed by **Kurt Lewin**

(*Principles of Topological Psychology*) in 1936. The psychological situations in which individual or group behavior occurs can be diagrammed by using concepts of physics, chemistry (*see* **valence**), and mathematics. Lewin combined topology (for mapping the "life space") and **vector** analysis for study of motives; for example, the behavioral environment is diagrammed as the life space while forces impelling the individual toward or away from goals are considered as vectors. Also called **field theory**.

topology Study of (-logy) place (topo-). Nonmetric geometry concerned not with the shape of objects or direction of lines but with their modes of contact. For example, a drinking straw and a doughnut are topologically identical. *See* **topological psychology**.

toposcope A viewing instrument (-scope) of things in place (topo-). An elaborate **electroencephalographic** (EEG) viewing or **display** device with spatially arranged cathode ray tubes corresponding to various electrode positions on the head for purposes of making detailed studies of EEG relationships (Brown, p. 116).

Developed in 1951 by English physiologist William Grey Walter (born 1910) and H. W. Shipton (born 1920), an electronics engineer.

TOTE (Test-Operate-Test-Exit) unit The fundamental **cognitive** unit of behavior, designed to replace the **reflex arc** or S-R associationism. *See* **Barker, ecological psychology, intelligence**, (also G. A. Miller, E. Galanter, and K. H. Pribram, *Plans and the Structure of Behavior*. New York: Holt, Rinehart, and Winston, 1960).

toxic disorders Brain damage resulting from poisonous agents.

trace The hypothetical **construct** of memories supposed to exist in the brain. *See* **mneme**.

trace conditioning A form of **conditioning** in which the **unconditioned stimulus** (UCS) is paired with the trace of the **conditioned stimulus** (CS) rather than with the CS itself, or in which the CS is presented first but terminates before the UCS begins. (B. Reynolds, "The Acquisition of a Trace Conditioned Response as a Function of the Magnitude of the Stimulus Trace," *Journal of Experimental Psychology*, 1945, 35, 15-30).

tracts *See* **axon**.

training group (T group) A T group consists of persons who meet in a relatively unstructured psychological atmosphere and participate as learners. Participants are thereby enabled to test out new ways of behaving without fear of criticism from parents or friends while receiving immediate feedback. Participants must be willing to explore openly their own **motivations** and feelings, their **needs**, values, and behavioral patterns. *See* **intensive group experience**.

trait A relatively enduring characteristic or distinguishable dimension of **personality**, which frequently can be tested or measured. A specific, typical reaction. A psychological **construct** used to explain a seemingly enduring general attribute based upon clusters of related ways of behaving and thinking. **Allport** believes traits are generalized dispositions of people by which they can be profitably compared. He has organized traits into classes: morphological (including anthropometric measurements), physiological, aptitudes, skills and achievements, drives, interests (opinions and beliefs), and values (G. W. Allport, "Traits Revisited," *American Psychologist*, 1966, **21**, 1-10).

trait profile A **psychograph** or chart based on a person's scores obtained from a rating of his various **traits** which are plotted in parallel rows with the peak scores connected by pencil marks, leaving a profile pattern of traits.

tranquilizer An agent (-er) that calms the mind; a drug such as a **meprobromate** (Miltown, Equanil) and **phenothiazone** (Compazine, Stelazine) that has replaced the use of **barbiturates** in the control of mental illness,

and acts differently from a sedative by calming the upset person without affecting alertness. **Reserpine** was the first drug tranquilizer and the most effective one is generally acknowledged to be **chlorpromazine**.

The term tranquilizer entered psychiatry in 1812 with American physician Benjamin Rush's (1745-1813) introduction of a wooden chair with straps to hold down patients. In his *Diseases of the Mind* he said: "If all the means that have been mentioned (blisters, emetics, and purgatives) should prove ineffectual to establish a government over deranged patients, recourse should be had to certain modes of coercion: (1) confinement by means of a strait waistcoat or of a chair which I have called a tranquilizer, (2) showers—cold water up the coat sleeve so that it may go over the patient's armpits and down his trunk, then he should be threatened with death, thereby eliminating chains and whips."

The term became popular in the United States when **Miltown** was introduced about 1955, being the butt of many television jokes for years afterward.

trans- A prefix meaning across, over, beyond, through, surpassing.

transducer That which (-er) leads (-duc-) across (trans-). An extremely sensitive, miniature, amplifying resistor (with a single input and a single output channel) that converts energy or information of one form into another, usually for measurement purposes. Hence, though a powerhouse dynamo and a strain gauge (as a mechanical-electrical transducer) both convert mechanical movements into electrical signals, only the latter is classed as a transducer. **Receptors** for monitoring respiratory movements are considered transducers because they transform physical energy into **nerve impulses**. *Transduction* is the process of converting one kind of energy into another, such as the coding process involved in the transformation by various sensory receptors of physical stimuli into nerve impulses that can carry the message(s) to the **brain**. *See* **biological transducer system, quantizer**.

transferase *See* **galactosemia**.

transference phenomenon A carry (-fer-) over (trans-) condition (-ence). **Identification** of a figure in the present with significant figures in the past. In psychoanalysis, one of the more important tools of therapy, with which the unconscious, emotional attitudes of the patient are transferred (on) to the psychoanalyst. In this way the therapist is made the object of emotional response (love or hatred)—originally directed, in most cases without reward or recognition, to parents or other significant people. Often, by this symbiotic relationship, the psychoanalyst is able to help provide the patient with a better understanding of his basic emotional attitudes.

transfer of training The carryover value of learning an old task upon the learning of a new one; if facilitative, it is *positive transfer*; if not, it is *negative transfer*. New learning is facilitated or transferred from prior learning when principles or generalizations are conceptualized and then applied specifically to the new learning experience.

transfer RNA (tRNA) Ribonucleic acid that plays a role in transferring amino acids into cell-specialization enzymes. There are about sixty different kinds of tRNA in each cell. In protein synthesis, after the **messenger RNA** (mRNA) has located itself in one of the **ribosomes** in the cell cytoplasm, a tRNA molecule from the cytoplasm attaches itself to a special amino acid molecule. It then transfers it to a ribosome, its position being dictated by the mRNA. A similar procedure follows for each amino acid until a chain of amino acids forms a protein molecule.

transformation The process (-tion) of transforming or changing. A mathematical alteration or substitution in a **set** of scores.

transformational grammar A linguistic approach to grammar in which language is linked with the mind by conceptualizing language as having a surface structure (observable pattern of speech) and a deeper structure (consisting of basic patterns of language fixed in the brain). It emphasizes the skills of a speaker and not the system involved in use of the language.

Developed by Noam Chomsky. *See* **generative theory of language acquisition**.

transient situational disturbances Adjustment reactions characteristic of certain life periods, such as of *infancy* (crying spells and severe social withdrawal); of *childhood* (enuresis, attention-getting behavior, etc.); of *adolescence* (school failure, brooding, etc.); of *adult life* (resentment and depression associated with unwanted pregnancy, suicidal attempts, etc.); and of *late life* (feelings of rejection associated with forced retirement, accompanied often by social withdrawal).

transitional cortex A band of the **cerebral cortex** extending from the side of the **frontal lobe** to the **temporal lobe**, antedating phylogenetically the **allocortex** but older than the **neocortex**. Stimulation of it produces visceral responses.

translocation In genetics, the change in location of one chromosome to another, both chromosomes usually becoming fused in the transfer (trans-). Translocation may result in a special form of mongolism (such as occurs, for example, when chromosome #21 fuses with #15 or #22) or in Turner's syndrome (in which the male sex chromosome is missing). *See* **Down's disease**.

transmitter substance A chemical substance or agent (-er) such as **acetylcholine** that is released at the **axon** terminal of a **neuron** and sent (-mitt) across (trans-) the **synaptic gap**. The substance is excitatory or inhibitory in function, depending upon whether it produces or prevents occurrence of an impulse in the next neuron. *See* **synapse, synaptosome, synaptic transmission**.

The first direct evidence that nervous transmission was mediated by a chemical substance was provided in 1904 by the English physician Thomas R. Elliott (1877-1961), who observed that effects resulting from **adrenalin** and the stimulation of sympathetic nerves were similar, hinting that an adrenalin-like stimulant probably was liberated at a smooth muscle cell upon the arrival of a sympathetic impulse. Two years later Elliott's substance turned out to be **acetylcholine** when its pharmacological effects upon nerve tissue were discovered. Acetylcholine, however, was not isolated until 1929 by **Dale** and his associates. *See* **Vagusstoff**.

transverse plane (Horizontal plane in man); a crosswise (transverse) cut through the body at right angles to the **cephalocaudal axis**, dividing the body or any part of it into upper and lower parts. *See* **anatomical directions**.

transvestism A persistent practice (-ism) of cross (trans-) dressing (-vest-), or desire to wear clothes of the opposite sex, with associated feelings of sexuality and excitement, but with uncomfortable feelings when dressed in garments of one's own sex.

traumatic disorders Brain damage resulting from physical injury.

traumatic neuroses Neuroses precipitated by extreme stress or catastrophic experiences in an otherwise normal person.

Traumdeutung (Ger., dream interpretation) The psychological significance of dreams, developed by **Freud**.

traveling wave theory of hearing A modification of the place theory of hearing developed by Békésy. *See* **hearing theories**.

treatment Subjecting something or someone to an action or influence. The term treatment in statistics has its origins in the early use of **analysis of variance** and other statistics in agricultural research (for example, fertilizer is one form of treatment applied to a plot of ground, the variations in yield due to such

t

treatments being called effects). A treatment is interpreted as one of the **treatment levels** or results of combined **independent variables** that have been subjected to a well-constructed and meaningful **experimental design**. In general, a treatment is any variation in the experimental conditions whose effects are to be observed and evaluated. It may be a method used, an experienced response, a dosage of a drug, or the independent variable itself. In *social psychology*, a treatment encompasses the induced stimulus patterns to which a subject is allowed to respond. In clinical psychology and psychiatry, a treatment refers to the assistance given by a therapist to a patient in the therapeutic relationship.

treatment combination The combining of various **independent variables** within a well-constructed **experimental design**.

treatment levels Appropriate randomly selected levels of the different kinds of the **independent variable** that may be applied in an experiment. They should be chosen to cover as wide a range as necessary for detecting any real effects of the independent variable, and the spacing and number of the levels should sufficiently define the shape of the function relating the independent and **dependent variables**. Distinctions should be carefully made between qualitative and quantitative treatments (Kirk, pp. 6-7).

tremorgraph A recording device (-graph) that registers tremors mechanically (via a pneumatic system).

It was developed in 1932 by the Russian psychologist **A. R. Luria.**

triad A three-person group engaged in encounter meetings, **group therapy** sessions, or small group studies.

trial and error A type of learning in which the subject begins a task with apparently nonsystematic or random activity. As the behavior becomes more relevant and successful, random movements tend to drop out with eventual **reinforcement** of the correct response. The correctness can be verified only by actual trial. Contrasted with **insight** learning, where the subject "sees through" the problem or discovers a principle for its solution. *See* **heuristic method, Köhler.**

The phrase is traceable to Alexander Bain who used it in *The Senses and the Intellect* (1855), in discussing the creative or inventive intellect; trial and error as the "grand and final resort" for trying to solve all difficult problems (Woodworth and Schlosberg, 1965, p. 446).

trichromatism State (-ism) of having three (tri-) color (-chromat-) systems. Normal or nearly normal color vision, requiring three primary lights (such as black-white, blue-yellow, and red-green) to duplicate the colors viewed. A *trichromat* is a person with normal color vision.

Tridione (trimethadione) A drug used in the treatment of *petit mal*, but which unfortunately can also produce other forms of **epilepsy.**

trigeminal nerve Relating to (-al) a triple (tri-) paired (-gemin-) nerve. **Cranial nerve V**, with three paired sensory branches (ophthalmic, maxillary, and mandibular nerves) that carry **afferent** impulses from the face and tongue. Its motor functions are concerned with chewing.

Described first by **Fallopius**, Italian anatomist. In 1748 it was more carefully described by German anatomist Johan Friedrich Meckel (1714-1774). French physician Francois Chaussier (1746-1828) called the nerve trifacial. The trigeminal name was coined in 1732 by Dutch anatomist Jacob (Jacques) Benignus Winslow (1669-1760).

trisome (trisomy) A three (tri-) bodied (-somes) chromosome. An aberration (a **nondisjunctive** type of error in cell division) in the **autosomes** of the body so that there are three rather than the usual two **chromosomes**, resulting in the total number of 47 chromosomes instead of 46. In man, three often mentioned trisomics are: trisomy-15 of Group D (chromosomes numbered from 13-15 in the Denver System of chromosomal count), another from Group E (chromosomes 16-18), and a third from group G (21-22, plus the telocentric Y-chromosome), usually called *trisomy-21*.

People with trisomic aberrations are generally severely **mentally retarded**, trisomy-21, for example, being the genetic cause of **Down's syndrome.**

tritanopia *See* **color blindness.**

tRNA Transfer RNA.

trochlear nerve Pertaining to (-ar) the pulley-shaped (trochlea) **cranial nerve** IV, controlling certain eye movements.

About 1503, Italian anatomist Alessandro Achillini (1463-1512) discovered this nerve.

trophotropic function Relating to (-ic) a tropism concerned with nutritive (tropho-) functions (e.g., digestion, cell maintenance) that are largely controlled by the **parasympathetic nervous system** centers of the **hypothalamus.** Appetite is apparently a trophotropic function when associated with relaxation. **Serotonin** plays an as yet undefined role in the trophotropic system. *See* **ergotropic system.**

tropism A condition (-ism) of turning or changing (trop-) the direction of an organism. Involuntary, unlearned primitive **orienting reactions** moving the organism either away from or toward a **stimulus.** For example, phototropism is a reaction to light, *positive* (as when a moth is attracted to light) or *negative* (as when a cockroach or spider avoids light and seeks the dark). In motile organisms, often used interchangeably with **taxis.**

Andrew Knight (1758-1838), English horticulturist, apparently conducted first experiments (1802) on direction of growth of roots and stems. In 1890, **Jacques Loeb** made extensive studies on animal cell tropisms, comparing results with Knight's work.

tropostereoscope A stereoscope that turns (tropo-) or adjusts, usually consisting of two adjustable, adjoining tubes provided with a mechanism to hold observed images in place. Designed to demonstrate the influence of double images in depth perception.

Trousseau, Armand (1801-1867) French physician. *See* **aphasia, adrenal gland.**

tryptophan(e) A crystalline **amino acid** appearing like (-phane) and actually being a product of tryptic (trypsin) digestion derived from proteins, and one of the first amino acids demonstrated to be needed in the diet (as a **pellagra** preventive); also important as raw material necessary for production of niacinamide. *See* **serotonin.**

In 1890, German chemist Richard Neumeister (1854-1903) hypothesized that such a substance existed, naming it tryptophane. It was isolated in 1901 by English chemist Frederick G. Hopkins (1861-1947) and his colleagues.

T-score transformation A standard score transformed to a scale with a **mean** of 50 and a **standard deviation** of 10.

TSH Thyroid Stimulating Hormone, or **thyrotrophic hormone.**

T statistic *See* **Wilcoxon T statistic.**

t-test (t-ratio) A test of **significance** in which the ratio of a value (such as the difference between two means) to its **standard error** is computed. *See* **Student's t,** Table 6a.

tuberous sclerosis (epiloia, Bourneville's disease) A disease, characterized by **mental retardation** and formation of multiple skin and brain tumors. Retarded development and seizures may appear early and increase in severity along with tumor growth. It is transmitted by a single dominant autosomal gene arising by new mutation.

Désiré M. Bourneville (1840-1909), French physician, in collaboration with Edouard Brissaud (1852-1909), French neurologist, described in 1880 various degenerative mental disorders and named them tuberous sclerosis of the brain.

Tukey's honestly significant difference test (HSD) A multiple comparison test designed for making all pairwise comparisons among means. It demands the same statistical assumptions as a *t* ratio. (Kirk, p. 88).

John Wilder Tukey. Born Massachusetts, 1915. Ph.D. Princeton 1939 (mathematics). Research interests: communication principles and mathematical statistics. *See* **a posteriori.**

Turner's syndrome *See* **translocation.**

twins, fraternal *See* **fraternal twins.**

twins, identical *See* **identical twins.**

two-factor theory C. E. Spearman's (1904) theory of the structure of **intelligence** demonstrating that two processes derived from test scores by **factor analysis** make up intelligence: (*a*) the *g* or *general factor*, entering into all intellectual functions, and (*b*) specific *s* factors contributing to *special abilities*. Technically, however, these so-called "two" factors may be reduced to one, or, as Spearman himself later suggested, they may be proliferated to multifactors. Multifactor theory dominates Thurstone's concepts (involving from six to ten **primary mental abilities)** and Guilford's (in which at least 120 kinds of "testable" abilities are postulated).

In learning theory, two-factors refer to an assumption that two different learning processes exist, one requiring **reinforcement** and the other occurring solely by **association.** In interference theory of forgetting, forgetting results from two factors: (*1*) *unlearning* and (*2*) *response competition.*

two sample tests (*See* Tables 25b, 25c, and 26.)

tympanic cavity *Same as* **middle ear.**

tympanic membrane (typanum) Eardrum. Drum-(tympan-)like (-ic) membrane, separating the outer from the **middle ear,** that receives sound vibrations and transmits them to the **ossicles,** to which it is attached.

type I conditioning (type I CR) Classical conditioning. The **conditioned response** (CR) is similar to the **unconditioned response** (UR) and training follows a procedure where the **unconditioned stimulus** (US) always follows the **conditioned stimulus** (CS), whether or not the CR occurs. For example, training a dog to salivate to a bell (CS) by feeding (US) him each time the bell is rung (Thompson, p. 579).

type I error The error made of rejecting the **null hypothesis** (H_O) when H_O is true. The probability of committing this error is symbolized by alpha (α), which measures the risk of falsely rejecting the null hypothesis, after the experimenter has adopted a particular **level of significance.** If H_O is false, the **probability** of making a type I error is zero.

type theory *See* **constitutional types.**

type II conditioning (type II CR) Instrumental conditioning. The conditioned response (CR) differs from the unconditioned response (UR) and is necessary for occurrence of the unconditioned stimulus (US). For example, a rat learns to press a lever (CR) to obtain food (US) (Thompson, p. 579).

type II error The error made when the experimenter fails to reject the **null hypothesis** (H_O) when it is false. The probability of such error is symbolized by beta (β), indicating the risk taken, and determined by the magnitude of the experimental effect, random error, size of sample, **level of significance,** etc. If H_O is true, the **probability** of making a type II error is zero.

typewriter maze A **maze** in which the subject must continually press a series of letters on a typewriter when a signal sounds until the correct letter is hit by **trial and error.** Errors are related to sequential position. It was devised to investigate serial phenomena in sequential learning of motor tasks, utilizing different elements throughout the series.

Developed by F. H. Lumley in 1932.

typology *See* **constitutional types.**

tyrosine A crystalline amino acid or chemical (-ine) formed as a protein cleavage product obtained from cheese (tyros-). It is converted by the enzyme tyrosine hydroxylase to **dopa**, an amino acid found only in those cells carrying out catecholamine metabolism, the enzyme dopa decarboxylase converting the dopa to **dopamine**. Not essential for nutrition. It supplies effects of **phenylalanine** in its absence or reduces its effects when present.

It was discovered by **Liebig** in 1846, and synthesized in 1883 by German chemist Emil Erlenmeyer (1825-1909).

U

UCR (UR) Unconditioned response.

UCS (US) Unconditioned stimulus.

Umweg (Ger., roundabout) *Same as* **detour problem.**

Umwelt (Ger., world around) The **biological world** or environment that must be contended with. One of the ways (the others being **Mitwelt, Eigenwelt, Merkwelt**) of conceiving of the world, each view being necessary to a total existence. The plural connotation should not convey separate places or conditions. The human being must live simultaneously in *Umwelt, Mitwelt*, and *Eigenwelt* along with wholesome *Merkwelt*. They are all interdependent. *See* **existence.**

unbiased estimate The **mean** of a random **sample** is an unbiased estimate of the population mean, μ. An estimate of a **parameter** is unbiased if its expected value is equal to the parameter.

uncertainty In statistics, a condition described with mathematical precision under the laws of **probability**. Probability by nature must deal with uncertainty, and *statistics* itself may be defined as a technique for making decisions under conditions of uncertainty. A formula for a measure of uncertainty, $\hat{H}$, is given:

$$\hat{H} = \log_2 A$$

where A is the number of equally likely alternatives. $\hat{H}$, as a measure of uncertainty, is usually expressed in **binary digits**. In **information theory**, uncertainty becomes a function of the number of things that can happen as well as a function of the equal likelihood of the alternatives happening. Uncertainty may also be construed as a drive to seek information.

The uncertainty principle (or indeterminancy) was used first (1927) in reference to quantum mechanics by Werner Heisenberg (born 1901, Ph.D. Munich, 1923, German philosopher.

unconditional positive regard *See* **free.**

unconditioned (primary) reinforcer A reinforcer (such as a **stimulus**) that operates as an **operant** without prior conditioning.

unconditioned response (UCR or UR) In **classical conditioning** the natural (not reflexively trained), reliable, innate response elicited by the **unconditioned stimulus**. It is used as a basis for establishing a **conditioned response** to a previously neutral stimulus. For example, an electric shock (unconditioned stimulus) applied to a dog's paw causes a paw movement (unconditioned response).

unconditioned stimulus (UCS or US) Classical conditioning in which a **stimulus** (such as food in the mouth) reliably elicits a specific **response** (salivation) without conditioning or training, or which does not depend upon its pairing with another like stimulus.

unconscious Unaware; not realizing the existence of something; temporarily insensible. According to psychoanalysts, the unconscious comes to light in dreams, in slips of the tongue, and in such modes of expression as art and literature; the unconscious is due to **repression** of early memories, conflicts, and unacceptable feelings (1909). Unconscious conflicts causing **neurosis** may be uncovered and resolved in psychoanalysis.

Freud said that the unconscious is "any mental process the existence of which we are obliged to assume . . . was active at a certain time, although not aware of it at that time. We infer it from its effects."

Herbart antedated Freud 75 years in development of a concept of the unconscious. Karl Gustav (1789-1869) an obstetrician turned **psychologist**, considered his concept of the "unconscious" to be a creative life force, somewhat similar to Freud's Eros, and that as the child matures his conscious ideas progressively move into the forgetfulness of the unconscious. **Janet** used the word to describe the "value of a truly dynamic psychological factor," but failed to develop the idea. Freud and **Breuer** introduced their concept of the unconscious in 1893.

Existentially, the unconscious cannot exist as it splits the indivisible being into separate lives (the conscious and the unconscious). In some neo-Freudian interpretations, the **id** has replaced the "unconscious."

unconscious motivation The **Freudian** premise that unconscious motives affect people's behavior. Inferred dynamic processes (**needs**, desires, and goals) not readily apparent to consciousness but accounting for many forms of behavior. For example, a person might have various conscious **motives** as to the choice of a profession, but the basic unconscious motive might be the desire to outshine his father.

uncontrolled variable A vagrant condition in an experiment that operates outside of the investigator's design of measurement or procedures of control.

uncus A hook-like (uncus) structure. The hooked end of the **hippocampal** convolution.

union of sets A and B $A \cup B$ (being the set of elements each belonging to A or B or both). Ex: Set $A = \{1, 2, 3\}$; Set $B = \{4, 5, 6\}$; $\therefore A \cup B = \{1, 2, 3, 4, 5, 6\}$; Set $A = \{1, 2, 3, 5\}$; Set $B = \{4, 5, 6, 9\}$ $\therefore A \cup B = \{1, 2, 3, 4, 5, 6, 9\}$. *See* **Boolean algebra, set theory.**

universal set *See* **set, Boolean algebra.**

universe (population) In statistics, the total group under consideration in a study or experiment from which **samples** are drawn. Some statistical writers (for example, Diamond and O'Toole) distinguish between universe and population by referring to the population as "collections of real persons or objects" and the universe as a hypothetical grouping or accumulation of **data** (test scores, etc.) (Diamond, pp. 14, 33; O'Toole, p. 10).

unrestricted sampling A type of **sampling** drawn from a **population** in which all possible samples have the same chance of being selected.

Unzer, Johann August (1727-1799) German physician. Helped popularize concept of **reflex**, using verb "to reflect" frequently in reference to reflex action. He introduced (1771) the German words *aufleitend*, which became **afferent** in translation, and *ableitend* (**efferent**).

UR Unconditioned response.

uracil A crystalline solid obtained from **nucleic acid**. *See* **genetic code.**

US Unconditioned stimulus.

U-shaped curve A **distribution curve** consisting of relatively few measures in the middle ranges but relatively many at the two extremes.

U statistic *Same as* **U test.**

U test A nonparametric rank-sum test (Mann-Whitney) used for testing the **null hypothesis** that two independent samples come from identically distributed **populations**. *See* Table 29.

utility program A **computer** program designed for performing testing and operating functions. (Sometimes called maintenance program).

utricle Little (-icle) bag (ut(e)r-). A liquid-filled saclike structure in the **vestibule** at the base of the **semicircular canals** of the inner ear; contains **receptors** that respond to head movements or position in a gravitational field.

u-variable A standardized, continuous, normal **variable** with a mean of 0 and a **standard deviation** and **variance** of 1.

V

V Coefficient of variability; also **variance.**

vagus nerve The wandering (vagus) nerve, either of the pair of **cranial nerve** X, arising from the **medulla** and branching off to various organs (such as lungs, stomach) throughout the body. It has an inhibiting effect upon heart action. *See* **cranial nerves.**

About 65 A.D., Roman physician and anatomist Marinus (or Marinos) (40-110) described the nerve as the 6th. About 1655, the term was coined by Italian anatomist Domenico de Marchetti (1626-1688).

Vagusstoff The "stuff" that **Loewi's** experiments (from 1921-1924) indicated to be involved in chemical transmission in the **parasympathetic nervous system**, identified in 1914 by Ewins and by **Dale** and Loewi in the late 20's as **acetylcholine**. The first evidence, however, that a specific chemical substance was responsible for transmission of the **nerve impulse** came from Thomas R. Elliott's (1904) observations that acetylcholine is a parasympathetic mediator and that **adrenalin** is a sympathetic mediator. *See* **transmitter substance.** Conclusive evidence that acetylcholine was definitely involved in nerve transmission came in 1933 by German physiologist Wilhelm Feldberg (born 1900) and John H. Gaddum (1898-1962), British physiologist.

valence The quality (-ence) of power (val-). The strength of attraction (positive) or repulsion (negative) of goals, which may also have mixed (ambi-) valences. For example, one may be ambivalent about striving for success in business for, although the high salary holds positive valence, the long hours and hard work hold negative valence. *See* **topological psychology.**

The word was borrowed by **Kurt Lewin** (1939) from chemistry and used in his **field theory**. The term valence in chemistry, named 1852 by English chemist Edward Frankland (1825-1899), referred to his description of atoms as having hooks that had combining power (valence) to hang on to other atoms.

In an experiment on the forgetting of intentions, reported by Lewin, the subject was required to sign and date the paper used at the end of each task. Subjects forgot to sign their names for various reasons, such as extended pauses, change in occasions, etc.

Lewin points out that a subject will often "forget" to sign his name if required later to sign on a paper larger or of a different color. "Obviously, the paper reminds the subject of the intention, as does the mailbox of the letter to be mailed, or the knot in the handkerchief of something not to be forgotten: they have what I would like to call a valence." In cases of specific intentions, "a whole varied series of events and objects had valences (mailbox-friend). The valence may be fixated, however, as in the example of the paper, to a very specific object." (Intention, Will, and Need, *Vorsatz, Wille, und Beduerfnis. Psychologische Forschung*, 7, 1926; David Rapaport, *Organization and Pathology of Thought. Selected Sources*. New York: Columbia University Press, 1951, p. 109).

V

validity Quality (-ity) of being strong or well-grounded (valid-); the property of being legitimately derived from premises by logical inference. The degree to which a test actually measures what it was designed to measure. (A so-called **personality** or temperament scale should not measure, for instance, character.) The validity correlation or coefficient (r_v) is the **correlation** between scores on a measurement instrument and the **criterion** scores that the instrument is supposed to measure.

Other than **construct validity** and **predictive validity**, which are defined separately in their proper alphabetical listings, there are other types of validity usually associated with validation of tests. *Content validity* of a test is determined by systematically analyzing samples of the test items to assure that adequate coverage and representation of the items (such as words for spelling test or history items for a history test) are made. Content validity is used frequently in the evaluation of achievement tests. *Empirical (true) validity* demonstrates the relation between test scores and a criterion (which is an independent and direct measure of that characteristic or quality the test is designed to predict). Such validation must compare two sets of data (for example, test scores and criterion measures) on the same person. *Factorial validity* expresses the correlation between the test under consideration and the factor(s) common to a group of tests or other measures of behavior, as determined by the statistical technique of **factor analysis**. (Hays, 1964, pp. 66, 75; Cronbach, 1970, pp. 121-150).

value system The hierarchical ordered system in which one person ranks, consciously or unconsciously, one value or ideal over another. Many aspects of **attitudes** and values overlap, but values are culture-bound and fairly limited and inherent within the self. A person's value system, as an ordering of values, is usually determined from a measure of attitude. Attitudes and values commingle with properties of what is expected and what is desired. Stability of values is partly due to their existence as guiding influences within the culture. They also reflect the culture of a society and are widely shared by its members.

Values emerge when an emotion joins a **cognition**. A value, as a long-range **motive**, may become a goal. Values frequently underly attitude. Men die for values (freedom, duty, honor) but not *for* attitudes. However, men have died *because* of their attitudes. *See* **study of values**.

variability The degree to which phenomena are subject to change or become variable. The amount of spread or variation of scores in a **distribution**, as measured by the **standard deviation** (most common measure of variability), **interquartile range**, **mean deviation**, **variance**, etc. In social psychology, the degree to which a person (because of social influences) rather unpredictably displays both conformity and anticonformity.

variable One of the conditions of an experiment that is changed or can be changed; that is, **independent variables** are conditions that may be manipulated by the experimenter and **dependent variables** are the behavioral consequences dependent upon the experimental conditions.

The term was introduced in 1816 by the French mathematician **Lacroix** in his *"Traité Élémentaire du Calcul des Probabilities."* Lacroix was also the first to use the term Napierian logarithm.

variable interval schedule (VI) A simple **schedule of reinforcement** in which the first response receives reinforcement after a variable time interval (seconds or minutes) between successive reinforcements, disregarding the in-between correct responses, if any. The time variation makes it impossible for the subject to predict when the reinforcement will occur. *See* **variable ratio schedule**; *compare* **fixed interval schedule**.

variable ratio schedule (VR) A simple ratio schedule of reinforcement in which the **response** is reinforced after a varying number of responses. However, the sequence is varied so that the reinforced response does not occur (at the same point) simultaneously in the sequence each time. An effective method for obtaining and maintaining a constant and high rate of response. The ratio is determined by the average number of responses that precede a reinforcement.

variance (V) The square of the **standard deviation**, representing the **variance** of a population only. When described as the mean squared deviation, variance may be applied to either a sample or a population.

variance ratio (F) A ratio between two estimates of **variance** in the same population, reached by different methods. *See* **F distribution**.

Varolio (Varolius), Contanzio (1543-1575) Italian physician and anatomist. By being the first to separate the **brain** from the skull he thus became the first (1568) to describe a hitherto unseen area which he compared to a bridge (the **pons**) crossing a canal; thus, the **pons Varolii**.

vasomotor Action (-motor) of ducts or vessels (vaso-). One of the regulatory functions of the **autonomic nervous system**. Refers to the action of nerves or hormones causing expansion (vasodilation) or contraction (vasoconstriction) of the blood vessels.

vasopressin (ADH) Antidiuretic hormone. Vaso-constricting (-press-) agent (-in); vessel-compressing. A hormone manufactured in certain nuclei of the **hypothalamus**, eventually stored in the pituitary gland's neural lobe, which upon proper stimulation is released into the blood stream controlling body tissue water usage (kidney mainly). Also increases blood pressure slightly. Damage to the vasopressin area in the hypothalamus produces diabetes insipidus. *See* **oxytocin, neurohypophysis**. (V. Du Vigneaud, *Hormones of the Posterior Pituitary Gland: Oxytocin and Vasopressin*. New York, Academic Press, 1954-55, pp. 1-26 in the Harvey Lectures).

vasopressor That which (-or) compresses (-press-) blood vessels (vaso-). *See* **pressor substance**.

vector An agent (-or) that carries (vect-) forces toward a goal. An ordered set of quantities (variables) that, for example, describes a condition of a system or its specific **input** or **output**. In physics and mathematics, a quantity having direction and magnitude; a matrix having either a single row or a single column.

The term was used in field theory by Lewin in 1938 to denote impelling psychological forces sometimes varying in magnitude but having defined directions. For example, a drive toward a goal might be represented by an arrow in one direction, and the force opposing it (social, practical, etc.) as an arrow in the opposite direction.

vegetative nervous system Same as **sympathetic nervous system**.

venia legendi Permission (venia) to lecture (legendi) in German universities. An elective position, after having been elected **Privatdozent** from *Ärztliche* Approbation, which entitled one to lecture in his specialized field, making him equivalent to about assistant professor or instructor in American universities. No official salary was given but the *Privatdozent* was eligible to receive fees from his students as well as continuing as **Assistent**. *See* **German higher education**.

Venn diagrams A diagram using circles, squares, or other closed geometrical figures to represent infinite **sets** and their relationships. Named after John Venn (1834-1923), English logician. *See* **Euler diagrams**.

ventral Pertaining to (-al) the belly (vent-) region. Contrasted with **dorsal**. Now generally substituted for **anterior**. *See* **anatomical directions**.

ventricle *See* **brain ventricles**.

ventrodorsal Proceeding from anterior to posterior, from the front to the back; *same as* **dorsoventral**.

ventromedial nucleus (satiety center) A nucleus that is located close to the mid (-medial) ventral area of the **hypothalamus** (also called ventromedial hypothalamus—VMH). It apparently plays an inhibitory role in eating since, by its destruction in animals, satiety is not reached and **hyperphagia** results; such destruction also causes rage and viciousness. When the intact area is electrically stimulated, however, satiety does result (Morgan, pp. 380-381).

verbal aphasia *See* **speech aphasia**.

verbal conditioning A procedure in which special verbal responses (such as the singular "I" followed by the plural "We") are reinforced so as to increase the subject's facility in responding with the plural when the singular is given (or some other such verbal stimulus).

verbal summator A device that repeats samples of meaningless and elementary speech sounds (primarily vowels) at low intensities, to which the subject responds with his own invented but meaningful short statements. The stimulus words are no more than mumbled vowels, which in a sense force the subject, in his search for attaching meaning to everything, to find significance. **Skinner** claimed that his verbal summator "evokes latent verbal responses through summation with imitative responses to skeletal samples of speech" (B. F. Skinner, "The Verbal Summator and a Method for the Study of Latent Speech," *Journal of Psychology*, 1936, **2**, 71-107).

verbal test Any test that measures verbal ability or facility in handling verbal symbols, such as vocabulary items, comprehension, arithmetic, and general information. *See* **Wechsler Adult Intelligence Scale** and **Binet test**.

verbigeration The act of (-ation) driving (-iger-) words out of one's mouth meaninglessly. Stereotyped, meaningless, repetitive outbursts of words or sentences without reference to questions asked or subject matter under discussion. Recognized as one of the symptoms of hebephrenic reactions. Coined by **Kahlbaum** 1874.

Verdrängung *See* **repression**.

veridical perception Relating to (-al) a perception said (-dic-) to be true (veri-) and confirmed as a result of continued exposure to the perceived subjects, being especially reinforced by precise descriptions and measurements. Veridical **hallucinations** and dreams correspond to a real situation (as when the apparition of a distant person coincides temporally with his death reported at a later time).

Veronal Relating to (-al) Verona. The first clinically useful **barbiturate**, named by **Fischer** and German chemist Josef von **Mehring** in 1902 after the Italian city of Verona, which to them was symbolic of tranquillity. Veronal became "barbitone" in England and "barbital" in the United States.

vertical axis Pertaining to (-al) the upright (vertic-) position; perpendicular to the horizontal plane. From the head to toe in erect man; comparable to **cephalocaudal** axis in quadruped animals. *See* **anatomical directions**.

Vesalius, Andreas (1514-1564) Latinized version of Andre Wesal, Belgian anatomist. Author of first comprehensive work on human anatomy. Studied the organization of the human body through dissection and overthrew the authority of **Galen** by disproving many of his assumptions, particularly in denying the hollowness of nerves. *See* **corpus callosum, labyrinth, malleus**.

vesania (madness) Insanity, in general, used by French botanist and physician Francois Sauvages (1706-1767) in his *Nosologia Methodica*, 1763.

vestibular nerve A sensory offshoot of the auditory nerve.

vestibular sense Pertaining to (-ar) the sense of body movement and position, mediated by end organs in the vestibule of the **inner ear**, which are activated by gravitational pull and rectilineal head movements.

vestibule An entrance or antechamber (vestibul-) in the **inner ear**. The central cavity of the bony **labyrinth** of the middle ear, and the anatomical parts (**utricle** and **saccule**) of the membranous labyrinth containing receptors for the equilibrium sense.

Vicq d'Azyr, Felix (1748-1794) French comparative anatomist. *See* **fissure, hippocampus.**

Vieussens, Raymond de (1641-1715). French physician. His *Neurographia Universalis*, 1685, was the most complete text on the spinal cord and brain up to that time, showing functional independence of the brain from the spinal cord. *See* **ganglion.**

Vineland Social Maturity Scale A series of items in progressive order of difficulty based on the person's past performance and arranged in a **Binet**-type age scale designed to measure the successive stages of social competence from infancy to adult life. The scale has been used as a record of developmental history, as a measure of growth, improvement or deterioration, as a guide for child training, as a method for mental diagnosis and vocational or educational guidance, and as a measure of insight in mentally abnormal patients. There are 117 items in several major categories in the scale: self help (generally, in eating and dressing); self direction; occupation; communication; socialization; and locomotion. The scale covers a range from birth to over 25 years, but it has been found most useful with children from infancy to 5 years and with mentally retarded persons of all ages. Responses for scoring are usually obtained from an informant, customarily a parent. Scores are reported as S.A. (social age) and S.Q. (social quotient), analogous to **mental age** and **intelligence quotient.**

viral RNA Transferable nucleic acids presumably ancestral to the viruses.

Virchow, Rudolph (1821-1902) German anatomist and pathologist. Developed modern theory of disease. He was the first to describe and name the **neuroglia**. *See* **myelin sheath, glia cells.**

visceral brain *See* **central theory.**

visceral nervous system Same as **sympathetic nervous system.**

viscerogenic needs *See* **Murray.**

viscerotonia Visceral tone (-tonia). According to **Sheldon**, a cluster of traits or temperamental components in which digestive and related visceral functions are predominant. Viscerotonia is associated with the **endomorph** body type and expressed by gluttony, greed for affection, love of comfort, deep-sleep, sociability, and need of people when troubled. *See* **cerebrotonia, somatotonia.**

visible spectrum The range of that part of the electromagnetic spectrum whose radiations are usually visible, having wavelengths extending from about 3800 angstroms (one ten-billionth of a meter) for violet light to about 7800 for

red light. On the **nanometer** scale, wavelengths are expressed in billionths of a meter, the visible spectrum extending from about 380 to 780 nanometers. Colors of the visible spectrum result from sunlight being passed through a prism which separates and converts the beam of white light into bands of color (four being most prominent: red, green, yellow, and blue).

vision theories *See* **color vision theories.**

visual agnosia *See* **agnosia.**

visual aphasia A disorder (-ia) of not (a-) being able to see words (-phas-) visually; word blindness. Perceptual disturbances in understanding meaning of language as read. *See* **alexia.**

visual cliff An apparatus for studying depth perception in animals and infants. It is so constructed that a baby can crawl along a raised normal-appearing, solid floor and approach the edge of an apparent drop or "cliff," which is covered with a large sheet of reinforced glass. If the child hesitates or fails to crawl onto the "glass cliff," it is assumed that he has a perception of depth. It has been determined that babies at the crawling stage have a full appreciation of a drop, and consequently have depth perception during infancy.

The experiment was designed by the psychologist Mrs. Eleanor Gibson, after wondering about children's perceptions while picnicking one day near the edge of a cliff of the Grand Canyon. Mrs. Gibson was born in Illinois, 1910. Ph.D. Yale, 1938. Special studies: experimental and theoretical aspects of **perception.** DSC Award 1968.

visual convergence A binocular cue in depth perception, effective at distances less than about 60 feet, that arises from inward turning (convergence) of both eyes for near objects and the divergence of the eyes for far objects, so that axes meet at the point of fixation. The closer the object, the greater the angle of convergence.

visual cycle The sequence of chemical changes occurring in the **rods** of most vertebrate animals when visible electromagnetic energy stimulates **rhodopsin**, causing it to break down into **retinene** and **opsin** which then immediately and spontaneously change back again into rhodopsin.

visual purple (rod pigment, rhodopsin) A photosensitive substance, the major pigment in the **rods.**

Visual purple was first noticed (1851) by German anatomist Heinrich Müller (1820-1864), and in 1876 German physiologist Franz Boll (1849-1879) observed that a frog's retina exposed to the dark turned purplish but that it became yellowish (thus "visual yellow") upon being exposed to light. It was isolated from the retina in 1877 by German physician and physiologist Wilhelm F. Kuhne (1837-1900). *See* **rhodopsin.**

Vives, Juan de (1492-1540) A humanistic Spanish philosopher, psychologist, and educator. A champion of treating mentally ill people with gentility and understanding rather than mocking and ridiculing them. He said that man's behavior is the criterion for understanding him rather than dismissing his actions as functions of the soul or mind. In 1538 (*De Anima et Vita*), he described relationships between memory and emotions, discussing behavior in terms that anticipated **Freud's** dynamics and those of current behavioral psychologists, touching upon a theory of the unconscious.

vocational guidance The process of helping a person to choose, prepare for, enter upon, and progress in an occupation, with the aid of a professional vocational counselor. *See* **counselor.**

Frank Parsons (1869-1921) an American educator and social worker is recognized as being the founder of organized vocational guidance, which was an outgrowth of voluntary civic, educational, and social work.

He first expressed his ideas in 1908, publishing a book, *Choosing a Vocation*, in 1909. He was the originator of the term vocational guidance which he first used in 1908 in a report to the Vocation Bureau of Boston.

Vogts, the Refers to the joint work of German neurologist Oskar Vogt (1870-1959) and his French psychiatrist wife, Cecile (Mugnier) Vogt (1875-1962). Did extensive work on mapping of cortical areas, using their own student's (**Brodmann**) divisions of the **brain** as a guide. They coined the terms **allocortex, isocortex,** and **juxtallocortex,** which **Karl Pribram** refers to often in his references to the brain cortex. *See* **cytoarchitectonics.**

volley theory of hearing A modified frequency theory of hearing (proposed by Wever and Bray, 1930) stating that the frequency of the stimulus is represented in bundles of fibers in the **auditory nerve** responding somewhat independently, so that the frequency is represented by the composite volley, even though no single fiber carries impulses at that rate. It adequately explains frequencies up to 5000, but the resonance (or place) theory is needed to explain higher frequencies. Both theories used jointly are called the "place-volley" theory. *Compare* **frequency theory, place theory,** Békésy's traveling wave theory **of hearing.**

volt (V) The SI unit of electromotive force, equal to the difference of electrical potential between two points of a conducting wire carrying a constant current of 1 **ampere** with the power lost between these two points being equal to 1 **watt.**

Named after Alessandro Volta (1745-1827), Italian physicist.

Von Restorff effect The tendency of unusual-appearing items (such as a few printed words in red ink on a page of black words) to be so prominent and distinctive that they are more readily learned and longer retained.

Originally demonstrated and reported on by the German psychologist H. von Restorff ("*Über die Wirkung von Bereithabildungen in Spurenfeld,*" in W. Köhler and H. von Restorff, "*Analyse von Vergangen in Spurenfeld,*" *Psychologische Forschung* 1933, 18, 299-342).

voodoo death Widespread phenomenon of sudden death among some primitive peoples in which the person, after violating a taboo or feeling that he is bewitched, actually wills himself to die. The term has also been used in referring to the sudden deaths occurring with United States prisoners of war in Korea who were "brainwashed" to become hopelessly isolated from their pals and buddies. Experimentally, it has been shown to occur in many animals other than man, resulting from feelings of utter hopelessness, causing an over-activity of the **parasympathetic** system and a state of shock produced by excessive **adrenalin** release (Walter B. Cannon, "Voodoo Death." *American Anthropology,* 1942, 44, 169-181; C. P. Richter, On the Phenomenon of Sudden Death in Animals and Man. *Psychosomatic Medicine,* 1957, 19, 191-198).

Vor-diplom The German student's first (*vor-*) major examination.

Vorexamen A preliminary (*vor-*) examination in the German higher educational system (in medicine, for example) that is a prerequisite for taking terminal examinations (*Abschlussexamen*), which, if passed, result in a diploma, a state examination, a doctorate, or some other degree or examination.

voyeurism Seeking of sexual gratification by watching others undress. *Same as* **scopophilia.**

vRNA Viral RNA.

Vygotskii (Vygotsky), Lev Semenovich (1896-1934) Russian psychologist (influenced by Ach) who played an important role in developing Russian clinical psychology and in showing the importance of speech in the organization of mankind's behavioral patterns.

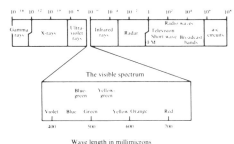

Wave length in meters

The visible spectrum

Wave length in millimicrons

The total electromagnetic spectrum, only a very small part of it producing the sensation called light.

Vygotskii-Sakharov method A method proposed by **Vygotskii** and Sakharov (his pupil) for practical investigation of concept formation. The method led to implicating the inhibited state of the **cerebral cortex** during **schizophrenia** as underlying the cause of disruption in connecting word meanings (semantic disorganization) and thereby upsetting concept-formation (Cole and Maltzman, p. 283).

W w

WAIS Acronym for **Wechsler Adult Intelligence Scale.**

Waldeyer-Hartz, Wilhelm von (1836-1921) German neurologist and anatomist, known for his work on the histology of the nervous system. Introduced the term **neuron** (1891) to describe the independent nerve unit, leading to the concept of the **neuron doctrine,** largely developed by **Ramon y Cajal.** He also originated the word **chromosome.**

Wald-Wolfowitz "runs" test A large sample **nonparametric** test of randomness based upon serial covariance. *See* **runs test** (also Table 26).

Abraham Wald (1902-1950). A Rumanian-born mathematician and statistician, naturalized American 1943. Ph.D. (mathematics) Vienna.

Jacob Wolfowitz. A Polish-born (1910) American statistician and mathematician. Ph.D. New York University 1942. Specialities: information theory, probability theory, measurement theory.

wall-eye *See* **strabismus.**

want As used by **cognitive** psychologists, the subjective experience of desire and intent as a motivational force in man.

Warner-Warden maze *See* **alley maze.**

Warren Medal Granted by the **Society of Experimental Psychologists** (SEP). The Award was established in 1936 by Mrs. Catherine C. Warren to be given to those who have made outstanding contributions to psychology through service, research, or writings. It was named in honor of Howard Crosby Warren (1867-1934), American (New Jersey) psychologist. Ph.D., Johns Hopkins 1917. Made many studies in experimental psychology, including reflexes, emotions, instincts, and illusions; also developed an **alley maze.** His psychological dictionary was popular for many years. APA President 1913.

Recipients of the Warren Medal

1936	E. G. Wever and C. W. Bray. *See* **hearing theories.**
1937	K. S. Lashley. *See* **Lashley.**
1938	Elmer A. Culler
1939	Carlyle Jacobsen
1940	Ernest R. Hilgard
1941	Clarence H. Graham
1942	B. F. Skinner. *See* **Skinner.**
1943	S. S. Stevens. *See* **Stevens.**
1944	No award
1945	Clark L. Hull. *See* **Hull's behavior system.**
1946	No award
1947	Wolfgang Köhler. *See* **Köhler.**
1948	H. K. Hartline
1949	Walter R. Miles
1950	Curt P. Richter
1951	Frank A. Beach
1952	James J. Gibson
1953	Kenneth W. Spence. *See* **Spence.**
1954	Neal E. Miller. *See* **Miller, Neal E.**
1955	Georg von Békésy. *See* **Békésy.**
1956	Harry F. Harlow. *See* **love.**
1957	Lorrin A. Riggs
1958	Donald O. Hebb
1959	Harry Helson. *See* **Helson.**
1960	Carl Pfaffmann
1961	Carl I. Hovland
1962	James Olds. *See* **Olds.**
1963	William K. Estes. *See* **Estes.**

1964	Benton J. Underwood
1965	William C. Young
1966	Floyd Ratliff
1967	Eliot Stellar
1968	Richard L. Solomon
1969	Roger W. Sperry
1970	Daniel S. Lehrman
1971	Leo Hurvich and Dorothea Jameson Hurvich. *See* opponent-process theory under **color-vision theories.**

Watson, John Broadus (1878-1958) American (South Carolina) animal psychologist; later, applied psychologist (executive in an advertising agency). Ph.D., Chicago 1903. His **behaviorism** denied the usefulness of the introspective methods of the time, reduced thought to subvocal speech, and insisted that the proper subject matter of psychology is behavior that is observable, objective, verifiable, and subject to conditioning. In 1913, his paper, "Psychology as a Behaviorist Views it," formally launched behaviorism. APA President, 1915. *See* **Bekhterev.**

watt (W) The **SI** unit of power, being equal to the power giving rise to the production of energy at the rate of 1 **joule** per second.

Named after the Scottish engineer and inventor, James Watt (1736-1819).

waxy flexibility *Same as* **cerea flexibilitas.**

weber (Wb) The **SI** unit of *magnetic flux* (total number of lines of induction through a given cross section of a surface), equal to a flux that produces an electromotive force of one volt in a single turn of wire as the flux is uniformly reduced to zero in 1 second.

Named after Wilhelm Eduard Weber (1804-1891), German physicist (brother of Ernst).

Weber-Fechner law *See* **Fechner.**

Weber's law An inexact formulation of the constant relation between changes in stimulus-intensity and perception. It is expressed as the mathematical rule that the difference threshold between two sensations in the same **modality** is a constant fraction of the original or reference stimulus. The constant fraction may vary considerably for different attributes and senses. The law is limited in accuracy to the middle range of intensity, and does not hold for extreme values.

$$\text{Weber's law:} \quad \frac{\Delta I}{I} = k$$

where ΔI = the difference threshold
I = intensity of the stimulus
k = a constant fraction

After Ernst Heinrich Weber (1795-1878), German physiologist and anatomist. Known for research on sensation, especially touch, and for developing Weber's law in 1834.

Wechsler tests Individually administered tests of intelligence for children (**Wechsler Intelligence Scale for Children, Wechsler Preschool and Primary Scale of Intelligence**) and for adolescents and adults (**Wechsler Adult Intelligence Scale**).

These tests are point scales rather than age scales (such as the **Binet**). Each of the subtest items, arranged in ascending order of difficulty, is grouped under verbal or performance categories.

Statistically, the **Wechsler** tests use standard scores with a **mean** of 10 and a **standard deviation** of 3. The scaled subtest scores are converted into a deviation IQ with a mean of 100 and a σ of 15. Thus, the IQ normal range of intelligence on this scale is from 85-115 (for a plus and minus 1 sigma).

Named after David Wechsler, Rumanian-born (1896) American psychologist. Ph.D., Columbia, 1925. Chief psychologist for many years at the Bellevue Psychiatric Hospital, New York.

Wechsler Adult Intelligence Scale (WAIS) The first form of this test was published in 1939 as the Wechsler-Bellevue Intelligence Scale. It was supplanted by the WAIS in 1958, with six subtests comprising the verbal scale (general information, vocabulary, arithmetic, etc.) and five the performance scale (block design, picture completion, etc.). Each subtest is individually administered and yields scores that are converted to **standard scores,** summed, and transformed into IQ's by reference to tables which consider the age of the examinee. Speed and accuracy are both considered in scoring arithmetic, digit symbol, block design, picture arrangement, and object assembly. The standardization sample consisted of 1700 cases, with an equal number of men and women distributed over seven age levels between 16 and 75 years.

Wechsler Intelligence Scale for Children (WISC). A downward extension of the original Wechsler-Bellevue, distributed in 1949, but consisting of twelve subtests, two of which (digit span and coding and/or mazes) can be used if desired as alternates or supplementary tests. These subtests yield an IQ based on scaled scores for each age level—not on a **mental age.** The IQ can be derived from either the verbal or performance scale, but also yields separate verbal and performance IQ's and a full scale IQ. The standardization sample included 100 boys and 100 girls at each age from 5 through 15 years, totaling 2200 cases. Only white school children were included, but there were also 55 mental retardates tested.

Wechsler Preschool and Primary Scale of Intelligence (WPPSI). Another modification of the earlier Wechsler test, and designed for ages 4 to 6½ years overlapping the WISC in the 5-6½ range. This test has eleven subtests (1 an alternate), ten of which are used in finding the IQ. Three new tests (sentences—a memory test; animal house—similar to WAIS digital-symbol and coding subtests; and geometric design—requires copying of 10 simple designs) have been added, but the others are merely downward extensions and adaptations of WISC subtests. The WPPSI, published in 1967, was standardized on 100 boys and 100 girls in each of half-year age groups from 4 to 6½ (six in all), totaling 1200 children. It was stratified against the 1960 census and controlled for geographical location, urban-rural residence, sex, father's occupational level, and also, white-nonwhite proportion. Like the WAIS and WISC, WPPSI yields separate verbal, performance, and full scale IQ's. *See* **apraxia.**

wedge photometer An instrument for measuring differential sensitivity to **brightness** changes. A wedge of glass (or optical wedge), with one side illuminated by a constant source of light while the other half's light source is finely adjusted, that enables the observer to differentiate between small differences in stimulation. Generally, a **photometer** measures **candlepower, illuminance,** and **luminance.** A flicker photometer is used to compare stimuli that are successively shown in the same visual area.

weighted item An item in a test multiplied by numbers that reflect the relative importance or usefulness of the item in predicting a **criterion.**

Weltanschauung (*Weltansicht*) World view or outlook. Originally used in the literary sense but has become associated with an attitude toward life or the world (the medieval *Weltanschauung,* for example), and has become articulated into a philosophical system. Although often used as a synonymous term, *Weltansicht* more strictly refers to a feeling of apprehension about the world in general. In his *New Introductory Lectures on Psychoanalysis* (1933), Freud described *Weltanschauung* "as an intellectual construction which solves all the problems of our existence uniformly on the basis of one overriding hypothesis, which, accordingly leaves no question unanswered and in which everything that interests us finds its fixed place."

Wernicke's syndrome An **organic psychosis** characterized by degeneration of the **central nervous system** (midbrain in particular) and marked by **ataxia**, memory loss, clouding of consciousness, and paralysis of eye muscles, sometimes coma. Onset is insidious. Especially common in chronic alcoholics with nutritional deficiency, but may also occur in others not alcoholic (e.g., from vitamin deficiency).

After German neurologist Karl Wernicke (1848-1905). *See* **aphasia**.

Wertheimer, Max (1880-1943) Czech-born psychologist. Graduated from Würzburg under Külpe in 1904. Rejected the concepts of distinct psychic units of associationist and analytic psychology. In 1910-1912, with Köhler and Koffka formulated the conceptual approach that became **Gestalt psychology**. Wertheimer's study of apparent movement led to his famous paper (published in the *Zeitschrift für Psychologie*, 1912) on the **phi phenomenon**, which formally inaugurated Gestalt psychology.

Wever-Bray theory of hearing *See* **volley theory** under **hearing theories**.

Wheatstone, Sir Charles (1802-1875) English physicist and inventor. Research in electricity, light, vision, and sound. Developed the **chronoscope** in practical form (1840), which Hipp improved upon in 1842 (**Hipp chronoscope**). It is still used in modified form in psychological laboratories. He invented the **stereoscope** in 1838, which made it possible for Helmholtz and others to advance their study on binocular vision. His so-called *Wheatstone bridge* was designed to measure unknown electrical resistances, consisting of a diamond-shaped "bridge" circuit with adjustable resistors on three sides (the unknown resistance making the fourth side). After the three resistors are adjusted to bring the circuit into balance, the unknown resistance can be calculated from the values indicated by the three adjustable resistances. (Venables and Martin, pp. 12-13).

wheel network *See* **group network**.

white noise A complex mixture of sound waves used for experimental purposes, containing all frequencies of sound presented simultaneously at an equal loudness so that no one frequency predominates. It sounds like a "whoosh" or low-pitched hiss, like steam escaping. Analogous to white light, which is a mixture of all wavelengths of light.

G. A. Miller and his colleagues used "white noise" at various noise levels to study word-identifications and the effects of context on psychological performance (G. A. Miller, G. A. Heise, and W. Lichten, "The Intelligibility of Speech as a Function of the Context of the Test Materials," *Journal of Experimental Psychology*, 1951, **41**, 329-335).

whole learning Learning a task in total or as a unit. For example, memorizing a poem from beginning to end without recourse to breaking it up into more manageable units or stanzas. *Contrasted with* **part learning**.

whole-part method of learning A combination of two methods of learning, especially in memory experiments. *Whole learning* (**massed practice**) means learning a whole sequence of material; *part learning* (**distributed practice**) involves learning the sequence in parts, then combining the parts.

Whytt, Robert (1714-1766) Scottish vitalist physician. Played a major role in clarifying the concept of the spinal reflex. *See* **pupillary reflex, reflex**.

Wilcoxon, Frank (1892-1963) Ph.D. in organic chemistry, Cornell 1924. A chemist and consulting statistician for the American Cyanamid Company for many years. Developed new statistical procedures for testing fungicides and insecticides, which have been found to be valuable in other sciences as well.

The *Wilcoxon signed-ranks test* is a **nonparametric** test of homogeneity on ordinal scale properties, designed to determine the mean difference significance in matched pairs of scores, utilizing both the magnitude and the direction of the difference between pairs. The underlying variable is assumed to be continuously distributed. A version of the test for two samples was proposed by Wilcoxon ("Individual Comparisons by Ranking Methods," *Biometrics Bulletin*, 1945, **I**, 80-83), but it was later developed by Mann and Whitney. (*See* Table 28).

The *Wilcoxon T statistic* tests the **null hypothesis** that the frequency distribution of the original measurements is identical for treated and untreated pair members but without need for specifying the shape of the frequency distribution. Each rank is therefore equally likely to have a + or a − sign. The *T* statistic usually requires that the original measurements be made on **an interval scale**. It is used for small samples when the difference scores come from other than a normally distributed population. The test's rationale assumes that if no real differences exist between two sets of measurements, then the differences might be expected to balance each other out. If they don't, then chance is causing the inequality. (See Table 28; also Hays, 1963, pp. 633-635).

wild children *See* **feral child**.

Willis, Thomas (1621-1675) English philosopher and physician who followed the **iatrochemical** school of thinking. Made many contributions to the anatomy and physiology of the nervous system. His book *Cerebri Anatome*, 1664, summarized most of the anatomical information (mostly **Galenic**) known up to that time. *See* **accessory nerve, dementia praecox, glossopharyngeal nerve, ophthalmic nerve, cranial nerves**.

Wirklicher Geheimer Rat (actual privy councillor) An honorary title conferred by the German government or Austrian government (*Wirklicher Geheimer Hofrat*) on a professor (and other professional workers) after having served many years of distinguished service and entitled to be called Exzellenz (your excellency).

WISC Acronym for **Wechsler Intelligence Scale for Children**.

Witmer, Lightner *See* **clinical psychologist**.

Wolff, Christian (1679-1754) German philosopher, influenced primarily by **Leibniz**. He made a distinction between empirical psychology (which depended upon sensation) and rational psychology (dependent upon reason), indicating that rational psychology was the better of the two for clarity of ideas. He was the first to espouse German faculty psychology, expressing the idea that the soul consists of various faculties or powers ("potencies of action"). *See* **monism, ontology, psychometry, dualism, empirical, monad**.

Woodworth, Robert Sessions (1869-1962) American (Massachusetts) experimental psychologist. Ph.D., Columbia 1899. Trained under **James, G. S. Hall**, and **Sherrington**. Performed many studies on **personality** (first personality questionnaire), learning, and thinking. Exponent of dynamic and **functional psychology**. APA President 1914. Received first **Gold Medal Award** 1956. (Boring, pp. 564-565, 580; Vinacke, p. 6; *American Psychologist*, March, 1963, 131-33).

word An ordered set of characters treated by the **computer** as a unit, regardless of its being a number, an address code, a machine instruction, or any combination of the above. The number of **bits** used to make up a computer "word" may be fixed or variable. In fixed word computers, word length remains constant although it may differ from one type of computer to another. In variable word computers, word length may be varied by program instructions or other means; the content of one storage position.

word association test A technique that requests the subject, from a list of presented words, to respond to each word with the first word that comes to mind. Reaction time as well as quality of response is noted. Long reaction time and no response (**blocking**), as well as the word associated with, supposedly reveal repressions, complexes, or other hidden aspects of the **personality**.

A testing technique introduced by **Jung** in 1910 as an aid in investigating personality.

word blindness A condition, often associated with **brain** injuries, in which the person cannot recognize the words he sees.

First described in 1869 by English neurologist Henry C. Bastian (1837-1915). German physician Adolf Kussmaul (1822-1902), called the condition word-blindness in 1877 (named **dyslexia** in 1887 by **Rudolph Berlin**).

Wundt, Wilhelm (1832-1920) German physiologist and psychologist. During his early academic life he associated with and was influenced by **Helmholtz** and **Fechner**. Founded the first journal on experimental psychology in 1881. Performed much research on experience and sensation (mental elements), detection thresholds, and **reaction time**. Trained many early experimentalists. Some of his students were: **Baldwin, Bekhterev, J. McK. Cattell, G. S. Hall, Angell, Kraepelin, Külpe, Münsterberg, Titchener**. Wrote extensively on folk psychology. *See* **act psychology, apperception, Anaxagoras, psychological laboratory** (also Boring, pp. 316-327, 461-462; Vinacke, p. 62).

Würzburg School The university at Würzburg as well as the school of thought that prospered there at the turn of century. **Külpe** inspired and sponsored much of the psychological thinking at the school, leading to many studies on thought processes, particularly **imageless thought**. Külpe at first used the introspective method as a base for experimentation and elaboration, but when it proved to be inadequate in explaining content in consciousness, Külpe introduced *Bewusstseinlagen*, or conscious attitudes, thought elements other than sensations or ideas. Another concept that emerged from the Würzburg school was the *Aufgabe*, or the purpose, task, or set one has that precedes a conscious chain of events. The research produced at Würtzburg was not convincing, but it served to shift the emphasis of psychology away from the "conscious" in thinking to set and attitude, eventually leading to **Lewin's** tension systems. *See* **Ach, Bühler, determining tendency**, *Einstellung*.

X

X-chromosome (McClung's chromosome) The female sex-determining **chromosome**. If paired with another X-chromosome, the resulting individual will be a female. If combined with a Y-chromosome, a male results, The female carries two X-chromosomes, while the male has an X and a Y.

The X-chromosome was called "X" in 1891 by Rudolph Henking (1854-1917), American bacteriologist, as a result of finding a nondividing chromosome in his investigations of sperm formation. In 1902, Clarence Erwin McClung (1870-1946), American zoologist suggested that the X-chromosome could be the sex-determiner, although he erroneously thought that the X-chromosome was male-producing.

XXY *See* **Klinefelter's syndrome**.

XYY A chromosomal aberration in which there is an extra Y-chromosome. It was found originally (1965) to be present in a chromosomal study of extremely tall men (averaging over 6 feet) incarcerated in a mental institution for the criminally insane. However, other studies have indicated that the XYY condition and criminality are not necessarily highly correlated. The XYY chromosome develops either by fertilization of a normal ovum by a YY sperm, resulting from **nondisjunction** at the second **meiotic** division or from failure of a normal, fertilized XY ovum to separate in the early stages of **mitosis**.

X

Evidence, thus far shows that XYY fathers do not transmit the chromosomal arrangement to their sons. Although affected males are not necessarily predisposed to aggressive behavior studies indicate that they do have a greater chance of committing crimes and of behaving antisocially than normal XY males. Prominent conditions associated with the XYY male are mental dullness, brain dysfunction, large genitalia, and severe cases of acne. Incidence in the general population reportedly runs from about 0.5 to 3.5 per thousand persons.

Y

Yang *See* **T'ai Chi Ch'uan, dualism.**

Yates correction An adjustment by Yates (1934) in calculating χ^2 with one **degree of freedom** for a 2 × 2 table. It helps bring the distribution (based on a discontinuous frequency) nearer to the continuous χ^2 distribution from which published tables for testing χ^2 are derived. (See Table 8).

Frank Yates (born 1902), British research statistician and associate of **Fisher.** Specialized in sampling and computer research.

Y-chromosome Carrier of male sex-linked **genes.** Females carry two X-chromosomes while males presumably have an X- and a Y-chromosome. However, there are strong indications that factors for maleness exist primarily in the **autosomes.**

Yin *See* **T'ai Chi Ch'uan, dualism.**

Y-maze A box-like laboratory device consisting of a walled-in series of pathways in the shape of a Y. Usually, the base of the Y is the starting point with one of the arms serving as the end point (goal box) where the experimental subject (usually a rat) may obtain his reward. The Y-maze is often used to measure comparative strengths of different **drives.** For example, an animal deprived of, say, food and water, is placed in a Y-maze with food located in one arm and water in the other. Consistent selection of one (say, water) over the other (food) indicates the subject's greater drive for water. *See* **maze.**

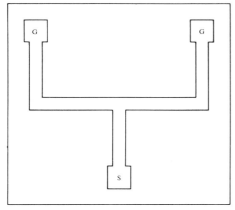

A simple Y-maze. Donald J. Lewis, Scientific Principles of Psychology, © *1963. Reprinted by permission of Prentice-Hall, Inc., Englewood Cliffs, New Jersey*

Young, Paul Thomas Born 1892, California. Ph.D. (psychology), Cornell 1918. His **pseudophone** study showed that sound and visual cues are needed to localize sound. Also made studies on motivation and hedonic processes in behavior. Received **DSC Award** 1965.

Young, Thomas (1773-1829) English physician and physicist. First to measure and describe astigmatism. First (1807) to explain sensation of color as being due to presence in retina of some structures corresponding to red, green, and violet. Discovered interference of light, leading to establishment of wave theory of light. *See* **accommodation, Helmholtz.**

Young-Helmholtz theory *See* **color-vision theories.**

Z

Zeigarnik effect A tendency to recall uncompleted tasks more readily than completed ones (despite the greater amount of time spent and repetitiveness involved in such completion). The trend is reversed, however, if interruption signifies failure and completion symbolizes success, or if tasks are performed under stress. A "tension system" or felt need seems to exist for return to such tasks. (A. J. Marrow, "Goal Tensions and Recall," *Journal of General Psychology,* 1938, **19**, 3-35, 37-64).

After Blyuma Vulfovna Zeigarnik, Russian-born (1900) but German practicing psychologist, who first reported the phenomenon in 1927.

Zeitgeber (Ger., clock, watch or time giver) An external event that gives a cue as to the passage of time.

Zeitgeist (Ger., spirit of the times) World view; emotional outlook.

Zeitschrift (Ger., journal, periodical)

Zener cards A deck of five cards each of which has five different symbols (cross, circle, rectangle, star, and wavy lines) used in **extrasensory** experiments.

Karl Edward Zener (1903-1964), American (Indiana) psychologist. Ph.D. 1926, Harvard.

Zielvorstellung (Ger., idea of a goal, end, or purpose) *See* **Ach, *Absicht.***

zoetrope *See* **stroboscope.**

Zöllner's lines *See* **illusion.**

zone digit (zone bit) The **bits** or digits other than the four used to represent the digits in a **binary code.**

zoophilia A disorder (-ia) involving an extreme degree of love (-phil-) for animals by a human being. The word is loosely defined and depends for its meaning on the educational, intellectual, and cultural background of the person using it. Generally, it refers to a person's fixation on an animal that may result in sexual excitement because of real or imagined contact. In the *medical sense* (including psychiatric), the condition is construed to have pathological significance, thus requiring medical or psychiatric treatment. *Legally,* zoophilia is sometimes considered as being synonymous with *sodomy* (from Sodom, one of the twin sin cities of the Bible destroyed by "the Lord who . . . rained brimstone and fire" upon them because of their wickedness). Sodomy involves "unnatural intercourse with a human or animal." Originally, sodomy referred to animal or homosexual anal intercourse only, but legal interpretations have sometimes included *fellatio* and *cunnilingus.* Gomorrah, the other wicked twin city, is memorialized by the word gomorrhean, a synonym for lesbian.

Zoophilia is often used synonymously with *bestiality,* both words stretching in meaning from (1) merely showing deep concern about the welfare of animals; to (2) fondling and cuddling animals excessively without obvious or conscious sexual arousal; to (3) actual kissing, masturbation, and/or sexual penetration of any available body orifices. An earlier term, *zooerastia,* describes the condition (-ia) found among Greek shepherds who were lovers (-erast-) of animals, particularly sheep.

Females reportedly seldom engage in sexual intercourse with animals, although clinical reports indicate that some women have successfully manipulated liaisons with male dogs and donkeys. Males tend to have coitus more often with domestic animals, chickens, or sheep.

z-score A **standard score,** showing the relative location of the score in the distribution, that has been transformed from a raw score (X) by use of the **mean** and **standard deviation** (S.D.) of a distribution. Negative z-scores represent scores below the mean. The z-score expresses the number of standard deviations X is away from the mean. It is computed by

$$z = \frac{X - \bar{X}}{S} \text{ or } z = \frac{X - \mu}{\sigma}$$

depending upon the data under consideration.

For example, a student received a score of 40 on two consecutive tests. The first test had a mean of 30 and a S.D. of 5, with a mean of 44 and a S.D. of 3 on the second test. The respective z-scores are:

$$z_1 = \frac{40 - 30}{5} = 2.00$$

$$z_2 = \frac{40 - 44}{3} = 1.33$$

showing that the student had a higher standing on the first test (z_1) although he had received the same raw score on each test.

Conversion to standardized scores creates a new distribution having a mean of 0 and a S.D. of 1.00. (See Table 2).

Z-score A **standard score** converted to a scale with a **mean** of 50 and a **standard deviation** of 10. *See* **T-score** (also Hays, 1963, pp. 32-44, 53, 64).

Z-transformation (z_r transformation) *See* **Fisher r-to-Z transformation.**

Zwaardemaker olfactometer Apparatus for the control and measurement of odorous stimuli. First constructed in 1889 by the Dutch physiologist, Hendrik Zwaardemaker (1857-1930), and improved by him for many years afterward.

zygote Yoke. The fertilized egg or cell produced by the union of ovum and spermatozoon. *See* **gamete.**

Some Symbols and Notations Used in Statistics

In this section there are three special groupings:

1. A list of mathematical symbols and operators, the symbols being listed according to the alphabetical order of their verbal translations.

2. An alphabetized glossary of symbols, abbreviations, and notations. Definitions are based upon those used in the textbooks as listed in the bibliography. Some definitions are truncated, altered, or combined with others. Any definition not followed by numbers in parentheses is generally accepted by statisticians. Parenthesized numbers indicate a somewhat specialized treatment of the entry as used in the textbook listed by that number in the bibliography. The order of listing follows this convention: Capital letters are listed first, with boldface lettering preceding Roman, and with superscripts coming prior to subscripts. One capital letter (A, B, etc.) precedes two (AB, BD, etc.), which, in turn, precedes three (ABD, XYZ, etc.). Next in order, after all forms of capital letters are listed, are small letters which follow the same order as for capital letters. For both upper and lower case, qualifying letters (such as a^b) precede qualifying digits (a^2), all in alphabetical or ordinal sequence.

3. A glossary of those statistical terms (usually parameters) whose symbols are letters of the Greek alphabet. Although population parameters are usually denoted by Greek letters (and sample values by Roman letters), there are some exceptions, which are indicated when they occur.

1. Some Mathematical Symbols and Operators

$\vert\ \vert$	Absolute value of deviations, disregarding signs as $\vert-5\vert = 5$.
Σ	Algebraic sum.
$\rightarrow\infty$	Approaches infinity.
$\rightarrow$	Approaches limit.
$\doteq$	Approximately equal to.
$-$	Bar over a letter refers to a sample as well as to the average of the statistic, as $\overline{X}$ is the arithmetic mean of $\overline{X}$ values.
$\therefore$	Because; since.
$\{\ \}$	Braces. Encloses elements of a set, as in $\{a\ b\}$, set of all a such that the statement b is true.
$[\ ]$	Brackets.

$\subset$	Is a proper subset of.
$\subseteq$	Is a subset of.
$\wedge$	Circumflex; an estimator; uncertainty in a sample, such as $\hat{H}$.
$\prod$	Continued product of all terms.
$\degree$	Degree.
$/$	Diagonal or shilling bar means divided by.
$\propto$	Directly proportional to; varies directly as; varies with infinity.
$\div$	Divided by
$-$	Divided by, as a divided by b in $\dfrac{a}{b}$.
$''$	Double prime, such as a'' (read as a double prime); second.
$\ldots$	Ellipsis.
$\simeq$	Estimated by.
$!$	Factorial, such as $N!$, which is the factorial of integer N.
Δ	Finite difference; in calculus, an increment, as $\Delta y =$ an increment of y.
$\equiv$	Identical.
∞	Infinity.
$\int$	Integration. Shows that the expression following it is to be integrated, such as $\int f(x)\ dx$ means the indefinite integral of $f(x)$ with respect to x.
$\cap$	Intersection, indicating both; as in: $P(A \cap B) =$ intersection of A and $B =$ probability of both A and B occurring.
M	Is measured by.
$\sim$	Is similar to, as $\Delta ABC \sim \Delta DEF$.
$\log_e m$	Logarithm to the base e for the value m.
$-$	Minus; negative.
$\times$; $\cdot$	Multiplied by, as $6 \times 7 = 42$, or $6\cdot 7 = 42$.
$(\ )$	Parentheses.
$+$	Plus; positive.
$\pm$	Plus or minus.
$\mp$	Minus or plus.
$'$	Prime; minute.
$:$	Ratio of; ratio; is to.
r^n	r to the power of n.
$\sqrt{\ }$	Root; radical sign; square root.
$\sqrt[3]{\ }$	Square root; $\sqrt[3]{\ }$ cube root.
$\ni$	Such that.
$\exists$	There exists.
$\therefore$	Therefore; hence.
$\cup$	Union; indicating either or both; as in: $P(A \cup B) =$ union of A and $B =$ probability of either A or B occurring.

$-$	Vinculum (as a symbol of aggregation) placed over two or more members of a compound quantity, as $a-\overline{b-c} = a-(b-c)$, equivalent to parentheses or brackets.

2. Glossary of Symbols and Notations

$A...Z$	Any italicized capital letter may be used to identify a variable, although many capital letters have other special uses. When a letter identifies a variable, X, then the use of the many variants of this letter follow certain conventions, such as the following, modified from Diamond (20). The italicized large letter $-X$, for example$-$stands for the variable or dimension as such. The Roman type large letter $-X-$indicates an original or raw score on the dimension. The boldface capital $\mathbf{X}$ stands for the set of scores on the dimension. The overlined capital $\overline{X}$ indicates the arithmetic mean of a set of scores. The large letter, prime, X' stands for a regressed score in the original scale units. The italicized small letter x indicates a deviation from the mean. The italicized small letter prime x' stands for a deviation from an assumed mean. The small boldface letter $\mathbf{x}$ stands for a standard score, more commonly represented as z_x.
A	(Also $\mathbf{X}$, $\mathbf{Z}$). A rectangular matrix consisting of rows and columns. The transpose of $\mathbf{A}$ is denoted by $\mathbf{A}'$; the inverse by $\mathbf{A}^{-1}$
A	Constant term, or parameter in regression equation; a variable; arbitrary origin value in computing mean; upper left-hand cell in a 2×2 table; the set itself.

Mathematical Symbols and Operators*

Symbols for Equality, Inequality, Comparison				Geometric Symbols	
$\doteq$	Approximately.	$>$	Greater than ($a>b$ indicating a is greater than b).	$(\angle)$	Angle
$\sim ; \doteqdot , \triangleq$	Approximately equal to.			$\angle s$	Angles
$::$	As equals; equality between ratios.	$\equiv$	Identical.	$(\frown)$	Arc of a circle
		$<$	Less than ($a<b$ indicates a is less than b).	$\bigcirc ; \odot$	Circle
$\cong ; \simeq ; \equiv$	Congruent; is congruent to.			$\circledS$	Circles
$\sim$	Difference between; of the order of; a deviation; e.g., $x\sim z$ indicates a difference between x and z without stating which is greater.	$\gg$	Much greater than.	$(\bigcirc)$	Circumference
		$\ll$	Much less than.	$\diagup\!\!\!\!\diagdown$	Parallelogram
		$\mp ; \neq$	Not equal to.	$\perp$	Perpendicular to
$=$	Equal to.	$\not>$	Not greater than.	$\perp s$	Perpendiculars
$\geqslant ; \geq ; \overline{>} ; \geqq$	Equal to or greater than.	$\not<$	Not less than.	$\square$	Rectangle
$\leqslant ; \leq ; \overline{<} ; \leqq$	Equal to or less than.	$\parallel$	Parallel to.	$\llcorner$	Right angle
$\sim\!\sim ; \circeq$	Equivalent to.	$\sim\!\!\sim$	Similar to.	$\square$	Square
				$\triangle$	Triangle

*Symbols are listed according to the alphabetical order of the first letter occurring in their verbal translation.

$\bar{A}$	Set of elements not in set A, called the complement of Set A.
A'	The transpose of matrix A. A matrix formed by interchanging the rows and columns of matrix A.
$A = \{a,b,c,d\}$	Set A includes the elements of a, b, c, and d.
AB	The interaction between treatments A and B.
A−B	The difference between sets A and B.
A=B	Sets A and B are equivalent.
A×B	Cartesian (set) product.
A⊆B...	A is a subset of B.
A⊂B...	A is a proper subset of B; at least one element of B is not an element of A.
A⊄B	A is not a subset of B.
A∪B	Union of sets A and B, defined as the set of elements that belong to A or to B.
A∩B...	Intersection of sets A and B, defined as the set of elements that belong to both A and B.
ABC	Set of sample points; triple interaction of treatments A, B, and C.
a	Y intercept; upper left cell in a fourfold table; observed frequency in one class of double dichotomy (93); constant term in regression equation (78); used with subscripts as σyx and σxy, the first subscript denoting the predicted variable, second the observed variable (24); the number of levels of factor A of a factorial experiment; element in matrix A, the element in the ith and jth column is denoted as a_{ij}; a particular member of the set (33).
$\left\{{a \atop b}\right\}$	Constants of a regression equation in simple correlation.
(a, b)	An ordered pair of elements, a from set A, and b from set B; a member of AxB.
a∈A	a is a member of the set A (33).
a∉A	a is not a member of the set A (33).
B	Term in Bartlett's test for homogeneity of variance (93); population regression coefficient; factor in a factorial experiment; upper righthand cell in a 2 × 2 table, or the value therein.
b	Sample regression weight (coefficient); upper right cell in a fourfold table; frequency observed in one class of a double dichotomy (93); as subscript: below, in a formula for the median, between, in symbols for variance, sums of squares, etc. (20).
$b_{12:34}$	Regression coefficient of variable X_2 on X_1 excluding X_3 and X_4.
C	Contingency coefficient, a measure of strength of association between two categorical variables; in two-way analysis of variance experimental design the number of columns in the data table for a two-factor experiment (33); centile; lower lefthand cell in a 2 × 2 contingency table, or the value therein; number of treatments on one of the variables in a factorial design experiment (20).
CE	The constant error: CE = PSE−I_N.
C_{25}	The 25th centile, Q_1.
C_{50}	The 50th centile, median, Q_2.
C_{75}	The 75th centile, Q_3.
c	Difference between arbitrary origin and mean or median; lower left cell of a fourfold table; constant in trend or regression equation; number of columns in a contingency table (78); as subscript: of columns, to identify subsum, etc. (20).
C^N	See $\binom{N}{r}$
cum f	Cumulative frequency.
cum %	Cumulative percent.
D	Symbol for decile. Difference between two measures expressed as ranks, between two weighted means, between two numbers of a pair of scores, or between two cumulative frequency polygons in the Kolmogorov-Smirnoff test; lower righthand cell in a 2 × 2 table, or the value therein.
$\bar{D}$	Mean of the differences between paired scores (78).
d	Deviation value or M. P. of a class interval from line of trend $(Y − Y_c)$, or arbitrary origin, or G. M., or average other than A. M.; difference between two observations or between paired ranks (24); constant in trend or regression equation; deviation of a difference score (D) from $\bar{D}$ (78); lower right cell of a fourfold table, or the value therein.
d′	Deviation of the M. P. of a class from an arbitrary origin in class interval units.
|d|	Absolute value of d.
df, d.f.	Degrees of freedom.
E	An efficiency ratio; expected frequency or theoretical value in the calculation of χ^2; an event. In sensory discrimination, the dimension representing the magnitude of the central effect of a stimulus used in selecting the response; the 'decision axis'.
E[ ]	Same as E( ).
E( )	Expected value of term(s) within the parentheses, e.g., E(X) is the expectation of random variable X (33).
E_i	Expected number (frequency) in a category under a given probability distribution.
E_{xy}, E_{yx}	Correlation ratio in a sample.
$E(MS_B)$	Expected value of the treatment mean square for a fixed effects model (44).
$E(MS_{BG})$	Expected value of the between-groups mean square (44).
$E(MS_{WG})$	Expected value of the within-groups mean square (44).
$E(MS_{res})$	Expected value of the residual mean square (44).
e	A mathematical constant = 2.71828, base of Napierian or natural system of logarithms; in deviation form, the random error component of a variable (e = x − a); as subscript: expected (20).
F	Factor matrix consisting of correlations of each variance in R with each of the extracted factors; F ratio computed from a sample.
F	A ratio of two variances; used with subscript to denote value of F that cuts off the upper α portion of the sampling distribution of F. See F.
F_σ	
FCP	Forced choice procedure.
$f(E|I_j)$	The probability density function on E given that stimulus I_j is presented.
$f(E_i|I_j)$	The probability density of E_i when I_j is presented.
$f(I_j|I_N)$	The probability density that I_j will occur as a reproduction of I_N.
F_{max}	A test for homogeneity of variance equal to the ratio of the largest to the smallest variance.
f	Frequency of items in a distribution or a subgroup. Subscripts denote interval or subclass (f_i); or row frequencies (f_r); or column frequencies (f_c); or cell frequencies (f_{xy}); or observed frequencies (f_o); or expected frequencies (f_e).
fX	A score multiplied by its corresponding frequency.
$f(X)$	Density function; frequency function of the random variable X.
$F(X)$	Distribution function; cumulative distribution function.
G	Geometric mean; grand total of observations.
G. M.	Guessed mean.
G_m	Geometric mean.
g_1	Measure of skewness (24).
g_2	Measure of kurtosis (24).
H	Indicator of a statistical hypothesis, as in H: μ=4, the hypothesis that the population mean is equal to four; a test statistic for comparing samples by means of the sums of ranks; the uncertainty in a population; in the Kruskal-Wallis test, a statistic approximating χ^2.
$\hat{H}$	The uncertainty in a sample; a biased (smaller) estimator of H.
H_0	The null hypothesis, as in: $H_0: \mu_1 − \mu_2 = 0$, or as in $H_0: p = q$, the hypothesis that no difference exists between p and q; hypothesis actually being tested (33, 78). A statement concerning one or more parameters that is subjected to a statistical test.
H_1	The alternative hypothesis that remains tenable if H_0 is rejected.
H_m	Harmonic mean.
HSD	Honestly Significant Difference test, Tukey's multiple comparison test.
h	The hypothetical frequency in the chi-square test of goodness of fit or the chi-square test of independence; a variable subscript; size of a class interval; length of a vector in cosine model of correlation (20).
h^2	Communality.
h_i^2	Common variance of an observed variable.
I	Identity matrix, item identity; a physical dimension of intensity or magnitude, such as luminance, weight, or temporal duration.
I_M	The mean of the productions or reproductions of a standard stimulus.
I_S	The stimulus intensity serving as "signal+noise" in a given experiment.

IU	The interval of uncertainty; the range between the stimuli given (P(G) = 0·50 and P(L) = 0·50) when three categories of response are used.
I_0	The absolute threshold: $I_0 = I_{0·50}$, $I_N = 0$.
$I_{0·50}$	The stimulus magnitude such that $P(Y|I_{0·50}) = 0·50$.
$I_{0·50(G)}$	The stimulus magnitude such that $P(G|I_{0·50(G)}) = 0·50$.
i	Width of a class (or step) interval; subscript along with j, k, l, etc., used to identify particular observations in a group.
i_{md}	Class interval in which the median falls.
i_{mo}	Class interval in which the mode falls.
J	Number of different experimental treatments or groups in an experiment.
j	Variable subscript often denoting the jth treatment group or factor level, or denoting columns.
K	Kendall's coefficient of consistency; in a two-factor experiment, number of treatment groups or levels of the second factor; number of "blocks" of observations in an experiment (33); the number of observations in the K-S test which are equal to or less than X.
K-S Test	Kolmogorov-Smirnoff Test.
k	A constant; number of samples or treatments or times a test is lengthened in an experiment (24); number or size of groups, classes, variables, strata, etc., or subgroups in a sample; number of arrays in correlation table; a variable (running) subscript (33); an arbitrarily positive number (33); coefficient of alienation; as subscript: of the cell (20).
L	Lower confidence limit; in defining range, lowest score of a sample.
LL	Lower limit of the class in which the median falls; the lower limen; $I_{0·50(L)}$, or the analogous measure for ML.
L_{Md}	Lower limit of class interval containing median.
L_{me}	Same as L_{Md}.
L_{mo}	Lower limit of modal group or class.
LSD	Least significant difference between two means (44).
$Log^{-1}a$	Number whose log is a.
$Log_e m$	Logarithm to the base e for the value of m.
l	A linear function of random variables; lower limit of a class interval.
l_m	Lower limit of a modal group.
M	Sample arithmetic mean.
M'	Assumed mean.
MCS	Method of constant stimuli.
M. D.	Mean deviation.
M_D	Mean difference between N matched pairs.
Md	The median.
ML	Method of limits.
M. P.	Midpoint.
MS	Mean square in the analysis of variance.
MS_{error}	Unbiased estimate of the population error variance (44).
M_2	Second moment about the mean (variance).
M_3	Third moment about the mean.
M_4	Fourth moment about the mean.
m	Moment about the mean (value of nth moment is $\Sigma x^n/N$); number of items in a test (93); value of M.P. of a class of a population distribution; in the sign test, the frequency of the less frequent sign (20).
N	Total number of independently drawn cases, observations, or elements in a population when n is the number in a sample; alternative symbol to n_N.
N! !N	Factorial of integer N (read as N factorial): N! = (N-1) (N-2) ... 1; !N is read as factorial N.
N_p	Number of cases in one of two categories, the other being N_q. See N_p.
N_q	Number of unordered combinations of N things taken r at a time.
(N_r)	
$\binom{N}{r}$	Number of unordered combinations of N things taken r at a time, $0 \leqslant r \leqslant N$; a binomial coefficient.
N. S.	Not significant, in a statistical test.
n	Number of cases (values) of a variable in a sample from a universe of size N; number of items in a test; number of times a test is lengthened; number of degrees of freedom (93); numbers of pairs; number (size) of any one of several samples containing the same number of observations (33).
$\binom{n}{m}$	Number of ways in which subsets, each consisting of m elements can be formed from a set of n elements (20). See $\binom{N}{r}$.
$\binom{n}{r}$	
n_1	Number of d. f. for the numerator mean square of a variance ratio (93).
n_2	Number of d. f. for denominator mean square of variance ratio (93).
O	Observed frequency as in the calculation of χ^2.
ϕ	The empty set (33).
o	As subscript: obtained or observed.
P	Percentile (subscripts indicate which percentile is meant); probability level of occurrence of an event; proportion (percentage or fraction) of elements in one class of a dichotomous population; sample proportion of "successes" in sampling from a Bernoulli distribution (33).
P( )	Probability of event(s) within parentheses.
P(. . .)	Probability of . . .; as in: P(A) = probability of A occurring.
P(A|B)	Conditional probability; probability of A occurring given that B occurs.
P(A<X<B)	Probability of X falling between the fixed values A and B.
P. E.	Probable error of a statistic.
P_i	Percentile point (subscript denotes particular percentile point, as P_{10}, P_{40}, etc.).
P_r^n	Number of permutations of n things taken r at a time.
P(R)	The probability of the response R.
$P(R|I_j)$	The probability of the response R on trials on which I_j is presented.
P(R|R)	The probability of R given the response R was made on the preceding trial.
nP_n	Number of permutations of n things taken altogether.
p	Sample proportion or probability estimate in one of two mutually exclusive classes; parameter of a binomial; number of independent variables in the multiple regression; probability of a given event size; probability of "success" in a single Bernoulli trial (33); as subscript: of the proportion (20).
p(A)	Probability associated with a particular event A in a probability function (33).
p'	Sample proportion or percentage.
$\hat{p}$	Estimator of p, the parameter of a binomial population.
p_i	Sample proportion in the ith class; estimate of the probability of the occurrence of the ith event; parameter of a binomial population.
p_k	The proportion of scores in a set that belong to a subset, k.
Q	Semi-interquartile range (quartile deviation), defined as $(P_{75} - P_{25})/2$ or $(Q_3-Q_1)/2$; percentage where $Q = 100 - P$ or fraction where $Q = 1.00$; probability of nonoccurrence of an event (78); proportion of cases in the other class of a dichotomous population (the other being P) (78).
Q_I	Interquartile range equals $Q_3 - Q_1$.
Q_1	The first quartile, equivalent to the 25th percentile.
Q_2	The second quartile, equivalent to the median and 50th percentile.
Q_3	The third quartile, equivalent to the 75th percentile.
QD	Quartile deviation or semi-interquartile range (Q).
Q_m	Quadratic mean.
q	Probability of failure; proportion of nonoccurrences: $1 - p$; proportion of cases in a category; arbitrary symbol designating one or more variables partialed out of the primary variable(s).
q_α	Tabled value for degrees of freedom and α level of significance.
R	A matrix of correlations. A given response which may be defined, for example, as Y, N or D; number of runs in a sequence associated with the runs test; rank-order coefficient of correlation; multiple correlation (product moment r between unmodified variable(s) and the weighted sum of two or more variables); in a scoring formula the number of right answers; the range of values of a set of measurements; in two-way analysis of variance experimental design, the number of rows in the data table for a two-factor experiment (compare C) (33).
R'	The set of responses allowed in a given experimental design.
R'_N	The number of elements in R'.

$\bar{R}_1$ and R_2 — The sum of ranks for the group having a sample size of n_1 or n_2. R_1 and R_2 are used in a wide variety of nonparametric tests involving ranks, e.g., Mann-Whitney U-formula (78), Wilcoxon Matched Pairs Signed Ranks test, Kruskal-Wallis one-way anova, Friedman Two-Way anova, etc.

$R_{1 \cdot 234}$ — Multiple correlation coefficient for variable X_1 and variables X_2, X_3, and X_4.

$(R_{1 \cdot 23 \ldots n})$ — Coefficient of multiple correlation between dependent variable X, and the independent variables X_2, $X_3 \ldots X_n$.

$R_{x \cdot yy}$, $R_{1 \cdot 23}$ — See $r_{x \cdot yz}$, $r_{1 \cdot 23}$.

r — Pearson product-moment correlation coefficient; used with subscripts to denote variables correlated, e.g., r_{xy}, r_{21}, etc; designates the number of steps separating ordered means (44); number of rows in a contingency table; as subscript of the correlation; of rows; of ranks (20).

r! — r factorial; product of the integers from r to 1.

r' — Coefficient of rank correlation.

r_b — See r_{bis}.

r_{bi}, r_{bis} — Biserial correlation coefficient.

r_c — Intraclass correlation coefficient.

r_{hh} — Reliability coefficient for half a test.

r_{pR} — Reliability coefficient for a test lengthened R times.

r_{pb} ($r_{pt\ bis}$) — Point biserial correlation; the product moment r between a dichotomous and a continuous variable.

r_{rho} — Spearman rank-order correlation coefficient.

$p^r xx$ — Spearman-Brown reliability coefficient for a test whose length is increased p times.

$pq^r xy$ — Estimate of correlation between two tests (x and y) when one is lengthened p times and the other q times.

r_s — Serial correlation coefficient; Spearman rank correlation, this symbol r_s used in preference to ρ to avoid confusion with the population correlation (33).

r_t — Tetrachoric correlation coefficient.

r_{tet} — Same as r_t.

r_{tt} — Reliability coefficient.

r_{xx} — See r_{tt}.

$r_{x \cdot yz}$, $r_{1 \cdot 23}$ — Multiple correlation coefficient.

$r_{xy \cdot z}$, $r_{12 \cdot 3}$ — Partial correlation coefficient for X_1 and X_2, excluding X_3.

r^2 — Coefficient of determination.

r_{11} — Reliability coefficient.

$12^r 34$ — Partial correlation coefficient for X_1 and X_2 and expected X_3 and X_4.

S — Sample space of an experiment; set of all possible outcomes of an experiment; sum of squares used in anova and covariance (93); sample standard deviation; number of subjects in a repeated measurements design; a statistic in the Kendall (tau) test maximum likelihood estimator.

$\bar{S}$ — Arithmetic mean of two or more standard deviations.

S' — The set of stimulus values used in a given experimental design.

S. D. — Standard deviation.

SD_L — The standard deviation of a set of estimates of UL (or of LL) obtained by ML.

S_k — Skewness.

S^2_{yx} — Variance of y residuals from regression line.

SS — Standard score; sum of squares in anova (33).

SS_{BG} — Sum of squares between groups.

SS_{WG} — Sum of squares within groups.

s — Sample (estimate) of a standard deviation defined as $\sqrt{\Sigma x^2 / N}$, used with subscript to denote variable, s_x, s_y, etc. (24, 78); estimate of the standard error of a statistic (24); number of subjects in a repeated measurements design.

s^2 — Variance, or square of the standard deviation, used with subscripts as indicated under s (24, 93); estimate of variance (20); biased estimator of σ^2.

$\hat{s}$ — Sample standard deviation based on unbiased variance estimate, expressed as s = $\sqrt{\Sigma x^2 / N - 1}$.

$\hat{s}^2$ — Unbiased estimate of the population variance, expressed as s^2 = $\Sigma x^2 / N - 1$.

$s_{\bar{D}}$ or $\hat{s}_D$ — Standard error of the difference (20); estimated S. E. of the difference between means, direct-difference method (78).

$s_{\bar{D}}$ — Standard deviation of the difference scores (78).

s_p — Standard error of the proportion (20).

s_r — Standard error of the correlation (20).

$s_{\bar{X}}$ — Standard error of the mean (20); estimated standard error of a sample mean, defined as $s_{\bar{X}}$ = $\hat{s}/\sqrt{N}$ = s/$\sqrt{N} - 1$ (78).

s_y — Sample standard deviation; standard error of estimate of Y variable.

s_z — Standard error of z (20).

$\hat{s}^2_B$ or s^2_b — Between-group variance estimate (78) and (20).

$\hat{s}^2_W$ or s^2_w — Within-group variance estimate (78) and (20).

$s_{p_1 - p_2}$ — Standard error of the difference in proportions (20).

$s_{\bar{X}_1 - \bar{X}_2}$ — (Estimated) standard error of the difference between means (20, 78).

$s_{y \cdot x}$ — Standard error of estimate for a sample (93).

$s_{est\ y}$ — Standard error of estimate when predictions are made from X to Y (78).

$s_{est\ x}$ — Standard error of estimate when predictions are made from Y to X (78).

$s_{y \cdot x}$, $s_{x \cdot y}$ — Standard error of estimate (24).

$s_{y'}$, $s_{x'}$ — Standard deviation of predicted values of Y and X (24).

T — Smaller sum of ranks with the least frequent sign; in Wilcoxon matched pairs signed-ranks test and in the Mann-Whitney test the sum of the scores T within a set (or sum of ranks in groups with smaller sums); McCall's T score, a standard score with arbitrary mean of 50 and arbitrary S. D. of 10; a correction factor for ties.

$\hat{T}$ — A (larger) biased estimate of T.

T_i — The sum of all scores in group i (93); a true score of an observation.

Ts — True score on a test for an individual subject (33).

t — Student's t: the ratio of any statistic to an unbiased estimate of its standard error; a random variable following the distribution of t with v degrees of freedom (33); number of trials in a repeated measurements design; statistic for testing a null hypothesis or estimating confidence limits when σ is unknown; as subscript: total (20). Value of t that cuts off the upper portion of the sampling distribution of t.

U — Upper confidence limit; symbol for the Mann-Whitney U nonparametric test statistic; the universal set.

U' — Mann-Whitney U test statistic.

UL — The upper limen; $I_{0 \cdot 50}(G)$, or the analogous measurement for ML.

u — Upper limit of a class interval; ordinate of unit normal curve (93).

V — Coefficient of variation.

v — Number of runs in a sample; degrees of freedom for MS error (experimental error in various anova tests).

W — Kendall's coefficient of concordance; width of a confidence interval; universal set; number of wrong answers on a test; weight used in obtaining a weighted mean; the Weber fraction: W = $\Delta I / I_N$, or W = σ_I / I_N.

W_r — The difference that a comparison must exceed in order to be declared significant in Newman-Keuls and Duncan's tests.

w — Width of a confidence interval; weight assigned each value of a variable; as subscript: within.

X — The boldfaced capital symbolizes set of scores on the dimension.

$\bar{X}$ — Arithmetic mean of a sample or set of scores.

X · — The most common symbol for a variable or score dimension (20); a matrix value of an independent variable in a correlation matrix; the horizontal axis or dimension in a scatter diagram (20).

X' — A coded variable; a score predicted by a regression equation; a transformed score; a regressed score in the original scale units (20).

$\tilde{X}$ — Predicted value of X.

$\tilde{X}$, $\tilde{x}$ — Sample estimate computed from a regression equation.

X', Y' — Scores predicted by regression equations (78).

$X_{\ell\ell}$ — Score at lower limit of interval containing X.

X_{ul} — Score at upper limit of interval containing X.

X_1 — Value of the dependent variable in multiple correlation and partial correlation.

$X_2, X_3 \ldots X_m$ — Values of independent variables in multiple correlation and partial correlation.

X_o — Assumed origin.

X_p — Percentile, a score X that exceeds the proportion p of a set of ordered scores.

(X,Y) — A joint event, consisting of a value for variable X paired with a value for variable Y (33).

x   A column matrix or vector; number of objects in one category or the number of successes (78); deviation of an individual value from its sample mean, $x = X - \overline{X}$; midpoint of a class interval.

$\tilde{x}$ *Same as* $\tilde{X}$.

x'   Deviation from an assumed mean.

Y   A random variable; the vertical axis in a scatter diagram (20); the value of a dependent variable in a correlation matrix; the response YES, in sensory discrimination experiments.

Y'   Y score predicted from X; a coded score.

$\overline{Y}$ Mean of a sample.

$\hat{Y}$ Predicted value of Y.

Y_c   Y value determined from trend or regression line.

y   The dependent variable; an observation; deviation of individual Y value from its arithmetic mean $\overline{Y}$; height of the ordinate of the normal distribution.

$\overline{y}$ $\overline{Y}$.

$\hat{y}$ Deviation of Y from $\overline{Y}$.

YNP   YES-NO-procedure in sensory discrimination experiments.

Z   Fisher's logarithmic transformation of r (value corresponding to r_{xy} in Fisher's r to Z transformation), which varies without limit and is approximately normally distributed (33).

Z_r   Fisher's logarithmic transformation used in testing significance of a correlation coefficient (93).

z   Standard score with a mean of zero and a standard deviation of unity; the ratio of a normally distributed statistic to its standard error (20); the abscissa of a normal curve; deviation of a sample mean or of a specific score from the population mean expressed in standard deviation units (78); a standard normal variable; a statistic for testing the null hypothesis when σ is known (78); as subscript: refers to transformations of r (20); the standardized normal deviate cutting on a tail of the normal distribution equal in area to ϵ.

|z| Absolute value of a standardized score.

$z_y{'}$ Y' expressed in terms of a z-score (78).

$z_{0.01} = \pm 2.58$ Critical value of z, minimum z required to reject H_0 at the 0.01 level of significance, two-tailed test (78).

$z_{0.05} = \pm 1.96$ Minimum value of z required to reject H_0 at the 0.05 level of significance, two-tailed test (78).

3. *Greek Letters Used in Statistics*

Ordinarily parameters are denoted by Greek letters and sample statistics by Roman letters. However, chi-squared (χ^2) denotes a statistic, and F, P, and Q indicate frequency and proportion in a population.

Many of the Greek capital letters (A, B, E, H, etc.) are not used in statistics because of their identity and consequent confusion with English capitals. The symbols included here follow the Greek order for alphabetizing.

Greek Alphabet

A α alpha
B β beta
Γ γ gamma
Δ δ delta
E ϵ epsilon
Z ζ zeta
H η eta
Θ θ theta
I ι iota
K κ kappa
Λ λ lambda
M μ mu
N ν nu
Ξ ξ xi
O o omicron
Π π pi
P ρ rho
Σ σ sigma
T τ tau
Υ υ upsilon
Φ ϕ phi
X χ chi
Ψ ψ psi
Ω ω omega

alpha
a   (Capital A; small letter a). Probability of rejecting an actually true (correct) H_0 when it is true; risk of making a type I error. *See* **alpha** in dictionary section.

a^3   Measure of skewness.

beta
β   (Capital B; small letter β). Probability of accepting H_0 when it is actually false (risk of type II error); regression weight in a multiple regression equation applied to an independent variable or predictor in standard score form (24). The critical likelihood ratio.

β_y   Population regression coefficient.

$1 - \beta$ Power of a statistical test against some given true alternative to the null hypothesis (33).

$\beta_{Y \cdot X}$ Regression coefficient for prediction of Y from X in the population (33).

$\beta_1, \beta_2, ..., \beta_{J-1}...$ Population regression coefficients for linear and curvilinear trends between Y and X.

$\left. \begin{array}{l} \beta_{12 \cdot 3}, \beta_{12 \cdot 34} \\ \beta_{13 \cdot 24}, \beta_{24 \cdot 23} \end{array} \right\}$ Beta coefficients

β_1   Measure of relative skewness.

β_2   Measure of relative kurtosis.

gamma
γ   (Capital Γ; small letter γ). Coefficient of predictive association between sets of ordered classes (33).

delta
$\Delta = \dfrac{|\mu_1 - \mu_2|}{\sigma Y|X}$ (Capital Δ; small letter δ). Absolute difference between two population means, relative to the standard deviation for either population. Mean square successive difference.

$\Delta^2 (D^2)$

δ   The number of degrees of freedom associated with a chi square value; a determinant; also difference between two population means, $\mu_1 \mu_2$. Noncentrality parameter for noncentral t or noncentral F (33).

epsilon
ϵ   (Capital E; small letter ϵ). A member of, as "a ϵ A" reads as "a is a member of A"; an acceptable limiting false positive rate.

ϵ^2   Differentiation ratio without bias (20).

zeta
ζ   (Capital Z; small letter ζ). Test for linearity of regression, value in the Fisher r to Z transformation corresponding to the population correlation (33).

ζ_r   Population value corresponding to the statistic z_r.

eta
η   (Capital H; small letter η). The population value of the correlation ratio, measuring the fit of the observations to the means of the vertical or horizontal arrays.

$\eta_{xy} \eta_{yx}$ Correlation ratio in the population.

$\eta^2_{Y \cdot X}$ Correlation ratio for relation of Y to X (33).

theta
θ   (Capital Θ; small letter θ). Population value of a proportion (24); any statistic.

θ_0   Value of θ specified by the null hypothesis (33).

kappa
κ   (Capital K; small letter κ). A curve criterion.

lambda
λ_1   (Capital Λ; small letter λ). A constant appearing in the ith orthogonal polynomial.

λ_B   Asymmetric measure of predictive association for a contingency table (33).

λ_{AB}   Symmetric measure of predictive association in a contingency table (33).

mu
μ   (Capital M; small letter μ). Population arithmetic mean; assumed value of (used in H_0 testing); used with subscript to indicate variable: μ_x.

$\mu = E(X)$ Mean of the probability distribution of the random variable X (33).

μ_0   Value of population mean under H_0.

μ_1   Value of population mean under H_1.

$\mu_{\overline{X}}$ Mean of the distribution of sample means (78).

μ_D   Mean of the difference between paired scores (78).

$\mu_1{'}, \mu_2{'}, \mu_3{'}$, etc.   First, second, third, etc., moment of a distribution.

$\mu_1 \ \mu_2, \mu_3$, etc.   First, second, third, etc., moment about the mean.

nu
ν   (Capital N; small letter ν). Number of degrees of freedom for a t or chi-square variable; $\nu_1 \nu_2 \nu_3$ (nu$_1$, nu$_2$, nu$_3$); moments about arbitrary origin; the true score of an individual on Y.

ν_1, ν_2   Number of degrees of freedom for numerator and denominator, respectively, for an F ratio; the parameters of the F distribution (33).

xi
ξ_{50}   (Capital Ξ; small letter ξ). Median of a population.

ξ_j   Effect associated with treatment j, in the general regression model (33).

pi
π   (Capital Π; small letter π). A mathematical constant (3.1415926+), the ratio of the circumference of a circle to its diameter.

rho
ρ   (Capital P; small letter ρ). Correlation coefficient in a population; the Spearman rho or rank-order variable, being a variant of the product moment correlation

$$P = \frac{COV\,(x, y)}{\sigma_x \sigma_y}.$$

P_1 — Intraclass correlation coefficient for a population (33).

sigma Σ — (Capital Σ; small letter σ). Summation sign for a series of values. *See* **summation** in dictionary section.

Σ_{XY} — The sum of paired products of X and Y measures, each in deviation form.

σ — The population standard deviation of a random variable of measures; standard error of a statistic (followed by a subscript indicating the statistic).

σ — Maximum likelihood estimate of σ (24).

σ^2 — Population variance [E $(x - \mu)^2$] on a complete enumeration of all items, with subscripts as for σ.

$\sigma^2(...)$ — Variance of.

σ_D — The standard deviation of the distribution of the differences between the central effects of two stimuli.

σ_M — True standard error of the mean, given samples of size N from some population (33).

$\sigma_{med.}$ — Standard error of median.

σ_P — Standard error of percentage.

σ_r — Standard error of coefficient of correlation.

σ_u — Standard deviation of regression.

σ_v — Standard error of coefficient of variation.

σ_σ — Standard error of standard deviation.

σ_σ^2 — Standard error of variance.

$\sigma_{\bar{x}}$ — Standard error of the arithmetic mean.

σ_X — Standard deviation of scores on X.

σ_Y — Standard deviation of scores on Y.

$\sigma_{x \cdot y}$ — True standard error of estimate for predictions of X from Y.

$\sigma_{y \cdot x}$ — True standard error of estimate for predictions of Y from X in some populations.

σ_{x-y} — Standard error of difference between two statistics X and Y.

σ_Z — The standard error of the Z transformation of r or σ.

tau τ — (Capital T small letter τ). Kendall's tau, a measure of relationship between pairs of ranks. Not actually a coefficient of correlation, but primarily an index that shows rank-order agreement, or the tendency of two rank-orders to be alike.

upsilon v — (Capital Υ; small letter v). The so-called "true" score of an individual (score) on Y.

phi ϕ — (Capital Φ; small letter ϕ). The phi coefficient, a product moment r based on two dichotomous variables; the null (empty) set; measure of fourfold point correlation; transformation of percents to angles.

ϕ^2 — Index of mean square contingency for a population or a sample contingency table (33).

chi χ^2 — (Capital X; small letter χ). The usual usage for chi; a variable with a chi square distribution; used to determine probability that a distribution of frequencies within categories is in accordance with a stated hypothesis; the Pearson chi-square statistic (33); value used in test for goodness of fit; variable distributed as probability distribution.

psi ψ — (capital Ψ; small letter ψ). Value of a particular comparison among population means (33).

omega ω^2 — (capital Ω; small letter ω). Population index showing the relative or proportional reduction in the variance of Y given the X value for an observation (33).

UNITS OF MEASURE: SI PREFIXES, UNITS, AND CONVERSION FACTORS

Prefixes: Multiples and Submultiples of SI Units

The most likely prefixes to be used in APA journals are kilo-, milli-, micro-, and nano-. The prefixes hecto-, deka-, deci-, and centi- are to be restricted to instances where there is a strongly felt need, such as using the centimeter as the unit of length in certain biological and physiological measurements. Compound prefixes should not be used; for example 10^{-9} meter is represented by 1 nm (nanometer), not 1 mμm. Attaching a prefix to a unit essentially constitutes a new unit, for example: 1 km^2 = 1 (km)^2 = 10^6 m^2 and not 1 k(m^2) = 10^3 m^2. Where possible, any numerical prefix should appear in the numerator of an expression.

The prefixes femto (10^{-15}) and atto (10^{-18}) are not likely to be used in psychological measurement. The prefix nano- has largely replaced the use of the millimicron and pico- has done likewise for micromicro. *See* **International System of Units**

Prefix and symbol		Meaning	Multiples and submultiples
tera-	(T)	one trillion	$1,000,000,000,000 = 10^{12}$
giga-	(G)	one billion	$1,000,000,000 = 10^9$
mega-	(M)	one million	$1,000,000 = 10^6$
kilo-	(k)	one thousand	$1,000 = 10^3$
hecto-	(h)	one hundred	$100 = 10^2$
deka-	(da, dk)	ten	$10 = 10^1$
Unit = one			$1 = 10^0$
deci-	(d)	one-tenth	$0.1 = 10^{-1}$
centi-	(c)	one-hundredth	$0.01 = 10^{-2}$
milli-	(m)	one-thousandth	$0.001 = 10^{-3}$
micro	(μ)	one-millionth	$0.000\ 001 = 10^{-6}$
nano-	(n, mμ)	one-billionth	$0.000\ 000\ 001 = 10^{-9}$
pico-	(p, $\mu\mu$)	one-trillionth	$0.000\ 000\ 000\ 001 = 10^{-12}$
femto	(f)	one-quadrillionth	10^{-15}
atto	(a)	one-quintillionth	10^{-18}

Derived SI Units

Name of unit and symbol	Physical quantity
ampere per meter (A/m^{-1})	magnetic field strength
candela per square meter (cd/m^{-2})	luminance
cubic meter (m^3)	volume
kilogram per cubic meter (kg/m^{-3})	density
meter per second (m/s^{-1})	velocity
meter per second squared (m/s^{-2})	acceleration
newton per square meter (N/m^{-2})	pressure
newton second per square meter (N s/m^{-2})	dynamic viscosity
radian per second (rad/s^{-1})	angular velocity
square meter (m^2)	area
square meter per second (m^2/s^{-1})	kinematic viscosity, diffusion coefficient
volt per meter (V/m^{-1})	electric field strength

Derived SI Units with Special Names

Name of unit and symbol	Physical quantity	Definition of unit
coulomb (C)	electric charge	A s
degree Celsius (°C)	customary temperature	$t/°C = T/°K - 273.15$
farad (F)	electric capacitance	$A^2 \, s^4 \, kg^{-1} \, m^{-2} = A \, s \, V^{-1}$
henry (H)	inductance	$kg \, m^2 \, s^{-2} \, A^{-2} = V \, s \, A^{-1}$
hertz (Hz)	frequency	cycle per second
joule (J)	energy	$kg \, m^2 \, s^{-2}$
lumen (lm)	luminous flux	cd sr
lux (lx)	illumination	$cd \, sr \, m^{-2}$
newton (N)	force	$kg \, m \, s^{-2} = J \, m^{-1}$
ohm (Ω)	electric resistance	$kg \, m^2 \, s^{-3} \, A^{-2} = V \, A^{-1}$
tesla (T)	magnetic flux density	$kg \, s^{-2} \, A^{-1} = V \, s \, m^{-2}$
volt (V)	electric potential	$kg \, m^2 \, s^{-3} \, A^{-1} = J \, A^{-1} \, s^{-1}$
watt (W)	power	$kg \, m^2 \, s^{-3} = J \, s^{-1}$
weber (Wb)	magnetic flux	$kg \, m^2 \, s^{-2} \, A^{-1} = V \, s$

Conversion Factors for SI Units

The table provides exact numerical multiples of SI units and multiplying factors for conversion to corresponding new numbers and SI units.
The first two digits represent a power of 10; thus for an acre to be converted to square meters (m^2), the first two digits (03) indicate that the following sequence of digits is to be multiplied by 10 to the third power: hence, 1 acre = $4.046\,856\,422\,4 \times 10^3$ meter^2 exactly. Asterisks represent an exact definition. *See* **International System of Units** as defined in the dictionary section.

To convert from:	To:	Multiply by:
acre	meter^2	+03 4.046 856 422 4 *
ampere (international of 1948)	ampere	-01 9.998 35
angstrom	meter	-10 1.000*
Celsius (temperature)	kelvin	$t_K = t_C + 273.15$
coulomb (1948)	coulomb	-01 9.998 35
erg	joule	-07 1.00*
Fahrenheit	kelvin	$t_K = (5/9)(t_F + 459.67)$
Fahrenheit	Celsius	$t_C = (5/9)(t_F - 32)$
farad (1948)	farad	-01 9.995 05
foot	meter	-01 3.048*
foot candle	lumen/meter^2	+01 1.076 391 0
foot lambert	candela/meter^2	+00 3.426 259
grain	kilogram	-05 6.479 891*
gram	kilogram	-03 1.00*
henry (1948)	henry	+00 1.000 495
inch	meter	-02 2.54*
joule (1948)	joule	+00 1.000 165
lambert	candela/meter^2	+04 1/π*
micron	meter	-06 1.00
mile (U.S. statute)	meter	+03 1.609 344*
minute (mean solar)	second (mean solar)	+01 6.00*
minute (sidereal)	second (mean solar)	+01 5.983 617 4
ohm (1948)	ohm	+00 1.000 495
ounce (U.S. fluid)	meter^3	-05 2.957 352 956 25*
Rankine (temperature)	kelvin	$t_K = (5/9)t_R$
rayleigh (rate of photon emission)	1/second meter^2	+10 1.00*
second (ephemeris)	second	+00 1.000 000 000
second (sidereal)	second (mean solar)	-01 9.972 695 7
volt (1948)	volt	+00 1.000 330
watt (1948)	watt	+00 1.000 165

According to the APA, the journal policy on units of measurement (American Psychologist, 1971, 26, 12, p. 1099) is that they will accept measurements in traditional units but with "SI equivalents in parentheses," until such time that "experimenters become accustomed to the system." The following table, based on information provided in the *American Psychologist* article and in the *American Scientist* previously referred to, represents some of the traditional units and their equivalent SI units, which might, at some time, conceivably be used in psychology. Figures reprinted from *American Psychologist* are in parentheses.

Examples of Units Contrary to SI, with Their Equivalents

Physical Quantity	Traditional Unit	Equivalent SI Units
length	1 inch	0.0254 m (25.4 mm)
	1 foot	0.3048 m
	1 ångstrom	10^{-10} m (0.1 nm)
area	1 square inch	6.4516×10^{-4} m^2
	1 square foot	0.092 903 m^2
	1 square yard	0.836 127 m^2
volume	1 cubic inch	$1.638\,71 \times 10^{-5}$ m^3 (16.3871 cm^3)
	1 cubic foot	0.028 316 8 m^3 (28.316 8 cm^3)
capacity	1 fluid ounce	2.95737×10^{-5} m^3
mass	1 U.S. grain	6.479891×10^{-5} kg
	1 ounce	2.834952×10^{-2} kg
	1 U. S. pound	0.453 592 37 kg (.4536 kg)
temperature	degree Rankine	5/9 °K
	degree Fahrenheit	$t/°F = 9/5 \, T/°C + 32$
illumination	1 foot candle	10.763 9 lx (lux)
luminance	1 foot lambert	3.426 26 cd/m^2
	millilambert	3.1831 cd/m^2
energy	erg	10^{-7} J
	calorie (thermochemical)	4.184 J
	calorie (15°C)	4.1858 J

Statistical Tables

Table 1a

Cumulative Binomial Probabilities: One-Tailed

N \ x	0	1	2	3	4	5	6	7	8	9	10	11	12	13	14	15
5	031	188	500	812	969	†										
6	016	109	344	656	891	984	†									
7	008	062	227	500	773	938	992	†								
8	004	035	145	363	637	855	965	996	†							
9	002	020	090	254	500	746	910	980	998	†						
10	001	011	055	172	377	623	828	945	989	999	†					
11		006	033	113	274	500	726	887	967	994	†	†				
12		003	019	073	194	387	613	806	927	981	997	†	†			
13		002	011	046	133	291	500	709	867	954	989	998	†	†		
14	001	006	029	090	212	395	605	788	910	971	994	999	†	†		
15		004	018	059	151	304	500	696	849	941	982	996	†	†	†	
16		002	011	038	105	227	402	598	773	895	962	989	998	†	†	
17		001	006	025	072	166	315	500	685	834	928	975	994	999	†	
18		001	004	015	048	119	240	407	593	760	881	952	985	996	999	
19			002	010	032	084	180	324	500	676	820	916	968	990	998	
20			001	006	021	058	132	252	412	588	748	868	942	979	994	
21			001	004	013	039	095	192	332	500	668	808	905	961	987	
22				002	008	026	067	143	262	416	584	738	857	933	974	
23				001	005	017	047	105	202	339	500	661	798	895	953	
24				001	003	011	032	076	154	271	419	581	729	846	924	
25					002	007	022	054	115	212	345	500	655	788	885	

To save space, decimal points are omitted in the p's.

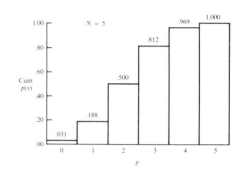

The above figure represents the probabilities, p, of the occurrence of an event (0 ≤ 1, 2, 3, 4, and 5) for an N = 5.

Discussion

Statistical Background (See binomial distribution)

Table Explanation

Given in the body of this table are *one-tailed probabilities* under H_O for the binomial test only when $P = Q = ½$. Let $p =$ the smaller of the observed frequencies. For a *two-tailed test* the p is doubled, but reference should also be made to Table 1b. For N larger than 25, Table 2 may be used. Also, since the binomial distribution approaches the normal distribution as N increases, Table 5 also may be used, but under special circumstances. (See Siegel, pp. 40-42.)

In a coin-tossing experiment, for example, what are the chances of obtaining so many successes out of so many trials? For an N of 5 the probability for 0 successes is .031 or approximately 3%. For 1 success it is .188 (but this value also includes the likelihood of either this 1 occurring *or* also 0, since this is a cumulative scale). For two successes to occur from the remaining four trials the probability is .500 or ½, but at this stage of the game the chances are also .500 for either 1 *or* 0 successes. On the third toss of a coin the probability is .812 or 81% of the times for there to be 3 successes, *or* 2 successes, *or* 1 success, *or* 0 successes. In other words, with each succeeding toss of a coin the probability, p, (on the horizontal axis) must also include the previous probabilities.

Example and Use of Table

In an experiment in which 14 dogs were trained by two different methods to see how well they would learn certain tasks, half (randomly selected from the 14) were chosen to be subjected to Method A (involving praise and reward) and half to Method B (involving punishment for errors). It was predicted that Method A would be the best approach.

Null and Alternative Hypotheses

H_O: $p_1 = p_2 = ½$. That is, there is no difference between the probability of using Method A (p_1) and Method B (p_2); that any differences which do exist might ordinarily be expected.
H_1: $p_1 > p_2$

Test Chosen

The binomial test is chosen because the data are in two discrete categories with the design being one-sample in nature.

Significance Level

Let $a = .01$ for an N of 14.

Rejection Region

The region is one-tailed, since the direction of the difference was predicted. The region consists of all values of p (p representing the number of subjects under Method B) which are so small that their probability occurrence under H_O is ≤ than $a = .01$.

Decision

The test results showed that of the 14 dogs, only 4 responded better (that is, learned their tasks more efficiently) to punishment (method B) than to praise and reward (method A). Entering Table 1a with an $N = 14$ and a p (the smaller frequency) of 2, it is seen that the probability associated with $p ≤ 2$ is p .006. Therefore, since this p is smaller than the a of .01, the decision is to reject H_O for H_1. The conclusion is that $p_1 > p_2$, or that dogs when praised and rewarded will perform certain tasks better than dogs that are punished.

Table 1b

Cumulative Binomial Probabilities: Two-Tailed

N	X	.01	.05	.10	.15	.20	.25	.30	1/3	.35	.40	.45	.50
2	0	.9801	.9025	.8100	.7225	.6400	.5625	.4900	.4444	.4225	.3600	.3025	.2500
	1	.0198	.0950	.1800	.2550	.3200	.3750	.4200	.4444	.4550	.4800	.4950	.5000
	2	.0001	.0025	.0100	.0225	.0400	.0625	.0900	.1111	.1225	.1600	.2025	.2500
3	0	.9703	.8574	.7290	.6141	.5120	.4219	.3430	.2963	.2746	.2160	.1664	.1250
	1	.0294	.1354	.2430	.3251	.3840	.4219	.4410	.4444	.4436	.4320	.4084	.3750
	2	.0003	.0071.	.0270	.0574	.0960	.1406	.1890	.2222	.2389	.2880	.3341	.3750
	3	.0000	.0001	.0010	.0034	.0080	.0156	.0270	.0370	.0429	.0640	.0911	.1250
4	0	.9606	.8145	.6561	.5220	.4096	.3164	.2401	.1975	.1785	.1296	.0915	.0625
	1	.0388	.1715	.2916	.3685	.4096	.4219	.4116	.3951	.3845	.3456	.2995	.2500
	2	.0006	.0135	.0486	.0975	.1536	.2109	.2646	.2963	.3105	.3456	.3675	.3750
	3	.0000	.0005	.0036	.0115	.0256	.0469	.0756	.0988	.1115	.1536	.2005	.2500
	4	.0000	.0000	.0001	.0005	.0016	.0039	.0081	.0123	.0150	.0256	.0410	.0625
5	0	.9510	.7738	.5905	.4437	.3277	.2373	.1681	.1317	.1160	.0778	.0503	.0312
	1	.0480	.2036	.3280	.3915	.4096	.3955	.3602	.3292	.3124	.2592	.2059	.1562
	2	.0010	.0214	.0729	.1382	.2048	.2637	.3087	.3292	.3292	.3456	.3369	.3125
	3	.0000	.0011	.0081	.0244	.0512	.0879	.1323	.1646	.1811	.2304	.2757	.3125
	4	.0000	.0000	.0004	.0022	.0064	.0146	.0284	.0412	.0488	.0768	.1128	.1562
	5	.0000	.0000	.0000	.0001	.0003	.0010	.0024	.0041	.0053	.0102	.0185	.0312
6	0	.9415	.7351	.5314	.3771	.2621	.1780	.1176	.0878	.0754	.0467	.0277	.0156
	1	.0571	.2321	.3543	.3993	.3932	.3560	.3025	.2634	.2437	.1866	.1359	.0938
	2	.0014	.0305	.0984	.1762	.2458	.2966	.3241	.3292	.3280	.3110	.2780	.2344
	3	.0000	.0021	.0146	.0415	.0819	.1318	.1852	.2195	.2355	.2765	.3032	.3125
	4	.0000	.0001	.0012	.0055	.0154	.0330	.0595	.0823	.0951	.1382	.1861	.2344
	5	.0000	.0000	.0001	.0004	.0015	.0044	.0102	.0165	.0205	.0369	.0609	.0938
	6	.0000	.0000	.0000	.0000	.0001	.0002	.0007	.0014	.0018	.0041	.0083	.0156
7	0	.9321	.6983	.4783	.3206	.2097	.1335	.0824	.0585	.0490	.0280	.0152	.0078
	1	.0659	.2573	.3720	.3960	.3670	.3115	.2471	.2048	.1848	.1306	.0872	.0547
	2	.0020	.0406	.1240	.2097	.2753	.3115	.3177	.3073	.2985	.2613	.2140	.1641
	3	.0000	.0036	.0230	.0617	.1147	.1730	.2269	.2561	.2679	.2903	.2918	.2734
	4	.0000	.0002	.0026	.0109	.0287	.0577	.0972	.1280	.1442	.1935	.2388	.2734
	5	.0000	.0000	.0002	.0012	.0043	.0115	.0250	.0384	.0466	.0774	.1172	.1641
	6	.0000	.0000	.0000	.0001	.0004	.0013	.0036	.0064	.0084	.0172	.0320	.0547
	7	.0000	.0000	.0000	.0000	.0000	.0001	.0002	.0005	.0006	.0016	.0037	.0078
8	0	.9227	.6634	.4305	.2725	.1678	.1001	.0576	.0390	.0319	.0168	.0084	.0039
	1	.0746	.2793	.3826	.3847	.3355	.2670	.1977	.1561	.1373	.0896	.0548	.0312
	2	.0026	.0515	.1488	.2376	.2936	.3115	.2965	.2731	.2587	.2090	.1569	.1094
	3	.0001	.0054	.0331	.0839	.1468	.2076	.2541	.2731	.2786	.2787	.2568	.2188
	4	.0000	.0004	.0046	.0185	.0459	.0865	.1361	.1707	.1875	.2322	.2627	.2734
	5	.0000	.0000	.0004	.0026	.0092	.0231	.0467	.0683	.0808	.1239	.1719	.2188
	6	.0000	.0000	.0000	.0002	.0011	.0038	.0100	.0171	.0217	.0413	.0703	.1094
	7	.0000	.0000	.0000	.0000	.0001	.0004	.0012	.0024	.0033	.0079	.0164	.0312
	8	.0000	.0000	.0000	.0000	.0000	.0000	.0001	.0002	.0002	.0007	.0017	.0039
9	0	.9135	.6302	.3874	.2316	.1342	.0751	.0404	.0260	.0207	.0101	.0046	.0020
	1	.0830	.2985	.3874	.3679	.3020	.2253	.1556	.1171	.1004	.0605	.0339	.0176
	2	.0034	.0629	.1722	.2597	.3020	.3003	.2668	.2341	.2162	.1612	.1110	.0703
	3	.0001	.0077	.0446	.1069	.1762	.2336	.2668	.2731	.2716	.2508	.2119	.1641
	4	.0000	.0006	.0074	.0283	.0661	.1168	.1715	.2048	.2194	.2508	.2600	.2461
	5	.0000	.0000	.0008	.0050	.0165	.0389	.0735	.1024	.1181	.1672	.2128	.2461
	6	.0000	.0000	.0001	.0006	.0028	.0087	.0210	.0341	.0424	.0743	.1160	.1641
	7	.0000	.0000	.0000	.0000	.0003	.0012	.0039	.0073	.0098	.0212	.0407	.0703
	8	.0000	.0000	.0000	.0000	.0000	.0001	.0004	.0009	.0013	.0035	.0083	.0176
	9	.0000	.0000	.0000	.0000	.0000	.0000	.0000	.0001	.0001	.0003	.0008	.0020
10	0	.9044	.5987	.3487	.1969	.1074	.0563	.0282	.0173	.0135	.0060	.0025	.0010
	1	.0914	.3151	.3874	.3474	.2684	.1877	.1211	.0867	.0725	.0403	.0207	.0098
	2	.0042	.0746	.1937	.2759	.3020	.2816	.2335	.1951	.1757	.1209	.0763	.0439
	3	.0001	.0105	.0574	.1298	.2013	.2503	.2668	.2601	.2522	.2150	.1665	.1172
	4	.0000	.0010	.0112	.0401	.0881	.1460	.2001	.2276	.2377	.2508	.2384	.2051
	5	.0000	.0001	.0015	.0085	.0264	.0584	.1029	.1366	.1536	.2007	.2340	.2461
	6	.0000	.0000	.0001	.0012	.0055	.0162	.0368	.0569	.0689	.1115	.1596	.2051
	7	.0000	.0000	.0000	.0001	.0008	.0031	.0090	.0163	.0212	.0425	.0746	.1172
	8	.0000	.0000	.0000	.0000	.0001	.0004	.0014	.0030	.0043	.0106	.0229	.0439
	9	.0000	.0000	.0000	.0000	.0000	.0000	.0001	.0003	.0005	.0016	.0042	.0098
	10	.0000	.0000	.0000	.0000	.0000	.0000	.0000	.0000	.0000	.0001	.0003	.0010

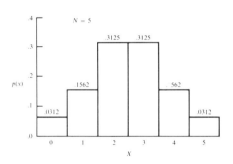

The above figure represents the two-tailed probabilities for $P \mp Q = \frac{1}{2}$ or .50 (last column) when N = 5. Note that the distribution is symmetrical and that when each value of $p(X)$ at 0 (.0312), 1 (.1562), and 2 (.3125) is added it totals approximately .50 (.4999) for one tail and 1.00 (.9998) for both tails.

Discussion

Statistical Background (See **binomial distribution.**)

Table Explanation

Given in the body of this table are *two-tailed probabilities* under H_0 for the binomial test when P equals any of a number of probabilities ranging from .01 to .50. Note that the total of X values for any N or p is always 1.00. For example, an N of 2 and a p of .10 gives .8100 + .1800 + .0100, which totals 1.00.

Example and Use of Table

Over a number of years the male proportion of births to female is approximately 100 to 103. If due to radiation poisoning the probability of male births became ¼, what would the probabilities be of boys and girls in families with five children?
P = ¼ or .25
Q = ¾ or .75
N = 5
What would the chance distribution be for the following?
0 boys (all girls); 1 boy; 2 boys; 3 boys; 4 boys; 5 boys
By referring to Table 1b for an N of 5 and a p of ¼ or .25, the probabilities are:
0 boys (.2373), or about a 24% chance of getting all girls
1 boy (.3955), or about a 40% chance of getting 1 boy *or* 0 boys
2 boys (.2637), or about 26% chance, etc.
3 boys (.0879), or about 9% chance, etc.
4 boys (.0146), or about 1½ chances out of 100
5 boys (.0010), or 0 chances

What are the probabilities for a mother with four boys and one girl to have come from a population in which $P_{male} = \frac{1}{4}$? The chances of having four or more boys out of five children in such a population would be .0010 + .0146 = .0156 or slightly more than $1\frac{1}{2}\%$ or $1\frac{1}{2}$ chances out of 100 for such an occurrence. The null hypothesis could be rejected at .05 level, indicating that the mother did not come from a population in which $P_{male} = \frac{1}{4}$. However, the null hypothesis would not be rejected at the .01 level.

Table 1c

Binomial Coefficients (Including Pascal's Triangle)

N	$\binom{N}{0}$	$\binom{N}{1}$	$\binom{N}{2}$	$\binom{N}{3}$	$\binom{N}{4}$	$\binom{N}{5}$	$\binom{N}{6}$	$\binom{N}{7}$	$\binom{N}{8}$	$\binom{N}{9}$	$\binom{N}{10}$
0	1										
1	1	1									
2	1	2	1								
3	1	3	3	1							
4	1	4	6	4	1						
5	1	5	10	10	5	1					
6	1	6	15	20	15	6	1				
7	1	7	21	35	35	21	7	1			
8	1	8	28	56	70	56	28	8	1		
9	1	9	36	84	126	126	84	36	9	1	
10	1	10	45	120	210	252	210	120	45	10	1
11	1	11	55	165	330	462	462	330	165	55	11
12	1	12	66	220	495	792	924	792	495	220	66
13	1	13	78	286	715	1287	1716	1716	1287	715	286
14	1	14	91	364	1001	2002	3003	3432	3003	2002	1001
15	1	15	105	455	1365	3003	5005	6435	6435	5005	3003
16	1	16	120	560	1820	4368	8008	11440	12870	11440	8008
17	1	17	136	680	2380	6188	12376	19448	24310	24310	19448
18	1	18	153	816	3060	8568	18564	31824	43758	48620	43758
19	1	19	171	969	3876	11628	27132	50388	75582	92378	92378
20	1	20	190	1140	4845	15504	38760	77520	125970	167960	184756

The binomial coefficient is the number that appears before each term of the binomial expansion. The binomial coefficients for an N of 2, for example, are 1, 2, and 1; for an N of 3 the coefficients are 1, 3, 3, and 1. Each coefficient tells the number of combinations of n objects taken r at a time. When two coins are tossed, for example, there is one way of getting 0 heads, two ways of getting 1 head, and 1 way of getting two heads.

If p and q approximate .50, the distribution of binomial coefficients more nearly approximates the normal as n increases beyond 20. A table of binomial coefficients is useful up to about an n of 20, but beyond 20 the normal curve more usefully determines the probability. In many psychological experiments there are numerous instances with 50 : 50 chances of occurring. A table of binomial coefficients is useful in such instances, as it is for any chance distributions, gambling or otherwise. Table 1c can be easily converted into Pascal's triangle by shifting each succeeding row to the left one column more than the row above it, so that each row begins with a 1 and ends with a 1 and each other entry is the sum of the two entries immediately above it. Notice the triangle drawn within the Pascal triangle below. The Pascal triangle and Table 1c are used in the same manner.

N													Sum
1						1	1						2
2					1	2	1						4
3				1	3	3	1						8
4			1	4	6	4	1						16
5		1	5	10	10	5	1						32
6	1	6	15	20	15	6	1						64
7	1	7	21	35	35	21	7	1					128
8	1	8	28	56	70	56	28	8	1				256
9	1	9	36	84	126	126	84	36	9	1			512
10	1	10	45	120	210	252	210	120	45	10	1		1,024

Table 1d

CONFIDENCE BELTS FOR p (CONFIDENCE COEFFICIENT · ·95)

SCALE OF p

SCALE OF $\frac{X}{n}$

The numbers located on the curved lines indicate the sample size for which the confidence belt applies. For any given confidence coefficient the belt narrows with increase in sample size.

The chart (Table 1d) gives boundary lines for the rejection regions for $\alpha = .05$ or 5% and for the confidence coefficient of .95 for $N = 10, 15, 20, 30, 50, 100, 250,$ and 1000.

For a confidence level of 95%, the sample proportion, p, is given on the x axis and the population proportion on the y axis.

Each one of the curves corresponds to a different sample size, with an upper and a lower limit for each sample size. For sample sizes not listed it is necessary to interpolate.

These charts (Tables 1d and 1e) provide rapid answers to problems such as (1) in which a sample has been drawn (n and x known) in order to obtain the confidence interval for p, (2) in which it is necessary to plan in advance the size of sample required to give a desired degree of accuracy in estimation, and (3) so as to determine sampling variation limits expected to occur in x when p is known, thereby enabling determination of sample size needed.

As n decreases significantly from 1000, the curves cut the axis $x/n = 0$ at a greater distance from $p = 0$. In both charts, the points of intersection correspond to those values of p for which the first term of the binomial $q^n = (1-p)^n$ equals .025 and .005 respectively. The end points on the axis $x/n = 1$ correspond to values of p for which the last term, p^n, equals .025 and .005.

Table 1e

CONFIDENCE BELTS FOR p (CONFIDENCE COEFFICIENT · ·99)

SCALE OF p

SCALE OF $\frac{X}{n}$

Example and Use of Chart

In order to use the chart for testing significance, read horizontally; for finding confidence intervals, read vertically.

Example: Assume that out of 100 architects in Los Angeles, all 100 of them specify Bobrick washroom equipment, a Los Angeles-based firm, in their specifications for new buildings. The Bobrick company claims that they have 65% of the soap dispenser business in the U.S. because of the recognized superiority of their product. What would the results be in a sampling of architects outside of Los Angeles? Let the population proportion, P, be the proportion of architects that specify Bobrick equipment. To test whether or not P = 65%, the hypotheses are:

$$H_0: \quad P = 0.65$$
$$H_1: \quad P = 0.65$$

A random sample of 1000 architects outside of Los Angeles is obtained and the sample proportion of those specifying Bobrick equipment is found to be $p = 0.60$. Examining the two curves that correspond to $n = 1000$, the lower and upper values for .60 (on the horizontal axis) are found to be approximately .55 and .68. Therefore, if the population proportion were P = 0.65, the probability of p falling outside the two limits of 0.55 and 0.68 is $\alpha = 5\%$. Assuming a significance level of .05, the null hypothesis is not rejected. that is, the P, or population proportion of architects does truly = 65% of all architects specifying Bobrick washroom equipment.

Table 2

Z-Scores and the Proportions of Area under the Normal Curve

(A) z	(B) area between mean and z	(C) area beyond z	(A) z	(B) area between mean and z	(C) area beyond z	(A) z	(B) area between mean and z	(C) area beyond z
0.00	.0000	.5000	0.55	.2088	.2912	1.10	.3643	.1357
0.01	.0040	.4960	0.56	.2123	.2877	1.11	.3665	.1335
0.02	.0080	.4920	0.57	.2157	.2843	1.12	.3686	.1314
0.03	.0120	.4880	0.58	.2190	.2810	1.13	.3708	.1292
0.04	.0160	.4840	0.59	.2224	.2776	1.14	.3729	.1271
0.05	.0199	.4801	0.60	.2257	.2743	1.15	.3749	.1251
0.06	.0239	.4761	0.61	.2291	.2709	1.16	.3770	.1230
0.07	.0279	.4721	0.62	.2324	.2676	1.17	.3790	.1210
0.08	.0319	.4681	0.63	.2357	.2643	1.18	.3810	.1190
0.09	.0359	.4641	0.64	.2389	.2611	1.19	.3830	.1170
0.10	.0398	.4602	0.65	.2422	.2578	1.20	.3849	.1151
0.11	.0438	.4562	0.66	.2454	.2546	1.21	.3869	.1131
0.12	.0478	.4522	0.67	.2486	.2514	1.22	.3888	.1112
0.13	.0517	.4483	0.68	.2517	.2483	1.23	.3907	.1093
0.14	.0557	.4443	0.69	.2549	.2451	1.24	.3925	.1075
0.15	.0596	.4404	0.70	.2580	.2420	1.25	.3944	.1056
0.16	.0636	.4364	0.71	.2611	.2389	1.26	.3962	.1038
0.17	.0675	.4325	0.72	.2642	.2358	1.27	.3980	.1020
0.18	.0714	.4286	0.73	.2673	.2327	1.28	.3997	.1003
0.19	.0753	.4247	0.74	.2704	.2296	1.29	.4015	.0985
0.20	.0793	.4207	0.75	.2734	.2266	1.30	.4032	.0968
0.21	.0832	.4168	0.76	.2764	.2236	1.31	.4049	.0951
0.22	.0871	.4129	0.77	.2794	.2206	1.32	.4066	.0934
0.23	.0910	.4090	0.78	.2823	.2177	1.33	.4082	.0918
0.24	.0948	.4052	0.79	.2852	.2148	1.34	.4099	.0901
0.25	.0987	.4013	0.80	.2881	.2119	1.35	.4115	.0885
0.26	.1026	.3974	0.81	.2910	.2090	1.36	.4131	.0869
0.27	.1064	.3936	0.82	.2939	.2061	1.37	.4147	.0853
0.28	.1103	.3897	0.83	.2967	.2033	1.38	.4162	.0838
0.29	.1141	.3859	0.84	.2995	.2005	1.39	.4177	.0823
0.30	.1179	.3821	0.85	.3023	.1977	1.40	.4192	.0808
0.31	.1217	.3783	0.86	.3051	.1949	1.41	.4207	.0793
0.32	.1255	.3745	0.87	.3078	.1922	1.42	.4222	.0778
0.33	.1293	.3707	0.88	.3106	.1894	1.43	.4236	.0764
0.34	.1331	.3669	0.89	.3133	.1867	1.44	.4251	.0749
0.35	.1368	.3632	0.90	.3159	.1841	1.45	.4265	.0735
0.36	.1406	.3594	0.91	.3186	.1814	1.46	.4279	.0721
0.37	.1443	.3557	0.92	.3212	.1788	1.47	.4292	.0708
0.38	.1480	.3520	0.93	.3238	.1762	1.48	.4306	.0694
0.39	.1517	.3483	0.94	.3264	.1736	1.49	.4319	.0681
0.40	.1554	.3446	0.95	.3289	.1711	1.50	.4332	.0668
0.41	.1591	.3409	0.96	.3315	.1685	1.51	.4345	.0655
0.42	.1628	.3372	0.97	.3340	.1660	1.52	.4357	.0643
0.43	.1664	.3336	0.98	.3365	.1635	1.53	.4370	.0630
0.44	.1700	.3300	0.99	.3389	.1611	1.54	.4382	.0618
0.45	.1736	.3264	1.00	.3413	.1587	1.55	.4394	.0606
0.46	.1772	.3228	1.01	.3438	.1562	1.56	.4406	.0594
0.47	.1808	.3192	1.02	.3461	.1539	1.57	.4418	.0582
0.48	.1844	.3156	1.03	.3485	.1515	1.58	.4429	.0571
0.49	.1879	.3121	1.04	.3508	.1492	1.59	.4441	.0559
0.50	.1915	.3085	1.05	.3531	.1469	1.60	.4452	.0548
0.51	.1950	.3050	1.06	.3554	.1446	1.61	.4463	.0537
0.52	.1985	.3015	1.07	.3577	.1423	1.62	.4474	.0526
0.53	.2019	.2981	1.08	.3599	.1401	1.63	.4484	.0516
0.54	.2054	.2946	1.09	.3621	.1379	1.64	.4495	.0505

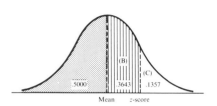

Explanation of Table

Since the total area covered under the normal curve shown above is 1.00 or 100%, one-half of it is .5000 or 50%. In the table, proportions for only one-half of the total area are given, since negative z values (for the left half of the curve) have identical proportions to positive ones (the right half).

Example and Use of Table

Given: z-score of 1.10. Locate 1.10 in (A) column, then line up with column (B) to obtain the value for the area between z and the mean, which is .3643 or 36.43% of the area.

The area below or to the left of z above gives .3643 + .5000 = .8643 (adding both shaded areas) or 86.43% of the total area.

Column (C), for figure above, provides the value for the area beyond or to the right of z, equalling .1357 or 13.57%. (See unshaded area above.)

(A) z	(B) area between mean and z	(C) area beyond z	(A) z	(B) area between mean and z	(C) area beyond z	(A) z	(B) area between mean and z	(C) area beyond z
1.65	.4505	.0495	2.22	.4868	.0132	2.79	.4974	.0026
1.66	.4515	.0485	2.23	.4871	.0129	2.80	.4974	.0026
1.67	.4525	.0475	2.24	.4875	.0125	2.81	.4975	.0025
1.68	.4535	.0465	2.25	.4878	.0122	2.82	.4976	.0024
1.69	.4545	.0455	2.26	.4881	.0119	2.83	.4977	.0023
1.70	.4554	.0446	2.27	.4884	.0116	2.84	.4977	.0023
1.71	.4564	.0436	2.28	.4887	.0113	2.85	.4978	.0022
1.72	.4573	.0427	2.29	.4890	.0110	2.86	.4979	.0021
1.73	.4582	.0418	2.30	.4893	.0107	2.87	.4979	.0021
1.74	.4591	.0409	2.31	.4896	.0104	2.88	.4980	.0020
1.75	.4599	.0401	2.32	.4898	.0102	2.89	.4981	.0019
1.76	.4608	.0392	2.33	.4901	.0099	2.90	.4981	.0019
1.77	.4616	.0384	2.34	.4904	.0096	2.91	.4982	.0018
1.78	.4625	.0375	2.35	.4906	.0094	2.92	.4982	.0018
1.79	.4633	.0367	2.36	.4909	.0091	2.93	.4983	.0017
1.80	.4641	.0359	2.37	.4911	.0089	2.94	.4984	.0016
1.81	.4649	.0351	2.38	.4913	.0087	2.95	.4984	.0016
1.82	.4656	.0344	2.39	.4916	.0084	2.96	.4985	.0015
1.83	.4664	.0336	2.40	.4918	.0082	2.97	.4985	.0015
1.84	.4671	.0329	2.41	.4920	.0080	2.98	.4986	.0014
1.85	.4678	.0322	2.42	.4922	.0078	2.99	.4986	.0014
1.86	.4686	.0314	2.43	.4925	.0075	3.00	.4987	.0013
1.87	.4693	.0307	2.44	.4927	.0073	3.01	.4987	.0013
1.88	.4699	.0301	2.45	.4929	.0071	3.02	.4987	.0013
1.89	.4706	.0294	2.46	.4931	.0069	3.03	.4988	.0012
1.90	.4713	.0287	2.47	.4932	.0068	3.04	.4988	.0012
1.91	.4719	.0281	2.48	.4934	.0066	3.05	.4989	.0011
1.92	.4726	.0274	2.49	.4936	.0064	3.06	.4989	.0011
1.93	.4732	.0268	2.50	.4938	.0062	3.07	.4989	.0011
1.94	.4738	.0262	2.51	.4940	.0060	3.08	.4990	.0010
1.95	.4744	.0256	2.52	.4941	.0059	3.09	.4990	.0010
1.96	.4750	.0250	2.53	.4943	.0057	3.10	.4990	.0010
1.97	.4756	.0244	2.54	.4945	.0055	3.11	.4991	.0009
1.98	.4761	.0239	2.55	.4946	.0054	3.12	.4991	.0009
1.99	.4767	.0233	2.56	.4948	.0052	3.13	.4991	.0009
2.00	.4772	.0228	2.57	.4949	.0051	3.14	.4992	.0008
2.01	.4778	.0222	2.58	.4951	.0049	3.15	.4992	.0008
2.02	.4783	.0217	2.59	.4952	.0048	3.16	.4992	.0008
2.03	.4788	.0212	2.60	.4953	.0047	3.17	.4992	.0008
2.04	.4793	.0207	2.61	.4955	.0045	3.18	.4993	.0007
2.05	.4798	.0202	2.62	.4956	.0044	3.19	.4993	.0007
2.06	.4803	.0197	2.63	.4957	.0043	3.20	.4993	.0007
2.07	.4808	.0192	2.64	.4959	.0041	3.21	.4993	.0007
2.08	.4812	.0188	2.65	.4960	.0040	3.22	.4994	.0006
2.09	.4817	.0183	2.66	.4961	.0039	3.23	.4994	.0006
2.10	.4821	.0179	2.67	.4962	.0038	3.24	.4994	.0006
2.11	.4826	.0174	2.68	.4963	.0037	3.25	.4994	.0006
2.12	.4830	.0170	2.69	.4964	.0036	3.30	.4995	.0005
2.13	.4834	.0166	2.70	.4965	.0035	3.35	.4996	.0004
2.14	.4838	.0162	2.71	.4966	.0034	3.40	.4997	.0003
2.15	.4842	.0158	2.72	.4967	.0033	3.45	.4997	.0003
2.16	.4846	.0154	2.73	.4968	.0032	3.50	.4998	.0002
2.17	.4850	.0150	2.74	.4969	.0031	3.60	.4998	.0002
2.18	.4854	.0146	2.75	.4970	.0030	3.70	.4999	.0001
2.19	.4857	.0143	2.76	.4971	.0029	3.80	.4999	.0001
2.20	.4861	.0139	2.77	.4972	.0028	3.90	.49995	.00005
2.21	.4864	.0136	2.78	.4973	.0027	4.00	.49997	.00003

Some tables include the larger portion of the area under the curve. Such values can be readily obtained from this table by subtracting any given value in the (C) column from 1.00.

Percentiles are obtained from any z value by adding the value in column (B) to .5000. Thus, for a z of 0.33, column (B) gives .1293, and .1293 + .5000 = .6293 or .63, the percentile value.

Table 3

Functions of p, q, z, and y Where p and q are Proportions (p + q = 1.00)
and z and y are Constants of the Unit Normal Distribution Curve*

p (or q)	A pq	B $\sqrt{pq}$	C pq/y	D $\sqrt{pq}/y$	E p/y	F y/p	G zy/p	H y	I zy/q	J y/q	K q/y	L $\sqrt{p/q}$	M $\sqrt{q/p}$	q (or p)
.99	.0099	.0995−	.3715	3.733	37.15−	.02692	−.06262	.02665	6.2002	2.665	.3752	9.950	.1005	.01
.98	.0196	.1400	.4048	2.892	20.24	.04941	−.1015	.04842	4.9719	2.421	.4131	7.000	.1429	.02
.97	.0291	.1706	.4277	2.507	14.26	.07015	−.1319	.06804	4.2657	2.268	.4409	5.686	.1759	.03
.96	.0384	.1960	.4456	2.274	11.14	.08976	−.1571	.08617	3.7717	2.154	.4642	4.899	.2041	.04
.95	.0475	.2179	.4605	2.113	9.211	.1086	−.1786	.1031	3.3928	2.063	.4848	4.359	.2294	.05
.94	.0564	.2375−	.4735	1.994	7.891	.1267	−.1970	.1191	3.0868	1.985	.5037	3.958	.2526	.06
.93	.0651	.2551	.4848	1.900	6.926	.1444	−.2131	.1343	2.8307	1.918	.5213	3.645	.2743	.07
.92	.0736	.2713	.4951	1.825	6.188	.1616	−.2271	.1487	2.6110	1.858	.5381	3.391	.2949	.08
.91	.0819	.2862	.5043	1.762	5.604	.1785	−.2393	.1624	2.4191	1.804	.5542	3.180	.3145	.09
.90	.0900	.3000	.5128	1.709	5.128	.1950	−.2499	.1755	2.2491	1.755	.5698	3.000	.3333	.10
.89	.0979	.3129	.5206	1.664	4.733	.2113	−.2591	.1880	2.0966	1.709	.5850	2.844	.3516	.11
.88	.1056	.3250	.5279	1.625	4.399	.2273	−.2671	.2000	1.9587	1.667	.5999	2.708	.3693	.12
.87	.1131	.3363	.5346	1.590	4.112	.2432	−.2739	.2115	1.8330	1.627	.6145	2.587	.3865	.13
.86	.1204	.3470	.5409	1.559	3.864	.2588	−.2796	.2226	1.7175	1.590	.6290	2.478	.4035	.14
.85	.1275	.3571	.5468	1.532	3.646	.2743	−.2843	.2332	1.6110	1.554	.6433	2.380	.4201	.15
.84	.1344	.3666	.5524	1.507	3.452	.2896	−.2880	.2433	1.5123	1.521	.6576	2.291	.4365	.16
.83	.1411	.3756	.5576	1.484	3.280	.3049	−.2909	.2531	1.4203	1.489	.6718	2.210	.4525	.17
.82	.1476	.3842	.5625	1.464	3.125	.3200	−.2929	.2624	1.3344	1.458	.6860	2.134	.4685	.18
.81	.1539	.3923	.5671	1.446	2.985	.3350	−.2941	.2714	1.2538	1.428	.7002	2.065	.4844	.19
.80	.1600	.4000	.5715	1.429	2.858	.3500	−.2946	.2800	1.1781	1.400	.7144	2.000	.5000	.20
.79	.1659	.4073	.5756	1.413	2.741	.3648	−.2942	.2882	1.1067	1.372	.7287	1.940	.5156	.21
.78	.1716	.4142	.5796	1.399	2.634	.3796	−.2931	.2961	1.0393	1.346	.7430	1.883	.5311	.22
.77	.1771	.4208	.5832	1.386	2.536	.3943	−.2913	.3036	.9754	1.320	.7575	1.830	.5465	.23
.76	.1824	.4271	.5867	1.374	2.445	.4090	−.2889	.3109	.9149	1.295	.7720	1.780	.5620	.24
.75	.1875	.4330	.5900	1.363	2.360	.4237	−.2858	.3178	.8573	1.271	.7867	1.732	.5774	.25
.74	.1924	.4386	.5931	1.352	2.281	.4384	−.2820	.3244	.8026	1.248	.8016	1.687	.5928	.26
.73	.1971	.4440	.5961	1.343	2.208	.4529	−.2775	.3306	.7504	1.225	.8166	1.644	.6082	.27
.72	.2016	.4490	.5989	1.334	2.139	.4675	−.2725	.3366	.7006	1.202	.8318	1.604	.6236	.28
.71	.2059	.4538	.6015	1.326	2.074	.4822	−.2668	.3423	.6532	1.180	.8472	1.565	.6391	.29
.70	.2100	.4583	.6040	1.318	2.013	.4967	−.2605	.3477	.6078	1.159	.8628	1.528	.6547	.30
.69	.2139	.4625−	.6063	1.311	1.956	.5113	−.2535	.3528	.5643	1.138	.8787	1.492	.6703	.31
.68	.2176	.4665−	.6085	1.304	1.902	.5259	−.2460	.3576	.5227	1.118	.8949	1.458	.6860	.32
.67	.2211	.4702	.6106	1.298	1.850	.5405	−.2378	.3621	.4828	1.097	.9112	1.425	.7018	.33
.66	.2244	.4737	.6124	1.293	1.801	.5552	−.2290	.3664	.4445	1.078	.9279	1.393	.7178	.34
.65	.2275	.4770	.6142	1.288	1.755	.5698	−.2196	.3704	.4078	1.058	.9449	1.363	.7338	.35
.64	.2304	.4800	.6158	1.283	1.711	.5845	−.2095	.3741	.3725	1.039	.9623	1.333	.7500	.36
.63	.2331	.4828	.6174	1.279	1.669	.5993	−.1989	.3776	.3387	1.020	.9800	1.305	.7663	.37
.62	.2356	.4854	.6188	1.275	1.628	.6141	−.1876	.3808	.3061	1.002	.9980	1.277	.7829	.38
.61	.2379	.4877	.6200	1.271	1.590	.6290	−.1757	.3837	.2748	.9938	1.016	1.251	.7996	.39
.60	.2400	.4899	.6212	1.268	1.553	.6439	−.1631	.3863	.2447	.9659	1.035	1.225	.8165	.40
.59	.2419	.4918	.6223	1.265	1.518	.6589	−.1499	.3888	.2158	.9482	1.055	1.200	.8336	.41
.58	.2436	.4936	.6232	1.263	1.484	.6739	−.1361	.3909	.1879	.9307	1.074	1.175	.8510	.42
.57	.2451	.4951	.6240	1.260	1.451	.6891	−.1215	.3928	.1611	.9134	1.095	1.151	.8686	.43
.56	.2464	.4964	.6247	1.259	1.420	.7043	−.1063	.3944	.1353	.8964	1.116	1.128	.8864	.44
.55	.2475	.4975−	.6253	1.257	1.390	.7196	−.09043	.3958	.1105	.8796	1.137	1.106	.9045	.45
.54	.2484	.4984	.6258	1.256	1.360	.7351	−.07382	.3969	.0867	.8629	1.159	1.083	.9229	.46
.53	.2491	.4991	.6262	1.255	1.332	.7506	−.05650	.3978	.0637	.8464	1.181	1.062	.9417	.47
.52	.2496	.4996	.6264	1.254	1.305	.7662	−.03843	.3984	.0416	.8301	1.205	1.041	.9608	.48
.51	.2499	.4999	.6266	1.253	1.279	.7820	−.01960	.3988	.0204	.8139	1.229	1.020	.9802	.49
.50	.2500	.5000	.6267	1.253	1.253	.7979	−.00000	.3989	.0000	.7979	1.253	1.000	1.0000	.50

*When *p* is less than .50, interchange *p* and *q* as the headings of the first and last columns indicate.

The above table provides *p*, *q*, *z*, and *y* values where *p* and *q* = *p* − 1 are proportions and *z* and *y* are normal distribution standard scores and ordinates corresponding to *p* (or *q*) when *p* is regarded as a cumulative probability. The value $\sqrt{pq}$ is useful for calculations of point-biserial correlation coefficients. Point biserial correlations may be converted to a biserial coefficient by multiplication with $\sqrt{pq}/y$. Values in the table also facilitate use of the phi coefficient (used for test-item intercorrelations). In the table, for given values of *p*, corresponding values of *pq/y*, *p/y*, and *pq/y* are supplied for computing biserial *r* and its standard error.

Table 4

Percent of Cases Under Portions of the Normal Curve
(Including Scores and Scale Equivalents)

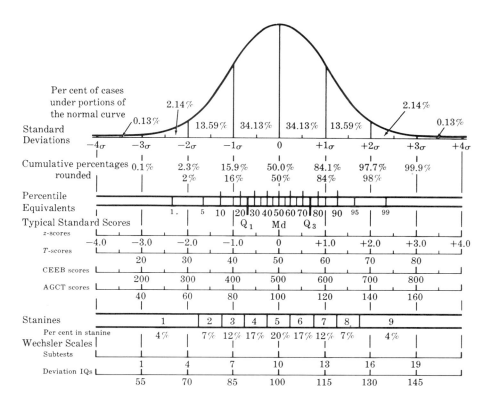

Explanation and Use of the Table

Assume that the mean IQ of 8th grade children in Notown, USA, is 100 and the standard deviation is 15 (a value used by Wechsler in his tests). What portion of these children will have IQ's below 115 (which includes the total area under the curve to the left of 1)? Adding these percentages under the curve: 13.59% 34.13% 34.13% 13.59% .13% gives a total of 84.12%. The same approximate figure may be obtained by referring to the rows next following standard deviations. For example, cumulative percentages give 84.1% and the percentile equivalents also may be read as approximately 84%. Therefore, approximately 84% of the children will have an IQ below 115.

Other score values may be read in similar fashion.

The Normal Curve, Percentiles, and Standard Scores

Distribution of scores on many standardized educational and psychological tests approximate the form of the *Normal Curve* shown at the top of this chart. Below it are shown some of the systems that have been developed to facilitate the interpretation of scores by converting them into numbers which indicate the examinee's relative status in a group.

The zero (0) at the center of the baseline shows the location of the mean (average) raw score on a test, and the symbol σ (sigma) marks off the scale of raw scores in *Standard Deviation* units.

Cumulative percentages are the basis of the *Percentile Equivalent* scale.

Several systems are based on the standard deviation unit. Among these *standard score* scales, the z-score, the *T*-score and the *stanine* are general systems which have been applied to a variety of tests. The others are special variants used in connection with tests of the *College Entrance Examination Board*, the World War II *Army General Classification Test*, and the *Wechsler* tests.

Tables of *Norms*, whether in percentile or standard score form, have meaning only with reference to a specified test applied to a specified population. The chart does not permit one to conclude, for instance, that a percentile rank of 84 on one test necessarily is equivalent to a z-score of +1.0 on another; this is true only when each test yields essentially a normal distribution of scores and when both scales are based on identical or very similar groups of people.

Table 5

Poisson Distribution

μ	0.1		0.2		0.3		0.4		0.5		0.6		0.8	
r	$P\{r\}$	$\Sigma P\{r\}$	$P\{r\}$	$\Sigma P\{r\}$	$P\{r\}$	$\Sigma P\{r\}$	$P\{r\}$	$\Sigma P\{r\}$	$P\{r\}$	$\Sigma P\{r\}$	$P\{r\}$	$\Sigma P\{r\}$	$P\{r\}$	$\Sigma P\{r\}$
0	.9048	.9048	.8187	.8187	.7408	.7408	.6703	.6703	.6065	.6065	.5488	.5488	.4493	.4493
1	.0905	.9953	.1637	.9824	.2222	.9630	.2681	.9384	.3033	.9098	.3293	.8781	.3595	.8088
2	.0045	.9998	.0164	.9988	.0333	.9963	.0536	.9920	.0758	.9856	.0988	.9769	.1438	.9526
3	—	—	.0011	.9999	.0033	.9996	.0072	.9992	.0126	.9982	.0198	.9967	.0383	.9909
4	—	—	—	—	.0003	.9999	.0007	.9999	.0016	.9998	.0030	.9997	.0077	.9986
5									—	—	—	—	.0012	.9998
6									—	—	—	—	.0002	1.0000

μ	1.0		1.2		1.4		1.6		2.0		2.5		3.0	
r	$P\{r\}$	$\Sigma P\{r\}$	$P\{r\}$	$\Sigma P\{r\}$	$P\{r\}$	$\Sigma P\{r\}$	$P\{r\}$	$\Sigma P\{r\}$	$P\{r\}$	$\Sigma P\{r\}$	$P\{r\}$	$\Sigma P\{r\}$	$P\{r\}$	$\Sigma P\{r\}$
0	.3679	.3679	.3012	.3012	.2466	.2466	.2019	.2019	.1354	.1354	.0821	.0821	.0498	.0498
1	.3679	.7458	.3614	.6626	.3452	.5918	.3230	.5249	.2707	.4061	.2052	.2873	.1494	.1992
2	.1839	.9197	.2169	.8795	.2417	.8335	.2584	.7833	.2707	.6768	.2565	.5438	.2241	.4233
3	.0613	.9810	.0867	.9662	.1128	.9463	.1378	.9211	.1805	.8573	.2138	.7576	.2241	.6474
4	.0153	.9963	.0260	.9924	.0395	.9858	.0551	.9762	.0902	.9475	.1336	.8912	.1680	.8154
5	.0031	.9994	.0062	.9986	.0111	.9967	.0176	.9938	.0361	.9836	.0668	.9580	.1008	.9162
6	.0005	.9999	.0012	.9998	.0026	.9993	.0047	.9985	.0120	.9956	.0278	.9858	.0504	.9666
7			—	—	.0005	.9998	.0011	.9996	.0032	.9988	.0099	.9957	.0216	.9882
8			—	· —	.0001	.9999	.0002	.9998	.0009	.9997	.0031	.9988	.0081	.9963
9			—	—	—	—	—	—	.0002	.9999	.0009	.9997	.0027	.9990
10											.0002	.9999	.0008	.9998
11											—	—	—	—
12														

μ	3.5		4.0		4.5		5.0	
r	$P\{r\}$	$\Sigma P\{r\}$	$P\{r\}$	$\Sigma P\{r\}$	$P\{r\}$	$\Sigma P\{r\}$	$P\{r\}$	$\Sigma P\{r\}$
0	.0302	.0302	.0183	.0183	.0111	.0111	.0067	.0067
1	.1057	.1359	.0733	.0916	.0500	.0611	.0337	.0404
2	.1850	.3209	.1466	.2832	.1125	.1736	.0842	.1246
3	.2158	.5367	.1954	.4336	.1688	.3424	.1404	.2650
4	.1888	.7255	.1954	.6290	.1898	.5322	.1755	.4405
5	.1322	.8577	.1563	.7853	.1708	.7030	.1755	.6160
6	.0771	.9348	.1042	.8895	.1281	.8311	.1462	.7622
7	.0385	.9733	.0596	.9491	.0824	.9135	.1045	.8667
8	.0169	.9902	.0298	.9789	.0463	.9598	.0653	.9320
9	.0066	.9968	.0132	.9921	.0232	.9830	.0363	.9683
10	.0023	.9991	.0053	.9974	.0104	.9934	.0181	.9864
11	.0007	.9998	.0019	.9993	.0043	.9977	.0082	.9946
12	—	—	.0006	.9999	.0016	.9993	.0034	.9980
13					.0006	.9999	.0013	.9993
14					—	—	.0005	.9998

P = the proportion of the population in the designated category
n = the sample size
r = the number of individuals in the stated category in the sample
$P\{r\}$ = the probability of a sample containing r individuals in the stated category
$\Sigma P\{r\}$ = the probability of a sample containing r or fewer individuals in the stated category
$\mu = Pn$ = the population mean value of r

Example and Use of Table

   Assume that an air force wants to discover the most economical way to obtain successful pilots from its training program. Limits are set down. Every pilot trainee must belong in either the successful or unsuccessful mutually exclusive category, dictated by life or death. The successful pilot survives to serve his air force, the unsuccessful pilot fails to do either. To prevent waste of men and money the air force sets up a training program wishing to eliminate the likely unsuccessful ones before it is too late. No trainee shall be permitted to fail more than 1.0% (.010) of the preliminary tests, prior to flying solo. The null hypothesis is set up with $H_0 : \geqslant 0.010$, that is, the trainee pilot will never make it. But if the hypothesis can be rejected at an appropriate early enough alpha risk, then the pilot can be allowed to proceed with confidence of success. An alpha of 0.05 is set. The sample of trainees will be tested and the null hypothesis rejected only if the number of unsuccessful trainees, x, would be in the best .05 end of the sampling distribution if P = 0.010. Since no flying errors will be tolerated, r = 0. Follow the line r = 0 in the table until a value approximating a p(0) = .05 is obtained, indicating the 95% level of confidence. The closest to .05 is 0.0498 where μ = 3.0. Since P = 0.010, $n = \mu/P = 3.0/0.10 = 300$, suggesting that 300 trainees will fall from the program before 1 is permitted to go on. Therefore, the null hypothesis is accepted and something has to be done about the training program as their standards are too high.

Table 6a

Critical Values of *t*

df	α .25 2α .50	.20 .40	.15 .30	.10 .20	.05 .10	.025 .05	.01 .02	.005 .01	.0005 .001
1	1.000	1.376	1.963	3.078	6.314	12.706	31.821	63.657	636.619
2	.816	1.061	1.386	1.886	2.920	4.303	6.965	9.925	31.598
3	.765	.978	1.250	1.638	2.353	3.182	4.541	5.841	12.924
4	.741	.941	1.190	1.533	2.132	2.776	3.747	4.604	8.610
5	.727	.920	1.156	1.476	2.015	2.571	3.365	4.032	6.869
6	.718	.906	1.134	1.440	1.943	2.447	3.143	3.707	5.959
7	.711	.896	1.119	1.415	1.895	2.365	2.998	3.499	5.408
8	.706	.889	1.108	1.397	1.860	2.306	2.896	3.355	5.041
9	.703	.883	1.100	1.383	1.833	2.262	2.821	3.250	4.781
10	.700	.879	1.093	1.372	1.812	2.228	2.764	3.169	4.587
11	.697	.876	1.088	1.363	1.796	2.201	2.718	3.106	4.437
12	.695	.873	1.083	1.356	1.782	2.179	2.681	3.055	4.318
13	.694	.870	1.079	1.350	1.771	2.160	2.650	3.012	4.221
14	.692	.868	1.076	1.345	1.761	2.145	2.624	2.977	4.140
15	.691	.866	1.074	1.341	1.753	2.131	2.602	2.947	4.073
16	.690	.865	1.071	1.337	1.746	2.120	2.583	2.921	4.015
17	.689	.863	1.069	1.333	1.740	2.110	2.567	2.898	3.965
18	.688	.862	1.067	1.330	1.734	2.101	2.552	2.878	3.922
19	.688	.861	1.066	1.328	1.729	2.093	2.539	2.861	3.883
20	.687	.860	1.064	1.325	1.725	2.086	2.528	2.845	3.850
21	.686	.859	1.063	1.323	1.721	2.080	2.518	2.831	3.819
22	.686	.858	1.061	1.321	1.717	2.074	2.508	2.819	3.792
23	.685	.858	1.060	1.319	1.714	2.069	2.500	2.807	3.767
24	.685	.857	1.059	1.318	1.711	2.064	2.492	2.797	3.745
25	.684	.856	1.058	1.316	1.708	2.060	2.485	2.787	3.725
26	.684	.856	1.058	1.315	1.706	2.056	2.479	2.779	3.707
27	.684	.855	1.057	1.314	1.703	2.052	2.473	2.771	3.690
28	.683	.855	1.056	1.313	1.701	2.048	2.467	2.763	3.674
29	.683	.854	1.055	1.311	1.699	2.045	2.462	2.756	3.659
30	.683	.854	1.055	1.310	1.697	2.042	2.457	2.750	3.646
40	.681	.851	1.050	1.303	1.684	2.021	2.423	2.704	3.551
60	.679	.848	1.046	1.296	1.671	2.000	2.390	2.660	3.460
120	.677	.845	1.041	1.289	1.658	1.980	2.358	2.617	3.373
∞	.674	.842	1.036	1.282	1.645	1.960	2.326	2.576	3.291

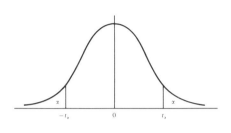

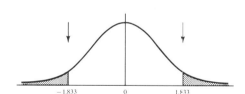

Table Explanation

Table 6a is an abbreviated table showing only selected percentage points for various *t* distributions in terms of the degrees of freedom involved. Alpha levels are given for both directional (one-tailed) and nondirectional (two-tailed) tests of significance, although most significance tests are nondirectional. Note that as the degrees of freedom approach infinity (beyond 120), the probabilities approach the normal curve. The *t* distribution is unimodal, symmetric about 0, and it is flatter than the normal distribution, that is, its tail area is larger and its peak is not as high. In using the *t* test the population standard deviations are not known. There are various considerations to take into account in calculating the *t*. For example:

1. $t = \dfrac{\overline{X} - \mu_0}{S_{\overline{X}}}$ *Significance test for a single mean:* degrees of freedom $N - 1$. μ_0 is the expected value as stated in the null hypothesis.

2. $t = \dfrac{(\overline{X}_1 - \overline{X}_2) - (\mu_1 - \mu_2)}{S_{\overline{X}_1 - \overline{X}_2}}$ *Significance test for the difference between means for two independent samples:* df = $N_1 + N_2 - 2$. $\mu_1 - \mu_2$ is the expected value as stated in the null hypothesis. If this hypothesis is that both samples come from the same population, this difference is equal to zero.

     For a *one-tailed test:* $\begin{aligned} &H_0 : \mu_1 \geqslant \mu_2 \ or \ H_0 : \mu_1 \leqslant \mu_2 \\ &H_1 : \mu_1 < \mu_2 \ or \ H_1 : \mu_1 > \mu_2 \end{aligned}$

     For a *two-tailed test:* $\begin{aligned} &H_0 : \mu_1 = \mu_2 \\ &H_1 : \mu_1 \neq \mu_2 \end{aligned}$

3. $t = \dfrac{\overline{D} - \mu_0}{S_{\overline{b}}}$ *Significance test for the difference between means for two correlated samples:* df = the number of pairs minus one $(N - 1)$, is the difference stated in the H_0. The probability values for this example can be more readily computed by using Table 6b.

Use of Table

In using a *t* table certain assumptions must be made: (a) The difference between means in the sampling distribution should be normally distributed. (b) The denominator of the *t* statistic is an unbiased estimate of the population value. In the examples of 2 and 3 above, the assumption is that the samples are drawn from populations whose variances are equal (which can be checked against an F test).

Assume the following: an M_1 of 98.4, an M_2 of 72, a standard error of the difference of .94, and 28 degrees of freedom. To determine if the difference between the two means is a true difference rather than due to chance, enter the *t* table and discover that a *t* of 2.048 is needed for significance at the 5 per cent level and a *t* of 2.763 at the 1 (one) per cent level. With the previously assumed values, a *t* of 4.68 was obtained by working out the *t* formula. It may be reasonably certain then, with the *t* of 4.68 exceeding both the 5 and 1 per cent levels of significance, that the difference in means is a real difference.

Table 6b

Critical Values for Sandler's A-Statistic
(An Alternate for Student's *t* When Correlated Samples are Used)

$n - 1$*	Level of significance for one-tailed test					$n - 1$*
	.05	.025	.01	.005	.0005	
	Level of significance for two-tailed test					
	.10	.05	.02	.01	.001	
1	0.5125	0.5031	0.50049	0.50012	0.5000012	1
2	0.412	0.369	0.347	0.340	0.334	2
3	0.385	0.324	0.286	0.272	0.254	3
4	0.376	0.304	0.257	0.238	0.211	4
5	0.372	0.293	0.240	0.218	0.184	5
6	0.370	0.286	0.230	0.205	0.167	6
7	0.369	0.281	0.222	0.196	0.155	7
8	0.368	0.278	0.217	0.190	0.146	8
9	0.368	0.276	0.213	0.185·	0.139	9
10	0.368	0.274	0.210	0.181	0.134	10
11	0.368	0.273	0.207	0.178	0.130	11
12	0.368	0.271	0.205	0.176	0.126	12
13	0.368	0.270	0.204	0.174	0.124	13
14	0.368	0.270	0.202	0.172	0.121	14
15	0.368	0.269	0.201	0.170	0.119	15
16	0.368	0.268	0.200	0.169	0.117	16
17	0.368	0.268	0.199	0.168	0.116	17
18	0.368	0.267	0.198	0.167	0.114	18
19	0.368	0.267	0.197	0.166	0.113	19
20	0.368	0.266	0.197	0.165	0.112	20
21	0.368	0.266	0.196	0.165	0.111	21
22	0.368	0.266	0.196	0.164	0.110	22
23	0.368	0.266	0.195	0.163	0.109	23
24	0.368	0.265	0.195	0.163	0.108	24
25	0.368	0.265	0.194	0.162	0.108	25
26	0.368	0.265	0.194	0.162	0.107	26
27	0.368	0.265	0.193	0.161	0.107	27
28	0.368	0.265	0.193	0.161	0.106	28
29	0.368	0.264	0.193	0.161	0.106	29
30	0.368	0.264	0.193	0.160	0.105	30
40	0.368	0.263	0.191	0.158	0.102	40
60	0.369	0.262	0.189	0.155	0.099	60
120	0.369	0.261	0.187	0.153	0.095	120
∞	0.370	0.260	0.185	0.151	0.092	∞

*n = number of pairs

For any given value of n − 1, the table shows the values of A corresponding to various levels of probability. A is significant at a given level if it is equal to or <u>less than</u> the value shown in the table.

Discussion

See *Sandler's A-Statistic* under appropriate alphabetical entry for description of this test. Also see example 3 under Table 6a.

The A-statistic is defined as:

$$A = \frac{\Sigma D^2}{(\Sigma D)^2}$$

where ΣD^2 is the sum of the squares of the difference and $(\Sigma D)^2$ is the square of the sum of the differences. Under $n - 1$ degrees of freedom, the obtained A value is equal to or less than the tabled values at various significance levels.

Example and Use of Table

In a "before and after" problem an experiment is conducted to see if 25 people change in their beliefs toward God after being exposed to special films and lectures designed to impress people about the values of God. More favorable beliefs are anticipated as a result of such exposure.

Null Hypothesis H_0: There is no difference in beliefs before and after the exposure; that is, $r_D = 0$.

Alternative Hypothesis H_1: Beliefs are more favorable after the exposure, that is, $\mu_D < 0$. Since H_1 is directional only one-tailed values are necessary.

Statistical test: For a before-after type of design, the *t*-ratio for correlated samples or Sandler's A-statistic is applicable.

Significance level and sampling distribution: An alpha (α) of 0.01 is set as the significance level with a df of $n - 1$, or $25 - 1 = 24$.

Assuming that the $D^2 = 88$ and $D = -14$, with 24 degrees of freedom, $A = 88/196 = .449$. For 24 df at the 0.01 level (one-tailed test), therefore, an A equal to or less than 0.195 is required for significance. Since .449 is greater, the null hypothesis—that is, there is no difference in beliefs—is acceptable.

Table 7

Arcsin Transformation

$$\phi = 2 \arcsin \sqrt{X}$$

X	φ	X	φ	X	φ	X	φ	X	φ
.001	.0633	.041	.4078	.36	1.2870	.76	2.1177	.971	2.7993
.002	.0895	.042	.4128	.37	1.3078	.77	2.1412	.972	2.8053
.003	.1096	.043	.4178	.38	1.3284	.78	2.1652	.973	2.8115
.004	.1266	.044	.4227	.39	1.3490	.79	2.1895	.974	2.8177
.005	.1415	.045	.4275	.40	1.3694	.80	2.2143	.975	2.8240
.006	.1551	.046	.4323	.41	1.3898	.81	2.2395	.976	2.8305
.007	.1675	.047	.4371	.42	1.4101	.82	2.2653	.977	2.8371
.008	.1791	.048	.4418	.43	1.4303	.83	2.2916	.978	2.8438
009	.1900	.049	.4464	.44	1.4505	.84	2.3186	.979	2.8507
.010	.2003	.050	.4510	.45	1.4706	.85	2.3462	.980	2.8578
.011	.2101	.06	.4949	.46	1.4907	.86	2.3746	.981	2.8650
.012	.2195	.07	.5355	.47	1.5108	.87	2.4039	.982	2.8725
.013	.2285	.08	.5735	.48	1.5308	.88	2.4341	.983	2.8801
.014	.2372	.09	.6094	.49	1.5508	.89	2.4655	.984	2.8879
.015	.2456	.10	.6435	.50	1.5708	.90	2.4981	.985	2.8960
.016	.2537	.11	.6761	.51	1.5908	.91	2.5322	.986	2.9044
.017	.2615	.12	.7075	.52	1.6108	.92	2.5681	.987	2.9131
.018	.2691	.13	.7377	.53	1.6308	.93	2.6062	.988	2.9221
.019	.2766	.14	.7670	.54	1.6509	.94	2.6467	.989	2.9315
.020	.2838	.15	.7954	.55	1.6710	.95	2.6906	.990	2.9413
.021	.2909	.16	.8230	.56	1.6911	.951	2.6952	.991	2.9516
.022	.2978	.17	.8500	.57	1.7113	.952	2.6998	.992	2.9625
.023	.3045	.18	.8763	.58	1.7315	.953	2.7045	.993	2.9741
.024	.3111	.19	.9021	.59	1.7518	.954	2.7093	.994	2.9865
.025	.3176	.20	.9273	.60	1.7722	.955	2.7141	.995	3.0001
.026	.3239	.21	.9521	.61	1.7926	.956	2.7189	.996	3.0150
.027	.3301	.22	.9764	.62	1.8132	.957	2.7238	.997	3.0320
.028	.3363	.23	1.0004	.63	1.8338	.958	2.7288	.998	3.0521
.029	.3423	.24	1.0239	.64	1.8546	.959	2.7338	.999	3.0783
.030	.3482	.25	1.0472	.65	1.8755	.960	2.7389		
.031	.3540	.26	1.0701	.66	1.8965	.961	2.7440		
.032	.3597	.27	1.0928	.67	1.9177	.962	2.7492		
.033	.3654	.28	1.1152	.68	1.9391	.963	2.7545		
.034	.3709	.29	1.1374	.69	1.9606	.964	2.7598		
.035	.3764	.30	1.1593	.70	1.9823	.965	2.7652		
.036	.3818	.31	1.1810	.71	2.0042	.966	2.7707		
.037	.3871	.32	1.2025	.72	2.0264	.967	2.7762		
.038	.3924	.33	1.2239	.73	2.0488	.968	2.7819		
.039	.3976	.34	1.2451	.74	2.0715	.969	2.7876		
.040	.4027	.35	1.2661	.75	2.0944	.970	2.7934		

Discussion

(See *arcsin transformation* under alphabetical listing for definition.) The notation $\sin^{-1}$ (inverse sine) is equivalent to arcsin. Since Table 7 provides values of ϕ (or X') from .0633 (for an X of .001), it is not necessary to use the formula ϕ (or X') = 2 arcsin $\sqrt{X}$.

Note: The values in Table 7 are in radians, which correspond to a given p other than 0 or 1. Its variance is approximately $\sigma^2 = 1/N$. (For arcsin transformations for proportions see Snedecor, Table A16, page 569 ff.)

Arcsin transformations are of value when the distribution is binomial in nature and when the mean and variances are proportional.

In general, where relationships between *mean* and *variance* are not evident the researcher can by trial and error find a transformation, such as the time-saving arc sin one here, which will stabilize the within-groups variances. Arcsin transformations are applicable when scores are proportions, such as percentage correct or where the percentage predictions of one event are involved, or when there are a fixed number of trials with the proportion (X) representing the likelihood of a correct response varying from one treatment level to another.

Table 8

Upper Percentage Points of the χ^2 Distribution

df	.99	.98	.95	.90	.80	.70	.50	.30	.20	.10	.05	.02	.01	.001
1	.0³157	.0³628	.00393	.0158	.0642	.148	.455	1.074	1.642	2.706	3.841	5.412	6.635	10.827
2	.0201	.0404	.103	.211	.446	.713	1.386	2.408	3.219	4.605	5.991	7.824	9.210	13.815
3	.115	.i85	.352	.584	1.005	1.424	2.366	3.665	4.642	6.251	7.815	9.837	11.345	16.266
4	.297	.429	.711	1.064	1.649	2.195	3.357	4.878	5.989	7.779	9.488	11.668	13.277	18.467
5	.554	.752	1.145	1.610	2.343	3.000	4.351	6.064	7.289	9.236	11.070	13.388	15.086	20.515
6	.872	1.134	1.635	2.204	3.070	3.828	5.348	7.231	8.558	10.645	12.592	15.033	16.812	22.457
7	1.239	1.564	2.167	2.833	3.822	4.671	6.346	8.383	9.803	12.017	14.067	16.622	18.475	24.322
8	1.646	2.032	2.733	3.490	4.594	5.527	7.344	9.524	11.030	13.362	15.507	18.168	20.090	26.125
9	2.088	2.532	3.325	4.168	5.380	6.393	8.343	10.656	12.242	14.684	16.919	19.679	21.666	27.877
10	2.558	3.059	3.940	4.865	6.179	7.267	9.342	11.781	13.442	15.987	18.307	21.161	23.209	29.588
11	3.053	3.609	4.575	5.578	6.989	8.148	10.341	12.899	14.631	17.275	19.675	22.618	24.725	31.264
12	3.571	4.178	5.226	6.304	7.807	9.034	11.340	14.011	15.812	18.549	21.026	24.054	26.217	32.909
13	4.107	4.765	5.892	7.042	8.634	9.926	12.340	15.119	16.985	19.812	22.362	25.472	27.688	34.528
14	4.660	5.368	6.571	7.790	9.467	10.821	13.339	16.222	18.151	21.064	23.685	26.873	29.141	36.123
15	5.229	5.985	7.261	8.547	10.307	11.721	14.339	17.322	19.311	22.307	24.996	28.259	30.578	37.697
16	5.812	6.614	7.962	9.312	11.152	12.624	15.338	18.418	20.465	23.542	26.296	29.633	32.000	39.252
17	6.408	7.255	8.672	10.085	12.002	13.531	16.338	19.511	21.615	24.769	27.587	30.995	33.409	40.790
18	7.015	7.906	9.390	10.865	12.857	14.440	17.338	20.601	22.760	25.989	28.869	32.346	34.805	42.312
19	7.633	8.567	10.117	11.651	13.716	15.352	18.338	21.689	23.900	27.204	30.144	33.687	36.191	43.820
20	8.260	9.237	10.851	12.443	14.578	16.266	19.337	22.775	25.038	28.412	31.410	35.020	37.566	45.315
21	8.897	9.915	11.591	13.240	15.445	17.182	20.337	23.858	26.171	29.615	32.671	36.343	38.932	46.797
22	9.542	10.600	12.338	14.041	16.314	18.101	21.337	24.939	27.301	30.813	33.924	37.659	40.289	48.268
23	10.196	11.293	13.091	14.848	17.187	19.021	22.337	26.018	28.429	32.007	35.172	38.968	41.638	49.728
24	10.856	11.992	13.848	15.659	18.062	19.943	23.337	27.096	29.553	33.196	36.415	40.270	42.980	51.179
25	11.524	12.697	14.611	16.473	18.940	20.867	24.337	28.172	30.675	34.382	37.652	41.566	44.314	52.620
26	12.198	13.409	15.379	17.292	19.820	21.792	25.336	29.246	31.795	35.563	38.885	42.856	45.642	54.052
27	12.879	14.125	16.151	18.114	20.703	22.719	26.336	30.319	32.912	36.741	40.113	44.140	46.963	55.476
28	13.565	14.847	16.928	18.939	21.588	23.647	27.336	31.391	34.027	37.916	41.337	45.419	48.278	56.893
29	14.256	15.574	17.708	19.768	22.475	24.577	28.336	32.461	35.139	39.087	42.557	46.693	49.588	58.302
30	14.953	16.306	18.493	20.599	23.364	25.508	29.336	33.530	36.250	40.266	43.773	47.962	50.892	59.703

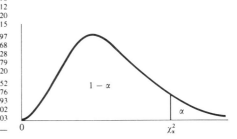

For $v > 30$, the expression $\sqrt{2\chi^2} - \sqrt{2v - 1}$ may be used as a normal deviate with unit variance.

H_O: observed distribution = theoretical distribution; $f_O = f_e$
H_1: observed distribution $\neq$ theoretical distribution; $f_O \neq f_e$
The null hypothesis may be tested by:

$$\chi^2 = \sum_{i=1}^{k} \frac{(f_O - f_e)^2}{f_e}$$

where

f_O = the observed number in a given category,
f_e = the expected number in that category,
$\sum_{i=1}^{k}$ means to sum this ratio over all k categories.

(Note: In cases with only one degree of freedom, i.e. a 2 × 2 table, use:

$$\chi^2 = \sum_{r=1}^{2} \sum_{c=1}^{2} \frac{(1f_O - f_e) - 0.5)^2}{f_e}$$

Null and Alternative Hypotheses

Use of Table

The table is used to test hypotheses for the form: $H_O: \sigma^2 = \sigma_O^2$ where σ_O^2 is the variance value under the null hypothesis, and also of the form

$$\Sigma \frac{(O - E)^2}{E}, \frac{(A - D)^2}{A + D}, \text{etc.,}$$

to mention only two test statistics that are distributed as chi-square. This table gives values of χ^2 corresponding to percentage points in various distributions determined by df. The left margin gives various degrees of freedom. The column headings give two-tailed probabilities frequently used. The tabled values are χ^2 values; the computed χ^2 must be as large or larger than the tabled value to be significant at the stated df and level.

Note: The test is a two-tailed test due to the squaring process. The alpha probabilities may be halved if one-tailed probabilities are desired. Many sets of data are too complex for a one-tailed test, and this table should be so used only if there is a single outcome which could go in one of two opposite directions. It is unusual to have a need for testing the significance of sample chi-squares with more than 30 degrees of freedom, but if such occasion arises a normal approximation can be attained by calculating the normal deviate $z = \sqrt{2\chi^2} - \sqrt{2df - 1}$, and referring to the normal curve for the needed values.

Table 9

Values of $-p(i) \log_2 p(i)$ from 0.00 to 0.999

p		0	1	2	3	4	5	6	7	8	9
.00	0.0	000	100	179	251	319	382	443	501	557	612
.01		664	716	766	814	862	909	955	999	*043*	*086*
.02	0.1	129	170	211	252	291	330	369	407	444	481
.03		518	554	589	624	659	693	727	760	793	825
.04		858	889	921	952	983	*013*	*043*	*073*	*103*	*132*
.05	0.2	161	190	218	246	274	301	329	356	383	409
.06		435	461	487	513	538	563	588	613	637	662
.07		686	709	733	756	780	803	826	848	871	893
.08		915	937	959	980	*002*	*023*	*044*	*065*	*086*	*106*
.09	0.3	127	147	167	187	207	226	246	265	284	303
.10		322	341	359	378	396	414	432	450	468	485
.11		503	520	537	555	571	588	605	622	638	654
.12		671	687	703	719	734	750	766	781	796	811
.13		826	841	856	871	886	900	915	929	943	957
.14		971	985	999	*012*	*006*	*040*	*053*	*066*	*079*	*092*
.15	0.4	105	118	131	144	156	169	181	194	206	218
.16		230	242	254	266	278	289	301	312	323	335
.17		346	357	368	379	390	401	411	422	432	443
.18		453	463	474	484	494	504	514	523	533	543
.19		552	562	571	581	590	599	608	617	626	635
.20		644	653	661	670	678	687	695	704	712	720
.21		728	736	744	752	760	768	776	783	791	798
.22		806	813	821	828	835	842	849	856	863	870
.23		877	883	890	897	903	910	916	923	929	935
.24		941	948	954	960	966	971	977	983	989	994
.25	0.5	000	006	011	017	022	027	032	038	043	048
.26		053	058	063	068	073	077	082	087	091	096
.27		100	105	109	113	118	122	126	130	134	138
.28		142	146	150	154	158	161	165	169	172	176
.29		179	183	186	189	192	196	199	202	205	208
.30		211	214	217	220	222	225	228	230	233	235
.31		238	240	243	245	248	250	252	254	256	258
.32		260	262	264	266	268	270	272	273	275	277
.33		278	280	281	283	284	286	287	288	289	291
.34		292	293	294	295	296	297	298	299	300	300
.35		301	302	302	303	304	304	305	305	306	306
.36		306	306	307	307	307	307	307	307	307	307
.37		307	307	307	307	307	306	306	306	305	305
.38		305	304	304	303	302	302	301	300	300	299
.39		298	297	296	295	294	293	292	291	290	289
.40		288	287	285	284	283	281	280	278	277	276
.41		274	272	271	269	267	266	264	262	260	258
.42		257	255	253	251	249	247	244	242	240	238
.43		236	233	231	229	226	224	222	219	217	214
.44		212	209	206	204	201	198	195	193	190	187
.45		184	181	178	175	172	169	166	163	160	157
.46		153	150	147	144	140	137	133	130	127	123
.47		120	116	112	108	105	102	098	094	090	086
.48		083	079	075	071	067	063	059	055	051	047
.49		043	039	034	030	026	022	018	013	009	004

Discussion

In determining the uncertainty involved when alternatives are and are not equally likely (such as in certain types of guessing games or in choice-reaction-time experiments) the use of logarithms is used in the uncertainty formula

$$\hat{H} = -p(i) \log_2 p(i)$$

where

$\hat{H}$ = the uncertainty symbol

$p(i)$ = the proportion of cases in an individual category

Ordinarily, the logarithm of the proportion of cases is located in logarithmic tables and multiplied by the proportion, $p(i)$, for each of the several categories and then summed (Σ). Table 9, however, gives the product of the proportion and its logarithm $-p(i) \log_e p(i)$. The proportions are looked up for each category in the table for their corresponding value of $-p(i) \log_2 p(i)$ and summed, such sums being usually expressed in *binary digits* (bits). It has been applied only to two-valued series on the assumption that the data occur in discrete steps disregarding time factors.

Special Note

Close examination of Table 9 reveals that there are certain table entries in italics, these being in the row immediately above a printed value in the second column. These italicized numbers indicate that the first digit (in the second column) that is ordinarily used to make up a $p(i)$ value is to be obtained from one line below the one for $p(i)$. For example, the $-p(i) \log_2 p(i)$ for a $p(i)$ of .145 is 0.4040 rather than 0.3040 as it might usually be read. That is, 0.4 is prefixed to the .040 of column 5 in the row above.

Table 9 (continued)

p		0	1	2	3	4	5	6	7	8	9
.50	0.5	000	996	991	987	982	978	973	968	964	959
.51	0.4	954	950	945	940	935	930	926	921	916	911
.52		906	901	896	891	886	880	875	870	865	860
.53		854	849	844	839	833	828	823	817	812	806
.54		801	795	789	784	778	772	767	761	755	750
.55		744	738	732	726	720	714	709	702	697	691
.56		684	678	672	666	660	654	648	641	635	629
.57		623	616	610	604	597	591	584	578	571	565
.58		558	551	545	538	532	515	518	511	505	498
.59		491	484	477	471	464	457	450	443	436	429
.60		422	415	408	401	393	386	379	372	365	357
.61		350	343	335	328	321	313	306	298	291	283
.62		276	268	261	253	246	238	230	223	215	207
.63		200	192	184	176	168	160	152	145	137	129
.64		121	113	105	097	089	081	072	064	056	048
.65		040	032	023	015	007	998	990	982	973	965
.66	0.3	957	948	940	931	923	914	906	897	888	880
.67		871	862	854	845	836	828	819	810	801	792
.68		783	774	766	757	748	739	730	721	712	703
.69		694	685	675	666	657	648	639	630	621	611
.70		602	593	583	574	565	556	546	537	527	718
.71		508	499	489	480	470	461	451	441	432	422
.72		412	403	393	383	373	364	354	344	334	324
.73		315	305	295	285	275	265	255	245	235	225
.74		215	204	194	184	174	164	154	144	133	123
.75		113	102	092	082	072	061	051	040	030	020
.76		009	999	988	978	967	957	946	935	925	914
.77	0.2	903	893	882	872	861	850	839	828	818	807
.78		796	785	774	764	752	742	731	720	708	697
.79		686	676	665	654	642	631	620	609	598	587
.80		576	564	553	542	530	519	508	497	485	474
.81		462	451	440	428	417	405	394	383	371	359
.82		348	336	325	313	301	290	278	266	255	243
.83		231	219	208	196	184	172	160	148	137	125
.84		113	101	089	077	065	053	041	029	017	005
.85	0.1	993	981	969	957	944	932	920	908	896	884
.86		871	859	847	834	822	810	798	785	773	760
.87		748	735	723	712	698	686	673	661	648	635
.88		623	610	598	585	573	560	547	534	522	509
.89		496	484	471	458	445	432	420	407	394	381
.90		368	355	342	329	316	303	290	277	264	251
.91		238	225	212	199	186	173	159	146	133	120
.92		107	094	080	067	054	040	027	014	000	987
.93	0.0	974	960	947	934	920	907	893	880	866	853
.94		839	826	812	799	785	771	758	744	730	717
.95		703	689	675	662	648	635	621	607	593	579
.96		565	552	538	524	510	496	482	468	454	441
.97		426	412	398	384	370	356	342	328	314	300
.98		285	271	257	243	229	215	200	186	172	158
.99		144	129	115	101	086	072	058	043	029	014

Example and Use of Table

Assume that it is known that half (.50) the foul balls hit in a baseball game fall behind the home plate area while ¼ (.25) each fall toward first and third base respectively. What would be the uncertainty, H, of guessing about the location of a foul ball if a blind-folded psychologist at a ball game said he could pinpoint its location merely by listening to the tick of the bat against the ball?

A table such as the following can be set up:

Category (i)	$p(i)$	$-p(i)\log_e p(i)$
1st base	.25	.50
3rd base	.25	.50
Home plate	.50	.50

How were these figures arrived at? The $p(i)$ values were already established by the assumption. The $-p(i)\log_e p(i)$ values were obtained by referring to the respective digits of .25 and .50. On the previous page it is seen that .25 gives 0.5 in the second column. The digit .50 in the first column at the top of this page also has a value of 0.5 in the second column, so whether the $p(i)$ is .25 or .50 makes no difference since the $-p(i)\log_e p(i)$ for each is identical. Summing the obtained values (.50 + .50 + .50) gives 1.5 or 1½ bits, indicating that 1½ guesses will be needed to guess where the foul ball will fall.

For a $-p(i)$ with digits, such as .791, the same procedure is followed, except that there is a value for the additional digit to locate. A p of .791 reveals 0.2 as the value for the first digit of $-p(i)\log_e p(i)$. The second, third, and fourth digits of $-p(i)\log_e p(i)$ are obtained by reading across the row for .79 to the column under 1 which gives 676, which when added to the first digit of 0.2 results in .2676.

Table 10

Critical Values of Pearson *r*

df = n − 2*	Level of significance for one-tailed test			
	.05	.025	.01	.005
	Level of significance for two-tailed test			
	.10	.05	.02	.01
1	.9877	.9969	.9995	.9999
2	.9000	.9500	.9800	.9900
3	.8054	.8783	.9343	.9587
4	.7293	.8114	.8822	.9172
5	.6694	.7545	.8329	.8745
6	.6215	.7067	.7887	.8343
7	.5822	.6664	.7498	.7977
8	.5494	.6319	.7155	.7646
9	.5214	.6021	.6851	.7348
10	.4973	.5760	.6581	.7079
11	.4762	.5529	.6339	.6835
12	.4575	.5324	.6120	.6614
13	.4409	.5139	.5923	.6411
14	.4259	.4973	.5742	.6226
15	.4124	.4821	.5577	.6055
16	.4000	.4683	.5425	.5897
17	.3887	.4555	.5285	.5751
18	.3783	.4438	.5155	.5614
19	.3687	.4329	.5034	.5487
20	.3598	.4227	.4921	.5368
25	.3233	.3809	.4451	.4869
30	.2960	.3494	.4093	.4487
35	.2746	.3246	.3810	.4182
40	.2573	.3044	.3578	.3932
45	.2428	.2875	.3384	.3721
50	.2306	.2732	.3218	.3541
60	.2108	.2500	.2948	.3248
70	.1954	.2319	.2737	.3017
80	.1829	.2172	.2565	.2830
90	.1726	.2050	.2422	.2673
100	.1638	.1946	.2301	.2540

Discussion

This table provides critical values of *r* for determining significance at various one- and two-tailed alpha (*a*) levels. The critical values depend upon degrees of freedom (df) equal to the number of pairs of scores under consideration minus two (N − 2). As *r* moves away from 0.00 toward 1.00, a relationship may be indicated leading to the rejection of the null hypothesis. Smaller degrees of freedom require larger values of *r* for significance.

Null and Alternative Hypotheses

H_0: $\rho = 0$; there is no association between the pairs of scores, i.e., the population correlation coefficient, ρ, is equal to 0.00.

H_1: $\rho \neq 0$; there is an association between the pairs of scores, i.e., they are not equal.

Example and Use of the Table

To use Table 10, first locate the appropriate degrees of freedom for the correlation coefficient in the N − 2 (or df) column. Scan to the right fixing at the desired alpha level. The value in the body of the table located at the intersection is the minimum *r* value needed for significance. For example, with 15 degrees of freedom an *r* of .4821 or greater is needed for significance at the .05 level, two-tailed test.

Table 11

Functions of *r*

r	$\sqrt{r}$	r^2	$\sqrt{r-r^2}$	$\sqrt{1-r}$	$1-r^2$	$\sqrt{1-r^2}$ / k	$100(1-k)$ / % Eff.	r
1.00	1.0000	1.0000	0.0000	0.0000	0.0000	0.0000	100.00	1.00
.99	.9950	.9801	.0995	.1000	.0199	.1411	85.89	.99
.98	.9899	.9604	.1400	.1414	.0396	.1990	80.10	.98
.97	.9849	.9409	.1706	.1732	.0591	.2431	75.69	.97
.96	.9798	.9216	.1960	.2000	.0784	.2800	72.00	.96
.95	.9747	.9025	.2179	.2236	.0975	.3122	68.78	.95
.94	.9695	.8836	.2375	.2449	.1164	.3412	65.88	.94
.93	.9644	.8649	.2551	.2646	.1351	.3676	63.24	.93
.92	.9592	.8464	.2713	.2828	.1536	.3919	60.81	.92
.91	.9539	.8281	.2862	.3000	.1719	.4146	58.54	.91
.90	.9487	.8100	.3000	.3162	.1900	.4359	56.41	.90
.89	.9434	.7921	.3129	.3317	.2079	.4560	54.40	.89
.88	.9381	.7744	.3250	.3464	.2256	.4750	52.50	.88
.87	.9327	.7569	.3363	.3606	.2431	.4931	50.69	.87
.86	.9274	.7396	.3470	.3742	.2604	.5103	48.97	.86
.85	.9220	.7225	.3571	.3873	.2775	.5268	47.32	.85
.84	.9165	.7056	.3666	.4000	.2944	.5426	45.74	.84
.83	.9110	.6889	.3756	.4123	.3111	.5578	44.22	.83
.82	.9055	.6724	.3842	.4243	.3276	.5724	42.76	.82
.81	.9000	.6561	.3923	.4359	.3439	.5864	41.36	.81
.80	.8944	.6400	.4000	.4472	.3600	.6000	40.00	.80
.79	.8888	.6241	.4073	.4583	.3759	.6131	38.69	.79
.78	.8832	.6084	.4142	.4690	.3916	.6258	37.42	.78
.77	.8775	.5929	.4208	.4796	.4071	.6380	36.20	.77
.76	.8718	.5776	.4271	.4899	.4224	.6499	35.01	.76
.75	.8660	.5625	.4330	.5000	.4375	.6614	33.86	.75
.74	.8602	.5476	.4386	.5099	.4524	.6726	32.74	.74
.73	.8544	.5329	.4440	.5196	.4671	.6834	31.66	.73
.72	.8485	.5184	.4490	.5292	.4816	.6940	30.60	.72
.71	.8426	.5041	.4538	.5385	.4959	.7042	29.58	.71
.70	.8367	.4900	.4583	.5477	.5100	.7141	28.59	.70
.69	.8307	.4761	.4625	.5568	.5239	.7238	27.62	.69
.68	.8246	.4624	.4665	.5657	.5376	.7332	26.68	.68
.67	.8185	.4489	.4702	.5745	.5511	.7424	25.76	.67
.66	.8124	.4356	.4737	.5831	.5644	.7513	24.87	.66
.65	.8062	.4225	.4770	.5916	.5775	.7599	24.01	.65
.64	.8000	.4096	.4800	.6000	.5904	.7684	23.16	.64
.63	.7937	.3969	.4828	.6083	.6031	.7766	22.34	.63
.62	.7874	.3844	.4854	.6164	.6156	.7846	21.54	.62
.61	.7810	.3721	.4877	.6245	.6279	.7924	20.76	.61
.60	.7746	.3600	.4899	.6325	.6400	.8000	20.00	.60
.59	.7681	.3481	.4918	.6403	.6519	.8074	19.26	.59
.58	.7616	.3364	.4936	.6481	.6636	.8146	18.54	.58
.57	.7550	.3249	.4951	.6557	.6751	.8216	17.84	.57
.56	.7483	.3136	.4964	.6633	.6864	.8285	17.15	.56
.55	.7416	.3025	.4975	.6708	.6975	.8352	16.48	.55
.54	.7348	.2916	.4984	.6782	.7084	.8417	15.83	.54
.53	.7280	.2809	.4991	.6856	.7191	.8480	15.20	.53
.52	.7211	.2704	.4996	.6928	.7296	.8542	14.58	.52
.51	.7141	.2601	.4999	.7000	.7399	.8602	13.98	.51
.50	.7071	.2500	.5000	.7071	.7500	.8660	13.40	.50

Discussion

Table 11 presents functions of *r* found in various test statistics. In determining the standard error of the estimate, for example, in the formula

$$S_{est\ y} = S_y\sqrt{1 - r^2},$$

the function $\sqrt{1 - r^2}$ may be found in the seventh column above. The function $1 - r^2$, the proportion of the Y variance not attributable to the relation of Y to X, is located in column six. This function is often found in regression analysis, analysis of variance, point biserial correlation, and the *t* statistic.

Values for an *r* of .50 to .01 are found on the following page.

r	$\sqrt{r}$	r^2	$\sqrt{r-r^2}$	$\sqrt{1-r}$	$1-r^2$	$\sqrt{1-r^2}$ k	$100(1-k)$ % Eff.	r
.50	.7071	.2500	.5000	.7071	.7500	.8660	13.40	.50
.49	.7000	.2401	.4999	.7141	.7599	.8717	12.83	.49
.48	.6928	.2304	.4996	.7211	.7696	.8773	12.27	.48
.47	.6856	.2209	.4991	.7280	.7791	.8827	11.73	.47
.46	.6782	.2116	.4984	.7348	.7884	.8879	11.21	.46
.45	.6708	.2025	.4975	.7416	.7975	.8930	10.70	.45
.44	.6633	.1936	.4964	.7483	.8064	.8980	10.20	.44
.43	.6557	.1849	.4951	.7550	.8151	.9028	9.72	.43
.42	.6481	.1764	.4936	.7616	.8236	.9075	9.25	.42
.41	.6403	.1681	.4918	.7681	.8319	.9121	8.79	.41
.40	.6325	.1600	.4899	.7746	.8400	.9165	8.35	.40
.39	.6245	.1521	.4877	.7810	.8479	.9208	7.92	.39
.38	.6164	.1444	.4854	.7874	.8556	.9250	7.50	.38
.37	.6083	.1369	.4828	.7937	.8631	.9290	7.10	.37
.36	.6000	.1296	.4800	.8000	.8704	.9330	6.70	.36
.35	.5916	.1225	.4770	.8062	.8775	.9367	6.33	.35
.34	.5831	.1156	.4737	.8124	.8844	.9404	5.96	.34
.33	.5745	.1089	.4702	.8185	.8911	.9440	5.60	.33
.32	.5657	.1024	.4665	.8246	.8976	.9474	5.25	.32
.31	.5568	.0961	.4625	.8307	.9039	.9507	4.93	.31
.30	.5477	.0900	.4583	.8367	.9100	.9539	4.61	.30
.29	.5385	.0841	.4538	.8426	.9159	.9570	4.30	.29
.28	.5292	.0784	.4490	.8485	.9216	.9600	4.00	.28
.27	.5196	.0729	.4440	.8544	.9271	.9629	3.71	.27
.26	.5099	.0676	.4386	.8602	.9324	.9656	3.44	.26
.25	.5000	.0625	.4330	.8660	.9375	.9682	3.18	.25
.24	.4899	.0576	.4271	.8718	.9424	.9708	2.92	.24
.23	.4796	.0529	.4208	.8775	.9471	.9732	2.68	.23
.22	.4690	.0484	.4142	.8832	.9516	.9755	2.45	.22
.21	.4583	.0441	.4073	.8888	.9559	.9777	2.23	.21
.20	.4472	.0400	.4000	.8944	.9600	.9798	2.02	.20
.19	.4359	.0361	.3923	.9000	.9639	.9818	1.82	.19
.18	.4243	.0324	.3842	.9055	.9676	.9837	1.63	.18
.17	.4123	.0289	.3756	.9110	.9711	.9854	1.46	.17
.16	.4000	.0256	.3666	.9165	.9744	.9871	1.29	.16
.15	.3873	.0225	.3571	.9220	.9775	.9887	1.13	.15
.14	.3742	.0196	.3470	.9274	.9804	.9902	.98	.14
.13	.3606	.0169	.3363	.9327	.9831	.9915	.85	.13
.12	.3464	.0144	.3250	.9381	.9856	.9928	.72	.12
.11	.3317	.0121	.3129	.9434	.9879	.9939	.61	.11
.10	.3162	.0100	.3000	.9487	.9900	.9950	.50	.10
.09	.3000	.0081	.2862	.9539	.9919	.9959	.41	.09
.08	.2828	.0064	.2713	.9592	.9936	.9968	.32	.08
.07	.2646	.0049	.2551	.9644	.9951	.9975	.25	.07
.06	.2449	.0036	.2375	.9695	.9964	.9982	.18	.06
.05	.2236	.0025	.2179	.9747	.9975	.9987	.13	.05
.04	.2000	.0016	.1960	.9798	.9984	.9992	.08	.04
.03	.1732	.0009	.1706	.9849	.9991	.9995	.05	.03
.02	.1414	.0004	.1400	.9899	.9996	.9998	.02	.02
.01	.1000	.0001	.0995	.9950	.9999	.9999	.01	.01
.00	.0000	.0000	.0000	1.0000	1.0000	1.0000	.00	.00

Table 12
Equivalent Values of r and z

z	·00	·01	·02	·03	·04	·05	·06	·07	·08	·09	Mean Diff.
·0	·0000	·0100	·0200	·0300	·0400	·0500	·0599	·0699	·0798	·0898	100
·1	·0997	·1096	·1194	·1293	·1391	·1489	·1586	·1684	·1781	·1877	98
·2	·1974	·2070	·2165	·2260	·2355	·2449	·2543	·2636	·2729	·2821	94
·3	·2913	·3004	·3095	·3185	·3275	·3364	·3452	·3540	·3627	·3714	89
·4	·3800	·3885	·3969	·4053	·4136	·4219	·4301	·4382	·4462	·4542	82
·5	·4621	·4699	·4777	·4854	·4930	·5005	·5080	·5154	·5227	·5299	75
·6	·5370	·5441	·5511	·5580	·5649	·5717	·5784	·5850	·5915	·5980	68
·7	·6044	·6107	·6169	·6231	·6291	·6351	·6411	·6469	·6527	·6584	60
·8	·6640	·6696	·6751	·6805	·6858	·6911	·6963	·7014	·7064	·7114	53
·9	·7163	·7211	·7259	·7306	·7352	·7398	·7443	·7487	·7531	·7574	46
1·0	·7616	·7658	·7699	·7739	·7779	·7818	·7857	·7895	·7932	·7969	39
1·1	·8005	·8041	·8076	·8110	·8144	·8178	·8210	·8243	·8275	·8306	33
1·2	·8337	·8367	·8397	·8426	·8455	·8483	·8511	·8538	·8565	·8591	28
1·3	·8617	·8643	·8668	·8692	·8717	·8741	·8764	·8787	·8810	·8832	24
1·4	·8854	·8875	·8896	·8917	·8937	·8957	·8977	·8996	·9015	·9033	20
1·5	·9051	·9069	·9087	·9104	·9121	·9138	·9154	·9170	·9186	·9201	17
1·6	·9217	·9232	·9246	·9261	·9275	·9289	·9302	·9316	·9329	·9341	14
1·7	·9354	·9366	·9379	·9391	·9402	·9414	·9425	·9436	·9447	·9458	12
1·8	·94681	·94783	·94884	·94983	·95080	·95175	·95268	·95359	·95449	·95537	95
1·9	·95624	·95709	·95792	·95873	·95953	·96032	·96109	·96185	·96259	·96331	79
2·0	·96403	·96473	·96541	·96609	·96675	·96739	·96803	·96865	·96926	·96986	65
2·1	·97045	·97103	·97159	·97215	·97269	·97323	·97375	·97426	·97477	·97526	53
2·2	·97574	·97622	·97668	·97714	·97759	·97803	·97846	·97888	·97929	·97970	44
2·3	·98010	·98049	·98087	·98124	·98161	·98197	·98233	·98267	·98301	·98335	36
2·4	·98367	·98399	·98431	·98462	·98492	·98522	·98551	·98579	·98607	·98635	30
2·5	·98661	·98688	·98714	·98739	·98764	·98788	·98812	·98835	·98858	·98881	24
2·6	·98903	·98924	·98945	·98966	·98987	·99007	·99026	·99045	·99064	·99083	20
2·7	·99101	·99118	·99136	·99153	·99170	·99186	·99202	·99218	·99233	·99248	16
2·8	·99263	·99278	·99292	·99306	·99320	·99333	·99346	·99359	·99372	·99384	13
2·9	·99396	·99408	·99420	·99431	·99443	·99454	·99464	·99475	·99485	·99495	11

	·0	·1	·2	·3	·4	·5	·6	·7	·8	·9	
3	·99505	·99595	·99668	·99728	·99777	·99818	·99851	·99878	·99900	·99918	—
4	·99933	·99945	·99955	·99963	·99970	·99975	·99980	·99983	·99986	·99989	—

Table 12 gives the transformation of r to z and z to r. If z = 1.47, for example, the equivalent value of r is 0.8996. And by examining the tabled values close enough to a desired r, an equivalent value of z can be obtained. For example, an r of .67 (the closest value to it being .6696) gives a corresponding z value of .81 (combining the .8 under z and the .01 value in the second column).

Table 13a

Confidence Limits for the Population Correlation Coefficient ρ Given the Sample Coefficient r.
Confidence Coefficient, $1 - 2a = 0.95$

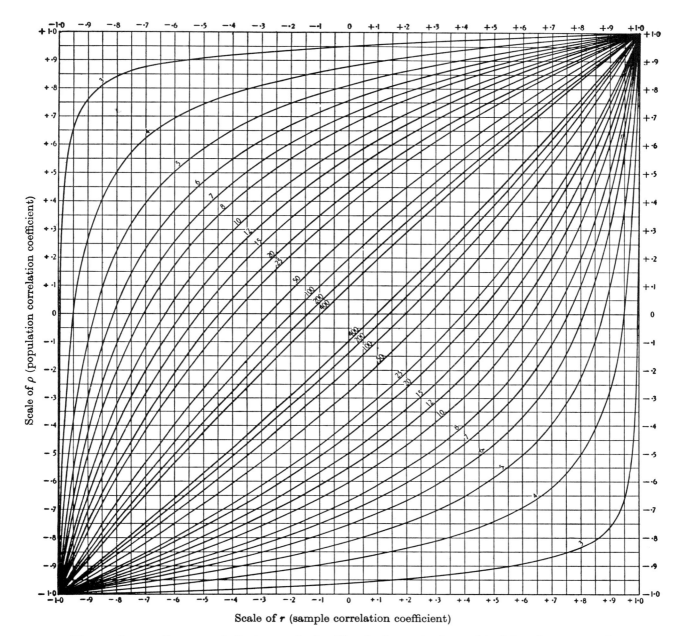

Scale of r (sample correlation coefficient)

The numbers on the curves indicate sample size. The chart can also be used to determine upper and lower 2·5 % significance points for r, given ρ.

Use of the Table and Example

The technique for using this table is identical to that for using Table 1d, which gives the confidence limits of a proportion.
Assume a sample r of $-.20$ with a sample size of 25. At the x axis a $-.20$ intersects the p scale at $-.55$. That is the lower confidence limit of p. For the upper limit continue up the vertical line until the second curved line for a sample size of 25 is reached, which shows a ρ of .20. We may, therefore, be 95 per cent confident that the population correlation lies between $-.55$ and .20.

Table 13b

Confidence Limits for the Population Correlation Coefficient ρ Given the Sample Coefficient r.
Confidence Coefficient, $1 - 2a = 0.99$

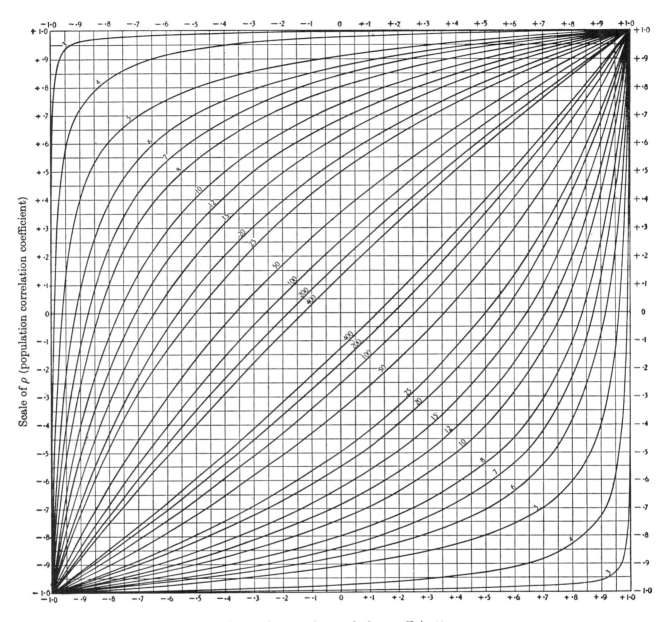

Scale of r (sample correlation coefficient)

The numbers on the curves indicate sample size. The chart can also be used to determine upper and lower 0·5 % significance points for r, given ρ.

The statistic r is an estimator of the parameter (rho), the correlation coefficient which measures the closeness of the population relation between X_1 and X_2. This table is used exactly like Table 13a. It differs only in the value of α.

Table 14
Estimates of r_t for Various Values of bc/ad

r_t	$\dfrac{bc}{ad}$	r_t	$\dfrac{bc}{ad}$	r_t	$\dfrac{bc}{ad}$
.00	0–1.00	.35	2.49–2.55	.70	8.50–
.01	1.01–1.03	.36	2.56–2.63	.71	8.91–
.02	1.04–1.06	.37	2.64–2.71	.72	9.36–
.03	1.07–1.08	.38	2.72–2.79	.73	9.83–
.04	1.09–1.11	.39	2.80–2.87	.74	10.34–
.05	1.12–1.14	.40	2.88–2.96	.75	10.91–
.06	1.15–1.17	.41	2.97–3.05	.76	11.52–
.07	1.18–1.20	.42	3.06–3.14	.77	12.17–
.08	1.21–1.23	.43	3.15–3.24	.78	12.90–
.09	1.24–1.27	.44	3.25–3.34	.79	13.71–
.10	1.28–1.30	.45	3.35–3.45	.80	14.59–
.11	1.31–1.33	.46	3.46–3.56	.81	15.58–
.12	1.34–1.37	.47	3.57–3.68	.82	16.66–
.13	1.38–1.40	.48	3.69–3.80	.83	17.89–
.14	1.41–1.44	.49	3.81–3.92	.84	19.29–
.15	1.45–1.48	.50	3.93–4.06	.85	20.86–
.16	1.49–1.52	.51	4.07–4.20	.86	22.69–
.17	1.53–1.56	.52	4.21–4.34	.87	24.77–
.18	1.57–1.60	.53	4.35–4.49	.88	27.23–
.19	1.61–1.64	.54	4.50–4.66	.89	30.10–
.20	1.65–1.69	.55	4.67–4.82	.90	33.61–
.21	1.70–1.73	.56	4.83–4.99	.91	37.80–
.22	1.74–1.78	.57	5.00–5.18	.92	43.07–
.23	1.79–1.83	.58	5.19–5.38	.93	49.84–
.24	1.84–1.88	.59	5.39–5.59	.94	58.80–
.25	1.89–1.93	.60	5.60–5.80	.95	70.96–
.26	1.94–1.98	.61	5.81–6.03	.96	89.02–
.27	1.99–2.04	.62	6.04–6.28	.97	117.55–
.28	2.05–2.10	.63	6.29–6.54	.98	169.68–
.29	2.11–2.15	.64	6.55–6.81	.99	293.13–
.30	2.16–2.22	.65	6.82–7.10	1.00	938.98–
.31	2.23–2.28	.66	7.11–7.42		
.32	2.29–2.34	.67	7.43–7.75		
.33	2.35–2.41	.68	7.76–8.11		
.34	2.42–2.48	.69	8.12–8.49		

Discussion

The tetrachoric correlation requires the setting up of data into a four-fold table, with both of the variables assumed to be continuous but which are nevertheless treated as a dichotomy.

The tetrachoric r provides an estimate of the parameter, ρ. Its interpretation is identical to the Pearson r, but it is a less reliable measurement.

Table 14 is entered with the value of ad/bc (or its reciprocal if it is larger). If the reciprocal is used the resulting r_t will be negative. Interpolation for between values of ad/bc is not recommended since accuracy of the values does not extend beyond the second decimal. The author (Davidoff) of this table advises that it is not necessary to only use proportions in computing ad/bc; the raw proportions may be used directly. However, if proportions are used, there is little need to carry out the values beyond two places.

Example and Use of the Table

Assume that it is desired to find the correlation between the upper half and the lower half of a class of 100 students on their performance of a particularly difficult test item. Results can be segregated into the top 50 and lower 50, with right and wrong answers counted, and then set up in a fourfold table, with a, b, c, and d being the cell frequencies. The ratio ad/bc or bc/ad (whichever numerator is larger) is used, and the correlation coefficient value is read directly from Table 14.

	Right	Wrong	Total
Upper 50	24 (a)	26 (b)	50
Lower 50	5 (c)	45 (d)	50
Total	29	71	100

To enter Table 14 it is necessary to follow the value arrangement of ad/bc, thus:

$$ad/bc = \frac{(24)(45)}{(26)(5)} = \frac{1080}{130} = 8.31$$

The value of 8.31 is located in the ad/bc column between the range of 8.12–8.49, which gives an r_t of .69, and although only an approximation it can be proved to be quite close to the r_t solved by a quadratic equation of the second power, all higher powers being ignored. If ad is less than bc, the ratio bc/ad is used, since the larger of the two products is always placed in the numerator.

Table 15

Complete Sets of Orthogonal Latin Squares

3×3

I				II		
1	2	3		1	2	3
2	3	1		3	1	2
3	1	2		2	3	1

4×4

I

1	2	3	4
2	1	4	3
3	4	1	2
4	3	2	1

AC, BD

II

1	2	3	4
3	4	1	2
4	3	2	1
2	1	4	3

ACD, BC

III

1	2	3	4
4	3	2	1
2	1	4	3
3	4	1	2

AD, BCD

5×5

I

1	2	3	4	5
2	3	4	5	1
3	4	5	1	2
4	5	1	2	3
5	1	2	3	4

II

1	2	3	4	5
3	4	5	1	2
5	1	2	3	4
2	3	4	5	1
4	5	1	2	3

III

1	2	3	4	5
4	5	1	2	3
2	3	4	5	1
5	1	2	3	4
3	4	5	1	2

IV

1	2	3	4	5
5	1	2	3	4
4	5	1	2	3
3	4	5	1	2
2	3	4	5	1

7×7

I

1	2	3	4	5	6	7
2	3	4	5	6	7	1
3	4	5	6	7	1	2
4	5	6	7	1	2	3
5	6	7	1	2	3	4
6	7	1	2	3	4	5
7	1	2	3	4	5	6

II

1	2	3	4	5	6	7
3	4	5	6	7	1	2
5	6	7	1	2	3	4
7	1	2	3	4	5	6
2	3	4	5	6	7	1
4	5	6	7	1	2	3
6	7	1	2	3	4	5

III

1	2	3	4	5	6	7
4	5	6	7	1	2	3
7	1	2	3	4	5	6
3	4	5	6	7	1	2
6	7	1	2	3	4	5
2	3	4	5	6	7	1
5	6	7	1	2	3	4

IV

1	2	3	4	5	6	7
5	6	7	1	2	3	4
2	3	4	5	6	7	1
6	7	1	2	3	4	5
3	4	5	6	7	1	2
7	1	2	3	4	5	6
4	5	6	7	1	2	3

V

1	2	3	4	5	6	7
6	7	1	2	3	4	5
4	5	6	7	1	2	3
2	3	4	5	6	7	1
7	1	2	3	4	5	6
5	6	7	1	2	3	4
3	4	5	6	7	1	2

VI

1	2	3	4	5	6	7
7	1	2	3	4	5	6
6	7	1	2	3	4	5
5	6	7	1	2	3	4
4	5	6	7	1	2	3
3	4	5	6	7	1	2
2	3	4	5	6	7	1

8×8

I

1	2	3	4	5	6	7	8
2	1	4	3	6	5	8	7
3	4	1	2	7	8	5	6
4	3	2	1	8	7	6	5
5	6	7	8	1	2	3	4
6	5	8	7	2	1	4	3
7	8	5	6	3	4	1	2
8	7	6	5	4	3	2	1

AD, BE, CF

II

1	2	3	4	5	6	7	8
5	6	7	8	1	2	3	4
2	1	4	3	6	5	8	7
6	5	8	7	2	1	4	3
7	8	5	6	3	4	1	2
3	4	1	2	7	8	5	6
8	7	6	5	4	3	2	1
4	3	2	1	8	7	6	5

AEF, BD, CE

III

1	2	3	4	5	6	7	8
7	8	5	6	3	4	1	2
5	6	7	8	1	2	3	4
3	4	1	2	7	8	5	6
8	7	6	5	4	3	2	1
2	1	4	3	6	5	8	7
4	3	2	1	8	7	6	5
6	5	8	7	2	1	4	3

ADE, BEF, CD

IV

1	2	3	4	5	6	7	8
8	7	6	5	4	3	2	1
7	8	5	6	3	4	1	2
2	1	4	3	6	5	8	7
4	3	2	1	8	7	6	5
5	6	7	8	1	2	3	4
6	5	8	7	2	1	4	3
3	4	1	2	7	8	5	6

ADEF, BDE, CEF

V

1	2	3	4	5	6	7	8
4	3	2	1	8	7	6	5
8	7	6	5	4	3	2	1
5	6	7	8	1	2	3	4
6	5	8	7	2	1	4	3
7	8	5	6	3	4	1	2
3	4	1	2	7	8	5	6
2	1	4	3	6	5	8	7

ADF, BDEF, CDE

VI

1	2	3	4	5	6	7	8
6	5	8	7	2	1	4	3
4	3	2	1	8	7	6	5
7	8	5	6	3	4	1	2
3	4	1	2	7	8	5	6
8	7	6	5	4	3	2	1
2	1	4	3	6	5	8	7
5	6	7	8	1	2	3	4

AF, BDF, CDEF

VII

1	2	3	4	5	6	7	8
3	4	1	2	7	8	5	6
6	5	8	7	2	1	4	3
8	7	6	5	4	3	2	1
2	1	4	3	6	5	8	7
4	3	2	1	8	7	6	5
5	6	7	8	1	2	3	4
7	8	5	6	3	4	1	2

AE, BF, CDF

Orthogonal Latin squares (or Graeco-Latin squares) are those formed from two superimposed Latin squares, one square being of Greek and the other of Latin letters, so arranged that the same Latin letter is never paired more than once with the same Greek letter. Complete sets of orthogonal squares exist for all prime numbers (power values of p) and powers of primes. Table 15 here includes a complete set of orthogonal Latin squares (3 × 3, 4 × 4, 5 × 5, 8 × 8, 9 × 9, and 10 × 10, as well as one of a set of five 12 × 12 squares). (See Kirk for many references and uses of Latin squares and their variations.)

Table 15 (continued)

9×9

I

```
1 2 3 4 5 6 7 8 9
2 3 1 5 6 4 8 9 7
3 1 2 6 4 5 9 7 8
4 5 6 7 8 9 1 2 3
5 6 4 8 9 7 2 3 1
6 4 5 9 7 8 3 1 2
7 8 9 1 2 3 4 5 6
8 9 7 2 3 1 5 6 4
9 7 8 3 1 2 6 4 5
```
$AC(J), BD(J),$
$AC(J) \times BD(J).$

II

```
1 2 3 4 5 6 7 8 9
7 8 9 1 2 3 4 5 6
4 5 6 7 8 9 1 2 3
2 3 1 5 6 4 8 9 7
8 9 7 2 3 1 5 6 4
5 6 4 8 9 7 2 3 1
3 1 2 6 4 5 9 7 8
9 7 8 3 1 2 6 4 5
6 4 5 9 7 8 3 1 2
```
$BC(J), AD(I),$
$BC(J) \times AD(I).$

III

```
1 2 3 4 5 6 7 8 9
9 7 8 3 1 2 6 4 5
5 6 4 8 9 7 2 3 1
6 4 5 9 7 8 3 1 2
2 3 1 5 6 4 8 9 7
7 8 9 1 2 3 4 5 6
8 9 7 2 3 1 5 6 4
4 5 6 7 8 9 1 2 3
3 1 2 6 4 5 9 7 8
```
$ABC(Y), ABD(W),$
$BCD(Y), ACD(Z).$

IV

```
1 2 3 4 5 6 7 8 9
8 9 7 2 3 1 5 6 4
6 4 5 9 7 8 3 1 2
9 7 8 3 1 2 6 4 5
4 5 6 7 8 9 1 2 3
2 3 1 5 6 4 8 9 7
5 6 4 8 9 7 2 3 1
3 1 2 6 4 5 9 7 8
7 8 9 1 2 3 4 5 6
```
$ABC(X), ABD(Y),$
$ACD(X), BCD(Z).$

V

```
1 2 3 4 5 6 7 8 9
3 1 2 6 4 5 9 7 8
2 3 1 5 6 4 8 9 7
7 8 9 1 2 3 4 5 6
9 7 8 3 1 2 6 4 5
8 9 7 2 3 1 5 6 4
4 5 6 7 8 9 1 2 3
6 4 5 9 7 8 3 1 2
5 6 4 8 9 7 2 3 1
```
$AC(I), BD(I),$
$AC(I) \times BD(I).$

VI

```
1 2 3 4 5 6 7 8 9
4 5 6 7 8 9 1 2 3
7 8 9 1 2 3 4 5 6
3 1 2 6 4 5 9 7 8
6 4 5 9 7 8 3 1 2
9 7 8 3 1 2 6 4 5
2 3 1 5 6 4 8 9 7
5 6 4 8 9 7 2 3 1
8 9 7 2 3 1 5 6 4
```
$BC(I), AD(J),$
$BC(I) \times AD(J).$

VII

```
1 2 3 4 5 6 7 8 9
5 6 4 8 9 7 2 3 1
9 7 8 3 1 2 6 4 5
8 9 7 2 3 1 5 6 4
3 1 2 6 4 5 9 7 8
4 5 6 7 8 9 1 2 3
6 4 5 9 7 8 3 1 2
7 8 9 1 2 3 4 5 6
2 3 1 5 6 4 8 9 7
```
$ABC(Z), ABD(X),$
$BCD(X), ACD(W).$

VIII

```
1 2 3 4 5 6 7 8 9
6 4 5 9 7 8 3 1 2
8 9 7 2 3 1 5 6 4
5 6 4 8 9 7 2 3 1
7 8 9 1 2 3 4 5 6
3 1 2 6 4 5 9 7 8
9 7 8 3 1 2 6 4 5
2 3 1 5 6 4 8 9 7
4 5 6 7 8 9 1 2 3
```
$ABC(W), ABD(Z),$
$ACD(Y), BCD(W).$

Use of Orthogonal Latin Squares

Complete sets of orthogonal squares are used in factorial design as well as in quasi-factorial and quasi-Latin square designs. From these squares other designs in balanced incomplete blocks may be generated, as may other designs utilizing analysis of variance techniques.

Table 16

Coefficients of Orthogonal Polynomials

k	Polynomial	Coefficients										Σc_{ij}^2
3	Linear	-1	0	1								2
	Quadratic	1	-2	1								6
	Linear	-3	-1	1	3							20
4	Quadratic	1	-1	-1	1							4
	Cubic	-1	3	-3	1							20
	Linear	-2	-1	0	1	2						10
5	Quadratic	2	-1	-2	-1	2						14
	Cubic	-1	2	0	-2	1						10
	Quartic	1	-4	6	-4	1						70
	Linear	-5	-3	-1	1	3	5					70
6	Quadratic	5	-1	-4	-4	-1	5					84
	Cubic	-5	7	4	-4	-7	5					180
	Quartic	1	-3	2	2	-3	1					28
	Linear	-3	-2	-1	0	1	2	3				28
7	Quadratic	5	0	-3	-4	-3	0	5				84
	Cubic	-1	1	1	0	-1	-1	1				6
	Quartic	3	-7	1	6	1	-7	3				154
	Linear	-7	-5	-3	-1	1	3	5	7			168
	Quadratic	7	1	-3	-5	-5	-3	1	7			168
8	Cubic	-7	5	7	3	-3	-7	-5	7			264
	Quartic	7	-13	-3	9	9	-3	-13	7			616
	Quintic	-7	23	-17	-15	15	17	-23	7			2184
	Linear	-4	-3	-2	-1	0	1	2	3	4		60
	Quadratic	28	7	-8	-17	-20	-17	-8	7	28		2772
9	Cubic	-14	7	13	9	0	-9	-13	-7	14		990
	Quartic	14	-21	-11	9	18	9	-11	-21	14		2002
	Quintic	-4	11	-4	-9	0	9	4	-11	4		468
	Linear	-9	-7	-5	-3	-1	1	3	5	7	9	330
	Quadratic	6	2	-1	-3	-4	-4	-3	-1	2	6	132
10	Cubic	-42	14	35	31	12	-12	-31	-35	-14	42	8580
	Quartic	18	-22	-17	3	18	18	3	-17	-22	18	2860
	Quintic	-6	14	-1	-11	-6	6	11	1	-14	6	780

Discussion

Basically, a polynomial is an algebraic expression containing more than one term. In the analysis of data for trend, polynomials must be expressed so that the successive terms are uncorrelated, such as in the form of

$$X'_j = a + b_1 c_{1j} + b_2 c_{2j} + \dots + b_m c_{mj}$$

The b's are regression coefficients and the c's are orthogonal coefficients. In Table 16, it is seen that the sum of products is zero, that is, the c_{1j}'s equal zero. For example, for $k = 3$ the linear polynomial of -1 0 1 (considering signs) equals zero as do any of the other coefficients. The number of times the signs change determines the degree of the polynomial.

Table Explanation

Because the sum of the products of the coefficients in Table 16 equals zero, the polynomials are said to be orthogonal, being independent of each other. The number of times the signs change determines the degree of the polynomial. In the linear set above one sign changes, in the quadratic there are two (from 1 to -2 is one change, plus back to 1 again is two), while the cubic has three changes (for $k = 4$, for example, the sign changes from -1 to 3, then to a -3 for the second change, and back to one for the third change).

The k column refers to the number of components being compared. For example, if $k = 4$ groups to be analyzed, the coefficients in the linear component are -3 for group 1, -1 for 2, 1 for 3, and 3 for the fourth group, whereas the cubic components would be -1, 3, -3, and 1 respectively.

Use of Table

These polynomial coefficients are needed in polynomial regression analysis and trend. All treatment levels must be equally spaced with an equal number of observations in each treatment level. The tabled coefficients assure that each set represents only one trend of relationship. (For more details see Kirk, pp. 116-118; Ferguson, pp. 346-352; Myers, pp. 352-357; and Snedecor and Cochran, pp. 349-351, 460-464).

Table 17

Upper Percentage Points of Cochran's
Test for Homogeneity of Variance

$$C = \frac{\text{largest } \hat{\sigma}_j^2}{\Sigma \hat{\sigma}_j^2}$$

df for $\hat{\sigma}_j^2$	α	\(k = number of variances\) 2	3	4	5	6	7	8	9	10	15	20
1	.05	.9985	.9669	.9065	.8412	.7808	.7271	.6798	.6385	.6020	.4709	.3894
	.01	.9999	.9933	.9676	.9279	.8828	.8376	.7945	.7544	.7175	.5747	.4799
2	.05	.9750	.8709	.7679	.6838	.6161	.5612	.5157	.4775	.4450	.3346	.2705
	.01	.9950	.9423	.8643	.7885	.7218	.6644	.6152	.5727	.5358	.4069	.3297
3	.05	.9392	.7977	.6841	.5981	.5321	.4800	.4377	.4027	.3733	.2758	.2205
	.01	.9794	.8831	.7814	.6957	.6258	.5685	.5209	.4810	.4469	.3317	.2654
4	.05	.9057	.7457	.6287	.5441	.4803	.4307	.3910	.3584	.3311	.2419	.1921
	.01	.9586	.8335	.7212	.6329	.5635	.5080	.4627	.4251	.3934	.2882	.2288
5	.05	.8772	.7071	.5895	.5065	.4447	.3974	.3595	.3286	.3029	.2195	.1735
	.01	.9373	.7933	.6761	.5875	.5195	.4659	.4226	.3870	.3572	.2593	.2048
6	.05	.8534	.6771	.5598	.4783	.4184	.3726	.3362	.3067	.2823	.2034	.1602
	.01	.9172	.7606	.6410	.5531	.4866	.4347	.3932	.3592	.3308	.2386	.1877
7	.05	.8332	.6530	.5365	.4564	.3980	.3535	.3185	.2901	.2666	.1911	.1501
	.01	.8988	.7335	.6129	.5259	.4608	.4105	.3704	.3378	.3106	.2228	.1748
8	.05	.8159	.6333	.5175	.4387	.3817	.3384	.3043	.2768	.2541	.1815	.1422
	.01	.8823	.7107	.5897	.5037	.4401	.3911	.3522	.3207	.2945	.2104	.1646
9	.05	.8010	.6167	.5017	.4241	.3682	.3259	.2926	.2659	.2439	.1736	.1357
	.01	.8674	.6912	.5702	.4854	.4229	.3751	.3373	.3067.	.2813	.2002	.1567
16	.05	.7341	.5466	.4366	.3645	.3135	.2756	.2462	.2226	.2032	.1429	.1108
	.01	.7949	.6059	.4884	.4094	.3529	.3105	.2779	.2514	.2297	.1612	.1248
36	.05	.6602	.4748	.3720	.3066	.2612	.2278	.2022	.1820	.1655	.1144	.0879
	.01	.7067	.5153	.4057	.3351	.2858	.2494	.2214	.1992	.1811	.1251	.0960
144	.05	.5813	.4031	.3093	.2513	.2119	.1833	.1616	.1446	.1308	.0889	.0675
	.01	.6062	.4230	.3251	.2644	.2229	.1929	.1700	.1521	.1376	.0934	.0709

Discussion

Somewhat similar to the F_{max} statistic, this test is relatively simple for determining homogeneity of variance, and is also sensitive for testing departures from normality.

Null and Alternative Hypotheses

H_0: the variances of all treatment groups are the same, that is, homogeneous.

H_1: the variances are not all the same, that is, they are heterogeneous.

The null hypothesis can be rejected at the specified alpha level (.05) if the computed C is equal to or greater than the tabled value for a given k and $N - 1$.

Use of Table and Example

Using the same data as presented with the Hartley F_{max} statistic (Table 19), the form becomes

$$C = \frac{\hat{S}^2 \text{ largest variance}}{\Sigma \hat{S}^2 \text{ total variance}} = \frac{7.5}{8.5} = .8824, \text{ with } \begin{matrix} k=3 \\ N-1=4 \end{matrix}$$

Table 17 is then entered at the row marked 4 and reading down from the $k = 3$ column, it is noted that the value of C needed for significance at the 5 per cent level is .7457 and at the 1 per cent level .8335. The C value .8824 is therefore significant at both levels, indicating that the variance of all treatment groups is homogeneous; i.e., the H_0 is retained or accepted.

Table 18

Percentage Points of the Studentized Range

Error df	α	\multicolumn{10}{c}{r = number of means or number of steps between ordered means}									
		2	3	4	5	6	7	8	9	10	11
5	.05	3.64	4.60	5.22	5.67	6.03	6.33	6.58	6.80	6.99	7.17
	.01	5.70	6.98	7.80	8.42	8.91	9.32	9.67	9.97	10.24	10.48
6	.05	3.46	4.34	4.90	5.30	5.63	5.90	6.12	6.32	6.49	6.65
	.01	5.24	6.33	7.03	7.56	7.97	8.32	8.61	8.87	9.10	9.30
7	.05	3.34	4.16	4.68	5.06	5.36	5.61	5.82	6.00	6.16	6.30
	.01	4.95	5.92	6.54	7.01	7.37	7.68	7.94	8.17	8.37	8.55
8	.05	3.26	4.04	4.53	4.89	5.17	5.40	5.60	5.77	5.92	6.05
	.01	4.75	5.64	6.20	6.62	6.96	7.24	7.47	7.68	7.86	8.03
9	.05	3.20	3.95	4.41	4.76	5.02	5.24	5.43	5.59	5.74	5.87
	.01	4.60	5.43	5.96	6.35	6.66	6.91	7.13	7.33	7.49	7.65
10	.05	3.15	3.88	4.33	4.65	4.91	5.12	5.30	5.46	5.60	5.72
	.01	4.48	5.27	5.77	6.14	6.43	6.67	6.87	7.05	7.21	7.36
11	.05	3.11	3.82	4.26	4.57	4.82	5.03	5.20	5.35	5.49	5.61
	.01	4.39	5.15	5.62	5.97	6.25	6.48	6.67	6.84	6.99	7.13
12	.05	3.08	3.77	4.20	4.51	4.75	4.95	5.12	5.27	5.39	5.51
	.01	4.32	5.05	5.50	5.84	6.10	6.32	6.51	6.67	6.81	6.94
13	.05	3.06	3.73	4.15	4.45	4.69	4.88	5.05	5.19	5.32	5.43
	.01	4.26	4.96	5.40	5.73	5.98	6.19	6.37	6.53	6.67	6.79
14	.05	3.03	3.70	4.11	4.41	4.64	4.83	4.99	5.13	5.25	5.36
	.01	4.21	4.89	5.32	5.63	5.88	6.08	6.26	6.41	6.54	6.66
15	.05	3.01	3.67	4.08	4.37	4.59	4.78	4.94	5.08	5.20	5.31
	.01	4.17	4.84	5.25	5.56	5.80	5.99	6.16	6.31	6.44	6.55
16	.05	3.00	3.65	4.05	4.33	4.56	4.74	4.90	5.03	5.15	5.26
	.01	4.13	4.79	5.19	5.49	5.72	5.92	6.08	6.22	6.35	6.46
17	.05	2.98	3.63	4.02	4.30	4.52	4.70	4.86	4.99	5.11	5.21
	.01	4.10	4.74	5.14	5.43	5.66	5.85	6.01	6.15	6.27	6.38
18	.05	2.97	3.61	4.00	4.28	4.49	4.67	4.82	4.96	5.07	5.17
	.01	4.07	4.70	5.09	5.38	5.60	5.79	5.94	6.08	6.20	6.31
19	.05	2.96	3.59	3.98	4.25	4.47	4.65	4.79	4.92	5.04	5.14
	.01	4.05	4.67	5.05	5.33	5.55	5.73	5.89	6.02	6.14	6.25
20	.05	2.95	3.58	3.96	4.23	4.45	4.62	4.77	4.90	5.01	5.11
	.01	4.02	4.64	5.02	5.29	5.51	5.69	5.84	5.97	6.09	6.19
24	.05	2.92	3.53	3.90	4.17	4.37	4.54	4.68	4.81	4.92	5.01
	.01	3.96	4.55	4.91	5.17	5.37	5.54	5.69	5.81	5.92	6.02
30	.05	2.89	3.49	3.85	4.10	4.30	4.46	4.60	4.72	4.82	4.92
	.01	3.89	4.45	4.80	5.05	5.24	5.40	5.54	5.65	5.76	5.85
40	.05	2.86	3.44	3.79	4.04	4.23	4.39	4.52	4.63	4.73	4.82
	.01	3.82	4.37	4.70	4.93	5.11	5.26	5.39	5.50	5.60	5.69
60	.05	2.83	3.40	3.74	3.98	4.16	4.31	4.44	4.55	4.65	4.73
	.01	3.76	4.28	4.59	4.82	4.99	5.13	5.25	5.36	5.45	5.53
120	.05	2.80	3.36	3.68	3.92	4.10	4.24	4.36	4.47	4.56	4.64
	.01	3.70	4.20	4.50	4.71	4.87	5.01	5.12	5.21	5.30	5.37
∞	.05	2.77	3.31	3.63	3.86	4.03	4.17	4.29	4.39	4.47	4.55
	.01	3.64	4.12	4.40	4.60	4.76	4.88	4.99	5.08	5.16	5.23

Table Explanation

Table 18 contains values of q, the studentized range statistic, that are used in the Tukey HSD (honestly significant difference) test (see Kirk, pp. 88-90 for description and use) and the Newman-Keuls test (see Kirk, pp. 91-93). Both of these are *a posteriori* multiple comparison tests.

The distribution of q, the studentized range, is obtained by dividing R by S:

R (the range for a set of a independent and normally distributed values)

S (the estimate of the S.D. of the values where the range is being considered)

The sampling distribution of q is that of R/S which depends upon a (the number of values ranged over) and upon the df's associated with S.

In order to enter the table for q, it is necessary to have both the degrees of freedom for MS_{error} and k, the number of treatment levels in the experiment. At least the .01 level of significance is considered if the experimenter considers making a Type I error more undesirable than making a Type II error. (For more details, see Kirk, p. 88; Winer, p. 77; Snedecor and Cochran, pp. 272-3; Myers, pp. 334-5; Pearson and Hartley, 1966).

r = number of means or number of steps between ordered means										Error
12·	13	14	15	16	17	18	19	20	α	df
7.32	7.47	7.60	7.72	7.83	7.93	8.03	8.12	8.21	.05	5
10.70	10.89	11.08	11.24	11.40	11.55	11.68	11.81	11.93	.01	
6.79	6.92	7.03	7.14	7.24	7.34	7.43	7.51	7.59	.05	6
9.48	9.65	9.81	9.95	10.08	10.21	10.32	10.43	10.54	.01	
6.43	6.55	6.66	6.76	6.85	6.94	7.02	7.10	7.17	.05	7
8.71	8.86	9.00	9.12	9.24	9.35	9.46	9.55	9.65	.01	
6.18	6.29	6.39	6.48	6.57	6.65	6.73	6.80	6.87	.05	8
8.18	8.31	8.44	8.55	8.66	8.76	8.85	8.94	9.03	.01	
5.98	6.09	6.19	6.28	6.36	6.44	6.51	6.58	6.64	.05	9
7.78	7.91	8.03	8.13	8.23	8.33	8.41	8.49	8.57	.01	
5.83	5.93	6.03	6.11	6.19	6.27	6.34	6.40	6.47	.05	10
7.49	7.60	7.71	7.81	7.91	7.99	8.08	8.15	8.23	.01	
5.71	5.81	5.90	5.98	6.06	6.13	6.20	6.27	6.33	.05	11
7.25	7.36	7.46	7.56	7.65	7.73	7.81	7.88	7.95	.01	
5.61	5.71	5.80	5.88	5.95	6.02	6.09	6.15	6.21	.05	12
7.06	7.17	7.26	7.36	7.44	7.52	7.59	7.66	7.73	.01	
5.53	5.63	5.71	5.79	5.86	5.93	5.99	6.05	6.11	.05	13
6.90	7.01	7.10	7.19	7.27	7.35	7.42	7.48	7.55	.01	
5.46	5.55	5.64	5.71	5.79	5.85	5.91	5.97	6.03	.05	14
6.77	6.87	6.96	7.05	7.13	7.20	7.27	7.33	7.39	.01	
5.40	5.49	5.57	5.65	5.72	5.78	5.85	5.90	5.96	.05	15
6.66	6.76	6.84	6.93	7.00	7.07	7.14	7.20	7.26	.01	
5.35	5.44	5.52	5.59	5.66	5.73	5.79	5.84	5.90	.05	16
6.56	6.66	6.74	6.82	6.90	6.97	7.03	7.09	7.15	.01	
5.31	5.39	5.47	5.54	5.61	5.67	5.73	5.79	5.84	.05	17
6.48	6.57	6.66	6.73	6.81	6.87	6.94	7.00	7.05	.01	
5.27	5.35	5.43	5.50	5.57	5.63	5.69	5.74	5.79	.05	18
6.41	6.50	6.58	6.65	6.73	6.79	6.85	6.91	6.97	.01	
5.23	5.31	5.39	5.46	5.53	5.59	5.65	5.70	5.75	.05	19
6.34	6.43	6.51	6.58	6.65	6.72	6.78	6.84	6.89	.01	
5.20	5.28	5.36	5.43	5.49	5.55	5.61	5.66	5.71	.05	20
6.28	6.37	6.45	6.52	6.59	6.65	6.71	6.77	6.82	.01	
5.10	5.18	5.25	5.32	5.38	5.44	5.49	5.55	5.59	.05	24
6.11	6.19	6.26	6.33	6.39	6.45	6.51	6.56	6.61	.01	
5.00	5.08	5.15	5.21	5.27	5.33	5.38	5.43	5.47	.05	30
5.93	6.01	6.08	6.14	6.20	6.26	6.31	6.36	6.41	.01	
4.90	4.98	5.04	5.11	5.16	5.22	5.27	5.31	5.36	.05	40
5.76	5.83	5.90	5.96	6.02	6.07	6.12	6.16	6.21	.01	
4.81	4.88	4.94	5.00	5.06	5.11	5.15	5.20	5.24	.05	60
5.60	5.67	5.73	5.78	5.84	5.89	5.93	5.97	6.01	.01	
4.71	4.78	4.84	4.90	4.95	5.00	5.04	5.09	5.13	.05	120
5.44	5.50	5.56	5.61	5.66	5.71	5.75	5.79	5.83	.01	
4.62	4.68	4.74	4.80	4.85	4.89	4.93	4.97	5.01	.05	∞
5.29	5.35	5.40	5.45	5.49	5.54	5.57	5.61	5.65	.01	

Table 19

Upper Percentage Points of the F_{max} Statistic

$$F_{max} = (\hat{\sigma}^2_{largest})/(\hat{\sigma}^2_{smallest})$$

df for $\hat{\sigma}^2_j$	α	\multicolumn{11}{c}{k = number of variances}
		2	3	4	5	6	7	8	9	10	11	12
4	.05	9.60	15.5	20.6	25.2	29.5	33.6	37.5	41.4	44.6	48.0	51.4
	.01	23.2	37.	49.	59.	69.	79.	89.	97.	106.	113.	120.
5	.05	7.15	10.8	13.7	16.3	18.7	20.8	22.9	24.7	26.5	28.2	29.9
	.01	14.9	22.	28.	33.	38.	42.	46.	50.	54.	57.	60.
6	.05	5.82	8.38	10.4	12.1	13.7	15.0	16.3	17.5	18.6	19.7	20.7
	.01	11.1	15.5	19.1	22.	25.	27.	30.	32.	34.	36.	37.
7	.05	4.99	6.94	8.44	9.70	10.8	11.8	12.7	13.5	14.3	15.1	15.8
	.01	8.89	12.1	14.5	16.5	18.4	20.	22.	23.	24.	26.	27.
8	.05	4.43	6.00	7.18	8.12	9.03	9.78	10.5	11.1	11.7	12.2	12.7
	.01	7.50	9.9	11.7	13.2	14.5	15.8	16.9	17.9	18.9	19.8	21.
9	.05	4.03	5.34	6.31	7.11	7.80	8.41	8.95	9.45	9.91	10.3	10.7
	.01	6.54	8.5	9.9	11.1	12.1	13.1	13.9	14.7	15.3	16.0	16.6
10	.05	3.72	4.85	5.67	6.34	6.92	7.42	7.87	8.28	8.66	9.01	9.34
	.01	5.85	7.4	8.6	9.6	10.4	11.1	11.8	12.4	12.9	13.4	13.9
12	.05	3.28	4.16	4.79	5.30	5.72	6.09	6.42	6.72	7.00	7.25	7.48
	.01	4.91	6.1	6.9	7.6	8.2	8.7	9.1	9.5	9.9	10.2	10.6
15	.05	2.86	3.54	4.01	4.37	4.68	4.95	5.19	5.40	5.59	5.77	5.93
	.01	4.07	4.9	5.5	6.0	6.4	6.7	7.1	7.3	7.5	7.8	8.0
20	.05	2.46	2.95	3.29	3.54	3.76	3.94	4.10	4.24	4.37	4.49	4.59
	.01	3.32	3.8	4.3	4.6	4.9	5.1	5.3	5.5	5.6	5.8	5.9
30	.05	2.07	2.40	2.61	2.78	2.91	3.02	3.12	3.21	3.29	3.36	3.39
	.01	2.63	3.0	3.3	3.4	3.6	3.7	3.8	3.9	4.0	4.1	4.2
60	.05	1.67	1.85	1.96	2.04	2.11	2.17	2.22	2.26	2.30	2.33	2.36
	.01	1.96	2.2	2.3	2.4	2.4	2.5	2.5	2.6	2.6	2.7	2.7
∞	.05	1.00	1.00	1.00	1.00	1.00	1.00	1.00	1.00	1.00	1.00	1.00
	.01	1.00	1.00	1.00	1.00	1.00	1.00	1.00	1.00.	1.00	1.00	1.00

Discussion

For statistical background of the F_{max} statistic see appropriate alphabetical entry. This test is often called Hartley's test for determining homogeneity of variance in analysis of variance, in which the statistic

$$F_{max} = \frac{\text{largest of k variances}}{\text{smallest of k variances}} = \frac{\hat{\sigma}_j^2 \text{ largest}}{\hat{\sigma}_j^2 \text{ smallest}}$$

where

k = no. of variances
n = no. of observations within each treatment level
with df = to k and $N - 1$.

The null hypothesis can be rejected at the specified alpha level (.05) if the computed F_{max} statistic is equal to or greater ($\geqslant$) than the tabled value for a given k and $N - 1$.

Null and Alternative Hypotheses

H_0: the variances of all treatment groups are the same
H_1: the variances are not the same

Use of Table with Example

Let A_1, A_2, and A_3 represent three treatment groups yielding the following X scores on the observations in each group. Do these groups show homogeneity of variance ($a = .05$)?

\multicolumn{2}{c}{A_1}	\multicolumn{2}{c}{A_2}	\multicolumn{2}{c}{A_3}
X_1	X_1^2	X_2	X_2^2	X_3	X_3^2
0	0	2	4	4	16
0	0	2	4	3	9
0	0	3	9	3	9
5	25	3	9	4	16
5	25	4	16	4	16
10	50	14	42	18	66

$$\hat{\sigma}_j^2 = \frac{\Sigma x^2 - (\Sigma x)^2/N}{N-1}$$

$$\hat{\sigma}_1 = \left(50 - \frac{(10)^2}{5}/4\right) = 7.5$$

$$\hat{\sigma}_2 = \left(42 - \frac{(14)^2}{5}/4\right) = .70$$

$$\hat{\sigma}_3 = \left(66 - \frac{(18)^2}{5}/4\right) = .30$$

$$F_{max} = \frac{\hat{\sigma}_j^2 \text{ largest}}{\hat{\sigma}_j^2 \text{ smallest}} = \frac{7.5}{.30} = 25 \quad \begin{array}{l} K=3 \\ N-1=4 \end{array}$$

Entering the table at the row marked 4 and reading down from the $k = 3$ column, it is noted that the .05 value is 15.5 and the .01 value is 37. The $F_{max} = 25$, which is significant at the .05 level but not at the .01 level. The null hypothesis is therefore retained; i.e., the variances of all treatment groups are the same.

Table 20
Upper Percentage Points of the F Distribution

df for denominator	α	df for numerator											
		1	2	3	4	5	6	7	8	9	10	11	12
1	.25	5.83	7.50	8.20	8.58	8.82	8.98	9.10	9.19	9.26	9.32	9.36	9.41
	.10	39.9	49.5	53.6	55.8	57.2	58.2	58.9	59.4	59.9	60.2	60.5	60.7
	.05	161	200	216	225	230	234	237	239	241	242	243	244
2	.25	2.57	3.00	3.15	3.23	3.28	3.31	3.34	3.35	3.37	3.38	3.39	3.39
	.10	8.53	9.00	9.16	9.24	9.29	9.33	9.35	9.37	9.38	9.39	9.40	9.41
	.05	18.5	19.0	19.2	19.2	19.3	19.3	19.4	19.4	19.4	19.4	19.4	19.4
	.01	98.5	99.0	99.2	99.2	99.3	99.3	99.4	99.4	99.4	99.4	99.4	99.4
3	.25	2.02	2.28	2.36	2.39	2.41	2.42	2.43	2.44	2.44	2.44	2.45	2.45
	.10	5.54	5.46	5.39	5.34	5.31	5.28	5.27	5.25	5.24	5.23	5.22	5.22
	.05	10.1	9.55	9.28	9.12	9.01	8.94	8.89	8.85	8.81	8.79	8.76	8.74
	.01	34.1	30.8	29.5	28.7	28.2	27.9	27.7	27.5	27.3	27.2	27.1	27.1
4	.25	1.81	2.00	2.05	2.06	2.07	2.08	2.08	2.08	2.08	2.08	2.08	2.08
	.10	4.54	4.32	4.19	4.11	4.05	4.01	3.98	3.95	3.94	3.92	3.91	3.90
	.05	7.71	6.94	6.59	6.39	6.26	6.16	6.09	6.04	6.00	5.96	5.94	5.91
	.01	21.2	18.0	16.7	16.0	15.5	15.2	15.0	14.8	14.7	14.5	14.4	14.4
5	.25	1.69	1.85	1.88	1.89	1.89	1.89	1.89	1.89	1.89	1.89	1.89	1.89
	.10	4.06	3.78	3.62	3.52	3.45	3.40	3.37	3.34	3.32	3.30	3.28	3.27
	.05	6.61	5.79	5.41	5.19	5.05	4.95	4.88	4.82	4.77	4.74	4.71	4.68
	.01	16.3	13.3	12.1	11.4	11.0	10.7	10.5	10.3	10.2	10.1	9.96	9.89
6	.25	1.62	1.76	1.78	1.79	1.79	1.78	1.78	1.78	1.77	1.77	1.77	1.77
	.10	3.78	3.46	3.29	3.18	3.11	3.05	3.01	2.98	2.96	2.94	2.92	2.90
	.05	5.99	5.14	4.76	4.53	4.39	4.28	4.21	4.15	4.10	4.06	4.03	4.00
	.01	13.7	10.9	9.78	9.15	8.75	8.47	8.26	8.10	7.98	7.87	7.79	7.72
7	.25	1.57	1.70	1.72	1.72	1.71	1.71	1.70	1.70	1.69	1.69	1.69	1.68
	.10	3.59	3.26	3.07	2.96	2.88	2.83	2.78	2.75	2.72	2.70	2.68	2.67
	.05	5.59	4.74	4.35	4.12	3.97	3.87	3.79	3.73	3.68	3.64	3.60	3.57
	.01	12.2	9.55	8.45	7.85	7.46	7.19	6.99	6.84	6.72	6.62	6.54	6.47
8	.25	1.54	1.66	1.67	1.66	1.66	1.65	1.64	1.64	1.63	1.63	1.63	1.62
	.10	3.46	3.11	2.92	2.81	2.73	2.67	2.62	2.59	2.56	2.54	2.52	2.50
	.05	5.32	4.46	4.07	3.84	3.69	3.58	3.50	3.44	3.39	3.35	3.31	3.28
	.01	11.3	8.65	7.59	7.01	6.63	6.37	6.18	6.03	5.91	5.81	5.73	5.67
9	.25	1.51	1.62	1.63	1.63	1.62	1.61	1.60	1.60	1.59	1.59	1.58	1.58
	.10	3.36	3.01	2.81	2.69	2.61	2.55	2.51	2.47	2.44	2.42	2.40	2.38
	.05	5.12	4.26	3.86	3.63	3.48	3.37	3.29	3.23	3.18	3.14	3.10	3.07
	.01	10.6	8.02	6.99	6.42	6.06	5.80	5.61	5.47	5.35	5.26	5.18	5.11

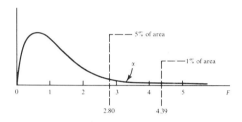

Example

For $df_1 = 9$, $df_2 = 12$
$P[F > 2.80] = 0.05$ or 5% of area
$P[F > 4.39] = 0.01$ or 1% of area

Null and Alternative Hypotheses

H_0: $\sigma_1^2 \leq \sigma_2^2$
H_1: $\sigma_1^2 > \sigma_2^2$

Discussion

The distribution of F depends upon two parameters associated with the degrees of freedom of the numerator and the df of the denominator of the F ratio. Table 20 presents certain α levels for the *upper* (right-side) tail. The columns give the df for the numerator; the rows give the df for the denominator. The computed F (see *F Distribution* in alphabetical listing of this book for formula) must be equal to or greater than the tabled values to be significant at the one-tailed α level chosen.

Table 20 (continued)

15	20	24	30	40	50	60	100	120	200	500	∞	α	df for denominator
— df for numerator														
9.49	9.58	9.63	9.67	9.71	9.74	9.76	9.78	9.80	9.82	9.84	9.85	.25	1
61.2	61.7	62.0	62.3	62.5	62.7	62.8	63.0	63.1	63.2	63.3	63.3	.10	
246	248	249	250	251	252	252	253	253	254	254	254	.05	
3.41	3.43	3.43	3.44	3.45	3.45	3.46	3.47	3.47	3.48	3.48	3.48	.25	2
9.42	9.44	9.45	9.46	9.47	9.47	9.47	9.48	9.48	9.49	9.49	9.49	.10	
19.4	19.4	19.5	19.5	19.5	19.5	19.5	19.5	19.5	19.5	19.5	19.5	.05	
99.4	99.4	99.5	99.5	99.5	99.5	99.5	99.5	99.5	99.5	99.5	99.5	.01	
2.46	2.46	2.46	2.47	2.47	2.47	2.47	2.47	2.47	2.47	2.47	2.47	.25	3
5.20	5.18	5.18	5.17	5.16	5.15	5.15	5.14	5.14	5.14	5.14	5.13	.10	
8.70	8.66	8.64	8.62	8.59	8.58	8.57	8.55	8.55	8.54	8.53	8.53	.05	
26.9	26.7	26.6	26.5	26.4	26.4	26.3	26.2	26.2	26.2	26.1	26.1	.01	
2.08	2.08	2.08	2.08	2.08	2.08	2.08	2.08	2.08	2.08	2.08	2.08	.25	4
3.87	3.84	3.83	3.82	3.80	3.80	3.79	3.78	3.78	3.77	3.76	3.76	.10	
5.86	5.80	5.77	5.75	5.72	5.70	5.69	5.66	5.66	5.65	5.64	5.63	.05	
14.2	14.0	13.9	13.8	13.7	13.7	13.7	13.6	13.6	13.5	13.5	13.5	.01	
1.89	1.88	1.88	1.88	1.88	1.88	1.87	1.87	1.87	1.87	1.87	1.87	.25	5
3.24	3.21	3.19	3.17	3.16	3.15	3.14	3.13	3.12	3.12	3.11	3.10	.10	
4.62	4.56	4.53	4.50	4.46	4.44	4.43	4.41	4.40	4.39	4.37	4.36	.05	
9.72	9.55	9.47	9.38	9.29	9.24	9.20	9.13	9.11	9.08	9.04	9.02	.01	
1.76	1.76	1.75	1.75	1.75	1.75	1.74	1.74	1.74	1.74	1.74	1.74	.25	6
2.87	2.84	2.82	2.80	2.78	2.77	2.76	2.75	2.74	2.73	2.73	2.72	.10	
3.94	3.87	3.84	3.81	3.77	3.75	3.74	3.71	3.70	3.69	3.68	3.67	.05	
7.56	7.40	7.31	7.23	7.14	7.09	7.06	6.99	6.97	6.93	6.90	6.88	.01	
1.68	1.67	1.67	1.66	1.66	1.66	1.65	1.65	1.65	1.65	1.65	1.65	.25	7
2.63	2.59	2.58	2.56	2.54	2.52	2.51	2.50	2.49	2.48	2.48	2.47	.10	
3.51	3.44	3.41	3.38	3.34	3.32	3.30	3.27	3.27	3.25	3.24	3.23	.05	
6.31	6.16	6.07	5.99	5.91	5.86	5.82	5.75	5.74	5.70	5.67	5.65	.10	
1.62	1.61	1.60	1.60	1.59	1.59	1.59	1.58	1.58	1.58	1.58	1.58	.25	8
2.46	2.42	2.40	2.38	2.36	2.35	2.34	2.32	2.32	2.31	2.30	2.29	.10	
3.22	3.15	3.12	3.08	3.04	3.02	3.01	2.97	2.97	2.95	2.94	2.93	.05	
5.52	5.36	5.28	5.20	5.12	5.07	5.03	4.96	4.95	4.91	4.88	4.86	.01	
1.57	1.56	1.56	1.55	1.55	1.54	1.54	1.53	1.53	1.53	1.53	1.53	.25	9
2.34	2.30	2.28	2.25	2.23	2.22	2.21	2.19	2.18	2.17	2.17	2.16	.10	
3.01	2.94	2.90	2.86	2.83	2.80	2.79	2.76	2.75	2.73	2.72	2.71	.05	
4.96	4.81	4.73	4.65	4.57	4.52	4.48	4.42	4.40	4.36	4.33	4.31	.01	

Example of Use of Table (One-Tailed Test)

Given: $N_1 = 6$, $\Sigma x_1^2 = 125$; $N_2 = 11$, $\Sigma x_2^2 = 25$.

The numbers of degrees of freedom for the numerator are 15 and for the denominator 9, so the estimated population variances, separately derived, are $125/15 = 8.3$ and $25/9 = 2.78$. The variance ratio, F, is $8.3/2.78 = 3$. To be significant at the .01 level with 15 degrees of freedom in the numerator (see Table 20) and 9 df in the denominator, an F of 4.96 or larger is required. Since 3 falls below this value the H_0 is retained or accepted. It is likely that the two samples at this level came from the same population or from two populations with equal variances. The same conclusion holds true at the .05 level where the obtained F of 3 is still below the value found there (3.01).

Table 20 (continued)

df for denominator	α	df for numerator											
		1	2	3	4	5	6	7	8	9	10	11	12
10	.25	1.49	1.60	1.60	1.59	1.59	1.58	1.57	1.56	1.56	1.55	1.55	1.54
	.10	3.29	2.92	2.73	2.61	2.52	2.46	2.41	2.38	2.35	2.32	2.30	2.28
	.05	4.96	4.10	3.71	3.48	3.33	3.22	3.14	3.07	3.02	2.98	2.94	2.91
	.01	10.0	7.56	6.55	5.99	5.64	5.39	5.20	5.06	4.94	4.85	4.77	4.71
11	.25	1.47	1.58	1.58	1.57	1.56	1.55	1.54	1.53	1.53	1.52	1.52	1.51
	.10	3.23	2.86	2.66	2.54	2.45	2.39	2.34	2.30	2.27	2.25	2.23	2.21
	.05	4.84	3.98	3.59	3.36	3.20	3.09	3.01	2.95	2.90	2.85	2.82	2.79
	.01	9.65	7.21	6.22	5.67	5.32	5.07	4.89	4.74	4.63	4.54	4.46	4.40
12	.25	1.46	1.56	1.56	1.55	1.54	1.53	1.52	1.51	1.51	1.50	1.50	1.49
	.10	3.18	2.81	2.61	2.48	2.39	2.33	2.28	2.24	2.21	2.19	2.17	2.15
	.05	4.75	3.89	3.49	3.26	3.11	3.00	2.91	2.85	2.80	2.75	2.72	2.69
	.01	9.33	6.93	5.95	5.41	5.06	4.82	4.64	4.50	4.39	4.30	4.22	4.16
13	.25	1.45	1.55	1.55	1.53	1.52	1.51	1.50	1.49	1.49	1.48	1.47	1.47
	.10	3.14	2.76	2.56	2.43	2.35	2.28	2.23	2.20	2.16	2.14	2.12	2.10
	.05	4.67	3.81	3.41	3.18	3.03	2.92	2.83	2.77	2.71	2.67	2.63	2.60
	.01	9.07	6.70	5.74	5.21	4.86	4.62	4.44	4.30	4.19	4.10	4.02	3.96
14	.25	1.44	1.53	1.53	1.52	1.51	1.50	1.49	1.48	1.47	1.46	1.46	1.45
	.10	3.10	2.73	2.52	2.39	2.31	2.24	2.19	2.15	2.12	2.10	2.08	2.05
	.05	4.60	3.74	3.34	3.11	2.96	2.85	2.76	2.70	2.65	2.60	2.57	2.53
	.01	8.86	6.51	5.56	5.04	4.69	4.46	4.28	4.14	4.03	3.94	3.86	3.80
15	.25	1.43	1.52	1.52	1.51	1.49	1.48	1.47	1.46	1.46	1.45	1.44	1.44
	.10	3.07	2.70	2.49	2.36	2.27	2.21	2.16	2.12	2.09	2.06	2.04	2.02
	.05	4.54	3.68	3.29	3.06	2.90	2.79	2.71	2.64	2.59	2.54	2.51	2.48
	.01	8.68	6.36	5.42	4.89	4.56	4.32	4.14	4.00	3.89	3.80	3.73	3.67
16	.25	1.42	1.51	1.51	1.50	1.48	1.47	1.46	1.45	1.44	1.44	1.44	1.43
	.10	3.05	2.67	2.46	2.33	2.24	2.18	2.13	2.09	2.06	2.03	2.01	1.99
	.05	4.49	3.63	3.24	3.01	2.85	2.74	2.66	2.59	2.54	2.49	2.46	2.42
	.01	8.53	6.23	5.29	4.77	4.44	4.20	4.03	3.89	3.78	3.69	3.62	3.55
17	.25	1.42	1.51	1.50	1.49	1.47	1.46	1.45	1.44	1.43	1.43	1.42	1.41
	.10	3.03	2.64	2.44	2.31	2.22	2.15	2.10	2.06	2.03	2.00	1.98	1.96
	.05	4.45	3.59	3.20	2.96	2.81	2.70	2.61	2.55	2.49	2.45	2.41	2.38
	.01	8.40	6.11	5.18	4.67	4.34	4.10	3.93	3.79	3.68	3.59	3.52	3.46
18	.25	1.41	1.50	1.49	1.48	1.46	1.45	1.44	1.43	1.42	1.42	1.41	1.40
	.10	3.01	2.62	2.42	2.29	2.20	2.13	2.08	2.04	2.00	1.98	1.96	1.93
	.05	4.41	3.55	3.16	2.93	2.77	2.66	2.58	2.51	2.46	2.41	2.37	2.34
	.01	8.29	6.01	5.09	4.58	4.25	4.01	3.84	3.71	3.60	3.51	3.43	3.37
19	.25	1.41	1.49	1.49	1.47	1.46	1.44	1.43	1.42	1.41	1.41	1.40	1.40
	.10	2.99	2.61	2.40	2.27	2.18	2.11	2.06	2.02	1.98	1.96	1.94	1.91
	.05	4.38	3.52	3.13	2.90	2.74	2.63	2.54	2.48	2.42	2.38	2.34	2.31
	.01	8.18	5.93	5.01	4.50	4.17	3.94	3.77	3.63	3.52	3.43	3.36	3.30
20	.25	1.40	1.49	1.48	1.46	1.45	1.44	1.43	1.42	1.41	1.40	1.39	1.39
	.10	2.97	2.59	2.38	2.25	2.16	2.09	2.04	2.00	1.96	1.94	1.92	1.89
	.05	4.35	3.49	3.10	2.87	2.71	2.60	2.51	2.45	2.39	2.35	2.31	2.28
	.01	8.10	5.85	4.94	4.43	4.10	3.87	3.70	3.56	3.46	3.37	3.29	3.23

How to Handle a Two-Tailed Test

Null and Alternative Hypotheses

$H_0: \sigma_1^2 = \sigma_2^2$; $H_1: \sigma_1^2 \neq \sigma_2^2$

Placing the larger variance arbitrarily in the numerator of the F ratio doubles the probability of the test. Thus the probability value for any given region is doubled and the .05 and .01 regions become .10 and .02 respectively.

To find F values corresponding to two-tailed rejection regions two values (the upper and lower) must be found. The *upper value* is obtained as in the example on the previous page; the *lower value* is found by finding the corresponding value required on the upper tail of a distribution with numerator and denominator df's reversed and then taking the reciprocal. For example, for a two-tailed test, with an α = .05 and $df_1 = 12$, $df_2 = 15$ and a sample value of 2.00, what are the limits of the rejection region? Table 20 for α = .05 shows that F (.05: 12, 15) = 2.48. This is the boundary for the upper rejection region. Next the value for F (.05: 15, 12) = 2.62 is located, and its reciprocal obtained (1/2.62) which equals .38. If the sample F ratio is larger than 2.48 or smaller than .38, the sample value falls within the rejection region. Since the assumed sample value is 2.00, it falls within the acceptance region, and therefore the null hypothesis is retained $H_0: \sigma_1^2 = \sigma_1^2$.

Table 20 (continued)

15	20	24	30	40	50	60	100	120	200	500	∞	α	df for denominator
1.53	1.52	1.52	1.51	1.51	1.50	1.50	1.49	1.49	1.49	1.48	1.48	.25	
2.24	2.20	2.18	2.16	2.13	2.12	2.11	2.09	2.08	2.07	2.06	2.06	.10	10
2.85	2.77	2.74	2.70	2.66	2.64	2.62	2.59	2.58	2.56	2.55	2.54	.05	
4.56	4.41	4.33	4.25	4.17	4.12	4.08	4.01	4.00	3.96	3.93	3.91	.01	
1.50	1.49	1.49	1.48	1.47	1.47	1.47	1.46	1.46	1.46	1.45	1.45	.25	
2.17	2.12	2.10	2.08	2.05	2.04	2.03	2.00	2.00	1.99	1.98	1.97	.10	11
2.72	2.65	2.61	2.57	2.53	2.51	2.49	2.46	2.45	2.43	2.42	2.40	.05	
4.25	4.10	4.02	3.94	3.86	3.81	3.78	3.71	3.69	3.66	3.62	3.60	.01	
1.48	1.47	1.46	1.45	1.45	1.44	1.44	1.43	1.43	1.43	1.42	1.42	.25	
2.10	2.06	2.04	2.01	1.99	1.97	1.96	1.94	1.93	1.92	1.91	1.90	.10	12
2.62	2.54	2.51	2.47	2.43	2.40	2.38	2.35	2.34	2.32	2.31	2.30	.05	
4.01	3.86	3.78	3.70	3.62	3.57	3.54	3.47	3.45	3.41	3.38	3.36	.01	
1.46	1.45	1.44	1.43	1.42	1.42	1.42	1.41	1.41	1.40	1.40	1.40	.25	
2.05	2.01	1.98	1.96	1.93	1.92	1.90	1.88	1.88	1.86	1.85	1.85	.10	13
2.53	2.46	2.42	2.38	2.34	2.31	2.30	2.26	2.25	2.23	2.22	2.21	.05	
3.82	3.66	3.59	3.51	3.43	3.38	3.34	3.27	3.25	3.22	3.19	3.17	.01	
1.44	1.43	1.42	1.41	1.41	1.40	1.40	1.39	1.39	1.39	1.38	1.38	.25	
2.01	1.96	1.94	1.91	1.89	1.87	1.86	1.83	1.83	1.82	1.80	1.80	.10	14
2.46	2.39	2.35	2.31	2.27	2.24	2.22	2.19	2.18	2.16	2.14	2.13	.05	
3.66	3.51	3.43	3.35	3.27	3.22	3.18	3.11	3.09	3.06	3.03	3.00	.01	
1.43	1.41	1.41	1.40	1.39	1.39	1.38	1.38	1.37	1.37	1.36	1.36	.25	
1.97	1.92	1.90	1.87	1.85	1.83	1.82	1.79	1.79	1.77	1.76	1.76	.10	15
2.40	2.33	2.29	2.25	2.20	2.18	2.16	2.12	2.11	2.10	2.08	2.07	.05	
3.52	3.37	3.29	3.21	3.13	3.08	3.05	2.98	2.96	2.92	2.89	2.87	.01	
1.41	1.40	1.39	1.38	1.37	1.37	1.36	1.36	1.35	1.35	1.34	1.34	.25	
1.94	1.89	1.87	1.84	1.81	1.79	1.78	1.76	1.75	1.74	1.73	1.72	.10	16
2.35	2.28	2.24	2.19	2.15	2.12	2.11	2.07	2.06	2.04	2.02	2.01	.05	
3.41	3.26	3.18	3.10	3.02	2.97	2.93	2.86	2.84	2.81	2.78	2.75	.01	
1.40	1.39	1.38	1.37	1.36	1.35	1.35	1.34	1.34	1.34	1.33	1.33	.25	
1.91	1.86	1.84	1.81	1.78	1.76	1.75	1.73	1.72	1.71	1.69	1.69	.10	17
2.31	2.23	2.19	2.15	2.10	2.08	2.06	2.02	2.01	1.99	1.97	1.96	.05	
3.31	3.16	3.08	3.00	2.92	2.87	2.83	2.76	2.75	2.71	2.68	2.65	.01	
1.39	1.38	1.37	1.36	1.35	1.34	1.34	1.33	1.33	1.32	1.32	1.32	.25	
1.89	1.84	1.81	1.78	1.75	1.74	1.72	1.70	1.69	1.68	1.67	1.66	.10	18
2.27	2.19	2.15	2.11	2.06	2.04	2.02	1.98	1.97	1.95	1.93	1.92	.05	
3.23	3.08	3.00	2.92	2.84	2.78	2.75	2.68	2.66	2.62	2.59	2.57	.01	
1.38	1.37	1.36	1.35	1.34	1.33	1.33	1.32	1.32	1.31	1.31	1.30	.25	
1.86	1.81	1.79	1.76	1.73	1.71	1.70	1.67	1.67	1.65	1.64	1.63	.10	19
2.23	2.16	2.11	2.07	2.03	2.00	1.98	1.94	1.93	1.91	1.89	1.88	.05	
3.15	3.00	2.92	2.84	2.76	2.71	2.67	2.60	2.58	2.55	2.51	2.49	.01	
1.37	1.36	1.35	1.34	1.33	1.33	1.32	1.31	1.31	1.30	1.30	1.29	.25	
1.84	1.79	1.77	1.74	1.71	1.69	1.68	1.65	1.64	1.63	1.62	1.61	.10	20
2.20	2.12	2.08	2.04	1.99	1.97	1.95	1.91	1.90	1.88	1.86	1.84	.05	
3.09	2.94	2.86	2.78	2.69	2.64	2.61	2.54	2.52	2.48	2.44	2.42	.01	

df *for numerator*

df *for denominator*

df for denominator	α	df for numerator											
		1	2	3	4	5	6	7	8	9	10	11	12
22	.25	1.40	1.48	1.47	1.45	1.44	1.42	1.41	1.40	1.39	1.39	1.38	1.37
	.10	2.95	2.56	2.35	2.22	2.13	2.06	2.01	1.97	1.93	1.90	1.88	1.86
	.05	4.30	3.44	3.05	2.82	2.66	2.55	2.46	2.40	2.34	2.30	2.26	2.23
	.01	7.95	5.72	4.82	4.31	3.99	3.76	3.59	3.45	3.35	3.26	3.18	3.12
24	.25	1.39	1.47	1.46	1.44	1.43	1.41	1.40	1.39	1.38	1.38	1.37	1.36
	.10	2.93	2.54	2.33	2.19	2.10	2.04	1.98	1.94	1.91	1.88	1.85	1.83
	.05	4.26	3.40	3.01	2.78	2.62	2.51	2.42	2.36	2.30	2.25	2.21	2.18
	.01	7.82	5.61	4.72	4.22	3.90	3.67	3.50	3.36	3.26	3.17	3.09	3.03
26	.25	1.38	1.46	1.45	1.44	1.42	1.41	1.39	1.38	1.37	1.37	1.36	1.35
	.10	2.91	2.52	2.31	2.17	2.08	2.01	1.96	1.92	1.88	1.86	1.84	1.81
	.05	4.23	3.37	2.98	2.74	2.59	2.47	2.39	2.32	2.27	2.22	2.18	2.15
	.01	7.72	5.53	4.64	4.14	3.82	3.59	3.42	3.29	3.18	3.09	3.02	2.96
28	.25	1.38	1.46	1.45	1.43	1.41	1.40	1.39	1.38	1.37	1.36	1.35	1.34
	.10	2.89	2.50	2.29	2.16	2.06	2.00	1.94	1.90	1.87	1.84	1.81	1.79
	.05	4.20	3.34	2.95	2.71	2.56	2.45	2.36	2.29	2.24	2.19	2.15	2.12
	.01	7.64	5.45	4.57	4.07	3.75	3.53	3.36	3.23	3.12	3.03	2.96	2.90
30	.25	1.38	1.45	1.44	1.42	1.41	1.39	1.38	1.37	1.36	1.35	1.35	1.34
	.10	2.88	2.49	2.28	2.14	2.05	1.98	1.93	1.88	1.85	1.82	1.79	1.77
	.05	4.17	3.32	2.92	2.69	2.53	2.42	2.33	2.27	2.21	2.16	2.13	2.09
	.01	7.56	5.39	4.51	4.02	3.70	3.47	3.30	3.17	3.07	2.98	2.91	2.84
40	.25	1.36	1.44	1.42	1.40	1.39	1.37	1.36	1.35	1.34	1.33	1.32	1.31
	.10	2.84	2.44	2.23	2.09	2.00	1.93	1.87	1.83	1.79	1.76	1.73	1.71
	.05	4.08	3.23	2.84	2.61	2.45	2.34	2.25	2.18	2.12	2.08	2.04	2.00
	.01	7.31	5.18	4.31	3.83	3.51	3.29	3.12	2.99	2.89	2.80	2.73	2.66
60	.25	1.35	1.42	1.41	1.38	1.37	1.35	1.33	1.32	1.31	1.30	1.29	1.29
	.10	2.79	2.39	2.18	2.04	1.95	1.87	1.82	1.77	1.74	1.71	1.68	1.66
	.05	4.00	3.15	2.76	2.53	2.37	2.25	2.17	2.10	2.04	1.99	1.95	1.92
	.01	7.08	4.98	4.13	3.65	3.34	3.12	2.95	2.82	2.72	2.63	2.56	2.50
120	.25	1.34	1.40	1.39	1.37	1.35	1.33	1.31	1.30	1.29	1.28	1.27	1.26
	.10	2.75	2.35	2.13	1.99	1.90	1.82	1.77	1.72	1.68	1.65	1.62	1.60
	.05	3.92	3.07	2.68	2.45	2.29	2.17	2.09	2.02	1.96	1.91	1.87	1.83
	.01	6.85	4.79	3.95	3.48	3.17	2.96	2.79	2.66	2.56	2.47	2.40	2.34
200	.25	1.33	1.39	1.38	1.36	1.34	1.32	1.31	1.29	1.28	1.27	1.26	1.25
	.10	2.73	2.33	2.11	1.97	1.88	1.80	1.75	1.70	1.66	1.63	1.60	1.57
	.05	3.89	3.04	2.65	2.42	2.26	2.14	2.06	1.98	1.93	1.88	1.84	1.80
	.01	6.76	4.71	3.88	3.41	3.11	2.89	2.73	2.60	2.50	2.41	2.34	2.27
∞	.25	1.32	1.39	1.37	1.35	1.33	1.31	1.29	1.28	1.27	1.25	1.24	1.24
	.10	2.71	2.30	2.08	1.94	1.85	1.77	1.72	1.67	1.63	1.60	1.57	1.55
	.05	3.84	3.00	2.60	2.37	2.21	2.10	2.01	1.94	1.88	1.83	1.79	1.75
	.01	6.63	4.61	3.78	3.32	3.02	2.80	2.64	2.51	2.41	2.32	2.25	2.18

Table 20 (continued)

15	20	24	30	40	50	60	100	120	200	500	∞	α	df for denominator
				df *for numerator*									df *for denominator*
1.36	1.34	1.33	1.32	1.31	1.31	1.30	1.30	1.30	1.29	1.29	1.28	.25	
1.81	1.76	1.73	1.70	1.67	1.65	1.64	1.61	1.60	1.59	1.58	1.57	.10	22
2.15	2.07	2.03	1.98	1.94	1.91	1.89	1.85	1.84	1.82	1.80	1.78	.05	
2.98	2.83	2.75	2.67	2.58	2.53	2.50	2.42	2.40	2.36	2.33	2.31	.01	
1.35	1.33	1.32	1.31	1.30	1.29	1.29	1.28	1.28	1.27	1.27	1.26	.25	
1.78	1.73	1.70	1.67	1.64	1.62	1.61	1.58	1.57	1.56	1.54	1.53	.10	24
2.11	2.03	1.98	1.94	1.89	1.86	1.84	1.80	1.79	1.77	1.75	1.73	.05	
2.89	2.74	2.66	2.58	2.49	2.44	2.40	2.33	2.31	2.27	2.24	2.21	.01	
1.34	1.32	1.31	1.30	1.29	1.28	1.28	1.26	1.26	1.26	1.25	1.25	.25	
1.76	1.71	1.68	1.65	1.61	1.59	1.58	1.55	1.54	1.53	1.51	1.50	.10	26
2.07	1.99	1.95	1.90	1.85	1.82	1.80	1.76	1.75	,1.73	1.71	1.69	.05	
2.81	2.66	2.58	2.50	2.42	2.36	2.33	2.25	2.23	2.19	2.16	2.13	.01	
1.33	1.31	1.30	1.29	1.28	1.27	1.27	1.26	1.25	1.25	1.24	1.24	.25	
1.74	1.69	1.66	1.63	1.59	1.57	1.56	1.53	1.52	1.50	1.49	1.48	.10	28
2.04	1.96	1.91	1.87	1.82	1.79	1.77	1.73	1.71	1.69	1.67	1.65	.05	
2.75	2.60	2.52	2.44	2.35	2.30	2.26	2.19	2.17	2.13	2.09	2.06	.01	
1.32	1.30	1.29	1.28	1.27	1.26	1.26	1.25	1.24	1.24	1.23	1.23	.25	
1.72	1.67	1.64	1.61	1.57	1.55	1.54	1.51	1.50	1.48	1.47	1.46	.10	30
2.01	1.93	1.89	1.84	1.79	1.76	1.74	1.70	1.68	1.66	1.64	1.62	.05	
2.70	2.55	2.47	2.39	2.30	2.25	2.21	2.13	2.11	2.07	2.03	2.01	.01	
1.30	1.28	1.26	1.25	1.24	1.23	1.22	1.21	1.21	1.20	1.19	1.19	.25	
1.66	1.61	1.57	1.54	1.51	1.48	1.47	1.43	1.42	1.41	1.39	1.38	.10	40
1.92	1.84	1.79	1.74	1.69	1.66	1.64	1.59	1.58	1.55	1.53	1.51	.05	
2.52	2.37	2.29	2.20	2.11	2.06	2.02	1.94	1.92	1.87	1.83	1.80	.01	
1.27	1.25	1.24	1.22	1 21	1 20	1.19	1.17	1.17	1.16	1.15	1.15	.25	
1.60	1.54	1.51	1.48	1.44	1.41	1.40	1.36	1.35	1.33	1.31	1.29	.10	60
1.84	1.75	1.70	1.65	1.59	1.56	1.53	1.48	1.47	1.44	1.41	1.39	.05	
2.35	2.20	2.12	2.03	1.94	1.88	1.84	1.75	1.73	1.68	1.63	1.60	.01	
1.24	1.22	1.21	1.19	1.18	1.17	1.16	1.14	1.13	1.12	1.11	1.10	.25	
1.55	1.48	1.45	1.41	1.37	1.34	1.32	1.27	1.26	1.24	1.21	1.19	.10	120
1.75	1.66	1.61	1.55	1.50	1.46	1.43	1.37	1.35	1.32	1.28	1.25	.05	
2.19	2.03	1.95	1.86	1.76	1.70	1.66	1.56	1.53	1.48	1.42	1.38	.01	
1.23	1.21	1.20	1.18	1.16	1.14	1.12	1.11	1.10	1.09	1.08	1.06	.25	
1.52	1.46	1.42	1.38	1.34	1.31	1.28	1.24	1.22	1.20	1.17	1.14	.10	200
1.72	1.62	1.57	1.52	1.46	1.41	1.39	1.32	1.29	1.26	1.22	1.19	.05	
2.13	1.97	1.89	1.79	1.69	1.63	1.58	1.48	1.44	1.39	1.33	1.28	.01	
1.22	1.19	1.18	1.16	1.14	1.13	1.12	1.09	1.08	1.07	1.04	1.00	.25	
1.49	1.42	1.38	1.34	1.30	1.26	1.24	1.18	1.17	1.13	1.08	1.00	.10	∞
1.67	1.57	1.52	1.46	1.39	1.35	1.32	1.24	1.22	1.17	1.11	1.00	.05	
2.04	1.88	1.79	1.70	1.59	1.52	1.47	1.36	1.32	1.25	1.15	1.00	.01	

Table 21

Power Function for Analysis of Variance

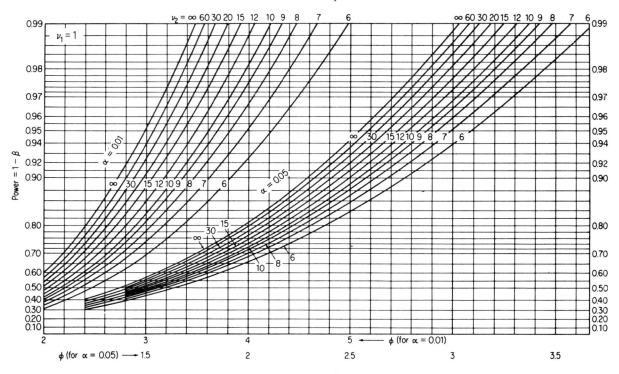

Discussion

In general, power efficiency refers to the increase in sample size necessary to make one test as powerful as another. Power may vary as a function of alpha level, sample size, the value of the alternate hypothesis, the use of correlated measures, and the nature of the statistical test itself. In order to reduce the likelihood of an experiment's sample size being either too small or too large it is important to make power calculations before rather than after an experiment. The power $(1 - \beta)$ of the F test in analysis of variance helps determine the probability of rejecting the null hypothesis when it is false. Table 21 simplifies the calculation of power. The parameter ϕ is used to enter the table and is given by

$$\phi = \sqrt{\frac{\sum_{j=1}^{k} \beta_j^2 / k}{\sigma_\epsilon^2 / \sqrt{n}}}$$

Table 21 (continued)

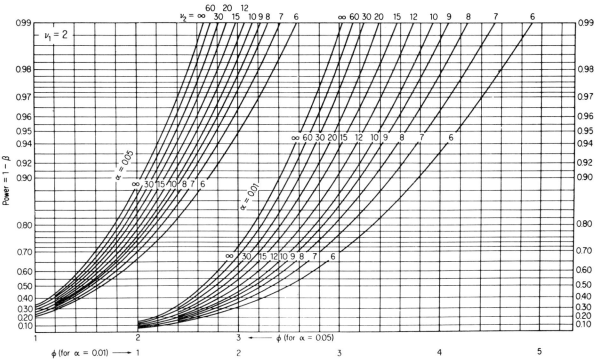

Table 21 (continued)

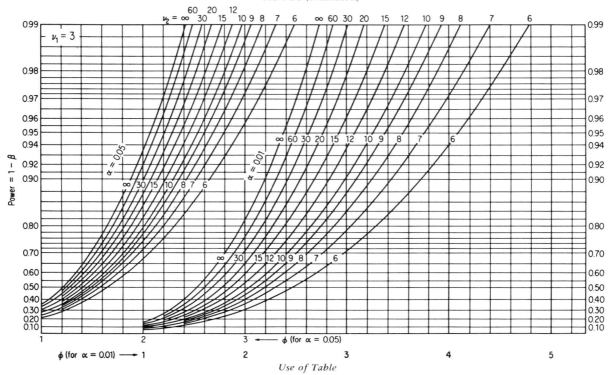

Use of Table

The power functions of Table 21 give the foundation for making decisions as to how many subjects are to be included in the experiment for effective results. Use of Table 21 requires the following information: (1) The a level, indicating willingness to risk Type I errors (the probability of rejecting the null hypothesis when it is true). Although the sizes of population treatment effects are unknown, a probability of rejecting H_0 can be selected, given that ϕ is $\geqslant$ some critical value, say ϕ. (2) n = the size of the jth sample. (3) The error variance, σ_ϵ^2, such estimate obtained from the desired dependent variable of a previous experiment.

(4) where $\displaystyle\sum_{j=1}^{k} \beta_j^2 / k$ = sum of squared treatment effects,

n = size of the jth sample,

σ_ϵ^2 = error variance.

(5) v_1 and v_2 degrees of freedom for treatment and error effects, respectively. (For more detailed information concerning use of these charts, see Kirk, pp. 107-109; Myers, pp. 77-79; Pearson and Hartley, volume 2, 1972).

Table 21 (continued)

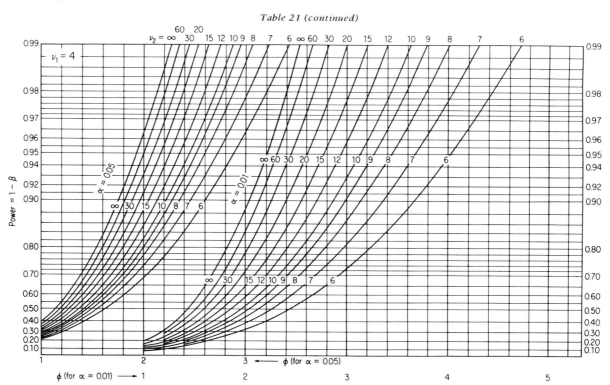

Table 21 (continued)

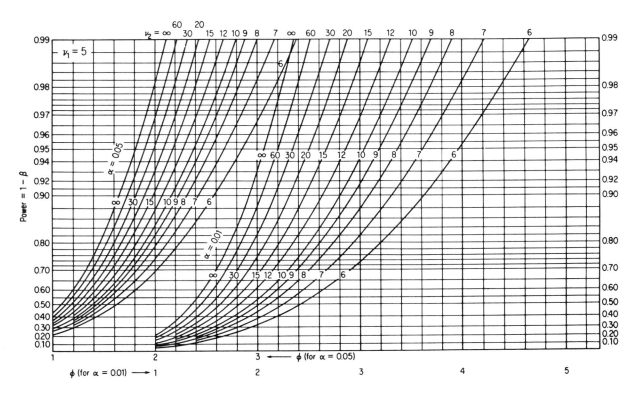

Table 21 (continued)

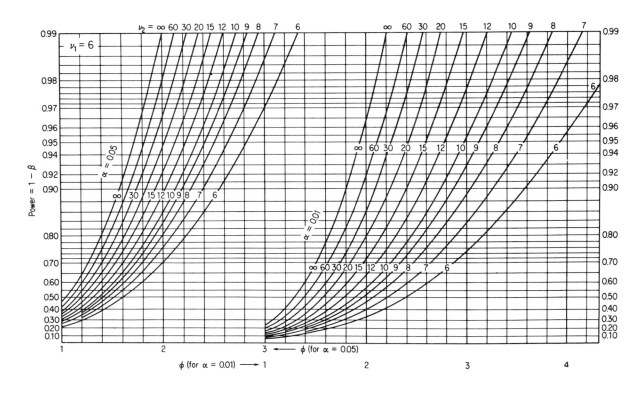

Table 21 (continued)

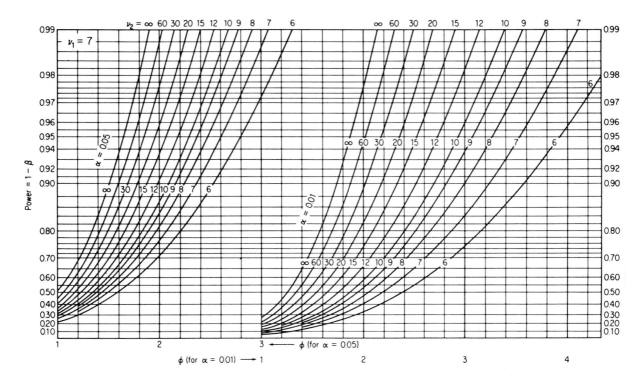

Table 21 (continued)

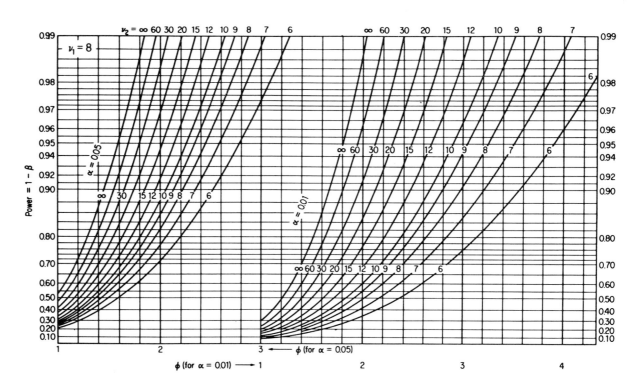

Table 22

Percentage Points of the Dunn
Multiple Comparison Test

Number of Compari- sons (C)	α	Error df											
		5	7	10	12	15	20	24	30	40	60	120	∞
2	.05	3.17	2.84	2.64	2.56	2.49	2.42	2.39	2.36	2.33	2.30	2.27	2.24
	.01	4.78	4.03	3.58	3.43	3.29	3.16	3.09	3.03	2.97	2.92	2.86	2.81
3	.05	3.54	3.13	2.87	2.78	2.69	2.61	2.58	2.54	2.50	2.47	2.43	2.39
	.01	5.25	4.36	3.83	3.65	3.48	3.33	3.26	3.19	3.12	3.06	2.99	2.94
4	.05	3.81	3.34	3.04	2.94	2.84	2.75	2.70	2.66	2.62	2.58	2.54	2.50
	.01	5.60	4.59	4.01	3.80	3.62	3.46	3.38	3.30	3.23	3.16	3.09	3.02
5	.05	4.04	3.50	3.17	3.06	2.95	2.85	2.80	2.75	2.71	2.66	2.62	2.58
	.01	5.89	4.78	4.15	3.93	3.74	3.55	3.47	3.39	3.31	3.24	3.16	3.09
6	.05	4.22	3.64	3.28	3.15	3.04	2.93	2.88	2.83	2.78	2.73	2.68	2.64
	.01	6.15	4.95	4.27	4.04	3.82	3.63	3.54	3.46	3.38	3.30	3.22	3.15
7	.05	4.38	3.76	3.37	3.24	3.11	3.00	2.94	2.89	2.84	2.79	2.74	2.69
	.01	6.36	5.09	4.37	4.13	3.90	3.70	3.61	3.52	3.43	3.34	3.27	3.19
8	.05	4.53	3.86	3.45	3.31	3.18	3.06	3.00	2.94	2.89	2.84	2.79	2.74
	.01	6.56	5.21	4.45	4.20	3.97	3.76	3.66	3.57	3.48	3.39	3.31	3.23
9	.05	4.66	3.95	3.52	3.37	3.24	3.11	3.05	2.99	2.93	2.88	2.83	2.77
	.01	6.70	5.31	4.53	4.26	4.02	3.80	3.70	3.61	3.51	3.42	3.34	3.26
10	.05	4.78	4.03	3.58	3.43	3.29	3.16	3.09	3.03	2.97	2.92	2.86	2.81
	.01	6.86	5.40	4.59	4.32	4.07	3.85	3.74	3.65	3.55	3.46	3.37	3.29
15	.05	5.25	4.36	3.83	3.65	3.48	3.33	3.26	3.19	3.12	3.06	2.99	2.94
	.01	7.51	5.79	4.86	4.56	4.29	4.03	3.91	3.80	3.70	3.59	3.50	3.40
20	.05	5.60	4.59	4.01	3.80	3.62	3.46	3.38	3.30	3.23	3.16	3.09	3.02
	.01	8.00	6.08	5.06	4.73	4.42	4.15	4.04	3.90	3.79	3.69	3.58	3.48
25	.05	5.89	4.78	4.15	3.93	3.74	3.55	3.47	3.39	3.31	3.24	3.16	3.09
	.01	8.37	6.30	5.20	4.86	4.53	4.25	4.1*	3.98	3.88	3.76	3.64	3.54
30	.05	6.15	4.95	4.27	4.04	3.82	3.63	3.54	3.46	3.38	3.30	3.22	3.15
	.01	8.68	6.49	5.33	4.95	4.61	4.33	4.2*	4.13	3.93	3.81	3.69	3.59
35	.05	6.36	5.09	4.37	4.13	3.90	3.70	3.61	3.52	3.43	3.34	3.27	3.19
	.01	8.95	6.67	5.44	5.04	4.71	4.39	4.3*	4.26	3.97	3.84	3.73	3.63
40	.05	6.56	5.21	4.45	4.20	3.97	3.76	3.66	3.57	3.48	3.39	3.31	3.23
	.01	9.19	6.83	5.52	5.12	4.78	4.46	4.3*	4.1*	4.01	3.89	3.77	3.66
45	.05	6.70	5.31	4.53	4.26	4.02	3.80	3.70	3.61	3.51	3.42	3.34	3.26
	.01	9.41	6.93	5.60	5.20	4.84	4.52	4.3*	4.2*	4.1*	3.93	3.80	3.69
50	.05	6.86	5.40	4.59	4.32	4.07	3.85	3.74	3.65	3.55	3.46	3.37	3.29
	.01	9.68	7.06	5.70	5.27	4.90	4.56	4.4*	4.2*	4.1*	3.97	3.83	3.72
100	.05	8.00	6.08	5.06	4.73	4.42	4.15	4.04	3.90	3.79	3.69	3.58	3.48
	.01	11.04	7.80	6.20	5.70	5.20	4.80	4.7*	4.4*	4.5*		4.00	3.89
250	.05	9.68	7.06	5.70	5.27	4.90	4.56	4.4*	4.2*	4.1*	3.97	3.83	3.72
	.01	13.26	8.83	6.9*	6.3*	5.8*	5.2*	5.0*	4.9*	4.8*			4.11

For a brief statistical description of this test see the entry of *Dunn Multiple Comparison Test* under its appropriate alphabetical listing in this book. For details concerning procedures and use of Table 22, see Kirk, pp. 79-81.

Table 23

Percentage Points of the Duncan New
Multiple Range Test

Error df	Protection Level	r = number of means for range being tested													
		2	3	4	5	6	7	8	9	10	12	14	16	18	20
1	.05	18.0	18.0	18.0	18.0	18.0	18.0	18.0	18.0	18.0	18.0	18.0	18.0	18.0	18.0
	.01	90.0	90.0	90.0	90.0	90.0	90.0	90.0	90.0	90.0	90.0	90.0	90.0	90.0	90.0
2	.05	6.09	6.09	6.09	6.09	6.09	6.09	6.09	6.09	6.09	6.09	6.09	6.09	6.09	6.09
	.01	14.0	14.0	14.0	14.0	14.0	14.0	14.0	14.0	14.0	14.0	14.0	14.0	14.0	14.0
3	.05	4.50	4.50	4.50	4.50	4.50	4.50	4.50	4.50	4.50	4.50	4.50	4.50	4.50	4.50
	.01	8.26	8.5	8.6	8.7	8.8	8.9	8.9	9.0	9.0	9.0	9.1	9.2	9.3	9.3
4	.05	3.93	4.01	4.02	4.02	4.02	4.02	4.02	4.02	4.02	4.02	4.02	4.02	4.02	4.02
	.01	6.51	6.8	6.9	7.0	7.1	7.1	7.2	7.2	7.3	7.3	7.4	7.4	7.5	7.5
5	.05	3.64	3.74	3.79	3.83	3.83	3.83	3.83	3.83	3.83	3.83	3.83	3.83	3.83	3.83
	.01	5.70	5.96	6.11	6.18	6.26	6.33	6.40	6.44	6.5	6.6	6.6	6.7	6.7	6.8
6	.05	3.46	3.58	3.64	3.68	3.68	3.68	3.68	3.68	3.68	3.68	3.68	3.68	3.68	3.68
	.01	5.24	5.51	5.65	5.73	5.81	5.88	5.95	6.00	6.0	6.1	6.2	6.2	6.3	6.3
7	.05	3.35	3.47	3.54	3.58	3.60	3.61	3.61	3.61	3.61	3.61	3.61	3.61	3.61	3.61
	.01	4.95	5.22	5.37	5.45	5.53	5.61	5.69	5.73	5.8	5.8	5.9	5.9	6.0	6.0
8	.05	3.26	3.39	3.47	3.52	3.55	3.56	3.56	3.56	3.56	3.56	3.56	3.56	3.56	3.56
	.01	4.74	5.00	5.14	5.23	5.32	5.40	5.47	5.51	5.5	5.6	5.7	5.7	5.8	5.8
9	.05	3.20	3.34	3.41	3.47	3.50	3.52	3.52	3.52	3.52	3.52	3.52	3.52	3.52	3.52
	.01	4.60	4.86	4.99	5.08	5.17	5.25	5.32	5.36	5.4	5.5	5.5	5.6	5.7	5.7
10	.05	3.15	3.30	3.37	3.43	3.46	3.47	3.47	3.47	3.47	3.47	3.47	3.47	3.47	3.48
	.01	4.48	4.73	4.88	4.96	5.06	5.13	5.20	5.24	5.28	5.36	5.42	5.48	5.54	5.55
11	.05	3.11	3.27	3.35	3.39	3.43	3.44	3.45	3.46	4.46	3.46	3.46	3.46	3.47	3.48
	.01	4.39	4.63	4.77	4.86	4.94	5.01	5.06	5.12	5.15	5.24	5.28	5.34	5.38	5.39
12	.05	3.08	3.23	3.33	3.36	3.40	3.42	3.44	3.44	3.46	3.46	3.46	3.46	3.47	3.48
	.01	4.32	4.55	4.68	4.76	4.84	4.92	4.96	5.02	5.07	5.13	5.17	5.22	5.24	5.26
13	.05	3.06	3.21	3.30	3.35	3.38	3.41	3.42	3.44	3.45	3.45	3.46	3.46	3.47	3.47
	.01	4.26	4.48	4.62	4.69	4.74	4.84	4.88	4.94	4.98	5.04	5.08	5.13	5.14	5.15
14	.05	3.03	3.18	3.27	3.33	3.37	3.39	3.41	3.42	3.44	3.45	3.46	3.46	3.47	3.47
	.01	4.21	4.42	4.55	4.63	4.70	4.78	4.83	4.87	4.91	4.96	5.00	5.04	5.06	5.07
15	.05	3.01	3.16	3.25	3.31	3.36	3.38	3.40	3.42	3.43	3.44	3.45	3.46	3.47	3.47
	.01	4.17	4.37	4.50	4.58	4.64	4.72	4.77	4.81	4.84	4.90	4.94	4.97	4.99	5.00
16	.05	3.00	3.15	3.23	3.30	3.34	3.37	3.39	3.41	3.43	3.44	3.45	3.46	3.47	3.47
	.01	4.13	4.34	4.45	4.54	4.60	4.67	4.72	4.76	4.79	4.84	4.88	4.91	4.93	4.94
17	.05	2.98	3.13	3.22	3.28	3.33	3.36	3.38	3.40	3.42	3.44	3.45	3.46	3.47	3.47
	.01	4.10	4.30	4.41	4.50	4.56	4.63	4.68	4.72	4.75	4.80	4.83	4.86	4.88	4.89
18	.05	2.97	3.12	3.21	3.27	3.32	3.35	3.37	3.39	3.41	3.43	3.45	3.46	3.47	3.47
	.01	4.07	4.27	4.38	4.46	4.53	4.59	4.64	4.68	4.71	4.76	4.79	4.82	4.84	4.85
19	.05	2.96	3.11	3.19	3.26	3.31	3.35	3.37	3.39	3.41	3.43	3.44	3.46	3.47	3.47
	.01	4.05	4.24	4.35	4.43	4.50	4.56	4.61	4.64	4.67	4.72	4.76	4.79	4.81	4.82
20	.05	2.95	3.10	3.18	3.25	3.30	3.34	3.36	3.38	3.40	3.43	3.44	3.46	3.46	3.47
	.01	4.02	4.22	4.33	4.40	4.47	4.53	4.58	4.61	4.65	4.69	4.73	4.76	4.78	4.79
22	.05	2.93	3.08	3.17	3.24	3.29	3.32	3.35	3.37	3.39	3.42	3.44	3.45	3.46	3.47
	.01	3.99	4.17	4.28	4.36	4.42	4.48	4.53	4.57	4.60	4.65	4.68	4.71	4.74	4.75
24	.05	2.92	3.07	3.15	3.22	3.28	3.31	3.34	3.37	3.38	3.41	3.44	3.45	3.46	3.47
	.01	3.96	4.14	4.24	4.33	4.39	4.44	4.49	4.53	4.57	4.62	4.64	4.67	4.70	4.72
26	.05	2.91	3.06	3.14	3.21	3.27	3.30	3.34	3.36	3.38	3.41	3.43	3.45	3.46	3.47
	.01	3.93	4.11	4.21	4.30	4.36	4.41	4.46	4.50	4.53	4.58	4.62	4.65	4.67	4.69
28	.05	2.90	3.04	3.13	3.20	3.26	3.30	3.33	3.35	3.37	3.40	3.43	3.45	3.46	3.47
	.01	3.91	4.08	4.18	4.28	4.34	4.39	4.43	4.47	4.51	4.56	4.60	4.62	4.65	4.67
30	.05	2.89	3.04	3.12	3.20	3.25	3.29	3.32	3.35	3.37	3.40	3.43	3.44	3.46	3.47
	.01	3.89	4.06	4.16	4.22	4.32	4.36	4.41	4.45	4.48	4.54	4.58	4.61	4.63	4.65
40	.05	2.86	3.01	3.10	3.17	3.22	3.27	3.30	3.33	3.35	3.39	3.42	3.44	3.46	3.47
	.01	3.82	3.99	4.10	4.17	4.24	4.30	4.34	4.37	4.41	4.46	4.51	4.54	4.57	4.59
60	.05	2.83	2.98	3.08	3.14	3.20	3.24	3.28	3.31	3.33	3.37	3.40	3.43	3.45	3.47
	.01	3.76	3.92	4.03	4.12	4.17	4.23	4.27	4.31	4.34	4.39	4.44	4.47	4.50	4.53
100	.05	2.80	2.95	3.05	3.12	3.18	3.22	3.26	3.29	3.32	3.36	3.40	3.42	3.45	3.47
	.01	3.71	3.86	3.93	4.06	4.11	4.17	4.21	4.25	4.29	4.35	4.38	4.42	4.45	4.48
∞	.05	2.77	2.92	3.02	3.09	3.15	3.19	3.23	3.26	3.29	3.34	3.38	3.41	3.44	3.47
	.01	3.64	3.80	3.90	3.98	4.04	4.09	4.14	4.17	4.20	4.26	4.31	4.34	4.38	4.41

Use of Table

The df and the range of the pairs of groups being compared must be located within the table at appropriate levels of significance. For example, assume a df of 20, that the range of the pair being compared is equal to 5, and the computed critical value is 5.05 at the .01 significance level. Referring to the table it is seen that 4.40 is the critical value for a df of 20, an r of 5, and a .01 level of significance. Since the computed value of 5.05 is larger, the conclusion is that the difference between the groups is significant beyond the .01 level. (For further explanations and mechanics of this test, see Kirk, pp. 91-95.)

Table 24

Percentage Points for the Comparison of
$k-1$ Treatment Means With a Control

One-tailed comparisons

| Error df | α | \multicolumn{9}{c}{k = number of treatment means, including control} |
		2	3	4	5	6	7	8	9	10
5	.05	2.02	2.44	2.68	2.85	2.98	3.08	3.16	3.24	3.30
	.01	3.37	3.90	4.21	4.43	4.60	4.73	4.85	4.94	5.03
6	.05	1.94	2.34	2.56	2.71	2.83	2.92	3.00	3.07	3.12
	.01	3.14	3.61	3.88	4.07	4.21	4.33	4.43	4.51	4.59
7	.05	1.89	2.27	2.48	2.62	2.73	2.82	2.89	2.95	3.01
	.01	3.00	3.42	3.66	3.83	3.96	4.07	4.15	4.23	4.30
8	.05	1.86	2.22	2.42	2.55	2.66	2.74	2.81	2.87	2.92
	.01	2.90	3.29	3.51	3.67	3.79	3.88	3.96	4.03	4.09
9	.05	1.83	2.18	2.37	2.50	2.60	2.68	2.75	2.81	2.86
	.01	2.82	3.19	3.40	3.55	3.66	3.75	3.82	3.89	3.94
10	.05	1.81	2.15	2.34	2.47	2.56	2.64	2.70	2.76	2.81
	.01	2.76	3.11	3.31	3.45	3.56	3.64	3.71	3.78	3.83
11	.05	1.80	2.13	2.31	2.44	2.53	2.60	2.67	2.72	2.77
	.01	2.72	3.06	3.25	3.38	3.48	3.56	3.63	3.69	3.74
12	.05	1.78	2.11	2.29	2.41	2.50	2.58	2.64	2.69	2.74
	.01	2.68	3.01	3.19	3.32	3.42	3.50	3.56	3.62	3.67
13	.05	1.77	2.09	2.27	2.39	2.48	2.55	2.61	2.66	2.71
	.01	2.65	2.97	3.15	3.27	3.37	3.44	3.51	3.56	3.61
14	.05	1.76	2.08	2.25	2.37	2.46	2.53	2.59	2.64	2.69
	.01	2.62	2.94	3.11	3.23	3.32	3.40	3.46	3.51	3.56
15	.05	1.75	2.07	2.24	2.36	2.44	2.51	2.57	2.62	2.67
	.01	2.60	2.91	3.08	3.20	3.29	3.36	3.42	3.47	3.52
16	.05	1.75	2.06	2.23	2.34	2.43	2.50	2.56	2.61	2.65
	.01	2.58	2.88	3.05	3.17	3.26	3.33	3.39	3.44	3.48
17	.05	1.74	2.05	2.22	2.33	2.42	2.49	2.54	2.59	2.64
	.01	2.57	2.86	3.03	3.14	3.23	3.30	3.36	3.41	3.45
18	.05	1.73	2.04	2.21	2.32	2.41	2.48	2.53	2.58	2.62
	.01	2.55	2.84	3.01	3.12	3.21	3.27	3.33	3.38	3.42
19	.05	1.73	2.03	2.20	2.31	2.40	2.47	2.52	2.57	2.61
	.01	2.54	2.83	2.99	3.10	3.18	3.25	3.31	3.36	3.40
20	.05	1.72	2.03	2.19	2.30	2.39	2.46	2.51	2.56	2.60
	.01	2.53	2.81	2.97	3.08	3.17	3.23	3.29	3.34	3.38
24	.05	1.71	2.01	2.17	2.28	2.36	2.43	2.48	2.53	2.57
	.01	2.49	2.77	2.92	3.03	3.11	3.17	3.22	3.27	3.31
30	.05	1.70	1.99	2.15	2.25	2.33	2.40	2.45	2.50	2.54
	.01	2.46	2.72	2.87	2.97	3.05	3.11	3.16	3.21	3.24
40	.05	1.68	1.97	2.13	2.23	2.31	2.37	2.42	2.47	2.51
	.01	2.42	2.68	2.82	2.92	2.99	3.05	3.10	3.14	3.18
60	.05	1.67	1.95	2.10	2.21	2.28	2.35	2.39	2.44	2.48
	.01	2.39	2.64	2.78	2.87	2.94	3.00	3.04	3.08	3.12
120	.05	1.66	1.93	2.08	2.18	2.26	2.32	2.37	2.41	2.45
	.01	2.36	2.60	2.73	2.82	2.89	2.94	2.99	3.03	3.06
∞	.05	1.64	1.92	2.06	2.16	2.23	2.29	2.34	2.38	2.42
	.01	2.33	2.56	2.68	2.77	2.84	2.89	2.93	2.97	3.00

Discussion

For definition of this test see the entry *Dunnett's Multiple Comparison Test* at the appropriate alphabetical listing in this book.

The *parameters* for Dunnett's *t* are:

k = number of treatments (including the control)

df (or v) = degrees of freedom for MS_{error} (which is the unbiased estimate of the population error variance).

The following formula provides d' or the difference that a comparison must exceed to be considered significant:

$$d' = tD_{a/2; \, k, \, v} \sqrt{\frac{2(MS_{error})}{n}}$$

where

$tD_{a/2; \, k, \, v}$ = the two-tailed value in Table 24

v = degrees of freedom associated with MS_{error}

Example and Use of Table

The above table is for *one-tailed comparisons.* Assume a *k* of 5 and a *v* of .20; then for a one-tailed test the value obtained from the table at .01 level of significance is 3.08. For an example of two-tailed comparisons, see the following page of Table 24. (See Kirk, pp. 94-5; Roscoe, pp. 241-2; Winer, pp. 90-1; and Myers, p. 337 for more extensive coverage on this test.)

Table 24 (continued)

Two-tailed comparisons

Error df	α	\multicolumn{9}{c}{k = number of treatment means, including control}
		2	3	4	5	6	7	8	9	10
5	.05	2.57	3.03	3.29	3.48	3.62	3.73	3.82	3.90	3.97
	.01	4.03	4.63	4.98	5.22	5.41	5.56	5.69	5.80	5.89
6	.05	2.45	2.86	3.10	3.26	3.39	3.49	3.57	3.64	3.71
	.01	3.71	4.21	4.51	4.71	4.87	5.00	5.10	5.20	5.28
7	.05	2.36	2.75	2.97	3.12	3.24	3.33	3.41	3.47	3.53
	.01	3.50	3.95	4.21	4.39	4.53	4.64	4.74	4.82	4.89
8	.05	2.31	2.67	2.88	3.02	3.13	3.22	3.29	3.35	3.41
	.01	3.36	3.77	4.00	4.17	4.29	4.40	4.48	4.56	4.62
9	.05	2.26	2.61	2.81	2.95	3.05	3.14	3.20	3.26	3.32
	.01	3.25	3.63	3.85	4.01	4.12	4.22	4.30	4.37	4.43
10	.05	2.23	2.57	2.76	2.89	2.99	3.07	3.14	3.19	3.24
	.01	3.17	3.53	3.74	3.88	3.99	4.08	4.16	4.22	4.28
11	.05	2.20	2.53	2.72	2.84	2.94	3.02	3.08	3.14	3.19
	.01	3.11	3.45	3.65	3.79	3.89	3.98	4.05	4.11	4.16
12	.05	2.18	2.50	2.68	2.81	2.90	2.98	3.04	3.09	3.14
	.01	3.05	3.39	3.58	3.71	3.81	3.89	3.96	4.02	4.07
13	.05	2.16	2.48	2.65	2.78	2.87	2.94	3.00	3.06	3.10
	.01	3.01	3.33	3.52	3.65	3.74	3.82	3.89	3.94	3.99
14	.05	2.14	2.46	2.63	2.75	2.84	2.91	2.97	3.02	3.07
	.01	2.98	3.29	3.47	3.59	3.69	3.76	3.83	3.88	3.93
15	.05	2.13	2.44	2.61	2.73	2.82	2.89	2.95	3.00	3.04
	.01	2.95	3.25	3.43	3.55	3.64	3.71	3.78	3.83	3.88
16	.05	2.12	2.42	2.59	2.71	2.80	2.87	2.92	2.97	3.02
	.01	2.92	3.22	3.39	3.51	3.60	3.67	3.73	3.78	3.83
17	.05	2.11	2.41	2.58	2.69	2.78	2.85	2.90	2.95	3.00
	.01	2.90	3.19	3.36	3.47	3.56	3.63	3.69	3.74	3.79
18	.05	2.10	2.40	2.56	2.68	2.76	2.83	2.89	2.94	2.98
	.01	2.88	3.17	3.33	3.44	3.53	3.60	3.66	3.71	3.75
19	.05	2.09	2.39	2.55	2.66	2.75	2.81	2.87	2.92	2.96
	.01	2.86	3.15	3.31	3.42	3.50	3.57	3.63	3.68	3.72
20	.05	2.09	2.38	2.54	2.65	2.73	2.80	2.86	2.90	2.95
	.01	2.85	3.13	3.29	3.40	3.48	3.55	3.60	3.65	3.69
24	.05	2.06	2.35	2.51	2.61	2.70	2.76	2.81	2.86	2.90
	.01	2.80	3.07	3.22	3.32	3.40	3.47	3.52	3.57	3.61
30	.05	2.04	2.32	2.47	2.58	2.66	2.72	2.77	2.82	2.86
	.01	2.75	3.01	3.15	3.25	3.33	3.39	3.44	3.49	3.52
40	.05	2.02	2.29	2.44	2.54	2.62	2.68	2.73	2.77	2.81
	.01	2.70	2.95	3.09	3.19	3.26	3.32	3.37	3.41	3.44
60	.05	2.00	2.27	2.41	2.51	2.58	2.64	2.69	2.73	2.77
	.01	2.66	2.90	3.03	3.12	3.19	3.25	3.29	3.33	3.37
120	.05	1.98	2.24	2.38	2.47	2.55	2.60	2.65	2.69	2.73
	.01	2.62	2.85	2.97	3.06	3.12	3.18	3.22	3.26	3.29
∞	.05	1.96	2.21	2.35	2.44	2.51	2.57	2.61	2.65	2.69
	.01	2.58	2.79	2.92	3.00	3.06	3.11	3.15	3.19	3.22

Example and Use of Table (Two-tailed)

For a k = 5 and v = 20, the tabled value at the .01 level of significance is 3.40. For a hypothetical critical difference (d') for a comparison, assume a control mean ($\overline{X}_1$) of 40.1 and four treatment means, $\overline{X}_2$ = 45.8, $\overline{X}_3$ = 43.2, $\overline{X}_4$ = 50.0, and $\overline{X}_5$ = 49.4. The difference between $\overline{X}_1$ and each of the four treatment means exceeds the d' except in the case of $\overline{X}_3$, where the difference is only 3.1. Therefore, all differences among population means are significant at the .01 level except the difference between μ and μ_3.

Table 25a

Critical Values of D (Maximum Difference) in the Kolmogorov-Smirnov Goodness of Fit Test

Sample size (N)	Level of significance for $D = maximum |F_0(X) - S_N(X)|$				
	.20	.15	.10	.05	.01
1	.900	.925	.950	.975	.995
2	.684	.726	.776	.842	.929
3	.565	.597	.642	.708	.828
4	.494	.525	.564	.624	.733
5	.446	.474	.510	.565	.669
6	.410	.436	.470	.521	.618
7	.381	.405	.438	.486	.577
8	.358	.381	.411	.457	.543
9	.339	.360	.388	.432	.514
10	.322	.342	.368	.410	.490
11	.307	.326	.352	.391	.468
12	.295	.313	.338	.375	.450
13	.284	.302	.325	.361	.433
14	.274	.292	.314	.349	.418
15	.266	.283	.304	.338	.404
16	.258	.274	.295	.328	.392
17	.250	.266	.286	.318	.381
18	.244	.259	.278	.309	.371
19	.237	.252	.272	.301	.363
20	.231	.246	.264	.294	.356
25	.21	.22	.24	.27	.32
30	.19	.20	.22	.24	.29
35	.18	.19	.21	.23	.27
Over 35	$\dfrac{1.07}{\sqrt{N}}$	$\dfrac{1.14}{\sqrt{N}}$	$\dfrac{1.22}{\sqrt{N}}$	$\dfrac{1.36}{\sqrt{N}}$	$\dfrac{1.63}{\sqrt{N}}$

Steps to Follow

1. Researcher establishes from his data a hypothetical frequency distribution from which a relative cumulative frequency distribution is made with as many score intervals as score levels.
2. A random sample is drawn and its relative frequency distribution is determined.
3. Each interval of sampling distribution is then paired with its corresponding interval of the hypothetical distribution, and differences for each interval between the two distributions are determined. Let D = maximum deviation. D is compared to the tabled value for appropriate sample and significance level.

Null and Alternative Hypotheses

Assume that it is desired to determine if one group (A) is distributed similarly to Group B.

H_0: Group A is distributed the same as Group B.

H_1: Group A is not distributed the same.

Example and Use of Table

Assume that an obtained D is .15. If this calculated value of D equals or exceeds the tabled value, the null hypothesis is rejected, the finding is considered significant, and the population distribution differs from the hypothetical one at the stated significance level. Thus, for an N of 50 at the .05 level (two-tail value), the D is .18841. Since the computed D of .15 is less than .188, the null hypothesis is retained and no significant difference is considered to exist between the two distributions.

(See *Kolmogorov-Smirnov Goodness of Fit Test* under appropriate alphabetical entry; also Roscoe, pp. 209-213; Siegel, pp. 47-52; O'Toole, pp. 180-188).

Table 25b

Critical Values of K_D in the Kolmogorov-Smirnov Test for Two Samples of Equal Size
(N is the size of each sample)

N	One-tailed test*		Two-tailed test†	
	$\alpha = .05$	$\alpha = .01$	$\alpha = .05$	$\alpha = .01$
3	3	—	—	—
4	4	—	4	—
5	4	5	5	5
6	5	6	5	6
7	5	6	6	6
8	5	6	6	7
9	6	7	6	7
10	6	7	7	8
11	6	8	7	8
12	6	8	7	8
13	7	8	7	9
14	7	8	8	9
15	7	9	8	9
16	7	9	8	10
17	8	9	8	10
18	8	10	9	10
19	8	10	9	10
20	8	10	9	11
21	8	10	9	11
22	9	11	9	11
23	9	11	10	11
24	9	11	10	12
25	9	11	10	12
26	9	11	10	12
27	9	12	10	12
28	10	12	11	13
29	10	12	11	13
30	10	12	11	13
35	11	13	12	
40	11	14	13	

Explanation and Use of Table

Table 25b may be used in the test of the null hypothesis when n_1 equals n_2 and when both n_1 and n_2 are of equal size, with $N \leq 40$. Data is required to be on an ordinal scale and continuously distributed. If data are grouped, this test is not as powerful as the chi-square statistic.

In general, the procedure to follow is similar to that in Table 25a, except for two independent random samples of equal size being drawn to determine if the populations differ, and also that the largest of the differences in the cumulative frequencies is designated as K_D instead of D.

Null and Alternative Hypotheses

H_0: there is no difference between the distributions.
H_1: there is a difference between the distributions.

If the calculated value of $K_D \geq$ the tabled value, the finding is significant, the H_0 is rejected, and the two distributions are considered to differ. If the calculated value is less than the tabled value, the H_0 is retained and the conclusion is drawn that no significant difference exists between the two distributions.

For example, in a one-tailed test where N equals 10, if the $K_D = 7$, the null hypothesis can be rejected at the $\alpha = 0.1$ level, and, of course, at the $\alpha = .05$ level (where a K_D of 6 is the critical value).

Table 25c
Table of Critical Values of D in the Kolmogorov-Smirnov Test for Two Large Samples

Level of significance	Value of D so large as to call for rejection of H_0 at the indicated level of significance, where $D = maximum \ |S_{n_1}(X) - S_{n_2}(X)|$
.10	$1.22 \sqrt{\dfrac{n_1 + n_2}{n_1 n_2}}$
.05	$1.36 \sqrt{\dfrac{n_1 + n_2}{n_1 n_2}}$
.025	$1.48 \sqrt{\dfrac{n_1 + n_2}{n_1 n_2}}$
.01	$1.63 \sqrt{\dfrac{n_1 + n_2}{n_1 n_2}}$
.005	$1.73 \sqrt{\dfrac{n_1 + n_2}{n_1 n_2}}$
.001	$1.95 \sqrt{\dfrac{n_1 + n_2}{n_1 n_2}}$

Table 25c may be used to test the null hypothesis when both n_1 and n_2 are larger than 20, but it is not necessary for n_1 to equal n_2. Data must be continuously distributed. Numerous tie scores or grouped data vitiate the use of this statistic.

Although Table 25c is two-tailed it may be adapted to one-tailed use by entering the table with twice the level of significance. For example, to obtain the value at the .05 level for a one-tailed test, use .10.

Null and Alternative Hypotheses

H_0: no difference exists in the two distributions under consideration.
H_1: a difference between the two distributions does exist.

Explanation and Use of Table

In order to use the table it is necessary to determine the value of D by using the formula

$$D = maximum \ |S_{n_1}(X) - S_{n_2}(X)| \text{, the maximum absolute value of D.}$$

where $S_{n_1}(X) =$ the observed cumulative step function of one of the samples, or K/n_1, where K equals the number of scores equal to or less than X.
where $S_{n_1}^{n_2}(X) = K/n_2$, or the observed cumulative step function of the other sample.

After obtaining this value of D compare it with the critical one which is obtained by entering the observed values of n_1 and n_2 in the expression given in the table. If the observed D is equal to or larger than that computed from the expression in the table, the finding is considered to be significant and H_0 may be rejected at the two-tailed significance level. The H_0 is retained, of course, if the calculated value is smaller than the tabled value.

For example, assume an n_1 of 40 and an n_2 of 50, with a researcher wanting to make a two-tailed test at $\alpha = .01$. The researcher enters the table at $\alpha = .01$ and finds that the value of D in the second column is $1.63 \sqrt{n_1 + n_2 / n_1 n_2}$. He uses this value of D, thus

$$1.63 \sqrt{\frac{n_1 + n_2}{n_1 n_2}}$$

$$1.63 \sqrt{\frac{n_1 + n_2}{n_1 n_2}} = 1.63 \sqrt{\frac{40 + 50}{(40)(50)}} = 1.63 \sqrt{\frac{90}{2000}} = 1.63 \sqrt{.045} = .345$$

The obtained D, from the formula above, must be larger than .345 for H_0 to be rejected.

Table 26

Critical Values of r in the Runs Test

n_1 \ n_2	2	3	4	5	6	7	8	9	10	11	12	13	14	15	16	17	18	19	20
2											2	2	2	2	2	2	2	2	2
3					2	2	2	2	2	2	2	2	2	3	3	3	3	3	3
4				2	2	2	3	3	3	3	3	3	3	3	4	4	4	4	4
5			2	2	3	3	3	3	3	4	4	4	4	4	4	4	5	5	5
6		2	2	3	3	3	3	4	4	4	4	5	5	5	5	5	5	6	6
7		2	2	3	3	3	4	4	5	5	5	5	5	6	6	6	6	6	6
8		2	3	3	3	4	4	5	5	5	6	6	6	6	6	7	7	7	7
9		2	3	3	4	4	5	5	5	6	6	6	7	7	7	7	8	8	8
10		2	3	3	4	5	5	5	6	6	7	7	7	7	8	8	8	8	9
11		2	3	4	4	5	5	6	6	7	7	7	8	8	8	9	9	9	9
12	2	2	3	4	4	5	6	6	7	7	7	8	8	8	9	9	9	10	10
13	2	2	3	4	5	5	6	6	7	7	8	8	9	9	9	10	10	10	10
14	2	2	3	4	5	5	6	7	7	8	8	9	9	9	10	10	10	11	11
15	2	3	3	4	5	6	6	7	7	8	8	9	9	10	10	11	11	11	12
16	2	3	4	4	5	6	6	7	8	8	9	9	10	10	11	11	11	12	12
17	2	3	4	4	5	6	7	7	8	9	9	10	10	11	11	11	12	12	13
18	2	3	4	5	5	6	7	8	8	9	9	10	10	11	11	12	12	13	13
19	2	3	4	5	6	6	7	8	8	9	10	10	11	11	12	12	13	13	13
20	2	3	4	5	6	6	7	8	9	9	10	10	11	12	12	13	13	13	14

n_1 \ n_2	2	3	4	5	6	7	8	9	10	11	12	13	14	15	16	17	18	19	20
2																			
3																			
4				9	9														
5			9	10	10	11	11												
6			9	10	11	12	12	13	13	13	13								
7				11	12	13	13	14	14	14	14	15	15	15					
8				11	12	13	14	14	15	15	16	16	16	16	17	17	17	17	17
9					13	14	14	15	16	16	16	17	17	18	18	18	18	18	18
10					13	14	15	16	16	17	17	18	18	18	19	19	19	20	20
11					13	14	15	16	17	17	18	19	19	19	20	20	20	21	21
12					13	14	16	16	17	18	19	19	20	20	21	21	21	22	22
13						15	16	17	18	19	19	20	20	21	21	22	22	23	23
14						15	16	17	18	19	20	20	21	22	22	23	23	23	24
15						15	16	18	18	19	20	21	22	22	23	23	24	24	25
16							17	18	19	20	21	21	22	23	23	24	25	25	25
17							17	18	19	20	21	22	23	23	24	25	25	26	26
18							17	18	19	20	21	22	23	24	25	25	26	26	27
19							17	18	20	21	22	23	23	24	25	26	26	27	27
20							17	18	20	21	22	23	24	25	25	26	27	27	28

Given in the bodies of the two sections of Table 26 are critical values of r for various values of n_1 and n_2. For the *one-sample* runs test, any value of r which is ≤ than that shown in the top section or ≥ than that shown in the bottom section is significant at the .05 level. For the *Wald-Wolfowitz two-sample* runs test, any value of r which is ≤ than that shown in the top section is significant at the .05 level.

If either n_1 or n_2 or both n_1 and n_2 are larger than 20 these tables cannot be used for tests of randomness. However, since the sampling distribution under H_0 for r is approximately normal for such large samples a normal distribution table may be used.

In using Table 26:

Let n_1 = the number of elements of one kind (heads)

  n_2 = the number of elements of other kind (tails)

  N = the total number of observed events ($n_1 + n_2$)

Both sections of Table 26 have to be used if a two-tailed test is involved. For example, in a coin-tossing experiment, assume the following run: HHHHHHHTTHHHHTTTTTTTT, which gives 4 runs or $r = 4$, making the material subject to use by the first section with n_1 being 9 (heads) and n_2 being 10 (tails), thereby totaling 19. Reference to the first section for an n_1 of 9 and an n_2 of 10 gives a value of 5; the value of 16 is located in the second section for an n_2 of 10 and an n_1 of 9. A random sample, therefore, would be expected to contain more than 5 runs but less than 16. Any observed r of 5 or less or of 16 or more is in the region of rejection. Since the observed $r = 4$ is smaller than 5, the H_0 is rejected at the .05 level; that is, since the H_0 specifies that the fall of the coins is random, the H_1 stating that the fall of the coins is not random is accepted instead.

Table 27

Critical Lower-Tail Values of r for Binomial Distribution with $p = \frac{1}{2}$

n	$\alpha = 0.005$		$\alpha = 0.01$		$\alpha = 0.025$		$\alpha = 0.05$	
5							0	(.0313)
6					0	(.0156)	0	(.0156)
7			0	(.0078)	0	(.0078)	0	(.0078)
8	0	(.0039)	0	(.0039)	0	(.0039)	1	(.0352)
9	0	(.0020)	0	(.0020)	1	(.0195)	1	(.0195)
10	0	(.0010)	0	(.0010)	1	(.0107)	1	(.0107)
11	0	(.0005)	1	(.0059)	1	(.0059)	2	(.0327)
12	1	(.0032)	1	(.0032)	2	(.0193)	2	(.0193)
13	1	(.0017)	1	(.0017)	2	(.0112)	3	(.0461)
14	1	(.0009)	2	(.0065)	2	(.0065)	3	(.0287)
15	2	(.0037)	2	(.0037)	3	(.0176)	3	(.0176)
16	2	(.0021)	2	(.0021)	3	(.0106)	4	(.0384)
17	2	(.0012)	3	(.0064)	4	(.0245)	4	(.0245)
18	3	(.0038)	3	(.0038)	4	(.0154)	5	(.0481)
19	3	(.0022)	4	(.0096)	4	(.0096)	5	(.0318)
20	3	(.0013)	4	(.0059)	5	(.0207)	5	(.0207)
21	4	(.0036)	4	(.0036)	5	(.0133)	6	(.0392)
22	4	(.0022)	5	(.0085)	5	(.0085)	6	(.0262)
23	4	(.0013)	5	(.0053)	6	(.0173)	7	(.0466)
24	5	(.0033)	5	(.0033)	6	(.0113)	7	(.0320)
25	5	(.0020)	6	(.0073)	7	(.0216)	7	(.0216)
26	6	(.0047)	6	(.0047)	7	(.0145)	8	(.0378)
27	6	(.0030)	7	(.0096)	7	(.0096)	8	(.0261)
28	6	(.0019)	7	(.0063)	8	(.0178)	9	(.0436)
29	7	(.0041)	7	(.0041)	8	(.0121)	9	(.0307)
30	7	(.0026)	8	(.0081)	9	(.0214)	10	(.0494)
31	7	(.0017)	8	(.0053)	9	(.0147)	10	(.0354)
32	8	(.0035)	8	(.0035)	9	(.0100)	10	(.0251)
33	8	(.0023)	9	(.0068)	10	(.0175)	11	(.0401)
34	9	(.0045)	9	(.0045)	10	(.0122)	11	(.0288)
35	9	(.0030)	10	(.0083)	11	(.0205)	12	(.0448)
36	9	(.0020)	10	(.0057)	11	(.0144)	12	(.0326)
37	10	(.0038)	10	(.0038)	12	(.0235)	13	(.0494)
38	10	(.0025)	11	(.0069)	12	(.0168)	13	(.0365)
39	11	(.0047)	11	(.0047)	12	(.0119)	13	(.0266)
40	11	(.0032)	12	(.0083)	13	(.0192)	14	(.0403)
41	11	(.0022)	12	(.0058)	13	(.0138)	14	(.0298)
42	12	(.0040)	13	(.0098)	14	(.0218)	15	(.0442)
43	12	(.0027)	13	(.0069)	14	(.0158)	15	(.0330)
44	13	(.0048)	13	(.0048)	15	(.0244)	16	(.0481)
45	13	(.0033)	14	(.0080)	15	(.0178)	16	(.0362)
46	13	(.0023)	14	(.0057)	15	(.0129)	16	(.0270)
47	14	(.0040)	15	(.0093)	16	(.0200)	17	(.0395)
48	14	(.0028)	15	(.0066)	16	(.0147)	17	(.0297)
49	15	(.0047)	15	(.0047)	17	(.0222)	18	(.0427)
50	15	(.0033)	16	(.0077)	17	(.0164)	18	(.0325)

Note: Exact probabilities are shown in parentheses.

Discussion

For statistical background of the sign test see the appropriate alphabetical listing of the term in this handbook. The value for p most frequently hypothesized by the sign test is 1/2. Table 27 gives the critical values of r for N's from 5-50 when $p = 1/2$. When the H_0 states that $p = 1/2$, r is significant approximately at the 0.05 level for a two-tailed test if the absolute difference between the number of successes and the number of failures equals or exceeds 2 = N.

For two-tailed values from .01 through .50, see Table 2. Table 1 may also be used for other values that can be applied in the sign test.

Table 27 Null and Alternative Hypotheses

H_0: The two matched samples N_1 and N_2 are drawn from populations with identical distributions, $p(+) = p(-) = 0.5$; an equal number of positive and negative differences between pairs is expected if only chance determines these differences, i.e. the theoretical probability of a plus = probability of a minus = 0.5.

H_1: The parent populations represented by the matched samples are different: $p(+) \neq p(-) \neq 0.5$.

Steps in Procedure for Using the Test

1. A series of paired observations is required. Find the sign of the difference between each pair of scores.
2. Count the number of times a plus appears and a minus appears. If ties occur in a few pairs, eliminate the pairs and reduce N accordingly. Many ties make the test undesirable.
3. If plus signs outnumber minus, the number of minus signs is labeled "r." If minus signs outnumber plus signs, plus signs are labeled "r." The result, r, is referred to Table 27, which gives the probabilities of obtaining r's as small as the ones listed for a two-tailed test. For a one-tailed test, the probabilities are divided by 2.

Use of the Table and Example

The value calculated in the above steps must be equal to or smaller than the value listed in Table 27 under the desired alpha level (two-tailed) when N matched pairs have been considered in the calculation.

Pair	Treatment	Control	Sign of difference (T−C)
A	25	16	+
B	22	19	+
C	23	7	+
D	16	18	−
E	10	10	0
F	21	24	−
G	20	9	+
H	14	16	−
I	26	30	−
J	27	21	+
K	29	24	+

Here there are ten comparisons which show differences ($N = 10$); 6 are positive, 4 are negative. If $a = 0.05$, two tailed test for $N = 10$ matched pairs, the tabled value is 1. Since the smaller of the calculated values is larger than this, H_0 can *not* be rejected.

Table 28
Critical Values of Wilcoxon's T Statistic at Various Levels of Probability

	Level of significance for one-tailed test					Level of significance for one-tailed test			
	.05	.025	.01	.005		.05	.025	.01	.005
	Level of significance for two-tailed test					Level of significance for two-tailed test			
N	.10	.05	.02	.01	N	.10	.05	.02	.01
5	0	--	--	--	28	130	116	101	91
6	2	0	--	--	29	140	126	110	100
7	3	2	0	--	30	151	137	120	109
8	5	3	1	0	31	163	147	130	118
9	8	5	3	1	32	175	159	140	128
10	10	8	5	3	33	187	170	151	138
11	13	10	7	5	34	200	182	162	148
12	17	13	9	7	35	213	195	173	159
13	21	17	12	9	36	227	208	185	171
14	25	21	15	12	37	241	221	198	182
15	30	25	19	15	38	256	235	211	194
16	35	29	23	19	39	271	249	224	207
17	41	34	27	23	40	286	264	238	220
18	47	40	32	27	41	302	279	252	233
19	53	46	37	32	42	319	294	266	247
20	60	52	43	37	43	336	310	281	261
21	67	58	49	42	44	353	327	296	276
22	75	65	55	48	45	371	343	312	291
23	83	73	62	54	46	389	361	328	307
24	91	81	69	61	47	407	378	345	322
25	100	89	76	68	48	426	396	362	339
26	110	98	84	75	49	446	415	379	355
27	119	107	92	83	50	466	434	397	373

Discussion

The symbol T denotes the smaller sum of ranks associated with differences that are all of the same sign. For any given N (number of ranked differences), the obtained T is significant at a given level if it is equal to or less than the tabled value. (See Wilcoxon's Signed Ranks Test under Wilcoxon for definition under alphabetical listing).

Null and Alternative Hypotheses

H_0: The two matched samples N_1 and N_2 are drawn from populations with identical distributions: the sum of the positive ranks is approximately equal to the sum of the negative ranks.

H_1: The parent populations represented by the matched samples are different: the sum of the ranks will be significantly positive or negative.

Example and Use of Table

Assume that in an experiment concerned with 11 pairs there were the following distribution of scores for "treatment" and for "control."

Pair	Treatment	Control	Score Differences	Rank	Signed Rank
A	25	16	9	8	8
B	22	19	3	3.5	3.5
C	23	7	16	10	10
D	16	18	-2	1.5	-1.5
E	10	10	(0)	—	—
F	21	24	-3	3.5	-3.5
G	20	9	11	9	9
H	14	16	-2	1.5	-1.5
I	26	30	-4	5	-5
J	27	21	6	7	7
K	29	24	5	6	6

If $a = 0.05$, two-tailed test, for N = 10 matched pairs (note that the zero difference, pair E, was dropped from the calculation), T = 8. The computed T for this example is:

$$T = -1.5 + -3.5 + -1.5 + -5 = -11.5$$

Since the computed value (−11.5) is larger than the tabled value (8), H_0 can *not* be rejected.

Table 28 gives the critical absolute values for T when N matched pairs have been considered in the calculation. The smaller sum must be equal to or less than the tabled value to be significant at the level given.

Steps to Follow in the Procedure of the Test

1. Find the difference between each pair of scores, keeping the order of subtraction constant (in this example "control" is subtracted from "treatment").
2. Rank these scores from smallest to largest, disregarding algebraic signs. If ties or zero differences occur each difference receives the average rank for the set, with half being given positive signs, half negative signs. (Note: if the number of ties in a set is odd, one may be randomly discarded. This, of course, reduces the number of pairs being ranked by one. It is often considered to be poor practice, however, to eliminate any ties since ties are considered evidence for retention of the H_0.)
3. Attach the sign of the difference to each rank and so signify in a signed rank column.
4. Compute T, the sum of the ranks with the smaller sum (−1.5, −3.5, −1.5, and −5, totaling 11.5 as opposed to the larger sum which is 43.5).

Table 29

Critical Values of *U* and *U'* for a One-tailed Test at *a* = 0.00 or a Two-tailed Test at *a* = 0.01

To be significant for any given n_1 and n_2: Obtained U must be equal to or less than the value shown in the table. Obtained U' must be equal to or greater than the value shown in the table.

n_2 \ n_1	1	2	3	4	5	6	7	8	9	10	11	12	13	14	15	16	17	18	19	20
1	--	--	--	--	--	--	--	--	--	--	--	--	--	--	--	--	--	--	--	--
2	--	--	--	--	--	--	--	--	--	--	--	--	--	--	--	--	--	--	0/38	0/40
3	--	--	--	--	--	--	--	--	0/27	0/30	0/33	1/35	1/38	1/41	2/43	2/46	2/49	2/52	3/54	3/57
4	--	--	--	--	--	0/24	0/28	1/31	1/35	2/38	2/42	3/45	3/49	4/52	5/55	5/59	6/62	6/66	7/69	8/72
5	--	--	--	--	0/25	1/29	1/34	2/38	3/42	4/46	5/50	6/54	7/58	7/63	8/67	9/71	10/75	11/79	12/83	13/87
6	--	--	--	0/24	1/29	2/34	3/39	4/44	5/49	6/54	7/59	9/63	10/68	11/73	12/78	13/83	15/87	16/92	17/97	18/102
7	--	--	--	0/28	1/34	3/39	4/45	6/50	7/56	9/61	10/67	12/72	13/78	15/83	16/89	18/94	19/100	21/105	22/111	24/116
8	--	--	--	1/31	2/38	4/44	6/50	7/57	9/63	11/69	13/75	15/81	17/87	18/94	20/100	22/106	24/112	26/118	28/124	30/130
9	--	--	0/27	1/35	3/42	5/49	7/56	9/63	11/70	13/77	16/83	18/90	20/97	22/104	24/111	27/117	29/124	31/131	33/138	36/144
10	--	--	0/30	2/38	4/46	6/54	9/61	11/69	13/77	16/84	18/92	21/99	24/106	26/114	29/121	31/129	34/136	37/143	39/151	42/158
11	--	--	0/33	2/42	5/50	7/59	10/67	13/75	16/83	18/92	21/100	24/108	27/116	30/124	33/132	36/140	39/148	42/156	45/164	48/172
12	--	--	1/35	3/45	6/54	9/63	12/72	15/81	18/90	21/99	24/108	27/117	31/125	34/134	37/143	41/151	44/160	47/169	51/177	54/186
13	--	--	1/38	3/49	7/58	10/68	13/78	17/87	20/97	24/106	27/116	31/125	34/135	38/144	42/153	45/163	49/172	53/181	56/191	60/200
14	--	--	1/41	4/52	7/63	11/73	15/83	18/94	22/104	26/114	30/124	34/134	38/144	42/154	46/164	50/174	54/184	58/194	63/203	67/213
15	--	--	2/43	5/55	8/67	12/78	16/89	20/100	24/111	29/121	33/132	37/143	42/153	46/164	51/174	55/185	60/195	64/206	69/216	73/227
16	--	--	2/46	5/59	9/71	13/83	18/94	22/106	27/117	31/129	36/140	41/151	45/163	50/174	55/185	60/196	65/207	70/218	74/230	79/241
17	--	--	2/49	6/62	10/75	15/87	19/100	24/112	29/124	34/136	39/148	44/160	49/172	54/184	60/195	65/207	70/219	75/231	81/242	86/254
18	--	--	2/52	6/66	11/79	16/92	21/105	26/118	31/131	37/143	42/156	47/169	53/181	58/194	64/206	70/218	75/231	81/243	87/255	92/268
19	--	0/38	3/54	7/69	12/83	17/97	22/111	28/124	33/138	39/151	45/164	51/177	56/191	63/203	69/216	74/230	81/242	87/255	93/268	99/281
20	--	0/40	3/57	8/72	13/87	18/102	24/116	30/130	36/144	42/158	48/172	54/186	60/200	67/213	73/227	79/241	86/254	92/268	99/281	105/295

(Dashes in the body of the table indicate that no decision is possible at the stated level of significance.)

Discussion

The Mann-Whitney U-test uses the actual ranks of the observations. It assumes that the two groups are being compared on a continuously distributed underlying variable and that the two groups represent independent samples. This is a very powerful nonparametric test.

Null and Alternative Hypotheses

H_0: the two samples N_1 and N_2 are drawn from populations with identical distributions (the order of n_1 scores preceding n_2 scores when they are ranked together is random).

H_1: the two samples N_1 and N_2 are not drawn from identical populations (the order of n_1 scores preceding n_2 scores is not that which one would expect by chance at the *a* level of significance).

Steps to Follow

1. Combine the N_1 and N_2 observations, keeping their sample origin identifiable.
2. Rank these observations (with rank of 1 to the smallest value) until all observations have been assigned ranks. Ties may be given an average rank.
3. Compute U = the smaller sum of ranks or U' = $N_1 N_2$ − U = the larger sum. Either one of the above statistics (U or U') may be used because of the design of Table 29. For most samples there is less chance of error if these sums of ranks are calculated by the following formulas:

(a) $N_1 N_2 + \dfrac{N_1 (N_1 + 1)}{2} - R_1 =$ N_1 sum of ranks

(b) $N_1 N_2 + \dfrac{N_2 (N_2 + 1)}{2} - R_2 =$ N_2 sum of ranks

where R_x = sum of ranks assigned to a group with a sample size of N_x. The smaller of the above calculations (a or b) is U.

Table 29 (continued)

To be significant for any given n_1 and n_2: Obtained U must be equal to or <u>less than</u> the value shown in the table.
Obtained U′ must be equal to or <u>greater than</u> the value shown in the table.

Values shown as U (top) / U′ (bottom).

n_2 \ n_1	1	2	3	4	5	6	7	8	9	10	11	12	13	14	15	16	17	18	19	20
1	--	--	--	--	--	--	--	--	--	--	--	--	--	--	--	--	--	--	--	--
2	--	--	--	--	--	--	--	--	--	--	--	--	0/26	0/28	0/30	0/32	0/34	0/36	1/37	1/39
3	--	--	--	--	--	--	0/21	0/24	1/26	1/29	1/32	2/34	2/37	2/40	3/42	3/45	4/47	4/50	4/52	5/55
4	--	--	--	--	0/20	1/23	1/27	2/30	3/33	3/37	4/40	5/43	5/47	6/50	7/53	7/57	8/60	9/63	9/67	10/70
5	--	--	--	0/20	1/24	2/28	3/32	4/36	5/40	6/44	7/48	8/52	9/56	10/60	11/64	12/68	13/72	14/76	15/80	16/84
6	--	--	--	1/23	2/28	3/33	4/38	6/42	7/47	8/52	9/57	11/61	12/66	13/71	15/75	16/80	18/84	19/89	20/94	22/93
7	--	--	0/21	1/27	3/32	4/38	6/43	7/49	9/54	11/59	12/65	14/70	16/75	17/81	19/86	21/91	23/96	24/102	26/107	28/112
8	--	--	0/24	2/30	4/36	6/42	7/49	9/55	11/61	13/67	15/73	17/79	20/84	22/90	24/96	26/102	28/108	30/114	32/120	34/126
9	--	--	1/26	3/33	5/40	7/47	9/54	11/61	14/67	16/74	18/81	21/87	23/94	26/100	28/107	31/113	33/120	36/126	38/133	40/140
10	--	--	1/29	3/37	6/44	8/52	11/59	13/67	16/74	19/81	22/88	24/96	27/103	30/110	33/117	36/124	38/132	41/139	44/146	47/153
11	--	--	1/32	4/40	7/48	9/57	12/65	15/73	18/81	22/88	25/96	28/104	31/112	34/120	37/128	41/135	44/143	47/151	50/159	53/167
12	--	--	2/34	5/43	8/52	11/61	14/70	17/79	21/87	24/96	28/104	31/113	35/121	38/130	42/138	46/146	49/155	53/163	56/172	60/180
13	--	0/26	2/37	5/47	9/56	12/66	16/75	20/84	23/94	27/103	31/112	35/121	39/130	43/139	47/148	51/157	55/166	59/175	63/184	67/193
14	--	0/28	2/40	6/50	10/60	13/71	17/81	22/90	26/100	30/110	34/120	38/130	43/139	47/149	51/159	56/168	60/178	65/187	69/197	73/207
15	--	0/30	3/42	7/53	11/64	15/75	19/86	24/96	28/107	33/117	37/128	42/138	47/148	51/159	56/169	61/179	66/189	70/200	75/210	80/220
16	--	0/32	3/45	7/57	12/68	16/80	21/91	26/102	31/113	36/124	41/135	46/146	51/157	56/168	61/179	66/190	71/201	76/212	82/222	87/233
17	--	0/34	4/47	8/60	13/72	18/84	23/96	28/108	33/120	38/132	44/143	49/155	55/166	60/178	66/189	71/201	77/212	82/224	88/234	93/247
18	--	0/36	4/50	9/63	14/76	19/89	24/102	30/114	36/126	41/139	47/151	53/163	59/175	65/187	70/200	76/212	82/224	88/236	94/248	100/260
19	--	1/37	4/53	9/67	15/80	20/94	26/107	32/120	38/133	44/146	50/159	56/172	63/184	69/197	75/210	82/222	88/235	94/248	101/260	107/273
20	--	1/39	5/55	10/70	16/84	22/98	28/112	34/126	40/140	47/153	53/167	60/180	67/193	73/207	80/220	87/233	93/247	100/260	107/273	114/286

(Dashes in the body of the table indicate that no decision is possible at the stated level of significance.)

Note

Under the null hypothesis the number of times an n_1 precedes an n_2 should approximate the number of times an n_2 precedes an n_1. Thus U should be similar to U′ in value. If H_0 is not maintained, then the bulk of the N_1 sample should fall on one side of the bulk of the N_2 cases, as the rankings would not be random.

Use of the Table and Example

For a given N_1 and N_2, the tabled values give the upper and lower limits at or outside of which the computed U or U′ value must fall in order to be significant at the a level specified in the table.

Example:

Sample 1	Ranks	Sample 2	Ranks
9	6	2	1
3	2.5	7	5
3	2.5	11	7
6	4	13	8
		14	9
$R_1 = 15$		$R_2 = 30$	

$U = 4(5) + 4(5)/2 - 15 = 20 + 10 - 15 = 15$
$U' = 4(5) + 5(6)/2 - 30 = 20 + 15 - 30 = 5$

If $a = 0.05$, two-tailed test, for $N_1 = 4$ and $N_2 = 5$, the calculated value must be equal to or less than 1 for U, or equal to or greater than 19 for U′ (by reference to Table 29). Since the calculated values fall *within* these limits, the H_0 is retained or not rejected.

To be significant for any given n_1 and n_2: Obtained U must be equal to or <u>less than</u> the value shown in the table. Obtained U' must be equal to or <u>greater than</u> the value shown in the table.

n_2\\n_1	1	2	3	4	5	6	7	8	9	10	11	12	13	14	15	16	17	18	19	20
1	--	--	--	--	--	--	--	--	--	--	--	--	--	--	--	--	--	--	--	--
2	--	--	--	--	--	--	--	0/16	0/18	0/20	0/22	1/23	1/25	1/27	1/29	1/31	2/32	2/34	2/36	2/38
3	--	--	--	--	0/15	1/17	1/20	2/22	2/25	3/27	3/30	4/32	4/35	5/37	5/40	6/42	6/45	7/47	7/50	8/52
4	--	--	--	0/16	1/19	2/22	3/25	4/28	4/32	5/35	6/38	7/41	8/44	9/47	10/50	11/53	11/57	12/60	13/63	13/67
5	--	--	0/15	1/19	2/23	3/27	5/30	6/34	7/38	8/42	9/46	11/49	12/53	13/57	14/61	15/65	17/68	18/72	19/76	20/80
6	--	--	1/17	2/22	3/27	5/31	6/36	8/40	10/44	11/49	13/53	14/58	16/62	17/67	19/71	21/75	22/80	24/84	25/89	27/93
7	--	--	1/20	3/25	5/30	6/36	8/41	10/46	12/51	14/56	16/61	18/66	20/71	22/76	24/81	26/86	28/91	30/96	32/101	34/106
8	--	0/16	2/22	4/28	6/34	8/40	10/46	13/51	15/57	17/63	19/69	22/74	24/80	26/86	29/91	31/97	34/102	36/108	38/111	41/119
9	--	0/18	2/25	4/32	7/38	10/44	12/51	15/57	17/64	20/70	23/76	26/82	28/89	31/95	34/101	37/107	39/114	42/120	45/126	48/132
10	--	0/20	3/27	5/35	8/42	11/49	14/56	17/63	20/70	23/77	26/84	29/91	33/97	36/104	39/111	42/118	45/125	48/132	52/138	55/145
11	--	0/22	3/30	6/38	9/46	13/53	16/61	19/69	23/76	26/84	30/91	33/99	37/106	40/114	44/121	47/129	51/136	55/143	58/151	62/158
12	--	1/23	4/32	7/41	11/49	14/58	18/66	22/74	26/82	29/91	33/99	37/107	41/115	45/123	49/131	53/139	57/147	61/155	65/163	69/171
13	--	1/25	4/35	8/44	12/53	16/62	20/71	24/80	28/89	33/97	37/106	41/115	45/124	50/132	54/141	59/149	63/158	67/167	72/175	76/184
14	--	1/27	5/37	9/47	13/57	17/67	22/76	26/86	31/95	36/104	40/114	45/123	50/132	55/141	59/151	64/160	67/171	74/178	78/188	83/197
15	--	1/29	5/40	10/50	14/61	19/71	24/81	29/91	34/101	39/111	44/121	49/131	54/141	59/151	64/161	70/170	75/180	80/190	85/200	90/210
16	--	1/31	6/42	11/53	15/65	21/75	26/86	31/97	37/107	42/118	47/129	53/139	59/149	64/160	70/170	75/181	81/191	86/202	92/212	98/222
17	--	2/32	6/45	11/57	17/68	22/80	28/91	34/102	39/114	45/125	51/136	57/147	63/158	67/171	75/180	81/191	87/202	93/213	99/224	105/235
18	--	2/34	7/47	12/60	18/72	24/84	30/96	36/108	42/120	48/132	55/143	61/155	67/167	74/178	80/190	86/202	93/213	99/225	106/236	112/248
19	--	2/36	7/50	13/63	19/76	25/89	32/101	38/114	45/126	52/138	58/151	65/163	72/175	78/188	85/200	92/212	99/224	106/236	113/248	119/261
20	--	2/38	8/52	13/67	20/80	27/93	34/106	41/119	48/132	55/145	62/158	69/171	76/184	83/197	90/210	98/222	105/235	112/248	119/261	127/273

(Dashes in the body of the table indicate that no decision is possible at the stated level of significance.)

Table 29 (continued)

To be significant for any given n_1 and n_2: Obtained U must be equal to or <u>less than</u> the value shown in the table.
Obtained U' must be equal to or <u>greater than</u> the value shown in the table.

$n_2 \backslash n_1$	1	2	3	4	5	6	7	8	9	10	11	12	13	14	15	16	17	18	19	20
1	--	--	--	--	--	--	--	--	--	--	--	--	--	--	--	--	--	--	0/19	0/20
2	--	--	--	--	0/10	0/12	0/14	1/15	1/17	1/19	1/21	2/22	2/24	2/26	3/27	3/29	3/31	4/32	4/34	4/36
3	--	--	0/9	0/12	1/14	2/16	2/19	3/21	3/24	4/26	5/28	5/31	6/33	7/35	7/38	8/40	9/42	9/45	10/47	11/49
4	--	--	0/12	1/15	2/18	3/21	4/24	5/27	6/30	7/33	8/36	9/39	10/42	11/45	12/48	14/50	15/53	16/56	17/59	18/62
5	--	0/10	1/14	2/18	4/21	5/25	6/29	8/32	9/36	11/39	12/43	13/47	15/50	16/54	18/57	19/61	20/65	22/68	23/72	25/75
6	--	0/12	2/16	3/21	5/25	7/29	8/34	10/38	12/42	14/46	16/50	17/55	19/59	21/63	23/67	25/71	26/76	28/80	30/84	32/88
7	--	0/14	2/19	4/24	6/29	8/34	11/38	13/43	15/48	17/53	19/58	21/63	24/67	26/72	28/77	30/82	33/86	35/91	37/96	39/101
8	--	1/15	3/21	5/27	8/32	10/38	13/43	15/49	18/54	20/60	23/65	26/70	28/76	31/81	33/87	36/92	39/97	41/103	44/108	47/113
9	--	1/17	3/24	6/30	9/36	12/42	15/48	18/54	21/60	24/66	27/72	30/78	33/84	36/90	39/96	42/102	45/108	48/114	51/120	54/126
10	--	1/19	4/26	7/33	11/39	14/46	17/53	20/60	24/66	27/73	31/79	34/86	37/93	41/99	44/106	48/112	51/119	55/125	58/132	62/138
11	--	1/21	5/28	8/36	12/43	16/50	19/58	23/65	27/72	31/79	34/87	38/94	42/101	46/108	50/115	54/122	57/130	61/137	65/144	69/151
12	--	2/22	5/31	9/39	13/47	17/55	21/63	26/70	30/78	34/86	38/94	42/102	47/109	51/117	55/125	60/132	64/140	68/148	72/156	77/163
13	--	2/24	6/33	10/42	15/50	19/59	24/67	28/76	33/84	37/93	42/101	47/109	51/118	56/126	61/134	65/143	70/151	75/159	80/167	84/176
14	--	2/26	7/35	11/45	16/54	21/63	26/72	31/81	36/90	41/99	46/108	51/117	56/126	61/135	66/144	71/153	77/161	82/170	87/179	92/188
15	--	3/27	7/38	12/48	18/57	23/67	28/77	33/87	39/96	44/106	50/115	55/125	61/134	66/144	72/153	77/163	83/172	88/182	94/191	100/200
16	--	3/29	8/40	14/50	19/61	25/71	30/82	36/92	42/102	48/112	54/122	60/132	65/143	71/153	77/163	83/173	89/183	95/193	101/203	107/213
17	--	3/31	9/42	15/53	20/65	26/76	33/86	39/97	45/108	51/119	57/130	64/140	70/151	77/161	83/172	89/183	96/193	102/204	109/214	115/225
18	--	4/32	9/45	16/56	22/68	28/80	35/91	41/103	48/114	55/123	61/137	68/148	75/159	82/170	88/182	95/193	102/204	109/215	116/226	123/237
19	0/19	4/34	10/47	17/59	23/72	30/84	37/96	44/108	51/120	58/132	65/144	72/156	80/167	87/179	94/191	101/203	109/214	116/226	123/238	130/250
20	0/20	4/36	11/49	18/62	25/75	32/88	39/101	47/113	54/126	62/138	69/151	77/163	84/176	92/188	100/200	107/213	115/225	123/237	130/250	138/262

(Dashes in the body of the table indicate that no decision is possible at the stated level of significance.)

Table 30

Critical Values of r_{rho}: The Spearman
Rank-Order Correlation Coefficient

N	Significance level (one-tailed test)	
	.05	.01
4	1.000	
5	.900	1.000
6	.829	.943
7	.714	.893
8	.643	.833
9	.600	.783
10	.564	.746
12	.506	.712
14	.456	.645
16	.425	.601
18	.399	.564
20	.377	.534
22	.359	.508
24	.343	.485
26	.329	.465
28	.317	.448
30	.306	.432

Discussion

The distribution of r_{rho} (or ρ) is symmetrical about the value of zero. As n becomes larger, r_{rho} approaches the normal curve and is cut off at -1 and 1, as shown here:

The curve shows the distribution of r_{rho}, assuming that the population ρ is zero.

The Spearman rank-order correlation coefficient is designed for use with variables which are ordinally scaled. Table 30 can be used to test the null hypothesis that: $H_0 : \rho = 0, \rho \leq 0$, or $\rho \geq 0$ where ρ is the population rank-difference correlation coefficient. To obtain r_{rho} it is necessary first to rank the N observations independently on the two variables before computing. The r_{rho} represents the extent to which the rankings between the two samples are the same. The use of r_{rho} entails consideration of certain assumptions: that the measures are continuously distributed; that there are not many tie scores; that the number of cases is small; and that no two subjects have identical quantities on a specific characteristic.

Null and Alternative Hypotheses

H_0: $r_{rho} = 0$; there is no association between the pairs of scores.
H_1: $r_{rho} \neq 0$; there is an association between the pairs of scores.

Use of Table and Example

Table 30 gives critical values required for determining significance at various one- and two-tailed alpha levels. Critical values of r_{rho} depend on degrees of freedom equal to the number of pairs (N) under consideration. Larger values of r_{rho} are required for significance if smaller degrees of freedom are involved.

To use Table 30, first locate the appropriate df for the problem in the N column. Scan to the right locating the desired alpha level. The value in the body of the table located at the intersection of the appropriate row and column is the minimum r_{rho} value needed for determining significance. The table provides one- and two-tailed probabilities corresponding to various values of r_{rho} and n. For example, if N = 9, a r_{rho} of .600 is required for significance at the .05 level (one-tailed test) and a value of .683 is needed for significance at the .05 level, two-tailed test. Interpretation is the same as for the Pearson r. For N > 30 a t test statistic can be used to determine if ρ is different from zero. The test statistic

$$t = r_{rho} \sqrt{\frac{N-2}{1-r_{rho}^2}}$$

is approximately distributed as the t distribution with df = N − 2.

Table 31a

Critical Values for Kendall's Coefficient of Concordance

k	N					Additional values for N = 3	
	3†	4	5	6	7	k	s
Values at the .05 level of significance							
3			64.4	103.9	157.3	9	54.0
4		49.5	88.4	143.3	217.0	12	71.9
5		62.6	112.3	182.4	276.2	14	83.8
6		75.7	136.1	221.4	335.2	16	95.8
8	48.1	101.7	183.7	299.0	453.1	18	107.7
10	60.0	127.8	231.2	376.7	571.0		
15	89.8	192.9	349.8	570.5	864.9		
20	119.7	258.0	468.5	764.4	1,158.7		
Values at the .01 level of significance							
3			75.6	122.8	185.6	9	75.9
4		61.4	109.3	176.2	265.0	12	103.5
5		80.5	142.8	229.4	343.8	14	121.9
6		99.5	176.1	282.4	422.6	16	140.2
8	66.8	137.4	242.7	388.3	579.9	18	158.6
10	85.1	175.3	309.1	494.0	737.0		
15	131.0	269.8	475.2	758.2	1,129.5		
20	177.0	364.2	641.2	1,022.2	1,521.9		

Discussion

For a definition and formula for this coefficient see appropriate alphabetical listing in this handbook for *Kendall's coefficient of concordance.*

Table 31a provides critical values for 0.05 and 0.01 levels of significance assuming that the k (3 or more) sets of rankings are statistically independent. Additional values for N = 3 are listed in the extreme right two columns. For larger values of N, the quantity $k(N-1)W$ is distributed approximately as a χ^2 variate with $N - 1$ df.

Example

Assume that 5 senior professors are to rank the overall effectiveness of 7 junior professors for consideration of promotion, and that they are also interested in determining the relationship among the ratings of all 5 professors.

Null and Alternative Hypotheses

H_0: k sets of ranks are statistically independent, i.e., there is no agreement among the raters.
H_1: k sets of ranks are not independent, i.e., there is agreement among the judges or raters.

Steps to Follow

A table can be set up with the 7 junior professors listed in the first column, and their respective rankings by each of the 5 raters noted in the second column. Rankings for each of the 7 are then summed for the rows to make up the third column (Rj). Sum the Rj column and divide by N to get mean value of Rj. In a fourth column (D), the difference of the sum of ranks of each row is obtained by subtracting from the mean, disregarding signs. This D column is squared to give the s column (or D^2), and then summed. Since N is less than 7, Table 31a will give critical values of s associated with W's significant at the .05 and .01 levels. N = the number of cases to be ranked; k = the number of judges assigning ranks; and s = sum of squares of deviations from the Rj mean. The value of W is obtained by the formula

$$W = \frac{s}{1/12k^2(N^3 - N)}$$

Use of Table

Assume that for the k of 5 and N of 7 that a W of .295 is obtained. Since perfect agreement is indicated by W = 1 and lack of agreement by W = 0, this is a relatively low measure of agreement. Significance of the W may be determined by obtaining the probability associated with the occurrence under H_0 of a value as large as the s with which it is associated. Let us assume that the s under consideration here is 35. Table 31a, for a k of 5 and an N of 7 shows that an s of 35 is not even significant at the .05 level (since it would have to be at least 276.2). Therefore, the H_0 is maintained; there is no agreement among the raters.

Table 31b

Probabilities in the Kendall Rank Correlation Coefficient

S	Values of N 4	5	8	9	S	Values of N 6	7	10
0	.625	.592	.548	.540	1	.500	.500	.500
2	.375	.408	.452	.460	3	.360	.386	.431
4	.167	.242	.360	.381	5	.235	.281	.364
6	.042	.117	.274	.306	7	.136	191	.300
8		.042	.199	.238	9	.068	.119	.242
10		.0083	.138	.179	11	.028	.068	.190
12			.089	.130	13	.0083	.035	.146
14			.054	.090	15	.0014	.015	.108
16			.031	.060	17		.0054	.078
18			.016	.038	19		.0014	.054
20			.0071	.022	21		.00020	.036
22			.0028	.012	23			.023
24			.00087	.0063	25			.014
26			.00019	.0029	27			.0083
28			.000025	.0012	29			.0046
30				.00043	31			.0023
32				.00012	33			.0011
34				.000025	35			.00047
36				.0000028	37			.00018
					39			.000058
					41			.000015
					43			.0000028
					45			.00000028

Table 31b lists S values for N between 4 and 10, assuming that the two sets of rankings are statistically independent. Kendall's tau has a -1 value when paired ranks are in inverse order and a $+1$ value if in normal order. The table is used to determine the exact probability associated with the occurrence under H_0 of any value as extreme as an observed S, the S representing the summed results, obtained in the following manner: In two sets of rankings, one being in natural sequence and the other in disarray, S is calculated by comparing each rank on, say Y, with every other rank, there being $N(N-1)/2$ such comparisons for N ranks. A weight of $+1$ is assigned to a pair ranked in sequence, say 3 and 4, but a -1 is assigned to a pair ranked in inverse order, say 4 and 3. S is the sum of such weights over all $N(N-1)/2$ such comparisons. (See alphabetical entry of *Kendall's Rank-Correlation Coefficient, tau*, for formula and additional statistical information).

In determining the significance of an observed relation between two samples of ranks it is necessary to obtain S and then refer to Table 31b for determining the one-tailed probability associated with that particular value. The null hypothesis may be rejected if the $p \leqslant a$. For example, with an $N = 5$ and an obtained S of 8, Table 31b shows that an $S = 8$ for $N = 5$ has probability of occurrence under H_0 of $p = .042$. Thus H_0 could be rejected at significance level $a = .042$, and conclude that the two variables under consideration are associated in the population from which the assumed sample was drawn.

If N is larger than 10, tau may be considered to be normally distributed and the probability associated with the occurrence under H_0 of any value as extreme as an observed value of r may be determined by computing the value of z and determining its significance by referring to a normal distribution table. (See Siegel, pp. 213-223; Ferguson, pp. 220-225, 365-369.)

Table 32

Probabilities Associated with Values as Large as Observed Values of H
in the Kruskal-Wallis One-Way Analysis of Variance by Ranks

Sample sizes			H	p	Sample sizes			H	p
n_1	n_2	n_3			n_1	n_2	n_3		
2	1	1	2.7000	.500	4	3	2	6.4444	.008
								6.3000	.011
2	2	1	3.6000	.200				5.4444	.046
								5.4000	.051
2	2	2	4.5714	.067				4.5111	.098
			3.7143	.200				4.4444	.102
3	1	1	3.2000	.300	4	3	3	6.7455	.010
								6.7091	.013
3	2	1	4.2857	.100				5.7909	.046
			3.8571	.133				5.7273	.050
3	2	2	5.3572	.029				4.7091	.092
			4.7143	.048				4.7000	.101
			4.5000	.067					
			4.4643	.105	4	4	1	6.6667	.010
								6.1667	.022
3	3	1	5.1429	.043				4.9667	.048
			4.5714	.100				4.8667	.054
			4.0000	.129				4.1667	.082
3	3	2	6.2500	.011				4.0667	.102
			5.3611	.032	4	4	2	7.0364	.006
			5.1389	.061				6.8727	.011
			4.5556	.100				5.4545	.046
			4.2500	.121				5.2364	.052
3	3	3	7.2000	.004				4.5545	.098
			6.4889	.011				4.4455	.103
			5.6889	.029	4	4	3	7.1439	.010
			5.6000	.050				7.1364	.011
			5.0667	.086				5.5985	.049
			4.6222	.100				5.5758	.051
4	1	1	3.5714	.200				4.5455	.099
4	2	1	4.8214	.057				4.4773	.102
			4.5000	.076	4	4	4	7.6538	.008
			4.0179	.114				7.5385	.011
4	2	2	6.0000	.014				5.6923	.049
			5.3333	.033				5.6538	.054
			5.1250	.052				4.6539	.097
			4.4583	.100				4.5001	.104
			4.1667	.105	5	1	1	3.8571	.143
4	3	1	5.8333	.021	5	2	1	5.2500	.036
			5.2083	.050				5.0000	.048
			5.0000	.057				4.4500	.071
			4.0556	.093				4.2000	.095
			3.8889	.129				4.0500	.119

The Kruskal-Wallis test utilizes a statistic H derived from the formula explained under the alphabetical listing of Kruskal-Wallis ranks test. For more than 5 cases the H statistic has a chi-square distribution with $k - 1$ degrees of freedom, k being the number of independent samples. If the observed value of H is $\geqslant$ the chi square value for the previously set significance level and for the observed value of $df = k - 1$, then H_0 may be rejected at that selected level of significance. However, for $k = 3$ and N in each of the three samples being equal to or less than 5, the chi-square approximation to the sampling distribution of H does not hold. Exact probabilities for such sample sizes may then be obtained from Table 32.

The first column in Table 32 gives the number of cases for the various possible values of n_1, n_2, and n_3. The second column gives various values of H. The third column gives the probability (p) associated with the occurrence under H_0 of values as large as an observed H.

Null and Alternative Hypotheses

H_0: the k independent samples have been drawn from a common population. The null hypothesis is rejected for large values of H.

H_1: the k independent samples come from different populations.

The significance levels in the table give the probabilities of obtaining an observed value of H as large or larger than the associated value when the null hypothesis is true.

Table 32 (continued)

Sample sizes			H	p	Sample sizes			H	p
n_1	n_2	n_3			n_1	n_2	n_3		
5	2	2	6.5333	.008				5.6308	.050
			6.1333	.013				4.5487	.099
			5.1600	.034				4.5231	.103
			5.0400	.056	5	4	4	7.7604	.009
			4.3733	.090				7.7440	.011
			4.2933	.122				5.6571	.049
5	3	1	6.4000	.012				5.6176	.050
			4.9600	.048				4.6187	.100
			4.8711	.052				4.5527	.102
			4.0178	.095	5	5	1	7.3091	.009
			3.8400	.123				6.8364	.011
5	3	2	6.9091	.009				5.1273	.046
			6.8218	.010				4.9091	.053
			5.2509	.049				4.1091	.086
			5.1055	.052				4.0364	.105
			4.6509	.091	5	5	2	7.3385	.010
			4.4945	.101				7.2692	.010
5	3	3	7.0788	.009				5.3385	.047
			6.9818	.011				5.2462	.051
			5.6485	.049				4.6231	.097
			5.5152	.051				4.5077	.100
			4.5333	.097	5	5	3	7.5780	.010
			4.4121	.109				7.5429	.010
5	4	1	6.9545	.008				5.7055	.046
			6.8400	.011				5.6264	.051
			4.9855	.044				4.5451	.100
			4.8600	.056				4.5363	.102
			3.9873	.098	5	5	4	7.8229	.010
			3.9600	.102				7.7914	.010
5	4	2	7.2045	.009				5.6657	.049
			7.1182	.010				5.6429	.050
			5.2727	.049				4.5229	.099
			5.2682	.050				4.5200	.101
			4.5409	.098	5	5	5	8.0000	.009
			4.5182	.101				7.9800	.010
5	4	3	7.4449	.010				5.7800	.049
			7.3949	.011				5.6600	.051
			5.6564	.049				4.5600	.100
								4.5000	.102

Example and Use of Table

Assume that there are three samples which contain 5, 2, 2 cases respectively, and that an *H* has been computed and found to be 6.8555. Since, according to the table, the null hypothesis may be rejected at the .008 level of significance for an $H \geqslant 6.5333$, and since the hypothetical *H* of 6.8555 is larger than this value, then the null hypothesis may be rejected at this level: the samples do come from different populations.

(See Siegel, pp. 184-194 for additional examples and use of the Kruskal-Wallis test.)

Table 33 (continued)

n	n²	√n	√10n	n³	∛n	∛10n	∛100n
50	2 500	7.071 068	22.36068	125 000	3.684 031	7.937 005	17.09976
51	2 601	7.141 428	22.58318	132 651	3.708 430	7.989 570	17.21301
52	2 704	7.211 103	22.80351	140 608	3.732 511	8.041 452	17.32478
53	2 809	7.280 110	23.02173	148 877	3.756 286	8.092 672	17.43513
54	2 916	7.348 469	23.23790	157 464	3.779 763	8.143 253	17.54411
55	3 025	7.416 198	23.45208	166 375	3.802 952	8.193 213	17.65174
56	3 136	7.483 315	23.66432	175 616	3.825 862	8.242 571	17.75808
57	3 249	7.549 834	23.87467	185 193	3.848 501	8.291 344	17.86316
58	3 364	7.615 773	24.08319	195 112	3.870 877	8.339 551	17.96702
59	3 481	7.681 146	24.28992	205 379	3.892 996	8.387 207	18.06969
60	3 600	7.745 967	24.49490	216 000	3.914 868	8.434 327	18.17121
61	3 721	7.810 250	24.69818	226 981	3.936 497	8.480 926	18.27160
62	3 844	7.874 008	24.89980	238 328	3.957 892	8.527 019	18.37091
63	3 969	7.937 254	25.09980	250 047	3.979 057	8.572 619	18.46915
64	4 096	8.000 000	25.29822	262 144	4.000 000	8.617 739	18.56636
65	4 225	8.062 258	25.49510	274 625	4.020 726	8.662 391	18.66256
66	4 356	8.124 038	25.69047	287 496	4.041 240	8.706 588	18.75777
67	4 489	8.185 353	25.88436	300 763	4.061 548	8.750 340	18.85204
68	4 624	8.246 211	26.07681	314 432	4.081 655	8.793 659	18.94536
69	4 761	8.306 624	26.26785	328 509	4.101 566	8.836 556	19.03778
70	4 900	8.366 600	26.45751	343 000	4.121 285	8.879 040	19.12931
71	5 041	8.426 150	26.64583	357 911	4.140 818	8.921 121	19.21997
72	5 184	8.485 281	26.83282	373 248	4.160 168	8.962 809	19.30979
73	5 329	8.544 004	27.01851	389 017	4.179 339	9.004 113	19.39877
74	5 476	8.602 325	27.20294	405 224	4.198 336	9.045 042	19.48695
75	5 625	8.660 254	27.38613	421 875	4.217 163	9.085 603	19.57434
76	5 776	8.717 798	27.56810	438 976	4.235 824	9.125 805	19.66095
77	5 929	8.774 964	27.74887	456 533	4.254 321	9.165 656	19.74681
78	6 084	8.831 761	27.92848	474 552	4.272 659	9.205 164	19.83192
79	6 241	8.888 194	28.10694	493 039	4.290 840	9.244 335	19.91632
80	6 400	8.944 272	28.28427	512 000	4.308 869	9.283 178	20.00000
81	6 561	9.000 000	28.46050	531 441	4.326 749	9.321 698	20.08299
82	6 724	9.055 385	28.63564	551 368	4.344 481	9.359 902	20.16530
83	6 889	9.110 434	28.80972	571 787	4.362 071	9.397 796	20.24694
84	7 056	9.165 151	28.98275	592 704	4.379 519	9.435 388	20.32793
85	7 225	9.219 544	29.15476	614 125	4.396 830	9.472 682	20.40828
86	7 396	9.273 618	29.32576	636 056	4.414 005	9.509 685	20.48800
87	7 569	9.327 379	29.49576	658 503	4.431 048	9.546 403	20.56710
88	7 744	9.380 832	29.66479	681 472	4.447 960	9.582 840	20.64560
89	7 921	9.433 981	29.83287	704 969	4.464 745	9.619 002	20.72351
90	8 100	9.486 833	30.00000	729 000	4.481 405	9.654 894	20.80084
91	8 281	9.539 392	30.16621	753 571	4.497 941	9.690 521	20.87759
92	8 464	9.591 663	30.33150	778 688	4.514 357	9.725 888	20.95379
93	8 649	9.643 651	30.49590	804 357	4.530 655	9.761 000	21.02944
94	8 836	9.695 360	30.65942	830 584	4.546 836	9.795 861	21.10454
95	9 025	9.746 794	30.82207	857 375	4.562 903	9.830 476	21.17912
96	9 216	9.797 959	30.98387	884 736	4.578 857	9.864 848	21.25317
97	9 409	9.848 858	31.14482	912 673	4.594 701	9.898 983	21.32671
98	9 604	9.899 495	31.30495	941 192	4.610 436	9.932 884	21.39975
99	9 801	9.949 874	31.46427	970 299	4.626 065	9.966 555	21.47229
100	10 000	10.00000	31.62278	1 000 000	4.641 589	10.00000	21.54435

Table 33

Squares, Square Roots, Cubes, Cube Roots

(See p. 237 for explanations of tables.)

n	n²	√n	√10n	n³	∛n	∛10n	∛100n
1	1	1.000 000	3.162 278	1	1.000 000	2.154 435	4.641 589
2	4	1.414 214	4.472 136	8	1.259 921	2.714 418	5.848 035
3	9	1.732 051	5.477 226	27	1.442 250	3.107 233	6.694 330
4	16	2.000 000	6.324 555	64	1.587 401	3.419 952	7.368 063
5	25	2.236 068	7.071 068	125	1.709 976	3.684 031	7.937 005
6	36	2.449 490	7.745 967	216	1.817 121	3.914 868	8.434 327
7	49	2.645 751	8.366 600	343	1.912 931	4.121 285	8.879 040
8	64	2.828 427	8.944 272	512	2.000 000	4.308 869	9.283 178
9	81	3.000 000	9.486 833	729	2.080 084	4.481 405	9.654 894
10	100	3.162 278	10.00000	1 000	2.154 435	4.641 589	10.00000
11	121	3.316 625	10.48809	1 331	2.223 980	4.791 420	10.32280
12	144	3.464 102	10.95445	1 728	2.289 428	4.932 424	10.62659
13	169	3.605 551	11.40175	2 197	2.351 335	5.065 797	10.91393
14	196	3.741 657	11.83216	2 744	2.410 142	5.192 494	11.18689
15	225	3.872 983	12.24745	3 375	2.466 212	5.313 293	11.44714
16	256	4.000 000	12.64911	4 096	2.519 842	5.428 835	11.69607
17	289	4.123 106	13.03840	4 913	2.571 282	5.539 658	11.93483
18	324	4.242 641	13.41641	5 832	2.620 741	5.646 216	12.16440
19	361	4.358 899	13.78405	6 859	2.668 402	5.748 897	12.38562
20	400	4.472 136	14.14214	8 000	2.714 418	5.848 035	12.59921
21	441	4.582 576	14.49138	9 261	2.758 924	5.943 922	12.80579
22	484	4.690 416	14.83240	10 648	2.802 039	6.036 811	13.00591
23	529	4.795 832	15.16575	12 167	2.843 867	6.126 926	13.20006
24	576	4.898 979	15.49193	13 824	2.884 499	6.214 465	13.38866
25	625	5.000 000	15.81139	15 625	2.924 018	6.299 605	13.57209
26	676	5.099 020	16.12452	17 576	2.962 496	6.382 504	13.75069
27	729	5.196 152	16.43168	19 683	3.000 000	6.463 304	13.92477
28	784	5.291 503	16.73320	21 952	3.036 589	6.542 133	14.09460
29	841	5.385 165	17.02939	24 389	3.072 317	6.619 106	14.26043
30	900	5.477 226	17.32051	27 000	3.107 233	6.694 330	14.42250
31	961	5.567 764	17.60682	29 791	3.141 381	6.767 899	14.58100
32	1 024	5.656 854	17.88854	32 768	3.174 802	6.839 904	14.73613
33	1 089	5.744 563	18.16590	35 937	3.207 534	6.910 423	14.88806
34	1 156	5.830 952	18.43909	39 304	3.239 612	6.979 532	15.03695
35	1 225	5.916 080	18.70829	42 875	3.271 066	7.047 299	15.18294
36	1 296	6.000 000	18.97367	46 656	3.301 927	7.113 787	15.32619
37	1 369	6.082 763	19.23538	50 653	3.332 222	7.179 054	15.46680
38	1 444	6.164 414	19.49359	54 872	3.361 975	7.243 156	15.60491
39	1 521	6.244 998	19.74842	59 319	3.391 211	7.306 144	15.74061
40	1 600	6.324 555	20.00000	64 000	3.419 952	7.368 063	15.87401
41	1 681	6.403 124	20.24846	68 921	3.448 217	7.428 959	16.00521
42	1 764	6.480 741	20.49390	74 088	3.476 027	7.488 872	16.13429
43	1 849	6.557 439	20.73644	79 507	3.503 398	7.547 842	16.26133
44	1 936	6.633 250	20.97618	85 184	3.530 348	7.605 905	16.38643
45	2 025	6.708 204	21.21320	91 125	3.556 893	7.663 094	16.50964
46	2 116	6.782 330	21.44761	97 336	3.583 048	7.719 443	16.63103
47	2 209	6.855 655	21.67948	103 823	3.608 826	7.774 980	16.75069
48	2 304	6.928 203	21.90890	110 592	3.634 241	7.829 735	16.86865
49	2 401	7.000 000	22.13594	117 649	3.659 306	7.883 735	16.98499
50	2 500	7.071 068	22.36068	125 000	3.684 031	7.937 005	17.09976

Table 33 (continued)

n	n^2	$\sqrt{n}$	$\sqrt{10n}$	n^3	$\sqrt[3]{n}$	$\sqrt[3]{10n}$	$\sqrt[3]{100n}$
150	22 500	12.24745	38.72983	3 375 000	5.313 293	11.44714	24.66212
151	22 801	12.28821	38.85872	3 442 951	5.325 074	11.47252	24.71680
152	23 104	12.32883	38.98718	3 511 808	5.336 803	11.49779	24.77125
153	23 409	12.36932	39.11521	3 581 577	5.348 481	11.52295	24.82545
154	23 716	12.40967	39.24283	3 652 264	5.360 108	11.54800	24.87942
155	24 025	12.44990	39.37004	3 723 875	5.371 685	11.57295	24.93315
156	24 336	12.49000	39.49684	3 796 416	5.383 213	11.59778	24.98666
157	24 649	12.52996	39.62323	3 869 893	5.394 691	11.62251	25.03994
158	24 964	12.56981	39.74921	3 944 312	5.406 120	11.64713	25.09299
159	25 281	12.60952	39.87480	4 019 679	5.417 502	11.67165	25.14581
160	25 600	12.64911	40.00000	4 096 000	5.428 835	11.69607	25.19842
161	25 921	12.68858	40.12481	4 173 281	5.440 122	11.72039	25.25081
162	26 244	12.72792	40.24922	4 251 528	5.451 362	11.74460	25.30298
163	26 569	12.76715	40.37326	4 330 747	5.462 556	11.76872	25.35494
164	26 896	12.80625	40.49691	4 410 944	5.473 704	11.79274	25.40668
165	27 225	12.84523	40.62019	4 492 125	5.484 807	11.81666	25.45822
166	27 556	12.88410	40.74310	4 574 296	5.495 865	11.84048	25.50954
167	27 889	12.92285	40.86563	4 657 463	5.506 878	11.86421	25.56067
168	28 224	12.96148	40.98780	4 741 632	5.517 848	11.88784	25.61158
169	28 561	13.00000	41.10961	4 826 809	5.528 775	11.91138	25.66230
170	28 900	13.03840	41.23106	4 913 000	5.539 658	11.93483	25.71282
171	29 241	13.07670	41.35215	5 000 211	5.550 499	11.95819	25.76313
172	29 584	13.11488	41.47288	5 088 448	5.561 298	11.98145	25.81326
173	29 929	13.15295	41.59327	5 177 717	5.572 055	12.00463	25.86319
174	30 276	13.19091	41.71331	5 268 024	5.582 770	12.02771	25.91292
175	30 625	13.22876	41.83300	5 359 375	5.593 445	12.05071	25.96247
176	30 976	13.26650	41.95235	5 451 776	5.604 079	12.07362	26.01183
177	31 329	13.30413	42.07137	5 545 233	5.614 672	12.09645	26.06100
178	31 684	13.34166	42.19005	5 639 752	5.625 226	12.11918	26.10999
179	32 041	13.37909	42.30839	5 735 339	5.635 741	12.14184	26.15879
180	32 400	13.41641	42.42641	5 832 000	5.646 216	12.16440	26.20741
181	32 761	13.45362	42.54409	5 929 741	5.656 653	12.18689	26.25586
182	33 124	13.49074	42.66146	6 028 568	5.667 051	12.20929	26.30412
183	33 489	13.52775	42.77850	6 128 487	5.677 411	12.23161	26.35221
184	33 856	13.56466	42.89522	6 229 504	5.687 734	12.25385	26.40012
185	34 225	13.60147	43.01163	6 331 625	5.698 019	12.27601	26.44786
186	34 596	13.63818	43.12772	6 434 856	5.708 267	12.29809	26.49543
187	34 969	13.67479	43.24350	6 539 203	5.718 479	12.32009	26.54283
188	35 344	13.71131	43.35897	6 644 672	5.728 654	12.34201	26.59006
189	35 721	13.74773	43.47413	6 751 269	5.738 794	12.36386	26.63712
190	36 100	13.78405	43.58899	6 859 000	5.748 897	12.38562	26.68402
191	36 481	13.82027	43.70355	6 967 871	5.758 965	12.40731	26.73075
192	36 864	13.85641	43.81780	7 077 888	5.768 998	12.42893	26.77732
193	37 249	13.89244	43.93177	7 189 057	5.778 997	12.45047	26.82373
194	37 636	13.92839	44.04543	7 301 384	5.788 960	12.47194	26.86997
195	38 025	13.96424	44.15880	7 414 875	5.798 890	12.49333	26.91606
196	38 416	14.00000	44.27189	7 529 536	5.808 786	12.51465	26.96199
197	38 809	14.03567	44.38468	7 645 373	5.818 648	12.53590	27.00777
198	39 204	14.07125	44.49719	7 762 392	5.828 477	12.55707	27.05339
199	39 601	14.10674	44.60942	7 880 599	5.838 272	12.57818	27.09886
200	40 000	14.14214	44.72136	8 000 000	5.848 035	12.59921	27.14418

Table 33 (continued)

n	n^2	$\sqrt{n}$	$\sqrt{10n}$	n^3	$\sqrt[3]{n}$	$\sqrt[3]{10n}$	$\sqrt[3]{100n}$
100	10 000	10.00000	31.62278	1 000 000	4.641 589	10.00000	21.54435
101	10 201	10.04988	31.78050	1 030 301	4.657 010	10.03322	21.61592
102	10 404	10.09950	31.93744	1 061 208	4.672 329	10.06623	21.68703
103	10 609	10.14889	32.09361	1 092 727	4.687 548	10.09902	21.75767
104	10 816	10.19804	32.24903	1 124 864	4.702 669	10.13159	21.82786
105	11 025	10.24695	32.40370	1 157 625	4.717 694	10.16396	21.89760
106	11 236	10.29563	32.55764	1 191 016	4.732 623	10.19613	21.96689
107	11 449	10.34408	32.71085	1 225 043	4.747 459	10.22809	22.03575
108	11 664	10.39230	32.86335	1 259 712	4.762 203	10.25986	22.10419
109	11 881	10.44031	33.01515	1 295 029	4.776 856	10.29142	22.17220
110	12 100	10.48809	33.16625	1 331 000	4.791 420	10.32280	22.23980
111	12 321	10.53565	33.31666	1 367 631	4.805 896	10.35399	22.30699
112	12 544	10.58301	33.46640	1 404 928	4.820 285	10.38499	22.37378
113	12 769	10.63015	33.61547	1 442 897	4.834 588	10.41580	22.44017
114	12 996	10.67708	33.76389	1 481 544	4.848 808	10.44644	22.50617
115	13 225	10.72381	33.91165	1 520 875	4.862 944	10.47690	22.57179
116	13 456	10.77033	34.05877	1 560 896	4.876 999	10.50718	22.63702
117	13 689	10.81665	34.20526	1 601 613	4.890 973	10.53728	22.70189
118	13 924	10.86278	34.35113	1 643 032	4.904 868	10.56722	22.76638
119	14 161	10.90871	34.49638	1 685 159	4.918 685	10.59699	22.83051
120	14 400	10.95445	34.64102	1 728 000	4.932 424	10.62659	22.89428
121	14 641	11.00000	34.78505	1 771 561	4.946 087	10.65602	22.95770
122	14 884	11.04536	34.92850	1 815 848	4.959 676	10.68530	23.02078
123	15 129	11.09054	35.07136	1 860 867	4.973 190	10.71441	23.08350
124	15 376	11.13553	35.21363	1 906 624	4.986 631	10.74337	23.14589
125	15 625	11.18034	35.35534	1 953 125	5.000 000	10.77217	23.20794
126	15 876	11.22497	35.49648	2 000 376	5.013 298	10.80082	23.26967
127	16 129	11.26943	35.63706	2 048 383	5.026 526	10.82932	23.33107
128	16 384	11.31371	35.77709	2 097 152	5.039 684	10.85767	23.39214
129	16 641	11.35782	35.91657	2 146 689	5.052 774	10.88587	23.45290
130	16 900	11.40175	36.05551	2 197 000	5.065 797	10.91393	23.51335
131	17 161	11.44552	36.19392	2 248 091	5.078 753	10.94184	23.57348
132	17 424	11.48913	36.33180	2 299 968	5.091 643	10.96961	23.63332
133	17 689	11.53256	36.46917	2 352 637	5.104 469	10.99724	23.69285
134	17 956	11.57584	36.60601	2 406 104	5.117 230	11.02474	23.75208
135	18 225	11.61895	36.74235	2 460 375	5.129 928	11.05209	23.81102
136	18 496	11.66190	36.87818	2 515 456	5.142 563	11.07932	23.86966
137	18 769	11.70470	37.01351	2 571 353	5.155 137	11.10641	23.92803
138	19 044	11.74734	37.14835	2 628 072	5.167 649	11.13336	23.98610
139	19 321	11.78983	37.28270	2 685 619	5.180 101	11.16019	24.04390
140	19 600	11.83216	37.41657	2 744 000	5.192 494	11.18689	24.10142
141	19 881	11.87434	37.54997	2 803 221	5.204 828	11.21346	24.15867
142	20 164	11.91638	37.68289	2 863 288	5.217 103	11.23991	24.21565
143	20 449	11.95826	37.81534	2 924 207	5.229 322	11.26623	24.27236
144	20 736	12.00000	37.94733	2 985 984	5.241 483	11.29243	24.32881
145	21 025	12.04159	38.07887	3 048 625	5.253 588	11.31851	24.38499
146	21 316	12.08305	38.20995	3 112 136	5.265 637	11.34447	24.44092
147	21 609	12.12436	38.34058	3 176 523	5.277 632	11.37031	24.49660
148	21 904	12.16553	38.47077	3 241 792	5.289 572	11.39604	24.55202
149	22 201	12.20656	38.60052	3 307 949	5.301 459	11.42165	24.60719
150	22 500	12.24745	38.72983	3 375 000	5.313 293	11.44714	24.66212

Table 33 (continued)

n	n^2	$\sqrt{n}$	$\sqrt{10n}$	n^3	$\sqrt[3]{n}$	$\sqrt[3]{10n}$	$\sqrt[3]{100n}$
250	62 500	15.81139	50.00000	15 625 000	6 299 605	13.57209	29.24018
251	63 001	15.84298	50.09990	15 813 251	6 307 994	13.59016	29.27911
252	63 504	15.87451	50.19960	16 003 008	6 316 360	13.60818	29.31794
253	64 009	15.90597	50.29911	16 194 277	6 324 704	13.62616	29.35667
254	64 516	15.93738	50.39841	16 387 064	6 333 026	13.64409	29.39530
255	65 025	15.96872	50.49752	16 581 375	6 341 326	13.66197	29.43383
256	65 536	16.00000	50.59644	16 777 216	6 349 604	13.67981	29.47225
257	66 049	16.03122	50.69517	16 974 593	6 357 861	13.69760	29.51058
258	66 564	16.06238	50.79370	17 173 512	6 366 097	13.71534	29.54880
259	67 081	16.09348	50.89204	17 373 979	6 374 311	13.73304	29.58693
260	67 600	16.12452	50.99020	17 576 000	6 382 504	13.75069	29.62496
261	68 121	16.15549	51.08816	17 779 581	6 390 677	13.76830	29.66289
262	68 644	16.18641	51.18594	17 984 728	6 398 828	13.78586	29.70073
263	69 169	16.21727	51.28353	18 191 447	6 406 959	13.80337	29.73847
264	69 696	16.24808	51.38093	18 399 744	6 415 069	13.82085	29.77611
265	70 225	16.27882	51.47815	18 609 625	6 423 158	13.83828	29.81366
266	70 756	16.30951	51.57519	18 821 096	6 431 228	13.85566	29.85111
267	71 289	16.34013	51.67204	19 034 163	6 439 277	13.87300	29.88847
268	71 824	16.37071	51.76872	19 248 832	6 447 306	13.89030	29.92574
269	72 361	16.40122	51.86521	19 465 109	6 455 315	13.90755	29.96292
270	72 900	16.43168	51.96152	19 683 000	6 463 304	13.92477	30.00000
271	73 441	16.46208	52.05766	19 902 511	6 471 274	13.94194	30.03699
272	73 984	16.49242	52.15362	20 123 648	6 479 224	13.95906	30.07389
273	74 529	16.52271	52.24940	20 346 417	6 487 154	13.97615	30.11070
274	75 076	16.55295	52.34501	20 570 824	6 495 065	13.99319	30.14742
275	75 625	16.58312	52.44044	20 796 875	6 502 957	14.01020	30.18405
276	76 176	16.61325	52.53570	21 024 576	6 510 830	14.02716	30.22060
277	76 729	16.64332	52.63079	21 253 933	6 518 684	14.04408	30.25705
278	77 284	16.67333	52.72571	21 484 952	6 526 519	14.06096	30.29342
279	77 841	16.70329	52.82045	21 717 639	6 534 335	14.07780	30.32970
280	78 400	16.73320	52.91503	21 952 000	6 542 133	14.09460	30.36589
281	78 961	16.76305	53.00943	22 188 041	6 549 912	14.11136	30.40200
282	79 524	16.79286	53.10367	22 425 768	6 557 672	14.12808	30.43802
283	80 089	16.82260	53.19774	22 665 187	6 565 414	14.14476	30.47395
284	80 656	16.85230	53.29165	22 906 304	6 573 138	14.16140	30.50981
285	81 225	16.88194	53.38539	23 149 125	6 580 844	14.17800	30.54557
286	81 796	16.91153	53.47897	23 393 656	6 588 532	14.19456	30.58126
287	82 369	16.94107	53.57238	23 639 903	6 596 202	14.21109	30.61686
288	82 944	16.97056	53.66563	23 887 872	6 603 854	14.22757	30.65238
289	83 521	17.00000	53.75872	24 137 569	6 611 489	14.24402	30.68781
290	84 100	17.02930	53.85165	24 389 000	6 619 106	14.26043	30.72317
291	84 681	17.05872	53.94442	24 642 171	6 626 705	14.27680	30.75844
292	85 264	17.08801	54.03702	24 897 088	6 634 287	14.29314	30.79363
293	85 849	17.11724	54.12947	25 153 757	6 641 852	14.30944	30.82875
294	86 436	17.14643	54.22177	25 412 184	6 649 400	14.32570	30.86378
295	87 025	17.17556	54.31390	25 672 375	6 656 930	14.34192	30.89873
296	87 616	17.20465	54.40588	25 934 336	6 664 444	14.35811	30.93361
297	88 209	17.23369	54.49771	26 198 073	6 671 940	14.37426	30.96840
298	88 804	17.26258	54.58938	26 463 592	6 679 420	14.39037	31.00312
299	89 401	17.29162	54.68089	26 730 899	6 686 883	14.40645	31.03776
300	90 000	17.32051	54.77226	27 000 000	6 694 330	14.42250	31.07233

Table 33 (continued)

n	n^2	$\sqrt{n}$	$\sqrt{10n}$	n^3	$\sqrt[3]{n}$	$\sqrt[3]{10n}$	$\sqrt[3]{100n}$
200	40 000	14.14214	44.72136	8 000 000	5 848 035	12.59921	27.14418
201	40 401	14.17745	44.83302	8 120 601	5 857 766	12.62017	27.18934
202	40 804	14.21267	44.94441	8 242 408	5 867 464	12.64107	27.23436
203	41 209	14.24781	45.05552	8 365 427	5 877 131	12.66189	27.27922
204	41 616	14.28286	45.16636	8 489 664	5 886 765	12.68265	27.32394
205	42 025	14.31782	45.27693	8 615 125	5 896 369	12.70334	27.36852
206	42 436	14.35270	45.38722	8 741 816	5 905 941	12.72396	27.41295
207	42 849	14.38749	45.49725	8 869 743	5 915 482	12.74452	27.45723
208	43 264	14.42221	45.60702	8 998 912	5 924 992	12.76501	27.50138
209	43 681	14.45683	45.71652	9 129 329	5 934 472	12.78543	27.54538
210	44 100	14.49138	45.82576	9 261 000	5 943 922	12.80579	27.58924
211	44 521	14.52584	45.93474	9 393 931	5 953 342	12.82609	27.63296
212	44 944	14.56022	46.04346	9 528 128	5 962 732	12.84632	27.67655
213	45 369	14.59452	46.15192	9 663 597	5 972 093	12.86648	27.72000
214	45 796	14.62874	46.26013	9 800 344	5 981 424	12.88659	27.76331
215	46 225	14.66288	46.36809	9 938 375	5 990 726	12.90663	27.80649
216	46 656	14.69694	46.47580	10 077 696	6 000 000	12.92661	27.84953
217	47 089	14.73092	46.58326	10 218 313	6 009 245	12.94653	27.89244
218	47 524	14.76482	46.69047	10 360 232	6 018 462	12.96638	27.93522
219	47 961	14.79865	46.79744	10 503 459	6 027 650	12.98618	27.97787
220	48 400	14.83240	46.90416	10 648 000	6 036 811	13.00591	28.02039
221	48 841	14.86607	47.01064	10 793 861	6 045 944	13.02559	28.06278
222	49 284	14.89966	47.11688	10 941 048	6 055 049	13.04521	28.10505
223	49 729	14.93318	47.22288	11 089 567	6 064 127	13.06477	28.14718
224	50 176	14.96663	47.32864	11 239 424	6 073 178	13.08427	28.18919
225	50 625	15.00000	47.43416	11 390 625	6 082 202	13.10371	28.23108
226	51 076	15.03330	47.53946	11 543 176	6 091 199	13.12309	28.27284
227	51 529	15.06652	47.64452	11 697 083	6 100 170	13.14242	28.31448
228	51 984	15.09967	47.74935	11 852 352	6 109 115	13.16169	28.35600
229	52 441	15.13275	47.85394	12 008 989	6 118 033	13.18090	28.39739
230	52 900	15.16575	47.95832	12 167 000	6 126 926	13.20006	28.43867
231	53 361	15.19868	48.06246	12 326 391	6 135 792	13.21916	28.47983
232	53 824	15.23155	48.16638	12 487 168	6 144 634	13.23821	28.52086
233	54 289	15.26434	48.27007	12 649 337	6 153 449	13.25721	28.56178
234	54 756	15.29706	48.37355	12 812 904	6 162 240	13.27614	28.60259
235	55 225	15.32971	48.47680	12 977 875	6 171 006	13.29503	28.64327
236	55 696	15.36229	48.57983	13 144 256	6 179 747	13.31386	28.68384
237	56 169	15.39480	48.68265	13 312 053	6 188 463	13.33264	28.72430
238	56 644	15.42725	48.78524	13 481 272	6 197 154	13.35136	28.76464
239	57 121	15.45962	48.88763	13 651 919	6 205 822	13.37004	28.80487
240	57 600	15.49193	48.98979	13 824 000	6 214 465	13.38866	28.84499
241	58 081	15.52417	49.09175	13 997 521	6 223 084	13.40723	28.88500
242	58 564	15.55635	49.19350	14 172 488	6 231 680	13.42575	28.92489
243	59 049	15.58846	49.29503	14 348 907	6 240 251	13.44421	28.96468
244	59 536	15.62050	49.39636	14 526 784	6 248 800	13.46263	29.00436
245	60 025	15.65248	49.49747	14 706 125	6 257 325	13.48100	29.04393
246	60 516	15.68439	49.59839	14 886 936	6 265 827	13.49931	29.08339
247	61 009	15.71623	49.69909	15 069 223	6 274 305	13.51758	29.12275
248	61 504	15.74802	49.79960	15 252 992	6 282 761	13.53580	29.16199
249	62 001	15.77973	49.89990	15 438 249	6 291 195	13.55397	29.20114
250	62 500	15.81139	50.00000	15 625 000	6 299 605	13.57209	29.24018

Table 33 (continued)

$\sqrt[3]{100n}$	$\sqrt{10n}$	$\sqrt{n}$	n^3	$\sqrt{10n}$	$\sqrt{n}$	n^2	n
32.71066	15.18294	7.047 299	42 875 000	59.16080	18.70829	122 500	**350**
32.74179	15.19739	7.054 004	43 243 551	59.24525	18.73499	123 201	351
32.77285	15.21181	7.060 697	43 614 208	59.32959	18.76166	123 904	352
32.80386	15.22620	7.067 377	43 986 977	59.41380	18.78829	124 609	353
32.83480	15.24057	7.074 044	44 361 864	59.49790	18.81489	125 316	354
32.86569	15.25490	7.080 699	44 738 875	59.58188	18.84144	126 025	355
32.89652	15.26921	7.087 341	45 118 016	59.66574	18.86796	126 736	356
32.92730	15.28350	7.093 971	45 499 293	59.74948	18.89444	127 449	357
32.95801	15.29775	7.100 588	45 882 712	59.83310	18.92089	128 164	358
32.98867	15.31198	7.107 194	46 268 279	59.91661	18.94730	128 881	359
33.01927	15.32619	7.113 787	46 656 000	60.00000	18.97367	129 600	**360**
33.04982	15.34037	7.120 367	47 045 881	60.08328	19.00000	130 321	361
33.08031	15.35452	7.126 936	47 437 928	60.16644	19.02630	131 044	362
33.11074	15.36864	7.133 492	47 832 147	60.24948	19.05256	131 769	363
33.14112	15.38274	7.140 037	48 228 544	60.33241	19.07878	132 496	364
33.17144	15.39682	7.146 569	48 627 125	60.41523	19.10497	133 225	365
33.20170	15.41087	7.153 090	49 027 896	60.49793	19.13113	133 956	366
33.23191	15.42489	7.159 599	49 430 863	60.58052	19.15724	134 689	367
33.26207	15.43889	7.166 096	49 836 032	60.66300	19.18333	135 424	368
33.29217	15.45286	7.172 581	50 243 409	60.74537	19.20937	136 161	369
33.32222	15.46680	7.179 054	50 653 000	60.82763	19.23538	136 900	**370**
33.35221	15.48073	7.185 516	51 064 811	60.90977	19.26136	137 641	371
33.38215	15.49462	7.191 966	51 478 848	60.99180	19.28730	138 384	372
33.41204	15.50849	7.198 405	51 895 117	61.07373	19.31321	139 129	373
33.44187	15.52234	7.204 832	52 313 624	61.15554	19.33908	139 876	374
33.47165	15.53616	7.211 248	52 734 375	61.23724	19.36492	140 625	375
33.50137	15.54996	7.217 652	53 157 376	61.31884	19.39072	141 376	376
33.53105	15.56373	7.224 045	53 582 633	61.40033	19.41649	142 129	377
33.56067	15.57748	7.230 427	54 010 152	61.48170	19.44222	142 884	378
33.59024	15.59121	7.236 797	54 439 939	61.56298	19.46792	143 641	379
33.61975	15.60491	7.243 156	54 872 000	61.64414	19.49359	144 400	**380**
33.64922	15.61858	7.249 505	55 306 341	61.72520	19.51922	145 161	381
33.67863	15.63224	7.255 842	55 742 968	61.80615	19.54482	145 924	382
33.70800	15.64587	7.262 167	56 181 887	61.88699	19.57039	146 689	383
33.73731	15.65947	7.268 482	56 623 104	61.96773	19.59592	147 456	384
33.76657	15.67305	7.274 786	57 066 625	62.04837	19.62142	148 225	385
33.79578	15.68661	7.281 079	57 512 456	62.12890	19.64688	148 996	386
33.82494	15.70014	7.287 362	57 960 603	62.20932	19.67232	149 769	387
33.85405	15.71366	7.293 633	58 411 072	62.28965	19.69772	150 544	388
33.88310	15.72714	7.299 894	58 863 869	62.36986	19.72308	151 321	389
33.91211	15.74061	7.306 144	59 319 000	62.44998	19.74842	152 100	**390**
33.94107	15.75405	7.312 383	59 776 471	62.52999	19.77372	152 881	391
33.96999	15.76747	7.318 611	60 236 288	62.60990	19.79899	153 664	392
33.99885	15.78087	7.324 829	60 698 457	62.68971	19.82423	154 449	393
34.02766	15.79424	7.331 037	61 162 984	62.76942	19.84943	155 236	394
34.05642	15.80759	7.337 234	61 629 875	62.84903	19.87461	156 025	395
34.08514	15.82092	7.343 420	62 099 136	62.92853	19.89975	156 816	396
34.11381	15.83423	7.349 597	62 570 773	63.00794	19.92486	157 609	397
34.14242	15.84751	7.355 762	63 044 792	63.08724	19.94994	158 404	398
34.17100	15.86077	7.361 918	63 521 199	63.16645	19.97498	159 201	399
34.19952	15.87401	7.368 063	64 000 000	63.24555	20.00000	160 000	**400**

Table 33 (continued)

$\sqrt[3]{100n}$	$\sqrt{10n}$	$\sqrt{n}$	n^3	$\sqrt{10n}$	$\sqrt{n}$	n^2	n
31.07233	14.42250	6.694 330	27 000 000	54.77226	17.32051	90 000	**300**
31.10681	14.43850	6.701 759	27 270 901	54.86347	17.34935	90 601	301
31.14122	14.45447	6.709 173	27 543 608	54.95453	17.37815	91 204	302
31.17556	14.47041	6.716 570	27 818 127	55.04544	17.40690	91 809	303
31.20982	14.48631	6.723 951	28 094 464	55.13620	17.43560	92 416	304
31.24400	14.50218	6.731 315	28 372 625	55.22681	17.46425	93 025	305
31.27811	14.51801	6.738 664	28 652 616	55.31727	17.49286	93 636	306
31.31214	14.53381	6.745 997	28 934 443	55.40758	17.52142	94 249	307
31.34610	14.54957	6.753 313	29 218 112	55.49775	17.54993	94 864	308
31.37999	14.56530	6.760 614	29 503 629	55.58777	17.57840	95 481	309
31.41381	14.58100	6.767 899	29 791 000	55.67764	17.60682	96 100	**310**
31.44755	14.59666	6.775 169	30 080 231	55.76737	17.63519	96 721	311
31.48122	14.61229	6.782 423	30 371 328	55.85696	17.66352	97 344	312
31.51482	14.62788	6.789 661	30 664 297	55.94640	17.69181	97 969	313
31.54834	14.64344	6.796 884	30 959 144	56.03570	17.72005	98 596	314
31.58180	14.65897	6.804 092	31 255 875	56.12486	17.74824	99 225	315
31.61518	14.67447	6.811 285	31 554 496	56.21388	17.77639	99 856	316
31.64850	14.68993	6.818 462	31 855 013	56.30275	17.80449	100 489	317
31.68174	14.70536	6.825 624	32 157 432	56.39149	17.83255	101 124	318
31.71492	14.72076	6.832 771	32 461 759	56.48008	17.86057	101 761	319
31.74802	14.73613	6.839 904	32 768 000	56.56854	17.88854	102 400	**320**
31.78106	14.75146	6.847 021	33 076 161	56.65686	17.91647	103 041	321
31.81403	14.76676	6.854 124	33 386 248	56.74504	17.94436	103 684	322
31.84693	14.78203	6.861 212	33 698 267	56.83309	17.97220	104 329	323
31.87976	14.79727	6.868 285	34 012 224	56.92100	18.00000	104 976	324
31.91252	14.81248	6.875 344	34 328 125	57.00877	18.02776	105 625	325
31.94522	14.82766	6.882 389	34 645 976	57.09641	18.05547	106 276	326
31.97785	14.84280	6.889 419	34 965 783	57.18391	18.08314	106 929	327
32.01041	14.85792	6.896 434	35 287 552	57.27128	18.11077	107 584	328
32.04291	14.87300	6.903 436	35 611 289	57.35852	18.13836	108 241	329
32.07534	14.88806	6.910 423	35 937 000	57.44563	18.16590	108 900	**330**
32.10771	14.90308	6.917 396	36 264 691	57.53260	18.19341	109 561	331
32.14001	14.91807	6.924 356	36 594 368	57.61944	18.22087	110 224	332
32.17225	14.93303	6.931 301	36 926 037	57.70615	18.24829	110 889	333
32.20442	14.94797	6.938 232	37 259 704	57.79273	18.27567	111 556	334
32.23653	14.96287	6.945 150	37 595 375	57.87918	18.30301	112 225	335
32.26857	14.97774	6.952 053	37 933 056	57.96551	18.33030	112 896	336
32.30055	14.99259	6.958 943	38 272 753	58.05170	18.35756	113 569	337
32.33247	15.00740	6.965 820	38 614 472	58.13777	18.38478	114 244	338
32.36433	15.02219	6.972 683	38 958 219	58.22371	18.41195	114 921	339
32.39612	15.03695	6.979 532	39 304 000	58.30952	18.43909	115 600	**340**
32.42785	15.05167	6.986 368	39 651 821	58.39521	18.46619	116 281	341
32.45952	15.06637	6.993 191	40 001 688	58.48077	18.49324	116 964	342
32.49112	15.08104	7.000 000	40 353 607	58.56620	18.52026	117 649	343
32.52267	15.09568	7.006 796	40 707 584	58.65151	18.54724	118 336	344
32.55415	15.11030	7.013 579	41 063 625	58.73670	18.57418	119 025	345
32.58557	15.12488	7.020 349	41 421 736	58.82176	18.60108	119 716	346
32.61694	15.13944	7.027 106	41 781 923	58.90671	18.62794	120 409	347
32.64824	15.15397	7.033 850	42 144 192	58.99152	18.65476	121 104	348
32.67948	15.16847	7.040 581	42 508 549	59.07622	18.68154	121 801	349
32.71066	15.18294	7.047 299	42 875 000	59.16080	18.70829	122 500	**350**

Table 33 (continued)

n	n²	$\sqrt{n}$	$\sqrt{10n}$	n³	$\sqrt[3]{n}$	$\sqrt[3]{10n}$	$\sqrt[3]{100n}$
450	202 500	21.21320	67.08204	91 125 000	7.663 094	16.50964	35.56893
451	203 401	21.23676	67.15653	91 733 851	7.668 766	16.52186	35.59526
452	204 304	21.26029	67.23095	92 345 408	7.674 430	16.53406	35.62155
453	205 209	21.28380	67.30527	92 959 677	7.680 086	16.54624	35.64780
454	206 116	21.30728	67.37952	93 576 664	7.685 733	16.55841	35.67401
455	207 025	21.33073	67.45369	94 196 375	7.691 372	16.57056	35.70018
456	207 936	21.35416	67.52777	94 818 816	7.697 002	16.58269	35.72632
457	208 849	21.37756	67.60178	95 443 993	7.702 625	16.59480	35.75242
458	209 764	21.40093	67.67570	96 071 912	7.708 239	16.60690	35.77848
459	210 681	21.42429	67.74954	96 702 579	7.713 845	16.61897	35.80450
460	211 600	21.44761	67.82330	97 336 000	7.719 443	16.63103	35.83048
461	212 521	21.47091	67.89698	97 972 181	7.725 032	16.64308	35.85642
462	213 444	21.49419	67.97058	98 611 128	7.730 614	16.65510	35.88233
463	214 369	21.51743	68.04410	99 252 847	7.736 188	16.66711	35.90820
464	215 296	21.54066	68.11755	99 897 344	7.741 753	16.67910	35.93404
465	216 225	21.56386	68.19091	100 544 625	7.747 311	16.69108	35.95983
466	217 156	21.58703	68.26419	101 194 696	7.752 861	16.70303	35.98559
467	218 089	21.61018	68.33740	101 847 563	7.758 402	16.71497	36.01131
468	219 024	21.63331	68.41053	102 503 232	7.763 936	16.72689	36.03700
469	219 961	21.65641	68.48357	103 161 709	7.769 462	16.73880	36.06265
470	220 900	21.67948	68.55655	103 823 000	7.774 980	16.75069	36.08826
471	221 841	21.70253	68.62944	104 487 111	7.780 490	16.76256	36.11384
472	222 784	21.72556	68.70226	105 154 048	7.785 993	16.77441	36.13938
473	223 729	21.74856	68.77500	105 823 817	7.791 488	16.78625	36.16488
474	224 676	21.77154	68.84766	106 496 424	7.796 975	16.79807	36.19035
475	225 625	21.79449	68.92024	107 171 875	7.802 454	16.80988	36.21578
476	226 576	21.81742	68.99275	107 850 176	7.807 925	16.82167	36.24118
477	227 529	21.84033	69.06519	108 531 333	7.813 389	16.83344	36.26654
478	228 484	21.86321	69.13754	109 215 352	7.818 846	16.84519	36.29187
479	229 441	21.88607	69.20983	109 902 239	7.824 294	16.85693	36.31716
480	230 400	21.90890	69.28203	110 592 000	7.829 735	16.86865	36.34241
481	231 361	21.93171	69.35416	111 284 641	7.835 169	16.88036	36.36763
482	232 324	21.95450	69.42622	111 980 168	7.840 595	16.89205	36.39282
483	233 289	21.97726	69.49820	112 678 587	7.846 013	16.90372	36.41797
484	234 256	22.00000	69.57011	113 379 904	7.851 424	16.91538	36.44308
485	235 225	22.02272	69.64194	114 084 125	7.856 828	16.92702	36.46817
486	236 196	22.04541	69.71370	114 791 256	7.862 224	16.93865	36.49321
487	237 169	22.06808	69.78539	115 501 303	7.867 613	16.95026	36.51822
488	238 144	22.09072	69.85700	116 214 272	7.872 994	16.96185	36.54320
489	239 121	22.11334	69.92853	116 930 169	7.878 368	16.97343	36.56815
490	240 100	22.13594	70.00000	117 649 000	7.883 735	16.98499	36.59306
491	241 081	22.15852	70.07139	118 370 771	7.889 095	16.99654	36.61793
492	242 064	22.18107	70.14271	119 095 488	7.894 447	17.00807	36.64278
493	243 049	22.20360	70.21396	119 823 157	7.899 792	17.01959	36.66758
494	244 036	22.22611	70.28513	120 553 784	7.905 129	17.03108	36.69236
495	245 025	22.24860	70.35624	121 287 375	7.910 460	17.04257	36.71710
496	246 016	22.27106	70.42727	122 023 936	7.915 783	17.05404	36.74181
497	247 009	22.29350	70.49823	122 763 473	7.921 099	17.06549	36.76649
498	248 004	22.31591	70.56912	123 505 992	7.926 408	17.07693	36.79113
499	249 001	22.33831	70.63993	124 251 499	7.931 710	17.08835	36.81574
500	250 000	22.36068	70.71068	125 000 000	7.937 005	17.09976	36.84031

Table 33 (continued)

n	n²	$\sqrt{n}$	$\sqrt{10n}$	n³	$\sqrt[3]{n}$	$\sqrt[3]{10n}$	$\sqrt[3]{100n}$
400	160 000	20.00000	63.24555	64 000 000	7.368 063	15.87401	34.19952
401	160 801	20.02498	63.32456	64 481 201	7.374 198	15.88723	34.22799
402	161 604	20.04994	63.40347	64 964 808	7.380 323	15.90042	34.25642
403	162 409	20.07486	63.48228	65 450 827	7.386 437	15.91360	34.28480
404	163 216	20.09975	63.56099	65 939 264	7.392 542	15.92675	34.31314
405	164 025	20.12461	63.63961	66 430 125	7.398 636	15.93988	34.34143
406	164 836	20.14944	63.71813	66 923 416	7.404 721	15.95299	34.36967
407	165 649	20.17424	63.79655	67 419 143	7.410 795	15.96607	34.39786
408	166 464	20.19901	63.87488	67 917 312	7.416 860	15.97914	34.42601
409	167 281	20.22375	63.95311	68 417 929	7.422 914	15.99218	34.45412
410	168 100	20.24846	64.03124	68 921 000	7.428 959	16.00521	34.48217
411	168 921	20.27313	64.10928	69 426 531	7.434 994	16.01821	34.51018
412	169 744	20.29778	64.18723	69 934 528	7.441 019	16.03119	34.53815
413	170 569	20.32240	64.26508	70 444 997	7.447 034	16.04415	34.56607
414	171 396	20.34699	64.34283	70 957 944	7.453 040	16.05709	34.59395
415	172 225	20.37155	64.42049	71 473 375	7.459 036	16.07001	34.62178
416	173 056	20.39608	64.49806	71 991 296	7.465 022	16.08290	34.64956
417	173 889	20.42058	64.57554	72 511 713	7.470 999	16.09578	34.67731
418	174 724	20.44505	64.65292	73 034 632	7.476 966	16.10864	34.70500
419	175 561	20.46949	64.73021	73 560 059	7.482 924	16.12147	34.73266
420	176 400	20.49390	64.80741	74 088 000	7.488 872	16.13429	34.76027
421	177 241	20.51828	64.88451	74 618 461	7.494 811	16.14708	34.78783
422	178 084	20.54264	64.96153	75 151 448	7.500 741	16.15986	34.81535
423	178 929	20.56696	65.03845	75 686 967	7.506 661	16.17261	34.84283
424	179 776	20.59126	65.11528	76 225 024	7.512 572	16.18534	34.87027
425	180 625	20.61553	65.19202	76 765 625	7.518 473	16.19806	34.89766
426	181 476	20.63977	65.26868	77 308 776	7.524 365	16.21075	34.92501
427	182 329	20.66398	65.34524	77 854 483	7.530 248	16.22343	34.95232
428	183 184	20.68816	65.42171	78 402 752	7.536 122	16.23608	34.97958
429	184 041	20.71232	65.49809	78 953 589	7.541 987	16.24872	35.00680
430	184 900	20.73644	65.57439	79 507 000	7.547 842	16.26133	35.03398
431	185 761	20.76054	65.65059	80 062 991	7.553 689	16.27393	35.06112
432	186 624	20.78461	65.72671	80 621 568	7.559 526	16.28651	35.08821
433	187 489	20.80865	65.80274	81 182 737	7.565 355	16.29906	35.11527
434	188 356	20.83267	65.87868	81 746 504	7.571 174	16.31160	35.14228
435	189 225	20.85665	65.95453	82 312 875	7.576 985	16.32412	35.16925
436	190 096	20.88061	66.03030	82 881 856	7.582 787	16.33662	35.19618
437	190 969	20.90454	66.10598	83 453 453	7.588 579	16.34910	35.22307
438	191 844	20.92845	66.18157	84 027 672	7.594 363	16.36156	35.24991
439	192 721	20.95233	66.25708	84 604 519	7.600 139	16.37400	35.27672
440	193 600	20.97618	66.33250	85 184 000	7.605 905	16.38643	35.30348
441	194 481	21.00000	66.40783	85 766 121	7.611 663	16.39883	35.33021
442	195 364	21.02380	66.48308	86 350 888	7.617 412	16.41122	35.35689
443	196 249	21.04757	66.55825	86 938 307	7.623 152	16.42358	35.38354
444	197 136	21.07131	66.63332	87 528 384	7.628 884	16.43593	35.41014
445	198 025	21.09502	66.70832	88 121 125	7.634 607	16.44826	35.43671
446	198 916	21.11871	66.78323	88 716 536	7.640 321	16.46057	35.46323
447	199 809	21.14237	66.85806	89 314 623	7.646 027	16.47287	35.48971
448	200 704	21.16601	66.93280	89 915 392	7.651 725	16.48514	35.51616
449	201 601	21.18962	67.00746	90 518 849	7.657 414	16.49740	35.54257
450	202 500	21.21320	67.08204	91 125 000	7.663 094	16.50964	35.56893

Table 33 (continued)

n	n²	√n	√10n	n³	∛n	∛10n	∛100n
550	302 500	23.45208	74.16198	166 375 000	8.193 213	17.65174	38.02952
551	303 601	23.47339	74.22937	167 284 151	8.198 175	17.66243	38.05256
552	304 704	23.49468	74.29670	168 196 608	8.203 132	17.67311	38.07557
553	305 809	23.51595	74.36397	169 112 377	8.208 082	17.68378	38.09854
554	306 916	23.53720	74.43118	170 031 464	8.213 027	17.69443	38.12149
555	308 025	23.55844	74.49832	170 953 875	8.217 966	17.70507	38.14442
556	309 136	23.57965	74.56541	171 879 616	8.222 899	17.71570	38.16731
557	310 249	23.60085	74.63243	172 808 693	8.227 825	17.72631	38.19018
558	311 364	23.62202	74.69940	173 741 112	8.232 746	17.73691	38.21302
559	312 481	23.64318	74.76630	174 676 879	8.237 661	17.74750	38.23584
560	313 600	23.66432	74.83315	175 616 000	8.242 571	17.75808	38.25862
561	314 721	23.68544	74.89993	176 558 481	8.247 474	17.76864	38.28138
562	315 844	23.70654	74.96666	177 504 328	8.252 372	17.77920	38.30412
563	316 969	23.72762	75.03333	178 453 547	8.257 263	17.78973	38.32682
564	318 096	23.74868	75.09993	179 406 144	8.262 149	17.80026	38.34950
565	319 225	23.76973	75.16648	180 362 029	8.267 029	17.81077	38.37215
566	320 356	23.79075	75.23297	181 321 496	8.271 904	17.82128	38.39478
567	321 489	23.81176	75.29940	182 284 263	8.276 773	17.83177	38.41737
568	322 624	23.83275	75.36577	183 250 432	8.281 635	17.84224	38.43995
569	323 761	23.85372	75.43209	184 220 009	8.286 493	17.85271	38.46249
570	324 900	23.87467	75.49834	185 193 000	8.291 344	17.86316	38.48501
571	326 041	23.89561	75.56454	186 169 411	8.296 190	17.87360	38.50750
572	327 184	23.91652	75.63068	187 149 248	8.301 031	17.88403	38.52997
573	328 329	23.93742	75.69676	188 132 517	8.305 865	17.89444	38.55241
574	329 476	23.95830	75.76279	189 119 224	8.310 694	17.90485	38.57482
575	330 625	23.97916	75.82875	190 109 375	8.315 517	17.91524	38.59721
576	331 776	24.00000	75.89466	191 102 976	8.320 335	17.92562	38.61958
577	332 929	24.02082	75.96052	192 100 033	8.325 148	17.93599	38.64191
578	334 084	24.04163	76.02631	193 100 552	8.329 954	17.94634	38.66422
579	335 241	24.06242	76.09205	194 104 539	8.334 755	17.95669	38.68651
580	336 400	24.08319	76.15773	195 112 000	8.339 551	17.96702	38.70877
581	337 561	24.10394	76.22336	196 122 941	8.344 341	17.97734	38.73100
582	338 724	24.12468	76.28892	197 137 368	8.349 126	17.98765	38.75321
583	339 889	24.14539	76.35444	198 155 287	8.353 905	17.99794	38.77539
584	341 056	24.16609	76.41989	199 176 704	8.358 678	18.00823	38.79755
585	342 225	24.18677	76.48529	200 201 625	8.363 447	18.01850	38.81968
586	343 396	24.20744	76.55064	201 230 056	8.368 209	18.02876	38.84179
587	344 569	24.22808	76.61593	202 262 003	8.372 967	18.03901	38.86387
588	345 744	24.24871	76.68116	203 297 472	8.377 719	18.04925	38.88593
589	346 921	24.26932	76.74634	204 336 469	8.382 465	18.05947	38.90796
590	348 100	24.28992	76.81146	205 379 000	8.387 207	18.06969	38.92996
591	349 281	24.31049	76.87652	206 425 071	8.391 942	18.07989	38.95195
592	350 464	24.33105	76.94154	207 474 688	8.396 673	18.09008	38.97390
593	351 649	24.35159	77.00649	208 527 857	8.401 398	18.10026	38.99584
594	352 836	24.37212	77.07140	209 584 584	8.406 118	18.11043	39.01774
595	354 025	24.39262	77.13624	210 644 875	8.410 833	18.12059	39.03963
596	355 216	24.41311	77.20104	211 708 736	8.415 542	18.13074	39.06149
597	356 409	24.43358	77.26578	212 776 173	8.420 246	18.14087	39.08332
598	357 604	24.45404	77.33046	213 847 192	8.424 945	18.15099	39.10513
599	358 801	24.47448	77.39509	214 921 799	8.429 638	18.16111	39.12692
600	360 000	24.49490	77.45967	216 000 000	8.434 327	18.17121	39.14868

Table 33 (continued)

n	n²	√n	√10n	n³	∛n	∛10n	∛100n
500	250 000	22.36068	70.71068	125 000 000	7.937 005	17.09976	36.84031
501	251 001	22.38303	70.78135	125 751 501	7.942 293	17.11115	36.86486
502	252 004	22.40536	70.85196	126 506 008	7.947 574	17.12253	36.88937
503	253 009	22.42766	70.92249	127 263 527	7.952 848	17.13389	36.91385
504	254 016	22.44994	70.99296	128 024 064	7.958 114	17.14524	36.93830
505	255 025	22.47221	71.06335	128 787 625	7.963 374	17.15657	36.96271
506	256 036	22.49444	71.13368	129 554 216	7.968 627	17.16789	36.98709
507	257 049	22.51666	71.20393	130 323 843	7.973 873	17.17919	37.01144
508	258 064	22.53886	71.27412	131 096 512	7.979 112	17.19048	37.03576
509	259 081	22.56103	71.34424	131 872 229	7.984 344	17.20175	37.06004
510	260 100	22.58318	71.41428	132 651 000	7.989 570	17.21301	37.08430
511	261 121	22.60531	71.48426	133 432 831	7.994 788	17.22425	37.10852
512	262 144	22.62742	71.55418	134 217 728	8.000 000	17.23548	37.13271
513	263 169	22.64950	71.62402	135 005 697	8.005 205	17.24669	37.15687
514	264 196	22.67157	71.69379	135 796 744	8.010 403	17.25789	37.18100
515	265 225	22.69361	71.76350	136 590 875	8.015 595	17.26908	37.20509
516	266 256	22.71563	71.83314	137 388 096	8.020 779	17.28025	37.22916
517	267 289	22.73763	71.90271	138 188 413	8.025 957	17.29140	37.25319
518	268 324	22.75961	71.97222	138 991 832	8.031 129	17.30254	37.27720
519	269 361	22.78157	72.04165	139 798 359	8.036 293	17.31367	37.30117
520	270 400	22.80351	72.11103	140 608 000	8.041 452	17.32478	37.32511
521	271 441	22.82542	72.18033	141 420 761	8.046 603	17.33588	37.34902
522	272 484	22.84732	72.24957	142 236 648	8.051 748	17.34696	37.37290
523	273 529	22.86919	72.31874	143 055 667	8.056 886	17.35804	37.39675
524	274 576	22.89105	72.38784	143 877 824	8.062 018	17.36909	37.42057
525	275 625	22.91288	72.45688	144 703 125	8.067 143	17.38013	37.44436
526	276 676	22.93469	72.52586	145 531 576	8.072 262	17.39116	37.46812
527	277 729	22.95648	72.59477	146 363 183	8.077 374	17.40218	37.49185
528	278 784	22.97825	72.66361	147 197 952	8.082 480	17.41318	37.51555
529	279 841	23.00000	72.73239	148 035 889	8.087 579	17.42416	37.53922
530	280 900	23.02173	72.80110	148 877 000	8.092 672	17.43513	37.56286
531	281 961	23.04344	72.86975	149 721 291	8.097 759	17.44609	37.58647
532	283 024	23.06513	72.93833	150 568 768	8.102 839	17.45704	37.61005
533	284 089	23.08679	73.00685	151 419 437	8.107 913	17.46797	37.63360
534	285 156	23.10844	73.07530	152 273 304	8.112 980	17.47889	37.65712
535	286 225	23.13007	73.14369	153 130 375	8.118 041	17.48979	37.68061
536	287 296	23.15167	73.21202	153 990 656	8.123 096	17.50068	37.70407
537	288 369	23.17326	73.28028	154 854 153	8.128 145	17.51156	37.72751
538	289 444	23.19483	73.34848	155 720 872	8.133 187	17.52242	37.75091
539	290 521	23.21637	73.41662	156 590 819	8.138 223	17.53327	37.77429
540	291 600	23.23790	73.48469	157 464 000	8.143 253	17.54411	37.79763
541	292 681	23.25941	73.55270	158 340 421	8.148 276	17.55493	37.82095
542	293 764	23.28089	73.62065	159 220 088	8.153 294	17.56574	37.84424
543	294 849	23.30236	73.68853	160 103 007	8.158 305	17.57654	37.86750
544	295 936	23.32381	73.75636	160 989 184	8.163 310	17.58732	37.89073
545	297 025	23.34524	73.82412	161 878 625	8.168 309	17.59809	37.91393
546	298 116	23.36664	73.89181	162 771 336	8.173 302	17.60885	37.93711
547	299 209	23.38803	73.95945	163 667 323	8.178 289	17.61959	37.96025
548	300 304	23.40940	74.02702	164 566 592	8.183 269	17.63032	37.98337
549	301 401	23.43075	74.09453	165 469 149	8.188 244	17.64104	38.00646
550	302 500	23.45208	74.16198	166 375 000	8.193 213	17.65174	38.02952

Table 33 (continued)

n	n²	√n	√10n	n³	∛n	∛10n	∛100n
650	422 500	25.49510	80.62258	274 625 000	8.662 391	18.66256	40.20726
651	423 801	25.51470	80.68457	275 894 451	8.666 831	18.67212	40.22787
652	425 104	25.53429	80.74652	277 167 808	8.671 266	18.68168	40.24845
653	426 409	25.55386	80.80842	278 445 077	8.675 697	18.69122	40.26902
654	427 716	25.57342	80.87027	279 726 264	8.680 124	18.70076	40.28957
655	429 025	25.59297	80.93207	281 011 375	8.684 546	18.71029	40.31009
656	430 336	25.61250	80.99383	282 300 416	8.688 963	18.71980	40.33059
657	431 649	25.63201	81.05554	283 593 393	8.693 376	18.72931	40.35108
658	432 964	25.65151	81.11720	284 890 312	8.697 784	18.73881	40.37154
659	434 281	25.67100	81.17881	286 191 179	8.702 188	18.74830	40.39198
660	435 600	25.69047	81.24038	287 496 000	8.706 588	18.75777	40.41240
661	436 921	25.70992	81.30191	288 804 781	8.710 983	18.76724	40.43280
662	438 244	25.72936	81.36338	290 117 528	8.715 373	18.77670	40.45318
663	439 569	25.74879	81.42481	291 434 247	8.719 760	18.78615	40.47354
664	440 896	25.76820	81.48620	292 754 944	8.724 141	18.79559	40.49388
665	442 225	25.78759	81.54753	294 079 625	8.728 519	18.80502	40.51420
666	443 556	25.80698	81.60882	295 408 296	8.732 892	18.81444	40.53449
667	444 889	25.82634	81.67007	296 740 963	8.737 260	18.82386	40.55477
668	446 224	25.84570	81.73127	298 077 632	8.741 625	18.83326	40.57503
669	447 561	25.86503	81.79242	299 418 309	8.745 985	18.84265	40.59526
670	448 900	25.88436	81.85353	300 763 000	8.750 340	18.85204	40.61548
671	450 241	25.90367	81.91459	302 111 711	8.754 691	18.86141	40.63568
672	451 584	25.92296	81.97561	303 464 448	8.759 038	18.87078	40.65585
673	452 929	25.94224	82.03658	304 821 217	8.763 381	18.88013	40.67601
674	454 276	25.96151	82.09750	306 182 024	8.767 719	18.88948	40.69615
675	455 625	25.98076	82.15838	307 546 875	8.772 053	18.89882	40.71626
676	456 976	26.00000	82.21922	308 915 776	8.776 383	18.90814	40.73636
677	458 329	26.01922	82.28001	310 288 733	8.780 708	18.91746	40.75644
678	459 684	26.03843	82.34076	311 665 752	8.785 030	18.92677	40.77650
679	461 041	26.05763	82.40146	313 046 839	8.789 347	18.93607	40.79653
680	462 400	26.07681	82.46211	314 432 000	8.793 659	18.94536	40.81655
681	463 761	26.09598	82.52272	315 821 241	8.797 968	18.95465	40.83655
682	465 124	26.11513	82.58329	317 214 568	8.802 272	18.96392	40.85653
683	466 489	26.13427	82.64381	318 611 987	8.806 572	18.97318	40.87649
684	467 856	26.15339	82.70429	320 013 504	8.810 868	18.98244	40.89643
685	469 225	26.17250	82.76473	321 419 125	8.815 160	18.99169	40.91635
686	470 596	26.19160	82.82512	322 828 856	8.819 447	19.00092	40.93625
687	471 969	26.21068	82.88546	324 242 703	8.823 731	19.01015	40.95613
688	473 344	26.22975	82.94577	325 660 672	8.828 010	19.01937	40.97599
689	474 721	26.24881	83.00602	327 082 769	8.832 285	19.02858	40.99584
690	476 100	26.26785	83.06624	328 509 000	8.836 556	19.03778	41.01566
691	477 481	26.28688	83.12641	329 939 371	8.840 823	19.04698	41.03546
692	478 864	26.30589	83.18654	331 373 888	8.845 085	19.05616	41.05525
693	480 249	26.32489	83.24662	332 812 557	8.849 344	19.06533	41.07502
694	481 636	26.34388	83.30666	334 255 384	8.853 599	19.07450	41.09476
695	483 025	26.36285	83.36666	335 702 375	8.857 849	19.08366	41.11449
696	484 416	26.38181	83.42661	337 153 536	8.862 095	19.09281	41.13420
697	485 809	26.40076	83.48653	338 608 873	8.866 338	19.10195	41.15389
698	487 204	26.41969	83.54639	340 068 392	8.870 576	19.11108	41.17357
699	488 601	26.43861	83.60622	341 532 099	8.874 810	19.12020	41.19322
700	490 000	26.45751	83.66600	343 000 000	8.879 040	19.12931	41.21285

Table 33 (continued)

n	n²	√n	√10n	n³	∛n	∛10n	∛100n
600	360 000	24.49490	77.45967	216 000 000	8.434 327	18.17121	39.14868
601	361 201	24.51530	77.52419	217 081 801	8.439 010	18.18130	39.17041
602	362 404	24.53569	77.58866	218 167 208	8.443 688	18.19137	39.19213
603	363 609	24.55606	77.65307	219 256 227	8.448 361	18.20144	39.21382
604	364 816	24.57641	77.71744	220 348 864	8.453 028	18.21150	39.23548
605	366 025	24.59675	77.78175	221 445 125	8.457 691	18.22154	39.25712
606	367 236	24.61707	77.84600	222 545 016	8.462 348	18.23158	39.27874
607	368 449	24.63737	77.91020	223 648 543	8.467 000	18.24160	39.30033
608	369 664	24.65766	77.97435	224 755 712	8.471 647	18.25161	39.32190
609	370 881	24.67793	78.03845	225 866 529	8.476 289	18.26161	39.34345
610	372 100	24.69818	78.10250	226 981 000	8.480 926	18.27160	39.36497
611	373 321	24.71841	78.16649	228 099 131	8.485 558	18.28158	39.38647
612	374 544	24.73863	78.23043	229 220 928	8.490 185	18.29155	39.40795
613	375 769	24.75884	78.29432	230 346 397	8.494 807	18.30151	39.42940
614	376 996	24.77902	78.35815	231 475 544	8.499 423	18.31145	39.45083
615	378 225	24.79919	78.42194	232 608 375	8.504 035	18.32139	39.47223
616	379 456	24.81935	78.48567	233 744 896	8.508 642	18.33131	39.49362
617	380 689	24.83948	78.54935	234 885 113	8.513 243	18.34123	39.51498
618	381 924	24.85961	78.61298	236 029 032	8.517 840	18.35113	39.53631
619	383 161	24.87971	78.67655	237 176 659	8.522 432	18.36102	39.55763
620	384 400	24.89980	78.74008	238 328 000	8.527 019	18.37091	39.57892
621	385 641	24.91987	78.80355	239 483 061	8.531 601	18.38078	39.60018
622	386 884	24.93993	78.86698	240 641 848	8.536 178	18.39064	39.62143
623	388 129	24.95997	78.93035	241 804 367	8.540 750	18.40049	39.64265
624	389 376	24.97999	78.99367	242 970 624	8.545 317	18.41033	39.66385
625	390 625	25.00000	79.05694	244 140 625	8.549 880	18.42016	39.68503
626	391 876	25.01999	79.12016	245 314 376	8.554 437	18.42998	39.70618
627	393 129	25.03997	79.18333	246 491 883	8.558 990	18.43978	39.72731
628	394 384	25.05993	79.24645	247 673 152	8.563 538	18.44958	39.74842
629	395 641	25.07987	79.30952	248 858 189	8.568 081	18.45937	39.76951
630	396 900	25.09980	79.37254	250 047 000	8.572 619	18.46915	39.79057
631	398 161	25.11971	79.43551	251 239 591	8.577 152	18.47891	39.81161
632	399 424	25.13961	79.49843	252 435 968	8.581 681	18.48867	39.83263
633	400 689	25.15949	79.56130	253 636 137	8.586 205	18.49842	39.85363
634	401 956	25.17936	79.62412	254 840 104	8.590 724	18.50815	39.87461
635	403 225	25.19921	79.68689	256 047 875	8.595 238	18.51788	39.89556
636	404 496	25.21904	79.74961	257 259 456	8.599 748	18.52759	39.91649
637	405 769	25.23886	79.81228	258 474 853	8.604 252	18.53730	39.93740
638	407 044	25.25866	79.87490	259 694 072	8.608 753	18.54700	39.95829
639	408 321	25.27845	79.93748	260 917 119	8.613 248	18.55668	39.97916
640	409 600	25.29822	80.00000	262 144 000	8.617 739	18.56636	40.00000
641	410 881	25.31798	80.06248	263 374 721	8.622 225	18.57602	40.02082
642	412 164	25.33772	80.12490	264 609 288	8.626 706	18.58568	40.04162
643	413 449	25.35744	80.18728	265 847 707	8.631 183	18.59532	40.06240
644	414 736	25.37716	80.24961	267 089 984	8.635 655	18.60495	40.08316
645	416 025	25.39685	80.31189	268 336 125	8.640 123	18.61458	40.10390
646	417 316	25.41653	80.37413	269 586 136	8.644 585	18.62419	40.12461
647	418 609	25.43619	80.43631	270 840 023	8.649 044	18.63380	40.14530
648	419 904	25.45584	80.49845	272 097 792	8.653 497	18.64340	40.16598
649	421 201	25.47548	80.56054	273 359 449	8.657 947	18.65298	40.18663
650	422 500	25.49510	80.62258	274 625 000	8.662 391	18.66256	40.20726

Table 33 (continued)

n	n²	√n	√10n	n³	∛n	∛10n	∛100n
750	562 500	27.38613	86.60254	421 875 000	9.085 603	19.57434	42.17163
751	564 001	27.40438	86.66026	423 564 751	9.089 639	19.58303	42.19037
752	565 504	27.42262	86.71793	425 259 008	9.093 672	19.59172	42.20909
753	567 009	27.44085	86.77557	426 957 777	9.097 701	19.60040	42.22779
754	568 516	27.45906	86.83317	428 661 064	9.101 727	19.60908	42.24647
755	570 025	27.47726	86.89074	430 368 875	9.105 748	19.61774	42.26514
756	571 536	27.49545	86.94826	432 081 216	9.109 767	19.62640	42.28379
757	573 049	27.51366	87.00575	433 798 093	9.113 782	19.63505	42.30243
758	574 564	27.53180	87.06320	435 519 512	9.117 793	19.64369	42.32105
759	576 081	27.54995	87.12061	437 245 479	9.121 801	19.65232	42.33965
760	577 600	27.56810	87.17798	438 976 000	9.125 805	19.66095	42.35824
761	579 121	27.58623	87.23531	440 711 081	9.129 806	19.66957	42.37681
762	580 644	27.60435	87.29261	442 450 728	9.133 803	19.67818	42.39536
763	582 169	27.62245	87.34987	444 194 947	9.137 797	19.68679	42.41390
764	583 696	27.64055	87.40709	445 943 744	9.141 787	19.69538	42.43242
765	585 225	27.65863	87.46428	447 697 125	9.145 774	19.70397	42.45092
766	586 756	27.67671	87.52143	449 455 096	9.149 758	19.71256	42.46941
767	588 289	27.69476	87.57854	451 217 663	9.153 738	19.72113	42.48789
768	589 824	27.71281	87.63561	452 984 832	9.157 714	19.72970	42.50634
769	591 361	27.73085	87.69265	454 756 609	9.161 687	19.73826	42.52478
770	592 900	27.74887	87.74964	456 533 000	9.165 656	19.74681	42.54321
771	594 441	27.76689	87.80661	458 314 011	9.169 623	19.75535	42.56162
772	595 984	27.78489	87.86353	460 099 648	9.173 585	19.76389	42.58001
773	597 529	27.80288	87.92042	461 889 917	9.177 544	19.77242	42.59839
774	599 076	27.82086	87.97727	463 684 824	9.181 500	19.78094	42.61675
775	600 625	27.83882	88.03408	465 484 375	9.185 453	19.78946	42.63509
776	602 176	27.85678	88.09086	467 288 576	9.189 402	19.79797	42.65342
777	603 729	27.87472	88.14760	469 097 433	9.193 347	19.80647	42.67174
778	605 284	27.89265	88.20431	470 910 952	9.197 290	19.81496	42.69004
779	606 841	27.91057	88.26098	472 729 139	9.201 229	19.82345	42.70832
780	608 400	27.92848	88.31761	474 552 000	9.205 164	19.83192	42.72659
781	609 961	27.94638	88.37420	476 379 541	9.209 096	19.84040	42.74484
782	611 524	27.96426	88.43076	478 211 768	9.213 025	19.84886	42.76307
783	613 089	27.98214	88.48729	480 048 687	9.216 950	19.85732	42.78129
784	614 656	28.00000	88.54377	481 890 304	9.220 873	19.86577	42.79950
785	616 225	28.01785	88.60023	483 736 625	9.224 791	19.87421	42.81769
786	617 796	28.03569	88.65664	485 587 656	9.228 707	19.88265	42.83586
787	619 369	28.05352	88.71302	487 443 403	9.232 619	19.89107	42.85402
788	620 944	28.07134	88.76936	489 303 872	9.236 528	19.89950	42.87216
789	622 521	28.08914	88.82567	491 169 069	9.240 433	19.90791	42.89029
790	624 100	28.10694	88.88194	493 039 000	9.244 335	19.91632	42.90840
791	625 681	28.12472	88.93818	494 913 671	9.248 234	19.92472	42.92650
792	627 264	28.14249	88.99438	496 793 088	9.252 130	19.93311	42.94458
793	628 849	28.16026	89.05055	498 677 257	9.256 022	19.94150	42.96265
794	630 436	28.17801	89.10668	500 566 184	9.259 911	19.94987	42.98070
795	632 025	28.19574	89.16277	502 459 875	9.263 797	19.95825	42.99874
796	633 616	28.21347	89.21883	504 358 336	9.267 680	19.96661	43.01676
797	635 209	28.23119	89.27486	506 261 573	9.271 559	19.97497	43.03477
798	636 804	28.24889	89.33085	508 169 592	9.275 435	19.98332	43.05276
799	638 401	28.26659	89.38680	510 082 399	9.279 308	19.99166	43.07073
800	640 000	28.28427	89.44272	512 000 000	9.283 178	20.00000	43.08869

Table 33 (continued)

n	n²	√n	√10n	n³	∛n	∛10n	∛100n
700	490 000	26.45751	83.66600	343 000 000	8.879 040	19.12931	41.21285
701	491 401	26.47640	83.72574	344 472 101	8.883 266	19.13842	41.23247
702	492 804	26.49528	83.78544	345 948 408	8.887 488	19.14751	41.25207
703	494 209	26.51415	83.84510	347 428 927	8.891 706	19.15660	41.27164
704	495 616	26.53300	83.90471	348 913 664	8.895 920	19.16568	41.29120
705	497 025	26.55184	83.96428	350 402 625	8.900 130	19.17475	41.31075
706	498 436	26.57066	84.02381	351 895 816	8.904 337	19.18381	41.33027
707	499 849	26.58947	84.08329	353 393 243	8.908 539	19.19286	41.34977
708	501 264	26.60827	84.14274	354 894 912	8.912 737	19.20191	41.36926
709	502 681	26.62705	84.20214	356 400 829	8.916 931	19.21095	41.38873
710	504 100	26.64583	84.26150	357 911 000	8.921 121	19.21997	41.40818
711	505 521	26.66458	84.32082	359 425 431	8.925 308	19.22899	41.42761
712	506 944	26.68333	84.38009	360 944 128	8.929 490	19.23800	41.44702
713	508 369	26.70206	84.43933	362 467 097	8.933 669	19.24701	41.46642
714	509 796	26.72078	84.49852	363 994 344	8.937 843	19.25600	41.48579
715	511 225	26.73948	84.55767	365 525 875	8.942 014	19.26499	41.50515
716	512 656	26.75818	84.61678	367 061 696	8.946 181	19.27396	41.52449
717	514 089	26.77686	84.67585	368 601 813	8.950 344	19.28293	41.54382
718	515 524	26.79552	84.73488	370 146 232	8.954 503	19.29189	41.56312
719	516 961	26.81418	84.79387	371 694 959	8.958 658	19.30084	41.58241
720	518 400	26.83282	84.85281	373 248 000	8.962 809	19.30979	41.60168
721	519 841	26.85144	84.91172	374 805 361	8.966 957	19.31872	41.62093
722	521 284	26.87006	84.97058	376 367 048	8.971 101	19.32765	41.64016
723	522 729	26.88866	85.02941	377 933 067	8.975 241	19.33657	41.65938
724	524 176	26.90725	85.08819	379 503 424	8.979 377	19.34548	41.67857
725	525 625	26.92582	85.14693	381 078 125	8.983 509	19.35438	41.69775
726	527 076	26.94439	85.20563	382 657 176	8.987 637	19.36328	41.71692
727	528 529	26.96294	85.26429	384 240 583	8.991 762	19.37216	41.73606
728	529 984	26.98148	85.32292	385 828 352	8.995 883	19.38104	41.75519
729	531 441	27.00000	85.38150	387 420 489	9.000 000	19.38991	41.77430
730	532 900	27.01851	85.44004	389 017 000	9.004 113	19.39877	41.79339
731	534 361	27.03701	85.49854	390 617 891	9.008 223	19.40763	41.81247
732	535 824	27.05550	85.55700	392 223 168	9.012 329	19.41647	41.83152
733	537 289	27.07397	85.61542	393 832 837	9.016 431	19.42531	41.85056
734	538 756	27.09243	85.67380	395 446 904	9.020 529	19.43414	41.86959
735	540 225	27.11088	85.73214	397 065 375	9.024 624	19.44296	41.88859
736	541 696	27.12932	85.79044	398 688 256	9.028 715	19.45178	41.90758
737	543 169	27.14774	85.84870	400 315 553	9.032 802	19.46058	41.92655
738	544 644	27.16616	85.90693	401 947 272	9.036 886	19.46938	41.94551
739	546 121	27.18455	85.96511	403 583 419	9.040 966	19.47817	41.96444
740	547 600	27.20294	86.02325	405 224 000	9.045 042	19.48695	41.98336
741	549 081	27.22132	86.08136	406 869 021	9.049 114	19.49573	42.00227
742	550 564	27.23968	86.13942	408 518 488	9.053 183	19.50449	42.02115
743	552 049	27.25803	86.19745	410 172 407	9.057 248	19.51325	42.04002
744	553 536	27.27636	86.25543	411 830 784	9.061 310	19.52200	42.05887
745	555 025	27.29469	86.31338	413 493 625	9.065 368	19.53074	42.07771
746	556 516	27.31300	86.37129	415 160 936	9.069 422	19.53948	42.09653
747	558 009	27.33130	86.42916	416 832 723	9.073 473	19.54820	42.11533
748	559 504	27.34959	86.48699	418 508 992	9.077 520	19.55692	42.13411
749	561 001	27.36786	86.54479	420 189 749	9.081 563	19.56563	42.15288
750	562 500	27.38613	86.60254	421 875 000	9.085 603	19.57434	42.17163

Table 33 (continued)

n	n²	√n	√10n	n³	∛n	∛10n	∛100n
800	640 000	28.28427	89.44272	512 000 000	9.283 178	20.00000	43.08869
801	641 601	28.30194	89.49860	513 922 401	9.287 044	20.00833	43.10664
802	643 204	28.31960	89.55445	515 849 608	9.290 907	20.01665	43.12457
803	644 809	28.33725	89.61027	517 781 627	9.294 767	20.02497	43.14249
804	646 416	28.35489	89.66605	519 718 464	9.298 624	20.03328	43.16039
805	648 025	28.37252	89.72179	521 660 125	9.302 477	20.04158	43.17828
806	649 636	28.39014	89.77750	523 606 616	9.306 328	20.04988	43.19615
807	651 249	28.40775	89.83318	525 557 943	9.310 175	20.05816	43.21400
808	652 864	28.42534	89.88882	527 514 112	9.314 019	20.06645	43.23185
809	654 481	28.44293	89.94443	529 475 129	9.317 860	20.07472	43.24967
810	656 100	28.46050	90.00000	531 441 000	9.321 698	20.08299	43.26749
811	657 721	28.47806	90.05554	533 411 731	9.325 532	20.09125	43.28529
812	659 344	28.49561	90.11104	535 387 328	9.329 363	20.09950	43.30307
813	660 969	28.51315	90.16651	537 367 797	9.333 192	20.10775	43.32084
814	662 596	28.53069	90.22195	539 353 144	9.337 017	20.11599	43.33859
815	664 225	28.54820	90.27735	541 343 375	9.340 839	20.12423	43.35633
816	665 856	28.56571	90.33272	543 338 496	9.344 657	20.13245	43.37406
817	667 489	28.58321	90.38805	545 338 513	9.348 473	20.14067	43.39177
818	669 124	28.60070	90.44335	547 343 432	9.352 286	20.14889	43.40947
819	670 761	28.61818	90.49862	549 353 259	9.356 095	20.15710	43.42715
820	672 400	28.63564	90.55385	551 368 000	9.359 902	20.16530	43.44481
821	674 041	28.65310	90.60905	553 387 661	9.363 705	20.17349	43.46247
822	675 684	28.67054	90.66422	555 412 248	9.367 505	20.18168	43.48011
823	677 329	28.68798	90.71935	557 441 767	9.371 302	20.18986	43.49773
824	678 976	28.70540	90.77445	559 476 224	9.375 096	20.19803	43.51534
825	680 625	28.72281	90.82951	561 515 625	9.378 887	20.20620	43.53294
826	682 276	28.74022	90.88454	563 559 976	9.382 675	20.21436	43.55052
827	683 929	28.75761	90.93954	565 609 283	9.386 460	20.22252	43.56809
828	685 584	28.77499	90.99451	567 663 552	9.390 242	20.23066	43.58564
829	687 241	28.79236	91.04944	569 722 789	9.394 021	20.23880	43.60318
830	688 900	28.80972	91.10434	571 787 000	9.397 796	20.24694	43.62071
831	690 561	28.82707	91.15920	573 856 191	9.401 569	20.25507	43.63822
832	692 224	28.84441	91.21403	575 930 368	9.405 339	20.26319	43.65572
833	693 889	28.86174	91.26883	578 009 537	9.409 105	20.27130	43.67320
834	695 556	28.87906	91.32360	580 093 704	9.412 869	20.27941	43.69067
835	697 225	28.89637	91.37833	582 182 875	9.416 630	20.28751	43.70812
836	698 896	28.91366	91.43304	584 277 056	9.420 387	20.29561	43.72556
837	700 569	28.93095	91.48770	586 376 253	9.424 142	20.30370	43.74299
838	702 244	28.94823	91.54234	588 480 472	9.427 894	20.31178	43.76041
839	703 921	28.96550	91.59694	590 589 719	9.431 642	20.31986	43.77781
840	705 600	28.98275	91.65151	592 704 000	9.435 388	20.32793	43.79519
841	707 281	29.00000	91.70605	594 823 321	9.439 131	20.33599	43.81256
842	708 964	29.01724	91.76056	596 947 688	9.442 870	20.34405	43.82992
843	710 649	29.03446	91.81503	599 077 107	9.446 607	20.35210	43.84727
844	712 336	29.05168	91.86947	601 211 584	9.450 341	20.36014	43.86460
845	714 025	29.06888	91.92388	603 351 125	9.454 072	20.36818	43.88191
846	715 716	29.08608	91.97826	605 495 736	9.457 800	20.37621	43.89922
847	717 409	29.10326	92.03260	607 645 423	9.461 525	20.38424	43.91651
848	719 104	29.12044	92.08692	609 800 192	9.465 247	20.39226	43.93378
849	720 801	29.13760	92.14120	611 960 049	9.468 966	20.40027	43.95105
850	722 500	29.15476	92.19544	614 125 000	9.472 682	20.40828	43.96830

Table 33 (continued)

n	n²	√n	√10n	n³	∛n	∛10n	∛100n
850	722 500	29.15476	92.19544	614 125 000	9.472 682	20.40828	43.96830
851	724 201	29.17190	92.24966	616 295 051	9.476 396	20.41628	43.98553
852	725 904	29.18904	92.30385	618 470 208	9.480 106	20.42427	44.00275
853	727 609	29.20616	92.35800	620 650 477	9.483 814	20.43226	44.01996
854	729 316	29.22328	92.41212	622 835 864	9.487 518	20.44024	44.03716
855	731 025	29.24038	92.46621	625 026 375	9.491 220	20.44821	44.05434
856	732 736	29.25748	92.52027	627 222 016	9.494 919	20.45618	44.07151
857	734 449	29.27456	92.57429	629 422 793	9.498 615	20.46415	44.08866
858	736 164	29.29164	92.62829	631 628 712	9.502 308	20.47210	44.10581
859	737 881	29.30870	92.68225	633 839 779	9.505 998	20.48005	44.12293
860	739 600	29.32576	92.73618	636 056 000	9.509 685	20.48800	44.14005
861	741 321	29.34280	92.79009	638 277 381	9.513 370	20.49593	44.15715
862	743 044	29.35984	92.84396	640 503 928	9.517 052	20.50387	44.17424
863	744 769	29.37686	92.89779	642 735 647	9.520 730	20.51179	44.19132
864	746 496	29.39388	92.95160	644 972 544	9.524 406	20.51971	44.20838
865	748 225	29.41088	93.00538	647 214 625	9.528 079	20.52762	44.22543
866	749 956	29.42788	93.05912	649 461 896	9.531 750	20.53553	44.24246
867	751 689	29.44486	93.11283	651 714 363	9.535 417	20.54343	44.25949
868	753 424	29.46184	93.16652	653 972 032	9.539 082	20.55133	44.27650
869	755 161	29.47881	93.22017	656 234 909	9.542 744	20.55922	44.29349
870	756 900	29.49576	93.27379	658 503 000	9.546 403	20.56710	44.31048
871	758 641	29.51271	93.32738	660 776 311	9.550 059	20.57498	44.32745
872	760 384	29.52965	93.38094	663 054 848	9.553 712	20.58285	44.34440
873	762 129	29.54657	93.43447	665 338 617	9.557 363	20.59071	44.36135
874	763 876	29.56349	93.48797	667 627 624	9.561 011	20.59857	44.37828
875	765 625	29.58040	93.54143	669 921 875	9.564 656	20.60643	44.39520
876	767 376	29.59730	93.59487	672 221 376	9.568 298	20.61427	44.41211
877	769 129	29.61419	93.64828	674 526 133	9.571 938	20.62211	44.42900
878	770 884	29.63106	93.70165	676 836 152	9.575 574	20.62995	44.44588
879	772 641	29.64793	93.75500	679 151 439	9.579 208	20.63778	44.46275
880	774 400	29.66479	93.80832	681 472 000	9.582 840	20.64560	44.47960
881	776 161	29.68164	93.86160	683 797 841	9.586 468	20.65342	44.49644
882	777 924	29.69848	93.91486	686 128 968	9.590 094	20.66123	44.51327
883	779 689	29.71532	93.96808	688 465 387	9.593 717	20.66904	44.53009
884	781 456	29.73214	94.02127	690 807 104	9.597 337	20.67684	44.54689
885	783 225	29.74895	94.07444	693 154 125	9.600 955	20.68463	44.56368
886	784 996	29.76575	94.12757	695 506 456	9.604 570	20.69242	44.58046
887	786 769	29.78255	94.18068	697 864 103	9.608 182	20.70020	44.59723
888	788 544	29.79933	94.23375	700 227 072	9.611 791	20.70798	44.61398
889	790 321	29.81610	94.28680	702 595 369	9.615 398	20.71575	44.63072
890	792 100	29.83287	94.33981	704 969 000	9.619 002	20.72351	44.64745
891	793 881	29.84962	94.39280	707 347 971	9.622 603	20.73127	44.66417
892	795 664	29.86637	94.44575	709 732 288	9.626 202	20.73902	44.68087
893	797 449	29.88311	94.49868	712 121 957	9.629 797	20.74677	44.69756
894	799 236	29.89983	94.55157	714 516 984	9.633 391	20.75451	44.71424
895	801 025	29.91655	94.60444	716 917 375	9.636 981	20.76225	44.73090
896	802 816	29.93326	94.65728	719 323 136	9.640 569	20.76998	44.74756
897	804 609	29.94996	94.71008	721 734 273	9.644 154	20.77770	44.76420
898	806 404	29.96665	94.76286	724 150 792	9.647 737	20.78542	44.78083
899	808 201	29.98333	94.81561	726 572 699	9.651 317	20.79313	44.79744
900	810 000	30.00000	94.86833	729 000 000	9.654 894	20.80084	44.81405

Table 33 (continued)

$\sqrt[3]{100n}$	$\sqrt[3]{10n}$	$\sqrt[3]{n}$	n^3	$\sqrt{10n}$	$\sqrt{n}$	n^2	n
45.62903	21.17912	9.830 476	857 375 000	97.46794	30.82207	902 500	**950**
45.64503	21.18655	9.833 924	860 085 351	97.51923	30.83829	904 401	951
45.66102	21.19397	9.837 369	862 801 408	97.57049	30.85450	906 304	952
45.67701	21.20139	9.840 813	865 523 177	97.62172	30.87070	908 209	953
45.69298	21.20880	9.844 254	868 250 664	97.67292	30.88689	910 116	954
45.70894	21.21621	9.847 692	870 983 875	97.72410	30.90307	912 025	955
45.72489	21.22361	9.851 128	873 722 816	97.77525	30.91925	913 936	956
45.74082	21.23101	9.854 562	876 467 493	97.82638	30.93542	915 849	957
45.75675	21.23840	9.857 993	879 217 912	97.87747	30.95158	917 764	958
45.77267	21.24579	9.861 422	881 974 079	97.92855	30.96773	919 681	959
45.78857	21.25317	9.864 848	884 736 000	97.97959	30.98387	921 600	**960**
45.80446	21.26055	9.868 272	887 503 681	98.03061	31.00000	923 521	961
45.82035	21.26792	9.871 694	890 277 128	98.08160	31.01612	925 444	962
45.83622	21.27529	9.875 113	893 056 347	98.13256	31.03224	927 369	963
45.85208	21.28265	9.878 530	895 841 344	98.18350	31.04835	929 296	964
45.86793	21.29001	9.881 945	898 632 125	98.23441	31.06445	931 225	965
45.88376	21.29736	9.885 357	901 428 696	98.28530	31.08054	933 156	966
45.89959	21.30470	9.888 767	904 231 063	98.33616	31.09662	935 089	967
45.91541	21.31204	9.892 175	907 039 232	98.38699	31.11270	937 024	968
45.93121	21.31938	9.895 580	909 853 209	98.43780	31.12876	938 961	969
45.94701	21.32671	9.898 983	912 673 000	98.48858	31.14482	940 900	**970**
45.96279	21.33404	9.902 384	915 498 611	98.53933	31.16087	942 841	971
45.97857	21.34136	9.905 782	918 330 048	98.59006	31.17691	944 784	972
45.99433	21.34868	9.909 178	921 167 317	98.64076	31.19295	946 729	973
46.01008	21.35599	9.912 571	924 010 424	98.69144	31.20897	948 676	974
46.02582	21.36329	9.915 962	926 859 375	98.74209	31.22499	950 625	975
46.04155	21.37059	9.919 351	929 714 176	98.79271	31.24100	952 576	976
46.05727	21.37788	9.922 738	932 574 833	98.84331	31.25700	954 529	977
46.07298	21.38518	9.926 122	935 441 352	98.89388	31.27299	956 484	978
46.08868	21.39247	9.929 504	938 313 739	98.94443	31.28898	958 441	979
46.10436	21.39975	9.932 884	941 192 000	98.99495	31.30495	960 400	**980**
46.12004	21.40703	9.936 261	944 076 141	99.04544	31.32092	962 361	981
46.13571	21.41430	9.939 636	946 966 168	99.09591	31.33688	964 324	982
46.15136	21.42156	9.943 009	949 862 087	99.14636	31.35283	966 289	983
46.16700	21.42883	9.946 380	952 763 904	99.19677	31.36877	968 256	984
46.18264	21.43608	9.949 748	955 671 625	99.24717	31.38471	970 225	985
46.19826	21.44333	9.953 114	958 585 256	99.29753	31.40064	972 196	986
46.21387	21.45058	9.956 478	961 504 803	99.34787	31.41656	974 169	987
46.22948	21.45782	9.959 839	964 430 272	99.39819	31.43247	976 144	988
46.24507	21.46506	9.963 198	967 361 669	99.44848	31.44837	978 121	989
46.26065	21.47229	9.966 555	970 299 000	99.49874	31.46427	980 100	**990**
46.27622	21.47952	9.969 910	973 242 271	99.54898	31.48015	982 081	991
46.29178	21.48674	9.973 262	976 191 488	99.59920	31.49603	984 064	992
46.30733	21.49396	9.976 612	979 146 657	99.64939	31.51190	986 049	993
46.32287	21.50117	9.979 960	982 107 784	99.69955	31.52777	988 036	994
46.33840	21.50838	9.983 305	985 074 875	99.74969	31.54362	990 025	995
46.35392	21.51558	9.986 649	988 047 936	99.79980	31.55947	992 016	996
46.36943	21.52278	9.989 990	991 026 973	99.84989	31.57531	994 009	997
46.38492	21.52997	9.993 329	994 011 992	99.89995	31.59114	996 004	998
46.40041	21.53716	9.996 666	997 002 999	99.94999	31.60696	998 001	999
46.41589	21.54435	10.000 000	1 000 000 000	100.00000	31.62278	1 000 000	**1000**

Table 33 (continued)

$\sqrt[3]{100n}$	$\sqrt[3]{10n}$	$\sqrt[3]{n}$	n^3	$\sqrt{10n}$	$\sqrt{n}$	n^2	n
44.81405	20.80084	9.654 894	729 000 000	94.86833	30.00000	810 000	**900**
44.83064	20.80854	9.658 468	731 432 701	94.92102	30.01666	811 801	901
44.84722	20.81623	9.662 040	733 870 808	94.97368	30.03331	813 604	902
44.86379	20.82392	9.665 610	736 314 327	95.02631	30.04996	815 409	903
44.88034	20.83161	9.669 176	738 763 264	95.07891	30.06659	817 216	904
44.89688	20.83929	9.672 740	741 217 625	95.13149	30.08322	819 025	905
44.91341	20.84696	9.676 302	743 677 416	95.18403	30.09983	820 836	906
44.92993	20.85463	9.679 860	746 142 643	95.23655	30.11644	822 649	907
44.94644	20.86229	9.683 417	748 613 312	95.28903	30.13304	824 464	908
44.96293	20.86994	9.686 970	751 089 429	95.34149	30.14963	826 281	909
44.97941	20.87759	9.690 521	753 571 000	95.39392	30.16621	828 100	**910**
44.99588	20.88524	9.694 069	756 058 031	95.44632	30.18278	829 921	911
45.01234	20.89288	9.697 615	758 550 528	95.49869	30.19934	831 744	912
45.02879	20.90051	9.701 158	761 048 497	95.55103	30.21589	833 569	913
45.04522	20.90814	9.704 699	763 551 944	95.60335	30.23243	835 396	914
45.06164	20.91576	9.708 237	766 060 875	95.65563	30.24897	837 225	915
45.07805	20.92338	9.711 772	768 575 296	95.70789	30.26549	839 056	916
45.09445	20.93099	9.715 305	771 095 213	95.76012	30.28201	840 889	917
45.11084	20.93860	9.718 835	773 620 632	95.81232	30.29851	842 724	918
45.12721	20.94620	9.722 363	776 151 559	95.86449	30.31501	844 561	919
45.14357	20.95379	9.725 888	778 688 000	95.91663	30.33150	846 400	**920**
45.15992	20.96138	9.729 411	781 229 961	95.96874	30.34798	848 241	921
45.17626	20.96896	9.732 931	783 777 448	96.02083	30.36445	850 084	922
45.19259	20.97654	9.736 448	786 330 467	96.07289	30.38092	851 929	923
45.20891	20.98411	9.739 963	788 889 024	96.12492	30.39737	853 776	924
45.22521	20.99168	9.743 476	791 453 125	96.17692	30.41381	855 625	925
45.24150	20.99924	9.746 986	794 022 776	96.22889	30.43025	857 476	926
45.25778	21.00680	9.750 493	796 597 983	96.28084	30.44667	859 329	927
45.27405	21.01435	9.753 998	799 178 752	96.33276	30.46309	861 184	928
45.29030	21.02190	9.757 500	801 765 089	96.38465	30.47950	863 041	929
45.30655	21.02944	9.761 000	804 357 000	96.43651	30.49590	864 900	**930**
45.32278	21.03697	9.764 497	806 954 491	96.48834	30.51229	866 761	931
45.33900	21.04450	9.767 992	809 557 568	96.54015	30.52868	868 624	932
45.35521	21.05203	9.771 485	812 166 237	96.59193	30.54505	870 489	933
45.37141	21.05954	9.774 974	814 780 504	96.64368	30.56141	872 356	934
45.38760	21.06706	9.778 462	817 400 375	96.69540	30.57777	874 225	935
45.40377	21.07456	9.781 946	820 025 856	96.74709	30.59412	876 096	936
45.41994	21.08207	9.785 429	822 656 953	96.79876	30.61046	877 969	937
45.43609	21.08956	9.788 909	825 293 672	96.85040	30.62679	879 844	938
45.45223	21.09706	9.792 386	827 936 019	96.90201	30.64311	881 721	939
45.46836	21.10454	9.795 861	830 584 000	96.95360	30.65942	883 600	**940**
45.48448	21.11202	9.799 334	833 237 621	97.00515	30.67572	885 481	941
45.50058	21.11950	9.802 804	835 896 888	97.05668	30.69202	887 364	942
45.51668	21.12697	9.806 271	838 561 807	97.10819	30.70831	889 249	943
45.53276	21.13444	9.809 736	841 232 384	97.15966	30.72458	891 136	944
45.54883	21.14190	9.813 199	843 908 625	97.21111	30.74085	893 025	945
45.56490	21.14936	9.816 659	846 590 536	97.26253	30.75711	894 916	946
45.58095	21.15680	9.820 117	849 278 123	97.31393	30.77337	896 809	947
45.59698	21.16424	9.823 572	851 971 392	97.36529	30.78961	898 704	948
45.61301	21.17168	9.827 025	854 670 349	97.41663	30.80584	900 601	949
45.62903	21.17912	9.830 476	857 375 000	97.46794	30.82207	902 500	**950**

METHODS AND EXAMPLES FOR FINDING SQUARE ROOTS AND CUBE ROOTS

SQUARE ROOTS

Finding the Square Root When the Exact Number is an Integer Between 1 and 1000. Locate the number for which the square root is desired (in the first column), say 17, and refer to the third column for its square root, which is 4.1231.

Finding the Square Root of Numbers Not Given in the Table

Method

Step 1: Adjust the decimal point an even number of places to the right or left of its original position until either one of the two following numbers is attained:
(a) A three digit whole number that can be located under the $\sqrt{n}$ column, or
(b) A four digit whole number with the last digit zero (necessitating use of the $\sqrt{10n}$ column).

Step 2: Locate the square root under the appropriate column for the number obtained under either (a) or (b) above. Then move the decimal place for this entry one-half as many places in the opposite direction as had been moved originally under Step 1.

Examples

Find the Square Root of .0133

Step 1: Adjusting the decimal point four places to the *right* of .0133 gives an *n* of 133.

Step 2: Under $\sqrt{n}$ for an *n* of 133, find 11.53256. By moving the decimal point two places (½ of 4) to the *left* gives the square root of .0133 as .1153256.

Find the Square Root of 268,000

Step 1: Adjusting the decimal point two places to the *left* of 268,000 gives a four digit number with the last digit zero, 2680. (See Step 1b above under *Method.*) Since 2680 is 10 times the tabled value of 268 available under the *n* column, column $\sqrt{10n}$ must be used.

Step 2: Under $\sqrt{10n}$ for an *n* of 268, the tabled value is 51.76872. Hence, the decimal point is moved one place (½ of 2) to the *right,* thus giving 517.6872, the square root of 268,000.

CUBE ROOTS

Finding the Cube Root When the Exact Number is an Integer Between 1 and 1000. Locate the number for which the cube root is desired (in the first column), say 167. In the fifth column, (n^3), the cube of 167 is found to be 4,657,463. The following procedure lists the steps to follow:

Finding the Cube Root of a Given Number

Method

Step 1: Adjust the decimal point of a given number by a multiple of 3 to the *right* or *left* until the number reached is one of the following:
(a) A *three* digit whole number (called *n*, to be located under the *n* column), or
(b) A *four* digit whole number with the last digit zero (called 10*n*), or
(c) A *five* digit whole number with the last two digits zero (called 100*n*).

Step 2: Find the entry in the respective columns of n^3, $\sqrt[3]{10n}$, or $\sqrt[3]{100n}$. Then move the decimal point one-third as many places in the opposite direction as had been moved originally under Step 1.

Examples

Find the Cube Root of .133

Step 1: By moving the decimal point of .133 three places to the *right* an *n* value of 133. is obtained.

Step 2: Under the $\sqrt[3]{n}$ column, find 5.104469 for the *n* of 133. For proper replacement of decimal, move the decimal point one place (1/3 of 3) to the *left*, thus obtaining .5104469, the cube root of .133.

Find the Cube Root of 1,330,000

Step 1: By moving the decimal point of 1,330,000. three places to the *left* a value of 1330. is obtained. By dropping off the one zero to obtain an *n* of 133, resort to the use of the $\sqrt[3]{10n}$ column is necessary.

Step 2: Under $\sqrt[3]{10n}$ for the *n* of 133, find 10.99724. For proper replacement of decimal, move the decimal point one place (1/3 of 3) to the *right*, thus obtaining 109.9724, the cube root of 1,330,000.

Find the Cube Root of .0133

Step 1: By moving the decimal point of .0133 six places to the *right*, an *n* value of 013300, or 133 (by dropping out zeros) is obtained, necessitating use of the $\sqrt[3]{100n}$ column.

Step 2: Under $\sqrt[3]{100n}$ for the *n* of 133, find 23.69285. For proper replacement of decimal, move the decimal point two places (1/3 of 6) to the *left*, thus obtaining .2369285, the cube root of .0133.

Table 34

Random Numbers

	1 2 3 4 5	6 7 8 9 10	11 12 13 14 15	16 17 18 19 20	21 22 23 24 25
1	10 27 53 96 23	71 50 54 36 23	54 31 04 82 98	04 14 12 15 09	26 78 25 47 47
2	28 41 50 61 88	64 85 27 20 18	83 36 36 05 56	39 71 65 09 62	94 76 62 11 89
3	34 21 42 57 02	59 19 18 97 48	80 30 03 30 98	05 24 67 70 07	84 97 50 87 46
4	61 81 77 23 23	82 82 11 54 08	53 28 70 58 96	44 07 39 55 43	42 34 43 39 28
5	61 15 18 13 54	16 86 20 26 88	90 74 80 55 09	14 53 90 51 17	52 01 63 01 59
6	91 76 21 64 64	44 91 13 32 97	75 31 62 66 54	84 80 32 75 77	56 08 25 70 29
7	00 97 79 08 06	37 30 28 59 85	53 56 68 53 40	01 74 39 59 73	30 19 99 85 48
8	36 46 18 34 94	75 20 80 27 77	78 91 69 16 00	08 43 18 73 68	67 69 61 34 25
9	88 98 99 60 50	65 95 79 42 94	93 62 40 89 96	43 56 47 71 66	46 76 29 67 02
10	04 37 59 87 21	05 02 03 24 17	47 97 81 56 51	92 34 86 01 82	55 51 33 12 91
11	63 62 06 34 41	94 21 78 55 09	72 76 45 16 94	29 95 81 83 83	79 88 01 97 30
12	78 47 23 53 90	34 41 92 45 71	09 23 70 70 07	12 38 92 79 43	14 85 11 47 23
13	87 68 62 15 43	53 14 36 59 25	54 47 33 70 15	59 24 48 40 35	50 03 42 99 36
14	47 60 92 10 77	88 59 53 11 52	66 25 69 07 04	48 68 64 71 06	61 65 70 22 12
15	56 88 87 59 41	65 28 04 67 53	95 79 88 37 31	50 41 06 94 76	81 83 17 16 33
16	02 57 45 86 67	73 43 07 34 48	44 26 87 93 29	77 09 61 67 84	06 69 44 77 75
17	31 54 14 13 17	48 62 11 90 60	68 12 93 64 28	46 24 79 16 76	14 60 25 51 01
18	28 50 16 43 36	28 97 85 58 99	67 22 52 76 23	24 70 36 54 54	59 28 61 71 96
19	63 29 62 66 50	02 63 45 52 38	67 63 47 54 75	83 24 78 43 20	92 63 13 47 48
20	45 65 58 26 51	76 96 59 38 72	86 57 45 71 46	44 67 76 14 55	44 88 01 62 12
21	39 65 36 63 70	77 45 85 50 51	74 13 39 35 22	30 53 36 02 95	49 34 88 73 61
22	73 71 98 16 04	29 18 94 51 23	76 51 94 84 86	79 93 96 38 63	08 58 25 58 94
23	72 20 56 20 11	72 65 71 08 86	79 57 95 13 91	97 48 72 66 48	09 71 17 24 89
24	75 17 26 99 76	89 37 20 70 01	77 31 61 95 46	26 97 05 73 51	53 33 18 72 87
25	37 48 60 82 29	81 30 15 39 14	48 38 75 93 29	06 87 37 78 48	45 56 00 84 47
26	68 08 02 80 72	83 71 46 30 49	89 17 95 88 29	02 39 56 03 46	97 74 06 56 17
27	14 23 98 61 67	70 52 85 01 50	01 84 02 78 43	10 62 98 19 41	18 83 99 47 99
28	49 08 96 21 44	25 27 99 41 28	07 41 08 34 66	19 42 74 39 91	41 96 53 78 72
29	78 37 06 08 43	63 61 62 42 29	39 68 95 10 96	09 24 23 00 62	56 12 80 73 16
30	37 21 34 17 68	68 96 83 23 56	32 84 60 15 31	44 73 67 34 77	91 15 79 74 58
31	14 29 09 34 04	87 83 07 55 07	76 58 30 83 64	87 29 25 58 84	86 50 60 00 25
32	58 43 28 06 36	49 52 83 51 14	47 56 91 29 34	05 87 31 06 95	12 45 57 09 09
33	10 43 67 29 70	80 62 80 03 42	10 80 21 38 84	90 56 35 03 09	43 12 74 49 14
34	44 38 88 39 54	86 97 37 44 22	00 95 01 31 76	17 16 29 56 63	38 78 94 49 81
35	90 69 59 19 51	85 39 52 85 13	07 28 37 07 61	11 16 36 27 03	78 86 72 04 95
36	41 47 10 25 62	97 05 31 03 61	20 26 36 31 62	68 69 86 95 44	84 95 48 46 45
37	91 94 14 63 19	75 89 11 47 11	31 56 34 19 09	79 57 92 36 59	14 93 87 81 40
38	80 06 54 18 66	09 18 94 06 19	98 40 07 17 81	22 45 44 84 11	24 62 20 42 31
39	67 72 77 63 48	84 08 31 55 58	24 33 45 77 58	80 45 67 93 82	75 70 16 08 24
40	59 40 24 13 27	79 26 88 86 30	01 31 60 10 39	53 58 47 70 93	85 81 56 39 38
41	05 90 35 89 95	01 61 16 96 94	50 78 13 69 36	37 68 53 37 31	71 26 35 03 71
42	44 43 80 69 98	46 68 05 14 82	90 78 50 05 62	77 79 13 57 44	59 60 10 39 66
43	61 81 31 96 82	00 57 25 60 59	46 72 60 18 77	55 66 12 62 11	08 99 55 64 57
44	42 88 07 10 05	24 98 65 63 21	47 21 61 88 32	27 80 30 21 60	10 92 35 36 12
45	77 94 30 05 39	28 10 99 00 27	12 73 73 99 12	49 99 57 94 82	96 88 57 17 91
46	78 83 19 76 16	94 11 68 84 26	23 54 20 86 85	23 86 66 99 07	36 37 34 92 09
47	87 76 59 61 81	43 63 64 61 61	65 76 36 95 90	18 48 27 45 68	27 23 65 30 72
48	91 43 05 96 47	55 78 99 95 24	37 55 85 78 78	01 48 41 19 10	35 19 54 07 73
49	84 97 77 72 73	09 62 06 65 7.	87 12 49 03 60	41 15 20 76 27	50 47 02 29 16
50	87 41 60 76 83	44 88 96 07 80	83 05 83 38 96	73 70 66 81 90	30 56 10 48 59

Random Numbers and Use of Table

To obtain an empirical sampling distribution, a random selection procedure demands that each population element has an equal chance of being an element in a given sample. Table 34, for example, is an abbreviated table of random numbers which provides a source for obtaining such random samples for most experimental and theoretical purposes.

Each number in the table has an equal chance of being selected at each position in the table. However, each population sampling element must be assigned a unique number. Then the table can be entered at some arbitrary point with the necessary amount of random numbers being selected in some predetermined order.

Assume that it has become necessary in a research project to randomly assign 150 subjects to three treatment groups of 50 each. The following procedure is one of several that may be followed:

1. Enumerate all the subjects in any arbitrary order. Since three-digit labels will be required for some, three-digit labels must be given to all, assuring them of having an equal chance, *a priori*, of appearing at any point in the table.

2. Turn to any of the three blocks of random numbers, and, starting at a chance-selected point, read successive three-digit numbers. Follow any predetermined pattern, up or down, forwards or backwards, etc. Varying the pattern, in effect, creates a larger table. Once the pattern is established and followed, the previously *enumerated* elements of the population are now *ordered* according to the *random order* in which their numbers occur in this reading.

3. The first 50 elements so selected may constitute Group A, the second Group B, the remainder Group C.

	1	2	3	4	5	6	7	8	9	10	11	12	13	14	15	16	17	18	19	20	21	22	23	24	25
1	22	17	68	65	84	68	95	23	92	35	87	02	22	57	51	61	09	43	95	06	58	24	82	03	47
2	19	36	27	59	46	13	79	93	37	55	39	77	32	77	09	85	52	05	30	62	47	83	51	62	74
3	16	77	23	02	77	09	61	87	25	21	28	06	24	25	93	16	71	13	59	78	23	05	47	47	25
4	78	43	76	71	61	20	44	90	32	64	97	67	63	99	61	46	38	03	93	22	69	81	21	99	21
5	03	28	28	26	08	73	37	32	04	05	69	30	16	09	05	88	69	58	28	99	35	07	44	75	47
6	93	22	53	64	39	07	10	63	76	35	87	03	04	79	88	08	13	13	85	51	55	34	57	72	69
7	78	76	58	54	74	92	38	70	96	92	52	06	79	79	45	82	63	18	27	44	69	66	92	19	09
8	23	68	35	26	00	99	53	93	61	28	52	70	05	48	34	56	65	05	61	86	90	92	10	70	80
9	15	39	25	70	99	93	86	52	77	65	15	33	59	05	28	22	87	26	07	47	86	96	98	29	06
10	58	71	96	30	24	18	46	23	34	27	85	13	99	24	44	49	18	09	79	49	74	16	32	23	02
11	57	35	27	33	72	24	53	63	94	09	41	10	76	47	91	44	04	95	49	66	39	60	04	59	81
12	48	50	86	54	48	22	06	34	72	52	82	21	15	65	20	33	29	94	71	11	15	91	29	12	03
13	61	96	48	95	03	07	16	39	33	66	98	56	10	56	79	77	21	30	27	12	90	49	22	23	62
14	36	93	89	41	26	29	70	83	63	51	99	74	20	52	36	87	09	41	15	09	98	60	16	03	03
15	18	87	00	42	31	57	90	12	02	07	23	47	37	17	31	54	08	01	88	63	39	41	88	92	10
16	88	56	53	27	59	33	35	72	67	47	77	34	55	45	70	08	18	27	38	90	16	95	86	70	75
17	09	72	95	84	29	49	41	31	06	70	42	38	06	45	18	64	84	73	31	65	52	53	37	97	15
18	12	96	88	17	31	65	19	69	02	83	60	75	86	90	68	24	64	19	35	51	56	61	87	39	12
19	85	94	57	24	16	92	09	84	38	76	22	00	27	69	85	29	81	94	78	70	21	94	47	90	12
20	38	64	43	59	98	98	77	87	68	07	91	51	67	62	44	40	98	05	93	78	23	32	65	41	18
21	53	44	09	42	72	00	41	86	79	79	68	47	22	00	20	35	55	31	51	51	00	83	63	22	55
22	40	76	66	26	84	57	99	99	90	37	36	63	32	08	58	37	40	13	68	97	87	64	81	07	83
23	02	17	79	18	05	12	59	52	57	02	22	07	90	47	03	28	14	11	30	79	20	69	22	40	98
24	95	17	82	06	53	31	51	10	96	46	92	06	88	07	77	56	11	50	81	69	40	23	72	51	39
25	35	76	22	42	92	96	11	83	44	80	34	68	35	48	77	33	42	40	90	60	73	96	53	97	86
26	26	29	13	56	41	85	47	04	66	08	34	72	57	59	13	82	43	80	46	15	38	26	61	70	04
27	77	80	20	75	82	72	82	32	99	90	63	95	73	76	63	89	73	44	99	05	48	67	26	43	18
28	46	40	66	44	52	91	36	74	43	53	30	82	13	54	00	78	45	63	98	35	55	03	36	67	68
29	37	56	08	18	09	77	53	84	46	47	31	91	18	95	58	24	16	74	11	53	44	10	13	85	57
30	61	65	61	68	66	37	27	47	39	19	84	83	70	07	48	53	21	40	06	71	95	06	79	88	54
31	93	43	69	64	07	34	18	04	52	35	56	27	09	24	86	61	85	53	83	45	19	90	70	99	00
32	21	96	60	12	99	11	20	99	45	18	48	13	93	55	34	18	37	79	49	90	65	97	38	20	46
33	95	20	47	97	97	27	37	83	28	71	00	06	41	41	74	45	89	09	39	84	51	67	11	52	49
34	97	86	21	78	73	10	65	81	92	59	58	76	17	14	97	04	76	62	16	17	17	95	70	45	80
35	69	92	06	34	13	59	71	74	17	32	27	55	10	24	19	23	71	82	13	74	63	52	52	01	41
36	04	31	17	21	56	33	73	99	19	87	26	72	39	27	67	53	77	57	68	93	60	61	97	22	61
37	61	06	98	03	91	87	14	77	43	96	43	00	65	98	50	45	60	33	01	07	98	99	46	50	47
38	85	93	85	86	88	72	87	08	62	40	16	06	10	89	20	23	21	34	74	97	76	38	03	29	63
39	21	74	32	47	45	73	96	07	94	52	09	65	90	77	47	25	76	16	19	33	53	05	70	53	30
40	15	69	53	82	80	79	96	23	53	10	65	39	07	16	29	45	33	02	43	70	02	87	40	41	45
41	02	89	08	04	49	20	21	14	68	86	87	63	93	95	17	11	29	01	95	80	35	14	97	35	33
42	87	18	15	89	79	85	43	01	72	73	08	61	74	51	69	89	74	39	82	15	94	51	33	41	67
43	98	83	71	94	22	59	97	50	99	52	08	52	85	08	40	87	80	61	65	31	91	51	80	32	44
44	10	08	58	21	66	72	68	49	29	31	89	85	84	46	06	59	73	19	85	23	65	09	29	75	63
45	47	90	56	10	08	88	02	84	27	83	42	29	72	23	19	66	56	45	65	79	20	71	53	20	25
46	22	85	61	68	90	49	64	92	85	44	16	40	12	89	88	50	14	49	81	06	01	82	77	45	12
47	67	80	43	79	33	12	83	11	41	16	25	58	19	68	70	77	02	54	00	52	53	43	37	15	26
48	27	62	50	96	72	79	44	61	40	15	14	53	40	65	39	27	31	58	50	28	11	39	03	34	25
49	33	78	80	87	15	38	30	06	38	21	14	47	47	07	26	54	96	87	53	32	40	36	40	96	76
50	13	13	92	66	99	47	24	49	57	74	32	25	43	62	17	10	97	11	69	84	99	63	22	32	98

References

1. Alexander, Franz G., & Sheldon T. Selesnick. *The history of psychiatry.* New York: A Mentor Book, The New American Library, 1966.

2. Alpern, Mathew, Merle Lawrence, & David Wolsk. *Sensory processes.* Belmont, Calif.: Brooks/Cole, 1968.

3. Anastasi, Ann. *Psychological testing.* New York: Macmillan, 1968.

4. Barker, Roger G. *Ecological psychology.* Stanford, Calif.: Stanford University Press, 1968.

5. Bell, Eric T. *Men of mathematics.* New York: Simon and Schuster, 1937.

6. Birch, David, & Joseph Veroff. *Motivation: A study of action.* Belmont, Calif.: Brooks/Cole, 1966.

7. Bischof, Ledford J. *Interpreting personality theories.* New York: Harper and Row, 1964.

8. Blum, Gerald S. *Psychodynamics: The science of unconscious mental forces.* Belmont, Calif.: Wadsworth, 1966.

9. Boring, Edwin G. *A history of experimental psychology.* New York: Appleton-Century-Crofts, 1957.

10. Brown, Clinton C. *Methods in psychophysiology.* Baltimore: Williams & Wilkins, 1967.

11. Brown, Roger. *Social psychology.* New York: The Free Press, 1965.

12. Butter, Charles M. *Neuropsychology: The study of brain and behavior.* Belmont, Calif.: Brooks/Cole, 1968.

13. Caldwell, Anne E., M. D. *Origins of psychopharmacology: From CPZ to LSD.* Springfield, Ill.: Charles C. Thomas, 1970.

14. Chase, Clinton I. *Elementary statistical procedures.* New York: McGraw-Hill, 1967.

15. Clarke, Edwin, & C. D. O'Malley. *The human brain and spinal cord.* Berkeley and Los Angeles: University of California Press, 1968.

16. Cole, Michael, & Irving Maltzman (eds.). *Handbook of contemporary Soviet psychology.* New York: Basic Books, 1969.

17. Cronbach, Lee J. *Essentials of psychological testing.* New York: Harper and Row, 1970.

18. D'Amato, M. R. *Experimental psychology: Methodology, psychophysics and learning.* New York: McGraw-Hill, 1970.

19. Diamond, Solomon. *Personality and temperament.* New York: Harper and Brothers, 1957.

20. Diamond, Solomon. *Information & error.* New York: Basic Books, 1959.

21. Downie, N. M., & R. W. Heath. *Basic statistical methods* (2nd ed.) New York: Harper and Row, 1965.

22. Du Bois, Phillip H. *An introduction to psychological statistics.* New York: Harper and Row, 1965.

23. Edwards, Allen L. *Statistical methods* (2nd ed.) New York: Holt, Rinehart and Winston, 1967.

24. Ferguson, George A. *Statistical analysis in psychology and education* (2nd ed.) New York: McGraw-Hill, 1966.

25. Fisher, R. A. *Statistical methods for research workers* (12th ed.) Edinburgh: Oliver and Boyd, 1952.

26. Fitts, Paul M., & Michael I. Posner. *Human performance.* Belmont, Calif.: Brooks/Cole, 1967.

27. Freund, John E., & Frank J. Williams. *Elementary business statistics.* Englewood Cliffs, N. J.: Prentice-Hall, 1964.

28. Gergen, Kenneth J. *The psychology of behavior exchange.* Reading, Mass.: Addison-Wesley, 1969.

29. Guilford, J. P. *Fundamental statistics in psychology and education* (4th ed.) New York: McGraw-Hill, 1965.

30. Haymaker, Webb, & Francis Schiller. *The founders of neurology* (2nd ed.) Springfield: Charles C. Thomas, 1970.

31. Hays, William L. *Statistics for psychologists.* New York: Holt, Rinehart and Winston, 1963.

32. Hays, William L. *Basic statistics.* Belmont, Calif.: Brooks/Cole, 1967.

33. Hays, William L. *Quantification in psychology.* Belmont, Calif.: Brooks/Cole, 1968.

34. Hilgard, Ernest R., & Richard C. Atkinson. *Introduction to psychology* (4th ed.) New York: Harcourt, Brace, and World, 1967.

35. Hilgard, Ernest R., & Gordon H. Bower. *Theories of learning* (3rd ed.) New York: Appleton-Century-Crofts, 1966.

36. Hollander, Edwin P. *Principles and methods of social psychology.* New York: Oxford University Press, 1967.

37. Hollander, Edwin P., & Raymond G. Hunt. *Current perspectives in social psychology.* New York: Oxford University Press, 1967.

38. Hull, L. L. *Principles of behavior: An introduction to behavior theory.* New York: Appleton-Century-Crofts, 1943.

39. Hunter, Richard, & Ida Macalpine. *Three Hundred Years of Psychiatry, 1535-1860.* London and New York: Oxford University Press, 1963.

40. Jaeger, Edmund C. *A source-book of medical terms.* Springfield: Charles C. Thomas, 1953.

41. Jones, Edward E., & Harold B. Gerard. *Foundations of social psychology.* New York: Wiley, 1967.

42. Kelly, E. Lowell. *Assessment of human characteristics.* Belmont, Calif.: Brooks/Cole, 1967.

43. Kessler, Jane W. *Psychopathology of childhood.* Englewood Cliffs, N. J.: Prentice-Hall, 1966.

44. Kirk, Roger E. *Experimental design: Procedures for the behavioral sciences.* Belmont, Calif.: Brooks/Cole, 1968.

45. Klein, D. B. *A history of scientific psychology: Its origins and philosophical backgrounds.* New York: Basic Books, 1970.

46. Kolstoe, Ralph H. *Introduction to statistics for the behavioral sciences.* Homewood, Ill.: The Dorsey Press, 1969.

47. Leukel, Francis. *Introduction to physiological psychology.* St. Louis: C. V. Mosby, 1963.

48. Lewis, E. Vernon. *Statistical analysis: Ideas and methods.* Princeton, N. J.: Van Nostrand, 1963.

49. Lindquist, E. F. *Design and analysis of experiments in psychology and education.* Boston: Houghton Mifflin, 1956.

50. Logan, Frank A. *Fundamentals of learning and motivation.* Dubuque, Iowa: Wm. C. Brown, 1970.

51. Lordahl, Daniel S. *Modern statistics for behavior sciences.* New York: Ronald Press, 1967.

52. Lundin, Robert W. *Personality: A behavioral analysis.* Toronto: Macmillan, 1969.

53. Maddi, Salvatore R. *Personality theories: A comparative analysis.* Homewood, Ill.: Dorsey Press, 1968.

54. Manis, Melvin. *Cognitive processes.* Belmont, Calif.: Brooks/Cole, 1968.

55. McDavid, John W., & Herbert Harari. *Social psychology: Individuals, groups, societies.* New York: Harper & Row, 1968.

56. McNemar, Quinn. *Psychological statistics.* New York: Wiley, 1962.

57. Mendenhall, William. *Introduction to statistics.* Belmont, Calif.: Wadsworth, 1964.

58. Milner, Peter M. *Physiological psychology.* New York: Holt, Rinehart and Winston, 1970.

59. Morgan, Clifford T. *Physiological psychology.* New York: McGraw-Hill, 1965.

60. Murray, H. A. *Explorations in personality.* New York: Oxford University Press, 1938.

61. Mussen, Paul H. *The psychological development of the child.* Englewood Cliffs, N. J.: Prentice-Hall, 1963.

62. Myers, Jerome L. *Fundamentals of experimental design.* Boston: Allyn & Bacon, 1969.

63. Nash, John. *Developmental psychology, a psychobiological approach.* Englewood Cliffs, N. J.: Prentice-Hall, 1970.

64. O'Toole, A. L. *Elementary practical statistics.* New York: Macmillan, 1964.

65. Partington, J. R. *A history of chemistry* (4 vols.) New York: Macmillan, 1964.

66. Pearson, Egon S., & H. O. Hartley (Eds.), *Biometrika tables for statisticians*, vol. I (3rd ed.) New York: Cambridge University Press, 1966.

67. Pearson, Egon S., & H. O. Hartley (Eds.), *Biometrika tables for statisticians*, vol. II. New York: Cambridge University Press, 1972.

68. Pepper, O. H. Perry. *Medical etymology.* Philadelphia: Saunders, 1949.

69. Piéron, Henri. *Vocabulaire de la psychologie.* Paris: Presses Universitaires de France, 1963.

70. Pronko, N. H. *Panorama of psychology.* Belmont, Calif.: Brooks/Cole, 1969.

71. *Psychology today: An introduction* (Contributing consultants). Del Mar, Calif.: CRM Books, 1970.

72. Quarton, Gardner C., Theodor Melnechuk, Francis O. Schmitt, & the associates of the Neurosciences Research Program. *The neurosciences.* New York: Rockefeller University Press, 1967.

73. Quincy's Lexicon-Medicum. *A New Medical Dictionary by Robert Hooper, M.D. of the University of Oxford and the Royal College of Physicians of London.* Philadelphia: M. Carey and Son, Benjamin Warner and Edward Parker, Publishers, 1817.

74. *Readings in clinical psychology today.* (Contributing consultants). Del Mar, Calif.: CRM Books, 1970.

75. Robinson, Halbert B., & Nancy M. Robinson. *The mentally retarded child: A psychological approach.* New York: McGraw-Hill, 1965.

76. Rogers, Carl R., & Barry Stevens. *Person to person.* Walnut Creek, Calif.: Real People Press, 1967.

77. Ruch, Floyd, & Philip G. Zimbardo. *Psychology and life* (8th ed.) Glenview, Ill.: Scott, Foresman, 1971.

78. Runyon, Richard, & Audrey Haber. *Fundamentals of behavioral statistics.* Reading, Mass.: Addison-Wesley, 1967.

79. Sanford, Fillmore H., & Lawrence S. Wrightsman, Jr. *Psychology: A scientific study of man* (3rd ed.) Belmont, Calif.: Brooks/Cole, 1970.

80. Senders, Virginia. *Measurement and statistics.* New York: Oxford University Press, 1958.

81. Siegel, Sidney. *Nonparametric statistics for the behavioral sciences.* New York: McGraw-Hill, 1956.

82. Skinner, B. F. *The behavior of organisms: An experimental analysis.* New York: Appleton-Century, 1938.

83. Snedecor, George W., & William G. Cochran. *Statistical methods* (2nd ed.) Ames: Iowa University Press, 1968.

84. Talbott, John H. *A biographical history of medicine: Excerpts and essays on the men and their works.* New York: Grune and Stratton, 1970.

85. Thompson, Richard F. *Foundations of physiological psychology*. New York: Harper and Row, 1967.
86. Thompson, Travis, & Charles R. Schuster. *Behavioral pharmacology*. Englewood Cliffs, N.J.: Prentice-Hall, 1968.
87. Tolman, Edward C. *Purposive behavior in animals and men*. New York: Century, 1932.
88. Venables, P. H., & I. Martin (Eds.) *A manual of psychophysiological methods*. Amsterdam: North-Holland, 1967.
89. Vinacke, N. Edgar. *Foundations of psychology*. New York: American Book, 1968.
90. Wain, Harry, M. D. *The story behind the word*. Springfield, Ill.; Charles C. Thomas, 1958.
91. Walker, Edward L. *Psychology as a natural and social science*. Belmont, Calif.: Brooks/Cole, 1967.
92. Walker, Edward L. *Conditioning and instrumental learning*. Belmont, Calif.: Brooks/Cole, 1968.
93. Walker, Helen M., & Joseph Lev. *Statistical inference*. New York: Holt, Rinehart, and Winston, 1953.
94. Wechsler, David. *The measurement and appraisal of adult intelligence*. Baltimore: Williams and Wilkins, 1958.
95. Weinberg, George H., & John A. Schumaker. *Statistics. An intuitive approach* (2nd ed.) Belmont, Calif.: Brooks/Cole, 1969.
96. Weintraub, Daniel J., & Edward L. Walker. *Perception*. Belmont, Calif.: Brooks/Cole, 1968.
97. Williams, Roger J., & Edwin M. Lansford. *Encyclopedia of biochemistry*. New York: Reinhold, 1967.
98. Williams, Trevor I. (Ed.) *A biographical dictionary of scientists*. London: Adam and Charles Black, 1969.
99. Winer, B. J. *Statistical principles on experimental design*. New York: McGraw-Hill, 1962.
100. Woodworth, Robert S., & Harold Schlosberg. *Experimental psychology* (Rev. ed.) New York: Holt, Rinehart and Winston, 1965.
101. Yamane, Taro. *Statistics: An introductory analysis*. New York: Harper and Row, 1967.
102. Zajonc, Robert B. *Social psychology: An experimental approach*. Belmont, Calif.: Brooks/Cole, 1968.

Supplementary References

103. Arnau, L. Earle. *Introduction to physiological and pathological chemistry* (8th ed.) St. Louis: The C. V. Mosby Company, 1972.
104. Bishop, Gale B., and Winfred F. Hill. *Dimensions of psychology: Introductory readings*. New York: J. B. Lippincott Company, 1972.
105. Bonaparte, Marie, Anna Freud, and Ernst Kris (Eds.). *The origins of psychoanalysis: Sigmund Freud's letters to Wilhelm Fliess during 1887-1902*. New York: Basic Books, 1954.
106. Bowman, Robert E., and Surinda P. Datta (Eds.). *Biochemistry of brain and behavior*. New York: Plenum Press, 1970.
107. Brill, A. A. *The basic writings of Sigmund Freud*. New York: The Modern Library, 1938.
108. Clinard, Marshall B. *Anomie and deviant behavior*. New York: The Free Press, 1964.
109. Eiduson, Samuel, Edward Geller, Arthur Yuwiler, and Bernice T. Eiduson. *Biochemistry and behavior*. Princeton: D. Van Nostrand Company, 1964.
110. Freud, Sigmund. *New introductory lectures on psychoanalysis*. New York: W. W. Norton and Company, 1933.
111. Gardner, William I. *Behavior modification in mental retardation*. New York: Aldine-Atherton, 1971.
112. Johnson, Ronald C. *Conscience, contract, and social reality: Theory and research in behavioral science*. New York: Holt, Rinehart and Winston, 1972.
113. Konorski, Jerzy. *Integrative activity of the brain. An interdisciplinary approach*. Chicago: University of Chicago Press, 1967.
114. Lewis, William C. *Why people change: The psychology of influence*. New York: Holt, Rinehart and Winston, 1972.
115. McLaughlin, Barry. *Learning and social behavior*. New York: The Free Press, 1971.
116. Mortensen, C. David. *Communication: The study of human interaction*. New York: McGraw-Hill Book Company, 1972.
117. Murphy, Gardner. *Personality: A biosocial approach to origins and structure*. New York: Harper and Brothers, 1947.
118. Piaget, Jean. *The language and thought of the child* (2nd ed.). London: Routledge, 1932.
119. Proshansky, Harold M., William H. Ittelson, and Leanne G. Rivlin. *Environmental psychology: Man and his physical setting*. New York: Holt, Rinehart and Winston, 1970.
120. Rapaport, David (Ed.). *Organization and pathology of thought: Selected sources*. New York: Columbia University Press, 1951.
121. Sahakian, William S. *History of psychology: A source book in systematic psychology*. Itaska: F. E. Peacock, 1968.
122. Wertheimer, Michael (General Ed.). *Confrontation: Psychology and the problems of today*. Glenview: Scott, Foresman and Company, 1970.